ENCYCLOPEDIA OF AMERICAN HISTORY

The Great Depression and World War II
1929 to 1945

VOLUME VIII

ENCYCLOPEDIA OF AMERICAN HISTORY

ENCYCLOPEDIA OF AMERICAN HISTORY

The Great Depression
and World War II
1929 to 1945

VOLUME VIII

John W. Jeffries, Editor
Katherine Liapis Segrue, Assistant Editor
Gary B. Nash, General Editor

Facts On File, Inc.

Encyclopedia of American History:
The Great Depression and World War II (1929 to 1945)

Editorial Director: Laurie E. Likoff
Editor in Chief: Owen Lancer
Chief Copy Editor: Michael G. Laraque
Associate Editor: Dorothy Cummings
Production Director: Olivia McKean
Production Manager: Rachel L. Berlin
Production Associate: Theresa Montoya
Art Director: Cathy Rincon
Interior Designer: Joan M. Toro
Desktop Designers: Erika K. Arroyo and David C. Strelecky
Maps and Illustrations: Dale E. Williams and Jeremy Eagle

Facts On File, Inc.
132 West 31st Street
New York NY 10001

Library of Congress Cataloging-in-Publication Data

Encyclopedia of American history / Gary B. Nash, general editor.
p.   cm.
Includes bibliographical references and indexes.
Contents: v. 1. Three worlds meet — v. 2. Colonization and settlement —
v. 3. Revolution and new nation — v. 4. Expansion and reform — v. 5. Civil War
and Reconstruction — v. 6. The development of the industrial United States —
v. 7. The emergence of modern America — v. 8. The Great Depression and
World War II — v. 9. Postwar United States — v. 10. Contemporary
United States. — v. 11 Comprehensive index
ISBN 0-8160-4371-X (set)   ISBN 0-8160-4368-X (v. 8)
1. United States—History—Encyclopedias. I. Nash, Gary B.
E174 .E53 2002
973′.03—dc21   2001051278

Contents

★

List of Entries

About the Editors

General Editor: Gary B. Nash received a Ph.D from Princeton University. He is currently director of the National Center for History in the Schools at the University of California, Los Angeles, where he teaches American history of the colonial and Revolutionary era. He is a published author of college and precollegiate history texts. Among his best-selling works is *The American People: Creating a Nation and Society* (Addison Wesley, Longman), now in its fifth edition.

Nash is an elected member of the Society of American Historians, American Academy of Arts and Sciences, and the American Philosophical Society. He has served as past president of the Organization of American Historians, 1994–95, and was a founding member of the National Council for History Education, 1990.

Volume Editor: John W. Jeffries, University of Maryland, Baltimore County, received a Ph.D. from Yale University. He is the author of several books, including *Wartime America: The World War II Homefront* (Ivan Dee, 1996).

Foreword

The Encyclopedia of American History series is designed as a handy reference to the most important individuals, events, and topics in U.S. history. In 10 volumes, the encyclopedia covers the period from the 15th century, when European explorers first made their way across the Atlantic Ocean to the Americas, to the present day. The encyclopedia is written for precollegiate as well as college students, for parents of young learners in the schools, and for the general public. The volume editors are distinguished historians of American history. In writing individual entries, each editor has drawn upon the expertise of scores of specialists. Articles contributed by the various volume editors are uncredited. This ensures the scholarly quality of the entire series.

This 10-volume encyclopedia of "American history" is broadly conceived to include the historical experience of the various peoples of North America. Thus, in the first volume, many essays treat the history of a great range of indigenous people before contact with Europeans. In the same vein, readers will find essays in the first several volumes that sketch Spanish, Dutch, and French explorers and colonizers who opened up territories for European settlement that later would become part of the United States. The venues and cast of characters in the American historical drama are thus widened beyond traditional encyclopedias.

In creating the eras of American history that define the chronological limits of each volume, and in addressing major topics in each era, the encyclopedia follows the architecture of *The National Standards for United States History, Revised Edition* (Los Angeles: National Center for History in the Schools, 1996). Mandated by the U.S. Congress, the national standards for U.S. history have been widely used by states and school districts in organizing curricular frameworks and have been followed by many other curriculum-building efforts.

Entries are cross-referenced, when appropriate, with *See also* citations at the end of articles. At the end of most entries, a listing of articles and books allows readers to turn to specialized sources and historical accounts. In each volume, an array of maps provide geographical context, while numerous illustrations help vivify the material covered in the text. A time line is included to provide students with a chronological reference to major events occurring in the given era. The selection of historical documents in the back of each volume gives students experience with the raw documents that historians use when researching history. A comprehensive index to each volume also facilitates the reader's access to particular information.

In each volume, long entries are provided for major categories of American historical experience. These categories may include: African Americans, agriculture, art and architecture, business, economy, education, family life, foreign policy, immigration, labor, Native Americans, politics, population, religion, urbanization, and women. By following these essays from volume to volume, the reader can access what might be called a mini-history of each broad topic, for example, family life, immigration, or religion.

— Gary B. Nash
University of California, Los Angeles

Introduction

The years from 1929 to 1945 were by any reckoning among the most eventful and important in American history. In barely more than a decade and a half, the United States experienced the Great Depression and World War II—the worst period of hard times in the nation's history and then the worst war in world history. Having a large and ramifying impact on the United States, the events of the depression and war deeply influenced national life and directions in the decades to follow. For most of the period, moreover, Franklin D. Roosevelt, the most important American president of the 20th century, was in the White House. The Roosevelt administration implemented the New Deal and, with it, the modern American regulatory-welfare state; it made the Democratic Party the nation's majority party for a generation and more; it managed the wartime mobilization that not only helped win the war but also ended the depression; and it led the United States into a new era of global activism and leadership.

The Great Depression and World War II thus brought pivotal economic, political, diplomatic, and military developments, and the entries in this volume of the Encyclopedia of American History reflect that fact. But the period was also one of important social and cultural developments. Demographic patterns; popular culture; the arts and literature; the status and roles of African Americans, women, and immigrant groups—these and other areas of American life also underwent change crucial to the shape of postwar America and receive significant attention in the entries that follow. And in addition to illuminating the importance and impact of the 1929 to 1945 era, the entries in this volume help to explain the period's important continuities and connections to the pre-1929 past as well as to the post-1945 future.

I am grateful to the many people who helped make this volume possible. Gary Nash of UCLA and Owen Lancer of Facts On File gave me the opportunity to work on the project. Katherine Liapis Segrue, my assistant editor, wrote a number of entries, helped edit the others, and performed a variety of crucial administrative duties. Several officials at the University of Maryland, Baltimore County, made important contributions—Provost Art Johnson, by making essential space available; Policy Sciences Director Marv Mandell and Dean of Arts and Sciences Rick Welch, by enabling Kathy Segrue to work with me; and my department chair, Jim Grubb, by offering numerous kindnesses. Perhaps my greatest debt is to the contributors to this volume, many of them my present and former students. Working with UMBC undergraduate and graduate students on this project has been a special and rewarding pleasure.

In this enterprise, my family—happily now a larger one—again sustained me and enriched my life. My gratitude for everything they have given to me goes to my wife, Renate; to our children, Martha and Bill, and their spouses, Scott and Amy; and to our grandchildren, Sarah, Julia, and Savannah.

—John W. Jeffries
Catonsville, Md.

ENTRIES
A TO Z

advertising

Advertising from 1929 to 1945 experienced the challenges of other BUSINESS enterprises in coping with the GREAT DEPRESSION and in adjusting to the priorities and changed circumstances of the WORLD WAR II HOME FRONT.

Advertising revealed important aspects of American culture as well. Both appealing to and influencing the hopes and fears of the American people, advertising patterns also reflected the emergence of RADIO as a central component of both the NEWS MEDIA and the POPULAR CULTURE. Newspapers remained by far the largest venue for advertising, accounting for close to half of advertising expenditures in the 1930s and for about one-third during the war. Direct mail was second for most of the period. By 1939, however, radio had passed magazines for third place, and then by 1944 overtook direct mailing. (After the war, direct mailing reclaimed second place in advertising dollars and television advertising became a major factor in the 1950s.)

As the ECONOMY plummeted in the early 1930s (and advertising expenditures dropped from $3.4 billion in 1929 to just $1.3 billion in 1933), advertisers tried various tactics to stimulate buying. Some pursued a tactic of boosterism, hoping to increase purchases by raising morale and confidence in the economy; others took a different tack, trying to capitalize on fears of declining economic and social status by pointing out such perils as an unappealing complexion or unstylish clothing; still others simply tried to enhance the allure of their products. Advertisers also turned increasingly to sophisticated market research and to scientific PUBLIC OPINION POLLS to determine public preferences and how to appeal to them.

The depression brought increased criticism of advertising, consistent with the declining image of business more generally. Some critics suggested that there needed to be truth in advertising regulations similar to the stock market reforms that required full and accurate disclosure. Consumers Research, Inc., was formed to test products and advertising claims, and a splinter group from that organization established the Consumers Union. The FOOD, DRUG, AND COSMETIC ACT of 1938 gave the Food and Drug Administration additional power over labeling and advertising.

Advertising picked up by the middle of the decade and spending on ads rose to $2.1 billion by 1940, with some of the increase going to marketing the electrical appliances—refrigerators, for example, and washing machines—that continued to transform American homes. (The importance and appeal of such TECHNOLOGY-based consumer goods were reflected in displays at the 1939–40 NEW YORK WORLD'S FAIR.) The federal GOVERNMENT also did its own form of advertising in the 1930s, from the "Blue Eagle" campaign of the NATIONAL RECOVERY ADMINISTRATION, to publicity for the SOCIAL SECURITY ACT, to the posters for such agencies as the WORKS PROGRESS ADMINISTRATION and the FARM SECURITY ADMINISTRATION. Political parties and candidates for office continued election-time advertising as well.

Expenditures on advertising increased further as the economy recovered because of defense MOBILIZATION, but the American entry into WORLD WAR II raised issues for advertisers. Despite the return of prosperity, they worried that there might be little need for advertising when consumer goods were restricted because of war production. Concerned also that the government might take steps to limit advertising for fear that it would contribute to inflation by increasing product costs and consumer demand, advertisers formed the Advertising Council soon after PEARL HARBOR to protect the industry.

The Advertising Council worked with the OFFICE OF WAR INFORMATION and other government agencies to support the war effort. Facilitated by the Ad Council, advertising firms donated time and expertise to a sort of domestic PROPAGANDA that promoted WAR BONDS, victory gardens, scrap and fat drives, conservation of food and vital materials, and recruitment of men and women for the armed forces and defense industries. Such contributions to the war effort, which the Ad Council said amounted to some $1 billion in services, paid off in continued visibility, increased prestige, and even tax write-offs.

Product advertising continued as well, and painted an appealing picture of the nation as well as of the goods the ads promoted. Expenditures on advertising rose to $2.9 billion by 1945, and surely would have risen more without the constraints of the war years. Wartime ads depicted American GIs as innocent and decent idealists who would do their duty and win the war, and the home front as a place of hard work, common cause, sacrifice, and old-fashioned values that sustained the GIs and helped speed victory. As the end of the war neared, advertisements portrayed an America rooted in values and patterns of the past but propelled by the free enterprise system into a postwar future of economic abundance and wonderful new consumer goods. As it so often does, advertising both reflected and influenced the culture, for polls showed that most Americans wanted an era in which traditional American ways would continue but the American standard of living would be much better. It was a compelling picture, one that wartime and postwar Americans eagerly pursued.

Further reading: Stephen R. Fox, *The Mirror Makers: A History of American Advertising and Its Creators* (New York: Morrow, 1984); Roland Marchand, *Advertising the American Dream: Making Way for Modernity, 1920–1940* (Berkeley: University of California Press, 1985).

African Americans

For African Americans, the era of the GREAT DEPRESSION and WORLD WAR II was one of continuing and sometimes increased difficulties, but also one of achievement and change that laid important groundwork for the postwar CIVIL RIGHTS movement.

During and after World War I, southern blacks in significant numbers left the Jim Crow discrimination, segregation, disfranchisement, and brutality of the SOUTH for the "Promised Land" of the North and the factory jobs that offered a higher standard of living and greater autonomy from whites. This "Great Migration" forever changed the nature of black America. By the mid-20th century African Americans were becoming predominantly urban and nonsouthern, and a solid, though still small, black middle class had begun to emerge.

Urbanization was crucial to bringing down the wall restraining African Americans from full and equal access to the opportunities and benefits of American life. In 1928, Oscar DePriest, a Chicago Republican, became the first African American elected to CONGRESS from the North and the first black member of Congress since 1901. Grow-

Most Americans suffered greatly during the depression of the 1930s, but blacks, especially those in rural areas, were the hardest hit. Shown here is an evicted sharecropper with her baby. *(Library of Congress)*

ing political clout was further demonstrated when in 1930 the NATIONAL ASSOCIATION FOR THE ADVANCEMENT OF COLORED PEOPLE (NAACP) helped turn back President HERBERT HOOVER's nomination to the SUPREME COURT of John J. Parker, who had made racially prejudiced statements. Parker's defeat prompted African Americans to focus on other unfriendly politicians, often effectively. The NAACP also had some significant successes with lawsuits and Supreme Court decisions in the 1930s and 1940s that began to erode legalized Jim Crow. The NAACP and other black leaders failed, however, to get federal antilynching legislation through Congress.

By 1932, black voters were well along in the shift that had begun in 1928 from the REPUBLICAN PARTY to the DEMOCRATIC PARTY, and by 1936 they had become an integral part of the "Roosevelt Coalition" that made the Democrats the new majority party of the country. Symbolic of this change in party allegiance, a black Democrat, Arthur W. Mitchell, won DePriest's congressional seat in 1934. This shift reflected dissatisfaction with the inattention, if not open hostility, of the party of Lincoln to the racial situation in America. Where Hoover had seemingly tried to build a "lily-white" Republican Party in the South, President FRANKLIN D. ROOSEVELT appointed more African Americans to significant GOVERNMENT positions than any prior president. An unofficial "BLACK CABINET" emerged in the Roosevelt administration to give advice on issues critical to African Americans and to recruit other blacks to government.

Indicative, however, of the ambivalent attitude and actions of the NEW DEAL on racial issues, the Black Cabinet was sometimes rebuffed by FDR and forced to see his subordinates. At other times, they sought access through the president's wife, ELEANOR ROOSEVELT. She made her most famous gesture of support for African Americans in 1939, when she resigned from the Daughters of the American Revolution after the DAR refused to allow the singer Marian Anderson to give a concert recital in its Constitution Hall in Washington. Secretary of the Interior HAROLD ICKES offered an alternative site, and Anderson sang instead on Easter Sunday on the steps of the Lincoln Memorial. Mrs. Roosevelt was especially close to MARY MCLEOD BETHUNE, leader of the Black Cabinet and head of the National Council of Negro Women, inviting her to the White House over the protest of white southern Democrats.

Although the Harlem Renaissance that defined "the New Negro" as poised and self-reliant was winding down by the end of the 1920s, it prompted many writers to continue producing. Writer and folklorist Zora Neale Hurston published her best works during the depression decade of the 1930s, most importantly *Their Eyes Were Watching God* in 1937. The saga of the strong-willed, independent Janie's journey of self-discovery attracted considerable attention. Even better known was RICHARD WRIGHT's 1940 novel *Native Son,* a gripping examination of the effects of racial oppression upon a hapless young man named Bigger Thomas and the black community around him. The jazz that flourished during the Harlem Renaissance continued to influence American MUSIC as more and more whites listened to the swing music of DUKE ELLINGTON, Count Basie, Cab Calloway, and many others.

Despite such obvious achievements, life was often grim for African Americans. In the infamous 1931 SCOTTSBORO BOYS case, nine black youths were unjustly accused of raping two white women while riding a freight train through Alabama. Their hasty convictions and death sentences illustrated the inequalities of the justice system, especially but not exclusively in the South, where lynch law remained a problem. (Twice, however, the Supreme Court overturned the Alabama decisions and ordered retrials, and eventually all nine regained their freedom.) During the 1930s and 1940s, black workers encountered continu-ing resistance from LABOR unions in gaining admission. The new CONGRESS OF INDUSTRIAL ORGANIZATIONS (CIO) was often helpful, however, and black workers were able, for example, to gain increased entry in the AUTOMOBILE INDUSTRY with the support of the United Automobile Workers.

The depression that caused so much havoc hit African Americans well before it descended upon the rest of the country. By the time the stock market crashed in 1929, many black workers were already experiencing hard times—and things then got worse, as black Americans were laid off from jobs in disproportionately high numbers. By 1932, half the black workers in the urban South were out of work. In 1934, roughly two of every five black workers were unemployed, twice the national level. Black farmers and farm workers in the South similarly saw a bad situation turn worse.

New Deal programs aided distressed blacks and reestablished federal government support of African Americans, though typically with limits and discrimination. The CIVILIAN CONSERVATION CORPS (CCC), for example, maintained segregated facilities but, nevertheless, employed young black men. The NATIONAL YOUTH ADMINISTRATION (NYA) had programs for black youths, though kept them separate from whites. The NATIONAL RECOVERY ADMINISTRATION (some blacks said NRA stood for "Negroes Ruined Again") countenanced racial disparities in wages. Agencies granting mortgages and business loans extended them to blacks with the proviso they live and operate in segregated areas. The Agricultural Adjustment Administration (AAA) gave little support to black farmers in the South. Blacks were included in New Deal RELIEF programs, though often the help given was not commensurate with need.

Given the status of race relations at the time, New Deal support of African Americans, limited and uneven though it may have been, provided an important start for government intervention on behalf of blacks. Racial discrimination in New Deal programs often came at the local level, in the North as well as the South, and New Deal officials found it difficult to overcome resistance—though many did not try. Important members of the Roosevelt administration, including Harold Ickes and HARRY HOPKINS, did, however, urge more attention to blacks and to racial prejudice, as did Eleanor Roosevelt.

World War II brought more and better jobs to black workers. First fired during the Depression, blacks were typically last hired during wartime economic MOBILIZATION, but the shortage of workers did eventually lead to their increased presence in the industrial work force. Roughly one million black men and women served in the armed forces, and the U.S. ARMY and U.S. NAVY began to relax some of the discrimination and segregation that

Shown here are Negro Air Corps cadets in an advanced flying class. *(National Archives)*

marked the wartime military. Black GIs fought with distinction under General GEORGE S. PATTON. Best known were the Tuskegee Airmen, the "Fighting 99th" Pursuit Squadron, organized in 1941, and the 332nd Fighter Group. Trained under separate and adverse conditions, these airmen proved their abilities time and again, both as escorts and active fighters. In Europe, the army experimented with platoon-level troop integration. Despite its success, the policy was largely abandoned until President Harry S. Truman desegregated the military.

On the home front, A. PHILIP RANDOLPH, president of the Brotherhood of Sleeping Car Porters, pressured Roosevelt to end discrimination in the defense mobilization effort with his 1941 MARCH ON WASHINGTON MOVEMENT (MOWM). Randolph threatened a march of as many as 100,000 black protestors in the nation's capital if the president did not take corrective action against discrimination in defense hiring and the armed forces. Not wanting international embarrassment, FDR issued EXECUTIVE ORDER 8802 in June 1941, banning discrimination in government

and government contractors and establishing the FAIR EMPLOYMENT PRACTICES COMMITTEE (FEPC) to enforce the order. The wartime labor shortage probably made more difference in increasing black employment, but these were important steps.

In other ways, too, black protest increased during the war. Such protest was fueled by the irony African Americans felt in the nation fighting a war against the Nazis and their master race philosophy under America's own system of racial supremacy. Black newspapers thus publicized the "Double-V" campaign—victory abroad over the AXIS but also victory at home over Jim Crow. The NAACP grew from 50,000 to 450,000 members during the war. Though some protest took place in the South, the renewed migration of blacks out of the rural South and toward the centers of defense industry in the North and on the West Coast gave blacks more opportunity for activism than in the repressive South. And given prejudice and discrimination in the North as well as the South, they had reason for protest.

Black-white tensions remained high, and sometimes increased, as African Americans moved to crowded war-boom cities. Municipal police forces often acted more like occupying armies in the "colored sections" of American cities. Whenever blacks left these ghettos, even for employment or school, they were regarded with suspicion and harassment. Vicious race riots broke out in 1943 that left many dead in Harlem and Detroit over discrimination that underscored the reluctance of white America to accede to any more than minimal racial opportunity. The massive and enormously important examination of America's racial problem in the 1944 two-volume study by the Swedish economist GUNNAR MYRDAL, *An American Dilemma,* put the onus for racial problems squarely on white shoulders and set the tone for racial inquiry for years to come.

The difficulties, disappointments, and frustrations of the Great Depression and World War II, and also the progress, changes, and hopes of the era, contributed to a surge of determination that World War II had provided the opportunity for equality for which blacks had long been waiting. The result was the postwar Civil Rights movement. The first signal accomplishment of the decades-long struggle to reverse legalized Jim Crow came with the unanimous Supreme Court decision in *Brown v. Board of Education* (1954) reversing *Plessy v. Ferguson* (1896) that had sanctioned racial segregation.

See also AGRICULTURAL ADJUSTMENT ACT; CITIES AND URBAN LIFE; POLITICS IN THE ROOSEVELT ERA; RACE AND RACIAL CONFLICT.

Further reading: Dan T. Carter, *Scottsboro: A Tragedy of the American South* (New York: Oxford University Press, 1969); Richard M. Dalfiume, *Desegregation of the U.S. Armed Forces: Fighting on Two Fronts, 1939–1953* (Columbia: University of Missouri Press, 1969); John Hope Franklin and Alfred A. Moss Jr, *From Slavery to Freedom: A History of Negro Americans,* 6th ed. (New York: Knopf, 1988); John B. Kirby, *Black Americans in the Roosevelt Era: Liberalism and Race* (Knoxville: University of Tennessee Press, 1980); Harvard Sitkoff, *A New Deal for Blacks: The Emergence of Civil Rights as a National Issue* (New York: Oxford University Press, 1978); Nancy J. Weiss, *Farewell to the Party of Lincoln: Black Politics in the Age of FDR* (Princeton, N.J.: Princeton University Press, 1983); Neil A. Wynn, *The Afro-American and the Second World War,* rev. ed. (New York: Holmes & Meier, 1993).

—Howard Smead

Agricultural Adjustment Act (1933)

President FRANKLIN D. ROOSEVELT signed the Agricultural Adjustment Act into law on May 12, 1933, during the first Hundred Days of the NEW DEAL. The resulting Agricul-

tural Adjustment Administration was, together with the NATIONAL RECOVERY ADMINISTRATION for industry, central to the effort of the FIRST NEW DEAL of 1933 to achieve economic recovery by means of planning and controls.

By 1933, American AGRICULTURE was in crisis. Overproduction and declining foreign markets after World War I had resulted in low prices and profits for American farmers during the 1920s. The 1929 AGRICULTURAL MARKETING ACT of the HOOVER PRESIDENCY proved unable to curtail production or protect prices, and then the GREAT DEPRESSION produced disastrous conditions for farmers. By 1933, farm income had fallen by some 60 percent from 1929, hundreds of thousands of farm mortgages were being foreclosed, and small farmers were in an especially desperate situation. The farmers' plight had become so desperate that loud and sometimes violent protests erupted throughout rural America, and a number of agricultural states passed moratorium laws preventing farm foreclosures.

With farmers roughly one-fourth of the work force and agriculture vital to the nation's ECONOMY, a variety of solutions were suggested to ease the farmer's plight. One idea was to use the protective tariff to reserve the U.S. agricultural market for American farmers, and have a government agency "dump" surplus crops onto foreign markets. A second idea was simply to have farmers cut back on production in order to free themselves from surpluses that depressed prices, with the federal GOVERNMENT "advising" the agricultural sector. Some argued for currency inflation to raise the price of farm goods. Montana State College economist M. L. Wilson offered another approach, the domestic allotment plan, in which the federal government would pay farmers who voluntarily reduced acreage of certain crops and would finance the program by taxing the processors of farm products.

Roosevelt and his incoming administration had a particular concern about agriculture in order to achieve a balanced economy and restore prosperity. FDR had endorsed the domestic allotment plan during the ELECTION OF 1932, influenced by agricultural advisers HENRY A. WALLACE and REXFORD G. TUGWELL. After his election, Roosevelt met with farm leaders, expressed his support for wide-ranging agricultural legislation, and directed Wallace to draft a bill for introduction into CONGRESS. Wallace drew up legislation that incorporated a variety of approaches, and soon after its submission in March, the House of Representatives passed the bill without change. To head off efforts by Senate inflationists to include the unlimited coinage of silver in the bill, Roosevelt endorsed legislation introduced by Democratic senator Elmer Thomas of Oklahoma giving discretionary authority to increase the money supply by reducing the gold content of the dollar, by coining silver, or by issuing up to $3 billion in paper money not backed by precious metal of any kind. With the Thomas amendment, Congress passed the Agricultural Adjustment Act on April 28, 1933, and Roosevelt signed the bill on May 12.

The Agricultural Adjustment Act had three sections. Title I was the domestic allotment plan, in which the government entered into agreements with growers of basic commodities (corn, cotton, hogs, milk, rice, tobacco, wheat) to reduce production. Producers would receive a "parity" price, which provided the same purchasing power farmers had enjoyed during the so-called golden age of agriculture from 1909 to 1914. This would be financed initially by $100 million and then by taxes on farm processors (millers, canners, and the like). Title II provided for federally funded emergency, low-interest mortgage payments to farmers who faced foreclosure and eviction from their homes and land, an issue of immediate importance because of growing agricultural debt, attempts to "stave off the sheriff," and threats of a nationwide farmers' strike. Title III incorporated the Thomas amendment, and in addition, the bill created the Agricultural Adjustment Administration (AAA), which would oversee New Deal farm policy.

Secretary of Agriculture Henry Wallace named George N. Peek, a farm implements manufacturer who had championed the plan to dump farm surpluses abroad, as AAA administrator. Following disagreements with Wallace over AAA policy, Peek was fired in December 1933 and replaced by Chester Davis, who supported the acreage reduction approach. By 1934, more than three million farmers were participating in AAA programs, organized into more than 4,000 local associations at the county level, especially in Midwestern states, to implement production controls. Together with other New Deal farm programs—the FARM CREDIT ADMINISTRATION to save farm mortgages, for example—the AAA helped stabilize American agriculture.

From the beginning, however, the AAA was embroiled in controversy involving both external criticism and internal dissension. With AAA payments going largely to big farmers and landlords, who often took land out of production that was being farmed by tenants, sharecroppers, and other small farmers, a number of critics complained that the AAA ignored suffering small farmers. NORMAN THOMAS, other SOCIALISTS, and the SOUTHERN TENANT FARMERS UNION that they helped found, criticized the AAA for neglecting the rural Southern poor, especially sharecroppers. Inside the AAA, a group of liberal reformers led by Legal Division head Jerome Frank attempted to shift policy to give more help to tenant farmers but were fired in 1935 by Chester Davis, who feared alienating big farmers and their powerful (largely southern) allies in Congress.

Critics of the AAA also included agricultural processors, who objected to the processing tax. The constitutionality of the levy was at issue when the SUPREME COURT, in January 1936, struck down the processing tax— and the Agricultural Adjustment Act itself—ruling that such a tax was an improper exercise of the federal government's power. The Court also held that agriculture was local production and did not fall under the regulatory power of Congress, which had authority only over interstate commerce, not local production or intrastate commerce.

Congress moved quickly to pass a new farm bill in 1936, the Soil Conservation and Domestic Allotment Act, that provided benefits to farmers who practiced soil conservation (and limited the production of staple cash crops) by growing such soil-building crops as grasses rather than soil-depleting crops like wheat and cotton. In 1938, Congress passed another Agricultural Adjustment Act, which eliminated processing taxes, allowed compulsory production controls (if they were approved by the farmers themselves), established the ever-normal granary plan allowing the government to advance loans on surplus crops at prices slightly below parity levels, and implemented federal crop insurance.

Though the Agricultural Adjustment Act helped big farmers more than small ones and though the recovery of farm prices and the agricultural sector owed at least as much to drought and then to heightened demand during WORLD WAR II as it did to AAA policy, the Agricultural Adjustment Act of 1933 and its successors laid the foundations for American farm policy in the postwar era.

Further reading: Van L. Perkins, *Crisis in Agriculture: The Agricultural Adjustment Administration and the New Deal* (Berkeley: University of California Press, 1964); Theodore Saloutos, *The American Farmer and the New Deal* (Ames: Iowa State University Press, 1982).

—William J. Thompson

Agricultural Marketing Act (1929)

The Agricultural Marketing Act of 1929 was the effort, ultimately unsuccessful, of the HOOVER PRESIDENCY to solve the problem of overproduction and declining prices that had afflicted American AGRICULTURE in the 1920s.

As he had promised during his 1928 campaign for the White House, President HERBERT C. HOOVER made addressing the farm problem one of the priorities of his administration. He convened a special session of CONGRESS in April 1929 and asked for a new agricultural policy, but one that would not rely on GOVERNMENT taxes and subsidies as had the proposed McNary-Haugen bills of the 1920s. Consistent with his philosophy of government, Hoover also wanted a farm policy that rested upon private and voluntary efforts, with government providing assistance but not imposing controls.

On June 15, the Agricultural Marketing Act was signed into law. It created a Federal Farm Board, funded at $500 million, to provide technical assistance to farmers and to lend money to support existing agricultural cooperatives and establish new ones. The cooperatives could buy equipment more cheaply than individual farmers; they could coordinate voluntary production agreements among farmers; and they could manage sales to keep prices up and middlemen charges down. The cooperatives could also form crop stabilization corporations that were eligible for Farm Board loans to enable them to buy surplus crops, store them, and put them on the market in an orderly fashion that would keep prices as high as possible.

The Agricultural Marketing Act was a creative and unprecedented effort to address the problems of farmers, and one that avoided direct government intervention to curtail production or support prices. Yet it failed because it lacked adequate power over production—and also sufficient funds for the stabilization corporations to take the mounting farm surpluses off the market, despite what seemed the huge sum of $500 million. The situation was made more difficult by the fact that in such staple crops as wheat and cotton there was a glut on the world, not just the national, market. American farmers (and also those abroad) continued to produce at high levels, the onset of the GREAT DEPRESSION reduced consumer spending, and the Farm Board's resources were soon overwhelmed. In 1931, the Farm Board and key stabilization corporations abandoned efforts to keep surpluses off the markets. Prices plunged still further, and the crisis in agriculture grew worse. With the defeat of Hoover in the ELECTION OF 1932, it fell to the new president, FRANKLIN D. ROOSEVELT, and the AGRICULTURAL ADJUSTMENT ACT of 1933 to deal with the problem of farm production and farm prices.

Further reading: David E. Hamilton, *From New Day to New Deal: American Farm Policy from Hoover to Roosevelt, 1928–1933* (Chapel Hill: University of North Carolina Press, 1991).

agriculture

The period from 1929 to 1945 brought major changes to American agriculture. The onset of the GREAT DEPRESSION dramatically worsened the difficulties that many American farmers had experienced in the 1920s. From 1929 to 1933, despite efforts of the HOOVER PRESIDENCY, farm income plummeted and small farmers in particular experienced great hardship. The AGRICULTURAL ADJUSTMENT ACT and other NEW DEAL measures provided assistance and created a new and permanent role of the federal GOVERNMENT in agriculture. WORLD WAR II then brought recovery to the agricultural sector as well as to the ECONOMY overall. The events of the depression and the war also hastened MIGRATION out of rural America, spurred technological change, and augmented the economic and political power of large agribusiness. Thus, in a number of ways, American agriculture was significantly different in 1945 from what it had been in 1929.

When the Great Depression struck in 1929, many farmers were already suffering from hard times that had marked much of the 1920s. After World War I, increased domestic agricultural production, growing competition in world markets, and declining demand for American agricultural products, combined to drive many agricultural prices, especially in such staple products as cotton and wheat, to extremely low levels. Farmers who saw their incomes shrink typically attempted to make up the difference by increasing production, which, in the absence of new markets, only drove down prices even further. Many small farmers had difficulties paying taxes and mortgages, and foreclosures and tenancy increased.

By the mid-1920s, most analysts realized that the best way to increase agricultural prices was to reduce or eliminate the growing agricultural surpluses. CONGRESS twice passed versions of the McNary-Haugen bill, designed to reduce agricultural surpluses and raise domestic prices by creating a government corporation to purchase surplus agricultural products and sell them on the world market at greatly reduced prices. President Calvin Coolidge vetoed both McNary-Haugen bills on the grounds that they involved improper federal subsidy of agriculture and would invite economic retaliation from other nations.

Coolidge's successor, President HERBERT C. HOOVER, then made the agricultural problem an early top priority of his administration. In June 1929, Hoover signed the AGRICULTURAL MARKETING ACT, which authorized the president to appoint a Federal Farm Board, funded at $500 million, to help farmers create marketing cooperatives that might regulate production and sales of farm goods and thus keep prices up. Although the legislation marked a significant new departure, it relied upon voluntary action by farmers and lacked sufficient funds. Production therefore continued to rise and commodity prices and farmer incomes continued to fall—disastrously so, once the depression hit.

The net income of American farmers plummeted from $7 billion in 1929 to only $2.5 billion in 1932. By 1930, more than 25 percent of farmers produced less than $600 worth of farm products a year, and an even higher percentage lived in primitive and isolated conditions. Few farmers even had electricity or running water. Farm tenancy rose sharply again in the early 1930s with new waves of foreclosures because of farmers' inability to pay their taxes and mortgages. By 1933, banks were foreclosing on some 20,000 farm mortgages monthly, and thousands of small, undercapitalized country banks had failed, while thousands were barely solvent. With farmer incomes dropping and with land values down by 40 percent, the chances that farmers would be able to secure additional sources of funding quickly vanished. As the Great Depression worsened, farmers experienced abandoned homesteads, collapsing prices, longer working hours, buildings and equipment in disrepair, a lack of cash or credit, and a rising wave of political discontent.

By the time FRANKLIN D. ROOSEVELT assumed the presidency in March 1933, the economic crisis of American agriculture had thus reached crisis proportions. The centerpiece of the New Deal agricultural policy of Roosevelt and Secretary of Agriculture HENRY A. WALLACE was the Agricultural Adjustment Administration (AAA). Created in 1933 by the Agricultural Adjustment Act, this agency attempted to raise agricultural prices to what was called "parity." This meant that prices of agricultural and non-agricultural goods would have the same relation as they did in the "golden age of agriculture" baseline years from 1909 to 1914, and thus farmers would gain more actual purchasing power. To accomplish this, the AAA made benefit payments to farmers for limiting acreage under production—in effect paying farmers not to produce the surpluses as well as raising prices by limiting production. AAA helped reduce surpluses and raise prices, though it assisted large farmers more than small ones, and tenants, sharecroppers, and farm laborers often got little or no help.

In January 1936, the SUPREME COURT invalidated the Agricultural Adjustment Act, on grounds that the processing tax used to raise money for the benefit payments was unconstitutional and that agricultural production was local production beyond the power of the federal government to regulate. In February 1936, Congress responded by passing the Soil Conservation and Domestic Allotment Act, which paid farmers to take land out of production—but ostensibly to conserve soil, not limit production—with the money to come from the government's general fund rather than from a processing tax.

In February 1938, Congress passed another Agricultural Adjustment Act. This new law expanded the soil conservation programs under the Soil Conservation and Domestic Allotment Act. It offered crop insurance to wheat producers to protect them against drought, and gave the secretary of agriculture power to authorize crop loans and impose marketing quotas. It also approved the idea of Secretary of Agriculture Wallace to develop an "ever-normal granary," which would be used to store surplus crops, thereby taking surpluses off the market and ensuring adequate food in the event of a crop failure.

A number of other New Deal programs also sought to help farmers. In May 1933, President Roosevelt created

the FARM CREDIT ADMINISTRATION to help increase the amount of credit available to farmers and make it easier for farmers to pay off debts. That same month Congress established the TENNESSEE VALLEY AUTHORITY, which built dams, improved flood control, implemented better land-use practices, and brought cheap hydroelectric power to farmers in the Tennessee Valley. In October 1933, the president created the Commodity Credit Corporation, which allowed farmers to borrow money from the federal government with the understanding that if commodity prices did not rise, the government would take a farmer's crops in lieu of the unpaid loans and would still be willing to lend money to the farmer in the following year.

In April 1935, Roosevelt established the RESETTLEMENT ADMINISTRATION to relocate struggling farmers from submarginal land that had been depleted by overfarming, mining, and drought, to new land with fertile soil. In 1937, the Resettlement Administration was absorbed into the FARM SECURITY ADMINISTRATION, which also provided farmers with debt reduction assistance, technical support, and loans to buy land or equipment. The RURAL ELECTRIFICATION ADMINISTRATION, which the president established in May 1935, brought electrical power to millions of farmers by making low interest loans to private electrical companies if they agreed to extend their power lines into thinly populated rural areas.

Ultimately, the expansion of electric service revolutionized life in rural America. In 1934, only 10 percent of American farms had electricity; by 1950, more than 90 percent did. Nonetheless, chronic difficulties, the depression, the DUST BOWL, and then the new industrial jobs produced by World War II led to a significant migration of people from rural to urban America that reinforced the long-term redistribution of the population toward urban areas. From 1930 to 1950, the number of people working in agriculture fell from 10.3 million to 7.5 million—and from 23 percent to 12 percent of the nation's workers.

Advances in SCIENCE, TECHNOLOGY, and MEDICINE AND PUBLIC HEALTH in the 1929–45 era helped to resolve problems that had long beset agriculture. Traditionally, farmers could only watch as diseases killed their animals and crops, insects ate their harvests, and weeds overtook their pastures. Drought, frost, or storms could easily destroy an entire year's harvest in a matter of days. These situations cost American farmers millions of dollars each year, and for the growing number of farmers living on the verge of financial ruin in the 1930s, a natural disaster could easily mean the difference between impoverishment and economic prosperity.

In 1928, Alexander Fleming discovered penicillin, which by the end of World War II had replaced sulfa drugs as the principal antibiotic used in America and allowed the United States to bring under control many diseases, such as bovine tuberculosis, that had ravaged livestock as well as people for centuries. In 1943, a Swiss company also introduced the insecticide DDT to America, and two years later, the United States began marketing the herbicide 2,4-dichlorophenoxyacetic acid (shortened to 2,4,-D in 1945). Furthermore, the development of better plant varieties and fertilizers allowed American farmers to double, and in some cases even triple, the yields of some crops. Improved livestock care and breeding techniques also increased the amount of meat and milk animals produced. And the use of tractors and other labor-saving devices not only sharply reduced the need for manual labor, but also reduced the time needed for planting, harvesting, and general upkeep—and contributed to the migration of farm workers from rural to urban areas.

Lastly, advances in TRANSPORTATION—along with new food processing techniques, such as the large-scale use of metal cans and frozen foods—made it easier to preserve food for long trips. This helped to produce new food distribution methods, such as the emergence of large supermarket chains, as well as changes in the nation's diet. Because of these transformations, agricultural production continued to rise even as the number of people engaged in agriculture continued to fall. By the end of World War II, a farmer in the United States could produce enough food to feed 12 people, up from only 7 people in 1910.

World War II had a powerful impact on American agriculture. Millions of poor farmers looking for new opportunities left the farm and entered the military or took jobs in the nation's rapidly growing defense plants and shipyards. Moreover, after years of urging farmers to reduce production, the government, using draft exemptions as well as subsidies and exhortation, now found it necessary to encourage farmers to increase production in order to ensure that America had enough food for military and civilian needs. Indeed, the war did what two decades of federal farm policies had been unable to do—eliminate agricultural surpluses and raise commodity prices.

Congress passed the LEND-LEASE ACT in March 1941, which sent Great Britain much-needed food and material. In May 1941, Great Britain and the United States formed the Anglo-American Food Committee, and in June 1942, the Combined Food Board, to coordinate food shipments to the Allies. Soon the federal government became the chief food buyer in the United States. The rise in demand caused agricultural prices to rise sharply during the war, and farm income more than doubled. For the first time since World War I, American farmers enjoyed the financial freedom to pay off debts, restore their credit, purchase needed and wanted goods, and put money in the bank.

However, most farmers remembered how agricultural surpluses after World War I had driven down commodity prices, and wanted some assurance that they would be pro-tected from falling prices at the end of the war. Congress provided the first of many such assurances in May 1941 when Senator John H. Bankhead of Alabama pushed an amendment through Congress guaranteeing farmers that prices for corn, wheat, cotton, rice, and tobacco would be at least 85 percent of what they had been during the AAA's "parity" baseline years. Two months later, Congress extended this guarantee to include all agricultural goods produced for the war effort. The U.S. government also used cash incentives and subsidies to encourage farmers to produce scarce commodities and keep the cost of living down. Nevertheless, because the need for food was so high and supply could not keep up with demand, the government used price controls to combat inflation—though, pressured by the "farm bloc," Congress exempted farm goods from price controls until they had reached 110 percent of the parity level.

Traditionally, rural poverty has been a chronic problem in the United States. But the economic developments of the depression and World War II together with new federal programs begun by the New Deal helped raise commodity prices and lift millions of rural people out of poverty, often by means of migration to metropolitan areas. After World War II, Washington continued to play an important and increasing role in American food production as new challenges and changing world markets began to confront American farmers.

Further reading: Gilbert Fite, *American Farmers: The New Minority* (Bloomington: University of Indiana Press, 1981); David Hamilton, *From New Deal to New Deal: American Farm Policy from Hoover to Roosevelt, 1928–1933* (Chapel Hill: University of North Carolina Press, 1991); Richard S. Kirkendall, *Social Scientists and Farm Politics in the Age of Roosevelt* (Columbia: University of Missouri Press, 1982); Theodore Saloutos, *The American Farmer and the New Deal* (Ames: Iowa State University Press, 1982); Walter Wilcox, *The Farmer in the Second World War* (Ames: Iowa State University Press, 1947); Donald Worster, *Dust Bowl: The Southern Plains in the 1930s* (New York: Oxford University Press, 1979).

—David W. Waltrop

aircraft industry

After the growth of aviation for both business and pleasure during the 1920s, the aircraft industry was hit hard by the onset of the GREAT DEPRESSION. Passenger travel nonetheless increased during the decade, and as WORLD WAR II approached, growing military demands for aircraft began the enormous wartime expansion of the industry. By the end of World War II, the importance of AIR POWER in modern warfare had been established, and aviation was poised to become an increasingly important component of American TRANSPORTATION.

The so-called Lindbergh Boom in the civil aircraft industry, associated with the famous transatlantic flight, peaked in 1929. Just a few years later, many aircraft manufacturers were bankrupt, and the total value of industry production plummeted from $91 million in 1929 to $33 million in 1933. GOVERNMENT policy then played an increasingly important part in the operations of the aircraft and airline industries during the 1930s. Government mail contracts were a major source of airline revenue, and the military purchases helped sustain aircraft production. New technologies developed by the National Advisory Committee for Aeronautics brought improvements in aircraft manufacturing. Better airframe construction enabled airlines to expand their passenger business and rely less on government contracts. In 1938, the federal government established the Civil Aeronautics Authority to oversee aviation, while the government also built and operated ground facilities for air traffic control.

By the late 1930s, the aircraft industry had begun to recover economically. The value of industry production increased to nearly $200 million in 1938 and $370 million by 1940. This was due in part to increased passenger travel, which grew from fewer than 400,000 passengers in 1930 to more than 2.5 million in 1940. In the mid-1930s, Douglas Aircraft began producing the venerable DC-3 airliner, which accounted for the great majority of air passengers by the end of the decade. But by 1940, the rise in industry sales came mostly from the demand for military aircraft. In November 1938, President FRANKLIN D. ROOSEVELT told advisers that he wanted the aircraft industry to expand production to supply the British and the French and to provide the American air corps with 10,000 aircraft. Despite criticisms from ISOLATIONISTS and others worried about possible violations of the NEUTRALITY ACTS, American aviation helped meet the needs of the British and the French.

In January 1939, Roosevelt asked Congress for a $300 million special appropriation for aircraft construction, sig-

One of the most important World War II contractors was the Boeing Company of Seattle, Washington. In this photograph two assembly line workers are seen completing the fuselage framework of a B-17 Flying Fortress bomber. *(Library of Congress)*

naling the start of the American rearmament program. After the Nazi BLITZKRIEG overran western Europe in the spring of 1940, Roosevelt in May set a stunning production goal of 50,000 planes a year, in part to cover French and British requirements. Following PEARL HARBOR and American entry into the war, FDR increased his goals still further—to 60,000 aircraft in 1942 and 125,000 in 1943.

Although Roosevelt's goals at first seemed fantastic, the aircraft industry by the end of the war had produced some 300,000 aircraft—about the same number as Germany, Britain, and Japan combined. It took an unprecedented and monumental effort to reach such totals. Manufacturers had to expand current plants, create new facilities and production processes, subcontract smaller parts out to other industries, and recruit qualified workers. Dozens of new aircraft plants were created in the United States, many of them in the SUNBELT states. Cooperation within the aircraft industry in the sharing of manpower, materials, new techniques, and technologies also contributed to the remarkable production totals.

Though never matching the efficiency and productivity of HENRY J. KAISER in wartime SHIPBUILDING, Henry Ford conceived and carried out the creation of an enormous aircraft facility near Detroit in Willow Run, Michigan, that utilized the assembly line process. After early difficulties, "the Run" produced 500 bombers a month and at peak efficiency in 1944 could turn out a new B-24 Liberator bomber every 63 minutes. The standardization of parts in the industry allowed for certain components to be manufactured at smaller facilities and shipped for final assembly elsewhere. The switch to the assembly line process in aircraft plants not only increased efficiency and productivity but also allowed the use of unskilled and semiskilled workers.

As the value of industry production soared to $5.8 billion in 1942, $12.5 billion in 1943, and the wartime peak of $16 billion in 1944, employment within the aircraft industry burgeoned from some 50,000 in 1939 to over 2 million by 1943. AFRICAN AMERICANS comprised more than 6 percent of employees, while the employment of women, found to be highly efficient and more dexterous than men while welding in small spaces, increased to a peak of nearly one-half million. (Despite the enduring image of ROSIE THE RIVETER, relatively few women were trained as riveters or other higher-skilled jobs.) Facility managers counteracted low morale and high turnover among assembly line workers with the use of on-site nurseries, music, and lunchtime entertainment as well as appeals to patriotism.

Government planning for RECONVERSION helped cushion the impact of the war's end on aviation as it did for other industries in the early postwar period. The aircraft industry—which had effectively demonstrated the importance of air power, established the ease of air transport for passengers and cargo, and continued to create such new technologies as jet engines and helicopters—would continue to grow in size and importance in the postwar era.

See also ARMY AIR FORCES, U.S.

Further reading: Roger E. Bilstein, *Enterprise of Flight: The American Aviation and Aerospace Industry* (Washington, D.C.: Smithsonian Institution Press, 2001); Donald Pattillo, *Pushing the Envelope: The American Aircraft Industry* (Ann Arbor: University of Michigan Press, 1998).
                                        —Traci L. Siegler

air power

WORLD WAR II was the first conflict in history to see the daily use of strategic and tactical air power. Air power thus played a major role in the war, not only in support of ground operations but also in naval combat in the WORLD WAR II PACIFIC THEATER.

Japanese air forces, divided into army and naval forces, contained the most sophisticated aircraft in the world by 1941, and scored triumphs against the United States at PEARL HARBOR in December 1941, and during campaigns in the Pacific early in 1942. But Japan suffered major defeats at the hands of the U.S. NAVY at the BATTLE OF THE CORAL SEA in May 1942 and at the BATTLE OF MIDWAY in June 1942—encounters that underscored the new importance of air power in naval warfare, for the surface fleets never came in contact. The BATTLE OF THE PHILIPPINE SEA in 1944 brought the effective end of Japanese air power. The Japanese air forces, and Japan's smaller aircraft industry, were overwhelmed by more numerous and mobile American air forces to the point that air defenses of the home islands were practically nonexistent when the American bombing campaign began in mid-1944.

In the EUROPEAN THEATER, the Germans demonstrated air power in a ground support role in Poland in September 1939. The German Luftwaffe quickly destroyed the Polish air force, enabling attacks at will on depots, factories, transportation centers, and enemy forces. This same pattern, using aircraft as "flying artillery," was used in every German BLITZKRIEG campaign in Europe between 1940 and mid-1942. However, the BATTLE OF BRITAIN in 1940 and subsequent military operations severely strained the Luftwaffe, as did demands for home air defense after Allied bombings campaigns began in 1942. Although the Anglo-American strategic air campaigns encountered heavy Luftwaffe resistance, this threat ended by early 1944, as did Germany's ability to provide air support for German troops in the field.

The Allies developed sophisticated tactical air forces. As they prepared for the INVASION OF NORMANDY, the British Royal Air Force and the U.S. ARMY AIR FORCES gained air superiority over Europe and destroyed transportation and communications networks vital to counterattacking enemy forces. When the Normandy invasion took place, Anglo-American air power was overwhelming, numbering approximately 12,000 aircraft, compared to 300 Luftwaffe aircraft. On D day, the Allies flew 15,000 sorties, the Luftwaffe only 100. For the remainder of the war, Allied air forces controlled European skies.

The Anglo-American strategic air campaigns against Germany and Japan were controversial and involved questions of effectiveness versus costs in money, material, and manpower, as well as the military value and morality of bombing urban areas. The British began the strategic bombing of Germany in 1940, but discovered that daylight long-range missions were costly and bombing inaccurate, prompting the start of night areas attacks on nonindustrial targets. When the U.S. Eighth Army Air Force arrived in Britain in 1942, its leaders emphasized daylight precision bombing in the erroneous belief that B-17 Flying Fortresses, using the Norden bombsight, could obtain significant results with acceptable losses. They asserted bombers could reach and destroy "choke points" in the German economy that would shut down the enemy war effort. Operations against ball bearing plants in 1943 had little impact, but the discovery that petroleum was the vital "choke point" quickly brought Germany to grief. In addition, the early 1944 advent of long-range escort fighters such as the U.S. P-51 Mustang and the P-47 Thunderbolt assured the survival of the bomber and made the Allied Combined Bomber Offensive more lethal. Although it failed to destroy enemy morale, strategic bombing reduced war production, snarled transportation and communications, and diverted significant resources from the fronts to home defense. Allied raids killed an estimated 600,000 German civilians.

In the Pacific, American raids on Japan, using the B-29 Superfortress, had little effect until bases were established in the MARIANA ISLANDS, and carpet bombing with napalm was substituted for high-level bombing in March 1945. Between March and August 1945, an estimated 60 percent of Japan's urban areas were burned out, killing an estimated 500,000 people. In August 1945, American aircraft used the new ATOMIC BOMB on HIROSHIMA AND NAGASAKI and World War II came to an end.

A country's capacity for developing air power depended on the availability of a large industrial base, scientific and technical knowledge, a skilled workforce, secure training and base areas, and ample raw materials and fuel. Between 1939 and 1945, the United States, with its productive AIRCRAFT INDUSTRY, produced some 300,000 aircraft. During the same period, the Soviet Union produced 157,000 aircraft; the United Kingdom, 131,000; Germany, 120,000; and Japan, 77,000. Aircraft losses were greatest for Germany (95,000), followed by the Soviet Union, the United States (59,000), Japan (49,000), and Great Britain (49,000).

Further reading: John Buckley, *Air Power in the Age of Total War* (Bloomington: Indiana University Press, 1999); Conrad C. Crane, *Bombs, Cities, and Civilians: American Air Power Strategy in World War II* (Lawrence: University of Kansas Press, 1993); Michael Sherry, *The Rise of American Air Power: The Creation of Armageddon* (New Haven, Conn.: Yale University Press, 1987).

—Clayton D. Laurie

America First Committee

The America First Committee was the most prominent organization opposing American intervention in Europe and the Pacific and challenging the FOREIGN POLICY of President FRANKLIN D. ROOSEVELT during the 15 months leading up to PEARL HARBOR and the U.S. entry into WORLD WAR II. It was the brainchild of R. Douglas Stuart, Jr., a Yale Law School student, who during the summer of 1940 enlisted the support of a number of businessmen and politicians, primarily from the Midwest, where ISOLATIONISTS were especially numerous.

The formation of the America First Committee was announced in Chicago on September 4, 1940, following the announcement of the DESTROYERS-FOR-BASES DEAL with England. General Robert E. Wood, the chairman of the board of Sears, Roebuck, & Company, became the national chairman; Stuart became the national director; and a five-member executive committee, mostly of midwestern businessmen, was established. A larger national committee included such prominent individuals as Alice Roosevelt Longworth, the daughter of Theodore Roosevelt; George N. Peek, the former head of the Agricultural Adjustment Administration; Eddie Rickenbacker, the noted aviator and World War I flying ace; and Lillian Gish, the famous silent film actress. Henry Ford served on the national committee for several months, but was dropped by America First because of his suspected ANTI-SEMITISM. The celebrated aviator Charles A. Lindbergh became a national committee member in April 1941, after declining an offer to replace Wood as chairman.

Many prominent Americans in business, labor, and politics spoke at America First rallies and lent their names to committee activities. The list included HERBERT C. HOOVER, BURTON K. WHEELER, Gerald P. Nye (chairman of the NYE COMMITTEE), ROBERT M. LA FOLLETTE, JR., NORMAN THOMAS, HUGH S. JOHNSON, and JOHN L. LEWIS. While most America First members and their allies were affiliated with the REPUBLICAN PARTY, a broad range of political ideologies were represented, including neofascists, members of the DEMOCRATIC PARTY, SOCIALISTS, and even a few COMMUNISTS. At its peak, the America First Committee had a membership of between 800,000 and 850,000, with the greatest concentration of members in the Midwest—especially within a 300-mile radius of Chicago. It was weakest in the interventionist SOUTH.

To the embarrassment of many America First leaders, the committee, its local chapters, and its activities, attracted some neo-Nazi elements, as well as followers of the vitriolic radio priest FATHER CHARLES E. COUGHLIN. Opponents of America First, including the Roosevelt administration, accused the committee of being a "Nazi transmission belt." Roosevelt himself authorized wiretaps and FEDERAL BUREAU OF INVESTIGATION probes and urged his attorney general to investigate the America First Committee. While most members of America First were loyal, patriotic Americans who hated German tyranny, doubts lingered, especially after Lindbergh gave an inflammatory and, some believed, anti-Semitic speech under committee auspices at Des Moines, Iowa, in September 1941.

The America First Committee believed that it was more important for the United States to stay out of the European conflict than to assist a British victory over the AXIS powers. In early 1941, the America First Committee fought vigorously against LEND-LEASE ACT aid to Great Britain. After Roosevelt signed the Lend-Lease bill, the America First Committee opposed naval escorts for shipping convoys across the Atlantic Ocean, fearing that the sinking of American vessels would draw the nation into war. The committee also objected to sending U.S. military draftees outside the Western Hemisphere. Unsuccessful in those efforts, the America First Committee also failed to prevent the repeal of the provisions of the NEUTRALITY ACTS forbidding the arming of American vessels and allowing them access to belligerent ports.

The America First Committee nonetheless continued its efforts up until the attack on Pearl Harbor on December 7, 1941. Over the next month, the America First Committee ceased all noninterventionist activity, postponing rallies and halting the distribution of literature, and the national committee voted to dissolve the organization. By April 1942, the America First Committee had ceased to exist.

Further reading: Wayne S. Cole, *America First: The Battle against Intervention, 1940–1941* (Madison: University of Wisconsin Press, 1953).

—William J. Thompson

American Civil Liberties Union (ACLU)

In 1920, members of the National Civil Liberties Bureau, which had defended conscientious objectors and other dissidents in World War I, founded the American Civil Liber-
ties Union. For most of the 1920s, the ACLU was a small group of lawyers and other activists that fought primarily for freedom of political speech and occasionally for academic freedom, as in the famous Scopes trial of 1925. In 1929, the ACLU began contesting limits on other types of expression, such as CENSORSHIP of books and MOVIES.

Throughout the 1930s and 1940s, the ACLU's conception of CIVIL LIBERTIES became even broader and went beyond first amendment rights. The organization became especially active in cases involving issues of race and minority rights. In 1932, it issued a report entitled "Black Justice," which detailed the extent of institutional racism in America, and it took part in *Powell v. Alabama,* a U.S. SUPREME COURT case that arose out of the SCOTTSBORO BOYS incident. In 1934, the ACLU lobbied for the INDIAN REORGANIZATION ACT. During WORLD WAR II, it opposed the relocation of JAPANESE AMERICANS on the basis of race and argued for the desegregation of the armed forces.

At the same time, the ACLU continued to defend political dissenters in the 1930s and 1940s. For example, it fought the loyalty oaths required of teachers by law in more than 20 states. The organization opposed the Alien Registration Act (known as the SMITH ACT) of 1940, which required all resident aliens to be fingerprinted and made it illegal to advocate violent overthrow of the U.S. GOVERNMENT. It also defended American Nazi groups' right to rally. Though it did not oppose the SELECTIVE SERVICE system, it did fight for the rights of CONSCIENTIOUS OBJECTORS in various court cases.

In other instances, the positions adopted by the ACLU sometimes seemed to contradict its professed ideals. In 1940, for example, the ACLU declared that persons belonging to "political organizations that support totalitarian governments" could no longer serve on any of its committees, a stipulation many considered analogous to the loyalty oaths previously denounced by the organization. And while ACLU lawyers represented Japanese Americans who claimed that internment during World War II was based on their race, and therefore illegal, they did not, as a group, challenge the constitutionality of EXECUTIVE ORDER 9066.

Despite being criticized by some for being too radical and by others for being too timid, the ACLU was an important organization in the 1930s and 1940s. Most significant were its efforts to prevent a repeat of the widespread abuses of civil liberties that had occurred during World War I and its willingness to broach the subject of racial injustice at a time when few Americans would.

Further reading: Samuel Walker, *In Defense of American Liberties: A History of the ACLU* (New York: Oxford University Press, 1990).

—Pamela J. Lauer

American Federation of Labor (AFL)

The American Federation of Labor (AFL), had long been the preeminent LABOR organization by the onset of the GREAT DEPRESSION. Founded in 1886 and led until his death in 1924 by Samuel Gompers, the AFL was an association of craft unions, including carpenters, clothing and garment workers, electricians, machinists, meat cutters, and teamsters, along with coal miners.

The AFL shunned radical politics in favor of conservative unionism, which emphasized volunteerism without GOVERNMENT interference in labor-management relations, and focused on the bread and butter goals of wages, hours, and working conditions of union members. Its membership primarily comprised native-born, "old-stock" skilled craftsmen, rather than the "new-immigrant" (southern and eastern European) and African American unskilled workers who toiled in mass production industries such as automobiles, coal, and steel. In the heavy industries where the AFL had a presence, they impeded organizing, prevented strikes, and often ignored workers. The 1920s were not good years for organized labor, as prosperity, the hostility of BUSINESS toward workers, government sympathy toward employers, and the rigidity of the AFL's leadership, helped thin the ranks to less than 3 million members on the eve of the Great Depression.

Important AFL leaders, including its president, William Green, and JOHN L. LEWIS, had backed HERBERT C. HOOVER for president in 1928 and 1932. However, the election of FRANKLIN D. ROOSEVELT in 1932, and then such NEW DEAL legislation as the NATIONAL INDUSTRIAL RECOVERY ACT and the NATIONAL LABOR RELATIONS ACT, shifted labor support to the DEMOCRATIC PARTY. In the ELECTION OF 1936, AFL unions contributed significant amounts of money to Roosevelt and the Democrats and union members voted overwhelmingly Democratic.

By the mid-1930s, however, conflict was growing within the labor movement between the craft unionists, who wanted workers organized according to skill, and leaders like Lewis and SIDNEY HILLMAN, who believed in "industrial unionism"—gathering *all* workers in an industry into a single union. The tensions within the AFL reached a boiling point at the federation's convention in October 1935. There, Lewis appealed to the delegates that they had a duty to support the struggling unions in the mass production industries because the labor movement, he said, was founded on the principle that "the strong shall help the weak." A resolution demanding industrial unionism in the AFL was decisively defeated, and Lewis got into a fistfight with "Big Bill" Hutcheson, the head of the carpenters' union.

On November 4, 1935, Lewis, Hillman, and several other union leaders met and formed the Committee for Industrial Organization, originally intended to be a branch within the AFL. The AFL leadership, however, opposed the organizational efforts by the committee in the mass production industries, and suspended 10 dissident unions in 1937. A year later, in November 1938, Lewis, Hillman, and the other suspended unionists broke away from the AFL, and formed a separate labor federation, the CONGRESS OF INDUSTRIAL ORGANIZATIONS (CIO).

Hostilities between the two groups persisted as the AFL began a "counterreformation," claiming to be the honest union, rather than the "radical-infested" CIO—points they made by testifying before the House Un-American Activities Committee and urging boycotts of CIO-made products. Between 1937 and 1945, the AFL claimed nearly 4 million new members, more than the CIO over the same period, and enjoyed remarkable growth in nonmanufacturing industries such as transportation, communication, construction, hotel, restaurant, and retail, and public service workers.

The onset of WORLD WAR II did not end the hostility between the two labor federations, despite efforts by some union leaders and Democratic Party politicians. Conflict occurred in defense industries such as aircraft and electrical plants, and the AFL was accused of red-baiting, corruption, and being cozy with business. Competition between the AFL and CIO continued after the war, until the two organizations came to a merger agreement as the AFL-CIO in 1955.

See also POLITICS IN THE ROOSEVELT ERA.

Further reading: Irving Bernstein, *The Turbulent Years: A History of the American Worker, 1933–1941* (Boston: Houghton Mifflin, 1969); Philip Taft, *The AFL: From the Death of Gompers to the Merger*, rev. ed. (New York: Octagon, 1970).

—William J. Thompson

American Liberty League

In August 1934, a number of conservative Democrats joined with important businessmen to form the American Liberty League for the purpose of opposing President FRANKLIN D. ROOSEVELT and the NEW DEAL. The Liberty League argued that the New Deal was an unconstitutional effort to enlarge GOVERNMENT and regulate BUSINESS and that it would impede recovery from the GREAT DEPRESSION and harm the nation's ECONOMY and political system. A significant voice of CONSERVATISM in the 1930s, this well-financed organization used speeches and publications to promote its message, but it never gained many followers and disbanded in 1940.

The league's leadership came largely from wealthy businessmen and members of the DEMOCRATIC PARTY who were unhappy with Roosevelt and the New Deal. The Du Pont family provided about one-third of the League's funding, but such major businessmen as Alfred Sloan of General Motors, Edward F. Hutton of General Foods, Sewell L. Avery of Montgomery Ward, and Nathan Miller of U.S. Steel contributed as well. Important conservative Democrats, including 1928 Democratic presidential candidate Al Smith, former Democratic Party chairman John J. Raskob, and 1924 Democratic presidential candidate John W. Davis, also joined the League and played important roles.

Though claiming to be nonpartisan and nonpolitical, the league spoke out against Roosevelt, New Deal programs and many of the people Roosevelt brought to government. Jouett Shouse, a former chairman of the Democratic Party Executive Committee who headed the Liberty League, explained that the league's goal was "to defend and uphold the Constitution, . . . [to] teach the duty of government to encourage and protect individual and group initiative and enterprise, to foster the right to work, earn, save, and acquire property and to preserve the ownership and lawful use of property when acquired." In league speeches and publications Roosevelt was characterized as a tyrant and the New Deal was characterized as fascistic, socialistic, or communistic. (Roosevelt said that the league seemed to him like a group formed to support just two or three of the Ten Commandments.)

In 1936, the Liberty League focused on unseating Roosevelt in that year's presidential election. At a league dinner in Washington, D.C., on January 25, 1936, Al Smith gave the keynote address, in which he accused the New Deal of causing class warfare and betraying both the Democratic platform of 1932 and the United States Constitution. He said that "there can be only one capital, Washington or Moscow." The Roosevelt administration turned this speech on the league, arguing that the league was merely representing big business and their selfish interests.

In the ELECTION OF 1936, the league supported REPUBLICAN PARTY presidential candidate ALFRED M. LANDON, who saw its endorsement as a liability. The league's membership (at its peak, reportedly 125,000) fell off following the landslide reelection of Roosevelt in 1936, and the league stopped its public activities and disbanded within a few years.

Further reading: George Wolfskill, *The Revolt of the Conservatives: A History of the American Liberty League, 1934–1940* (Boston: Houghton Mifflin, 1962).
— Edwin C. Cogswell

amphibious warfare

During WORLD WAR II, amphibious warfare, the practice of invading enemy-held territory from the sea by transporting troops, along with armor, artillery, and all material to sustain short-term operations, and then securing a beachhead, became a new operational art. Requiring the full integration of air, land, and sea forces, it also depended upon a degree of planning, organization, technical and operational competence, and flexibility of command and control rarely seen prior to 1942. Although methods were initially crude, by 1945 the art of amphibious warfare was brought to near perfection, especially by the U.S. MARINES and the U.S. ARMY. Although Japan and Germany carried out limited amphibious assaults between 1937 and 1942, it was the United States that first created a specific amphibious warfare doctrine, with specialized troops, landing craft, weapons, and equipment.

The U.S. Marine Corps began amphibious warfare experiments in the 1930s and subsequently tailored its weapons and units to fit the naval ships then under construction. In addition, the marines experimented with landing craft, based on the American Higgins boat, and with amphibious tracked vehicles and other larger types of craft developed in Britain. The marines also developed the concept of combat loading, ship-to-shore artillery support, as well as close air support. All six U.S. Marine divisions during World War II were trained in amphibious assault tactics, and marine instructors trained U.S. Army divisions that were used in the landings of the NORTH AFRICAN CAMPAIGN, at SICILY, in the ITALIAN CAMPAIGN, in the INVASION OF NORMANDY, and at the Aleutians, New Guinea, the PHILIPPINES, and OKINAWA.

The drive of the U.S. NAVY and Marine Corps across the central Pacific against Japan in the WORLD WAR II PACIFIC THEATER started with the assault on TARAWA in the Gilbert Islands in November 1943, which demonstrated the validity of amphibious warfare. Although marine forces encountered fierce opposition and heavy losses, amphibious assaults were subsequently carried out in the Marshall Islands (February 1944), in the MARIANA ISLANDS (June–July 1944), on Peleliu (September 1944), at IWO JIMA (February 1945), and at Okinawa (April 1945).

General Douglas MacArthur, commanding U.S. Army forces in the Southwest Pacific theater, became equally expert in amphibious operations and performed a series of leapfrog assaults in New Guinea and the Philippines between 1942 and 1945. Indeed, U.S. Army forces in the Pacific undertook more amphibious assaults than the Marine Corps, and between October 1944 and August 1945 alone, MacArthur conducted 52 amphibious landings against Japanese-held areas.

In the EUROPEAN THEATER, the British carried out amphibious operations at Dieppe in August 1942, and larger, more successful landings with U.S. Army forces in North Africa; at Sicily, Salerno, and Anzio in Italy; in southern France; and at Normandy. Amphibious operations became central to British and American strategic conduct of

The amphibious assault of Normandy beaches was a major part of the Allies' Operation Overlord. Seen here are men of the veteran U.S. First Infantry Division going ashore under enemy fire. *(Library of Congress)*

the war. The amphibious assault was shown at its most complex in the Normandy invasion on June 6, 1944, and the January 1945 invasion of Luzon Island in the Philippines, which were the largest operations of their kind in history.

Landing forces were usually divided into assault troops, reinforcing units, and occupation forces. Following a prelanding air and naval bombardment, landing craft carrying the assault formations were guided toward the beaches. Landing craft were loaded with supplies and equipment in such a way that they could be unloaded in the order they were needed ashore. The assault took place in waves using specially designed landing craft, each carrying a complete military unit. Each wave was timed to reach shore at a particular time to prevent an excessive buildup of forces on the beach and to assure landing in the correct tactical order. Landing forces were most vulnerable when hitting the beach, and it was vital to have the correct mix of air and naval gunfire available at H-Hour, the moment of landing on D day, to assure that troops would not be pushed back into the sea. Complications necessitated great command flexibility. Once troops had secured a beachhead, reinforcing units arrived with heavier equipment and weapons. When the beachhead was secure, occupation forces, usually comprised of logistical and construction personnel, landed to establish a base for further operations.

Further reading: Jeter A. Isley and Philip A. Crowl, *The U.S. Marines and Amphibious War: Its Theory and Prac-* *tice in the Pacific War* (Princeton, N.J.: Princeton University Press, 1951); John A. Lorelli, *To Foreign Shores: U.S. Amphibious Operations in World War Two* (Annapolis, Md.: U.S. Naval Institute Press, 1995).

—Clayton D. Laurie

Anglo-American relations

The era of WORLD WAR II brought the development of a uniquely close diplomatic relationship between the United States and Great Britain. Although the United States was absorbed by the GREAT DEPRESSION in the early 1930s and then sought insulation from global affairs with the NEUTRALITY ACTS of the mid-1930s, Anglo-American collaboration in World War II brought the two nations together in what came to be known as the "special relationship."

During the Great Depression and the resulting domestic turmoil, the United States largely withdrew from leadership in international affairs. President HERBERT C. HOOVER did attempt to maintain some American involvement in global affairs, cooperating for example with Great Britain and Japan to limit naval building at the LONDON NAVAL CONFERENCE of 1930. But other actions, such as the protectionist HAWLEY-SMOOT TARIFF ACT of 1930, weak American responses to the Japanese invasion of MANCHURIA and the Italian invasion of ETHIOPIA, and the lack of American cooperation at the LONDON ECONOMIC CONFERENCE OF 1933, during the HOOVER PRESIDENCY and the first term of FRANKLIN D. ROOSEVELT, reflected the U.S. reluctance to provide significant international leadership. The Neutrality Acts then confirmed the American effort to avoid entanglements in the events that ultimately led to World War II, and Roosevelt was essentially a bystander as British prime minister Neville Chamberlain concluded the MUNICH CONFERENCE with Nazi Germany. Such American policy, prompted in part by significant anti-British sentiment within sectors of the American public, contributed to an atmosphere of some suspicion between the two nations.

By the end of the 1930s, however, Roosevelt grew increasingly disturbed about events in Europe and, especially after the outbreak of war in 1939, sought to establish a closer relationship with Great Britain. In 1939, the president succeeded in ending the arms embargo of the Neutrality Acts and to have CASH-AND-CARRY apply to war goods, thus allowing belligerent nations (Britain, in particular) to obtain war supplies if they were paid for in cash and were not transported in American ships. Roosevelt further illustrated his belief that the United States and Great Britain had developed concurrent interests in FOREIGN POLICY by establishing a close personal relationship with new British prime minister Winston Churchill. Continued collaboration between the two world leaders would later play a crucial role in the course of Allied action in World War II.

American popular opinion began to shift significantly in favor of aiding England in wake of the German BLITZKRIEG offensive of spring 1940 and the ongoing BATTLE OF BRITAIN. Such measures as the DESTROYERS-FOR-BASES DEAL of 1940 and the LEND-LEASE ACT of 1941 authorized significant American assistance to the British in the war against Germany. Discussions began in early 1941 to make strategic plans in preparation for the possibility of American entrance into World War II, a cooperation that would continue throughout the course of the war. Roosevelt and Churchill met in person for the first time in August 1941 and produced the ATLANTIC CHARTER, which outlined Allied war principles and aims.

After PEARL HARBOR and the American entry into the war, the Soviet Union joined the United States and Great Britain in endorsing the terms of the Atlantic Charter, creating the GRAND ALLIANCE. Because the United States and Great Britain shared democratic views and values as well as mutual concerns and often similar visions of the postwar world, Anglo-American relations were always closer than SOVIET-AMERICAN RELATIONS. Significantly, the British were involved in the ATOMIC BOMB project and discussions about the bomb's potential use, while the Soviets were not notified of the bomb's existence until the POTSDAM CONFERENCE in July 1945—and even then cryptically. Shared interests between the United States and Great Britain often placed them in direct opposition with their Soviet allies. For much of the war, Roosevelt acquiesced in Churchill's desire to delay the opening of a SECOND FRONT in western Europe, much to the dismay of Soviet premier Joseph Stalin. These mutual interests also extended to preparations for the postwar world as both the British and Americans were concerned about Soviet efforts to create a sphere of influence in eastern Europe.

But there were differences as well, and some tensions in Anglo-American relations during the war. The British did not share the anticolonial views of the United States, and resisted American pressure to grant its colonial possessions—India in particular—independence. American strategists were much more eager than the British to open the second front as soon as possible. And as it became more apparent that Great Britain would no longer be able to maintain its previous stature in international affairs and that the United States and the Soviet Union would be the dominant postwar powers, Soviet-American relations became increasingly important in Roosevelt's priorities. At the TEHERAN CONFERENCE of late 1943, Roosevelt sided with Stalin in insisting on launching the Normandy invasion to open the second front in the spring of 1944.

Despite such differences and disagreements, and despite the shifts in global power, Anglo-American rela-

tions remained close. In the postwar world, Anglo-American relations would remain friendly as both nations would find themselves opposing their erstwhile Soviet ally in the developing cold war.

See also WORLD WAR II EUROPEAN THEATER.

Further reading: Warren F. Kimball, *Forged in War: Roosevelt, Churchill, and the Second World War* (New York: Morrow, 1997); David Reynolds, *The Creation of the Anglo-American Alliance, 1937–1941* (Chapel Hill: University of North Carolina Press, 1982).

—Mary E. Carroll-Mason

antimonopoly

The conviction that economic concentration harmed the economy and gave big BUSINESS excessive political power was an important part of 20th-century LIBERALISM going back to the Progressive Era and especially to the ideas of Louis Brandeis. But while Brandeis (a SUPREME COURT justice in the 1930s) and his views continued to have significant influence among liberals, antimonopoly (or antitrust) policy did not figure prominently in NEW DEAL reform and recovery programs until the mid- and late 1930s. Efforts to reduce the size and power of the corporate giants then lost momentum during WORLD WAR II.

The most important development in antimonopoly policy in the HOOVER PRESIDENCY involved LABOR rather than business. The 1932 Norris-LaGuardia Act, sponsored by Republican senator GEORGE NORRIS of Nebraska and Republican congressman FIORELLO LAGUARDIA of New York, prohibited the use of federal court injunctions under the antitrust laws to enforce "yellow dog" employment contracts forbidding workers to join unions. President HERBERT C. HOOVER, an opponent of monopoly and of suspending or easing antitrust laws for business trade associations, reluctantly signed the legislation.

With the election of FRANKLIN D. ROOSEVELT to the presidency in 1932, antitrust advocates, including Brandeis disciple FELIX FRANKFURTER, a Harvard Law School professor, tried to influence New Deal policy in an antimonopoly direction. But the so-called FIRST NEW DEAL of 1933 sought instead to combat the GREAT DEPRESSION by cooperating with big business in national planning and controls. The NATIONAL INDUSTRIAL RECOVERY ACT (NIRA) of 1933 suspended antitrust laws so that the NATIONAL RECOVERY ADMINISTRATION (NRA) could develop "codes" of fair competition with cartel-like arrangements in industry. The NRA, however, failed to bring economic recovery, and came under sharp criticism for breeding monopoly power from such progressive Republicans in CONGRESS as Gerald Nye and WILLIAM E. BORAH as well as from liberal Democrats. In 1935, the Supreme Court found the NRA unconstitutional in *SCHECHTER POULTRY CORPORATION V. UNITED STATES*.

Frankfurter and his protégés in the administration had more influence on the SECOND NEW DEAL of 1935. The PUBLIC UTILITY HOLDING COMPANY ACT sought to dismantle the giant corporations that dominated the electric power industry. New Deal TAXATION beginning with the REVENUE ACT OF 1935 aimed at taxing big business much more heavily than before, and the undistributed profits tax proposed in 1936 had an important antimonopoly dimension. The Robinson-Patman Act of 1936 prohibited manufacturers or wholesalers from giving special discounts to chain stores and other large purchasers, and the 1937 Miller-Tydings Act extended such "fair trade" protection of small retailers. Nonetheless, antitrust efforts remained secondary to other New Deal programs.

The RECESSION OF 1937–38 then gave antimonopoly policy a far more central place in administration priorities. A number of New Dealers, including LEON HENDERSON, maintained that concentrated economic power allowed business to restrict production and fix prices higher than they should be, which in turn led to depressed sales, unemployment, and insufficient consumer spending power. Brandeisians had long held that the depression itself could be ascribed in large part to such monopoly power—and the recession, they said, provided more evidence yet. In April

In June 1934, as part of President Franklin D. Roosevelt's New Deal, the Securities and Exchange Commission was established to regulate the stock market. Such measures were intended to protect consumers and the national economy, but as the cartoon shown here indicates, some felt the federal government's efforts to regulate trade were simply not powerful enough to destroy all the "roadblocks" facing small businesses. Cartoon by Philip Dorf *(Private Collection)*

1938, just after he had also announced an increase in federal spending, FDR asked CONGRESS to conduct an investigation into concentrations of economic power, and Congress created the TEMPORARY NATIONAL ECONOMIC COMMITTEE (TNEC).

The creation of the TNEC, with Henderson as its executive secretary, and the 1938 appointment of Thurman Arnold as assistant attorney general in charge of the Antitrust Division of the Justice Department gave antimonopoly efforts impressive new momentum. The TNEC undertook a massive investigation of the American economy from 1938 to 1941, calling some 552 witnesses and publishing several dozen volumes of testimony and analysis. Arnold enlarged his division's budget and staff fivefold, greatly stepped up its antitrust suits (some of them against labor unions), and had significant early successes. Yet the antimonopoly momentum was soon spent. When the TNEC issued its final report and recommendations in 1941, they attracted little attention, and Arnold encountered increasing resistance and difficulties.

World War II proved decisive in the ebbing of the new antimonopoly campaign, despite Arnold's efforts and the concern of liberals in Washington about the growing size and power of big business in wartime economic MOBILIZATION. Wartime spending and the resulting prosperity confirmed the doctrine of KEYNESIANISM that government compensatory spending could fire the economy, and antitrust policy lost appeal as a way to enhance consumption and bring prosperity. Conservatives and businessmen won increasing influence in national policy. By mid-1942, antitrust efforts were essentially called off for the duration of the war when business and the military persuaded the administration that antitrust efforts distracted business and impaired mobilization efforts. In early 1943, Roosevelt appointed Arnold to the Washington, D.C. Court of Appeals. By the end of the war, antimonopoly efforts had lost much of their force and support.

Further reading: Alan Brinkley, "The Antimonopoly Ideal and the Liberal State: The Case of Thurman Arnold," *Journal of American History* 80 (1993): 557–79; Ellis W. Hawley, *The New Deal and the Problem of Monopoly: A Study in Economic Ambivalence* (Princeton, N.J.: Princeton University Press, 1966); David Lynch, *The Concentration of Economic Power* (New York: Columbia University Press, 1946).

anti-Semitism

Anti-Semitism in America, present since the nation's founding and particularly virulent in the 1920s, remained high and in some ways intensified during the GREAT DEPRESSION and WORLD WAR II. Manifested not just in attitudes about JEWS but also in actions ranging from name-calling to discrimination to acts of vandalism and sometimes violence, anti-Semitism rose during the war before declining by the end of the war.

PUBLIC OPINION POLLS in the 1929–1945 era indicated that a significant minority of Americans accepted derogatory stereotypes of Jews. Such views held, for example, that Jews had too much political and economic power, and that they used this power to manipulate world and national events for their own benefit. The economic insecurities of the depression years sometimes led to scapegoating and reinforced anti-Semitic attitudes and behavior. Job discrimination, restrictive quotas in universities, and bans against Jews belonging to clubs or buying property in some developments remained common. Because President FRANKLIN D. ROOSEVELT included a number of Jewish officials in his NEW DEAL, anti-Semites called his administration the "Jew Deal." After the United States entered into World War II, many Americans erroneously accused Jews of shirking military duty and charged them with profiteering from the war. From 1941 until 1944, Americans consistently reported to pollsters that they were more suspicious of Jewish Americans than they were of either Japanese Americans or German Americans.

Anti-Semitism was frequently expressed in harsh rhetorical attacks against Jews, including those by the Silver Shirt League, a nativist group, and by the American Bund, a Nazi-funded group that the U.S. GOVERNMENT would later target after America's entry into the war. A single anti-Jewish demonstration in Madison Square Garden in 1939 by the Bund drew more than 20,000 people and little counterprotest. Millions of Americans listened as well to the RADIO programs of FATHER CHARLES E. COUGHLIN, a Catholic priest who accused Jews of being Communist sympathizers and of subversively plotting to draw America into World War II. In his broadcasts, Coughlin subtly advocated violence against Jews. He openly supported the Christian Front, a native fascist group, whose members physically assaulted Jewish children in cities across America and, in one instance, conspired to poison dozens of Jews in Detroit and to assassinate members of CONGRESS. Hostility toward Jews also led to vandalizing Jewish businesses and to desecrating synagogues in some cities.

Most tragically, anti-Semitism contributed to the refusal of most Americans to support admitting the mostly Jewish refugees fleeing from Hitler's regime and the unfolding HOLOCAUST in Europe into the United States. A poll in 1938, in fact, indicated that 60 percent of Americans objected to the presence of Jews in America. The anti-Semitism of high-ranking officers in the State Department and in consulates abroad helped produce restrictive IMMIGRATION procedures designed to drastically limit Jewish immigration into the United States. Fear of provoking a powerful anti-Jewish backlash inhibited pro-immigration organizations that might otherwise have more forcefully called for members of the United States Congress to liberalize immigration quotas.

Jewish organizations, including the Anti-Defamation League, formed the General Jewish Council to counter the real and perceived threats posed by widespread anti-Semitism and to debunk anti-Semitic rumors and stereotypes. The U.S. government used other evidence gathered by the council to pursue and dismantle the American Bund. Not until 1944, when Americans felt confident that the nation would emerge victorious from World War II, did anti-Semitic sentiment in the United States subside. After the war, anti-Semitism declined sharply, in part because of a horrified reaction to the Holocaust and the attitudes that had produced it.

Further reading: Leonard Dinnerstein, *Antisemitism in America* (New York: Oxford University Press, 1994).

—Julie Whitcomb

Army, U.S.

The U.S. Army in WORLD WAR II was the largest ground force ever fielded in the nation's history and was vital to the Allied victory in both the EUROPEAN THEATER and PACIFIC THEATER. In Europe, the army engaged AXIS forces beginning in November 1942 in the NORTH AFRICAN CAMPAIGN, and followed the victory there with successful operations in SICILY, the ITALIAN CAMPAIGN, the INVASION OF NORMANDY, and central Europe. In the Pacific theater, the army supported island-hopping advances of the U.S. NAVY and U.S. MARINES in the central Pacific and vanquished Japanese forces in the southwest Pacific and the PHILIPPINES.

The U.S. Army raised a force of more than 8.2 million men and women by March 1945, in both combat and support arms, including nearly 1.8 million personnel in the U.S. ARMY AIR FORCES. Under President FRANKLIN D. ROOSEVELT as commander in chief, the War Department, with headquarters at the newly constructed Pentagon, supervised the recruitment, training, deployment, and operations of the largest force in American history.

Roosevelt, like British prime minister Winston Churchill and Soviet leader Joseph Stalin, retained overall control of the nation's war effort, but he entrusted his civilian and military subordinates with greater responsibility for the conduct of affairs than did his contemporaries. Secretary of War HENRY L. STIMSON was responsible for the administration of the army from July 1940 until the end of the war. Stimson was assisted by Under Secretary of War Robert P. Patterson, who was primarily concerned with procurement; by Assistant Secretary of War John J.

McCloy, who acted as Stimson's deputy; and by Assistant Secretary of War for Air Robert A. Lovett, who supervised air force administrative functions.

This civilian team controlled subordinate military elements consisting of three separate, coequal, and autonomous components following the reorganization of the War Department in March 1942. The first component was the U.S. Army Ground Forces under Lieutenant General Lesley J. McNair, whose command trained and developed ground combat branches including armor, infantry, airborne, and artillery. Once units were raised, trained, and equipped, they were shipped overseas to one of seven theaters where they became the theater commander's responsibility.

The second component, and eventually the largest, was the Services of Supply (later Army Services Forces), under Lieutenant General Brehon B. Sommervell. This command bore responsibility for ground force logistics and procurement, and included the transportation and quartermaster corps, chemical warfare service, ordnance, medical, and signal corps, and the corps of engineers and military police. The third component was the army air forces under General HENRY H. "HAP" ARNOLD, which had its own organizations comparable to those of the ground forces.

The establishment of these commands left chief of staff GEORGE C. MARSHALL and the War Department General Staff free to plan and execute operations from the Operations and Plans Division at the Pentagon. Marshall controlled the theater commanders worldwide and coordinated U.S. Army operations with other military services represented on the Joint Chiefs of Staff, as well as British forces through the Combined Chiefs of Staff.

When the war started in 1939, the army consisted of 190,000 troops that were well trained and led, yet were understrength and lacking in modern equipment. The National Guard consisted of a mere 200,000 men. With the beginning of conscription, following passage of the SELECTIVE SERVICE Act in September 1940, the army ranks increased rapidly to approximately 1.4 million men by December 1941. During the war, 38.8 percent of personnel were volunteers and 61.2 percent were draftees. Although Marshall planned to raise 100 divisions, the army finally comprised 90 divisions. Approximately 73 percent served overseas, with an average duration of 33 months. At the beginning of the war, the army accepted AFRICAN AMERICANS only in limited numbers, usually in segregated noncombat units, but by 1945 the numbers and duties of black soldiers had expanded and some steps had been taken toward desegregation. Women served in the WOMEN'S ARMY CORPS (WAC).

The creation of the triangular infantry divisions in May 1940, each consisting of three regiments with three battalions and three companies, totaling 14,250 men, with supporting engineer, artillery, armor, service, and headquarters units, proved wise, as they were flexible in combat. The army was deployed in 11 field armies (First to Ninth, and 10th and 15th), containing 26 corps total. In addition to infantry divisions, the basic unit, the army created 16 heavy and light armored divisions, with 390 and 263 TANKS, respectively, and 60 nondivisional tank battalions, 326 artillery battalions, 400 antiaircraft batteries, and 86 tank destroyer battalions. In response to needs for specialized units, the army raised one mountain, five airborne, and two cavalry divisions. The army deployed 68 divisions to the European theater and 22 divisions to the Pacific theater.

It is generally accepted that the organization and administration of the army during World War II, both at home and abroad, was second to none. Critics do cite a faulty replacement system that tended to damage unit cohesion, and a lack of infantry replacements late in the war because of the draw of other branches of the military. American soldiers, however, were well trained, equipped, fed, and led. Their access to, and liberal use of, copious amounts of materiel, munitions, technically advanced weaponry, and firepower usually gave them a crucial edge. Overall, army personnel performed well under fire and aggressively took the initiative to the enemy in diverse terrain, weather, and battle conditions. Casualties (combat and noncombat losses) in the U.S. Army and U.S. Army Air Forces numbered approximately 820,000, including 234,874 dead.

Further reading: Geoffrey Perret, *There's a War to Be Won: The United States Army in World War II* (New York: Ballantine, 1997); Russell Weigley, *History of the United States Army* (New York: Macmillan, 1967).

—Clayton D. Laurie

Army Air Forces, U.S.

By the end of WORLD WAR II, the U.S. Army Air Forces comprised the largest and most powerful air armada ever created and dominated the skies in both the EUROPEAN THEATER and the PACIFIC THEATER. Vastly superior in size and technical sophistication to any other air force on either side of the conflict, the army air forces conducted decisive strategic bombing campaigns against both Nazi Germany and imperial Japan, significantly impairing Axis war production and morale. The army air forces also provided vital tactical close air support to American and Allied ground forces in every major campaign worldwide, especially after 1943, effectively denying enemy forces of their mobility and supplies.

In September 1939, the U.S. Army Air Corps was an administrative unit of the U.S. ARMY, under the command of Major General HENRY H. "HAP" ARNOLD. Many airmen, however, desired greater autonomy, believed that AIR

POWER would play a major role in any future conflict, and were dissatisfied by a chain of command dominated by ground officers. Their agitation prompted the army to create a nearly autonomous and coequal U.S. Army Air Forces within the larger army in June 1941. As commander of the later Army Air Forces Headquarters, Arnold sat on the Joint Chiefs of Staff and directed subsequent air operations without formally reporting through the army chain of command to the chief of staff.

With a separate headquarters, training establishment, bases, meteorological and intelligence services, communications and transport system, and procurement and supply structure, the army air forces expanded at an extraordinary rate following the outbreak of the European War in 1939. In that year the army possessed 17 air bases in the continental United States, a figure that grew to 345 main bases, 116 smaller bases, and 322 auxiliary fields by 1943 alone, not counting additional thousands of bomber bases, airstrips, and other tactical fighter bases in the combat theaters abroad. Manpower grew from 20,000 men in June 1938 to nearly 1.8 million by March 1945, eventually comprising about one-fifth of the U.S. Army's total strength. Barred from the army air forces at the beginning of the war, African Americans subsequently served in limited numbers as pilots and crewmembers, most notably in the 99th Pursuit Squadron of the Tuskegee Airmen. In addition to those in uniform, the air forces also employed a further 422,000 civilians performing a host of technical, administrative, and service duties such as ferrying aircraft or serving in the Civil Air Patrol. Some 1,000 women served in the WOMEN AIR-FORCE SERVICE PILOTS (WASP), a quasimilitary civilian organization that performed a variety of piloting tasks for the army air forces.

In September 1939 the air force possessed 2,470 aircraft, largely obsolescent types, although new state-of-the-art models, such as the B-29 Superfortress, were already in development. By its peak strength in July 1944, the air force had nearly 80,000 operational aircraft of all types and descriptions from fighters, reconnaissance and cargo aircraft to light, medium, and heavy bombers, many of them rated among the best in the world in terms of bomb load capacity, technical and mechanical performance, durability, and ability to deliver firepower in the air and on the ground.

During World War II the army developed 16 separate air forces (the First through 16th), 11 of these serving either in strategic, reconnaissance, patrol, or tactical roles in the European theater and the Pacific theater, or in Panama, the Caribbean, or Alaska. Four of these air forces remained in the United States for purposes of continental defense and training. The organization and equipping of the air forces varied widely depending on roles and missions, but each force most usually contained fighter, bomber, and air service commands. Other air forces, such as the Ninth Air Force in Europe, played a primarily tactical support role, while the Eighth and 15th Air Forces in Britain and the Mediterranean, respectively, and the 20th Air Force in the Marianas Islands conducted largely strategic bombardment missions. The 10th Air Force in India provided tactical ground support in the China-Burma-India theater and organized and flew the "Hump" supply route over the Himalayas to Nationalist China.

The combat units in an air force varied widely as well, with the group, roughly equivalent to an army ground unit, serving as the main administrative and operational unit. Altogether the air forces created 243 fully equipped groups, each consisting of three or four squadrons, the basic combat unit. Squadrons were described and numbered according to function, and they normally did their training together and fought together as a unit. In 1944, a squadron, which contained three or more flights or aircraft, contained from seven B-29 Superfortress bombers up to 25 fighter aircraft, numbering from 200 to 500 men.

By the end of the war, the U.S. Army Air Forces had taken delivery of some 158,000 aircraft out of the 300,000 produced by the United States for itself and for the GRAND ALLIANCE. The force included 51,221 bombers and 47,000 fighters, of which nearly 23,000 were lost in combat. During the war the air force flew over 2,363,000 combat sorties, dropped 2,057,000 tons of bombs (more than 75 percent of that on Germany), and expended 459,750,000 rounds of ammunition. Casualties numbered 115,383, including 40,061 dead, of whom 17,021 were officers.

Further reading: Geoffrey Perret, *Winged Victory: The Army Air Forces in World War II* (New York: Random House, 1993); John F. Shiner, *With Courage: The United States Air Force in World War II* (Washington, D.C.: Government Printing Office, 1995).

—Clayton D. Laurie

Arnold, Henry H. ("Hap") (1886–1950)

The commanding general of the U.S. ARMY AIR FORCES during World War II, an aviation pioneer, and a leading proponent of AIR POWER, Henry Harley "Hap" Arnold is considered the creator of the modern United States Air Force.

Born in Gladwyne, Pennsylvania, Arnold graduated from West Point in 1907. In 1911, he volunteered for flight training with the Wright Brothers, and was one of the first army aviators. During World War I, he served in Washington overseeing the training of flying units and the acquisition of air bases. In the 1920s and 1930s, Arnold served at a number of military posts where he developed his ideas on the uses of air power and the importance of technology. In 1938, he was promoted to the rank of major general and assumed command of the U.S. Army Air Corps (later the U.S. Army Air Forces).

Arnold played a vital role not only in building the U.S. Army Air Forces during World War II but also in furthering ANGLO-AMERICAN RELATIONS and the prosecution of the war. Recognizing the danger posed by the German Luftwaffe, Arnold began working in the late 1930s to impress upon President FRANKLIN D. ROOSEVELT the need to expand America's air strength. His efforts contributed to CONGRESS appropriating billions of dollars for the expansion of the army air forces from 1939 to 1941. Among Arnold's first tasks was to allocate aircraft production between expanding the U.S. forces and those of Allies under the LEND-LEASE ACT, and he served as President Roosevelt's air adviser at the ATLANTIC CHARTER conference of Roosevelt and British prime minister Winston Churchill in 1941. Early in 1942, Arnold agreed to a British-American strategic bombing offensive in Europe. As a member of the American Joint Chiefs of Staff and the British-American combined staffs, Arnold attended the CASABLANCA CONFERENCE and the POTSDAM CONFERENCE. In 1944 he was promoted to the rank of five-star general.

General Arnold was known for his brusque and demanding style of command. More an organizer and builder than a strategist, he realized technology's importance and sponsored research into advanced electronics and aeronautical design. By war's end, his command had grown from fewer than 20,000 men and 300 aircraft to some 1.8 million personnel and well over 60,000 aircraft. He retired in early 1946 because of a heart condition. Even in retirement his influence continued, as he pushed to make the air force a separate branch of the armed forces, and for the use of missiles. (The U.S. Air Force was created in 1947.) Arnold died in 1950.

Further reading: Henry Harley Arnold, *Global Mission* (New York: Harper, 1949).

—Robert J. Hanyok

art and architecture

From 1929 to 1945, American art and architecture underwent important developments that reflected both long-term trends and the momentous events of the era. Modernism (a broadly defined movement based upon the intentional rejection of traditional, classical methods of artistic expression) continued to profoundly influence American art, but the social and political context of the GREAT DEPRESSION and the NEW DEAL had a significant impact as well. Aided by a large influx of European artists, New York City especially revealed the growing accomplishments of American art and architecture and increasingly displaced Paris as the world capital of art.

Architectural achievement in the period included the continued prominence and productions of Frank Lloyd Wright and the emergence of urban skyscrapers, most notably in New York. A modernist architect with natural instincts, the Wisconsin-born Wright continued to build upon the legacy he had established in earlier decades. His most notable achievement of the era was the rustic Falling Water (constructed between 1936 and 1939), a blended, modernistic and Japanese-styled home built in the secluded woods of Pennsylvania near Pittsburgh.

Meanwhile, architecture in the New York City area in the interwar years came to epitomize the very notion of the modern big city. Especially in Manhattan, the 1920s and early 1930s witnessed the rise of the skyscraper as a powerful symbol of urban civilization. Relying upon an adapted French art deco style, the New York City skyline was expanded to include the Chrysler Building (designed by William Van Allen and completed in 1930) as well as the world-famous symbol of modern New York City itself, the towering Empire State Building (completed in 1931 under the direction of the architectural firm Shreve, Lamb and Harmon). The architect Raymond Hood, who had been at the forefront of early Manhattan skyscraper development in the 1920s (for example, the Daily News Building and the American Radiator Building), continued to be a powerful architectural force through the 1930s. While the McGraw-Hill Building was one of his notable achievements, he is best known for the Rockefeller Center, begun in 1929 and completed in 1939. Under the patronage of the powerful Rockefeller family, Hood designed the multipurpose area to include such notable venues as the RCA building and the popular Radio City Music Hall (conceptualized by Samuel Lionel "Roxy" Rothafel, and designed by Wallace Harrison).

The opening of the NEW YORK WORLD'S FAIR in 1939 further cemented the developing image of New York City as the world's cosmopolitan, architectural center. The modernistic obelisk Trylon and the soaring, triangular Perisphere (also designed by Wallace Harrison) complemented the prophetic Futurama exhibition, designed by Norman Bel Geddes under the sponsorship of the General Motors Corporation. Such international exposure gave New York City a creatively vibrant, cutting-edge feel, and helped to transform the image of Manhattan from one of a crowded destination for industrial immigrants to that of a center for cultural and artistic progressivism. With the construction of the Museum of Modern Art (1929) and the Whitney Museum (1931), New York City was poised to become the new world center for sculpture and painting as well. During World War II, war production and construction needs took priority over such architectural projects in New York and elsewhere.

The leading figure in American sculpture during the period was the innovative Alexander Calder (1898–1976).

The home and studio of Frank Lloyd Wright, Chicago, Illinois *(Library of Congress)*

The inventor of the "mobile" form of sculpture, Calder had studied and worked in Paris prior to coming back to America. Calder constructed abstract figures out of wire, wood, tin, and other materials, often placing ball-like shapes at the ends. Sometimes, his constructions were enormous (especially later creations, which could approach the size of an airplane), and at other times they were interconnected arcs or leaflike structures that moved with room air currents. Calder's mechanical engineering background doubtless enabled him to effectively manipulate materials and shapes in unique ways that greatly expanded the creative horizons of modern sculpting.

The Great Depression brought about major changes in the relationship between GOVERNMENT and the arts. Such New Deal programs as the Public Works of Art Project (PWAP) and the FEDERAL ART PROJECT (FAP), undertook various art ventures in order to provide work RELIEF jobs for unemployed artists. The resulting publicly funded paintings, sculptures, and murals often reflected populist and patriotic themes. These works sometimes displayed a noticeably chauvinistic emphasis upon displaying the strength of indigenous American character, as well as teaching the necessary public virtues to weather the economic crisis. Generally, the work produced by the federal programs was not highly regarded by art critics, although such subsequently renowned artists as Jackson Pollock and Willem de Kooning were at one time supported by the Federal Art Project.

The increasing role of government in the arts during the depression also offered opportunities to African American artists, particularly the New Jersey–born Jacob Lawrence. As a young man, Lawrence had traveled to New York City, where he was stimulated by the Harlem Renaissance. Lawrence focused on the contemporary Great Migration of AFRICAN AMERICANS from the southern poverty and racism to almost equally grim northern urban areas. During the

1930s and 1940s, Lawrence painted a series of 60 works that came to be known as the Migration Series (originally known as *The Migration of the Negro*). In these paintings, which were influenced by Cubism and the French painter Henri Matisse, Lawrence depicted the harsh realities of life for African Americans during the Great Depression. Even while depicting such themes as rural African-American poverty, urban slums, and prison life, however, Lawrence did not display a radical or overtly political ideology in his works, in contrast to more openly leftist artists of the period.

PHOTOGRAPHY continued to develop as an art form in the era, particularly in the Western School of Ansel Adams and others. Also of continuing importance was Alfred Stieglitz (1864–1946), a pioneer in the emergence of photography as a distinct art form who brought European avant-garde artistic styles to America in the late 1800s. Opening in New York City the most influential artistic photography studio in America, Stieglitz was highly active not only in photography but also in promoting modernist painting and sculpture and in lecturing widely, until his death in 1946.

But photography reached a larger audience through the photojournalism of *LIFE* MAGAZINE and the NEWS MEDIA. As with other aspects of art, photography also reflected the social and political currents of the era—not only in the photojournalism of the depression and war years, but also in the documentary photographs of the New Deal's FARM SECURITY ADMINISTRATION (FSA). Such accomplished FSA photographers as Dorothea Lange and Walker Evans provided graphic (and often carefully and purposefully composed) depictions of rural poverty designed to develop support for reform programs. During World War II, the FSA's photographic section was transferred to the OFFICE OF WAR INFORMATION, which sought to inspire patriotism as well as to document social change and progress.

During the Great Depression and World War II, three camps emerged that defined particular artistic styles and preoccupations: abstract artists, social realists, and region-alists. While the sculptor Alexander Calder clearly was one of the most notable representatives of the abstract wing, other important abstract artists of the period (overwhelmingly centered in New York City) included Fritz Glarner, Burgoyne Diller, Carl Holty, Ilya Bolotowsky, and Charmion von Wiegand. The abstract artists were influenced by Europeans (such as Piet Mondrian and others), and they often produced works of geometric and abstractly utopian construction. In general, however, this group received little attention at the time, perhaps because the economic and social difficulties of the Great Depression tended to point toward a focus upon more realistic themes.

Nighthawks, painting by Edward Hopper, 1942 *(The Art Institute of Chicago)*

The social realists of the time can themselves be broadly divided into two groups: those artists who were more overtly political from a liberal or leftist perspective and those who can best be characterized as apolitical. Strongly political and leftist themes were injected into the U.S. art scene by the Mexican artist Diego Rivera, whose mural, *Man at the Crossroads,* created a furor for its heroic depiction of Soviet leader Vladimir Lenin. Though commissioned by the Rockefeller family for inclusion in the new Rockefeller Center, the mural so offended the Rockefellers that they removed Rivera, and the mural, from the project. Other politically radical social realist artists included Ben Shahn, Jack Levine, and Philip Evergood, who generally displayed overtly marxist themes and social commentary in their works.

From a more apolitical perspective, artists such as Stuart Davis and Edward Hopper especially focused on urban scenes and the realities of life in the big city. Davis tended more toward abstraction in his later works, as he was increasingly influenced by the Cubist movement. Two of his most noteworthy works were both murals: *Men without Women* (1932) and *Swing Landscape* (1938), itself a piece created under the auspices of the New Deal's WORKS PROGRESS ADMINISTRATION. Davis often drew inspiration from his excursions into various New York City neighborhoods, including Chinatown and jazz clubs catering primarily to blacks.

Edward Hopper likewise portrayed landscape and cityscape works that often had the feel of a vignette, and a certain dreamlike character often pervaded his paintings. Hopper depicted the realities and complexities of both rural and especially urban life in 20th-century America, with a special attention given to lighting, shadow, and mood, which often provided his works with a mysterious or even lonely quality. Works such as *Early Sunday Morning* (1930), *Room in New York* (1932), and perhaps Hopper's most notable work, *Nighthawks* (1942), are primary examples of this particular style and emphasis.

From a completely different venue came the work of the regionalists, including such artists as Grant Wood, John Steuart Curry, and Thomas Hart Benton. These artists developed themes relating to small-town, rural, and farm life in the America of the period. Quintessentially American in their portrayal of heartland values, religion, and morality, these artists gained, perhaps surprisingly, a critical following in the sophisticated New York City art world of the day. Notable works of these artists include Wood's *Stone City, Iowa* (1930) and especially his well-known *American Gothic* (1930), Curry's *Baptism in Kansas* (1928), and Benton's *Social History of Missouri* (1935). In a somewhat different vein, the popular artist Norman Rockwell also gave attention to such themes in his mass-produced works. Rockwell's name became practically synonymous with the image of small-town Americana as exhibited in his productions, which provided reassurance in the trying days of depression and war, and his works were deeply beloved by the public at large.

Finally, the mid-1940s witnessed the emergence of the movement that would later become known as abstract expressionism, a phenomenon that would last into the 1950s and beyond. This movement would shift the artistic focus to the examination of Jungian-style concepts and themes, such as the primordial, the primitive, and archetypal explorations. Such notable figures as the "drip" artist Jackson Pollock (*Mural* and *Pasiphae,* both 1943), Willem de Kooning (*Seated Figure,* 1940), and Mark Rothko (*Baptismal Scene,* 1945), would all lay the foundations for this next influential period in American art in the postwar era.

See also CITIES AND URBAN LIFE.

Further reading: Ian Chilvers, *Dictionary of Twentieth-Century Art* (New York: Oxford University Press, 1998); Wayne Craven, *American Art: History and Culture* (New York: Harry N. Abrams, 1994); Helen Gardner et al., *Art through the Ages,* 11th ed. (New York: Harcourt Brace, 2000); Robert Hughes, *American Visions: The Epic History of Art in America* (New York: Knopf, 1997); H. W. Janson, *History of Art,* 6th ed. (New York: Harry N. Abrams, 2001).

—Haelim Allen

Asian Americans

Throughout the 1930s and 1940s, many Asian Americans struggled both to preserve their ethnic identity and customs and to deal with increased prejudice and win new opportunities. As it did for other groups, WORLD WAR II ultimately hastened their assimilation and acculturation, though only after severe trauma in the case of Japanese Americans.

Although the term "Asian Americans" can include a variety of peoples from throughout the Asian continent, Japan, and the Philippines, it typically refers to those from East Asia. (Only a few thousand immigrants from India lived in the United States in this period.) Among the East Asians, Chinese Americans and Japanese Americans were most numerous and prominent. By 1930, primarily as a result of immigration restrictions imposed during the late 19th century and early 20th century, culminating in the Johnson-Reed Act of 1924 that among other things essentially prohibited immigration from China and Japan, immigrants from East Asia represented only about 1 percent of the U.S. foreign-born population (and roughly one-tenth of 1 percent of the total population). East Asian immigrants were concentrated in the western states, particularly in California.

Like other immigrant groups, Asian Americans came in search of economic opportunities. Arriving at Angel Island in San Francisco Bay, many immigrants from East Asia looked for work in cities such as San Francisco where they established ethnic enclaves known as "Chinatowns" or "Japan towns." However, unlike European immigrants in the East, the majority of Asian Americans found employment not as industrial workers but as laborers in the developing agricultural economy of the West and in mining. During the GREAT DEPRESSION, the scarcity of jobs often confined Asian Americans, even those with professional training, to menial jobs in the service sector as domestics.

Opportunities for Asian Americans were limited not only by the depression but by prejudice as well. Nativist groups such as the Asian Exclusion League and the Native Sons and Daughters of the Golden West worked to bar Asian Americans from more desirable occupations. And although some Chinese American workers in the garment industry experienced limited success in the International Ladies Garment Workers Union of San Francisco, Asian Americans were largely kept out of LABOR unions. Federal law prevented Asian immigrants from becoming naturalized citizens, though the American-born children of Asian immigrants did have U.S. citizenship.

Because of the shortage of jobs and the growing extent and cost of RELIEF programs in the 1930s, GOVERNMENT officials wanted to limit additional IMMIGRATION. The prevailing hostility toward nonwhite groups prompted offi-cials to target MEXICAN AMERICANS and also Filipinos, who as residents of a U.S. territory had enjoyed unrestricted immigration. In 1934, after the Tydings-McDuffie Act pledged independence for the Philippines by 1945, Filipino nationals were classified as aliens, given an annual immigration quota of just 50 people, and disqualified from NEW DEAL programs.

Anti-Japanese sentiment escalated sharply after the bombing of PEARL HARBOR and U.S. entry into World War II. By February 1942, pressure from local political organizations and the military prompted President FRANKLIN D. ROOSEVELT to issue EXECUTIVE ORDER 9066 that led to the RELOCATION OF JAPANESE AMERICANS from the West Coast. Suffering considerable financial and personal losses, more than 110,000 Japanese Americans—roughly two-thirds of whom were U.S. citizens–were incarcerated in camps. The SUPREME COURT sustained the relocation policy, by far the worst violation of CIVIL LIBERTIES on the WORLD WAR II HOMEFRONT, in its 1944 decision in *KOREMATSU V. UNITED STATES*.

For Asian Americans, and especially Japanese Americans, World War II marked a turning point in which many communities worked to identify more closely with mainstream America. During the war, an estimated 25,000 or more Japanese Americans, many seeking to demonstrate their loyalty, served in the U.S. armed forces. In fact, the most decorated unit in the U.S. ARMY, with more than 9,000 casualties, was the Japanese-American 442nd Regimental Combat Team. China's suffering at the hands of Japanese militarism received considerable attention during the war, and Chinese Americans began to gain political influence and support from groups such as the AMERICAN CIVIL LIBERTIES UNION and prominent figures such as publisher HENRY LUCE in campaigns to permit Chinese immigration. After the war, the barriers facing Asian Americans did not disappear, but they began to steadily, if slowly, crumble as Asian Americans sought new opportunities and became more fully accepted members of American society.

Further reading: Roger Daniels, *Asian America: Chinese and Japanese in the United States Since 1850* (Seattle: University of Washington Press, 1988); Stephan Thernstrom ed., *Harvard Encyclopedia of American Ethnic Groups* (Cambridge, Mass.: Belknap Press of Harvard University, 1980).

—Shannon L. Parsley

U.S. Fifth Army commander Mark Clark is seen in this photo reviewing the 442nd Regimental Combat Team, composed entirely of Japanese Americans from the mainland U.S. and Hawaii. The unit, established in 1943, was one of the most highly decorated in U.S. history. *(National Archives)*

Atlantic, Battle of the (1940–43)

The Battle of the Atlantic involved the effort of German SUBMARINES to disrupt the shipping of American goods to Great Britain and the Soviet Union. During the most

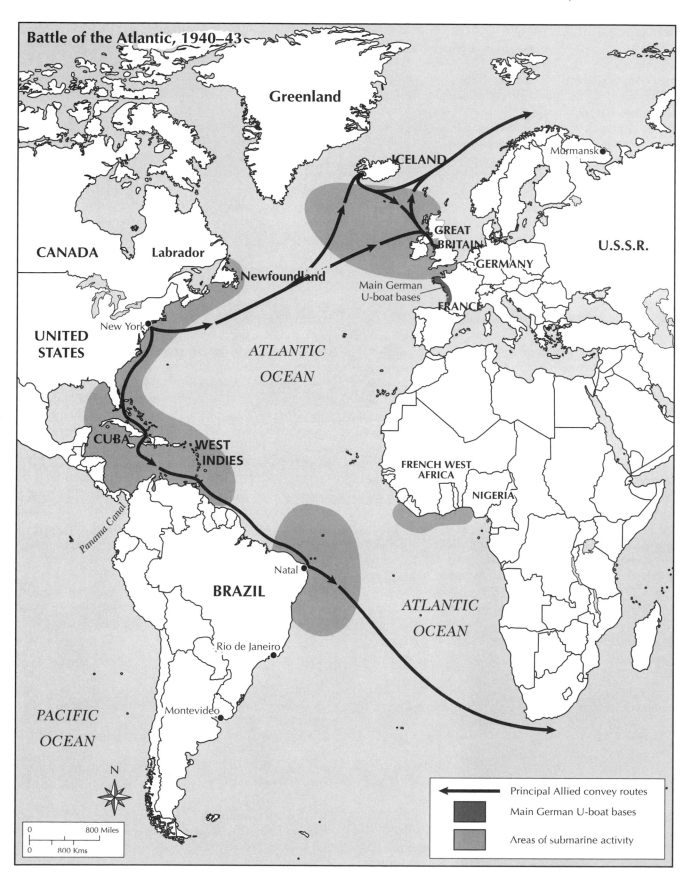

Battle of the Atlantic, 1940–43

Greenland

ICELAND

Murmansk

CANADA   Labrador

Newfoundland

GREAT
BRITAIN

GERMANY

U.S.S.R.

Main German
U-boat bases

FRANCE

New York

UNITED
STATES

ATLANTIC
OCEAN

CUBA

WEST
INDIES

FRENCH WEST
AFRICA

NIGERIA

Panama Canal

Natal

BRAZIL

ATLANTIC
OCEAN

Rio de Janeiro

PACIFIC
OCEAN

Montevideo

N

0   800 Miles

0   800 Kms

Principal Allied convey routes

Main German U-boat bases

Areas of submarine activity

intense period of the Battle of the Atlantic, from 1940 until early 1943, the Germans so threatened imports of American supplies and war materials to Great Britain that near crisis conditions existed. Yet the Allied ability to marshal technology, to organize and coordinate antisubmarine forces, and to produce ships, ultimately assured victory and enabled American LEND-LEASE ACT materials to reach their destinations in sufficient quantities.

Germany possessed 40 U-boats in September 1939, but these vessels could not access Atlantic shipping routes until the German conquest of Norway and France in April and June 1940. That summer, British antisubmarine resources were stretched thin, but convoys soon reduced losses. Grand Admiral Karl Doenitz then ordered U-boats to attack in "wolf packs" of up to 20 U-boats, and the wolf packs sank increasing tonnage from September 1940 into 1941, including 1,299 merchant ships in 1941 alone. Despite British and American successes in CODE BREAKING, and in using improved radio direction-finding equipment, radar, sonar, depth charges, and sea and air escorts, the wolf packs dominated in 1942. U-boats scored successes along the North Atlantic "Murmansk run" to the Soviet Union, in the Caribbean, and along the American coast.

The tide turned quickly between February and May 1943. Allied naval and air forces made better use of intelligence, and the American SHIPBUILDING industry provided more shipping and escort ships with improved antisubmarine weapons. Air cover provided by escort carriers of the U.S. NAVY and by U.S. ARMY AIR FORCES B-24 bombers equipped with radar and searchlights closed the "Atlantic gap." In February 1943, 22 U-boats were sunk, followed by 32 in March and April and 46 in May. Germany then suspended operations, tacitly admitting defeat, and convoys went unmolested to Europe after mid-1943. During the Battle of the Atlantic, the Germans lost 785 out of some 1,160 U-boats and sank nearly 2,600 Allied merchant ships.

See also WORLD WAR II EUROPEAN THEATER.

Further reading: Samuel Eliot Morrison, *The Battle of the Atlantic: September 1939–May 1943* (Champaign-Urbana: University of Illinois Press, 2001).

—Clayton D. Laurie

Atlantic Charter (1941)

The Atlantic Charter was a document of common principles issued by U.S. president FRANKLIN D. ROOSEVELT and British prime minister Winston Churchill on August 14, 1941, following a meeting on August 9–12 aboard U.S. and Royal Navy ships in Placentia Bay, off the coast of Newfoundland. The conference marked the first wartime meeting between Roosevelt and Churchill, but the two leaders had divergent aims. Churchill wanted a clear American commitment to join Britain in WORLD WAR II at a time when Britain was facing setbacks in North Africa, the Atlantic, and Southeast Asia. Already, the LEND-LEASE ACT of March 1941 had enabled increased material support of England, and Lend-Lease had been extended to the Soviet Union following her invasion by Germany in June 1941. But with most Americans still hoping to avoid entry into the war (the conference came just as the SELECTIVE SERVICE Act was being extended by only one vote in the House of Representatives), Roosevelt wanted to signal cooperation with Great Britain, but to stop well short of an explicit commitment to a military alliance. He also wanted a statement of principles to show that American principles would not be eroded by cooperation with the British or the Soviets.

The Atlantic Charter reflected principles stated in Woodrow Wilson's Fourteen Points of World War I, including self-determination, disarmament, and economic cooperation. It stated that neither country sought territorial aggrandizement. It acknowledged that all people had the right to choose their own form of government and not have territorial changes forced upon them, and called for free trade and freedom of the seas. The charter also vaguely indicated a desire for "the establishment of a wider and permanent system of general security." Though ISOLATIONISTS remained suspicious, most Americans felt that Roosevelt had successfully avoided a commitment of war, while many in Britain felt that Churchill had gotten too little and given up too much, including the possibility of losing its colonies. But the conference did serve to symbolize American-British cooperation. The Atlantic Charter itself became a basis of the Declaration of the United Nations in January 1942 and later a foundation of the UNITED NATIONS organization.

See also ANGLO-AMERICAN RELATIONS.

Further reading: Theodore A. Wilson, *The First Summit: Roosevelt and Churchill at Placentia Bay, 1941*, rev. ed. (Lawrence: University of Kansas Press, 1991).

—Charles Marquette

atomic bomb

The atomic bomb was a stunningly powerful new weapon developed during WORLD WAR II that relied upon nuclear fission—splitting the nucleus of a uranium or plutonium atom—to release a tremendous amount of energy. It played a vital role not only in the surrender of Japan in the PACIFIC THEATER of the war but also in the deteriorating relations of the GRAND ALLIANCE after the war.

The wartime race for an atomic weapon began in Germany in 1938 when two scientists discovered a way to split uranium atoms and produce atomic fission. The following year, with the threat of a potential Nazi nuclear arsenal in mind, the physicist Albert Einstein successfully persuaded President FRANKLIN D. ROOSEVELT to undertake an American-sponsored effort to build a bomb. In 1941, the U.S. government's OFFICE OF SCIENTIFIC RESEARCH AND DEVELOPMENT began secretly coordinating what became known as the MANHATTAN PROJECT. Scores of hand-picked researchers at universities across the country confirmed that a fission chain reaction was possible by isolating the rarer uranium isotope U-235 from the more common form, U-238, and later found that a new element, plutonium, behaved the same way. Between 1943 and 1945, army general Leslie R. Groves and physicist J. Robert Oppenheimer directed about 120,000 personnel in the $2 billion Manhattan Project at installations in 37 facilities in the United States and Canada. A laboratory at Los Alamos, in the New Mexico desert, was responsible for putting the weapon together.

In July 1945, as tests continued, and two months after Germany surrendered, President Harry S. Truman traveled to Germany to meet with his British and Soviet allies at the POTSDAM CONFERENCE. Among other issues, the "Big Three" leaders discussed how to prosecute the war against the sole remaining AXIS power, Japan. At the conclusion of the conference, Truman and new British prime minister Clement Attlee (the Soviets had not yet entered the war against Japan) issued the Potsdam Declaration, which called upon Japan to surrender unconditionally by August 3 or face "prompt and utter destruction," although not specifically mentioning the atomic bomb, which had just been successfully tested at Alamogordo. Nor did Truman explicitly inform Soviet leader Joseph Stalin about the bomb (the British had been involved in the project). Rather, as the conference neared its end, Truman (as he later wrote) "casually mentioned to Stalin that we had a new weapon of unusual destructive force." Stalin, who knew about the Manhattan Project because of Soviet ESPIONAGE, gave little reaction.

As the bomb moved from a potential weapon to an actual one in the spring and summer of 1945, questions arose over whether and how to use the bomb against Japan. It had generally been assumed by policymakers that the bomb would be a legitimate weapon of war, but the reality of the bomb and its immense power reopened the issue. Some of the very scientists who helped create the bomb, Oppenheimer among them, argued for restraint. Others advised Truman to demonstrate the bomb for spectators at a disclosed site or issue a warning to Tokyo. Army Chief of Staff General GEORGE C. MARSHALL, however, argued that using the awesome weapon was preferable to accepting a large number of Allied casualties in an invasion of Japan. The excessive brutality of the Pacific war, anger at Japan, and racial antagonisms also contributed to the decision. So did worsening SOVIET-AMERICAN RELATIONS, for some

American policymakers believed that using the bomb would impress the Soviets with American power and resolve and make them more amenable to cooperating on the host of postwar issues facing the Grand Alliance and causing disagreement and tension. Although he admitted "that an atomic bomb explosion would inflict damage and casualties beyond imagination," Truman went ahead with the prior decision to use it.

On August 6, 1945, the B-29 bomber *Enola Gay* dropped a uranium bomb on Hiroshima, devastating the city and killing up to 50,000 people immediately, with another 50,000 or more dying soon thereafter. Still, the Japanese refused to accept surrender terms. On August 8, the Soviet Union declared war against Japan. On August 9, the United States dropped a plutonium bomb, this time on the port city of Nagasaki, killing at least 50,000, and injuring another 60,000 (*see* HIROSHIMA AND NAGASAKI). In the face of the new atomic threat, the emperor intervened and offered surrender.

Almost immediately, the atomic bomb began to affect the postwar American economy, foreign policy, domestic affairs, and popular culture. Scientists, cultural critics, and government officials debated control over atomic know-how. Some cold war anticommunists saw the American atomic monopoly as a way to forestall Soviet aggression and intimidation. Idealistic opponents, however, believed that atomic power was so awesome that only international control could preserve the fragile peace. In 1949, the Soviets shocked Americans when they detonated their first atomic device. This event contributed to the United States adopting a more stringent form of containing communism, launched the development of a hydrogen bomb, and sparked investigations into spying at Los Alamos.

The atomic bomb also triggered conflicting feelings of optimism and fear. In the 1950s, the government promoted atomic energy as an efficient, clean, inexpensive form of power. Unrealistic innovators foresaw a nuclear utopia where atomic power fueled kitchen appliances and automobiles. Others acknowledged the potential danger of radiation fallout by building bomb shelters. All the while, the government's civil defense program assured Americans that fear had been exaggerated and that the peaceful atom could bring benefits to all.

Issues of control gradually gave way to the threat of proliferation. While the atomic bomb ignited the superpowers' nuclear arms race, other nations also sought atomic technology. Despite a global nuclear nonproliferation treaty, by the end of the 20th century no fewer than two dozen countries possessed nuclear weapons, many of which were used for leverage against old regional enemies.

Further reading: Richard Rhodes, *The Making of the Atomic Bomb* (New York: Simon & Schuster, 1986); Martin

J. Sherwin, *A World Destroyed: The Atomic Bomb and the Grand Alliance* (New York: Knopf, 1975); Allan M. Winkler, *Life Under a Cloud: American Anxiety about the Atom* (New York: Oxford University Press, 1993).

—Andrew J. Falk

automobile industry

By the 1920s, the American automobile industry had become one of the nation's most important big businesses, central to the nation's ECONOMY and to patterns of TRANSPORTATION. The secret to success for the "Big Three" manufacturers (Ford, General Motors, and Chrysler) that dominated the industry was to mass produce automobiles for a mass market, selling the product at a reasonable price and thereby assuring large profits. Workers were paid well, but were nonunion, a condition that Ford and the other corporate heads enforced through various means of infiltration and intimidation. In 1929 alone, nearly 4.5 million cars were sold—roughly one for every 25 Americans. The automobile industry then suffered during the GREAT DEPRESSION, was crucial to the efforts of LABOR to unionize mass production industries in the 1930s, and played a vital role in economic MOBILIZATION during WORLD WAR II.

The 1930s proved to be a trying decade for automobile industry leaders, who had to cope with the impact of the depression and with NEW DEAL regulatory and labor policies. As automobile sales dropped by three-fourths between 1929 and 1932, production, profits, and employment all plummeted as well. The New Deal's NATIONAL RECOVERY ADMINISTRATION (NRA) drafted codes of fair competition for automobiles as for other industries. Although Ford refused to cooperate, the auto codes were lenient, allowing for industry self-regulation and bypassing NRA Section 7(a)—the guarantee of collective bargaining between employers and workers—with a clause that enabled companies to hire and fire employees for union-related activities.

Another New Deal measure, the NATIONAL LABOR RELATIONS ACT of 1935, which guaranteed the right of collective bargaining and outlawed unfair labor practices, together with the emergence of the CONGRESS OF INDUSTRIAL ORGANIZATIONS (CIO) in the mid-1930s, then led to the unionization of much of the automobile industry. The key event in the automotive industry—and because of its significance, in mass production industries more generally—was the 44-day sit-down strike at General Motors' Fisher Body Plant in Flint, Michigan, the largest automobile industry plant in the world. The strike began on December 30, 1936, when workers refused to leave the plant until the demands of the new United Automobile Workers union were recognized, and ended on February 11, 1937, when GM gave in. During the brilliantly organized strike, neither Roosevelt nor Michigan's governor, Frank Murphy, used troops to break up the job action, and GM lost $175 million in sales as car production dropped from 15,000 per week to barely 150.

As a result of the General Motors strike, UAW membership increased from 98,000 to 400,000 in the first months of 1937. Buoyed by success at GM and Chrysler, the autoworkers' next objective was Ford, but the old carmaker and his vigilante police force—the "Service Department," which intimidated and physically roughed up labor organizers—kept the UAW out until May 1941. But the CIO success with GM and Chrysler in the automobile industry helped produce unionization in the STEEL INDUSTRY and elsewhere.

After the RECESSION OF 1937–38, when car sales dropped by half, the automobile industry recovered and was rolling out nearly 4 million vehicles by 1941, a million more than two years earlier. Remembering the lean years of the early 1930s, automakers worried about the consequences of converting to defense production at the expense of a growing consumer market and moved slowly and without urgency toward conversion to military production. They continued to produce new cars despite growing shortages of materials and the suspension of new model changes to allow the use of machine tools for military needs. After PEARL HARBOR, the WAR PRODUCTION BOARD ordered suspensions of passenger vehicle production for the duration of the war.

The automobile industry ultimately played a large and vital role in the war effort, despite such notable disappointments as the Ford-produced B-24 bomber. Not only did the automakers turn out trucks, jeeps, and TANKS, but they produced aircraft parts, machine guns, small arms ammunition, helmets, and binoculars as well—in all, an estimated one-fifth of national output. Conversion to military production led to the employment of new workers, including AFRICAN AMERICANS and women (who at one point constituted one-fourth of the workers in auto industry plants), and to a decline in factory control over workers, which increased workers' power and strikes.

Beginning in 1943, RECONVERSION of the auto plants was planned, but car makers took part in the so-called war within a war, in which companies still producing war goods opposed others converting to peacetime production. At war's end, with much of the existing passenger vehicle stock aging or lacking proper parts, the automobile industry began to make up for lost time, as more than 2 million new vehicles were produced in 1946 and nearly 7 million in 1950. In the immediate postwar years, the U.S. automotive industry produced 80 percent of all motor vehicles made in the world.

See also BUSINESS.

Further reading: Sidney Fine, *Sit-Down: The General Motors Strike of 1936–37* (Ann Arbor: University of Michigan Press, 1995); James J. Flink, *The Automobile Age* (Cambridge, Mass.: MIT Press, 1988).

—William J. Thompson

Axis

The Axis was a coalition of nations led by Germany, Italy, and Japan that fought against the United States and other nations of the GRAND ALLIANCE during World War II. (See WORLD WAR II EUROPEAN THEATER.)

Several treaties signed from 1936 to 1940 bound Germany, Italy, and Japan together. The first came on October 25, 1936, with the announcement of an "axis" connecting Germany and Italy. A month later, on November 25, 1936, Germany and Japan signed an anti-Comintern treaty aimed at the Soviet Union, and on November 6, 1937, Italy joined Germany and Japan in an anti-Comintern agreement. On May 22, 1939, the "Pact of Steel" brought Germany and Italy into a full military alliance. And then on September 27, 1940, the Rome-Berlin-Tokyo Axis was cemented when Germany, Italy, and Japan signed the Tripartite Pact.

In the Tripartite Pack, signed after Germany had overrun western Europe in the spring of 1940, Germany, Italy, and Japan declared they would assist each other by "all political, economic and military means" if one of them were attacked by a "Power at present not involved in the European War or in the Chinese-Japanese conflict." The two major nations not involved in combat in Europe or Asia in September 1940 were the United States and the Soviet Union. But since a separate article excluded the Soviet Union, which had signed a mutual nonaggression treaty with Germany (the NAZI-SOVIET PACT) in 1939, the treaty was really aimed at the United States and at deterring the U.S. from military action on behalf of Britain or China. By 1940, therefore, Germany and Italy were cooperating in military operations in Europe and North Africa, while Germany, Italy, and Japan had joined together in what amounted to a military treaty of defense against the United States.

As the 1936 and 1937 anti-Comintern treaties indicated, concerns about the Soviet Union helped to produce the Axis alliance. But each of the three major Axis nations also had broad territorial and political ambitions that lay behind their alliance. In particular, Germany aspired to conquer Europe, establish a "thousand-year Reich" of Nazi domination, and implement the HOLOCAUST to eliminate Jewry, while Japan sought to create and dominate what it called a "Greater East Asia Co-prosperity Sphere." One Axis strategy was to turn conquered territories into suppliers of their war machines, and in some cases Axis-con-

Benito Mussolini and Adolf Hitler (l to r) in Munich, Germany, 1940 *(Library of Congress)*

trolled nations contributed troops to the war effort. Such states as Hungary, Bulgaria, Romania, and Slovakia, as well as the Japanese-controlled government in Manchukuo, became part of the Axis alliance.

Despite growing American opposition to the ambitions and actions of the Axis nations from the late 1930s on, and despite its increasingly pro-Allied and anti-Axis policies in 1940 and 1941, the United States did not enter the war until the Japanese attack on PEARL HARBOR in December 1941. In response to America's declaration of war on Japan, Germany and Italy declared war on the United States. The American entry into the war against the three Axis nations helped create the Grand Alliance of the United States, the Soviet Union, and Britain that ultimately defeated the Axis.

In actuality, there was little collaboration and coordination between the Germans and Italians on the one hand and the Japanese on the other. Japan had been angered when Germany concluded the Nazi-Soviet Pact of 1939 despite the anti-Comintern treaties of 1936 and 1937. Germany subsequently did not inform Japan when it abrogated the Nazi-Soviet Pact and invaded the Soviet Union in June 1941, nor did the Japanese tell Germany of their plans to attack Pearl Harbor on December 7, 1941. Japan did not declare war on the Soviet Union after the German invasion of the USSR. During critical points in the war, moreover, Japan and Germany cooperated only minimally, and Hitler criticized the Japanese for not doing more to attack Allied merchant shipping in the Pacific delivering American LEND-LEASE ACT aid to the Soviets.

German and Italy did work together in the EUROPEAN THEATER, with Germany as the dominant partner. They jointly waged the NORTH AFRICAN CAMPAIGN, and Germans contributed in a major way to the defense of Italy during the ITALIAN CAMPAIGN. Italian troops went to the eastern front to support the Nazis in the German-Soviet campaign. But the Italian surrender to the Allies in September 1943 confirmed the German conviction that Italy was an unreliable partner.

The United States's entrance into the war turned the tide of the war in favor of the Grand Alliance and led to the defeat of the Axis. In the European theater, American lend-lease assistance and the U.S. ARMY and the U.S. NAVY contributed importantly to bringing the surrender of Germany in May 1945 and, with it, the effective end of the Axis alliance. In the PACIFIC THEATER, the United States played the major role in defeating Japan, and the Japanese surrender came soon after the use of the ATOMIC BOMB on HIROSHIMA AND NAGASAKI in early August 1945.

See also FOREIGN POLICY.

Further reading: Gerhard L. Weinberg, *A World at Arms: A Global History of World War II* (New York: Cambridge University Press, 1994).

—Michael Leonard

B

Banking Act of 1933

The Banking Act of 1933, also known as the Glass-Steagall Act, was the first piece of NEW DEAL legislation to bring significant reform to the banking system. Developed by CONGRESS and signed by President FRANKLIN D. ROOSEVELT on June 16, 1933, the act's main provisions were to separate commercial and investment banking, to create the FEDERAL DEPOSIT INSURANCE CORPORATION (FDIC), and to increase the power of the Federal Reserve Board. It played a major role in strengthening and stabilizing American banking.

Banking policy of the early 20th century allowed commercial banks to trade in stocks and bonds and underwrite securities. This practice was never seriously challenged until the STOCK MARKET CRASH of 1929, which wiped out billions of dollars in assets. Because banks could not turn their greatly devalued paper assets into cash, they were often unable to pay off panicked depositors. As the GREAT DEPRESSION deepened in the early 1930s, thousands of banks failed and countless individual bank accounts were lost. When President Roosevelt was inaugurated in March 1933, the banking system was in crisis and had been temporarily shut down by banking "holidays" declared in state after state. The EMERGENCY BANKING ACT OF 1933 restored confidence and brought the reopening of the banking system, but it did not bring fundamental change.

Although Roosevelt wanted to defer further banking legislation, members of Congress thought reform was essential. In mid-May, Senator Carter Glass (D-Va.) and Congressman Henry Steagall (D-Ala.) proposed their bill to address problems in banking. The prohibition against commercial banks from also engaging in investment banking ended a practice that had contributed not only to the liquidity crisis of the early 1930s but also to speculation that had helped bring on the stock market crash. The Glass-Steagall Act prohibited commercial banks from underwriting or dealing in corporate securities. The act's most important contribution to banking stability, at first opposed by Roosevelt and most bankers, was the creation of the FDIC (initially called the Temporary Deposit Insurance Corporation). The FDIC insured individual bank depositors up to $2,500 (raised to $5,000 in 1934), a crucial guarantee that eliminated the individual investor's fear of losing deposited money and thus prevented bank panics and resulting bank failures. The Glass-Steagall Act also gave the Federal Reserve Board new power over open-market operations (selling and buying government securities to affect interest rates), an important reform carried further by the BANKING ACT OF 1935.

The Glass-Steagall Act, especially the creation of the FDIC, brought stability to the banking industry and a sharp reduction in bank failures. In fact, fewer banks suspended operations between 1933 and 1940 than in any single year in the 1920s. Ironically, the Roosevelt administration received credit for a major and successful measure that really originated in Congress.

Further reading: Susan Estabrook, *The Banking Crisis of 1933* (Lexington: University Press of Kentucky, 1973).

—Michael Leonard

Banking Act of 1935

Recognized as the last major accomplishment of the SECOND NEW DEAL of 1935 and as the most important banking reform of the NEW DEAL, the Banking Act of 1935 produced the first substantial modification of the Federal Reserve system since its inception in 1913. It gave the federal GOVERNMENT effective control of the banking system and monetary policy.

In 1934, President FRANKLIN D. ROOSEVELT appointed MARRINER ECCLES to head the Federal Reserve Board, and Eccles then drafted a banking bill that would give the federal government more control over money and credit. Sent to CONGRESS in February 1935, the bill passed the House of Representatives relatively easily. It encountered resistance in the Senate, however, particularly from Virginia's Carter Glass, a principal architect of the 1913 Federal Reserve Act who opposed centralized federal control of banking, and from many private bankers, especially the big New York bankers. In June, FDR made the bill a "must" item of legislation. Despite the fact that Glass rewrote much of the bill, the final draft, though not as far-reaching as originally intended, kept many of Eccles's main objectives intact.

The banking act, signed by Roosevelt on August 23, 1935, had several key features. It created a strong, central board of governors of the Federal Reserve System that could control the operations of regional banks and manage discount and interest rates. The law centralized open market operations (the sales and purchases of government securities to affect interest rates) in the Federal Open Market Committee in order to reduce the influence of the private bankers and to consolidate control of the U.S. money market. The law also empowered the president to appoint seven members to this newly formed board of governors, with the consent of the Senate, for 14-year terms. Eccles was appointed chairman of the new board of governors. Finally, the act also completed the implementation of deposit insurance and the FEDERAL DEPOSIT INSURANCE CORPORATION (FDIC), which was initiated under the BANKING ACT OF 1933. State banks were required to join the Federal Reserve System before July 1, 1942, if they wanted the benefits from the FDIC.

Further reading: Helen M. Burns, *The American Banking Community and New Deal Banking Reforms, 1933–1935* (Westport, Conn.: Greenwood, 1974); Marriner Eccles, *Beckoning Frontiers: Public and Personal Recollections* (New York: Knopf, 1951).

—Michael T. Walsh

Baruch, Bernard M. (1870–1965)

A millionaire stock speculator, Bernard Baruch offered advice to the administration of President FRANKLIN D. ROOSEVELT, as he did to presidents from Woodrow Wilson to Lyndon B. Johnson. He assiduously cultivated the press and his own public image as the "park-bench statesman" and adviser to presidents.

Bernard Mannes Baruch was born in South Carolina, graduated from City College of New York, and became a millionaire by the time he was 30 by virtue of his success on the stock market. During World War I, President Wilson appointed Baruch head of the War Industries Board, and Baruch won a favorable public reputation for his role in helping to increase American war production. He was an influential member of the DEMOCRATIC PARTY during the 1920s, and gave financial support to many Democrats in

the CONGRESS, especially those sharing his pro-BUSINESS views.

In the ELECTION OF 1932, Baruch did not endorse Roosevelt until after FDR had won the Democratic nomination. Though a number of Roosevelt's advisers were wary of Baruch, his standing in the Democratic Party and the money he could bring to the campaign led Roosevelt to suggest that he consult with the BRAIN TRUST on industrial recovery policy. Baruch's protégé, General HUGH JOHNSON, became the first administrator of the NATIONAL RECOVERY ADMINISTRATION, a NEW DEAL agency modeled on the War Industries Board. Other Baruch associates, including George Peek, the first head of the Agricultural Adjustment Administration, also had significant roles in New Deal programs. Baruch himself remained close to conservative Democrats, had a good relationship with ELEANOR ROOSEVELT, and maintained his cordial relations with the press.

Baruch's relationship with FDR and other New Dealers remained strained, however, as his career in WORLD WAR II revealed. At first, Roosevelt attempted to keep him at arm's length, but Roosevelt eventually named him to lead an investigation of the rubber shortage. FDR then agreed that Baruch might become head of the WAR PRODUCTION BOARD (WPB), but the president backed away from the appointment and it never eventuated. Toward the end of the war, Baruch coauthored a report on RECONVERSION for the WPB that played an important role in shaping reconversion policy in a way favorable to business.

After the war, Baruch presented American recommendations on atomic energy to the UNITED NATIONS. But President Harry S. Truman, like others, thought Baruch self-serving and cut ties with him after Baruch refused to serve on Truman's 1948 reelection committee. Nonetheless, Baruch's public reputation remained such that Presidents John F. Kennedy and Lyndon B. Johnson made a point of consulting with him in the 1960s.

Further reading: Jordan A. Schwarz, *The Speculator: Bernard Baruch in Washington, 1917–1965* (Chapel Hill: University of North Carolina Press, 1981).

Bataan Death March (1942)

On April 9, 1942, an estimated 10,000 American and 60,000 Filipino troops surrendered to the Japanese on the Bataan Peninsula of Luzon island in the PHILIPPINES. On the subsequent "Bataan Death March," the Japanese drove the 70,000 PRISONERS OF WAR (POWs), the largest seizure ever of American forces, on a brutal 65-mile journey to prison. Some 600 Americans and nearly 10,000 Filipinos died when the Japanese clubbed, bayoneted, or shot strag-

Photograph taken of American and Filipino soldiers during the Bataan Death March *(National Archives)*

glers. Thousands more died in prison camps. The Bataan Death March was one of the events producing a fierce animosity toward Japan during WORLD WAR II.

The Japanese had landed in northern Luzon in December 1941 after the attack on PEARL HARBOR, and pushed American forces south to Bataan and Corregidor Island. On April 9, the embattled and weakened American and Filipino contingent, without sufficient ammunition, food, or medicine to continue effective resistance, surrendered. The Japanese, who were unprepared for so many prisoners and who did not respect them because they had surrendered, forced the POWs to march northward to Camp O'Donnell in the hot sun without food and water. Along the way, the Japanese subjected their captives to a variety of cruel humiliations, and to death by decapitation, beating, gunfire, or bayonets if they were to stop.

After reaching Camp O'Donnell, the remaining prisoners died at the rate of one person every 45 minutes. With only three badly working water taps, diseases such as malaria and dysentery along with starvation and dehydration took their toll. Another 1,500 Americans and at least 25,000 Filipinos died by July 1942. Beginning in June, the Americans were moved to a better-equipped POW camp on the other side of Manila Bay with those who had surrendered on Corregidor on May 6. Gradually, these prisoners would be split up and put to work for the Japanese until their eventual liberation at the end of the war. The Filipinos who remained behind at Camp O'Donnell were released at the end of July.

Further reading: Donald Knox, *Death March: The Survivors of Bataan* (New York: Harcourt Brace Jovanovich, 1985); John W. Whitman, *Bataan Our Last Ditch: The Bataan Campaign, 1942* (New York: Hippocrene, 1990).
—Ronald G. Simon

Berle, Adolf A., Jr. (1895–1917)

Adolf Augustus Berle, a member of the BRAIN TRUST of FRANKLIN D. ROOSEVELT and later an assistant secretary of state, was born January 29, 1895, in Boston, Massachusetts, to devoutly Christian and socially active parents. Berle graduated from high school at age 12 and earned his bachelor's, master's, and law degrees from Harvard University by the time he was 21. He practiced law and taught at Harvard Business School, developing expertise in corporate law and Latin American affairs, before joining the faculty of Columbia Law School in 1927. Heavily influenced by the Social Gospel movement, he entered public life through service with New York City's Henry Street Settlement House.

In 1932, RAYMOND C. MOLEY introduced Berle to Roosevelt, and Moley, Berle, and REXFORD G. TUGWELL formed the nucleus of FDR's Brain Trust. Also in 1932, *The Modern Corporation and Private Property* appeared, coauthored with the economist Gardiner C. Means. The book became Berle's most influential publication and articulated his intellectual contribution to the Brain Trust. He believed that the modern corporate economy had concentrated power in the hands of a professional managerial class, out of reach of stockholders and public control, a situation that required federal intervention through reform of the banking system and securities markets. As the most moderate of the Brain Trusters, and still steeped in his Social Gospel roots, Berle believed businessmen could be "converted" to a more responsible brand of capitalism rather than being forced to do so by the GOVERNMENT.

After Roosevelt's victory in the ELECTION OF 1932, Berle did not immediately take up a post in the administration, although he continued as a presidential adviser. He advised FIORELLO LaGUARDIA in his successful 1933 New York City mayoral race and served as city chamberlain for three years. In 1938, Berle became an assistant secretary of state for Latin American affairs, and in this position played a crucial role in implementing Roosevelt's GOOD NEIGHBOR POLICY and advocating collective security in the Western Hemisphere after the outbreak of WORLD WAR II in 1939. During the war, his duties included coordinating the INTELLIGENCE activities of the State Department. By 1944, however, Berle had lost much of his earlier influence with Roosevelt, and his notorious arrogance had alienated most of his State Department colleagues. In November 1944, he resigned his position as assistant secretary of state.

Berle then served for a year as ambassador to Brazil before returning full-time to his law practice and teaching. In later years, he remained active in public life, and although never regaining his earlier influence, served with such organizations as Radio Free Europe and John F. Kennedy's Interdepartmental Task Force on Latin America. Berle died in New York City on February 17, 1971.

See also NEW DEAL.

Further reading: Jordan A. Schwarz, *Liberal: Adolf A. Berle and the Vision of an American Era* (New York: Free Press, 1987).

—Mary E. Carroll-Mason

Bethune, Mary McLeod (1875–1955)

Mary McLeod Bethune, an educator and the leading member of the BLACK CABINET of the NEW DEAL era, was an advocate for CIVIL RIGHTS and education for the black community and for New Deal efforts to assist AFRICAN AMERICANS. One of 17 children born to an illiterate sharecropper in South Carolina, Bethune was schooled at the Presbyterian Mission School, graduated from Scotia Seminary in North Carolina in 1893, and then received two years of higher education at Moody Bible Institute in Chicago. In 1898 she married Albertus Bethune, and they had one son, Albert. After leaving Moody, Bethune went to teach in the SOUTH and in 1904 founded the Daytona Normal and Industrial School for Negro Girls, which later became Bethune-Cookman College in Daytona Beach, Florida.

In 1927, Bethune began an important personal friendship with ELEANOR ROOSEVELT after a meeting of the National Council of Women, where Bethune was the only black woman invited. She introduced Roosevelt to influential African Americans and educated her about race relations and racial inequalities. In 1935 she helped found the National Council of Negro Women, and throughout the 1930s fought for racial justice on a variety of issues, including the effort to free the black youths convicted in the SCOTTSBORO BOYS case. She also supported antilynching legislation, demonstrated against the poll tax, worked for extended employment and educational opportunities for blacks, and urged federal support of the SOUTHERN TENANT FARMERS UNION, which sought to help tenant farmers and sharecroppers.

Bethune's formal relationship with FRANKLIN D. ROOSEVELT and the New Deal began in 1936, when she asked to meet with FDR regarding the impact of the NATIONAL YOUTH ADMINISTRATION (NYA) on minority groups. Roosevelt appointed Bethune as head of the NYA's Division of Negro Affairs, which made her the highest-ranking African American in the government. She became the leader of the

Mary McLeod Bethune *(National Archives)*

Black Cabinet, an informal but significant group of black federal officials who worked to increase New Deal attention and assistance to African Americans.

Bethune received numerous honorary degrees and awards, and her writings include *What the Negro Wants*, *Spiritual Autobiographies*, weekly columns in newspapers, and articles in publications of the National Council of Negro Women. She continued her civil rights work until her death in 1955.

Further reading: Rackman Holt, *Mary McLeod Bethune* (Garden City, N.J.: Doubleday, 1964); B. Joyce Ross, "Mary McLeod Bethune and the National Youth Administration: A Case Study of Power Relationships in the Black Cabinet of Franklin D. Roosevelt," *Journal of Negro History* 60 (January 1975): 1–28.

—Anne Rothfeld

Black, Hugo L. (1886–1971)

Hugo Lafayette Black was a United States senator from Alabama (1927–1937) and the first SUPREME COURT justice appointed by President FRANKLIN D. ROOSEVELT.

Black was born on February 27, 1886, in Clay County, Alabama. He attended the University of Alabama Law

School, graduating in 1906. Black's practice in Birmingham focused on the concerns of working-class whites, including personal injury litigation. He also served as a police court judge and public prosecutor, where he demonstrated great concern for CIVIL LIBERTIES. After army service in the United States during World War I, Black returned to an expanding law practice. To make contacts, he joined several organizations, including the Ku Klux Klan. Black was first elected to the Senate in 1926.

Reelected to a second term in 1932, Black became one of the strongest supporters of the NEW DEAL and gained significant attention for his investigation of public utility corporations. His dramatic style during legislative hearings delighted the press, but overshadowed his hard work in winning passage of significant legislation including the FAIR LABOR STANDARDS ACT, the PUBLIC UTILITY HOLDING COMPANY ACT, and the TENNESSEE VALLEY AUTHORITY. Black also supported some of President Roosevelt's less successful ventures, including the 1937 COURT-PACKING PLAN proposed after the Supreme Court overturned major New Deal programs in the mid-1930s.

Roosevelt nominated Black to the Supreme Court in August 1937, and after confirmation by the Senate, Black took his seat on the Court that month. Shortly thereafter, reports of his membership in the Klan made headlines. A storm of controversy raged until Black addressed the nation, admitting his past Klan membership but repudiating the Klan and declaring the matter closed. Though Black wrote the majority decision in *KOREMATSU V. UNITED STATES* (1944) that upheld the RELOCATION OF JAPANESE AMERICANS—he maintained that military necessity justified the policy—any doubts about his commitment to justice for Americans of all races were dispelled during the remainder of his career.

In his early years on the Court, Black joined the new liberal majority in decisions sustaining activist federal policy. During his 34 years as justice, Black became known especially for his belief in absolute freedom of speech; for his strict, literal interpretation of the Constitution; and for his view that the Fourteenth Amendment required the states to abide by the limitations set by the first eight amendments.

After several strokes, Black retired from the Supreme Court on September 17, 1971. He died eight days later.

Further reading: Roger K. Newman, *Hugo Black: A Biography* (New York: Pantheon, 1994).

—Jill Frahm

Black Cabinet

An informal, self-organized advisory group in the administration of President FRANKLIN D. ROOSEVELT, the "Black Cabinet" worked to improve the impact of NEW DEAL programs on AFRICAN AMERICANS. Sometimes also referred to by the press as the "black brain trust," though participants called themselves the Federal Council on Negro Affairs, the Black Cabinet included a changing group of African Americans holding official positions in the GOVERNMENT. The most important members of the Black Cabinet included MARY MCLEOD BETHUNE, director of the Division of Negro Affairs in the NATIONAL YOUTH ADMINISTRATION (NYA); William H. Hastie, assistant solicitor in the Department of the Interior (and later appointed by FDR as the first black federal judge); Robert C. Weaver, adviser for Negro affairs in the PUBLIC WORKS ADMINISTRATION; and Robert Vann, assistant to the attorney general.

Often meeting at Bethune's home, the Black Cabinet sought to identify and recruit gifted black men and women to serve in government positions, to make the Roosevelt administration more sensitive to the problems of black communities, and to influence federal policies affecting African Americans. Their recommendations ranged from avoiding racial slurs in speeches and stories, to desegregating government cafeterias, to ensuring that African Americans got their fair and needed share of government programs. In such efforts, the Black Cabinet sometimes found ready allies from administration figures, including ELEANOR ROOSEVELT, Secretary of the Interior HAROLD ICKES, relief administrator HARRY L. HOPKINS, and NYA director Aubrey Williams. The Black Cabinet also fielded complaints and inquiries from black constituents, with some being forwarded to the White House's attention, and they provided information to the press on discriminatory aspects of the New Deal and of government programs.

The impact of the Black Cabinet was both significant and limited. It marked a distinct break from the absence of a significant black voice in the federal government and served to raise the consciousness of FDR and New Deal officials. In part because of its efforts, Roosevelt appointed many more African Americans to federal positions than had previous administrations. And the Black Cabinet had some impact on New Deal programs. Thanks to Bethune and Aubrey Williams, the NYA gave substantial assistance to African Americans, while Harold Ickes worked to ensure that Public Works Administration projects hired black workers. Other New Deal agencies—the WORKS PROGRESS ADMINISTRATION and the CIVILIAN CONSERVATION CORPS, for example—were less discriminatory that they might otherwise have been. Yet New Deal programs frequently did discriminate against African Americans, often but not always because of local implementation; and in view of their disproportionate unemployment and poverty blacks rarely got their full share of New Deal help despite the continuing efforts of the Black Cabinet.

Despite such limits, the Black Cabinet had both real and symbolic importance. It represented a change from past administrations, and it helped push the New Deal further than it would otherwise have gone in giving attention and help to African Americans. Many black Americans recognized and appreciated such change, and both by its efforts in Washington and by its active campaigning, the Black Cabinet helped Roosevelt win black votes as African Americans began to shift decisively to the DEMOCRATIC PARTY in the ELECTION OF 1936. By the end of the 1930s, as WORLD WAR II approached and attention went increasingly to FOREIGN POLICY and defense issues, the Black Cabinet became less active and influential.

See also CIVIL RIGHTS; POLITICS IN THE ROOSEVELT ERA.

Further reading: B. Joyce Ross, "Mary McLeod Bethune and the National Youth Administration: A Case Study of Power Relationships in the Black Cabinet of Franklin D. Roosevelt," *Journal of Negro History* 60 (January 1975): 1–28; Nancy J. Weiss, *Farewell to the Party of Lincoln: Black Politics in the Age of FDR* (Princeton, N.J.: Princeton University Press, 1983 [esp. chapter 7]).

black market

In order to allocate consumer goods fairly during WORLD WAR II, the OFFICE OF PRICE ADMINISTRATION (OPA) administered the RATIONING program of the federal GOVERNMENT. To prevent inflation, the OPA regulated prices in the wartime system of WAGE AND PRICE CONTROLS. Though generally successful, rationing and restrictions on consumer spending proved unpopular in a nation just emerging from the GREAT DEPRESSION and with money to spend again after a decade of hard times. As a consequence, an illegal "black market" existed on the WORLD WAR II HOME FRONT.

Home front Americans understood the need for rationing and controls, but even though overall consumer spending increased during the war, the public did not enjoy or always abide by the rules. In order to buy additional amounts of coveted but scarce and rationed goods—gasoline, for example, or meat, or sugar, or shoes—people sometimes would pay prices above the established limits or buy items without using the required rationing coupons. Most black market violations took place in established retail operations between merchants and customers, and proved difficult for the OPA to prevent. Up to one-fourth of Americans surveyed said that it could be justifiable to purchase goods on the black market. One study estimated that one in five businesses received warnings about such activities and that one in 15 were charged with illegal operations. By some estimates, up to half of all businesses were involved in black market activities of various kinds. The court system generally gave no more than light fines to the few who were prosecuted and convicted.

Some of the rationed items proved especially susceptible to flourishing black market activities. Gasoline rationing, particularly unpopular because it limited the use of automobiles for both necessary and recreational driving, gave rise to an extensive black market. Here, organized criminals played an important role by producing counterfeit ration coupons that they sold both to gasoline station operators and to drivers. Legitimate coupons were stolen from OPA offices (coupons for 20 million gallons were lifted from the Washington, D.C., office) and sold at a premium. Motorists sometimes sold excess coupons to service stations or to other drivers—or gave them to friends, which was also an infraction of the rules. Working with the FEDERAL BUREAU OF INVESTIGATION, the OPA took such measures at it could to stop these and other black market activities, but the agency estimated that 5 percent of all gasoline sold was sold illegally. Similarly, an active black market existed for tires.

Food was another source of widespread black market activities, especially when shortages occurred. Meat gave rise to especially serious black market operations, including the resurgence of cattle rustling in some places and selling the stolen beef to cooperating packers and butchers. Wholesalers and retailers would sell meat and poultry above ceiling prices in a variety of ways, including taking side payments, or giving short weights. Another practice was the so-called red market, whereby a low grade of meat was sold for higher-grade prices or where more bone or fat than allowable was included. "Tie-in" sales, requiring customers to purchase an unpopular item in order to get a desired one, also took place in meat as with other items. Expensive restaurants apparently turned to the black market to ensure meat for their customers. Sugar, coffee, and other desirable scarce items also experienced black market operations.

The majority of home front Americans participated only incidentally at most in black market activities and supported efforts to end them—partly because the black market often siphoned goods away from legitimate sales. Some communities organized campaigns that reduced such operations. Even so, the black market was a reality on the World War II American home front, an indication that many people were unwilling to experience sacrifice that they thought excessive or unfair or even inconvenient, and that many merchants were willing to profit from scarcity.

Further reading: Richard Lingeman, *Don't You Know There's a War On? The American Home Front, 1941–1945* (New York: Putnam, 1970).

blitzkrieg

Blitzkrieg, or "lightning war," was the tactic of rapid attack with massive numbers of mechanized infantry and tank divisions covered by close air support that enabled the German army to quickly invade and overrun Poland, Scandinavia, the Low Countries, and France in the early stages of WORLD WAR II. Blitzkrieg doctrine was to use highly mechanized armored forces to win quick victories, robbing the enemy of time to mobilize their forces and resources, and thus avoid a war of attrition that Germany was ill prepared to win.

Blitzkrieg tactics were developed from the traditional German military doctrine of encirclement and annihilation, and from the high losses during the static trench warfare during World War I. During the interwar period, the German general staff adopted the idea that TANKS should be separated from traditional infantry units and be used with motorized infantry units or operate independently. Tanks could be used to destroy the enemy's front lines, and then penetrate deep into the rear areas, destroying the enemy's command and control infrastructure and its will to fight. In theory, the use of mechanized forces in unison with tactical AIR POWER would allow movement of some 250 miles per day and devastate the enemy before they could form any resistance.

Europe got its first taste of blitzkrieg warfare on September 1, 1939, when 50 divisions of the German army rolled across the German-Polish border, and Poland surrendered by the end of the month. The true power of blitzkrieg was demonstrated in the spring of 1940. Using amphibious landings, paratroopers, and panzer divisions, the German army swept into Scandinavia in April 1940 with such speed that Denmark surrendered within a few hours and Norway was subdued in a few weeks. Then, on May 10, 1940, Germany invaded the Low Countries of Belgium, Holland, and Luxembourg. Four days later, German forces moved through the Ardennes Forest, north of the useless Maginot line, and pivoted north toward the English Channel, eventually trapping the majority of the Allied army in the port of Dunkirk. The remaining French forces crumbled in front of the German onslaught and France surrendered in less than 40 days from the start of the invasion.

The greatest asset of blitzkrieg proved to be its largest drawback. While blitzkrieg gave the German army the ability to drive large distances over a relatively short period of time, it required huge amounts of supply and support to sustain such long-distance drives. It could not be successful against an enemy that could trade soldiers and space for time, a lesson that Germany would learn from the ultimately disastrous invasion of the Soviet Union in 1941.

See also WORLD WAR II EUROPEAN THEATER.

Further reading: James S. Corum, *The Roots of Blitzkrieg: Hans von Seeckt and German Military Reform* (Lawrence: University Press of Kansas, 1992).

—George Michael Curry

Bonus Army (1932)

As the GREAT DEPRESSION deepened in the early 1930s, UNEMPLOYMENT reached at least one-fourth of the workforce and impoverished Americans increasingly looked to the federal GOVERNMENT for help. Asking for prepayment of a bonus due them beginning in 1945, World War I veterans constituted one group asking for federal assistance. In 1931, CONGRESS enacted (over the veto of President HERBERT C. HOOVER) legislation allowing the veterans to borrow up to half the value of their bonus. Then in 1932, some 20,000 veterans and family members—the "Bonus Army"—went to Washington, D.C., to demand full payment of their bonus. Hoover's response in not just opposing the bonus but having the military forcibly disperse the Bonus Army contributed to his landslide defeat in the ELECTION OF 1932.

The "Bonus Expeditionary Force," as the bonus marchers called themselves (after the American Expeditionary Force of World War I), came from across the country to urge Congress to pay their benefits immediately. Traveling by car, on trucks, in empty railroad cars, and even by foot, the Bonus Army arrived in Washington, D.C., in the late spring of 1932. Most lived in tents and huts in a makeshift camp in Anacostia Flats just outside the city. Some moved into empty federal buildings in downtown Washington.

President Hoover, who insisted that a balanced budget was essential for recovery from the depression, opposed accelerating the bonus payment. He also objected to prepaying the bonus because he thought it would set a bad precedent and encourage other groups to seek RELIEF assistance from the federal government—something the HOOVER PRESIDENCY firmly opposed. Many members of Congress, however, supported the veterans' request. The Patman Bonus Bill, proposed in June 1932, called for immediate payment to the veterans and passed the House of Representatives. It was then defeated in the Senate, as Republicans and many Democrats agreed with Hoover that the bill would further harm the ECONOMY by seriously unbalancing the budget.

Following the failure of the Patman Bonus Bill, several thousand marchers departed, but others stayed on. Hoover, who never met with the veterans, had the White House put under armed guard, and in late July his administration ordered the veterans removed from the unused federal buildings they occupied. On July 28, the Washington police took over the buildings, and in one confrontation two marchers were shot and killed. Hoover then directed the army to remove the marchers from the downtown area. Commanded by General Douglas MacArthur, some 600 troops, using tear gas, rifles affixed with bayonets, and light tanks, cleared downtown Washington and, with men, women, and children fleeing before them, moved on to empty and burn the Anacostia camp. One baby died from the tear gas.

MacArthur's use of force went beyond Hoover's orders, but the country blamed the president, who defended the army's actions and held the marchers themselves responsible for the consequences. Other administration officials claimed that the Bonus Army had been dominated by criminals and by radicals. But, as most people understood, the bonus marchers were in fact dispirited, down-and-out people who had served their country and wanted help from the government in the hard times of the Great Depression. In Washington, the marchers organized committees to operate the camp safely, disavowed Communist efforts, and with rare exceptions proved peaceful and law-abiding. The military action against the Bonus Army was an appalling episode that sent Hoover's popularity plummeting still further and spelled his certain defeat in the coming election.

The dispersal of the Bonus Army did not end the bonus issue. In May 1933, roughly 1,000 veterans came to Washington, hoping that the new president, FRANKLIN D. ROOSEVELT, would support their cause. Roosevelt also opposed accelerating the bonus payments (although he did implement federal relief programs for the unemployed and destitute), but he was able to handle the protest far more adeptly than Hoover had the year before. His wife, ELEANOR ROOSEVELT, met the marchers to discuss their concerns, showing that the administration cared about their needs. Realizing that Roosevelt would veto any bonus bill, this second bonus march dispersed peacefully. Veterans finally succeeded in securing their bonus early in 1936, when Congress passed a bonus bill over Roosevelt's veto.

Further reading: Roger Daniels, *The Bonus March: An Episode of the Great Depression* (Westport, Conn.: Greenwood, 1971).

—Katherine Liapis Segrue and Justin Taylor

Borah, William E. (1865–1940)

William E. Borah was one of the most visible progressive Republicans of the interwar years and one of the staunchest ISOLATIONISTS in FOREIGN POLICY. Known as the Lion of Idaho for his forthright and eloquent stands, he was also called the "spearless leader" by one colleague because his independence left him with little influence among fellow senators.

Born near Fairfield, Illinois, on June 29, 1865, Borah settled in Idaho on the advice of a fellow train passenger as he headed west to pursue a legal career. Borah became a successful prosecuting attorney, married an Idaho governor's daughter, and became involved in local REPUBLICAN PARTY politics. Elected by the Idaho legislature to the U.S. Senate in 1906, Borah served five and a half terms as senator until his death.

In the Senate, Borah became a progressive Republican, supporting regulation of big business and other reforms. He supported American entry into World War I, but opposed U.S. membership in the League of Nations and remained a firm isolationist in the 1920s in his position as chairman of the Foreign Relations Committee. Borah backed HERBERT C. HOOVER for president in 1928, but along with other Republican progressives became disillusioned with the HOOVER PRESIDENCY and its response to the GREAT DEPRESSION. He refused to support Hoover for reelection in 1932, and was hopeful that the new president, FRANKLIN D. ROOSEVELT, would pursue a progressive agenda.

Borah endorsed much of the early NEW DEAL, but his steadfast individualism and distrust of big GOVERNMENT led him into vocal opposition by the time of Roosevelt's 1937 COURT-PACKING PLAN. In 1936, although 71 years old, Borah briefly ran for president, dropping out after winning the Wisconsin primary but doing poorly elsewhere; in the fall, he refused to support Republican nominee ALFRED M. LANDON in the ELECTION OF 1936. He remained among the ardent isolationists in the 1930s, supporting the NEUTRALITY ACTS and opposing American military aid to Great Britain and France after WORLD WAR II erupted in Europe in 1939. Borah died in Washington, D.C., on January 19, 1940.

Further reading: Marian C. McKenna, *Borah* (Ann Arbor: University of Michigan Press, 1961).

—William J. Thompson

Bradley, Omar N. (1893–1981)

General Omar Nelson Bradley's tactical skills and firm but low-key leadership helped secure the Allied victory in the EUROPEAN THEATER of WORLD WAR II. His concern for his soldiers, celebrated by the journalist ERNIE PYLE, won him the reputation as the "G.I.'s general."

Born on February 12, 1893, in Clark, Missouri, Bradley graduated from the U.S. Military Academy at West Point in the famed class of 1915, which included Dwight D. Eisenhower. He remained on the home front during World War I and served in a variety of posts, including a number of U.S. ARMY schools, in the interwar period. In 1941, General GEORGE C. MARSHALL offered Bradley the position of

Commandant of the Infantry School at Fort Benning, Georgia. This assignment brought Bradley the rank of brigadier general, and in 1942 he was promoted to Major General. In February 1943, Bradley was sent to North Africa, and in April he assumed command of the U.S. Army II Corps, directing important victories in the successful NORTH AFRICAN CAMPAIGN. Later in 1943, Bradley helped plan and implement the invasion of SICILY, and he was promoted to lieutenant general.

Bradley's greatest contributions came during and after the 1944 INVASION OF NORMANDY. After commanding the U.S. First Army at Normandy, Bradley was put in charge of the 12th Army Group, which comprised the Ninth, First, and Third Armies and included roughly one million soldiers. Bradley led the 12th Army Group in the Allied advance across France and helped win the Ardennes campaign and the BATTLE OF THE BULGE in the winter of 1944–45. He then played a leading role in the drive westward through the Rhineland and the Ruhr area that ended with the surrender of Germany in May 1945. He was promoted to full general in 1945.

In 1948, President Harry S. Truman named Bradley army chief of staff. He then served as chairman of the Joint Chiefs of Staff from 1949 to 1953 and was promoted to five-star rank—general of the army—in 1950. Bradley retired in 1953.

Further reading: Omar N. Bradley, and Clay Blair, *A General's Life: An Autobiography* (New York: Simon & Schuster, 1983).

—Daniel J. Fury

Brain Trust

The "Brain Trust" was the collective name given to a small group of academics who advised FRANKLIN D. ROOSEVELT and provided ideological foundations for the FIRST NEW DEAL of 1933. Assembled at Roosevelt's request in 1932 by RAYMOND C. MOLEY, a professor of government at Columbia University's Barnard College, the original and most important members of the Brain Trust were Moley, Columbia University economist REXFORD G. TUGWELL, and Columbia Law School professor ADOLF A. BERLE, JR. Roosevelt referred to these advisers as his "privy council," and then a newspaper reporter dubbed them the "Brains Trust" in September 1932.

While the members of the Brain Trust often disagreed about what specific policy measures would end the GREAT DEPRESSION, they did agree that the depression was the result of structural flaws in the American ECONOMY, that antitrust and other efforts to restore an economy of small units were misguided, and that the economy should function, with appropriate planning, as an organic structure of interdependent parts. Corporate interests, in their view, had gained a disproportionate amount of power over the American economy in the years preceding the depression and had upset the balance of parts. Borrowing from the English economic theorist J. A. Hobson, the Brain Trusters held that, left unchecked, this imbalance had caused a crisis of "underconsumption" in which consumers could no longer afford to buy enough products and services to sustain prosperity. Moley and Berle believed this imbalance would be best remedied by allowing BUSINESS to regulate itself to eliminate unfair business practices. Tugwell, who believed that depressed farm prices caused by agricultural overproduction were central to problems in the domestic economy, maintained that a GOVERNMENT-planned economy was required for economic recovery and balanced prosperity.

The First New Deal, as it took shape under the leadership of the Brain Trust, combated the Great Depression much differently from previous attempts by the HOOVER PRESIDENCY. In its insistence that the causes *and* solutions for the depression were domestic in nature, the Brain Trust rejected Hoover's internationalist approach. The ideas of the Brain Trust contributed to the NATIONAL RECOVERY ADMINISTRATION (NRA) and the Agricultural Adjustment Administration (AAA), both of which involved economic planning and controls coordinated by the government. The NRA, created to implement the NATIONAL INDUSTRIAL RECOVERY ACT (NIRA) in 1933, sought to implement industry-wide codes of fair competition and improve employment practices in the manufacturing sector, while the AAA sought to raise agricultural prices by reducing output and granting subsidies to farmers who cut production. In practice, both the NRA and the AAA faced significant obstacles in achieving their established goals and had disappointing and sometimes unintended results.

The Brain Trust was most influential during 1932–33 in creating philosophical foundations of the First New Deal, but was less successful in directing the subsequent implementation of NEW DEAL policy. Many DEMOCRATIC PARTY politicians were suspicious of the Brain Trust and feared that their status as nonelected advisers to the president gave them undue influence in policy decisions without the accountability of having to answer to constituents. Political considerations made Roosevelt reluctant to associate himself with any specific economic philosophy for fear of alienating the conservatives within his own party. The problems of the NRA and the AAA only heightened Roosevelt's increasing tendency to turn to other advisers and ideas. The Brain Trust was effectively disbanded when Raymond Moley left the Roosevelt administration in 1933. The other two original members, Tugwell and Berle, continued to work closely with Roosevelt until 1936 and 1944, respectively; but like Moley, although not for the same reasons, they would express disappointment with the subsequent path of the New Deal.

Despite the limits on their actual influence on policy-making, the Brain Trust left an important legacy, for their proximity to Roosevelt helped inspire a generation of idealistic and ambitious young liberal lawyers and scholars to enter careers with the federal government.

Further reading: Elliot A. Rosen, *Hoover, Roosevelt, and the Brains Trust: From Depression to New Deal* (New York: Columbia University Press, 1977).

—Mary E. Carroll-Mason

Bretton Woods Conference (July 1944)

The United Nations Monetary and Financial Conference, commonly known as the Bretton Woods Conference, took place in New Hampshire in July 1944. It resulted in the establishment of two organizations: the International Monetary Fund (IMF), to facilitate international monetary cooperation; and the International Bank for Reconstruction and Development (IBRD, usually called the World Bank), to provide loans to individual nations and to the United Nations Relief and Rehabilitation Administration (UNRRA) for postwar rebuilding and development. The IMF and IBRD were designed to underwrite world peace and prosperity by preventing another global depression and the economic nationalism that many thought had contributed to the coming of WORLD WAR II.

Several dozen nations met at Bretton Woods, with the United States leading the discussions. The American position reflected long-term concerns of Secretary of State CORDELL HULL about the dangers of high tariffs and other forms of economic nationalism. But the principal American figures in creating the Bretton Woods system, with its emphasis on currency convertability, expanded trade, development loans, and a healthy, cooperative world economy, were Secretary of the Treasury HENRY T. MORGENTHAU, JR., and his assistant secretary, the economist Harry Dexter White.

The United States emerged from World War II with a large accumulation of gold and credits and a strong industrial economy. This great economic strength, together with American power in wartime and postwar global politics, made it virtually inevitable that the United States would dominate the Bretton Woods conference and the instrumentalities it created. The U.S. Senate approved the Bretton Woods agreements in July 1945, and by December 1945 the required number of governments had ratified the treaties establishing the IMF and the IBRD. The Soviet Union took part in the conference but did not participate in the Bretton Woods system because of worsening SOVIET-AMERICAN RELATIONS as the cold war developed.

The main objective of the International Monetary Fund was to prevent the currency devaluations of the 1930s that had seemed so harmful to international economic and political stability. It sought to protect and stabilize short-term foreign exchange rates without jeopardizing a country's domestic economic goals and production levels, and to standardize international monetary transactions in a smooth, efficient system that would promote free trade, stability, and prosperity. The U.S. plan that emerged from Bretton Woods protected the gold standard and established the dollar as the world's dominant currency. IMF operations were disappointing in the early postwar period, but the agency did help to establish the principle that currency devaluations not be used in international economic competition.

The International Bank for Reconstruction and Development was to provide loans at reasonable interest rates to underwrite the reconstruction of economies damaged by World War II and to promote investments and growth in developing countries. The goal was a healthy, growing world economy. The United States, as the largest subscriber to the World Bank, had the principal voice in its operations, and in the early postwar period saw that it channeled assistance to European countries whose economic difficulties made them vulnerable to communist inroads. Such assistance was connected to American "containment" policy in the cold war and prefigured the Marshall Plan assistance to Europe. Smaller developing nations did not get the sort of assistance envisioned in the initial agreements.

Like the American leadership in creating and implementing the UNITED NATIONS, the Bretton Woods system reflected the new role and power of the United States in global affairs and its determination to use its power in pursuing its own interests and principles as well as global peace and prosperity. In the early postwar era, the IMF and IBRD became tied to American containment policy in the cold war, but both would play larger roles in subsequent decades in fostering currency convertability and stability and in providing loans for economic development.

Further reading: Alfred E. Eckes Jr., *A Search for Solvency: Bretton Woods and the International Monetary System, 1944–1971* (Austin: University of Texas Press, 1979); Richard N. Gardner, *Sterling-Dollar Diplomacy* (New York: McGraw-Hill, 1969).

—Anne Rothfeld

Bridges, Harry (1901–1977)

An Australian-born maritime worker who identified with the radical and militant elements of the LABOR movement, Harry Bridges played an important role in the resurgence of organized labor in the United States during the GREAT DEPRESSION.

Bridges was born on July 28, 1901, into a middle-class household near Melbourne, Australia, and went by the name Alfred Renton Bridges. A number of experiences and people in his early life exposed him to dissenting ideas, including his uncle Harry, an official of Australia's main labor party, whose name Bridges adopted. Bridges left home when he was 16 to pursue adventure as a sailor, and journeys to the slums of Bombay and London impressed upon him the degree to which capitalism could materially and spiritually impoverish working people. Bridges also learned of protest tactics and strategies as a participant in the massive 1917 general strike in Australia and as a brief recruit of the International Workers of the World (IWW) while unemployed in New Orleans.

In 1922, Bridges found work as a longshoreman on the San Francisco waterfront and experienced its dreadful working conditions. Longshoremen who did not belong to the company union had to endure the humiliation of the morning "shape-up" in which throngs of men waited on the docks in hopes of gaining temporary employment. Blacklists, kickbacks, and favoritism often influenced hiring decisions, and speedups rendered already dangerous work even more threatening to life and limb. Bridges joined the International Longshoremen's Association (ILA), but its conservative leadership refused to seek change. The Great Depression severely aggravated these hardships, leaving Bridges without work and his family on RELIEF and pushing him and many other longshoremen toward unionism and radicalism.

GOVERNMENT sanction of union organizing under the NATIONAL INDUSTRIAL RECOVERY ACT (NIRA) of the NEW DEAL inspired longshoremen to act. When 12,000 Pacific Coast longshoremen went on strike in May 1934, area seamen and teamsters joined them, as did more than 100,000 San Francisco workers who waged a general strike to protest police violence against unionists. Bridges became an effective union organizer and a major spokesperson for the longshoremen. Despite the use of strikebreakers, the longshoremen won union recognition, a pay increase, a shorter workweek, and an end to the hated shape-up.

The solidarity displayed by various maritime workers during the strike quickly crumbled. Seamen returned to the tradition of craft-oriented and racially discriminatory unionism, while Bridges and his ILA supporters championed industrial unionism. This conflict mirrored larger splits occurring within the labor movement during the 1930s between the AMERICAN FEDERATION OF LABOR (AFL) and the CONGRESS OF INDUSTRIAL ORGANIZATIONS (CIO). In 1937, Bridges led an overwhelming majority of Pacific Coast longshoremen into the CIO to form the International Longshoremen's and Warehousemen's Union

(ILWU). Emphasizing common economic interests among workers, he welcomed AFRICAN AMERICANS into the ILWU and helped to organize a multiethnic force of sugar and pineapple plantation workers in Hawaii.

Between 1934 and 1962, Bridges fought a number of attempts on the part of his enemies in BUSINESS, government, and organized labor to force his deportation on the grounds that he sought to overthrow the government by force. These legal battles intensified considerably with the revival of anticommunism following WORLD WAR II. Although he apparently joined the Communist Party, according to his biographer, Bridges always denied membership, and he avoided deportation. In any event, he was guided less by communist ideology than by a commitment to addressing the needs and desires of longshoremen.

By the 1960s, rapid technological changes undermined the bargaining power of skilled workers. Bridges accepted mechanization in return for a hefty pension benefit for older longshoremen, an agreement that contributed to high unemployment, unsafe working conditions, and a large temporary workforce on the docks. He died in 1977.

Further reading: Charles P. Larrowe, *Harry Bridges: The Rise and Fall of Radical Labor in the United States,* 2d ed. (Westport, Conn.: L. Hill, 1977); Bruce Nelson, *Workers on the Waterfront: Seamen, Longshoremen, and Unionism in the 1930s* (Urbana: University of Illinois Press, 1988).

—Theresa Ann Case

Britain, Battle of (1940)

The Battle of Britain, waged between Great Britain and Germany in the summer and fall of 1940, was the first battle in history conducted entirely by AIR POWER, as Germany attempted to gain air supremacy over Britain in preparation for an invasion. Although the German effort was ultimately unsuccessful, the threat to Great Britain, following the success of the German BLITZKRIEG in overrunning western Europe in the previous months, was instrumental in the shift of American FOREIGN POLICY to anti-AXIS intervention through such measures as the DESTROYERS-FOR-BASES DEAL.

The German Luftwaffe forces based in France, the Low Countries, Norway, and Denmark consisted of 1,260 medium bombers, 320 dive-bombers, and over 1,000 fighters. Continental bases were a mere 20 minutes from England, but German fighters had a short range, and Luftwaffe twin-engine fighters and dive-bombers could not match the RAF Supermarine Spitfire or Hawker Hurricane. In addition, German bombers carried small bomb loads.

The British Royal Air Force (RAF) Fighter Command operated over home ground, which allowed longer times in the air and rapid pilot recovery. Increases in fighter production in 1939, an efficient ground-to-air communications network, and a radar system along the southern coast, gave a slight advantage to the 600 RAF pilots flying 900 fighters.

Early skirmishes in the Battle of Britain began in July 1940, with combat beginning in earnest on August 13, called "Eagle Day," when the Luftwaffe attacked in strength. The period of mid- to late August was one of heavy fighting, with RAF pilots flying multiple sorties each day. Yet both sides overestimated the other's casualties and their own successes. German intelligence failures caused a shift in tactics based on the assumption that the RAF had suffered irreplaceable losses. The Luftwaffe starting attacking airfields, but then shifted to terror bombings of cities, particularly London, in retaliation for an RAF raid on Berlin on August 25. Regular daylight attacks on London, known as the Blitz, began on September 7. The RAF responded quickly against Luftwaffe bombers over London on September 15, known as "Battle of Britain Day," and downed 175 aircraft in one week, prompting a suspension of daylight raids. While the Blitz continued with decreasing intensity through May 1941, attacks on airfields never resumed, and the planned German invasion was canceled on September 17. Between July 31 and October 31, the RAF lost 788 aircraft compared to 1,295 Luftwaffe aircraft destroyed. Referring to the RAF's successful defense of Britain, Churchill memorably said that "Never in the field of human conflict was so much owed by so many to so few."

See also WORLD WAR II EUROPEAN THEATER.

Further reading: Richard Collier, *Eagle Day: The Battle of Britain, August 6–September 15, 1940* (New York: Dutton, 1982).

—Clayton D. Laurie

Bulge, Battle of the (December 1944–January 1945)
In the six months after the INVASION OF NORMANDY in June 1944, American and British forces drove the German army from France and began threatening the German border. In December 1944, the Germans launched a counteroffensive in the Ardennes Forest in Belgium in a desperate effort to halt the Allied advance and capture the vital Belgian port of Antwerp. This last German major thrust in the EUROPEAN THEATER of WORLD WAR II was named the Battle of the Bulge, because of the wedge that the Germans drove into the Allied lines before American forces repelled the German attack.

Early in the morning of December 16, 1944, the Germans attacked vulnerable American positions in the Ardennes Forest, sending them reeling back in surprise and confusion. But the German army soon encountered fierce American resistance. When the Germans demanded

the surrender of the key town of Bastogne on December 22, General Anthony McAuliffe, personifying the courage and resiliency of American troops in the battle, replied with his famous single-word message: "Nuts!"

The tide turned for the Allies by December 23. In a remarkable feat of generalship, General GEORGE S. PATTON, JR., had wheeled his Third Army northward from the Moselle to attack the German flank from the south. The fog and heavy clouds that grounded Allied air forces lifted, and Allied planes resupplied isolated garrisons and began to attack the German troops and supply lines. The German advance was halted just miles from the Meuse River by the U.S. First Army on December 26. The extent of the "bulge" that the Germans created was some 60 miles deep and 50 miles wide at the base—a considerable salient, but well short of Hitler's ambitious objectives. By mid-January, the battle had been won, and by end of the month the Allies were ready to press ahead into Germany.

The Battle of the Bulge was the largest engagement on the western front, and the largest that American soldiers—who did almost all of the fighting—had ever been part of. More than a half million American troops were involved, and the American casualties of at least 70,000 (virtually the entire Allied total and more than in any other battle of the war) included some 20,000 dead. British prime minister Winston Churchill said that the Battle of the Bulge would "be regarded as an ever-famous American victory." Turning back this final German offensive and depleting the Germans' reserves of manpower and equipment, this victory effectively secured the fate of Nazi Germany and led to its surrender in May 1945.

Further reading: Charles B. MacDonald, *A Time for Trumpets: The Untold Story of the Battle of the Bulge* (New York: Morrow, 1985).

—Michael Leonard

Bush, Vannevar (1890–1974)
Vannevar Bush, born in Everett, Massachusetts, the son of a Universalist minister, is best known for directing the massive effort to mobilize American SCIENCE and TECHNOLOGY for WORLD WAR II. His classic manifesto, *Science: The Endless Frontier,* written at the request of President FRANKLIN D. ROOSEVELT as a proposal for continuing this mobilization during peacetime, inspired the creation of the National Science Foundation and other GOVERNMENT funding organizations of the cold war.

During undergraduate work at Tufts College, doctoral studies in electrical engineering at the Massachusetts Institute of Technology, and various work with industry and the military, Bush developed an early faith in technology and its potential for public good. He held strong beliefs on ethics and public responsibility for engineers. As a professor in electrical engineering and later dean of engineering at MIT (1919–1939), he was at the center of curricular reforms in this fast-developing field so closely connected with industry. Known for his administrative acumen, he also won respect as an able and innovative researcher in engineering science for his work in solving difficult quantitative engineering problems using graphical methods and analog computers.

In 1939, Bush became president of the Carnegie Institution of Washington, and also served as chairman of the National Advisory Committee on Aeronautics. Soon after arriving in Washington, he was at the center of mobilizing science and technology for the war effort. He instigated and chaired the National Defense Research Committee, which was quickly succeeded in 1941 by the OFFICE OF SCIENTIFIC RESEARCH AND DEVELOPMENT (OSRD) as the war MOBILIZATION effort expanded. Enjoying a close and trusted relationship with President Roosevelt, personal acquaintance with numerous industry leaders, familiarity with and respect in the university world, and knowledge of the military establishment, Bush masterfully led and defended OSRD during challenging and often chaotic times. The impressive number of major wartime inventions (radar, radio-inertial navigation, amphibious vehicles, the proximity fuse, penicillin, and of course the ATOMIC BOMB, to cite just a few) that issued from OSRD-sponsored research crowned Bush's already substantial reputation.

Bush's July 1945 report, *Science: The Endless Frontier,* became the blueprint for instituting what some scholars have called the "permanent mobilization" of science and technology for the cold war, and has been reprinted and studied continuously since, often forming the starting point for periodic review of the subject by government. Bush also arranged for an extensive history of OSRD to be written and published in a series of popular books—and proved to be as masterful in crafting and controlling the remembrance of OSRD as he was in building and operating it in the first place.

Bush believed that it was the peculiarly American democratic character and institutions that made science and technology successful in the United States and correspondingly hindered it in totalitarian states. He therefore wished to dismantle the OSRD as quickly as possible, viewing it as an effective but undemocratic emergency measure for the war effort. In its place he envisioned a National Research Foundation that would support science and technology with public money, but place funding decisions and accountability in the meritocracy of science and technology leadership rather than in a government body. The National Science Foundation was established by President Harry S. Truman in 1950, one of a number of postwar government agencies with responsibilities for science and technology.

Vannevar Bush *(Library of Congress)*

Further reading: Daniel J. Kevles, "The National Science Foundation and the Debate over Postwar Research Policy, 1942–1945: A Political Interpretation of *Science—The Endless Frontier,*" *Isis* 68 (1977): 5–26; G. Pascal Zachary, *Endless Frontier: Vannevar Bush, Engineer of the American Century* (New York: Free Press, 1997).

—Joseph N. Tatarewicz

business

Few business enterprises, small or large, fully escaped the consequences of the GREAT DEPRESSION of the 1930s. Between 1929 and 1933, industrial production was halved and UNEMPLOYMENT soared from three percent to 25 percent. In these four years, 110,000 businesses failed and more than 5,000 banks went under. For many businesses that survived the initial collapse of the ECONOMY, the problems of these early years of the depression—reduced markets and low profits—dragged on for the rest of the 1930s. General conditions only improved following the increased demand brought about by GOVERNMENT spending for military preparedness in Europe and the United States in the late 1930s, and then for MOBILIZATION for WORLD WAR II in the early 1940s. World War II then had important consequences for business.

Nevertheless, during the depression and war, experiences varied among businesses in different industries and sectors. Generally, larger businesses did better than smaller, manufacturing suffered less than banking and finance, consumer goods manufacturers performed better than makers of capital goods. The country's biggest businesses—those among the 100 largest industrial enterprises in the country in terms of employees, total assets, and gross receipts—probably did best. There were no bankruptcies within this group, although most initially faced reduced sales, profits, and dividends. The biggest enterprises were apt to be in oligopolistic industries—such as the AUTOMOBILE INDUSTRY, the STEEL INDUSTRY, chemicals, and electrical products—where the few firms in an industry had the market power and financial reserves to stay in business despite the difficult times. They cut back on operations, reduced workforces, repositioned resources, and concentrated on producing those products for which markets still existed. General Motors, for example, experienced a 75 percent drop in sales between 1929 and 1933. Sales declined precipitously for the company's most inexpensive vehicles, so GM focused on its more expensive lines of automobiles designed for the middle and upper classes.

Among the largest companies, managers took advantage of low labor, material, and equipment costs. Some stockpiled raw materials, upgraded equipment, repaired idle plant, and invested in improving manufacturing processes. Firms with established research laboratories—General Electric, AT&T, Du Pont, Alcoa, General Motors, RCA, Merck & Co., Eli Lilly, Standard Oil of New Jersey, Shell Oil—were able to hire large numbers of engineers and scientists with advanced degrees because of the low wages for university graduates. Such highly trained personnel also found jobs in industries such as glass making and food processing, where they had not been so well represented before.

Managers also embraced strategies of product diversification that moved businesses into new markets. A long-term consequence of diversification and larger research and development (R and D) operations was that many enterprises were well positioned to meet the needs of the World War II economy. During the war, many firms proved adept at moving far afield from their accustomed markets. Workers at the consumer products company Procter & Gamble, for example, filled almost 25 percent of the country's artillery shells with explosives. Stepped up R and D in the 1930s led Alcoa to develop several alloys later widely used in military aircraft. Similarly, advances in petroleum refining TECHNOLOGY prepared the industry to meet increased wartime demands for petroleum products, including high-octane aviation fuel.

Small businesses—defined as firms employing fewer than 100 workers—experienced the depression very differently. Historically, such enterprises had faced a precarious existence, enduring high rates of failure. The depression years were no exception. Even so, there was an increase in the numbers of small businesses formed during the 1930s. In the retail sector, there were almost 1.8 million stores in 1939, an increase of 300,000 from 1929. But most of these new enterprises were products of the troubled times, small operations in labor intensive, service-oriented businesses. Unemployed workers turned to small-scale, low capital retailing to eke out some kind of a living.

In contrast, larger businesses producing consumer goods fared best during the depression. Consumption spending (in "constant" dollars corrected for the deflation of the early depression) declined only about 20 percent between 1928 and 1932, whereas investment fell nearly 90 percent. Consequently, consumer goods manufacturers were apt to be more "depression proof" than those engaged in producing machinery and equipment. Households continued to purchase everyday items (groceries, beverages, cigarettes, soaps, medicines, detergents, personal hygiene products, work clothes, newspapers, magazines). Moreover, while most families could not afford new automobiles or new homes, they needed to fuel and service the cars, and maintain and repair the houses, they already had. Thus, sales of petroleum products, automobile parts, and tires remained strong. By 1936, for example, petroleum sales exceeded those of 1929. New home building plummeted during the depression, making the HOUSING construction sector one of the most troubled of the decade, along with AGRICULTURE and mining. Those already owning homes, though, continued to make improvements. In 1930, for example, only 51 percent of homes had flush toilets; by 1940 the proportion was 60 percent.

Further belying the general view that the 1930s were a period of unrelieved doom for business were examples of new companies that achieved later success. Entrepreneurs established companies in the 1930s that were destined to become household names to a later generation: Hewlett-Packard, Polaroid Camera, Texas Instruments, and Ryder Truck. Fledgling companies established earlier also took off in the 1930s. Because the SOCIAL SECURITY ACT of 1935 meant that the federal government needed to keep information about almost every wage earner, for example, IBM's electromechanical punchcard equipment gave the company a new market and positioned it for even more rapid growth during the war and postwar periods.

The 1930s were also a period of important business innovations with far-reaching consequences for American life. New firms emerged, and established businesses grew, in industries that commercialized new technology, products, and services. Developments in industries related to aviation, supported in part by federal funding for their military applications, led to improvements in avionics, aircraft engines, aviation fuel, and aluminum alloys. These advances proved vital to the United States's capabilities in fighting World War II. Commercial RADIO broadcasting, and the growth of the MOVIES, structured a mass entertainment industry with profound long-run consequences, both good and ill, in creating a more national, less regional, American POPULAR CULTURE. Chemical and petroleum companies engaged in research focused on carbon (found in petroleum), which served as the basis for the making of numerous synthetic materials. The most famous result of these efforts was Du Pont's commercialization of nylon, first created in 1934. Such work on polymers (the building blocks of this chemical revolution) in the 1930s paid off in the war years with the production of many new materials, including synthetic rubber.

The retail sector also saw innovations in the 1930s. A particularly vibrant area of growth was in gasoline service stations, funded in part by the major petroleum companies to spur on retail sales of gasoline. Chain grocery stores (which had over a third of the market for grocery sales in 1933) continued to grow during the 1930s, as did supermarkets, stores that sold a larger number and variety of goods than the chain stores. Between 1935 and 1939, the number of supermarkets increased from about 300 to almost 5,000.

Advances in grocery chain and supermarket retailing resulted from innovations in the food processing industry. Major food processing companies, such as General Foods and General Mills, invested heavily in improving processing, packaging, and distribution, and launched heavily advertised new products and product lines. The industry, for example, introduced pasteurized fruit juices and individually packaged baked goods. In adding zinc to can coatings, food processors made canned goods safer. By 1939, the output of these products had doubled from the 160 million units produced in 1931. Progress in bottling soft drinks, along with innovations in vending machines, increased the market for a growing variety of these popular products. General Foods Corporation introduced frozen foods in the 1930s, although it was not until after World War II that household refrigerators had freezers able to store such products safely.

Business also had to face up to the growing presence of the federal government in the economy during the 1930s. NEW DEAL legislation fundamentally altered the structure and behavior of key industries by creating new independent regulatory agencies or granting increased authority to already established government departments. Industries affected included banking, securities, telephone, aviation, railroads, broadcasting, electric power, petroleum, lumber, mining, and agriculture. These changes affected businesses differently, and generated differing responses from business leaders, many of them hostile to the New Deal, but others more supportive. Perhaps the most significant piece of legislation from a general business point of view was the 1935 NATIONAL LABOR RELATIONS ACT. By conferring on workers a right to organize unions, the New Deal altered the fundamental relationship between workers and owners/managers. LABOR relations became for many businesses one of the most contentious matters of the time, an issue that for many firms lasted well into the postwar years.

World War II had a profound impact on American business. Wartime government spending of more than $300 billion to finance MOBILIZATION ended the depression. This sum was 10 times greater than that expended on World War I. Indeed, it was about double what the federal government had spent in its entire history. The rapid economic turnaround provided a robust stimulus to employment, sales, and business profits. But, as with the depression, the consequences of the war for businesses varied among industries and economic sectors. The requirements of a government geared to total war had a greater positive impact on the largest enterprises than the smallest. Federal officials needed the expertise of mass production manufacturers to produce great quantities of war materials, and businessmen often played key roles in mobilization agencies. Government also employed the research and development skills of the largest businesses, enterprises capable of developing and producing highly sophisticated, technologically advanced products and weapons.

A high level of collaboration with technologically advanced companies continued into the cold war years, forming what became known as the military-industrial-university complex. Government-business cooperation during World War II was closest in munitions, aviation, electronics, metals, chemicals, and nuclear power. The most famous collaboration occurred in the MANHATTAN PROJECT that produced the ATOMIC BOMB. Perhaps less well known was the government's enlisting the pharmaceutical companies in a crash program to produce large quantities of penicillin to reduce combat deaths attributable to infection.

New technologies emerging from World War II had long-lasting effects on American business. In the postwar decades, many of the largest companies commercialized the new technologies. Wartime advances in aviation, nuclear power, radar, jet propulsion, antibiotics, synthetic materials, and computers eventually all found their way into products for industry and households. World War II also solidified the position of big business in the American economy. During the war, over half of the government's $175 billion in prime defense contracts went to 33 companies. While many of them subcontracted work to smaller enterprises, about three-quarters of subcontracts went to enterprises employing more than 500 employees. Businesses employing more than 10,000 people increased their share of industrial employment from 13 to 30 percent between 1939 and 1944. Small businesses, employing 100 or fewer people, dropped from 26 to 19 percent of industrial employment in the same years. These trends toward industrial concentration were to continue in the postwar period.

The Great Depression and World War II thus had important consequences for American business. Few enterprises escaped the problems created by the collapse in

1929 or the effects of the U.S. involvement in World War II, and all had to deal with a federal government that had vastly increased powers because of the New Deal and wartime mobilization. This new environment often created problems for the owners of small firms, as well as for the managers of giant enterprises. But economic collapse and a wartime economy also prompted among the largest businesses a greater commitment to developing and commercializing technology, and to diversifying their operations. Smaller businesses had a more difficult time adjusting to the economic changes and challenges, but some also found opportunity in these years—especially during the war—by supplying goods and services to government and big business.

From the perspective of more than half a century, the business losses, failures, and disruption of the depression and war provide only part of the story. The 1930s were also a time of innovation and experiment that prepared business to meet the demands of a global war. And World War II also positioned business, mainly large enterprises, to meet the government's needs in the cold war and to take advantage of the boom times that followed the most destructive war in history.

Further reading: Michael Bernstein, *The Great Depression: Delayed Recovery and Economic Change in America, 1929–1939* (New York: Cambridge University Press, 1987); Mansel Blackford, *A History of Small Business in America* (New York: Twayne, 1991); Alfred D. Chandler, Jr., *Scale and Scope: The Dynamics of Industrial Capitalism* (Cambridge, Mass.: Belknap Press of Harvard University Press, 1990); Margaret Graham, "The Threshold of the Information Age: Radio, Television, and Motion Pictures Mobilize the Nation," in *A Nation Transformed by Information: How Information Has Shaped the United States from Colonial Times to the Present*, Alfred D. Chandler Jr. and James W. Cortada, eds. (New York: Oxford University Press, 2000); Thomas K. McCraw, *American Business, 1920–2000: How It Worked* (Wheeling, Ill.: Harlan Davidson, 2000).

—William H. Becker

Byrnes, James F. (1882–1972)

As a United States senator from South Carolina, SUPREME COURT justice, wartime administrator, and secretary of state, James F. Byrnes was one of the most influential political figures of the 1929–1945 period. Byrnes, who earned a reputation as sly and able, was perhaps the most important southern politician between John C. Calhoun and Lyndon B. Johnson.

James Francis Byrnes was born on May 2, 1882, in Charleston, South Carolina, seven weeks after his civil servant father died of tuberculosis. Though he dropped out of school at age 14 to help support his mother and sister, Byrnes was an ambitious young man who received his education in law and politics by running errands for a prominent Charleston attorney and working as a court stenographer.

By 1910, Byrnes had settled in Aiken, South Carolina, married (converting from the Roman Catholic to the Episcopal Church), and become a successful attorney and prosecutor. He was elected that year, at age 28, to the U.S. House of Representatives, where he would serve for 14 years. As a congressman, Byrnes gained several patrons important to his political career, including BERNARD M. BARUCH, the financier and DEMOCRATIC PARTY insider who owned a South Carolina estate, and FRANKLIN D. ROOSEVELT, who met Byrnes while assistant secretary of the navy. Byrnes ran unsuccessfully for the U.S. Senate in 1924, his refusal to join the Ku Klux Klan being a factor in his defeat, and returned to Aiken to practice law.

In 1930, Byrnes was elected to the U.S. Senate, and immediately became an important figure in Washington. He was an early supporter of Roosevelt's presidential candidacy in 1932, and served as consultant and sometimes speechwriter during the campaign. After Roosevelt's election, Byrnes was a staunch supporter of the NEW DEAL, helping to draft some legislation and to shepherd through CONGRESS such measures as the AGRICULTURAL ADJUSTMENT ACT, the NATIONAL INDUSTRIAL RECOVERY ACT, the CIVILIAN CONSERVATION CORPS, and the FEDERAL EMERGENCY RELIEF ADMINISTRATION. During the SECOND NEW DEAL of 1935, Byrnes helped win passage of the NATIONAL LABOR RELATIONS ACT despite his links to South Carolina textile interests and his growing antipathy toward organized LABOR.

In 1936, Byrnes easily won reelection to the Senate, defeating an opponent in the Democratic primary who attempted to tie the New Deal and Roosevelt to racial equality. Byrnes emphasized economic issues and how the New Deal benefited all—especially white—South Carolinians. After Roosevelt's reelection in 1936, Byrnes backed the president's COURT-PACKING PLAN, but broke with FDR on labor issues, including sit-down strikes by the CONGRESS OF INDUSTRIAL ORGANIZATIONS. Byrnes also opposed Roosevelt's attempted "purge" of anti–New Deal Democrats (including his South Carolina colleague "Cotton Ed" Smith) in 1938, but he remained on friendly terms personally with the president. He worked against CIVIL RIGHTS for AFRICAN AMERICANS and helped defeat antilynching legislation.

Although ambitious for the presidency himself, Byrnes backed Roosevelt for a third term in the ELECTION OF 1940, but was disappointed when he was passed over for the vice presidency, due to opposition from labor and northern liberals. In 1941, Roosevelt appointed Byrnes to the Supreme Court, but the South Carolinian found the job too constraining. After the American entry into WORLD WAR II, Byrnes resigned from the Court in 1942 to direct the Office of Economic Stabilization. A year later, Roosevelt named Byrnes to head the OFFICE OF WAR MOBILIZATION, a position so important that he had an office in the White House East Wing, and became known as the "assistant president."

In 1944, Byrnes was again passed over for the vice presidency, and again Roosevelt placated his old friend, this time by having him accompany the president to the YALTA CONFERENCE in February 1945. Rumors persisted that Roosevelt would name Byrnes as either secretary of state or UNITED NATIONS ambassador. After Roosevelt died in April 1945, the new president, Harry S. Truman, a former Senate colleague, named Byrnes secretary of state. Byrnes served in that position until 1947, when personal and philosophical differences with Truman, and growing disillusionment with the Democratic Party on labor and racial issues, led to his resignation.

In 1950, Byrnes was elected governor of South Carolina on a conservative, segregationist platform; he served one term. In 1952, although still nominally a Democrat, he made little secret of his preference for Republican Dwight D. Eisenhower in the presidential race. Byrnes lived out his final years in South Carolina as a wayward Democrat who in 1968 endorsed Richard M. Nixon for president. James F. Byrnes died in Key West, Florida, on April 9, 1972.

Further reading: David Robertson, *Sly and Able: A Political Biography of James F. Byrnes* (New York: W. W. Norton, 1994).

—William J. Thompson

C

Cairo Conference (November 1943)

The Cairo Conference, involving the United States, Great Britain, and China, was held in late November 1943 to discuss strategy and objectives for the Far Eastern arena of the PACIFIC THEATER of WORLD WAR II.

American president FRANKLIN D. ROOSEVELT and British prime minister Winston Churchill scheduled this conference to take place before they met with Soviet leader Joseph Stalin at the TEHERAN CONFERENCE, which would focus on Allied strategy in Europe. Originally Roosevelt had planned to meet only with Stalin at Teheran; however, Churchill insisted that he attend the Teheran Conference and also that he and Roosevelt meet beforehand at Cairo, Egypt, to coordinate their approach to the Teheran meeting and decisions about Europe. Roosevelt suggested that the Soviets and Chinese join the Cairo Conference and discuss Allied strategy in the Pacific. China agreed, but the Soviets demurred, preferring not to meet with the Chinese because of the Soviet nonaggression pact with Japan.

Roosevelt intended that the Cairo Conference focus especially on discussions with Chinese leader Jiang Jieshi (Chiang Kai-shek) about the war in Asia. Besides wanting to keep China in the war, Roosevelt thought China should be added to the "Big Three" (the United States, Soviet Union, and Britain) and as one of the major powers should have a significant voice in wartime and postwar policies. Roosevelt also attempted to get Churchill to pledge postwar independence to Britain's Asian colonies, as the United States had for the Philippines. Churchill tried unsuccessfully to ignore Jiang, whom he considered unimportant, and to pressure Roosevelt into agreeing upon a united diplomatic front to present to the Soviets at Teheran.

Despite tensions between Roosevelt and Churchill, the Cairo Conference did come to some agreements about the Pacific war before the two men flew on to their meeting with Stalin at Teheran. The conferees decided that Japan would be stripped of territorial gains it had made since World War I and would return to China territory taken before and during the war, and they agreed that the Allies would require an unconditional surrender from Japan. These points, along with other decisions, were made public in December in the Cairo Declaration. Roosevelt also promised Chiang and his Nationalist Chinese forces continued assistance, including LEND-LEASE ACT aid and American support of an attack on Burma, although he came to the conclusion previously reached by others that Jiang was a weak and indecisive leader.

Roosevelt and Churchill met again less formally at Cairo in early December 1943, just after the Teheran Conference, in what is sometimes known as the Second Cairo Conference. Here they unsuccessfully tried to coax neutral Turkey into the war on the Allied side, and decided to delay the Burma offensive in order to shift needed resources into the cross-Channel invasion of France set at Teheran for the spring of 1944.

See also ANGLO-AMERICAN RELATIONS; GRAND ALLIANCE.

Further reading: Robert Dallek, *Franklin D. Roosevelt and American Foreign Policy, 1932–1945* (New York: Oxford University Press, 1979); Keith Sainsbury, *The Turning Point: Roosevelt, Stalin, Churchill, and Chiang Kai-Shek, 1943. The Moscow, Cairo, and Teheran Conferences* (Oxford, U.K.: Oxford University Press, 1985).

—Nicholas Fry

Capra, Frank (1897–1991)

Frank Capra was perhaps the most famous motion picture director of the 1930s and 1940s. His celebration of democracy and the common man permeated his most important Hollywood MOVIES of the 1930s as well as his *Why We Fight* films of World War II, produced in collaboration with the U.S. GOVERNMENT. Capra's focus on the dignity and decency of ordinary people reflected not only his own views but also themes often found elsewhere in the ART, PHOTOGRAPHY, LITERATURE, and POPULAR CULTURE of the GREAT DEPRESSION.

Capra himself lived a version of the American dream after his family moved to the United States from Sicily when he was six years old. Working his way through college, Capra earned a degree in engineering before beginning his career in Hollywood. His 1934 comedy, *It Happened One Night*, won five Academy Awards, including both best picture and best director. Capra's celebration of American democracy and the American dream shaped his subsequent films of the 1930s, especially *Mr. Deeds Goes to Town* (1936) and *Mr. Smith Goes to Washington* (1939). Deeds, after inheriting a fortune and moving to the city, gives his money away and returns to his small-town home, disillusioned by greed and the power of money. Smith, a newly elected senator, sees the corruption of money and power in the U.S. Senate when he arrives in Washington and fights to expose it and return to the democratic ideal.

In 1941 Capra joined the U.S. ARMY Signal Corps and was asked by the War Department to create a series of films explaining the significance of the war and depicting the dangers of fascism and Nazism. Though much different in format from Capra's fictional Hollywood movies and really part of the government's wartime PROPAGANDA effort, the seven-film *Why We Fight* series also expressed his strong patriotism and his belief in the ideal of democratic government and the strength of ordinary people. The films were shown to soldiers going overseas to impress upon them the meaning of the war. The first film in the series was also released for general distribution and, while faring poorly at the box office, won a 1942 Academy Award.

After the war, Capra continued to make films designed to celebrate American values and inspire optimism in his audiences. His most famous work, *It's a Wonderful Life* (1946) is now considered to be the peak of Capra's career, though it was not a commercial success. By the 1950s and 1960s, audiences and their tastes changed, and Capra's films became relics of an older generation.

Further reading: Frank Capra, *The Name above the Title: An Autobiography* (New York: Macmillan, 1971); Charles J. Maland, *Frank Capra*, rev. ed. (New York: Twayne, 1995).

—Ann Adams

Casablanca Conference (January 1943)

With victory near in the NORTH AFRICAN CAMPAIGN by early 1943, a meeting of the Allied leaders seemed desirable to discuss the next steps to be taken against the AXIS powers in the EUROPEAN THEATER of WORLD WAR II. President FRANKLIN D. ROOSEVELT wanted the conference to

include Soviet premier Joseph Stalin, but Stalin insisted that the military situation in the Soviet Union was too delicate for him to leave. British prime minister Winston Churchill and Roosevelt then decided to meet in the small seaside city of Casablanca in North Africa.

Roosevelt, Churchill, and their staffs met from January 13 to 23, 1943. Much of the conference was given over to debate between the British military, which wanted next to invade SICILY, and the smaller and less well-prepared American military contingent, which wanted to launch a cross-Channel invasion of German-occupied France as soon as possible and thus open a true SECOND FRONT in Europe. The joint communiqué of January 23 indicated that Sicily was to be the next target for the Allies and said that the BATTLE OF THE ATLANTIC would be given top priority in order to end the German U-boat threat to Allied shipping. Roosevelt and Churchill also pledged to fulfill LEND-LEASE ACT agreements with the Soviet Union and to launch the round-the-clock Combined Bomber Offensive against Germany. They agreed to put 30 percent of the American total war effort to operations in the PACIFIC THEATER, thus allowing the U.S. NAVY to remain on the offensive against the Japanese.

Roosevelt and Churchill understood that Stalin would be angry about the decision not to open the second front by a cross-Channel invasion of France that would relieve German pressure on the Soviet Union. To help ease Stalin's suspicions after his inability to deliver the cross-Channel invasion, and after agreement to the negotiated surrender of Vichy French forces in North Africa, President Roosevelt announced at a January 24 press conference that the Allied powers would accept nothing less than unconditional surrender from the Axis powers. This doctrine of unconditional surrender was enunciated chiefly to reassure Stalin and solidify the GRAND ALLIANCE and SOVIET-AMERICAN RELATIONS. Aiming also to prevent a future German leader from claiming, as Hitler had, that civilian leadership had "sold out" the military, it committed the Allied powers to totally defeat the Axis powers, possibly extending the duration and cost of the war.

See also ANGLO-AMERICAN RELATIONS.

Further reading: Robert Dallek, *Franklin D. Roosevelt and American Foreign Policy, 1932–1945* (New York: Oxford University Press, 1979).

—George Michael Curry

cash-and-carry

As global tensions increased in the 1930s, CONGRESS enacted a series of NEUTRALITY ACTS between 1935 and 1941 aimed at preventing the United States from entering war again as it had during World War I. To maintain American neutrality, yet permit sales of raw materials and other nonmilitary goods that might help the U.S. ECONOMY, a "cash-and-carry" provision was included in the 1937 Neutrality Act. It permitted nations at war to buy nonmilitary goods from the United States if paid for in advance by cash and carried away on ships not under United States registry. The cash-and-carry provision was set to expire in two years.

By the beginning of WORLD WAR II in 1939, cash-and-carry, like the Neutrality Acts generally, fit uncomfortably with the growing anti-AXIS sentiment in the United States. In the Atlantic, cash-and-carry helped Britain and France, which had significant trade contacts with the United States as well as ample shipping. In the Pacific conflict between China and Japan, however, the cash-and-carry principle favored Japan, with its shipping capacity and trade with the United States. And even for Britain and France the requirements of cash-and-carry had the potential to limit the acquisition of needed materials.

The Neutrality Acts had imposed an embargo on military items to nations at war, but these goods were also included under cash-and-carry after the beginning of the war in Europe in September 1939. Over the objections of ISOLATIONISTS, pro-Allied interventionists helped President FRANKLIN D. ROOSEVELT eliminate the arms embargo from the Neutrality Act of November 1939. Those opposed to intervention succeeded, however, in renewing cash-and-carry, which had expired in the spring and which now applied to the sale of military as well as nonmilitary items. The new legislation also continued the ban on loans to nations at war.

By late 1940, England was no longer able to pay cash for the war materials and other goods it needed. The BATTLE OF THE ATLANTIC, moreover, was reducing British shipping at an alarming rate. In his annual address to Congress, on January 6, 1941, Roosevelt announced that he was sending LEND-LEASE ACT legislation to Congress for action, so that England could acquire the materials it needed for its defense. Passage of the Lend-Lease Act removed the cash requirement of cash-and-carry, and the subsequent Neutrality Act of November 1941 allowed American ships to carry cargo to nations at war.

See also FOREIGN POLICY.

Further reading: William L. Langer, and S. Everett Gleason, *The Challenge to Isolation, 1937–1940* (New York: Harper & Row, 1952); ———, *The Undeclared War, 1940–1941* (New York: Harper & Row, 1953).

—Edwin C. Cogswell

Catholics

Throughout the era of the GREAT DEPRESSION and WORLD WAR II, the United States GOVERNMENT restricted IMMI-GRATION in accordance with legislation of the 1920s. But previous Roman Catholic immigration, especially to larger CITIES, laid the foundation for such Catholic groups as IRISH AMERICANS, ITALIAN AMERICANS, and POLISH AMERICANS to become religious, social, and political forces in American life. Although the Roman Catholic Al Smith's failed presidential run in 1928 exposed persistent strands of anti-Catholic nativism in America, ethnic Catholics would became key components in the political success of the NEW DEAL programs of President FRANKLIN D. ROOSEVELT in the 1930s and beyond. By far the largest religious group in the United States, Catholics generally became more "respectable" and accepted from 1929 to 1945, particularly in urban areas.

Roman Catholic lay people played an increasingly large role in American life in the era. JAMES A. FARLEY and EDWARD J. FLYNN served as chairmen of the DEMOCRATIC PARTY National Committee and as important political advisers to President Roosevelt, and other Catholics held important offices in federal, state, and local government. JOSEPH P. KENNEDY served as the first head of the SECURITIES AND EXCHANGE COMMISSION and as ambassador to Great Britain. Partly because of the unprecedented number of Catholics appointed to government positions by Roosevelt, though especially because of New Deal programs that helped the heavily working-class Catholic population, Catholic voters were a key part of the new Democratic majority forged in the elections of the 1930s. Catholics also figured prominently in such diverse areas as LABOR, LITERATURE, and SPORTS.

Roman Catholics began to effectively utilize mass media, especially the RADIO. For instance, the popular bishop Fulton J. Sheen possessed keen intellectual abilities, but became known as a great preacher and orator who could connect personally and spiritually with the general American public. Later a television personality, Sheen is often credited with being a key founder of the so-called electronic church in America. A far more controversial Roman Catholic broadcaster was Father CHARLES E. COUGHLIN, who became as much known for his political and social commentary as for his purely doctrinal messages. His fierce anticommunist stances quickly became mixed with overtly anti-Semitic diatribes and global conspiracy theories. Coughlin opposed Franklin Roosevelt, the New Deal, and American involvement in World War II, as well as displaying pro-Nazi sympathies—and the church brought about an end to his public pronouncements.

Another notable Catholic figure of the era was Archbishop (later, Cardinal) Francis Joseph Spellman, who was simultaneously an ardent anticommunist, archbishop of New York, and diplomatic representative of Pope Pius XII during World War II. Serving as U.S. military vicar and unofficial envoy for Franklin Roosevelt during wartime,

Spellman was also involved in promoting conservative social positions on such issues as birth control, movie CENSORSHIP, and the relationship between government funding and private EDUCATION.

Other Catholic leaders became advocates of LIBERALISM. Such women as Dorothy Day, who was a founding figure in the Catholic Worker movement, became active in the public arena. A pacifist, Day surprisingly had converted to Roman Catholicism from a secular, socialist past, and she pursued radical social and political change through the church. Another influential Roman Catholic figure of the period was Father John A. Ryan. Trained in political and economic theory, Ryan served as director of the Social Action Department of the influential National Catholic Welfare Council. He was a fierce critic of the economic policies of President HERBERT C. HOOVER and one of Franklin Roosevelt's staunchest New Deal supporters. Ryan became a key figure in forging a progressive social and political image for the 20th-century Catholic Church in America.

The period also witnessed a developing focus upon issues involving AFRICAN AMERICANS, as demonstrated by the urban missionary priest William McCann in Harlem, and the Jesuit priest William Markoe in St. Louis, who functioned as a type of proto-CIVIL RIGHTS spokesman there. While Roman Catholicism did not generally appeal to African Americans, emerging groups like the Federation of Colored Catholics demonstrated that African American Catholics were attempting to shape the religious, political, and social debates of a stormy era. The Jesuit priest John LaFarge helped establish the Catholic Interracial Council in 1934, and by the 1940s, local chapters were located in cities throughout the North and South, thus providing key lay and clerical support for the future Civil Rights movement of the 1950s and beyond.

World War II saw Catholics patriotically supporting the war effort, further reinforcing their sociocultural legitimacy, though they were still perceived as "ethnics" by the broader Anglo-American culture. While continuing to hold important government positions, Catholics also served in large numbers in the U.S. military and constituted a significant part of the labor force in the defense industry. By the end of the war, MEXICAN AMERICAN Catholic immigrants were moving in substantial numbers into already Hispanic areas of the American Southwest, especially around Los Angeles. These Hispanic Catholics imported a unique style of Catholicism, which often led to hostilities with already established Catholic communities.

From the depression to the end of World War II, Catholics continued to influence the evolving face of urban environments in America. At the grassroots level, Catholic laypeople displayed increased interest in Marian devotion and neighborhood festivals. Dynamic priests at the parish level often functioned as much as social and economic spokesmen and activists as they did as purely spiritual leaders.

See also POLITICS IN THE ROOSEVELT ERA; RELIGION.

Further reading: Jay P. Dolan, *The American Catholic Experience: A History from Colonial Times to the Present* (Notre Dame, Ind.: University of Notre Dame Press, 1992); James J. Hennesey, *American Catholics: A History of the Roman Catholic Community in the United States* (New York: Oxford University Press, 1981).

—J. Henry Allen, Jr.

censorship

Censorship is the prior review of all forms of expression in order to suppress or restrain, in part or entirely, anything considered objectionable. The era of the GREAT DEPRESSION and WORLD WAR II was marked by a number of efforts by the GOVERNMENT and by private organizations to censor objectionable speech, publications, and other forms of expression. The period also brought some state and federal court rulings that overturned or eased censorship laws and practices. During World War II, government censorship, while extensive and pervasive, was nonetheless less onerous than during World War I.

In the first part of the 20th century, censorship clashed with the prohibition in the First Amendment of the Constitution of laws abridging the freedom of speech or of the press. During World War I, for example, the Espionage Act and the Sedition Act sharply restricted opposition to the war or criticism of the government, and in 1919 the SUPREME COURT upheld such censorship in *Abrams v. the United States*. In 1925, the Supreme Court (*Gitlow v. New York*) ruled that even speeches that posed no immediate danger to public order could be punished. The 1930 HAWLEY-SMOOT TARIFF ACT prohibited the import of anything immoral or obscene.

New forms of expression, such as MOVIES and RADIO encountered censorship during this period. Following several scandals, the Motion Picture Association of America adopted a strict code for the film industry in the 1920s to head off government censorship. Private groups, notably the Roman Catholic Legion of Decency, had their own film rating system, lobbied against a number of movies, and contributed to the film industry strengthening its self-censorship with the Production Code Administration, established in 1934. Many states and municipality censorship boards banned totally, or in part, a number of films. Such actions did not apply only to obscenity or "immoral" behavior, but also to portrayals of violence, crime, and social problems. The Chicago Board of Censors refused to allow the showing of a 1937 Paramount newsreel of the Republic Steel Memorial Day Massacre, for example, while a

Memphis board blocked a film showing black and white children going to school together.

Because radio stations were licensed, strict government controls could be enforced on this medium. Programs considered inflammatory or immoral, such as those of FATHER CHARLES E. COUGHLIN and Mae West were reviewed by the FEDERAL COMMUNICATIONS COMMISSION or cancelled by the radio stations. Radio and film self-censorship came partly for economic reasons. Since so many Americans attended movies or listened to the radio, continued income from admissions and ADVERTISING depended upon the widest possible audience appeal. Controversial programs or films would reduce industry profitability.

During the 1930s and 1940s, court decisions overturned some censorship laws and practices. In 1931, the Supreme Court (*Near v. Minnesota ex rel. Olson*) ruled that a Minnesota statute preventing the publication of "scandalous and malicious" material was an unconstitutional prior restraint of the press. In 1934, a New York federal judge lifted the ban on James Joyce's *Ulysses*, seized under the Hawley-Smoot Tariff Act, although other courts upheld bans of the novels *Tropic of Cancer* (1934) by Henry Miller and *Lady Chatterley's Lover* (1944) by D. H. Lawrence. The Supreme Court also struck down a Georgia law prohibiting speeches by COMMUNISTS (1937).

The approach of World War II caused the U.S. government to take actions to ensure domestic security and to protect military secrets. The U.S. ARMY and U.S. NAVY began planning for censorship by the late 1930s, and during the war censored communications and also correspondence of armed forces personnel. In 1940, CONGRESS passed the SMITH ACT, which among other things outlawed advocating the overthrow of the government and authorized deporting aliens who belonged to revolutionary organizations or expressed revolutionary sentiments.

On December 19, 1941, President FRANKLIN D. ROOSEVELT issued Executive Order 8985 creating the federal Office of Censorship under Associated Press editor Byron Price. The office eventually grew to 90 offices across the country staffed by more than 14,000 examiners who scanned radio and movie scripts, magazine and newspapers stories, listened to telephone conversations, monitored radio broadcasts, checked for invisible inks, banned crossword puzzles, and reviewed more than a million overseas letters a day. Letters marked with the sticker *Opened by Censor* became a common sight during the war.

While primarily meant to protect wartime secrets and uncover ESPIONAGE, censorship also shaped how Americans perceived the war and served PROPAGANDA purposes. Censors restricted the publication of brutal images of the war and problems on the domestic front. Not until 1943 were photos of dead Americans released for publication; before then, such images were thought harmful to morale,

but as the Allies clearly gained the upper hand, the government wanted to avoid home-front overconfidence. The armed forces censored their own photographers and filmmakers—and used their products for public relations purposes. The OFFICE OF WAR INFORMATION and its Bureau of Motion Pictures ensured that the content of Hollywood films during the war fit with the administration's war aims through appeals to patriotism and threats to restrict distribution. Like war reporters and photographers, filmmakers cooperated with government wishes.

Still, whatever the tensions with First Amendment rights, wartime censorship never seemed excessive, especially in comparison with the other nations at war or with the World War I home front. In part this was due to the unwillingness of many leaders, especially President Roosevelt, to repeat the excesses of World War I. Only two cases were brought to trial during the war under the Smith Act. Moreover, Byron Price exercised his power with restraint, while American journalists adhered to a system of self-censorship. The Office of Censorship was terminated at the end of the war.

See also AMERICAN CIVIL LIBERTIES UNION; CIVIL LIBERTIES.

Further reading: Leon Hurwitz, *The Historical Dictionary of Censorship in the United States* (Westport, Conn.: Greenwood Press, 1985); Clayton R. Koppes, and Gregory D. Black, *Hollywood Goes to War: How Politics, Profits, and Propaganda Shaped World War II Movies* (New York: Free Press, 1987); George H. Roeder, Jr., *The Censored War: American Visual Experience during World War II* (New Haven: Yale University Press, 1993); Michael S. Sweeney, *Secrets of Victory: The Office of Censorship and the American Press and Radio in World War II* (Chapel Hill: University of North Carolina Press, 2001).

—Robert J. Hanyok

children

The dramatic events engaging Americans from 1929 to 1945 deeply shaped the lives of children, and young people made their own important contributions to the American experience during these significant years. Together with demographic shifts and other POPULATION TRENDS, these events also contributed to growing debates about the role of public policy for children and their families.

The census of 1930 showed the median age of Americans as 26.4 and counted approximately 24 million individuals of less than 20 years of age. This significant group constituted 38 percent of the total population. Although the numbers suggest that America's youngest citizens were statistically important, the 1930 census also revealed that children and adolescents comprised a shrinking proportion of the total U.S. population. One hundred years earlier, people under 20 made up a majority of the total population (56 percent), and the country's median age was only 17.2. Over the next century, life expectancy lengthened and families became smaller, thereby reducing children's share of the total population.

Despite the fact that young people were a smaller part of the total, by the 1930s and 1940s social policies directed at children combined with a revised cultural definition of childhood to bring positive changes for America's youngest citizens. Beginning in the mid-19th century Americans moved toward a new middle-class definition of childhood and adolescence that was firmly grounded in law and culture by the 1930s and 1940s. In this new formulation, the average family (4.3 members) was approximately half of what it had been in 1830. Smaller families allowed parents to focus more attention on their offspring. Health care improved and overall life expectancy lengthened. A declining number of youngsters worked for wages and children spent more years in school. Compulsory school attendance fostered age segregation that increased the influence of peer groups and the development of a separate youth culture.

The GREAT DEPRESSION and World War II then presented different but difficult hurdles for America's youngest citizens and produced ambivalence among adults toward expanded public policies for young people in the postwar years. As the U.S. Children's Bureau noted in its 1933 report, the onset of the Great Depression often hit children the hardest. One-third of Americans were ill-housed, ill-clothed, and ill-fed—and of those, the majority were children. In addition, young people eligible to work found it very difficult to get a job. Americans 16 to 20 years of age had UNEMPLOYMENT rates twice those of adults, and an estimated 23,000 homeless teens rode the nation's railways and hitchhiked along its highways looking for work.

Several NEW DEAL programs sought to help young people. The CIVILIAN CONSERVATION CORPS, a work RELIEF program open to males 16 through 23 years of age, but closed to females, provided jobs for unemployed young men. The NATIONAL YOUTH ADMINISTRATION offered part-time jobs and tuition assistance to help young people remain in high school and college (and off the job market). The NYA included a division focused on the needs of young AFRICAN AMERICANS, a foreshadowing of postwar efforts to end racial inequality.

New Deal policymakers also took advantage of the fact that the economic crisis of the 1930s eroded opposition to federal legislation to regulate child labor and increased pressure on the government to keep young people under eighteen out of the paid labor force. Child labor regulations of the NATIONAL RECOVERY ADMINISTRATION (NRA) immediately removed 150,000 young workers from payrolls. After the NRA was declared unconstitutional in 1935,

child labor provisions of the 1938 FAIR LABOR STANDARDS ACT outlawed the employment of individuals under 16 in the manufacture of materials shipped across state lines. The law also regulated the hiring of young people aged 16 and 17, although AGRICULTURE and domestic service were exempted from the law. The new legislation did not end the exploitation of all young workers, but it combined with the decade's labor crisis and existing compulsory school attendance laws to force the vast majority of individuals under 18 years of age out of the wage-labor market and into school.

During the 1930s, even Hollywood MOVIES reflected the new social status of children based on the middle-class model emphasizing EDUCATION. Films featuring the "Our Gang" kids, and child stars such as Mickey Rooney, Judy Garland, and Shirley Temple idealized childhood and adolescence as a time of schooling and fun absent from adult responsibilities. For the first time in American history a majority of 17-year-olds attended high school.

Young people also experienced greater independence. Dating moved adolescent boys and girls far from the watchful eyes of parents. Youth clubs such as the Boy Scouts, Girl Scouts, YMCA, YWCA, and 4-H gained new members. Racial and ethnic segregation persisted, but comic books and other "kid"-centered aspects of POPULAR CULTURE crossed such social lines. Reflecting the evolution of a separate youth culture, a 1941 article in *Popular Science* introduced the word "teenager" into the American print vocabulary for the first time.

Some of the programs involving children and youth begun during the New Deal era took on new aspects when the United States entered World War II. For example, nursery schools begun by the WORKS PROGRESS ADMINISTRATION to provide unemployed teachers with relief jobs during the Great Depression expanded as a growing pool of mothers entered the wartime labor force. Many parents and child welfare advocates worried that day care was not good for children, but the wartime demand for women's labor overrode such concerns.

The Title V program for maternal and child health of the SOCIAL SECURITY ACT was also transformed by wartime needs. As more men enlisted or were drafted into the military, authorities became concerned about maintaining high morale among the troops. Many soldiers and sailors worried about pregnant wives and newborns unable to get good health care. In response, CONGRESS expanded Title V to include the Emergency Maternity and Infant Care program (EMIC), which provided free prenatal, delivery, postnatal, and infant health care to the wives and children of enlisted men. This far-reaching effort meant that one out of every seven children born in the United States from 1943 to 1949 could be called a "government baby." And just in time, for overall birth rates rose during the war years—

and then continued to climb for the next two decades. EMIC appears to have contributed to the continued decline in the U.S. infant mortality rate, which fell from 47.0 deaths per 1,000 live births in 1940 to 29.2 in 1950. However, despite the program's popularity and the rising U.S. birth rate, Congress had designed EMIC only as a wartime measure to enhance morale among the troops. The program ended with the conclusion of DEMOBILIZATION in 1949.

Some child welfare advocates argued that the demise of EMIC reflected the growing ambivalence among adults about programs for children as the war came to a close. As more mothers worked outside the home, young people gained autonomy that some viewed as a threat to society. The postwar worry about juvenile delinquency actually began on the WORLD WAR II HOME FRONT. The population exploded near military bases and war production centers, and critics raised concerns about unsupervised children and adolescents judged to be "out of control." The 1943 riots against ZOOT-SUITERS in Los Angeles where U.S. sailors and soldiers attacked Mexican-American adolescents, ironically underscored for many adults their perception of rising delinquency among young people. A 1950 report by the U.S. Children's Bureau declared that such conclusions were false, but during the 1940s and 1950s adults became increasingly concerned about juvenile delinquency.

Of course, most children and adolescents did not engage in antisocial behavior during the war. Instead, they participated in scrap drives, WAR BONDS sales, and other patriotic endeavors. Some youths took factory, service, or agricultural jobs. Older siblings cared for younger brothers and sisters while parents worked. The military draft included a deferment for all males through age 19 attending high school, but many younger boys lied about their age and joined up anyway.

Further reading: Robert H. Bremner, ed., *Children and Youth in America: A Documentary History*, vol. III (Cambridge, Mass.: Harvard University Press, 1970); Joseph M. Hawes, *Children between the Wars: American Childhood, 1920–1940* (New York: Twayne, 1997); Kriste Lindenmeyer, *"A Right to Childhood": The U.S. Children's Bureau and Child Welfare, 1912–1946* (Urbana: University of Illinois Press, 1997); William Tuttle, *"Daddy's Gone to War": The Second World War in the Lives of America's Children* (New York: Oxford University Press, 1993).

—Kriste Lindenmeyer

cities and urban life

In 1929, America's cities basked in the glow of nearly three decades of rapid growth and general prosperity. By 1932,

cities were foundering and sliding toward bankruptcy as they attempted to deal with the massive UNEMPLOYMENT of the GREAT DEPRESSION. The continuation of the depression for another eight years affected cities in several fundamental ways. First, urban growth nearly halted. Population stagnated and did not rebound until WORLD WAR II, while new construction did not reach 1920s levels until the postwar era. Second, the depression created a municipal fiscal crisis that forced cities to cut back drastically on basic urban services and facilities, leaving many of them with serious problems in these areas by 1945. Deteriorating conditions and inadequate HOUSING in central cities helped lead to the burgeoning of SUBURBS in the postwar era. Finally, urban unemployment and fiscal problems caused cities to turn to the federal GOVERNMENT for aid, producing long-term alliances between cities and both the federal government and the DEMOCRATIC PARTY. The Second World War then created so many new war-related jobs that rural and small-town people flocked to metropolitan areas. A number of southern and western cities expanded rapidly, laying foundations for a major shift in urban population centers away from the Northeast and Middle West toward SUNBELT areas of the SOUTH, the West, and especially the Pacific Coast.

The most visible impact of the Great Depression in the nation's cities was the huge decline in new construction. Housing starts fell to one-tenth of the peak years of the 1920s, and commercial or industrial construction likewise almost halted. Cities that had been growing rapidly for many decades suddenly seemed frozen in time, looking in 1940 much as they had in 1930. In the residential areas of cities and in their suburbs, miles of streets and sidewalks seemed to disappear as grass and weeds grew up in thousands of vacant lots. By 1940 almost all the major cities faced serious problems that stemmed in part from the depression: an aging and neglected physical plant, increased TAXATION made necessary by the decline of property values, and reduced urban services. War production demands created a substantial construction boom of new factories and other facilities in a number of cities and their suburbs; but there was little spending on the urban infrastructure.

Urban population during the 1929–1945 era followed a pattern that was dictated by the economic health of each city. Prior to the 1930s, city populations had increased steadily through in-migration and the annexation of outlying suburbs. The Great Depression halted both these trends, and urban population growth slowed dramatically and in some cities was reversed. Among the nation's largest 15 cities, only New York and Los Angeles showed any significant gains, and even their growth rates were far below those of the 1920s. World War II then reversed the population trend of the 1930s. Between 1940 and 1945, many

A tenement in Pittsburgh, Pennsylvania, 1938 *(Library of Congress)*

cities experienced huge influxes of war workers and their families. The arrival of so many new residents created extremely overcrowded housing conditions and increased social problems.

During the 1930s, unemployment and destitution became a familiar part of urban life, most visibly in the big cities. During the depths of the depression, from 1931 to 1933, the nation's largest cities held hundreds of thousands of unemployed people, and RELIEF rolls exceeded anything ever seen before. In some manufacturing cities like Detroit, up to half and sometimes higher proportions of the labor force found themselves unemployed or working part-time. By 1931, private charitable agencies were overwhelmed, and municipal governments began to spend ever larger portions of their funds to aid the unemployed.

While NEW DEAL programs brought help from 1933 to 1941, the economic atmosphere of cities remained grim. Even in the late 1930s, unemployment remained high, and city dwellers who did hold jobs lived in fear of losing them. Yet without the New Deal's massive job programs, the his-

tory of the nation's cities during the depression years could have been quite turbulent. The only major urban violence arising from economic conditions occurred during the middle and late 1930s in connection with the formation of the new industrial LABOR unions; but even these disturbances fell far short of anything like a general uprising of the urban working class.

The continuing sluggishness of the urban economy throughout the 1930s also had an impact on the movement of people within cities, and from the city to the suburbs. Both types of movement slowed considerably. Very few people could afford to buy new homes on the urban fringe, and so they remained in houses and neighborhoods that in the normal course of events would have been turned over to a new generation of upwardly mobile families leaving overcrowded, substandard housing. World War II brought rising incomes and an influx of new residents, but little new housing. Thus, by 1945, cities contained a large number of people who had been living for over a decade in undesirable housing conditions, but whose savings were now sufficient to allow them to buy new homes.

In the postwar era, home builders, some of whom had learned how to mass-produce relatively good, inexpensive houses for the federally financed war worker housing projects, responded by constructing huge numbers of houses, mostly in the suburbs. Suburban housing was especially attractive because it allowed families to escape the problems that bedeviled the central cities and which they had been nearly powerless to deal with since 1930. The outflow of the city's middle classes, which had begun in a limited way in the 1910–30 era, now commenced on a much larger scale.

Only the federal government in the 1930s might have been able to help America's cities sustain themselves as places where a large portion of the middle- and upper-income groups would have wished to live, but it proved unwilling to undertake such an ambitious (and perhaps impossible) task. Although the New Deal was quite active in cities, its spending, with the exception of low-income housing projects, was aimed primarily at relieving urban unemployment and only secondarily at efforts to improve the basic fabric of city life. Even so, the assistance that the New Deal brought to cities and city residents brought Roosevelt and the Democratic Party great support, and the urban vote played a major role in the emergence of the Democrats as the nation's new majority party in the POLITICS IN THE ROOSEVELT ERA.

The United States Conference of Mayors, formed in 1932 to seek federal aid for the unemployed, helped draw President FRANKLIN D. ROOSEVELT and the New Deal into their relationship with the nation's cities. Led by Mayor Frank Murphy of Detroit, the conference pleaded with the Roosevelt administration to give cities money to employ the jobless—a financial burden that cities like Detroit could no longer carry. Indeed, by 1933 most of the nation's cities were headed toward bankruptcy or already in the hands of receivers. The municipal fiscal crisis of 1931–33 arose from the fact that property tax revenues fell sharply at the same time that unemployment relief added a large new item to municipal budgets. Few state governments had the resources, or, dominated by unsympathetic rural legislators, the desire to give cities much if any assistance.

The New Deal responded to the mayors' requests for help by providing millions of dollars for urban employment projects. Almost all the federally funded projects—through such agencies as the FEDERAL EMERGENCY RELIEF ADMINISTRATION, the CIVIL WORKS ADMINISTRATION, and the WORKS PROGRESS ADMINISTRATION—made improvements in the urban environment. These included such activities as street repairs, urban highway and bridge construction, the embellishment of park lands, and the expansion of water and sewer systems; but the projects were never large enough or numerous enough to make a major impact on the overall quality of city life. More important, the Roosevelt administration never conceived of these activities as anything like a coordinated or comprehensive attack on the basic urban problems of poverty, lack of education and skills, social disorganization, crime, pollution, and traffic congestion.

The only long-range, permanent urban improvement undertaken by the New Deal was its slum clearance and low-income housing program embodied in the United States Housing Act of 1937. Under the UNITED STATES HOUSING AUTHORITY, terrible slums were cleared and replaced by safe, sanitary public housing projects. The chief drawbacks to the program were its late start and small scale. Still in operation today, it has never come close to replacing all the substandard dwellings in America's cities and has played only a small role in housing the urban poor.

In contrast to the economic stagnation and nearly static nature of the urban physical plant, the social and cultural life of cities retained a real vitality for their heterogeneous populations. City life was grim for the unemployed and impoverished, but for many working-class families and those of middle and upper income, the cities still offered a cornucopia of moderately priced or free entertainments and diversions: parks, playgrounds, professional SPORTS teams, movie theaters, department stores, soda fountains, dance halls, night clubs, amusement parks, and dozens of other attractions. Crime, vice, juvenile delinquency, and poverty continued to plague cities, but were accepted as part of the price of urban living—balanced by the big and little pleasures of city life.

A significant long-term trend often obscured by the economic problems of cities was that ethnic differences and antagonisms began to fade as the immigrants of the 1890–1920 era were gradually replaced by the second and third generations. Most cities still had their Little Italy or Polish Town; saloons (brought back by the end of prohibition) still catered to particular ethnic groups; and urban political machines still based much of their strength on ethnic allegiances. But dance halls, cabarets, and amusement parks became places where younger people of all backgrounds were thrown together. Both neighborhood theaters and downtown movie palaces showed Hollywood MOVIES that largely ignored the distinctiveness of America's ethnic cultures and thus tended to undermine them. City park and RECREATION departments sponsored a variety of sports and recreational programs that also brought people from different ethnic groups into contact. Tensions and even conflict persisted, and AFRICAN AMERICANS and MEXICAN AMERICANS remained isolated—but important change was under way.

World War II turned attention to the use of America's cities as war production centers. The huge task of economic MOBILIZATION for war ended urban unemployment and actually created a greater demand for workers than the local labor force could supply. Extraordinarily heavy wartime MIGRATION added a new layer of in-migrants to American cities, particularly in rapidly growing Sunbelt cities. Despite some tensions between in-migrants and old-timers, the wartime emphasis on national unity, the breakdown of ethnic (and to some degree racial) barriers in war plants, and the intermingling of peoples at USO centers and other recreational facilities further reduced ethnic suspicions and differences. However, the renewed influx of African Americans, and a substantial immigration of Mexican immigrants into the cities of the West Coast, often heightened racial animosities and in some cities brought a wave of racial violence.

In conclusion, America's cities suffered significantly during the Great Depression from massive unemployment and financial problems that forced them to cut back drastically on municipal facilities and services. The New Deal made its major contribution to the nation's cities by giving work relief to the unemployed. Despite federal construction projects in the cities, the urban physical plant as a whole, and especially urban housing, was in poor condition by 1945. There was never any major attempt to address the basic social, economic and physical problems of the cities, problems sometimes exacerbated by World War II. When the war ended, the central cities appeared increasingly unattractive to many of its middle- and upper-income residents. They began to move to the suburbs and new housing as quickly as possible—creating problems for central cities that ultimately became even more serious than the ones they faced during the 1930s.

See also POPULATION TRENDS.

Further reading: Lizabeth Cohen, *Making a New Deal: Industrial Workers in Chicago, 1919–1939* (New York: Cambridge University Press, 1990); Philip Funigiello, *The Challenge to Urban Liberalism: Federal-City Relations during World War II* (Knoxville: University of Tennessee Press, 1978); Mark I. Gelfand, *A Nation of Cities: The Federal Government and Urban America, 1933–1965* (New York: Oxford University Press, 1975).

—Joseph L. Arnold

civil liberties

The term *civil liberties* refers to individual rights guaranteed in the federal Constitution, particularly in the Bill of Rights, and often refers especially to First Amendment rights of speech, religion, the press, assembly, and petitioning the GOVERNMENT. From 1929 to 1945, civil liberties issues sometimes involved efforts at CENSORSHIP in such areas as MOVIES, the NEWS MEDIA, and LITERATURE, but they more often arose out of efforts to clamp down on

radicalism and to protect national security. Despite challenges to civil liberties, the era also helped lay foundations for protecting and expanding civil liberties in the postwar era.

During the 1930s, government policies that raised worries about abridging First Amendment rights were largely responses to perceived threats from political groups on the far left and far right. In 1938, the House Committee on Un-American Activities was formed, and in 1939, CONGRESS passed the Hatch Act, denying federal employment to anyone belonging to a revolutionary group. The loyalty board of the Civil Service Commission subsequently increased its investigations of the political backgrounds and beliefs of potential employees. COMMUNISTS were often under surveillance and their literature was subject to confiscation, but the government also watched American Bundists and other pro-Nazi or pro-Fascist groups.

The economic impact of the GREAT DEPRESSION also led to concerns about civil liberties. High UNEMPLOYMENT levels and stiff competition for jobs, for example, led government officials to deport thousands of MEXICAN AMERICANS, many of whom were U.S. citizens, in the MEXICAN REPATRIATION PROGRAM. The growth and increased activism of organized LABOR raised worries about civil liberties, for during previous times of labor conflict, government had often taken the side of management and disregarded the civil liberties of workers and their leaders. By the mid-1930s, however, workers had gained significant protection under the law to organize, bargain collectively, and conduct strikes, especially with the passage of the NATIONAL LABOR RELATIONS ACT of 1935.

With the U.S. entrance into WORLD WAR II, some feared a renewal of the repressive governmental policies of World War I. The SMITH ACT of 1940 had authorized the deportation of any alien belonging to a "revolutionary" organization or expressing revolutionary sentiments, and it outlawed speech attempting to breed disloyalty in the military or advocating the overthrow of the government. But only two cases were brought under the Smith Act during the war, and fears of a repressive home front proved generally to be unfounded. Widespread popular support for the war effort and a dearth of outspoken protestors, as well as the memory of World War I excesses, helped prevent widespread violations of civil liberties.

Even the draft did not ignite extensive protest, as it had in World War I and would years later during the Vietnam War. Groups such as the AMERICAN CIVIL LIBERTIES UNION, which championed civil liberties in a number of important episodes in the era, failed to protest the passage of the SELECTIVE SERVICE Act of 1940, although it tried to ensure that the draft was implemented democratically. The act provided alternatives for CONSCIENTIOUS OBJECTORS, and men who refused to participate in combat for religious reasons were offered noncombatant or civilian duties. However, those who objected for purely political reasons or for religious reasons deemed illegitimate were not excused, and more than 5,000 objectors were imprisoned over the course of the war.

But the WORLD WAR II HOME FRONT did witness one of the most egregious violations of civil liberties in American history, the relocation of JAPANESE AMERICANS, citizens and noncitizens alike, and their incarceration in internment camps. The SUPREME COURT let the relocation policy stand in the case of *KOREMATSU V. UNITED STATES*. Unnaturalized German-American and Italian-American immigrants were also labeled ENEMY ALIENS and subjected to various regulations, but these did not involve violations of the civil liberties of citizens.

Further reading: Kermit L. Hall, ed., *Civil Liberties in American History: Major Historical Interpretations* (New York: Garland, 1987); Michael Linfield, *Freedom under Fire: U.S. Civil Liberties in Times of War* (Boston: South End Press, 1990).

—Pamela J. Lauer

civil rights

Civil rights means, in effect, citizenship rights, including the rights to move about freely, to have economic opportunity, to obtain an education, to rent or own a home wherever personal fortune permits, to have access to public accommodations, and to vote and hold public office. The U.S. Constitution and its Bill of Rights incorporated civil rights into the nation's fundamental law. The extension of civil rights to all citizens has become a central tenet of American political culture and embodies the idea that "the people" have certain basic rights that may not be violated.

Until the era of the Civil War and Reconstruction, however, and the adoption of the Thirteenth, Fourteenth, and Fifteenth Amendments to the Constitution, the civil rights of AFRICAN AMERICANS were denied by slavery or abridged by law and custom. By the early 20th century, a series of "Jim Crow" laws and practices producing segregation, disfranchisement, and discrimination in the SOUTH had eliminated most of the civil rights gained during Reconstruction. In other regions, custom and law also abridged the rights of African Americans and sometimes those of ASIAN AMERICANS and MEXICAN AMERICANS. The post–World War I period did not produce much progress toward safeguarding civil rights despite growing black protest, the activities of the NATIONAL ASSOCIATION FOR THE ADVANCEMENT OF COLORED PEOPLE (NAACP), and the "Great Migration" of blacks from the rural South to urban areas of the nation.

The 1930s brought some limited gains in the area of civil rights for African Americans. The 1931 SCOTTSBORO BOYS case, in which Alabama authorities jailed and prosecuted nine young black men wrongly accused of raping two white women, brought national attention to civil rights, and ultimately federal court decisions overturned the convictions. During the decade, the NAACP and its executive secretary, WALTER WHITE lobbied heavily for the Costigan-Wagner antilynching bill from its introduction in CONGRESS in 1933 until its final failure late in the decade. Fear of the bill's passage did help reduce lynchings, and the bill won significant support from the public and northern congressmen and senators, but President FRANKLIN D. ROOSEVELT, fearing alienating southern Democrats he thought crucial to his NEW DEAL programs, refused to sponsor it or other corrective federal legislation. The New Deal itself did little for civil rights, though its programs were extended to African Americans and ELEANOR ROOSEVELT, HAROLD ICKES, and others supported efforts to safeguard civil rights, as did the unofficial BLACK CABINET that advised the president.

Meanwhile, the NAACP and other groups continued chipping away at the wall of legal segregation. During the HOOVER PRESIDENCY, the NAACP had helped block the nomination to the SUPREME COURT of John J. Parker, a foe of civil rights for blacks. The all-white Democratic primary, which prevented blacks from taking part in the most important elections in the one-party Democratic South, remained a particular target of the NAACP Legal Defense Fund, which pursued a number of cases, culminating in *Smith v. Allwright* in 1944 that found the all-white primary unconstitutional. The NAACP's efforts in the 1930s and 1940s also produced decisions against segregation in higher EDUCATION that laid groundwork for the 1954 decision of *Brown v. Board of Education of Topeka* that overturned the legal sanction given segregation by *Plessy v. Ferguson* in 1896.

As WORLD WAR II approached, blacks remained largely excluded from economic opportunity. In 1941, the black activist A. PHILIP RANDOLPH organized the MARCH ON WASHINGTON MOVEMENT and threatened a mass march on Washington to protest discrimination in defense plant hiring and in the armed forces. To head off the march, FDR issued EXECUTIVE ORDER 8802, which forbade discrimination on grounds of race, nationality, and religion in defense industry and government hiring and established the FAIR EMPLOYMENT PRACTICES COMMITTEE (FEPC) to implement the new rules.

The war years nonetheless saw continued denials of the civil rights of African Americans and other minorities. The most notable wartime violation of civil rights and CIVIL LIBERTIES was the relocation of JAPANESE AMERICANS, citizens and noncitizens alike. The South denied black

A drinking fountain on the county courthouse lawn, Halifax, North Carolina, 1938 *(Library of Congress)*

servicemen civil rights that it granted German PRISONERS OF WAR, and despite Executive Order 8802, blacks only slowly were offered jobs in defense industry. The armed forces remained segregated for most of the war. Mexican Americans encountered discrimination in the West and Southwest. Wartime patterns of RACE AND RACIAL CONFLICT included race riots in the summer of 1943 between whites and African Americans and Mexican Americans.

Even so, World War II marked a turning point for civil rights. Black protest increased—the NAACP mushroomed from some 50,000 members to 450,000 members, for example, and many blacks talked about a double victory over the AXIS abroad and Jim Crow at home. White Americans outside the South became more aware of discrimination against African Americans and other racial minorities, in part because of the highly-influential and best-selling 1944 study of American race relations by GUNNAR MYRDAL, *An American Dilemma.* Executive Order 8802 was a significant initiative, and by the end of the war a number of northern states had adopted interracial commissions and civil rights had won a new place on the agenda of liberals

and northern Democrats. The armed forces had begun to move toward desegregation. And the wartime rhetoric of democracy and of opposing the master race philosophy of Nazi Germany resonated in postwar America and helped build more support for civil rights.

Further reading: John Kirby, *Black Americans in the Roosevelt Era: Liberalism and Race* (Knoxville: University of Tennessee Press, 1980); Harvard Sitkoff, *A New Deal for Blacks: The Emergence of Civil Rights as a National Issue* (New York: Oxford University Press, 1978).

—Howard Smead

Civil Works Administration (CWA)

The Civil Works Administration (CWA) was a NEW DEAL program that provided work RELIEF in the winter of 1933–34. In the autumn of 1933, relief administrator HARRY HOPKINS persuaded President FRANKLIN D. ROOSEVELT that millions of Americans would suffer during the coming winter without major new action. The ECONOMY was not recovering sufficiently to provide jobs for the unemployed, the PUBLIC WORKS ADMINISTRATION (PWA) could not produce a significant number of jobs until the spring of 1934, and the FEDERAL EMERGENCY RELIEF ADMINISTRATION (FERA) could not provide sufficient assistance for the jobless. UNEMPLOYMENT remained at over one-fifth of the labor force.

Early in November 1933, Roosevelt transferred $400 million from the PWA and authorized Hopkins to establish the Civil Works Administration, which would implement work-relief projects to hire unemployed workers. Unlike the FERA, the CWA was entirely a federally supported program and was from the first a work-relief agency that hired needy people to work on specific projects, an approach that Hopkins and Roosevelt much preferred to dispensing direct relief. Half of the CWA workers came from existing relief rolls, but the other were unemployed and were not subjected to a means test. CWA workers were paid at regional average minimum wages, well above prevailing relief payments.

Harry Hopkins implemented the new agency with his characteristic energy. By late November, nearly 1 million workers had received their first checks from the CWA, and its height in mid-January, the agency employed more than 4 million people. Spending some $900 million in just a few months, the CWA inevitably involved some inefficiencies and slipshod or seemingly unnecessary work (often called "boondoggles"), but it also enriched the nation's infrastructure. CWA built or improved 40,000 schools, 1,000 airports, 3,500 parks and playgrounds, and hundreds of thousands of miles of roads. It laid more than 10 million feet of sewer pipe and built 150,000 outhouses for rural families. It employed 50,000 teachers and some 3,000 artists and writers. And it helped the nation through the winter of 1933–34, providing the dignity of work instead of a handout and raising both the income and the spirits of millions of Americans, not only in the Christmas season of 1933 but through the rest of the winter as well.

The CWA nonetheless came to seem too expensive and too vulnerable to President Roosevelt, who terminated it in the spring of 1934. It had served its essential function of seeing the country through the winter of 1933–34; it was increasingly criticized for inefficiency and political manipulation (although, as with other New Deal relief efforts, corruption and graft were remarkably small); and by the spring, the administration hoped that economic improvement and PWA projects would provide jobs for CWA workers. Always concerned about the psychological impact as well as the costs of GOVERNMENT relief, moreover, Roosevelt was worried about creating a permanent group of people dependent upon government jobs and money. As early as February, Hopkins began reducing CWA rolls in the South, where warm weather returned first; and by early

April he had let some 4 million workers go throughout the nation. A number of CWA projects were taken over by the FERA in 1934, and beginning in 1935, the WORKS PROGRESS ADMINISTRATION would begin an even more expansive work-relief program. Although a short-lived agency, CWA was nonetheless an important one, not only in the help it gave and in the projects it undertook but also in the precedents it established for work relief and federal responsibility for economic security.

Further reading: Bonnie Fox Schwartz, *The Civil Works Administration, 1933–1934: The Business of Emergency Employment in the New Deal* (Princeton, N.J.: Princeton University Press, 1984).

Civilian Conservation Corps (CCC)

Established in March 1933 during the first Hundred Days of the FRANKLIN D. ROOSEVELT administration, the Civilian Conservation Corps (CCC) was an important part of both the conservation and the RELIEF efforts of the NEW DEAL. One of the most popular New Deal agencies, it was also especially close to the heart of Roosevelt himself. Deeply troubled by the plight of hundreds of thousands of youthful transients at the depth of the GREAT DEPRESSION, Roosevelt and others saw the CCC as a way to conserve not only the nation's land and natural resources but also the spirits of young men by providing them income and new opportunities and experiences. The CCC peaked at roughly a half million workers in 1935, ultimately employed a total of some three million young men over its 1933–1942 lifetime, and accomplished a large and imaginative assortment of projects.

At its inception, the CCC was authorized to employ some 250,000 young men in a variety of conservation efforts. Jobless young men between 18 and 25 years old were to enlist for a period of six months (renewable for three more terms, or up to two years) and were paid $30 a month ($25 of which they were to send home) for working on a variety of conservation projects. The program worked through established GOVERNMENT agencies, coordinated by the CCC director, with the Labor Department selecting the young men, the War Department transporting them to camps, and the Agriculture and Interior Departments supervising the projects. The CCC did not enroll women, and it imposed a quota on AFRICAN AMERICANS and operated segregated camps.

Perhaps most noted of the CCC accomplishments were its reforestation projects, which accounted for some 75 percent of all trees planted in the nation down to 1942. But the CCC did far more than this—in implementing other forms of erosion control; in protecting wildlife and building some 300,000 wildlife shelters; in stocking nearly

1 billion fish; in developing trails, campgrounds, and other infrastructure in national parks; in preserving and restoring national historical sites; in building dams for flood control; in building firebreaks, lookout towers, and trails for fire control; and in other ways protecting, preserving, and beautifying the nation's natural and built environment. And in accomplishing such tasks, the CCC also pioneered in work relief that brought needed money to destitute young people and their families. Like subsequent New Deal programs aimed at work relief, training, and education for young people, it also had the desired effect of keeping them off the job market, so that jobs might go to unemployed adults.

As a work-relief agency, the CCC seemed increasingly unnecessary and was vulnerable to conservative opposition as prosperity returned with WORLD WAR II. Even before the off-year election of 1942 gave a clear ideological majority to the congressional CONSERVATIVE COALITION of Republicans and conservative Democrats, Congress stepped up its opposition to such holdover 1930s agencies as the WORKS PROGRESS ADMINISTRATION (WPA) and the CCC. The CCC's numbers had been falling steadily since the late 1930s in any event, and by 1942 it was to focus its efforts on those related to the war effort. Even public support for the CCC waned in these new circumstances. In July 1942, Roosevelt unhappily terminated the agency after Congress cut off its appropriations.

See also ENVIRONMENTAL ISSUES.

Further reading: John Salmond, *The Civilian Conservation Corps, 1933–1942: A New Deal Case Study* (Durham, N.C.: Duke University Press, 1967).

code breaking

Code breaking played an important role in WORLD WAR II. Codes are systems of words, letters, or symbols that represent others. A code substitutes groups of two or more numbers or letters for words, phrases, or sentences making up a message. A cipher substitutes a letter or number for each letter of the message. After Samuel Morse invented his code of dots and dashes for telegraph communication in the 1830s, hundreds of different ways were soon invented to encode and decode the messages, and the invention of cipher machines and computers in the 20th century made the process of encoding and decoding faster and more complex. The German Enigma machine and the Japanese "J" or Type 97 Alphabetical Typewriter, or Purple machine, are the most famous examples.

Codes and ciphers were used during the American Civil War, the Russo-Japanese War of 1904–05, and World War I, but greater attention was devoted to code breaking following Britain's founding of the Code and Cypher School at Bletchley Park in 1919. Numbering 150 people in 1939, the Bletchley Park staff increased to 3,500 in 1942 and to 10,000 by 1945. Approximately 65 Americans worked at Bletchley Park, working almost exclusively on the German Enigma machine ciphers, which produced Ultra INTELLIGENCE, the code name for decrypted German and Italian radio messages. The British first deciphered German Enigma codes in May 1940.

The American code word *Magic* represented intelligence derived from Japanese diplomatic communications using the Purple machine, while *Ultra* referred to intercepted and decoded military communications. Unlike Great Britain and the USSR but like the AXIS nations, the United States did not have a central code and cipher school and operated separate offices within the military services. The U.S. NAVY Operations Division (N-2) and the War Department General Staff (G-2) began code and cipher operations (known as cryptanalysis, which was distinct from traffic analysis) in 1924 and 1929, respectively. Americans working for the U.S. ARMY Signal Intelligence Service, later known as the Special Intelligence Branch, Military Intelligence Service, under Colonel William F. Friedman, first broke the Japanese Purple diplomatic code in September 1940 and provided a machine to the British in 1941. Although only occasionally deciphered through 1940 and 1941, the Japanese Purple code was read with increasingly regularity by 1942. By spring 1942, American code breakers working for the U.S. Navy Communications Security Unit formed by Commander Laurence F. Safford, were also reading messages enciphered in the Japanese naval code, known as JN-25. Breaking the JN-25 code was an extraordinary feat as the code comprised some 45,000 five-digit groups, each signifying a word or phrase, further embedded in additional five-digit groups taken from a continually changing list of 50,000 random numbers. Perhaps the greatest triumph of this navy unit during the war, under Commander Joseph P. Rochefort, Jr., was the accurate prediction of the Japanese attack at the BATTLE OF MIDWAY in time for Americans forces to take effective countermeasures and turn the tide of the war in the PACIFIC THEATER in June 1942.

The Germans and Japanese used many codes and ciphers during the war, some of which were never broken. The Japanese had more than 50 codes, while the Allies knew of 200 German codes by 1945. The Axis powers were convinced that their systems were unbreakable, as were the Allies, although both sides were successful in breaking each other's code to some extent. The Allied emphasis on strict security, especially between the Americans and British, prevented the Axis, and the Soviet Union, from breaking their codes following 1943, while Allied intelligence services had increasingly regular and direct knowledge of Axis plans through decrypted enemy communications after 1942.

Further reading: Stephen Budransky, *Battle of Wits: The Complete Story of Codebreaking in World War II* (New York: Free Press, 2000); Ronald Lewin, *American Magic: Codes, Ciphers, and the Defeat of Japan* (New York: Farrar, Straus & Giroux, 1982); Thomas D. Parrish, *The Ultra Americans: The U.S. Role in Breaking the Nazi Codes* (New York: Stein & Day, 1986).

—Clayton D. Laurie

Communists

While they were never a major force in American politics, the high point of influence for Communists came during the 1930s, when the GREAT DEPRESSION gave them hope that the impending collapse of capitalism would create favorable conditions for Marxist revolution in the United States. The Communist Party of the United States (CPUSA) attracted disappointingly small political support and membership gains from 1929 to 1945, but Communists did play important roles in LABOR and other reform efforts in the 1930s. As directed by the Soviet Union, Communists also sometimes infiltrated GOVERNMENT agencies during the NEW DEAL and WORLD WAR II.

In the early years of the Great Depression, Communists established Unemployed Councils, which acted as local RELIEF agencies, and organized protest demonstrations and marches against poverty, joblessness, and hunger. Communists also fought for AFRICAN AMERICANS, as in the SCOTTSBORO BOYS case, although blacks never comprised over 10 percent of CPUSA membership. In the ELECTION OF 1932, however, Communist Party candidate William Z. Foster (and his African-American running mate, James Ford) received just 103,000 votes (three-tenths of 1 percent of the total popular vote), despite UNEMPLOYMENT of at least one-fourth of the labor force and the failure of the HOOVER PRESIDENCY and private enterprise to improve economic conditions.

From 1933 to mid-1935, Communists denounced new President FRANKLIN D. ROOSEVELT and his New Deal legislation, labeling FDR "a social fascist" who was worse than his predecessor, HERBERT C. HOOVER, and whose programs were "the same as [Adolf] Hitler's." Communists were especially critical of such key New Deal legislation as the NATIONAL INDUSTRIAL RECOVERY ACT, calling it a "slave program"; the AGRICULTURAL ADJUSTMENT ACT, which rewarded large farmers at the expense of sharecroppers, tenants, and migrant workers; and the NATIONAL LABOR RELATIONS ACT, termed an "antistrike" bill.

In the summer of 1935, the Communist line changed, when Soviet leader Joseph Stalin ordered a POPULAR FRONT strategy, with the Communist Party to forge alliances with SOCIALISTS, other left-wing groups, and liberals in the fight against fascism. American Communists were told to stop criticizing Roosevelt and the New Deal and work to gain influence within mainstream labor unions, peace, and youth groups. Socialists remained skeptical and often hostile to CPUSA motives, while the Roosevelt administration took a largely benign attitude toward Communists, believing that they were no threat to domestic order and had little influence as a political party.

During the Popular Front period from 1935 to 1939, Communists had their greatest impact in the industrial unions. When JOHN L. LEWIS and the mass production unions separated from the AMERICAN FEDERATION OF LABOR to create the CONGRESS OF INDUSTRIAL ORGANIZATIONS (CIO), Communists helped organize automotive and steel workers, resulting in control of a third of CIO unions by the late 1930s, and party influence in the national organization. With considerably less success, but with great personal courage, Communists attempted biracial organization of southern sharecroppers and tenant farmers and of California agricultural workers, an effort which was crushed by planters and growers.

Although Communists were active in the political life of the 1930s, they had little success in building membership or political power. While an estimated 200,000 to 250,000 people joined the CPUSA during the decade, few stayed for more than a year, resulting in low membership numbers. Actual membership figures of the CPUSA ranged from about 9,000 in 1929 to roughly 80,000 ten years later. The CPUSA evolved from being a party of the unemployed with a largely foreign-born, Jewish, and New York–based leadership to a more middle-class, union-affiliated, and native-born membership. Few blacks or women were members, and even fewer had leadership roles. In the ELECTION OF 1936, Communist Party national chairman Earl Browder received only some 80,000 votes for president—just two-tenths of 1 percent—and he attracted barely more than half that total in 1940.

The Popular Front strategy remained the Moscow-directed policy for American Communists until August 1939, when the NAZI-SOVIET PACT was signed. For the next two years, Communists joined ISOLATIONISTS in criticizing Roosevelt's anti-AXIS defense and foreign policy, including the SELECTIVE SERVICE Act and the LEND-LEASE ACT, and some party members spoke at AMERICA FIRST COMMITTEE rallies. Hitler was treated as an ally of the Soviet Union by the CPUSA until Germany invaded Russia in mid-1941, when the Communists reversed themselves again and attacked fascism. After PEARL HARBOR, Communists supported the war effort, endorsing universal military training and no-strike pledges by labor and calling for national unity.

In addition to the visible public world of American communism, a covert world also existed. The CPUSA was used by the Soviet Union to infiltrate federal government agencies from the Agricultural Adjustment Administration and NATIONAL LABOR RELATIONS BOARD, to the State and Treasury Departments, and even the White House staff. Communists also engaged in ESPIONAGE during World War II, including gathering information on the nation's most closely guarded secret, the MANHATTAN PROJECT to produce the ATOMIC BOMB. Although the extent and impact of Soviet-sponsored espionage has often been exaggerated, it was nonetheless significant, as the release of documents in Moscow and Washington in the 1990s demonstrated.

The CPUSA, whose membership peaked at 80,000 in 1939, declined rapidly after World War II, as the cold war and domestic anticommunism so depleted the party that American communism had nearly ceased to exist by the late 1950s.

Further reading: Irving Howe and Lewis Coser, *The American Communist Party: A Critical History* (New York: Praeger, 1962); Harvey Klehr, *The Heyday of American Communism: The Depression Decade* (New York: Basic Books, 1984).

—William J. Thompson

Congress

Reflecting the political developments of the era, control of Congress from 1929 to 1945 shifted from the REPUBLICAN PARTY to the DEMOCRATIC PARTY, and Congress enacted major programs increasing the size, cost, and power of the federal government. Changes in American GOVERNMENT arising from the NEW DEAL and WORLD WAR II significantly enhanced the power of the PRESIDENCY, but Congress nonetheless played a significant role in shaping domestic and foreign policy, particularly in the 1930s. Within Congress, power typically resided more with committee chairmen, the "barons" of Capitol Hill, than with the Speaker of the House or the Senate majority leader.

The election of 1928 that sent HERBERT C. HOOVER to the White House by an overwhelming margin also continued the control of Congress that Republicans had enjoyed in the 1920s. (See the table for the composition of Congress from 1929 to 1946.) Hoover called Congress into special session in the spring of 1929 to deal with economic issues facing farmers, and within two months, Congress passed the AGRICULTURAL MARKETING ACT. In 1930, Congress also passed the HAWLEY-SMOOT TARIFF ACT, a much-criticized tariff that went beyond Hoover's wishes by raising protection to the highest levels ever. In the remainder of the year, Congress generally acquiesced in the president's program to deal with the early stages of the GREAT DEPRESSION.

In the off-year congressional elections of 1930, the Democrats made striking gains. Losing eight senators, Republicans held only a 48–47 edge in the Senate (a Farmer-Labor senator held the other seat). Each party won 217 seats in the House, with one Farmer-Labor representative as the potential decisive vote; but by the time Congress assembled in late 1931, deaths and replacements favoring the Democrats gave them a 220-214 seat majority. Despite the swing to the Democrats, the 1930 election results did not reflect quite such a rejection of Hoover and the Republicans as the totals might suggest, for the turnover of some 50 seats in the House was only about 15 more than the average loss for the incumbent president's party in off-year elections since 1900. Moreover, the Republicans, who won some 54 percent of the total popular vote for Congress, remained clearly the majority party outside the SOUTH. The loss of eight Senate seats, on the other hand, was about twice the usual number for the party holding the presidency and provided an early indication of the impact of the depression on the Republican Party.

The 72nd Congress that met in the final two years of the HOOVER PRESIDENCY only slowly staked out positions much different from Hoover's. A number of key Democratic leaders were southern conservatives who shared Hoover's concern about the federal government doing and spending too much. Early in 1932, Congress established at Hoover's request the RECONSTRUCTION FINANCE CORPORATION to lend money to banks and other financial institutions to help them weather the depression.

But as the ECONOMY continued down and as UNEMPLOYMENT continued its sharp rise, Congress became more active. A coalition of Democrats and progressive Republicans, often led in the Senate by New York Democrat ROBERT F. WAGNER, Wisconsin Republican ROBERT M. LA FOLLETTE, JR., and Nebraska Republican GEORGE W. NORRIS, pushed for public works and RELIEF spending. Partly to embarrass Hoover, conservative Democrats also became more assertive and critical of his policies. When Hoover vetoed the Garner-Wagner relief bill, Congress virtually forced upon him the RELIEF AND RECONSTRUCTION ACT of 1932, a compromise measure enabling the federal government to lend states money for relief and public works. Still, neither Congress nor the Democrats were ready to move much beyond Hoover, as revealed by their refusal to mandate direct relief assistance to the unemployed and by their approval of a record peacetime tax increase in 1932, supported by an emotional plea for balancing the budget by Speaker of the House JOHN NANCE GARNER.

Democrats overwhelmingly controlled the 73rd Congress following their landslide victory in the ELECTION OF 1932. Though southern Democrats dominated leadership posts because of their seniority, the new Congress nonetheless proved exceptionally responsive to the agenda of new president FRANKLIN D. ROOSEVELT—and, in any case, southerners in the House and Senate tended to be more liberal than northerners on domestic economic policy in the early and mid-1930s. Not only did Democrats want to make a positive record to contrast with that of Hoover and the Republicans, but over half of the Democrats in Congress has been elected in 1930 and 1932, and were disposed to following the president and his more liberal policies. Roosevelt effectively used his personal leadership and patronage power to win support in Congress. Above all, the collapse of the economy—unemployment was at least 25 percent by early 1933 and national production and income were down by about 50 percent—compelled action. In the hundred days that produced the so-called FIRST NEW DEAL of 1933, Congress enacted a host of major programs, focusing especially on recovery and relief and including the NATIONAL INDUSTRIAL RECOVERY ACT, the AGRICULTURAL ADJUSTMENT ACT, and the FEDERAL EMERGENCY RELIEF ADMINISTRATION.

The election of 1934 then registered great public support for the New Deal. Counter to the usual trend in off-year elections, Democrats picked up seats in both the House and the Senate. Democratic gains came especially in urban areas, and in the 74th Congress urban liberal Democrats, led by Robert F. Wagner, had more power than before. The SECOND NEW DEAL enacted by Congress in 1935 reflected the greater strength of liberal Democrats and included such landmark reform legislation as the EMERGENCY RELIEF APPROPRIATIONS ACT, the NATIONAL LABOR RELATIONS ACT (also called the Wagner Act), the SOCIAL SECURITY ACT, and the REVENUE ACT OF 1935 (or "Wealth Tax"). But while Congress remained remarkably responsive to the president, it also asserted its own priorities. The Wealth Tax, for example, was more limited than Roosevelt had wanted, and Congress (especially Senator Wagner) was much more responsible than Roosevelt for the Wagner Act supporting organized labor.

The ELECTION OF 1936 gave Democrats their most top-heavy control of Congress ever. Yet even though voters had ratified the New Deal and reelected Roosevelt by a record landslide, Roosevelt achieved little of the expansive program he had in mind for his second term. A CONSERVATIVE COALITION of Republicans and conservative Democrats in Congress began to cooperate across party lines to oppose liberal measures. The coalition arose partly from the changing nature of the Democratic Party, increasingly dominated by northern liberals pursuing the agenda of urban LIBERALISM and eclipsing southern, conservative, and rural leaders in the party. The coalition also reflected the continuing strength of CONSERVATISM in the nation, a

prevailing "antimetropolitan" ideology in a Congress where rural constituencies retained a disproportionate influence, and also a sense that power was shifting too far to the presidency at the expense of the Congress. Roosevelt's heavy-handed, and ultimately successful, effort to have the Senate elect Kentucky's Alben Barkley as majority leader over Mississippi's Pat Harrison further disaffected southern and conservative Democrats in Congress.

A series of events in 1937–38—especially Roosevelt's COURT-PACKING PLAN, sit-down strikes by LABOR, and the RECESSION OF 1937–38—brought the formation of the conservative coalition. In November 1937, a bipartisan group led by southern Democrats issued a "Conservative Manifesto," criticizing the New Deal welfare state and insisting upon lower taxes, balanced budgets, states' rights, and small government. A varying coalition of Republicans and conservative (mostly southern) Democrats cooperated to oppose key administration proposals beginning with the 1937 court-packing bill. The president did have some limited successes in his second term—the UNITED STATES HOUSING AUTHORITY, the FARM SECURITY ADMINISTRATION, the FAIR LABOR STANDARDS ACT, and the EXECUTIVE REORGANIZATION ACT, for example—but even they were weaker than proposed. Angered at anti–New Deal Democrats, Roosevelt tried to defeat a number of them in the party's 1938 primaries. This largely unsuccessful "purge" attempt deepened party divisions and further emboldened conservative Democrats to oppose the president. Then, in the election of 1938, Republicans gained more than 70 seats in the House and seven in the Senate, strengthening not only the GOP's presence in Congress but also the power of the conservative coalition that stymied Roosevelt's domestic program.

By the end of the 1930s, FOREIGN POLICY increasingly commanded attention of Roosevelt and the Congress. Earlier in the decade, Congress had demonstrated its power in foreign policy. With ISOLATIONISTS holding substantial power, the Senate rejected American participation in the World Court, the NYE COMMITTEE carried out its critical investigation of the munitions industry, and Congress passed the NEUTRALITY ACTS that went further than Roosevelt had wanted. As Roosevelt turned to more active and clearly anti-AXIS defense and foreign policies during his second term, he needed the support of southern Democrats in Congress, particularly as much of the midwestern and western delegations of both parties remained anti-interventionist. (The priority Roosevelt gave international affairs by the late 1930s and his dependence upon southern Democratic support further limited chances for domestic reform.) After the outbreak of World War II in the late summer of 1939, isolationists lost influence and Congress supported Roosevelt's initiatives, beginning with the repeal of the arms embargo in 1939. In the next two years, Congress agreed to such key measures as the National Defense Appropriations Act of 1940, the SELECTIVE SERVICE Act of 1940, and the LEND-LEASE ACT of 1941.

For the remainder of Roosevelt's presidency, Congress largely followed the patterns established from 1937 to 1941. Democrats remained the majority party, but the conservative coalition continued to thwart domestic reform. In the ELECTION OF 1940, Roosevelt won an unprecedented third term, but Democrats picked up only seven House seats and lost three more senators. Then in the election of 1942, Republicans picked up nearly 50 congressional seats and nine seats in the Senate, paring the Democratic majority in the House to just 218–208. Those gains partly reflected the typical off-year pattern of losses by the incumbent party, but they also reflected the more limited appeal of New Deal issues in the context of wartime priorities and prosperity. By the early 1940s, moreover, southern Democrats in Congress had become distinctly more conservative than they had been in the early and mid-1930s and were instrumental in opposing liberal programs.

In this context, such New Deal relief programs as the WORKS PROGRESS ADMINISTRATION and the CIVILIAN CONSERVATION CORPS that now seemed unnecessary were eliminated or slashed. Proposals to expand the New Deal went nowhere, and the NATIONAL RESOURCES PLANNING BOARD, which proposed a far-reaching liberal agenda, was terminated. The most important social legislation Congress passed was the GI BILL OF RIGHTS, but that was enacted more as a politically popular reward to veterans than as a piece of domestic reform. As the war came to an end, Congress also ensured generous RECONVERSION policies

for BUSINESS. Yet even the conservative 78th Congress that met from 1943 to 1944 did not seriously attack the heart of the New Deal regulatory welfare state. Democrats gained two dozen House seats but lost two more in the Senate in the ELECTION OF 1944, but neither those results nor Roosevelt's fourth-term reelection altered domestic policymaking.

In defense and foreign policy, Congress continued largely to go along with the president's requests during World War II. Although often justifiably critical of early disorganization and inefficiency in the MOBILIZATION programs, and frequently complaining about excessive executive power, Congress nonetheless gave Roosevelt great leeway to establish agencies and implement policies to spur production, mobilize manpower, and check inflation. Such important new agencies as the WAR PRODUCTION BOARD, the OFFICE OF WAR MOBILIZATION, and the OFFICE OF PRICE ADMINISTRATION had little congressional involvement. Congress played an even smaller role in military and foreign policy, whereas commander in chief Roosevelt had extraordinary authority. In planning postwar foreign policy, on the other hand, Roosevelt did have to play close attention to the Senate's authority over treaties in working toward such postwar international organizations as the UNITED NATIONS and the economic agencies coming out of the BRETTON WOODS CONFERENCE.

Trends established during Roosevelt's presidency persisted after 1945. Particularly in foreign policy, Congress typically responded to the president's agenda rather than taking the lead itself. The executive branch was larger, better organized, and more powerful than before. Changes in the NEWS MEDIA contributed to enhancing the power of

		House			Senate		
PARTY STRENGTH IN CONGRESS, 1929–1946*							
Congress	Years	Dem.	Repub.	Other	Dem.	Repub.	Other
71st	1929–31	167	267	1	39	56	1
72nd	1931–33	220	214	1	47	48	1
73rd	1933–34	310	117	5	60	35	1
74th	1935–36	319	103	10	69	25	2
75th	1937–38	331	89	13	76	16	4
76th	1939–40	261	164	4	69	23	4
77th	1941–42	268	162	5	66	28	2
78th	1943–44	218	208	4	58	37	1
79th	1945–46	242	190	2	56	38	1

*Source: *The Statistical History of the United States, from Colonial Times to the Present* (Stamford, Conn.: Fairfield Publishers, 1965)

the presidency, for RADIO (and later television) allowed the president to address the nation and mobilize support more effectively than could the Congress or its individual members. But while the dynamics of policymaking shifted toward the presidency in the 1929–45 era, Congress had by no means been eclipsed. It retained its essential legislative authority on both foreign and domestic policy, and the conservative coalition continued during Harry Truman's presidency and after (until briefly in the mid-1960s) to thwart liberal efforts to expand the regulatory-welfare state established in the 1930s.

Further reading: Richard N. Chapman, *Contours of Public Policy, 1939–1945* (New York: Garland, 1981); James T. Patterson, *Congressional Conservatism and the New Deal: The Growth of the Conservative Coalition in Congress, 1933–1939* (Lexington: University Press of Kentucky, 1967); David L. Porter, *Congress and the Waning of the New Deal* (Port Washington, N.Y.: Kennikat Press, 1980); Howard L. Reiter, "The Building of a Bifactional Structure: The Democrats in the 1940s." *Political Science Quarterly,* 116, no. 1 (Spring 2001): 107–29; Clyde P. Weed, *Nemesis of Reform: The Republican Party during the New Deal* (New York: Columbia University Press, 1994); Roland Young, *Congressional Politics in the Second World War* (New York: Columbia University Press, 1956).

Congress of Industrial Organizations (CIO)

The Congress of Industrial Organizations (CIO) was formed in November 1938 by leaders of 10 dissident unions within the AMERICAN FEDERATION OF LABOR (AFL) who had created its predecessor, the Committee for Industrial Organization, three years earlier. Organizing workers by industry instead of by craft, the CIO quickly became a major LABOR organization with significant economic and political power.

The AFL, which had been the dominant labor organization in the United States since its founding in the 1880s, organized skilled workers according to craft or trade rather than seeking the mass organization of all workers in a particular industry. By the early 1930s, the AFL's approach increasingly frustrated union leaders in mass production industries, such as JOHN L. LEWIS of the United Mine Workers and SIDNEY HILLMAN of the Amalgamated Clothing Workers of America, who believed that their members as well as other unskilled, immigrant, and African American workers in big industry were being treated like second-class citizens.

Beginning in 1934, Lewis and other unhappy labor leaders called on the AFL at their annual convention to organize mass production workers into industrial unions.

The first year, about one-third of the convention delegates agreed, and Lewis repeated his demands in October 1935, but the rank-and-file delegates voted down industrial unionism by an 18,464 to 10,987 margin. Three weeks later, Lewis, Hillman, David Dubinsky of the International Ladies Garment Workers Union, and seven other union leaders formed the Committee for Industrial Organization as a branch within the AFL.

Immediately, Lewis set out to organize the AUTOMOBILE INDUSTRY, the STEEL INDUSTRY, and the rubber industry by using United Mine Workers money and key lieutenants such as PHILIP MURRAY, who set up the Steelworkers Organizing Committee (SWOC). After "heresy" hearings, the AFL suspended the Committee for Industrial Organization unions in September 1937, and in November 1938, the committee formally became the Congress of Industrial Organizations, with Lewis as its president.

Between 1935 and 1938, the Committee for Industrial Organization achieved major successes in organizing unions in the mass production industries. In 1936, rubber workers went on strike at Goodyear Tire and Rubber, and Murray and the SWOC traveled throughout the Pennsylvania steel mills signing up new members. In late December 1936, the United Auto Workers (UAW) began a six-week sit-down strike against General Motors

This cartoon of September 1937 depicts the angry Congress of Industrial Organizations leader John L. Lewis after the Supreme Court's ruling in *Jones and Laughlin Steel v. NLRB* (1937), which upheld the National Labor Relations Act. *(Library of Congress)*

at the large Flint, Michigan, plant, which resulted in the automaker's capitulation to the union's demands for recognition and wage and hour benefits in February 1937. The United States Steel Corporation recognized the SWOC in March 1937, and agreed to their demands.

By late 1937, both the automotive and steel unions had grown to over 350,000 members. The CIO helped set up the Non-Partisan League, which worked for the reelection of FRANKLIN D. ROOSEVELT in the ELECTION OF 1936, and Lewis, a lifelong Republican, endorsed FDR in 1936. The CIO's progress was slowed in late 1937 and 1938 by several factors, the RECESSION OF 1937–38 that raised unemployment, the mobilization of moderate and conservative forces against "radical" sit-down strikes, and company police forces preventing union organizing at Republic, Bethlehem, and other "Little Steel" plants, and at the Ford Motor Company.

By the early 1940s, however, even Little Steel and Henry Ford could not stop the CIO organizing drive, as membership increased to 2.6 million. A factor that both helped and hurt the CIO was the presence by the early 1940s of active COMMUNISTS or those with pro-communist sympathies, who led several unions and maintained a strong and influential minority in others, including the UAW. Lewis resigned as head of the CIO after the ELECTION OF 1940, when his brief truce with Roosevelt ended and he endorsed Republican WENDELL L. WILLKIE, a decision opposed by his fellow union leaders, the majority of whom backed Roosevelt. Philip Murray succeeded Lewis as president of the CIO.

After PEARL HARBOR, the CIO, along with the AFL, agreed to a no-strike pledge for the duration of the war—although Lewis led the miners out on strike, independent of either large labor organization. During World War II, the CIO organized AIRCRAFT INDUSTRY and SHIPBUILDING workers, and increased its membership by nearly 2 million. Through its political action committee (PAC), the CIO helped forge a strong link in the postwar years between the American labor movement and the DEMOCRATIC PARTY. Strife between the CIO and AFL continued until the two organizations merged in 1955.

Further reading: Irving Bernstein, *The Turbulent Years: A History of the American Worker, 1933–1941* (Boston: Houghton Mifflin, 1969); Nelson Lichtenstein, *Labor's War at Home: The CIO in World War II* (New York: Cambridge University Press, 1982); Robert H. Zieger, *The CIO: 1935–1955* (Chapel Hill: University of North Carolina Press, 1995).

—William J. Thompson

conscientious objectors

During WORLD WAR II, religiously motivated conscientious objectors (COs) received exemptions from serving in combat roles in the armed forces. More than half of the roughly 70,000 men who applied for CO status received it, with some 25,000 serving as noncombatants in the military and 12,000 serving in alternative civilian public service positions.

Anticipating America's entry into World War II, CONGRESS in June 1940 held hearings on what would become the Selective Training and Service Act. Representatives of CIVIL LIBERTIES, religious, and pacifist groups testified at these hearings. They advocated a broad definition of conscientious objection to include a nonreligious exemption as well as provisions for alternative civilian service.

Signed into law by President FRANKLIN D. ROOSEVELT in September 1940, the act provided CO exemption from combat service only for a person who "by reason of religious training and belief is conscientiously opposed to participation in war in any form." Moral or ethical objection to war did not qualify. The act classified COs as noncombatants in the armed forces and also authorized a new status allowing COs to perform alternative work under civilian administration.

To influence the design of civilian service, historic peace churches (Quakers, for example) together with other religious organizations formed the National Service Board for Religious Objectors (NSBRO). NSBRO representatives, SELECTIVE SERVICE, and President Roosevelt agreed in December that NSBRO would be responsible for administering and financing civilian service COs, with the work performed under Selective Service direction. Unlike the noncombatant COs serving in uniform, COs performing civilian service were not paid any wages or benefits by the federal GOVERNMENT.

The plan called for civilian service COs to work in Civilian Public Service (CPS) camps and to continue CIVILIAN CONSERVATION CORPS projects. Projects at new CPS camps as well as in hospitals and on farms were later included. Some 500 COs volunteered as human guinea pigs in medical experiments, and more than 2,000 worked as attendants in hospitals for the mentally ill. Many COs spent the war performing such chores as digging ditches rather than performing work to benefit humanity as they desired.

Originally, noncombatant COs in the military served in medical or supply units around the world. After January 1943, noncombatant assignments were confined to the medical corps, where they often served with great bravery and distinction.

Between 5,500 and 6,000 people went to prison rather than perform duties in civilian service or in the military as noncombatants. Most of those imprisoned were Jehovah's Witnesses, who had unsuccessfully sought deferments as ministers. Sentences generally ranged from one to three years imprisonment at federal penitentiaries.

Further reading: Mulford Q. Sibley and Philip F. Jacob, *Conscription of Conscience: The American State and the Conscientious Objector, 1941–1947* (Ithaca, N.Y.: Cornell University Press, 1952).

—D. K. Yates

conservatism

Conservatism from 1929 to 1945 was concerned with what conservatives saw as the erosion of economic freedom, individual liberty, and moral values, resulting from the growth of a stronger federal GOVERNMENT and changes in traditional American institutions. Above all, conservatism in the era of the GREAT DEPRESSION, the NEW DEAL, and WORLD WAR II focused on limiting the growing power of the federal government. For most of the period it was primarily reactive, critical of the New Deal and of President FRANKLIN D. ROOSEVELT and their impact upon the country.

The rise of industrial capitalism in America during the decades after the Civil War engendered a debate about the right and capacity of government to regulate BUSINESS in the nation's general interest. In the 19th century, protecting individual liberty and economic freedom and otherwise limiting the power of the state was labeled "classical" or "laissez-faire" LIBERALISM. During the early 20th century, this limited-government approach to economic freedom and individual liberty became the domain of conservatives. Progressives (later redefined as liberals) called for a strong state to restrain the growing economic and political power of big business, to protect individuals from corporate power and political corruption, and to provide for social welfare and moral uplift. Conservatives defended the status quo: limited government, economic and individual freedom, government by elites, and fundamentalist religion.

In the 1920s, conservatism and the REPUBLICAN PARTY regained power because of a backlash against progressivism, the tensions of World War I, and challenges to traditional patterns of American life. Prosperity during the decade enabled business to reassert itself, the Republican administrations of the 1920s pursued pro-business policies and opposed social and economic reform, and a cautious and even docile LABOR movement made little impact on workers' lives. Cultural conservatism was manifest in several ways. The growth of urban immigrant populations threatened the "old stock" base of traditional America, and CONGRESS passed the National Origins Act in 1924, which restricted immigration, especially from southern and eastern Europe. Prohibition was to a significant degree a response to the drinking habits of an "un-American America." The controversy over evolution and the Scopes Trial was part of a larger debate between liberal Christianity, urban and with a somewhat secular outlook, and a mainly rural Protestant fundamentalism. The presidencies of Warren G. Harding, Calvin Coolidge, and HERBERT C. HOOVER reflected the economic and cultural conservatism of the times.

When the HOOVER PRESIDENCY began in 1929, there seemed little doubt that conservatism would be the governing mandate for the foreseeable future. Then in 1929 came the calamitous Great Depression. Conservatives held that there were no structural flaws in the national ECONOMY, and that prosperity would return if the market were allowed to correct itself. But despite Hoover's efforts—which some conservatives criticized as going too far—the economy continued to fall and UNEMPLOYMENT soared. Conservatism seemed discredited, and certainly unsuccessful, and a new liberalism emerged in the 1930s, similar in ideas and programs to the old progressivism, with the goal of reforming capitalism.

After the election of Franklin D. Roosevelt in the ELECTION OF 1932, conservatism was defensive and sometimes confused, partly because of the new president's adroitness in moving around the center of the ideological spectrum. The major measures of the FIRST NEW DEAL of 1933—the NATIONAL INDUSTRIAL RECOVERY ACT, the AGRICULTURAL ADJUSTMENT ACT, the FEDERAL EMERGENCY RELIEF ADMINISTRATION, the TENNESSEE VALLEY AUTHORITY, and the CIVILIAN CONSERVATION CORPS—were looked upon first with skepticism, then outright hostility by conservatives. By 1934, conservatives were harshly critical of the New Deal. Former president Hoover led the critics, calling for a return to the philosophy of individualism. A number of business and other conservative organizations, ranging from the U.S. Chamber of Commerce and the National Association of Manufacturers to the Sentinels of the Republic and the National Taxpayers League, all weighed in against the New Deal.

The most visible and vocal of the conservative organizations was the AMERICAN LIBERTY LEAGUE, a diverse group of businessmen, industrialists, and conservative Democrats, who were bankrolled with Du Pont money and led by dissident Democrats including former presidential nominees John W. Davis and Alfred E. Smith. For a brief time, the Liberty League raised nearly as much money as both major parties to support their message that the New Deal was an unconstitutional peril to the nation's economy and institutions. However, for all their financial resources and organizational planning, the American Liberty League failed to stop Roosevelt and the New Deal, or for that matter, even to attract a wide group of conservatives under their banner. Hoover and other small-town, heartland conservatives, for example, distrusted the Wall Street–oriented leadership of the league.

Further conservative attacks on Roosevelt and the New Deal came from two additional sources. One was a small but committed group of intellectuals and journalists, some of whom could be classed as libertarians, who believed in government noninterference in both the economic and social spheres and retained a belief in social Darwinism; the other was a small but loud group of neofascists who came from the far right. The first group included such intellectuals as Irving Babbitt, Paul Elmer More, and George Santayana, and journalists such as Henry L. Mencken and Albert Jay Nock. Mencken, who had been a hero to liberals and civil libertarians for his attacks on CENSORSHIP and closed-minded thinking in the 1920s, became a caustic critic of the New Deal and of Roosevelt.

On the far right, the best known was Gerald L. K. Smith (a former associate of HUEY P. LONG), who saw the New Deal as either a "Red" or "Jewish" plot. Combining fundamentalist Christianity with ANTI-SEMITISM, the neofascists labeled the New Deal as the "Jew Deal," because of the visible number of JEWS in the administration. Until he was later silenced by the Catholic Church, FATHER CHARLES E. COUGHLIN became notorious for his anti-Semitism mixed with harsh denunciations of the New Deal and Wall Street.

The programs of the SECOND NEW DEAL in 1935, such as the SOCIAL SECURITY ACT, the NATIONAL LABOR RELATIONS ACT, and the WORKS PROGRESS ADMINISTRATION, made labor and the working class central to liberal policy (and to the politics of the DEMOCRATIC PARTY). These measures further antagonized business conservatives as well as upper-class easterners who believed that Roosevelt, one of their own, was a "traitor to his class." The REVENUE ACT OF 1935 and other New Deal efforts to reform TAXATION also alienated conservatives, business, and the wealthy.

With Congress dominated by liberal Democrats in the mid-1930s, only one branch of government, the SUPREME COURT, remained a bastion of conservatism at the federal level. To the delight of conservatives, the court upheld economic liberty by invalidating the NRA in 1935 and the AAA in 1936. Overturning other New Deal measures as well, the Court seemed to be sharply restricting the role of government and was due to rule on cases involving the National Labor Relations Act and Social Security.

In 1936, conservative forces geared up to defeat Roosevelt. The Liberty League gave money to Republican Party nominee ALFRED M. LANDON, but seemed more interested in attacking Roosevelt directly. The Coughlin–Gerald Smith faction formed the UNION PARTY, which won fewer than 900,000 votes. Roosevelt, in seeking reelection, relished attacking his conservative and well-heeled opponents, saying that he "welcomed their hatred." He won a landslide victory, and Democrats controlled the Congress by enormous majorities in both the House and the Senate.

The ELECTION OF 1936 did not still the forces of conservative opposition. Roosevelt, angry about the Supreme Court overturning New Deal legislation (and denouncing the justices as "nine old men"), sent to Congress a court reorganization bill, called the COURT-PACKING PLAN by opponents. Conservatives in Congress, particularly southern Democrats and Republicans, joined by progressives from the GOP and maverick Democrats, eviscerated the court bill, although Roosevelt claimed to have lost the battle but won the war, as several of the justices retired and were replaced by liberals.

But perhaps Roosevelt won only a campaign and lost the larger struggle, for the court-packing episode helped change the dynamics of Congress and increase the influence of conservative legislators on Capitol Hill. Only a few years earlier, conservatives in Congress chiefly comprised eastern Republicans and a few southern Democrats. By the late 1930s, large Republican gains in the 1938 elections and the defection of a number of southern Democrats and progressive Republicans helped create a powerful CONSERVATIVE COALITION that emerged as a barrier to the New Deal's expansion of liberal reform. The court-packing plan played a role in that, as did labor unrest, the RECESSION OF 1937–38, and, for the southerners, concerns about the growing strength of urban northern Democrats in the party and their CIVIL RIGHTS efforts. As outlined in the "Conservative Manifesto" of November 1937, the conservative coalition opposed the New Deal regulatory welfare state and championed the core conservative issues of the era: limited central government, lower taxes, balanced budgets, individual responsibility, economic freedom, states' rights, and property rights.

By the late 1930s, FOREIGN POLICY became an issue that affected all Americans as World War II approached. Conservatives, as with every political and ideological group, were divided between intervention and nonintervention. Conservative southern Democrats often supported anti-AXIS policies. A number of important conservatives were ISOLATIONISTS, however, as indicated by the leadership of the AMERICA FIRST COMMITTEE and by such important voices in Congress as ROBERT A. TAFT. Those on the far right, the neofascists, were thinly veiled Nazi sympathizers.

World War II strengthened conservatism in a number of ways. Wartime prosperity made liberal programs seem unnecessary, and wartime priorities made them seem diversionary. Business had more influence in Washington during the war than in the New Deal years as government MOBILIZATION agencies used businessmen in important positions. In 1942, the Republicans nearly won numerical control of the House of Representatives, and the conservative coalition strengthened its control of Congress. Such liberal Depression-era RELIEF programs as the CCC and the WPA were terminated. The strike by JOHN L. LEWIS's miners in 1943 gave antilabor conservatives the impetus to pass the Smith-Connally Act, which placed restrictions on certain union activities and presaged the postwar Taft-Hartley Act. The wartime Congresses did not roll back the heart of the New Deal, but conservatism plainly was resurgent.

In 1944, an important book was published that helped guide the postwar conservative movement—*The Road to Serfdom,* written by economist and Austrian émigré Friedrich A. von Hayek. In his book, Hayek contended that centralized state planning (such as the New Deal) inevitably led to totalitarianism. A free market would guarantee freedom; economic planning and social welfare in the hands of government would lead to dictatorship. Despite the general moderation of the Truman and Eisenhower presidencies, what has been called the "liberal consensus" generally characterized early postwar America. But the antistatist ideas of Hayek and of the 1937 "Conservative Manifesto," joined to fierce anticommunism in the cold war, continued to dominate conservative thought. By the 1960s, beginning especially with the movement associated with Arizona senator Barry Goldwater, conservatism gained significant new strength and influence.

Further reading: Russell Kirk, *The Conservative Mind: From Burke to Eliot,* 7th ed. (Washington, D.C.: Regnery, 1986); James T. Patterson, *Congressional Conservatism and the New Deal: The Growth of the Conservative Coalition in Congress, 1933–1939* (Lexington: University of Kentucky Press, 1967); Clinton Rossiter, *Conservatism in America* (New York: Knopf, 1962); Clyde P. Weed, *The Nemesis of Reform: The Republican Party during the New Deal* (New York: Columbia University Press, 1994); George Wolfskill and John A. Hudson, *All but the People: Franklin D. Roosevelt and His Critics* (New York: Macmillan, 1969).

—William J. Thompson

conservative coalition

The conservative coalition was an informal alliance of Republicans and conservative Democrats in CONGRESS that formed during the second term of President FRANKLIN D. ROOSEVELT to oppose the NEW DEAL. Such opposition had been minimal in the first term. The devastating collapse of the ECONOMY in the early years of the GREAT DEPRESSION from 1929 to 1933 made decisive action seem essential. Democrats, in control of the national GOVERNMENT after the ELECTION OF 1932, wanted the party to make a positive record. Party loyalty and their generally good personal relationships with Roosevelt brought support from most conservative as well as liberal Democrats, including southern Democrats who recognized also that New Deal aid was crucial to their region and popular among their constituents. Roosevelt could count as well on support from progressive Republicans, and liberal Democrats gained even more power in Congress in the election of 1934. With the overwhelming Democratic victory in the ELECTION OF 1936 that produced top-heavy Democratic majorities of nearly 4-1 in the House and 5-1 in the Senate, Roosevelt and the New Deal seemed to have little effective opposition.

Yet within a year, a group of Republican and conservative Democrats, dominated by southern Democrats, had issued a "Conservative Manifesto" enunciating major themes of CONSERVATISM in the Roosevelt years. The manifesto insisted upon balanced budgets, lower taxes, limited central government, states' rights, and property rights, and it sharply criticized the emerging welfare state of the New Deal. Republicans and conservative Democrats increasingly cooperated across party lines in support of those principles and succeeded in thwarting much of Roosevelt's second-term agenda. The conservative coalition, a loose working alliance varying from issue to issue, included at its core most Republicans, frequently joined by a large number of southern Democrats and a scattering of rural and conservative Democrats from other areas. With half or more of the membership of both houses coming from rural constituencies, an "antimetropolitan" ideology, affronted by the growing urban liberalism of New Deal policy, helped bring congressional conservatives together.

A number of circumstances and events gave rise to the conservative coalition. A key factor was the changing nature of the national DEMOCRATIC PARTY during Roosevelt's presidency. Democrats became the party of the big-government regulatory welfare state and increasingly pursued the agenda of urban liberalism. Northern liberals began eclipsing southerners in party councils and decisions, and government money and programs seemed to go increasingly to labor, to the urban unemployed and impoverished, to ethnic groups and to AFRICAN AMERICANS. Not only did rural constituencies and interests have less power and influence, but New Deal RELIEF, LABOR, SOCIAL SECURITY, and AGRICULTURE programs threatened to upset traditional economic and political patterns in the SOUTH. Southerners were further provoked by the 1938 antilynching bill that was supported by northern Democrats before being killed by a filibuster by southern Democrats. Most Republicans shared concerns about the size, cost, and focus of government programs with conservative Democrats, and they shared as well a sense that under Roosevelt and the New Deal excessive power was gravitating toward the executive branch at the expense of the Congress.

A series of developments in 1937 and 1938 then brought the coalition into being and led to the November 1937 "Conservative Manifesto." Roosevelt's 1937 inaugural address was a ringing call to expand the New Deal. Early in the year, he introduced an executive reorganization bill, which threatened further to increase presidential power at the expense of the Congress. Then he proposed the COURT-PACKING PLAN, which aroused conservatives (and many liberals as well). As one conservative Texas Democrat put it, "Boys, here's where I cash in"; and conservative Democrats worked across party lines with Republicans to oppose the bill. The sit-down strikes conducted by the CONGRESS OF INDUSTRIAL ORGANIZATIONS, in which strikers occupied plants seeking union recognition, seemed a radical assault on property that was enabled by New Deal policy. The RECESSION OF 1937–38 sent the economy spiraling downward again in the fall, suggesting that New Deal economic policy had failed and leading conservatives to insist upon small-government, budget-balancing approaches.

Court-packing, labor unrest, and the "Roosevelt recession" also weakened public support for the president, emboldening New Deal opponents, as did the reelection in the mid-1930s of key conservative Democrats, which made them feel more secure in opposing FDR. Angered at the anti–New Deal Democrats, Roosevelt worked to defeat a number of them in the 1938 party primaries—but his "purge" attempt was largely an embarrassing failure and deepened the fissures in the party. In the election of 1938, Republicans gained some 70 seats in the House and seven in the Senate, significantly enlarging the Republican contingent in the Congress and strengthening the conservative coalition. By the late 1930s, moreover, the coming of WORLD WAR II shifted Roosevelt's priorities to defense and foreign policy, where he needed support from southern Democrats. For the remainder of Roosevelt's presidency, indeed well beyond it, Republicans and conservative Democrats effectively produced a sort of stalemate in domestic policy, in which the New Deal would not be significantly expanded or rolled back.

Further reading: James T. Patterson, *Congressional Conservatism and the New Deal: The Growth of the Conservative Coalition in Congress, 1933–1939* (Lexington: University Press of Kentucky, 1967); Roland Young, *Congressional Politics in the Second World War* (New York: Columbia University Press, 1956).

Coral Sea, Battle of the (May 1942)

The Battle of the Coral Sea took place from May 3 to May 8, 1942. The Imperial Japanese Navy had been on the offensive since the attack on PEARL HARBOR in December 1941, and by the spring of 1942 was threatening Australia. Suffering from what has been called the "victory disease," the Japanese overreached themselves. At the Battle of the Coral Sea, the U.S. NAVY was able to check Japanese expansion to the south; and although tactically neither side achieved full victory, strategically the battle was a significant American success. The battle was also important for revealing the new realities of naval warfare in which aircraft carriers, not battleships, were the major force: Surface ships never encountered each other, and the battle was fought entirely by planes from the two fleets' aircraft carriers.

To cut off Australia from U.S. support, the Japanese aimed to win control of the Coral Sea, bordering Australia to the north, by taking over Port Moresby, on the southwest tip of New Guinea, and Tulagi in the SOLOMON ISLANDS. But American INTELLIGENCE was able to track movements of the Japanese fleet and to break the Japanese code, thus allowing Admiral CHESTER W. NIMITZ to have two carrier groups ready to meet the Japanese. The battle began on May 3, with the Japanese invasion of Tulagi, though it did not reach full scale until May 7. On that day, the Americans were able to sink a Japanese light carrier and force the Japanese to abort their Port Moresby invasion. The battle ended on May 8, 1942, after a fierce naval air battle. The Japanese temporarily lost use of two of their most valuable ships, the badly damaged carriers *Shokaku* and *Zuikaku,* on this day, and retreated from the Coral Sea, ending their attempt on Port Moresby and their pressure on Australia. Because the American carrier *Lexington* was lost as a result of the action (and the carrier *Yorktown* damaged), the Japanese had something of a tactical edge in the battle; and the Japanese control of Tulagi would be significant in later combat in the Solomons. But the Japanese advance south toward Australia had been halted, and because of the Battle of the Coral Sea, the Japanese could not use their damaged carriers *Shokaku* and *Zuikaku* a month later at the pivotal BATTLE OF MIDWAY.

See also AIR POWER; WORLD WAR II PACIFIC THEATER.

Further reading: Ronald Spector, *Eagle against the Sun: The American War with Japan* (New York: Free Press, 1985).

—Michael Moore

Coughlin, Father Charles E. (1891–1979)

Father Charles Edward Coughlin, the controversial "radio priest," was an important figure in American politics in the

1930s and organized an unsuccessful political challenge to President FRANKLIN D. ROOSEVELT in the ELECTION OF 1936.

Coughlin was born on October 25, 1891, in Hamilton, Ontario, Canada, and at the urging of his mother decided to enter the Roman Catholic priesthood. He taught at Assumption College in Ontario and then received his first, and only, parish—the Shrine of the Little Flower outside Detroit in Royal Oak, Michigan. Using the relatively new medium of RADIO in an effort to raise funds for his struggling parish and increase its membership, Father Coughlin gave his first radio sermon on October 17, 1926. The program quickly became popular, and the donations sent to Father Coughlin allowed him to syndicate his show in 1929 and reach listeners throughout most of the Midwest. When he began broadcasting *The Golden Hour of the Little Flower* on CBS in 1930, Coughlin was heard by up to 40 million Americans every Sunday night.

Until 1930, Father Coughlin's radio program was primarily religious in nature. But as the GREAT DEPRESSION deepened, his sermons became more overtly political, as he denounced President HERBERT C. HOOVER and the group he blamed for the depression—international bankers. By 1932, Coughlin had become an enthusiastic supporter of Franklin D. Roosevelt, whom he believed would radically reform the American economy. "Roosevelt or Ruin," he told his audience. Roosevelt, aware that Coughlin reached millions of listeners, cultivated the radio priest's support. However, although Coughlin saw himself as a critical component to Roosevelt's victory in the ELECTION OF 1932, the relationship was never a close or personal one. By 1934, frustrated by his lack of influence and by the banking policy of the FIRST NEW DEAL and the administration's efforts to regulate rather than dismantle big business, Coughlin broke with Roosevelt.

In November 1934, Coughlin created the National Union for Social Justice (NUSJ) and used the organization to increase his following and challenge Roosevelt and the NEW DEAL. At the heart of the NUSJ platform were its demands for establishing a central bank, nationalizing public utilities, and increasing the coinage of silver. Attracting a following dominated by working-class and lower-middle-class CATHOLICS who found Coughlin's populist message appealing, the NUSJ claimed to have 8 million members at its peak in 1936. In addition, millions more were sympathetic to Coughlin's message attacking international bankers and political parties and calling for radical monetary reform.

An apparent test of Coughlin's power came in the Senate debate of early 1935 over the United States joining the World Court. Coughlin saw the World Court as dominated by the same international bankers he blamed for the

Father Charles Coughlin *(Library of Congress)*

depression, and he urged his listeners to call, telegram, and write to their senators to vote against the World Court. When the Senate voted against membership, it seemed that Coughlin had proven his political muscle. But the unsuccessful political party that he created in the presidential election of 1936 revealed how limited the radio priest's power really was.

In 1936, Coughlin, Dr. FRANCIS TOWNSEND, and Gerald L. K. Smith, who had taken over the Share Our Wealth program following the death of HUEY LONG, joined to form the UNION PARTY. The new party nominated North Dakota congressman William Lemke for president, but it lacked both unity and organization and Lemke won less than 2 percent of the popular vote. The results reflected the facts that Coughlin's followers also tended to support Roosevelt and that they overwhelmingly preferred Roosevelt to Coughlin's candidate. Coughlin himself hurt the Union Party by denouncing the popular FDR as "anti-God" and as "Franklin Double-Crossing Roosevelt." Rejected by the voters, denounced by superiors in the Catholic hierarchy, and likening himself to the martyred Jesus Christ, Coughlin announced his retirement from public life after the election.

Unhappy out of the spotlight, Coughlin resumed his radio show in January 1937, but his popularity was never the same. He became increasingly anti-Semitic; when he began speaking favorably of Adolf Hitler and Benito Mussolini in 1940, he lost all but his diehard supporters and his radio show was taken off the air. A fringe figure by the time the United States entered WORLD WAR II, Coughlin left the public arena for good in 1942. As part of the government's CENSORSHIP of far right- and left-wing groups, the postmaster general prohibited delivery of Coughlin's magazine, *Social Justice,* and the attorney general arranged to have Coughlin's archbishop silence him. Father Coughlin then retreated back to his parish. He retired in 1966 and died an obscure figure in 1979.

See also ANTI-SEMITISM.

Further reading: Alan Brinkley, *Voices of Protest: Huey Long, Father Coughlin, and the Great Depression* (New York: Knopf, 1982); Donald I. Warren, *Radio Priest: Charles Coughlin, the Father of Hate Radio* (New York: Free Press, 1996).

—Katherine Liapis Segrue

court-packing plan

The "court-packing plan" of 1937 was the controversial attempt by President FRANKLIN D. ROOSEVELT to enlarge the SUPREME COURT so that it would make more favorable rulings on NEW DEAL programs.

In a remarkable period from May 1935 to May 1936, the Supreme Court had invalidated a number of major New Deal measures, including the NATIONAL INDUSTRIAL RECOVERY ACT and the AGRICULTURAL ADJUSTMENT ACT. The reasoning in those decisions suggested, moreover, that the SOCIAL SECURITY ACT and the NATIONAL LABOR RELATIONS ACT (Wagner Act) were likely to be overturned as well, and that a federal wages and hours law that President Roosevelt had in mind would stand no chance. One obvious possibility to protect the New Deal from judicial veto was a constitutional amendment to limit the Court's power or to augment the authority of the CONGRESS in economic and social areas. But agreeing upon wording proved difficult, and any amendment would need approval by two-thirds majorities in each house of Congress and then ratification by 36 states—a slow and uncertain process at best, especially when the Roosevelt administration believed that quick action was needed in order to safeguard programs made necessary by the GREAT DEPRESSION.

Congress also had the authority to alter the number of judges on the Supreme Court and other federal benches, and had done so in the past. Many of the unfavorable decisions, moreover, had been decided by narrow 5-4 and 6-3 votes, with four conservative justices—Willis Van Devanter, James C. McReynolds, George Sutherland, and Pierce Butler—consistently voting against the New Deal, often joined by Owen J. Roberts and Chief Justice Charles Evans Hughes. The liberal wing of the Court—Justices Louis D. Brandeis, Harlan Fiske Stone, and Benjamin N. Cardozo—believed that the Constitution was expansive enough to support most New Deal programs and that in any case the Court should more prudently exercise its power of judicial review.

On February 5, 1937, Roosevelt announced his Judicial Procedures Reform Bill, which was quickly dubbed the "court-packing bill." If a federal judge who had served at least 10 years did not retire six months after reaching age 70, the president could appoint a new judge to the bench—up to as many as six to the Supreme Court and 44 to lower federal courts. (The average age of Supreme Court justices, not coincidentally, was 71.)

Roosevelt's proposal set off a furor. He had launched the bill with no advance warning to key congressional leaders and with no public mention in the 1936 presidential campaign or otherwise. He claimed he wanted a younger and more efficient judiciary, when he plainly wanted a more responsive and liberal one. Conservatives feared that the bill was part of an administration plan to subordinate the legislative and judicial branches to the executive branch. Many liberals were also unhappy, upset not only by Roosevelt's tactics but worried about what a different kind of president might do with such powers. Even so, it was widely assumed that the court-packing bill would pass, given Roosevelt's landslide victory in the ELECTION OF 1936 just a few months earlier and his apparent power in the overwhelmingly Democratic Congress.

But the proposal encountered insuperable obstacles. Conservative Democrats joined with Republicans in working against it, and liberal Democrats often were passive at best. Chief Justice Hughes made it plain that the Court was neither inefficient nor behind in its work. In the famous "switch in time that saved nine," Hughes and Roberts joined in 5-4 decisions that upheld the National Labor Relations Act in April and the Social Security Act in May, and in May conservative justice Van Devanter retired. With a liberal Supreme Court evidently assured, the court-packing bill's chances faded quickly, even after FDR agreed to a slightly revised version and became more forthright about his real purpose. Public opinion, so far as it can be measured, evidently turned against the proposal, too. Roosevelt, uncharacteristically politically tone-deaf, persevered nonetheless, but met humiliating defeat.

In the aftermath, Roosevelt claimed that he lost the battle (the court-packing bill) but won the war (a more liberal Supreme Court). He was partly right, for the Court would not invalidate another piece of New Deal legislation; and as vacancies occurred on the Supreme Court, Roosevelt was able to form a more liberal "Roosevelt Court." But Roosevelt lost more than the court-packing bill. He also lost a cooperative Congress that would approve liberal legislation, as the disaffection of conservative Democrats over court-packing helped produce the CONSERVATIVE COALITION in Congress that would stymie and limit the New Deal for the remainder of Roosevelt's presidency. And although the Court had apparently changed direction in 1937 (some scholars believe that the Court was trending toward a more expansive view of GOVERNMENT policy in any event), and ratified the modern regulatory welfare state, it retained its powers of judicial review and would exercise them robustly in the years and decades to follow.

Further reading: Joseph Alsop and Turner Catledge, *The 168 Days* (Garden City, N.Y.: Doubleday, 1938); William E. Leuchtenburg, *The Supreme Court Reborn: The Constitutional Revolution in the Age of Roosevelt* (New York: Oxford University Press, 1995).

D

demobilization

The surrenders of Germany and Japan in the spring and late summer of 1945 marked the beginning of the demobilization of the massive military and industrial machine that the United States had assembled to fight WORLD WAR II. The demobilization of the armed forces proceeded at a rapid pace. During the two-year period from June 1945 to June 1947, the number of military personnel dropped from 12 million to 1.5 million.

Almost immediately after V-J DAY in mid-August 1945, and weeks before Japan's formal surrender in early September aboard the USS *Missouri,* pressure began to mount to reduce the size of the armed services and to reconvert the nation's industry to peacetime production. Within a few months, disgruntled U.S. servicemen stationed overseas were protesting for Washington to bring them home so they could get on with their lives, especially to take civilian jobs and raise families. Idle and bored GIs in Manila booed top brass during one demonstration. Others, who were fed up with regulations and regimentation, protested in Frankfurt and also in Paris, where they marched down the Champs Elysees and yelled "scab" and "slacker" at American soldiers who refused to join the march. Some even purchased advertising space in American newspapers to voice their demands. Many civilians joined the protests, organizing into clubs and petitioning Washington for the immediate release of their husbands, sons, and loved ones from active duty.

The pressure at home and abroad forced the military to scrap its plans for an orderly partial demobilization. Originally the War Department had planned discharges based on a point system that recognized the length and difficulty of service. The department, however, decided to release all men with two years' service. U.S. ARMY Chief of Staff Dwight D. Eisenhower soon ordered his commanders to return home any men "for whom there is no military need."

The demobilization of U.S. forces proceeded at an alarming rate, one that President Truman admitted amounted virtually to a "disintegration." Soon after Japan's surrender, the president announced that the army and the U.S. ARMY AIR FORCES would be cut to 1.95 million by June 1946. By spring 1946, he had further reduced the number to one million as of July 1946. The U.S. NAVY was reduced to less than 500,000 by 1947, the U.S. MARINES to less than 100,000. Along with the release of service members came training camp closures and the destruction and sale to private industry of ships and unneeded war equipment. The hasty discharge of seasoned specialists and combat veterans particularly damaged military readiness. Because of global instability, and at the president's request, Congress extended the SELECTIVE SERVICE Act to March 31, 1947.

The war's sudden end caught the Truman administration unprepared for peace and without a plan for confronting changing and potentially volatile domestic and global situations. Fears that the rapid demobilization and RECONVERSION would disrupt the economy and perhaps mean a return to depression conditions proved unfounded. Wartime savings, quick reconversion, pent-up demand for consumer goods, the return of many women to the home from industry jobs, and the 1944 GI BILL OF RIGHTS that sent many veterans to college kept unemployment low and the economy strong.

In foreign affairs, the president's immediate problem was twofold. He had to find a way to maintain a military force sufficient both for the occupation of Germany and Japan and for ensuring global stability and national security. Balancing these requirements proved difficult, especially considering public pressure and Truman's tight fiscal policies.

Compounding his task was residual, although hardly dominant, isolationist sentiment in Congress. Believing that AIR POWER and the exclusive possession of the ATOMIC BOMB would ensure the nation's security, some conservative lawmakers wanted the president to leave the world's problems to the UNITED NATIONS. Taking this approach, they believed, would require only limited U.S. military participation. Their sentiments changed, however, as tensions between the United States and Soviet Union intensified in mid- and late 1940s. The reduction of military strength finally ended with the outbreak of war in Korea in June 1950.

Although Americans did not realize it at the time, a good deal of the regimentation and wartime way of life that had developed with the MOBILIZATION for World War II would not completely disappear with the end of the war. During the next few years, policymakers would find themselves having to come to grips with exactly how much of the wartime apparatus and system of doing things they should retain in order to confront new postwar problems.

Further reading: Jack S. Ballard, *The Shock of Peace: Military and Economic Demobilization after World War II* (Washington, D.C.: University Press of America, 1983); James M. Gerhardt, *The Draft and Public Policy: Issues in Military Manpower Procurement, 1945–1970* (Columbus: Ohio State University Press, 1971); John C. Sparrow, *History of Personnel Demobilization in the United States Army* (Washington, D.C.: Center of Military History, 1994).

—Edwin D. Miller

Democratic Party

From 1929 to 1945, the Democratic Party went from a disorganized minority party to the majority party of the nation. As the decade of the 1920s neared its end, the prospects of the Democratic Party in national politics seemed dim. Only two Democrats had won the presidency since 1860; the REPUBLICAN PARTY had been the normal majority party since the mid-1890s; and Republicans had dominated national politics throughout the 1920s. In the election of 1928, HERBERT C. HOOVER defeated the Democratic presidential nominee, Alfred E. Smith, by 58.2 to 40.9 percent of the popular vote. In the CONGRESS elected that year, Republicans outnumbered Democrats by 267-167 in the House of Representatives and by 56-39 in the Senate. The Republican Party's organizational strength, longstanding majority status, and identification with the prosperity of the 1920s seemed to promise its continued dominance.

The Democratic Party did have some areas of significant strength. The SOUTH, where few AFRICAN AMERICANS could vote, had been solidly Democratic since the era of the Civil War and Reconstruction, and Democrats controlled a number of CITIES outside the South because of strong organizations and support from Catholic immigrant groups (especially IRISH AMERICANS). But the party had severe weaknesses as well. It was more a collection of state and local machines than an organized national party. Its two major areas of strength, old-stock rural Protestants in the Midwest and South and ethnic urban CATHOLICS in the North, were bitterly at odds on the polarizing social issues of the 1920s (Prohibition and immigration restriction, for example), and it had taken the divided Democrats 103 ballots to decide upon a compromise presidential nominee in 1924. Al Smith, the Irish-American Catholic governor of New York, won the party's nomination in 1928; but while he rallied millions of new urban voters to the Democratic Party, he carried only six states in the deep South plus heavily Catholic Massachusetts and Rhode Island. In addition to its deep cultural and geographical divisions, the Democratic Party offered little real policy alternative to the Republicans and no common position on most big issues. "I don't belong to an organized political party," quipped the humorist Will Rogers. "I'm a Democrat."

The GREAT DEPRESSION provided the Democrats the opportunity to regain national power. The two parties essentially broke even in the election of 1930, and when the new Congress met, Democrats had a narrow majority in the House and a coalition of Democrats and progressive Republicans were able to control the Senate when they wished. But the Democrats were unified only in their efforts to blame the collapse of the ECONOMY on Hoover and the Republicans. A number of leading congressional Democrats from the South, including Speaker of the House JOHN NANCE GARNER of Texas, were traditional small-government conservatives, as unwilling as Hoover to support expensive or expansive new federal programs. Others in the party wanted more GOVERNMENT action, but progressive southern and western rural Democrats typically emphasized assistance to AGRICULTURE, while liberal urban Democrats focused on help for workers and the cities.

As the Democrats prepared for the ELECTION OF 1932, many supported the popular and progressive governor of New York, FRANKLIN D. ROOSEVELT. Roosevelt had ties to both rural and urban Democrats, partly through his efforts in the 1920s to have the party establish an effective national organization, and he understood that Democrats had to stress the economic problems that might unite the party. Although opposed by leading Democratic conservatives, and by Al Smith, who wanted renomination, Roosevelt was the early front-runner. He won the necessary two-thirds of the convention delegates on the fourth ballot, when John Nance Garner, subsequently nominated for vice president, helped deliver enough votes to ensure Roosevelt's nomination.

The election of 1932 was in many ways a transitional one for the Democratic Party. Roosevelt and the Democrats swept to landslide victory, with 57.4 percent of the presidential vote and with margins of 310-117 in the House and 60-35 in the Senate. But the election marked more a rejection of Hoover and the Republicans than an affirmation of Roosevelt and the Democrats, who waged a campaign that was inconsistent and unclear, criticizing

Hoover for doing and spending too much as well as for doing too little to deal with the depression. The Democrats' forthright opposition to Prohibition was perhaps the most obvious distinction between the two parties. Yet if Roosevelt did not clearly or consistently outline what would become the NEW DEAL, his greater emphasis on providing action for the economy and RELIEF for the unemployed distinguished him from Hoover. And the election had transferred power to the Democrats and given them a chance to govern—and to build a new coalition of voters that would keep them in power.

Once in office, Roosevelt began to implement the New Deal and, helped by new national chairman JAMES A. FARLEY, to build the organizational strength and voter support that made Democrats the majority party. Democrats gained strength in both houses of Congress in the election of 1934, a significant departure from the usual pattern of the incumbent president's party losing substantial ground in off-year elections and a telling confirmation of public support for Roosevelt and the New Deal. The Democratic gains, moreover, came especially from northern and urban constituencies increasingly central to the party's voter base and policy agenda. The social reform programs of 1935 came in significant measure from the greater strength of urban liberals in Congress, typified in many ways by Senator ROBERT F. WAGNER of New York. The new directions of the party upset conservative Democrats, some of whom joined Al Smith in the anti–New Deal AMERICAN LIBERTY LEAGUE.

The ELECTION OF 1936 confirmed the Democratic Party's new urban, liberal orientation and established it as the nation's new majority party. At their national convention, the Democrats abolished their requirement of a two-thirds majority for nomination, which ended the veto power that southern Democrats had long enjoyed. Roosevelt tried to rally the working class and lower middle class behind him and his party with rhetoric castigating "economic royalists." Democrats made particular efforts to turn out the vote among ethnic groups and LABOR, and unions in 1936 provided the party unprecedented financial and organizational support. Led by ELEANOR ROOSEVELT and MARY W. "MOLLY" DEWSON of the Democratic National Committee, the party made special efforts to bring women to the polls. Secretary of Labor FRANCES PERKINS was the first woman cabinet member ever, and the New Deal's WOMEN'S NETWORK brought political dividends. Roosevelt's appointments of Catholics and JEWS to important government positions in unprecedented numbers helped solidify the support of those groups. Similarly, Roosevelt named many African Americans, such as MARY MCLEOD BETHUNE, to significant posts, and the resulting informal BLACK CABINET as well as assistance from New Deal programs led black Americans to vote Democratic in unprece-

dented numbers. New Deal programs, relief especially, also helped Democratic urban politicians build or strengthen powerful organizations that brought voters to the polls.

In November, FDR won more than three-fifths of the presidential vote, losing (as Farley had predicted) only Maine and Vermont, and Democrats swept to even more top-heavy control of the Congress, with margins of nearly 4 to 1 in the House and 5 to 1 in the Senate. Unlike 1932, the electorate had voted not just against the Republicans, but for Roosevelt, the Democrats, and the New Deal. The Democratic Party's new majority came from the Roosevelt Coalition of voters, based partly on the South but even more on overwhelming support in northern metropolitan areas from working-class and lower-income voters, Catholic and Jewish ethnic groups, and African Americans. And the realignment of the 1930s had not only made the Democratic Party the majority party at the national level but, in varying degrees, had also built substantial new Democratic strength in many states and cities.

Yet the Democratic Party's new top-heavy majority status carried its own difficulties. A coalition so broad was hard to keep together, as subsequent years would show. Many voters in 1936 had supported Roosevelt but did not necessarily think of themselves as Democrats. Democratic politicians and officials at the state and local levels, particularly in the South, were often lukewarm at best toward New Deal policy and at odds with liberal Democrats in Washington. Rural Democrats thought too much attention and money were going to urban areas and industrial workers. Southerners feared also that too much power was going to the North and that New Deal programs were undermining traditional social, political, and even racial patterns in the South. Senator JAMES F. BYRNES of South Carolina complained that the introduction of antilynching legislation meant that southerners had "been deserted by the Democrats of the North," and by the end of the decade southern Democrats in Washington increasingly opposed social and economic reform. Conservative Democrats retained their small-government preferences and feared the growing size, power, and costs of the federal government. At times, Roosevelt seemed inclined to try to reorient the party system along clear liberal/conservative lines, but it was never a priority and was probably impossible given the exigencies of the era and the obstacles of the American political system.

Democratic factionalism flared in 1937 and 1938, when conservative, most southern and rural, Democrats in the Congress, began joining with Republicans to form a CONSERVATIVE COALITION that would stymie much of Roosevelt's domestic agenda for the remainder of his presidency. In addition to their concerns about the federal government doing and spending too much, congressional conservatives feared that the executive branch was aggrandizing power, diminishing states' rights, and giving excessive attention to the agenda of urban liberals. The COURT-PACKING PLAN of 1937, sit-down strikes by CIO workers, and the RECESSION OF 1937–38 fueled public criticism of Roosevelt and led conservative Democrats to ally with Republicans in defeating proposals to extend the New Deal. Angered, Roosevelt sought to "purge" anti–New Deal Democrats by opposing them in party primaries in 1938—but his efforts at punishing them and liberalizing the party were on balance an embarrassing failure that deepened party divisions. In the election of 1938, Republicans picked up substantial strength in the Congress.

For the remainder of the Roosevelt years, the Democratic Party remained divided along ideological and geographical lines, with the majority liberal wing unable to control Congress because of the strength of the conservative coalition. As the economy recovered during World War II, New Deal programs aimed at the unemployed and impoverished were eliminated or cut back, and liberal proposals to extend the New Deal stood no chance. Though the heart of the New Deal regulatory welfare state remained intact, Democratic liberals were often distressed not just by the party's conservatives, but even by Franklin Roosevelt, who many thought did not provide enough leadership for domestic programs in the war years. Yet liberals themselves typically changed their programmatic emphasis as LIBERALISM changed in the late 1930s and 1940s, emphasizing KEYNESIANISM to produce economic growth via fiscal policy rather than the regulation and redistribution of the early New Deal. As liberal northern Democrats also increasingly championed CIVIL RIGHTS, southern Democrats became all the more worried about the party's direction; and although the South remained solidly Democratic in 1944, seeds were laid for the "Dixiecrat" revolt of 1948. In Congress, Southern Democrats in the House and Senate were clearly more conservative than Democrats from the North by the early 1940s, a geographical split in the party that would continue in the postwar years.

Despite their ongoing divisions and tensions, however, Democrats remained the majority party for the remainder of Roosevelt's presidency, and for decades beyond. In the ELECTION OF 1940, Roosevelt decisively won an unprecedented third term, with the party division in Congress changing little. James Farley resigned as national chairman, upset by FDR's decision to seek a third term as well as by the party's liberal direction, but EDWARD J. FLYNN proved an able successor. Republicans cut sharply into Democratic margins in Congress in the election of 1942; but in the ELECTION OF 1944, Roosevelt won another decisive victory and Democrats increased their control of Congress. Democrats thus retained their majority status in the new politics of prosperity and global war. The core of the Roosevelt Coalition, like the core of the New Deal regulatory-welfare state, emerged largely intact from World War II, as did the party issues and images of the realignment of the 1930s. POLITICS IN THE ROOSEVELT ERA had not just transformed the Democratic Party but had profoundly changed the American political system.

Further reading: John M. Allswang, *The New Deal and American Politics* (New York: Wiley, 1978); David Burner, *The Politics of Provincialism: The Democratic Party in Transition, 1918–1932* (New York: Knopf, 1968); Otis L. Graham, Jr., "The Democratic Party, 1932–1945" in *The History of U.S. Political Parties,* ed. Arthur M. Schlesinger, Jr. (New York: Chelsea House, 1973), pp. 1939–2006; James T. Patterson, *Congressional Conservatism and the New Deal* (Lexington: University of Kentucky Press, 1967); Sean J. Savage, *Roosevelt: The Party Leader, 1932–1945* (Lexington: University Press of Kentucky, 1991).

destroyers-for-bases deal (1940)

The "destroyers-for-bases" deal of 1940 resulted from negotiations between Great Britain and the United States over sending 50 U.S. World War I–vintage destroyers to Britain in return for British bases in the Atlantic and the Caribbean.

British prime minister Winston Churchill made the request for destroyers to President FRANKLIN D. ROOSEVELT in order to augment the British fleet while production of new British warships was under way. The destroyers would be used to protect British convoys from German U-boat attacks in the BATTLE OF THE ATLANTIC. The fall of France and the BATTLE OF BRITAIN in the spring and summer of 1940 brought additional concerns about the defense of Britain.

Because any such agreement to help Britain would make U.S. FOREIGN POLICY more interventionist and anti-AXIS, Roosevelt knew that it would provoke outcries from ISOLATIONISTS. He was also concerned that it would encounter resistance from others in CONGRESS and the American public who still believed it more important not to get involved in another war than it was to help the British. Roosevelt thus knew that he would have to proceed carefully, especially since 1940 was an election year.

At first, FDR thought that congressional approval might be needed for transferring the ships, but after consultation with advisers, he concluded that he could use his authority as commander in chief to exchange materials the military declared surplus if the result enhanced national security. Acquiring British bases in the Western Hemisphere could be justified in terms of national security, and Roosevelt announced the exchange on September 3. As he had expected, the agreement outraged isolationists, who formed the AMERICA FIRST COMMITTEE; but the public, increasingly supportive of helping Britain short of directly entering the war, generally endorsed it, and it had relatively little impact on the ELECTION OF 1940.

The 50 destroyers eventually transferred to the Royal Navy after refitting provided some help to the British, though their importance was more symbolic than military. In return for the destroyers, the United States received naval bases in Bermuda and Newfoundland and leases to bases in the Caribbean. A major step away from the NEUTRALITY ACTS and toward a more anti-Axis foreign policy, the destroyers-for-bases deal prepared the way for the LEND-LEASE ACT.

See also ANGLO-AMERICAN RELATIONS.

Further reading: Warren F. Kimball, *Forged in War: Roosevelt, Churchill, and the Second World War* (New York: Morrow, 1997); William L. Langer and S. Everett Gleasan, *The Challenge to Isolation, 1937–1940* (New York: Harper, 1952).

Dewey, Thomas E.   See Volume IX

Dewson, Mary ("Molly") (1874–1962)
Mary "Molly" Dewson, a DEMOCRATIC PARTY official and Social Security Board member during the administration of President FRANKLIN D. ROOSEVELT, was born on February 18, 1874, in Quincy, Massachusetts. Educated at nearby Wellesley College, she used her liberal arts education to enter the Progressive Era social reform movement in New England. She served in a number of positions, including superintendent of probation for Lancaster State Industrial School for Girls and executive secretary of the Massachusetts Commission on the Minimum Wage. In addition, Dewson also became involved in politics during this time through activity in the woman's suffrage movement.

Dewson moved to New York in 1920 to take a position with the National Consumers' League. Through the league, Dewson became a part of New York's social reform movement, making lifelong friendships with women such as ELEANOR ROOSEVELT and FRANCES PERKINS. It was during this time that Dewson became involved in Democratic Party activity, and she played a role in resolving disputes among women's groups during Al Smith's 1928 presidential campaign.

By 1932, Dewson was committed to Franklin D. Roosevelt's candidacy for president, and he appointed Dewson as director of the Women's Division of the Democratic National Campaign Committee, in charge of organizing and mobilizing female Democratic Party voters. While dedicated to mobilizing women voters, Dewson, along with Eleanor Roosevelt, also worked during the next five years

to secure prominent appointments for women in the Roosevelt administration. Their major success was the appointment of Frances Perkins as secretary of labor, the first female cabinet member. Dewson was an important member of the WOMEN'S NETWORK, which sought to advance women and women's interests in the administration.

By 1937 Dewson, anticipating that Roosevelt would serve only two terms, and becoming less interested in political activity, was ready to leave the Women's Division to a capable successor. She was appointed to the Social Security Board in 1937 and promptly resigned her directorship of the Women's Division to accept the new position. But for health reasons, Dewson served on the board for only a short time. In June 1938 she resigned from the board, but not before making sure that her successor was a woman (Ellen S. Woodward). Dewson spent her remaining years in retirement at her home in Castine, Maine, where she suffered a stroke and died five days later on October 12, 1962.

Further reading: Susan Ware, *Partner and I: Molly Dewson, Feminism, and New Deal Politics* (New Haven, Conn.: Yale University Press, 1987).

—Katherine Liapis Segrue

DiMaggio, Joe (Joseph Paul) (1914–1999)
Joe DiMaggio, the "Yankee Clipper," was one of the greatest and most revered baseball players ever. Voted the American League's most valuable player in 1939, 1941, and 1947, he had a lifetime batting average of .325, batted in 1,537 runs, hit 361 home runs, and in 1941 set the amazing record of hitting safely in 56 consecutive games. He made the All-Star team every year he played, and was elected to the Baseball Hall of Fame in 1955.

Born in San Francisco in 1914, the son of an immigrant ITALIAN-AMERICAN fisherman, Joseph Paul DiMaggio was expected to carry on the family trade. However, he had little interest in fishing—or in school, for he dropped out at age 15—and preferred sandlot baseball. He was signed by the San Francisco Seals of the Pacific Coast League and began playing minor league baseball with the Seals in 1932 at age 17.

In 1936, he joined the New York Yankees, batting .323 and leading the league in triples. He led the league in home runs, total bases, and runs scored in his second year. But DiMaggio was not just a great hitter—he excelled in every phase of the game and was one of the most graceful and talented center fielders in baseball history as well. A man of enormous pride, he always played to the best of his ability—because, he said, there might be someone in the stands who had never seen him play. He led the Yankees' return to the eminence of the Babe Ruth era (the team won the American League pennant 10 times and the World

Series nine times in DiMaggio's 13 seasons), and helped make SPORTS such an important diversion as the GREAT DEPRESSION lingered on. Baseball was the national pastime, and "Joltin' Joe" DiMaggio was its new hero.

DiMaggio enlisted in the U.S. ARMY during WORLD WAR II, and when he left the service in 1945, having missed three seasons, he was no longer the same player. But although troubled by a bone spur in his heel, he had several more productive seasons before retiring in 1951. After retiring, DiMaggio remained in the public eye, partly because of his marriage to the fabled movie star Marilyn Monroe, but also because of the grace and dignity that had marked his baseball days as well. Recent biographical studies have pointed to a less appealing private side of Joe DiMaggio, but it is the remarkable public figure that the nation celebrated and remembers.

Further reading: Richard Ben Cramer, *Joe DiMaggio: The Hero's Life* (New York: Simon & Schuster, 2000).

—Anthony Lavin

dollar-a-year men

"Dollar-a-year men" was a term used to describe businessmen who volunteered their services during WORLD WAR II for a token salary of one dollar (although they usually retained their corporate pay) to head or serve in GOVERNMENT agencies that oversaw wartime economic MOBILIZATION. Although they played a significant role in organizing the massive American wartime production, some of their activities were criticized for favoring large BUSINESS interests.

Dollar-a-year men first appeared during World War I when President Woodrow Wilson attempted to mobilize the American economy for the First World War with the War Industries Board (WIB). After Wilson appointed BERNARD M. BARUCH, an independent Wall Street investor, to head the WIB, it became more effective, but was criticized by progressives for allowing businesses to serve their own interests.

Early in World War II, NEW DEAL liberals sought ways to mobilize the economy without business interests again dominating. But since the government lacked enough experienced bureaucrats to direct the mammoth project of economic mobilization, President FRANKLIN D. ROOSEVELT turned to businessmen to help direct and staff mobilization agencies. These included such dollar-a-year men as William Knudsen of General Motors, who chaired the National Defense Advisory Commission, and DONALD NELSON of Sears Roebuck, who headed the WAR PRODUCTION BOARD.

Several thousand corporate executives, financial officers, technical experts, and lawyers took positions as dollar-a-year men in the wartime mobilization agencies and the War Department. Together with military procurement officers, they dominated the award of contracts, and they favored large corporations as the fastest way to achieve large-scale, high-quality war production. In the first year of the war, about 60 percent of contracts went to just 20 firms; in the first four years more than half of all contracts were awarded to only 33 companies. This approach was sometimes criticized despite the extraordinary totals of wartime production.

Although the economic mobilization agencies were dissolved at war's end, the close relationship between business and the military continued after the war in the so-called military-industrial complex.

Further reading: Bruce Catton, *The War Lords of Washington* (New York: Harcourt, 1948); Jeffery Dowart, *Forrestal and Eberstadt: A National Security Partnership, 1909–1949* (College Station: Texas A & M University Press, 1991).

—Robert J. Hanyok

Douglas, William O. (1898–1980)

William O. Douglas was the third chairman of the SECURITIES AND EXCHANGE COMMISSION (SEC) and a SUPREME COURT justice appointed by President FRANKLIN D. ROOSEVELT.

Born in Maine, Minnesota, on October 16, 1898, Douglas moved with his family to Washington State when he was three. As a child, he contracted polio, which left him weak and sickly. Hiking helped regain his strength and made him a lifelong advocate for the environment. Douglas attended Whitman College and returned home to teach. Dissatisfied after a year, Douglas entered Columbia Law School, graduating in 1925. After two unhappy years at a Wall Street law firm, he returned to Columbia Law School to teach. Within a year he resigned to join the faculty at Yale University, where his research focused on corporate bankruptcy law.

Douglas's connection with the SEC began in 1934 while he was still at Yale, when he was selected to perform a study of the reorganization of bankrupt corporations. During this assignment, Douglas impressed SEC chairman JOSEPH P. KENNEDY, and was introduced to President Roosevelt. Kennedy arranged for Douglas to be named to the commission in 1936 and Roosevelt made him the SEC chairman a year later. Under Douglas, the SEC took significant steps to protect investors and compel stockbrokers to abide by SEC regulations.

While on the SEC, Douglas, a staunch advocate of the NEW DEAL, became part of the president's trusted inner circle. In 1939, Roosevelt offered Douglas the seat on the Supreme Court vacated by Louis D. Brandeis. Douglas accepted the nomination, which was confirmed that April, and became part of the liberal "Roosevelt Court."

Douglas, the longest serving justice ever, remained on the Supreme Court for over 36 years. Although he supported the majority when the Supreme Court upheld the legality of the relocation of JAPANESE AMERICANS during World War II, he later proved to be a strong defender of free speech, the right to privacy, CIVIL RIGHTS, and CIVIL LIBERTIES. His extreme liberal positions on some issues and unorthodox behavior outside the Court led to an impeachment investigation by the Judiciary Committee of the House of Representatives in 1970. He was exonerated when no impeachable offense was found.

Douglas suffered a stroke in 1974. Although he tried to return to the bench, his condition led to his retirement in November 1975. William O. Douglas died on January 19, 1980.

Further reading: James F. Simon, *Independent Journey: The Life of William O. Douglas* (New York: Harper & Row, 1980).

—Jill Frahm

Du Bois, William Edward Burghardt   See Volume VII

Dust Bowl

In the 1930s, a large area in the southwestern plains of the United States came to be known as the "dust bowl." Years of farming using environmentally damaging techniques, combined with economic depression and severe drought, produced environmental disaster and human tragedy. The geographical boundaries of the dust bowl were never clear-cut, but most often the term was used to describe the area bordered by western Kansas and southeastern Colorado on the north and by northeastern New Mexico and the Oklahoma and Texas panhandles on the south. At its worst, the Dust Bowl included some 100 million acres of land.

Throughout much of the 19th century, the Great Plains had been considered by many to be a wasteland, the "Great American Desert." By the early 20th century, however, advances in agricultural technology led to a reassessment of the region. Farmers began growing drought-resistant crops, primarily wheat, while mechanized farming equipment made it possible to farm enormous plots of land. High wheat prices during World War I encouraged further cultivation. This cultivation entailed the removal of the area's native grasses and the sod formed by the grasses' roots, both of which had held the dry, powdery soil of the plains in place. "Sod-busting" did not by itself cause the Dust Bowl, but it left the land vulnerable

Dust storms compounded the problem of the depression when they swept across the Midwest. *(National Archives)*

to environmental damage and when drought struck, disaster ensued.

Nearly every region of the continental United States was affected by drought in the 1930s, but the plains states were particularly hard hit. In Boise City, Oklahoma, for example, an average of less than 12 inches of rain fell per year from 1931 to 1936. Farmers, desperate to stay afloat financially, continued to plow and plant each year, but crop yields were dismal. With no roots to hold it in place and no rain to tamp it down, the soil simply blew away, forming the massive dust storms from which the Dust Bowl got its name. Between 1930 and 1941, the region was plagued by more than 325 dust storms, 72 of them in 1937 alone. Skies were often darkened in the plains states and the Midwest by such storms, and some reached still further east, depositing grit as they did so. One particularly fierce storm in May 1934 removed an estimated one-third of a billion tons of topsoil—and dropped dust as far east as Washington, Boston, and even on ships hundreds of miles offshore in the Atlantic Ocean.

Heavily in debt, in part because of farm machinery bought on credit, and unable to eke out a living under such adverse climatic conditions, thousands of farmers lost their land and moved elsewhere to look for work. These dis-

placed farmers were part of a large MIGRATION to the West Coast, particularly to California, that took place during the GREAT DEPRESSION. More than 300,000 left from Oklahoma alone, and for this reason the term "Okie" was applied to all of the new migrants, even though large numbers also left from Texas, Kansas, and Colorado. Photographer Dorothea Lange recorded the plight of the Okies in her book, *An American Exodus: A Record of Human Erosion* (1939). Lange's stark images remain well known, as do those of JOHN STEINBECK in his novel about an Oklahoma family's journey west, *The Grapes of Wrath* (1939).

The federal GOVERNMENT recognized the difficulties faced by farmers in the Dust Bowl, and a number of NEW DEAL agencies attempted to relieve the suffering of those who remained in the region. In 1934, the Soil Erosion Service was developed to teach new farming methods that minimized erosion. These methods included terracing the land, contour plowing, planting wind-resistant crops, and regrowing native grasses in some areas. A year later, the Soil Erosion Service became the Soil Conservation Service. In its new guise, this agency took an even more active role, paying farmers cash to plant soil-conserving crops. The Forest Service, at the urging of President FRANKLIN D. ROOSEVELT, planted a 2,000 mile-long "shelterbelt" of trees down the center of the Great Plains, in an attempt to reduce wind-related erosion. The RESETTLEMENT ADMIN-ISTRATION proposed a more radical solution to soil erosion in the plains states: Stop cultivating the land altogether and resettle the farmers in more productive agricultural areas. Resettlement plans were not popular with farm families, and many chose to stay put and "tough it out"—although they often accepted help in the form of government relief checks.

Soil-conserving farming techniques, along with improved irrigation, did help restore fertility to the soil in some areas of the southwestern plains. Still, the situation for farmers in that region did not get appreciably better until 1941. At that time, the drought ended and WORLD WAR II caused an increase in demand for crops. As soon as these factors made farming the plains profitable again, much of the land was put back into cultivation. Because of the marginal quality of the soil in this region, dust bowls have recurred, although never again on the scale seen in the 1930s.

See also AGRICULTURE; ENVIRONMENTAL ISSUES.

Further reading: James Gregory, *American Exodus: The Dust Bowl Migration and Okie Culture in California* (New York: Oxford University Press, 1989); Donald Worster, *Dust Bowl: The Southern Plains in the 1930s* (New York: Oxford University Press, 1979).

—Pamela J. Lauer

E

Eccles, Marriner S. (1890–1977)

Serving as governor (1934–36) and chairman (1936–48) of the Federal Reserve Board, Marriner Stoddard Eccles was one of the most important individuals in shaping the economic policy of the United States in the era of the NEW DEAL and WORLD WAR II. An early advocate of substantially increasing government spending to promote recovery, he became one of the strong supporters of KEYNESIANISM in the administration of FRANKLIN D. ROOSEVELT.

Born in Logan, Utah, on September 9, 1890, Eccles was the eldest son of a Scottish immigrant and prominent Utah industrialist, David Eccles. As a boy, Marriner worked at his father's companies, and in 1909 his formal education ended after three and a half years of high school. He then traveled to Glasgow, Scotland, to fulfill his duties as a missionary of the Mormon Church. Two years later, David Eccles's death shifted a tremendous responsibility to Marriner, who took control of his family's portion of the Eccles estate.

Throughout the 1920s, Marriner Eccles adhered to his father's belief in thriftiness and the principles of laissez-faire as he honed his administrative and analytical skills. By 1928, he had consolidated more than 17 banks and lending institutions into the First Security Corporation. Under Eccles's leadership First Security withstood runs on its central branch in Ogden as well as other branches during the early years of the GREAT DEPRESSION, and Eccles negotiated a merger to rescue the failing Deseret National Bank in Salt Lake City.

Eccles also began reading the work of the economists William T. Foster and Waddill Catchings, who argued that the economic orthodoxy of the 1920s failed to address the deficiencies in consumer demand created by excessive saving and insufficient wage increases. Foster and Catchings concluded that in order to compensate for declining demand, GOVERNMENT must increase its spending. By the early 1930s, Eccles had adopted Foster and Catchings's views and spoke out for the need for compensatory fiscal and monetary policy. He went to Washington to present his views to the Senate, and was asked to assist in drafting the EMERGENCY BANKING ACT OF 1933 and the legislation creating the FEDERAL HOUSING ADMINISTRATION. In 1934 Eccles was appointed special assistant to Secretary of the Treasury HENRY MORGENTHAU, and in November was appointed governor of the Federal Reserve by President Roosevelt.

As governor of the Federal Reserve, Eccles began to press Roosevelt for substantial increases in spending for public works projects. He also set himself to the task of reorganizing the Federal Reserve System as the primary sponsor of the BANKING ACT OF 1935. Throughout his service in the Roosevelt administration, Eccles encountered numerous challenges from Secretary Morgenthau, who advised the president to curb spending and work toward a balanced budget. However, after the RECESSION OF 1937–38, New Deal policymakers turned toward deficit spending to promote recovery; and, during World War II, widespread prosperity provided evidence of the efficacy of Keynesianism and the fiscal policies championed by Eccles.

Continuing to serve as chairman of the Federal Reserve Board until 1948, Eccles also contributed after the war to the development of the World Bank and the International Monetary Fund created by the BRETTON WOODS CONFERENCE. He served as Federal Reserve Board vice chairman until 1951, when he resigned and returned to his personal business interests. Later he wrote articles and spoke in public on the Vietnam War, communism in China, and world overpopulation. Marriner Eccles died on December 18, 1977.

Further reading: Marriner Eccles, *Beckoning Frontiers: Public and Personal Recollections* (New York: Knopf, 1951).

—Shannon L. Parsley

Economic Bill of Rights

In his State of the Union message of January 11, 1944, President FRANKLIN D. ROOSEVELT called for a "second Bill of Rights under which a new basis of security and prosperity can be established for all. . . ." This new "Economic Bill of Rights," as it came to be called, included the rights to a useful and remunerative job, to income enough for adequate food, clothing, and recreation, to a decent home, to a good education, to adequate medical care, and to economic protection against old age, sickness, accident, and unemployment. Roosevelt again called for an economic bill of rights at the end of his campaign in the ELECTION OF 1944. Although it remained rhetoric more than concrete policy prescriptions, the economic bill of rights indicated the direction that many liberals wanted GOVERNMENT policy to take after WORLD WAR II.

Roosevelt's January 1944 declaration of the new bill of rights came as a surprise, because he made it two weeks after a much-heralded press conference in December 1943 in which he had suggested that "old Dr. New Deal" with his internal medicine had largely completed his job and was giving way to "Dr. Win-the-War." Most listeners understood this to be a signal that the president would not pursue further liberal reform during the war. Yet at that same press conference Roosevelt also talked about a "new program" that would "result in more security, in more employment, in more recreation, in more education, in more health, in better housing for all of our citizens."

In fact, Roosevelt had been hearing and thinking about such an economic bill of rights for some time. The idea had been discussed by the NATIONAL RESOURCES PLANNING BOARD (NRPB) as early as 1939 and communicated several times to the president. The NRPB's important 1943 report, *Post-War Plan and Program,* included such goals as adequate and decent jobs, good wages, housing, health care, education, and other aspects of a good and secure life in what it called a "new bill of rights" as part of its far-reaching liberal postwar program.

But while Roosevelt and many liberals talked in such expansive terms, they had little chance of implementing the economic bill of rights. The NRPB reports fell on indifferent public ears and hostile congressional ones, and CONGRESS terminated the agency in 1943. Nor did Roosevelt's January 1944 State of the Union message have much impact, and though FDR again advocated the economic bill of rights in his reelection campaign, the political context of the mid-1940s was not conducive to major new reform measures. Even the FULL EMPLOYMENT BILL of 1945, which addressed the widespread public concern about postwar jobs and called for fiscal policy to ensure the right to a job for everyone willing and able to work, became the watered-down Employment Act of 1946. The Economic Bill of Rights did, however, provide an agenda for LIBERALISM in the postwar era.

Further reading: John W. Jeffries, "The 'New' New Deal: FDR and American Liberalism, 1937–1945," *Political Science Quarterly* 105 (Fall 1990): 397–418.

economy

The period from 1929 to 1945 was one of the most eventful in the history of the American economy. Following the expansion of the 1920s, the nation's economy at 1929 had achieved unprecedented levels of production and income as well as widespread expectations of continuing growth and prosperity. Then in late 1929, the GREAT DEPRESSION struck, sending the economy plummeting. By 1933, UNEMPLOYMENT had reached some 25 percent or more of the labor force. The NEW DEAL of President FRANKLIN D. ROOSEVELT helped bring some improvement, but the Depression lasted for a decade. As late as 1940, unemployment stood at nearly 15 percent. MOBILIZATION for WORLD WAR II then ended the depression, took production, income, and employment to record highs, and set the stage for two decades more of extraordinary economic growth and prosperity. The modern "mixed economy" of increasing GOVERNMENT regulation of BUSINESS and responsibility for economic security emerged in the era. (See the table for data on the gross national product, national income, and unemployment from 1929 to 1945.)

After recovery from the 1921–22 recession, the economy had grown prodigiously in the 1920s. From 1922 to 1929, the gross national product rose by just over 40 percent, from $74 billion to $104.4 billion; national income increased by close to 40 percent, from $63.1 to $87.8 billion; and unemployment stabilized at about 4 percent by late in the decade. Home and road construction and the AUTOMOBILE INDUSTRY paced the economy, though such newer industries as electrical appliances contributed as well. It appeared to many as though the United States had developed a "new economy," in which productivity and living standards would continue to rise because of modern technology and management practices.

Impressive as the economic performance of the 1920s was, however, there were underlying problems that became clearer later. The distribution of income was such that there was not enough money in the hands of workers and farmers to sustain the consumer spending necessary for continued growth. Such "sick industries" as coal and textiles experienced difficulties in the decade. AGRICULTURE faced overproduction and low prices, which bore especially heavily on small farmers. Construction and automobile production could not maintain their growth by the late 1920s because of saturated markets, and unsold inventories began

SELECTED ECONOMIC DATA, 1929–1945

Year	Gross National Product (Billions of Dollars)		National Income (Billions of Dollars)	Unemployment (% Civilian Labor Force)
	Current Prices	1929 Prices	Current Prices	
1929	104.4	104.4	87.8	3.2
1930	91.1	95.1	75.7	8.7
1931	76.3	89.5	59.7	15.9
1932	58.5	76.4	42.5	23.6
1933	56.0	74.2	40.2	24.9
1934	65.0	80.8	49.0	21.7
1935	72.5	91.4	57.1	20.1
1936	82.7	100.9	64.9	16.9
1937	90.8	109.1	73.6	14.3
1938	85.2	103.2	67.6	19.0
1939	91.1	111.0	72.8	17.2
1940	100.6	121.0	81.6	14.6
1941	125.8	138.7	104.7	9.9
1942	159.1	154.7	137.7	4.7
1943	192.5	170.2	170.3	1.9
1944	211.4	183.6	182.6	1.2
1945	213.6	180.9	181.2	1.9

Note: Under Gross National Product, "current dollars" means GNP as measured by the value of the dollar each year; "1929 dollars" means that the GNP for each year is given in the value of 1929 dollars. In looking at the columns, one can see that the decline in the GNP from 1929 to 1933 as measured in "current dollars" exaggerates the decline in the GNP, because of the *deflation* of that period, which increased the value of the dollar. Conversely, the rise in GNP during World War II as measured in current dollars exaggerates the increase, because of the *inflation* of that period, which decreased the value of the dollar.

Source: *The Statistical History of the United States, from Colonial Times to the Present.* Stamford, Conn.: Fairfield Publishers, 1965.

to mount in other industries. Newer industries, including electrical appliances, aviation, petrochemicals and plastics, and processed foods, had not developed enough to carry the economy. Questionable practices and a lack of coordination and regulation marked the banking system. By the end of the decade, uncontrolled speculation characterized the stock market. Conventional economic thought lacked the tools for adequate analysis of or prescription for such economic problems. In short, for all its strengths and successes in the 1920s, the American economy had important weaknesses.

The economy began to show signs of decline by mid-1929, and then fell sharply in the winter of 1929–30. The STOCK MARKET CRASH of October 1929 is often taken as the beginning of the Great Depression, but the crash was no more than a contributing factor to the economic collapse and the decade-long duration of the depression. Year by year from 1929 to 1933, the economy spiraled down and unemployment grew worse, despite occasional rallies and

plateaus. By 1933, the gross national product stood at just 54 percent of the 1929 high, and national income at only 46 percent. Industrial production was down by more than half, and manufacturing wages and farm income by about 60 percent. The New York Stock Exchange was at 17 percent of 1929 levels, foreign trade was off by 70 percent, and unemployment was at least one-fourth and perhaps as high as one-third of the labor force. The consumer price index had fallen by about 25 percent, for the depression was a profoundly deflationary event—but income had fallen even more, so there was no ability to increase spending and consumption and (with profits down catastrophically, too) no incentive for new investment. Never had the nation's economy sunk so low.

The ELECTION OF 1932 brought President Franklin D. Roosevelt to the White House, and his New Deal programs aimed to produce economic recovery as well as RELIEF for the unemployed and impoverished and reform to the nation's economic and social institutions. The major programs of the FIRST NEW DEAL, the AGRICULTURAL ADJUSTMENT ACT and the NATIONAL INDUSTRIAL RECOVERY ACT, sought recovery for the agricultural and manufacturing sectors. While helping to arrest the decline and stabilizing the economy, they had small success at best in bringing expansion. New Deal relief programs, which contributed to unwanted budget deficits, had more impact on the economy, and expansionary monetary policies evidently played some role, too. And while New Deal reforms strengthened banking, the stock market, and other segments of the economy, New Deal regulation, TAXATION, and LABOR policy worried and angered business and worked against investments needed to stimulate the economy.

In any event, the economy did show improvement from 1933 to 1937. The gross national product grew by more than 60 percent, national income increased by over 80 percent, and unemployment fell from roughly 25 to 14 percent. By 1937, in fact, the GNP as measured in constant 1929 dollars had exceeded 1929 levels. But although those figures represent one of the most impressive peacetime expansions ever, they really reflect how far the economy had fallen by 1933, not the health of the economy in 1937. The economy remained far below full-employment, full-production prosperity.

Despite the continuing slack in the economy, Roosevelt was heartened by the gains and turned to more restrictive fiscal and monetary policy in 1937, out of a desire to avoid budget deficits and a worry about inflation. The result was the fierce RECESSION OF 1937–38 (sometimes called the "Roosevelt Recession"). From the late summer of 1937 to the spring of 1938, economic indexes fell faster than at the beginning of the depression, although not as far or for as long. By the spring of 1938, industrial production and payrolls were off by more than one-third, and unemployment rose to 19 percent for the year. The recession caused a searching reevaluation of economic policy within the administration, and in April 1938 Roosevelt increased spending and asked for a study of monopoly. Especially important was the new importance by the late 1930s of KEYNESIANISM—which argued for government deficit spending to produce economic growth—among New Deal economists and policymakers.

The return to expansionary fiscal and monetary policy helped stimulate the economy. Between 1938 and 1940, GNP and national income both increased by about 20 percent and unemployment fell from 19 to 14.6 percent. But it was the economic mobilization and massive spending for World War II, not New Deal policies or spending, that at last took the American economy out of the Great Depression. The figures are remarkable: from 1940 to 1944 (the peak year of wartime prosperity), GNP more than doubled, rising by 110 percent; national income increased by 124

percent; and unemployment shriveled from 14.6 to an amazing 1.2 percent. Even when corrected for wartime inflation, the gains in production, income, and living standards were extraordinary. Personal savings increased rapidly, too. World War II—and the huge federal budget deficits of some $50 billion per year in each of three years—ended the depression and began a quarter century of unprecedented growth and prosperity.

But World War II did not just galvanize the economy; it also brought important change that laid foundations for the postwar era. Newer industries, such as aviation, electronics, and petrochemicals, took off. Winning the lion's share of war contracts, established or emerging giants in the STEEL INDUSTRY, the AIRCRAFT INDUSTRY, automobiles, and other industries expanded and modernized their plants and increased their economic (and political) power. Big agribusiness, boosted by new applications of mechanization, grew more important, too. Military needs and SCIENCE produced new breakthroughs in TECHNOLOGY —with atomic power, aerospace, synthetic rubber and other petrochemical products, pharmaceuticals, communications, and electronics especially prominent. New patterns of subsidizing research and development tied government, universities, and the military together, contributing to what President Dwight D. Eisenhower would later call the "military-industrial complex." The GI BILL OF RIGHTS helped lay foundations for home construction, business enterprise, and education that would spark the postwar economy. Wartime military and economic mobilization stimulated economic growth and change in SUNBELT areas of the SOUTH and the West Coast. Keynesian economic analysis, confirmed by wartime prosperity, became much more widely accepted, and, together with wartime changes in taxation, laid the basis for postwar economic policy.

Not everything changed during the war, of course, and much wartime change reinforced or accelerated change already under way. The distribution of income and wealth remained much the same, for example (as it had in the New Deal years as well), but the much higher incomes of the war years and beyond meant that most people enjoyed rising income and more spending power. The economy had long been trending toward concentrations of industrial and economic power, and new industries had begun to emerge in the interwar years. The striking wartime growth in California industry built on prewar developments, as did the larger role of the government in the economy. Nonetheless, the war had a large and lasting impact on the American economy—and set the stage for the remarkable expansion and prosperity that would characterize the next two decades.

Finally, the war also changed the nation's status in the global economy. By 1929, the United States had already become the world's most important economic power. But by 1945, its global status was even more dominant. Not only had the war produced growth and prosperity in the United States, but it had also skewed and damaged—sometimes virtually destroyed—the economies of the other major industrial nations. In 1947, the United States produced almost half the world's manufactured goods, nearly 60 percent of the world's oil and steel, and some 80 percent of the world's automobiles. The United States also played a more important role in world economic policies, as reflected by the BRETTON WOODS CONFERENCE and the International Monetary Fund and the World Bank that stemmed from it. As Alan M. Milward has written, "by 1945 the foundations of the United States' economic domination over the next quarter of a century had been secured"—and that "may have been the most influential consequence of the Second World War for the post-war world."

Further reading: Michael Bernstein, *The Great Depression: Delayed Recovery and Economic Change in America, 1929–1939* (New York: Cambridge University Press, 1987); Lester Chandler, *America's Greatest Depression* (New York: Harper & Row, 1970); Peter Fearon, *War, Prosperity, and Depression: The U.S. Economy, 1917–1945* (Oxford, U.K.: Oxford University Press, 1987); Alan S. Milward, *War, Economy and Society: 1939–1945* (Berkeley: University of California Press, 1977); Harold G. Vatter, *The U.S. Economy in World War II* (New York: Columbia University Press, 1985); *The Statistical History of the United States from Colonial Times to the Present* (Stamford, Conn.: Fairfield Publishers, 1965).

education

The American education system, like other aspects of society from 1929 to 1945, reflected the impact first of the GREAT DEPRESSION and then of WORLD WAR II. As it typically does, education in the era also reflected the nation's social structure and societal priorities. During the 1930s this meant a public education system based upon the individual-centered "progressive" pedagogy to train good citizens. With the coming of World War II, the progressive approach gave way to an emphasis on patriotism and to education aimed at preparing students for whatever roles their nation needed them to fill. By the end of the war, educational priorities changed to more functional, "life-adjustment" objectives, reflecting the new global state of affairs and the transition from a wartime to a peacetime economy. For a variety of reasons, enrollments in schools and colleges generally increased during the 1930s, declined during the war, and then shot up in the postwar era.

Throughout the 20th century, the American education system broadened its reach, with public education growing increasingly accessible and uniform. By 1929, education was becoming the province of professional teachers who were more concerned with the social value of knowledge than with the scholarly pursuit of it for its own sake. Professional associations and state and local governments had expanded their influence and authority over both content and methodology. For elementary school students, this meant an education in how to become a productive member of society. Still influenced by the progressive educator John Dewey, progressive pedagogy came to dominate educational thought by the early 1920s and reached its greatest level of influence in the 1930s.

Progressive education emphasized the basics of reading, writing, and arithmetic, as well as social studies, which encompassed not only national history but also civics. This broadened emphasis on all the social sciences was a result of the progressive philosophy of educating the citizen and of the particular early-20th-century concern about "Americanizing" immigrant youth. In 1931, the state of Virginia created a new progressive curriculum that quickly became a model for 31 other states. This new curriculum was based on the specific progressive principles of protection and conservation of life, property, and natural resources; production, distribution, transportation, and consumption of goods and services; exploration; recreation; extension of freedom; and expression of aesthetic and religious impulses. Termed "social reconstructionism," this approach also reflected the economic turmoil of the depression and the political liberalism of the NEW DEAL.

At the same time that they addressed their curricula, school systems found themselves struggling with budget cuts resulting from the onset of the depression. Average annual expenditures per pupil in public day schools dropped from $87 in 1930 to $67 in 1934 before slowly rebounding to $88 in 1940 and to $117 in 1944. As a result, some public schools began charging tuition to meet basic needs while others were forced to close their doors—with either solution depriving some American CHILDREN of ready access to education. On the other hand, the depressed job market helped keep many youth in school, and the percentage of young people aged 5 through 17 in public day schools rose from 81 percent in 1930 to 85 percent in 1940. (Counting nonpublic schools, more than 90 percent of the 5- through 17-year-old population attended school in 1940.)

During the war years, progressive pedagogy lost ground as emphasis shifted toward the encouragement of nationalism and support for the war effort. Those on the left fringe of progressive education who took aim at capitalism as a root cause of social ills found themselves targets of criticism from educational and noneducational groups alike. Patriotic organizations such as the Daughters of the American Revolution issued positions and statements on classroom content and textbook selection during World War II aimed at promoting nationalism and rooting out what they saw as subversive material. Such concerns resulted in changing goals even by the Educational Policies Commission of the National Educational Association. This body's 1944 report of top 10 objectives changed from the community-minded list set forth in its 1938 report to more conservative and national goals six years later. This conservative trend then gave way by the middle of the 1940s to a more functional approach to education emphasizing "life-adjustment" in such areas as citizenship, home and family life, use of leisure, health, tools of learning, work experience, and occupational adjustments.

By the end of the 1930s, more than 7 million students were enrolled in secondary schools. Just between 1930 and 1934, the percentage of school-aged youth in secondary schools increased by more than 25 percent, a testimony to family, local, state, and national efforts to educate American youth in the face of the Great Depression as well as a product of the lack of employment opportunities for young people. The percentage of high school graduates among 17-year-olds increased from 29 percent in 1930 to 51 percent in 1942.

In a major departure from the early years of the century when the chief function of secondary schools was to serve as college preparatory institutions for a select few, high schools of the 1930s and 1940s focused on becoming

Rural school near Tipler, Wisconsin, May 1937 *(Library of Congress)*

comprehensive schools for all American youth. The typical curriculum, which had previously stressed preparation for college and white-collar jobs, was broadened considerably to include a wider array of vocational training. Perhaps even more than in the primary grades, emphasis shifted during the war from the individual and his or her role in society to war aims and service to society. By the end of this era, more students than ever were attending and graduating from high school, but a smaller percentage—about one-third—of high school graduates were attending college, reflecting the change in educational goals and the broadening student population in high schools.

College enrollments rose from 1.1 million to 1.5 million between 1930 and 1940 (after falling off for a few years early in the decade), and from 12.4 percent to 15.7 percent of the 18 to 21 age group. By 1944, college enrollments had fallen back almost to 1930 levels because of the demands of the armed forces and war MOBILIZATION. Similarly, the number of degrees conferred by institutions of higher education rose from 140,000 in 1930 to 217,000 in 1940, before declining to 142,000 in 1944. Where male graduates had typically far outnumbered women before the war and would do so again afterward, women earned a majority of degrees conferred in the mid-1940s. The college population did remain overwhelmingly upper and upper middle class, and the majority of courses taught therefore emphasized preparation for white-collar and professional occupations.

As part of the larger role of the federal GOVERNMENT during the presidency of FRANKLIN D. ROOSEVELT, federal programs provided assistance to education. The NATIONAL YOUTH ADMINISTRATION, in addition to giving out-of-school youth part-time employment, also gave more than 2 million students financial assistance to stay in school from 1935 to 1943. Direct aid to colleges and universities also helped address the needs of higher education, and the Bankhead-Jones Act of 1935 added money to higher education institutions that were already receiving federal funds under the Morrill Act of 1890. On average, the Bankhead-Jones Act added some $2 million dollars per year between 1937 and 1945 to the $2.5 million annually received from Morrill for colleges of agriculture and mechanical arts. During World War II, the Student War Loans Program was established, and through the Interior Department's Office of Education the federal government subsidized courses in engineering, chemistry, physics, and production supervision, all essential to the war effort.

Even with federal aid to address financial concerns, institutions sometimes found it difficult to find or retain qualified faculty to teach those enrolled. Colleges also responded to the war effort by shortening holidays, eliminating summer breaks, and often housing officer training programs. While the majority of secondary school programs and many college programs stressed training to prepare youth for their part in the war effort, graduate school came to be viewed as having the role of promoting and preserving democracy in a world perceived to be increasingly threatened by totalitarian states.

As the end of the war neared, attention turned toward the returning soldiers who would flood the job market possibly leading to a resumption of depression-era problems. Education was once again the preferred solution, and the GI BILL OF RIGHTS included grants to help veterans afford a college education—and also slow their reentrance into the workforce. In the postwar era, education once again would respond to the changing societal conditions in which it operated and to the needs of the students whom it educated.

Further reading: Lawrence A. Cremin, *American Education: The Metropolitan Experience, 1887–1980;* Edgar B. Gumbert and Joel H. Spring, *The Superschool and the Superstate: American Education in the 20th Century, 1918–1970* (New York: John Wiley & Sons, 1974); Richard Wayne Lykes, *Higher Education and the United States Office of Education (1867–1953)* (Washington, D.C.: Bureau of Postsecondary Education, 1975).

—Thomas Campbell

Eisenhower, Dwight D.   See Volume IX

elderly

The GREAT DEPRESSION and WORLD WAR II had a significant impact on the lives of people over the age of 65. As the nation entered the depression years, the elderly found themselves a particularly vulnerable age group economically. Campaigns to provide a national old-age pension, notably the one led by Dr. FRANCIS TOWNSEND, brought their plight to national attention, and the SOCIAL SECURITY ACT of 1935 addressed the economic insecurity of old age. MOBILIZATION for World War II finally ended the depression, and the need for war workers opened up job opportunities for the elderly. By the postwar period, the elderly constituted a growing proportion of the nation's population, had an expanding safety net, and formed an increasingly important political constituency.

The elderly as a group had been growing since the turn of the 20th century, as advances in MEDICINE AND PUBLIC HEALTH helped to increase life expectancy from 47 in 1900 to 60 in 1930. By 1930, those over age 65 were estimated at 6.5 million people, or about 5 percent of the United States's population. But the elderly were a vulnerable group, disproportionately likely to live in poverty. Most did not have access to private pensions (only an estimated 150,000 elderly lived on private pensions in the 1930s), and

for those who planned to live on their savings, the banking crisis of the depression wiped out many accounts. State old-age assistance programs were in no better shape—by 1934, only about 180,000 elderly were receiving state elderly aid, with an average monthly payment of less than $20. Families, who had been the traditional safety net for the elderly, found themselves increasingly unable to assist elderly parents and relatives as the UNEMPLOYMENT rate continued to rise. Compounding this was the fact that the elderly tended to be among those first fired, and their unemployment rates were consistently higher than the national average.

The condition of the elderly became part of the national agenda during the NEW DEAL of President FRANKLIN D. ROOSEVELT. As the depression continued, several grass-roots movements of the elderly began gaining momentum. The largest was the Townsend Movement, begun by a California physician, Dr. Francis Townsend. Townsend's impracticable but popular program proposed a $200 per month pension to every person over age 60, to be spent by the end of the month and financed by a national sales tax. Townsend clubs began springing up around the nation and by 1935 had almost 500,000 dues-paying members. Concurrently, the President's Committee on Economic Security, created in 1934, was working on its recommendations that included addressing old-age poverty, and became the Social Security Act of 1935.

In the long run, the most significant part of the Social Security Act was the Old-Age Insurance program (OAI, changed to Old-Age and Survivors' Insurance in 1939), popularly known as Social Security. A federally administered retirement program, OAI was funded through employer and employee payroll taxes, with the amount of benefits tied to the worker's employment history. But benefits were not scheduled to begin until 1942 (changed to 1940), and the elderly needed immediate relief. Partly to address this gap, the Social Security Act also created a public assistance program, the Old-Age Assistance program (OAA), which absorbed the estimated 700,000 elderly receiving aid from the FEDERAL EMERGENCY RELIEF ADMINISTRATION and provided financial assistance to the elderly not covered under OAI. At its peak, OAA supported over 2.7 million elderly persons in 1950, though by 1951 the number of OASI recipients exceeded those under OAA.

World War II showed that the elderly could be, and often wanted to be, productive members of the workforce. The war years saw a critical shortage of workers and the elderly helped to fill this need. The number of elderly receiving old-age assistance declined each year as they reentered the workforce, although DEMOBILIZATION put many back into retirement after 1945. The number of persons over 65 on OAA and OASI climbed once more, even as the elderly were becoming a larger proportion of the population (8 percent by 1950). A by-product was that the economic independence OAA and OASI provided the elderly meant that they were less dependent on their families and were increasingly less likely to live with their adult children or other relatives.

Through the efforts to provide them with economic security, the elderly also found their political voice by the postwar period. Social Security, as it was expanded over the decades to include most workers and benefits were also increased, became one of the "sacred cows" of American politics, and any perceived threat to the program could bring out large numbers of voters. The years 1929–1945, then, ameliorated the economic plight of the elderly and helped create one of the strongest political lobbying groups in the United States.

Further reading: Carole Haber and Brian Gratton, *Old Age and the Search for Security: An American Social History* (Bloomington: Indiana University Press, 1994); *Report of the Committee on Economic Security of 1935 and Other Basic Documents Relating to the Development of the Social Security Act* (Washington, D.C.: National Conference on Social Welfare, 1985).

—Katherine Liapis Segrue

election of 1932

Taking place in the depths of the GREAT DEPRESSION, the election of 1932 transferred power from the REPUBLICAN PARTY to the DEMOCRATIC PARTY and sent FRANKLIN D. ROOSEVELT to the White House.

Although they had been the nation's majority party since the 1890s and had dominated the politics of the 1920s, the Republicans faced dismal prospects in 1932. In 1930, the GOP had lost some 50 seats in the House and eight in the Senate and failed to control CONGRESS for the first time in more than a decade. As the depression worsened in 1931 and 1932, the popularity of President HERBERT C. HOOVER and the Republicans had plummeted as well, all the more after the BONUS ARMY episode in the summer of 1932. With little hope of victory, the dispirited Republican Party renominated Hoover and his running mate, Vice President Charles Curtis.

The Democrats nominated Franklin D. Roosevelt, the popular activist governor of New York, for president, and Texan JOHN NANCE GARNER, Speaker of the House of Representatives, for vice president. (Garner had enabled Roosevelt's nomination on the fourth ballot by releasing delegates pledged to him, Garner, thus avoiding a deadlocked convention.) Wanting to symbolize his desire for change, Roosevelt broke longstanding political precedent by appearing in person at the convention to accept his nomination. He said that Democrats should be "a party of liberal thought, of planned action," and declared that "I

pledge you, I pledge myself, to a new deal for the American people."

Neither at the convention nor during the campaign, however, did Roosevelt clearly say just what the NEW DEAL would be. He and the Democrats criticized Hoover both for doing and spending too much and for doing and spending too little, and were perhaps most forthright in pledging to end Prohibition. Nevertheless, a real difference did emerge between the sunny, confident Roosevelt, with his obvious readiness to use the federal GOVERNMENT to address the social and economic problems of the depression, and the dour, discredited Hoover, who warned that Roosevelt was a dangerous radical and stubbornly defended his own unpopular and unsuccessful policies.

Election day brought a landslide victory for the Democrats. In the greatest four-year reversal ever at the presidential level, Roosevelt won 57.4 percent of the popular vote and 472 votes in the electoral college. (In 1928, Hoover had won 58.2 percent of the popular vote and 444 votes in the electoral college.) The first Democrat in 56 years to win a majority of the popular vote for president, Roosevelt lost only six states (Delaware, Pennsylvania, Connecticut, New Hampshire, Vermont, and Maine). Roosevelt added Protestant middle-class, working-class, and farm voters to his party's traditional urban, ethnic, and white southern strength, though as compared to the full-blown Roosevelt Coalition in the ELECTION OF 1936, which culminated the transformation of POLITICS IN THE ROOSEVELT ERA, Roosevelt's 1932 vote was based less on massive strength in urban, working-class, ethnic, and AFRICAN AMERICAN areas. Picking up another 90 seats in the House of Representatives and 13 in the Senate from 1930, Democrats also took overwhelming control of the Congress, with a margin of 310-117 in the House and 60-35 in the Senate.

The 1932 election was a decisive rejection of the HOOVER PRESIDENCY and the Republicans, who were identified with the Great Depression and with policies that seemed unresponsive to national and human needs. Despite unemployment of at least one-fourth of the labor force, voters also rejected radical alternatives: the Socialist candidate, NORMAN THOMAS, won just 2.2 percent of the vote, and the COMMUNISTS garnered a scant three-tenths of 1 percent. Although more a rejection of Hoover and the GOP than an affirmation of Roosevelt and the Democrats, the election was a call for change that gave Roosevelt and his party the chance to deal effectively with the depression and earn reelection in their own right. Only after 1932 did it become clear that Roosevelt's presidency would bring the transformation of American government and the realignment of American politics.

Further reading: Frank Freidel, "The Election of 1932" in *History of American Presidential Elections, 1789–1968,*

Vol. 3, edited by Arthur M. Schlesinger, Jr. (New York: Chelsea House, 1971), pp. 2,707–2,806.

election of 1936

In the election of 1936, FRANKLIN D. ROOSEVELT was reelected to his second term as president in one of the largest landslide victories in American political history. The election served to ratify Roosevelt's NEW DEAL, and it culminated the realignment of American politics that made the DEMOCRATIC PARTY the new majority party. It was therefore not only the most significant election of the POLITICS IN THE ROOSEVELT ERA, but also one of the most important in American political history.

To run against Roosevelt and Vice President JOHN NANCE GARNER, the Republicans nominated ALFRED M. LANDON, the governor of Kansas, for president and Frank Knox, a Chicago newspaper publisher, for vice president. Landon won the GOP nomination partly because of his apparent electoral appeal (in elections in which Republicans had few successes, he defeated an incumbent Democrat in 1932 and then won reelection in 1934), partly because he seemed able to bridge the differences between the conservative and progressive wings of the REPUBLICAN PARTY. A significant new third party also appeared in the 1936 election, the UNION PARTY, which had been created by FATHER CHARLES E. COUGHLIN and which nominated Congressman William "Liberty Bill" Lemke of North Dakota for president.

Neither Landon nor Lemke proved able to wage an effective campaign against Roosevelt and the New Deal. By autumn, the Union party had fallen into disarray, with Coughlin making increasingly intemperate attacks on the president, and Lemke having little impact. Landon tried to provide a moderate alternative to the New Deal, pledging support for AGRICULTURE, LABOR, and the ELDERLY, while saying that he would provide more careful management of government programs and budgets than did FDR. But he generated neither excitement nor much support and proved unable to distance himself from anti–New Deal conservatives in the party. He became increasingly critical of the New Deal as the campaign wore on and called the popular SOCIAL SECURITY ACT a "cruel hoax."

For his part, Roosevelt tried to rally working-class and middle-class voters behind the New Deal and against what he called "economic royalists" opposing it. Such rhetoric reached its height on October 31, when he said that the forces of "organized money" are "unanimous in their hate for me—and I welcome their hatred." He continued that he hoped it would be said that "the forces of selfishness and of lust for power met their match" in his first term—and that they "met their master" in his second. Yet despite such words (demagoguery, his critics said), Roosevelt offered little in the way of new programs and campaigned especially on the nonideological slogan of "Four Years Ago and Now." Asking voters to look at the increase in jobs, production, national income, and economic security between 1932 and 1936, he wanted the election to be a referendum on his presidency and its programs to deal with the GREAT DEPRESSION.

The voters returned a smashing verdict for Roosevelt and the New Deal. The president won 27,752,869 votes, 60.8 percent of the total, as against Landon's 16,674,665 and 36.5 percent. (Lemke carried but 1.9 percent; Socialist NORMAN THOMAS not even half of 1 percent.) As Democratic national chairman JAMES FARLEY had predicted, Roosevelt lost only Maine and Vermont in winning 523 electoral votes to Landon's eight. And Democrats swept to top-heavy control of the CONGRESS, picking up another dozen seats in the House and seven in the Senate. When the 75th Congress met early in 1937, Democrats would control the House by a nearly 4 to 1 margin (331-89) over the Republicans, and the Senate by nearly 5 to 1 (76-16).

Democrats won such a stunning victory because the Roosevelt Coalition, formed in the political realignment of the 1930s, reached its apex in 1936. To the traditionally Democratic "Solid South," Roosevelt added massive support among working-class and lower-middle-class voters and among ethnic CATHOLICS and JEWS, especially in the big CITIES of the industrial North. Roosevelt won nearly four out of five lower-income voters, three out of five middle-income voters, and even an impressive two out of every five upper-income voters. AFRICAN AMERICANS shifted from the party of Lincoln to the party of Roosevelt in 1936. Roosevelt also won some 80 percent of the union vote, and LABOR contributed to Democratic coffers in unprecedented amounts.

Yet the meaning of the 1936 election was complicated. Democrats had become the majority party, and the voters had resoundingly approved the New Deal. Yet as the remainder of FDR's presidency would show, CONSERVATISM remained a powerful force because of the entrenched power of small-government, anti-statist, and individualist attitudes and values, and the Republican Party would rally from the rout of 1936. The election of 1936 thus proved to be more an endorsement of FDR himself and of the specific programs of the New Deal than an ideological conversion to LIBERALISM or a mandate to extend the New Deal.

Further reading: William E. Leuchtenburg, "The Election of 1936" in *History of American Presidential Elections, 1789–1968*, Vol. 3, edited by Arthur M. Schlesinger, Jr. (New York: Chelsea House, 1971), pp. 2,809–2,904.

election of 1940

The early stages of WORLD WAR II in Europe gave the presidential election of 1940 a much different context from that of the earlier POLITICS IN THE ROOSEVELT ERA, when the domestic issues of the GREAT DEPRESSION and the NEW DEAL had dominated presidential politics. Yet despite the impact of the war on national life and politics, and the new salience of defense and FOREIGN POLICY, party images and voting patterns proved strikingly consistent with those of the 1930s. In November, the American people elected FRANKLIN D. ROOSEVELT to an unprecedented third term.

Perhaps the greatest impact of the war on the politics of 1940 came in shaping the presidential nominations. The early front-runners for the Republican nomination were Ohio's conservative senator ROBERT A. TAFT and New York district attorney Thomas E. Dewey. But the war made Taft seem too isolationist to be president, and Dewey too young. WENDELL L. WILLKIE, a utilities magnate who had made a name for himself in the late 1930s as an engaging, articulate critic of New Deal regulatory policy (although he endorsed much New Deal social reform) came from far behind, backed by influential eastern internationalists, to win the Republican nomination on the sixth ballot. Charles McNary of Oregon, the minority leader in the Senate, was nominated for vice president.

On the Democratic side, Roosevelt's intentions were unclear down to 1940, and PUBLIC OPINION POLLS suggested that a majority of voters opposed a third term. The Nazi BLITZKRIEG that overran western Europe in the spring of 1940 then helped to reverse public opinion on the third-term issue and led Roosevelt to seek reelection in order to ensure an active, pro-Allied foreign policy. After renominating Roosevelt, the Democratic convention reluctantly acquiesced in FDR's choice for vice president, Secretary of Agriculture HENRY A. WALLACE.

The war also affected the presidential campaign. At first, Willkie supported Roosevelt's defense and foreign policy; but as the campaign wore on, with Roosevelt clearly ahead, Willkie became more and more critical of Roosevelt. He claimed that FDR intended to take the nation to war and warned that a third term would lead the country to dictatorship. Worried that Willkie might make inroads into isolationist voters and ethnic groups opposed to his pro-Allied policy, Roosevelt near the end of the campaign issued his famous pledge: "I have said this before, but I shall say it again and again and again: Your boys are not going to be sent into any foreign wars." Yet even though questions of national defense and foreign policy affected American politics more in 1940 than in a generation, domestic issues and party images from the 1930s were central to the campaign. Again in 1940, Roosevelt ran especially as the candidate of reform and economic security—and also of recovery as well, as defense spending produced economic growth and more jobs. Again he portrayed the Republicans as the party of the rich and of hard times.

Roosevelt won another decisive victory, with 54.8 percent of the popular vote as against Willkie's 44.8 percent, and 449 of the 531 votes in the electoral college. Democrats also retained clear control of the CONGRESS, with margins of 268-162 in the House and 66-28 in the Senate. But where Roosevelt had carried 60.8 percent of the vote in 1936, winning by 27.8 million to 16.7 million votes, his margin of victory in 1940 fell from 11 million to five million votes (27.3 million to 22.3 million), and he lost 10 states (much of the isolationist Midwest as well as Maine and Vermont). Despite their commanding control of CONGRESS, moreover, Democrats regained little of the ground lost in the House of Representatives in the 1938 election, when Republicans had picked up some 70 seats. And the Democrats lost three more seats in the Senate after dropping seven in 1938.

To some extent, the reduced Democratic totals reflected defections among well-off and more conservative voters, but losses came also from ISOLATIONISTS and from ethnic groups (especially IRISH AMERICANS, ITALIAN AMERICANS, and GERMAN AMERICANS) concerned about FDR's pro-Allied and anti-AXIS bent. Roosevelt retained or increased his support among internationalists and such pro-Allied ethnic groups as JEWS and POLISH AMERICANS, while many voters simply found his experience reassuring. But continuity in voting patterns was more important than change, and the continued Democratic dominance was more important than the erosion of Democratic strength. Most voters cast their ballots as they had in the ELECTION OF 1936, and polls showed that voting decisions turned more on Roosevelt's domestic record and image than on foreign policy. The principal sources of Democratic strength—the SOUTH, CITIES, and ethnic, black, and working-class voters—remained the same. The new majority Roosevelt Coalition, forged in the 1930s, had clearly withstood its first challenge, despite the new circumstances and concerns of 1940.

Further reading: Robert E. Burke, "The Election of 1940" in *History of American Presidential Elections, 1789–1968,* Vol. 3, edited by Arthur M. Schlesinger, Jr. (New York: Chelsea House, 1971), pp. 2,917–3,006.

election of 1944

In 1944, FRANKLIN D. ROOSEVELT was elected to his fourth term as president, and there was less change in voting patterns between 1940 and 1944 than between any other pair of elections of the 1930s and 1940s. Yet despite the stability in the presidential vote, the 1944 election was a significant one. Not only did it show the continuing strength of the Democratic majority forged by POLITICS IN THE ROO-SEVELT ERA, but it illuminated national attitudes and priorities that would be important to early postwar politics and policy.

The most important choices that each party had to make in 1944 had both short-term and long-term significance. For Democrats, the decision involved who would run for vice president with Roosevelt. The incumbent was HENRY A. WALLACE, but he was far too liberal, on both domestic and FOREIGN POLICY issues, for most party leaders, and Roosevelt did little to support him. The nomination went to Missouri senator Harry S. Truman, who seemed a good political fit: he was a loyal but moderate New Dealer; he got on well with organization leaders; and he was from a border state at a time when the DEMOCRATIC PARTY was showing increasing strains between the its northern and southern wings.

For the REPUBLICAN PARTY, the issue was the presidential nomination. The initial front-runner was 1940 nominee WENDELL L. WILLKIE, but by 1944 Willkie was far more liberal than his party, especially on CIVIL RIGHTS, social reform, and foreign policy. The nomination went instead to the young governor of New York, Thomas E. Dewey, a moderate on both foreign and domestic policy. For vice president, the Republicans selected conservative Ohio governor John Bricker. Both parties thus rejected the more liberal candidates, and in Truman and Dewey chose men well within the consensus of their parties, and the nation, on foreign and domestic policy—and who, as things turned out, would be the presidential nominees in 1948.

Once more, the presidential campaign centered on Roosevelt. Although FDR advocated a far-reaching ECONOMIC BILL OF RIGHTS in 1944, he ran essentially as the candidate of prosperity and peace—issues that PUBLIC OPINION POLLS showed to be central to public concerns as the war neared its end. Despite assurances on both issues, neither Dewey nor the GOP could convince voters that they could better ensure jobs and peace than the experienced Roosevelt. Republican charges that Roosevelt was too old and infirm to serve as president had little impact upon the voters, even though Roosevelt was in fact suffering from serious heart disease by late 1944. Nor did GOP claims that COMMUNISTS had infiltrated the Democratic Party have much resonance in 1944, although they anticipated an important postwar issue.

Roosevelt won reelection by nearly the same margin and with the essentially the same sources of support as in 1940. He won the popular vote with 25,606,585 votes and 53.5 percent to Dewey's 22,014,745 and 46 percent, and he carried 36 of the 48 states and 432 of the 531 votes in the electoral college. Again, working-class, lower-middle-class, ethnic, and black voters in metropolitan areas provided the heaviest Democratic vote, while the SOUTH remained solidly Democratic one last time. Organized LABOR played a major role in the campaign and election. Democrats also regained some of the ground lost in the House of Representatives in the election of 1942 in winning control of CONGRESS by 242-190 in the House and 56-38 in the Senate. To an important extent, the election of 1944, like wartime politics and policymaking more generally, showed that both the NEW DEAL and the Roosevelt Coalition had endured the new circumstances of the war years and would continue to be central to American politics and policies in the postwar era. But the politics of 1944 also revealed a continuing ebbing of the reformist impulse and of the top-heavy Democratic strength of the mid-1930s, trends that would be apparent as well in postwar politics.

Further reading: Leon Friedman, "The Election of 1944" in *History of American Presidential Elections, 1789–1968*, Vol. 4, edited by Arthur M. Schlesinger, Jr. (New York: Chelsea House, 1971), pp. 3,009–3,096.

Ellington, Duke (Edward Kennedy) (1899–1974)

Duke Ellington, pianist, bandleader, and composer, was one of the most influential figures in 20th-century American MUSIC. Although he disliked the term "jazz" applied to his work, preferring the term "Negro folk music," Ellington had a major impact on the development of jazz as an art form in the United States by combining elements of African-American musical forms with Euro-American styles. His body of work includes such immediately recognizable titles as "Mood Indigo," "Sophisticated Lady," and "It Don't Mean a Thing (If It Ain't Got That Swing)," all written in the early 1930s. But he also wrote longer, concerto-like, pieces such as *Black, Brown and Beige* (1943) that marked the range and sophistication of his musicianship. More than a thousand compositions carry his copyright, three-fourths of them written by him alone.

Edward Kennedy Ellington was born in 1899 in Washington, D.C. Middle-class AFRICAN AMERICANS, his parents stressed to their children that they should be "representatives of a great and proud race." The manners and bearing that developed from this idea inspired a friend to give young Edward the nickname "Duke," a name that endured for the rest of his life. His music, like his demeanor, was characterized by a sophistication and elegance that led some to call him "Duke Elegant."

Basic piano lessons during elementary school were Ellington's only formal musical training. Later, he experimented independently and began to write original compositions. While a teenager, he decided to make music his career. Ellington's primary concern throughout most of his life was his music, which often overshadowed his personal life. This is implied by the title of his autobiography, *Music*

Is My Mistress, and by the early end to his 1918 marriage. By 1923, Ellington's first band, the Washingtonians, had landed a job in New York. They spent over four years with the Hollywood (later Kentucky) Club. A subsequent five years at the famous Cotton Club in Harlem included regular RADIO broadcasts and along with recordings and tours brought Ellington national and international prominence and helped Ellington and his band endure the hard times of the early years of the GREAT DEPRESSION.

In the mid- to late 1930s, the big swing bands partly eclipsed Ellington, who refused to compromise his more complex and artistic music despite the popularity of commercial big band swing music. Yet Ellington remained popular and influential, partly with small-group performances but also with his own orchestra, enriched by new compositions and arrangements by Billy Strayhorn, including "Take the A Train" (1941), which became Ellington's signature song. Like Ellington, Strayhorn preferred to focus on more artistic, less commercial music, but Ellington's bands continued to perform and record popular songs as well as extended compositions and concert suites. Some critics consider Ellington's late-1930s and early-1940s output perhaps the peak of his career and creativity and one of the

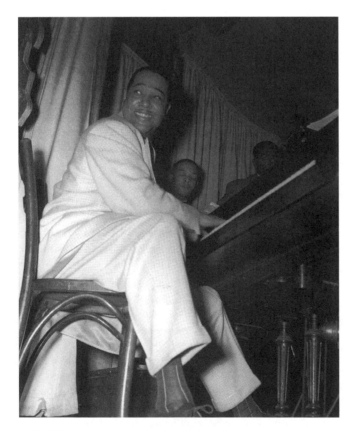

Duke Ellington directing his band from the piano at the Hurricane Club, New York City *(Library of Congress)*

extraordinary pinnacles not just of jazz but of American music. In 1943, Ellington gave his first of nine performances at Carnegie Hall.

The decline of the big bands, changing musical tastes, and new directions in jazz in the postwar era diminished Ellington's public popularity, but after his band's exciting performance at the 1956 Newport Jazz Festival, Ellington and his music reclaimed some of their earlier prominence. Certainly Ellington's own reputation as a giant of American music soared, and he received many honors in later life, including honorary degrees from Yale and Columbia Universities, the President's Gold Medal from Lyndon Johnson, and the Medal of Freedom from Richard Nixon.

Further reading: John Edward Hasse, *Beyond Category: The Life and Genius of Duke Ellington* (New York: Simon & Schuster, 1993).

—Joanna Smith

Emergency Banking Act of 1933

The Emergency Banking Act of 1933 was the first piece of NEW DEAL legislation enacted to strengthen the nation's banking system. When FRANKLIN D. ROOSEVELT took office on March 4, 1933, more than 5,000 banks had failed since the beginning of the GREAT DEPRESSION, and banking operations had been suspended by most states to prevent panicked depositors from making withdrawal demands that would shut down still more banks. The banking system was paralyzed—and it faced collapse.

During the "interregnum" between Roosevelt's election and his inauguration, CONGRESS and the Hoover administration had unsuccessfully sought remedies for the banking system. Toward the end of the HOOVER PRESIDENCY, Hoover contemplated an executive order declaring a national banking "holiday" to close the banks to protect them from runs, but refrained from such action without Roosevelt's support. Roosevelt refused to give such an endorsement, maintaining that he had no authority (and clearly wanting no responsibility) until he became president. Hoover's and Roosevelt's advisers nonetheless worked together toward finding a solution. On March 5, the day after his inauguration, Roosevelt authorized two proclamations: the first called Congress into a special session on March 9; and the second, drawing on documents earlier prepared for Hoover, suspended transactions in gold and declared a national banking holiday from March 6 to March 9. Later, Roosevelt extended the banking holiday until March 13.

On March 9, following round-the-clock meetings at the Treasury Department, FDR submitted to Congress the Emergency Banking Bill, drafted in substantial part by Hoover administration officials. Because printed copies of

The "banking holiday" extended the influence of the federal government on the U.S. economy. This cartoon expresses the hope that American banks would come out of the holiday refreshed and revitalized. Cartoon by Bolte Gibson
(Library of Congress)

the bill were not immediately available, the bill's provisions were read to the House of Representatives, which passed the bill by unanimous voice vote. The Senate overwhelmingly approved the bill a few hours later, and that evening, just eight hours after the bill was introduced, Roosevelt signed the Emergency Banking Act into law.

The Emergency Banking Act permitted the RECONSTRUCTION FINANCE CORPORATION to purchase preferred stock of banks that were in trouble but basically sound in order to put needed money in their hands, authorized issuing new currency, and took the nation off the gold standard. It also provided for the reopening of banks that were deemed financially stable by federal examiners and for the reorganization of others. On the evening of Sunday, March 12, in the first of his fireside chats, Roosevelt told the nation that it was safe to return money to banks. On March 13, eight days after FDR's inauguration, deposits exceeded withdrawals in the first reopened banks. The banking system had survived the crisis.

In one sense, the Emergency Banking Act was profoundly conservative, for it did not nationalize the banks or implement far-reaching new GOVERNMENT power over the banking system. Rather, it enabled the government to shore up the existing system. Subsequent legislation would bring

real reform. But the act was, together with Roosevelt's public reassurances, remarkably effective in meeting the emergency of early March 1933. Understandably, although with exaggeration, RAYMOND MOLEY, a member of the president's famous BRAIN TRUST, would say later that "Capitalism was saved in eight days."

See also BANKING ACT OF 1933; BANKING ACT OF 1935.

Further reading: Helen M. Burns, *The American Banking Community and New Deal Banking Reforms, 1933–1935* (Westport, Conn.: Greenwood, 1974); Susan Estabrook, *The Banking Crisis of 1933* (Lexington: University Press of Kentucky, 1973).

Emergency Relief Appropriation Act (1935)

Called the "Big Bill" by President FRANKLIN D. ROOSEVELT when he proposed it early in 1935, the Emergency Relief Appropriation Act was signed into law on April 8, 1935. It funded nearly $5 billion for work RELIEF and public works programs—to that point, the largest single appropriation in American history—and marked new directions for NEW DEAL relief efforts.

The legislation resulted from the continuing ravages of the GREAT DEPRESSION, with UNEMPLOYMENT still at roughly one-fifth of the work force early in 1935, and from growing political pressure for more vigorous federal GOVERNMENT programs to assist jobless and impoverished Americans. The Emergency Relief Appropriation Act involved a restructuring as well as an expansion of New Deal programs and reflected Roosevelt's insistence that the federal government stop giving direct relief payments to the unemployed. "To dole out relief in this way," he said, "is to administer a narcotic, a subtle destroyer of the human spirit."

The Emergency Relief Appropriation Act thus entailed work-relief projects that would put people to work on projects that would give them a sense of accomplishment and self-respect and add to the nation's infrastructure. Projects were to be labor-intensive, contribute to building useful projects that would if possible (like toll bridges) ultimately help pay for themselves, and pay a "security wage" higher than direct relief payments but lower than prevailing wages in private employment. The federal government would provide work-relief to employable workers then on relief rolls (then about 3.5 million—of some 10 million unemployed), but would return to the states responsibility for the roughly 1.5 million unemployable (aged, handicapped, and infirm) relief recipients. (The SOCIAL SECURITY ACT passed later in 1935 would provide some matching federal-state assistance for unemployables in addition to its programs for old-age retirement and unemployment compensation.)

Under the leadership of HARRY HOPKINS, the Emergency Relief Appropriation Act provided some additional funds to such existing programs as the CIVILIAN CONSERVATION CORPS and the PUBLIC WORKS ADMINISTRATION and supported a number of major new programs, including the RURAL ELECTRIFICATION ADMINISTRATION and the RESETTLEMENT ADMINISTRATION. By far the largest and most important of the new work-relief programs was the WORKS PROGRESS ADMINISTRATION (and its important subprograms, including the NATIONAL YOUTH ADMINISTRATION before it became independent in 1939), which ultimately employed some 5 million workers in an innovative variety of jobs and projects. Funding those new programs marked a victory for Hopkins and others wanting quickly implemented, labor-intensive work relief over HAROLD ICKES and those advocating instead large-scale, long-term, capital-intensive public works programs that would employ fewer workers.

Further reading: Searle F. Charles, *Minister of Relief: Harry Hopkins and the Depression* (Syracuse, N.Y.: Syracuse University Press, 1963); Donald S. Howard, *The WPA and Federal Relief Policy* (New York: Russell Sage Foundation, 1943).

enemy aliens

After the United States entered WORLD WAR II in December 1941, unnaturalized immigrants from AXIS nations were officially classified as enemy aliens by the U.S. government. Concerns about ITALIAN AMERICANS, GERMAN AMERICANS, and JAPANESE AMERICANS had been rising since at least 1940, as the nation became increasingly anti-Axis in its sympathies. In this atmosphere, the loyalty of aliens came under scrutiny, and efforts to designate these groups as enemy aliens began in 1940 and 1941. In the case of the Italian Americans and Japanese Americans, suspicions stemmed also from ethnic and racial antipathies unrelated to the war. As the war progressed, what had begun as a suspicion of all enemy aliens shifted to focus almost exclusively on Japanese Americans.

By 1940, the number of unnaturalized persons living in the United States was approximately 3 percent of the U.S. population. There were 599,000 unnaturalized Italian immigrants (more than one-third of the total 1.6 million Italian American immigrants in the country). Among German Americans, there were 264,000 aliens. Of the 127,000 Japanese Americans in the United States, most (80,000) were American-born, while 47,000 were aliens and prohibited by law from obtaining U.S. citizenship. Although relatively few in number, aliens living in the United States increasingly came under surveillance during 1940, particularly as some GOVERNMENT officials feared the possibility of "fifth column" immigrants with loyalties to their home nation who might be engaged in ESPIONAGE or sabotage activities for the Axis nations.

The first official act to single out these groups came when President Roosevelt authorized the attorney general to use wiretaps to monitor aliens suspected of subversion in May 1940. Next came the SMITH ACT, passed by CONGRESS in June 1940 and intended to prevent espionage and acts of sabotage by agents of Axis nations in the United States. The Smith Act required that aliens from Germany, Italy, and Japan register with the federal government annually at their local post office, keep the government informed of any change of address, provide fingerprints, and report any organizational affiliations. In addition, any alien who had been part of a communist or fascist group could be deported.

Public opinion supported this restrictive policy, for many Americans had suspicions about the loyalties of Italians, Germans, and Japanese living in the United States. This could be seen in the job discrimination against these groups in 1940 and 1941, and some defense industry employers reported that they did not hire workers who were from these ethnic groups, whether alien or American-born. Chiefly in response to pressure from the MARCH ON WASHINGTON MOVEMENT to open up defense jobs to AFRICAN AMERICANS, Roosevelt issued EXECUTIVE ORDER 8802 in June 1941, prohibiting ethnic as well as racial discrimination in employment by industries contracting with the federal government. This government action increased the hiring of German Americans and Italian Americans and also helped to ease suspicions of their loyalties.

After the attack on PEARL HARBOR on December 7, 1941, unnaturalized German, Japanese, and Italian immigrants were officially categorized as enemy aliens. In addition to the restrictions already imposed, this status restricted their movements from areas designated "sensitive military areas" and their ability to possess items that could be used for sabotage, such as short-wave radios; it required enemy aliens to have special identification; and it subjected them to possible detention and/or deportation. Policymakers then began discussing detaining all German, Italian, and Japanese aliens in the United States. In the months following Pearl Harbor, some enemy aliens already under surveillance were detained—about 8,000 Germans, 2,300 Japanese, and several hundred Italians.

As 1942 wore on, fear of espionage by German and Italian aliens receded, and the idea of relocating all Germans and Italians was discarded. Reflecting the larger numbers and greater assimilation of these groups, German Americans especially, this was partly a political decision. In particular, Italian Americans were a major component of the DEMOCRATIC PARTY coalition but had defected from the party in significant numbers in the ELECTION OF 1940. On Columbus Day, 1942, just before the November elections, Roosevelt removed Italians from the enemy alien classification.

On the other hand, the movement to detain and relocate Japanese Americans gained momentum. Pushed by West Coast politicians and the military, FDR issued EXECUTIVE ORDER 9066 on February 19, 1942, which authorized the RELOCATION OF JAPANESE AMERICANS, moving approximately 110,000 from the West Coast to camps further inland. Though there is no evidence that Japanese Americans took part in any espionage or sabotage, Japanese Americans thus bore the brunt of enemy alien policy, reflecting their lack of political power and assimilation as well as the racism of the time.

Further reading: John W. Jeffries, *Wartime America: The World War II Home Front* (Chicago: Ivan R. Dee, 1996); Richard Polenberg, *War and Society: The United States, 1941–1945* (New York: J. B. Lippincott, 1972).

—Katherine Liapis Segrue

environmental issues

By the early 20th century, a growing number of Americans had become concerned about the rapid consumption, and possible depletion, of the nation's natural resources, and the Progressive Era included efforts to address such problems. After ebbing in the 1920s, GOVERNMENT involvement in environmental issues increased during the 1930s as part of the agendas of presidents HERBERT C. HOOVER and FRANKLIN D. ROOSEVELT.

Hoover had sought with some success to promote conservation and resource management in the 1920s during his tenure as secretary of commerce in the cabinets of Warren Harding and Calvin Coolidge. He had advocated legislation that regulated aspects of the fishing industry, for example, and approved construction of Boulder Dam. As president, Hoover continued to work for environmental protection by such efforts as supporting the development of flood control measures and encouraging oil conservation.

Like Hoover, Franklin Roosevelt had a long-standing interest in environmental issues. As governor of New York, he campaigned for responsible forestry and sponsored a number of reforestation initiatives. Forest preservation remained an integral part of Roosevelt's conservation program during his presidency. More forestland—more than 11 million acres—was added to the government's holdings by FDR's administration than had been added under any previous administration. Roosevelt's secretary of the interior, HAROLD ICKES, worked to establish a number of new national parks, including Shenandoah National Park in Virginia and Olympic National Park in Washington State.

Roosevelt and Ickes also supported various state reforestation plans.

Although forest management continued to be important to conservationists, natural disaster helped bring another environmental issue to the forefront during the 1930s. In the southwestern plains, prolonged drought coupled with soil-depleting farming techniques left the land barren and exposed. The resultant environmental damage in the DUST BOWL heightened awareness of soil erosion and the need for soil conservation. In 1933, FDR established the Soil Erosion Service as an emergency measure. Soil conservation efforts were expanded when the Soil Conservation Service (SCS), a permanent agency housed under the Department of Agriculture, was created in 1935. These agencies oversaw a number of conservation initiatives, including scientific research, flood control, reforestation, grazing and pasture regulations, and farmer education and cooperation programs.

Some environmental projects undertaken by the government during this period were designed to control the environment rather than protect it, and to allow expansion into previously inhospitable areas. The Reclamation Service became the Bureau of Reclamation in 1933 and experienced enormous growth in the 1930s. Through the building of massive dams, the bureau provided vast areas of the American West with water for irrigation and hydroelectric power for industrial development. The dams were also designed to control flooding and soil erosion. Even more ambitious were the goals of the TENNESSEE VALLEY AUTHORITY (TVA), an agency formed to spearhead the revitalization of the Tennessee Valley, one of the country's most depressed areas. TVA planners hoped to combine reclamation and conservation projects with education and social programs in order to stimulate economic growth.

To accomplish his environmental goals, Roosevelt also incorporated conservation work into initiatives designed primarily to alleviate the nation's economic woes. One of the most popular NEW DEAL programs, the CIVILIAN CONSERVATION CORPS (CCC), established in 1933, furnished much of the labor for FDR's forest and soil conservation programs. CCC enrollees planted over a billion trees, fought forest fires, and built roads, campgrounds, and recreation facilities in the national parks. They worked on flood control projects for the Army Corps of Engineers and carried out agricultural demonstrations for the SCS. They also worked on a number of reclamation projects carried out by the Bureau of Reclamation and assisted in improving wildlife habitats and grazing lands. Another program, the PUBLIC WORKS ADMINISTRATION, also provided laborers for a number of conservation projects.

The environmentalism of Hoover and Roosevelt, like that of their predecessors, was based largely on a belief in the importance of wise usage of the nation's resources and a persuasion that the fundamental purpose of conservation was to ensure the availability of natural resources for future use and development. But government efforts in the 1930s also led to increased national consciousness about environmental issues. Private organizations such as the Sierra Club, Friends of the Land, and the National Wildlife Federation grew in size and number, helping build the foundation for a more preservationist environmentalism in the decades to follow.

Ironically, some of the very projects hailed as breakthroughs in environmental management in the 1930s and 1940s subsequently provoked criticism from environmentalists for being sources of ecological damage. Dam building, for instance, has frequently been blamed for a myriad of environmental problems in the American Southwest, including loss of wildlife habitat and increased salinity of the water supply. Similarly, some characterize the soil conservation programs of the era as misguided and overly expensive efforts to sustain commercial AGRICULTURE in areas essentially unfit for farming. And some developments of the war years, such as the increasing use of chemical pesticides, the harnessing of atomic power, and the expansion of SUBURBS, also presented significant environmental problems that would become issues in the postwar era.

Further reading: A. L. Riesch Owen, *Conservation under FDR* (New York: Praeger, 1983); John Salmand, *The Civilian Conservation Corps, 1935–1942: A New Deal Case Study* (Durham, N.C.: Duke University Press, 1967); Donald Worster, *Dust Bowl: The Southern Plains in the 1930s* (New York: Oxford University Press, 1979).

—Pamela J. Lauer

espionage

Espionage is the systematic clandestine collection of information on other nations. Traditionally human agents (spies) collected such information; but since WORLD WAR II, technical methods, although less romantic, exciting, and glamorous, have produced far more reliable and timely INTELLIGENCE.

Before and during World War II, the intelligence services of the AXIS nations, especially those of Nazi Germany, were reputed to have legions of spies and saboteurs operating in the United States and South America organized into a centrally directed "fifth column," capable of damaging not only war industries but also national unity. In the United States, the task of countering this reputedly well-entrenched clandestine force was the job of the FEDERAL BUREAU OF INVESTIGATION, which expanded from fewer than 400 agents in 1933 to nearly 5,000 agents by 1944. During the war itself, the FBI conducted more than 19,000

investigations of alleged Axis sabotage and espionage, although none was proven definitively. Thirty-three Axis agents residing in the United States in 1941 were quickly identified and imprisoned, as were thousands of Axis nationals who were taken into custody and deported by 1942. Indeed, postwar analysis found that no coherent Axis fifth column ever existed in the United States, or the Americas, and the few attempts to infiltrate agents were amateurish failures. The FBI apprehended eight German saboteurs who landed on Long Island in June 1942, and two who landed in Maine in November 1944, within days of their arrival.

Nazi espionage failures in the United States were shared by the Japanese military Special Service Organizations, which included units for decoding, recruiting foreign spies, and conducting propaganda and fifth column activities. The espionage agents attached to the Japanese diplomatic posts abroad did score some notable successes, such as gathering information about U.S. NAVY forces at PEARL HARBOR before December 1941. But Japanese ignorance of Allied successes in CODE BREAKING resulted in a massive security breach revealing tremendous amounts of vital Axis tactical and strategic information. Although most Americans assumed that Japanese Americans living on the Pacific coast constituted a fifth column force, a fear that contributed to the RELOCATION OF JAPANESE AMERICANS, no credible evidence existed at that time or later to support this fear and no Japanese espionage activities were uncovered in the United States during the war.

The USSR conducted far more successful espionage operations against the United States and Great Britain than did the Axis powers. Indeed, Soviet intelligence and espionage services, consisting of the Red Army GRU, and its Communist Party counterpart, the NKVD, later known as the KGB, enjoyed enormous wartime success against the Allies and Axis alike, that carried over well into the postwar era. The GRU had extensive agent networks in Europe, including the Rote Kapelle, or Red Orchestra, that controlled the Lucy ring in Switzerland that handled spies within the Nazi military and political high command in Berlin. In Japan, Richard Sorge, another GRU agent, provided copious information on Japanese military and political activities until his capture and execution in 1944. Soviet espionage operations against the Allies included successful NKVD efforts in recruiting double agents within the British MI organizations that operated into the postwar years and by the GRU in recruiting spies working on the American MANHATTAN PROJECT that produced the ATOMIC BOMB.

Espionage efforts by Great Britain were equally sophisticated during the war. In July 1940 the British created the Special Operations Executive (SOE) to conduct

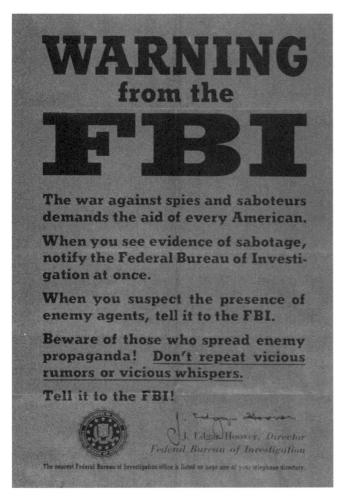

As Americans became more fearful that the United States would become involved in World War II, many citizens began to worry that there were spies among us. The FBI poster shown here warns Americans to be on the lookout for evidence of sabotage or rumormongering. *(National Archives)*

espionage operations and to control a growing body of agents belonging to resistance groups in Nazi-occupied Europe. The British had extraordinary success in running clandestine organizations in Europe, consisting largely of SOE administered guerrilla organizations and individually recruited and trained agents. The XX or 20 Committee managed to identify and recruit all German agents sent to Great Britain to become double agents for the purpose of feeding the Nazis false information. The British intelligence agencies also excelled at deception operations, such as the 1943 operation that led the Germans to think that an invasion of the Balkans was imminent.

The United States formed the OFFICE OF STRATEGIC SERVICES in June 1942 to conduct espionage operations abroad. However, with the British SOE dominating in Europe, and given the geographic expanses of the Pacific,

the Americans came to rely on technical means of intelligence collection and their agent networks remained relatively small and of secondary importance.

Further reading: Jeffrey T. Richelson, *A Century of Spies: Intelligence in the Twentieth Century* (New York: Oxford University Press, 1995).

—Clayton D. Laurie

Ethiopia

On October 3, 1935, Italian troops invaded the independent African country of Ethiopia. Italian dictator Benito Mussolini hoped that the conquest of Ethiopia would be the first step toward establishing a new Roman Empire around the Mediterranean. Like the 1931 Japanese invasion of MANCHURIA, Italy's invasion of Ethiopia revealed the inability of the League of Nations to halt aggression and the lack of American readiness to take decisive action. This encouraged the AXIS nations to continue their paths of aggression in Europe and Asia that ultimately led to WORLD WAR II.

The invasion of Ethiopia demonstrated the failure of the League of Nations to protect the territory and independence of its members. Although the league imposed economic sanctions against Italy, it refused to place an embargo against oil shipments, which were essential to the Italian military, partly because the United States would not agree to honor the embargo. France and Britain also feared that Italy might declare war in retaliation to an oil embargo, or threaten British economic and strategic interests in Malta, Alexandria, or the Suez Canal.

President FRANKLIN D. ROOSEVELT sympathized with Ethiopia's plight. But the first of the NEUTRALITY ACTS, which CONGRESS had passed only five weeks earlier, prevented him from intervening in the conflict or even joining the league's proposed oil embargo. Roosevelt also wanted to avoid antagonizing ISOLATIONISTS in the United States. FDR did quickly invoke the neutrality legislation to impose a strict arms embargo against Italy and Ethiopia, and the administration called for a "moral embargo" on oil and other goods for Italy. Nevertheless, U.S. sales of oil, scrap iron, and copper to Italy rose sharply, until Secretary of State CORDELL HULL threatened to release the names of American businesses engaged in this trade.

On May 5, 1936, Italian troops under Field Marshal Pietro Badoglio captured Addis Ababa, the capital of Ethiopia. The Ethiopian emperor, Haile Selassie, fled to Britain and asked the League of Nations to intervene directly on Ethiopia's behalf, but Britain and France opposed taking military action. On July 15, 1936, the League lifted all sanctions against Italy, effectively recognizing Italy's annexation of Ethiopia.

See also FOREIGN POLICY.

Further reading: Robert Dallek, *Franklin D. Roosevelt and American Foreign Policy, 1932–1945* (New York: Oxford University Press, 1979).

—David W. Waltrop

European theater   See World War II European theater

Executive Order 8802 (1941)

Executive Order 8802, signed by President FRANKLIN D. ROOSEVELT on June 25, 1941, called for an end to discrimination in employment practices by the GOVERNMENT and by defense contractors because of race, creed, color, or national origin, and established the FAIR EMPLOYMENT PRACTICES COMMITTEE (FEPC), the first federal agency devoted to CIVIL RIGHTS since Reconstruction. Although responding chiefly to the circumstances and demands of AFRICAN AMERICANS, the executive order applied to white ethnic groups as well.

Discrimination against blacks in defense industry and the armed forces in the early stages of the MOBILIZATION effort of WORLD WAR II produced protests from black leaders and efforts to change existing policy and practices. A. PHILIP RANDOLPH organized the MARCH ON WASHINGTON MOVEMENT (MOWM) early in 1941 to demand equal opportunity. He insisted that Roosevelt take tangible action or see 100,000 African Americans march on Washington to protest for change and a fair share in the war effort.

Roosevelt, worried also about discrimination against white immigrants with skills needed in defense production, and concerned that such a march might be embarrassing to the country, eventually responded by issuing Executive Order 8802. In addition to stating that "there shall be no discrimination in the employment of workers in the defense industries or government because of race, creed, color or national origin," the executive order went on to say that both employers and labor unions had a responsibility "to provide for the full and equitable participation of all workers in the defense industries" and mandated that all further defense contracts contain a clause prohibiting discrimination. Perhaps the most important section of the executive order was the creation of the FEPC to investigate complaints and take remedial action. Although the order did not apply to the military, as Randolph and other black leaders had desired, the march on Washington was not held.

Executive Order 8802 and the FEPC helped to bring new opportunity to black Americans and to reduce job discrimination against other minority groups. During World War II, the number of African-American civilians employed by the federal government more than tripled, to some 200,000, while the proportion of blacks in defense industry jobs rose from 3 to 8 percent. Insuffi-cient authority for penalizing noncompliance and an inadequate budget nonetheless limited the FEPC, and black employment gains came to a significant degree from the labor shortage created by the millions of men who joined the armed forces. Other problems, such as the continued practice of hiring blacks only for menial jobs and the denial of necessary training for advancement, eventually led to stronger support from Roosevelt. Whatever its limitations, Executive Order 8802 set a new precedent for government involvement in civil rights and helped encourage a new public responsibility among leaders of American industry.

See also RACE AND RACIAL CONFLICT.

Further reading: Herbert Garfinkel, *When Negroes March: The March on Washington Movement in the Organizational Politics for FEPC* (New York: Atheneum, 1969); Paula F. Pfeffer, *A. Philip Randolph, Pioneer of the Civil Rights Movement* (Baton Rouge: Louisiana State University Press, 1990).

—Ronald G. Simon

Executive Order 9066 (1942)

Executive Order 9066, issued by President FRANKLIN D. ROOSEVELT on February 19, 1942, authorized the War Department to designate "military areas" and to exclude "any and all persons" from them. Although the executive order did not specify any individual group, it led to the RELOCATION OF JAPANESE AMERICANS from the West Coast and to the incarceration of more than 110,000 Japanese Americans, about two-thirds of them American citizens, during WORLD WAR II.

A number of factors accounted for the much different treatment given Japanese Americans than GERMAN AMERICANS and ITALIAN AMERICANS, the other two ethnic groups whose unnaturalized immigrants were designated as ENEMY ALIENS. By contrast to Italian Americans and German Americans, who played important roles in the ECONOMY and had political influence, mainland Japanese Americans were few in number, often isolated and unassimilated, and politically powerless. Such factors also help to explain why the large numbers of people (up to 200,000) of Japanese ancestry who made up more than one-third of the population of militarily vulnerable Hawaii were not relocated.

The reason given for Executive Order 9066 and the relocation and incarceration of Japanese Americans was military security. And indeed there were fears and rumors of attacks, sabotage, and espionage on the West Coast, although never any evidence of them. But racism and racial prejudice were at the heart of what happened. Anti-Japanese sentiment and restrictions had shaped the Japanese experience in America. On the West Coast,

Japanese Americans had faced not only prejudice and discrimination in jobs and housing but also legal sanctions barring them from the full enjoyment of CIVIL RIGHTS. National law prevented Japanese immigrants from becoming American citizens.

The attack on PEARL HARBOR inflamed anti-Japanese feelings and triggered fear of Japanese Americans. Local citizens (some of them also harboring economic resentments against the Japanese) and politicians pressed for action, and the military agreed. Speaking for such groups, the army general in charge of the Western Defense Command said of the Japanese Americans: "A Jap's a Jap. . . . It makes no difference whether he is an American citizen or not. . . . Racial affinities are not severed by migration. The Japanese race is an enemy race."

Pressed by local and military officials, President Roosevelt agreed to Executive Order 9066 over the objections of Justice Department officials. Secretary of War HENRY L. STIMSON implemented the order only on the West Coast and only against Japanese Americans. Some 15,000 Japanese Americans moved of their own accord before such voluntary relocation was stopped, and more than 110,000 were relocated by the GOVERNMENT and incarcerated in internment camps run by the War Relocation Authority. Stimson understood that the policy made a "tremendous hole in our constitutional system." Nonetheless, the SUPREME COURT upheld the policy in *KOREMATSU V. UNITED STATES* (1944).

Some compensatory and corrective action was taken after the war. In 1948, CONGRESS approved some reparations to internees—$37 million for the relocation and the loss of an estimated $400 million in property. In 1988, Congress acknowledged the "fundamental injustice" of the policy and awarded $20,000 to each living survivor of the relocation.

Further reading: Roger Daniels, *The Decision to Relocate the Japanese Americans* (Philadelphia: Lippincott, 1975); Peter Irons, *Justice at War: The Story of the Japanese Internment Cases* (New York: Oxford University Press, 1983).

Executive Reorganization Act (1939)

The Executive Reorganization Act, passed in April 1939, authorized the creation of the Executive Office of the President, to include six presidential assistants. It also enabled President FRANKLIN D. ROOSEVELT to transfer the Bureau of the Budget to the Executive Office, to establish the NATIONAL RESOURCES PLANNING BOARD within the Executive Office, and to create a liaison officer for personnel management to enlarge the president's control over the federal bureaucracy. Reflecting Roosevelt's desire to streamline the executive branch and enable better policy planning and coordination by the White House, the Act was an important step in strengthening and modernizing the PRESIDENCY.

Yet the Executive Reorganization Act was significantly weaker than the executive reorganization bill Roosevelt had sent to CONGRESS in January 1937, and it thus marked not only a significant milestone in the development of the presidency but also a compromise reflecting the vicissitudes of Roosevelt's second term. Wanting to improve the administrative and management capacity of the presidency as the federal bureaucracy expanded rapidly and often confusingly with the proliferation of NEW DEAL agencies, Roosevelt established the President's Committee on Administrative Management in 1936. The committee proposed a number of reforms including: expanding the president's staff; moving the Bureau of the Budget from the Treasury Department to the White House; establishing a powerful planning agency in the executive branch; consolidating the many independent GOVERNMENT agencies into 12 cabinet departments reporting directly to the president; reorganizing the civil service and greatly extending the merit system. Taken together, the proposals would not simply have strengthened the executive branch but also would have substantially freed executive reorganization from congressional control and created a far more powerful administrative state controlled by the White House. Some scholars have seen in the executive reorganization bill the central aim of a THIRD NEW DEAL in which the administration sought to add enhancing the capacity of the executive branch to the FIRST NEW DEAL of 1933 and the SECOND NEW DEAL of 1935 that had created the modern regulatory welfare state.

But in the political context of Roosevelt's second term, the executive reorganization bill stood little chance. It was followed soon thereafter by the COURT-PACKING PLAN, which provoked great public and congressional resistance. Together, the two proposals raised the specter among conservatives of dangerous executive aggrandizement at the expense of both the legislative and the judicial branches. As other events of 1937 and 1938 diminished Roosevelt's influence in Washington and helped create a CONSERVATIVE COALITION in Congress, and as the course of Nazi Germany enabled critics to warn of an American dictatorship, the executive reorganization bill encountered growing opposition. In April 1938 the overwhelmingly Democratic House of Representatives defeated the president's proposal by eight votes. The bill was revived in much weaker form in 1939, lacking such important features as civil service reform and creation of new executive departments, exempting key independent agencies from reorganization, and enabling Congress to veto reorganization plans. The Executive Reorganization Act then won passage in April and took effect July 1, 1939. On September 8, Roosevelt established the Executive Office of the President.

Further reading: Barry D. Karl, *Executive Reorganization and Reform in the New Deal* (Cambridge, Mass.: Harvard University Press, 1963); Richard Polenberg, *Reorganizing Roosevelt's Government: The Controversy over Executive Reorganization, 1936–1939* (Cambridge, Mass.: Harvard University Press, 1966).

F

Fair Employment Practices Committee (FEPC)

On June 25, 1941, EXECUTIVE ORDER 8802 established the Fair Employment Practices Committee (FEPC), officially known as the President's Committee on Fair Employment Practice, to investigate and take action against discrimination based on race, creed, color, or national origin in the GOVERNMENT and defense industry. Created by President FRANKLIN D. ROOSEVELT under pressure from A. PHILIP RANDOLPH and the MARCH ON WASHINGTON MOVEMENT, the FEPC was the first federal agency established to address the CIVIL RIGHTS of AFRICAN AMERICANS since Reconstruction. The FEPC was also instituted to address employment bias against white ethnic groups, but the great majority of the FEPC's caseload involved discrimination against blacks.

Throughout the GREAT DEPRESSION, black workers suffered from extremely high levels of UNEMPLOYMENT due to the shattered ECONOMY and widespread discrimination in the labor market. The percentage of African-American workers in some industries was lower in 1940 than it had been in 1910. As MOBILIZATION for WORLD WAR II began to pour billions of dollars into the economy and to create hundreds of thousands of new jobs, the overwhelming majority of black workers continued to be excluded from all but a small percentage of the lowest paid and most onerous work in defense industries. Additionally, segregation and the denial of skilled and leadership positions for African Americans persisted throughout the military. Randolph and other black leaders, including WALTER WHITE, the secretary of the NATIONAL ASSOCIATION FOR THE ADVANCEMENT OF COLORED PEOPLE (NAACP), had been unable to gain any tangible concessions on the protection of the rights of African Americans from Roosevelt. Finally, with an all-black march on Washington, D.C., scheduled for July 1, 1941, the president issued Executive Order 8802, forbidding discrimination in many areas of the federal government and in companies with war contracts with the federal government and the unions they worked with. The directive did not include the armed forces.

The FEPC was authorized to conduct mediation and advise the government on employment discrimination but had little enforcement power. The only punitive measure it wielded was to suggest the discontinuation of war labor contracts with companies it found had violated the Executive Order—a suggestion quite unlikely to be taken because of the wartime need for defense production. In mid-1942, the FEPC was placed under the authority of the WAR MANPOWER COMMISSION, which proved reluctant to have the agency pursue complaints. A year later, upon the urging of civil rights leaders, Roosevelt established a new version of the FEPC in the Executive Office of the President, where it had more autonomy and authority.

Despite the variety of problems that plagued it during its five-year tenure, including insufficient funding, chronic understaffing, and the lack of real enforcement power, the FEPC was able to make some headway against employment bias as it urged unions to accept African Americans, pressured corporations in the defense industry to change their hiring policies, helped to resolve dozens of race-related strikes when white workers refused to work with blacks, held national public hearings, and received thousands of complaints yearly. Additionally, even as difficulties in the arena of RACE AND RACIAL CONFLICT continued to afflict the country, the FEPC and Executive Order 8802 contained great symbolic value as part of the struggle for civil rights.

The percentage of defense industry jobs filled by African Americans rose from 3 percent to 8 percent between 1942 and 1945, and the number of blacks employed by the federal government more than tripled. It is very difficult, however, to quantify the effectiveness of the committee as the heavy MIGRATION of blacks from the rural SOUTH to industrial centers and the tight labor market of wartime were also important factors in the increased employment and wage levels of African Americans. By one accounting, the FEPC successfully resolved only about one-third of the complaints it received, and only about one-fifth from the South.

By 1946, when the Fair Employment Practices Committee was dissolved because of opposition from CONGRESS, several states had created their own agencies to monitor discrimination, but an attempt to establish a permanent federal FEPC was killed by conservative and southern legislators. It was only with the Civil Rights Act of 1964 that many of the aims of the Fair Employment Practices Committee became national law.

Further reading: Merl E. Reed, *Seedtime for the Modern Civil Rights Movement: The President's Committee on Fair Employment Practice, 1941–1946* (Baton Rouge: Louisiana State University Press, 1991); Louis Ruchames, *Race, Jobs and Politics: The Story of FEPC* (New York: Columbia University Press, 1953).

—Aimee Alice Pohl

Fair Labor Standards Act (1938)

Signed by President FRANKLIN D. ROOSEVELT on June 25, 1938, the FAIR LABOR STANDARDS ACT (sometimes known as the Wages and Hours Act) established national minimum wage and maximum hours standards in manufacturing and prohibited employing child labor in interstate commerce. Although the CONSERVATIVE COALITION in CONGRESS succeeded in significantly limiting the bill's initial coverage, it marked a significant beginning for further reform.

The campaign for the Fair Labor Standards Act (FLSA) arose from the need to replace the wages, hours, and child labor provisions of the NATIONAL RECOVERY ADMINISTRATION (NRA) that were invalidated when the SUPREME COURT ruled the NRA unconstitutional in 1935 in the case of *SCHECHTER POULTRY CORPORATION V. UNITED STATES*. Regulating wages and hours and ending child labor had long been on the agenda of many liberals, and were reforms that Roosevelt and Secretary of Labor FRANCES PERKINS sought. The president also thought such legislation would help produce economic recovery, for higher wages would help create a market for both manufactured goods and agricultural products.

Several groups opposed the wages, hours, and child labor reforms. Conservatives and BUSINESS disliked such an extension of GOVERNMENT power over business. Many southerners feared that by creating a national minimum wage, the SOUTH would lose an attractive enticement for industry to locate there—low-wage labor. These southern congressmen wanted a wage differential that would create different minimum wage levels for each region of the nation, with the lowest minimum in the South. Conserva-

tive southerners also feared the impact on the region's social and racial patterns. Some LABOR leaders in the AMERICAN FEDERATION OF LABOR opposed the legislation, for they worried that the new minimum wage would eventually become the maximum wage and preferred to win better wages and other demands through collective bargaining rather than government regulations.

In May 1937, liberal Alabama senator HUGO BLACK introduced a federal wages and hours bill into the Senate. The Senate approved it within two months, but the bill faced much stiffer opposition and made much slower progress in the House of Representatives. Opponents who wanted to weaken the act by exempting industries and workers covered proposed dozens of limiting amendments. Not until May 1938 did a version pass the House; it then took another month for the House and Senate to agree upon the final bill.

In its final form, the Fair Labor Standards Act exempted agricultural workers, retail and service employees, domestic workers, fishermen, and others from the regulations. Many of these activities employed AFRICAN AMERICANS at wages much lower than the proposed minimum wage. The final version also limited application of the child labor provisions, exempting CHILDREN under 16 in such areas as AGRICULTURE and various retail and service employment where child labor was concentrated. Consequently the FLSA child labor provisions applied to only about 50,000 of the 850,000 child workers under 16 in 1938.

The FLSA set minimum wages at 25¢ per hour and maximum hours at 44 per week, with a provision that the minimum wage would rise to 40¢ per hour by 1945 and maximum hours would fall to 40 hours per week by 1940. The bill also provided for payment of wages at time and a half for overtime, and it established the Wage and Hour Division of the Department of Labor to supervise and enforce the FLSA. In the case of *United States v. Darby Lumber Co.* (1941), the Supreme Court upheld the FLSA as constitutional under the commerce clause of the Constitution.

Further reading: Irving Bernstein, *The Turbulent Years: A History of the American Worker, 1933–1941* (Boston: Houghton Mifflin, 1970).

—Courtney D. Mattingly

Farley, James A. (1888–1976)

With Louis McHenry Howe and EDWARD J. FLYNN, James A. Farley completed the triumvirate of FRANKLIN D. ROOSEVELT's closest political strategists. Like Flynn, Farley also served as chairman of the Democratic National Committee (DNC) during Roosevelt's presidency.

A second generation IRISH AMERICAN, Farley was born on May 30, 1888, in Grassy Point, New York, and even as a boy he expressed an interest in party politics. By his early 20s, he was actively involved in electioneering for the DEMOCRATIC PARTY. In 1911, Farley successfully ran for the office of town clerk in the predominantly Republican township of Stony Point, and by 1918, he was elected Democratic county chairman for Rockland County, New York. As chairman, he developed contacts with county party leaders, as well as with Tammany Hall, the prominent political machine of New York, and learned the effective use of patronage and the value of local organization.

In 1928, Farley was elected state secretary of New York's Democratic Party and managed Franklin Roosevelt's successful gubernatorial campaign, and then as state chairman managed Roosevelt's reelection campaign in 1930. Farley first achieved national recognition as the director of Roosevelt's bid for the presidency in the ELECTION OF 1932. He not only toured the country on behalf of FDR, but also assisted in securing Roosevelt's nomination by helping to persuade JOHN NANCE GARNER to release his delegates at the Chicago convention (Garner then received the vice presidential nomination). In 1932, Farley was appointed DNC chairman; after Roosevelt's inauguration, he was named postmaster general of the United States, holding both posts simultaneously.

Known by thousands simply as "Jim," Farley was an affable and engaging man. His personal style of campaigning, from his extensive use of correspondence to whirlwind tours of the country, helped him to develop a keen sensitivity to current sentiment among party leaders. As chairman of the DNC and as U.S. postmaster general, Farley used his influence over patronage during the 1930s to reward party members who supported the president and penalize those who did not. During the ELECTION OF 1936, his use of PUBLIC OPINION POLLS allowed him to concentrate on doubtful sections of the country and to accurately predict Roosevelt's landslide victory over ALFRED M. LANDON, who carried only Maine and Vermont.

During Roosevelt's second term, a rift developed between Farley and the president as FDR attempted to extend the power of the executive branch and pursued policies that conflicted with Farley's more conservative views. In 1938, Roosevelt attempted to punish his conservative opponents within the Democratic Party by using his influence to bring about their defeat in the congressional primaries. This "purge" strategy disturbed Farley, who felt it inappropriate for the president to interfere in local matters such as primary elections. In 1940, after Roosevelt's decision to run for an unprecedented third term, Farley resigned his cabinet post and his position as DNC chairman. At the Democratic convention in Chicago, he publicly protested FDR's decision by allowing his own name to be placed before the convention. Farley was nominated by Virginia senator Carter Glass, but won only 72 1/2 votes. However, despite his differences with the president, Farley reluctantly endorsed Roosevelt's candidacy in the ELECTION OF 1940.

After leaving the DNC, Farley turned to private industry, taking a post as chairman of the Coca Cola Export Corporation. He remained in politics as New York state party chairman, and in the ELECTION OF 1944 again opposed FDR's nomination but supported the president during the campaign. Retiring from politics after the 1944 election, he largely confined his efforts to business. On June 9, 1976, Jim Farley died one week before he was to be named chairman emeritus of the party at the Democratic national convention.

See also POLITICS IN THE ROOSEVELT ERA.

Further reading: James A. Farley, *Jim Farley's Story: The Roosevelt Years* (New York: Whittlesey House, 1948).
—Shannon L. Parsley

Farm Credit Administration (FCA)

On March 27, 1933, President FRANKLIN D. ROOSEVELT issued an executive order creating the Farm Credit Administration (FCA). The FCA increased the amount of credit available to farmers during the GREAT DEPRESSION, made it easier for farmers to refinance their farm mortgages and pay off their debts, helped shore up struggling rural banks, and more effectively coordinated the government's increasingly large and complex farm credit system.

After the STOCK MARKET CRASH of October 1929, many people who had deposited money in banks began withdrawing their money. In order to get cash for depositors, banks responded to the accelerating number of withdrawals by calling in their loans. But in many rural communities, falling land and commodity prices during the 1920s made it difficult for farmers to meet their loan payments. Consequently, thousands of small rural banks ran out of money and shut down, while many more were barely solvent. The failure of so many rural banks caused a severe credit shortage for farmers; the number of mortgage foreclosures rose sharply; and many farmers lost their life savings as well as their farms.

To resolve the financial crisis gripping America's banking system, President HERBERT C. HOOVER created the RECONSTRUCTION FINANCE CORPORATION, which was designed to help struggling banks increase their liquidity. But such efforts largely ignored the problems of farmers. Instead, Hoover relied on two institutions to extend credit to farmers: the Federal Farm Loan Board, which President Woodrow Wilson had created in 1916; and the Federal Farm Board, which Hoover created in 1929 when he signed the AGRICULTURAL MARKETING ACT. Yet, despite the efforts of the HOOVER PRESIDENCY, the credit shortage facing American farmers continued to worsen.

When the FCA became operational on May 27, 1933, it disbanded the Federal Farm Loan Board and Federal Farm Board and took over their remaining activities. On June 16, 1933, CONGRESS passed the Farm Credit Act, which gave congressional approval to Roosevelt's executive order creating the FCA. The chairman of the Federal Farm Board became the governor of the FCA, and a 13-member Federal Farm Credit Board was appointed to serve as the FCA's policymaking body. Roosevelt appointed HENRY T. MORGENTHAU, JR., as the first governor of the FCA, a position he held until early 1934 when he became secretary of the treasury.

The FCA supervised the operation of the nation's federal land banks, intermediate credits banks, farm loan associations, and the central bank for cooperatives. On an average day, the FCA could refinance more than 300 mortgages; within its first 18 months of operation, the FCA refinanced more than 20 percent of all farm mortgages in the United States. Through the Crop Loan Act, the FCA also gave loans to farmers for crop production and harvesting, and under the Farm Mortgage Refinancing Act, issued up to $2 billion in bonds for refinancing farm debts. By the end of 1940, the FCA had made a total of nearly $7 billion in loans, saved hundreds of thousands of struggling farms from foreclosure, and stopped thousands of small rural banks from declaring bankruptcy.

Although originally established as an independent GOVERNMENT agency, the FCA lost its independent status in 1939, when FDR, as part of his EXECUTIVE REORGANIZATION ACT, transferred it to the Department of Agriculture. It remained part of the Department of Agriculture until the Farm Credit Act of 1953 reestablished it as an independent agency.

See also AGRICULTURE; HOME OWNERS LOAN CORPORATION.

Further reading: David E. Hamilton, *From New Day to New Deal: American Farm Policy from Hoover to Roosevelt, 1928–1933* (Chapel Hill: University of North Carolina Press, 1991); Theodore Saloutos, *The American Farmer and the New Deal* (Ames: Iowa State University Press, 1982).

—David W. Waltrop

Farm Security Administration (FSA)

The Farm Security Administration (FSA) was a NEW DEAL agency created in 1937 to help sharecroppers, tenant farmers, migrant workers, and other American farmers cope with the problems of rural poverty during the GREAT DEPRESSION. However, because it adopted several approaches that alarmed conservatives, it quickly became one of President FRANKLIN D. ROOSEVELT's most controversial GOVERNMENT programs and had only limited success.

In early 1934, HARRY HOPKINS, director of the FEDERAL EMERGENCY RELIEF ADMINISTRATION (FERA), established a special division within the FERA to address the chronic problem of rural poverty in the United States. In 1935, President Roosevelt consolidated many of FERA's antipoverty efforts, as well as pieces of several other programs, into a new agency called the RESETTLEMENT ADMINISTRATION (RA). Headed by REXFORD G. TUGWELL, the RA provided disadvantaged farmers with technical support, debt reduction assistance, money for land rehabilitation, and loans to buy land and equipment. It also planned to give struggling farmers a fresh start by moving them from substandard land to new land with good soil, adequate equipment, and expert guidance. But because the RA lacked sufficient funds, it moved fewer than 4,500 of the planned half-million families it hoped to relocate, and hardly made a dent in alleviating the problem of rural poverty.

In early 1937, the President's Farm Tenancy Committee issued a report recommending that CONGRESS expand the rural antipoverty programs that had been developed by FERA and the RA. In July 1937, Congress approved the Bankhead-Jones Farm Tenant Act, which extended long-term, low-interest loans to poor farmers so that they could purchase their own farms. But because the farm tenancy report made it clear that struggling farmers needed much more assistance than the Bankhead-Jones Act provided, Secretary of Agriculture HENRY A. WALLACE established the Farm Security Administration with instructions to take over the remaining activities of the RA, implement the provisions of the Bankhead-Jones Act, and develop a unified approach to combat rural poverty.

From its inception through fiscal year 1947, the FSA's tenant-purchase program made available nearly $300 million in loans to just over 47,000 farmers, and as of May 1941, the FSA and its predecessor organization, the RA, helped work out debt reductions totaling almost $100 million for approximately 145,000 farmers. Under the leadership of Will W. Alexander, its first director, the FSA encouraged farmers to save money by pooling their financial resources, creating cooperatives, and selling their crops collectively. It helped migrant workers by maintaining a series of safe, sanitary, labor camps throughout the country. Because poor health often prevented farmers from working, the FSA worked with state and local authorities to establish special medical and dental care programs across the nation. The FSA also tried to treat AFRICAN AMERICANS fairly.

Despite the FSA's efforts and achievements, the dimensions of the problem were simply too great for the agency to solve. The FSA also faced fierce political opposition. The American Farm Bureau Federation feared that if poor farmers received too much assistance they might have the financial resources to open their own business, thus increasing the number of competitors, tightening the labor market, and raising the wages of workers. The American Medical Association opposed the FSA because it worried that the medical and dental cooperatives would reduce physicians' fees. Large farm corporations and southern landowners argued that the FSA undermined traditional landholding patterns. And congressional conservatives maintained that the FSA's relief efforts sounded too much like socialism, and viewed the entire agency as a liberal attempt to redistribute the nation's wealth. Even many of the FSA's own clients resented the agency, claiming that it was overly paternalistic and insisting that its loan management system interfered with their private lives.

During WORLD WAR II, the FSA took part in the RELOCATION OF JAPANESE AMERICANS. But with Roosevelt preoccupied with the war, congressional resistance to the President stiffening, and the need to cut nondefense spending growing, the power of the FSA rapidly declined. As a result, in 1941, Congress began to cut funding to the FSA, and by 1943 the agency was struggling for survival. President Harry S. Truman abolished the FSA in 1946 when he signed the Home Administration Act, and created the Farmers Home Administration in its place.

See also AGRICULTURE.

Further reading: Sidney Baldwin, *Poverty and Politics: The Rise and Decline of the Farm Security Administration* (Chapel Hill: University of North Carolina Press, 1968); Michael R. Grey, *New Deal Medicine: The Rural Health Programs of the Farm Security Administration* (Baltimore: Johns Hopkins University Press, 1999).

—David W. Waltrop

Faulkner, William (1897–1962)

Winner of the Nobel Prize in literature and the Pulitzer Prize in fiction, William Cuthbert Faulkner is one of the most celebrated American authors. His novels, poems, and short stories made Faulkner perhaps the most prominent figure in the LITERATURE of the American SOUTH. Among his best-known works are the novels *The Sound and the Fury* (1929), *As I Lay Dying* (1930), *Sanctuary* (1931), *Absalom! Absalom!* (1936), and *Intruder in the Dust* (1948).

William Cuthbert Faulkner was born on September 25, 1897, in New Albany, Mississippi, and grew up in the nearby town of Oxford, where he would spend much of his life. Oxford eventually provided the background for many of Faulkner's works. His education was not lengthy, for he left high school before graduating and later spent only a little over a year at the University of Mississippi. He joined the Royal Canadian Air Force during World War I, but returned home after a short stint during which he never saw combat. Faulkner's first published work was a poem, "L'Apres-Midi d'un Faune." The following years resulted in the appearance of several pieces in the University of Mississippi newspaper, as well as the release of a book of poetry entitled *The Marble Faun* (1924). His first novel, *Soldiers' Pay*, was published in 1926.

In 1932, Faulkner began working as a contract writer for MGM studios in Hollywood. Deciding that film was not his preferred medium, he asked on more than one occasion for a release from his contract, but it was not granted. For more than two decades, he continued to write screenplays for Hollywood MOVIES, as well as working on his own projects. He was awarded the 1949 Nobel Prize in literature for his accumulated works, and he won the Pulitzer Prize in 1955 for *A Fable* (1954), which also won the National Book Award for Fiction. In the 1950s, he spent a few semesters as writer in residence at the University of Virginia, where he was appointed to the faculty in 1960. In 1962, he died of a heart attack in Oxford.

In his writings, Faulkner created the fictional Yoknapatawpha County, Mississippi, based on Oxford and surrounding Lafayette County. He drew inspiration from people and experiences that he encountered in his life and created a community that seemed almost real, with many characters appearing in more than one work. Each family had its own history, and several generations might appear in one book or throughout several. The Snopes family, for example, was developed over the course of a trilogy. Quentin Compson, whose family's downfall is the subject of *The Sound and the Fury*, tells the story of Thomas Sutpen in *Absalom! Absalom!* Faulkner depicted the South as an area deeply rooted its the past, frequently with tragic results for the characters in his works.

Faulkner's writing style was dark and emotional. His narratives often contained aspects of the South's racial and class divisions, and of violence and immorality, including rape, incest, theft, and the heavy drinking to which he himself sometimes succumbed. Frequently making use of a stream-of-consciousness format, he switched thoughts and even timelines suddenly, sometimes even in the middle of a sentence. He tended to write in the vernacular, particularly for the characters in the lower classes. All of these characteristics make his writing difficult to understand for many, and unpalatable to others. Many, however, in Faulkner's own time and into the present, view him as one of the greatest authors in American history and as the greatest and most illuminating writer of the American South.

Further reading: Richard J. Gray, *The Life of William Faulkner: A Critical Biography* (Cambridge, Mass.: Blackwell, 1994); David L. Minter, *William Faulkner: His Life and Work* (Baltimore: Johns Hopkins University Press, 1980).

—Joanna Smith

Federal Art Project (FAP)

The Federal Art Project (FAP), which provided work for unemployed artists, was part of a revised effort by the NEW DEAL in 1935 to provide work RELIEF for the unemployed. Under the provisions of the EMERGENCY RELIEF APPROPRIATION ACT of April 1935, President FRANKLIN D. ROOSEVELT in May created the WORKS PROGRESS ADMINISTRATION (WPA), with HARRY HOPKINS as its administrator. Hopkins decided that part of the WPA's funds should be used to create federal programs to employ jobless artists and writers. The separate programs of the FEDERAL THEATRE PROJECT, FEDERAL WRITERS' PROJECT, FEDERAL MUSIC PROJECT, and Federal Art Project were collectively referred to as Federal One. Ultimately, some $40 million went to FAP, which helped an estimated 9,000 artists.

Hopkins appointed Holger Cahill as director of the FAP. Cahill's professional credentials were not as an artist but rather as a museum curator, art buyer, and prolific writer on American art. Preserving the skills of America's artists at all levels of proficiency and providing a source of income to impoverished artists were only part of the program's objectives. Cahill also desired that FAP artists feel a sense of participation in American life and that art be integrated into the lives of the American people by means of increased exposure to the arts.

Achieving such goals proved difficult despite the genuine concern of those involved in the FAP. At its peak in 1936, the FAP employed more than 5,000 artists nationwide, but spreading the program beyond the urban centers in which artists typically were concentrated proved a challenge. In November 1936, New York City and Chicago accounted for roughly half of all FAP employment. The most common operation of the FAP outside of urban areas involved community art centers, more than 100 of which were set up in 38 different states by 1940 in an attempt to achieve Cahill's dream of an art-conscious America. Inexpensive to operate and usually run by a small staff, the art centers provided classes for children and adults as well as exhibitions open to the entire neighborhood.

Most of the artists employed by the FAP were involved in the production of artistic works. FAP workers used many different media types. An estimated 2,500 murals, 18,000 sculptures, 108,000 paintings, 200,000 prints of 11,000 designs, and 2,000,000 silkscreen posters of 35,000 designs were produced throughout the life of the project. Region-

Poster for a Federal Art Project exhibition of art by WPA Federal Art Project artists at the Albany Institute of History and Art *(Library of Congress)*

alism and social consciousness were common themes in the art produced, which was often influenced by Mexican muralists as well as by LABOR rights organizations. The FAP's Index of American Design, an ambitious attempt to compile a pictorial survey of American art, involved research rather than original art. Traveling exhibitions of American art work reproduced as part of the index and exhibitions of FAP production pieces had attendance figures in the millions, including presentations at the World's Fairs in San Francisco and New York in 1939 and 1940. FAP murals and sculptures appeared in public buildings throughout the country.

Unlike the strong political criticism faced by the Federal Theatre Project, and, to a lesser degree, the Federal Writers' Project, criticism of the FAP focused on the skill level of the artists employed. Although the FAP nurtured such important artists as Jackson Pollock and Willem de Kooning, much of the original FAP art was of indifferent quality and was disdained by the professional and academic art communities.

By the beginning of WORLD WAR II, federal funding for the Federal One programs was eliminated, and control of the projects was transferred from Washington, D.C., to state administrations. With the transfer of control to state governments, community centers disappeared due to lack of funds, and the FAP dissolved in the face of wartime priorities and economic recovery. Cahill and his colleagues had failed to convince CONGRESS that federal support of the arts was a legitimate function of GOVERNMENT. During its lifetime, however, the FAP not only provided employment to artists during the GREAT DEPRESSION but apparently also contributed to an increase in public awareness of the arts.

See also ART AND ARCHITECTURE.

Further reading: William F. McDonald, *Federal Relief Administration and the Arts: The Origins and Administrative History of the Arts Projects of the Works Project Administration* (Columbus: Ohio State University Press, 1969); Richard D. McKinzie, *The New Deal for Artists* (Princeton, N.J.: Princeton University Press, 1973).

—Courtney D. Mattingly

Federal Bureau of Investigation (FBI)

The expansion of GOVERNMENT programs under the NEW DEAL went beyond social and economic reform to other areas, including crime control. To emphasize the expansion of the federal government in the area of law enforcement, the word "federal" was added to the title of the Justice Department's Bureau of Investigation in 1935, making it the Federal Bureau of Investigation (FBI). Legislation enacted in 1934 and 1935 also gave the FBI broader authority to seek fugitives, investigate bank robberies, and follow interstate thefts. During WORLD WAR II, its duties were expanded to include national security investigations.

This expansion in jurisdiction brought with it expansion in the FBI's staff and budget. In 1934, the agency had 391 special agents to conduct investigations; by 1935, it had 568. The FBI then grew to 1,596 special agents in 1941, and during World War II reached 4,886 special agents in 1944, with no further significant increases until 1952. The bureau's budget rose from $2.5 million in 1934 to $14.7 million in 1941, and peaked in 1945 at $44 million.

J. Edgar Hoover led the FBI during this period. Appointed in 1924 to straighten out the bureau's internal problems, Hoover had built an agency that was widely respected and he had developed significant political power himself. President FRANKLIN D. ROOSEVELT considered replacing Hoover, but decided to keep him, intending to use the FBI to lead a national effort to crack down on crime.

Hoover, ever aware of public image and the use of the NEWS MEDIA, sought with the Roosevelt administration's help to build an agency that would be recognized as the nation's premier crime control agency. Publicizing the bureau's exploits fighting gangsters such as Bonnie and Clyde and John Dillinger boosted its visibility. The agents were popularized in American culture as G-men—which stood for "Government Men"—when George "Machine Gun" Kelly shouted "Don't shoot G-men, don't shoot" during his arrest by the FBI.

As part of its expanded role, the bureau developed a central reporting system for fingerprint records, and its national forensic crime laboratory provided service to local law enforcement agencies that lacked detailed arrest records and evidence examination capabilities. To assist in further professionalizing law enforcement agencies, the bureau opened the FBI National Academy in 1935 to provide training in modern investigative methods and police management to law enforcement officers around the country.

As tension in Europe increased in the late 1930s, worries about fascists and COMMUNISTS led to investigation of people associated with such groups, and the bureau went beyond criminal investigations to establish a domestic INTELLIGENCE-gathering apparatus. National security concerns led to surveillance of dissidents and to infiltration of LABOR unions, political groups, and other organizations. Hoover even opened a file on the president's wife, ELEANOR ROOSEVELT, for her alleged association with communists.

While Hoover reported the resulting information to his direct boss, the attorney general, he was aware that it was also shared with the president. Through Attorney General Homer Cummings, Roosevelt requested Hoover to report on Earl Browder, the head of the Communist Party U.S.A., as well as individuals critical of the administration. At the direction of the White House, Hoover in 1937 and 1938 ordered investigations of the American Youth Congress, the Workers' Alliance, and some WORKS PROGRESS ADMINISTRATION employees, with investigative reports being forwarded to the White House.

In 1939, Roosevelt directed the FBI to coordinate ESPIONAGE investigations for the federal government. Its intelligence-gathering authority led the bureau to examine AXIS activities in the Western Hemisphere, with Hoover placing a number of agents in South American countries. The FBI exposed the largest spy ring in 1941, when 33 people were arrested in New York. The following year, 1942, eight German saboteurs were arrested shortly after they landed in New York and Florida.

While expansion in the 1930s and 1940s improved addressing national crime problems in a mobile society, it also increased the prestige of the FBI and the political influence of Hoover himself, whose conservative political purposes were often quite different from those of the Roosevelt administration. The broadened wartime authority of the agency to eliminate security threats also enabled the Roosevelt administration to keep tabs on troublesome foreign policy critics and political opponents. Both the salutary and the troubling features of the FBI and its practices would continue into the postwar era.

Further reading: Ronald Kessler, *The FBI* (New York: Pocket Star Books, 1994); Richard Gid Powers, *G-Men: Hoover's FBI in American Popular Culture* (Carbondale: Southern Illinois University Press, 1983).

—Edwin C. Cogswell

Federal Communications Commission (FCC)

The Federal Communications Commission (FCC) was established by the Communications Act of 1934 to regulate wired and wireless communications—RADIO and the telephone system especially—in the United States. One of the regulatory agencies established as part of the NEW DEAL, the FCC helped bring order and establish standards in the communications industry.

The FCC was created after a quarter-century of failed attempts by the federal GOVERNMENT to regulate the growing commercial radio broadcast industry. The latest effort had been the Radio Act of 1927 that established the Federal Radio Commission (FRC) under the Department of Commerce. The FRC reorganized licensing and frequency assignment and reduced some of the chaos produced by radio stations that changed frequencies, operated at whatever power and schedules suited them, and interfered with each other's operations. However, there were many problems with the FRC. CONGRESS approved the commission for only one year of operation, and annually had to renew its charter. Its authority was limited to radio. Other government agencies, such as the Interstate Commerce Commission, the Post Office, and the Department of State had responsibilities that overlapped those of the FRC. The advances in radio technology, the development of television, and the need to regulate telegraph and telephone communications also put pressure on the government to create a more centralized and responsive agency.

The Federal Communications Commission was one of a number of new federal agencies created during the presidency of Franklin D. Roosevelt. Shown here is the FCC's logo.
(Federal Communications Commission)

Late in the HOOVER PRESIDENCY, Congress proposed legislation to assign additional regulatory functions to the FRC, but President HERBERT C. HOOVER killed this bill with a pocket veto. A 1933 interagency government panel appointed by President FRANKLIN D. ROOSEVELT then recommended a single agency to regulate all communications. Roosevelt proposed such an agency in the Communications Act, which was easily passed by Congress in 1934. The FCC was part of a series of New Deal measures that brought the creation of new regulatory agencies (for example, the SECURITIES AND EXCHANGE COMMISSION and the NATIONAL LABOR RELATIONS BOARD) and the strengthening of existing ones (for example, the Interstate Commerce Commission and the Food and Drug Administration).

Early in its existence, the FCC faced many issues created by the commercial and technological advances of the communications industry. Commercial radio was entering its "golden age" of broadcasting, and the medium filled a large public need for information and entertainment. In addition to assigning specific frequencies to stations and establishing technical operating standards, the FCC in 1937 issued its first guidelines for radio program content and balance, ADVERTISING, and obscenity. It also initiated investigations into the industry practice of one company owning multiple radio networks and examined AT&T's telephone rate structure. The FCC worked closely with the new and developing communications technologies of the time and by 1940 had established the transmission standards for the dozen experimental television stations in the United States, and had approved the initial broadcasts of the first FM radio stations. The FCC also was asked to investigate the controversial *War of the Worlds* radio broadcast by ORSON WELLES.

When WORLD WAR II began, commercial radio station construction was halted and restrictions were placed on amateur radio use. The FCC performed radio INTELLIGENCE work in conjunction with the FEDERAL BUREAU OF INVESTIGATION (FBI), the State Department, and the military. This effort grew out of the FCC's Field Division, which had a nationwide net of monitoring stations supplemented by mobile units that measured the field strength of radio transmissions and located illicit stations. In 1940, the FBI asked the FCC to monitor German radio transmissions from the Western Hemisphere. In early 1942, the commission was asked to review the army's claim of ESPIONAGE content in radio transmissions by Japanese Americans, a charge it disproved. Later that year, a presidential order restricted the FCC from further work in radio intelligence with the military.

The FCC's principal contribution to the war was its work in Latin America. The Rio Conference of American Republics of January 1942 issued a resolution that called for the elimination of clandestine AXIS radio stations in the

Western Hemisphere. The FCC, in conjunction with the State Department and FBI, sent technical experts and equipment to 10 Latin American countries to help establish their own radio monitoring organizations. By the beginning of 1943, all clandestine Axis radio stations, except in Argentina, were shut down and their agents arrested.

The FCC proved to be an important regulatory agency for the communications industry in ensuring order and setting technical standards and content guidelines. Its efforts would facilitate the postwar explosion in commercial radio and television.

Further reading: Erwin Krasnow et al., *The Politics of Broadcast Regulation*, 3d ed. (New York: St. Martin's Press, 1982); Philip Rosen, *The Modern Stentors: Radio Broadcasters and the Federal Government, 1920–1934* (Westport, Conn.: Greenwood Press, 1980).

—Robert J. Hanyok

Federal Deposit Insurance Corporation (FDIC)

The Federal Deposit Insurance Corporation (FDIC) was created in 1933 to protect bank deposits in the event of a bank failure by insuring deposits up to a specified amount (which has increased over the succeeding decades). Established in the wake of the banking crisis of the early 1930s, the FDIC played a major role in restoring the stability of the banking system and public confidence in banks.

The first years of the GREAT DEPRESSION brought thousands of bank failures, and the number of closings accelerated in the winter of 1932–33. Banks failed in such numbers because their assets—mortgages and other loans, for example—had lost value to the point where they could not be converted into enough cash to cover deposit withdrawals. When one bank failed and depositors lost their money, panicked depositors of other banks tried to recover their money. This led to "bank runs" that only aggravated the situation and brought still more failures.

After President FRANKLIN D. ROOSEVELT was inaugurated in March 1933, he declared a bank holiday that closed all banks temporarily while his administration and CONGRESS worked on the EMERGENCY BANKING ACT OF 1933. Congress passed the act on March 9, and the banks began reopening on March 13. The emergency measures helped to restore some public confidence in the nation's banking system, but deposits remained vulnerable to runs and banks to possible failures.

Although Roosevelt wanted to defer further banking legislation, Congress initiated the push for federal insurance for bank deposits and passed the BANKING ACT OF 1933 in June. Separating commercial and investment banking and strengthening the Federal Reserve System, the act also created federal deposit insurance. Over the initial

objections of Roosevelt and his secretary of the treasury, the Federal Deposit Insurance Corporation was to begin operation on July 1, 1934; in the meantime, the Temporary Deposit Insurance Corporation (TDIC) was established to provide insurance protection for depositors. Deposit insurance guaranteed depositors their first $2,500, and all banks that were part of the Federal Reserve System were required to participate in TDIC by January 1, 1934. Non–Federal Reserve banks could join TDIC if they could prove the financial well-being of their institution. Overall, 90 percent of commercial banks and more than one-third of savings banks joined the TDIC.

FDIC was scheduled to succeed the TDIC in July 1934 under the Banking Act of 1933. Instead, at the urging of TDIC officials, Congress extended the TDIC through the summer of 1935. The BANKING ACT OF 1935 then strengthened the FDIC system created in 1933, and the FDIC began operations in August 1935. The major changes since 1933 included an increase in the amount insured to $5,000 per account, while the insurance fund was raised by a levy on the total bank deposits in an institution (one-twelfth of 1 percent). To address the fear that insuring deposits might be too expensive, FDIC was also given more power to supervise and ensure the financial health of member banks, including making loans to troubled banks, purchasing their assets, and helping mergers between institutions by issuing guarantees. Nearly all of the banks that had been part of the TDIC joined the FDIC and by 1941, almost all American banks were FDIC members.

The FDIC was one of the most successful reforms of the NEW DEAL. Between 1934 and 1941 there were only 370 bank failures, with the FDIC paying out almost $23 million to cover lost deposits. The failure rate in subsequent years was even lower (just 28 failures from 1942 through 1945, for example). By insuring the money Americans deposited in their banks, the FDIC helped to restore confidence in the banking system, worked to reverse the trend toward more bank failures, and contributed to the financial stability of banking institutions.

Further reading: Milton Friedman, and Anna Jacobsen Friedman, *A Monetary History of the United States* (Princeton, N.J.: Princeton University Press, 1963).

—Katherine Liapis Segrue

Federal Emergency Relief Administration (FERA)

By the winter of 1932–33, at the depths of the GREAT DEPRESSION, the UNEMPLOYMENT rate had soared to at least one-fourth of the labor force. Chief among the priorities of President FRANKLIN D. ROOSEVELT and his NEW DEAL administration upon talking office in March 1933 was the provision of financial assistance—or RELIEF—to unemployed Americans. On May 12, 1933, CONGRESS created the Federal Emergency Relief Administration (FERA) and authorized it to distribute $500 million to state and local governments. A week later Roosevelt named HARRY HOPKINS to head the new agency. The FERA was an important part of the FIRST NEW DEAL enacted during the first Hundred Days of the Roosevelt administration and of the New Deal's efforts to support unemployed and impoverished Americans until economic recovery could provide jobs.

Unlike the relief funds authorized by the 1932 RELIEF AND RECONSTRUCTION ACT of the HOOVER PRESIDENCY, the FERA granted rather than lent money to states and localities. Of the $500 million authorized by Congress, half would be granted directly on the basis of need and half would be spent on a matching basis of one federal dollar for every three state dollars. Hopkins, who had headed New York's Temporary Emergency Relief Administration when Roosevelt was governor of New York, was from the beginning a key adviser and policy maker in Roosevelt's administration and the central figure in New Deal relief policy.

Hopkins implemented the FERA with dispatch, spending some $5 million in his first two hours on the job and hundreds of millions more in the next weeks and months. Dispensing the money as quickly and flexibly as possible and having to rely upon an underdeveloped and inexperienced organizational structure, FERA invited criticism from opponents for inefficiency—and for the inevitable political use, especially by local officials, of relief spending. Hopkins and the FERA encountered additional difficulties in the reluctance of state officials to provide the money for matching grants. Sometimes that was because state constitutions forbade such spending or because poorer states simply lacked the fiscal capacity; but it was also because of fiscal conservatism and a disinclination to provide money to what some officials thought were the "undeserving" poor who were supposedly responsible for their plight despite the collapse of the ECONOMY. Racial and ethnic biases, not only in the SOUTH, also shaped distribution of FERA funds at the local level. To circumvent such resistance, to avoid inequity, and to reduce local political use of FERA funds, Hopkins increasingly relied on direct grants—and then often encountered criticism that the federal GOVERNMENT was interfering with state policymaking and subverting the American federal system.

At first, the FERA emphasized payments directly to the poor (the "dole"), which seemed essential to getting it to the unemployed needy as quickly as possible. But the process often seemed demeaning or degrading in a number of ways. After presenting themselves at a public "intake" room for screening, potential recipients had to undergo a "means" test whereby officials would closely examine income and spending habits prior to certifying applicants

for aid. Many FERA clients received only food or clothing or specific food orders instead of cash to spend as they desired. But while such direct relief disbursements in cash or kind continued for otherwise unemployable recipients (the aged, handicapped, and dependent children, for example), FERA funds increasingly went for work relief projects, which would hire the unemployed for such projects as constructing roads and buildings, and sometimes hired middle-class professionals as well. In this way, the FERA continued projects begun by the CIVIL WORKS ADMINISTRATION in the winter of 1933–34 and anticipated the efforts of the New Deal's major work relief program, the WORKS PROGRESS ADMINISTRATION, begun in 1935.

FERA projects erected some 5,000 public buildings and 7,000 bridges, built nearly a quarter million miles of new roads, and taught an estimated 1.5 million adults how to read. Project workers had to be on relief rolls and undergo the means test, and received on average only some $6.50 per week. Despite its limitations and difficulties, and the criticisms of politics, inefficiency, and useless but expensive "boondoggle" projects, the FERA was an important agency that helped hundreds of thousands of Americans and marked the federal government's acceptance of direct relief to the unemployed. It was phased out after the WPA, the SOCIAL SECURITY ACT, and other programs of the SECOND NEW DEAL of 1935 further defined the emerging American welfare state.

Further reading: Searle E. Charles, *Minister of Relief: Harry Hopkins and the Depression* (Syracuse, N.Y.: Syracuse University Press, 1963).

Federal Housing Administration (FHA)

The National Housing Act of 1934 created the Federal Housing Administration (FHA) to revive the HOUSING industry by ensuring long-term mortgages and stimulating the construction of new homes. Prior to the 1930s, home mortgages usually required a down payment of 35 percent or more, with the loan lasting only five to 10 years and necessitating a large "balloon" payment at the end. Many working- and lower-class Americans could not meet these stringent requirements to qualify for a home mortgage, and for the middle-class families who had bought homes in the 1920s, the economic collapse of the GREAT DEPRESSION created havoc in their ability to pay their mortgage. Compounding this problem was the fact that new home construction had nearly ground to a halt by 1933 because of the depression's impact on incomes and the housing industry.

NEW DEAL housing policy developed over the 1930s. In 1933, the first priority was to stop the avalanche of home foreclosures, and the HOME OWNERS LOAN CORPORATION was created in June 1933 to help by providing assistance in refinancing existing mortgages. The PUBLIC WORKS ADMINISTRATION also provided money at the local level to build new housing and provide jobs in construction, but the PWA, headed by HAROLD ICKES, was very cautious in granting money and the agency built little new housing by 1937. In 1937, the UNITED STATES HOUSING AUTHORITY was created to build urban public housing.

The FHA had two functions: to guarantee home mortgages by providing lenders insurance against default and to provide money for home modernization and construction. FHA initially proved disappointing in stimulating new home construction, but its insurance aspect had an immediate, discernible impact. Together with the HOLC's refinancing of existing mortgages, the FHA helped to stabilize the foreclosure rate on existing mortgages, which had reached 1,000 per day in early 1933. The FHA had clear rules on what condition homes needed to be in to qualify for an FHA guarantee, and this clarity provided standardization in the inspection of homes across the mortgage industry, including private inspections. The FHA also stimulated the issuance of new mortgages, as the agency was able to convince lenders to reduce the down payment needed to purchase a home and stretch payment terms to a more affordable 20- or 30-year period.

But the policies of the FHA had some unintended and negative consequences, particularly for America's central CITIES. Following the practices of private banks, FHA "red-lined" high risk areas of cities, refusing to insure homes in declining or blighted urban neighborhoods. Rental properties and home improvement loans were also viewed as high-risk investments. Rental unit construction dropped off markedly in the next several decades, from about 40 percent of all new home construction in 1927 to less than 10 percent in 1956. The FHA chiefly financed single-family home units in the SUBURBS, and this became one of the contributing factors to the acceleration of white, middle-class suburbanization during the post–WORLD WAR II period.

Further reading: Mark I. Gelfand, *A Nation of Cities: The Federal Government and Urban America, 1933–1965* (New York: Oxford University Press, 1975); Kenneth T. Jackson, *Crabgrass Frontier: The Suburbanization of the United States* (New York: Oxford University Press, 1985).

— Katherine Liapis Segrue

Federal Music Project (FMP)

The Federal Music Project (FMP) was one of several NEW DEAL projects that provided work RELIEF for a variety of people in the arts. Organized as part of the WORKS PROGRESS ADMINISTRATION (WPA) in 1935, these projects, collectively known as Federal One, also included the FEDERAL THEATRE PROJECT, the FEDERAL WRITERS' PROJECT, and the FEDERAL ART PROJECT. The FMP allowed thousands of musicians and MUSIC workers to continue their crafts and to enhance the cultural life of the nation through performances, instruction, composition, and the preservation of American musical traditions.

Even before the GREAT DEPRESSION struck, American musicians had experienced difficult times. Such innovations in TECHNOLOGY as the phonograph, RADIO, and the introduction of sound in MOVIES had replaced live with "canned" music and displaced thousands of performers. Prohibition caused many nightclubs and other musical venues to close down. With the additional impact of the depression, up to two-thirds of the nation's musicians were unemployed by 1933 by one estimate.

The choice of Nikolai Sokoloff, the Russian-born director of the Cleveland Orchestra, as national director of the Federal Music Project lent the project immediate prestige. Emphasizing orchestral over popular or folk music during his 1935–39 tenure, Sokoloff ensured that the FMP met the highest standards of musical competence as assessed by required auditions. Under his leadership of the FMP, the number of symphony orchestras in the United States expanded significantly, and a much larger segment of the public had access to "serious" music. A number of CITIES held composers' forums, where the performance of a new work was followed by discussions between composer and audience. The FMP sponsored compositions by such masters as Aaron Copland and Roy Harris and often broadcast its compositions over the radio.

But the FMP did much more than support and stimulate symphonic music. It put on free concerts across the nation, sponsored glee clubs, dance bands, and jazz ensembles, commissioned operas, and provided social music to communities in rural and small-town America. The FMP gave thousands of performances in hospitals and schools, sponsored music festivals across the country, and conducted workshops and panel discussions. The project also provided work for music teachers, music librarians, music therapists, and repairers of musical implements.

The FMP preserved not only the skills of musicians and music workers but also the nation's musical traditions. In 1938, it began cooperating with the WPA's committee on the folk arts, and recorded and studied music by AFRICAN AMERICANS, MEXICAN AMERICANS, and NATIVE AMERICANS, as well as other regional folk music. It employed thousands of music copyists to transcribe music for easier use by schools and libraries. And it launched the ambitious Index of American Composers project, which although never completed or published (it remains stored in the Library of Congress), includes some 20,000 entries on 7,300 compositions by more than 2,000 composers.

The FMP did not encounter the sharp ideological and political opposition of other Federal One projects, the Federal Theatre Project in particular, but it faced the same struggle for adequate appropriations from CONGRESS as did the others. When the Federal Theatre Project was terminated in 1939, the FMP and the artists and writers projects were allowed to continue under state and local sponsorship. Budget cuts reduced FMP rolls from their high of 16,000 to just 5,500 in 1939. With the coming of WORLD WAR II, the WPA Music Program (as it was called under local control) organized bands to play at armed forces training camps and worked with the military, until it was terminated in 1943 together with the other remaining arts programs.

Further reading: William F. McDonald, *Federal Relief Administration and the Arts: The Origins and Administrative History of the Arts Projects of the Works Project Administration* (Columbus: Ohio State University Press, 1969).

—Timothy Arnquist

Federal Theatre Project (FTP)

From its inception in 1935 until its demise in 1939, the Federal Theatre Project (FTP), created as a way to provide work RELIEF for an estimated 13,000 unemployed theater workers, faced challenges different from those encountered by most other NEW DEAL relief programs. Formed as a part of the WORKS PROGRESS ADMINISTRATION (WPA), the Federal Theatre Project, together with the FEDERAL WRITERS' PROJECT, the FEDERAL ART PROJECT, and the FEDERAL MUSIC PROJECT, made up an effort known collectively as Federal One to provide work relief for the arts. The FTP became the most controversial of these programs.

Hallie Flanagan, a Grinnell College classmate of New Deal relief administrator HARRY HOPKINS and head of Vassar College's Experimental Theatre, was chosen to lead the Federal Theatre Project. Enthusiastic about the FTP and its possibilities from the very beginning, the dynamic Flanagan believed that the project could and should be used for the creation of a socially relevant theater. She and the other project organizers intended to spread the FTP across the United States. Each region would have its own center, with local theaters established in the surrounding communities. Personnel would be recruited locally.

A thriving federal theater took root only in three cities. New York City had the most important programs, but Los Angeles and Chicago also built successful projects and loyal audiences. Actors of varied backgrounds and experience shared the stage. Successful productions resulted, including ORSON WELLES's production of *Mac-beth* with an all-black cast and *It Can't Happen Here,* Sinclair Lewis's controversial play about fascism. FTP audiences ultimately totaled an estimated 30 million people, and the program provided employment for thousands of theater people.

Despite its successes and the public support it gained, the Federal Theatre Project encountered a variety of challenges and problems. One of the most important issues faced by the FTP was whether the chief goal was to provide work relief or to create a quality theater, a debate that was never satisfactorily settled. Facing pressure from Washington to place workers on the payroll as quickly as possible in order to meet relief needs, many regional projects hired actors without auditioning them first. The result was typically an underqualified or inexperienced workforce. Challenges also came from the unions, which demanded that specific hours limitations be placed on workers; consequently, opening dates were often pushed back to allow for further rehearsals. In addition, commercial theater criticized the federal productions, claiming that they led to unfair competition.

Another problem that Flanagan faced was that she frequently lost well-qualified staff members because of the frustrations of working with uncooperative or unsympathetic GOVERNMENT officials. Within six months after the creation of the Federal Theatre Project, two-thirds of the original 24 regional directors had resigned their posts. Bureaucrats or relief workers with little or no interest in the artistic attributes of the project often replaced these valuable personnel.

A significant aspect of Hallie Flanagan's plan for a socially relevant theater was the creation of what were called Living Newspapers. The goal of these productions was to draw the public's attention to contemporary social or political issues. All were commercially successful, but each one also faced criticism from people in government. Members of Congress who were quoted in one production felt that they had been misrepresented by the context in which their words were placed.

In 1938, the project came under investigation by the House Un-American Activities Committee, led by the conservative Texas Democratic congressman Martin Dies. Accusations of New Deal propaganda and Communist sympathies in the FTP had been leveled for some time, from both inside and outside sources. For several weeks, witnesses were brought before the committee to testify about alleged—and sometimes real—radical and Communist activities within the FTP. When Hallie Flanagan appeared before the committee to defend the FTP, she was only allowed one morning in which to make her case, and was not permitted to complete her argument. By the time the investigations closed in late 1938, national public support for the Federal Theatre Project was dwindling.

Despite the negative publicity of the period during and immediately following the Dies committee hearings, successful shows continued to be produced in the major centers. However, the Federal Theatre Project was an endangered institution. It encountered not only ideological opposition but also criticism that its operations (and money) were focused too narrowly on New York and a few other big cities. In 1939, when the other Federal One arts projects were placed under state control, the Federal Theatre Project was abolished completely. Subsequent attempts to reinstate the project in 1940 and 1941 proved unsuccessful.

Further reading: Jane DeHart Mathews, *The Federal Theatre 1935–1939: Plays, Relief, and Politics* (Princeton, N.J.: Princeton University Press, 1967); William F. McDonald, *Federal Relief Administration and the Arts: The Origins and Administrative History of the Arts Projects of the Works Project Administration* (Columbus: Ohio State University Press, 1969).

—Joanna Smith

Federal Writers' Project (FWP)

The Federal Writers' Project (FWP) was one of four NEW DEAL arts projects, collectively known as Federal One, that were created as part of the WORKS PROGRESS ADMINISTRATION (WPA) in 1935 to provide work RELIEF for the unemployed. After conducting an occupational survey of families on relief, New Deal relief administrator HARRY HOPKINS realized the need for specific relief programs for white-collar workers, including writers and other artists. In addition to the FWP, the other arts projects were the FEDERAL THEATRE PROJECT, the FEDERAL ART PROJECT, and the FEDERAL MUSIC PROJECT. Congressional hostility and defense spending priorities during WORLD WAR II eventually led to the termination of the Federal Writers' Project and the other Federal One programs.

The FWP, under the direction of former journalist Henry Alsberg, gave thousands of unemployed writers work on over a thousand publications on American topics during the GREAT DEPRESSION. Early questions arose as to what a government-sponsored writers' project should do. The idea that FWP writers would simply work on government manuals and reports was quickly discarded as bureaucratic and mundane. Another option would have given writers freedom to select their own projects, including novels, short stories, and poems. This was seen as risky, however, because of the potential for controversial content. Ultimately, the FWP focused chiefly on nonfiction.

But the FWP was characterized by ambiguity of aims from its inception and was often criticized for pedestrian work. Bringing together ambitious young writers, librarians, journalists, and teachers, once-talented writers past their literary prime, and writers with very little talent or experience, the FWP involved a peculiar and precarious mix of individuals. Relatively few of its participants were creative writers, and pressure for instant results hastened the writing process, generating numerous books and pamphlets that later often made for dull reading, even though good editing in Washington improved much of the submitted work. The writers' project was never intended to produce great LITERATURE, although a number of notable writers worked on the FWP, including RICHARD WRIGHT. Peak FWP employment came in April 1936, with nearly 6,700 women and men on its payrolls, and the project employed some 10,000 writers in all.

FWP writers produced a popular collection of guidebooks, the American Guide series, for each of the states, major cities and counties, regions of the country, and interstate highway routes. As the published volumes of the American guides delved deeper below the surface of American life, the FWP progressed from a set of tour books, almanacs, educational pamphlets, and natural history books to introductory essays of the state guides, county and local histories, ethnic studies, and folklore studies that added to national self-knowledge. The FWP's Life in America series contained some 150 volumes on a range of topics. Interviews with former slaves and life histories of southern black tenant farmers, farm and cotton-mill owners, and workers published in *These Are Our Lives* (1939) gave new perspectives to American history and more knowledge about the plight of the marginalized and dispossessed. Such attention to the downtrodden was a common theme in depression-era art and literature, and the FWP's most productive period, 1935–40, was a time when the Great Depression inclined Americans to seek knowledge about the past and each other.

The need for a larger defense budget in the years leading up to World War II siphoned off federal dollars from the FWP, as did criticism from conservatives, including the House Committee on Un-American Activities and its chairman Texas Democratic congressman Martin Dies. The Dies committee targeted the FWP as a "Red nest" and "a festering sore of communism." By 1939, budget cuts had forced the project to scale down to 3,500 workers, although it was so popular that every state provided money to keep it alive when CONGRESS reduced funding in 1939. The Federal Writers' Project was eliminated along with the WPA in 1943 and much of its unpublished work was lost or destroyed. Even so, the FWP left a substantial legacy in its American Guide and Life in America series and in its compilations of folklore and oral histories.

Further reading: Jerre Mangione, *The Dream and the Deal: The Federal Writers' Project, 1935–1943* (Boston: Little, Brown, 1972); William F. McDonald, *Federal Relief*

Administration and the Arts: The Origins and Administrative History of the Arts Projects of the Works Project Administration (Columbus: Ohio State University, 1969).

—Joseph C. Gutberlet

First New Deal

The first Hundred Days of the administration of President FRANKLIN D. ROOSEVELT marked the beginning of what scholars have come to call the First New Deal of 1933, which emphasized economic recovery from the GREAT DEPRESSION and RELIEF assistance to the unemployed.

Historians have long used a "two New Deals" framework to impose order on the myriad agencies and pieces of legislation of the NEW DEAL, and to understand the changes in the policies and legislative agenda of between the First New Deal of 1933 and the SECOND NEW DEAL of 1935, which emphasized social reform. Although the first- and second New Deal model tends to exaggerate change in policy and ideology between 1933 and 1935 while often overlooking continuities, it has nonetheless proven a useful conceptual framework. (Recently scholars have also identified a THIRD NEW DEAL in Roosevelt's second and third terms.)

Unlike his predecessor, HERBERT C. HOOVER, Roosevelt, counseled by members of his BRAIN TRUST, attributed the causes of the Great Depression to structural flaws in the American economy and to a failure to regulate BUSINESS. The Roosevelt administration thus turned toward an enlarged role for the federal GOVERNMENT in regulating and stabilizing the ECONOMY. In addition to programs designed to provide relief, the most prominent of which was the FEDERAL EMERGENCY RELIEF ADMINISTRATION, the administration implemented programs to use national government planning to prevent further economic decline and promote recovery through the coordination and regulation of private industry and AGRICULTURE.

The two key agencies that embodied this philosophy behind the First New Deal were the Agricultural Adjustment Administration (AAA) created by the AGRICULTURAL ADJUSTMENT ACT, and the NATIONAL RECOVERY ADMINISTRATION (NRA) developed in 1933 to carry out the provisions of the NATIONAL INDUSTRIAL RECOVERY ACT. The AAA used subsidies and taxes to control farm production and raise prices on agricultural goods. The NRA suspended antitrust laws for those companies that complied with its codes for production, prices, and employment practices. By 1935, however, after the Supreme Court decision in *SCHECTER POULTRY CORPORATION V. UNITED STATES* declared the NRA unconstitutional, policymakers began to turn away from efforts to advance recovery through planning and controls, and looked toward social reform to provide both immediate relief and long-term security during the Second New Deal.

Further reading: William E. Leuchtenburg, *Franklin D. Roosevelt and the New Deal, 1932–1940* (New York: Harper, 1963); William H. Wilson, "The Two New Deals: A Valid Concept?" *The Historian* 28 (February 1966): 268–88.

—Shannon L. Parsley

Flynn, Edward J. (1891–1953)

Edward Joseph Flynn, a New York lawyer and leader of the Bronx County [New York] Democratic organization, rose to national prominence as a political adviser to FRANKLIN D. ROOSEVELT. Flynn was a close associate of Roosevelt's during the 1920s, and in 1928 helped to persuade FDR to run for governor of New York. Throughout the 1930s and 1940s, Flynn continued to serve Roosevelt as an informal adviser, and in 1940 succeeded JAMES A. FARLEY as chairman of the DEMOCRATIC PARTY National Committee.

Flynn was born on September 22, 1891, to a well-to-do IRISH AMERICAN family in New York, and in 1912 graduated from Fordham Law School. He entered politics in 1917 as a member of the New York State Legislature, where he remained for four years. Flynn was then elected sheriff of Bronx County and in 1922 was elected chairman of the Bronx Democratic committee. After Roosevelt was elected governor of New York in 1928, Flynn accepted an appointment as New York secretary of state. In 1932, Flynn worked with James Farley and Louis Howe in helping to win the presidential nomination for Roosevelt. Flynn continued to use his influence as Bronx County leader and as national committeeman for New York to garner support for the president throughout the 1930s. In 1938, during FDR's attempt to "purge" the Democratic Party of conservative opponents to the NEW DEAL, Flynn campaigned on behalf of pro–New Deal candidates for the president. Although, concerned for the president's health, he urged Roosevelt not to seek a third term in the ELECTION OF 1940, Flynn helped HARRY HOPKINS to organize the efforts to renominate Roosevelt at the Chicago convention.

In 1943, FDR appointed Flynn minister to Australia and ambassador-at-large for the South Pacific. This appointment provided fodder for Roosevelt's critics in the Senate, who argued that Flynn was unqualified for the job. In order to stave off the developing controversy Flynn withdrew his name. Although Flynn, anticipating his appointment, had resigned his position as Democratic National Committee chairman, he returned to the DNC until he was succeeded by Robert Hannegan in 1944.

With the ELECTION OF 1944, Flynn was assigned the task of finding a suitable vice-presidential candidate. He settled on Missouri senator Harry S. Truman and helped secure his nomination. After FDR's death, Flynn largely retired from national politics. He remained involved in local politics and emerged as a champion of the liberal wing of the Democratic Party in New York during the postwar struggle between liberals and conservatives, led by James Farley. In 1953, Edward Flynn died while on vacation in Ireland.

See also POLITICS IN THE ROOSEVELT ERA.

Further reading: Edward J. Flynn, *You're the Boss* (New York: Viking, 1947).

—Shannon L. Parsley

Food, Drug, and Cosmetic Act (1938)

The Food, Drug, and Cosmetic Act of 1938 strengthened the power of the Food and Drug Administration, a federal regulatory agency created in 1906 to protect American consumers from harmful food and drug products. Strengthening the FDA was consistent with NEW DEAL efforts to increase the regulatory power of the federal GOVERNMENT. It was also consistent with New Deal efforts to better balance consumers' and producers' interests and to include consumers as a constituency in the agencies of the federal government, beginning with the establishment of the Consumer Advisory Board of the NATIONAL RECOVERY ADMINISTRATION in 1933.

In working to protect the public from unsafe food and drugs in the 1930s, the Food and Drug Administration was constrained by inadequate statutory power and by limited funding and staffing. Products continued to come on the market that harmed, and sometimes killed, consumers, despite the best efforts of the FDA's modest staff of fewer than 250 chemists and inspectors. In 1937, the Massengil Company distributed a new drug for syphilis, Elixir of Sulfanilamide, which contained an untested lethal solvent that caused more than 100 deaths. The ensuing stir revealed the FDA's weaknesses and spurred the passage of a stronger statute the following year.

The resulting law, the 1938 Food, Drug, and Cosmetic Act, one of the last New Deal successes in strengthening the regulatory powers of the federal government, gave the FDA new power to eliminate abuses in production, labeling, and advertising, as well as additional authority over cosmetics and medical devices. The law also gave the FDA power to establish legally enforceable food standards, to conduct factory inspections, to enforce injunctions on seized products and companies, and to require the premarket approval of drugs.

In the years after 1938, the FDA enjoyed enhanced power, activity, and success, even though wartime priorities brought some decrease in the agency's staffing. SUPREME COURT decisions in the 1940s and 1950s upheld FDA actions on ADVERTISING and confirmed its power in overseeing and regulating food, drugs, and cosmetics.

Further reading: Charles O. Jackson, *Food and Drug Legislation in the New Deal* (Princeton, N.J.: Princeton University Press, 1970).

—David Slak

foreign policy

The foreign policy of the United States from 1929 to 1945 was marked by the gradual reemergence of a major American presence in world political and military affairs. The domestic problems wrought by the GREAT DEPRESSION and a continuing adverse reaction to World War I and the nation's participation in it limited the U.S. role in international politics throughout much of the 1930s. The coming of WORLD WAR II compelled the United States to take an active part in the global geopolitical arena. Producing a national consensus for ongoing American involvement and leadership in world affairs and making the United States the world's great superpower, rivaled only by the Soviet Union, World War II dramatically changed the nation's foreign policy and world role.

After World War I, many Americans believed that large corporations who desired lucrative military contracts had orchestrated U.S. involvement in the war, and suspicion of big business and of internationalism deepened after the STOCK MARKET CRASH of 1929. President HERBERT C. HOOVER, a firm believer in international cooperation, economic and otherwise, attempted to alleviate the global crisis through collaboration with European nations to restore the international economy as well as working for arms reduction agreements at the LONDON NAVAL CONFERENCE and the WORLD DISARMAMENT CONFERENCE. A number of factors, including German and Japanese ambitions for arms parity, prevented the success of these efforts at international peace and prosperity. The protectionist HAWLEY-SMOOT TARIFF ACT, signed by Hoover in 1930, worked against international cooperation and contributed to the failure to halt the downward spiral of the American and world economies.

As the United States struggled in the depths of the depression, the international scene grew increasingly more ominous. Imperial Japan invaded MANCHURIA in September 1931, and Hoover adopted the policy of "nonrecognition" by refusing to acknowledge diplomatically the Japanese conquest of Manchuria. This essentially passive policy, called the Stimson Doctrine after Secretary of State HENRY L. STIMSON, would be representative of American foreign policy toward global turmoil for much of the next decade.

FRANKLIN D. ROOSEVELT succeeded Hoover as president in 1933, and while Roosevelt never withdrew from international affairs as much as American ISOLATIONISTS hoped, the foreign policy of his first term was marked by noninterventionism. Global affairs took second place to Roosevelt's primary concerns with American domestic troubles, as shown by his action during the LONDON ECONOMIC CONFERENCE of 1933. While Roosevelt initially seemed eager to cooperate in an agreement on currency stabilization, he abruptly withdrew American support from the tentative settlement after being convinced that global currency stabilization could harm American economic recovery. Other examples of the administration's approach to foreign policy include American recognition of the Soviet Union in November 1933 (partly in hopes of economic benefits for the United States) and the concurrent development of the GOOD NEIGHBOR POLICY toward Latin America. Although SOVIET-AMERICAN RELATIONS did not change much in the short run, restraint in Latin America allowed the United States to avoid active intervention while developing relationships with nations whose goodwill would later become important.

Nonintervention remained the most distinguishing feature of American foreign policy through the mid-1930s. The emergence of expansionist aggressor governments in Europe and Asia seemed at first to be disturbing but unrelated phenomena that posed little threat to the United States, as the Japanese continued their assault on China and Italy invaded ETHIOPIA. The outbreak of the SPANISH CIVIL WAR in 1936 changed this situation, however, when Germany and Italy sided with General Francisco Franco's Fascist regime in their attempts to oust the Soviet-aided republican government of Spain. In addition, Germany, Italy, and Japan signed an anti-Comintern (really an anti-Soviet) pact in November 1937. While the treaty indicated the possibility of conflict between totalitarian nations of the right and left that were often hostile to American interests, it also signaled the more ominous prospect of cooperation among Germany, Japan, and Italy, the three militarily aggressive nations on two separate continents.

In 1935, the United States enacted the first of the NEUTRALITY ACTS, and then extended them in subsequent years to avoid American involvement in the conflicts in Europe. Roosevelt did exert some authority by not cutting the Chinese off from American arms after the Sino-Japanese War began. By 1939, however, the situation in Europe had grown even more menacing. At the September 1938 MUNICH CONFERENCE, the British and French made unsuccessful attempts to appease Nazi Germany by acquiescing in its seizure of part of Czechoslovakia, but Hitler took the remainder of Czechoslovakia in March 1939.

With the signing of the NAZI-SOVIET PACT in August 1939 and the formal beginning of World War II the following month with the German invasion of Poland, the United States began slowly, but steadily, moving toward anti-AXIS intervention. The United States had already begun a naval buildup, and then, in the autumn of 1939 enabled the British and French to purchase American arms by amending the Neutrality Acts so that the CASH-AND-CARRY provisions would allow belligerents to buy arms as long as they paid in cash and transported their purchases in non-American vessels. The United States was more assertive with Japan, abrogating the commerce treaty between the two nations.

The beginning of World War II thus found the United States sympathetic to the Western democracies and China, but still hoping that the nation might stay out of the war. Hostility toward Germany and Japan grew, however, especially after the Nazi attack on western Europe in the spring of 1940, and American opinion increasingly turned toward actively supporting the Allies. Roosevelt continued to seek ways to help the British and French, including the DESTROYERS-FOR-BASES DEAL of September 1940 in which the United States exchanged 50 overage destroyers for British naval bases in the Western Hemisphere. This new initiative came just before Germany, Italy, and Japan signed the Tripartite Pact on September 27, cementing the Rome-Berlin-Tokyo Axis.

In the meantime, the United States continued to prepare for the possibility of war. The SELECTIVE SERVICE System was begun in the autumn of 1940. Moral embargoes against the Japanese were extended into mandatory bans on the sale of aviation fuel and scrap iron outside the Western Hemisphere. The United States also began to plan strategy with the British, who had been left alone to fight the Axis powers after the French surrender to Germany in June 1940. American leaders believed that the Nazi-Soviet alliance was doomed to failure, but were not certain when the split might come. It occurred in June 1941, when Germany abrogated the nonaggression pact and invaded the Soviet Union.

The United States and Japan undertook talks in the summer of 1941 that proved to be a final, fruitless attempt to prevent war. The Americans insisted that the Japanese, who had concluded a neutrality treaty with the Soviets in April 1941, should respect the territorial integrity of China and restore the status quo of 1937, while the Japanese hoped to use American influence to generate a settlement with the Chinese legitimating Japanese encroachment in China. Cut off from American oil by embargo and believing that additional territorial expansion in pursuit of more oil would invite American retaliation, the Japanese began to prepare the December 7, 1941, attack on the United States at PEARL HARBOR, Hawaii.

Meanwhile, Roosevelt continued to do what he could to aid the nations fighting Germany in Europe. He extended military aid to the Soviets as well as to the British under the LEND-LEASE ACT of 1941, and U.S. warships patrolled the Atlantic. After one of these ships, the *Greer,* was attacked by a German submarine in September 1941, FDR issued a "shoot on sight" order toward Axis vessels that entered American "defensive" waters of the Atlantic. Continued submarine attacks on American ships prompted Roosevelt to authorize merchant vessels to carry arms. The United States conducted these activities as an undeclared war until the Japanese attack on Pearl Harbor. Following the American declaration of war on Japan on December 8, Germany declared war on the United States on December 11. The United States was now at war against the Axis Powers.

American entrance into World War II solidified the GRAND ALLIANCE of the United States, Great Britain, and the Soviet Union. The alliance grew out of the closer ANGLO-AMERICAN RELATIONS created by cooperation between Roosevelt and the new British prime minister, Winston Churchill beginning in 1940. The Soviet Union joined the alliance after endorsing the objectives of the war as outlined in Roosevelt and Churchill's ATLANTIC CHARTER of August 1941. The three nations concluded that Nazi Germany posed much the greatest threat and that war strategy should thus focus on defeating Germany first.

Wartime strategy nonetheless became a sticking point for the various members of the alliance. The Soviets desperately wanted the Americans and British to open a SECOND FRONT in western Europe to relieve German pressure on the eastern front that was causing enormous death and destruction in the Soviet Union, but neither the Americans nor the British were ready for such a move in 1942. Despite this delay, the Soviets were able to turn the tide of the war in favor of the Allies by repulsing the German siege of Leningrad and forcing a German surrender at Stalingrad. Although Stalin continued to demand a second front, the Soviet successes allowed the Americans and British to postpone the opening of this second front until spring 1944.

From the beginning of the war, Franklin Roosevelt thought about the postwar world as well as wartime strategy. He hoped that the members of the wartime alliance, along with China, would emerge as global leaders that could preserve the peace. Especially at the late 1943 TEHERAN CONFERENCE and the early 1945 YALTA CONFERENCE, the Allies discussed both military strategy and the restructuring of the postwar world. The mechanisms for international political and economic cooperation included not only the new UNITED NATIONS, but also the International Monetary Fund (IMF) and the World Bank agreed to at the BRETTON WOODS CONFERENCE. In working for the creation of such organizations, Roosevelt was supported by a dramatic wartime transformation in public and congressional opinion away from the isolationism and noninterventionism of the 1930s and toward overwhelming agreement that the United States should play a leading role in the postwar world and in a collective security organization to keep the peace. Roosevelt hoped to achieve a post-

Prime Minister Winston Churchill addressing the U.S. Congress, December 1941 *(University of Kentucky Libraries)*

war world order in which all peoples would have the right to peaceful self-determination and in which the United Nations, led by the United States, Great Britain, the Soviet Union, and China, would provide a means by which stronger, more prosperous nations could keep the peace and assist weaker nations with military protection or economic development.

The Soviet Union and Great Britain, however, did not always share Roosevelt's vision of the world to come, causing tensions to emerge between the Allies once victory appeared inevitable. The British were reluctant to dismantle their colonial empire, but a far more serious source of discord was the Soviet desire for a sphere of influence in eastern Europe to address their security concerns. The Allies managed to come to agreement on tentative general principles governing the new power structure, but it was clear that serious ideological differences and divergent national aims were straining the Grand Alliance.

A number of other events then accelerated the deterioration of the Grand Alliance, including Roosevelt's death in April 1945 and Germany's surrender in May. Without Roosevelt and without a mutual enemy, the alliance lost important cementing forces. In addition, the development of the ATOMIC BOMB by the United States promised to change global politics forever. The tensions caused by these events were evident at the last of the wartime conferences of the Grand Alliance, the POTSDAM CONFERENCE. Issues that had been major points of conflict at Yalta, such as the independence of Poland and German reparations, remained so at Potsdam. The Allies were able to agree on the course the rest of the Japanese war would take, but discussion on European questions only illustrated how much the Grand Alliance had deteriorated. The British shared enough common interests with the United States that their relationship was not seriously affected by disagreements, but Soviet-American relations continued to worsen.

The Japanese surrender in August 1945 brought an end to World War II, leaving the United States and Soviet Union as the unquestioned leaders of the new global order. This position, however, presented a whole host of new problems for American diplomacy and the new determination by the United States to play a leading role in global affairs on behalf of international peace and prosperity and American interests and principles. The United States found itself in a developing cold war with its former ally, the Soviet Union, in a world where the specter of nuclear war made global conflict more dangerous than ever before.

Further reading: Warren I. Cohen, *Empire without Tears: America's Foreign Relations, 1921–1933* (Philadelphia: Temple University Press, 1987); Robert Dallek, *Franklin D. Roosevelt and American Foreign Policy, 1932–1945* (New York: Oxford University Press, 1979); Robert A. Divine, *Second Chance: The Triumph of Internationalism in America during World War II* (New York: Atheneum, 1971); Robert A. Divine, *The Illusion of Neutrality* (Chicago: University of Chicago Press, 1962); Robert A. Divine, *The Reluctant Belligerent: American Entry into World War II,* 2d ed. (New York: Wiley, 1979); Akira Iriye, *The Globalizing of America, 1913–1945* (New York: Cambridge University Press, 1993); David M. Kennedy, *Freedom from Fear: The American People in Depression and War, 1929–1945* (New York: Oxford University Press, 1999).

—Mary E. Carroll-Mason

Forrestal, James V. (1892–1949)

James Vincent Forrestal, who helped transform the U.S. NAVY into the largest and most powerful naval force in the world during World War II, served as undersecretary of the navy (1940–44), secretary of the navy (1944–47), and then as the nation's first secretary of defense (1947–49).

Forrestal was born on February 15, 1892, in what is now Beacon, Dutchess County, New York, to IRISH AMERICAN parents. He attended Princeton University, but left weeks before his graduation in 1915 (after failing an English course) and went to work as a bond salesman for a Wall Street investment firm. With the U.S. entry into World War I in 1917, Forrestal enlisted in the navy and became a naval aviator, although he never went overseas. He returned to Wall Street in 1920 and was a prominent figure there for two decades.

Embittered by a power struggle in his company, Forrestal left Wall Street to work as a special assistant to President FRANKLIN D. ROOSEVELT in 1940 to aid in the war MOBILIZATION effort. Within two months, he was appointed undersecretary of the navy, where he helped build the massive U.S. fleet by coordinating procurement and contracts. He became the secretary of the navy after William Franklin Knox died in April 1944, and worked hard to impress the navy's achievements upon the public. Forrestal also toured the battlefronts, including IWO JIMA; what he saw, according to Rear Admiral Ellis M. Zacharias, "turned his dislike of war into hatred of war." As victory in the war came closer in 1944–45, Forrestal turned his attention to the potential threat from the Soviet Union in a postwar world. At the POTSDAM CONFERENCE, Forrestal argued against using the ATOMIC BOMB without warning, and against requiring unconditional surrender from Japan.

President Harry S. Truman named Forrestal the nation's first secretary of defense in 1947, despite Forrestal's opposition to the unification of the armed forces under the National Security Act of 1947. As defense secretary, Forrestal aided in shaping the cold war policy of containment to limit the growth and power of the Soviet Union and communism. Forrestal opposed some of Truman's administration policies, including low defense budgets and the emphasis on AIR POWER. In March 1949, Truman asked for Forrestal's resignation. Suffering from physical and mental exhaustion, Forrestal was hospitalized in April. He committed suicide on May 22, 1949, jumping from the 16th floor of the Bethesda Naval Hospital where he was undergoing psychiatric treatment.

Further reading: Townsend Hoopes and Douglas Brinkley, *Driven Patriot: The Life and Times of James Forrestal* (New York: Knopf, 1992).

—Michael T. Walsh

Four Freedoms

In his State of the Union address of January 6, 1941, President FRANKLIN D. ROOSEVELT stressed the importance of opposing the AXIS nations in WORLD WAR II and preserving democracy. Outlining measures that included the increased production of war materials, he announced his decision to send CONGRESS his proposal for the LEND-LEASE ACT, which, if passed, would allow the United States to significantly increase aid to Britain's war efforts. Roosevelt supported his position on these issues by introducing the concept of "a world founded upon four essential human freedoms." He defined these freedoms as the freedom of speech, freedom of religion, freedom from want, and freedom from fear.

The freedoms of speech and religion paralleled those set forth in the Bill of Rights of the U.S. Constitution. Roosevelt characterized freedom from want as "economic

Poster for the Four Freedoms *(Library of Congress)*

Frankfurter, Felix (1882–1965)

Felix Frankfurter was a distinguished law professor, an important adviser to President FRANKLIN D. ROOSEVELT and the NEW DEAL, and an associate justice of the United States SUPREME COURT.

Frankfurter was born on November 15, 1882, in Vienna, Austria, and immigrated at age 12 with his parents to the United States. Although he spoke no English when he arrived in the United States, he went on to study at the City College of New York and then Harvard Law School where he edited the *Harvard Law Review*. While a law student at Harvard, Frankfurter developed a lifelong friendship with Louis D. Brandeis, later a Supreme Court justice. He came to share especially Brandeis's ANTI-MONOPOLY conviction that economic concentration should be limited because of the economic and political harm it produced.

When he became a professor at Harvard Law School, Frankfurter took a keen interest in his students, seeking to place them in clerkships with leading judges and later in important GOVERNMENT posts. While teaching administrative law, Frankfurter also advised then New York governor Franklin D. Roosevelt on public utilities regulation and recommended individuals for various state positions.

After Roosevelt was elected president in 1932, Frankfurter continued to advise him on a wide range of issues, including personnel appointments. Frankfurter's counsel to Roosevelt was generally in the areas of antitrust policy, securities regulation, TAXATION reform, and public utility regulation. Although Frankfurter was offered the post of solicitor general, he declined it, believing it would limit his ability to influence liberal reforms. Frankfurter also served as an informal placement bureau, assisting bright, liberal, young lawyers in finding government positions—and those who came to Washington on Frankfurter's recommendation were referred to as the "happy hot dogs."

The death of Justice Benjamin Cardozo in 1938 left a vacancy on the Supreme Court, and Roosevelt nominated Frankfurter as his successor. Many applauded his nomination because of Frankfurter's work for CIVIL LIBERTIES and his support of liberal causes. On the Court, he proved reluctant to overturn policy, and concurred with the majority in *KOREMATSU V. UNITED STATES* (1944), which upheld the RELOCATION OF JAPANESE AMERICANS by the government. Although sometimes disappointing his liberal supporters, Frankfurter's philosophy of judicial restraint was consistent with liberal criticism of the Supreme Court's invalidation of New Deal programs in the mid-1930s.

After 23 years on the Court, Frankfurter retired in poor health in 1962. He died three years later in Washington, D.C.

understandings which will secure to every nation a healthy peacetime life for its inhabitants," and freedom from fear as "a world-wide reduction of armaments to such a point and in such a thorough fashion that no nation will be in a position to commit an act of physical aggression against any neighbor." He maintained that it was possible to create a world in which these Four Freedoms predominated, and indicated that the United States should support those who sought such a world.

The concept of the Four Freedoms, a powerful image that was simply expressed and that had clear philosophical similarities to the NEW DEAL, came to represent American views of the war and why it was being fought. The Four Freedoms became the subject of an extremely popular illustration by the artist Norman Rockwell that was distributed by the OFFICE OF WAR INFORMATION. Yet despite the role of the Four Freedoms in wartime rhetoric and in shaping memories and understandings of the war's meaning, just 13 percent of military personnel asked about them during the war could name three of the Four Freedoms, and one-third could not name one. Americans believed in the Four Freedoms, but they fought the war especially to achieve victory and to enjoy better days at home.

—Joanna Smith

Further reading: Michael E. Parrish, *Felix Frankfurter and His Times: The Reform Years* (New York: Free Press, 1982).

—Edwin C. Cogswell

Full Employment Bill (1945)

The Full Employment Bill proposed in 1945 called for the federal GOVERNMENT to ensure a full-employment economy. It reflected both the new emphasis of LIBERALISM on Keynesian fiscal policy to underwrite full-employment prosperity as well as the prevailing public concern about jobs once the economic stimulus provided by the MOBILIZATION for WORLD WAR II had ended. The bill faced substantial opposition from conservatives and BUSINESS, and in its final form was enacted as the watered down, though still important, Employment Act of 1946.

The Full Employment Bill embodied the new importance in the liberal agenda of KEYNESIANISM that had emerged as central to the THIRD NEW DEAL during and after the RECESSION OF 1937–38 and that had been confirmed and enhanced by the wartime prosperity produced by heavy government spending. As liberals and LABOR planned postwar domestic policy, they came to focus especially on full employment, an emphasis that dovetailed with the concern among most Americans about sufficient postwar jobs. The POSTWAR PLANNING reports of the NATIONAL RESOURCES PLANNING BOARD reflected this emphasis on full employment, as did other postwar initiatives by liberals and by the FRANKLIN D. ROOSEVELT administration. The ECONOMIC BILL OF RIGHTS that Roosevelt espoused in 1944 included the right to a job, and in the ELECTION OF 1944 both Roosevelt and Republican nominee Thomas E. Dewey indicated their support of a full-employment economy. PUBLIC OPINION POLLS showed that postwar jobs ranked highest in public priorities.

In early 1945, liberals in CONGRESS introduced the Full Employment Bill, to commit the government to sufficient spending to ensure jobs for all Americans. But the bill, the centerpiece of the mid-1940s liberal agenda, encountered opposition from the powerful CONSERVATIVE COALITION in Congress, and as prosperity continued after the end of the war it commanded relatively little support from the public. In 1946, Congress enacted and President Harry S. Truman signed the Employment Act of 1946, an attenuated measure that called for "maximum" rather than "full" employment, did not provide for the "right to a useful and remunerative job" that the original bill had specified for all Americans able and willing to work, and lacked explicit Keynesian provisions for mandatory compensatory fiscal policy to ensure full employment. But the employment act did create the new Council of Economic Advisors, and it did reflect not only the new importance of Keynesian perspectives but also the government's new responsibility since the GREAT DEPRESSION and the NEW DEAL for the performance of the economy and the economic welfare of the American people.

Further reading: Stephen Kemp Bailey, *Congress Makes a Law: The Story behind the Employment Act of 1946* (New York: Columbia University Press, 1950).

G

Garner, John Nance (1868–1967)

John Nance Garner served two terms as vice president of the United States under President FRANKLIN D. ROOSEVELT, from 1933 to 1941. Prior to becoming vice president, Garner had represented southern Texas in the House of Representatives for more than 30 years, and had been elected speaker of the House in 1931. Nicknamed "Cactus Jack," Garner came to regret leaving the House for an office he regarded as powerless, or in his well-known words, "not worth a pitcher of warm spit."

Born in western Texas on November 22, 1868, Garner had little formal education and left Vanderbilt University after less than a year to study law on his own in Clarksville, Texas. Admitted to the bar at 22, Garner was elected to the Texas House of Representatives in 1898, and in 1902 won a seat in CONGRESS. Best known for his expertise in taxes, tariffs, and poker, he had a command of legislative process that led to his selection as Speaker of the House in 1931. As Speaker, Garner's support for a national sales tax to balance the budget during the GREAT DEPRESSION reflected his deeply conservative views. But he was also a fierce DEMOCRATIC PARTY partisan who as the ELECTION OF 1932 approached exerted his influence to thwart Republican president HERBERT HOOVER's programs and embarrass the president.

Garner became a candidate for the Democratic nomination for president in the spring of 1932. Falling far short, he released his delegates to Roosevelt, who then offered Garner the vice presidential nomination. As vice president, Garner's amiable style and political savvy made him a useful liaison with Congress, and he facilitated passage of early NEW DEAL programs. But Garner was never personally or philosophically close to the president. Like other conservative southern and rural Democrats, Garner increasingly objected to the emerging New Deal regulatory welfare state—especially its spending and LABOR policies. Following Roosevelt's controversial COURT-PACKING PLAN of 1937, Garner became a leader of the CONSERVATIVE COALITION in Congress opposing the New Deal, although he did so privately rather than publicly, winning the title, "con-niver-in-chief."

Garner's conservative allies convinced him to consider running for president in 1940. But he had no real chance at the Democratic nomination, and he left Washington in 1941, after 38 years in government, vowing to never again come east of the Potomac. John Nance Garner died in Uvalde, Texas, on November 7, 1967, days before his 99th birthday.

Further reading: Timothy Walch, ed., *At the President's Side: The Vice Presidency in the Twentieth Century* (Columbia: University of Missouri Press, 1997).

—Joseph C. Gutberlet

gays and lesbians

The period from 1929 to 1945 brought significant developments for gays and lesbians in the United States. Despite societal disapproval and sanctions, the emergence of a more active homosexual subculture in such major CITIES as New York and Los Angeles in the late 1920s and 1930s helped gays and lesbians find new opportunities to pursue their sexuality and to achieve a greater collective consciousness. Then MOBILIZATION and MIGRATION during WORLD WAR II uprooted millions of Americans, contributed to greater sexual permissiveness in American society, and produced nonfamilial and often sex-segregated environments in urban areas and the military where gays and lesbians could meet others like themselves and find support and solidarity. Although the military undertook efforts to winnow out homosexuals, gay men and lesbians served in all branches of the armed forces during the war.

During the interwar years, gays and lesbians increasingly developed friendship networks and meeting places, particularly in big cities, and often gained greater acceptance among younger city dwellers. But a society and legal system rooted in the Judeo-Christian tradition remained hostile to homosexuality, which was widely condemned as immoral, and to homosexual acts, which were typically made criminal under the law. Doctors supported a medical model that understood homosexuality as congenital disease, and some performed sterilization to prevent carriers from passing the disease on to future generations. Meeting places for gays and lesbians, often controlled by organized crime and situated in out-of-the-way locations, remained open at the pleasure of police. Patrons of gay bars risked entrapment and arrest, and gays and lesbians typically pleaded guilty to avoid further embarrassment in court proceedings that aimed to inculcate shame. Despite the development of gay communities in urban areas, then, the interwar years also meant continuing dangers and proscriptions and public socializing remained unusual.

Complexity also characterized gay and lesbian history during World War II. As young gays and lesbians joined the armed forces and relocated to urban settings to help with mobilization efforts, they found in the unusually sex-segregated arrangements of wartime America opportunities to encounter other homosexuals and forge personal ties and supportive networks. Some found that wartime mobilization reinforced the greater freedom they had already experienced before the war. On the other hand, the war years also brought new sanctions against homosexuality by the military and produced in many communities efforts to enforce old standards of behavior against what seemed improper sexual permissiveness among both homosexuals and heterosexuals.

Prior to World War II, the armed forces had not screened for homosexuality. But by 1943, military psychiatrists convinced the U.S. NAVY and the U.S. ARMY to establish policies banning gays and lesbians from military service. For the first time—and unlike the policies of other nations at war—the military medical examination forced homosexuals, previously accustomed to a measure of privacy, to face public inquiry. Few gay or lesbian inductees revealed their homosexual identity in these examinations, and only superficial and stereotypical signs of homosexuality were noticed by psychiatrists, who because of time constraints typically conducted hasty, perfunctory screenings. Only a tiny number of homosexuals were denied entry into the military or were subsequently discharged, but in the postwar era proscriptions against homosexuals in the military became routine, and some gay veterans who had been discharged were denied benefits under the GI BILL OF RIGHTS. Many gay men nonetheless served with distinction on the battlefronts. Lesbians generally experienced fewer difficulties in the military than did gay men.

For gays and lesbians, the events of the 1930s and the war years thus brought continuing and sometimes increased scrutiny and sanctions, but they also brought new opportunities and experiences that helped lay foundations for the more cohesive and assertive gay subculture of the postwar era.

Further reading: Allan Bérubé, *Coming Out Under Fire: The History of Gay Men and Women in World War II* (New York: Free Press, 1990); George Chauncey, *Gay New York: Gender, Urban Culture, and the Makings of the Gay Male World, 1890–1940* (New York: Basic Books, 1994); John D'Emilio, *Sexual Politics, Sexual Communities: The Making of a Homosexual Minority in the United States, 1940–1970* (Chicago: University of Chicago Press, 1983).

—Joseph C. Gutberlet

German Americans

German Americans represented one of the largest and oldest ethnic groups in the United States. An upwardly mobile group that was largely assimilated by the 1930s, German Americans' experiences during the GREAT DEPRESSION differed from those of newer immigrants. During World War II, the striking differences between the experiences of German Americans and of other ENEMY ALIENS underscored the degree to which German Americans had become accepted members of society.

While the immigration of Germans to America dates back to the colonial period, the largest influx of Germans began in the mid-19th century. Although German IMMIGRATION declined after 1890, first- and second-generation German Americans represented about 6 percent of the total U.S. population by 1930, and all Americans of German descent accounted for a significantly larger proportion of the population. In the mid-1930s, German immigration rates again began to rise as political and Jewish REFUGEES, among them many educated professionals, arrived from Germany.

German Americans in the 1930s and 1940s were scattered in rural and urban areas throughout the country and had established a strong occupational structure. Although many German Americans remained concentrated in the manufacturing industries, German Americans by the 1930s increasingly occupied positions not only as skilled workers but also in white-collar and professional jobs. Given their range of occupations, the experiences of German Americans varied considerably with the onset of the depression.

During the depression, however, the political response of many Germans to the failures of the HOOVER PRESIDENCY in dealing with the depression had a significant impact on the balance of party power in the United States. Traditionally supporters of the REPUBLICAN PARTY for the most part, German Americans had slowly begun to break away from the GOP in the 1920s. However, with the depression and the ELECTION OF 1932, greater numbers of German Americans began to shift their support to FRANKLIN D. ROOSEVELT and the DEMOCRATIC PARTY, and with the ELECTION OF 1936, they continued generally to endorse the NEW DEAL policies of the Roosevelt administration.

As FOREIGN POLICY began increasingly important in the late 1930s and U.S. policy became increasingly anti-AXIS, many German Americans recalled their experiences during World War I, when they were viewed with suspicion and were often the victims of persecution—a shocking experience that had led them to assimilate still further in the aftermath of the war. In the late 1930s, German ethnic ties became important again as the Nazi Party received support from groups such as the German American Bund. Roosevelt's anti-Axis policies alienated a substantial number of German-American voters during the ELECTION OF 1940. But very few German Americans supported the Bund or Nazi Germany, and during World War II, German Americans, unlike ITALIAN AMERICANS and Japanese Americans, experienced little discrimination or difficulty. Despite some concerns about the loyalty of German Americans and such "fifth column" activities as sabotage and ESPIONAGE, the idea of relocating German aliens was quickly abandoned. German Americans contributed vitally to the war effort, both on the home front and in the armed forces.

If the World War II experience clearly signified the acceptance of German Americans, it also revealed the continued erosion of a distinct German-American ethnic identity. As newer German and Austrian immigrants arrived, they quickly adopted American customs. By the 1940s, many of the elements that bound ethnic Germans together, including the German-language press and mutual aid societies were gone or disappearing, either as a result of the depression or due to concerted efforts among Germans to assimilate.

Further reading: Ronald H. Bayor, *Neighbors in Conflict: The Irish, Germans, Jews, and Italians of New York City, 1929–1941* (Baltimore: Johns Hopkins University Press, 1978); Stephan Thernstrom, ed., *Harvard Encyclopedia of American Ethnic Groups* (Cambridge, Mass.: Belknap Press of Harvard University, 1980).

—Shannon L. Parsley

GI Bill of Rights

Officially entitled the Serviceman's Readjustment Act, the GI Bill of Rights provided a wide array of benefits designed to help veterans back into the civilian mainstream after WORLD WAR II. It turned out to be one of the landmark pieces of social legislation of the mid-20th century.

The GI Bill had multiple origins. In part, it came from proposals in 1943 of the NATIONAL RESOURCES PLANNING BOARD (NRPB) and of President FRANKLIN D. ROOSEVELT. As CONGRESS was working on several bills to assist veterans, the American Legion recommended an omnibus bill early in 1944 that after being modified and somewhat weakened by conservatives gained widespread support and was signed into law by Roosevelt in June 1944. Though a significant piece of reform legislation that underwrote upward mobility for veterans in the postwar era, and the only such reform measure passed by the conservative 78th Congress, it was supported not so much as a reform but as a reward for veterans and their service. Its passage also reflected the lobbying efforts of the American Legion and the political power of the millions of servicemen and their families and friends. The press immediately dubbed the law the GI Bill of Rights, with the "GI" standing for Government Issue, the label soldiers had given themselves.

An estimated 16 million people were eligible to participate in the GI Bill programs administered by the Veterans Administration (VA). More than 10 million veterans ultimately collected benefits. The law did not discriminate on the basis of race or sex. Although originally intended to expire in 1956, the popularity and success of the GI Bill moved Congress to extend the law to allow veterans from virtually every conflict since World War II to benefit from the program.

The GI Bill included direct benefits for unemployment and job assistance, as well as business and farm loans and aid to disabled veterans and their dependents. The most significant elements of the law, however, were the benefits that helped veterans further their EDUCATION and acquire homes. Veterans were free to attend the educational institution of their choice. While attending class, the VA paid the veteran's full tuition and up to $500 per year for related school costs. They also received a monthly stipend of $50 if they were single and $75 if married for living expenses and to ease other financial burdens. Congress later increased the stipend amounts.

By 1948, nearly half of all male college students participated in the education benefits program, and in the 10 years that the full education benefits were made available, nearly 7 million veterans received tuition and training through the GI Bill. This unprecedented increase in college enrollment strained the resources of many universities, often resulting in shortages of student housing, classrooms, and faculty. Despite such problems, the GI Bill had a major impact on higher education by reshaping the popular image of college and helping to democratize higher education in America.

The GI Bill also helped veterans get their piece of the American dream by offering low interest mortgages. The law empowered the VA to issue payment guarantees for home lenders who made mortgages to veterans, and it capped the interest rate on these loans. With such liberal financing terms, veterans could buy a home without a down payment and make monthly payments that were less than prevailing rentals. By 1947, more than $4 billion in mortgages had VA guarantees, and 15 years later the figure exceeded $50 billion. Furthermore, the increase in mortgage funds resulted in thousands of houses built specifically for veterans and their families.

The VA mortgage program helped increase the level of homeownership significantly after World War II. Within ten years of the creation of the GI Bill, 57 percent of all nonfarm homes were owner-occupied, a dramatic increase from the 1940 level of just 41 percent. Furthermore, because much of this new HOUSING was in the SUBURBS, the GI Bill had a major effect on how Americans lived. Of the 13 million new homes built in the 1950s, 85 percent were in suburbs. Because many of these new homeowners were white, the GI Bill indirectly contributed to the so-called white flight from the CITIES.

Further reading: Keith W. Olson, *The G.I. Bill, the Veterans, and the Colleges* (Lexington: University Press of Kentucky, 1974); Davis R. B. Ross, *Preparing for Ulysses: Politics and Veterans during World War II* (New York: Columbia University Press, 1969).

—Dave Mason

Goodman, Benny (Benjamin David) (1909–1986)

Benny Goodman was one of the greatest jazz clarinet players of all time and the leader of one of the most important and famous big bands of the 1930s and 1940s. Known as "the King of Swing" because of his contributions to swing MUSIC, Goodman was a stylistic and technical innovator in big-band jazz.

Benjamin David Goodman was born the eighth of 12 children to a poor immigrant Jewish family in Chicago, Illinois. He enjoyed a gift for music, and studied under both classically trained and popular musicians in Chicago. Throughout the 1920s, Goodman was fascinated by the music of the jazz bands that dominated the Chicago entertainment scene. Although he became an accomplished classical clarinetist, it was in jazz that Goodman made his towering contributions. He began full-time professional employment in music at age 16 when he joined Ben Pollack's band in Venice, California. In the fall of 1929, Goodman left the band and began to perform as a freelance sideman with a variety of groups on RADIO and records.

In 1934, Goodman began developing a revolutionary musical style when he organized his own band to make records for release in England. He based his band's organization on the traditional jazz band of the time, but wanted every musician in his band to be able to solo at any given moment while at the same time having the capability to play in harmony with the rest of the band. This produced a band that could perform both jazz and the standard dance numbers of the day. In combining the two forms, building a remarkably strong rhythm section, and incorporating some of the "hotter" jazz of Fletcher Henderson's music, Goodman helped create a style of music called swing.

The Goodman band performances of the 1930s and 1940s became sensations, to popular audiences and jazz aficionados alike. Hiring extraordinarily talented musicians and getting the most from them, Goodman helped to give jazz a new legitimacy in 1938 when his band played in New York's Carnegie Hall to rave reviews. In addition to his big band performances and recordings, he also led important smaller groups and ensembles. And Goodman (himself influenced heavily by black musicians, including Henderson and DUKE ELLINGTON) took the unusual step of giving public performances with integrated groups, although he was motivated more by a desire for good music than by social reform.

With the decline of big band jazz after WORLD WAR II and the rise of such star attraction singers as FRANK SINATRA and the emergence of rock and roll, Goodman and the other swing era bandleaders lost much of their popularity. Goodman died, still a legend, in 1986 of a heart attack at age 77.

Further reading: James Lincoln Collier, *Benny Goodman and the Swing Era* (New York: Oxford University Press, 1989); Ross Firestone, *Swing, Swing, Swing: The Life and Times of Benny Goodman* (New York: Norton, 1993).

—Nicholas Fry

Good Neighbor policy

Most closely identified with the administration of President FRANKLIN D. ROOSEVELT, the Good Neighbor policy established the practice of nonintervention as the hallmark of United States FOREIGN POLICY toward Latin America. American policymakers hoped that ending U.S. intervention (especially military and political intervention) in the domestic affairs of Latin American countries would create healthy economic and political ties among the nations of the Western Hemisphere and combat the challenges presented by the GREAT DEPRESSION and by the increasing global tensions that would culminate in WORLD WAR II.

Historians disagree about the degree to which the Good Neighbor policy had its origins in the Republican administrations of the 1920s but agree that the first significant steps toward a noninterventionist policy toward Latin America occurred during the HOOVER PRESIDENCY. President HERBERT C. HOOVER rejected Theodore Roosevelt's "corollary" to the Monroe Doctrine, which had asserted the right of the United States to intervene in the affairs of nations in the Western Hemisphere if necessary to maintain order. Hoover ended American occupation of Nicaragua and committed to do the same in Haiti, but these good-faith attempts at ending military intervention were largely overshadowed by widespread dissatisfaction in Latin America at the passage of the HAWLEY-SMOOT TARIFF ACT in 1930, which reduced imports to the United States.

Franklin Roosevelt's actions toward Latin America expanded Hoover's noninterventionist policy into what is now known as the Good Neighbor policy. FDR's first major step toward this end came in his support for a resolution stating that "no state has the right to intervene in the internal or external affairs of another." This resolution, passed at the 1933 Pan-American Conference held in Montevideo, Uruguay, where the American delegation was led by Secretary of State CORDELL HULL and Assistant Secretary of State SUMNER WELLES, was followed by a number of substantive actions to implement the policy, ending 30 years of armed intervention by the United States in Latin America. Roosevelt honored Hoover's commitment to withdraw the United States military from Haiti, leaving troops in the Panama Canal Zone as the last American military forces remaining outside United States territory. In 1934, FDR abrogated the Cuban constitution's Platt Amendment, a stipulation that authorized United States intervention in Cuban domestic affairs. Roosevelt maintained the policy of the "good neighbor" even when it was put to its greatest test when the Mexican government nationalized the Mexican oil industry, including property belonging to several American oil firms, in 1938. Rejecting pressure from BUSINESS interests to use armed force to reclaim the American property, Roosevelt negotiated a compensatory settlement between the Mexican government and the oil corporations.

The Good Neighbor policy reflected an increasing tendency toward hemispheric regionalism in foreign policy. This regional approach allowed the United States to pursue international measures for economic recovery and, later, defense, while maintaining a safe distance from increasingly complicated European affairs. The good faith generated by the approach of the "good neighbor" allowed the United States to establish economic agreements with many Latin American nations under the auspices of the RECIPROCAL TRADE AGREEMENTS ACT. Diplomatically, the Good Neighbor policy achieved its most notable success in December 1938, when the United States joined with the other republics of the American continents to sign the Declaration of Lima, agreeing to consult each other if war threatened any portion of the Western Hemisphere. This expression of solidarity was the first of its kind among the nations of the Western Hemisphere. After

the U.S. entrance into World War II, this cooperation continued among the republics of North and South America as all but Argentina agreed to sever diplomatic relations with the AXIS powers at the Rio de Janeiro Conference of January 1942. Throughout the war, the nations of the Western Hemisphere collaborated in mutual defense against potential German submarine attack and sent troops to aid Allied forces.

While many of the connections initiated in this era between the United States and its Latin American neighbors were maintained after World War II, the Good Neighbor pledge of nonintervention was not sustained in the postwar era. The beginning of the cold war and fears of the spread of communism once again brought American military presence into Latin America to quell political instability.

Further reading: Irwin F. Gellman, *Good Neighbor Diplomacy: United States Policies in Latin America, 1933–1945* (Baltimore: Johns Hopkins University Press, 1979); Bryce Wood, *The Making of the Good Neighbor Policy* (New York: Columbia University Press, 1961).

—Mary E. Carroll-Mason

government

From 1929 to 1945, the American federal government grew enormously in size, power, and cost in order to cope with the GREAT DEPRESSION and then to mobilize the nation for WORLD WAR II. Particularly in the 1930s, state and local governments also took on new responsibilities.

Although the changed contours of American government by 1945 were largely a product of the exigencies of depression and war and of the leadership of President FRANKLIN D. ROOSEVELT, the preexisting structure, culture, and heritage of the American political system also shaped—and limited—what government did. Structurally, the American political system was characterized by a federal state of national, state, and local governments, and by a separation of executive, legislative, and judicial power. Ideologically, the American political culture included strong antistatist concerns about a powerful national government and corresponding emphases on states' rights, individualism, and a market economy. State and local governments were limited by their own legal authority and traditions—and by SUPREME COURT decisions that had also restrained the power of the federal government. As American government at all levels had expanded since the late 19th century in response to the challenges of modernizing change, its growth and authority had been constrained by such factors.

At the onset of the Great Depression, American government thus lacked the capacity—the size, authority, and expertise—to cope with such an economic and social calamity. Soaring UNEMPLOYMENT quickly outstripped the ability of private agencies and of local and state governments to deal with widespread impoverishment, while the federal government did not have the tools to meet the economic and social problems of the depression. President HERBERT C. HOOVER was in any case opposed to federal RELIEF programs or other extensions of federal authority that might create a powerful regulatory or welfare state. Partly because of action by CONGRESS, the HOOVER PRESIDENCY nonetheless did do more than any previous administration to deal with hard times. New agencies and programs were initiated, the number of federal employees rose slightly, and federal expenditures rose by about 40 percent from 1929 to 1933. (See table.) Plainly, however, government had barely begun to respond to the enormous challenge of the Great Depression.

The presidency of Franklin D. Roosevelt from 1933 to 1945 then proved to be a decisive turning point for American government. As the NEW DEAL sought to achieve economic recovery, effect social and economic reform, and provide assistance to the unemployed, it greatly increased the size and scope of the federal government. Assuming federal responsibility for relief assistance to the poor and jobless, implementing regulation of banking and BUSINESS, and enacting such landmark social legislation as the SOCIAL SECURITY ACT, the NATIONAL LABOR RELATIONS ACT, and the FAIR LABOR STANDARDS ACT, the New Deal created the modern American regulatory welfare state. As the role of the federal government expanded under the New Deal, the number of federal employees increased by almost 75 percent and federal expenditures nearly doubled between 1933 and 1940.

The expansion of the size and power of the federal government was by the late 1930s accompanied by—and enabled by—apparent change in Supreme Court rulings. After at first allowing federal and local governments some leeway in dealing with the emergency of the depression, the Court in 1935 and 1936 seemed intent on halting the growth of government power when it overturned a number of major New Deal programs and invalidated a New York state minimum wage law. But then after the COURT-PACKING PLAN and controversy of 1937, the Court upheld another state minimum wage law and approved the Social Security Act and the National Labor Relations Act. The Supreme Court did not subsequently invalidate another piece of New Deal social or economic reform, thus ratifying the powerful American state that emerged in the 1930s.

Another key change in American government during the New Deal years was that the PRESIDENCY became far more than before the center of policymaking in Washington, framing agendas and sending bills to Congress for approval and then using a much-expanded bureaucracy to implement policy. Roosevelt's personality and his adept use of RADIO and press conferences to communicate with the public further enhanced presidential power, as did his efforts to enlarge and improve the administrative capacity of the White House. Under the terms of the EXECUTIVE REORGANIZATION ACT of 1939, a new Executive Office of the President was established, including six administrative assistants, the Bureau of the Budget, and the NATIONAL RESOURCES PLANNING BOARD. Many scholars hold that Roosevelt fundamentally redefined the presidency—indeed, virtually invented the modern presidency and its role in the American political system.

But though the dynamics of executive-legislative relations changed in the 1930s, Congress remained a powerful force in American government. Throughout his presidency, Roosevelt had to take account of the "barons" on Capitol Hill, and Congress did more than simply respond to the president's agenda. Some of the major New Deal programs—the National Labor Relations Act, for example—came from Congress rather than from the White House. In the late 1930s, a CONSERVATIVE COALITION, opposing the further growth of the regulatory welfare state, and emphasizing states' rights and local authority, emerged in Congress to assert congressional authority and thwart Roosevelt's efforts to expand the New Deal. Congress also used the investigative powers of its committees to watch the activities of the increasingly powerful executive branch.

The New Deal also marked a turning point in federal-state and federal-city relations. Many states adopted "little New Deals" to deal with the depression, not only by administering new federal programs but also by implementing their own social and economic programs, often supported at least in part by federal money. State social services, taxes, and bureaucracies expanded, though at different rates in different areas. But while the size and the expenses of state and local governments increased, so as well did their dependence on the federal government for funds and ideas, and state and local governments often had to answer to Washington for how they carried out programs and spent money.

The structure and culture of the American political system nonetheless also constrained the power of the national government in its relationships with state and local governments. Because of the limited capacity of the federal government even after 1933, Roosevelt had to depend upon state and local officials—often conservative or otherwise opposed to expanding federal authority—to administer many New Deal programs. Together with congressional conservatives, state and local governments frequently continued to resist the burgeoning power of the federal government. In the SOUTH, for example, particular care was taken to prevent New Deal measures from upsetting the established social structure, especially in race relations—although conservative opponents of New Deal programs could be found in all sections of the nation. Still, as the national government grew during the 1930s, so did its reach and its authority over state and local governments. The decade was thus in many ways a crucial one for American government.

Yet the impact of the Great Depression and New Deal on the federal government was in some respects eclipsed by that of World War II. Between 1940 and 1945, the number of civilian employees of the federal government nearly quadrupled, and federal expenditures increased nearly elevenfold. Federal expenditures were somewhat less than those of state and local government at the end of the 1930s; by 1945, federal expenditures were about ten times as large. The demands of economic and military MOBILIZA-TION for war both underlay such growth and overcame objections to a larger and more costly government. Some 16 million people served in the military, and during and after the war American FOREIGN POLICY was transformed as the United States became the world's most powerful

nation and played a leading role in world affairs. As commander in chief, Roosevelt further expanded presidential power by exercising unprecedented influence in military and diplomatic affairs. The war effort also brought into clearer definition what President Dwight D. Eisenhower later called the "military-industrial complex," in which military and business officials worked closely with each other and with government officials in shaping and implementing national policy.

World War II brought great expansion of the federal government's role at home. With extraordinary delegations of authority from Congress to the executive branch, the presidency and the federal government took on powers far beyond those of the New Deal—to control material priorities and production (the WAR PRODUCTION BOARD and the OFFICE OF WAR MOBILIZATION), to regulate manpower (SELECTIVE SERVICE and the WAR MANPOWER COMMISSION), to fix prices and wages and ration consumer goods (the OFFICE OF PRICE ADMINISTRATION and the OFFICE

SIZE AND COST OF AMERICAN GOVERNMENT, 1925–1950

	Federal Government Civilian Employees	State/Local Government Non-Teaching Employees	Federal Government Expenses	State/Local Expenses
1925	553,045		$3,063,105,000	
1927			2,974,030,000	$7,810,000,000
1928	560,772		3,103,265,000	
1929	579,559	1,411,000	3,298,859,000	
1930	601,319	1,472,000	3,440,269,000	
1931	609,746	1,544,000	3,577,434,000	
1932	605,496	1,518,000	4,659,203,000	8,403,000,000
1933	603,587	1,479,000	4,622,865,000	
1934	698,649	1,525,000	6,693,900,000	7,842,000,000
1935	780,582	1,577,000	6,520,966,000	
1936	867,432	1,668,000	8,493,486,000	8,501,000,000
1937	895,993	1,717,000	7,756,021,000	
1938	882,226	1,815,000	6,791,838,000	9,988,000,000
1939	953,891	1,823,000	8,858,458,000	
1940	1,042,420	1,907,000	9,062,032,000	11,240,000,000
1941	1,437,682	1,957,000	13,262,204,000	
1942	2,296,384	1,887,000	34,045,679,000	10,914,000,000
1943	3,299,414	1,813,000	79,407,131,000	
1944	3,332,356	1,764,000	95,058,708,000	10,499,000,000
1945	3,816,310	1,784,000	98,416,220,000	
1950	1,960,708	2,454,000	39,617,003,000	27,905,000,000

Source: *The Statistical History of the United States, from Colonial Times to the Present* (Stamford, Conn.: Fairfield Publishers, 1965)

OF ECONOMIC STABILIZATION), to coordinate defense-related scientific and technological advances (the OFFICE OF SCIENTIFIC RESEARCH AND DEVELOPMENT). Although much of the cost of wartime mobilization was met by deficit spending, corroborating KEYNESIANISM and its emphasis on fiscal policy, the federal government extended the income tax far more broadly than before and inaugurated the withholding system. The number of taxable returns soared more than tenfold, from some 4 million in 1939 to nearly 43 million by 1945; personal income taxes exceeded corporate taxes for the first time; and the groundwork was laid for the far more important role of federal fiscal policy in the postwar era.

The size and cost of the federal government fell sharply once the war was over, but the combination of ongoing international role and the "ratcheting" effect whereby not all the increased size and cost of government were eliminated left the federal government much more powerful than before. In 1950, the federal government had nearly twice as many employees and it spent four times as much as in 1940—and its size was three times greater than in 1930 and its expenditures more than 11 times higher. In 1930, the federal government had spent only about half the amount of state and local government expenditures, and even in 1940 had spent 20 percent less; in 1950, the federal government spent 40 percent more than state and local government. As late as 1940, there were about two times as many employees of state and local government (excluding teachers) as there were federal civilian workers; in 1950, the ratio was just 5 to 4.

The era of the Great Depression and World War II, especially the Roosevelt years, thus produced signal changes in American government. The federal government grew far larger, more powerful, and more costly as it implemented the regulatory welfare state in the 1930s, mobilized the nation for war, and increasingly overshadowed state and local government. After 1937, the Supreme Court approved such expansions of federal authority. The presidency gained power relative to the Congress and became far more central than before to national policy. Yet such changes did not transform basic features of the nation's political structure and political culture. The federal structure and the separation of powers remained at the heart of American government, and antistatist and individualist sentiments continued to slow the growth of the federal government. But the unparalleled demands of depression and war and the leadership of Franklin D. Roosevelt had nonetheless brought large and lasting change to American government.

Further reading: Anthony Badger, *The New Deal: The Depression Years, 1933–1940* (New York: Hill & Wang, 1989); Ballard Campbell, *The Growth of American Gov-ernment: Governance from the Cleveland Era to the Present* (Bloomington: Indiana University Press, 1995); John W. Jeffries, *Wartime America: The World War II Home Front* (Chicago: Ivan R. Dee, 1996); Barry D. Karl, *The Uneasy State: The United States from 1915 to 1945* (Chicago: University of Chicago Press, 1983); William E. Leuchtenburg, *The Supreme Court Reborn: The Constitutional Revolution in the Age of Roosevelt* (New York: Oxford University Press, 1995); James T. Patterson, *Congressional Conservatism and the New Deal: The Growth of the Conservative Coalition in Congress, 1933–1939* (Lexington: University Press of Kentucky, 1967); James T. Patterson, *The New Deal and the States: Federalism in Transition* (Princeton, N.J.: Princeton University Press, 1969).

Grand Alliance

The Grand Alliance is the name given to the anti-AXIS coalition of nations headed by the United States, Great Britain, and the Soviet Union during World War II. This wartime collaboration of the three nations not only presented a united front against Nazi Germany (the Soviets did not declare war on Japan until August 8, 1945) and deliberated on military strategy but also helped create the geopolitical power structure of the postwar world. A product of the common need to defeat Adolf Hitler and Nazi Germany, the Alliance was troubled from the beginning by a history of American and British discord with the Soviet Union and by divergent worldviews and war aims. Disagreements between the Soviet Union on the one hand and the United States and Britain on the other as the war drew to an end led to the dissolution of the partnership and the onset of the cold war.

The Grand Alliance had its origins in the development of strong ANGLO-AMERICAN RELATIONS beginning in 1939. In August 1941, American president FRANKLIN D. ROOSEVELT and British prime minister Winston Churchill met and produced the ATLANTIC CHARTER, which outlined war aims and principles. A number of other events paved the way for the Soviets to join the United States and Great Britain in the alliance. Germany invaded the Soviet Union in June 1941, allowing the three nations to unite against their common Nazi enemy and opening the opportunity for the United States to provide the Soviets with assistance under the LEND-LEASE ACT. With Soviet endorsement of the Atlantic Charter and American entrance into the war in December 1941, the Grand Alliance was formed. The partners made the defeat of Nazi Germany their top priority, both because the Allies agreed that Hitler posed the greatest danger and because the Soviet Union had concluded a neutrality agreement with Japan in April 1941, which it did not formally abrogate until August 1945.

Throughout the war, the Allies consulted each other in a series of conferences to decide on both military strategy and how to reconstruct the global order in Europe and Asia. These conferences allowed the Allies to coordinate their military efforts, but also illuminated key issues producing conflict in the alliance both during and after the war. From the beginning, moreover, suspicions and tensions going back to the formation of the Soviet Union in 1917, divergent war aims, and ideological differences between the democracies and the totalitarian-communist USSR strained the alliance.

Initially, the opening of a SECOND FRONT in western Europe proved to be the most significant issue for the Grand Alliance, and it remained a source of suspicion and resentment for the Soviets. The German invasion of the Soviet Union had inflicted catastrophic destruction and loss of human life, and the Soviets badly wanted immediate relief on the eastern front. Stalin began to demand a second front as early as 1942, but the Americans and especially the British, concerned about their own military readiness, resisted early attempts to open the second front. Finally, in late 1943 at the TEHERAN CONFERENCE, Roosevelt sided with Soviet premier Joseph Stalin against Churchill in favor of opening the second front in the spring of 1944. For Roosevelt, a central priority, to which he eventually won Stalin's agreement, was the formation of the UNITED NATIONS as a guardian of international peace and a forum for continued big-power cooperation.

Throughout the war, a shifting balance of power among the members of the Grand Alliance also affected their deliberations. As the ravages of war left the British bankrupt and diminished their stature as a global power, SOVIET-AMERICAN RELATIONS became increasingly important as a priority for Roosevelt, sometimes even at the cost of relations with Churchill. This situation did not substantially harm the special relationship between Great Britain and the United States, built on a foundation of shared democratic ideals and values, and both the British and Americans found that their dealings with the Soviets were often marked by mutual suspicion and mistrust. Indeed, the United States did not even inform the Soviets about the MANHATTAN PROJECT that produced the ATOMIC BOMB, while including the British in developing and discussing the new weapon.

Despite tensions, the members of the Grand Alliance appeared willing to try to work through their differences to create a peaceful, postwar geopolitical structure. But disagreements within the Alliance were plain at the YALTA CONFERENCE of early 1945, with the defeat of Germany in sight and questions about the postwar world becoming more pressing by the day. At Yalta, Roosevelt, Churchill, and Stalin gathered for what proved to be the last time to discuss the terms of German surrender, the postwar status of eastern Europe, especially Poland, and the conditions of Soviet entrance into the war with Japan. A compromise settlement was reached that included a Soviet commitment to join the Asian war after the surrender of Germany and a tentative decision about Poland's border and government, but not without concern from Roosevelt and Churchill about the implications of a Soviet presence in eastern Europe. It appears, however, that Roosevelt understood Stalin's concerns about Soviet security on the western borders and hoped his willingness to compromise would convince Stalin that Soviet control of Poland was unnecessary.

The already fragile Grand Alliance continued to deteriorate after the conclusion of the Yalta Conference. The Americans and British complained that the Soviets were not living up to agreements about the creation of independent governments in eastern Europe. President Roosevelt died in April 1945; Germany surrendered in May, eliminating the reason the Alliance had been formed. Much American public opinion opposed Roosevelt's compromise at Yalta concerning Soviet influence in Poland, as the new president, Harry S. Truman, knew. In addition, the successful development of the first atomic bomb suddenly gave the United States more leverage than ever before but ultimately also increased Soviet-American tensions.

The POTSDAM CONFERENCE of July 1945, the last of the Grand Alliance's wartime conferences, marked the final semblance of cooperation among the Allies. By the end of the conference, Joseph Stalin was the single remaining original leader of the Grand Alliance; Clement Attlee replaced Winston Churchill as British prime minister partway through the conference. With Great Britain badly weakened by the war, Truman and Stalin were the primary actors at Potsdam, and Truman proved to be less willing to negotiate and compromise with Stalin than Roosevelt had been. The three nations were able to agree upon an unconditional surrender formula for the end of the war with Japan in the Potsdam Proclamation, and Truman notified Stalin for the first time, albeit in a cryptic manner, of the existence of the atomic bomb that the Americans had been working on with the British for some time. The Soviet Union agreed to enter the war against the Japanese in August, as it had promised at Yalta, but the atomic bomb made this pledge less significant than it had been just a few months before.

Truman was still on his way home from Potsdam when he heard the news that the first atomic bomb had been dropped on Hiroshima, Japan, heralding the beginning of the nuclear age (see HIROSHIMA AND NAGASAKI). The official end of the Japanese war came on September 2, 1945, an event that also brought the end of the Grand Alliance and a shift toward the postwar power structure. The United States and the Soviet Union emerged out of their alliance as the world's superpowers, and the ongoing tensions and disagreements between the two nations soon developed into the cold war.

See also FOREIGN POLICY.

Further reading: Herbert Feis, *Churchill, Roosevelt, and Stalin: The War They Waged and the Peace They Sought* (Princeton, N.J.: Princeton University Press, 1957); William Hardy McNeil, *America, Britain, and Russia: Their Cooperation and Conflict, 1941–1946* (New York: Oxford University Press, 1953); Martin J. Sherwin, *A World Destroyed: The Atomic Bomb and the Grand Alliance* (New York: Knopf, 1975).

—Mary E. Carroll-Mason

Great Depression

The Great Depression, the worst and longest contraction ever of the American ECONOMY, began in 1929 and lasted until 1941. For more than a decade, the American people experienced record levels of unemployment and poverty. At the depth of the Great Depression, in the winter of 1932–33, UNEMPLOYMENT was at least one-fourth of the workforce, and national income had dropped by more than 50 percent. From 1933 to 1937, significant economic expansion occurred, although it fell far short of full recovery; and then the RECESSION OF 1937–38 sent economic indexes plummeting again. Not until defense spending began to stimulate the economy in 1940–41 did the depression end. In addition to its economic and human impact, the Great Depression affected virtually every aspect of American life, and brought a transformation of American politics by enabling the victory of FRANKLIN D. ROOSEVELT in the presidential ELECTION OF 1932. Roosevelt's presidency produced the NEW DEAL and made the DEMOCRATIC PARTY the nation's majority party for decades to come. The depression of the 1930s was thus "great" not only in its magnitude but also in its widespread and far-reaching consequences.

But while the course and impact of the Great Depression are clear enough, there remains much disagreement about its causes and the reasons for its unprecedented depth and length. Scholars agree that a distinction must be made between the STOCK MARKET CRASH of late October 1929 and the Great Depression that engulfed the economy for more than a decade. Because economic indexes turned down so sharply after the stock market crash, that event has often seemed the cause of the Great Depression. But while the market crash played some role in the development of the Great Depression, the economy was already in trouble and evidently heading for at least a recession before the crash. By the late 1920s, construction and automobiles, the two key industries that had supported much of the prosperity of the 1920s, had begun to fall off,

and unsold business inventories were increasing in other industries as well. Layoffs and declining production followed. AGRICULTURE had experienced problems throughout the decade. To an important degree, in fact, early signs of difficulty on the stock market in the summer and fall of 1929 apparently reflected concern about the larger economy. Why had the economy begun to stumble, and why did the downturn become the Great Depression of the 1930s?

Although those questions elude clear consensus, a number of factors seem important. Much of the economic expansion of the 1920s had been solidly based, but there were flaws in the economy that limited both the extent and the duration of the decade's prosperity. One significant problem was the distribution of income in the United States. Simply put, too little money was in the hands of too many people, and too much money was in the hands of too few. In 1929, the bottom 40 percent of families earned just one-eighth of personal income, while the top 20 percent of families earned more than half—and the top 5 percent alone earned nearly one-third of national income. The average family income of the bottom 40 percent was just $725, a subsistence level or worse. The key issue in the income distribution data involves economic efficiency, not social equity: There was not enough disposable income in the hands of most workers and farmers to help carry the economy. Even for those in the middle-income ranges, there was no longer sufficient money—or credit—to continue the purchases that had sparked the 1920s boom. And for those at the top, who had plenty, money increasingly was saved instead of spent—or was put into the stock market, contributing to the price rise that helped to bring on the stock market crash. The maldistribution of income thus contributed to troubles in the economy evident by 1929.

The economic slowdown of the late 1920s was connected to another important pattern: the dependence of 1920s prosperity on housing and automobiles, and the failure of new industries to emerge that might have sustained the economy. Some important older industries—coal, textiles, and railroads in particular—had struggled throughout the decade. Such new industries as electronics and electrical appliances, aviation, processed foods, and petrochemicals had not developed far enough to attract sufficient investment and consumer spending that might have compensated for the saturated housing and automobile industries. Nor was there sufficient government spending at the local or national levels to make up for inadequate private investment.

Financial issues comprised a third major set of causes for the Great Depression. The nation's credit and banking system was shaky. Because so many farmers were in debt, small country banks experienced growing difficulties by the late 1920s as their customers defaulted on loans. Many

Shown in this 1931 photograph is a breadline in Boston during the Great Depression, the most severe economic crisis in U.S. history. *(Library of Congress)*

businesses were in debt, too. Beyond that, the banking system itself was unsound—indeed, it was scarcely a system at all—with little real control or integration from the Federal Reserve Board, with no deposit insurance that might have reassured depositors, with undercapitalized small banks, and with unsound practices followed by a number of major banks in their loans and stock market investments. The international debt structure was also problematical. Because high American tariffs made it difficult for European nations to earn money by selling goods in the United States, American loans abroad were helping to maintain Germany's war reparation payments and Allied payments of World War I debts to the United States.

Finally, economic policy and prevailing economic ideas sustained or exacerbated economic problems and were inadequate for dealing with the depression. High tariffs during the 1920s not only made it difficult for foreign nations to earn credits to buy American goods or repay war debts, but also inhibited purchasing in the United States by propping up prices. The HAWLEY-SMOOT TARIFF ACT of 1930 made things worse. National farm and labor policies during the 1920s contributed to the low earnings and the inadequate purchasing power of many farmers and workers. The Federal Reserve Board, whose easy credit policies helped fuel borrowing and stock market speculation, could not discipline dangerous banking practices, and there was similarly no control over speculation and shady dealings on the stock market. When the depression did come and then continued to deepen, the conventional insistence on balanced budgets and preserving the gold standard inhibited federal action, as did the orthodox view that downturns were inevitable and self-correcting. The Federal Reserve Board's tight money policies and higher interest rates in the early 1930s to protect the gold standard contributed to the worsening depression.

In a number of ways, then, the economy was unsound by late 1929. Scholars do not agree on precisely what role the stock market crash played in bringing on the Great Depression, but it was clearly a blow to the confidence that had helped support the economic expansion of the 1920s and it no doubt reduced some of the investment and consumer spending necessary for prosperity. The crash also helped bring down some financial institutions that had invested heavily in stocks and to dry up some of the loans supporting international finances. But the crash itself did not begin the economic downturn of the late 1920s, nor did it cause the Great Depression.

In fact, it took some time before the realization dawned that the slump was not a normal cyclical downturn in the economy. Spectacular though the stock market crash was, most observers agreed with President HERBERT C. HOOVER that the economy was fundamentally sound and would soon right itself and begin to expand. Temporary plateaus and rallies reinforced such expectations. Only as the depression deepened year after year, and as it became obviously a worldwide depression by 1931, with the collapse of the European trade and financial system that further damaged the American economy, did the gravity and the distinctiveness of this depression become obvious. By 1933, unemployment was at least one-fourth and perhaps one-third of the labor force, and many who were employed were working part-time or at reduced wages. National income had fallen by 54 percent, manufacturing wages and farm income by 60 percent. Industrial production was down by more than half (automobile production by 80 percent and steel production by 90 percent); foreign trade was off by 70 percent; and new capital investment in plants and equipment had plummeted by 98 percent. Business profits fell sharply, with estimates of the decline ranging from 60 to 90 percent. More than 5,000 banks had failed, and millions of savings accounts were lost or decimated. More than 100,000 businesses failed. The New York Stock Exchange was down to only about one-fifth of 1929 levels. The consumer price index fell by about 25 percent—but income had fallen much more than that, and declining prices further inhibited business investment.

Such catastrophic figures meant human calamity. Jobs were lost, income shriveled, hundreds of thousands of home and farm mortgages were foreclosed, and decent food, clothing, and shelter often could not be purchased. People starved, or were weakened by malnutrition—while unsold foodstuffs piled up or went bad on the nation's farms for want of enough money to buy them. Breadlines,

soup kitchens, and shantytowns dotted CITIES. Industrial workers and small farmers suffered especially, as did AFRICAN AMERICANS, MEXICAN AMERICANS, and other minority groups on the lower rungs of the economic ladder. Young people and the ELDERLY also had particular trouble getting or keeping jobs. The loss of income, houses, bank accounts, and white-collar jobs brought distress and suffering to middle-class Americans, too. Private and public RELIEF was altogether inadequate in the first years of the DEPRESSION, and New Deal relief programs, although a major change from the HOOVER PRESIDENCY, never brought help to everyone in need.

The Great Depression ramified through American society in other ways as well, especially in the first half of the 1930s. POPULATION TRENDS clearly reflected the depression's impact. Despite the highly visible transients, internal MIGRATION fell off, and IMMIGRATION totals plummeted to their lowest levels in a century. MARRIAGE AND FAMILY LIFE was affected too. Marriage and birth rates declined in the early years of the depression, and hard times increased strains within families, which often experienced role reversals as unemployed men lost their status as breadwinner and wives necessarily played a larger economic and decision-making role. Following as it did the high expectations and growing prosperity of the 1920s, the depression was an especially heavy psychological blow. Indeed, economic depression could bring personal depression, as unemployed and impoverished Americans often blamed themselves for their plight. Such areas of POPULAR CULTURE as SPORTS, RECREATION, and MOVIES were affected by the depression, as were LITERATURE and ART AND ARCHITECTURE.

The Great Depression also had enormous consequences for the American political system. In the election of 1932, voters overwhelmingly turned Hoover and the REPUBLICAN PARTY out of office and elected Franklin D. Roosevelt and the Democrats. Particularly in his first term from 1933 to 1937, Roosevelt's presidency produced the New Deal programs that created the modern American regulatory welfare state and transformed American GOVERNMENT. In POLITICS IN THE ROOSEVELT ERA, voters responded to Roosevelt and the New Deal by making the Democratic Party the nation's new majority party.

Finally, it must be emphasized that the Great Depression lasted for more than a decade, until defense spending brought recovery and full employment in the early 1940s. Not until 1941 did unemployment, which averaged some 20 percent throughout the decade, fall below 14 percent; by 1944, unemployment had plummeted to just 1 percent. Not until 1937 did the volume of gross national product (GNP) equal that of 1929, and then it fell again with the recession of 1937–38, which helped turn the administration toward KEYNESIANISM. Not until 1941 did the dollar value of GNP attain 1929 levels, and it soared to new record levels in the next few years. The New Deal contributed to some economic improvement and brought help and hope to tens of millions of Americans in the 1930s, but it was WORLD WAR II, not the New Deal, that at last ended the Great Depression.

Further reading: Michael Bernstein, *The Great Depression: Delayed Recovery and Economic Change in America, 1929–1939* (New York: Cambridge University Press, 1987); Michael D. Bordo, Claudia Goldin, and Eugene N. White, eds., *The Defining Moment: The Great Depression and the American Economy in the Twentieth Century* (Chicago: University of Chicago Press, 1998); Lester V. Chandler, *America's Greatest Depression, 1929–1941* (New York: Harper & Row, 1970); Richard Lowitt and Maurine Beasley, eds., *One-Third of a Nation: Lorena Hickok Reports the Great Depression* (Urbana: University of Illinois Press, 1981); Peter Temin, *Did Monetary Forces Cause the Great Depression?* (New York: Norton, 1976); Studs Terkel, *Hard Times: An Oral History of the Great Depression* (New York: Pantheon, 1970).

Guadalcanal

The campaign for Guadalcanal, an island located in the southern part of the SOLOMON ISLANDS, consisted of dozens of separate naval and land engagements between August 1942 and February 1943. The first significant joint operation of the U.S. NAVY, the U.S. ARMY, and the U.S. MARINES during WORLD WAR II, the campaign led to the withdrawal of the Japanese army from Guadalcanal by early 1943 and secured Allied supply routes to Australia. After the BATTLE OF THE CORAL SEA in May 1942 and the BATTLE OF MIDWAY in June had halted the Japanese advance south and west, Guadalcanal began the three-year campaign in the PACIFIC THEATER to push the Imperial Japanese forces back to the home islands.

Following the landing of marines on the beaches of Guadalcanal on August 7, 1942, the Japanese quickly responded by reinforcing their troops on the island. At the Battle of Savo Island of August 8–9, the U.S. Navy suffered perhaps its worst defeat in history, and in mid-August the Japanese landed more forces on Guadalcanal in an effort to drive the marines off the island and recapture the prized airstrip renamed Henderson Field by the marines. But by October, some 27,000 Americans were on Guadalcanal and nearby Tulagi.

Meanwhile, the navy fought an increasingly successful series of actions against the Imperial Japanese Navy from late August 1942 to January 1943, deterring Japanese efforts to strengthen their foothold on Guadalcanal. In the decisive naval battles of Guadalcanal (November 12–13 and November 14–15, 1942), the U.S. Navy, under Vice Admiral WILLIAM F. "BULL" HALSEY, stalled the "Tokyo Express" and left Japanese forces stranded on Guadalcanal without reinforcements and supplies.

By the end of 1942, American forces on Guadalcanal numbered nearly 60,000, almost triple the opposing Japanese strength, and American naval and AIR POWER in the area doomed the Japanese efforts. In early February 1943, the Imperial Japanese Army executed one of the rare Japanese retreats of the war, pulling all forces off Guadalcanal and conceding the island to the Americans. The campaign for the Solomons continued for the rest of the year, but the victory at Guadalcanal was a key breakthrough that put U.S. forces on the offensive.

Further reading: Richard B. Frank, *Guadalcanal* (New York: Random House, 1990); Edwin P. Hoyt, *Guadalcanal* (New York: Stein & Day, 1982).

—Michael Leonard

H

Halsey, William F., Jr. ("Bull")
(1882–1959)

Admiral William Frederick "Bull" Halsey, Jr., whose personality, penchant for action, and aggressive leadership earned him his nickname, helped the U.S. NAVY turn the tide in the PACIFIC THEATER of WORLD WAR II.

Halsey was born in Elizabeth, New Jersey, on October 30, 1882, and graduated from the U.S. Naval Academy in 1904. His obvious abilities brought him rapid promotion to command of destroyers before and during World War I. After a variety of assignments in the 1920s and 1930s, he qualified as a naval aviator in 1935 at the age of 52—the oldest man ever to do so. He won promotions to rear admiral in 1938 and to vice admiral in 1940.

Halsey was instrumental in the American victory over the Imperial Japanese Navy in the Pacific theater. His performance was characterized not only by bold leadership but also by the hostility toward the Japanese common after the attack on PEARL HARBOR. His mission, he said, was to "Kill Japs, kill Japs, kill more Japs." Early in 1942, he directed carrier attacks on Japanese positions in the Marshall and Gilbert Islands. Made commander of the Allied naval forces in the South Pacific in October 1942 (and promoted to full admiral in November), Halsey energized and brought success to the pivotal campaign in the SOLOMON ISLANDS that included the crucial victory at GUADALCANAL.

In June 1944, Halsey took command of the U.S. Third Fleet, and played a controversial role in the BATTLE FOR LEYTE GULF off the PHILIPPINES in October. As part of the large and complex battle, the Japanese positioned several aircraft carriers north of the main action, wanting to lure Halsey and his Third Fleet to the north so that a Japanese force could pass through the San Bernardino Strait and attack the U.S. Seventh Fleet. Eager to sink the Japanese carriers, Halsey took the bait and steamed north, permitting Vice Admiral Takeo Kurita's surface ships to enter Leyte Gulf through the San Bernardino Strait and inflict damage on the American forces. Ultimately, the Japanese

experienced a disastrous defeat at Leyte Gulf, one marking the end of the Japanese navy as a serious threat, but Halsey's reputation was tarnished. His impulsive decision to seek out the Japanese carriers, leaving the San Bernardino Strait unguarded, became known as "the Battle of Bull's Run." Halsey's record throughout the war nonetheless brought him appointment to admiral of the fleet—five-star rank—in December 1945. He retired from the navy in 1947.

Further reading: E. B. Potter, *Bull Halsey* (Annapolis, Md.: Naval Institute Press, 1985).

Harriman, W. Averell (1891–1986)

William Averell Harriman, businessman, NEW DEAL administrator, ambassador to the Soviet Union, secretary of commerce, and governor of New York, was born in New York City in 1891. He was the son of Edward Harriman, a powerful railroad financier who organized the Union Pacific Railroad. After graduating from Yale in 1913, Harriman trained to take over his father's firm but soon struck out on his own. During the 1920s he created one of the world's largest shipping fleets and developed businesses in the Soviet Union before being elected chairman of the board of Union Pacific in 1932.

Despite his BUSINESS background, Harriman had switched to the DEMOCRATIC PARTY in 1928 and he supported FRANKLIN D. ROOSEVELT in the ELECTION OF 1932. In 1933, presidential adviser HARRY HOPKINS helped Harriman win a post in the NATIONAL RECOVERY ADMINISTRATION. Harriman left the GOVERNMENT in 1937 to head the Business Advisory Council.

WORLD WAR II brought Harriman back to the Roosevelt administration in 1941, when he joined the OFFICE OF PRODUCTION MANAGEMENT. With the passage of the LEND-LEASE ACT in March 1941, Harriman went to London to oversee that program in England. He traveled to various battlefronts and expedited war material shipments to the British. He often bypassed the American ambassador and communicated directly to the White House, usually through Hopkins. In September 1941, Harriman traveled to Moscow to arrange Lend-Lease shipments to the Soviet Union; he later returned to the USSR with British prime minister Winston Churchill to discuss allied strategy with Joseph Stalin. In 1943, President Roosevelt named him ambassador to the Soviet Union, and Harriman was a member of the American delegation at the wartime CAIRO CONFERENCE, TEHERAN CONFERENCE, and YALTA CONFERENCE.

Harriman's work as ambassador was noteworthy for a meticulous attention to details. He won Stalin's respect with a blunt, face-to-face candor and a serious consideration of Soviet demands for Allied cooperation. He held no illusions about Soviet postwar aims and reported on Soviet methods to establish Communist regimes in Eastern Europe. By war's end, however, Harriman's influence in FOREIGN POLICY had diminished, and he played a smaller role at the Yalta Conference than he had at previous wartime meetings. He left Moscow in 1946.

Harriman subsequently served in the Truman administration as ambassador to Great Britain in 1946, secretary of commerce from 1946 to 1948, and as U.S. administrator of the Marshall Plan from 1948 to 1950. He was elected governor of New York in 1954, negotiated the 1963 Nuclear Test Ban Treaty under President John F. Kennedy, and served as President Lyndon B. Johnson's ambassador to the Paris peace talks with North Vietnam. He died in 1986.

See also GRAND ALLIANCE; SOVIET-AMERICAN RELATIONS.

Further reading: W. Averell Harriman and Elie Abel, *Special Envoy to Churchill and Stalin, 1941–1946* (New York: Random House, 1975).

—Robert J. Hanyok

Hawley-Smoot Tariff Act (1930)

Signed into law in June 1930 during the HOOVER PRESIDENCY, the Hawley-Smoot Tariff, coauthored by Oregon congressman Willis Hawley and Utah senator Reed Smoot, increased U.S. tariffs on imports to the highest levels in history. Often described as an "infamous" piece of legislation, the Hawley-Smoot Act has been blamed for prompting a worldwide increase in tariffs and for helping turn a moderate recession into the full-blown GREAT DEPRESSION. Although historians and economists have disagreed about the extent to which it contributed to the Great Depression, the Hawley-Smoot Tariff nonetheless had important political and economic consequences during the early 1930s.

Traditionally the REPUBLICAN PARTY had advocated a policy of high tariffs in an effort to protect American indus-

try and workers from an influx of inexpensive foreign goods. In 1922, a Republican Congress passed the Fordney-McCumber Tariff, which established high protectionist rates, and throughout the 1920s the GOP championed protective tariffs. During the election of 1928, the Republican platform called for a reexamination of Fordney-McCumber, and an upward revision of the tariff. As the tariff became a primary subject of debate in Congress in 1930, a number of special interests worked to secure high duties on foreign goods.

President HERBERT C. HOOVER, who favored high duties on agricultural imports in order to protect farmers, but increases on industrial products only when made necessary by increased unemployment, argued against a general increase in the tariff. He also felt that lobbyists had an excessive amount of influence in tariff legislation. He desired a more flexible tariff to be controlled by a tariff commission operating under the authority of the president, which could raise or lower tariffs by up to 50 percent. Although Congress acquiesced in Hoover's demand for greater flexibility through a strengthened tariff commission, it nonetheless passed a bill with high tariff levels for both industrial and agricultural goods, after 44 days and five nights of testimony and debate. Despite the protests of nearly a thousand economists who warned against continued restriction of trade through such high tariffs, and against his better judgment, President Hoover signed the Hawley-Smoot Act into law.

Politically, the Hawley-Smoot Tariff weakened the president. Ultimately losing the struggle with Congress, Hoover had demonstrated that he did not have the political skill to maintain control over his party. While the precise economic effects of the tariff remain difficult to gauge, its adoption in 1930 was interpreted by other nations as America's turn toward even more stringent protectionist policies. As a result, many other nations also increased tariff levels. Between 1930 and 1932, the retaliation of at least 25 trading partners would play a part in the decline of U.S. exports that would continue until the NEW DEAL and the passage of the RECIPROCAL TRADE AGREEMENTS ACT of 1934.

Further reading: Alfred E. Eckes, "Revisiting Hawley-Smoot," *Journal of Policy History* 7 (1995): 295–310; Douglas Irwin, "The Hawley-Smoot Tariff: A Quantitative Assessment," *Review of Economics and Statistics* 80 (May 1998): 326–35.

—Shannon L. Parsley

Henderson, Leon (1895–1986)

Leon Henderson, one of the NEW DEAL's most influential administrators, served in a number of significant posts under President FRANKLIN D. ROOSEVELT between 1934 and 1942.

Born in Millville, New Jersey, on May 26, 1895, Leon Henderson graduated from Swarthmore College, and after postgraduate work taught economics at the University of Pennsylvania and the Carnegie Institute of Technology. After serving two years as deputy secretary of Pennsylvania, he became director of consumer credit research for the Russell Sage Foundation in 1925.

Henderson joined the Roosevelt administration in 1934, when he became consumer affairs adviser and then director of the Research and Planning Division of the NATIONAL RECOVERY ADMINISTRATION (NRA). A persistent consumer advocate, Henderson criticized the NRA's industry-written codes, claiming they increased BUSINESS concentration and prevented recovery by permitting production restrictions and price increases. Originally an advocate of national industrial planning, Henderson became one of the New Deal's foremost advocates of ANTIMONOPOLY policy.

After the SUPREME COURT declared the NRA unconstitutional in 1935, Henderson became economic adviser to the DEMOCRATIC PARTY National Committee, and consultant to HARRY L. HOPKINS at the WORKS PROGRESS ADMINISTRATION. Influenced by Hopkins and MARRINER ECCLES, Henderson by 1938 had become a convert to KEYNESIANISM, the idea that GOVERNMENT deficit spending could stimulate the economy.

The RECESSION OF 1937–38 led the Roosevelt administration to turn both to additional spending and to increased emphasis on antimonopoly policy. At Roosevelt's request, CONGRESS established the TEMPORARY NATIONAL ECONOMIC COMMITTEE (TNEC) in 1938, and Henderson became TNEC's executive director, urging investigations of all forms of economic concentration and continuing his opposition to monopoly. Roosevelt appointed Henderson to the SECURITIES AND EXCHANGE COMMISSION (SEC) in 1939, further antagonizing opponents in BUSINESS and industry.

In 1941, Roosevelt selected Henderson to head the OFFICE OF PRICE ADMINISTRATION (OPA), which administered RATIONING during WORLD WAR II and set maximum prices on nonfarm consumer goods. The OPA became one of the most unpopular wartime agencies, and Henderson, always outspoken and often abrasive, became a lightning rod for public discontent and a target for unhappy interest groups. DEMOCRATIC PARTY officials were also upset with Henderson's refusal to use OPA for political patronage appointments. Henderson resigned as OPA director after Democratic setbacks in the 1942 elections, citing illness and overwork.

After the war, Henderson worked as an economist in both the public and private sectors, and served as chairman of Americans for Democratic Action (ADA), the liberal, anticommunist advocacy group. Henderson retired in the middle 1960s, settled on the West Coast, and died in Oceanside, California, on October 19, 1986.

Further reading: Ellis W. Hawley, *The New Deal and the Problem of Monopoly* (Princeton, N.J.: Princeton University Press, 1966).

—William J. Thompson

Hillman, Sidney (1887–1946)

Sidney Hillman, president of the Amalgamated Clothing Workers of America (ACW) for over 30 years, and a cofounder of the CONGRESS OF INDUSTRIAL ORGANIZATIONS (CIO) was a politically influential LABOR leader of the 1930s and 1940s.

Born in Zagare, Lithuania, then part of Russia, on March 23, 1887, "Simcha" Hillman was sent by his parents to study for the rabbinate, but instead turned to socialist politics and labor agitation, which led to his arrest and imprisonment for protesting in favor of a 10-hour working day. Fleeing Russia in 1906, Hillman lived in England with an uncle before moving to the United States and settling in Chicago. In Chicago, Hillman went to work as a cloth cutter, and led a successful 1910 strike of women garment workers.

Over the next several years, Hillman became a prominent union organizer among garment workers in Chicago and New York, and in 1914 became the first president of the Amalgamated Clothing Workers of America. During World War I, he served in Washington, D.C., on the Board of Control and Labor Standards for Army Clothing. Hillman organized clothing workers in the 1920s, maneuvering his way around COMMUNISTS and labor gangsters, and became a leader of the "new unionism"—the effort to improve every aspect of workers' lives, not merely to seek higher wages.

The election of FRANKLIN D. ROOSEVELT to the presidency in 1932 changed the position of organized labor in America and brought union leaders such as Hillman into greater public prominence and political influence. Hillman welcomed the NEW DEAL, and he served on the Labor Advisory Board of the NATIONAL RECOVERY ADMINISTRATION (NRA) and on other New Deal agencies. Hillman's association with labor leader JOHN L. LEWIS led to the ACW being admitted to the AMERICAN FEDERATION OF LABOR (AFL), and he joined with David Dubinsky of the International Ladies Garment Workers Union (ILGWU) to organize clothing workers.

Hillman, along with Lewis and others, grew increasingly frustrated with the AFL's neglect of workers in the mass production industries such as automobiles, coal, steel, and, of course, clothing. Beginning in 1934, Hillman, Lewis, and the other dissident leaders called on the AFL to organize mass production workers into industrial unions. Along with Lewis, Dubinsky, and seven other union leaders, Hillman cofounded the Committee for Industrial Organization in 1935 as a branch within the AFL. When the AFL suspended the dissident unionists in 1937, Hillman and the others formally separated in 1938, changing the group's name to Congress of Industrial Organizations (CIO).

In 1936, Hillman, who had previously been an active Socialist for many years, endorsed Roosevelt, and as treasurer of Labor's Non-Partisan League, raised over $1 million for the president's reelection. In the latter 1930s, Hillman organized the Textile Workers Organizing Committee, attempting unsuccessfully to break into the nonunion SOUTH and in the process earning the enmity of southern politicians such as JAMES F. BYRNES (whom Hillman may have prevented from being FDR's running mate in 1940 and 1944). In contrast to Lewis, who broke with Roosevelt after 1936, Hillman moved closer politically to the president, supporting, for example, the FAIR LABOR STANDARDS ACT.

In 1940, with WORLD WAR II having begun in Europe, Roosevelt named Hillman as associate director general (with General Motors chairman William Knudson) of the OFFICE OF PRODUCTION MANAGEMENT, and as labor member of the National Defense Advising Commission. After PEARL HARBOR, Roosevelt named Hillman as labor member of the WAR PRODUCTION BOARD, and unlike Lewis, he and the ACW abided by the president's "no-strike pledge" request. In 1943, Hillman became chairman and director of the CIO-Political Action Committee, which would help pro-labor DEMOCRATIC PARTY candidates.

At the Democratic National Convention in 1944, Hillman played a visible but mysterious role in the nomination of Harry S. Truman for vice president, as Roosevelt instructed aides to "clear it (Truman's nomination) with Sidney." In the fall campaign, the REPUBLICAN PARTY used "Clear It with Sidney" to portray Roosevelt as a tool of Hillman and the CIO-PAC as a haven for COMMUNISTS, and some Republicans engaged in Red-baiting and ANTI-SEMITISM to smear the union leader. The tactics backfired as Hillman and labor played a significant role in Roosevelt's victory in the ELECTION OF 1944.

After Roosevelt's death in 1945, Hillman remained influential with Truman and the Democrats, while locked in a struggle with Communist elements in the CIO. In ill health since 1942, Hillman suffered a series of heart attacks, and died on July 10, 1946, at his Point Lookout, New York, summer cottage.

Further reading: Steve Fraser, *Labor Will Rule: Sidney Hillman and the Rise of American Labor* (New York: Free Press, 1991).

—William J. Thompson

Hiroshima and Nagasaki

On August 6, 1945, an American B-29 bomber, the *Enola Gay*, dropped the first operational ATOMIC BOMB on Hiroshima, Japan, incinerating the heart of the city of a quarter million people. A second atomic bomb was dropped three days later with comparable damage on Nagasaki, and the Japanese offer of surrender came on August 10. The bombing of the two cities, Hiroshima especially, has come to symbolize the end of WORLD WAR II and the beginning of the atomic age. The American use of the atomic bomb has also provoked continuing inquiry and debate among scholars and the public—as the furor about the proposed *Enola Gay* exhibit at the Smithsonian Institution in the mid-1990s revealed.

The atomic bomb was developed by the American MANHATTAN PROJECT and was successfully tested at Alamogordo, New Mexico, on July 16, 1945. The light from the test could be seen some 200 miles away, sand was fused into glass pellets, and a mushroom cloud rose eight miles into the sky. J. Robert Oppenheimer, the chief scientist on the Manhattan Project, quoted from the Hindu *Bhagavad Gita:* "I am become Death, destroyer of worlds." In the aftermath of the test, the Potsdam Declaration, issued on July 26 at the end of the POTSDAM CONFERENCE, demanded that Japan surrender unconditionally by August 3 or face "prompt and utter destruction."

The Japanese did not surrender, and destruction promptly came. Much of Hiroshima was obliterated by the "Little Boy" uranium bomb, with perhaps as many as 50,000 deaths almost instantaneously and estimates of additional deaths by the end of the year from injury, burns, and radiation poison ranging as high as 100,000. President Harry S. Truman announced to the world that the atomic bomb involved the "harnessing of the basic power of the universe." The Japanese still did not surrender, even after the Soviet Union entered the war against Japan on August 8. Another American bomber, the *Bockscar,* then dropped the "Fat Man" plutonium bomb on Nagasaki on August 9, with another 50,000 deaths and eventually tens of thousands more. At last Japan surrendered.

Jubilant V-J DAY celebrations erupted when the news of the Japanese surrender became public. American servicemen in or heading toward the PACIFIC THEATER and their families rejoiced that the war was over and that the atomic bombs had evidently saved the GIs from a bloody invasion of the Japanese home islands. The overwhelming majority of the American public endorsed the use of the bombs. Truman told sailors as he returned home from Potsdam that the bombing of Hiroshima was "the greatest thing in history."

But while all Americans were glad to see the war end with no more peril to U.S. servicemen, and while most continued to approve using the atomic bomb, reservations, regrets, and questions about the bomb soon began to emerge. Truman himself, on hearing the news from Alamogordo, had written in his diary about "the most terrible thing ever discovered." Some religious leaders and scientists, and even a few military leaders, asked whether it had been necessary or right to use so awful a weapon. So did some critics, conservatives and liberals alike, in politics and the press. The author John Hersey's compelling and graphic account of several survivors of the Hiroshima bombing written for the *New Yorker* magazine and then published in his best-selling 1946 book, *Hiroshima,* had a huge impact on perceptions of the bomb. And for the following half century and more, the decision to use the atomic bomb has been discussed and often debated.

In fact, Truman did not so much make a decision to use the bomb as he did not reverse a longstanding decision to use it if necessary. From the beginning of the Manhattan Project, it had been assumed, implicitly and explicitly, that the bomb would be a legitimate weapon of war to be used if needed against the AXIS nations to end the war. Some support for developing and using the bomb ebbed after it became plain that Germany would not develop an atomic bomb, and even more support waned after Germany's surrender; but the original assumptions remained in place.

As the Manhattan Project neared completion, some scientists and GOVERNMENT officials suggested alternatives to using the atomic bomb—for example, an explicit warning to Japan; a demonstration of the bomb; agreeing to conditional surrender. U.S. NAVY and U.S. ARMY AIR FORCES leaders believed that a continuation of the naval blockade and air campaign against Japan would bring surrender. But there were counterarguments to such views, and Truman did not reverse the prior decision to use the bomb.

Some explanations for Truman's choice point to the difficulty the new president might have had in not following the unconditional surrender policy identified with President FRANKLIN D. ROOSEVELT, who had died only a few months earlier. Others suggest that the administration might have feared criticism for not using a weapon that cost $2 billion to develop. Some critics maintain that the bomb was dropped out of racism and revenge for PEARL HARBOR, the BATAAN DEATH MARCH, and other Japanese acts of war—although officials from the beginning had contemplated using the weapon on Germany, and anti-Japanese sentiment was at least as high among such Asian peoples as the Chinese and Filipinos who had suffered atrocities under the Japanese. The brutality of the war, and the bombing and killing of civilians by both the Allies and the Axis powers, contributed to a certain hardening of sensitivities among policymakers. In the several months prior to Hiroshima, for example, the American firebombing of Japanese cities, including Tokyo, took an estimated half million Japanese lives.

The aerial photo shows the aftermath of the atomic bomb explosion over Hiroshima. *(National Archives)*

Simple bureaucratic momentum also played a role, and helps to answer the question of why the second bomb was dropped, on Nagasaki. Once authorization was given to use the bomb after August 3, the timing of the bombings and the target of the second bomb were in the hands of military officials in the Pacific. Four cities, chosen for their shock value in demonstrating the destructive power of the bomb, were on the list of approved target cities. Hiroshima was designated for the first bomb because it was an undamaged industrial city lying on a plain surrounded by mountains, so that the bomb would cause maximum damage. Nagasaki (put last on the list) became the second target on August 9 because of weather conditions and the unexpected speed of preparing the "Fat Man" for use.

While most scholars agree that the atomic bomb was used to bring the surrender of Japan as quickly as possible, less consensus exists on whether the bomb was necessary to end the war. Some historians believe that conventional military power, a demonstration of the bomb, the entry of the Soviet Union into the war, agreement to a conditional surrender, or some combination of these factors, might have brought the Japanese surrender. On the other hand, a number of scholars, including some in Japan, hold that the shock of the atomic bomb was necessary to produce surrender by Japan's military leaders.

Some recent scholarship also calls into question the widespread understanding that the only alternative to the use of the bomb was invasion of the Japanese home islands, with a half million or more American deaths. Not only do some historians emphasize evidence suggesting that surrender might have come without an invasion or the atomic bomb, but a few contemporary documents indicate an expectation of no more than several tens of thousands of American deaths were an invasion to be launched. But even

A dense column of smoke rises more than 60,000 feet into the air over the Japanese port city of Nagasaki, the result of the second atomic bomb that was dropped on Japan. *(Library of Congress)*

that would have been a high cost, especially after more than three bloody years of war in the Pacific theater; and other contemporary documents project much higher figures. Since Truman had become president three months earlier, moreover, the United States had experienced nearly half of its total casualties in the Pacific theater, and the brutal warfare and high casualties on both sides at IWO JIMA and OKINAWA weighed much on American minds. Certainly Truman would have had a hard time justifying extending the war and losing even a small number of additional American lives. In any case, there is no way to know just what would have happened without use of the atomic bombs on Hiroshima and Nagasaki.

If the primary reason for dropping the bomb was to compel the quick surrender of Japan, most scholars also agree that a secondary and reinforcing reason was that it might work to the advantage of the United States in SOVIET-AMERICAN RELATIONS. By the summer of 1945, as the YALTA CONFERENCE and the Potsdam Conference had revealed, the United States and the Soviet Union were increasingly at odds about significant postwar questions, including Eastern Europe. Some American policymakers concluded that the American possession and use of the

bomb might make the Soviet Union more tractable on postwar issues. In fact, the bomb evidently exacerbated Soviet-American tensions and contributed to the development of the cold war—and to the uncertainties of the nuclear age.

Further reading: Richard B. Frank, *Downfall: The End of the Imperial Japanese Empire* (New York: Random House, 1999); John Hersey, *Hiroshima* (New York: Knopf, 1946); Michael J. Hogan, *Hiroshima in History and Memory* (New York: Cambridge University Press, 1996); Philip Nobile, ed., *Judgment at the Smithsonian* (New York: Marlowe & Co., 1995); Richard Rhodes, *The Making of the Atomic Bomb* (New York: Simon & Schuster, 1986); J. Samuel Walker, *Prompt and Utter Destruction: President Truman and the Use of Atomic Bombs against Japan* (Chapel Hill: University of North Carolina Press, 1997).

Holiday, Billie (1915–1959)

Billie Holiday is widely considered to be the most significant jazz-blues singer of the 1930s and 1940s. Her innovative style of singing made her a major figure in the world of MUSIC.

Born Eleanora Fagan, she spent her childhood in Baltimore. She did not begin singing professionally until she and her mother, Sadie Fagan, moved to New York. Unable to find work dancing, as had been her plan, she agreed to sing for $18 a week. She took her working name, Billie Holiday, from her father, Clarence Holiday, and from the actress Billie Dove.

Throughout her career, she worked with many influential jazz musicians. Her friend Lester Young gave her the nickname "Lady Day," by which she was known in jazz circles for much of her life. She performed with BENNY GOODMAN, Teddy Wilson, Count Basie, and Artie Shaw, and counted Louis Armstrong and Bessie Smith as her most important inspirations. Her singular style of singing meant that her voice was most suited to a more intimate musical accompaniment than could be achieved with a big band. It was her unusual style—relaxed and smooth, with an extraordinary capability for communicating emotion—that appealed greatly to jazz connoisseurs. Despite her popularity in jazz clubs, however, she never gained a large following in the general listening public. Among her best-known songs is "Strange Fruit," an account of a lynching that she introduced to her repertoire in 1938.

Holiday had a difficult personal life. She spent her childhood in poverty. She married twice, with both marriages ending unhappily, and she faced the discrimination routinely faced by AFRICAN AMERICANS in the venues where she worked. In addition, Holiday struggled with heroin addiction. She was arrested in 1947 and voluntarily committed to a rehabilitation program. Her addiction contributed to the gradual decline in her health and the quality of her voice during the 1950s. She died in a hospital at the age of 44 while under arrest for possession of drugs.

Further reading: Leslie Gourse, *Billie Holiday: The Tragedy and Triumph of Lady Day* (New York: Grolier Publishers, 1995).

—Joanna Smith

Holocaust

The Holocaust was the methodical persecution and attempted annihilation of European Jewry and Roma (Gypsies) by Nazi Germany. Between 1933 and 1945, Nazi forces murdered some 5 to 6 million JEWS—about two-thirds of Europe's Jewry—and more than 500,000 Roma.

Nazi persecution of Jews within Germany began immediately after Adolf Hitler's ascension to power in January 1933. Between 1933 and 1939, the Nazis undertook systematic measures to isolate Jews and to confiscate their assets. The Nuremberg Laws, for instance, implemented by the Nazi Party in September 1935, stripped Jews of their citizenship. Ongoing Nazi violence against Jews first crested on November 9–10, 1938, during Kristallnacht, a planned campaign of destruction and terror that resulted in the destruction of synagogues and Jewish businesses throughout Germany.

Hitler's annexation of Austria in 1938, the conquest of most of western Europe by the summer of 1940, and the invasions of Poland in 1939 and of the Soviet Union in 1941 brought the vast majority of Europe's Jews under Nazi control. By mid-1941, Nazis succeeded in removing German and Austrian Jews and Roma from all arenas of civil life, and had begun to persecute Jews living in western Europe. Millions of Polish Jews struggled to survive disease, starvation, and Nazi brutality in greatly overcrowded urban ghettos. More than 500,000 Jews and thousands of Roma were killed in large-scale massacres in the Soviet Union by divisions of the Nazi's police and security apparatus, with the assistance of local police and civilian collaborators. Initially, victims were shot after being forced to dig their own graves; later, they were gassed in mobile vans by Einzatsgruppen units.

By mid-1941, Hitler made clear his intention to annihilate Europe's Jews. The decision to exterminate all Roma in Europe came in December 1941. Planning of the "Final Solution" of what Hitler termed "the Jewish problem in Europe" took place in Wannsee, Germany, in January 1942. Those gathered for the meeting drew up a plan to round up and deport Jews from Nazi-occupied western Europe to concentration camps in the East. Jews in Poland, already segregated in ghettos, were to be sent to extermination

This 1945 photo was taken at Buchenwald concentration camp by a member of the U.S. 80th Infantry. Photograph by Private H. Miller *(United States Army)*

camps such as Treblinka and Belzec in Poland, designed to gas Jews on a mass scale immediately upon arrival. More than 3 million Jews died in these camps between 1942 and 1944. More than 1 million western and central European Jews selected for immediate death died in the gas chambers of Auschwitz-Birkenau. Jews chosen for slave labor in the thousands of Nazi concentration camps were systematically degraded, tortured, and starved. Jews sometimes fought back, notably during a three-week uprising in the Warsaw ghetto, but they were invariably defeated by an enemy intent upon their total annihilation.

News of Nazi persecution of Jews between 1933 and 1941 reached an American public marked by significant anti-immigrant sentiment and ANTI-SEMITISM. Events in Germany such as Kristallnacht in 1938 did provoke temporary outrage and a movement to boycott German-made goods. Fearing competition for scarce jobs during the GREAT DEPRESSION, however, the majority of Americans strongly opposed allowing REFUGEES fleeing from Nazism to enter the United States. Most members of CONGRESS echoed this public sentiment, defeating the few proposals offered to make exceptions to the restrictive IMMIGRATION quotas established in the 1920s.

The U.S. State Department administered American refugee policy. These officials, notably Assistant Secretary of State Breckinridge Long and many consulate officers abroad, designed impediments to drastically limit the number of Jewish and other refugees entering the United States. Despite public and congressional hostility toward loosening immigration quotas, President FRANKLIN D. ROOSEVELT called for a conference, held in France in July 1938, to respond to the developing refugee crisis caused by hundreds of thousands of German and Austrian Jews fleeing Nazi terror. No attending nation, however, including the United States, agreed to change its immigration laws, and no nation agreed to resettle what all insisted were "political," not Jewish, refugees.

The United States entered WORLD WAR II one month before Hitler's lieutenants formalized plans to exterminate Europe's Jews. Credible reports indicating the existence of extermination camps and the death of more than 1 million Jews reached the State Department by mid-1942. The State Department essentially confirmed their accuracy by autumn 1942, yet over the next year attempted to conceal that information from the American public. Roosevelt, aware of the reports, continued to insist that the best means of helping all of Hitler's victims was to achieve quick victory in the war.

Although divided by ideology and questions of strategy throughout the war, America's Jewish leadership was largely responsible for bringing public attention to the unfolding tragedy of the Holocaust in late 1942 and throughout 1943. Their efforts contributed to some public criticism of the administration's inaction. In response, FDR agreed to a bilateral conference suggested by the British government. The April 1943 Bermuda Conference, however, did not yield any changes in refugee policy, nor was the ongoing annihilation of Jews explicitly discussed.

In the winter of 1943–44, Secretary of the Treasury HENRY MORGENTHAU, JR., provided Roosevelt with more evidence about Nazis' killing of millions of Jews and a report on the State Department's obstructionist actions. Turning refugee policy over to the Treasury Department, FDR in January 1944 created a War Refugee Board (WRB) to facilitate the rescue of those in imminent danger of death by Nazi forces. WRB efforts are believed to have been responsible for saving about 200,000 Jews.

Further reading: Rita S. Botwinick, *A History of the Holocaust: From Ideology to Annihilation.* (Upper Saddle River, N.J.: Prentice Hall, 1996); David S. Wyman, *The Abandonment of the Jews: America and the Holocaust, 1941–1945* (New York: Pantheon, 1984); ———, *Paper Walls: America and the Refugee Crisis, 1938–1941* (Amherst: University of Massachusetts Press, 1968).

—Julie Whitcomb

Home Owners Loan Corporation (HOLC)

Designed to provide relief for homeowners facing foreclosure and to rescue the mortgage industry, the Home Owners Loan Corporation (HOLC) was created during the first Hundred Days of the NEW DEAL.

The GREAT DEPRESSION had created grave troubles in the mortgage industry. Prior to the 1930s, mortgage loans typically required high down payments (typically 35 percent or more) and had terms of five to 10 years, with a large "balloon" payment at the end of the loan. As homeowners were increasingly unable to meet the balloon payment, they had to refinance the loan or face foreclosure. To meet their own debts, banks called in balloon payments and liquidated the mortgages. Foreclosures jumped from 150,000 in 1930 to 250,000 in 1932, and to 1,000 per day by early 1933. With banks needing liquid assets and no home insurance to protect the owners, the mortgage industry was in shambles.

President HERBERT C. HOOVER had tried to address the problem with the Federal Home Loan Bank Act in 1932. CONGRESS, however, weakened Hoover's proposal to allow homeowners to use their home as collateral for a refinancing loan by making the amount of collateral needed to secure the loan more than most homeowners could afford. The result was that the Federal Home Loan Banks proved unable to slow the rate of foreclosure. Faced with an accelerated number of home (and farm) foreclosures after his inauguration, President FRANKLIN D. ROOSEVELT proposed the Home Owners Refinancing Act in the spring of 1933;

the act passed Congress in June 1933, creating the Home Owners Loan Corporation. (The FARM CREDIT ADMINISTRATION was also created in June to refinance farm mortgages.)

The HOLC had two purposes. First, it provided help to homeowners in danger of losing their homes by refinancing their mortgages. Second, it assisted troubled banks holding the mortgages by insuring the loans, thus allowing the banks to liquefy defaulted mortgages rather than owning and trying to resell the homes themselves. Operating mostly in America's CITIES, the HOLC refinanced almost one out of every five mortgages during the agency's life. Just from 1933 to 1936, it spent some $3 billion and refinanced a million homes. But while the agency assisted with refinancing, it was really an insurance agency for banks, not for homeowners, and it also foreclosed on properties, especially during the RECESSION OF 1937–38, when it foreclosed on 100,000 homes.

The Home Owners Loan Corporation did not survive WORLD WAR II. It was a victim of Congress's budget-cutting in 1943, when many New Deal RELIEF agencies, such as the WORKS PROGRESS ADMINISTRATION and NATIONAL YOUTH ADMINISTRATION, were eliminated. But the HOLC left a lasting legacy on the mortgage industry. Together with other New Deal HOUSING programs, such as the FEDERAL HOUSING ADMINISTRATION and the Federal National Mortgage Association (known popularly as Fannie Mae), HOLC helped to stabilize and rationalize the mortgage process. Mortgage loans became more affordable for many more Americans, the appraisal of homes was standardized so that insured banks financed homes at their appropriate value, and banks were able to turn their mortgages into liquid assets quickly by reselling them for their current value. By 1945, the risk that had long been a part of the realty and home construction industry had largely been removed, greatly aiding in the home building explosion of the postwar period.

Further reading: Kenneth T. Jackson, "Race, Ethnicity, and Real Estate Appraisal: The Home Owners Loan Corporation and the Federal Housing Administration," *Journal of Urban History* 6:4 (1980): 419–452; Gail Radford, *Modern Housing for America: Policy Struggles in the New Deal Era* (Chicago: University of Chicago Press, 1997).

—Katherine Liapis Segrue

Hoover, Herbert C. (1874–1964)

Herbert Clark Hoover served from 1929 to 1933 as the 31st president of the United States. Following impressive successes in BUSINESS and GOVERNMENT, Hoover won an overwhelming majority in the presidential election of 1928. But as the HOOVER PRESIDENCY was barely under way, the

GREAT DEPRESSION struck, and Hoover's unsuccessful efforts to revive the ECONOMY and deal with UNEMPLOYMENT led to his landslide defeat in the ELECTION OF 1932.

Hoover was born on August 10, 1874, in the Quaker community of West Branch, Iowa. Orphaned at the age of nine, he went to live with the Minthorn family in Newberg, Oregon. In 1891, Hoover entered Stanford University as a member of the "pioneer class" and pursued an interest in engineering. After graduating in 1895 with a degree in geology, he went to work for several mining operations throughout the West. He married fellow Stanford geology major Lou Henry, an outgoing woman who compensated for some of Hoover's introverted reserve.

In 1897, Hoover took a position with the London-based mining firm Bewick, Moreing and Company. By 1902, he had become a partner in Bewick Moreing, and for the next five years he traveled throughout the world, developing international prominence as an entrepreneur and geologist and earning praise as "the great engineer." After leaving the firm in 1908, Hoover invested in a number of successful mining and oil ventures. By 1910, at the age of 36, Hoover had amassed a fortune estimated at $3 million.

Hoover's Quaker upbringing had instilled in him not only an optimism that society could be improved and ordered through cooperative efforts, but also a conviction that wealth brought an obligation to work toward such goals through public service. With the outbreak of World War I, Hoover was given several opportunities to pursue his interest in humanitarianism and to apply his managerial skills to large-scale public endeavors. He headed the international committee for the relief of Belgium, which was successful in feeding 11 million people in Belgium and northern France. President Wilson then appointed Hoover as U.S. food administrator to coordinate efforts to provide food for allies. As food administrator, Hoover sought to avoid rationing, and instead encouraged Americans to voluntarily help conserve food by observing "wheatless" and "meatless" meals. After the war, Hoover headed the American Relief Administration's European Children's Fund, which continued to feed children through the summer of 1922.

Hailed as "the great humanitarian" for his wartime efforts, Hoover was appointed Secretary of Commerce under President Warren G. Harding. Although a member of the REPUBLICAN PARTY, ideologically Hoover was a progressive, and his appointment prompted opposition within the GOP. Hoover believed, as he described in his 1922 essay "American Individualism," that the government should play an active role in coordinating private industry and promoting voluntary associational efforts that would improve the overall standard of living without crossing the boundary between the public and private sectors.

During his time as secretary of commerce, he transformed an insignificant department into one of the most

Herbert Hoover campaigning from the back of a railroad car during the 1928 U.S. presidential election *(Library of Congress)*

important in the executive branch. Hoover not only made efforts to open foreign markets for U.S. goods, but he also worked to promote efficiency throughout the private sector through the standardization of consumer items, the reduction of costly LABOR strikes, and the improvement of planning processes. Moreover, Hoover worked to develop projects for the irrigation of dry lands and flood control.

In 1928, after President Calvin Coolidge chose not to run for reelection, the GOP turned to its most capable administrator to maintain control of the White House. Receiving 58 percent of the popular vote and carrying 40 out of 48 states, Hoover won by one of the largest margins in history. But with the STOCK MARKET CRASH of 1929 and the onset of the Great Depression. Hoover's presidency encountered enormous economic and political difficulties and his reputation sank with the economy. Although

Hoover made efforts to stave off further economic decline and to encourage business confidence, including the creation of the RECONSTRUCTION FINANCE CORPORATION, his failure to take effective action to alleviate unemployment and provide adequate RELIEF led many to perceive him as inept and uncaring. Hoover's presidency ended with his overwhelming defeat at the hands of FRANKLIN D. ROOSEVELT in 1932.

In 1933, Hoover returned to his home in Palo Alto, California, but he never completely retired from public life. Although he wanted the 1936 GOP presidential nomination, the party turned instead to Kansas governor ALFRED M. LANDON. Hoover remained an outspoken critic of the NEW DEAL, characterizing several programs as "fascistic," and vehemently criticizing Roosevelt's 1937 COURT-PACKING PLAN. He generally sided with ISOLATIONISTS who criticized Roosevelt's increasingly interventionist FOREIGN

POLICY in the late 1930s and early 1940s, although he did not join the AMERICA FIRST COMMITTEE.

During WORLD WAR II, Hoover established the privately run Polish Relief Commission, which fed children in occupied Poland until 1941 and the U.S. entry into the war. In 1946, President Harry S. Truman asked Hoover to head the Famine Emergency Commission to address postwar famine in Europe. In 1947, Hoover asked Congress to appoint a commission to examine the reorganization of the executive branch and address inefficiency in the federal government. The resulting Hoover Commission offered nearly 300 recommendations for change, more than two-thirds of which were accepted and which enhanced the managerial powers of the president. Hoover died on October 20, 1964.

Further reading: David Burner, *Herbert Hoover: A Public Life* (New York: Knopf, 1979); Joan Hoff Wilson, *Herbert Hoover: Forgotten Progressive* (Boston: Little, Brown, 1975).

—Shannon L. Parsley

Hoover, J. Edgar   See Volume IX

Hoover presidency

In 1928, HERBERT C. HOOVER was elected president with nearly three-fifths of the popular vote in a landslide victory over his Democratic opponent, Alfred E. Smith. Four years later, in the depths of the GREAT DEPRESSION, Hoover lost to FRANKLIN D. ROOSEVELT by margins as sweeping as those of 1928. The ELECTION OF 1932 was not just a rejection of the REPUBLICAN PARTY but also a repudiation of Hoover. For decades afterward, Hoover's image was that of a do-nothing, even heartless, president who deserved the political fate of 1932. More recently, however, historians have reexamined the Hoover presidency and found it more complicated and innovative than the prevailing stereotype. Some have even claimed to find significant origins of Roosevelt's NEW DEAL in Hoover's policies.

Hoover entered the White House with high public expectations. A mining engineer educated at Stanford, Hoover was a millionaire by the time he was 40 and devoted the rest of his life to public service. He earned a glowing reputation administering important programs during World War I, and in the 1920s was an active and powerful secretary of commerce under Presidents Warren G. Harding and Calvin Coolidge. Apparently one of the architects of the decade's prosperity, Hoover came to the presidency hailed as "the great engineer" and (because of his leadership in World War I relief efforts) as "the great humanitarian." On his inauguration in March 1929, the journalist Anne O'Hare McCormick wrote that "We were in a mood for magic. . . . We had summoned a great engineer to solve our problems for us; now we sat back comfortably and confidently to watch the problems being solved."

And Hoover, a deeply thoughtful man committed to his ideas and principles, was prepared to act. Convinced that modern technocratic skills could be brought to bear on public problems, he envisioned a "New Day" of ongoing prosperity. He believed that GOVERNMENT had a role to play in sustaining economic growth and social progress, but he also believed that the role of government must be limited and that the federal government should not intrude upon the responsibilities of the private sector or local government. Public policy should help to catalyze and coordinate voluntary "associational" activities in the private sector to stabilize the economy by promoting cooperation and efficiency, and it should facilitate a "new individualism" devoted to service and social progress. But the federal government should not direct and control those efforts and must above all avoid moving toward a regulatory or welfare state. He brought to the executive branch a number of "Hoover men" who shared his view and aims and his confidence in establishing coordinating mechanisms for addressing economic and social issues.

The Hoover presidency opened with a number of initiatives. The new president called a special session of CONGRESS to deal with AGRICULTURE, and within two months won passage of the AGRICULTURAL MARKETING ACT of 1929 that created the Federal Farm Board to sustain prices in a number of commodities by means of farm cooperatives and stabilization corporations. The administration planned a series of conferences and studies on other economic and social problems, with the intent of coordinating efforts to address them, and it began action in other areas too. But the early energy and high promise of the Hoover presidency soon ebbed. Little ultimately came from the detailed social and economic studies in terms of policy. Congress turned Hoover's request for tariff revision to provide flexibility into the HAWLEY-SMOOT TARIFF ACT of 1930, which imposed the highest tariff ever. Signed by Hoover despite criticism from virtually all the experts, the tariff suggested Hoover's deficiencies as a political leader. So did his unsuccessful efforts to revise IMMIGRATION policy, to reach agreement on oil production policy, and to find solutions to the vexing problem of Prohibition.

But it was the Great Depression that came to dominate administration priorities and policymaking. The depression also exposed the shortcomings of Hoover's leadership and produced his crushing defeat in 1932 and his unenviable public reputation for years after. Contrary to that public reputation, however, Hoover rejected orthodox advice to let the economy recover by itself. Rather, he took quick action to try to restore confidence and reverse the economic downturn. He issued statements declaring that the ECONOMY was fundamentally sound; he held meetings with BUSINESS leaders urging them not to cut production, prices, wages, or employment; he met with LABOR leaders requesting them not to press new wage demands or to conduct strikes; he promised to maintain and increase public works spending and urged local government to do the same; he supported lower interest rates and lower taxes to stimulate investment and buying.

Although such steps were in the right direction and went well beyond what previous presidents had done during depressions, none went far enough to have significant effect, and economic indexes continued down. The Agricultural Marketing Act was also unsuccessful, for in relying on voluntary action it gave the Federal Farm Board no authority to restrict production, and mounting surpluses overwhelmed the board's capacity and helped send agricultural prices plummeting still further. And the Hawley-Smoot Tariff went in exactly the wrong direction: It helped keep prices of American manufactured goods too high, and it invited retaliation from other nations to restrict markets for American industrial and agricultural goods. As the depression deepened, Hoover became less innovative, more resistant to new federal initiatives, and increasingly insistent that the origins of the depression lay abroad and that his policies were correct.

Two areas of policy—RELIEF and banking—reveal how Hoover's ideology shaped and constrained his action. They reveal as well how a number of significant initiatives of his presidency—such as the Norris-LaGuardia Act of March 1932 that limited the use of court injunctions against labor unions—often came from Congress with Hoover's reluctant acquiescence. With UNEMPLOYMENT mounting catastrophically in the early 1930s and with private and local relief efforts entirely inadequate, pressure mounted in the nation and in Congress for federal action. But Hoover's principles were clear: The federal government might encourage, support, and coordinate local and private efforts, but the federal government must not take on direct responsibility for relief. He created two agencies to collect information and to encourage and assist private and local efforts—the President's Emergency Committee on Employment, and then the President's Organization on Unemployment Relief—but they had little impact. As the depression worsened, moreover, Hoover insisted all the more on limiting government spending and trying to balance the budget. (In June 1932 he signed, with Democratic support, the largest peacetime tax increase ever.) Finally, after rebuffing or vetoing congressional measures for public works and relief spending, Hoover reluctantly signed the compromise RELIEF AND RECONSTRUCTION ACT in July 1932, which authorized the RECONSTRUCTION FINANCE CORPORATION to lend (not grant) states up to $300 million for relief and up to $1.5 billion for self-liquidating public works projects (toll roads, for example). But the administration allowed little of that money to be spent, and federal unemployment relief did not come until the New Deal.

In banking, Hoover took more action than he did with relief. The great problem of banking in the early 1930s was one of liquidity: how to turn declining paper assets (mortgages and business loans, for example) into the cash needed to pay off depositors. The Glass-Steagall Act of February 1932 expanded the currency supply by permitting the use of government securities to back Federal Reserve notes. In July 1932 the Congress passed the Federal Home Loan Bank Act, which did less than Hoover had recommended but did allow home loan banks to accept mortgages as collateral for loans. But these significant measures could not provide the help needed by faltering and failing commercial banks. Pressured by Hoover, who preferred private cooperative action, a number of the nation's major banks organized the National Credit Corporation late in 1931, with a fund of $500 million to help banks in need. But the bankers had exacted from Hoover a promise of federal assistance if the NCC proved inadequate to the task, as indeed it did. At Hoover's request, Congress in January 1932 created the Reconstruction Finance Corporation, authorized to lend up to $2 billion to banks and other financial institutions. But although it marked a significant new departure, the RFC disbursed money slowly, advanced loans largely to the largest banks and institutions, and did little to shore up the banking system. Under Roosevelt, the RFC was used far more dynamically to spur lending and expansion, not just to protect financial institutions.

Although his presidency came to be all but consumed by domestic economic matters, Hoover also gave attention to FOREIGN POLICY. He sought to reduce American intervention in Latin America, anticipating Roosevelt's GOOD NEIGHBOR POLICY of the 1930s. At the LONDON NAVAL CONFERENCE in 1930, he succeeded in winning modest expansion and a five-year extension of naval arms limitations. But the growing global depression and advancing militarism in Europe and Asia became the major problems; and here Hoover, like other heads of state, had little success. He sought major reductions in armaments at the WORLD DISARMAMENT CONFERENCE in 1932, and tried to tie them to resolving economic problems, but nothing came of his proposals. As the collapse of the American economy dried up the American loans abroad that had helped finance German reparations, Allied war debts, and European purchases of American goods, pressure mounted to reduce American tariffs and implement a moratorium on intergovernmental debts. Hoover finally agreed to the latter in June 1931, but the moratorium, unpopular among many Americans, could not rescue the international financial system. Nor did the administration take effective action to check militarism and aggression. After Japan invaded MANCHURIA in 1931, Secretary of State HENRY L. STIMSON could only persuade Hoover to respond with an essentially toothless "nonrecognition" policy with respect to Japanese territorial gains that violated international treaties involving the United States.

By mid-1932, then, the Hoover presidency and its efforts at home and abroad were in disarray. For most Americans, it was the domestic, not the global, situation that mattered, with the Great Depression approaching its

nadir. By the fall election, Hoover's reputation was badly tarnished not only by the depression and by his unsuccessful policies to deal with hard times, but by what seemed his hard-hearted refusal even to grant relief assistance. His role in sending military troops in late July to evict the BONUS ARMY that came to Washington to seek prepayment of the bonus voted them in the 1920s came to symbolize Hoover's presidency. The widely respected "Great Humanitarian" of 1928 had become the butt of jokes by 1932, with the shantytowns of the unemployed called Hoovervilles.

With between 12 to 14 million people out of work during the early 1930s, many Americans sought shelter in towns constructed of cardboard shacks on vacant land. In a gesture aimed at the government's unwillingness to act on their plight, they ironically dubbed these towns Hoovervilles. Shown is the Hooverville outside of Seattle, Washington. *(Private Collection)*

In the election that fall, Hoover went down to overwhelming defeat, losing the popular vote by 57.4 to 39.7 percent and carrying just six of the 48 states.

Although the electoral verdict of 1932 is understandable, the lingering image of a reactionary, do-nothing Hoover—in part the result of artful Democratic politicking in the 1930s—needs revision. Hoover did more than any president previously in combating a depression, and he often went beyond orthodox economic thought. Few leading Democrats advocated more far-reaching policies, and a number criticized him for doing and spending too much. Some of Hoover's initiatives were continued and expanded by Franklin Roosevelt, who also shared Hoover's concern about deficit spending and about the corroding effect of relief on initiative and self-respect. But the differences between the New Deal's regulatory welfare state and Hoover's policies far outweigh the continuities and similarities; and while the New Deal failed to end the depression, it did bring a variety of highly visible programs to provide relief and to effect social and economic reform.

Above all, perhaps, Hoover was an ideologue and a technocrat, unwilling to violate his ideas and principles, often contemptuous of politics and politicians, and unsuited by his shy and aloof temperament to providing public leadership. Roosevelt by contrast was a politician and a leader, at ease with people and in touch with public opinion, and ready to experiment in using government to provide humanitarian assistance and to preserve the American democratic capitalist system. The depression pushed Hoover's ideas and leadership ability to their limits and beyond, and then brought his defeat and the demise of his reputation. Indeed, the very failure of Hoover's programs helped set the stage for the far more expansive use of the federal government by the Roosevelt presidency.

Further reading: William J. Barber, *From New Era to New Deal: Herbert Hoover, the Economists, and American Economic Policy, 1921–1933* (New York: Cambridge University Press, 1985); David Burner, *Herbert Hoover: A Public Life* (New York: Knopf, 1979); Martin L. Fausold, *The Presidency of Herbert Hoover* (Lawrence: University of Kansas Press, 1985); Albert U. Romasco, *The Poverty of Abundance: Hoover, the Nation, the Depression* (New York: Oxford University Press, 1965); Jordan Schwarz, *The Interregnum of Despair: Hoover, Congress, and the Depression* (Urbana: University of Illinois Press, 1970); Joan Hoff Wilson, *Herbert Hoover: Forgotten Progressive* (Boston: Little, Brown, 1975).

Hopkins, Harry L. (1890–1946)

Harry Lloyd Hopkins, RELIEF administrator for the NEW DEAL in the 1930s, was one of the principal advisers of FRANKLIN D. ROOSEVELT and during WORLD WAR II served as the president's personal ambassador on key FOREIGN POLICY and military issues. A wisecracking, practical, and sometimes cynical man who was as comfortable at the race tracks as at the White House, Hopkins was tenderhearted as well as tough-minded, and he brought to public service deep concern for underprivileged and destitute Americans and unflagging dedication to Roosevelt and the nation.

Born and raised in Iowa and educated at Iowa's Grinnell College, Hopkins moved to New York City in 1912, and for nearly two decades worked as a social worker and administrator. In those capacities he developed his convictions that public and private agencies needed to do more to alleviate poverty and ill health and that every American should "have access to the opportunity to provide for himself and his family a decent and American way of living." In 1931, Roosevelt, then governor of New York, named Hopkins to head the state's Temporary Emergency Relief Administration; in 1933, Roosevelt brought Hopkins to Washington to head the first major national relief program, the FEDERAL EMERGENCY RELIEF ADMINISTRATION (FERA).

From 1933 to 1938, Hopkins served as Roosevelt's relief administrator, heading not just the FERA but subsequently also the CIVIL WORKS ADMINISTRATION (CWA) and the WORKS PROGRESS ADMINISTRATION (WPA). Like Roosevelt, Hopkins preferred work relief, which preserved dignity and self-respect in addition to building the national infrastructure, over direct relief (cash payments or food and clothing) to the unemployed and needy. He took part throughout the decade in an often vitriolic and usually successful struggle for works projects money with Secretary of the Interior HAROLD ICKES, who headed the PUBLIC WORKS ADMINISTRATION and preferred carefully planned, capital-intensive public works projects over the labor-intensive work relief projects that could quickly get money into the economy. Hopkins's enormous energy and bureaucratic talents helped the relief programs accomplish what they did in the face of fiscal, ideological, and political obstacles. Despite the heavy and sometimes inefficient spending on relief, Hopkins's reputation for probity was never questioned—although he did come under fire, sometimes justified, for using relief spending for political purposes.

In Roosevelt's second term, Hopkins's role changed, and he became even more important in New Deal politics and policymaking. He had a significant part in Roosevelt's decision to try (with little success) to "purge" the DEMOCRATIC PARTY of anti–New Deal conservatives in the election of 1938, and by 1938 he was among the New Dealers pushing hardest to adopt fiscal policy based on KEYNESIANISM to lift the ECONOMY out of the RECESSION OF 1937–38. Late in 1938, he resigned as relief administrator to become secretary of commerce, and in the latter capacity not only tried to reconcile BUSINESS to the New Deal but also continued to push for Keynesian spending to underwrite recovery and reform. By the late 1930s, however, Hopkins was suffering from stomach cancer and a severe digestive disorder that led him to resign from the cabinet in 1940. But when Roosevelt decided to run for a third term in the ELECTION OF 1940, he relied on Hopkins to help assure his renomination and the somewhat unpopular nomination of HENRY A. WALLACE for vice president.

During World War II, Hopkins served as Roosevelt's adviser and personal envoy on diplomatic and military matters and lived for long spells in the White House. He worked especially to find ways to speed the defeat of the AXIS and to ensure the effectiveness of the GRAND ALLIANCE. Early in 1941, Hopkins visited England to help enhance coordination and cooperation between the two nations, and until August 1941 headed the LEND-LEASE ACT program sending assistance to Great Britain and later the Soviet Union. He worked with General GEORGE C. MARSHALL on military policy, served as FDR's envoy to British prime minister Winston Churchill and Soviet leader Josef Stalin, and played significant roles at the CASABLANCA CONFERENCE, the CAIRO CONFERENCE, and the TEHERAN CONFERENCE in 1943. At Teheran he helped persuade Churchill to agree to open a SECOND FRONT in the spring of 1944.

But cancer and his digestive disorder continued to ravage Hopkins and to diminish the energy of this once indefatigable man. His health kept him on the sidelines for much of 1944, and after participating in the February 1945 YALTA CONFERENCE he returned to the United States for treatment at the Mayo Clinic, where he was when Roosevelt died in April 1945. Although he resigned from the government in early May, he undertook at the request of new president Harry S. Truman another mission to Moscow later that month to try to persuade Stalin, with some limited success, to be more cooperative on a number of issues. Hopkins died in January 1946.

Further reading: Searle F. Charles, *Minister of Relief: Harry Hopkins and the Depression* (Syracuse, N.Y.: Syracuse University Press, 1963); George T. McJimsey, *Harry Hopkins: Ally of the Poor and Defender of Democracy* (Cambridge, Mass.: Harvard University Press, 1987).

housing

During the GREAT DEPRESSION and WORLD WAR II, the construction of private housing in the United States fell dramatically from the peak it had reached during the housing boom of the mid-1920s and did not recover fully until the postwar era. In 1925, 937,000 new housing units were constructed (more than 80 percent of them in urban areas). In 1933, the worst year of the Great Depression, only 93,000 units were built. Construction recovered slowly during the balance of the decade, but never approached the level reached in the 1920s.

In response to the collapse of the private housing industry during the 1930s, the NEW DEAL implemented legislation to stimulate the residential building and aid both middle- and lower-income families seeking better housing. Two of these acts, the National Housing Act of 1934 and the U.S. Housing Act of 1937, have survived to the present day. Also, during World War II the federal government built over 700,000 housing units to accommodate war workers, but only a relatively small number of them survived after 1945 to become permanent residences.

The long slump in new home construction crowded families and individuals into smaller, less attractive dwellings, and in the most extreme cases, into self-constructed shanties. For millions of Americans, the dream of buying their own home was shattered. In addition, hundreds of thousands of families who had purchased homes during the 1920s faced foreclosure when unemployment forced them to stop making their mortgage payments. Finally, the collapse of the home building industry threw construction workers out of jobs.

The Great Depression impelled millions of Americans to look to the federal GOVERNMENT, and to President FRANKLIN D. ROOSEVELT's New Deal, to help them survive the hard economic times. In response, FDR and the New Deal Democrats launched a host of programs to deal with the depression, and several focused on housing. Between 1933 and 1937, CONGRESS passed three major pieces of legislation that had varying degrees of influence on the housing sector. (Other New Deal programs, such as the RESETTLEMENT ADMINISTRATION, also involved housing.) The first of these measures was the Home Owners Refinancing Act of 1933 that prevented nearly a million homeowners from losing their houses. This was accomplished by the HOME OWNERS LOAN CORPORATION, a federal lending agency that allowed homeowners to refinance their mortgages, stretching them out for 20 years or longer, thus reducing the monthly payments.

By far the most important piece of housing legislation passed during the 1930s was the National Housing Act of 1934. Its goal was to stimulate new housing construction and reduce unemployment in the construction industry. It did this through another federal agency, the FEDERAL HOUSING ADMINISTRATION (FHA), which guaranteed loans for the construction of new houses if the dwellings met FHA guidelines involving the quality of construction, location, and the creditworthiness of the buyer. Mortgage lenders, now assured that they would bear no real risk in making loans on FHA-approved houses, offered low down

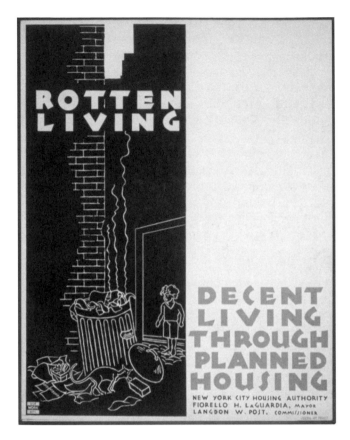

Poster for planned housing in New York City *(Library of Congress)*

payments and 20- to 30-year mortgages, terms far superior to those offered during the 1920s. Almost immediately, housing starts began to rise, and in 1939 over 500,000 private housing units were started. World War II brought private home construction to a temporary halt; but after the war, the long-term mortgages and housing standards established by the FHA, plus an even more generous financial package offered to veterans by the Veterans Administration, helped create the great postwar boom of the SUBURBS.

The FHA program also had the unintended effect of contributing to the decline of central CITIES. During the depressed 1930s, FHA administrators saw their overriding goals as creating the maximum number of new homes and assuring that these houses would retain their value and that owners would not default on their mortgages. Consequently, the FHA favored as prospective buyers middle-income families seeking homes built in white, middle-class areas on the fringes of central cities and out in the suburbs. New houses built in older neighborhoods, or in areas with more mixed populations, were generally not approved for FHA loans. As a result, FHA policy accelerated the outward movement of the white middle classes and denied

financial help to older, central city neighborhoods that had begun to decline, but were still far from slums.

The third major federal housing program of the New Deal, and the only one that generated real controversy, was the U.S. Housing Act of 1937 (also known as the Wagner Public Housing Act, after its chief sponsor, New York senator ROBERT F. WAGNER). Creating the UNITED STATES HOUSING AUTHORITY, the measure in its final form authorized direct federal funding for the construction of publicly owned, low-rent housing by local governments willing to create public housing authorities. Conservatives opposed all types of directly financed, publicly owned housing, but disagreement also existed among supporters of federally financed housing. One group, composed mainly of social workers, favored legislation that would construct federally subsidized housing within central cities exclusively for low-income families currently living in slum housing. Another group, composed more of architects and city planners, wanted legislation that would allow the federal government not only to help low-income families but also to provide financial aid to groups of moderate-income families that wished to build not-for-profit or cooperative housing. Since moderate-income people composed a much larger segment of the nation's population than the very poor, a federal housing program including them in publicly aided housing developments had the potential to create a far higher proportion of dwellings outside the traditional private housing market.

This more sweeping proposal alarmed the private housing industry. The U.S. Chamber of Commerce, the National Association of Real Estate Boards, and a number of other housing-related organizations were generally opposed to all types of publicly owned housing, but they lobbied most strenuously against the moderate-income housing proposals. As a result, the final version of the Wagner Housing Act authorized federal aid for housing projects open only to very low income families, and virtually guaranteed that these projects would be constructed only in central cities, on former slum sites. Suburban areas could keep public housing out by refusing to create public housing authorities. Finally, the act put a cap on per-unit construction costs that compelled local housing authorities to build dwellings or apartments that, while safe and sanitary, contained such a minimum amount of space and so few amenities that they would attract only those living in slum housing.

By 1941, hundreds of local housing authorities created under the Wagner Housing Act built approximately 160,000 housing units in the inner-city areas of the great metropolitan centers and in the poorer sections of smaller cities and towns. Because the housing in these projects was far safer and more sanitary than the typical slum dwelling, and because the federal subsidy allowed local housing authorities to charge very modest rent, waiting lists quickly developed. This new construction upgraded the housing conditions of many low-income families, but like FHA construction also reinforced the growing separation of lower- and middle-income groups from one another and accelerated the decline of central cities.

Quite separate from the New Deal housing programs of the 1930s were the housing units built by the federal government between 1940 and 1945 to house war workers and their families. The gigantic scale of war production brought millions of men and women to work in defense plants, often overwhelming the adjacent communities. Single family houses were divided up for three or four families, garages were converted into dwellings, and still there was not nearly enough space for the war workers. In June 1940, the federal government funded 20 housing developments for war workers; but the vast majority of war housing was built under the guidelines of the Lanham Defense Housing Act of October 1940. Congressman Lanham had been an opponent of the Wagner public housing program and wrote into the war housing legislation a section that prohibited the federal government from converting any of the war housing into public housing units for low-income families without the specific authorization of Congress.

By 1945, the federal government had spent approximately $2.5 billion constructing more than 700,000 housing units that ranged from trailer camps and temporary barracks-like housing units to entire residential communities. Some of these communities were designed by leading architects and achieved high standards, but most of the war housing developments were far more prosaic. No specific plan had been developed for disposing of the war housing units, so it took the federal government over a decade to dispose of them. Because of the provisions of the Lanham Act, only a tiny number of the housing units were conveyed to local public housing authorities. Approximately 250,000 temporary housing units were torn down and another 270,000 moved to college campuses to provide housing for veterans (and their families) attending school under the GI BILL. Approximately 182,000 permanent housing units, including a number of the most well-designed communities, were sold to veterans or to private investors. The government contractors who constructed some of the larger federal war housing projects gained valuable experience in the mass production of dwellings that they employed after the war in building communities such as the Levittowns.

Further reading: Gail Radford, *Modern Housing for America: Policy Struggles in the New Deal Era* (Chicago: University of Chicago Press, 1997); Kristin Szylvian, "The Federal Housing Program during World War II," in *From Tenements to Taylor Homes: In Search of an Urban Housing Policy in Twentieth-Century America,* edited by John

Bauman (University Park: Penn State University Press, 2000).

—Joseph L. Arnold

Hull, Cordell (1871–1955)

Cordell Hull served as a U.S. congressman (1907–21, 1923–31), senator (1931–33), and secretary of state (1933–44), and was the recipient of the 1945 Nobel Peace Prize. Born and raised in Tennessee, he attended Cumberland Law School and graduated in 1891. At age 21, Hull was elected to the Tennessee legislature, where he was a member from 1893 to 1897. After serving as a captain in the Spanish-American War, he presided as a circuit court judge from 1903 to 1907. In 1917, he married Rose Frances Whitney.

Hull was elected to the U.S. House of Representatives from Tennessee in 1906 and soon became an expert in economic policy. During Woodrow Wilson's presidency, Hull helped draft the first modern federal income tax as part of the Underwood Tariff Act (1913), and strongly supported U.S. membership in the League of Nations. He remained a devoted Wilsonian in his approach to international affairs throughout his career. Active in post–World War I world trade agreement efforts, Hull opposed the Republican Party's high tariffs and included a low-tariff program when writing portions of the DEMOCRATIC PARTY platform for the ELECTION OF 1932.

President FRANKLIN D. ROOSEVELT appointed Hull secretary of state in 1933, in part as a reward for Hull helping him win the 1932 Democratic nomination. Because of Roosevelt's own interest and involvement in FOREIGN POLICY, the president himself dominated major diplomatic decisions and initiatives with respect to Europe before and during WORLD WAR II. Hull was given more responsibility for Latin America and the Pacific, and for international trade negotiations. Hull and Roosevelt generally had good personal relations and shared many views, although some of Roosevelt's close advisers disparaged Hull. In 1937, SUMNER WELLES became undersecretary of state, an appointment that created friction between Roosevelt and Hull because FDR often preferred to work with Welles. Particularly during the war, Hull complained privately about being bypassed or ignored on key foreign policy decisions.

Throughout his tenure as secretary of state, Hull was a leading advocate of lower tariffs to stimulate international trade. At the LONDON ECONOMIC CONFERENCE of June and July 1933, Hull, who headed the American delegation, presented a plan to reduce trade barriers, only to be embarrassed by FDR's last minute decision not to back Hull's proposals or to participate in a new international economic program. Nonetheless, Hull was instrumental in having CONGRESS approve the RECIPROCAL TRADE AGREE-

MENTS ACT of 1934, which gave the president authority to lower tariff rates for countries trading with the United States. He had an important role in working for reduced trade barriers in the 1930s and the postwar era.

In addition to his efforts for freer international trade, Hull pursued other of Woodrow Wilson's aims, including better relations with Latin America. In November 1933 Hull was the chief American representative at the seventh Pan-American Conference in Montevideo, Uruguay, winning the confidence of Latin American leaders and laying foundations for the GOOD NEIGHBOR POLICY. The Montevideo conference was especially important for a protocol opposing intervention into the affairs of an independent country, an agreement that promised to change American policy in Latin America.

During the 1930s, Hull generally supported noninterventionist and neutrality policies, but he became by the end of the decade a proponent of rearmament, collective security, and aid to the Western democracies in order to resist AXIS aggression. Although Roosevelt rarely consulted with Hull about European affairs before or during the war, he did give Hull a larger role in trying to preserve peace and protect American interests in East Asia. Hoping to stop Japanese imperialism and aggression, Hull proposed the extension of oil, iron, and steel embargoes on the Japanese, as well as economic and military credit to the Chinese to build their defenses. Ultimately, of course, Hull and the United States proved unable to come to agreement with Japan, and war came at PEARL HARBOR in December 1941.

Consistent with Wilson's efforts to create the League of Nations, Hull throughout World War II sought to ensure an effective international organization to provide collective security and keep the peace in the postwar era. His work in helping to establish the UNITED NATIONS was perhaps the major achievement of Hull's career. Avoiding Wilson's mistakes, Hull carefully included Congress in planning for the United Nations, and in 1943 he visited Moscow to urge Soviet participation in the new organization. The longest serving secretary of state in American history, Hull resigned as secretary in November 1944 because of failing health. He continued to work as a senior adviser to the United Nations Conference in 1945.

Hull received the 1945 Nobel Peace Prize in honor of his work in Latin America and his efforts in the establishment of the United Nations. He devoted his remaining years to international peace issues, and died in July 1955 at the age of 84.

Further reading: Cordell Hull, *The Memoirs of Cordell Hull*, 2 vols. (New York: Macmillan, 1948); Julius Pratt, *Cordell Hull, 1933–1944*, 2 vols. (New York: Cooper Square, 1964).

—Anne Rothfeld

I

Ickes, Harold L. (1874–1952)

Harold LeClaire Ickes served as secretary of the interior from 1933 to 1946, longer than anyone has ever held that office. He also headed the PUBLIC WORKS ADMINISTRATION (PWA) of the NEW DEAL and served as petroleum administrator during WORLD WAR II. Despite his numerous differences with President FRANKLIN D. ROOSEVELT and other New Deal officials, Ickes, the self-described "old curmudgeon," was widely hailed for his honesty and efficiency.

Born on his grandfather's farm in Pennsylvania, Ickes moved to Chicago as a teenager. He became a reporter for the *Chicago Tribune* after graduating from the University of Chicago, where he earned a law degree in 1907. Originally a Republican, he joined the progressive Bull Moose movement of Theodore Roosevelt. Above all, Ickes was a government reformer. He fought corruption in both major parties, and, as a progressive, inveighed against graft and boss rule in Chicago. After heading the Western Independent Republican Committee for Roosevelt in 1932, Ickes became Roosevelt's secretary of the interior and served FDR in a number of key administrative capacities from 1933 to 1945. The irascible Ickes, characterized by his rugged honesty and referred to, with some sarcasm by his opponents, as "Honest Harold," was one of the more colorful and sometimes controversial figures of the Roosevelt administration.

From the beginning, Ickes was involved in a number of different policy areas. As secretary of the interior, he was responsible for the nation's natural resources, including federal land and mineral, water, fish, and wildlife resources. During the 1930s, he created a service aimed at fighting soil erosion, designed to improve conditions in parts of the Midwest and Southwest that became known as the DUST BOWL, crusaded for the preservation of domestic energy resources, worked on reforms involving public land in the West, sought to entice private investment into land preservation projects, and increased the stature of the national

park system. Intent on carrying out the work of national resource conservation, Ickes expanded the traditional role of the Interior Department.

As head of the Public Works Administration, a key New Deal agency established by the NATIONAL INDUSTRIAL RECOVERY ACT in 1933 to combat the GREAT DEPRESSION, Ickes controlled the expenditure of billions of dollars in federal money designed to boost the ECONOMY by constructing public works projects. His extreme frugality at the PWA significantly diminished the effectiveness of the program. In 1933, Ickes spent just $110 million of the more than $3 billion allocated to the PWA. Ickes differed sharply and often with RELIEF administrator HARRY HOPKINS, who held that government work funds should be spent more quickly and on labor-intensive projects that would give employment and income to workers rather than on capital-intensive projects. As a result of Ickes's cautious and penurious management, the PWA fell far short of delivering a badly needed economic boost in the early years of the Roosevelt administration—although the agency did earn a well-deserved reputation for honest, economical, and high-quality projects.

Roosevelt found Ickes a valuable asset as an administrator and a political adviser. He frequently called on Ickes for political help, particularly during the ELECTION OF 1936 and then during the controversial COURT-PACKING PLAN of 1937, which Ickes had encouraged. Mounting frustrations with New Deal opponents led Ickes in 1940 and 1944 to launch vituperative attacks on Republican presidential nominees WENDELL WILLKIE and THOMAS DEWEY, respectively. Ickes also quarreled with FDR and other New Dealers, feeling that his suggestions had not been given serious consideration, but his personal friendship with the president endured. As petroleum administrator during the war, Ickes played a key role in the wartime MOBILIZATION efforts on the American home front.

Ickes served one year as interior secretary under Harry S. Truman, before resigning from the GOVERNMENT in

1946 because of disagreements with the new administration. Upon leaving Washington, he settled on a farm near Olney, Maryland, working on his voluminous diary published as *The Secret Diary of Harold L. Ickes,* which serves as a valuable source on the politics of the New Deal. Ickes died in Washington, D.C., on February 3, 1952, at age 77.

See also ENVIRONMENTAL ISSUES.

Further reading: Graham White, and John Maze, *Harold Ickes and the New Deal: His Private Life and Public Career* (Cambridge, Mass.: Harvard University Press, 1985).

—Joseph C. Gutberlet

immigration

The most important developments in immigration from 1929 to 1945 were the sharp reduction in the number of immigrants because of the GREAT DEPRESSION and WORLD WAR II and the issue of what to do about REFUGEES, especially Jewish refugees from Nazi Germany and the HOLO-CAUST.

Immigration to the United States dropped off precipitously in the 1930s. The number of immigrants had averaged about 1 million per year in the decade before World War I, surged again once the war was over, and then fell off with the immigration restriction legislation of 1921 and 1924. Even so, immigration averaged nearly 300,000 annually from 1925 to 1930. The Great Depression then sent immigration plummeting to barely more than 50,000 per year from 1931 to 1940—the lowest rate since the 1820s. In the early years of the 1930s, in fact, more people left than entered the United States. Immigration picked up in the second half of the decade, before declining again, to only about 30,000 annually, during the war.

The social composition of immigration changed in the era too. Because the 1924 legislation imposed immigration quotas for nations outside the Western Hemisphere (and prevented most immigration from Asia), a higher proportion of immigrants than before came from Canada and Mexico. In terms of gender, immigration changed from about three-fifths male from 1900 to 1930 to three-fifths female in the next two decades.

While the decline in immigration in the 1920s had resulted from laws motivated in substantial part by nativist desires to keep out immigrants from southern and eastern Europe and from Asia, the low totals of the 1930s came largely because mass UNEMPLOYMENT made the United States a much less attractive destination. American policy also played a role, however. Concerned about the economic crisis, President HERBERT HOOVER insisted upon tight enforcement of national policy going back to the late 19th century preventing admission of immigrants who were likely to become public charges (the "LPC clause"). The

MEXICAN REPATRIATION PROGRAM of the 1930s begun in the HOOVER PRESIDENCY returned up to a half million MEXICAN AMERICANS to Mexico, many of them U.S. citizens, on the grounds that they might take scarce jobs or swell RELIEF rolls.

The administration of FRANKLIN D. ROOSEVELT brought little liberalization to immigration policy. The Tydings-McDuffie Act of 1934, in addition to setting independence for the Philippines for 1945, established a quota of just 50 per year on Filipino immigration. But the Mexican Repatriation Program slowed in the mid-1930s, the number of immigrants deported declined significantly, and during World War II the United States inaugurated the bracero program to bring Mexicans into the country to help alleviate the shortage of agricultural labor. In 1943, CONGRESS repealed the Chinese exclusion laws that went back to 1882 but established a yearly quota of just 105 for Chinese immigration. (It also made immigrant Chinese Americans eligible for citizenship, which paved the way for ultimately ending the ban on ASIAN AMERICAN immigrants becoming citizens.)

By the mid-1930s, the issue of refugees, especially Jewish refugees from Nazi Germany, began to emerge. In the contexts of the 1924 national quota law, the unemployment problem of the 1930s, and widespread ANTI-SEMITISM, the United States accepted only a small proportion of those who wanted to flee Nazi rule. Roosevelt did convene an unsuccessful conference in France in 1938 to discuss the refugee problem and also directed that refugees on temporary visas be allowed to remain in the United States and that the LPC clause not be rigidly enforced against refugees. He did not, however, make the refugee issue a major priority or take action to liberalize policy when German quotas were filled in the late 1930s. From 1933 through the end of World War II, the United States accepted an estimated quarter million refugees from Europe, most of them Jewish—but that total fell far below the quota limit even though it significantly exceeded what any other nation did.

During the war, immigration from outside the Western Hemisphere slowed to a trickle. Caused partly by the impact of wartime conditions on international travel, the decline also reflected State Department concerns about admitting immigrants who might be a threat to national security and by the anti-Semitic prejudices of some influential officials in the department. Secretary of the Treasury HENRY MORGENTHAU, JR., dismayed by the accumulating evidence of the Holocaust and the obstructionism of the State Department, helped persuade Roosevelt to create the War Refugee Board in January 1944, which may ultimately have helped rescue as many as 200,000 Jews. New U.S. policy on refugees and other displaced persons, and the resumption of significant immigration, did not occur until the early postwar era.

Further reading: Elliott Robert Barkan, *And Still They Come: Immigrants and American Society, 1920 to the 1990s* (Wheeling, Ill.: Harlan Davidson, 1996); Stephan Thernstrom, ed., *Harvard Encyclopedia of American Ethnic Groups* (Cambridge, Mass.: Belknap Press of Harvard University, 1980).

Indian Reorganization Act (1934)

The Indian Reorganization Act of 1934 was a major piece of NEW DEAL legislation aimed at reforming the relationship of the federal GOVERNMENT with NATIVE AMERICANS. The centerpiece of John Collier's "Indian New Deal," the act sought to restore self-government and cultural pride to Native Americans. While the act fell far short of Collier's initial intent, it reversed federal policy designed to assimilate Native Americans and provided a precedent for Indians to organize in later decades to demand full political and civil rights.

The Dawes Severalty Act of 1887 had guided federal policy toward Native Americans until the GREAT DEPRESSION. Providing for an allotment of 160 acres to family heads living on a federal reservation, the Dawes Act was intended to weaken tribal authority and to assimilate Indians through private property and individualism by providing them with land to make a living as farmers. By 1933, however, it was obvious that allotments had not improved the lives of Native Americans, whose economic and social circumstances were often dreadful.

The major advocate of reforming Indian policy was the commissioner of Indian affairs, John Collier. A social worker by education and training, Collier had been a major critic of federal Indian policy during the 1920s. Deeply influenced by Chief Justice John Marshall's 1832 decision that described Native American tribes as roughly comparable to foreign nations, meaning they should have limited self-government, and impressed by the Pueblo Indian reservation's agricultural success and cultural cohesiveness, Collier wanted to overhaul Indian policy to give tribes autonomy over their land, local politics, and cultural identity.

CONGRESS passed the Indian Reorganization Act, popularly known as the Wheeler-Howard Act, on June 18, 1934, though only with the personal intervention of Secretary of the Interior HAROLD L. ICKES and President FRANKLIN D. ROOSEVELT. The act effectively ended the allotment policy, allowing those who held land allotments to exchange them for shares in newly created tribal corporations. The corporations were able to hire legal counsel and oversee all issues arising from the communally held land, including disputes with state governments. For those who wanted to retain ownership of their land, inheritance rights were retained. Surplus land, meaning reservation land not allotted, reverted to the tribal corporation. Two million dollars were appropriated to allow reservations to acquire new lands to consolidate their land, while a $10 million fund was set up for tribes to modernize their reservations. For those tribes who voted to participate, a fund was set aside to assist them to set up a tribal corporation.

A tribal referendum was the mechanism to decide whether to participate in the Indian Reorganization Act. If a tribe rejected participation, it remained under the jurisdiction of the Bureau of Indian Affairs. If the referendum accepted the act, an election for tribal council members was then held; and once one-third of the members asked for a tribal corporation, a charter was written and a majority vote put the tribal corporation into effect. In the year following the act, tribes held referendums on whether to accept the act, with the larger reservations generally accepting the act and the smaller ones rejecting it. Only 71 tribes voted to participate and fully incorporate under the act.

The self-government that Collier had wanted through the Indian Reorganization Act did not work as effectively as he had envisioned. Many white westerners opposed the reform, and Native Americans were not unified in their support of the new policy. Many tribal leaders had been raised and educated under assimilation policy, and Collier could not convince them that the land reform would benefit them in the long term. A major blow came when the Navajo reservation voted in June 1935 to reject the act. Finally, Congress had weakened the legislation in 1934 to secure its passage, and provisions for an autonomous Indian court and another that made the tribal corporations the equivalent of municipalities were taken out of the act. Tribes who participated in the Indian Reorganization Act thus had something less than the self-government Collier had intended.

Opposition to significant reform began building as early as 1934. Funding for the Bureau of Indian Affairs and the Indian Reorganization Act was cut in each succeeding year, especially as Collier himself became more unpopular in Congress among opponents of the New Deal. He resigned as commissioner in 1945. In the 1950s, Congress tried to undo the Indian New Deal and return to assimilation with its "termination" policy of ending both public support of Indians and their special status under the law, but that policy was largely ignored and then ended in the 1960s.

Ultimately, the Indian Reorganization Act failed to significantly improve the economic and social conditions of Native Americans living on reservations, though it did have some residual success. It did end the allotment program, and by implication, reversed assimilation policy. And the tribal corporations that the act allowed for were able to reignite a sense of unity among Native Americans that would turn into a larger Pan-Indian movement in later decades.

Further reading: Kenneth Philp, *John Collier's Crusade for Indian Reform, 1920–1954* (Tucson: University of Arizona Press, 1977); Graham D. Taylor, *The New Deal and American Indian Tribalism: The Administration of the Indian Reorganization Act, 1934–1954* (Lincoln: University of Nebraska Press, 1980).

—Katherine Liapis Segrue

intelligence

Intelligence is information about other nations that has been carefully winnowed and analyzed for use by military and political leaders. The existence of permanent state institutions devoted to the collection and analysis of information on other nations, such as the Soviet Union's KGB or the American Central Intelligence Agency, is a recent phenomenon dating from WORLD WAR II. Before then, nations operated intelligence agencies only in wartime, and such agencies tended to be small military-affiliated ad hoc groups. Also beginning in World War II, the collection of information by technical means—for example, CODE BREAKING and intercepting communications—has far outweighed information gathered by human spies.

The United States greatly expanded its intelligence apparatus after 1941, having learned valuable lessons from the military disasters at PEARL HARBOR and in the PHILIPPINES. The major American intelligence organizations were affiliated with the military and included the U.S. Office of Naval Intelligence (ONI) and the War Department Military Intelligence Division (WDGS/MID or G-2). The War Department also created a Counter Intelligence Corps to ferret out spies in cooperation with the FEDERAL BUREAU OF INVESTIGATION, as well as a Special Branch in the Military Intelligence Service to conduct decoding operations, similar to the U.S. Navy's Communications Security Unit. Both army and navy groups excelled at code breaking, giving a significant strategic and tactical military advantage to Allied leaders. The United States also created the OFFICE OF STRATEGIC SERVICES (OSS) in June 1942, under the U.S. Joint Chiefs of Staff, to gather foreign intelligence. Although terminated in 1945, the OSS provided the basis for creating the Central Intelligence Agency in 1947.

In Great Britain, intelligence agencies were centralized in the military, were identified by the initials MI, and eventually numbered 19 organizations covering the full gamut of intelligence, counterintelligence, and ESPIONAGE operations. The two most famous included MI-5, the security service, and MI-6, the special or secret intelligence service, which were expanded during the war, although both had existed since 1909. MI-6 contained the Code and Cipher School at Bletchley Park, as well as the Radio Security Service.

The Soviet Union had two successful intelligence organizations during the war, the Red Army intelligence and espionage organization known as the GRU, and the Communist Party internal security apparatus known as the NKVD, which evolved into the postwar KGB. The GRU had important success with its espionage efforts in the American MANHATTAN PROJECT that produced the ATOMIC BOMB.

Japan alone among the major belligerents had a long history of organized intelligence operations, dating back to the Sino-Japanese War of 1895 and the Russo-Japanese War of 1904–05. In addition to the navy and army Special Service Organizations, Japan operated a secret state police force, the Kempei, which handled internal security and counterintelligence, as well as an intelligence service associated with the diplomatic service abroad. Surprisingly, considering Japan's long experience and extensive organizations, tactical intelligence gathering by military forces during World War II was exceptionally poor.

Nazi Germany suffered from a diffusion of intelligence efforts. Several state, Nazi Party, and military intelligence organizations existed during the Nazi era, although each tended to work in isolation and rarely shared information, a common handicap afflicting intelligence agencies in totalitarian states. The SS contained the Nazi Party intelligence service, the Sicherheitsdienst, or SD, which ran foreign and domestic intelligence branches. Germany had a Research Department prior to 1933, linked to the state of Prussia, that had intelligence gathering and analytical functions, as well as a secret state police, or Gestapo, for purposes of internal security. The primary military intelligence agency was the Abwehr, which provided assistance to German field units, and which coexisted with a separate military office for signals intelligence. The navy and air force had similar, smaller offices, focusing on tactical intelligence.

Further reading: Donald P. Steury, *The Intelligence War* (New York: Metro, 2000).

—Clayton D. Laurie

Irish Americans

One of the oldest and largest of the nation's immigrant groups, Irish Americans in the 1930s and 1940s achieved new prominence in the DEMOCRATIC PARTY, GOVERNMENT, literary and artistic circles, organized LABOR, and the Catholic Church. Irish Americans, now largely second-, third-, and even fourth-generation Americans, were increasingly accepted by others despite the persistence of anti-Catholic and anti-Irish prejudice well into the mid-20th century.

Most of the heavily urban Irish Americans were of the working class and lower middle class, often overrepresented in police and fire departments. Despite such obvious exceptions as JOSEPH P. KENNEDY, their economic circumstances often proved trying during the GREAT DEPRESSION. The *Studs Lonigan* trilogy of novelist James T. Farrell reflected the difficulties of working-class Irish-American life. But the Irish had grown accustomed to group self-reliance, could count on assistance from Irish-dominated city governments, and had a growing middle class able to weather the depression.

Irish neighborhoods were most prevalent and cohesive in the big CITIES of the Northeast, such as New York, Boston, and Philadelphia, although Chicago and San Francisco also had large and significant Irish-American populations. Elsewhere, Irish communities slowly dissolved in the early decades of the 20th century, partly because IMMIGRATION declined, especially after 1924, partly because of residential mobility, partly because younger Irish Americans were increasingly less inclined to marry someone of Irish extraction, particularly in the West and Midwest.

Irish Americans were inextricably tied to the Roman Catholic Church and were central to the role of CATHOLICS in American life. By the middle of the century, more than half of the bishops and one-third of all priests in the U.S. Catholic Church were Irish Americans. After the family, the parish was most important social unit in Irish America, and the church figured prominently in such areas as Irish-American education and politics as well. During the 1930s, the "radio priest" FATHER CHARLES E. COUGHLIN attracted millions of listeners for his political commentary and criticism of Roosevelt and the New Deal, while Monsignor John Ryan took an active role both in the church and in politics with his support of Roosevelt.

By 1932, only one Irish Catholic, Justice Pierce Butler, who had been appointed to the SUPREME COURT in 1922, had occupied a top-level position in the executive and judicial branches of the federal government in the 20th century. In 1928, Irish Americans were energized by the nomination of New York governor Al Smith, the first Irish Catholic nominated for president by a major party, but Americans were reluctant to disrupt the prosperity of the 1920s and Smith was also the target of virulent anti-Catholic prejudice. The election of President FRANKLIN D. ROOSEVELT in 1932 then presented the overwhelmingly Democratic Irish Americans with new opportunities. Two of FDR's closest political advisers, JAMES A. FARLEY and EDWARD J. FLYNN, served as Democratic National Committee chairmen during the Roosevelt presidency. Irish Americans were also named to influential positions in FDR's administration, including Thomas Walsh as attorney general and Farley as postmaster general. In 1938, Joseph P. Kennedy became the first Irish Catholic to be named American ambassador to Great Britain.

Roosevelt's election also had large implications for Irish-dominated big-city political organizations. NEW DEAL programs enabled Irish politicians to consolidate their power bases in the cities and provided new sources of federal patronage in the form of jobs for working-class and lower-middle-class citizens. Jobs and help dispensed under New Deal programs strengthened the standing of the Irish political bosses not only with Irish Americans but also with the southern and eastern European immigrant groups who became more solidly Democratic. Frank Hague of Jersey City, New Jersey, and Thomas Pendergast of Kansas City, Missouri, were among the most skilled at this style of politics. James Michael Curley, who served four nonconsecutive terms as mayor of Boston, exerted considerable control over party politics in Massachusetts and was revered among Boston's poor for his populism and patronage. Over the long run, however, the New Deal also sometimes eroded the power of urban bosses and local government, as federally directed programs displaced local ones as the chief source of assistance.

Irish Americans also took active leadership posts in American labor unions and played important roles in union organizing successes of the era. PHILIP MURRAY, the son of an Irish laborer, became president of the CONGRESS OF INDUSTRIAL ORGANIZATIONS (CIO) in 1940 and aided Roosevelt in establishing government labor policies during WORLD WAR II. George Meany, the grandson of a famine refugee, was active in the Roosevelt era and became president of the AFL-CIO after the 1955 merger.

For millions of Irish Americans, particularly in urban centers, the 1930s and 1940s represented a time of increased stature for the Irish collectively. In LITERATURE, F. Scott Fitzgerald remained a significant figure while James T. Farrell and John O'Hara also gained recognition; and in 1936, Eugene O'Neill became the only American playwright to win the Nobel Prize in literature. Though persisting antipathy toward Great Britain led many Irish Americans to resist supporting England in the early stages of World War II, full participation in economic MOBILIZATION and in the armed forces after the U.S. entry into the war provided both evidence and hope of greater acceptance and influence in American life.

Further reading: Ronald H. Bayor, *Neighbors in Conflict: The Irish, Germans, Jews, and Italians of New York City, 1929–1941* (Baltimore: Johns Hopkins University Press, 1978); Stephan Thernstrom, ed., *Harvard Encyclopedia of American Ethnic Groups* (Cambridge, Mass.: Belknap Press of Harvard University Press, 1980).

—Joseph C. Gutberlet

isolationists

Isolationists believed that the United States should avoid intervention in European wars, "entangling alliances" with other nations, and the use of military force except to defend American shores. The high point of isolationist sentiment and influence came during the 1930s, when noninterventionists kept the United States out of the worsening European situation, and prevented President FRANKLIN D. ROOSEVELT from taking action to oppose aggression. While not advocating a complete cutoff of trade and other relations with the rest of the world, isolationists believed that the United States should have self-determination in foreign affairs and limit spending on the military. Liberal isolationists wanted to curtail the power of BUSINESS to shape FOREIGN POLICY, while conservative isolationists wanted to restrict the power of the federal GOVERNMENT—especially the president (and in particular FDR)—to involve the United States in what they saw as international adventurism.

Isolationists in the 1930s included men and women from all walks of life. They were most numerous in the upper Midwest, and fewest in the SOUTH. While most isolationists were in the REPUBLICAN PARTY, a significant number were in the DEMOCRATIC PARTY, and some came from right- and left-wing groups as well. Isolationists were more prevalent in rural areas and small towns in the Midwest than in large eastern cities. Ethnically, isolationists were found primarily among GERMAN AMERICANS, IRISH AMERICANS, Scandinavian Americans, and ITALIAN AMERICANS. In religious affiliation, noninterventionists were mainly Lutherans and CATHOLICS, although it was much more their ethnic roots (German, Scandinavian, Irish, and Italian) than their religion that made them isolationists. Evidently more women than men were isolationist.

Isolationism reached its peak during Roosevelt's first term, from 1933 to 1937. Such progressive Republicans as GEORGE NORRIS, ROBERT M. LA FOLLETTE, JR., and WILLIAM E. BORAH supported much of the New Deal, and since most were isolationist, Roosevelt often acquiesced to them in matters of foreign policy in order to retain their support on domestic legislation. Under pressure from peace groups who blamed financially powerful "merchants of death" for American involvement in World War I, the Senate in 1934 created the NYE COMMITTEE, which investigated the munitions industry, its financial backers, and its role in influencing U.S. policy. Influenced by the Nye Committee, CONGRESS in 1935 passed the first of the NEUTRALITY ACTS, imposing an arms embargo and restricting American travel on belligerent ships.

After Roosevelt's reelection in 1936, which was supported by a number of congressional isolationists, the president's problems with the isolationists increased. Ironically, the troubles were exacerbated by a domestic issue, Roosevelt's COURT-PACKING PLAN, which alienated the Senate's largely isolationist progressive Republican bloc from the president. As events in Europe heated up, mistrust developed and an eventual break occurred. Roosevelt's "quarantine speech" of October 1937, when he warned of worsening international conditions, was criticized by isolationists, as was the president's attempt to block the Ludlow Amendment, which would have submitted any declaration of war to a national referendum.

Even after Germany's annexation of Austria, the MUNICH CONFERENCE in 1938, and Adolf Hitler's seizure of Czechoslovakia and invasion of Poland in 1939, most Americans remained noninterventionist. But within a year, Scandinavia, the Low Countries, and then France fell to the Nazis, a majority of Americans came to support the need to help Great Britain and defeat the AXIS powers. The isolationists responded by forming the AMERICA FIRST COMMITTEE in September 1940, and most prominent noninterventionists either were members or spoke at sponsored rallies. After Roosevelt's third-term victory over interventionist Republican WENDELL L. WILLKIE in the ELECTION OF 1940, the American First Committee and its allies attempted, without success, to prevent the passage of the LEND-LEASE ACT and the repeal of Neutrality Act provisions banning the arming of American vessels crossing the Atlantic.

The attack on PEARL HARBOR on December 7, 1941, effectively ended the efforts of isolationists. When war was declared, every isolationist in Congress, except Jeanette Rankin, a Republican representative from Montana (who had also voted against entry into World War I), voted yes. During World War II, some prewar isolationists were concerned about postwar American FOREIGN POLICY, especially membership in an international peacekeeping organization. But in July 1945, with only two dissenting votes, the Senate ratified the UNITED NATIONS charter, and the prominent isolationists in the Senate and elsewhere largely faded from the scene by the mid- to late 1940s. The lessons of the interwar years and the coming of WORLD WAR II, the enormous economic, military, and political power of the United States at the end of the war, worsening SOVIET-AMERICAN RELATIONS, and the world's entry into the nuclear age all made it impossible for the United States to retreat into isolationism. The events of 1929–45 had transformed American foreign policy, and the United States pursued a much-expanded role in international affairs in the post–World War II world.

Further reading: Wayne S. Cole, *Roosevelt and the Isolationists, 1932–45* (Lincoln: University of Nebraska Press, 1983); Robert Dallek, *Franklin D. Roosevelt and American Foreign Policy, 1932–1945* (New York: Oxford University Press, 1979); Manfred Jonas, *Isolationism in America, 1935–1941* (Ithaca, N.Y.: Cornell University Press, 1966).

—William J. Thompson

Italian Americans

With nearly 4 million Italians coming to the United States during the wave of IMMIGRATION between 1880 and 1920, Italian Americans represented the largest of the "new immigrant" groups from southern and eastern Europe. For Italian Americans, more than for most other ethnic groups, the events of the GREAT DEPRESSION and WORLD WAR II sometimes exacerbated ethnic tensions, but the war also hastened their assimilation and acceptance.

Italians tended to cluster in urban enclaves, often called "Little Italies," where they formed mutual aid societies and other community institutions and established local Italian-language newspapers. The Catholic Church also played an important role in Italian-American life. Although early Italian immigrants often resented Irish-American dominance of the church in America, by the 1930s the establishment of national parishes and the continuation of traditional religious celebrations in the form of feasts and festivals helped Italian Americans cultivate a unique ethnic and religious identity.

Coming primarily from the agricultural areas of southern Italy, the majority of Italian immigrants were peasants and arrived in the United States with relatively few industrial skills. Italian Americans had very high rates of transiency, as many sought only temporary employment and returned to Italy with their earnings. Generally, Italian immigrants were concentrated in lower-level industrial occupations. However, by the early 1930s, many Italian Americans had slowly begun to move into better jobs in manufacturing and into positions as clerks, mechanics, and carpenters. Often every able family member was expected to contribute to the family's budget, and by 1930 Italian women represented a substantial proportion of the labor force in the garment trades.

Italian Americans holding blue-collar jobs were hit hard by the Depression and many turned to NEW DEAL programs for support. During the 1930s, Italian Americans also became active members of LABOR unions and began to exert a greater influence in politics. Though national successes such as those of FIORELLO LA GUARDIA were exceptional, increasingly Italians reaped the benefits of political patronage and effectively mobilized support within their communities, gaining power as ward leaders and local officials. With the 1928 presidential candidacy of Al Smith—New York governor and fellow Catholic—Italian Americans went to the polls in much greater numbers than before in support of the DEMOCRATIC PARTY. In 1932 and 1936, Italian Americans comprised a substantial portion of the multiethnic coalition that supported FRANKLIN D. ROOSEVELT and the New Deal.

The approach of World War II created tensions for Italian Americans, as questions of FOREIGN POLICY began to overshadow domestic issues. Although many denounced fascism throughout the 1930s, other Italian Americans praised Benito Mussolini for his efforts to revitalize their homeland and create a respected "New Italy." Owing in part to an exaggerated association with organized crime, Italian Americans were often considered undesirable and untrustworthy—a sentiment reflected in a 1939 national opinion poll in which Italian Americans were rated the worst citizens among the immigrant groups. In 1940, when more than one-third of America's 1.6 million Italian immigrants were not naturalized U.S. citizens, FDR's denunciation of the Italian invasion of France as a "stab in the back" and his pursuit of anti-AXIS interventionist policies prompted many Italian Americans to desert the Democratic Party in the ELECTION OF 1940.

Although tension between the United States and Italy and their lack of acceptance in America caused many Italian Americans to be troubled by conflicting loyalties, after the attack on PEARL HARBOR in 1941 and the German and Italian declarations of war on the United States, Italian Americans wholeheartedly supported the war effort, demonstrating their loyalty by serving in the military and working in defense industries. Early in the war, however, unnaturalized Italian-American immigrants bore the stigma of being classified as ENEMY ALIENS and encountered suspicion and prejudice in employment. But unlike the massive RELOCATION OF JAPANESE AMERICANS, only a few hundred of the 600,000 Italian aliens in the United States were interned. In 1942, on the Italian-American holiday Columbus Day, Roosevelt removed Italian Americans from enemy alien status. While this was done partly out of concern for the upcoming midterm congressional elections and the declining support for Democrats among Italian Americans, it was also a recognition of Italian-American loyalty.

Although they continued to encounter prejudice, Italian Americans by the end of the war had taken important steps toward acceptance in American society. In addition to modest political and economic gains made during the depression and World War II, many of Italian Americans were able to take advantage after the war of the GI BILL OF RIGHTS in order to enter the middle class. Educational opportunities and loans from the FEDERAL HOUSING ADMINISTRATION helped to stimulate economic and social mobility among Italian Americans and allowed them opportunities to find the recognition and acceptance that earlier generations had been denied.

See also POLITICS IN THE ROOSEVELT ERA.

Further reading: Ronald H. Bayor, *Neighbors in Conflict: The Irish, Germans, Jews, and Italians of New York City, 1929–1941* (Baltimore: Johns Hopkins University Press, 1978); Stephen Fox, *The Unknown Internment: An Oral*

History of the Relocation of Italian Americans during World War II (Boston: Twayne, 1990).

—Shannon L. Parsley

Italian campaign

One of the most controversial enterprises in the EUROPEAN THEATER of WORLD WAR II, the Italian campaign began with high Allied hopes of quick victory but soon deteriorated into a relentless, slow-moving war of attrition. Because of a lack of Anglo-American agreement about opening a SECOND FRONT in France, a decision was reached at the CASABLANCA CONFERENCE in January 1943 to follow up the NORTH AFRICAN CAMPAIGN with an invasion of SICILY. As the Sicilian campaign proceeded in the summer of 1943, the western Allies decided to invade Italy. The goals were to divert AXIS forces from other fronts, to obtain bases for the Combined Bomber Offensive against Germany, and to force the ouster of Fascist dictator Benito Mussolini, while quelling Soviet leader Joseph Stalin's doubts about the cohesiveness of the GRAND ALLIANCE.

The Anglo-American Combined Chiefs of Staff did not anticipate a protracted fight for Italy, but planning for the invasion was hurried and based on numerous miscalculations—including, foremost, the belief that the Germans would retreat beyond the Alps and surrender Italy without a struggle. The invasion was delayed for weeks in the late summer of 1943 because of secret negotiations about the surrender of Italy following Mussolini's removal from office on July 25. Germany used this opportunity to move 16 divisions into Italy, occupying virtually the entire peninsula by the time the surrender of the Italian government was announced on September 8.

The British Eighth Army had already landed at Reggio, across the Straits of Messina from Sicily on September 3, and that was followed by an amphibious landing by the U.S. Fifth Army at Salerno and a British airborne landing at Taranto, both on September 9. The Allied actions convinced Hitler that his commander in Italy, Field Marshall Albert Kesselring, was correct in his strategy to fight for every inch of the peninsula, and a defensive belt across the country south of Rome, known as the Gustav Line, was constructed. Kesselring's defensive effort, conducted with ever decreasing numbers of troops and resources, was one of the most impressive aspects of the entire campaign. Although the Germans retreated throughout the fall, the Allied advance ground to a halt on reaching the Gustav Line. Facing poor weather, and rugged terrain that negated Allied air and armor advantages, the campaign developed into a series of small infantry actions in the mountains and valleys south of Rome. The Allies repeatedly attempted to find weak spots in the German line, but largely failed. Infantry assaults and air bombardments conducted on the abbey at Monte Cassino that dominated the strategic Liri Valley route toward Rome, and an amphibious invasion at Anzio north of the Gustav Line in January 1944, failed to dislodge the well-entrenched German forces.

A concerted offensive effort by the Allies in May 1944 succeeded in breaking the steadily weakening German forces in Italy. A well-ordered retreat, however, combined with an American diversion to capture Rome and a generally sluggish British advance, allowed German forces to retreat north where yet another series of fortifications, the Gothic Line, was constructed north of Florence. Although U.S. Fifth Army forces commanded by Lieutenant General Mark W. Clark liberated Rome on June 4, 1944, the triumph was incomplete, and by September the Allied advance halted at the Gothic Line. Following the June 1944 invasion of NORMANDY and the August 1944 invasion of southern France, the Allies in Italy were increasingly starved of troops and supplies diverted to swifter moving fronts in France. The Italian campaign continued much as it had the year before as Allied forces probed for weaknesses and attempted breakthroughs in the Gothic Line with only local success. The war in Italy degenerated into a grinding war of attrition, with the Allies attempting to hold down as many Axis troops as possible, at the lowest possible cost. By February 1945, both sides in Italy were conducting a frustrating holding operation, tying down similar numbers of troops on both sides.

The final Allied offensive in Italy launched between April 9 and 14, 1945, caused the greatly weakened Germany forces to retreat all along the line with Allied forces in rapid pursuit. A secretly negotiated surrender of Axis forces resulted in a cease-fire and surrender on May 2, 1945. Allied casualties during the campaign were 188,746 for the U.S. Fifth Army and 123,254 for the Eighth Army. German losses were estimated at 434,646.

Further reading: Richard Lamb, *The War in Italy, 1943–1945: A Brutal Story* (New York: DeCapo Press, 1996).

—Clayton D. Laurie

Iwo Jima (February–March 1945)

By the winter of 1944–45, particularly after their crushing defeat at the BATTLE FOR LEYTE GULF in October 1944, the Japanese were fighting desperately to protect the home islands from the relentless American advance in the final stages of the PACIFIC THEATER of WORLD WAR II. Because the tiny island of Iwo Jima lay between Japan and American B-29 bomber bases in the MARIANA ISLANDS, the United States planned to capture the island in order to eliminate a major Japanese radar and communication center and to enhance the American position for attacking mainland Japan.

Following more than two months of bombing and three days of naval gunfire shelling, U.S. MARINES landed on the soft volcanic ash of the Iwo Jima beach on February 19, 1945. At first, the Americans expected the battle would be over quickly, but the island was extraordinarily well defended—the bombing and naval gunfire had caused little damage—and the Japanese resisted fiercely. Savage combat on both sides continued until late March, often hand-to-hand and inch by inch, with the Japanese refusing to surrender and fighting almost literally to the last man. By the end of the battle in late March, more than 20,000 Japanese troops had been killed, with only a few hundred taken prisoner. The United States also suffered significant losses, with some 6,000 dead and 17,000 wounded. One-third of all marine deaths in the Pacific theater occurred on Iwo Jima.

Iwo Jima thus proved to be one of the most costly battles in the Pacific theater, and one with several ironies. In retrospect, many have thought it an unnecessary campaign, arguing that the island might simply have been bypassed. The fierce, many Americans thought fanatical, Japanese resistance on Iwo Jima and later on OKINAWA, had the effect of reinforcing the American readiness to use the ATOMIC BOMB on Japan to end the war without a bloody invasion of the home islands. And the battle produced one of the most famous photographs of the war, the flag raising on Mount Suribachi. Marines had captured Suribachi early in the battle and had planted an American flag there; but because the first flag was too small to be seen, a contingent was sent to raise a larger one. As this second flag was being raised, Associated Press photographer Joe Rosenthal took the picture that has come to be a

The raising of the Stars and Stripes atop Mount Suribachi, Iwo Jima *(National Archives)*

symbol not just of Iwo Jima but also of the U.S. Marine Corps and of the war in the Pacific.

Further reading: James Bradley, *Flags of Our Fathers* (New York: Bantam, 2000); Bill D. Ross, *Iwo Jima: Legacy of Valor* (New York: Vanguard, 1985).

J

Japanese Americans, relocation of

Following President FRANKLIN D. ROOSEVELT's issuance of EXECUTIVE ORDER 9066 on February 19, 1942, more than 110,000 Japanese Americans living along the West Coast of the United States were evacuated and then incarcerated in relocation camps. The process affected both the Issei, immigrants who were denied citizenship by federal law, and their American-born children, the Nisei, who were citizens.

Historically, Japanese immigrants to the United States had faced prejudiced treatment from non-Japanese Americans and from national and local GOVERNMENT, which limited IMMIGRATION, citizenship, and property ownership and other rights. Relatively few in number and mostly isolated from mainstream America, Japanese Americans were politically powerless. The bombing of PEARL HARBOR fueled the existing anti-Japanese sentiment, and led to unsubstantiated reports of sabotage against the United States.

The Wartime Civil Control Administration (WCCA) was established on March 11, 1942, and began to prepare for the evacuation of Japanese Americans from preestablished military zones. (Approximately 15,000 Japanese Americans had already moved voluntarily from the West Coast.) Sixteen temporary assembly centers in California, Washington, Oregon, and Arizona were quickly manufactured from existing facilities, usually racetracks or fair grounds. Given a week or less to prepare for an unknown destination, ill-equipped families hastily sold off their property and traveled by train to arbitrarily assigned assembly centers. There, they were subjected to roll calls, curfews, inspections, and armed guards for approximately three months.

Beginning in May 1942, the evacuees were moved to 10 relocation centers in California, Idaho, Wyoming, Utah, Arizona, Colorado, and Arkansas. Families were housed in barracks-style facilities divided into rooms averaging 20 x 16 feet per family and containing cots, a coal-burning stove, and a light bulb. Facilities within the camps included a mess hall, toilet and bathing areas, a laundry, and a recreation hall. Responsibility for the confined Japanese Americans was transferred to the War Relocation Authority (WRA), under the direction of Milton Eisenhower.

While in the camps, Japanese Americans attempted to create a sense of normalcy. Adults worked in agriculture, education, food preparation, and the creation of camouflage nets, although an individual's earnings were capped at $19 a month. Religious services conducted in English were allowed. Children attended schools with varying curriculums and materials. Much like the government education of NATIVE AMERICANS, these schools worked toward the assimilation of the young into American culture. Japanese Americans engaged in RECREATION such as baseball and organized dances, as well as in Boy Scouts activities.

Beginning in 1943, the adults were subjected to loyalty questions. This process was used to register the Nisei for the draft, which was reinstituted for Japanese Americans in January 1944. Although many resisted the draft and some Nisei renounced their citizenship, an estimated 25,000 or more served in the military, often with distinction. Nisei who passed the loyalty questions received clearance to leave the camps on the condition that they stay outside the military zones. Many took the one-way ticket and $25 and settled in cities such as Chicago, Denver, and New York, while others were recruited to work on farms. Distrust by non-Japanese Americans and bureaucratic paperwork slowed the process, but by June 1946 all of the camps except Tule Lake in northern California had been closed. Eventually two-thirds of the incarcerated would return to their original area of residence.

Despite being wronged, the Japanese community did not attempt widespread resistance to the evacuation process. Members of the Japanese American Citizens League and the Issei wished to demonstrate their loyalty to their adopted country by following the orders. Within the camp, traditional patterns of leadership were reversed. Typically,

This 1942 photograph shows the Mochida family awaiting the evacuation bus to an internment camp. *(National Archives)*

the head of the household had been detained by the FEDERAL BUREAU OF INVESTIGATION for questioning prior to evacuation and was reunited with the family only after a mother or an older son had taken charge. Also, the WRA disqualified Issei from holding offices such as block monitor within the camps, thereby shifting responsibility to the younger generation. A few individuals did take legal action against internment; however, as in *KOREMATSU V. UNITED STATES*, most judgments sided with the government and upheld the relocation policy.

Readjustment to the outside life proved difficult. The Issei lost the authority afforded them by Japanese culture; as a result, many became even more isolated from the American culture. Nisei were shocked that they had not been treated as citizens. In addition, there was a large loss of property. Japanese Americans sometimes had burned their artifacts and heirlooms prior to evacuation for fear of being suspected of disloyalty. In the haste of evacuation, homes and businesses had been sold off at extraordinarily low prices, and many more were repossessed due to non-payment of taxes. The Japanese Evacuation Claims Act of 1948 attempted to compensate for the loss of property incurred during confinement; eventually $37 million was distributed to settle $148 million worth of claims. In 1988, Congress provided $20,000 in restitution for surviving evacuees and acknowledged the injustice committed against them.

See also ASIAN AMERICANS; ENEMY ALIENS.

Further reading: Roger Daniels, *Prisoners without Trial: Japanese Americans in World War II* (New York: Hill & Wang, 1993); Roger Daniels, ed., *American Concentration Camps: A Documentary History of the Relocation and Incarceration of Japanese Americans, 1941–1945*, 9 vols (New York: Garland, 1989).

—Traci L. Siegler

Jews

For American Jews, the period between 1929 and 1945 marked a time of substantial change. Once divided by cultural and class differences, and by conflicts over theology and ZIONISM (the effort to establish a Jewish homeland in Palestine), Jews emerged from the GREAT DEPRESSION and WORLD WAR II unified by a stronger sense of group identity. The war years also helped reduce the barriers of ANTISEMITISM that Jews had long faced.

Arriving in America as early as 1654, Jews were a well-established, yet diverse ethnic group in the United States by the late 19th century. The period between 1880 and 1924 then witnessed the largest migration of Jews to the United States as more than 2.3 million Jews, largely from Russia and other eastern European nations, came to America. The majority of these immigrants came to escape religious persecution. The eastern European Jews crowded into urban enclaves, particularly in New York, and often had uneasy relations with the already established German Jews who had immigrated earlier. Like many other immigrants, Jews contributed to American POPULAR CULTURE including RADIO and MOVIES, yet also worked to preserve their customs and ethnic identity through the establishment of Hebrew and Yiddish weeklies, mutual aid societies, and fraternal associations such as B'nai B'rith and the Young Men's Hebrew Association.

By the 1930s, the roles and experiences of Jews in the workplace varied considerably. Jews placed a strong emphasis on the importance of education for economic advancement, and as a result, second-generation Jews often tended to be more successful than other ethnic groups in improving their occupational status, moving into skilled jobs and the professions including medicine and law. However, others worked as street peddlers with pushcarts in an effort to establish themselves in the retail trades, and many Jews who had arrived from Russia and eastern Europe worked as skilled laborers in the garment industry and other manufacturing industries.

The depression hit working-class Jews with particular force, and reinforced the important roles of Jewish leaders and members in LABOR unions. Throughout the 1930s, Jews often became active members and leaders of unions, including the Amalgamated Clothing Workers Union (ACW) and the International Ladies Garment Workers union. SIDNEY HILLMAN of the ACW helped found the CONGRESS OF INDUSTRIAL ORGANIZATIONS (CIO).

Along with unionization came an increase in political activity among American Jews during the depression.

Though Jewish representation among SOCIALISTS continued to be disproportionately high, Jews had by the ELECTION OF 1936 become a significant part of the emerging Democratic majority. Not only had Jewish voters endorsed FRANKLIN D. ROOSEVELT and the DEMOCRATIC PARTY, but like CATHOLICS, Jews held prominent positions as advisers and administrators in the NEW DEAL. At a time when economic strains sometimes intensified anti-Semitic attitudes and actions, Jews had particular reason to be grateful for the New Deal's inclusiveness.

With the expulsion of Jews from Nazi Germany throughout the 1930s, FOREIGN POLICY issues increasingly shaped the experiences and activities of American Jews. Organizations such as the American Jewish Congress (AJC), led by Rabbi Stephen Wise, encouraged boycotts of German goods and held demonstrations. In the ELECTION OF 1940, many American Jews, seeking to end the systematic persecution of European Jews, continued to endorse President Roosevelt. Many also supported U.S. intervention against Germany.

After U.S. entry into the war, PUBLIC OPINION POLLS indicated a substantial increase in hostility toward Jews. Throughout the war, Jews not only encountered prejudice and discrimination in employment, but Jewish businesses and synagogues also were sometimes vandalized. Jews were accused of profiting from the war and were perceived as more likely to evade service in the armed forces.

Anti-Semitism also hindered efforts to rescue European Jews from the HOLOCAUST. Throughout the 1930s and 1940s, efforts to assist REFUGEES by easing IMMIGRATION restrictions were thwarted in part by prejudice in the State Department and CONGRESS. Such attempts sometimes encountered obstacles within the Jewish community as well. Nevertheless, Jews worked aggressively on behalf of refugees, even if they achieved only limited success. In 1944, at the urging of Secretary of the Treasury HENRY MORGENTHAU, JR., Roosevelt established the War Refugee Board, which rescued more than 200,000 Jews. After the war, many Jews continued to work to provide support for displaced persons, and for the establishment of the Jewish state of Israel.

Despite the difficulties, World War II ultimately hastened the acceptance and assimilation of American Jews. Wartime anti-Semitism led to increased efforts by Jews and others to combat it, and anti-Semitism was further discredited as the ghastly evidence of the Holocaust became plain in 1945 and afterward. Jewish participation in the war effort also had an impact, as refugee scientists worked on the development of the ATOMIC BOMB, and more than a half million Jews served in the armed forces. Many others worked in defense industries. Although anti-Semitism did not vanish, American Jews in the postwar era encountered less prejudice and fewer obstacles than before.

See also POLITICS IN THE ROOSEVELT ERA.

Further reading: Ronald H. Bayor, *Neighbors in Conflict: The Irish, Germans, Jews, and Italians of New York City, 1929–1941* (Baltimore: Johns Hopkins University Press, 1978); Stephen Thernstrom, ed., *Harvard Encyclopedia of American Ethnic Groups* (Cambridge, Mass.: Belknap: Press of Harvard University Press, 1980).

—Shannon L. Parsley

Johnson, Hugh S. (1882–1942)

Hugh Samuel Johnson, first administrator of the NATIONAL RECOVERY ADMINISTRATION (NRA), was one of the early NEW DEAL's most visible and controversial officials.

Born in Fort Scott, Kansas, on August 5, 1882, Hugh S. Johnson grew up in rural Oklahoma, attended teachers college, and became the first Oklahoman to graduate from the United States Military Academy at West Point. Receiving his commission in 1903, Johnson served army stints in Texas, California, the Philippines, and Arizona, earned a law degree, participated in General John J. Pershing's pursuit of Mexican rebel Pancho Villa, and wrote several boys' adventure books.

Rising through the ranks to brigadier general, Johnson was assigned during World War I to implement selective service, and was director of the army's Bureau of Purchase and Supply. In that position, he served as liaison to the War Industries Board, where he met BERNARD M. BARUCH, who headed the agency. Retiring from the army in 1919, Johnson became vice president and general counsel for the Moline Plow Company, then board chairman of the Moline Implement Company. In 1927, Johnson joined Baruch as his assistant, became involved in DEMOCRATIC PARTY politics, and by 1932 was promoting industrial planning with the BRAIN TRUST of presidential candidate FRANKLIN D. ROOSEVELT.

In early 1933, Johnson helped draft the NATIONAL INDUSTRIAL RECOVERY ACT (NIRA), and then Roosevelt chose him to head the National Recovery Administration (NRA) and administer its industrial code system under Title I of the NIRA. Alternately blustery and profane, eloquent and reflective, the colorful Johnson traveled the country over the summer and fall of 1933 convincing business and industry to sign on to the "Blue Eagle" (the symbol of NRA, designed by Johnson). By early 1934, however, the NRA was under attack from BUSINESS, LABOR, and other critics, and Johnson's rash statements, fueled by anger and excessive use of alcohol, only worsened matters. Finally, in September 1934, Roosevelt requested Johnson's resignation.

After leaving the NRA, Johnson briefly headed the WORKS PROGRESS ADMINISTRATION in New York City, then left the New Deal altogether, becoming a syndicated columnist for the Scripps-Howard newspapers. Backing

Roosevelt in 1936, Johnson soon broke with the president over the COURT-PACKING PLAN, the RECESSION OF 1937–38, and FOREIGN POLICY. In the ELECTION OF 1940, Johnson backed WENDELL L. WILLKIE for president; and, as a leading isolationist, he helped launch the AMERICA FIRST COMMITTEE. After PEARL HARBOR, Roosevelt refused to restore Johnson's commission, which embittered the old general. Worn out and ravaged by alcohol, Hugh S. Johnson died in Washington, D.C., on April 15, 1942.

Further reading: John Kennedy Ohl, *Hugh S. Johnson and the New Deal* (DeKalb, Ill.: Northern Illinois University Press, 1985).

—William J. Thompson

Jones, Jesse H. (1874–1956)

Jesse Holman Jones, millionaire Texas businessman, chairman of the RECONSTRUCTION FINANCE CORPORATION (RFC) from 1933 to 1945, and secretary of commerce from 1940 to 1945, was one of the NEW DEAL's most powerful and influential officials.

Jones was born in Robertson County, Tennessee, on April 22, 1874. His family moved to Dallas, Texas, in 1883, and Jones graduated from Hill's Business College in 1891. Moving to Houston, Jones amassed a personal fortune in lumber, real estate, construction, and banking by the time he was 40. He became known as "Mr. Houston" for his role in the city's business and development. Prominent in the DEMOCRATIC PARTY, he almost single-handedly brought the Democrats' 1928 national convention to Houston, where he was Texas's "favorite son" presidential candidate. In 1932, President HERBERT C. HOOVER named Jones to the newly created Reconstruction Finance Corporation.

After FRANKLIN D. ROOSEVELT became president in 1933, he named Jones chairman of RFC, a position the Texan held for nearly 12 years. Jones transformed the RFC into arguably the most powerful agency in the federal government during the New Deal. Under Jones's leadership, the RFC, sometimes referred to as the "fourth branch of government," disbursed billions of dollars (the chairman's own estimate was nearly $50 billion) to businesses and financial institutions. Among New Deal officials, Jones was perhaps the most pro-BUSINESS and conservative. His pro-business outlook, however, was not cautious like that of the eastern financial elite, but represented a westerner's desire for expansion and new economic ventures.

In 1940, Roosevelt appointed Jones secretary of commerce after CONGRESS enacted special legislation to allow him to serve simultaneously as RFC chairman and as a cabinet officer. During WORLD WAR II, the RFC was given broad powers related to national defense, especially in war procurement and loans to build defense plants. Roosevelt was quoted as saying that Jones was "the only man in Washington who can say 'yes' or 'no' intelligently twenty-four hours a day."

Despite the president's confidence, the Roosevelt-Jones relationship grew strained, and in 1945, after Vice President HENRY A. WALLACE was replaced on the Democratic ticket by Harry S. Truman, FDR asked Jones to resign as commerce secretary in order to give Wallace a consolation position. Jones then resigned his other federal positions including RFC and returned to Houston. In retirement, Jones devoted most of his time to philanthropic activities, establishing the largest charitable foundation in Texas. Jesse H. Jones died in Houston, Texas, on June 1, 1956.

Further reading: Jordan A. Schwarz, *The New Dealers: Power Politics in the Age of Roosevelt* (New York: Knopf, 1993); Bascom M. Timmons, *Jesse H. Jones: The Man and the Statesman* (New York: Henry Holt, 1956).

—William J. Thompson

K

Kaiser, Henry J. (1882–1967)

Henry John Kaiser was a pioneering industrialist of great importance from the 1930s to the 1960s. His ability to bring large construction projects to completion allowed him to make important contributions in industrial development, and he played a vital role in the WORLD WAR II economic MOBILIZATION effort of the United States.

Kaiser was born to German immigrant parents in Spring Brook, New York, in 1882. He left school at the age of 13 and began to work full time to help support his family. Moving to the Pacific Northwest in 1906, he began working for a construction company. In 1914 he established his first company in Vancouver, British Columbia. He brought an uncanny ability to improvise and find solutions to various problems that allowed him to turn obstacles into opportunities. His company prospered, and Kaiser spent the next years earning a great deal of money building highways.

While building a highway in Cuba in 1928, Kaiser learned of the planned damming of the Colorado River. He was captivated by the idea of building such a large structure, and in 1931, he helped form Six Companies, Inc., and won the contract to build what became the Hoover Dam. After completion of the Hoover Dam (well under the deadline for completion mandated by the federal government), Kaiser went on to build the Grand Coulee and Bonneville Dams, naval facilities in the Pacific, and levees, aqueducts, and pipelines in the West.

During World War II, Kaiser won international fame for his achievements in SHIPBUILDING. He used his tried-and-true methods of economy of scale, centralized distribution of building materials, and assembly line methods to build ships at an amazing rate. These ships came to be known as liberty ships because they conveyed vital supplies and troops to the war fronts from the United States; early in the war, dozens were lost to enemy action. By war's end, Kaiser Shipbuilding had produced 1,490 cargo vessels and 50 small aircraft carriers. Overall, Kaiser built one-third of the total U.S. merchant ship production from 1941 through 1945.

After the war, Kaiser diversified into automobile, aluminum, and aircraft production. He received awards from organized LABOR for the generous health care benefits that were provided to his workers and that led to the incorporation of Kaiser Permanente in 1946. Kaiser died in Hawaii in 1967.

Further reading: Stephen M. Adams, *Mr. Kaiser Goes to Washington: The Rise of a Government Entrepreneur* (Chapel Hill: University of North Carolina Press, 1997); Mark S. Foster, *Henry J. Kaiser: Builder in the Modern American West* (Austin: University of Texas Press, 1989); Jordan A. Schwarz, *The New Dealers: Power Politics in the Age of Roosevelt* (New York: Knopf, 1993).

—Nicholas Fry

Kennedy, Joseph P. (1888–1969)

Joseph Patrick Kennedy was chairman of the SECURITIES AND EXCHANGE COMMISSION (1934–35) and ambassador to Great Britain (1938–41) in the administration of President FRANKLIN D. ROOSEVELT.

Kennedy was born on September 6, 1888, in Boston, Massachusetts. The son of an Irish Catholic saloonkeeper and politician, he worked his way through Harvard University and by his 30th birthday was a bank president and financial magnate who had amassed a personal fortune through banking, shipbuilding, and motion picture distribution. In 1915, he married Rose Fitzgerald, the daughter of colorful Boston mayor John Francis Fitzgerald, and the couple had nine children.

Kennedy joined Roosevelt's first presidential campaign in 1932 as an important financial contributor and fundraiser. After disappointing Kennedy by not appointing him secretary of the treasury, Roosevelt in 1934 named him the first chairman of the Securities and Exchange

Commission, a major NEW DEAL agency charged with regulating the stock market. Roosevelt was criticized for this nomination because of Kennedy's record of financial manipulation and profiteering on the market, but on resigning from the post in September 1935, Kennedy was hailed from all quarters as one of Roosevelt's most successful appointments. He also served as an effective contact with the BUSINESS community for the administration.

After working for Roosevelt again in the 1936 election, Kennedy became the first chairman of the United States Maritime Commission in 1937, and in 1938 was appointed ambassador to Great Britain, then the most prestigious diplomatic appointment and an especially striking one for an IRISH AMERICAN. But despite being the apparent pinnacle of Kennedy's public career, the ambassadorship to Great Britain put him in a position that ultimately damaged his reputation and his standing with Roosevelt. He supported British prime minister Neville Chamberlain's policy of appeasing Nazi Germany, and during the BATTLE OF BRITAIN in the early stages of WORLD WAR II sent cables to Washington arguing that the British cause was hopeless and urging President Roosevelt to rearm the United States rather than aid England. Although unhappy with Roosevelt's efforts to help Britain, he eventually supported FDR for a third term in 1940, but then resigned the ambassadorship. Despite his experience and contacts in GOVERNMENT and business, Kennedy was offered no significant position during the war and wartime economic MOBILIZATION.

The war took not only a public toll on Kennedy, but also a personal one. His oldest son, Joe Jr., was killed over Germany in a bombing campaign, and his daughter Kathleen was killed in a plane crash with her husband. After the war, Kennedy attached his political ambitions to the career of his second son, John Fitzgerald Kennedy, who was elected president in 1960. Joseph P. Kennedy died in 1969 at the age of 81.

Further reading: Michael R. Beschloss, *Kennedy and Roosevelt: The Uneasy Alliance* (New York: Norton, 1980); Doris Kearns Goodwin, *The Fitzgeralds and the Kennedys* (New York: Simon & Schuster, 1987).

—Julie F. Hanlon

Keynesianism

The term *Keynesianism* refers to the economic analysis and policies based on ideas advanced by the British economist John Maynard Keynes, especially in his *General Theory of Employment, Interest, and Money*, published in 1936. Keynesian ideas and policies had little impact on NEW DEAL policy until the late 1930s, but after the RECESSION OF 1937–38 and especially during WORLD WAR II, Keynesianism was increasingly embraced by liberal policymakers, played a major role in the redirection of LIBERALISM as part of the THIRD NEW DEAL, and came to be accepted at least in part by many economists and some businessmen as well.

At the heart of Keynes's ideas was his view that capitalist economies do not inevitably and automatically reach or sustain full-production, full-employment prosperity. This understanding led Keynes to focus on the dynamics of a market economy, which he said depend upon the sum total of private investment, consumer spending, and GOVERNMENT spending. If there were enough of these sources of spending taken together, an economy could reach and maintain full-employment, full-production prosperity; if not, the economy might languish at lower levels. This insight pointed to the importance of government spending, for if there were not sufficient private investment and consumer spending, then there was a clear role for additional, or compensatory, government spending to produce full-production full-employment prosperity. And to have its fullest impact, compensatory spending by the government should be deficit spending—for if the government raised revenues in order to balance the budget while spending more, it would take money from the hands of consumers and investors. Keynesianism had an important place for monetary policy (interest rates and the volume and value of currency); but it focused especially on fiscal policy (TAXATION and spending).

Down to the late 1930s, New Deal fiscal policy was not Keynesian. Though some New Dealers—MARRINER ECCLES, for example—had emphasized the importance of government spending and some knew about Keynes's ideas, President FRANKLIN D. ROOSEVELT, Treasury Secretary HENRY MORGENTHAU, and other important administration officials remained devoted to fiscal prudence and balanced budgets. The New Deal did of course incur deficits—but in order to finance essential programs, including RELIEF assistance to the unemployed and impoverished, rather than for the purpose of compensatory economic stimulus. The largest deficit was just some $4.4 billion dollars in 1936.

The recession of 1937–38 then led to a departure in economic thinking and policy. As some policymakers and economists looked at the pattern of the ECONOMY after 1933, they saw mild deficits and economic expansion from 1933 to 1937, followed by reduced spending and a plummeting economy in 1937 and 1938. Harvard economist Alvin Hansen was the foremost American mediator and proponent of Keynesian ideas, and he had a significant impact on key New Dealers, including HARRY L. HOPKINS, HENRY A. WALLACE, LEON HENDERSON, and others. In the policy debates over how to address the recession, proponents of spending won out over advocates of fiscal restraint and balanced budgets—and the economy began to recover from the 1937–38 downturn.

But World War II turned out to be the real proving grounds for Keynesianism. With less than half of the high costs of wartime MOBILIZATION financed by current revenues, deficits skyrocketed to some $50 billion per year from 1943 to 1945—more than 10 times the highest annual deficit during the 1930s. The result was full-production, full-employment prosperity, with the gross national product soaring, unemployment plummeting from 15 percent in 1940 to just 1 percent in 1944, and living standards rising. Massive deficits had produced economic recovery and prosperity. Although it is not clear that Roosevelt himself ever fully understood or accepted Keynesianism, many in his administration did, and Keynesian ideas increasingly shaped economic policy and analysis. The 1943 report of the NATIONAL RESOURCES PLANNING BOARD, *Post-War Plan and Program,* provided especially clear evidence that many liberals had come to understand that government spending on liberal programs could underwrite social reform as well as full-employment prosperity.

This liberal version of Keynesian compensatory spending on social reform did not, however, triumph in policymaking. Postwar fiscal policy (like that of the war years) was often more a "military Keynesianism" of national security spending in the cold war than it was "reform Keynesianism" of progressive taxation and spending on domestic reform programs. Postwar fiscal policy tended also to reflect the "commercial Keynesianism," preferred by BUSINESS, with deficits incurred by tax cuts more than by increased spending on liberal social programs. And the Keynesian FULL EMPLOYMENT BILL that was the centerpiece of the liberal agenda at the end of the war became the attenuated Employment Act of 1946 that did not commit the government to compensatory spending to ensure full employment. But if Keynesianism did not usually take the form preferred by liberals, Keynesian ideas had become central not only to the liberal agenda but also to economic analysis and policy more generally by the postwar era. The use of fiscal policy to manage the postwar economy was abetted by another wartime development, the REVENUE ACT OF 1942, which greatly expanded the number of Americans paying income taxes, led to implementation of the withholding system, and permitted more effective use of taxation in economic policy.

Further reading: Robert M. Collins, *The Business Response to Keynes, 1929–1964* (New York: Columbia University Press, 1981); Robert LeKachman, *The Age of Keynes* (New York: Random House, 1966); Herbert Stein, *The Fiscal Revolution in America* (Chicago: University of Chicago Press, 1969).

King, Ernest J. (1878–1956)

Admiral Ernest Joseph King served as chief of naval operations during WORLD WAR II. Born in Lorain, Ohio, on November 23, 1878, King graduated from the U.S. Naval Academy in 1901, having already seen combat on the USS *San Francisco* during the Spanish-American War. Commissioned as an ensign in 1903, he served on the USS *Cincinnati,* the USS *Alabama,* and the USS *New Hampshire,* and also as an instructor at the Naval Academy. In command of the USS *Terry,* King participated in operations at Vera Cruz, Mexico, in April 1914, and in 1916 joined the staff of Admiral Henry T. Mayo, commander, Atlantic Fleet, where he remained through World War I.

In the early 1920s, King commanded Submarine Divisions Three and 11, and the New London, Connecticut, submarine base. In 1928, at the age of 49, he underwent aviation training, one of the few senior naval officers to gain such qualifications. The next year he became the assistant chief of the Bureau of Aeronautics. In 1930 King took command of the aircraft carrier USS *Lexington.* After graduating from the Naval War College three years later, he was named chief of the Bureau of Aeronautics. Made vice admiral and commander of the five-carrier Aircraft Battle Force in 1938, King served on the General Board in 1939–40, and in February 1941 was appointed chief, Atlantic Fleet.

A few days after the Japanese attack on PEARL HARBOR in December 1941, King succeeded Admiral Husband E. Kimmel as commander in chief, U.S. Fleet, with the rank of admiral. In March 1942, he became the first officer to combine this post with the position of chief of naval operations, the top position in the U.S. NAVY. In the Atlantic, the navy took on the role of convoy protection, antisubmarine patrol, and amphibious operations support, which King undertook only after pressure was exerted by the president and the British. The WORLD WAR II PACIFIC THEATER was more clearly a naval conflict and was King's main interest, marked as it was by frequent fleet actions on sea and in the air, and by AMPHIBIOUS WARFARE assaults by the U.S. MARINES. The principal Pacific units under King's overall command, through his Pacific Ocean Area subordinate Admiral CHESTER W. NIMITZ, were the Third Fleet under Admiral WILLIAM F. HALSEY, the Fifth Fleet under Admiral Raymond A. Spruance, and the Seventh Fleet under Admiral Thomas C. Kincaid. By 1945, King commanded the largest naval armada ever created, consisting of some 4 million men and more than 92,000 ships and boats. Although directing the naval war from Washington, D.C., King was present during the landings of the INVASION OF NORMANDY in June 1944. That December he was given the temporary five-star rank of fleet admiral, which was made permanent in April 1946.

King also served as the chief naval adviser to President FRANKLIN D. ROOSEVELT and was involved in all of the major wartime Allied conferences. A gruff, fiercely-determined, and plainspoken man, he was a staunch advocate of sea power and a well-known Anglophobe, who constantly battled with the U.S. ARMY and the British to maintain U.S. Navy predominance in the Pacific. He vocally disapproved of the "Europe first" strategy and the secondary role the U.S. Navy played there.

The post of commander in chief, U.S. Fleet, was abolished in October 1945, and King relinquished his additional post of chief naval operations to Nimitz that December. On inactive status, King return to limited duty in 1950 as an adviser to the secretary of the navy and President Harry S. Truman. He died on June 25, 1956, at Portsmouth, New Hampshire.

Further reading: Thomas B. Buell, *Master of Sea Power: A Biography of Fleet Admiral Ernest J. King* (Boston: Little, Brown, 1980).

—Clayton D. Laurie

Korematsu v. United States

In the *Korematsu* case decided in December 1944, the SUPREME COURT upheld the RELOCATION OF JAPANESE AMERICANS implemented pursuant to EXECUTIVE ORDER 9066 of February 1942. The relocation and incarceration of Japanese Americans constituted the worst violation of CIVIL LIBERTIES in the United States during WORLD WAR II, and the *Korematsu* decision was overturned in 1984.

Before the *Korematsu* case, the Supreme Court had in June 1943 unanimously upheld the government's policy in two cases involving curfew orders. In one of them, *Hirabayashi v. United States*, the Court said that "residents having ethnic affiliations with an invading enemy may be a greater source of danger than those of different ancestry" and that it was "not for any court to sit in review of the wisdom" of military authorities. Despite the unanimous decision, however, there was concern within the Court. Justice Frank Murphy wrote in a concurring decision in *Hirabayashi* that the policy had "a melancholy resemblance to the treatment accorded to members of the Jewish race in Germany and in other parts of Europe" and involved "a substantial restriction of the personal liberty of citizens of the United States based upon the accident of race or ancestry."

The two 1943 cases were decided on narrow grounds that avoided a direct ruling on the forced removal of Japanese Americans. The case that would directly test the relocation policy involved Fred Korematsu, whose lawsuit was championed by the AMERICAN CIVIL LIBERTIES UNION. As the case worked its way through the judicial system to the Supreme Court, it created tension between the army, which insisted upon the military necessity of the relocations, and the Justice Department, which was convinced that the army's position was based to an important degree upon exaggerated or false evidence. Such doubts about military necessity might well have produced a majority decision by the Court that the relocation was unconstitutional, and under intense pressure from the army, the Justice Department brief removed a footnote indicating its strong doubts about the army's report. By a 6-3 margin, the Supreme Court on December 18, 1944, ruled in the *Korematsu* case (with Justice HUGO BLACK writing the majority decision) that the relocation policy was sufficiently justified by military necessity to meet constitutional strictures. In a bitter dissent, Justice Murphy called the decision a "legalization of racism." (Justices Owen Roberts and Robert Jackson also dissented.) On the same day, however, the Court also ruled unanimously in *ex parte Endo* that while temporary detention in relocation centers was constitutional, the government could not retain loyal American citizens (some two-thirds of the internees were citizens) in the centers.

The relocation policy upheld by the *Korematsu* decision was criticized and often condemned as unjust and unconstitutional from the beginning, and underwent searching review after the war. In 1948, Congress approved reparations to internees—some $37 million in compensation for the relocation and the estimated $400 million in property losses to Japanese Americans. In 1984, a federal court ruled that "fundamental error," including the government's fraudulent use of evidence, had tainted the *Korematsu* case and overturned the conviction. With other relocation cases pending, Congress in 1988 acknowledged the "fundamental injustice of evacuation, relocation and internment" and offered both apologies for the policy and reparations of $20,000 to living survivors of the internment. In 1998, President Bill Clinton awarded Fred Korematsu the Presidential Medal of Freedom, the nation's highest civilian honor.

Further reading: Peter H. Irons, *Justice at War* (New York: Oxford University Press, 1983); Peter H. Irons, ed., *Justice Delayed: The Record of the Japanese American Internment Cases* (Middleton, Conn.: Wesleyan University Press, 1989).

L

labor

The rise of the labor movement in America between 1929 and 1945 was one of the most important social and political phenomena of the era. NEW DEAL reforms helped American union membership grow fivefold between 1933 and 1945, from 2.7 million to 14.3 million workers. By the end of WORLD WAR II, more than one-third of nonfarm wage earners belonged to a labor union—the highest percentage ever.

In addition to the enormous overall growth of unions, other factors made the rise of organized labor an important part of the New Deal era. With the formation of the new CONGRESS OF INDUSTRIAL ORGANIZATIONS (CIO), unions expanded beyond the skilled trades into the mass production industries (for example, autos, electrical products, rubber, and steel). The newly organized mass production industrial unions recruited first- and second-generation immigrants from southern and eastern Europe and AFRICAN AMERICANS, who had largely been ignored by the long-established AMERICAN FEDERATION OF LABOR (AFL). The union movement formed a crucial component of the Roosevelt Coalition that made the DEMOCRATIC PARTY the nation's majority party in the 1930s and beyond.

Such growth in the size and significance of American unions did not seem possible in the years preceding the GREAT DEPRESSION. In the 1920s, growing prosperity, the hostility of BUSINESS toward unions, and GOVERNMENT sympathy for employers helped to thin the ranks of unions from 5 million to about 3.5 million members. Some prospering businesses, such as the AUTOMOBILE INDUSTRY, paid workers well, but kept them nonunion, a condition that Henry Ford and other corporate heads enforced through various means of infiltration and intimidation.

In addition, the AFL's conservative leadership emphasized "volunteerism"—no government interference in labor-management relations—and focused on wages, hours, and working conditions of union members. The AFL's membership of native-born, "old stock" skilled craftsmen ignored the growing southern and eastern European immigrant and African-American unskilled workers who toiled in the mass production industries of automobiles, coal, and steel. In heavy industry where the AFL had a presence, leaders often impeded organizing, prevented strikes, and ignored worker demands.

A number of powerful union leaders, among them AFL president William Green and JOHN L. LEWIS backed HERBERT C. HOOVER for president in both 1928 and 1932. But the Great Depression and the seeming indifference of the HOOVER PRESIDENCY and the REPUBLICAN PARTY to the plight of workers changed the thinking of many in the labor movement. By 1932, manufacturing UNEMPLOYMENT reached nearly one in three workers, and wages and hours were often reduced for those with jobs. Union membership fell still further, and work stoppages declined. Labor received needed help from CONGRESS in 1932 with the passage of the Norris–La Guardia Act, which forbade federal courts from issuing injunctions to enforce "yellow-dog" contracts prohibiting workers from joining unions and restricted the use of injunctions against strikes. Hoover reluctantly signed the bill, warning that only the courts could decide on the law's provisions.

Much change occurred after the election of FRANKLIN D. ROOSEVELT in 1932. Although the new president would often be ambivalent toward unions and their goals, his administration presided over the greatest legitimization of the labor movement yet in American history. An important early step in the New Deal for labor was the passage of the NATIONAL INDUSTRIAL RECOVERY ACT (NIRA) during the first Hundred Days at the start of Roosevelt's presidency. The NIRA contained section 7(a), the key provision of the act for labor, which stated that "employees shall have the right to organize and bargain collectively through representatives of their own choosing."

Section 7(a), which was erratically enforced by the NATIONAL RECOVERY ADMINISTRATION (NRA), became an area of conflict between government and employers. Business responded by setting up "company unions," which they claimed fulfilled the Section 7(a) mandate. Workers, however, disagreed, and responded by organizing into existing unions and forming new ones (typically not treated by the AFL leadership in the same manner as the established trades unions), and engaging in a series of confrontations with employers and local government authorities in 1933 and 1934.

Tensions between the AFL and leaders of mass production unions such as Lewis and SIDNEY HILLMAN boiled over beginning in 1934. At the AFL convention that year, Lewis, Hillman, and other dissidents called on the federation to organize mass production workers. The AFL's rank and file turned down industrial unionism in 1934; and when they did it again in 1935, Lewis, Hillman, David Dubinsky of the International Ladies Garment Workers Union (ILGWU), and seven other union leaders formed the Committee for Industrial Organization as a branch within the AFL. Immediately, Lewis set out to organize the automotive, rubber and steel industries by using money from his own United Mine Workers (UMW) union, and dispatching key lieutenants such as PHILIP MURRAY,

who set up the Steelworkers Organizing Committee (SWOC). After "heresy" hearings, the AFL suspended the committee unions in 1937, and in November 1938, the Committee for Industrial Organization formally became the Congress of Industrial Organizations, with Lewis as its head.

After the election of 1934, which brought more pro-labor members to the House of Representatives and the Senate, Congress moved toward greater protection of workers and their right to organize. A bill sponsored by Senator ROBERT F. WAGNER of New York would give a new NATIONAL LABOR RELATIONS BOARD (NLRB) the power to set union elections, define and prohibit unfair labor practices, and legally enforce its own decisions. Business leaders predictably opposed the bill, and Roosevelt, who had urged Wagner to shelve the bill in 1934, "never lifted a finger," recalled Secretary of Labor FRANCES PERKINS, for the legislation until after Senate passage.

In May 1935, while the House was deliberating the Wagner bill, the SUPREME COURT declared the NRA—and thus Section 7(a)—unconstitutional. The president now considered the Wagner bill "a must," and the House passed the NATIONAL LABOR RELATIONS ACT (NLRA), the most sweeping piece of workers' legislation in American history. The NLRA, or the Wagner Act, as it became commonly called, established a permanent NLRB to determine union representation and restrain business from committing "unfair labor practices" such as establishing company unions, espionage, blacklisting, strikebreaking, and yellow-dog contracts. The law would be challenged, but was upheld by the Supreme Court in 1937.

The peak years for CIO organizing in the mass production industries came from 1935 to 1938. During 1936, rubber workers went on strike at Goodyear Tire and Rubber, and Murray and the SWOC traveled throughout Pennsylvania signing up new members. In late December 1936, the United Auto Workers (UAW), led by Walter Reuther, began a six-week sit-down strike against General Motors at the large Flint, Michigan, plant, which resulted in the automaker's capitulation to the union's demands for recognition and wage and hour benefits in February, 1937. In the STEEL INDUSTRY, the United States Steel Corporation recognized the SWOC in March 1937, and agreed to its demands.

During the first half of 1937, at least a million and a half workers joined trade unions, most in the CIO-dominated mass production industries, but also in AFL-organized trades such as transportation (teamsters), construction, communication, and hotel and restaurant work. The CIO helped set up the Non-Partisan League, which worked for Roosevelt's reelection, and Lewis, a lifetime Republican, endorsed the president in the ELECTION OF 1936.

This cartoon shows President Roosevelt "peeking in" on a dispute between United Mine Workers of America president John L. Lewis and William Green, president of the American Federation of Labor. As the cartoon indicates, the New Deal increased government intervention in American labor. Cartoon by Walter Berryman *(Library of Congress)*

The organizing drive, especially by the CIO in the automobile and steel industries, was slowed in 1937 and 1938 by several factors, including the RECESSION OF 1937–38, which resulted in a 50 percent drop in production in the auto, rubber, and steel industries, and a corresponding rise in unemployment. Conservative forces mobilized against "radical" sit-down strikes, with company police preventing union organizing, at Bethlehem, Republic, and other "Little Steel" plants, and at Ford.

A factor that both helped and hurt labor—especially the CIO—was the presence by the late 1930s and early 1940s of active COMMUNISTS or those with pro-Communist sympathies, who led several unions or maintained a strong and influential minority in others. Communists played important roles in organizing efforts, but they also produced tensions in organized labor and damaged its reputation. Roosevelt distanced himself from such radicals, knowing it would hurt him, especially with southern politicians, if he became too closely identified with them.

The ELECTION OF 1940 also produced friction in organized labor. John L. Lewis broke with Roosevelt and endorsed Republican WENDELL L. WILLKIE, a decision opposed by Hillman, Murray, and most other union leaders. Lewis resigned as president of the CIO after Roosevelt's reelection victory, with Murray succeeding him.

The labor movement entered another significant period, and one of rapid growth, during World War II. Led by Hillman and Murray, most labor chiefs backed Roosevelt's moves toward anti-AXIS intervention, although Lewis was among the leading ISOLATIONISTS. An upsurge in strikes occurred in 1941, culminating in the army's breakup of the UAW-sponsored aircraft workers strike in June. To avoid being portrayed as unpatriotic, Hillman, as associate director of the OFFICE OF PRODUCTION MANAGEMENT, mediated nearly 250 disputes in 1941. After PEARL HARBOR, union membership increased from roughly 10 million to more than 14 million by 1945, including many more women and African Americans.

During the war, unions, particularly the CIO, not only grew but became "domesticated," caught between satisfying the demands of workers on the one hand and being perceived as patriotic and not disrupting the war effort on the other. The AFL, whose membership increased as rapidly as the CIO's, especially in defense construction, the AIRCRAFT INDUSTRY, and SHIPBUILDING, criticized government for favoritism and the CIO for radicalism. Labor leaders agreed to a no-strike pledge for the war's duration, and the NATIONAL WAR LABOR BOARD (NWLB), established to keep workers and management at peace, was as important as the Wagner Act in shaping industrial relations. Labor also received positions, typically as junior partners, in war MOBILIZATION agencies.

In 1942, the government made three policy decisions that significantly affected labor. The OFFICE OF PRICE ADMINISTRATION (OPA) issued in April its General Maximum Price Regulation (known as "General Max"), which capped prices to prevent inflation. In June, the NWLB issued the "maintenance of membership" rule, mandating that in any place of employment covered by union contract, new employees would automatically become union members unless they requested differently during the first fifteen days on the job; employers would collect dues and enforce the guidelines. And in July, the NWLB settled a dispute with "Little Steel" by imposing a settlement limiting wage increases to the rise in the cost of living between January 1941 and May 1942—about 15 percent.

By 1943, more aggressive management tactics and growing frustration and restiveness among many workers led to an increased wave of strikes, the longest and most significant of which was the Lewis-led walkout of the UMW in the spring. Although the strike ended peacefully, the miners' walkout led to the passage, over Roosevelt's veto, of the Smith-Connally Act. This legislation, a precursor to the 1947 Taft-Hartley Act, gave the president power to seize striking plants, barred unions from giving money to political candidates, required a secret ballot to strike, mandated a 30 day cooling off period, and authorized jailing of anyone suspected of encouraging other plants to strike. Labor's response was a further increase in strikes (some 5,000 in 1944, more than in the "radical" year of 1937), and the establishment of the CIO Political Action Committee (PAC) by Hillman and others, which supported primarily pro-union Democrats, and backed Roosevelt for a fourth term in the ELECTION OF 1944.

As World War II concluded in 1945, strikes continued, as labor, management, and government grappled over the issues of RECONVERSION. In the factories, workers who had won the right to collectively bargain in the 1930s had no intention of turning back the clock. The wave of postwar strikes, however, continued to fuel anti-labor sentiment in Congress and led to union-restricting action, especially passage of the Taft-Hartley Act in 1947.

Further reading: Irving Bernstein, *Turbulent Years: A History of the American Worker, 1933–1941* (Boston: Houghton Mifflin, 1970); Lizabeth Cohen, *Making a New Deal: Industrial Workers in Chicago, 1919–1939* (New York: Cambridge University Press, 1990); Nelson Lichtenstein, *Labor's War at Home: The CIO in World War II* (New York: Cambridge University Press, 1982); Philip Taft, *The AFL: From the Death of Gompers to the Merger* (New York: Octagon Books, 1959, 1970); Robert H. Zieger, *The CIO: 1935–1955* (Chapel Hill: University of North Carolina Press, 1995).

La Follette, Robert M., Jr. (1895–1953)

Born in Madison, Wisconsin, on February 6, 1895, Robert Marion La Follette, Jr., was the son of Robert M. La Follette, the governor and senator from Wisconsin whose name was identified with the early-20th-century Progressive movement. His college career at the University of Wisconsin cut short by illness, "Young Bob" became personal secretary in his father's Senate office and campaign manager of his 1924 Progressive Party candidacy for the presidency. When La Follette Senior died in early 1925, Robert Junior won a special election to fill the remainder of his father's term, and would win reelection three times. Once in the Senate, La Follette sought to link the older progressivism of his father with the growing strength of urban LIBERALISM.

La Follette was a harsh critic of the HOOVER PRESIDENCY during the GREAT DEPRESSION, and in the ELECTION OF 1932, he endorsed Democrat FRANKLIN D. ROOSEVELT for the White House. La Follette supported most of the NEW DEAL, and in 1934 left the REPUBLICAN PARTY to form the Progressive Party. He won reelection with Roosevelt's personal endorsement, a favor returned in the ELECTION OF 1936, when the senator supported the president's reelection. La Follette backed Roosevelt's 1937 COURT-PACKING PLAN, one of the few progressives to do so, and chaired a subcommittee of the Senate Committee on Education and Labor, known as the La Follette committee, to investigate harassment and intimidation against LABOR union organizers.

In foreign policy, La Follette remained firmly with the ISOLATIONISTS in the Senate, supporting the NEUTRALITY ACTS and a national referendum on war (which his father had once proposed) and opposing the SELECTIVE SERVICE Act and the LEND-LEASE ACT. After PEARL HARBOR, La Follette's influence began to wane, and he broke with Roosevelt over his opposition to American membership in any postwar international organization.

By 1945, La Follette decided to take the Progressive Party back into the Republican Party. This proved the undoing of his political career, for he lost the GOP senatorial primary in 1946 to an obscure circuit court judge, Joseph R. McCarthy. Devastated by his defeat, La Follette became increasingly depressed, and committed suicide in Washington, D.C., on February 24, 1953.

Further reading: Patrick J. Maney, *"Young Bob" La Follette: A Biography of Robert M. La Follette, Jr., 1895–1953* (Columbia: University of Missouri Press, 1978).

—William J. Thompson

La Guardia, Fiorello (1882–1947)

Fiorello Henry La Guardia, "the Little Flower," is remembered as one of New York City's most famous and beloved mayors. He had a political career as unique as his quirky personality. A Republican who worked on behalf of LABOR and campaigned for FRANKLIN D. ROOSEVELT, La Guardia was, at various times, elected as a Republican, a Progressive, a Republican-Democrat, and a Fusion candidate. Born to an Italian father and a Jewish mother, he was throughout his career a foe of racial, religious, and ethnic prejudice. He served as a U.S. congressman and as president of the New York City Board of Alderman as well as mayor of New York.

Born on December 11, 1882, in Greenwich Village, La Guardia spent most of his early life on army bases in the West, because of his father's job as an army bandmaster. In 1906 he returned to New York City, where he worked as an interpreter at Ellis Island and attended law school at night. He began practicing law in 1910, and soon got involved in local politics. Disgusted by graft and corruption in the Tammany-run Democratic Party, La Guardia registered as a Republican. Although he lost his first race for Congress in 1914, the margin was surprisingly close, and La Guardia was encouraged to run again. In 1916, he won election to Congress by a few hundred votes.

When the United States entered World War I, La Guardia enlisted in the Signal Corps, where he rose to the rank of major and earned a number of commendations. After the war, in 1919, he was elected president of the Board of Aldermen of New York. Following an unsuccessful bid for mayor in 1921, La Guardia was elected in 1922 to the House of Representatives, where he remained until 1933. In Congress, La Guardia earned a reputation as a liberal and a friend of labor. Most notably, he coauthored the Norris-La Guardia Act in 1932, a bill that protected workers' right to go on strike. After losing reelection to the House in the ELECTION OF 1932, La Guardia set his sights on becoming mayor of New York.

Although winning the nomination of the anti-Tammany Fusion Party required a fierce political battle, La Guardia won the general election and became the first Italian American elected to the city's highest post. After taking office on New Year's Day, 1934, he enthusiastically attempted to make good on his campaign promises to improve government efficiency, decrease corruption, end partisanship, increase social programs, and clean up the city, physically and morally. He cooperated with the Roosevelt administration and used NEW DEAL assistance in improving the city. Reelected in 1937 and 1941, La Guardia became New York's first three-term mayor.

Despite La Guardia's genuine devotion to New York, he never quite lost the desire for national influence. In the ELECTION OF 1940, he supported Roosevelt, and, in 1941, he was appointed director of the OFFICE OF CIVILIAN

DEFENSE, a position he resigned under fire in 1942 because of OCD's early missteps. He declined to run for another term as mayor in 1945, and returned to private life, although he remained visible in public affairs as a writer and speaker. In 1946, he became the director of the UNITED NATIONS Relief and Rehabilitation Administration. La Guardia died on September 21, 1947.

Further reading: Lawrence Elliott, *Little Flower: The Life and Times of Fiorello La Guardia* (New York: Morrow, 1983); Thomas Kessner, *Fiorello H. La Guardia and the Making of Modern New York* (New York: McGraw-Hill, 1989).

—Pamela J. Lauer

Landon, Alfred M. ("Alf") (1887–1987)

Alf Landon, who described himself as "an oilman who never made a million, a lawyer who never had a case and a politician who carried only Maine and Vermont," was governor of Kansas from 1933 to 1937 and achieved national prominence as the unsuccessful REPUBLICAN PARTY candidate for president in the ELECTION OF 1936.

Born Alfred Mossman Landon on September 9, 1887, in West Middlesex, Pennsylvania, he was the son of an oil prospector. In 1904, the Landon family moved to Kansas, where, at the insistence of his father, Landon attended the University of Kansas School of Law. Graduating in 1908, Landon chose not to enter the law profession, but instead decided to work as a bookkeeper in Independence. There he began investing in oil ventures, and by 1912 he had formed his own oil company.

During World War I, Landon received a commission in the U.S. Army's chemical warfare corps, but before he completed his training the war came to an end. Landon returned to Kansas and developed a successful oil business. He also took an active interest in party politics, and by 1928 was head of the Kansas Republican Party. Landon won the governorship of Kansas in 1932, appealing to common workers by appearing in work clothes, boots, and a battered brown fedora. In 1934, he was one of the few Republican governors to be elected as Democratic candidates were swept into state and federal offices throughout the nation. His success made him a frontrunner for the 1936 Republican presidential nomination.

The GOP selected Landon by acclamation in 1936 as the candidate to challenge FRANKLIN D. ROOSEVELT. Landon argued that a Republican administration would be able to implement needed social and economic reforms more efficiently and economically than could the NEW DEAL, and his success in balancing the budget in Kansas was touted by Republicans throughout the campaign. Although Democrats depicted Landon as a reactionary, labeling him the

"Kansas Coolidge," Landon represented the progressive wing of the GOP and agreed with many of the goals and programs of the Roosevelt administration. No match for the popularity of Roosevelt and the New Deal, however, Landon won only 36.5 percent of the popular vote and carried only the states of Maine and Vermont.

Although he never returned to public office, Landon remained active in the Republican Party and continued to voice his opinions. He continued to criticize the New Deal, but often supported Roosevelt's FOREIGN POLICY in the late 1930s. Though not among the Republican ISOLATIONISTS, he ultimately concluded that FDR's policies were too interventionist. After WORLD WAR II, he endorsed the Truman administration's efforts to provide aid to Europe. Later he supported many of the social welfare programs of the Johnson administration's "Great Society." In 1978, his daughter, Nancy Landon Kassebaum, was elected to the United States Senate, where she represented Kansas until 1997. Barely a month after his hundredth birthday, Alf Landon died at home in Topeka, on October 12, 1987.

Further reading: Donald R. McCoy, *Landon of Kansas* (Lincoln: University of Nebraska Press, 1966).

—Shannon L. Parsley

Leahy, William D. (1875–1959)

William Daniel Leahy was a distinguished American naval officer, a longtime friend of President FRANKLIN D. ROOSEVELT, and an important architect of Allied strategy during WORLD WAR II. He was born on May 6, 1875, in Hampton, Iowa. In 1882, his family moved to Wisconsin, where he lived until he entered the U.S. Naval Academy in 1893. After graduation in 1897, Leahy served on board the battleship *Oregon*, and saw action at the Battle of Santiago in July 1898 during the Spanish-American War. As a young officer, he also served in China during the Boxer Rebellion, and witnessed first hand America's colonial expansion into Latin America and the Pacific. In February 1904, he married Louise Tennent Harrington; they had one son, who also had a distinguished naval career.

During World War I, Leahy became an aide to Secretary of the Navy Josephus Daniels, and began a lifelong friendship with Franklin Roosevelt, who was then an assistant secretary of the navy. After World War I, Leahy held a number of important positions in Washington and in the fleet, was promoted to full admiral in 1936, and in 1937 became chief of naval operations (CNO), the top position in the U.S. NAVY. With World War II on the horizon, Leahy's main goal as CNO was to prepare the navy for conflict. He used his considerable political connections to persuade

CONGRESS to increase appropriations for the navy, and created contingency plans to be used in the event of war. Leahy remained CNO until 1939, when he reached the mandatory retirement age of 64.

After leaving the navy, Leahy became governor of Puerto Rico, a post he held until November 1940, when Roosevelt asked him to become America's ambassador to Vichy France. In 1942, Roosevelt recalled him to active duty, and he acted as both the chairman of the newly created Joint Chiefs of Staff and as the president's own personal chief of staff. As one of Roosevelt's most trusted advisers, Leahy took part in almost all top-level discussions during World War II, including the TEHERAN, YALTA, and POTSDAM CONFERENCES, and served as chairman of the combined British-American Chiefs of Staff whenever it met in the United States. On December 15, 1944, he became the first of only four U.S. naval officers ever to receive the rank of fleet (five star) admiral.

After Roosevelt's death, Leahy served as Truman's chief of staff until March 1949, when poor health caused his final retirement. As a staunch anti-communist, he supported Truman's efforts to block the expansion of communism into Iran, Greece, and Turkey, and argued against withdrawing American support to the Chinese Nationalists. In 1950, he published his autobiography, *I Was There.* He died on July 20, 1959, at Bethesda Naval Hospital.

Further reading: Henry H. Adams, *Witness to Power: The Life of Fleet Admiral William D. Leahy* (Annapolis, Md.: Naval Institute Press, 1985).

—David W. Waltrop

Lend-Lease Act (1941)

The Lend-Lease Act enabled the United States to supply its allies with much-needed war materials during WORLD WAR II. It authorized the president "to sell, transfer title to, exchange, lease, lend, or otherwise dispose of" defense articles to nations the president declared "vital to the defense of the United States." In all, Lend-Lease extended an estimated $50 billion worth of weapons, foodstuffs, and other supplies to some four dozen countries and played a significant role in the victory of the GRAND ALLIANCE over the AXIS.

The Lend-Lease Act came about because of the precarious situation of Great Britain at the end of 1940, when Prime Minister Winston Churchill informed President FRANKLIN D. ROOSEVELT that Britain's financial resources, and thus its ability to resist Germany, would soon be exhausted under the system of CASH-AND-CARRY. Roosevelt devised Lend-Lease as a way around existing FOREIGN POLICY constraints, including the NEUTRALITY ACTS, which barred loans to nations at war. In effect, Roosevelt's scheme proposed a neighborly system of lending needed supplies instead of charging for them. As the president put it at a December 17, 1940, press conference, Lend-Lease would be like a garden hose that would be lent to a neighbor to extinguish their burning home and to protect your home from burning, as well. The garden hose would then be returned. Roosevelt also gave a powerful defense of the proposed policy in a December 29 fireside chat where he called on the United States to be the "arsenal of democracy."

ISOLATIONISTS vigorously opposed the Lend-Lease proposal, viewing it as a means of pushing the United States into the war. But by the winter of 1940–41, American public opinion was shifting to a readiness to aid Great Britain even at the risk of war. The Lend-Lease bill, symbolically designated H.R.1776, passed by 317-71 votes in the House and by 60-31 in the Senate, and was signed into law by President Roosevelt on March 11, 1941. The office of Lend-Lease Administration, headed first by HARRY HOPKINS and then by Edward Stettinius, Jr., oversaw the distribution of funds.

Initial Lend-Lease expenditures not only provided Britain with essential material but also helped convert the United States from peacetime to wartime production. For the duration of the war, Britain requested the supplies that were needed and the U.S. provided as much as possible. For Britain, which received much the largest share of Lend-Lease assistance (about $30 billion), this meant an enormous flow of wartime goods that included aircraft, guns, bombs, ammunition, and foodstuffs. What Churchill called "the most unsordid act in the history of any nation" (though it did involve certain concessions by the British) helped Britain survive.

Lend-Lease was intended initially for Great Britain only, but was extended to dozens of other nations. Especially important were China and the Soviet Union. In the spring of 1941, Roosevelt declared the defense of China vital to the defense of the United States, and thus China was included in Lend-Lease aid. Supplies sent ranged from trucks, spare parts, lubricants, and gas to planes, guns, and ammunitions. However, a majority of funding to China was for the expansion of the Burma Road, a treacherous mountain passage that was the only overland route into China.

Lend-Lease aid was extended to the Soviets in the autumn of 1941, following the German invasion of the Soviet Union that summer. Because of American suspicions of the USSR, Lend-Lease for the Soviets was treated as a form of credit to be repaid beginning five years after the war. The U.S. promised the Soviets a fixed amount of supplies in a specified time period, typically a year. These supplies included planes, tanks, guns, and clothes. However, shipments were slow, and not all of the promised goods actually reached the Soviet Union. This complicated SOVIET-AMERICAN RELATIONS, as did the American and British delay until June 1944 of the opening of a SECOND FRONT in Europe to ease the burden of the Soviet Union resisting German forces. The Soviets complained that they were bearing the brunt of fighting Hitler's forces and not receiving enough aid from the United States. Many in America, however, saw it differently; the Soviets, they believed, were not sufficiently grateful for the aid they did receive, estimated to be a total of $10 billion by the end of the war.

Considering Lend-Lease a wartime policy for America's defense, not a measure to underwrite the costs of the war or to support postwar relief and reconstruction, CONGRESS wanted Lend-Lease ended as soon as possible. On May 11, 1945, three days after V-E DAY, the new president, Harry S. Truman, authorized cutbacks to nations receiving supplies under Lend-Lease. Shipments were confined to supplies that could be used in the WORLD WAR II PACIFIC THEATER until the defeat of Japan, at which time Lend-Lease would be terminated. The Soviet Union was again treated differently, for Truman stopped shipments to the Soviets immediately after V-E Day. After protests from the Soviet Union, he then allowed some shipments to continue. This episode increased (and reflected) the growing tension in Soviet-American relations, although the British, too, were unhappy about the quick termination of Lend-Lease after V-J DAY.

Whatever the disagreements about Lend-Lease and its termination, however, the Lend-Lease Act played a critical role supplying the Allies and bringing victory in the war, and it provided a model of sorts for postwar American foreign assistance programs.

See also ANGLO-AMERICAN RELATIONS.

Further reading: George C. Herring Jr., *Aid to Russia, 1941–1946: Strategy, Diplomacy, the Origins of the Cold War* (New York: Columbia University Press, 1973); Warren F. Kimball, *The Most Unsordid Act: Lend-Lease, 1939–1941* (Baltimore: Johns Hopkins University Press, 1969).

—Jonathan R. Mikeska

Lewis, John L. (1880–1969)

John Llewellyn Lewis, president of the United Mine Workers of America (UMW) for four decades, and cofounder and first president of the CONGRESS OF INDUSTRIAL ORGANIZATIONS (CIO), was the most important figure in American LABOR during the 1930s and 1940s.

Born in Lucas County, Iowa, on February 12, 1880, Lewis was the son of Welsh immigrants. He ended formal schooling at an early age and followed his father and broth-

ers into the mines of southern Iowa. After working for several years in western mines, Lewis returned to Iowa, married, and became head of the local UMW union. Skilled as a union organizer, he settled in Illinois and worked his way up the UMW ladder.

In 1917, Lewis became UMW vice president, and in 1920 became president of the United Mine Workers, a post he would hold until 1960. An imposing figure with large head, bushy eyebrows and booming voice, Lewis was given to biblical allusion and Shakespearean quotes. During the 1920s, Lewis established firm control of the UMW by beating back his opponents, though the union lost 80 percent of its membership in the decade. A Republican, Lewis backed HERBERT C. HOOVER for president in 1928, calling him the "foremost industrial statesman of modern times." That support, however, failed to gain for Lewis and the miners any advantage from the HOOVER PRESIDENCY. The coming of the GREAT DEPRESSION eroded Lewis's firm belief in free enterprise and led him toward the idea of national economic planning.

In the ELECTION OF 1932, Lewis publicly backed Hoover for reelection, but privately worked behind the scenes for FRANKLIN D. ROOSEVELT. After Roosevelt's

John L. Lewis (left) *(Library of Congress)*

election, Lewis backed NEW DEAL legislation benefiting labor, beginning with the NATIONAL INDUSTRIAL RECOVERY ACT (he served on the Labor Advisory Board of the NATIONAL RECOVERY ADMINISTRATION) and continuing with the NATIONAL LABOR RELATIONS ACT of 1935 and the Guffey-Snyder Bituminous Coal Act of 1936. Taking advantage of the NRA's Section 7(a) providing for collective bargaining, Lewis launched a massive organizing drive during the summer of 1933, resulting in 500,000 new UMW members.

Lewis became increasingly frustrated, however, with the neglect of workers by the AMERICAN FEDERATION OF LABOR (AFL) in mass production industries such as automobiles, clothing, steel, and coal. Beginning in 1934, Lewis, SIDNEY HILLMAN of the Amalgamated Clothing Workers (ACW), and other dissident leaders called on the AFL to organize mass production workers into industrial unions. After one-third of AFL members agreed the first year, Lewis in 1935 again repeated his demands for industrial unionism. Afterward, when words were exchanged, Lewis punched Carpenters Union head "Big Bill" Hutcheson, bloodying his face. Three weeks later, after being voted down again, Lewis, Hillman, David Dubinsky of the International Ladies Garment Workers Union (ILGWU), and several other union heads formed the Committee for Industrial Organization as a branch within the AFL.

Immediately, Lewis set out to organize the mass production industries, using UMW money, and dispatching his key lieutenant PHILIP MURRAY to organize the STEEL INDUSTRY. When the AFL suspended the Committee for Industrial Organization unions in 1937, Lewis and the other dissident leaders formally separated in 1938, changing the group's name to the CONGRESS OF INDUSTRIAL ORGANIZATIONS (CIO), with Lewis as first president.

Lewis also took an active role in the decade's politics. The United Mine Workers gave $500,000 to help set up the Non-Partisan League, which worked for Roosevelt's reelection, and Lewis, the lifelong Republican, endorsed the president in the ELECTION OF 1936. The Roosevelt-Lewis relationship soured quickly, however, over CIO involvement in sit-down strikes, COMMUNISTS in CIO unions, and Lewis's isolationist foreign policy views. By 1940, the break between Lewis and Roosevelt was complete, as the CIO president endorsed WENDELL L. WILLKIE for president, although most of his fellow union leaders again backed FDR's reelection.

After the ELECTION OF 1940, Lewis, who promised to quit if Roosevelt was reelected, resigned as CIO president and was replaced by Murray. Two years later, Lewis pulled the UMW out of the CIO. During WORLD WAR II, Lewis dissented from labor's no-strike pledge as the UMW went on strike in 1941 and 1943, the latter walkout leading to GOVERNMENT seizure of the mines. While the wartime strikes were successful in winning major concessions from mine operators, Lewis's imperious attitude alienated both the public and CONGRESS, while led to passage of the anti-union Smith-Connally Act in 1943 and the Taft-Hartley Act of 1947.

After the 1940s, Lewis's influence on national labor affairs diminished, and he retired as UMW president in 1960. John L. Lewis died in Washington, D.C., on June 11, 1969.

Further reading: Melvyn Dubofsky, and Warren VanTine, *John L. Lewis: A Biography* (New York: Quadrangle, 1977); Robert H. Zieger, *John L. Lewis: Labor Leader* (Boston: Twayne, 1988).

—William J. Thompson

Leyte Gulf, Battle for (October 1944)

The Battle for Leyte Gulf (October 23–25, 1944) was the largest naval engagement in history, involving four major actions between hundreds of ships of the U.S. NAVY and the Imperial Japanese Navy over a hundred thousand square miles of the Pacific Ocean. It marked the end of the Japanese navy as a significant fighting force in the PACIFIC THEATER of WORLD WAR II and ensured the success of the American invasion of Leyte Island in the PHILIPPINES.

Following American victories in the BATTLE OF THE PHILIPPINE SEA (which had destroyed Japan's naval air strength) and in the MARIANA ISLANDS in the summer of 1944, U.S. ARMY general Douglas MacArthur landed forces on Leyte Island on October 20. His assault was supported by the U.S. Third and Seventh Fleets, the largest naval force ever assembled. It included some 35 aircraft carriers, 12 battleships, 28 cruisers, 150 destroyers, plus other ships. At the same time, Japan implemented a complicated plan, involving four forces of its Combined Fleet, that was designed to lure U.S. ships away from Leyte and leave the American invasion force vulnerable to attack.

After contact was made with Japanese ships on October 23, aircraft from Admiral WILLIAM F. "BULL" HALSEY's Third Fleet launched attacks against Vice Admiral Kurita's force, sinking the superbattleship *Musashi* and other ships, though losing the light aircraft carrier USS *Princeton*. Two of the other Japanese forces encountered Vice Admiral Thomas Kinkaid's Seventh Fleet in the Surigao Strait, lost two battleships and three cruisers in a one-sided surface battle, and were forced to withdraw.

Meanwhile, airplanes from the Third Fleet had spotted the fourth Japanese force. The aggressive Halsey turned his fleet north to intercept what was really a decoy force of four aircraft carriers with few planes. Although Halsey sank all four Japanese carriers, he left the San Bernardino Strait unprotected, in what some derisively called the "Battle of Bull's Run." Elements of Kurita's force returned to the strait on October 25 and steamed toward Leyte Gulf, but were repelled by badly outnumbered ships from the American Seventh Fleet. The battered Japanese forces withdrew.

The heavy losses in the Battle for Leyte Gulf dealt the Japanese navy a lethal blow. In all, the Japanese lost four aircraft carriers, three battleships, 10 cruisers, and nine destroyers; the U.S. Navy lost three carriers, two destroyers, and one destroyer escort. But while the engagement meant the death of the Imperial Japanese Navy as a serious force, it also witnessed the birth of Japan's newest weapon—the kamikaze, the suicide airplane attack that would cause such enormous damage at the battle for OKINAWA in the spring of 1945. Though the destruction of its navy and the impending loss of the Philippines ended any realistic hopes in the war, Japan would fight on.

Further reading: Thomas J. Cutler, *The Battle of Leyte Gulf, 23–26 October, 1944* (New York: Harper, 1994).
—Michael Leonard

liberalism

Liberalism in the era of the GREAT DEPRESSION and the NEW DEAL was concerned especially with issues of political economy and economic security, above all with the role of the federal GOVERNMENT in reforming and strengthening the ECONOMY. But liberalism in America has never been unitary or unchanging. Not only were there various strands and emphases of liberalism from 1929 to 1945, but the dominant priority of liberal economic policy went from microeconomic regulation and control of the private sector in the early New Deal to macroeconomic fiscal policy to underwrite full-employment prosperity by the end of WORLD WAR II.

American liberalism changed in character in the early 20th century. In the 19th century, it had been "classical" or "laissez-faire" liberalism, concerned with protecting individual liberty and economic freedom and otherwise limiting the power of the state. During the early 20th century, and particularly in the New Deal era, that limited-government approach to protecting economic liberty became the domain of conservatives, as progressives and liberals called for a strong state to achieve their aims. Though reformers of the Progressive Era had important disagreements about government policy, most agreed that stronger government was necessary to restrain the growing economic and political power of big business, to protect individuals from corporate power and corrupt politics, and to ensure oppor-

tunity in the face of the powerful modernizing forces of industrialization, urbanization, and large organizations. An important segment of progressivism, especially in the urban North, wanted government to take on a stronger social welfare role as well. In addition to its concern with economic issues, progressivism also emphasized moral regeneration—thus the campaigns to end corruption in business and politics, or to combat individual as well as societal ills by such measures as Prohibition. And the Progressive Era saw efforts to integrate immigrants into American life and to advance the rights of women and African Americans. Some of these social and cultural priorities—the Americanization of immigrants, for example, or Prohibition—would often seemed later to be repressive programs of social control, but up until World War I they also involved moral uplift and efforts to enhance democracy.

During the 1920s, the social and cultural emphases of prewar progressivism ebbed, and reform—increasingly known as liberalism—came to focus more on economic issues. Partly that was because of the nationalistic and ethnic forces unleashed or illuminated by World War I that seemed so uncontrollable and harmful in international and national affairs. The fierce ethnocultural conflict of 1920s America helped prevent workers and farmers from making common cause and diverted attention from fundamental economic issues. Many liberal intellectuals thus came to distrust ethnic and racial passions and to believe that rational public activity could be focused more usefully on economic issues. For some, the exciting possibilities of the Russian Revolution and the new Soviet Union turned attention to the working class, industrial democracy, and economic reform. The growing power of BUSINESS, large disparities of wealth and living standards, and conservative Republican national governments also helped focus liberalism increasingly on economic issues—on taxes, tariffs, regulation, farm prices, and hydroelectric power, for example. Then in 1929 came the calamitous Great Depression, which for a decade commanded public attention and shaped politics and public policy.

A number of liberal approaches to the depression emerged, some of them drawing on ideas and economic programs of the progressives. These approaches included government planning and economic controls to produce equity and economic expansion, government spending to restore prosperity, and social welfare policies to help the unemployed and the impoverished. Some left-wing liberals were at times enticed by still more far-reaching ideas of state power and collectivism advocated by SOCIALISTS, COMMUNISTS, and other radicals; but in seeking to reform and sometimes to restructure economic institutions, liberalism sought to strengthen and preserve capitalism, not replace it. At the heart of early 1930s liberalism—and at the heart of the differences between liberals and conservatives—was a conviction that the depression had resulted from structural flaws in the domestic economy and that government must reform American capitalism in order to solve the nation's economic problems.

Although there was more to liberalism in the 1930s than the New Deal, and although the New Deal involved numerous and sometimes conflicting ideas and programs and seemed insufficient to many liberals, the principal policies and directions of the New Deal can nonetheless help to trace the focus and dynamics of liberalism during the presidency of FRANKLIN D. ROOSEVELT from 1933 to 1945. In Roosevelt's first term, the lineaments of the modern American regulatory welfare state were established, and liberalism's growing focus on economic security became apparent. The cornerstone measures of the FIRST NEW DEAL of 1933—the NATIONAL INDUSTRIAL RECOVERY ACT and the AGRICULTURAL ADJUSTMENT ACT—sought to produce economic recovery by means of government planning and controls. In 1933, the New Deal also accepted federal responsibility for RELIEF assistance to the unemployed and impoverished. Then the SECOND NEW DEAL of 1935 brought new programs with a social-democratic focus, such as the SOCIAL SECURITY ACT and the NATIONAL LABOR RELATIONS ACT, while the EMERGENCY RELIEF APPROPRIATIONS ACT reorganized and expanded relief policy. These programs of the Second New Deal made LABOR and the working class central to liberal policy and to the politics of the DEMOCRATIC PARTY.

Concerned primarily with economic issues and the role of government to address and resolve them, the New Deal thus focused on issues of political economy. Although 1930s liberals often did have an intensely moralistic concern about economic democracy and social welfare, New Deal liberalism for the most part did not share the focus on moral regeneration that had characterized much of prewar progressivism. New Deal liberals supported the repeal of Prohibition and often worked closely with political machines. They prided themselves on being practical and realistic, not sentimental. Northern liberals often cooperated with southern liberals on economic reform, despite the insistence of most southern liberals on maintaining their region's racial patterns. Women, AFRICAN AMERICANS, and ethnic groups, though important components of the majority coalition the Democrats forged in the 1930s and though given significant positions within the Roosevelt administration, did not receive the same policy priorities as did such economic groups as workers, farmers, and the unemployed. Particularly in New Deal efforts to enhance the administrative state, including the EXECUTIVE REORGANIZATION ACT of 1939, there was some effort at government reform, but it lacked the moral fervor of Progressive Era reform.

But although it commanded the support of most liberals, the emerging New Deal state had not solved the economic problem of the depression, as the severe RECESSION OF 1937–38 revealed. Sending economic indexes plummeting even faster than in 1929, the 1937–38 recession caused a reevaluation and ultimately a redirection of the New Deal and of mainstream liberalism in what some scholars have called the THIRD NEW DEAL. One important group of liberals wanted to effect structural reform and substantially to increase the regulatory power of the federal government, some by more vigorous ANTIMONOPOLY policy, others by enlarging the administrative capacity of the state in economic planning and control. Another group, believing with others that the recession had demonstrated that the American economy had become a mature economy lacking the ability to expand or sustain full-employment prosperity, called for enlarging public assistance and economic security programs to protect the unemployed and the impoverished. And yet another group (although there was overlap among all three approaches) advocated turning to KEYNESIANISM to revive the economy by means of fiscal policy. Keynesian liberals held that government spending on reform programs could not only bring economic recovery and full employment by compensating for inadequate private spending but could also underwrite social reform programs. The expansive liberal agenda for the postwar period developed by the NATIONAL RESOURCES PLANNING BOARD in the early 1940s reflected the new importance of Keynesianism in liberal policymaking.

By the end of the war, the Keynesian approach had largely triumphed among liberals and had come to define the political economy of wartime and postwar liberalism. The aims of thoroughgoing planning and controls to achieve structural reform by means of a far stronger administrative state had faded. There were a number of reasons for this. The heavy wartime deficit spending and the return to full-employment prosperity by the middle of the war confirmed Keynesian analysis. The wartime economic expansion also restored the faith of most liberals in the structure and growth capacity of the American economy and seemed to make an enlarged welfare state unnecessary. At the same time, microeconomic controls and planning fell out of favor among liberals, partly because wartime MOBILIZATION agencies had not seemed to work efficiently and had proved susceptible to "capture" by business and conservatives, partly because the examples of Nazism and communism made liberals increasingly wary about enlarging government power. Late-1930s antimonopoly efforts came to nothing, particularly as big business regained popularity and political power, and as antitrust action was abandoned during the war.

The political situation had changed, too, with the rise of the CONSERVATIVE COALITION in Congress, the return of prosperity, and the priorities given defense and foreign policy. In this changed context, the less intrusive macroeconomic fiscal policy to underwrite prosperity became far more politically feasible than planning, controls, and efforts to redistribute wealth and power. And PUBLIC OPINION POLLS showed that it was not economic or social welfare reform but, rather, prosperity and security—jobs, above all—that dominated public hopes for the postwar era at home. As a consequence, the far-reaching postwar program of the National Resources Planning Board developed in the early 1940s found little support, and Congress terminated the agency in 1943. Similarly, the ECONOMIC BILL OF RIGHTS based upon NRPB proposals and adumbrated by Roosevelt in 1944 had little resonance. By 1945, the principal aim of liberalism had become ensuring full-employment prosperity by means of Keynesian tools, as the emphasis on the FULL EMPLOYMENT BILL reflected.

But as liberalism became less aggressive on matters of political economy, it became more assertive on CIVIL RIGHTS and, eventually, CIVIL LIBERTIES. Intellectual and academic liberals had continued to chip away at the intellectual foundations of racism and ethnocentrism and thus to support efforts to respect minority groups and cultural liberalism. By the end of the 1930s, northern liberals were increasingly ready to promote civil rights for African Americans. The appalling treatment of JEWS by Nazi Germany caused more attention to combating racial and religious intolerance in America. The war years then greatly accelerated these dynamics. The notion of "Americans All" fighting a war for democracy against the master-race philosophy reinforced efforts for an inclusive cultural pluralism, and the mounting evidence about the HOLOCAUST had enormous impact. Prejudice and discrimination in wartime America, disturbing developments in RACE AND RACIAL CONFLICT, and the publication of the hugely important book by GUNNAR MYRDAL on American racial patterns, *An American Dilemma*, made civil rights much more a cause of liberals. By 1948, the growing insistence of northern Democrats on civil rights produced the "Dixiecrat" split in the Democratic Party. Though liberals in general did not take up women's rights in the 1940s and often acquiesced in wartime violations of civil liberties, the rights-based liberalism of the postwar era was clearly under way.

By 1945, then, liberalism was different from just a decade earlier. Still concerned mostly about the economy, liberalism had shifted from the emphasis of the early New Deal on planning and controls on behalf of structural reform, economic regulation, and industrial democracy to a focus on compensatory fiscal policy to sustain full employment prosperity. But as liberalism came to emphasize economic security in a full-employment econ-

omy, it also increasingly supported individual opportunity and freedom in the areas of civil rights and civil liberties. Finally, most liberals by 1945 had come to a conviction that the United States must pursue an active, internationalist FOREIGN POLICY, including participation in the new UNITED NATIONS. The emphasis on foreign policy would mean less attention on, and less money for, domestic policy, and, as in the case of SOVIET-AMERICAN RELATIONS, sometimes caused sharp disagreement among liberals.

See also POLITICS IN THE ROOSEVELT ERA.

Further reading: Alan Brinkley, *The End of Reform: New Deal Liberalism in Depression and War* (New York: Knopf, 1995); Steve Fraser, and Gary Gerstle, eds., *The Rise and Fall of the New Deal Order* (Princeton, N.J.: Princeton University Press, 1989); Gary Gerstle, "The Protean Character of American Liberalism." *American Historical Review* 99, no. 4 (October 1994): 1043–73; John W. Jeffries, "The 'New' New Deal: FDR and American Liberalism, 1937–1945," *Political Science Quarterly* 103 (Fall 1990): 397–418; David Plotke, *Building a Democratic Political Order: Reshaping American Liberalism in the 1930s and 1940s* (New York: Cambridge University Press, 1996).

Life magazine

HENRY LUCE, the head of Time, Inc., established *Life* as America's first picture magazine in 1936. *Life*'s use of PHOTOGRAPHY and its innovative photojournalistic approach quickly brought it astonishing success and made it one of the nation's most influential periodicals. Not only did *Life* make its mark in POPULAR CULTURE and the NEWS MEDIA, but the work of such accomplished staff photographers such as W. Eugene Smith, Margaret Bourke-White, and Peter Stackpole also found homes in many of the great art galleries, including the Museum of Modern Art in New York.

Life began its weekly publication on November 19, 1936, when it sold out its entire press run of 466,000. Within a few weeks, *Life* was selling a million copies, and improvements in advertising and printing technology soon turned the magazine into a profit-making publication of immense popularity. Containing weekly sections such as "Speaking of Pictures" and its "Picture of the Week," *Life* reported the news in pictures, offering a more vivid image of events than words could provide and opening the eyes of millions of Americans to the nation and world around them. Its photo essays became a staple of the magazine.

During WORLD WAR II, the popularity of *Life* increased still further. By one estimate, two out of every three Americans in the military read the magazine, as did tens of millions of civilians. In its coverage of the war, *Life* followed GOVERNMENT preferences in avoiding graphic pictures of American casualties, and waited until spring 1945 to show the blood of an American soldier.

After reaching its peak of some 24 million readers weekly, *Life*'s circulation declined as the growth of television in the 1950s provided America with a new medium for seeing current events. *Life*'s subscription rates dropped until the magazine closed down in 1972, marking the end of an era in photojournalism. (*Look* magazine, *Life*'s competitor going back to the 1930s, had folded the year before.) *Life* was reestablished as a monthly in 1978 but never had the same success and discontinued publication in March 2000. *Life* still releases special collections to commemorate important and historical events experienced throughout the world.

Further reading: James L. Boughman, *Henry R. Luce and the Rise of the American News Media* (Boston: Twayne, 1987); W. A. Swanberg, *Luce and His Empire* (New York: Scribner's, 1972).

—Ronald G. Simon

Lilienthal, David E. (1899–1981)

David Eli Lilienthal served as a member of the board of directors and then as chairman of the TENNESSEE VALLEY AUTHORITY (TVA), an important NEW DEAL agency, and later as director of the Atomic Energy Commission.

Lilienthal was born July 8, 1899, in Morton, Illinois, to parents who were immigrants from Austria-Hungary. He attended DePauw University, and then Harvard Law School, where he became friends with Professor FELIX FRANKFURTER. After Lilienthal graduated from law school, Frankfurter helped him find a position practicing law at a small firm in Chicago. Lilienthal's work with utility law brought him to the attention of Wisconsin Governor Philip La Follette, who asked him to join the state utility commission in 1931. He gained national recognition through this commission, with the result that President FRANKLIN D. ROOSEVELT appointed him one of the three original members of the TVA board of directors, along with Harcourt Morgan and board chairman Arthur Morgan.

Lilienthal's concept of the TVA's purpose contrasted greatly from that of Arthur Morgan. Whereas Lilienthal believed that the TVA should compete outright with private power companies, providing electricity at lower rates, Morgan maintained that the agency ought to cooperate with the utilities companies and be above all an instrument of planned social and economic change to end poverty and improve conditions in the region. Lilienthal's views ultimately prevailed, and in 1938 Roosevelt fired Morgan for

his public criticisms of Lilienthal and Harcourt Morgan. Lilienthal was named chairman of the TVA in 1941, and he led it during WORLD WAR II, when the TVA provided inexpensive power to the atomic energy installation at Oak Ridge, Tennessee, an important component of the MANHATTAN PROJECT that developed the ATOMIC BOMB. Some of TVA's manufacturing facilities also furnished munitions for the war effort.

Lilienthal was reappointed TVA chairman in 1945, but left soon after to work with a State Department committee on atomic energy and weapons. The resulting Acheson-Lilienthal report recommended international cooperation in the development of atomic energy. In 1946, President Truman appointed Lilienthal chairman of the new Atomic Energy Commission, making him the first civilian to head an effort previously run by the army. After resigning from the government in 1950, Lilienthal devoted his efforts especially to heading a private company involved in overseas economic development. He died of a heart attack in 1981.

Further reading: Thomas McCraw, *Morgan vs. Lilienthal: The Feud within the TVA* (Chicago: Loyola University Press, 1970); Steven M. Neuse, *David E. Lilienthal: The Journey of an American Liberal* (Knoxville: University of Tennessee Press, 1996).

—Joanna Smith

literature

During the 1920s, many Americans, but particularly writers and other intellectuals, felt estranged from the prevailing culture. While mainstream society found outlets in consumerism, booster clubs, or SPORTS events and professed faith in BUSINESS as much as RELIGION, the more rebellious indulged in gin and jazz, danced the jitterbug, experimented with sexuality, and read sarcastic criticisms of what H. L. Mencken derided as the "booboisie" culture. All of this contrasted considerably with the symbols of the period that followed: breadlines, shantytowns, and shovels.

The GREAT DEPRESSION led writers to formulate new perspectives and find new philosophies to describe and explain the conditions that enveloped the nation. Many authors looked disparagingly at the irresponsibility and intolerance that characterized the 1920s and promoted such themes as the strength of families and the ideals of social justice. In addition, writers in the 1930s unveiled sympathetic representations of destitute farmers, downtrodden immigrant laborers, and oppressed AFRICAN AMERICANS. Only a few years earlier such folks routinely had been regarded as inconsequential but now were depicted as resolute and striving to enjoy America's benefits.

Indeed, by the 1930s, old America—symbolized by Protestant villages and towns, small family farms, horses and buggies, and artisans—nearly was gone. In its place was a nation of impersonal, expanding CITIES characterized by ethnic enclaves, automobiles, and factory workers. Machines were more important to corporations than were the men who operated them, thus unskilled laborers became dependent on industrial barons. Likewise, motorized tractors enabled corporations to cobble together expansive farms from what had been the lifeline of some families for generations. As JOHN STEINBECK observed in *The Grapes of Wrath* (1939), unknown bankers in the East controlled Oklahoma farms. LABOR unions now were disparaged not for their affront to the American way but, as John Dos Passos illustrated in *The Big Money* (1933), for their ineffectiveness in effecting social change and improving working conditions for the people they supposedly championed. The most significant literature in the period following the STOCK MARKET CRASH, including WORLD WAR II, celebrated the common man and depicted those with power as the enemy.

Exploitation of the weak by the powerful hardly was a new concept in literature. However, in Edith Wharton's tales of wealthy New Yorkers and in such accomplished works as *Babbitt* (1922) by Sinclair Lewis, trampling the underclass had been akin to spending summers in Newport or scanning the business pages over breakfast—largely emblematic of a lifestyle. The themes espoused during the depression were fresh because the view and voice were altered and the suffering hidden beneath the boom, exposed now by the indignity of economic anguish, came to light in raw, undisguised portraits.

Many intellectuals repudiated democracy as a weapon used to dominate the minority, and a concentrated proletarian literary movement even emerged to capture the fiercest criticisms of usually marginal marxist writers. Few critics advocated such notions during the Roaring Twenties, but manifest changes in the ECONOMY and society during the 1930s inspired more grim and bitter criticism than the ironic and sarcastic skein of commentary in years past. Clifford Odets reflected this radical perspective in his noted play *Waiting for Lefty* (1935), as did such novelists as Michael Gold and Grace Lumpkin.

Dos Passos managed to blend rebuke of the 1920s and disillusion with the 1930s in three successive, connected works. Critics debate the significance of his *U.S.A.* trilogy (*The 42nd Parallel* [1930], *1919* [1932], and *The Big Money*), but the series remains an illuminating profile of social and cultural currents that shaped the age. Over the course of the novels, the characters changed from farm folks to urbanites, embraced the temptations of alcohol and artificial profits, encountered socialism, and gave birth to innovations or modern philosophies that later destroyed

them. In that way, the character Charlie Anderson, seen throughout the series, was an icon for the generation. He journeyed from the Midwest for work in New York and adventure in Florida; he became wealthy because of skill with machines, speculated in real estate, drank his dinners, and continuously moved farther from the fundamental things that anchored common men—family and work. Despite their limitations, the novels present an array of individuals who ably illustrate a vital cross-section of American culture and society.

Other novelists shared Dos Passos's disdain for the fruits of American capitalism. James T. Farrell examined the collapse of morality among working-class Irish youth in Chicago in his *Studs Lonigan* trilogy. In *The Grapes of Wrath,* Steinbeck memorably detailed the economic paradox of ripe fruit rotting on the vine as able-bodied men yearned for work and CHILDREN starved because inadequate profits would result from bringing the fruit to market. Erskine Caldwell's *Tobacco Road* (1932) conveyed the story of object poverty, ignorance, isolation, and hunger in the agricultural SOUTH. Earlier authors had regularly explored sin and oppression, yet no defined period in American literature invited so pervasive and persuasive a dissection of helplessness and despair as the depression era.

Perhaps nowhere is the tale of injustice and domination told more starkly than in *Native Son* (1940), by RICHARD WRIGHT. The novel conveyed without illusion the struggle, fear, and fate of one race at the mercy of another. Wright's juxtaposition of panic and control in his depiction of a black man, Bigger Thomas, who worked for an upper-middle-class white family in Chicago is both grim and distressing. Similarly, Wright's compelling autobiography, *Black Boy* (1945), depicted growing up in the oppressive racial conditions of the deep South.

Two works by Thomas Wolfe vividly reflected the awakening among intellectuals to social exploitation and the limits of democracy and capitalism. *Look Homeward, Angel* (1929), published within days of the stock market crash, is hopeful, idealistic, and lacking an awareness of broad social conflicts. By contrast, *You Can't Go Home Again* (1940) is a passionate acknowledgement of the nameless and powerless fellowship of laborers who were victimized by unforgiving social and economic systems.

If Wolfe spoke for those coming of age in the depression decade, Steinbeck gave voice to the unremarkable people who had long existed in the background of American society. He uncovered the experiences of the struggling poor—fruit pickers, common laborers, and especially farmers—and he traced the consequences of the era on them. Steinbeck's simple stories and elegant prose, evidenced in *Tortilla Flat* (1935) and *Of Mice and Men* (1937), masked the provocative and insightful social criticism they conveyed. His most acclaimed novel, *The Grapes of Wrath,* remains a powerful and enduring tribute to families, humanity, and the land as well as a coherent protest against an unjust system.

The enthusiasm and energy of the NEW DEAL notwithstanding, the onset of another world war was the fuel that finally fired the American economy. The war also sparked home-front changes that contributed to transitions in the social landscape of the nation. As one important example, large numbers of African Americans migrated from the rural South to northern cities for jobs. They earned wages, attended schools, and also fought for liberty. Indeed, the war years forged a foundation on which the advances of the next 20 years were constructed.

A simultaneous change is evident in the literature of the 1929–45 period. Blacks typically had appeared infrequently in major literary works and usually as stereotyped or one-dimensional characters, such as house servants. However, WILLIAM FAULKNER interwove and scrutinized race issues in three of his most celebrated novels, published during these years. Moreover, the voices of blacks themselves grew more prominent. In *Jonah's Gourd Vine* (1934) and *Their Eyes Were Watching God* (1937), Zora Neale Hurston shared forceful stories of black communities. Langston Hughes published poems, essays, and stories that revealed the daily life of poor blacks in cities. In addition, *Native Son,* the most significant novel by a black author during this period, also was one of the most momentous depictions of the period itself.

The most significant literature of World War II emerged in the years immediately after the war—written by men who served as soldiers—but clearly reflected the war years. Whereas novels regarding World War I largely had celebrated positive principles, major war fiction in this period frequently mirrored the themes found in contemporary social and political novels: the common man as hero and the powerful versus the powerless. *The Naked and the Dead* (1948), by Norman Mailer, involved an array of diverse men destined to die in a pointless conflict. Similarly, in *From Here to Eternity* (1951), James Jones made heroes of spirited enlisted men who refuse to conform and who defy the cruel indifference of officers and the system.

Two other significant works about the war examine the idea of power from the perspective of those wielding it. In *The Caine Mutiny* (1951), Herman Wouk examined the commitment of officers to the code of command and illustrates how that faithfulness fomented success as well as failure. Finally, James Gould Cozzens's *Guard of Honor* (1948), which includes a racial component, also detailed the motivations of senior officers and illuminated their efforts to meet the challenges of maintaining order, enforcing rules, and ensuring stability. All of these novels, however, reinforced the narrative pattern established before the war to tell harsh stories candidly.

The remarkable generation of writers who gave voice to and, at times, personified the 1920s lingered into the 1930s, but their predominant message became obsolete as the economy stalled—there was little materialism or complacency to denounce. Sinclair Lewis continued to publish but never matched his earlier form, and Scott Fitzgerald declined in health and then died in 1940. Ernest Hemingway remained productive, but even his notable successes of the decade (*To Have and Have Not* [1937] and *For Whom the Bell Tolls* [1940]) lacked the political immediacy and social resonance of such authors as Steinbeck and Faulkner.

Faulkner emerged from the 1930s as the country's literary champion. Grounding his work in his native Mississippi, he examined the implications of relationships and emotions using ordinary characters with unsophisticated problems and through them revealed a complex profile of social conditions. One consistent Faulkner theme is that a man often can be his own worst enemy. Thomas Sutpen, in *Absalom! Absalom!* (1936), is emblematic of that view; he seeks to achieve notoriety so that he can gain revenge against those whom he believes humiliated him as a youth. By homing in on traits and conditions that defined community, family, and sin in the South, as in *The Sound and the Fury* (1929) or *Light in August* (1932), Faulkner managed to outline social and economic conditions that circumscribed the nation. Faulkner was awarded the Nobel Prize in literature in 1949.

If there is a rival to Faulkner as the greatest American literary figure of the era, it probably is the playwright Eugene O'Neill, who received the Nobel Prize in literature in 1936. O'Neill probed psychological more than social themes in his arresting if often bleak portraits of families, relationships, and emotions. The play widely regarded as his greatest, *The Iceman Cometh,* which illustrates the need for hope to mask despair, was written in 1939 though not published until 1946. O'Neill also completed two more of his most important plays, *A Long Day's Journey into Night* and *A Touch of the Poet* in this period (although both were published years later).

Despite the prevalence of pessimistic themes, all literature between 1929 and 1945 was not negative. A number of poets—for example, Carl Sandburg and Robert Frost—celebrated American strengths and democracy and sought to inspire the nation during hard times. Likewise, history and biography became more popular during the depression, as Americans turned to them for guidance and for evidence of previous challenges—and successes.

A variety of novels emerged to satisfy popular demand for escapism during the melancholy era. A vast audience surfaced that was receptive to provocative but simple stories about amoral women or flawed but honest detectives in books like *The Big Sleep* (1939) by Raymond Chandler. Historical novels, such as *Gone with the Wind* (1936), by Margaret Mitchell, and *Drums Along the Mohawk* (1936), by Walter Edmonds, which both examine facets of survival as well as the bond between people and land, sold steadily to readers searching for a retreat into a more romantic age.

Ironically, the federal GOVERNMENT, long a disappointment to authors, also sponsored an innovative writing initiative amid the varied programs of the WORKS PROGRESS ADMINISTRATION. At its peak, the FEDERAL WRITERS' PROJECT (FWP) employed more than 6,500 writers, most often on nonfiction projects. The FWP supported authors pursuing fiction as well, including Saul Bellow, Zora Neale Hurston, and Richard Wright.

Through literature, readers as well as historians can glimpse the social arrangements, manners, aspirations, and values of an era in ways not usually possible with textbooks and monographs. Examining an era through its fiction can foster an understanding of imagery, motivations, and trends that standard historical analysis may not reveal. By 1945, America had accepted the concept of an active, centralized government; women and blacks entered a critical phase of their journeys toward equality; and the balance between capitalism and social progress was refashioned. Together, these factors and others formed new social, economic, and political systems, and literature evolved as well to capture the changes.

Further reading: Walter Blair, *American Literature, A Brief History* (New York: Scott, Foresman, 1964); Warren French, ed., *The Thirties: Fiction, Poetry, Drama* (Deland, Fla.: Everett Edwards, 1967); Michael Millgate, *American Social Fiction: James to Cozzens* (New York: Barnes & Noble, 1964); Jeffrey Walsh, *American War Literature, 1914 to Vietnam* (New York: St. Martin's Press, 1982).

—Douglas Propheter

London Economic Conference (1933)

The World Monetary and Economic Conference met in London, England, from mid June to late July 1933, to formulate cooperative economic policies to alleviate the global GREAT DEPRESSION. Sixty-six nations convened in London to discuss an international gold standard, currency stability, tariff reductions, and other international economic agreements that were thought to be potential solutions to the economic crisis. The London Economic Conference proved unsuccessful largely because of U.S.

president FRANKLIN D. ROOSEVELT and his preference for domestic rather than international action to deal with the depression.

The U.S. delegation to London was headed by Secretary of State CORDELL HULL, a staunch advocate of international economic cooperation who believed that he was sent to London to seek cooperation among nations and to negotiate a currency stabilization agreement. However, FDR had stated in his inaugural address that international economic commitments were secondary to the national economy, a belief that such members of his BRAIN TRUST as RAYMOND MOLEY and REXFORD G. TUGWELL shared. In the weeks leading up to the London conference, FDR's initial support of currency stabilization waned due to his fear that a stabilization agreement would thwart efforts to raise domestic prices, which he thought key to recovery. Hull had also been promised by FDR that he would ask CONGRESS for the authority to pursue reciprocal tariff agreements. Hull believed that such a proposal would reveal the U.S. commitment to ending the high tariffs in effect since the passage of the HAWLEY-SMOOT TARIFF ACT of 1930. On the eve of the conference, Roosevelt went back on his promise to Hull to seek a reciprocal trade bill.

In London, Moley, with Roosevelt's approval, issued a statement approving currency stabilization by the United States, Britain, and other gold-bloc countries. Then on July 1, FDR cabled Moley objecting to any premature currency stabilization agreement that would hinder his NEW DEAL agenda. On July 3, Roosevelt delivered what was called his "bombshell message" that the United States would not join in rate stabilization or a return to the gold standard. He declared that "old fetishes of so-called international bankers are being replaced by efforts to plan national currencies," and that "the sound internal economic system of a nation is a greater factor in its well being than the price of its currency in changing terms of the currencies of other nations." The United States would pursue a national, not an international, approach to solving its economic woes. Although this nationalistic approach was based on Moley's own ideas, Moley was surprised and embarrassed by this sudden reversal in Roosevelt's agenda, and resigned soon after as assistant secretary of state.

At the conference, Hull struggled to keep the other participating nations from denouncing Roosevelt and the United States for preventing a meaningful approach to the staggering international economy. Subsequently, the Roosevelt administration succeeded in enacting the RECIPROCAL TRADE AGREEMENTS ACT of 1934 that aimed at increasing foreign trade by decreasing high tariff rates and concluded an exchange stabilization agreement with Britain and France in 1936. Nonetheless, Roosevelt's action in July 1933 not only torpedoed the London conference but also contributed to the lack of common cause among the western democracies as WORLD WAR II approached during the 1930s.

See also FOREIGN POLICY.

Further reading: Robert Dallek, *Franklin D. Roosevelt and American Foreign Policy, 1932–1945* (New York: Oxford University Press, 1979); Lloyd Gardner, *Economic Aspects of New Deal Diplomacy* (Madison: University of Wisconsin Press, 1964).

—Michael T. Walsh

London Naval Conference (1930)

As part of his FOREIGN POLICY efforts at international cooperation to reduce armaments and prevent war, President HERBERT C. HOOVER helped arrange a naval arms limitation conference in London in 1930. By the time the conference opened, the GREAT DEPRESSION was in its early stages, and Hoover sought to link arms reduction with efforts to address the economic difficulties, as he would also during the WORLD DISARMAMENT CONFERENCE that convened in Geneva in 1932. He believed that by spending less on arms, nations might balance their budgets and stabilize economic conditions as well as reduce the chances of war. The London Naval Conference produced the first arms limitation agreement since the early 1920s, but subsequent attempts at arms control in the 1930s proved fruitless.

The Washington Naval Conference of 1921–22 had produced among the major naval powers a limitation agreement on capital ships (major combatant vessels including battleships, aircraft carriers, and heavy cruisers), using a ratio of 5:5:3:1.75:1.75 for the United States, Great Britain, Japan, Italy, and France, respectively. A 1927 conference in Geneva to extend controls to auxiliaries (light cruisers, destroyers, submarines) had failed. At London in 1930, the Americans, British, and Japanese agreed after hard bargaining to a six-year treaty with tonnage ratios for cruisers, destroyers, and submarines that amounted overall to roughly a 10:10:7 ratio on auxiliary ships. The conference maintained the 5:5:3 ratio of the Washington conference on capital ships.

Hopes that the agreement reached at London might lead to further arms control and international cooperation turned out to be false, however. In Tokyo, the Japanese military sharply criticized the treaty for maintaining American and British naval superiority. The 1932–34 World Disarmament Conference failed, as did efforts in the mid-1930s to sustain the naval arms limitation system of the Washington and London conferences. As Japan and Germany built their armed forces and pursued their paths of aggression, the world moved toward WORLD WAR II.

Further reading: L. Ethan Ellis, *Republican Foreign Policy, 1921–1933* (New Brunswick, N.J.: Rutgers University Press, 1968).

Long, Huey P. (1893–1935)

Huey Pierce Long, the controversial Louisiana governor (1928–32) and U.S. senator (1932–35), was born on August 30, 1893, in Winnfield, Louisiana, in the state's northern hill country. The second youngest of nine children, Long left school in 1910 to take a traveling sales position. In 1913, he married Rose Connell, whom he met when reentering school in Shreveport in 1911. In 1914, Long moved to New Orleans, where he enrolled at Tulane University Law School. Despite not finishing his classes at Tulane, he passed the bar exam in May 1915. The couple moved to Winnfield to set up Long's law practice, first with his brother Julius, then by Long alone. Not particularly interested in practicing law, Long used his practice as a stepping-stone to his long-held ambition: political office.

Long began his political career by winning election to the Louisiana Railroad Commission in 1918 (he served as chairman for several years in the 1920s), and his campaign foreshadowed his techniques in future statewide elections. Long's strategy was to portray himself as the candidate of the common man and win the vote of the rural, agricultural areas of Louisiana to make up for his lack of appeal in the urban areas. After winning the governorship in 1928, he dominated Louisiana politics until his death, and the state became polarized between pro- and anti-Longites. Although Long fulfilled many of his campaign promises, such as more paved roads and increased school spending, corruption in Louisiana politics also increased, with Long and his organization reaping the benefit. Following an unsuccessful attempt to impeach him in 1929, Long, known as "the Kingfish" in the state, consolidated his virtual total control over Louisiana politics and shifted his focus to national office.

Long was elected to the U.S. Senate in 1930, just as the GREAT DEPRESSION was beginning to deepen, but he did not take his seat until 1932 so that he could serve out his term as governor. A fierce critic of the HOOVER PRESIDENCY, Long at first supported FRANKLIN D. ROOSEVELT. But he soon soured on FDR and the NEW DEAL. Following such legislation of the FIRST NEW DEAL as the NATIONAL INDUSTRIAL RECOVERY ACT, Long saw the patrician Roosevelt as serving the interests of big business and Wall Street rather than the common man, whom Long claimed to represent. He became a vocal critic of Roosevelt, claiming that the New Deal did not do enough to end the Great Depression or to help the millions of Americans suffering due to the economic collapse.

In 1934, Long announced is own prescription for curing the depression, the Share Our Wealth plan. Long proposed a progressive income tax that would tax each million dollars of personal fortunes, exempting the first million, and would confiscate inheritances after the first million dollars. Money collected was to be redistributed to Americans with a one-time $5,000 payment to allow every American family to own a house, car, and radio. Each family would be assured of $2,500 per year for income maintenance, and Long also promised money for education, pensions, and other benefits. Long then used his plan, which was appealing to many, though deeply flawed in its numbers, to pursue his larger ambition: to be elected president. In February 1934, Long created the Share Our Wealth Society, made up of local clubs, to launch himself onto the national stage. He also made effective use of RADIO. By 1935, Long claimed to have 5 million Share Our Wealth members, a number that seems to have been inflated, and he published *My First Days in the White House,* a fictionalized account of a Long presidency. Long's sights were on the election of 1940; he believed that if he could split the Democratic vote in 1936, electing a Republican, he would then be a viable Democratic candidate in 1940.

Just as Long was positioning himself to challenge Roosevelt, he was assassinated on September 8, 1935, in Baton Rouge, Louisiana. The shooter was Carl A. Weiss, a doctor from Baton Rouge and a passionate anti-Longite. Without Long, the Share Our Wealth Society withered away, though Long's most ardent and ambitious follower, Gerald L. K. Smith, tried to keep it alive. In 1936, Smith allied the society with Father CHARLES E. COUGHLIN and Dr. FRANCIS TOWNSEND to form the UNION PARTY, which nominated North Dakota congressman William Lemke for president. But the followers of the three men were also largely supporters of Roosevelt, and most chose FDR over the Union Party in the ELECTION OF 1936.

Often portrayed as a demagogue, Long, at his peak in 1935, was the leading populist voice in a nation where many still feared that the Great Depression would never end. Without his voice, the movement for redistribution of wealth in America withered away, although the SECOND NEW DEAL of 1935 did begin to address some of the social issues that had fueled Long's appeal.

Further reading: Alan Brinkley, *Voices of Protest: Huey Long, Father Coughlin, and the Great Depression* (New York: Knopf, 1982); Harry T. Williams, *Huey Long* (New York: Knopf, 1969).

—Katherine Liapis Segrue

Louis, Joe (1914–1981)

Joe Louis, nicknamed "the Brown Bomber," was the premier American boxer and the heavyweight champion of the world from 1937 to 1949. In his career, he won 68 fights while losing only three. Because of the racial situation of the times, Louis, an African American, was an important figure in the social history of the United States during the era of the GREAT DEPRESSION and WORLD WAR II.

Louis was born Joseph Louis Barrow on May 13, 1914, near Lafayette, Alabama. In 1924, he moved to Detroit, where his father worked in a Ford plant. Louis started boxing while in vocational school, and by the time he was 20 years old he had won the national Amateur Athletic Union boxing title and had begun boxing professionally. Not quick on his feet, Louis was famous for his powerful and polished punching style. After winning some two dozen bouts, he fought the German boxer Max Schmeling in 1936, and lost in the 12th round in an upset. German Minister for Propaganda Joseph Goebbels hailed Schmeling's victory as a triumph for Nazism.

In 1937, Louis took the heavyweight title from James Braddock. Asked how it felt to be champion, Louis responded, "I don't want nobody to call me champ until I

Joe Louis *(Library of Congress)*

beat Schmeling." In a 1938 rematch, Louis beat Schmeling, knocking out the German two minutes into the first round. He remained heavyweight champion until 1949, when he retired. During the war, Louis staged a number of bouts to raise money for the Army and Navy Relief Societies before he joined the army. As a GI, he traveled more than 21,000 miles, helped with recruiting, and staged 96 boxing exhibitions before millions of soldiers and sailors.

In an era of harsh racial attitudes and institutionalized segregation, Joe Louis was one of the AFRICAN AMERICANS most easily recognized by white America. He was aware of his position as a symbol for all of black America. He maintained a dignified manner, claiming that this could make it easier for others who would follow him. He also would not accept stereotypes, once refusing to pose for photographers while holding a watermelon. To the black communities of the depression and war years, Joe Louis was a hero, and such African Americans as Malcolm X would subsequently write of their admiration for Louis's example. In later years, Louis twice returned to boxing, but with little success. He died in 1981 after years of poor health.

See also SPORTS.

Further reading: Chris Mead, *Champion—Joe Louis, Black Hero in White America* (New York: Scribner's, 1985).

—Robert J. Hanyok

Luce, Henry R. (1898–1967)

A prolific publisher and the cofounder and long-time editor in chief of Time, Inc., Henry Robinson Luce was one of the most influential journalists and shapers of American public opinion in the 20th century.

Luce's publishing empire, which included *Time, Life, Fortune,* and *Sports Illustrated,* allowed him the opportunity to send his generally conservative views on American society and America's role in the world into most of the nation's households. For decades, average Americans and national policymakers often looked to Luce to help make sense of a changing world and America's position in it. It was Luce who in 1941 described the 20th century as "the American Century."

Luce's childhood helps explain his zeal for his later work. He was born on April 3, 1898, in China, the oldest child of Presbyterian missionaries from Pennsylvania. He lived in China until he was 15 years old, visiting the United States only twice in that period. The contrasts between the relatively prosperous and ordered existence inside the compound in which he lived in China and the bleak situation outside its walls reinforced in Luce the sense of the spiritual superiority of Christianity and the

moral and cultural superiority of America. Luce later remarked that his "idealistic view of America came from the fact that the Americans I grew up with—all of them—were good people."

After study at Yale University in the United States and Oxford University in Great Britain, Luce worked briefly at two newspapers before founding *Time,* the first weekly news magazine, in 1923 with his college friend, Briton Hadden. In their prospectus to potential investors, they described *Time* as meeting the new needs of busy people to keep informed. They promised to provide readers with both sides of an issue and still "clearly indicate" *Time's* preference. Hadden died in 1929 and Luce became editor in chief of Time, Inc., until 1964. The *Time* publishing empire grew over the years. Luce founded *Fortune,* a business monthly, in 1930; LIFE MAGAZINE, a phenomenally popular pictorial news magazine, in 1936; and *Sports Illustrated* in 1954. By the end of WORLD WAR II, Time, Inc. was perhaps the most influential publishing house in the world.

Luce's landmark essay "The American Century" was published in *Life* in February 1941. By then, much of the world was engulfed in World War II, but the United States had not yet entered the conflict, and there were many ISOLATIONISTS who did not want the nation to intervene. Luce argued that the world was so interdependent, and the strength of the United States so great, that the United States had a responsibility to intervene in the war against the AXIS, assume world leadership, and share its economic power, technical skills, and political ideals—and in the process make the 20th century the "American century." Many newspapers and groups reprinted the article, and it soon became the basis for public and official debates about national policy.

Two of Luce's major lifelong concerns, reflected in the editorial views of *Time,* were combating communism in Asia and promoting the REPUBLICAN PARTY at home. After World War II, Luce actively pushed for American help for Chiang Kai-shek's army in his Chinese civil war with the communists led by Mao Zedong. After Mao proclaimed the People's Republic of China and Chiang retreated to Taiwan, Luce became a powerful advocate of resistance to China and aid to Taiwan. He also advocated a global strategy of massive United States resistance to communism in both Asia and Europe.

Luce called the Republican Party his "second church." He worked to rebuild and reorient the party after its disastrous showing in the ELECTION OF 1936, and was a leader of the eastern, internationalist Republicans who supported the successful effort of WENDELL L. WILLKIE for the GOP nomination in the ELECTION OF 1940. He actively promoted Dwight D. Eisenhower's candidacy and presidency in the 1950s. Luce's affection for John F. Kennedy led Time, Inc. to be somewhat less partisan in the 1960 election, and Luce had remarkable access to Kennedy during his term as president.

In his personal life, Luce was a deeply religious man who rarely missed church and prayed regularly. He had a large circle of friends, traveled widely, met with many foreign leaders, and had an ongoing friendly rivalry with his famous wife, Clare Boothe Luce, an accomplished playwright who served in CONGRESS from Connecticut during World War II. Henry Luce died in February 1967 from a sudden heart attack.

See also NEWS MEDIA; POPULAR CULTURE.

Further reading: James L. Boughman, *Henry R. Luce and the Rise of the American News Media* (Boston: Twayne, 1987); Robert Herzstein, *Henry R. Luce: A Political Portrait of the Man Who Created the American Century* (New York: Scribner's, 1994).

—John Day Tully

M

MacArthur, Douglas   See Volume IX

Manchuria

On the night of September 18, 1931, an explosion orchestrated by Japanese saboteurs destroyed a segment of track on the Japanese-controlled South Manchuria Railway near Mukden Station in the northern Chinese province of Manchuria. In the ensuing chaos, the Kwantung Army, the Japanese force that had occupied the area since 1905, advanced through the rest of the province, beginning the attempted Japanese conquest of Asia that would eventually culminate in the WORLD WAR II PACIFIC THEATER. As with the 1935 Italian invasion of ETHIOPIA, the failure of the United States to cooperate with the League of Nations in a firm effort to quell aggression reflected the American policy of noninterventionism produced by the adverse reaction to World War I and by the focus on domestic problems arising from the GREAT DEPRESSION.

Despite pleas for stronger action from his Secretary of State HENRY L. STIMSON, President HERBERT C. HOOVER expressed only moral disapproval of the Japanese actions. The United States adopted a policy of "nonrecognition," meaning that it would not recognize as legal any action that violated the administrative and territorial integrity of China or threatened the American commercial interests within China guaranteed by the Open Door Notes of 1899 and 1900 and the 1922 Nine-Power Treaty. The League of Nations, unable to pursue stronger action without American support, essentially adopted this same policy of nonrecognition, popularly known as the Stimson Doctrine. Not surprisingly, such a weak reaction encouraged the Japanese to pursue their expansionist agenda even more vigorously. In early 1932, Manchuria was converted into the Japanese puppet state of Manchukuo, and in 1933 Japan withdrew from the League of Nations. The defeat of the HOOVER PRESIDENCY in 1932 raised fears among American ISOLATIONISTS of a shift in policy towards Japan, but the new

president, FRANKLIN D. ROOSEVELT, and his secretary of state CORDELL HULL, continued to follow the Stimson Doctrine.

Throughout the 1930s, the Japanese grew increasingly more aggressive in East Asia and in asserting their military and diplomatic equality with the Western powers. Attempts to renew the naval limitation agreements signed at the 1930 LONDON NAVAL CONFERENCE failed in 1935 as the Japanese demanded arms parity in all categories of ships, a concession that neither the United States nor Great Britain was willing to make. In November 1936, Japan allied with Germany in the Anti-Comintern Pact. Despite evidence of increasing levels of Japanese militarism, the American government was caught by surprise when the Japanese conquest of Manchuria escalated into full-scale war with China in July of 1937. Roosevelt responded by refusing to intervene unless American citizens and property in China were threatened. This policy was tested when Japanese pilots sank the American gunboat *Panay* in the Yangtze River on December 12, 1937, killing two Americans in what seemed plainly a deliberate action. Public outcry about the incident within the United States was minimal, however; and after the Japanese government quickly offered apologies and indemnities, the episode blew over with no American retaliation or change in policy.

Tensions between the United States and Japan escalated as the Roosevelt administration began to move by the end of the decade toward more interventionist policies to stop German and Japanese aggression, including Japanese expansion in Manchuria. Negotiations in the autumn of 1941 offered a final opportunity to forestall hostilities between Japan and the United States. The Japanese requested the lifting of sanctions on materials such as iron ore, aviation gasoline, and scrap iron that Roosevelt had begun to impose the previous year, and demanded American acquiescence to their expansionism in East Asia. Roosevelt and Hull, believing that the conquest of Manchuria and war with China were part of larger Japanese designs on the rest of Asia, refused these terms and demanded that the Japanese withdraw from China and drop their expansionist campaign. On October 16, 1941, Japan's civilian government, led by Prime Minister Prince Fumimaro Konoye, fell and was succeeded by a militarist government led by General Hideki Tojo. While the civilian government had hoped to obtain international compliance with their expansionist aims through diplomacy, the militarists believed that this could only be achieved by force. The Japanese attack on PEARL HARBOR came on December 7, 1941.

While the Chinese regained direct control of Manchuria after World War II under terms established at the 1943 CAIRO CONFERENCE, the province continued to fall under foreign influence. In the wake of the Japanese surrender in 1945, the Soviet Union successfully demanded that several possessions in northern China lost by the Russians at the end of the Russo-Japanese War in 1905, including the South Manchuria Railway, should revert back to Russian control. After being liberated from the Japanese empire, Manchuria would quickly fall under the sphere of influence of the Soviet Union in the early years of the cold war.

See also FOREIGN POLICY.

Further reading: Robert Dallek, *Franklin D. Roosevelt and American Foreign Policy, 1932–1945* (New York: Oxford University Press, 1979); Armin Rappaport, *Henry L. Stimson and Japan, 1931–1933* (Chicago: University of Chicago Press, 1963).

—Mary E. Carroll-Mason

Manhattan Project

The Manhattan Project was the bland code name given to an effort of unprecedented scope and secrecy to produce the ATOMIC BOMB during WORLD WAR II. It began as a "uranium committee" under VANNEVAR BUSH's National Research Defense Council and its successor, the OFFICE OF SCIENTIFIC RESEARCH AND DEVELOPMENT (OSRD). Its expansion and secret existence approved personally by President FRANKLIN D. ROOSEVELT, the Manhattan Project expended nearly $2 billion, a cost about two-thirds that of all the conventional bombs, mines, and grenades procured for the entire war effort, and all without direct knowledge of CONGRESS. The result was a vast complex of "atomic cities" across the nation, where thousands of scientists and engineers worked in extreme secrecy, and which produced two operational bombs used on HIROSHIMA AND NAGASAKI in August 1945.

Shortly after the discovery of radioactivity in the 1890s, the possibility of liberating the enormous potential energy within matter motivated much theoretical and laboratory work. The so-called splitting of the atom in an experimental setting, with its implications for moving the weapons concept toward reality, was achieved by German physicists in late 1938, and perhaps in Italy a few years earlier. Leo Szilard, a Hungarian physicist living in New York and in communication with other refugee scientists from Germany and Russia, joined in 1939 with another émigré, Edward Teller, to persuade Albert Einstein to lend his name and influence to a letter informing President Roosevelt of the danger.

British and American physicists then worked on the problem without much progress beyond demonstrating the theoretical possibility of such a weapon. After PEARL HARBOR, and believing that the Germans were working effectively toward an atomic bomb, Vannevar Bush and others became convinced that developing an atomic bomb required a massive and organized effort that could produce a workable fission weapon within three years or so. Roosevelt agreed, and in the summer of 1942 the project was established within the U.S. Army Corps of Engineers, where its massive construction projects and funding could be most easily hidden. General Leslie Groves, a brusque organizational genius with graduate degrees in engineering who had just completed building the Pentagon, assumed control of what was termed the Manhattan Engineer District and attempted to maintain strict security within the project.

Six months later, barely a year after Pearl Harbor, a team of physicists directed by the Italian émigré Enrico Fermi, achieved the first sustained and controlled chain reaction with uranium, and construction was underway on several new sites. In Hanford, Washington, a plutonium extraction plant arose; in Oak Ridge, Tennessee, massive facilities were constructed to purify and extract, literally atom by atom, a specific isotope from uranium. Near isolated Los Alamos, New Mexico, thousands of physicists, chemists, and engineers gathered under the leadership of J. Robert Oppenheimer in hastily constructed military facilities to pursue the science and practical engineering of bomb design. At universities and industrial facilities throughout the country, other teams worked on various parts of the problem. Reflecting wartime tensions in SOVIET-AMERICAN RELATIONS and in the GRAND ALLIANCE against the AXIS, the British were privy to—and junior partners in—the Manhattan Project, while the Soviets were excluded from participation and knowledge (except through their own ESPIONAGE).

Both eventual bomb designs were fission weapons—designed to compress purified uranium or plutonium long enough (a split second) for the material to achieve critical mass and the subsequent chain reaction that would release the explosive power. The uranium weapon ("Little Boy") was relatively unproblematic and did not even need to be tested before its use on Hiroshima in August 1945. The plutonium weapon ("Fat Man") was used on Nagasaki, and was first tested at Alamagordo, New Mexico, in July 1945.

The atomic scientists, whom Groves called his bunch of "brilliant crackpots," initially worked together in patriotic unanimity. Deep rifts about the project and the use of the bomb developed after it became clear by 1944 that Germany would not be a contender in this race. Nonetheless, Groves, Oppenheimer, Bush, and others drove the project forward and presented it to a surprised President Truman shortly after Roosevelt's death in April 1945. The project and its leaders survived congressional and other scrutiny after the war largely because it was deemed a brilliant success that had won the final phase of the war and saved thousands of lives. The physical and personnel infrastructure became elements of an enormous and elaborate new cold war complex, with some of the laboratories under the civilian Atomic Energy Commission and others absorbed into the new Department of Defense.

Further reading: Richard G. Hewlett and Oscar E. Anderson Jr., *A History of the United States Atomic Energy Commission,* vol. 1: *The New World, 1939–1946* (University Park: Pennsylvania State University Press, 1962); Richard Rhodes, *The Making of the Atomic Bomb* (New York: Simon & Schuster, 1986).

—Joseph N. Tatarewicz

March on Washington Movement (MOWM)

A. PHILIP RANDOLPH organized the March on Washington Movement (MOWM) in 1941 to put pressure on President FRANKLIN D. ROOSEVELT to ensure a greater role for AFRICAN AMERICANS in the defense MOBILIZATION effort of WORLD WAR II. Tired of an established pattern of conferences, negotiations, and official statements but no advances on CIVIL RIGHTS, the MOWM aimed at forcing the administration to take action by organizing a protest march to be held in Washington, D.C. To head off the march, Roosevelt, on June 25, 1941, issued EXECUTIVE ORDER 8802, which established the FAIR EMPLOYMENT PRACTICES COMMITTEE and prohibited discrimination by GOVERNMENT and by defense contractors.

The MOWM grew out of continued economic discrimination facing African Americans. As the ECONOMY began to recover from the GREAT DEPRESSION in 1940 and 1941, blacks found themselves largely excluded from defense employment. For example, 56 St. Louis factories with government war contracts employed an average of three African Americans each, and a United States Employment Service poll showed that over 50 percent of defense industries questioned refused to hire blacks at all. African Americans were also excluded from federally organized training programs because it seemed a mistake to

train people for jobs they would not receive. The few who did find jobs in defense industry were typically restricted to positions at the lowest levels, despite their qualifications. Nor did the armed forces provide much opportunity, for the U.S. MARINES accepted no African Americans; the U.S. NAVY let them enlist only as cooks and stewards; and the U.S. ARMY accepted them only in restricted numbers, typically in segregated noncombat units.

Randolph, WALTER WHITE (the secretary of the NATIONAL ASSOCIATION FOR THE ADVANCEMENT OF COLORED PEOPLE [NAACP]), and T. Arnold Hill of the National Urban League met with Roosevelt in September 1940 to discuss these issues and to petition the president for defense jobs and desegregation of the armed forces. When the resulting press release indicated that there would be no policy change and seemed wrongly to imply their endorsement of this outcome, the black leaders took further action. The NAACP announced a two-day Conference on the Negro in National Defense at Hampton Institute and began organization of a 23-state National Defense Day to be held on January 26, 1941, to protest discrimination in defense industry.

For his part, Randolph began to sow the seeds of the MOWM. He declared that "a pilgrimage of 10,000 Negroes would wake up and shock official Washington as it has never been shocked before." The purpose of the march on Washington was to demand fair employment in defense jobs as well as desegregation and equality in the armed forces. Randolph's early support came from local black community groups, because established civil rights organizations thought the march too militant, while the black press believed it an impossible task. Undeterred, Randolph raised his original call for 10,000 marchers to 100,000 and established the March on Washington Committee (MOWC) to organize and supervise the march. As Randolph envisioned it, the March on Washington would be an exclusively African-American event: "We shall not call upon our white friends to march with us. There are some things Negroes must do alone. . . . Let the Negro masses speak!"

In an effort to prevent the march, Roosevelt enlisted his wife, ELEANOR ROOSEVELT, and New York mayor FIORELLO LA GUARDIA to discuss possible alternatives with Randolph, who refused to back down. Fearing the potential violence and political embarrassment that could occur if thousands of African Americans converged on Washington, Roosevelt invited Randolph and White back to the White House and offered a personal promise for better treatment of blacks if the march were called off. When Randolph demanded tangible action, FDR issued Executive Order 8802, which created the FEPC and forbade discriminatory employment practices by government and by defense contractors, but which did not apply to the armed forces. Randolph then agreed to call off the scheduled march, though he called it a postponement in order to retain leverage with the administration and avoid criticism from those who wanted no compromise.

Executive Order 8802 gave a measure of federal assistance in defense employment and contributed to a greater share of jobs for African Americans in the wartime economic boom. Although criticized by some more militant blacks for not going through with the march, Randolph continued with his objectives of nonviolent mass action protest and held a reorganization conference in Detroit in 1942. Following a poorly attended convention in Chicago in July 1943, the MOWM eventually disintegrated. But in addition to its success in bringing about Executive Order 8802 and the FEPC, the MOWM foreshadowed mass-action protest ideas and strategies used during the postwar Civil Rights movement.

Further reading: Herbert Garfinkel, *When Negroes March: The March on Washington Movement in the Organizational Politics for FEPC* (Glencoe, Ill.: Free Press, 1959); Paula F. Pfeffer, A. *Philip Randolph, Pioneer of the Civil Rights Movement* (Baton Rouge: Louisiana State University Press, 1990).

—Ronald G. Simon

Mariana Islands

Because of their strategic location, the Marianas were a major American objective in 1944 during the island-hopping campaign of the U.S. NAVY and U.S. MARINES across the Central Pacific in the WORLD WAR II PACIFIC THEATER. Once captured from the Japanese, the Marianas became an important staging point for air attacks on Japan.

The Marianas are a group of 15 Central Pacific Ocean islands stretching in a 500-mile curve midway between Japan and New Guinea. The four major islands, running north to south, are Saipan (the largest, at 14 miles long), Tinian, Rota, and Guam. The United States took control of Guam from Spain following the Spanish-American War in 1898 and subsequently used the island as a coaling station and naval base. Saipan, Tinian, and Rota had been under Japanese rule since World War I and had been fortified and made into significant military bases. On December 10, 1941, just days after the attack on PEARL HARBOR, Imperial Japanese forces from Saipan overcame the small U.S. Marines garrison on Guam. Saipan subsequently became a major military administrative center and the Marianas as a whole served as a defensive cornerstone of the Japanese empire in the Central Pacific.

The American invasion of Saipan began on June 15, 1944, with an amphibious assault by Admiral Richard "Kelly" Turner's Fifth Amphibious Force of 530 warships and 127,000 troops under U.S. Marine Corps Major General Holland M. "Howling Mad" Smith. The Second and Fourth Marine Divisions, following reinforcement by the U.S. Army 27th Infantry Division, succeeded in overcoming the 32,000-man Japanese garrison after a month of heavy fighting on July 13. Only 2,000 members of the enemy garrison survived the assault, and 3,126 Americans were killed and 13,160 wounded. Shockingly, hundreds of Japanese civilians resident on Saipan committed suicide by jumping off the cliffs into the sea at Marpi Point because of fear of what their fate might be in American hands.

Neighboring Tinian was assaulted on July 25, 1944, by the Second and Fourth Marine Divisions and was declared secured on August 2 with U.S. losses of 389 killed and 1,816 wounded. Virtually none of the Japanese garrison of 9,000 survived. The final invasion, of Guam, began on July 21 and lasted until August 10. It was undertaken by the Third Marine Division, First Marine Brigade, and 77th U.S. Army Infantry Division against some 11,000 Japanese defenders, all but a handful of whom died or committed suicide rather than surrender. Over 1,400 Americans were killed on Guam and a further 5,600 were wounded. Mopping-up and search operations against Japanese holdouts that had fled into the hills and jungles of the islands, especially on Guam, lasted well into the late 1940s. The last Japanese soldier on the island did not turn himself in to American authorities until the late 1970s.

The loss of the Marianas, combined with the stunning Japanese naval defeat in the BATTLE OF THE PHILIPPINE SEA of June 19 and 20, brought about the downfall of General Hideki Tojo as prime minister of the Japanese government and his retirement from public life. As expected, the Marianas played a major role in the subsequent American war effort. Strategically located some 1,200 miles south of Japan, Saipan, Tinian, and Guam, with their preexisting and rapidly improved airfields, proved vital for the American strategic air campaign against Japan. The first B-17 Flying Fortress and B-24 Liberator bombers of U.S. ARMY AIR FORCES arrived on the islands in August, and were joined in October 1944 by B-29 Superfortresses of the Twenty-first Bomber Command capable of reaching Japan. On August 6 and 9, 1945, B-29s flying from Tinian dropped the ATOMIC BOMB on the Japanese cities of HIROSHIMA AND NAGASAKI.

Following World War II, in 1947, the UNITED NATIONS designated the Mariana Islands as a trust territory of the United States. This relationship continued until 1978 when the people of the Marianas negotiated and signed a covenant with the United States, which granted the island's inhabitants the right to form a self-governing commonwealth. Residents of the Mariana Islands have U.S. citizenship, but they are not represented in Congress and do not have the right to vote in presidential elections.

Further reading: Philip A. Crowl, *Campaign in the Marianas* (Washington, D.C.: Office of the Chief of Military History, Department of the Army, 1960).

—Clayton D. Laurie

Marines, U.S.

The U.S. Marine Corps played a vital role in the U.S. NAVY's island-hopping campaign through the Central Pacific during WORLD WAR II. Excelling at AMPHIBIOUS WARFARE, the marines overwhelmed Imperial Japanese garrisons in the Gilbert, Marshall, MARIANA, Palau, SOLOMON, Bonin, and Ryukyu Islands between November 1943 and July 1945. Unlike the other and larger American combat services, the marines were largely confined to the WORLD WAR II PACIFIC THEATER and saw little action in the EUROPEAN THEATER.

A constituent part of the U.S. Navy, the Marine Corps has always been the smallest of the American combat services. Traditionally serving as the navy's land force, including providing guards at naval bases, ports, and aboard ships, the corps not only conducted amphibious operations during World War II but, unlike similar services elsewhere in the world, also had its own air force. The highest serving marine officer, the commandant of marines, had his own headquarters and staff, but he did not hold a position on the U.S. Joint Chiefs of Staff. Aboard ship, marine officers were subordinate to naval command.

Seeking an expanded combat role, the Marine Corps in 1933 created the Fleet Marine Force to undertake amphibious landings. By the time of the outbreak of World War II in 1939, about 25 percent of the corps' 19,400 men belonged to this assault force. The Fleet Marine Force was divided into two brigades, one stationed on the East Coast at Quantico, Virginia, and the other in San Diego, California. In February 1941, the two Fleet Marine Force brigades were expanded and renamed the First and Second Marine Divisions, each consisting of three infantry regiments, an artillery regiment, and various support units. Their supporting aviation units became the First and Second Marine Aircraft Wings. Other, much smaller marine units were scattered around the globe at the time of the attack on PEARL HARBOR in December 1941, in a total force numbering some 54,300 men.

Like the other military services, the U.S. Marine Corps expanded rapidly during the war. Although historically an all-volunteer force, the marines accepted draftees during World War II in order to maintain troop levels. The corps began accepting AFRICAN AMERICANS in 1942. Between August 1943 and September 1944, the marines formed six consecutively numbered divisions that totaled some 474,680 men by V-J DAY in 1945. The marines also formed raider and parachute battalions, a glider group, barrage balloon squadrons, and seven island defense battalions for guarding garrisons such as Wake Island and Guam. The marine aviation wings grew just as rapidly, from 641 pilots in 13 squadrons in December 1941, to 10,049 pilots in 128 squadrons formed into five aircraft wings, the First through Fourth and the Ninth plus a training wing. In addition, the aviation wings included 106,475 ground officers and enlisted men and women by 1945.

The First and Second Marine Divisions, and their attendant air wings, engaged in their first major operation at GUADALCANAL in August 1942 as part of the combined First Marine Amphibious Corps, which became the primary amphibious operations planning headquarters in the South Pacific area. Marines also saw service elsewhere in the central and Northern Solomon Islands and at New Britain, but were always outnumbered by U.S. ARMY troops, the predominant force in the Pacific theater.

Before Admiral CHESTER W. NIMITZ opened the Central Pacific offensive in November 1943, the Fifth Amphibious Corps was formed and saw service in the Gilbert Islands, landing on TARAWA on November 20, 1943, and on Eniwetok, Roi, and Namur in the Marshall Islands on February 1944. Later in 1944, both Marine Amphibious Corps came under the Fleet Marine Force, which was renamed the Fleet Marine Force, Pacific, commanded by Major General Holland M. "Howling Mad" Smith. The Second, Third, and Fourth Marine Divisions under Smith landed on Saipan, Guam, and Tinian in the Mariana Islands in June and July 1944. In October 1944, Smith relinquished his post to Major General Harry Schmidt. Following the marine assault on Peleliu in September, the marines invaded IWO JIMA in the Bonin Islands in February 1945. The bloodiest marine assault of the war, Iwo Jima cost the Third, Fourth, and Fifth Marine Divisions at least 6,000 dead and 17,000 wounded. Between April and June 1945, the First and Sixth Marine Divisions participated in the conquest of OKINAWA.

U.S. Marine Corps casualties during the war amounted to 86,940, of whom 19,733 were killed, with the vast majority of casualties incurred between July 1944 and July 1945.

Further reading: Robert Leckie, *Strong Men Armed: The U.S. Marines against Japan* (New York: Random House, 1962); Allan Reed Millett, *Semper Fidelis: The History of the United States Marine Corps* (New York: Free Press, 1991).

—Clayton D. Laurie

marriage and family life

The GREAT DEPRESSION and WORLD WAR II significantly affected marriage and family life in the United States. Reduced incomes during the 1930s forced families to adapt, as did wartime conditions. Although families might have been a bit more egalitarian at the end of the war, traditional family dynamics remained intact, with men typically the jobholders and women the homemakers.

There was hardly a family in the United States that did not suffer some financial loss during the depression. However, with most of the workforce employed even during the years of highest UNEMPLOYMENT, breadwinners typically did not lose their jobs. But jobholders frequently suffered pay cuts, shortened hours, or both, and adjustments had to be made at home to compensate. Women substituted their own labor for goods and services that were formerly purchased. Families turned to less expensive forms of RECREATION, such as listening to the RADIO or playing games at home. Endless little savings and sacrifices made by each member enabled straitened families to cope with the depression.

Even if the husband lost his job, families often had some resources to fall back on. Other family members might get jobs to supplement the household income. By the 1930s, the wife was more likely than the CHILDREN to look for work, despite societal pressure for her to remain at home. She might be able to find a job when her husband could not because some jobs were perceived as "women's work," which men would not usually take even during hard times. The wife might also take in boarders, sew, or bake to earn money. Although laws and changing values restricted their employment opportunities, children still might contribute to the family income by delivering newspapers, collecting bottles, or baby-sitting. If all else failed, the family went on RELIEF, which was widely viewed as failure.

Farm families, both white and AFRICAN AMERICAN, were especially hard hit by the depression. They had been suffering financially since the end of World War I because of overproduction, low prices, and debts incurred when trying to expand or mechanize. If farmers were unable to pay their bills, the banks foreclosed on their farms. Tenants and sharecroppers were sometimes forced off their farms when landlords cut production or mechanized. Many farm families, especially in the DUST BOWL, packed their meager belongings and traveled north to the industrial Midwest or west to California in search of a better life. These poor, desperate families, vividly depicted by JOHN STEINBECK's classic novel of the period, *The Grapes of Wrath*, became the symbol of the hopeless suffering of the depression.

Most families held up during the depression, despite fears that hard times might fragment them, and typically turned to one another for financial and emotional support. The ELDERLY might move in with younger relatives; families with jobs might assist unemployed cousins. The depression did force some families to break up either temporarily or permanently. A man might leave in search of work or

children might be placed in an institution if their family could no longer support them. The divorce rate dropped during the worst years of the depression because many couples could not afford to legally end their marriages. Although some broke up without a formal divorce, most marriages endured.

Traditional patterns of family roles and status survived the depression. Men remained the expected breadwinners and women the homemakers. Most of the time, the father retained his position as head of the household, even if he lost his job. At the same time, the mother's status frequently increased. Her savings around the house and, sometimes, her extra income helped the family cope. In some families, an unemployed husband lost status and respect. Marriages may have become more egalitarian during this period as the wife became more of a partner in the survival of the family.

The depression was a difficult time psychologically for young people. While the proportion of 14- to 18-year-olds in school increased from about 50 to 75 percent in the 1930s by one estimate, there was often little to look forward to after graduation from high school. College was frequently unaffordable, job prospects dim, and the possibility of marriage and families of their own uncertain. Marriage rates dropped significantly, falling from 67.6 per thousand unmarried women aged 15 and over in 1930 to 56 per thousand in 1932. Although the marriage rate rebounded after 1932, it is estimated that by 1938, 1.5 million couples had been forced to postpone marriage for financial reasons.

Similarly, birth rates fell as couples postponed children. The birthrate per thousand people fell from 21.3 in 1930 to 18.4 in 1933. It is possible that sexual relations may have declined due to depression-induced exhaustion, anxiety, and frustration. Pregnancy was sometimes seen as a misfortune, and the use of contraceptives increased, as did the number of abortions. However, the birth rate generally inched up after 1933.

Almost every New Deal program affected some families and mostly for the better. For example, the CIVIL WORKS ADMINISTRATION, WORKS PROGRESS ADMINISTRATION, CIVILIAN CONSERVATION CORPS, and other such programs provided income. The NATIONAL YOUTH ADMINISTRATION provided young men and women with part-time jobs and financial assistance to help keep them in school. SOCIAL SECURITY ACT benefits assisted the elderly. The HOME OWNERS LOAN CORPORATION helped families keep their homes, and the FEDERAL DEPOSIT INSURANCE CORPORATION protected their savings.

It took World War II to end the poverty of the depression. With an abundance of jobs available, unemployment disappeared and wages for most jobs increased significantly. However, the war brought families new challenges.

Marriage and birth rates increased with the start of World War II. With more money, couples who had postponed marriage and children could now afford them. Unmarried people far from home during the war sought companionship and these relationships frequently led to marriage. Whirlwind courtships were common as many couples married before the men went overseas. Between 1939 and 1942, the marriage rate increased by more than 25 percent. Following closely was the birth rate, which grew by about 20 percent between 1939 and 1943. The belief that husbands with children would not be drafted contributed to this increase in marriages and births, as did "goodbye babies." The increased marriage and birth rates were a precursor of the baby boom that lasted for nearly two decades following the war as well as of the family culture of the postwar era.

The war had a profound impact on family life. Roughly one-fifth of American families had at least one member serving in the armed forces. In addition to the 16 million people, mostly men, who served in the military, another 15 million civilians moved. Frequently, a family relocated to follow a military or civilian husband to military bases or war plants, and together military and civilian migrants totaled about one-fourth of the nation's population. This MIGRATION led to a shortage of housing, schools, and other services in war-boom communities, as well as an emotional toll on the migrants, especially if the move was far from home. Black families who left the South in search of war-related jobs found the change especially difficult because of prejudice and the vastly different lifestyle in other regions of the nation. Life grew even more complicated after the soldier husband went overseas. Wives suddenly found themselves head of the family, responsible for the finances and children, and accompanied by anxiety for her husband's safety.

For a variety of reasons, increasing numbers of married women took jobs during the war. Sometimes, the allotment military families received was not enough. Some women wanted to work for patriotic reasons or to help combat loneliness. The significant expansion of women workers during the war often had an impact on family life. Although women with small children were discouraged from seeking paid employment, some did take jobs. When child care was needed, it was usually provided by a neighbor or relative, partly because many mothers did not want to leave their children with strangers at day care centers, partly because such facilities were limited in numbers. While some school children had to return to empty homes because of working mothers, the extent of "latch-key" children was probably exaggerated, as most families found appropriate child care.

Physicians and child psychologists worried about the effects that a mother working outside the home had on her children, and believed it upset family stability. A small but significant rise in juvenile delinquency by both girls and boys led to national concern. However, these incidents of petty theft, minor violence, and sexual promiscuity were probably a response to the turbulent war years and not a serious problem. The emergence of a teenage culture separate from home and family did occur during this time, especially as young people also found new opportunities for earning money during the war years.

Even if the husband remained at home, a family had to make significant wartime adjustments. One or both of the parents might work long hours in a defense job. Many goods, including sugar, gasoline, clothing, and meat, were in short supply and limited through RATIONING. Other items like new cars were completely unavailable. Families grew victory gardens to supplement their diet and adapted to other shortages. Once again, the family pulled together to weather difficult times.

The end of the war brought new pressures as families tried to return to old ways. Many marriages were strained when the husband returned from the war. Couples had grown apart during the long separation or had barely known each other when they married. Sometimes a husband or wife changed because of wartime experiences. The divorce rate increased significantly in the years immediately following the war, peaking at 17.8 per thousand married women in 1946. However, most marriages and families survived. Indeed, postwar America was marked not only by the baby boom but also by an emphasis on marriage, family, and traditional family patterns.

See also WOMEN'S STATUS AND RIGHTS.

Further reading: D'Ann Campbell, *Women at War with America* (Cambridge, Mass.: Harvard University Press, 1984); William H. Chafe, *The Paradox of Change: American Women in the 20th Century* (New York: Oxford University Press, 1991); Susan Hartmann, *The Home Front and Beyond: American Women in the 1940s* (Boston: Twayne, 1982); William M. Tuttle Jr., *"Daddy's Gone to War": The Second World War in the Lives of America's Children* (New York: Oxford University Press, 1993); Susan Ware, *Holding Their Own: American Women in the 1930s* (Boston: Twayne, 1982).

—Jill Frahm

Marshall, George C. (1880–1959)

General George Catlett Marshall was chief of staff of the U.S. ARMY during WORLD WAR II, and served as secretary of state (1947–49) and secretary of defense (1950–51) after the war. A leader of formidable talents and unimpeachable integrity, steady, direct and plainspoken in demeanor, and a keen analyst of situations and people, Marshall was widely respected by the military and civilians alike. Twice named *Time* magazine's Man of the Year, he won the Nobel Peace Prize in 1953 for his work as secretary of state.

Marshall was born in Uniontown, Pennsylvania, on December 31, 1880. He graduated from the Virginia Military Institute in 1901 and in 1902 received a commission as a second lieutenant of infantry. After service in the Philippines and Oklahoma, he went to Fort Leavenworth, Kansas, where he attended the Infantry and Cavalry School and General Staff College. Between 1913 and 1916 Marshall began a series of staff assignments and went to the Philippines as an aide to General Hunter Liggett and, later, General James Franklin Bell.

Upon the American entry into World War I, Marshall went to France as a staff officer with the First Infantry Division, where he remained until July 1918. In August, he moved to the staff of the U.S. First Army. In September, Marshall supervised the movement of 500,000 troops and 2,700 guns from the St. Mihiel salient to the Argonne in preparation for the Meuse-Argonne offensive. In October, he was named First Army chief of operations, and, in November, Eighth Corps chief of staff.

General George C. Marshall   *(Hulton/Archive)*

Following the war, Marshall served as aide to the army chief of staff, General John J. Pershing, before going to Tientsin, China, with the Fifteenth Infantry. Returning to the United States in 1927, Marshall became assistant commandant of the Infantry School at Fort Benning, Georgia. While there, he came to personally know many of the junior officers who would one day become his principal lieutenants in World War II. Promoted to colonel in 1933, Marshall served as commander of the Eighth Infantry at Fort Moultrie, South Carolina, then as an instructor with the Illinois National Guard, becoming a brigadier general in 1936.

Two years later, in July 1938, Marshall joined the War Department General Staff. He became deputy chief of staff in October, acting chief of staff with the rank of major general in July 1939, and chief of staff of the army, with the rank of general, on the outbreak of war in Europe on September 1, 1939. In cooperation with President FRANKLIN D. ROOSEVELT and Secretary of War HENRY L. STIMSON, Marshall immediately began an expansion of the army and a reorganization of the War Department General Staff. Following the Japanese attack on PEARL HARBOR, he had the major responsibility for organizing, training, supplying, and deploying U.S. troops abroad. By his direction, the army in March 1942 was reorganized into three major commands: the U.S. Army Ground Forces, under Lieutenant General Lesley J. McNair; the U.S. Army Service Forces, under Lieutenant General Brehon B. Somervell; and the U.S. ARMY AIR FORCES, under Lieutenant General HENRY H. "HAP" ARNOLD. During the war, Marshall himself worked out of the War Plans Division.

Marshall was also a principal adviser to President Roosevelt on strategy and attended all of the major conferences of the GRAND ALLIANCE, from Casablanca to Potsdam. As senior member of the Allied Combined Chiefs of Staff, Marshall was the principal architect of the Allied strategy of fighting a two-theater war with a priority on defeating Germany first and opening a SECOND FRONT in France as early as possible. Although desiring the position of supreme Allied commander in Europe, Marshall deferred to Roosevelt's wish for him to remain in Washington, where he continued to manage both military and political aspects of a global war effort. In December 1944 he was promoted to the five-star rank of general of the army.

Soon after resigning as chief of staff in November 1945, Marshall was sent by President Harry S. Truman to mediate an end to the civil war in China, a mission that ended in failure. In January 1947, however, Marshall was appointed secretary of state, and he left the army the following month. In June of that year, in a speech at Harvard University, he proposed the European Recovery Program, a massive influx of aid benefiting a devastated Europe. The program was undertaken the following year and became known as the Marshall Plan. Marshall was instrumental in the founding of the North Atlantic Treaty Organization in 1949. In January 1949 he resigned from the cabinet, but returned in September 1950 as secretary of defense, a post he held until retiring from public life in September 1951. During 1949 and 1950 he served as president of the American Red Cross, and in 1953 he was awarded the Nobel Peace Prize, primarily for his European Recovery Plan. He died on October 16, 1959, in Washington, D.C.

Further reading: Forrest C. Pogue, *George C. Marshall,* 4 vols (New York: Viking, 1963–1987); Mark A. Stoler, *George C. Marshall: Soldier-Statesman of the American Century* (New York: Twayne, 1989).

—Clayton D. Laurie

Mauldin, Bill (born 1921)

Best known for his characters Willie and Joe, two war-weary infantrymen, the Pulitzer Prize–winning editorial cartoonist Bill Mauldin depicted the absurdities of military life and provided a realistic view of the American GI during WORLD WAR II.

William Henry Mauldin was born on October 29, 1921, in Mountain Park, New Mexico. He studied cartooning at the Chicago Academy of Fine Arts and in 1940 enlisted in the U.S. ARMY, where he served in the WORLD WAR II EUROPEAN THEATER with the Mediterranean edition of the army newspaper, *Stars and Stripes.* In 1942, Willie and Joe made their first appearance in *Stars and Stripes.* While the disheveled appearance and irreverent demeanor of Willie and Joe displeased officers as prominent as General GEORGE S. PATTON, JR., Mauldin's duo endeared themselves to GIs, who empathized with the pair, and to Americans at home, who found in them a way to understand the soldiers' experience and perspective.

Mauldin, much like journalist ERNIE PYLE, felt that GIs possessed a "nobility and dignity" that was shaped by the extraordinary circumstances in which they had been placed. His drawings not only gave a human face to America's citizen army but also provided poignant insights into the hardships of a soldier's life. Willie and Joe comics appeared in several papers and were presented in a number of books including *Star Spangled Banter* (1944), *Up Front* (1945), and *Back Home* (1945). In 1945, Mauldin became one of the youngest recipients ever of the Pulitzer Prize.

After the war, Mauldin continued to draw editorial cartoons addressing a range of social and political issues, including the difficulties encountered by many soldiers during their transition back to civilian life. Throughout his career, Mauldin produced drawings that spoke to important and often controversial issues, even when his editors

wanted him to avoid such topics. In the late 1950s and early 1960s, while working for the *St. Louis Post-Dispatch* and the *Chicago Sun-Times,* he published drawings that dealt with race relations and civil liberties, and won a second Pulitzer Prize in 1959. During the Persian Gulf War of 1991, he published cartoons that used a soldier's-eye view of the war to criticize the Bush administration. Although he effectively retired in 1992, he remained an influential presence in the cartooning profession into the 21st century.

Further reading: Bill Mauldin, *The Brass Ring* (New York: Norton, 1971).

—Shannon L. Parsley

medicine and public health

From 1929 to 1945, significant advances occurred in medical knowledge, treatment, and TECHNOLOGY, in employer-sponsored health insurance programs, and in the role of the federal GOVERNMENT in medical research and health care. WORLD WAR II played an especially important role in bringing such progress in medicine and public health, which contributed not only to increased life expectancy (from 57.1 years to 65.9 years between 1929 and 1945), but also to enhanced quality of life.

A number of important breakthroughs came in medical equipment, surgical procedures, and pharmaceuticals. In 1929, Philip Drinker invented the iron lung, an airtight metal tank using electrically powered bellows for artificial respiration for patients who could not breathe because of illnesses such as polio and a variety of injuries. X-ray machines enabled improved diagnosis and surgery. To reduce mortality from blood loss, Dr. Bernard Fantus of Chicago's Cook County Hospital established in 1937 the first repository in a hospital to store and preserve blood from donors, and called it a "blood bank." Then, in 1938, Dr. Charles Drew established a system to collect blood plasma, which the American Red Cross later relied upon to establish massive wartime blood drives and to distribute the blood needed for the war effort at home and abroad.

In cancer research, the most striking discovery of the era came from Dr. Charles B. Huggins, who in 1941 demonstrated the impact of the endocrine system in the functioning of the prostate gland. Enabling Huggins to successfully treat prostate cancer through hormone therapy in some patients, this pioneering research was a milestone in the use of chemotherapy for prostate and breast cancer and led to a significant drop in the mortality rate for these types of cancers.

In the early 1940s, Dr. Alfred Blalock and technician Vivien Thomas developed a shunt to bypass obstruction of the aorta. Using this technique, Dr. Blalock performed the first open-heart operation in 1944 at the Johns Hopkins

University Hospital in Baltimore, Maryland, on a 15-month-old baby girl (who successfully recovered from "blue baby" syndrome), thus opening the door to using the technique for other heart diseases.

During the World War II era, the U.S. made significant contributions in the production, packaging, and delivery of medical services, which led to saving countless numbers of lives throughout the world. The combination of wartime necessity and governmental support led to marked progress and innovation in many areas, particularly sanitation, infection control, pain management, evacuation procedures, blood collection and storage, and rehabilitative medicine. The progress in sanitation came in part as a response to the high incidence of malaria in the Pacific Islands. Antimalaria efforts included aggressive prevention and treatment measures. Because quinine, the traditional treatment, was unavailable (it was made from tree bark found in some Pacific islands, which were held by the Japanese), the United States used Atabrine, a substitute that sometimes caused violent side effects in the troops.

In the area of infection control, U.S. GIs carried sulfa powder to use on open wounds, which greatly reduced the rate of infection during the war. To fight bacteria, the government in 1941 challenged pharmaceutical companies to develop methods to mass-produce penicillin, the highly effective antibacterial drug discovered by the British bacteriologist Sir Alexander Fleming in 1928. Leading the way, Pfizer devoted three years to improve penicillin production using a deep-tank fermentation method, and the company produced 90 percent of the penicillin held by the Allies in 1944. The availability of penicillin, considered the first "wonder drug," helped save thousands of lives. In 1943, the microbiologist Selman Waksman discovered the natural antibiotic streptomycin in soil, which was effective against two debilitating and often fatal diseases of the day—tuberculosis and meningitis.

The United States also made great strides in alleviating the suffering of the wounded. The American pharmaceutical company Squibb developed a styrette for medics to use to quickly administer morphine, an addictive but potent painkiller. Because of new rapid evacuation techniques (primarily airlifting the wounded), almost all war casualties who were evacuated from northwest Europe recovered. Important advances also came in rehabilitative medicine, and in 1944 President FRANKLIN D. ROOSEVELT officially gave federal support to rehabilitation medicine for war casualties. Building upon work in rehabilitation in World War I, Dr. Howard Rush promoted a "whole person" aggressive "reconditioning" rehabilitation model that included acute care, physical and psychological rehabilitation, and vocational training designed to return the injured to civilian life as productive citizens.

With respect to more general government involvement in health care from 1929 to 1945, the federal government at first reduced and then expanded its role in public health, research, and health care, and became involved in controversy over the most hotly debated health care issue of the day—health insurance.

In health policy, partly because of criticism from the American Medical Association (AMA) that it was socialistic, the 1921 Sheppard-Towner Act providing funds for health care education for mothers and CHILDREN was allowed to expire in 1929. Soon after Roosevelt assumed the presidency in 1933, CONGRESS restored provisions of the Sheppard-Towner Act and began to make very limited provisions for assistance with medical expenses for people on RELIEF in the Federal Emergency Relief Act. Such assistance was expanded in 1935 in the SOCIAL SECURITY ACT, which gave grants-in-aid to states for maternity and child health care as well as for several categories of health-impaired groups.

Some growth also came in the role of the federal government in support for medical research during this period. In 1930, Congress created the National Institute of Health (NIH) to conduct medical research, and in 1937 it established the National Cancer Institute, which awarded grants for cancer research. In 1938, Congress established a grants-in-aid program to help states study and investigate venereal disease, and that same year the FOOD, DRUG, AND COSMETIC ACT extended the authority of the Food and Drug Administration (FDA) to monitor pharmaceuticals.

One government-funded study, however, became perhaps the most unethical and immoral program in the history of U.S. medical research. In 1932, the U.S. Public Health Service began a study on how syphilis would affect the cardiovascular and neurological systems of AFRICAN AMERICANS. This experiment, which included some 400 blacks in advanced stages of syphilis, was conducted at the Tuskegee Institute in Alabama. The men were told that they would be given medical treatment for "bad blood," yet were denied penicillin, a known cure, so that the experiment could continue. By 1972, when the study ended, 128 of the men had died of syphilis or complications from syphilis, and 40 wives and 19 children had become infected as a result of the participants not having received treatment.

As World War II approached, the NIH directed its attention to war-related issues. For the military, the NIH reported on categories of medical deferments, studied the effect of high altitude flying, prepared vaccines, and developed first-aid, burn, and trauma therapy for the injured. For the war effort at home, the agency researched hazardous substances and their effects on war-industry workers in order to improve working conditions. In 1944, Congress passed the Public Health Service Act, which included provisions to expand the National Cancer Institute's research grants program and made it part of the National Institute of Health. (In 1948, when Congress authorized the National Heart Institute and made it part of the NIH, it formally changed the agency's name to the National Institutes of Health to reflect the several research institutes it included.)

Perhaps the most controversial areas for health policy during this period involved national health insurance and prepaid health plans. The primary issue was whether the federal government or employers should sponsor or supplement health insurance. Employer-sponsored health insurance for hospitalization made a giant leap forward in 1929 when schoolteachers signed up for the first Blue Cross program, as did insurance for medical care in 1939 when the first Blue Shield plan was founded in California. In 1938, the industrialist HENRY J. KAISER enrolled 6,500 workers on the Grand Coulee Dam into his employer prepaid health insurance plan, entitled Permanente, a forerunner of today's HMOs. During the war buildup, more than 200,000 members of Kaiser's SHIPBUILDING plants in California and Washington enrolled in the plan.

Interest in government-funded, national health insurance increased during the GREAT DEPRESSION and World War II, particularly as advances in medicine caused corresponding increases in the cost of medical care. During the depression, President Roosevelt seemed to support national health insurance, at least in principle, but it was not included in the bill sent to Congress in January 1935 that became the Social Security Act. In 1944, FDR spoke of the right to adequate medical care as part of the ECONOMIC BILL OF RIGHTS, but again did not send Congress any legislation for national health insurance. Stronger support at the federal level came from such liberal Democrats in Congress as New York senator ROBERT F. WAGNER, and subsequently from President Harry S. Truman. In 1935, 1939, 1943, and 1945, Democrats introduced bills for federal subsidies of state medical care and national health insurance supported by taxes. In 1948 Truman, a strong and vocal supporter of national health insurance, proposed comprehensive national health insurance through a 4 percent increase in the Social Security tax. All these proposals sparked strong conservative opposition, led by the AMA, which vehemently argued that passage of national health insurance would be an "end to freedom" and would introduce socialized medicine. (The AMA also strongly opposed prepaid health plans and corporate medicine, both forerunners of HMOs.) National health insurance bills did not get through Congress, and the tradition of employer-sponsored health insurance in the United States continued.

By the late 1940s, the United States found itself a healthier nation, due to new discoveries, advances in technology, government sponsorship of medical research, and expanded private health insurance. In the postwar era, the

Poster promoting sanitary facilities as a means of halting the spread of disease. *(Library of Congress)*

government began to address new problems, such as the need for more medical facilities and personnel as demand for doctors, nurses, hospitals, and equipment increased because of the postwar baby boom, the increased life span of Americans, and rising expectations about medical care.

Further reading: George A. Bender and Robert A. Thom, *Great Moments in Medicine* (Detroit: Northwood Institute Press, 1966); James H. Jones, *Bad Blood: The Tuskegee Syphilis Experiment* (New York: Free Press, 1993); Theodor Litman et al., *Health Politics and Policy*, 2d ed. (Albany, N.Y.: Delmar Publishers, 1991); Irvine Loudon, ed., *Western Medicine: An Illustrated History* (Oxford, U.K.: Oxford University Press, 1997); Paul Starr, *The Social Transformation of American Medicine* (New York: Basic Books, 1982).

—Michele M. Hall

Mexican Americans

Mexican Americans faced many obstacles from 1929 to 1945. The GREAT DEPRESSION worsened their economic condition and intensified mistrust and resentment of them, particularly in the southwestern states. WORLD WAR II then brought change and new opportunities, but it sometimes exacerbated tensions as well.

There had long been a substantial Hispanic population in the United States, with the annexation of the Southwest from Mexico in the mid-19th century. But the beginning of the 20th century witnessed a surge in Mexican immigration. The search for economic opportunities accounted for most of the migration, first in railroad jobs, then as agricultural laborers by the 1910s. Roughly 500,000 Mexicans immigrated to the United States during the 1920s (Mexico was exempt from the stringent IMMIGRATION quotas of the decade), and thousands more immigrated illegally during the decade as well. Settling mainly in the Southwest, especially in California and Texas, the Mexican-American population also began to migrate to CITIES in California and the industrial Midwest. By 1930, Mexican Americans comprised about one-fifth of the population of Los Angeles, while their numbers in Chicago had grown from just over 3,000 in 1920 to almost 20,000 in 1930. The Mexican-American population in 1930 was at least 1.5 million people.

Overall, Mexican Americans remained undereducated and poor. In 1930, most were employed in unskilled jobs, with AGRICULTURE accounting for the largest occupational category (40 percent, with only 10 percent of Mexican Americans as farm owners). Manufacturing jobs in urban areas accounted for about 20 percent of Mexican American employment in 1930. Among women, domestic service employed nearly half the workers, while one-fifth worked as agricultural laborers. Mexican Americans' RELIGION set them apart not only from the larger Protestant majority but from other CATHOLICS as well, for the Catholic Church ignored the language barrier by appointing priests and bishops who did not speak Spanish and disdained Mexican Catholic traditions.

The scarcity of jobs during the 1930s heightened suspicion and resentment toward Mexican Americans, who were often assumed to be illegal immigrants and were accused of taking jobs and draining local RELIEF rolls. Mexican officials, who needed unskilled agricultural labor, and U.S. local, state, and the federal GOVERNMENT officials encouraged migration back to Mexico in the MEXICAN REPATRIATION PROGRAM. From 1929 to 1940, an estimated half million Mexican Americans were sent to Mexico, as many as half of them born in the United States or were legal residents. The pace of the repatriation slowed by the mid-1930s, but the experience contributed to Mexican Americans' suspicions of Anglo-Americans for decades, and

Mexican immigration to the United States dropped dramatically, to more than 30,000, in the 1930s.

For the Mexican Americans who remained, the Great Depression exacerbated their conditions. Living for the most part in rural or urban barrios, often in poor conditions, they experienced an UNEMPLOYMENT rate consistently higher than for most groups. The MIGRATION of other Americans to California, such as those escaping the DUST BOWL, increased the pool of agricultural workers, and Mexican Americans there found themselves losing jobs to the new arrivals. But they remained a significant number of the underpaid agricultural workforce, and Mexican Americans were leaders in the attempts to organize LABOR unions and force farm owners to pay higher wages and provide better working conditions. By the early 1930s there were about 40 agricultural union in California, with the largest the Confederation of Mexican Farm Workers' and Laborers' Union, consisting of 50 locals and 5,000 members. But with jobs scarce, competition from new migrants, and farm owners' stiff resistance to unionization, wages, hours and conditions did not improve significantly.

World War II brought new opportunities for Mexican Americans and increased their urbanization as well. About 350,000 Mexican Americans served in the military, while the recovering economy and MOBILIZATION for World War II opened up new jobs in war-related industries. The wartime urban migration of Mexican Americans also helped to create a labor shortage in agriculture. In response, the United States and Mexico initiated the bracero program, importing 220,000 seasonal workers from Mexico from 1942 to 1947.

For urban Mexican Americans, increased contact with Anglo society also led to tensions, culminating in the riots against ZOOT-SUITERS in June 1943, when navy personnel in Los Angeles assaulted Mexican Americans they saw wearing a zoot suit while city and military authorities did nothing. The experience showed the continued isolation of Mexican Americans, as their language, religion, and concentration in barrios continued to separate them from the larger society. Despite incidents like this, the war nonetheless proved to be a positive experience overall for Mexican Americans, and in the decades to follow, they would continue to urbanize, with the proportion engaged in agriculture in permanent decline.

Further reading: Mario T. Garcia, *Mexican Americans: Leadership, Ideology, and Identity, 1930–1960* (New Haven, Conn.: Yale University Press, 1989); Stephan Thernstrom, ed., *Harvard Encyclopedia of American Ethnic Groups* (Cambridge, Mass.: Belknap Press of Harvard University Press, 1980).

—Katherine Liapis Segrue

Mexican Repatriation Program

The Mexican Repatriation Program returned an estimated half million MEXICAN AMERICANS (often unwillingly) to Mexico during the GREAT DEPRESSION.

The number of Mexican Americans had swelled in the previous decades, as hundreds of thousands of Mexicans immigrated to the United States looking for better job opportunities. By 1930, there were approximately 1.5 million Mexican Americans in the United States (illegal immigration makes the number difficult to pinpoint), largely concentrated in the Southwest, particularly in California and Texas, and near the bottom of the economic ladder. When the Great Depression began in the United States in 1929, Mexican Americans found themselves vulnerable to still higher levels of unemployment and poverty than before. Some 85,000 Mexican Americans voluntarily returned to Mexico from 1929 to 1931.

The rising UNEMPLOYMENT rate exacerbated resentments toward Mexican Americans in the early 1930s. Typically assumed to be illegal immigrants, Mexican Americans were viewed as taking scarce jobs and draining RELIEF funds. In this atmosphere, and at the urging of Mexico (which had a critical shortage of agricultural workers), local, state, and federal GOVERNMENT officials moved to crack down on illegal residents, mainly in California and the Southwest but also in midwestern cities like Chicago.

Most of the repatriation was carried out at the local level, with relief officials taking their cue to initiate deportation from NEW DEAL programs requiring citizenship or legal residency for participation. Los Angeles, whose population was one-fifth Mexican American by 1930, took especially tough measures, subjecting Mexican Americans to harassment and detention, and providing relief recipients free one-way tickets to Mexico. By 1932, almost 75,000 Mexican Americans had left Southern California alone. But California was not alone in its efforts, and between 1929 and 1940, an estimated 500,000 Mexican Americans were sent to Mexico, up to half of them born in the United States or legal residents.

The rapid return of so many Mexican Americans created difficulties in absorbing them back into Mexico's economy and society. By 1937, the repatriation of Mexican Americans slowed considerably, and when WORLD WAR II opened up a need for industrial and agricultural workers, some returned to the United States. Then the U.S. government reversed the repatriation program and inaugurated the bracero program that imported some 220,000 Mexican agricultural workers on a temporary basis from 1942 to 1947. For many Mexican Americans, however, the experience of the repatriation program left a lingering suspicion of American authorities.

Further reading: Francisco E. Balderrama and Raymond Rodriguez, *Decade of Betrayal: Mexican Repatriation in the 1930s* (Albuquerque: University of New Mexico Press, 1995).

—Katherine Liapis Segrue

Midway, Battle of (June 1942)

The Battle of Midway, together with the BATTLE OF THE CORAL SEA a month earlier, marked a decisive turning point in the PACIFIC THEATER of WORLD WAR II. The Battle of the Coral Sea had halted the Japanese movement southward toward Australia; Midway stopped the Japanese advance eastward in the central Pacific. To this point, the Japanese had controlled the war in the Pacific; after Midway, the first important American victory in the Pacific, the Japanese were on the defensive. As in the Battle of the Coral Sea, surface combat ships never came in contact with each other, and the two engagements thus also demonstrated the new importance of aircraft carriers and AIR POWER in naval warfare. The two battles also reflected the importance of CODE BREAKING and INTELLIGENCE in the war.

The Japanese saw Midway as a major strategic site, particularly after the Americans had launched successful bombing raids on Tokyo and Japanese cities from the area in April 1942. They also hoped an attack on the island would draw the U.S. fleet into a decisive defeat. But with the help of "Magic," the intelligence system for breaking Japanese codes, the United States learned of the Japanese plans for attacking Midway, and Admiral CHESTER W. NIMITZ was able to prepare American forces accordingly. Early in the morning of June 4, 1942, planes from Japanese aircraft carriers—part of a huge attack force that included nearly three times as many combat ships as the U.S. NAVY could deploy—began the assault on Midway, although they caused only relatively minor damage on the island and experienced significant losses themselves. Planes from the American base on Midway found the Japanese fleet, and waves of planes from the American aircraft carriers *Enterprise, Hornet,* and *Yorktown* then struck the Japanese during rearmament operations, causing massive damage to ships and aircraft. By the end of the battle on June 7, Japan had lost some 300 planes and four of the six aircraft carriers involved in the attack on Pearl Harbor. The United States lost approximately 150 planes, but the only major American casualty was the carrier *Yorktown,* already damaged at the Battle of the Coral Sea. Though luck as well as intelligence information, planning, and skill accounted for the sweeping American victory, the Battle of Midway marked a decisive shift in the Pacific War. The U.S. Navy now had the upper hand, and U.S. forces soon were on the offensive.

Further reading: Gordon Prange, Donald M. Goldstein, and Katherine V. Dillon, *Miracle at Midway* (New York: Penguin, 1982).

—Charles Marquette

migration

From 1929 to 1945, migration within the United States produced significant redistribution of the population. Except for the early years of the GREAT DEPRESSION, the principal patterns of migration were highly consistent with previous trends. Americans moved especially from the rural Midwest, Southwest, and SOUTH toward metropolitan areas in the North and West. Within metropolitan areas, SUBURBS grew faster than central CITIES. SUNBELT areas of the West and South Coasts, California especially, grew even more rapidly than before. With the exception of armed forces personnel during the war, economic factors were as usual paramount in shaping patterns of population movement. And migration had important consequences not just for the migrants but also for the areas from and into which they moved and for the nation as a whole.

The period from 1929 to 1935 was different in two major ways from the years preceding and following: Migration levels were much lower, and urban-to-rural movement was far more pronounced. Both patterns resulted from the Great Depression and the dismal economic prospects in urban-industrial and rural-agricultural areas alike. Despite the highly visible unemployed transients of the depression years, there was a sharp decline in geographic mobility. Where net out-migration of the farm population had averaged more than one-half million per year during the 1920s and did so again from 1935 to 1940, for example, it fell to less than 60,000 annually from 1930 to 1935. Conversely, there was a noticeable back-to-the-land movement in urban-industrial states. Only California, Florida, and the Washington, D.C., area had net migration gains of more than 100,000 during this period, while Pennsylvania lost a quarter million people and Oklahoma nearly 120,000.

As the shock of the early depression years diminished and as economic prospects seemed to improve, migration picked up again from 1935 to 1940 and resumed patterns evident in the 1920s. In 1940, some 14 million people lived in a different county from the one in which they had lived in 1935. Migrants moved especially toward the Pacific Coast and out of the Midwest, Southwest, and South, with the rural-farm population diminishing rapidly and metropolitan areas, especially suburbs, gaining. The Great Plains states, where drought produced the DUST BOWL, had strikingly high out-migration; California and Florida had much the greatest population growth. As usual, people in their 20s and 30s predominated in the migrant streams. Native-born whites were significantly more likely to migrate than were AFRICAN AMERICANS or foreign-born whites, although blacks figured disproportionately among migrants from the South to such northern cities as New York, Philadelphia, Detroit, and Chicago. Among whites, men were somewhat more likely to move long distances, women more apt to move to cities (where they could more easily find jobs than in rural areas). People with more EDUCATION (particularly those with college degrees) and with higher-status professional and semiprofessional jobs were significantly more likely to migrate, especially between states or regions, than those with less education or lower-status jobs.

One particularly compelling migratory stream of the late 1930s, vividly portrayed in JOHN STEINBECK's novel *The Grapes of Wrath,* was that of the "Okies" moving from Oklahoma to California. Oklahoma lost 184,000 more migrants than it gained from 1935 to 1940, by far the highest net loss of any state; and the 95,000 Oklahomans who went to California easily topped the number arriving there from any other state. Yet the migrating Oklahomans were a more diverse group than the dispossessed Dust Bowl farmers of Steinbeck's novel who joined the agricultural workforce in California. Not much more than one-third of Oklahoma's migrants were farmers and perhaps nearly as many were professional, white-collar, and skilled workers. Just one out of eight Oklahomans who moved to California took up rural-farm residency. Like most other migrants, a majority of Oklahomans, including a majority of those who had been farmers, gravitated to metropolitan areas.

WORLD WAR II accelerated but otherwise did not fundamentally alter the migratory patterns of the late 1930s. More civilians—some 15 million in all—moved to a different county in just over three years from December 1941 to March 1945 than in the five years from 1935 to 1940. Another 16 million served in the armed forces in World War II; and adding them to the civilian migrants makes a total of more than 30 million Americans—nearly one out of every four—who experienced cross-county population movement during the war. Interstate migration increased significantly during the war, and an estimated 12 million people—almost one out of 10—moved permanently to another state.

Going to war plants and military bases on the packed trains and buses of wartime America, migrants moved especially to metropolitan areas and to the Pacific, Gulf, and South Atlantic Coasts, where war MOBILIZATION brought dramatic growth. Industrial areas in the upper Midwest also attracted large numbers of migrants, as did Washington, D.C., because of GOVERNMENT workers flocking in to staff the mobilization effort. Ongoing "depopulation" of rural America, especially in the South and Southwest, was particularly noticeable, as on average the farm population lost some 1.5 million people per year during the war, and the farm population fell by 20 percent. Between 1940 and 1950, by contrast, metropolitan areas grew by 21 percent and suburban areas by 35 percent. Overall, the geographic patterns of wartime migration correlated strongly with those of the 1920s and late 1930s, and those patterns persisted after the war. For example, California and the other Pacific Coast states grew spectacularly during the 1940s, by some 49 percent—but their population had increased by 47 percent in the 1920s.

Other characteristics of wartime migration were also significant. Particularly for the civilian migrants, it was far more optimistic, even vibrant, than depression era migration, for people counted on finding jobs rather than desperately searching for them. But opportunities opened more slowly for some groups than others, which in turn affected the timing of migrant streams. Young adults, the most employable and least rooted, dominated wartime migration. Because women slowly entered—and were slowly accepted into—the paid labor force, they were at first only a small fraction of the migrating workforce, although (especially as wives of workers and servicemen) women constituted a majority of all wartime civilian migrants.

As the supply of white male workers dried up with so many men entering the armed forces, employers necessarily turned to other sources of labor, including African Americans as well as women. The migration of African Americans peaked from 1943 to 1945, as more than 700,000 moved during the war, especially out of the rural South toward the burgeoning war production centers of the South, upper Midwest, and West. Black migration was much heavier than previously to West Coast cities, especially Los Angeles, and was relatively lighter than before to northeastern cities. The percentage of blacks living in the South declined from 77 to 68 percent from 1940 to 1950, while the percentage living in urban areas rose from 49 to 62 percent. MEXICAN AMERICANS resumed their movement away from rural barrios and toward urban areas in the West, where they found jobs in the booming SHIPBUILDING industry and AIRCRAFT INDUSTRY. Similarly, many NATIVE AMERICANS moved from tribal reservations to urban defense industries.

Wartime migration had important social consequences. For millions, it produced new opportunities and better lives. Migration also reduced barriers between groups and reinforced longstanding trends toward cultural diffusion and greater national homogeneity. Whether in the armed forces or in defense production centers, people from different backgrounds, regions, and experiences came together. But population movement also produced difficulties. Migrants who left homogeneous urban or rural communities often experienced disorientation in adjusting to new places and new people. Family strains sometimes developed, partly because decent HOUSING was often difficult to find.

For residents of war-boom areas inundated by immigrants, there were anxieties about rapid change and often animosity toward the unwanted newcomers—"riffraff" or "trailer trash"—who seemed to threaten community standards and existing racial or religious or class patterns, and whose presence created crowded conditions and higher taxes to provide essential services. Rural white southerners and African Americans caused particular distaste and apprehension, and race relations often deteriorated during the flux and tension of the war years. Particularly in the summer of 1943, race riots, involving also Mexican American ZOOT-SUITERS in California, broke out. But Americans also found common cause during the war, sometimes even across racial lines, and tensions typically abated as newcomers and old-timers alike adjusted to new circumstances and learned more about each other.

Migration from 1929 to 1945 thus had important consequences. Except at the outset of the depression, it continued, and during the war it accelerated, patterns long underway, redistributing the population away from the agricultural South, Southwest, and Midwest and toward metropolitan areas and their suburbs. Coastal and urban sunbelt areas, especially California and Florida, grew rapidly. That also in part continued existing trends, but the continuing importance of defense industry and military installations in sunbelt areas, together with their appealing climates and lifestyles signaled an important increase in the sunbelt's economic, political, and even cultural influence that would be felt in the postwar era. And despite wartime tensions and the persistence of regional and group differences, migration contributed to the ongoing social and cultural homogenization of American life.

Further reading: Philip J. Funigiello, *The Challenge to Urban Liberalism: Federal-City Relations during World War II* (Knoxville: University of Tennessee Press, 1978); James Gregory, *American Exodus: The Dust Bowl Migration and Okie Culture in California* (New York: Oxford University Press, 1989); John W. Jeffries, *Wartime America: The World War II Home Front* (Chicago: Ivan R. Dee, 1996); Henry S. Shryock Jr. and Hope Tisdale Eldridge, "Internal Migration in Peace and War," *American Sociological Review* 12, no. 1 (February 1947): 27–39.

mobilization

The American economic and military mobilization for WORLD WAR II made the United States the great "arsenal of democracy" that provided munitions, materials, and military power indispensable to victory over the AXIS. By 1944, the United States accounted for about 40 percent of all war goods produced in the world, and throughout the war the U.S. sent supplies to its allies under the provisions of the LEND-LEASE ACT.

Mobilization had important domestic consequences as well. It vanquished not only the Axis but also the GREAT DEPRESSION, as unemployment dropped from 15 percent to 1 percent between 1940 and 1944 and the gross national product more than doubled. It triggered massive MIGRATION, particularly to the SUNBELT states, which held so many military facilities and war plants. And it greatly increased the size, cost, and power of the federal GOVERNMENT.

Mobilization of the American military proceeded more easily than many had expected after passage of the initial SELECTIVE SERVICE legislation in September 1940. The draft got under way in October, and by 1945 the Selective Service System had administered the conscription of some 10 million of the 16 million men who served in the armed forces. Training camps and operational bases had to be enlarged and constructed, and a huge new military and civilian bureaucracy built. Inevitably there were problems and protests, but on balance the system worked well, providing the U.S. ARMY and U.S. NAVY sufficient personnel to carry out their operations in the EUROPEAN THEATER and the PACIFIC THEATER of the war. Together with the WAR MANPOWER COMMISSION—and sometimes in conflict with it—the Selective Service System tried to allocate manpower optimally between essential civilian tasks (especially in war industry) and the armed forces.

Economic mobilization underwent a disorganized and sometimes disheartening beginning before reaching the prodigious levels that underwrote the victory of the GRAND ALLIANCE over the Axis and the return of prosperity to the American ECONOMY. President FRANKLIN D. ROOSEVELT from the start set what seemed impossibly high production goals—in 1940, for example, he called for producing 50,000 airplanes per year—and his habits of administration made the organization of war mobilization less effective and orderly than it might have been. But the president also provided crucial leadership for both the WORLD WAR II HOME FRONT and the battlefronts and eventually hit upon an organizational framework that did the job.

Difficulties were inevitable, however, because economic mobilization involved such formidable challenges. Existing production facilities had to be converted to war production and new ones had to be built. Mechanisms had to be established for finding and allocating the raw materials, supplies, manpower, and money necessary for mobilization. Priorities and schedules had to be set for producing a bewildering variety of war and consumer goods. And there had to be enough production not just for American needs but for shipments of materials, munitions, and food to the Allies.

The real beginning of economic mobilization came with the National Defense Appropriation Act of 1940, which initiated the appropriation of billions of dollars for defense after the Nazi BLITZKRIEG had overrun western Europe that spring. In 1939 and 1940, Roosevelt had begun working toward an effective organizational and bureaucratic framework, and in January 1941 he established the OFFICE OF PRODUCTION MANAGEMENT (OPM) to coordinate conversion to defense production. The OPM, however, proved ineffective in mobilizing the economy, partly because prior to PEARL HARBOR many manufacturers (in the STEEL INDUSTRY and the AUTOMOBILE INDUSTRY, for example) resisted converting to war production as domestic markets began to revive after the long decade of the depression.

In January 1942, Roosevelt created the WAR PRODUCTION BOARD (WPB) to succeed the OPM. But the WPB lacked authority over manpower, and the military had final authority over contracts. WPB director DONALD M. NELSON, moreover, lacked the leadership skills necessary for the task. In May 1943, the president established the OFFICE OF WAR MOBILIZATION (OWM) as a sort of superagency to coordinate all the various mobilization agencies and efforts, including the "czars" established for such key materials as rubber and petroleum. FDR appointed former South Carolina senator and SUPREME COURT justice JAMES F. BYRNES as head of the OWM and invested him with such authority that he became known as the "assistant president."

By 1943, war production and its administration at last began to hit their stride. From the beginning, the government used such devices as subsidies, low-cost loans, tax write-offs, and guaranteed profits with "cost-plus" contracts to bring about conversion and expansion of production sites. The substantial slack in the ECONOMY in 1940 facilitated the initial stages of war production, since the need was to mobilize underutilized factories, labor supplies, and materials, rather than to squeeze more out of already mobilized resources. Subsequently, productivity gains and management efforts as well as government assistance helped raise output. The Controlled Materials Plan developed by the WPB in the fall of 1942 enabled an effective allocation of raw materials. The DOLLAR-A-YEAR MEN, brought into Washington from BUSINESS to staff the mobilization agencies because of an insufficient number of experienced government officials, helped too. And even in 1938, after the RECESSION OF 1937–38, American national income had been almost twice the combined national incomes of Germany, Japan, and Italy, so the United States could build upon a formidable economic base.

Contracts for the production of war goods went disproportionately to the old or emerging giants in autos, steel, the AIRCRAFT INDUSTRY, electronics, and other industries. Thirty-three firms garnered more than half of all prime war contracts awarded from 1940 to 1944. That was partly because representatives of big business played an important role in the war agencies, but mostly because it made sense to turn to the biggest, most experienced and productive companies to turn out the desperately needed war goods. The mobilization process also brought business and the military into closer contact, helping create what President Dwight D. Eisenhower would later call the "military-industrial complex."

The quality as well as the quantity of war goods was sometimes disappointing at first. Aircraft, torpedoes, tanks, and semiautomatic rifles, for example, had early problems and were sometimes inferior to Japanese and German counterparts. But inexorably, American production improved qualitatively as it surged quantitatively. Advances in SCIENCE and TECHNOLOGY made key contributions, and like production were often underwritten by government funds. In this, the OFFICE OF SCIENTIFIC RESEARCH AND DEVELOPMENT was instrumental, helping to develop items from proximity fuses to radar to the ATOMIC BOMB—and helping also to develop what some have called the "military-industrial-scientific complex."

A variety of other home-front efforts supported and supplemented the mobilization agencies. The OFFICE OF PRICE ADMINISTRATION (OPA) administered price controls and RATIONING of scarce civilian goods. WAGE AND PRICE CONTROLS helped keep wartime inflation under control, while rationing sought to ensure an equitable distribution of consumer goods in short supply. The NATIONAL WAR LABOR BOARD worked to achieve wage and other settlements that would satisfy LABOR and avoid strikes that would disrupt production. The RECONSTRUCTION FINANCE CORPORATION lent money for plant expansion. To staff this mammoth effort, the number of civilian employees of the federal government quadrupled, from about 1 million to roughly 4 million.

Mobilizing for war was extraordinarily expensive. In all, the federal government spent some $300 billion during the war—almost twice as much as in its previous history from 1789 to 1941—and annual expenses soared from $9 billion in 1939 to $98 billion in 1945, when government spending accounted for nearly half of gross national product. TAXATION provided essential revenues for the government as well as siphoning off money from consumer spending and thus reducing inflation. But taxes provided less than half of government expenses. Borrowing—including via WAR BONDS—accounted for the rest, and the combination of heavy deficits and returning prosperity confirmed the tenets of KEYNESIANISM and the importance of fiscal policy to the performance of the economy.

War production reached its peaks of output and efficiency by 1943 and 1944. Industrial output increased by about 15 percent yearly from 1940 to 1944, and by one esti-

mate American output per work hour was twice that of Germany and five times that of Japan. Perhaps no industry so well revealed American ingenuity and mass-production techniques as SHIPBUILDING, particularly by HENRY J. KAISER. The fabled wartime "prodigies of production" yielded (estimate vary) some 300,000 aircraft, 90,000 TANKS, 80,000 landing craft, 5,800 merchant ships, 1,500 navy ships, 2.6 million machine guns, 20 million small arms, 41 billion rounds of ammunition, and 6 million tons of bombs. Yet the United States never devoted its economy so heavily to war production as did other nations at war; about 40 percent of the U.S. GNP went to war goods, for example, whereas more than half did in Britain and Germany.

By 1944, with an Allied victory clearly in sight, attention began to turn to RECONVERSION to a peacetime economy and DEMOBILIZATION of the wartime military. In late 1944, the Office of War Mobilization was converted to the OFFICE OF WAR MOBILIZATION AND RECONVERSION, and the WPB and other agencies began to plan for (and sometimes squabble about) when and how to implement reconversion. War production declined in 1945, particularly after the surrender of Germany in May. With the surrender of Japan in August, reconversion and demobilization began in full force. The nation now had to deal with a new set of issues and problems, including achieving the paramount aim of most Americans—how to ensure a full-employment economy once the stimulus of war mobilization was gone.

Further reading: Keith E. Eiler, *Mobilizing America: Robert P. Patterson and the War Effort* (Ithaca, N.Y.: Cornell University Press, 1997); Eliot Janeway, *The Struggle for Survival: A Chronicle of Economic Mobilization in World War II* (New Haven, Conn.: Yale University Press, 1951); Donald M. Nelson, *Arsenal of Democracy: The Story of American War Production* (New York: Harcourt Brace, 1946); Harold G. Vatter, *The U.S. Economy in World War II* (New York: Columbia University Press, 1985).

Moley, Raymond C. (1886–1975)

Raymond Charles Moley, known for his role as leader of the BRAIN TRUST of FRANKLIN D. ROOSEVELT, was born on September 27, 1886, in Berea, Ohio. He received his bachelor's degree from Berea's Baldwin-Wallace College and a master's degree from Oberlin College before embarking on an initial career in education as a teacher and superintendent of schools. In 1914, he entered the doctoral program in political science at Columbia University.

After receiving his Ph.D. in 1918, Moley became an assistant professor of politics at Western Reserve University in Cleveland. In 1919, he accepted an appointment as director of the Cleveland Foundation, which undertook civic reform through research on urban problems, cooperation between business and government, and local philanthropy. Moley remained at this post until 1923 when he returned to Columbia as an associate professor of public law. Moley became an expert on criminal justice and it was in this capacity that he worked with Roosevelt when FDR was governor of New York from 1928 to 1932. In the brain trust that he was asked to form during Roosevelt's 1932 campaign for president, Moley advocated a policy of cooperation between BUSINESS and GOVERNMENT developed during his years with the Cleveland Foundation.

After Moley and the brain trust advised Roosevelt during the ELECTION OF 1932, Moley played a major role in shaping the FIRST NEW DEAL of 1933 that sought to achieve economic recovery by means of planning and controls worked out with business. He was appointed an assistant secretary of state in the new Roosevelt administration, but lasted less than a year in the position. His most famous assignment was as a delegate to the LONDON ECONOMIC CONFERENCE of June and July 1933, where he was instructed to negotiate a currency stabilization agreement. After concluding a seemingly innocuous agreement, Moley was heralded by the American press as the savior of American interests at the conference. This success was short-lived, however, as Roosevelt revoked the agreement on July 3 employing, in the ultimate of ironies, Moley's own idea that domestic economic reform should take precedence over international agreements.

Moley resigned from his State Department post in the autumn of 1933 to resume his teaching at Columbia and to assume the editorship of the political magazine *Today*. He continued as an occasional speechwriter for Roosevelt until 1939, when he publicly disengaged himself from the NEW DEAL, disillusioned with what he perceived as its increasing hostility to business. In later years, Moley became associated with the conservative wing of the REPUBLICAN PARTY. He died in Phoenix, Arizona, on February 18, 1975. While his direct political influence in the creation of the New Deal was limited, his accounts of the election of 1932 and the "Hundred Days" found in his books, *After Seven Years* (1939) and *The First New Deal* (1966), have made a significant contribution to historical understanding of Roosevelt's first administration.

Further reading: Raymond Moley, *After Seven Years* (New York: Harper, 1939).

—Mary E. Carroll-Mason

Morgenthau, Henry, T., Jr. (1891–1967)

A close friend and confidant of President FRANKLIN D. ROOSEVELT, Henry Morgenthau, Jr., served as secretary of the treasury from 1934 to 1945.

Morgenthau was born in New York City in 1891, into a wealthy family active in social justice efforts and the DEMOCRATIC PARTY. After studying at Cornell and working briefly at the Henry Street Settlement in New York, he used family money to purchase a farm that he managed himself in Dutchess County, New York, not far from Roosevelt's home in Hyde Park. Despite their much different personalities—Morgenthau tended to be an introverted and often insecure worrier who was not very articulate in public, while Roosevelt was just the reverse—the two became fast friends after meeting in 1915. Among other things, they shared a devotion to rural life and a conviction that GOVERNMENT should play an important role in ensuring the well-being of the American people.

After being elected governor of New York in 1928, Roosevelt named Morgenthau chairman of the state Agricultural Advisory Commission and then when reelected in 1930 appointed him state conservation commissioner. When FDR was elected president in 1932, he put Morgenthau in charge of the Federal Farm Board created by the AGRICULTURAL MARKETING ACT of the HOOVER PRESIDENCY. Morgenthau oversaw the transition of the Federal Farm Board into the new FARM CREDIT ADMINISTRATION, and when Secretary of the Treasury William H. Woodin, ill with cancer, could no longer perform his duties, Roosevelt named Morgenthau acting secretary in November 1933 and then secretary of the treasury in January 1934.

Serving as secretary of the treasury longer than anyone but Andrew Mellon, Morgenthau was deeply involved in NEW DEAL monetary and fiscal policy. In fiscal policy, he was always a staunch champion of the balanced budget. He vigorously objected when the administration turned to KEYNESIANISM and deficit spending as a result of the RECESSION OF 1937–38, and even threatened to resign. As always, however, he remained loyal to FDR, and in any case he supported the social reform priorities of New Deal spending even if he abhorred the deficits. He also supported New Deal efforts for more progressive TAXATION and was disappointed that CONGRESS kept tax reform from going further in closing loopholes and taxing the wealthy.

During WORLD WAR II, Morgenthau not only was instrumental in policies to finance economic MOBILIZATION efforts but also played a role in the development of the LEND-LEASE ACT, the BRETTON WOODS CONFERENCE, and the UNITED NATIONS. He opposed the RELOCATION OF JAPANESE AMERICANS and urged Roosevelt to do more to help European JEWS, particularly as evidence of the HOLOCAUST surfaced. Toward the end of the war, he helped to establish the War Refugee Board. An ardent foe of Hitler and Nazi Germany and an early advocate in the 1930s of a more vigorous FOREIGN POLICY to oppose the AXIS, he proposed the so-called Morgenthau Plan in 1944 that called for not only denazifying and demilitarizing but also dividing and deindustrializing Germany after the war. Seen by many as vindictive and misguided, the Morgenthau Plan and the reaction to it contributed to his difficult relationship with new president Harry S. Truman. Morgenthau resigned as secretary of the treasury in July 1945, and returned to his life as a farmer in Dutchess County until he died in 1967.

Further reading: John Morton Blum, *Roosevelt and Morgenthau: A Revision and Condensation of* From the Morgenthau Diaries (Boston: Houghton Mifflin, 1970); ———, *From the Morgenthau Diaries,* 3 vols. (Boston: Houghton Mifflin, 1959–1967).

movies

During the prosperous 1920s, the motion picture industry enjoyed success in keeping with the times. By 1930, 90 million filmgoers poured into theaters across America each week. Then, during the early years of the GREAT DEPRESSION, attendance dropped considerably and many studios struggled. Admissions expenditures fell from $732 million in 1930 to $482 million in 1933. However, as early as 1934, ticket sales began rising again as movies became for many the primary source of diversion during the depression and, after that, WORLD WAR II. Although attendance did not recover to the 1930 peak, it averaged 85 million weekly during the war. Theater receipts rose to $735 million by 1940 and then soared to almost $1.5 billion by 1945.

The depression decade accelerated development of the system conglomerate studios, which characterized the motion picture industry for decades. Between 1930 and 1933, 5,000 theaters closed and numerous small Hollywood studios folded or were absorbed by a few major film companies. Yet, as attendance and revenues climbed, big studios perfected an assembly-line production technique, and producers repeatedly returned to successful formulas to maximize returns. The dismal economic conditions fueled demand for escape, and a huge manufacturing system evolved to create standardized entertainment for the public.

With the development of talking pictures in the 1920s, sound itself often was the star and stories were less significant, but a simple underlying framework emerged nonetheless: violence did not exist, evil was punished, and sexuality was not acknowledged. Certainly, there were exceptions, but it was no coincidence that 6-year-old Shirley Temple was a major attraction. America on film was, generally, a utopian society filled with middle-class white families who wore nice clothes, lived in nice houses, and enjoyed nice lives. Through a variety of genres, such as comedies, westerns, and musicals, movies in the 1930s usually served as entertaining diversions from reality rather than as social or political statements. Historical biographies

and period dramas, such as *Gone With the Wind* (1939), held particular resonance because such films typically portrayed an era safely distant but which delivered a message that problems had arisen before and been overcome.

Nonetheless, considerable changes in the film industry accompanied the depression. Slapstick comedy, portrayed most notably by Charlie Chaplin, had been enormously popular during the silent age. But, with the economic despair that followed the STOCK MARKET CRASH, irreverent and cynical comedy by W. C. Fields and the Marx Brothers gained tremendous popularity in contrast to their goofy peers like Abbott and Costello or the pleasant team of Bob Hope and Bing Crosby. The Marx Brothers' skits often were nonsensical but bitter and sarcastic as well, and the five films they released between 1929 and 1933 garnered huge profits.

Not surprisingly, there were cinematic adaptations of suffering families, too, but since most people hoped to escape their daily lives, the number of poignant sagas about misery was small. The most highly regarded "depression" film was *The Grapes of Wrath* (1940), based on the novel by JOHN STEINBECK. Yet while the novel examined issues such as economic justice, humanity, and the control of land, the Hollywood version was more conservative and concentrated primarily on the family unit. Both the novel and the film affirmed positive messages despite the gloomy setting, but the film conveyed a more optimistic outlook at the expense of Steinbeck's most pointed social and political criticisms.

The decline in ticket sales in the early 1930s generated a range of responses by studios and theaters to retain their customers, including double features and instant-winner contests. Themes involving sexuality and immoral women also became more visible, and major female stars, such as Greta Garbo and Marlene Dietrich, played central roles. Typically, the women characters sinned, suffered indignities, and were punished or atoned, although Mae West starred in a succession of films that conveyed brash, confident sexuality and showed her having fun, which made her a sensation.

A second, more pronounced, change in movie content involved gangsters. Urbanization and IMMIGRATION, preoccupation with prohibition and organized crime, and cynicism about businessmen and politicians were bundled together into classic tales of bad guys and their thirst for power. The first important gangster film was *Little Caesar* (1930), which was followed the next year by some 50 imitations. Two others, *The Public Enemy* (1931) and *Scarface* (1932), complete the trio of films that set the standard for the genre. Most gangster films had similar plots: the bad guy was honorable in his way and used the corrupt system already in place to achieve success. Gangster films frequently mocked politicians and moralists and often depicted crime as the only avenue by which immigrants could rise out of poverty. Despite criticism from advocates for "decency," these movies were extremely popular.

Eventually, the moralists prevailed, however. Persistent pressure for virtuous film content persuaded the film industry to protect itself against potential CENSORSHIP or boycotts. In 1934, the motion picture industry adopted a code of practices that shaped filmmaking for the next 30 years. The basic tenets of the code ensured that dialogue was tame, criminals were not glorified, and violence and promiscuity were marginal. As a result, a second phase of gangster movies began in which the heroes were GOVERNMENT agents. Interestingly, the man who epitomized gangsters in the early films, James Cagney, became the leading star among those who played the crusading G-men.

Another genre of movies arose in which other good guys prevailed—screwball comedies. Conventional screwball comedies were witty and offbeat, and they followed basic thematic patterns: farcical misunderstandings that end happily ever after; love triangles in which the right guy ends up with the girl; the naive common man temporarily outmaneuvered who turns the tables on the corrupt sophisticate. *It Happened One Night* (1934), which starred Clark Gable as the guy who gets the girl (Claudette Colbert), established the model on which many subsequent comedies were based. As the depression continued, however, big stars like Gable were less important in the role of the common man who succeeds. Folksy Will Rogers was celebrated for his "country boy" charm and hopeful humanity. In a quite different genre, westerns also usually emphasized good guys who triumphed.

The war effort also prompted its share of cinematic productions, which were watched closely by the OFFICE OF WAR INFORMATION to ensure that appropriate messages were evident. Patriotism was pervasive, and movies about evil Nazis were numerous as the war in Europe unfolded. After the United States entered the conflict, war films illuminated the daring of pilots and the bravery of soldiers and sailors, but they tended to portray stereotypical characters and eschewed examinations of political issues. The most acclaimed war-themed film of the era was *Casablanca* (1942), which told the story of a cynical expatriate (played by Humphrey Bogart) who rediscovers his commitment to liberty and democracy.

The Hollywood community lent considerable support to the effort abroad as well as at home. Several leading men, such as Clark Gable and Jimmy Stewart, joined the military while numerous other performers served meals and visited hospitals. FRANK CAPRA, the premier director of screwball comedies as well as of movies celebrating the common man—perhaps most notably, *Mr. Smith Goes to Washington* (1939)—created an instructional and inspira-

tional series of films ("Why We Fight") for the War Department, part of which was released to the public. Walt Disney, famous for cartoons, produced an animated documentary about the effectiveness of aerial bombing. And Bob Hope led a parade of entertainers into combat zones across Europe, spreading goodwill and offering cheer for homesick GIs.

Films targeted at women were released with regularity throughout the 1940s. By 1944, women represented more than one-third of the workforce, and a significant portion of the male population was committed to military service. Producers recognized the change and devoted resources to capturing women's attention. In the 1930s, women often played supportive roles; however, throughout the war years, women not only were the leads but men sometimes were not a significant part of the story. Characters were mostly respected professionals (teacher, reporter) who wore elegant clothes and exuded matronly comfort. Women films revolved around concepts common in male-oriented films, such as bonding and justice, but typically involved emotions, attachment, and family, as in *Dark Victory* (1939) or *Meet Me in St. Louis* (1944).

The hundreds of films produced each year required dozens of stars to keep the movie machine functioning. Clark Gable was the favorite leading man; Jean Harlow was the original "blonde bombshell"; Fred Astaire's elegance defined musicals; and Greta Garbo's glamour and detachment made her a mysterious goddess. Gene Autry and Roy Rogers personified the cowboy until John Wayne created the classic western profile in *Stagecoach* (1939). Millions of boys emulated Mickey Rooney, who was the biggest box-office star in America before he turned 20.

Two men—James Cagney and Humphrey Bogart—were especially influential in the era and conveyed distinct personalities that illustrated societal conditions and changes. Cagney starred in 38 films between 1930 and 1941, but achieved stardom in *The Public Enemy*. His character, Tom Powers, became the template for nearly every subsequent gangster role. Cagney also symbolized much that was changing in American society. He was IRISH AMERICAN, and many of his roles involved urban tough guys who projected anger toward conventions of old America, such as naïve morality and Prohibition.

Humphrey Bogart was the archetype of the 1940s male star, whose three successive roles in *High Sierra* (1941), *The Maltese Falcon* (1941) and *Casablanca* (1942) established him as the preeminent actor in America. Bogart frequently played cynical, wry, and streetwise loners who exuded toughness and sexuality despite the actor's ordinary appearance.

Although male performers, directors, and producers dominated filmmaking in the era, many women also achieved fame and influence. Despite an undistinguished

Actor James Stewart (right) with British actor Claude Rains in a scene from *Mr. Smith Goes to Washington,* 1939 *(Hulton/Archive)*

early career, Bette Davis became a supremely confident and compelling attraction who dominated women's roles after her performance in *Of Human Bondage* (1934). Her fiery persona and captivating eyes made her a symbol of feminine strength. Katharine Hepburn became a symbol of evolving social conventions because her roles often challenged traditional norms regarding gender functions and responsibilities. Her controversial characters led many theaters to avoid her films in the 1930s, but she indisputably was Hollywood's leading actress following the release of *The Philadelphia Story* (1940).

Walt Disney began the 1930s as the creator of an animated mouse named Mickey, and emerged after the war as the leader of a worldwide entertainment enterprise crafted around children's fairy tales. Disney films originated as brief cartoons, but they possessed qualities that connected with audiences and impressed critics. In 1933, at the low point of the depression, Disney released *The Three Little Pigs*, which delivered through allegory complemen-

tary messages: work hard, do it right, don't give up, and stick together to defeat the enemy. Those old-fashioned virtues mirrored the optimism and confidence of President FRANKLIN D. ROOSEVELT, and the theme song from the film ("Who's Afraid of the Big Bad Wolf?") became a social anthem for the period. *Snow White and the Seven Dwarfs* (1937) was the company's first full-length feature film, and its success inspired the growth of a wholly new type of movie.

In part because of the depression, in part because of sound, and in part because of stars, the 1930s represent the period of Hollywood's greatest influence on American life. In the decade, spending on movie admissions accounted for roughly one of every five dollars spent on entertainment and RECREATION, and motion pictures also served as a powerful marketing tool for BUSINESS and industry. America's population had become preponderantly metropolitan, and the film industry helped sell a national urban culture to citizens across the country.

Still, dreams were the principal products of Hollywood's film factories. Some movies linked fantasy worlds with facts to engage the audience, such as *The Wizard of Oz* (1939), but many merely were replicas of a simple formula that had proved successful before. If the woeful economy eroded confidence, the film industry attempted to rebuild the American psyche one dream at a time. Hollywood embraced an audience that was confused, downtrodden, and widely divergent, and sold everyone the same hope: Ordinary people can survive and humanity will prevail over sinister forces. Whether as an escape from despair or a distraction from war, the people came. And, when the depression was over and the war won, the people stayed.

See also POPULAR CULTURE.

Further reading: Andrew Bergman, *We're in the Money: Depression America and Its Films* (New York: New York University Press, 1971); Charles Higham and Joel Greenberg, *Hollywood in the Forties* (New York: A. S. Barnes & Company, 1968); Charles Higham, *The Art of the American Film, 1900–1971* (Garden City, N.Y.: Press/Doubleday, 1974); Gerald Mast and Bruce Kawin, eds., *A Short History of the Movies,* 5th ed. (New York: Macmillan, 1992); John E. O'Connor and Martin A. Jackson, eds., *American History/American Film* (New York: Frederick Ungar, 1979).

—Douglas Propheter

Munich Conference (1938)

The Munich Conference of September 1938 has long symbolized the fruitless "appeasement" policy by which the western democracies sought to halt German aggression in the 1930s through negotiations and concessions. At Munich, British prime minister Neville Chamberlain and French premier Edouard Daladier agreed that Germany might take part of Czechoslovakia if the German führer, Adolf Hitler, agreed to make no further territorial demands. President FRANKLIN D. ROOSEVELT interposed no objection. In March 1939, Germany seized the remainder of Czechoslovakia. In September 1939, Germany invaded Poland, and WORLD WAR II began when Britain and France declared war on Germany.

The immediate context for the Munich Conference was Hitler's demand for the cession of the Sudentenland, a region of Czechoslovakia bordering on Germany that contained some 3 million ethnic Germans—and his clear intention to take the area by force if necessary. In late September 1938, Italian dictator Benito Mussolini proposed that a four-power conference involving himself, Hitler, Daladier, and Chamberlain convene in Munich, Germany, on September 29 and 30 to find a solution. On September 30, the four leaders released the Munich Agreement, which called for the Sudetenland to be handed over to Germany and for Hitler to forego additional territorial demands in Europe. Chamberlain came home to cheering crowds in London after the conference, claiming he achieved "peace in our time." More realistically, Winston Churchill, who would succeed Chamberlain as prime minister in May 1940, called the Munich Agreement a "total and unmitigated defeat."

The United States, reflecting the influence of ISOLATIONISTS who had helped produce the NEUTRALITY ACTS of the mid- and late 1930s, played no significant role in the Czech crisis or the Munich Conference. Although he had privately counseled British resistance to Germany, Roosevelt on hearing about plans for the Munich Conference sent Chamberlain a cable, saying, "Good man." The president also assured Hitler that "the United States has no political involvements in Europe, and will assume no obligations in the conduct of the present negotiations." PUBLIC OPINION POLLS showed that the American public overwhelmingly approved this hands-off policy; and in any case, the United States had neither the military power nor the diplomatic leverage to influence events in Europe. The nation could only remind the European powers of the toothless Kellogg-Briand Pact of 1928, the "international kiss" that had supposedly outlawed war, and urge a peaceful resolution of the crisis.

Privately, however, Roosevelt was appalled by the Munich Conference and deeply disturbed by the course of events as Germany, Japan, and Italy, soon to be joined in the AXIS alliance, pursued their paths of aggression. By 1939, the president began to increase American defense spending, to work to provide support for Britain and France should war come, and to forge a more interventionist American FOREIGN POLICY, including revision of the Neutrality Acts. A symbol of the weakness of the western democracies in the 1930s, the Munich Conference also marked a turning point of sorts, not only feeding Hitler's appetite for aggression but clarifying his intentions and leading to a more active and anti-Axis American defense and foreign policy.

Further reading: Robert Dallek, *Franklin D. Roosevelt and American Foreign Policy, 1932–1945* (New York: Oxford University Press, 1979); Robert Divine, *The Reluctant Belligerent* (New York: John Wiley & Sons, 1965); Arnold A. Offner, *American Appeasement: United States Foreign Policy and Germany, 1933–1938* (Cambridge, Mass.: Harvard University Press, 1969).

—Michael J. Leonard

Murray, Philip (1886–1952)

Philip Murray, a major LABOR leader of the 1930s and 1940s, became president of the CONGRESS OF INDUSTRIAL ORGANIZATIONS (CIO) in 1940 and led the CIO until his death in 1952. He also headed the Steelworkers Organizing Committee from 1936 to 1942 and then served as the first president of the United Steelworkers of America from 1942 to 1952.

The son of Irish Catholic parents, Murray was born in Scotland on May 25, 1886. Murray's father, a coal miner who became president of a local union, imbued in his son an appreciation for social and political liberalism, later reflected in his efforts to advance the lot of the working class. In 1902, Murray and his father left Scotland and came to America, where they settled in the coal-rich Pittsburgh area. Murray began working in the mines at age 16. He lost his job after a dispute with a weighmaster two years later, and 600 men followed Murray out of the mines on a strike that lasted four weeks. Although ultimately unsuccessful, the strike led Murray to become involved with organized labor. He was named to the international executive board of the United Mine Workers (UMW) in 1912, served on the War Labor Board during World War I, and by 1920, at age 34, was a vice president of the UMW.

The GREAT DEPRESSION and the NEW DEAL policies of President FRANKLIN D. ROOSEVELT brought Murray to national prominence, and he joined the ranks of other notable IRISH AMERICANS involved in the rise of industrial unionism. When JOHN L. LEWIS of the UMW and other leaders of the AMERICAN FEDERATION OF LABOR (AFL) formed the Committee for Industrial Organization in 1935, Lewis asked Murray to head the Steel Workers Organizing Committee (SWOC) to organize the STEEL INDUSTRY, and the UMW provided money and manpower for the effort. The SWOC won recognition from the powerful U.S. Steel Corporation in March 1937 following the sit-down strikes in the AUTOMOBILE INDUSTRY that led General Motors to recognize the United Auto Workers.

But Murray and the SWOC encountered difficulties with the so-called Little Steel firms (including Republic, Bethlehem, and others) that resisted unionization. Perhaps the worst conflict came in the "Memorial Day Massacre" in 1937 at a plant of the Republic Steel Company when police opened fire on union sympathizers, killing 10 men (seven of whom were shot in the back) and wounding 30 others, including one woman and three children. In all, 18 steelworkers died in organizing efforts during the summer of 1937, but Little Steel avoided unionization until the early 1940s.

Murray gradually surpassed Lewis's influence in the labor movement, and, by 1940, a rift had developed between the old friends. Lewis supported WENDELL L. WILLKIE, the Republican nominee for president in the ELECTION OF 1940, while Murray and most other CIO leaders continued to support Roosevelt. Keeping his promise to resign the CIO presidency if Roosevelt won, Lewis stepped down after the election, paving the way for Murray to succeed him.

During WORLD WAR II, Murray (now president of both the United Steelworkers of America and the CIO called for increases in production and controls on the nation's ECONOMY, although he did not support wage controls and continued to push throughout the war for increased wages for workers. He did agree to a no-strike pledge in order to avoid strikes that would harm production levels. Lewis rejected upholding the no-strike pledge, proving less cooperative with industry during wartime economic MOBILIZATION than Murray.

After the war, Murray successfully negotiated substantial wage increases for labor, forged even stronger links between the labor movement and the DEMOCRATIC PARTY, played an active role in shaping legislative priorities in Washington, and led the United Steelworkers in three national strikes in which workers successfully sought pensions and union security. Murray also worked in the postwar years to purge the CIO of COMMUNISTS, who dominated several unions. Philip Murray died of a heart attack in San Francisco, November 9, 1952, at the age of 66.

Further reading: Ronald Schatz, "Philip Murray and the Subordination of the Labor Unions to the United States Government" in *Labor Leaders in America,* edited by Melvyn Dubofsky and Warren Van Tine (Urbana: University of Illinois Press, 1987).

—Joseph C. Gutberlet

music

The period from 1929 to 1945 was a significant one for American music, particularly for the remarkable variety of indigenous music that flourished in the era and for the continued development and popularity of jazz. Music reflected the impact of both the GREAT DEPRESSION and WORLD WAR II on American life as well as the role played by TECHNOLOGY, especially RADIO, in American POPULAR CULTURE. Other important developments included the growing influence of AFRICAN AMERICANS on the nation's music and efforts to document and preserve traditional music. New York, Chicago, and New Orleans remained key centers of American music, though a number of other cities, including Kansas City, Memphis, and Nashville, were also important.

Perhaps the most notable patterns in American music in the 1930s involved the development, growing commercialization, and expanded audiences experienced by various forms of traditional and regional music. Much of this music was southern, ranging from African-American blues to white country and "hillbilly" music, and it included significant connections and even fusions among different ethnic, racial, and regional musical traditions, abetted in this era by the radio, phonograph records, and population movement. Reflecting the exigencies of the depression, protest songs also figured significantly in the decade, and gospel music became an important phenomenon in urban as well as rural areas. Though sales of phonographs and phonograph records fell off sharply early in the depression, radio had grown in extent and importance during the 1920s and provided an essential source of the expanding audiences for music in the 1930s.

White country music underwent developments in the 1930s with significant implications for the wartime and postwar periods. In the late 1920s and early 1930s, Jimmy Rodgers, like some other white country musicians, combined hillbilly with aspects of blues music. The Carter family gave traditional Appalachian folk music wider audiences with their recordings, as did Roy Acuff and his Smoky Mountain Boys for old-time country music and Bill Monroe and his Blue Grass Boys for bluegrass. The Grand Ole Opry broadcasts of Nashville radio station WSM and the National Barn Dance broadcasts of Chicago's WLS played key roles in building the popularity of such music.

The 1930s also saw the rise of "western music," particularly in Texas, with its stringband style and its impact on country music. The Cajun music of southern Louisiana, for example, was influenced by "western swing" music, including that of Bob Wills and the Texas Playboys. The popular movies of such cowboy singers as Roy Rogers and Gene Autry helped expand audiences for western music. And particularly in Texas, western music also developed what became known as "honky-tonk" music, with a harder sound, including electric guitars, and often with harder-edged lyrics than traditional country music.

The Great Depression of the 1930s, and the criticism of economic and political institutions that it often produced, contributed to a more protest-oriented folk music. Somewhat different from the lamentations of much blues and country music, this protest music was more self-consciously political and paralleled themes of social criticism in other artistic endeavors of the decade. Its best-known artist was Woody Guthrie, but there were others as well, and they sang songs of both rural and urban tribulation and protest. By the 1940s, and the American entry into the war and the return of prosperity, this folk music of social criticism sub-

Woody Guthrie   *(Library of Congress)*

sided, not to reemerge significantly until the 1950s and especially the 1960s.

One reason that folksingers in the 1960s revival could draw on earlier musicians was the remarkable effort made in the 1930s, particularly by various government agencies, to locate and preserve traditional American music. Two important agencies of the WORKS PROGRESS ADMINISTRATION, the FEDERAL WRITERS' PROJECT and especially the FEDERAL MUSIC PROJECT, with its field research on regional folk music and its Index of American Composers, sought to identify the indigenous music of America and the American people. The Library of Congress sent John Lomax and his son Alan to the South to locate and record the music of rural southerners, white and black. The Smithsonian Institution conducted similar efforts, as did various academic folklorists and aficionados of traditional music.

These efforts played an important role in helping to document traditional African-American music and musicians. The Lomaxes were instrumental in discovering (in Louisiana's Angola Penitentiary) Huddie Ledbetter, better known as "Leadbelly," who was more a singer of traditional black folk songs and "shouts" than of the blues with which he is also identified. The Lomaxes and others also helped to bring recognition to some of the black bluesmen of the 1930s and 1940s. Alan Lomax recorded McKinley Morganfield—later known as Muddy Waters—singing Delta blues on Stovall's Plantation in Mississippi in the early 1940s. Part of the wartime and postwar black MIGRATION north, Morganfield moved to Chicago in 1943 and, as Muddy Waters, began using an electric guitar. With Little Walter, Howlin' Wolf, and others, Waters developed the Chicago urban blues so important in the postwar era.

But many of the black blues singers of the 1930s did not have to be discovered by northern folklorists coming South. The radio and phonograph were already giving traditional bluesmen, including Charlie Patton, Son House, and Blind Lemon Jefferson, significant audiences. Radio and phonograph recordings also helped spread the music of such "boogie-woogie" blues pianists as Little Brother Montgomery, Jimmy Yancey, and Memphis Slim, who developed great popularity in northern cities. As blues singers and musicians migrated from the rural South to the urban North, they also influenced other genres from gospel to jazz and "swing" music, including the rhythmic, flowing Kansas City jazz popularized by Count Basie's band.

The most important development in jazz in this era was the emergence of the "Swing Era" big bands that dominated jazz, and much popular music, from the mid-1930s to just after World War II. Louis Armstrong and his "Hot Fives" and "Hot Sevens" recordings of the 1920s had revolutionized jazz and laid foundations for the Swing Era to follow. Early in the depression decade, jazz suffered from the general economic collapse, but especially with the rise to stardom of BENNY GOODMAN in 1935, jazz gained not only a new direction but a new popularity throughout the nation. Such black bands as those of DUKE ELLINGTON pioneered swing music, but with Goodman and other white bandleaders such as Tommy and Jimmy Dorsey and Glen Miller, jazz attained widespread new popularity.

A telling indication of the new stature of jazz and of the recognition of the importance of African-American music came from two landmark performances at New York's Carnegie Hall in 1938: One was Benny Goodman's now-legendary January jazz concert; the other was a December performance of traditional African-American music. And in 1943, Duke Ellington gave the first of what ultimately became nine Carnegie Hall concerts.

Other important developments marked jazz in the 1930s and 1940s. Duke Ellington, as composer as well as pianist and bandleader, produced remarkable music based in African-American and jazz traditions but taking it to a new and different level. BILLIE HOLIDAY, FRANK SINATRA, and others made individual singers more important than before, a factor contributing to the demise of the big bands

after World War II. And as big bands and their swing music began to dissolve after the war because of changing tastes and economic difficulties, "bebop," a harder-driving, less danceable jazz by smaller combos popularized by such artists as saxophonist Charlie Parker and trumpeter Dizzy Gillespie, began to reshape jazz in the postwar era.

Jazz as well as black and white traditional music also affected classical and other more "serious" music in the era—though such compositions by Duke Ellington as his 1943 concerto *Black, Brown and Beige* were serious music by any reckoning. George Gershwin worked jazz and African-American elements into his music, most famously in his 1935 opera *Porgy and Bess*. The composer Aaron Copland sometimes drew on jazz and African-American music, and in *Billy the Kid* (1938), *Rodeo* (1942), and *Appalachian Spring* (1944) on traditional white music as well.

Among the other significant developments in American classical music in the era were efforts to bring it to larger audiences. On Christmas Day, 1931, New York's Metropolitan Opera broadcast live on the radio, beginning the Saturday broadcasts of the "Met" that put opera in millions of American homes. In addition to its work documenting and preserving American music, the Federal Music Project of the NEW DEAL gave employment and income to professional musicians (perhaps two-thirds of whom were unemployed by 1933), provided musical education and instruction, and helped stage live performances of classical as well as popular music. While opera companies struggled and sometimes failed in the 1930s, the efforts of the Federal Music Project helped the number of symphony orchestras to increase significantly late in the decade.

A number of emigrés and exiles from Nazi-dominated Europe came to the United States in this era, with important consequences for American classical music. These artists included the Italian conductor Arturo Toscanini, the Polish pianist Arthur Rubenstein, and such composers as the Russian Igor Stravinsky, the Austrian Arnold Schoenberg, the Hungarian Béla Bartók, and the German Kurt Weill. With others, they brought additional vitality to American classical music in a way paralleling the impact of European expatriates on other aspects of American intellectual and artistic life. Yet even some of them, Stravinsky, for example, with his *Ebony Concerto* of the mid-1940s, also worked jazz and other indigenous American music into their compositions. The American John Cage, briefly a student of Schoenberg's, pursued decidedly untraditional music with his development of radical percussive compositions in the 1930s and 1940s.

American musical theater in the 1920s and 1930s was part of what became known as the "golden age" of the American musical, with talents such as Irving Berlin,

George Gershwin, Cole Porter, and Richard Rodgers leading the way. While the subject matter of musicals varied, they also reflected some of music's broader themes in the era and included such socially conscious productions in the 1930s as Gershwin's *Of Thee I Sing* (1931), a satire of the U.S. government that became the first musical to win a Pulitzer Prize, shows such as Richard Rodgers's *Oklahoma!* (1943) celebrating folk patterns, and such war-related musicals as Berlin's *This Is the Army* (1942) and Rodgers's *South Pacific* (1948).

The war had other effects on popular music. A number of snappy, chauvinistic anti-Japanese and anti-German songs were produced, but never really caught on. Rather, the big sellers were such patriotic standards as Kate Smith's version of "God Bless America," danceable songs such as "The Boogie-Woogie Bugle Boy of Company B," and sentimental ballads such as 1944's most popular song, "I'll Be Seeing You." With patriotism supplanting protest even among those who had produced or sung music of social criticism in the 1930s, Woody Guthrie's "This Land Is Your Land" became a hit during the war. The Andrews Sisters and other musical artists also visited overseas bases as part of the efforts of the UNITED SERVICE ORGANIZATIONS (USO) to lift morale. The best-selling record of the war years was Bing Crosby's "White Christmas," which reflected the sentimental focus on home characteristic of the war years. Much of this wartime music was evanescent, but such popular standards as "White Christmas," would have been hits in any era.

The really significant musical impact of World War II lay in how it continued or redirected many of the patterns of the 1930s, thus setting the stage for the postwar era. The big bands perhaps gained their peak of popularity, despite wartime restrictions and demands. (Glenn Miller was killed in an airplane crash on his way to entertain troops.) The frenzied reaction to Frank Sinatra ("Sinatramania") reflected not only the emergence of the first true "teen idol" but also the growing importance of individual singers at the expense of the big bands and thus heralded the postwar decline of big bands. By the end of the war, swing was giving way to bebop and big bands to smaller ensembles in more intimate settings. Blues singers, with other African Americans, continued their migration North, and particularly in Chicago developed electrified urban blues, based importantly on Delta blues and other rural traditions. Gospel music had increasing commercial success. White country music continued to grow in popularity, abetted by Grand Ole Opry tours and broadcasts. As rural whites moved toward cities and joined the armed forces, country music gained in popularity and geographic reach; honky-tonk emerged as the dominant strain of country music; and by the late 1940s Hank Williams had become a major national star. Based especially on such strands of African-American music as blues, jazz, and boogie-woogie, "rhythm and blues" began to emerge as important popular music. Rather than simply being "race" music aimed at black audiences, R&B became much more generally popular in the postwar era and contributed powerfully to the emergence of the rock 'n' roll that came to dominate American popular music.

See also ART AND ARCHITECTURE; FEDERAL ART PROJECT; FEDERAL THEATRE PROJECT; LITERATURE.

Further reading: Laura Browder and David McLean, "The Arts," in *American Decades, 1930–1939,* ed. Victor Bondi (Detroit: Gale Research, 1995); Ted Gioia, *The History of Jazz* (New York: Oxford University Press, 1997); Richard Lingeman, *Don't You Know There's a War On? The American Home Front, 1941–1945* (New York: Putnam's, 1970); Alan Lomax, *The Land Where the Blues Began* (New York: Pantheon, 1993); Bill C. Malone, *Country Music, U.S.A.* (Austin: University of Texas Press, 1985); John Warthen Struble, *The History of American Classical Music* (New York: Facts On File, 1995); Charles Reagan Wilson and William Ferris, eds. "Music" in *Encyclopedia of Southern Culture* (Chapel Hill: University of North Carolina Press, 1989).

Myrdal, Gunnar (1898–1987)

The Swedish scholar Gunnar Myrdal is best known in the United States for his enormously important 1,500-page study of American race relations—*An American Dilemma: The Negro Problem and Modern Democracy,* published in 1944. Myrdal's work provided one of the first in-depth examinations of America's racial system that kept its black citizens poor, uneducated, and deprived of most CIVIL RIGHTS. It played a major role in opening the eyes of white Americans to the plight and dissatisfaction of AFRICAN AMERICANS and in making civil rights a priority of many whites in the 1940s and 1950s. Its findings also contributed to the Supreme Court's landmark 1954 ruling against segregation in *Brown v. Board of Education.*

Born on December 6, 1898, in a small Swedish village, Gunnar Myrdal became one of his country's leading intellectuals and was active in Swedish politics before the Carnegie Corporation commissioned him in 1938 to head a study of what was called the "American Negro problem." Upon completing his research in 1942, he returned to Sweden and was elected to the Swedish Senate. Later he served as the executive secretary of the UNITED NATIONS Economic Commission for Europe and left that post to conduct an important study of the economic conditions in Asia. In 1974 he was awarded the Nobel Prize in economic science jointly with Austrian professor Frederich von

Hayek for work relating economic analysis to social and cultural conditions. His wife, Alva Myrdal, received the Nobel Peace Prize in 1982.

An American Dilemma was a highly ambitious project, involving historians, sociologists, psychologists, anthropologists, economists, and others—all creating a formidable body of work that led to one inescapable conclusion: The treatment of African Americans amounted to virtually a total denial of the fundamental principles upon which the United States had been founded. Myrdal's striking analysis of the history and consequences of slavery, white racism, and racial discrimination and segregation made a compelling case for immediate correction if America was to live up to its promise. The study became highly influential—and was a best-seller—at a time when the majority of white Americans supported racial segregation and turned a blind eye to the violence that supported it. Its impact was all the more remarkable considering that it came out during the tensions of WORLD WAR II. "I know of no other country where such a thing could have happened," Myrdal later remarked.

In conducting his study, Myrdal became one of the first scholars to connect racial conditions to repressive violence. He initiated his research by traveling by car through the SOUTH, meeting with white and black leaders. His African-American colleague, Ralph Bunche, was forced to pose as his chauffeur in order to avoid the wrath of affronted whites. Research lasted from 1939 through 1942. In addition to providing an incisive exploration of all facets of the African-American experience, including family life, RELIGION, and culture, *An American Dilemma* examined racial prejudice and its effects on the black community and its institutions. It described a broad pattern of lynching, riots, and individual acts of violence, perpetrated with the help or acquiescence of law enforcement, that amounted to little more that racial terrorism. The "dilemma" referred to in the title involved the tension between the high-minded idealism of the American creed of "liberty, equality, justice, and fair opportunity for everybody" and the racial prejudice that resulted in proscription, harassment, humiliation, and violence that characterized race relations. The true test of American greatness, Myrdal argued, would come in how it confronted and solved this dilemma.

Myrdal intended his study to force whites to see the sizable nature of the problem *they* had created, and through a systematic, detailed presentation of the facts, impel them to correct it. He placed the onus for the plight of black America squarely on the shoulders of whites. He called it the "principle of cumulation," which meant the inferior status of blacks forced upon them by whites, first by slavery and then by segregation, created a self-perpetuating cycle of low status that confirmed white prejudice and encouraged the status quo. Only by raising blacks to fully assimilated members of society could this problem be resolved. Myrdal hoped that a careful though passionate exploration of the facts offered in conjunction with the ongoing war against tyranny in World War II would convince whites to change their attitudes and practices. In this approach, he revealed a pronounced faith in the inherent integrity of the American system and in the essential goodness and strength of character of the American people—to which, ultimately, he made his appeal.

See also RACE AND RACIAL CONFLICT.

Further reading: Gunnar Myrdal, *An American Dilemma: The Negro Problem and Modern Democracy* (New York: Harper, 1944); David W. Southern, *Gunnar Myrdal and Black-White Relations: The Use and Abuse of an American Dilemma, 1944–1969* (Baton Rouge: Louisiana State University Press, 1987).

—Howard Smead

National Association for the Advancement of Colored People (NAACP)

During the era of the GREAT DEPRESSION and WORLD WAR II, the National Association for the Advancement of Colored People (NAACP) continued to play a central role in working for CIVIL RIGHTS for AFRICAN AMERICANS and combating the racial discrimination, segregation, and violence they faced, especially in the SOUTH. On the eve of the Great Depression, the NAACP had 325 branches in 44 states but just over 21,000 members nationwide. By 1945, due to a rigorous recruitment campaign and an expanded plan of attack, the NAACP had experienced unprecedented growth and included nearly a half million members.

Several significant events occurred in the early 1930s. In 1930, the NAACP led a successful protest to block the nomination of Judge John Parker to the United States SUPREME COURT because of Parker's racist statements. Later that year, James Weldon Johnson resigned as executive secretary of the association, and in March 1931 WALTER WHITE became his successor. A month into White's tenure, the trial of nine black teenagers accused of raping two young white women began in Scottsboro, Alabama. The case of the SCOTTSBORO BOYS tested the NAACP, which became involved in an unsuccessful struggle over representing the defendants with the International Labor Defense (ILD), a communist-led organization.

During the 1932 presidential election, most African Americans remained loyal to the REPUBLICAN PARTY, the party of Lincoln, although a minority viewed liberal northern Democrats and FRANKLIN D. ROOSEVELT's promise of a "new deal" as a hopeful alternative. In 1933, Robert C. Weaver and John P. Davis, together with the NAACP and a number of other black organizations, joined forces to create the Joint Committee on Economic Recovery (JCER). The JCER had some success in fighting against the racial wage differentials and for the inclusion of black Americans in NEW DEAL programs. White and the NAACP were unable, however, to persuade Roosevelt actively to support, or CONGRESS to enact, federal antilynching legislation.

By 1936, the association had become part of a New Deal political coalition consisting of liberal Democrats, LABOR, and civil rights organizations. The liberal-labor coalition helped FDR secure a landslide victory in the ELECTION OF 1936, and Walter White established a close relationship with ELEANOR ROOSEVELT that gave the NAACP some access to President Roosevelt. Such connections with the Roosevelt administration won little support for NAACP civil rights efforts, but they did bring help in 1939, when the Daughters of the American Revolution excluded the famed African-American singer Marian Anderson from performing at Constitution Hall in Washington. The NAACP quickly reacted and with the assistance of Eleanor Roosevelt, HAROLD ICKES, and other New Deal leaders, the concert was moved to the steps of the Lincoln Memorial, where Anderson performed before 75,000 people.

Throughout the depression, the NAACP experienced a number of internal conflicts, but none so important as that involving William E. B. Du Bois, one of the organization's founders and leaders. In 1934, Du Bois criticized the NAACP's program in the pages of its publication, the *Crisis,* suggesting that blacks organize among themselves and use self-segregation to defeat segregation and discrimination. Following those controversial remarks and his support of socialism, the board of directors denounced Du Bois and forced him to resign from the association. Du Bois later returned to the NAACP in 1944 as director of special research.

In 1935, Howard University law professor Charles Houston was appointed chief legal counsel of the NAACP. Assisted by his former student Thurgood Marshall, the two men began to lay the foundation for an extended and increasingly successful legal assault against school segregation. On November 5, 1935, the Maryland Court of Appeals ordered the University of Maryland to admit

Donald Murray, an African American. The following year, the NAACP initiated successful lawsuits against unequal salaries for African-American teachers. In 1938, Marshall replaced Houston as special counsel of the association, and other cases in education and voting rights brought by the NAACP in the late 1930s and war years led to further Supreme Court decisions eroding the legal edifice of Jim Crow and pointing toward the landmark 1954 decision in *Brown v. Board of Education of Topeka.* In 1938, in *Missouri ex rel. Gaines v. Canada,* the Supreme Court declared unconstitutional a state's refusal to provide a law school education to a qualified African American. In *Smith v. Allwright,* the Court in 1944 found the all-white primary used in the South unconstitutional.

As the United States drew nearer to involvement in World War II, African Americans remained in segregated military units and were barred from most defense jobs. In 1941, the NAACP supported A. PHILIP RANDOLPH and his MARCH ON WASHINGTON MOVEMENT that led FDR to sign EXECUTIVE ORDER 8802 in June 1941, which outlawed discrimination in government and war industries and created the FAIR EMPLOYMENT PRACTICES COMMITTEE. Subsequently, the NAACP joined and often led the growing activism of the war years on behalf of civil rights for African Americans. Under the leadership of Ella Baker, who joined the NAACP staff in 1941, southern membership increased from 18,000 in the late 1930s to 156,000 by the war's end. Nationwide, the association witnessed record growth and by 1946 had nearly half a million members in roughly 1,000 branches.

See also RACE AND RACIAL CONFLICT.

Further reading: Walter Francis White, *A Man Called White: The Autobiography of Walter White* (New York: Viking, 1948); Robert L. Zangrando, *The NAACP Campaign against Lynching, 1909–1950* (Philadelphia: Temple University Press, 1980).

—Anthony Ratcliff

National Industrial Recovery Act (NIRA) (1933)

The National Industrial Recovery Act (NIRA), signed by President FRANKLIN D. ROOSEVELT on June 16, 1933, was the central industrial recovery measure of the FIRST NEW DEAL of 1933. Though unsuccessful in lifting the ECONOMY out of the GREAT DEPRESSION, it did help to energize LABOR union organization, led to a reduction in child labor, and eventually underwrote major public works projects that strengthened the nation's infrastructure.

The legislation had multiple origins and many authors. The War Industries Board of World War I was a significant precursor. The NIRA drew on ideas from businessmen on how to avoid excessive competition and ensure stability by agreeing on production limits, prices, and other matters. Some labor leaders saw in such arrangements a way to safeguard wages and employment. Roosevelt's BRAIN TRUST had advocated planning and controls involving BUSINESS to address the depression. General HUGH S. JOHNSON, a former member of the War Industries Board, and New York senator ROBERT F. WAGNER, a liberal and an advocate of labor, played an especially important role in drafting the final legislation. Johnson felt that destructive competition was a central factor in the collapse of the economy and supported the principle of business self-regulation, while Wagner insisted upon provisions for labor's rights.

Title I of the NIRA authorized business and GOVERNMENT to create codes of fair competition regarding production quotas, prices, wages, and labor standards in an attempt to stabilize the market and prevent unfair competition. It also created the NATIONAL RECOVERY ADMINISTRATION (NRA), which would be led by Hugh Johnson and would oversee the formation and administration of the codes. The NIRA gave participating businesses exemption from antitrust laws and the NRA had power to license corporations. Section 7(a) of the NIRA provided for the right of workers to organize and bargain collectively as well as authorizing establishing maximum hours and minimum wages.

Title II of the NIRA established the PUBLIC WORKS ADMINISTRATION (PWA) and appropriated $3.3 billion dollars to fund the agency. Headed by HAROLD L. ICKES, the PWA was to stimulate the economy by means of public works projects and provide employment opportunities on the projects. The NIRA also included TAXATION on capital stock and excess profits to help finance public works spending.

The NIRA failed to bring about economic recovery. Especially at first, the PWA spent money too slowly to make much difference, and the NRA codes were unable to stimulate investment or expansion. The NRA proved increasingly unpopular as well as unsuccessful. Many businessmen resented government regulations, labor representatives were unhappy about the lack of enforcement of Section 7(a), consumers complained about high prices, and defenders of small business claimed that the codes promoted monopoly. Troubles for the NIRA culminated with the unanimous SUPREME COURT decision of May 1935 in *SCHECHTER POULTRY CORPORATION V. UNITED STATES* declaring the NIRA unconstitutional. Despite its denouement, however, the NIRA was one of the major NEW DEAL measures.

Further reading: Ellis W. Hawley, *The New Deal and the Problem of Monopoly* (Princeton, N.J.: Princeton University Press, 1966); Robert F. Himmelberg, *The Origins of* *the National Recovery Administration: Business, Government, and the Trade Association Issue, 1921–1933* (New York: Fordham University Press, 1976).

—Courtney D. Mattingly

National Labor Relations Act (NLRA) (1935)

The National Labor Relations Act (often called the Wagner Act, after its chief author, New York Democratic senator ROBERT F. WAGNER) was passed by CONGRESS in June 1935, and signed into law by President FRANKLIN D. ROOSEVELT on July 5, 1935. Often called the "Magna Carta" of organized labor, the NLRA was the most significant piece of LABOR rights legislation ever passed in the United States and enabled large-scale unionization of American industry over the next decade.

Although Section 7(a) of the 1933 NATIONAL INDUSTRIAL RECOVERY ACT of the NEW DEAL guaranteed collective bargaining, the National Labor Board established under the NATIONAL RECOVERY ADMINISTRATION had little enforcement power. Senator Wagner, a member of the NLB, introduced legislation in May 1934 to create a new board with enhanced enforcement powers in labor-management relations, including preventing acts of coercion by employers and requiring business to negotiate with union representatives. President Roosevelt, hopeful for management's cooperation with NRA and fearful of losing BUSINESS support over a stricter labor bill, asked Wagner to put his legislation aside and back a resolution allowing the president to create a new National Labor Relations Board. Wagner agreed to Roosevelt's request, despite opposition from progressive Republicans, and a new NLRB was created in June 1934.

Wagner was not satisfied, however, and he introduced a revised labor bill in February 1935 that would give a new NLRB the right to hold elections to determine union representatives and to define and prohibit specified unfair labor practices. It would also grant the NLRB legal power to enforce its decisions. Hearings were held before Wagner's Labor Committee in March, as the National Association of Manufacturers, U.S. Chamber of Commerce, and other pro-business groups testified against the bill, while labor representatives spoke in favor of the legislation. The Roosevelt administration, however, remained silent as Wagner almost single-handedly moved his bill through Congress, while neither the president, nor Secretary of Labor FRANCES PERKINS, nor NRA officials endorsed the legislation. Under Wagner's leadership, the Labor Committee unanimously reported out the bill on May 2. Southern Democrats, no friends of organized labor, asked Roosevelt to delay a final Senate vote, but Wagner convinced the president not to stall action on the legislation. On May 15, Wagner brought the labor bill to the Senate floor, where it was approved 63-12, after a pro-business amendment was defeated.

On May 27, the SUPREME COURT declared the National Industrial Recovery Act—and its Section 7(a)—unconstitutional, and Roosevelt reconsidered his earlier nonsupport of the labor bill. By mid-June, the House of Representatives had the legislation, with southern Democrats and business groups leading the opposition and liberal northern Democrats and the AFL leading support. On June 19, the House passed the bill. Eight days later, a House-Senate conference report approved the legislation, and Roosevelt signed the Wagner Bill on July 5.

The National Labor Relations Act was the most sweeping piece of workers legislation in American history. The act established the NATIONAL LABOR RELATIONS BOARD as a permanent, independent agency empowered to conduct elections to determine union representation, and restrain business from committing unfair labor practices, such as fostering company unions, discharging workers for union membership, and engaging in anti-union espionage, blacklisting, strikebreaking, yellow-dog contracts, or discrimination in wages. As with other New Deal legislation, the Wagner Act's constitutionality was tested in the courts, and on April 12, 1937, by a 5-4 decision, the Supreme Court, in *National Labor Relations Board v. Jones and Laughlin Steel Corporation,* upheld the NLRA in ruling that Congress had broad authority to regulate labor-management conflicts that affected interstate commerce.

The act's impact on union activity was apparent by 1940, as roughly 9 million workers were union members in the United States, three times the 1933 membership of some 3 million. The National Labor Relations Act, enacted at a critical time for American labor, provided legal and political protection for worker organization and contributed to a striking rise in union membership and power. Although the National Labor Relations Act has been amended subsequently, the fundamental features of the law still shape union organization and activities.

See also AMERICAN FEDERATION OF LABOR; CONGRESS OF INDUSTRIAL ORGANIZATIONS; *SCHECHTER POULTRY CORPORATION V. UNITED STATES.*

Further reading: Irving Bernstein, *The Turbulent Years: A History of the American Worker, 1933–1941* (Boston: Houghton Mifflin, 1970); J. Joseph Huthmacher, *Senator Robert F. Wagner and the Rise of Urban Liberalism* (New York: Atheneum, 1968).

—William J. Thompson

National Labor Relations Board (NLRB)

The National Labor Relations Board (NLRB) was established with passage of the NATIONAL LABOR RELATIONS

ACT (NLRA) of 1935, also known as the Wagner Act, during the SECOND NEW DEAL. The NLRB was intended to administer the NLRA's provisions that guaranteed workers' right to organize into independent unions to practice collective bargaining and that prohibited unfair labor practices by employers. The creation of the NLRB as a permanent, independent agency to protect the rights of workers and unions was a pivotal event in the history of American LABOR. Amendments to the NLRA in later years changed the duties of the NLRB to monitor unfair labor practices by unions and to restrict the involvement of COMMUNISTS.

The NLRB succeeded ineffectual agencies set up to monitor Section 7(a) of the NATIONAL INDUSTRIAL RECOVERY ACT (NIRA) of 1933, which provided for labor's right to collective bargaining and required employers to participate in good faith in such bargaining. These agencies (the National Labor Board, established in 1933, and the first version of a National Labor Relations Board, set up in 1934) had no real enforcement power. When the SUPREME COURT declared the NIRA, including section 7(a), uncon-

stitutional, CONGRESS passed the NLRA, and the new NLRB was created as a permanent, independent, quasijudicial agency.

The three-member NLRB had three major functions. Its first was to hold employee elections for the selection of union representation and to certify the unions winning a majority of the vote. Second, it reviewed charges and conducted hearings when necessary to determine whether management had violated the act by engaging in unfair labor practices, defined as employer conduct interfering with the right of employees to bargain collectively. The third function assigned to the NLRB was the authority to issue cease and desist orders against violators of the NLRA and also to take "affirmative action, including reinstatement of employees" in order to further enforce the act's provisions.

The NLRB had reduced responsibilities during WORLD WAR II, when the NATIONAL WAR LABOR BOARD had principal authority over labor relations. President FRANKLIN D. ROOSEVELT also appointed more conservative members to the NLRB during the war. With the passage

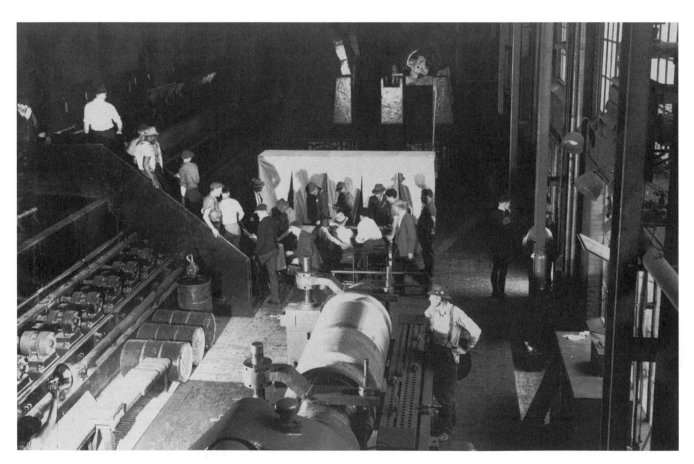

Shown here is a National Labor Relations Board election for union representation at the River Rouge Ford plant. *(Library of Congress)*

of the Taft-Hartley Act in 1947, union power was weakened as the NLRB's powers were extended to cover union practices considered unfair to employers, including the use of secondary boycotts and jurisdictional strikes. The Taft-Hartley Act also required union chiefs to file affidavits proving that they were not communists in order to obtain a hearing before the new five-member NLRB, a requirement repealed by the Landrum-Griffin Act of 1959.

In its early years, critics on the right complained that the NLRB sided with labor over management and with the CONGRESS OF INDUSTRIAL ORGANIZATIONS over the AMERICAN FEDERATION OF LABOR. Later, critics from the left often charged the NLRB with curbing union independence; widening the definition of workers not protected by the NLRA, which included agricultural and domestic employees; and being biased against labor, especially after the passage of the Taft-Hartley Act. But clearly the passage of the NLRA and the creation of the NLRB were crucial for the growth of organized labor and its power by affirming and protecting the rights of workers to organize and join unions.

Further reading: James A. Gross, *The Making of the National Labor Relations Board, 1933–1937* (Albany: State University of New York Press, 1974); ———, *The Reshaping of the National Labor Relations Board: National Labor Policy in Transition, 1937–1947* (Albany: State University of New York Press, 1981).

—Aimee Alice Pohl

National Recovery Administration (NRA)

Created by Title I of the NATIONAL INDUSTRIAL RECOVERY ACT (NIRA) of June 16, 1933, the National Recovery Administration (NRA) was one of the cornerstone agencies of the so-called FIRST NEW DEAL of 1933. It sought to lift the industrial sector of the ECONOMY out of the GREAT DEPRESSION by means of cartel-like agreements on production, prices, wages, and labor in various industries. Although the NRA proved unable to produce economic expansion, became increasingly unpopular, and was declared unconstitutional by the SUPREME COURT in 1935, it was nonetheless one of the important programs of the NEW DEAL.

Ideas leading to the NRA came from several sources. BUSINESS had long understood that agreements on prices and production limits might bring stability to an industry by eliminating price-cutting and overproduction, and trade associations in the 1920s had advocated exemption from antitrust laws to enable industry-wide production and marketing policies. The War Industries Board of World War I had involved production agreements worked out by GOVERNMENT and business organizations. A segment of LIBER-

Shown here is the logo of the National Recovery Administration (NRA), a New Deal Agency. *(New York Public Library)*

ALISM going back to the Progressive Era embraced economic concentration, with government planning and controls to make it more efficient and equitable. During the depression, a number of LABOR leaders, especially in the most troubled industries, believed that agreements on production and prices might stabilize employment and wages. The BRAIN TRUST of President FRANKLIN D. ROOSEVELT inclined toward accepting large organizations and planned economic activities as an approach to the depression. Such ideas sometimes differed considerably. Business wanted self-regulation approved by the government, for example, while such liberals as REXFORD G. TUGWELL wanted thoroughgoing government planning and controls over business. But these various approaches had in common some version of national planning to stabilize the industrial sector of the economy and produce expansion and recovery.

General HUGH S. JOHNSON, who had served on the War Industries Board and preferred the business self-government approach, was NRA's first administrator and together with New York senator ROBERT F. WAGNER had played a role in drafting the National Industrial Recovery Act. The NIRA suspended the antitrust laws for two years so that industrial organizations could draft, in conjunction with labor and consumer representatives as well as with government officials, codes of fair competition on prices, production, wages, and labor conditions. The complicated legislation was nearer to the business self-regulation than it was to the government-control model, but it did require presidential approval of codes and the government could impose codes when an industry did not come to agreement. In return for labor support, Section 7(a) of the NIRA authorized labor's right to organize and bargain collectively.

Johnson, a hard-drinking, mercurial, colorful figure, launched an aggressive publicity effort and conducted a frenetic "We Do Our Part" campaign to get industries to cooperate in approving codes—and winning the NRA Blue Eagle emblem. Until specific industry codes were approved, he asked employers to sign a "blanket code" with minimum, maximum hours, and the end of child labor, and he urged consumers to deal only with businesses displaying the Blue Eagle. Eventually, 541 hastily written codes were approved, many in industries where the codes were unnecessary, irrelevant, or simply not worth the time and effort. Other industries involved codes that seemed almost impossibly complicated and often inconsistent. A large bureaucracy inevitably emerged.

After an initial "NRA boom," caused largely by manufacturers trying to beat the implementation of the codes, industrial production briefly turned down again, and the NRA did little to stimulate economic expansion. Probably it did help arrest the economy's downward spiral, but it did not provide impetus for recovery, for it was restrictionist rather than expansionist. Prices were set too high to increase buying (and thus production and employment), while production quotas gave no incentive for businesses to cut costs, improve products, and create new demand. Moreover, the PUBLIC WORKS ADMINISTRATION, a companion agency created by the NIRA to pump money into the economy, spent too slowly to have any real economic stimulus. The NRA did, however, make significant progress in reducing child labor and increasing labor organization.

A failure at achieving recovery, NRA also became more and more unpopular. Business and conservatives increasingly disliked government regulation and bureaucracy. Liberals, labor, consumers, and small business thought big business and trade associations had too much say in drafting and implementing the codes. Small business and liberals believed that the NRA codes fostered and protected monopoly. Consumers, labor, and liberals thought prices too high. Labor was unhappy with employers for evading Section 7(a) and with Johnson and the NRA for not enforcing it. In 1934, Roosevelt prevailed upon Johnson to resign, but no improvement came in results or acceptance.

By 1935, the NRA seemed an unpopular failure, and its future was questionable. In May, in the case of *SCHECHTER POULTRY CORPORATION V. UNITED STATES,* the Supreme Court found the NIRA (and thus the NRA) unconstitutional for exceeding the power of the federal government by regulating intrastate commerce and for wrongly delegating legislative authority to the executive branch in the code-making process. The NRA was termi-

nated in 1936, though "little NRAs" were established in coal and some other industries in transportation, natural resources and service, and the NATIONAL LABOR RELATIONS ACT replaced and greatly expanded Section 7(a). The failure of the NRA led the New Deal to turn to other approaches at economic recovery, reform, and regulation.

Further reading: Bernard Bellush, *The Failure of the NRA* (New York: Norton, 1975); Ellis W. Hawley, *The New Deal and the Problem of Monopoly* (Princeton, N.J.: Princeton University Press, 1966).

National Resources Planning Board (NRPB)

The National Resources Planning Board (NRPB) was created under the provisions of the EXECUTIVE REORGANIZATION ACT of 1939. The successor to the 1933–34 National Planning Board, the 1934–35 National Resources Board, and the 1935–39 National Resources Committee, the NRPB reflected the desire of President FRANKLIN D. ROOSEVELT to enhance the policy planning and coordination capacity of the PRESIDENCY as part of the NEW DEAL. The NRPB developed a far-reaching liberal postwar program for the nation, though one that found little support among the public and much opposition in CONGRESS, which killed the agency in 1943.

The several predecessors of the NRPB had been concerned especially about the nation's resources, especially land and water resources. The NRPB quickly took on a far larger agenda, and building on some of the work of the National Resources Committee focused more broadly on social and economic conditions and policy. With the beginning of WORLD WAR II in Europe in 1939, the NRPB became the Roosevelt administration's principal agency for domestic POSTWAR PLANNING, and it produced a series of wide-ranging studies and reports.

Most important among the NRPB's reports were two that Roosevelt transmitted to Congress in March 1943 and that embodied the development of liberal policy ideas in the late 1930s and early 1940s. The first, *Security, Work, and Relief Policies,* which had largely been completed by December 1940, was based primarily on late 1930s fears of a chronically depressed ECONOMY with high levels of UNEMPLOYMENT. It called especially for comprehensive expansion of government public assistance, work RELIEF, and social insurance programs to ensure minimal economic security for all Americans.

The second, more important, and more recently developed report, *Post-War Plan and Program,* reflected the remarkable wartime expansion of the economy and the related acceptance by liberals of KEYNESIANISM, which stressed the importance of government fiscal policy for economic prosperity. This second report called for the

GOVERNMENT to ensure full employment in a "dynamic expanding economy" with "increasingly higher standards of living." It also contained the basis of the ECONOMIC BILL OF RIGHTS that Roosevelt would propose in 1944. Together, the two reports urged a much-enlarged government role in ensuring full-employment prosperity, rising living standards, and economic security.

Though reflecting expansive new wartime hopes and aims of LIBERALISM, the NRPB reports generated little support among an indifferent public enjoying wartime prosperity and focusing on the war. Rather, the reports encountered active opposition in the CONSERVATIVE COALITION that controlled the Congress after the election of 1942. As a result, the NRPB reports stood no real chance of implementation, were buried by Congress, and quickly faded from public view. Congress, as part of its effort to curb the power of the executive branch and to roll back New Deal programs that seemed unnecessary or vulnerable, terminated the agency a few months after its two landmark reports were made public.

Despite its relatively short career, however, the NRPB was an important agency. Its recommendations reflected the changing liberal program of the war years, especially the new importance of Keynesian fiscal policy to underwrite full-employment prosperity. Its demise reflected the more conservative atmosphere on the WORLD WAR II HOMEFRONT and the augmented power of conservatives in Congress. And although its proposals generally went unfulfilled in the short run, it provided an agenda for postwar liberalism and played a significant role in the development of the GI BILL OF RIGHTS enacted in 1944 and of the FULL EMPLOYMENT BILL proposed in 1945.

Further reading: Patrick D. Reagan, *Designing a New America: The Origins of New Deal Planning, 1890–1943* (Amherst: University of Massachusetts Press, 1999); Philip W. Warken, *A History of the National Resources Planning Board, 1933–1943* (New York: Garland, 1979).

National War Labor Board (NWLB)

One of a number of agencies created by the federal GOVERNMENT to mobilize the nation and its ECONOMY during WORLD WAR II, the National War Labor Board (NWLB) was established by President FRANKLIN D. ROOSEVELT in January 1942. Replacing the ineffective and shortlived National Defense Mediation Board, the 12-member board was composed equally of representatives from BUSINESS, LABOR, and the public and was directed to settle labor disputes in order to prevent disruption of the war effort. Other agencies with responsibility for labor included the WAR MANPOWER COMMISSION, created in April 1942 to ensure the efficient allocation of workers to necessary jobs,

and the NATIONAL LABOR RELATIONS BOARD, which had been established in 1935 to protect workers' rights to organize and bargain collectively.

In 1941, as MOBILIZATION brought increased industrial production, demands by workers for higher pay led to a wave of strikes around the nation. Soon after American entry into the war, in recognition of the need to curtail such disruptions of the war effort, Roosevelt helped negotiate a no-strike, no-lockout agreement between management and the two largest labor organizations, the AMERICAN FEDERATION OF LABOR (AFL) and the CONGRESS OF INDUSTRIAL ORGANIZATIONS (CIO). This pledge deprived the labor movement of its most powerful weapon, the strike, and placed workers' gains in the hands of the NWLB, which was empowered to impose binding agreements between labor and management. The NWLB was also given authority to recommend the government takeover of plants involved in work stoppages due to strikes or lockouts.

In an effort to slow inflation in 1942, the Roosevelt administration began to implement WAGE AND PRICE CONTROLS through caps on price increases by the OFFICE OF PRICE ADMINISTRATION. In a companion measure to keep wages from rising too quickly, and also in an attempt to resolve conflicts over pay, the NWLB established in July what became known as the "Little Steel" formula. Worked out to settle disputes in smaller steel companies but then applied broadly, the formula allowed for wage increases in accord with the rise in the cost of living between January 1941 and May 1942. This Little Steel formula was used to resolve pay disputes for the duration of the war and was a key part of the effort to combat inflation. Although workers' wages consistently rose less than farm income and corporate profits, the cap did not apply to overtime and incentive pay, job upgrades, and benefits, and workers' compensation and spending power did rise significantly during the war. And despite inevitable inequities and inefficiencies, the policy was generally successful.

Even as the no-strike pledge and wage controls placed a double burden on the labor movement's power, unions received what most considered an enormous bounty in June 1942 when the NWLB instituted the "maintenance of membership" rule. The maintenance of membership policy stipulated that every new worker hired into a place of employment with a union contract would automatically become a member of the union unless making a specific request to the contrary within 15 days of being hired. Additionally, the employer was required to collect union dues and to dismiss any employee who did not pay his or her dues and maintain good standing in the union. The rule kept nonunion workers from flooding war plants and reversing the gains of the strong union movement of the 1930s and contributed to a nearly 50 percent growth in union membership during the war.

Although most labor leaders were anxious to maintain a good relationship with the government and a positive image in the public eye in order to keep the gains they had won, including the maintenance of membership rule, not all leaders or workers were content to give up their bargaining power, and they continued to use strikes as a weapon. And some criticized the maintenance of membership rule as part of a general decline of the labor movement's independence. At the same time, many workers had real grievances that remained unresolved by the NWLB. The year 1943 saw a large increase over 1942 in the number of work stoppages, including strikes by miners led by United Mine Workers head JOHN L. LEWIS. These labor disturbances in the midst of the war were perceived as unpatriotic by many and helped lead to public support for an anti-union backlash, including the anti-labor Smith-Connally Act passed by CONGRESS in 1943.

During its tenure the National War Labor Board was an important force in labor relations, and was an example of the extended power of the executive branch in the nation's economy. It imposed some 20,000 wage-dispute settlements affecting 20 million workers and approved more than 4,000 wage agreements. The government took over several dozen plants shut down by labor disputes. Additionally, the NWLB had a policy mandating that women and minority workers receive equal pay for equal work. Although this was only rarely enforced, the idea continued in other government agencies and government guidelines. The NWLB was dissolved at the end of the war.

Further reading: Howell John Harris, *The Right to Manage: Industrial Relations Policies of American Business in the 1940s* (Madison: University of Wisconsin Press, 1982); James A. Gross, *The Reshaping of the National Labor Relations Board: National Labor Policy in Transition, 1937–1947* (Albany: State University of New York Press, 1981); Nelson Lichtenstein, *Labor's War at Home: The CIO in World War II* (New York: Cambridge University Press, 1982).

—Aimee Alice Pohl

National Youth Administration (NYA)

On June 26, 1935, President FRANKLIN D. ROOSEVELT created the National Youth Administration (NYA), as part of the SECOND NEW DEAL's effort to provide work RELIEF. NYA provided part-time work, schooling, and vocational training for unemployed youths between 16 and 25 years of age, and aimed at keeping youths in school and out of the saturated employment market.

In 1933, the FEDERAL EMERGENCY RELIEF ADMINISTRATION (FERA) inaugurated NEW DEAL efforts to help young people, who had one of the highest UNEMPLOYMENT rates in the GREAT DEPRESSION, with a successful pilot student aid program. (The CIVILIAN CONSERVATION CORPS also provided work for young men.) With FERA being phased out in 1935, President Roosevelt established the NYA after such figures as ELEANOR ROOSEVELT and HARRY L. HOPKINS urged him to address the problem of youth unemployment. Originally part of the WORKS PROGRESS ADMINISTRATION (WPA), the NYA was transferred to the Federal Security Agency in 1939 and was placed under the WAR MANPOWER COMMISSION in 1942 until it ceased operations in 1943. Aubrey Williams, a southern liberal, served as NYA director.

The NYA put a majority of its resources into keeping youth out of the workforce by providing high school and college students part-time jobs so they could remain in school, finish their education, and become productive assets for the American economy. For high school and pre-college youth who went to college, the NYA provided apprenticeships or internships in areas including public planning and research and also cooperated with state and local agencies who filled available positions with NYA youths. "Learning by doing" became an NYA motto.

Williams saw the NYA college aid programs as shaking up the existing educational establishments by having the schools accept working- and middle-class unemployed students, who would receive NYA money to pay their college costs. To qualify for NYA assistance, students had to have a strong academic background and be able to carry at least three-quarters of the normal academic course load. Participating institutions were required to supervise the NYA students' academic progress. NYA students worked in such diverse areas as surveys and statistical work, ground and building maintenance, and library services. The NYA college program later became one model for GI BILL OF RIGHTS educational provisions.

Williams's interest in promoting racial equality led the NYA to establish a Division Office of Negro Affairs, with educator MARY MCLEOD BETHUNE as its director. She used her prominent government position and her leadership of the BLACK CABINET to lobby for more inclusion of AFRICAN AMERICANS in the New Deal. The NYA was one of the first federal agencies to have racially integrated programs, teaching African Americans skills necessary for employment in the industrial economy and creating a college aid program for black students. Blacks who participated in NYA-sponsored programs were later commended for their efforts in defense industries.

In 1936, less than a year after its beginning, the NYA enrolled about 600,000 young people. Its peak came in April 1937 with 630,000 youths; the lowest point was in October 1937 (after Roosevelt had cut relief spending, helping to bring on the RECESSION OF 1937–38) with 360,000 youths. By 1943, the NYA had provided assistance to over 2 million young people. NYA students were divided fairly equally between the sexes and were racially proportionate to the nation's population. Males often worked in construction and technical workshops, females in "socially useful work" including assisting in libraries, holding clerical positions, and serving as school aides.

As UNEMPLOYMENT declined in the early 1940s because of the beginning stages of MOBILIZATION for WORLD WAR II, NYA programs shifted away from EDUCATION and toward vocational training for defense industry. Williams received high praise for his foresight and his contribution to the war effort, and student trainees, including blacks and females, were quickly hired in their vocational fields as positions became available. Student programs not involving the war effort were almost all dropped by 1942; and to trim federal expenditures and roll back New Deal relief programs, Congress terminated the NYA in 1943, deeming it no longer essential. But during its tenure, the NYA provided valuable financial assistance, education, and vocational training to young people and contributed to the pool of workers as the nation emerged from the Great Depression.

See also CHILDREN.

Further reading: Richard A. Reiman, *The New Deal and American Youth: Ideas and Ideals in a Depression Decade* (Athens: University of Georgia Press, 1992).

—Anne Rothfield

Native Americans

Despite efforts to ameliorate the poverty and isolation of Native Americans during the GREAT DEPRESSION and WORLD WAR II, conditions for the most part did not significantly improve. But in the longer run, the period provided new experiences and important changes in GOVERNMENT policy that laid the groundwork for later grassroots mobilization for CIVIL RIGHTS.

Native Americans in the United States made up a diverse group (approximately 170 distinct tribes, bands, or peoples) who lived mainly west of the Mississippi River, especially in Oklahoma, Arizona, and the upper Great Plains. The population, which had been declining since the first European contacts, began to experience growth after 1900 (237,000 in 1900; 366,000 in 1940). Different languages, cultures, and tribal rivalries had combined with the impact of federal policy to leave Native Americans isolated, internally fractured, and often living in desperate poverty.

The federal government had established reservations for Native Americans in the 19th century, and under the Dawes Severalty Act of 1887, reservation Indians were considered wards of the government, overseen by the Bureau

of Indian Affairs (BIA). The Dawes Act guided federal policy toward Native Americans into the 1930s, a policy sometimes called "coercive assimilation" for its emphasis on teaching American values such as individualism and private property through boarding schools for children and individual land allotments. The only significant change in federal policy between the 1880s and 1930s came when CONGRESS bestowed United States citizenship on Native Americans in 1924.

By the 1920s, a growing number of social reformers were denouncing assimilation policy as a failure. A significant 1928 Brookings Institution report, *The Problems of Indian Administration,* called on the federal government and the BIA to reject that approach in order better to address the economic, educational, and social needs of Native Americans. Economic and social indicators provided glaring proof that assimilation had indeed failed to help Native Americans. By the time of the Great Depression, more than half of all reservation Indians were landless (many had sold or rented their land allotments to white neighbors); more than half had incomes of under $200 per year; infant mortality was three times that of white Americans; and crime and alcoholism on reservations were well above the national averages. Native Americans were the most impoverished ethnic group in the United States, with overall poverty rates higher than those of AFRICAN AMERICANS in the SOUTH.

Reform of Indian policy was accomplished during the NEW DEAL under Secretary of the Interior HAROLD L. ICKES and the Commissioner of Indian Affairs John Collier. Collier especially had become a vocal critic of federal Indian policy during the 1920s, and with Ickes's support proposed what has been called the "Indian New Deal." The centerpiece was the INDIAN REORGANIZATION ACT of 1934, which aimed to restore self-government and cultural pride to Native Americans and ended land allotment. While only 71 tribes elected to participate in the act and it generally failed to achieve its goals, the seeds of self-government begun by the experience would be a precedent for Native American organization in later decades.

The New Deal also brought various RELIEF and work programs to the reservations. The CIVILIAN CONSERVATION CORPS (which had an Indian Division) and the WORKS PROGRESS ADMINISTRATION provided employment and agricultural improvements on reservations, and the PUBLIC WORKS ADMINISTRATION built much-needed new school and hospital facilities. The Indian boarding schools, the hated symbol of assimilation policy for most Native Americans, were gradually replaced by new day schools, with Collier giving preference to Native American teachers and trying to implement a more Indian-centered curriculum. And although the poverty rates among Native Americans did not significantly improve, the "Indian New Deal"

Two of the Navajo code talkers in World War II
(National Archives)

did bring desperately needed social services to reservations and at least stabilized their economic circumstances.

As it did for many other ethnic groups, World War II brought new opportunities for Native Americans. Some, including not only the well-known Navajo but also Hopi, Choctaws, and Cherokees, were "code talkers" for the military. Using their native languages, they made military messages unintelligible to AXIS code breakers. But Native American participation in the war was much broader than just the code talkers. About 25,000 Native Americans served in the armed forces, while another 40,000 found employment in defense work, migrating especially to the Los Angeles and San Francisco areas. The war provided the first major experience for many young Native Americans in the larger American culture.

During World War II, Native Americans also began efforts at organizing across tribal lines. With Collier's support, the National Congress of American Indians (NCAI) was created in 1944. Initially formed by major Oklahoma tribes, particularly the Cherokee, the NCAI became the leading intertribal political organization, lobbying for Indian rights and trying to dispel stereotypes about Native Americans.

The experience of Native Americans from 1929 through 1945 provided significant new departures. The Indian Reorganization Act and Collier's leadership reversed (at least temporarily) assimilation policy. World War II brought many Native Americans off the reservations and initiated the first significant urban migration, particularly among the younger generation. But the poverty and isolation of many Native Americans were only marginally alleviated. After the war, the "Indian New Deal" was rolled back, with the federal government replacing it with the "termination" policy of the 1950s that paid a lump sum to tribes to sever the "ward" relationship with the federal government. But the 1929–45 period helped to plant the seeds for the later Pan-Indian movement to demand full civil and political rights for Native Americans.

Further reading: Alison R. Bernstein, *American Indians and World War II* (Norman: University of Oklahoma Press, 1991); Kenneth R. Philp, *John Collier's Crusade for Indian Reform, 1920–1954* (Tucson: University of Arizona Press, 1977); Graham D. Taylor, *The New Deal and American Indian Tribalism: The Administration of the Indian Reorganization Act, 1934–1945* (Lincoln: University of Nebraska Press, 1980).

—Katherine Liapis Segrue

Navy, U.S.

The U.S. Navy played a decisive role in WORLD WAR II, particularly in the PACIFIC THEATER where, in a series of engagements from the BATTLE OF THE CORAL SEA and the BATTLE OF MIDWAY in 1942 to the BATTLE OF THE PHILIPPINE SEA and the BATTLE FOR LEYTE GULF in 1944, it destroyed the Imperial Japanese Navy. The new importance of naval AIR POWER was an especially significant feature of the Pacific war. In the EUROPEAN THEATER as well as the Pacific theater, the navy also supported AMPHIBIOUS WARFARE operations, including the invasion of NORMANDY and the battles of IWO JIMA and OKINAWA. With the British Royal Navy, the U.S. Navy prevailed in the BATTLE OF THE ATLANTIC against German SUBMARINES.

During World War II, the Navy Department was directed by a civilian secretary of the navy comparable to the secretary of the army heading the U.S. ARMY and responsible to President FRANKLIN D. ROOSEVELT, the commander in chief. From July 1940 until his death in May 1944, W. Franklin "Frank" Knox was secretary of the navy. JAMES V. FORRESTAL replaced Knox. Below the secretary were a variety of navy bureaus, which administered the service, and a Navy Board, which advised civilian leaders. The navy's highest military commander was the chief of naval operations, a position held in 1939 by Admiral Harold R. Stark. The preponderance of the navy's strength then rested in the Pacific Fleet, the U.S. Navy's largest, led by the commander in chief, U.S. Fleet, based at Pearl Harbor, Hawaii. The United States also had a small Asiatic Fleet based in Manila, in the PHILIPPINES, and a much smaller Atlantic Squadron. In February 1941, the Atlantic Squadron was upgraded to become the Atlantic Fleet, and a true two-ocean navy was created, with the Atlantic Fleet led by Vice Admiral ERNEST J. KING and the Pacific Fleet commanded by Vice Admiral Husband E. Kimmel. Following the Japanese attack on PEARL HARBOR, when Admiral Stark moved to Europe to command U.S. naval forces in that theater, King merged the posts of commander in chief, U.S. Fleet, and chief of naval operations, and held both positions himself. King thus had unprecedented power over the navy bureaus and reported directly to the president.

The U.S. Navy organized seven separate fleets during World War II, and these operated continuously in every ocean, including the Mediterranean, and along the American coastline. Following the attack at Pearl Harbor, the U.S. Navy also took administrative control of the 170,000 member U.S. Coast Guard and 1,150 coast guard ships and boats. The strengths of the navy's fleets varied according to their primary duties. The 10th Fleet was in charge of antisubmarine warfare along the U.S. coasts, but had no ships. Other fleets were often combined into much larger and more powerful task forces for specific operations. During the invasion of the MARIANA ISLANDS in June and July 1944, for example, Task Force 58 commanded by Rear Admiral Marc Mitscher, consisted of eight battleships, 15 fleet carriers, 24 cruisers, and smaller supporting vessels.

At the outbreak of war in Europe in 1939, the U.S. Navy, like most other naval powers, was still oriented toward capital ships, of which it had 15 of varying ages, most dating from the World War I era. In addition to its battleships, the navy also possessed five aircraft carriers, 18 heavy cruisers, 19 light cruisers, 61 submarines, and a variety of smaller craft including destroyers, patrol-torpedo boats, and gunboats; together, these totaled approximately 1,099 vessels, manned by 125,000 sailors. Thanks to SHIPBUILDING programs initiated in the 1930s, and especially in July 1940, the U.S. Navy was undergoing a major expansion by the time of the attack on Pearl Harbor in December 1941. That attack devastated the battleship fleet and hastened the new emphasis on aircraft carriers and air power. Between July 1, 1940, and August 31, 1945, the U.S. Navy, supported by the nation's remarkable shipbuilding program, completed or acquired an astounding 92,000 ships, boats, and craft of all varieties. In this total were 66,000 landing ships and landing craft, plus some 1,300 ships larger than destroyer escorts, including 138 aircraft carriers, 111 of which were escort carriers. The U.S. Navy lost through all causes, 157 ships, including submarines, destroyers, and larger vessels.

The U.S. Navy, like the army and U.S. MARINES, controlled its own air force, including carrier-based fighters, dive bombers, and torpedo bombers, as well as land-based patrol craft. Naval aviation grew tremendously between July 1940 and August 1945 as more than 75,000 aircraft were delivered; naval air personnel rose from 10,923, of whom 2,965 were pilots, to 437,524 personnel, of whom 60,747 were pilots.

The navy as a whole expanded from 161,000 personnel in 1940 to more than 3,400,000 in August 1945, including aviators but not counting the nearly half million marines. At the beginning of the war, AFRICAN AMERICANS could serve in the navy only as messmen; but during the war, the navy began using blacks not only in service and labor positions but also, in some cases, as radiomen, gunners' mates, and in other capacities. Particularly after racial unrest in 1944 arising from its treatment of black sailors, the navy also took steps toward desegregation. U.S. Navy casualties between December 7, 1941, and September 2, 1945, numbered approximately 37,000 killed and 38,000 wounded.

Further reading: Nathan Miller, *War at Sea: A Naval History of World War II* (New York: Scribner's, 1995); Samuel Eliot Morrison, *The Two-Ocean War: A Short History of the United States Navy in the Second World War* (Boston: Little, Brown, 1963); Ronald Spector, *Eagle against the Sun: The American War with Japan* (New York: Free Press, 1985).

—Clayton D. Laurie

Nazi-Soviet Pact (1939)

On August 23, 1939, the Soviet Union signed a nonaggression treaty with Nazi Germany. The Nazi-Soviet Pact gave Germany assurance it could attack Poland without fear of a Soviet military response—and barely more than a week later the German invasion of Poland began WORLD WAR II in Europe. The agreement also reflected important concerns that would continue to shape Soviet foreign policy during the war and after, including the Soviet Union's alienation from the United States and the other western democracies, its fear of Germany, and its territorial aspirations in eastern and northern Europe.

The treaty came as a shocking blow to many COMMUNISTS and others in the United States and elsewhere who had seen the Soviet Union as leading the opposition to Nazi Germany (though some lauded it as a brilliant piece of statecraft that saved the Soviet Union from attack). After signing the agreement, the Soviets abandoned the POPU-LAR FRONT effort to work with liberals against fascism. Increasing American suspicions of the Soviet Union, the Nazi-Soviet Pact contributed to troubled SOVIET-AMERI-CAN RELATIONS during and after World War II.

The nonaggression treaty between Germany and the Soviet Union reflected the circumstances, concerns, and calculations of German führer Adolf Hitler and Soviet premier Joseph Stalin. As Hitler planned his invasion of western Poland, which seemed certain to bring declarations of war from England and France, he feared provoking conflict also with the Soviet Union and having to fight a major war on two fronts. Stalin knew that his military was not ready for war with Germany, and he believed that Britain, France, and the United States would not come to the support of the Soviet Union. In addition, Stalin had his eyes on territories in eastern Poland, the Baltic states (Latvia, Lithuania, and Estonia), Finland, and Romania that had been part of the prerevolutionary Russian Empire.

Following several months of negotiations (while the Soviets were also talking with Britain and France about an alliance against Germany), Germany and the Soviet Union announced their nonaggression treaty on August 23, 1939. The pact included secret protocols that divided Poland between the two powers and allotted the Soviets spheres of influence in the Baltic states, Bessarabia (then part of Romania), and Finland. On September 1, 1939, Germany invaded Poland, and World War II officially began with the resulting declaration of war against Germany by Britain and France. The Soviet Union then seized the eastern part of Poland, invaded Finland later in the fall to take territorial and other concessions there, and annexed Bessarabia and the Baltic states in the summer of 1940.

After Germany abrogated the nonaggression treaty and attacked the Soviet Union in June 1941, the United States and Great Britain gave support to the Soviet Union that paved the way for the wartime GRAND ALLIANCE of the United States, Great Britain, and the Soviet Union against Germany. But the 1939 Nazi-Soviet Pact, a disturbing treaty that reinforced American suspicions of the Soviet Union, and the subsequent Soviet seizure of territory contributed to tensions within the Grand Alliance during the war. Soviet territorial aspirations evident in the secret protocols, and especially the issue of Poland, played a major role in the unraveling of the Grand Alliance and the onset of the cold war.

Further reading: Robert Dallek, *Franklin D. Roosevelt and American Foreign Policy, 1932–1945* (New York: Oxford University Press, 1979); Anthony Read and David Fisher, *The Deadly Embrace: Hitler, Stalin and the Nazi-Soviet Pact, 1939–1941* (New York: Norton, 1988).

Nelson, Donald M. (1888–1959)

After a successful career with Sears, Roebuck, Donald Marr Nelson headed the WAR PRODUCTION BOARD (WPB) during the economic MOBILIZATION for WORLD WAR II.

Nelson was born in Hannibal, Missouri, on November 17, 1888. After graduating from the University of Missouri with a B.S. degree in chemical engineering in 1911, Nelson became a chemist for Sears, Roebuck and Company in 1912. Made manager of the men's and boys' clothing department in 1921, he was promoted to head of merchandising in 1928, and in 1939 was appointed executive vice president and chairman of the executive committee.

Because of his business experience, his wide-ranging contacts gained through his work at Sears, and his support of President FRANKLIN D. ROOSEVELT and NEW DEAL policies, Nelson was asked to serve in several positions in defense mobilization agencies. He first came to Washington as one of the DOLLAR-A-YEAR MEN in 1940 to coordinate purchasing for the National Defense Advisory Committee and then headed the Division of Purchases of the OFFICE OF PRODUCTION MANAGEMENT (January 1941–January 1942) and the Supply, Priorities, and Allocations Board (July 1941–January 1942).

On January 16, 1942, FDR replaced the Office of Production Management with the WPB and named Nelson as chairman. The WPB's purpose was to oversee procurement, allocation, and production in the economic mobilization for war. However, Nelson was indecisive, lacked full authority over manpower and LABOR issues, and did not respond effectively to the military's refusal to surrender the power to control procurement and contracts. In the summer of 1944, Nelson battled unsuccessfully with military officials and big war contractors with respect to his program for limited RECONVERSION to civilian production. Nelson favored gradual reconversion as war production needs declined, so as to sustain full employment, while the large war contractors feared that competitors might get a head start on peacetime production and markets and the military opposed any reduction of war production capacity. Nelson resigned and went to China as the president's personal representative to discuss economic problems.

After the war ended, Nelson returned to private business. He died of a stroke in Los Angeles in 1959.

Further reading: Donald Marr Nelson, *Arsenal of Democracy: The Story of American War Production* (New York: Harcourt Brace, 1946).

—Michael T. Walsh

Neutrality Acts (1935–1941)

The Neutrality Acts were a series of laws passed by CONGRESS in 1935, 1936, and 1937, and then revised in

1939 and 1941, for the purpose of preventing American involvement in wars outside the Western Hemisphere. Sentiment for such legislation had been building since the 1920s because of an adverse reaction to U.S. participation in World War I and the subsequent rise of isolationist thinking in public opinion and FOREIGN POLICY. In response to pressure from peace groups seeking investigations into munitions makers and bankers, Congress established the NYE COMMITTEE in 1934 to probe corporate collusion in war.

In April 1935, Senator Gerald P. Nye, Republican of North Dakota and chairman of the Munitions Investigating Committee, introduced neutrality resolutions to restrict travel, loans, and export of arms by American citizens, businesses, and government. President FRANKLIN D. ROOSEVELT had encouraged neutrality legislation despite the opposition of Secretary of State CORDELL HULL, who was wary of bills being prepared by ISOLATIONISTS. After several months of debate, the Senate in August passed the Neutrality Act of 1935, which was signed by Roosevelt despite his strong preference for a discretionary arms embargo that would enable the president to help nations that had been attacked. The law imposed a mandatory arms embargo against any nation involved in armed conflict, prohibited the export of munitions without the government's permission, authorized the president to declare that Americans traveling on belligerents' ships did so at their own risk, restricted the use of U.S. ports by belligerent submarines, and established a munitions control board to license arms dealers.

Roosevelt invoked Neutrality Act provisions less than two months after passage when Italy invaded ETHIOPIA, and urged a "moral embargo" against each side, a request ignored as oil and other shipments to the Italians increased. In February 1936, Congress extended the act until May 1, 1937, keeping the arms embargo and now also prohibiting loans to belligerents. Roosevelt chose not to challenge the mandatory provisions of neutrality, fearing he might alienate the public, something he was unwilling to risk during an election year. When the SPANISH CIVIL WAR broke out in July 1936, Roosevelt urged a nondiscriminatory arms embargo against each side, which Congress enacted in January 1937.

With the 1936 Neutrality Act set to expire on May 1, 1937, congressional isolationists were determined to enact permanent legislation. Bills extending neutrality were introduced in both the Senate and House of Representatives, but were in disagreement over whether the president's authority to invoke cash-and-carry—permitting shipments of raw materials and nonmilitary items if paid for and carried in belligerents' ships—should be mandatory or discretionary. After a compromise was reached agreeing to the discretionary version, the Neutrality Act of 1937 was passed and signed by Roosevelt on May 1, 1937. The 1937 law made most of the 1935 act provisions ostensibly permanent, except for cash-and-carry, which would expire in 1939.

On January 4, 1939, Roosevelt told Congress that neutrality legislation "may actually give aid to an aggressor and deny it to a victim." Isolationists in Congress, however, wanted stricter legislation. When a compromise bill was introduced in March to revoke the arms embargo, noninterventionist senators in both parties killed the legislation. When Germany seized Czechoslovakia the same month, Roosevelt asked Congress to amend the 1937 law to eliminate the compulsory arms embargo. Attempts to eliminate the arms embargo in the House failed, and the Senate put off action until October, the month after WORLD WAR II began in Europe. Finally, on October 27, the Senate passed a revised neutrality bill as isolationists failed to keep the arms embargo provision in the legislation, and the House passed the bill in early November. Interventionist southern Democrats, though at odds with Roosevelt over NEW DEAL measures, helped secure passage of the bill. The Neutrality Act of 1939 lifted the arms embargo, but it retained cash-and-carry (which now applied to arms and munitions), continued the ban on loans to belligerents, and prohibited American vessels from transiting a broad "danger zone" that embraced most sea lanes to western European ports.

By the fall of 1941, with most of Europe in AXIS hands and Japan advancing on its neighbors in Asia, Roosevelt desired further changes in the neutrality laws, specifically to permit the arming of American merchant ships and allow them to transport goods to belligerent ports—and thus repeal the "carry" of cash-and-carry. (The "cash" part had been bypassed with congressional passage of the LEND-LEASE ACT enabling aid to Great Britain.) Despite opposition from the isolationist bloc, especially the AMERICA FIRST COMMITTEE, Congress passed a revised neutrality bill in November. The Neutrality Act of 1941 permitted the arming of American merchant vessels and allowed transportation of cargo to belligerent ports. Despite the alterations of 1939 and 1941, the Neutrality Act of 1937 remained in force until PEARL HARBOR, just three weeks after the last revisions, when the United States itself became a belligerent in World War II.

Further reading: Wayne S. Cole, *Roosevelt and the Isolationists, 1932–1945* (Lincoln: University of Nebraska Press, 1983); Robert A. Divine, *The Illusion of Neutrality* (Chicago: University of Chicago Press, 1962).

—William J. Thompson

New Deal

In accepting the Democratic nomination for president in 1932, FRANKLIN D. ROOSEVELT declared that "I pledge you, I pledge myself, to a new deal for the American people." Just what that "new deal" entailed never became clear during the ELECTION OF 1932, but the two words quickly became the identifying term for Roosevelt's candidacy and then his presidency. The New Deal's plethora of new programs and "alphabet" agencies to meet the crisis of the GREAT DEPRESSION had an enormous impact on the American people, ECONOMY, and political system. The New Deal created the modern American regulatory welfare state; it greatly increased the size, power, and cost of the federal GOVERNMENT; it reshaped LIBERALISM; it gave new voice and influence to LABOR, farmers, and other groups; and it underlay the transformation of American politics that made the DEMOCRATIC PARTY the new majority party of the country.

Efforts to understand and evaluate the New Deal by contemporaries and by scholars have taken a variety of forms and have produced a variety of interpretations. Three approaches have been especially fruitful. One is topical—to categorize and analyze New Deal programs in terms of their aims and substance. The second is chronological—to follow the unfolding of the New Deal year by year. The third is more judgmental and often ideological— to analyze just what difference the New Deal made and whether its impact was positive or negative.

Each of these three approaches has its shortcomings as well as its strengths, and there are other important ways to understand the New Deal. As one example, focusing on the personality and purposes of Franklin D. Roosevelt, one of the most important and powerful presidents ever, obviously helps in explaining the New Deal—although the New Deal was also shaped by other members of the administration, by the CONGRESS and the SUPREME COURT, by public opinion and politics, and by changing circumstances and unintended consequences. In any event, the three approaches sketched below have proved particularly useful in understanding and evaluating the complex set of programs that constituted the New Deal, and they can accommodate other perspectives.

The first interpretive or analytical framework is topical, to elucidate the aims and substance of New Deal programs. The New Deal was above all an attempt to cope with the Great Depression and it involved three clear goals: to achieve economic recovery from the depths of the depression; to provide humanitarian assistance—RELIEF—to the unemployed and destitute until recovery was achieved; and to enact social and economic reform to prevent another such depression from occurring and to shield citizens against its impact should another depression strike. This framework is often called the three R's—recovery, relief, and reform.

Some analysts might add a fourth goal, and a fourth *R*, to recovery, relief, and reform: reelection for Roosevelt and the Democrats. And not the least of the consequences of the New Deal was that the Democratic Party became the new majority party of the nation because of POLITICS IN THE ROOSEVELT ERA and would remain so for decades beyond the 1930s. But while politics and reelection were important priorities of Roosevelt and the Democrats, and while the New Deal had profoundly important political effects, the three-*R* framework involves the New Deal itself, not New Deal–era politics.

Economic recovery was the overriding priority of Roosevelt and the New Deal. When Roosevelt took office in March 1933, national income was down by more than half, and the gross national product by almost half, from 1929 levels. UNEMPLOYMENT was at least 25 percent, and perhaps as high as 33 percent, of the labor force. Millions more were impoverished because of reduced hours and wages. Yet as late as 1940, after 10 years of the Great Depression and seven years of the New Deal, unemployment remained at the depression level of 15 percent. WORLD WAR II, not the New Deal, ended the Great Depression.

But the New Deal did try to achieve recovery, and it did help bring some improvement in economic conditions. In 1933, the NATIONAL INDUSTRIAL RECOVERY ACT (NIRA) and the AGRICULTURAL ADJUSTMENT ACT (AAA) were implemented to use government planning and controls to bring recovery in the manufacturing and agricultural sectors. Both had important limits, failed to bring recovery, and were declared unconstitutional by the Supreme Court in the mid-1930s (the AAA was reinstituted in somewhat different form), but each contributed to stopping the downward slide.

From 1933 to 1936, economic indexes improved—not to prosperity levels, but to well above the 1933 lows. New Deal spending played a significant role in that expansion, though Roosevelt spent to finance his programs, not to produce Keynesian economic stimulus. On the other hand, New Deal regulation, TAXATION, and LABOR policy upset BUSINESS and inhibited private investment needed to stimulate the economy.

In 1937, Roosevelt turned to tighter fiscal and monetary policy, confident that the economy was on the right track and worried about budget deficits and inflation. Then the RECESSION OF 1937–38 struck, sending economic indexes down faster than—though not as far as— in the early years of the depression. This "Roosevelt Recession" caused a reconsideration of New Deal policy, and a turn toward KEYNESIANISM and purposeful government deficit spending to stimulate the economy. The economy began to turn up again, but not until wartime economic MOBILIZATION and massive deficit spending did the nation reach full-production, full-employment prosperity.

If the New Deal failed to achieve full recovery, it did provide relief assistance for millions of unemployed and impoverished Americans. The FEDERAL EMERGENCY RELIEF ADMINISTRATION (FERA) provided direct financial assistance beginning in 1933 and was supplemented by the CIVILIAN CONSERVATION CORPS (CCC) and the 1933–34 CIVIL WORKS ADMINISTRATION (CWA), both of which provided work relief in the form of jobs on government projects. In 1935, the largest New Deal relief agency, the WORKS PROGRESS ADMINISTRATION (WPA) superseded the FERA and provided work relief for millions. (At the same time, the SOCIAL SECURITY ACT provided public assistance as well as old age and unemployment insurance.) The New Deal never provided relief aid to all who needed it, and relief payments were typically low. But the acceptance of federal responsibility for relief assistance was a major change, and millions of Americans were helped through hard times by government relief programs.

In addition to jobs and assistance, Roosevelt and the New Deal provided another kind of relief—relief of the spirit and psyche. Partly by means of his "fireside chats" over the RADIO, FDR was able to communicate to Americans his concern and optimism, and New Deal programs provided tangible effort that the president and the government understood and cared. The lifting of American spirits after the worst days of the early 1930s was surely one of the administration's achievements.

Finally, the New Deal sought to implement reforms to prevent or cushion another depression. The BANKING ACTS of 1933 and 1935 and the FEDERAL DEPOSIT INSURANCE CORPORATION (FDIC) strengthened the banking system. The SECURITIES AND EXCHANGE COMMISSION (SEC) made the stock market sounder and safer, and other regulatory agencies such as the FEDERAL COMMUNICATIONS COMMISSION (FCC) sought to improve and stabilize sectors of the economy. The NATIONAL LABOR RELATIONS ACT (NLRA, or the Wagner Act) enabled labor to organize and bargain effectively. The REVENUE ACT OF 1935 and other New Deal tax legislation sought to make taxation fairer and to increase government revenues. Partly as a result of the EXECUTIVE REORGANIZATION ACT of 1939, the PRESIDENCY became more powerful.

The New Deal also brought important social as well as institutional reform, including accepting federal responsibility for relief. The Social Security Act included old age and unemployment insurance, and the FAIR LABOR STANDARDS ACT (FLSA) established minimum wages and maximum hours. The FARM SECURITY ADMINISTRATION (FSA) sought to help small farmers and migrant workers. The HOME OWNERS LOAN CORPORATION (HOLC), the FEDERAL HOUSING ADMINISTRATION (FHA), and the FARM CREDIT ADMINISTRATION (FCA), refinanced or insured home and farm mortgages (and rescued many banks that had made mortgage loans), while the UNITED STATES HOUSING AUTHORITY (USHA) began to provide public housing.

The three-R framework of recovery, relief, and reform thus provides a way to understand the New Deal as a whole and its efforts to ensure economic stability and security. But it is in an important sense a static framework, which does not trace the development and dynamics of New Deal policymaking. Here the second, or chronological framework, is useful. It helps to understand how and why New Deal priorities and programs evolved, and to link policymaking to politics and to the circumstances of the American people.

The chronological framework that has been used since the New Deal era itself distinguishes between the FIRST NEW DEAL of 1933 and the SECOND NEW DEAL of 1935. In this interpretation, the First New Deal was concerned above all with recovery and relief, with its cornerstone agencies being the NATIONAL RECOVERY ADMINISTRATION (NRA) and the Agricultural Adjustment Administration for recovery and the Federal Emergency Relief Administration for relief. The Second New Deal, by contrast, was concerned more with social reform, with its distinctive programs being the Works Progress Administration, the National Labor Relations Act, the Social Security Act, and the Revenue Act of 1935.

Critics of this framework complain, with reason, that it exaggerates differences and underestimates continuities. Early New Deal programs persisted into 1935 and after, for example, while some of the new 1935 programs either had precursors in the early New Deal (the Wagner Act had origins in Section 7(a) of the NIRA, for example), or had been in the planning stages for some time. The 1933 TENNESSEE VALLEY AUTHORITY (TVA) had been a reform, as had implementing relief programs. Throughout the 1930s, the New Deal sought recovery and relief and reform.

Still, there was a different focus to the 1933 and the 1935 legislation, and circumstances and politics can help to explain the change. In 1933, at the depths of the depression, the compelling need was to stop the economic collapse and get help to people. By 1935, the economy was doing better, and new reform measures had been developed. The political situation was also different by 1935. Such critics of the New Deal as HUEY LONG and FRANCIS TOWNSEND complained that Roosevelt had not done nearly enough for the poor and the ELDERLY. The Congress elected in 1934 was more liberal and far readier to accept reform programs for the poor and the working class—and, in the case of the Wagner Act, to insist upon such reform, despite little initial interest or support from Roosevelt and Secretary of Labor FRANCES PERKINS. The Second New Deal was thus to a significant degree a product of changing political dynamics.

The legislative achievements of the First and Second New Deals of 1933 and 1935 were extraordinary and laid the foundations of the modern regulatory welfare state. But after his landslide reelection in the ELECTION OF 1936, Roosevelt never again had such successes. The CONSERVATIVE COALITION in Congress thwarted much of his second-term agenda, and then FOREIGN POLICY and World War II changed the administration's focus and priorities.

Recently, however, scholars have identified a THIRD NEW DEAL in Roosevelt's second and third terms. This third stage of the New Deal was distinguished partly by a more conservative atmosphere in Washington and the nation, the result of the ongoing strength of American CONSERVATISM and adverse reactions to the 1937–38 recession, Roosevelt's COURT-PACKING PLAN, and labor unrest. But the Third New Deal was also characterized by the growing emphasis in liberal policy on macroeconomic fiscal policy to achieve full-production, full-employment prosperity instead of the earlier efforts at microeconomic regulation and control and at redistributive economic and social policies. (It also included a new ANTIMONOPOLY thrust, including the formation of the TEMPORARY NATIONAL ECONOMIC COMMITTEE, though this ultimately had little impact.) The Third New Deal, characterized by a more conservative political climate and by the new Keynesian agenda, was as important to postwar politics and government as were the First and Second New Deals, which produced the regulatory welfare state and the new Democratic majority.

Taken together, the topical approach of recovery, relief, and reform, and the chronological approach of the First, Second, and Third New Deals provide intersecting and complementary frameworks for understanding, analyzing, and explaining the New Deal and its development. Such understanding provides the essential basis for the third interpretive framework—evaluating or judging the New Deal. What difference did it make? Was it good or bad? Did it go too far or not far enough?

The basic viewpoints about the New Deal were largely established in the 1930s and have been reiterated and embellished since. Conservatives have called the New Deal a bad thing that went much too far. In this view, the New Deal harmed the American political system by making the federal government (and the presidency) too big and too powerful. It weakened the American economy by wasteful spending and by government intrusiveness and regulation that impaired the free enterprise system, and by labor and tax policies that prevented economic recovery by alienating BUSINESS. And the New Deal, it is said, had an adverse impact on the American people by making them dependent upon government and eroding principles of individualism. In the conservative interpretation, Roosevelt was an erratic, devious, and misinformed leader concerned more about politics and reelection than about the public good.

From the opposite perspective, analysts and scholars on the left have complained from the start that the New Deal merely shored up corporate capitalism, that it helped business and the upper class more than workers and the poor, that it did not redistribute wealth or income and only partly redistributed power, and that it did virtually nothing to advance AFRICAN AMERICANS or CIVIL RIGHTS. In this view, Roosevelt was a calculating president, protecting corporate capitalism with his programs while winning support from working-class and lower-middle-class Americans and from minority groups with his rhetoric. "New Left" scholars of the 1960s reprised such contemporary 1930s criticism. More recently, some scholars have also criticized the New Deal for doing little to improve WOMEN'S STATUS AND RIGHTS.

But if the New Deal and Franklin D. Roosevelt have been criticized from right and left, they have also been celebrated and defended. Liberals then and since have rejoiced in New Deal reform that accepted responsibility for assistance to the poor and unemployed, challenged business and the wealthy, enabled the organization of powerful labor unions, strengthened the nation's economic institutions, created a broker state where the power of business was rivaled by that of government and often by labor and farmers as well, and that gave African Americans, women, JEWS, CATHOLICS, and other groups a larger voice in American government. They have praised Roosevelt for championing such causes and achieving such results. In this view, the New Deal profoundly changed the nation—and for the better.

Each of these judgmental frameworks can adduce significant evidence in support of its views. But each also has shortcomings or blind spots. The conservative criticism, for example, often goes too far, with claims that the New Deal was socialist or fascist. In fact, most New Dealers wanted to strengthen and protect American capitalism by reforming it—and the modern mixed economy of government regulation and support of private enterprise did just that. Similarly, radical critiques point out shortcomings and limits of the New Deal, but often overlook successes and achievements. While correct that New Dealers, including FDR, were often cautious and even conservative reformers, operating within the traditions of American democratic capitalism, they often miss the degree to which the limits of the New Deal were imposed by the conservatism and antistatism of the culture, by opponents in Congress, by resistant, or racist, local officials who implemented New Deal programs, by events at home and abroad. And the admiring liberal accounts of the New Deal often exaggerate its virtues and successes and fail adequately to take into account significant criticisms from the right and the left.

Wherever one ultimately stands on the several evaluative frameworks of the New Deal, each raises important questions, rests on substantive evidence, and provokes reflection than can illuminate the New Deal and lead to still more questions and insights. Conflicting interpretations of the New Deal show no signs of ending, and scholars and others will continue to search for valid understandings and evaluations of the New Deal.

Further reading: Anthony J. Badger, *The New Deal: The Depression Years, 1933–1940* (New York: Hill & Wang, 1989); Alan Brinkley, *The End of Reform: New Deal Liberalism in Recession and War* (New York: Knopf, 1995); Paul Conkin, *The New Deal* 3d ed. (Arlington Heights, Ill.: Harlan Davidson, 1992); David E. Hamilton, ed, *The New Deal* (Boston: Houghton Mifflin, 1999); David M. Kennedy, *Freedom From Fear: The American People in Depression and War, 1929–1945* (New York: Oxford University Press, 1999); William E. Leuchtenburg, *Franklin D. Roosevelt and the New Deal, 1932–1940* (New York: Harper & Row, 1963); Arthur M. Schlesinger Jr., *The Age of Roosevelt*, 3 vols. (Boston: Houghton Mifflin, 1956–1960); Harvard Sitkoff, ed., *Fifty Years Later: The New Deal Evaluated* (Philadelphia: Temple University Press, 1985).

news media

During the 1930s and 1940s, the news media—newspapers, magazines, RADIO, and newsreels at the MOVIES—provided extensive coverage of the news and illuminated important issues. In their various ways, the news media gave Americans information on such diverse matters as the extent and nature of the GREAT DEPRESSION, the experiences of UNEMPLOYMENT and the DUST BOWL, the PRESIDENCY of FRANKLIN D. ROOSEVELT, the exploits of SPORTS stars, and the progress of WORLD WAR II.

Americans continued to rely upon the morning or evening newspaper for daily news. In addition to the major general circulation newspapers of the big cities—which typically still had several newspapers—an enormous variety of newspapers served the nation, from small town and rural journals to papers that catered specifically to particular groups. A number of newspapers were published by and for AFRICAN AMERICANS, with some—for example, the *Chicago Defender*—having widespread circulation. Such ethnic groups as GERMAN AMERICANS, ITALIAN AMERICANS, POLISH AMERICANS, and JEWS also had their own newspapers, often in foreign-language format.

In the 1930s, radio newscasts (either produced locally or through the major networks) increasingly brought news of the entire nation and world into American homes. By the end of the decade, radio was eclipsing newspapers as the most important source of daily news, and foreign-language broadcasts had a significant voice in ethnic communities. Some broadcasters—for example, Walter Winchell and Edward R. Murrow—became at least as well known as the leading print journalists. The importance of radio newscasts was vividly demonstrated on Sunday, December 7, 1941, when the Japanese attacked PEARL HARBOR. Millions of listeners were glued to their sets as the dreadful news came in, while newspapers were slower to cover the story.

Magazines had been relatively unimportant as sources of news down to the 1920s, being largely the realm of literature and specialty pieces. HENRY R. LUCE cofounded *Time,* the first weekly newsmagazine, in the early 1920s, however, and such competitors as *Newsweek* soon emerged as well. In the 1930s, moreover, the photo magazines such as LIFE MAGAZINE and *Look* appeared, using PHOTOGRAPHY to bring the events of the week to millions of readers.

Their access to large audiences gave newspapers, radio, and magazines the ability not only to increase the knowledge but also to sway the opinions of readers and listeners. While newspaper publishers in the 1930s generally reflected the conservative views of BUSINESS and often opposed Roosevelt and the NEW DEAL, reporters and columnists were typically more favorable to the administration. Roosevelt himself used his press conferences and his radio broadcasts to get his side of the story out and cultivated reporters to get friendly coverage.

Even before the attack on Pearl Harbor, the news media brought Americans the news of World War II. Edward R. Murrow reported via radio from London on the BATTLE OF BRITAIN and the British experience under German aerial attack, and he and other radio broadcasters followed the subsequent progress of the war. Among print journalists, ERNIE PYLE in particular won the loyalty and love of American GIs and professional acclaim at home for his unpretentious style in telling the story of the war through the eyes of ordinary soldiers. Like Pyle, other reporters carried friendly and positive accounts of American servicemen. Newsmagazines and newsreels also provided news and images of the war.

The news media, however, had to comply with CENSORSHIP by the GOVERNMENT, often in ways that advanced government PROPAGANDA efforts. The armed forces censored war reports and photographs, for example, while journalists frequently had to rely upon the military and the OFFICE OF WAR INFORMATION for information. Photographs of dead Americans were not released for publication until 1943, out of concern that they would harm morale, and the news media rarely provided information or images of the most grisly and brutal side of the war. Generally, however, the control of information and photographs was consistent with national security and humane concerns, and typically the news media willingly practiced self-censorship in such matters. They also pooled their resources during the war so that the various media outlets could share information and reports.

In the era of the Great Depression and World War II, the news media brought home the severity of the Great Depression, did generally a successful job of reporting the war, and provided insight into dominant personalities and dramatic events as well as into everyday life. Radical changes lay ahead, however, for the rapid development of television in the postwar era would profoundly affect the news media and the roles played by newspapers, magazines, newsreels, and radio.

See also POPULAR CULTURE.

Further reading: Erik Barnouw, *A Tower in Babel: A History of Broadcasting in the United States to 1933* (New York: Oxford University Press, 1966); ———, *The Golden Web: A History of Broadcasting in the United States, 1933–1953* (New York: Oxford University Press, 1968); Catherine L. Covert and John D. Stevens, eds., *Mass Media between the Wars: Perceptions of Cultural Tensions, 1918–1941* (Syracuse, N.Y.: Syracuse University Press, 1984); Alan Nourie and Barbara Nourie, eds., *American Mass-Market Magazines* (New York: Greenwood, 1990).

—Nicholas Fry

New York World's Fair (1939–1940)

The New York World's Fair of 1939–40 was the largest and most expensive world's fair ever to that point, and the most important of the world's fairs of the 1930s. Although attendance fell short of hopes, the fair reflected important aspects of American culture at the juncture of the GREAT DEPRESSION and WORLD WAR II.

Costing more than $150 million and covering more than 1,200 acres in the borough of Queens, the New York World's Fair was immense. Special highways, bridges, and subway stations were built to accommodate traffic to the fair, and 300 buildings were constructed on the fairgrounds. Two lakes were created, 10,000 trees were planted, and 25 miles of road were paved. Fifty-nine foreign nations and 33 U.S. states and territories participated. In addition, the fair corporation commissioned the creation of more than 100 murals and more than 60 sculptures.

The purported reason for the fair was the celebration of the 150th anniversary of George Washington's inaugural address. In reality, the fair of 1939 touched only lightly on historical themes. Far more obvious was the fair's emphasis on the future. The official guide book claimed that visitors would gain a "new and clearer view of today in preparation for tomorrow," and that the exhibits would "show the way toward the improvement of all the factors contributing to human welfare." This was reflected in the fair's official theme—"the World of Tomorrow."

This futuristic focus was also reflected in the architecture and layout of the fair. All of the physical elements were coordinated to impart a feeling of modernity and uniformity. Clean lines and bold shapes dominated in the buildings. The streets were arranged in an orderly manner, and even the color scheme was carefully planned. The only completely white buildings were the Perisphere and the Trylon, respectively a globe 200 feet in diameter and a 600-foot-tall three-sided obelisk that stood together at the center of the fair. The main thoroughfare, at one end of which these structures stood, also featured an 85-foot statue of Washington and an elaborate fountain called the Lagoon of Nations.

Many of the fair's exhibits shared this futuristic motif. Inside the Perisphere, revolving balconies afforded an aerial view of the model metropolis of the future, called Democracity. Similarly, the fair's most popular exhibit, General Motors's "Highways and Horizons," allowed visitors to travel through the America of 1960. Known as the Futurama, this exhibit showcased a time when the problems of society had been solved by new technologies, including superhighways, urban planning, and scientific agriculture. Other futuristic attractions included an electrified farm and the Town of Tomorrow, which featured single-family homes built with innovative materials and equipped with novel appliances. In the RCA building, crowds gathered around a seven-inch television screen to see the future of mass media. Westinghouse, Ford, Kodak, Nabisco, American Telephone & Telegraph, Heinz, Bethlehem Steel, and a host of other corporations also exhibited products at the fair.

In addition to the attractions offering education and enlightenment, the fair also provided pure entertainment. The amusement area of the fair contained elaborate attractions such as Jungleland, Old New York, Merrie England, and Children's World, as well as the more typical thrill rides, carnival games, and "girlie shows." Numerous parades and nightly fireworks shows were staged. Arenas housed Broadway plays, movies, and fashion shows. The Aquacade, which featured synchronized swimming productions, was one of the fair's most popular attractions.

Despite the time and effort that went into creating the fair, attendance failed to meet expectations. Instead of the projected 40 million to 50 million, only 25 million people visited the fair in its 1939 season, and the fair corporation lost money. As a result, some adjustments were planned for 1940. The admission price was dropped from 75¢ to 50¢. The official theme of the fair was also changed, evidently in response to increased qualms over the future and concern about the outbreak of World War II. Rather than "the World of Tomorrow," the planners now promised fairgoers refuge in patriotic celebrations of America's "Peace and

Shown here are the futuristic symbols of "the World of Tomorrow," the 600-foot-tall, needlelike Trylon and the Perisphere, a globe nearly 200 feet in diameter. *(Hulton/Archive)*

Freedom." In addition, advertisements emphasized the fun and escapism offered at the fair. While the fair corporation made money in 1940, turnout remained low, with only 18 million attending.

Although the New York World's Fair of 1939–40 was an economic failure, it was, and remains, an important icon of mid-20th-century America. The fair reflected a faith in TECHNOLOGY as a means of progress—a theme which, though tempered in later decades, continues to be an enduring element of American culture. Likewise, the fair's enthusiasm for new gadgets and material comforts reflected the emergence of the consumer culture, a ubiquitous, if often criticized, characteristic of modern American life. More poignantly, perhaps, the fair symbolized for many the possibility of hope in the midst of depression and international conflict.

See also POPULAR CULTURE.

Further reading: Helen A. Harrison, ed., *Dawn of a New Day: The New York World's Fair, 1939–40* (New York: Queens Museum, 1980); Larry Zim et al., *The World of Tomorrow: The 1939 New York World's Fair* (New York: Harper & Row, 1988).

—Pamela J. Lauer

Nimitz, Chester W. (1885–1966)

Admiral Chester William Nimitz served as the commander in chief of all United States land, sea, and air forces in the Pacific Ocean Areas during WORLD WAR II.

Nimitz was born in Fredricksburg, Texas, on February 24, 1885. He attended the U.S. Naval Academy and graduated in 1905. He was a submariner during the earliest days of the "silent service," and held a variety of assignments prior to World War I, including tours on the China station and as commander of the Atlantic Submarine Flotilla. In 1913 he traveled to Germany and Belgium to study advances in diesel engines; on his return to the United States, he supervised the construction of the first diesel ships built for the U.S. Navy, then undergoing the transition from coal to oil power.

In 1916, Nimitz was promoted to the rank of lieutenant commander. During World War I, he served as chief of staff to the commander of the submarine division, Atlantic Fleet. Various assignments followed after the war, including attendance at the U.S. Naval War College (1922–23), and staff assignments with the commander in chief of the Battle Fleet and the commander in chief of the U.S. Fleet. After attending the University of California (1926–29), Nimitz commanded Submarine Division 20 (1929–31) and the USS *Augusta* (1933–35), and served as assistant chief of the Bureau of Navigation (1935–38). He was promoted to rear admiral in 1938, and

for a year commanded a cruiser division before taking command of a battleship division. In June 1939 he was made chief of the Bureau of Navigation, where he remained until the Japanese attack on PEARL HARBOR in December 1941.

A senior commander with vast experience (although he never served aboard a ship in combat), extraordinary organizational and leadership talents, and a deliberate, low-key, but confident demeanor, Nimitz was named commander in chief of the U.S. Pacific Fleet in March 1942, with the rank of admiral. Soon thereafter, Nimitz was named commander of all land, sea, and air forces in the Pacific Ocean Areas. This included the North and Central Pacific Ocean Areas under his direct command, and supervision of the South Pacific Ocean Area, first commanded by Admiral Robert L. Ghormley and later Admiral WILLIAM F. HALSEY. As commander in chief of the Pacific Ocean Areas, Nimitz was responsible for the buildup, coordination, and overall direction of the PACIFIC THEATER campaign against Imperial Japan in cooperation with U.S. ARMY general Douglas A. MacArthur, commander of the Southwest Pacific Area. In addition, Nimitz commanded his own U.S. NAVY and U.S. MARINES subordinates including Admirals Halsey, Marc A. Mitscher, Raymond A. Spruance, Thomas C. Kincaid, John S. McCain, Sr., and Richard K. Turner.

Following a massive two-year buildup of naval, air, and land forces in Hawaii, Nimitz directed the sea battles and island-hopping AMPHIBIOUS WARFARE assaults across the Central Pacific toward the Japanese home islands. These included landings in the Gilbert Islands (November 1943), the Marshall Islands (January–February 1944), the MARIANA ISLANDS (June–July 1944), the Palaus (September 1944), the PHILIPPINES (October 1944), IWO JIMA (February 1945), and OKINAWA (April 1945). Nimitz also served as overall commander during the time his subordinates fought the BATTLE OF THE CORAL SEA (May 1942), the Battle of MIDWAY (June 1942), the Battle of the PHILIPPINE SEA (June 1944), and the Battle for LEYTE GULF (October 1944).

In December 1944, Nimitz was promoted to the newly created rank of admiral of the fleet, the naval equivalent to the U.S. Army five-star general-of-the-army rank. On September 2, 1945, the formal surrender of Japan was received aboard the battleship USS *Missouri* anchored in Tokyo Bay, then serving as Nimitz's flagship.

From December 1945 until his retirement from the U.S. Navy in December 1947, Nimitz served as chief of naval operations and then as special assistant to the secretary of the navy. In 1949 he was chosen to supervise the UNITED NATIONS plebiscite in Kashmir. He died on February 20, 1966.

Further reading: E. B. Potter, *Nimitz* (Annapolis, Md.: Naval Institute Press, 1976).

—Clayton D. Laurie

Normandy, invasion of (June 1944)

The June 6, 1944, invasion of Normandy, popularly known as D day, was the long-awaited opening of the SECOND FRONT in France with an amphibious assault across the English Channel. It was the largest AMPHIBIOUS WARFARE operation in history. When the Normandy campaign ended on September 1, 1944, Paris and most of France had been liberated, the Germans had lost a force of 700,000 men, and the western Allies were poised for the assault on Germany that together with the Soviet attack from the east would bring victory to the GRAND ALLIANCE in the WORLD WAR II EUROPEAN THEATER.

The Combined Chiefs of Staff decision to launch the invasion was made in spring 1943, with D day set for May 1, 1944, a decision made official at the TEHERAN CONFERENCE. Planning for Operation Overlord began under British lieutenant general Sir Frederic Morgan, whose small staff drew up an invasion plan approved at the Quebec Conference in August. It called for landing a force eventually consisting of 60 U.S. and 20 British and Canadian divisions, under the overall command of U.S. ARMY general Dwight D. Eisenhower as the supreme commander of the Allied Expeditionary Forces. Subordinate to Eisenhower was British field marshal Bernard Law Montgomery, who would command the 21st Army Group, the major ground force for the invasion. Admiral Sir Bertram

In this photo, taken in England a few hours before their jump into France, General Dwight D. Eisenhower urges men of the U.S. 101st Airborne Division to "Full victory—nothing else." *(Library of Congress)*

Ramsay of the British Royal Navy would command naval forces, and Air Chief Marshal Trafford Leigh-Mallory of the Royal Air Force would oversee the air units.

As the buildup of forces continued in Britain, Allied air forces began a bombing campaign aimed at transportation and communications centers in northern France and the Low Countries to deny counterattacking enemy forces access to the invasion area. Similarly, the air forces made an effort to clear the skies of the Luftwaffe, an effort that succeeded by March. Simultaneously, a massive deception campaign convinced the Germans that the Allied assault would be launched across the narrowest point of the English Channel at the Pas de Calais, rather than at Normandy.

To ensure the success of the landings, code-named Operation Neptune, planners increased the size of the invasion force from three to five divisions, to assault five beaches. Two beaches, code-named Utah and Omaha, would be assaulted by American divisions; one beach, Juno, by a Canadian division; and two beaches, Gold and Sword, by British divisions. Three airborne divisions, one British and two American, totaling 23,000 men, would land at opposite ends of the 50-mile-long invasion beachhead prior to the amphibious landings to block transportation routes at Ouistreham in the east and Ste. Mère Eglise in the west. By increasing the size of the invasion force, however, a postponement was necessary in order for the military to obtain more landing craft. D day was moved from May 1 to June 5, 1944.

The Germans knew the invasion was coming, but the Allied deception campaign kept them guessing as to where. A confused German chain of command, coupled with shortages of manpower, equipment, and resources, hindered German defensive preparations. Indeed, differing opinions between the commander in the west, Field Marshal Gerd von Rundstedt, and his subordinate commanding Army Group B in Normandy, Field Marshal Erwin Rommel, prevented coherent planning. Von Rundstedt hoped to defeat the Allies with a mobile counterattacking force once the Allies had moved inland, while Rommel, backed by Hitler, favored repelling the invaders on the beaches. In the end, neither plan was followed, although Rommel did clutter the beaches with obstacles.

Bad weather on June 5, 1944, prompted the recall of the 600-ship invasion force from mid-channel, but the decision was made to land the next day rather than waiting until June 19, the next date on which tidal conditions would again favor an assault. Following the dropping of airborne forces, and under naval shore fire, 176,000 Allied troops began landing at dawn on June 6, 1944. The Allies achieved tactical surprise; the landings on Utah, Gold, Juno, and Sword succeeded in establishing beachheads against moderate resistance, but the Americans landing on Omaha suffered heavy casualties fighting against a determined enemy. Nonetheless, by nightfall, more than 75,000 British and Canadian troops and 57,500 American troops were ashore. Casualties were approximately 4,300 British and Canadian soldiers, and about 6,000 Americans. When Operation Neptune ended on June 30, 1944, more than 850,000 Allied troops had landed, along with 148,000 vehicles, and 570,000 tons of supplies.

Although the Allies had hoped to quickly break out of the beachhead and move inland, increasingly stubborn German resistance against the British advance on Caen prompted American forces to divert south into the hedgerows of the Bocage country of Normandy, delaying the breakout until July 25–31.

Further reading: Stephen E. Ambrose, *D-Day, June 6, 1944: The Climactic Battle of World War II* (New York: Simon & Schuster, 1994); Max Hastings, *Overlord: D-Day and the Battle for Normandy* (New York: Simon & Schuster, 1984); Cornelius Ryan, *The Longest Day: June 6, 1944* (New York: Simon & Schuster, 1959).

—Clayton D. Laurie

Norris, George W. (1861–1944)

George William Norris, elected to five terms in the United States Senate from Nebraska, was a progressive and independent member of the REPUBLICAN PARTY who played a significant role in national politics in the 1920s and 1930s.

Born in Sandusky County, Ohio, on July 11, 1861, Norris worked from an early age to support his widowed mother and siblings, and attended Baldwin and Valparaiso Universities. He taught school in the Washington Territory, then moved to Nebraska, where he practiced law and entered local Republican politics.

Elected to Congress in 1902, Norris evolved from a conservative to progressive Republican during five terms in the House of Representatives, and broke with the GOP in 1912 to support the Progressive "Bull Moose" Party of Theodore Roosevelt. After he was elected to the U.S. Senate by the Nebraska legislature in 1912, he supported progressive reform legislation, but opposed American involvement in World War I and fought against membership in the League of Nations. During the 1920s, as chairman of the Agriculture Committee, Norris championed the development of hydroelectric power in the Tennessee Valley at Muscle Shoals, Alabama, and he also fought for the rights of organized LABOR. In 1928, Norris refused to back HERBERT C. HOOVER for president, preferring Democrat Al Smith instead, and four years later was an early advocate of FRANKLIN D. ROOSEVELT.

After Roosevelt became president, Norris staunchly supported most NEW DEAL legislation, including the TENNESSEE VALLEY AUTHORITY, the culmination of years of struggle for him. With Roosevelt's strong endorsement, Norris won reelection to a fifth term in 1936 after 40,000 Nebraskans signed petitions urging him not to retire. Norris eventually backed Roosevelt's COURT-PACKING PLAN, albeit with misgivings, but in FOREIGN POLICY he was among the ISOLATIONISTS opposing Roosevelt's interventionist aims. After voting against the SELECTIVE SERVICE Act in 1940, however, he moved away from the isolationists with his support of the LEND-LEASE ACT. Norris sought a sixth term in 1942, but despite another endorsement from Roosevelt, he lost reelection after 30 years in the Senate. In retirement, Norris wrote his memoirs and supported Roosevelt for a fourth term, praising his conduct of WORLD WAR II. Norris died in McCook, Nebraska, on September 2, 1944.

Further reading: Richard Lowitt, *George W. Norris: The Persistence of a Progressive, 1913–1933* (Urbana: University of Illinois Press, 1971); Richard Lowitt, *George W. Norris: The Triumph of a Progressive, 1933–1944* (Urbana: University of Illinois Press, 1978).

—William J. Thompson

North African campaign (November 1942– May 1943)

The Western Allies were facing a Japanese onslaught in the WORLD WAR II PACIFIC THEATER during the first half of 1942, yet President FRANKLIN D. ROOSEVELT and British prime minister WINSTON S. CHURCHILL agreed with their military advisers that it was important for them to engage the AXIS powers in the EUROPEAN THEATER at the earliest opportunity. (Germany and the Soviet Union had been fighting on the eastern front since June 1941.) While an indecisive seesaw battle had been raging in North Africa between British and Commonwealth forces and Axis forces since November 1940, it was decided that Morocco and Algeria, colonies of the nominally independent Vichy France government that was in fact subservient to Germany, would be suitable landing sites. Planning for Operation Torch, the invasion of Northwest Africa, began in the summer of 1942. Its ultimate goal was the destruction of Axis forces between two large east-west pincers.

The invasion plan called for landing three armies in Casablanca, Morocco, and in Oran and Algiers, Algeria. The Western Task Force, landing in Casablanca, embarked directly from Hampton Roads, Virginia, under command of Major General GEORGE S. PATTON, and consisted entirely of U.S. ARMY troops. The Central Task Force, also American, was commanded by U.S. Army major general Lloyd R. Fredendall. It would sail from Great Britain and land in Oran, Algeria. The Eastern Task Force, a composite British-American team, was commanded by U.S. Army

major general Charles W. Ryder, and would take Algiers. The invasion force totaled 65,000 men, accompanied by 650 British and American warships. The landings took place early on November 8, 1942, and achieved total surprise. Although Vichy French resistance was light, except at Casablanca, more than 1,400 Americans and 700 French soldiers were killed during the assault.

In spite of Allied efforts to decipher French reactions, the political situation in North Africa was initially far from clear. On November 10, however, the Allies gained the cooperation of a Vichy official, Admiral Jean Darlan, who called for a cease-fire, which ended the fighting. In response to this perceived betrayal by the Vichy regime, Adolf Hitler ordered German forces to occupy all of metropolitan France. Hitler then dispatched 17,000 men of the Fifth Panzer Army under General Jürgen von Arnim to Tunisia.

Although the Allies attempted a dash to Tunisia in December, logistical difficulties, American inexperience, poor Allied cooperation, bad weather, and mountainous terrain, as well as stubborn German resistance, halted the Allied advance. As German field marshal Erwin Rommel's Afrika Korps entered Tunisia in February, after a long retreat before advancing British and Commonwealth forces under Lieutenant General Bernard L. Montgomery, the Axis commanders decided to launch an offensive against inexperienced Allied troops in Tunisia, in particular Fredenall's U.S. II Corps. German forces attacked the Americans on February 14–15, 1943, at the Kasserine Pass and gained temporary successes. Determined British units, reinforced by the U.S. First Armored and U.S. Ninth Infantry Divisions stopped the German push, however, and the overextended Axis forces withdrew. On February 23, Rommel was appointed commander of the Panzer Army, Africa; but, tired and ill, he relinquished command to von Arnim and left Africa on March 9.

Following Kasserine, the Allies reorganized. British general Harold R. L. G. Alexander assumed command of Allied ground forces in North Africa with the 18th Army Group, under overall command of Lieutenant General Dwight D. Eisenhower, who directed the campaign from Allied Force Headquarters in Algiers. Below Alexander were three armies, one consisting of the American II Corps under General Patton, the British command in Tunisia coming under General Kenneth A. N. Anderson's First Army, and Montgomery's Eighth Army, now entering Tunisia. Following Montgomery's successful flanking attack on the last German defensive position (the Mareth line) in southern Tunisia in March, and with clear, dry weather and increasing material and manpower advantages, the Allies made rapid progress. Allied AIR POWER was especially telling, and more than 13,000 sorties were flown unopposed against Axis ground forces and the sea convoys

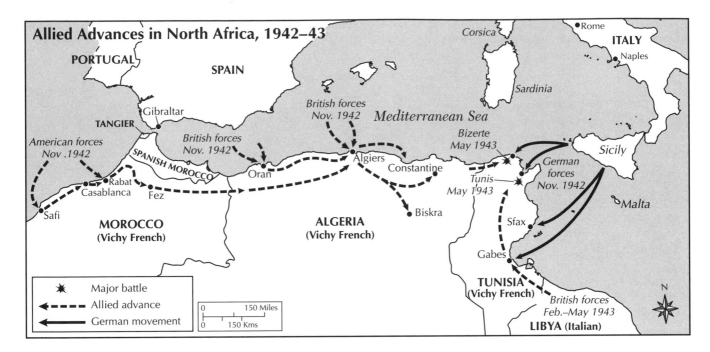

Allied Advances in North Africa, 1942–43

attempting their resupply. On May 7, 1943, the Americans took Bizerte, while British forces entered Tunis. With Allied aircraft dominating the skies and Allied navies blocking escape routes, Axis forces surrendered on May 13, 1943, giving the Allies control of the North African coast and jumping off points for the invasion of SICILY and the subsequent ITALIAN CAMPAIGN.

The 275,000 Axis prisoners taken spoke of the magnitude of the defeat, with other casualties, dead and wounded since February 1941, reaching a total of 345,000. Allied casualties since Torch included 12,200 British, American, and French troops killed, 42,000 wounded, and 20,000 captured or missing.

See also GRAND ALLIANCE.

Further reading: Norman Gelb, *Desperate Venture: The Story of Operation TORCH, the Allied Invasion of North Africa* (New York: Morrow, 1992); Alan Moorehead, *Desert War: The North African Campaign, 1940–1943* (New York: Penguin, 2001).

—Clayton D. Laurie

Nye committee (1934–1936)

The Nye committee, officially named the Special Committee Investigating the Munitions Industry, was created by the U.S. Senate on April 12, 1934. The widespread sense that participation in World War I had been a mistake led many Americans, especially isolationist and pacifist groups, to have suspicions about business-government complicity in the U.S. involvement in World War I. Peace groups called for congressional investigations of the munitions makers and their financial allies, and ISOLATIONISTS in the Senate succeeded in passing legislation that called for an investigation of munitions makers and their profits. Under the resolution, Vice President JOHN NANCE GARNER selected the committee members, including Senator Gerald P. Nye as chairman. Nye, a progressive Republican from North Dakota, was an ardent isolationist, as were the majority of the committee's other members.

After spending the summer of 1934 searching files of armament companies and subpoenaing witnesses, the committee held a first round of hearings in September. The committee interrogated BUSINESS leaders from companies engaged in the production and sale of armaments and munitions, with the star witnesses being the Du Pont brothers of E. I. Du Pont de Nemours and Company. The second round of hearings, held from December 1934 to April 1935, shifted focus from the armament makers themselves to the relationship between the munitions interests and the federal GOVERNMENT. In March 1935, the Nye committee met with President FRANKLIN D. ROOSEVELT, who urged the group to study and submit neutrality legislation to Congress, and Nye and his colleagues introduced legislation that led to the passage of the NEUTRALITY ACTS.

Chairman Nye, through speeches and radio addresses, generated a great deal of publicity for the committee, but he and his committee often sparked controversy as well. The committee issued two reports in late 1935, one urging a defensive navy built without profiteering or collusion, and the other proposing wartime taxes and price controls to take the profit out of war. The Nye committee's third round of hearings was held in January and February 1936, with testimony from representatives of firearms companies, steel companies, and financier J. P. Morgan. While interrogating Morgan, Nye accused President Woodrow Wilson of falsifying knowledge of Allied secret tactics during World War I—and was denounced by Senate Democrats for his attacks on Wilson.

In all, the Nye committee issued seven reports. In the reports, the committee accused munitions makers of bribery and influence peddling, proposed new approaches to wartime mobilization to eliminate profit, recommended permanent neutrality legislation, detailed the activities of J. P. Morgan and Company, and advocated government own-ership of the munitions industry. The two years of hearings, investigations, and reports of the Nye committee helped build public support for isolationism and led to passage of the restrictive neutrality laws of the mid-1930s.

See also FOREIGN POLICY.

Further reading: Wayne S. Cole, *Senator Gerald P. Nye and American Foreign Relations* (Minneapolis: University of Minnesota Press, 1962); Mathew Coulter, *The Senate Munitions Inquiry of the 1930s: Beyond the Merchants of Death* (Westport, Conn.: Greenwood Press, 1947); Paul A. C. Koistinen, *Planning War, Pursuing Peace: The Political Economy of American Warfare, 1920–1939* (Lawrence: University Press of Kansas, 1998).

—William J. Thompson

Office of Civilian Defense (OCD)

The federal Office of Civilian Defense (OCD) was created on May 20, 1941, and was initially headed by FIORELLO LA GUARDIA, the charismatic mayor of New York City. It had a twofold purpose: to protect civilians from enemy attack, and to maintain high morale on the WORLD WAR II HOME FRONT. By early 1942, more than 5½ million Americans had enrolled for such activities as coast watching, air raid defense and aircraft spotting, and enforcing blackouts.

At the time of the bombing of PEARL HARBOR in December 1941, the OCD comprised 1 million civil defense volunteers organized into 6,000 local councils. But the OCD fell far short of La Guardia's claims of effective organization. Local OCD councils bungled their assignments, and the air raid sirens that were supposed to warn city residents of air attacks often could be barely heard over the traffic. Soon, "wildcat" civilian defense organizations were begun by individual communities to compensate for the inefficient and ineffective local councils. The need for a comprehensive and effective civil defense organization became clearer after Pearl Harbor. False air raid alarms rippled across the country, particularly in San Francisco and Los Angeles as panicked citizens saw "Japanese" planes heading in all directions. As municipal and federal officials sought to bring some kind of order from the chaos, La Guardia maintained that the primary responsibility for the OCD was air raid defense and nothing more.

The OCD was not, however, completely inept. It added thousands of private pilots who had not joined the army air corps to its operations of the Civil Air Patrol, which supplemented and assisted army and navy antisubmarine patrols along the coasts. The air patrols, along with the coastal dim-outs, which eliminated light directed toward the sea, helped to diminish the U-boat threat along the East Coast.

Still, the OCD obviously needed improvement. President FRANKLIN D. ROOSEVELT sought to strengthen the agency by naming John Landis to the position of executive

director. La Guardia would remain involved with larger policy decisions, but Landis would run the day-to-day operations. La Guardia soon resigned and escaped the

Posters, such as the one above, were used by the Office of Civilian Defense to help Americans prepare for wartime *(Library of Congress)*

mounting criticism of his leadership coming from CONGRESS. Landis reorganized the OCD and eliminated some of the more superfluous programs such as the Arts Council of the Voluntary Participation Branch and the Children's Activities Section of the Physical Fitness Division of the OCD that had been suggested by ELEANOR ROOSEVELT. By the summer of 1942, although he was still facing a shortage of equipment and a poorly trained volunteer force, Landis had begun to enhance the operations and stature of the OCD.

By 1943, the OCD was better organized and fairly well equipped. By then, however, it was of little real use, for the tide of the war had shifted to the Allies and there was no real threat of an enemy attack on the United States. From 1943 to 1945 the OCD nonetheless continued to carry out air raid drills and blackouts and maintained its disaster preparedness programs.

Further reading: Richard Lingeman, *Don't You Know There's a War On? The American Home Front, 1941–1945* (New York: Putnam, 1970).

—Nicholas Fry

Office of Price Administration (OPA)

The Office of Price Administration (OPA) played a leading role in the WAGE AND PRICE CONTROLS of the WORLD WAR II HOME FRONT and also administered the federal GOVERNMENT program for RATIONING various goods in short supply.

By 1941, economic MOBILIZATION for World War II had begun to increase employment, income, and purchasing power and to divert materials and production to military goods. It thus raised the questions of how to combat the potentially large "inflationary gap" between limited supply and growing demand and of how to assure the equitable distribution of essential consumer goods. In April 1941, President FRANKLIN D. ROOSEVELT created the Office of Price Administration and Civilian Supply (OPACS), headed by LEON HENDERSON, an outspoken and sometimes abrasive and impolitic New Dealer. In August 1941, Roosevelt replaced the OPACS with the new Office of Price Administration, also under Henderson. The Emergency Price Control Act of January 1942 gave the OPA authority to set maximum prices on nonfarm consumer goods and rents.

It took more than a year for effective price controls on consumer goods to be implemented. Not only did a workable system have to be put in place, but the OPA lacked authority over farm prices, and Congress authorized farm prices to rise to 110 percent of the "parity" level established by the AGRICULTURAL ADJUSTMENT ACT of the NEW DEAL. Wage policy fell to the NATIONAL WAR LABOR BOARD. The

OPA's General Maximum Price Regulation ("General Max," in the parlance of wartime America) issued in April 1942 set maximum prices for consumer goods at the highest level reached in March 1942, but it was evaded in a number of ways and addressed only part of the wage/price problem. In October 1942, Congress passed the Economic Stabilization Act at Roosevelt's urging, and FDR appointed SUPREME COURT justice JAMES F. BYRNES to head the new Office of Economic Stabilization, with authority over farm prices and wages. In April 1943, FDR issued a "hold-the-line" order on wages and prices.

In this new framework, the OPA's efforts at price controls proved far more effective. Where the consumer price index had risen by some 24 percent from 1939 to 1943, it rose only about 4 percent more for the rest of the war. (It should be noted, however, that the official price index underestimated inflation and did not take into account the "hidden" inflation resulting from such factors as reduced quality and choice or the higher prices paid on the wartime BLACK MARKET.) The OPA rent control program proved generally successful from the outset.

The OPA administered rationing, its most unpopular function, as requested by supply agencies, with the WAR PRODUCTION BOARD ultimately acquiring authority to determine which goods would be rationed, and in what amounts and when. The OPA began rationing programs on 10 items in 1942, with additional items added to the rationing list later. Most Americans understood and accepted the need for rationing, as they did for wage and price controls, but they often disliked the implementation. The OPA relied upon local boards staffed by volunteers, which gave a certain local standing to the operations but also could produce favoritism and inefficiency. The rationing system was complicated and sometimes confusing, with coupons, certificates, stickers, stamps, and a changing point system for buying rationed items. Not all items in short supply were rationed, but a number of important ones were—gasoline, tires, meat, sugar, coffee, shoes, and canned goods, for example. And rationing seemed all the more frustrating when Americans had money to spend again after the long depression decade of the 1930s. Many consumers and merchants evaded OPA restrictions by black-market operations—and the FEDERAL BUREAU OF INVESTIGATION worked with the OPA to cut down on black market violations.

The OPA was most unpopular in 1942 when it was one of many home-front war agencies that had yet to find their stride, and public unhappiness with the OPA played a role in the sharp Republican gains in the election of 1942. OPA administrator Henderson had become a lightning rod for public discontent and the target of unhappy interest groups and of congressmen who thought him and his staff arrogant. He now became also a scapegoat for frustrated

Democrats already unhappy with his resistance to using the agency for political patronage appointments. Citing health issues, Henderson resigned under pressure.

Henderson's successors as OPA administrator, Prentiss Brown and Chester Bowles, fared much better. They were far more adept at public relations and assuaging constituencies and critics than Henderson had been. They also improved the agency's operations, especially in using local volunteers to administer price controls. And they had the good fortune of presiding over the OPA as the overall system of wage and price controls and rationing became more effective. The OPA and its programs were phased out after the war, though price controls and inflation again became a major political issue and a Democratic liability in the election of 1946.

Further reading: Lester V. Chandler, *Inflation in the United States, 1940–1948* (New York: Harper, 1951); Harold G. Vatter, *The U.S. Economy in World War II* (New York: Columbia University Press, 1985).

Office of Production Management (OPM)

The Office of Production Management (OPM) was created in January 1941 to coordinate the conversion of industry from civilian to defense production. It proved to be a weak and ineffectual agency for preparing the American ECONOMY for WORLD WAR II, and in January 1942 was folded into the new WAR PRODUCTION BOARD.

In order to facilitate economic MOBILIZATION and rearmament efforts, President FRANKLIN D. ROOSEVELT organized a National Defense and Advisory Commission (NDAC) in May 1940. NDAC had little success, and in January 1941, Roosevelt replaced that agency with the Office of Production Management. OPM was jointly directed by General Motors executive William S. Knudsen and Amalgamated Clothing Workers Union president SIDNEY HILLMAN in an effort to combine the interests of both BUSINESS and LABOR in mobilizing the economy for war. The primary objective of OPM was to coordinate the procurement and production of armaments and equipment. Its greatest legacy was its Division of Research and Statistics' compilation of "shopping lists" of estimates and production requirements for U.S. military needs.

Later in 1941, FDR diminished the potential effectiveness of OPM by creating two new agencies aimed at economic mobilization: the Office of Price Administration and Civilian Supply (OPACS) headed by LEON HENDERSON, and the Supply Priorities and Allocation Board (SPAB) led by DONALD M. NELSON. The existence of so many mobilization agencies enabled FDR to keep economic organization under his control, but the agencies often overlapped in complex and confusing ways that rendered many of them ineffectual and resulted in consolidations and the creation of still more agencies.

As production demands steadily increased, the OPM was to divert resources from civilian to military needs. But OPM encountered problems in purchasing and procurement of military equipment because the army and navy had divisions with those powers as well. Ironically, despite Knudsen's position, OPM also failed to in getting the AUTOMOBILE INDUSTRY to convert their factories from civilian production to war production. In January 1942, OPM, together with SPAB, was replaced by the War Production Board.

Further reading: Harold G. Vatter, *The U.S. Economy in World War II* (New York: Columbia University Press, 1985).

—Michael T. Walsh

Office of Scientific Research and Development (OSRD)

Directed by VANNEVAR BUSH, the Office of Scientific Research and Development (OSRD) became the chief GOVERNMENT arm for mobilizing SCIENCE and TECHNOLOGY for WORLD WAR II. Given unusual access and trust by President FRANKLIN D. ROOSEVELT, Bush masterfully directed and defended OSRD, quickly making it a major element of the war MOBILIZATION effort.

While enjoying only about a third of the overall wartime research and development funds, the OSRD's numerous projects nonetheless led to major inventions such as radar, radio-inertial navigation, new amphibious vehicles, the proximity fuse, mass production of penicillin, whole-blood substitutes, pesticides, and of course the ATOMIC BOMB. The OSRD was initially responsible for the "uranium" project, which rapidly became so large it was transferred to the U.S. ARMY Corps of Engineers' Manhattan Engineer District in 1942—the MANHATTAN PROJECT.

OSRD seemed a complete success, and Bush's final report, *Science: the Endless Frontier: A Report to the President on a Program for Postwar Scientific Research* (July 1945), was a blueprint for instituting what some scholars have called the "permanent mobilization" of science and technology for the cold war. Bush also arranged for an extensive history of the OSRD to be written and published in a series of popular books, *Science in World War II*, by the Atlantic Monthly Press.

The OSRD was the successor of the National Defense Research Committee (NDRC), established by Roosevelt in June 1940 with Bush as its head. The NDRC's membership, handpicked by Bush, constituted a who's who of research and development in the United States: Karl Compton, James Conant, Frank Jewett, Conway Coe,

Richard Tolman, Rear Admiral Harold Bowen, and Brigadier General George Strong. In May 1941, the NDRC became the OSRD, adding research in MEDICINE to its mandate. By the end of the war, the OSRD had spent half a billion dollars on some 2,000 contracts, with another $2 billion for the atomic bomb project.

Bush and his cadre of closest associates believed strongly in using existing private industrial and university capacities rather than creating new governmental ones. The leadership of the OSRD embodied or could easily tap the expertise and support of most major corporations and universities, had through Bush the sympathetic ear of the president, and found it relatively easy to impress even recalcitrant elements of the military services and congressional oversight committees. Bush and the OSRD were also adept at other, stronger organizational tactics that proved effective through the war but only partially so during RECONVERSION to peacetime and the cold war. The result was a highly productive scientific discovery and invention machine whereby the 1,500 or so employees of the OSRD could contract for research of promising utility for the war effort, select out those elements best suited for quick development, and get hardware into production and troops trained in time to be useful.

While the postwar institutions connecting science and technology with the government and military would diversify from rather than simply imitate the OSRD, it remained the exemplar and model of a successful relationship. The thousands of scientists and engineers mobilized in support of the war effort on OSRD contracts, many of them young men (and a few women) whose conventional training or careers had been interrupted, emerged with fundamentally changed notions and expectations when it came to science, technology, and government. While many of their mentors returned to university life glad to be done with intimate contact with military and government bureaucracy, they became the senior statesmen of science and technology, eager to perpetuate many aspects of the OSRD.

The OSRD also changed the fundamental relationships and institutions by which the military and civilian national security apparatus uses science and technology and fosters its development. In this case, however, to Bush's chagrin, science and technology units and advisory committees sprouted everywhere, in an undisciplined, decentralized, and duplicative manner. Finally, the atomic bomb project was only the largest and most unsettling of a host of OSRD-sponsored initiatives that had gone on hidden in secrecy from the institutions of democracy (even the vice president and most of Congress), that were based on esoteric and almost incomprehensible knowledge, and that produced powerful and sometimes terrifying weapons. As Congress and a new president emerged from the war, they had to face the problem of how the civilian trustees of

democracy could manage a government dependent on things they could not themselves comprehend.

Further reading: Carroll W. Pursell, "Science Agencies in World War II: The OSRD and Its Challengers," in *The Sciences in the American Context,* edited by Nathan Reingold (Washington, D.C.: Smithsonian Institution Press, 1979); Nathan Reingold, "Vannevar Bush's New Deal for Research; or the Triumph of the Old Order," *Historical Studies in the Physical and Biological Sciences* 17 (1987): 299–344.

—Joseph N. Tatarewicz

Office of Strategic Services (OSS)

The Office of Strategic Services (OSS) was created during WORLD WAR II to collect and analyze INTELLIGENCE information on the AXIS. The institutional predecessor of the Central Intelligence Agency, the OSS marked a significant change in American intelligence capabilities.

The OSS had its origins in the Coordinator of Information (COI), a civilian office attached to the White House and created in July 1941 by President FRANKLIN D. ROOSEVELT to force the various intelligence units of the U.S. NAVY, the U.S. ARMY, and the State Department to cooperate. Roosevelt chose New York attorney William J. "Wild Bill" Donovan to head this new office, which was to analyze data collected by other agencies. Soon, Donovan's operations included small espionage units from the Office of Naval Intelligence and the War Department and the State Department's overseas radio operation. After the attack on PEARL HARBOR in 1941, the COI was, at Donovan's request, assigned to the Joint Chiefs of Staff, while the OFFICE OF WAR INFORMATION took over the radio operations.

Despite the acquisition of the COI by the Joint Chiefs, Donovan and his personnel were involved in a struggle for power with the Office of Naval Intelligence and the U.S. Army's G-2 Branch. The FEDERAL BUREAU OF INVESTIGATION joined the resistance to Donovan's group by blocking it from operating in North and South America and from having any domestic counterintelligence capabilities.

Donovan nevertheless remained with the intelligence gathering and analysis unit, which was renamed the Office of Strategic Services in 1942. He immediately began acquiring personnel both to gather information in the field and to analyze it at home in the newly formed research and analysis unit. Donovan recruited some of the finest minds in American academia, particularly historians, political scientists, geographers, and psychologists, who carefully examined the information gathered by OSS agents to determine what the information meant and what should be done with it. Even so, the OSS by most reckonings did

William J. Donovan   *(Library of Congress)*

not contribute as much as did army and navy intelligence and the operations of the British.

The OSS also began to train agents to operate in the field and to train citizens of Axis-occupied territory to fight guerrilla wars against their conquerors. Members of the OSS helped train and supply members of the French Resistance as well as local anti-Japanese guerilla units in China and Southeast Asia. Other field agents were trained to gather intelligence from inside Germany and occupied Europe, although the dangerous assignments and the lack of experience and proper training of OSS agents sometimes resulted in casualties.

Aside from gathering and analyzing intelligence, the OSS undertook other important operations during the war. It had a special morale unit that tried to undermine the will of the Axis soldiers and citizens by creating antiwar PROPA-GANDA and dispersing it over enemy territory. The OSS also did conducted operations that were specific to particular theaters of the war. As one example, the agency ran a special bomb targeting office for the U.S. ARMY AIR FORCES in China that greatly enhanced the accuracy and effectiveness of air strikes against Japanese positions.

Following the surrender of the Axis powers in 1945, the Office of Strategic Services was disbanded and some of its departments were transferred to other agencies in the federal government, primarily the War Department. Two years later, the National Security Act of 1947 created the Central Intelligence Agency to oversee the nation's intelligence-gathering and analysis operations.

Further reading: Edward Hymoff, *The OSS in World War Two,* rev. ed. (New York: Richardson & Steirman, 1986); Bradley F. Smith, *The Shadow Warriors: OSS and the Origins of the CIA* (New York: Basic Books, 1983).
—Nicholas Fry

Office of War Information (OWI)

President FRANKLIN D. ROOSEVELT created the Office of War Information (OWI) in June 1942 to manage the dissemination of GOVERNMENT information during WORLD WAR II. Using publications, RADIO, and films to provide information about the nation's war effort and to give favorable portrayals of the American way of life, the OWI also carried out some CENSORSHIP functions. Elmer Davis, a respected CBS radio broadcaster, headed the agency.

The establishment of the OWI culminated administration efforts beginning in 1939 to organize the collection and dissemination of government information. As with other aspects of war MOBILIZATION, these efforts were marked by early confusion and bureaucratic conflict before a satisfactory structure was devised. Roosevelt wanted an agency that would both provide accurate information and serve government PROPAGANDA purposes at home and abroad—and without the troubling excesses of the Committee on Public Information during World War I. Stressing the principles of the ATLANTIC CHARTER and the FOUR FREEDOMS, the OWI sought above all to convey positive images of the United States and its war aims and to inspire confidence in an Allied victory. Although the goals of truth and propaganda sometimes worked at cross purposes, and although OWI had both shortcomings and critics, the agency generally was successful in meeting its objectives.

The OWI included a Domestic Branch and an Overseas Branch. The Domestic Branch was established to provide Americans information on the war and the war effort, to motivate them to greater efforts, and to convince them of the need for a leading American role in the world. It published pamphlets such as *Divide and Conquer* that illuminated the threat of fascism. It also published *Negroes and the War,* which in favorably depicting the circumstances and contributions of AFRICAN AMERICANS provoked criticism from white southern conservatives and African Americans alike for presenting what they saw, for different reasons, as a misleading portrayal of actual conditions.

The Overseas Branch produced materials for foreign audiences that illustrated the American contributions to the war, the accomplishments of democracy, and the virtues of America's people, institutions, and war aims. It published a magazine for overseas distribution titled *Victory*. This publication met opposition from its first issue, when a prominent article featured a large photograph of Roosevelt and an article portraying him and the NEW DEAL in very flattering terms. The magazine also contrasted the New Deal with such "reactionaries" as former Republican president HERBERT C. HOOVER. Such OWI material, some of it distributed to GIs as well, persuaded many in the REPUBLICAN PARTY that OWI was part of FDR's fourth-term campaign effort for the ELECTION OF 1944. It led to considerable opposition to some OWI activities in CONGRESS.

In addition to its informational and propaganda duties, the OWI included an Office of Censorship, under Associated Press news editor Byron Price, which monitored incoming and outgoing international communications, including films, that did not fall under armed forces censorship. And the OWI's Bureau of Motion Pictures not only produced and released its own films but also worked successfully to persuade Hollywood to portray acceptable themes in its wartime MOVIES.

As victory over the AXIS seemed increasingly likely, and the OWI thus less necessary, and as the agency provoked opposition among conservatives and Republicans, Congress cut off most Domestic Branch funding in 1943, sharply curtailing its activities, and continued to scrutinize the Overseas Branch. President Harry S. Truman dissolved the OWI at the end of the war in August 1945.

Further reading: Allan M. Winkler, *The Politics of Propaganda: The Office of War Information, 1942–1945* (New Haven, Conn.: Yale University Press, 1978).

Office of War Mobilization (OWM)

In May 1943, President FRANKLIN D. ROOSEVELT established the Office of War Mobilization (OWM) to more effectively coordinate America's MOBILIZATION efforts during WORLD WAR II. In order to accomplish this mission, Roosevelt gave the OWM and its director, JAMES F. BYRNES, significant power over America's wartime ECONOMY, so much so that people often called Byrnes "the assistant president."

In January 1942, more than a year before Roosevelt created the OWM, a well-publicized Senate report found that America's mobilization program was plagued by waste, inefficiency, and political self-interest, and recommended reorganizing the entire effort into a single authority. Immediately after this report, Roosevelt created the WAR PRODUCTION BOARD (WPB), which he hoped would effectively coordinate all aspects of America's wartime procurement and production. But because its director, DONALD M. NELSON, was not a decisive leader and lacked authority over important segments of the U.S. economy, such as rubber, petroleum, LABOR, and the military, the effectiveness of the WPB was limited from the beginning.

Roosevelt created the OWM because he realized that if he did not create an agency with more authority than the WPB, it would be extremely difficult for the United States to maximize its industrial and economic resources for wartime use. The OWM did not replace the WPB, but Byrnes quickly replaced Nelson as the real director of America's mobilization efforts and the WPB became one of OWM's subordinate agencies.

Byrnes, a former U.S. senator from South Carolina and SUPREME COURT justice, had exceptional political and administrative skills, which played a large part in the success of the OWM. Byrnes ensured that the OWM did not encroach on the jurisdiction of other agencies or become too involved in the details of wartime production and procurement, choosing instead to set larger national goals and coordinate the activities of the agencies under the OWM. But the fact that his office was located in the White House was an important reminder that his decisions carried full presidential authority.

America's mobilization program was initially poorly organized, but in part because of the efforts of the OWM, American wartime production rose steadily after mid-1943, so that by 1944, the United States was producing 60 percent of all Allied munitions and 40 percent of the world's arms. The OWM formally ended in October 1944 when CONGRESS reconstituted it as the OFFICE OF WAR MOBILIZATION AND RECONVERSION (OWMR).

Further reading: Herman Miles Somers, *Presidential Agency: OWMR, the Office of War Mobilization and Reconversion* (Cambridge, Mass.: Harvard University Press, 1950).

—David W. Waltrop

Office of War Mobilization and Reconversion (OWMR)

In October 1944, CONGRESS converted the OFFICE OF WAR MOBILIZATION (OWM) into the Office of War Mobilization and Reconversion (OWMR). Where the OWM had been responsible for coordinating the MOBILIZATION of America's economic and industrial resources for WORLD WAR II, the OWMR was charged with reconverting the ECONOMY to a peacetime basis.

In late 1943, as an Allied victory in World War II became more certain, Congress began to consider plans for an agency that could oversee the difficult problems of RECONVERSION and DEMOBILIZATION. Congress wanted an organization that could determine the best way to curtail wartime production, relax RATIONING and other wartime controls, settle wartime contracts that were no longer needed, dispose of surplus GOVERNMENT property, and help American industries resume producing civilian products. Moreover, Congress wanted this agency to be created through congressional legislation, not executive order, because the PRESIDENCY had grown extremely powerful during World War II, and Congress wanted to reassert many of the powers it had given to FRANKLIN D. ROOSEVELT during the war.

In what became known as the "war within the war," demobilization and reconversion involved extremely controversial issues. Liberals and LABOR hoped that an early and incremental reconversion would help protect workers' wartime jobs as production fell off. On the other hand, the military feared that reconversion would hamper wartime production and wanted to delay reconversion as long as possible, or at least until Germany was defeated. Large wartime contractors also wanted to delay reconversion, because they did not want to give competitors a head start in resuming civilian production. They also did not want to terminate wartime contracts without receiving generous compensation from the U.S. government.

As labor had feared, the so-called human side of reconversion, such as the training and placement of discharged workers and returning veterans, took a back seat to the interests of the military and big BUSINESS. The OWMR allowed war manufacturers to buy government-owned factories and other surplus property at greatly discounted rates, offered them lucrative bonuses to terminate wartime contracts, and protected them against competitors.

JAMES F. BYRNES, who had been the highly successful director of the OWM, became the first director of the OWMR, ensuring continuity in the agency's operations. The OWMR was effectively terminated in December 1946.

Further reading: Herman Miles Somers, *Presidential Agency: OWMR, the Office of War Mobilization and Reconversion* (Cambridge, Mass.: Harvard University Press, 1950).

—David W. Waltrop

Okinawa (April–June 1945)

On April 1, 1945, with Japan near defeat in the WORLD WAR II PACIFIC THEATER, the United States invaded the Japanese island of Okinawa. One thousand miles from

Tokyo and just 350 miles from the Japanese home islands, Okinawa could provide a base both for staging an anticipated amphibious attack on Kyushu (the southernmost home island) and for launching air attacks on Japan. Understanding Okinawa's strategic value for the defense of the home islands, Japan had heavily fortified the island and placed some 100,000 troops upon it. The battle became one of the bloodiest of the war, both on the island and in the waters offshore.

The American invasion, launched by an enormous U.S. NAVY fleet including more than three dozen aircraft carriers, came on April 1, 1945, with amphibious craft landing two divisions of U.S. MARINES and two divisions of U.S. ARMY troops. The bloody, brutal battle lasted nearly three months. Because the Japanese stayed entrenched in heavily fortified blockhouses, caves, and pillboxes, U.S. troops had to move inland before the fighting actually started. The Americans, who ultimately outnumbered the Japanese by roughly two to one, moved forward relentlessly, using their enormous arsenal of weaponry and firepower and both inflicting and taking huge losses. The navy and the U.S. ARMY AIR FORCES launched thousands of aircraft sorties in support of the ground troops before and during the invasion. By May, the Americans had pushed the Japanese back to the southern part of the island, and after weeks more of heavy fighting, U.S. forces broke through the Japanese fortifications. The battle officially ended on June 22, but some fighting continued beyond that date.

Two aspects of the Japanese resistance were especially dramatic. First, as at IWO JIMA, Japanese soldiers fought tenaciously to their deaths, typically refusing to surrender or be taken prisoner. Thousands committed suicide. Second, waves of Japanese kamikazes, suicide planes that dived into America ships, caused enormous damage. In all, the U.S. Navy took more losses than in any other battle of the war—one-fifth of its total wartime casualties—at Okinawa, losing 36 ships, 760 aircraft, and 4,900 men. Another 368 ships were damaged. On land, the U.S. took some 40,000 combat casualties, including more than 7,000 dead; one out of every seven Marines killed in the war died on Okinawa. The ferocious Japanese resistance and the large American losses at Okinawa, the last major battle of the war, reinforced the perception that an invasion of the Japanese home islands would be enormously costly in lives. It thus contributed to the American use of the ATOMIC BOMB to bring the war to an end.

Further reading: Gerald Astor, *Operation Iceberg: The Invasion and Conquest of Okinawa in World War II* (New York: D.I. Fine, 1995); Hiromichi Yahara, *The Battle for Okinawa* (New York: John Wiley & Sons, 1995).

Owens, Jesse (James Cleveland) (1913–1980)

Jesse Owens was a phenomenal track and field athlete who earned a lasting place in American history as the African American who embarrassed German chancellor Adolf Hitler and undermined his ideas of Aryan superiority at the 1936 Berlin Olympics. However, despite his exemplary performance at Berlin and the fame it brought him, Owens had to deal with racial prejudice and economic difficulties at home.

James Cleveland "Jesse" Owens was born in Alabama into a family of sharecroppers in 1913. He moved with his family to Cleveland, Ohio, in 1922. At age 13, Jesse ran in his first race; by the time he had graduated from high school he was a nationally recognized sprinter. He entered Ohio State University without a scholarship, and, in a remarkable performance as a sophomore in 1935, broke three world records and tied another in just 45 minutes of competition. That same year, Owens married his high school sweetheart, Ruth Solomon.

In his junior year, Owens won a place on the United States Olympic team for the 1936 Berlin Olympics. The Nazis had hoped to use the games to showcase their own racial superiority and they scoffed at the American team, especially the AFRICAN AMERICANS and JEWS on it, as being racially inferior. Owens undercut the Nazis' belief in their own racial superiority by capturing four gold medals. In winning three individual medals, he tied one Olympic record and broke two others, as well as breaking one world record. (Ironically, Owens and another African-American runner on the relay team that broke the world and Olympic records had replaced two Jewish athletes who had been removed to avoid offending the Germans.) After the Amer-

Jesse Owens winning the 220-yard low hurdles and setting a world record at the Big Ten meet in Ann Arbor, Michigan, on May 25, 1935 *(National Archives)*

ican victory, Hitler responded by snubbing the victorious American athletes—Owens in particular—at the medal presentations, refusing to shake their hands and later walking out during some events. Owens became an overnight celebrity as the American press lauded his victories and the consternation they caused the Nazis.

Despite his performances in Berlin, Owens never was able to turn his athletic fame into financial success. He was forced to leave Ohio State before graduating to help support his own family. To earn money he became a playground janitor just one year after his Olympic triumph, and he gave up amateur track and field competition for show races against horses, greyhounds, cars, and trucks. Later, Owens became a disc jockey, ran his own public relations and marketing firm, and was active as a professional speaker. In 1976, President Gerald Ford awarded Owens the Presidential Medal of Freedom for his lifetime accomplishments. Owens died of lung cancer in 1980 at age 66.

See also SPORTS.

Further reading: William J. Baker, *Jesse Owens: An American Life* (New York: Free Press, 1986).

—Nicholas Fry

P

Pacific theater See World War II Pacific theater

Patton, George S., Jr. (1885–1945)

George Smith Patton, Jr., was one of the most charismatic, effective, and controversial military leaders in American history. An active promoter of armored warfare in the 1920s and 1930s, he became famous for his aggressive and successful generalship of American armies in the WORLD WAR II EUROPEAN THEATER.

George Patton was born in San Gabriel, California, on November 11, 1885, and educated at the Virginia Military Institute and the United States Military Academy at West Point, from which he graduated in 1909. In World War I, Patton served in the infant American Tank Corps, leading an American tank brigade. During the interwar period, he served in various commands and continued his professional development by attending military schools such as the Army War College where he was a leader in promoting and developing armored warfare and tactics. In 1932, Patton took part in dispersing the BONUS ARMY of World War I veterans that came to Washington, D.C., seeking assistance from the government during the GREAT DEPRESSION.

After an important role in the invasion of Morocco during the NORTH AFRICAN CAMPAIGN, Patton was given command of the U.S. Seventh Army in the invasion of SICILY in July 1943. Visiting wounded soldiers during an inspection tour of local military hospitals, he slapped two soldiers suffering from battle fatigue because he felt they were malingering cowards. General Dwight D. Eisenhower temporarily removed Patton from command and directed him to apologize for his actions. When the incident was made public in the United States, Patton was removed from consideration for command of the Fifth Army in Italy, and it took Eisenhower's influence to keep Patton in the war at all.

Patton was sent to England to take command of the Third Army, which went into France after the invasion of NORMANDY. With the opportunity to restore his name, Pat-ton conducted an astonishingly rapid advance of his mechanized forces across France that continued into Germany through the vital Saar region. Producing one of the most impressive advances in the history of warfare, Patton's aggressive leadership also helped Allied forces turn the tide at the BATTLE OF THE BULGE. He was promoted to full general in 1945.

At the conclusion of the war, Patton was appointed as the military governor of Bavaria but was relieved of command in October 1945 because of his leniency in the denazification of German officials and his hostile attitude toward the Soviet Union. In December, he was involved in a serious car accident, and he died later in the month.

Further reading: Martin Blumenson, *Patton: The Man behind the Legend, 1885–1945* (New York: Morrow, 1985); Ladislas Farago, *Patton: Ordeal and Triumph* (New York: Van Obolensky, 1963).

—George Michel Curry

Pearl Harbor

The Imperial Japanese naval air attack on the U.S. NAVY Pacific Fleet base at Pearl Harbor on the Hawaiian island of Oahu on Sunday, December 7, 1941, was the event that brought the United States into WORLD WAR II.

Planned by the commander in chief of the Imperial Japanese Combined Fleet, Admiral Isoroku Yamamoto, in mid-1941, the attack was intended to cripple the U.S. Navy, the one force that could effectively intervene to halt Japanese conquests in the Pacific and Asia. With no means of challenging Japanese power with its Pacific Fleet strength destroyed, the United States, Yamamoto believed, would have to accept Japanese conquests as a fait accompli. Although U.S. INTELLIGENCE experts were expecting a Japanese attack in Asia in late 1941 or early 1942, their focus was on Malaya, Hong Kong, and the PHILIPPINES, then thought more vulnerable. Few even considered the possibility of a naval air attack on Pearl Harbor, more than 3,400 miles from Japan, although U.S. commanders there were put on alert on November 27. Admiral Husband E. Kimmel, the U.S. Navy commander, Pacific Fleet, and Lieutenant General Walter Short, the U.S. ARMY commander in Hawaii, interpreted the warnings to indicate possible sabotage or submarine attacks.

Intelligence failures contributed to the overall lack of preparedness. The United States was unable to read Japanese diplomatic codes that could have revealed espionage by their diplomats in Hawaii. In addition, military interservice rivalries, the lack of a centralized intelligence agency capable of analyzing available information, and sheer disbelief that Japan was capable of launching an attack of such magnitude from so far away all added to the eventual shock and surprise. Despite claims of revisionist historians, no credible evidence has surfaced to indicate that President Roosevelt, British prime minister Winston Churchill, or any other Allied military or political leaders had direct evidence of an attack on Pearl Harbor and deliberately failed to act in hope of creating a "back door" to war.

Strict radio silence hid the movements of the Japanese Combined Fleet of some 20 warships, including six

Seen here are two of the six U.S. battleships sunk in the attack on Pearl Harbor. *(National Archives)*

aircraft carriers with 360 warplanes, after it left the Kurile Islands Naval Base on November 26, under the command of Vice Admiral Chuichi Nagumo. Arriving 275 miles north of Hawaii early on December 7, the Japanese launched their first wave of 49 bombers, 40 torpedo-bombers, 51 dive-bombers, and 43 fighters at 6:00 A.M. A second wave of 54 bombers, 78 dive-bombers, and 36 fighters soon followed. The first contact with the incoming aircraft was reported by the Opana Mobile Radar Unit at Kahuku Point between 6:45 and 7:00, but the sightings were misinterpreted as an incoming flight of B-17s expected to arrive that morning from California, and no alert was sounded.

When the first wave arrived at 7:55, they found 70 ships in Pearl Harbor, including eight battleships. The American fleet's three aircraft carriers and its heavy cruiser force, however, were still at sea, having just delivered fighter aircraft to Wake Island. Following bombing and strafing runs that lasted until 8:25, a 20-minute lull took place before a second raid by the high-level bombers and dive-bombers began, lasting until 9:45. Three battleships were sunk, one capsized, and all the others were damaged. Three destroyers, three light cruisers, and four other ships were also sunk or damaged. On the airfields, of 231 army aircraft, only 166 remained intact, while only 54 navy and marine planes, out of some 250, were operable. Fearing a counterattack, Nagumo decided against a third attack on dry-docks, machine shops, repair facilities, and fuel depots.

American losses were significant nonetheless, and more than 2,400 servicemen were killed, about half of them dying aboard the USS *Arizona*. Nearly 1,200 were wounded. Encountering only a weak and ineffective defense, the Japanese suffered light casualties, and only 29 aircraft and six SUBMARINES, five of them midgets, were lost that day.

Although it was a major disaster for the United States (and cost Kimmel and Short their careers and reputations), the raid galvanized American public opinion for war. And while a short-term tactical victory for Japan, the attack on Pearl Harbor turned into a long-term strategic defeat. The Japanese contention that the United States would not intervene to contest Japanese conquests proved overwhelmingly false, as the Pearl Harbor attack so enraged the United States that American participation in the war until final victory was guaranteed. The failure to destroy the harbor's infrastructure also harmed Japan, because within a year all but two vessels damaged or sunk at Pearl Harbor were back in service. And the sinking and damaging of so many battleships accelerated the navy's emphasis on aircraft carriers and AIR POWER. Pearl Harbor continued to function as the headquarters of the U.S. Pacific Fleet throughout the war and was the starting point of all the major campaigns in the PACIFIC THEATER that led to Japan's ultimate defeat in 1945.

Further reading: Walter Lord, *Day of Infamy* (New York: Holt, 1957); Gordon Prange, *At Dawn We Slept: The Untold Story of Pearl Harbor* (New York: McGraw-Hill, 1981); ———, *Pearl Harbor: The Verdict of History* (New York: McGraw-Hill, 1986); John Toland, *Infamy: Pearl Harbor and Its Aftermath* (Garden City, N.Y.: Doubleday, 1982); Roberta Wohlstetter, *Pearl Harbor: Warning and Decision* (Stanford, Calif.: Stanford University Press, 1962).

—Clayton D. Laurie

Perkins, Frances (1880–1965)

Frances Perkins, secretary of labor from 1933 to 1945, was the first female cabinet member ever and played an important part in shaping key NEW DEAL policies, including the SOCIAL SECURITY ACT.

Born Fannie Coralie Perkins in Boston on April 10, 1880, Perkins grew up in Worcester, Massachusetts. Her interest in social activism developed when she was attending Mount Holyoke College and was introduced to Florence Kelley and the National Consumers League. After several years teaching at a girl's school in Chicago, Perkins became involved in the city's settlement house movement. She changed her name to Frances, which had a more formal sound, and began a career in social reform.

After moving to New York in 1910, Perkins, like many social reformers of her time, was deeply affected by the Triangle Shirtwaist Company fire in 1911, which killed 146 female workers. Following this tragedy, she forged a close working relationship with Al Smith, the governor of New York during much of the 1920s. Through Smith, Perkins received her first public sector job, an appointment to the state Industrial Commission, where she sought protective labor legislation and better safety protections. While Perkins worked to educate Smith on the problems of industrial working conditions, she also became involved in politics, taking part in Smith's unsuccessful presidential candidacy in 1928 by working to mobilize female voters. When FRANKLIN D. ROOSEVELT was elected governor of New York in 1928, he appointed Perkins as industrial commissioner.

Roosevelt's election to the presidency in 1932 brought Perkins to Washington, D.C., as secretary of labor in 1933, the first female cabinet member ever and the highest-ranking female in the executive branch. Her selection was opposed by the AMERICAN FEDERATION OF LABOR (AFL) and by other LABOR unions, who considered Perkins a social worker, not a union advocate. But at the urging of ELEANOR ROOSEVELT and MARY "MOLLY" DEWSON, director of the Women's Division of the DEMOCRATIC PARTY,

Roosevelt appointed Perkins to the cabinet post despite the misgivings of organized labor and of Perkins herself. Perkins did bring a labor agenda with her to Washington, though it was more to fulfill Progressive Era protective labor legislation proposals than to promote such interests of labor unions as collective bargaining. She also became an important member of the so-called WOMEN'S NETWORK of the Roosevelt administration. Highest on her agenda were old-age insurance and unemployment insurance, programs that Perkins wanted included in a social security system for Americans.

Perkins helped persuade Roosevelt in 1934 that the time was right for a plan for economic security. Like Roosevelt, Perkins favored insurance programs over RELIEF programs to provide financial support for the unemployed or destitute. In June 1934, Roosevelt created the Committee on Economic Security (CES) by executive order and charged the committee to formulate legislation. Perkins headed the CES, whose proposals led to the Social Security Act of 1935, a package of programs that mixed social insurance and public assistance and helped create the modern American welfare state. Social Security was the major achievement of Perkins's tenure as secretary of labor, but she also helped secure passage of the FAIR LABOR STANDARDS ACT of 1938, which prohibited child labor in interstate commerce and established for many industrial workers a 40-hour work week and the first federal minimum wage.

Perkins's role in the landmark labor legislation of the New Deal, the NATIONAL LABOR RELATIONS ACT (NLRA) of 1935, was far smaller. Concerned about protective legislation and raising workers' purchasing power rather than ensuring their rights to organize and engage in collective bargaining, Perkins initially opposed the NLRA. After the NATIONAL INDUSTRIAL RECOVERY ACT, with its provisions for labor organizations, was declared unconstitutional in May 1935, Perkins and the Roosevelt administration eventually gave their support to the NLRA.

Perkins remained secretary of labor until Roosevelt's death in April 1945, and resigned soon after Harry S. Truman assumed the presidency. She had been the only secretary of labor during Roosevelt's 12 years as president and had achieved many legislative successes in addition to breaking a gender barrier in high GOVERNMENT positions. Her goal as secretary of labor had been to achieve greater protection for workers, using the government to do what she felt private industry would not: setting hour and wage minimums and creating a system of economic protection against unemployment and old age. She went on to serve first as a civil service commissioner, then as a professor at Cornell University. Perkins died on May 14, 1965, following a series of strokes, at the age of 85.

See also WOMEN'S STATUS AND RIGHTS.

Further reading: George Whitney Martin, *Madam Secretary, Frances Perkins* (Boston: Houghton Mifflin, 1976); Frances Perkins, *The Roosevelt I Knew* (New York: Viking, 1945).

—Katherine Liapis Segrue

Philippines

The Philippine Islands were an important focus of military action in the WORLD WAR II PACIFIC THEATER. The Philippines had been a possession of the United States since the 1898 Spanish-American War. In 1936, the United States decided to grant the islands full independence by 1946, and the remainder of the 1930s saw efforts at nation building. Special emphasis was placed on raising a Philippine Commonwealth Army of 110,000 men, commanded by retired American general Douglas A. MacArthur, to protect the islands amid growing threats posed by Japan in Asia. At the request of President FRANKLIN D. ROOSEVELT, MacArthur came out of retirement in July 1941 and assumed command of the U.S. ARMY Forces, Far East, which included the Filipino army and 22,000 American troops. Although the War Department considered the 7,100-island Philippine archipelago indefensible, MacArthur convinced the high command that his preparations, when complete in April 1942, would deter or delay a Japanese attack until relief could arrive from the United States.

The Japanese air attack on the Philippines on December 8, 1941, caught MacArthur's command by surprise and resulted in the destruction of his 125 warplanes on the ground. Two days later, on December 10, Japanese forces from Formosa landed on Luzon, with Filipino forces offering only token resistance before retreating toward Manila. On December 20, additional Japanese forces landed on Mindanao and Jolo. Facing overwhelming odds, MacArthur declared Manila an open city and withdrew to the Bataan Peninsula, moving his headquarters to Corregidor Island. The precipitate retreat left no time to move food and supplies, and food rationing began in January 1942. Under constant attack between January and April, starving

After directing a stubborn but ultimately unsuccessful defense against the Japanese invasion of the Philippines in 1942, General Douglas MacArthur was evacuated from Bataan in March and taken by PT boat to Australia, vowing, "I shall return." On October 20, 1944, with the tide of war turned in the Allies' favor, MacArthur fulfilled his promise to the Philippine people by wading ashore at Luzon. *(Hulton/Archive)*

American and Filipino forces continued to await reinforcements, although relief was never a realistic possibility. Following MacArthur's evacuation to Australia on March 11, 1942, the Americans held Bataan until surrendering on April 9. Forces on Corregidor, under Major General Jonathan M. Wainwright, surrendered unconditionally on May 6. At least 10,000 Americans, and some 60,000 Filipinos, were brutalized by the Japanese during the infamous BATAAN DEATH MARCH to prisoner of war camps, compounding the tragedy that had already cost 20,000 American and Filipino lives.

Many American and Filipino soldiers escaped into the jungles and formed guerilla units, but not until 200,000 U.S. Army forces supported by some 700 vessels invaded Leyte Island between October 20 and 22, 1944, was any serious challenge to Japanese control of the Philippines mounted. The battle for Leyte Island lasted until December 31 and cost 15,500 American and 70,000 Japanese casualties. Neither significant Japanese reinforcements nor attempts by its navy to interfere with the landings altered the outcome, although the naval BATTLE FOR LEYTE GULF, October 23–25, 1944, was the largest of the war and destroyed Japan's remaining sea power.

The wisdom of liberating the entire Philippine archipelago rather than bypassing the remaining 300,000 Japanese troops there was hotly debated among American leaders. MacArthur's entreaties that the United States had a moral obligation to the Filipinos, however, won out, and the main island of Luzon was invaded on January 9, 1945, by 68,000 U.S. Army troops. While American forces made rapid progress, Japanese forces melted away into the jungles to mount further resistance, which lasted until August 15. The capital, Manila, was declared an open city by General Tomoyuki Yamashita in February, but his order was ignored by Imperial Navy Marines, and the city was largely destroyed in the subsequent liberation. The conquest of Luzon cost 41,000 American casualties and 192,000 Japanese dead. Elsewhere between February and August 1945, U.S. Army troops began the island-by-island liberation of the country, beginning with the Visayas, Mindanao, and other southern islands. This campaign cost 119,000 American casualties and 50,000 Japanese dead.

The final liberation of the Philippines was not accomplished until August 15, 1945, when Japanese forces were ordered to lay down their arms by the emperor. In keeping with American promises, the Philippines became an independent republic on July 4, 1946.

Further reading: M. Hamlin Cannon, *Leyte: The Return to the Philippines* (Washington, D.C.: Office of the Chief of Military History, Department of the Army, 1984); Robert Ross Smith, *The Approach to the Philippines* (Washington, D.C.: Office of the Chief of Military History, Department

of the Army, 1953); ———, *Triumph in the Philippines* (Washington, D.C.: Office of the Chief of Military History, Department of the Army, 1963).

—Clayton D. Laurie

Philippine Sea, Battle of the (June 1944)

The Battle of the Philippine Sea took place off the MARIANA ISLANDS on June 19 and 20, 1944. It resulted from the effort of the Imperial Japanese Navy to attack the U.S. NAVY Fifth Fleet of Admiral Raymond Spruance then supporting U.S. MARINES and U.S. ARMY amphibious landings on the islands of Saipan, Guam, Rota, and Tinian that had begun on June 15. The largest aircraft battle of the war, the Battle of the Philippine Sea was an overwhelming victory for the U.S. Navy, which destroyed what remained of Japanese naval aviation.

Admiral Jisaburo Ozawa's First Mobile Fleet consisted of five battleships, 13 cruisers, 28 destroyers, nine aircraft carriers and 473 aircraft. The larger, newer, and technologically superior U.S. Navy force, Task Force 58, consisted of seven battleships, 21 cruisers, 69 destroyers, and 15 aircraft carriers with 956 aircraft piloted by seasoned American airmen who were veterans of several prior combat actions.

The Japanese, whose location in the Philippine Sea was made known to Spruance well in advance by American SUBMARINES, radio-direction finding, and radar, launched four successive carrier air strikes toward the U.S. fleet on June 19. Surprised and intercepted 150 miles away from the American fleet by U.S. naval aviators, the outclassed Japanese fliers were annihilated in what became known as "the Great Marianas Turkey Shoot." Only 29 American warplanes were lost, compared to Japanese losses of 301 aircraft the first day. On June 20, Spruance launched a further devastating attack on the Japanese fleet, using aircraft and submarines, destroying a further 145 Japanese aircraft, sinking three aircraft carriers, damaging two others, and sinking and damaging numerous other smaller vessels. Of the 80 American aircraft lost during the battle, most were forced to ditch at sea after running out of fuel at the extreme limits of their range, and most of the downed American pilots were recovered.

Following the Battle of the Philippine Sea, the American landings continued without threat of interference from Imperial Japanese Naval forces and the Marianas were secured by August 1944.

See also AIR POWER; WORLD WAR II PACIFIC THEATER.

Further reading: William T. Y'Blood, *Red Sun Setting: The Battle of the Philippine Sea* (Annapolis, Md.: Naval Institute Press, 1981).

—Clayton D. Laurie

photography

Between 1929 and 1945, photography became increasingly important in art (see ART AND ARCHITECTURE), social reform, POPULAR CULTURE, and even military operations.

By the onset of the GREAT DEPRESSION, photography had become an effective agent of reform as well as an established form of art. The efforts of such photographers as Alfred Stieglitz and Edward Steichen had enabled photography to gain acceptance as an art form, while others had followed the lead of Jacob Riis and Lewis Hine in pursuing documentary photography on behalf of social reform.

In the early 1930s, the nature-oriented Western school of photographers further developed the place of photography in the art community. Led by Edward Weston, members of this school abandoned soft-focus effects for a sharper, more detailed study of nature. Guided by this principle, Weston went on to help establish the f.64 Group in 1932. This group derived its name and artistic objectives from the smallest f-stop on the camera, which allowed for the maximum sharpness necessary for landscape photography. The most accomplished member of the Western school and the f.64 Group was the famous photographer Ansel Adams.

Although photography was not included in the FEDERAL ART PROJECT of the NEW DEAL, it did find an important place in the FARM SECURITY ADMINISTRATION (FSA). Recognizing the power of photography in the cause of reform, FSA director Roy Stryker undertook an effort to create a photographic record of the dreadful conditions of farmers and migratory laborers who faced economic disaster brought on by the depression and the DUST BOWL. FSA photographers, including Dorothea Lange and Walker Evans, created some 270,000 negatives during this project. Lange (coauthor of *An American Exodus* with Paul S. Taylor, 1939) devoted much attention to migrant workers, while Evans (coauthor of *Let Us Now Praise Famous Men* with James Agee, 1941), spent two years with the FSA following the plight of sharecroppers. When the Farm Security Agency was terminated during WORLD WAR II, its photographic section was transferred to the OFFICE OF WAR INFORMATION (OWI).

In 1936, the introduction of *LIFE* and *Look* magazines established a popular outlet for the new genre of photojournalism, which combined photographers with researchers, writers, and editors. Photographers were briefed for their assignments and encouraged to take great quantities of photographs, so that the editors could develop a picture story with maximum impact on readers. *Life*'s W. Eugene Smith and Margaret Bourke-White quickly became recognized as top photojournalists for their ability to depict the drama of events while maintaining perfect composition. Photojournalism also produced one of the most memorable images of World War II, when Associ-

This classic photograph, *Migrant Mother, Nipuma, California* (1936), was taken by Dorothea Lange for the Farm Security Administration. (*Library of Congress*)

ated Press photographer Joe Rosenthal took his Pulitzer Prize–winning picture of U.S. MARINES raising the American flag atop Mount Suribachi on IWO JIMA in 1945.

During the war, OWI photographers sought to portray American life and culture to inspire patriotism as well as to document social change for AFRICAN AMERICANS, women, and other groups. Also responsible for coordinating the release of war news for domestic use, OWI controlled images produced by combat cameramen, who served on the battlefronts and whose work was essential to the historical record of the war. OWI wanted the photographs used to bolster home-front morale and to maintain popular approval for the America war effort, so images of American casualties and other photographs deemed inappropriate for release were kept at the Pentagon in a file known as the "Chamber of Horrors." By September 1943, concerned with public complacency as the war turned in favor of the Allies, the government released the first images of dead Americans and thereafter presented increasingly more graphic depictions in order to maintain the support needed for victory. Even so, *Life* did not show photographs of American blood being shed until 1945.

Photography also took on new roles for the military as it served as a primary source of INTELLIGENCE during World War II. In the two years following the bombing of PEARL HARBOR, U.S. airmen mapped some 21 million square kilometers of the earth's surface. General HENRY H. "HAP" ARNOLD, the commanding general of the U.S. ARMY AIR FORCES, declared that "a camera mounted on a P-38 often has proved more valuable than a P-38 with guns." The role of photography was especially evident in preparations for the invasion of NORMANDY, which relied on vital intelligence gathered from more than 4,500 photographic reconnaissance sorties. Photography thus served a variety of purposes in the era of the Great Depression and World War II.

Further reading: James Agee and Walker Evans, *Let Us Now Praise Famous Men* (Boston: Houghton Mifflin, 1941); Pete Daniel et al., *Official Images: New Deal Photography* (Washington, D.C.: Smithsonian Institution Press, 1987); Dorothea Lange and Paul Schuster Taylor, *An American Exodus: A Record of Human Erosion* (New York: Reynal & Hitchcock, 1939); George H. Roeder Jr., *The Censored War: American Visual Experience during World War Two* (New Haven, Conn.: Yale University Press, 1993); Alan Trachtenberg, *Reading American Photographs: Images as History, Mathew Brady to Walker Evans* (New York: Hill & Wang, 1989).

—Ronald G. Simon

Polish Americans

One of the largest ethnic groups in the United States, Polish Americans became increasingly assimilated into American society during the period of the GREAT DEPRESSION and WORLD WAR II. The depression had a particularly severe impact upon the predominantly working-class Polish-American population, and the NEW DEAL programs of President FRANKLIN D. ROOSEVELT made them staunch supporters of the DEMOCRATIC PARTY. During the war, the status of Poland deeply concerned them and affected their reaction to American FOREIGN POLICY.

Although there had been Poles in America since colonial times, the largest wave of IMMIGRATION occurred in the 30 years before World War I, when nearly 3 million ethnic Poles emigrated from eastern Europe. Most settled near industrial cities in the industrial and mining states of the Northeast and upper Midwest, and they typically took low-income jobs in mining and manufacturing. Polish Americans tended to live in their own enclaves, where language, culture, community institutions, and a devout Catholicism maintained their ethnic identity and slowed assimilation. A number of Polish JEWS also arrived during this period, but they experienced different geographic and economic patterns from those of the Catholic Polish population and generally identified themselves as Jews rather than as Poles.

World War I and the decade of the 1920s brought important developments for Polish Americans. The nation of Poland was reconstituted after the Versailles Treaty. Native-born individuals now often controlled the fraternal aid associations, and postwar prosperity enabled Polish Americans to begin leaving their initial urban neighborhoods. Polish Americans also had increasing political success; some won election to Congress, and many Poles enthusiastically supported the presidential candidacy of Catholic Democrat Al Smith.

The Great Depression hit Polish Americans particularly hard because so many were employed in the most heavily affected industries. The economic downturn overwhelmed the ability of self-help and fraternal aid associations to support the families of the unemployed workers, and threatened the traditional stability of Polish neighborhoods. In those ways and others, the depression probably hastened the assimilation of Polish Americans, who became a greater presence and force in the mainstream political and LABOR activities. Voting overwhelmingly for Roosevelt and the New Deal, Polish Americans proved to be an important component in the coalition of urban and southern voters that made the Democratic Party the nation's new majority party in the 1930s. Polish Americans were also active in the burgeoning of the LABOR movement. Historically involved in union activity, they accounted for a large portion of the growing membership of the unions in such blue-collar industries as steel, mining, and automobiles that played a crucial role in the emergence of the CONGRESS OF INDUSTRIAL ORGANIZATIONS.

Polish Americans supported the Allied cause from the beginning of World War II in September 1939, when Poland fell to Nazi Germany. They supported the LEND-LEASE ACT helping Britain and voted in even larger numbers than in 1936 for Roosevelt in the ELECTION OF 1940 because of his anti-AXIS interventionism as well as his domestic reform. An estimated 1 million Polish Americans or more joined the military. The war accelerated their assimilation as many Polish Americans mixed with other Americans in the armed forces and as workers in war industries, and they made impressive contributions to the war effort.

For Polish Americans, the fate of Poland was of crucial importance, especially regarding issues concerning the nation's postwar borders, the independence of its government, and its domination by the Soviet Union. Although their political support for FDR waned only slightly, many were critical of his actions at the YALTA CONFERENCE in 1945, where Roosevelt, keenly aware of the political clout of millions of Polish Americans, had tried unsuccessfully to ensure the independence of Poland. The end of the war also saw a growth of a pervasive anticommunist attitude among Polish Americans due to the actions of the USSR in Eastern Europe. This attitude was reinforced by the postwar arrival of thousands of refugees from Communist-dominated Poland, many of whom later came to have a large influence in Polish-American associations.

See also POLITICS IN THE ROOSEVELT ERA.

Further reading: John J. Bukowczyk, *And My Children Did Not Know Me: A History of the Polish-Americans* (Bloomington: Indiana University Press, 1987); Stephan Thernstrom, ed., *Harvard Encyclopedia of American Ethnic Groups* (Cambridge, Mass.: Belknap Press of Harvard University Press, 1980).

—Robert J. Hanyok

politics in the Roosevelt era

The DEMOCRATIC PARTY became the nation's majority party in the 1930s and retained its majority status during WORLD WAR II and after. This constituted a major turning point in American politics, for at the outset of the HOOVER PRESIDENCY in 1929, the REPUBLICAN PARTY seemed in a position of virtually unchallenged dominance. The normal majority party since the 1890s, Republicans had decisively won each of the three presidential elections in the 1920s and had controlled CONGRESS throughout the decade. In 1928, HERBERT C. HOOVER defeated Democratic nominee Alfred E. Smith by a margin of 58.2 percent to 40.9 percent in the popular vote for president and by 444 to 87 votes in the electoral college. Republicans controlled the 71st Congress that met in 1929 by 267-167 in the House and by 56-39 in the Senate. The Democratic Party was badly divided between its urban and rural wings and offered neither substantial policy alternatives nor serious political challenge to the Republicans.

Then came the STOCK MARKET CRASH of late 1929, and over the next three years the GREAT DEPRESSION sent the ECONOMY spiraling down, with UNEMPLOYMENT reaching at least one-fourth of the labor force and with national income down by more than 50 percent. The depression had devastating political consequences for Hoover and the Republican Party. In 1930, Democrats and Republicans virtually broke even in elections to the House of Representatives and the Senate. When the 72nd Congress met in 1931, Democrats controlled the House by 220-214 (because of the deaths and replacements that gave

Democrats a net gain of three seats). Although Republicans nominally controlled the Senate by 48-47, that body was effectively in the hands of a coalition of Democrats and progressive Republicans.

The ELECTION OF 1932 then completed the transfer of power from the Republicans to the Democrats. FRANKLIN D. ROOSEVELT defeated Hoover for the presidency by winning 42 of the 48 states, with 57.4 percent of the popular vote and 472 of the 531 votes in the electoral college. Democrats picked up some 90 additional seats in the House and 13 in the Senate and controlled the 73rd Congress that met in 1933 by 310-117 in the House and 60-35 in the Senate. The elections of 1930 and 1932 thus constituted a political turnaround of great magnitude—yet the electorate had voted much more against Hoover and the Republicans than for Roosevelt and the Democrats. Except for making it clear that he would be a more active president than Hoover, Roosevelt had not clearly or consistently said just what his policies would be. Voters also rejected truly radical alternatives in 1932, as they would throughout the depression decade, for NORMAN THOMAS, the Socialist Party candidate, won just 2.2 percent of the vote, and the COMMUNISTS just three-tenths of 1 percent.

In the off-year election of 1934 and then in the presidential ELECTION OF 1936, voters returned powerful affirmative verdicts on Roosevelt and the NEW DEAL to complete a realigning transformation of American politics that established the Democrats as the new majority party. In 1934, Democrats picked up nine additional House seats and another nine Senate seats—a significant departure from the previous off-year elections in the 20th century, when the incumbent president's party had lost on average some three dozen seats in the House and three or four in the Senate. Then, in 1936, Roosevelt won 60.8 percent of the popular vote and 523 of the 531 votes in the electoral college; only Maine and Vermont voted for Republican candidate ALFRED M. LANDON. All minor party candidates combined won less than 3 percent of the vote, with Socialist and Communist candidates together winning less than 1 percent. And the Democrats increased still further their already top-heavy control of the Congress, outnumbering Republicans by 331-89 in the House and 76-16 in the Senate when the 75th Congress met in 1937.

The Democrats owed their new majority status to the Roosevelt coalition of voters forged from 1928 to 1936. The coalition showed some continuities from past voting patterns, but also reflected the impact of the depression, New Deal, and Franklin Roosevelt on American politics. In part the Democratic majority was based on the party's continuing dominance of the "Solid South" that southern whites (most blacks remained disfranchised) had made reliably Democratic since the era of the Civil War and Reconstruction. Democrats also built upon and increased traditional strength among urban ethnic voters, with heavy support from CATHOLICS and JEWS. AFRICAN AMERICANS shifted to the Democratic Party in the mid-1930s. Decisive margins among working-class and middle-class voters also contributed to the new Democratic majority; in 1936, Roosevelt won roughly 4 out of every 5 working-class and union voters, and 3 out of every 5 middle-class voters. Such strength among urban ethnic, black, and working-class voters helped Roosevelt and the Democrats to win most metropolitan areas by margins of two-thirds and more. For their part, Republicans continued to find their greatest support among upper-income and old-stock Protestant voters. Farmers voted heavily for Roosevelt in 1932; but by 1936, midwestern farmers had begun to return to their more traditional Republican moorings.

The structure of the Roosevelt coalition reflected the dynamics of American politics from the late 1920s to the mid-1930s. For one thing, it depended upon the continuing importance of ethnic identities in the era and the Democrats' image as the more inclusive party. Democrats had nominated Al Smith for president in 1928, and millions of urban ethnic voters came to the polls for the first time, to rally behind Smith, a second-generation American and the first Catholic nominated for the presidency. Although he was soundly defeated, Smith's 15 million votes were almost as many as Democrats had won in the past two presidential elections combined. Most of the new voters evidently stayed with the Democratic Party, largely because these predominantly working-class people were especially vulnerable to the depression and were then helped by New Deal policies. But the Democrats continued after 1928 to offer more GOVERNMENT appointments and political nominations to Catholics and Jews and thus won their allegiance for ethnic as well as economic reasons.

But it was the depression and the New Deal, not ethnic or racial issues, that counted most in forging the new Democratic majority. In 1932, massive switching from the Republican to the Democratic Party because of the depression produced Roosevelt's landslide: Hoover had won 21.4 million votes in 1928, but just 15.8 million in 1932; by contrast, in 1932 Roosevelt won 22.8 million votes as against Smith's 15 million in 1928. In 1936, the entry of millions of new voters into the active electorate, rather than voter-switching, was the most important dynamic. Alf Landon actually won nearly a million more votes than Hoover had in 1932, but Roosevelt won almost 5 million votes more than in 1932 and increased his percentage of the popular vote from 57.4 to 60.8 percent. Some of Roosevelt's higher totals came from African-American and other voters switching from the GOP, but most came from young, ethnic, black, and working-class voters entering the active electorate for the first time and voting overwhelmingly for Roosevelt and the Democrats. Women, especially working-class, ethnic, and black women, also voted in much larger numbers beginning in 1928, and also to the benefit of the Democrats. From 1924 to 1936, voter turnout increased by almost three-fifths, from 29.1 million to 45.6 million voters, with the big surges coming in 1928 and 1936 and among working-class, ethnic, and urban voters flocking to the Democratic Party.

But while some feared for the two-party system after the 1936 election, the Republican Party retained major sources of real and potential strength. In addition to their own large core of supporters, Republicans could appeal to those concerned about the direction of the New Deal and the Democratic Party. Though the election of 1936 had obviously ratified the New Deal, voters generally seem to have supported specific programs for practical reasons rather than being converted ideologically to an expansive LIBERALISM. As subsequent events would show, traditional small-government and individualistic CONSERVATISM, opposed to a too-powerful central government, remained strong, even among many Democrats. Republicans made significant gains in the off-year election of 1938, especially because of the RECESSION OF 1937–38, but also because of the COURT-PACKING PLAN and LABOR unrest and the opposition they generated. In a striking return to the customary pattern of the incumbent president's party losing strength in off-year elections, the GOP gained 75 seats in the House and seven in the Senate. Democrats still easily controlled the Congress (261-164 in the House, 69-23 in the Senate), but an emerging CONSERVATIVE COALITION of Republicans and conservative (especially southern) Democrats increasingly thwarted Roosevelt and liberal Democrats in their efforts to expand the New Deal.

Despite Republican gains and Democratic setbacks in the late 1930s, however, Roosevelt won an unprecedented third term in the ELECTION OF 1940, and the new Democratic majority proved its durability. Roosevelt defeated Republican nominee WENDELL L. WILLKIE by 54.8 to 44.8 percent in the popular vote and by 449 to 82 in the electoral college. Although the beginning of WORLD WAR II in Europe produced a political context much different from the 1930s, the war figured less in the campaign and voting than did issues and party images from the depression and New Deal years. Accordingly, most voters voted as they had in 1936, and the Roosevelt coalition emerged largely intact from its first major test. To a significant degree, the victory was a personal one for Roosevelt himself, for Democrats picked up only a few seats in the House and lost three more in the Senate.

Republicans again made inroads into Democratic control of Congress in the off-year election of 1942, the first true wartime election in the United States. A number of things favored Republicans in 1942: prosperity had returned, diminishing the impact of New Deal issues,

PRESIDENTIAL ELECTIONS, 1928–1944

Year	Candidate	Party	Popular Vote		Electoral Vote
			Total	Percent	
1928					
	Herbert C. Hoover	Republican	21,391,993	58.2	444
	Alfred E. Smith	Democratic	15,016,169	40.9	87
	Norman Thomas	Socialist	267,835	.7	
	Other	(Socialist Labor;			
		Workers; Prohibition)	62,890	.2	
1932					
	Franklin D. Roosevelt	Democratic	22,809,638	57.4	472
	Herbert C. Hoover	Republican	15,758,901	39.7	59
	Norman Thomas	Socialist	881,951	2.2	
	William Z. Foster	Communist	102,785	.3	
	William D. Upshaw	Prohibition	81,869	.2	
	William H. Harvey	Liberty	53,425	.1	
	Other	(Socialist Labor)	33,276	.1	
1936					
	Franklin D. Roosevelt	Democratic	27,752,869	60.8	523
	Alfred M. Landon	Republican	16,674,665	36.5	8
	William Lemke	Union	882,479	1.9	
	Norman Thomas	Socialist	187,720	.4	
	Earl Browder	Communist	80,159	.2	
	Other	(Prohibition;			
		Socialist Labor)	50,624	.1	
1940					
	Franklin D. Roosevelt	Democratic	27,307,819	54.8	449
	Wendell L. Willkie	Republican	22,321,018	44.8	82
	Norman Thomas	Socialist	99,557	.2	
	Roger Q. Babson	Prohibition	57,812	.1	
	Other	(Communist;			
		Socialist Labor)	61,143	.1	
1944					
	Franklin D. Roosevelt	Democratic	25,606,585	53.5	432
	Thomas E. Dewey	Republican	22,014,745	46.0	99
	Norman Thomas	Socialist	80,518	.2	
	Claude A. Watson	Prohibition	74,758	.2	
	Other	(Socialist Labor)	45,336	.1	

*Source: The Statistical History of the United States, from Colonial Times to the Present (Stamford, Conn.: Fairfield Publisher, 1965). Only candidates with at least 50,000 votes are listed separately.

especially with Roosevelt off the ballot; many voters were angry at inflation, shortages, and RATIONING on the home front; and the war effort down to election day seemed ineffective, with red-tape snarls affecting MOBILIZATION and with the Germans and Japanese seemingly successful in both the EUROPEAN THEATER and the PACIFIC THEATER of the war. Republicans gained 46 seats in the House and another nine senators, paring Democratic control to 218-208 in the House and 58-37 in the Senate and placing ideological control clearly in the hands of the conservative coalition.

But the ensuing presidential ELECTION OF 1944 demonstrated the continuing dominance of Roosevelt and the Democrats. Roosevelt defeated Republican presidential nominee Thomas E. Dewey by 53.5 percent to 46 percent in the popular vote and by 432 to 99 votes in the electoral college, and Democrats increased their margin in the House (to 242-190) though dropping two more Senate seats (which pared their control there to 56-38). In the election, the chief issue was postwar prosperity and full employment, followed by postwar peace; and on both issues, Roosevelt and the Democrats enjoyed a clear margin in public confidence. Voting patterns changed less between 1940 and 1944 than in any other election in the 1930s and 1940s, with nine of 10 voters voting in 1944 as they had in 1940. The Roosevelt coalition had thus endured the test of new circumstances and issues during the war with relatively modest erosion. In fact, Democrats would remain the majority party for another quarter century, and issues, party images, and voting patterns from the Roosevelt era remained visible in the nation's politics at the turn of the 21st century.

Further reading: John M. Allswang, *The New Deal and American Politics* (New York: John Wiley & Sons, 1978); John W. Jeffries, *Testing the Roosevelt Coalition: Connecticut Society and Politics in the Era of World War II* (Knoxville: University of Tennessee Press, 1979); Everett C. Ladd Jr. with Charles D. Hadley, *Transformations of the American Party System: Political Coalitions from the New Deal to the 1970s*, 2d rev. ed. (New York: W. W. Norton, 1978); Samuel Lubell, *The Future of American Politics*, 3d rev. ed. (New York: Harper & Row, 1965); Clyde P. Weed, *The Nemesis of Reform: The Republican Party during the New Deal* (New York: Columbia University Press, 1994).

popular culture

Amidst the economic and political insecurity of the GREAT DEPRESSION and WORLD WAR II from 1929 to 1945, an unprecedented national popular culture emerged, expressing both an expanded sense of national unity and widespread feelings of dissent and discontent. The popular culture of this period had a reach beyond that of previous decades largely because of the new mass media, particularly RADIO and the MOVIES. The advent of new printing and recording technologies enabled other media and popular culture forms—magazine publishing, ADVERTISING, and popular MUSIC—to assume a new national scope and importance too. As Americans tuned their radios to the same national daily programs, flocked to the same Hollywood movies, and memorized the same Madison Avenue jingles and slogans, they came to share a common cultural experience.

More than that, thanks to these shared encounters, Americans experienced dramatic changes in social space. Radio waves invaded the intimate space of the home, blurring the boundaries between public and private. National broadcasts, along with the national distribution of movies, consumer goods, popular music, and professional SPORTS increasingly collapsed the nation into a single market and shrunk the distance between different social groups who now had access to the same popular culture vernacular.

One of the most striking things about the new mass-mediated popular culture of the period was its celebration of the mass audience that it catered to. The figure of "the people" was a central, if ambivalent symbol. In the context of the Great Depression, the still-new national mass media discovered "the people" as both a new audience and a new protagonist. "The people" consisted in large part of the millions of unionized laborers, immigrants, and unemployed who resonated so strongly with FRANKLIN D. ROOSEVELT's rhetoric of the "Forgotten Man."

In movies, advertisements, popular songs, and on the radio and playing fields, populist images abounded. Many of these images—the corrupt banker and honest outlaw of John Ford's classic western, *Stagecoach,* for example—tended to reinforce a left-leaning critique of capitalism, or, more broadly, to support the liberalism of the NEW DEAL. Indeed, the WORKS PROGRESS ADMINISTRATION itself subsidized a great deal of populist popular art, including theater, storytelling, and painting.

But the overall ideological message of this new sphere of popular culture and its embrace of "the people" is not at all clear. With its commercial financing and emphasis on romance, comedy, and happy endings, most of the popular narratives of Hollywood, network radio, and Broadway reinforced conformity and nonpolitical solutions to problems of poverty and oppression. And the very structure of the new media, with centrally produced messages directed to a largely passive mass audience, led some critics to fear that the fascist potential of mass-media, tapped so adeptly in Germany, could be exploited in the United States as well. For example, popular music, like big band swing, exuded a liberal urban ethos of racial diversity, use of illicit drugs, and increasingly frank expressions of sexuality. However, musicians and audiences were often constrained to conform to the segregated and conservative conditions of broadcast studios, record companies, and some nightclubs.

Nowhere were these contradictions more apparent than in Hollywood's "dream factory." By 1934, the motion picture industry had already begun to recover from the depression. Weekly attendance figures rose from some 60 million in 1932 to 85 million during the war. Weekend visits to the movie theater often included a newsreel, cartoons, and an A and a B feature—an impressive entertainment value at 25¢ a ticket. A significant fraction of this massive national audience comprised immigrants and laborers sympathetic to or affiliated with the new industrial unions. The highbrow settings common to the movies prior to the depression gave way after the STOCK MARKET CRASH

Actor, entertainer, and comedian Jack Benny plays the violin on stage during a radio broadcast. *(Hulton/Archive)*

to the demimonde of gangster, dancers, and prostitutes; to the devastated farms of the DUST BOWL; and to the streets, shop floors, and saloons of the CITIES, where the forgotten men and women, sang, danced, fought, and fell in love.

In 1934, with the advent of the Hays Commission, an industry-sponsored censorship bureau, Hollywood movies lost some of their brazen sexuality and subversive story-lines. Lovers became more chaste, and gangsters and other outlaws were required to pay for their crimes at the end of the film. Still, movies like *Goldiggers of 1933, The Grapes of Wrath,* and *Modern Times* depicted with sympathy the struggles of the forgotten people at the bottom of the economic pyramid. Movies like *Little Caesar, I Am a Fugitive from a Chain Gang,* and *All Quiet on the Western Front* revealed the ugly underside of the optimism and patriotism that had been so central to the popular and political culture of the 1920s. Hollywood stars Will Rogers and Charlie

Chaplin embodied the humble Everyman with comic flair that made them box-office favorites. And more than any other figure of the 1930s, the phenomenal popularity of Walt Disney's cartoon character Mickey Mouse epitomized the power of the motion pictures to generate loveable "underdog" characters.

Network radio achieved an even more impressive saturation, as daily broadcasts of *Amos 'n' Andy* and *The Goldbergs* and weekly broadcasts of *The Jack Benny Program* and *Fibber McGee and Molly* reached millions of Americans. When President Roosevelt addressed his public in his famous fireside chats, he set new audience records. During these highly popular broadcasts, cab drivers in big cities reported a drop-off in business, water utilities recorded a similar drop-off in water usage, and movie theater ushers confronted empty seats. These broadcasts were like national rituals, uniting Americans in simultaneous moments of shared experience. The fireside chats in particular emphasized the powerful connection between participation in a mass audience and citizenship, a link that proved to be crucial to Roosevelt's political power, given the fact that the majority of newspaper publishers were quite hostile to the New Deal and to Roosevelt himself.

Radio's power to unite was complicated—and undermined—by representations of AFRICAN AMERICANS and other racial and ethnic minorities that tended to reinforce existing segregation and prejudice. While *Amos 'n' Andy* brought the lives of black characters (played by white actors) into the homes of millions of Americans on a daily basis, the stereotypical representations of African Americans did little to challenge the racist notions behind segregation and racial violence.

Along with the advent of sound in motion pictures, radio broadcasts ushered in a new era in which voice was a powerful means of popular culture expression. The voice in talkies and on radio conveyed gender, ethnic, and class identities in ways that words and images could not. Voice—accent, intonation, timing, and pitch—conveyed subversive meanings that could not necessarily be captured by censors reviewing scripts. Through these media, Americans were brought into regular intimate contact with the untutored voices of "the people" in ways that often did undermine traditional class hierarchies. In an invisible medium like radio, voice carried the full burden of representing distinctions in race, gender, region, and socioeconomic background.

Documentary was another characteristic mode of the popular culture of the period. From the New Deal–funded arts projects, to movie newsreels and photojournalism, to the new science of PUBLIC OPINION POLLS, popular culture increasingly took the form of documenting the people. Following the lead of social scientists, advertisers and politicians invoked "the Great American Average" as a way to represent consumers and citizens, respectively. The Living Newspapers of the FEDERAL THEATRE PROJECT, films like Pare Lorentz's *The River* and *The Plow That Broke the Plains* and the PHOTOGRAPHY of Walker Evans and Margaret Bourke-White used the documentary form as social and political commentary about depression-era poverty and injustice. Audience participation broadcasts, *March of Time* newsreels, and print advertisements also employed documentary style to emphasize the immediacy and relevance of their messages and to achieve a kind of ersatz journalistic authenticity.

While much of the popular culture in the years 1929–45 centered on images of "the people," this was also an era in which supermen reached a new kind of iconic status in the United States. Superheroes such as the Shadow, Batman, the Green Hornet, and, of course, Superman himself burst onto the scene, achieving enormous popularity across a variety of media: comic books, pulp novels, radio, film, and newspaper cartoons. Sports figures like Babe Ruth, Lou Gehrig,

Dizzy Dean, Babe Didrikson, and JOE LOUIS became larger than life thanks in part to the perpetual glare of the news media, which celebrated their feats and recorded their every move. JESSE OWENS's victory over the Germans in the 1936 Olympics in Berlin carried layers of symbolic importance for Americans, especially for African Americans.

As the likelihood of U.S. entrance into WWII became ever clearer, the popular culture, along with the rest of the country, veered into war MOBILIZATION mode as early as 1939. Radio programs retuned their formats to promote the defense industry; motion pictures increasingly turned to plots sympathetic to the Allied cause, even cartoons began to incorporate comically exaggerated images—some of them racist—of AXIS leaders as the nemeses of popular heroes like Bugs Bunny. As some of the superstars of professional sports and Hollywood enlisted for one form or another of national service to the war effort, American popular culture increasingly embraced the war effort over themes of social diversity and critique.

Feeling the subtle but unmistakable pressure exerted by the OFFICE OF WAR INFORMATION, the Justice Department and other federal agencies, such cultural producers as broadcasters, filmmakers, publishers, and advertisers, avoided controversy and conflict in favor of morale-boosting images of wartime unity. The popular culture of the war years was marked by patriotic imagery and liberal pluralism, two concepts that were often joined in the multicultural foxhole scenes that became Hollywood clichés, to cite one example. In addition, popular films, radio programs, songs, and advertisements continually evoked lofty national goals, including the FOUR FREEDOMS, the virtues of the American people and their way of life, and the prospects of the good life of abundance once the war was over.

See also RECREATION; TECHNOLOGY.

Further reading: Lizabeth Cohen, *Making a New Deal: Industrial Workers in Chicago, 1919–1939* (New York: Cambridge University Press, 1990); Michael Denning, *The Cultural Front: The Laboring of American Culture in the Twentieth Century* (London and New York: Verso, 1996); John Jeffries, *Wartime America: The World War II Home Front* (Chicago: Ivan R. Dee, 1996); Lary May, *The Big Tomorrow: Hollywood and the Politics of the American Way* (Chicago: University of Chicago Press, 2000); Warren Susman, *Culture as History: The Transformation of American Society in the Twentieth Century* (New York: Pantheon, 1984).

—Jason Loviglio

Popular Front

In 1935, the Communist International, known as the Comintern, issued a statement urging COMMUNISTS around the world to postpone their revolutionary goals and work instead toward the eradication of fascism. Fascism, Moscow said, must be recognized as a distinct and serious threat, one that must be overcome before the broader struggle against bourgeois hegemony could continue. Communists were instructed to join forces with SOCIALISTS and others on the left in a "Popular Front" and to refrain from such anti-Socialist and antiliberal rhetoric as calling FRANKLIN D. ROOSEVELT and other liberals "social fascists."

Support for the new policy was most widespread among communists in France and Spain, and Popular Front coalitions gained control of the governments in both countries. French communists supported socialist Leon Blum, who was elected to head a Popular Front government in 1936. In Spain, a series of Popular Front governments ruled from 1936 to 1939, throughout the SPANISH CIVIL WAR between loyalist supporters of the government on the one hand and Francisco Franco and his Nationalist Party on the other. Although Popular Front candidates did not gain control of the government in Great Britain, they garnered support among substantial segments of the population.

The Popular Front was unable to acquire such influence in the United States, primarily because of the minor role traditionally played by the far left in American politics. In addition, the Popular Front initiative met with serious resistance from Socialist Party leaders. The Comintern instructed the Communist Party of the United States (CPUSA) to concentrate its efforts on building a new political party, the Farmer-Labor Party, which would function as an American Popular Front organization. When the Socialists refused to participate in a Farmer-Labor campaign for the presidency in 1936, the CPUSA, led by Earl Browder, petitioned the Comintern for permission to adapt the directive to the unique circumstances faced by communists in the United States. Moscow agreed that a new tactic was needed, and proposed that the CPUSA support Roosevelt's bid for reelection. This plan was also abandoned, when it was recognized that an endorsement by communists would likely hurt Roosevelt's campaign more than it would help. In the end, the CPUSA ran its own ticket headed by Browder, who railed against the REPUBLICAN PARTY but avoided criticizing Roosevelt or his NEW DEAL policies. He received just 80,000 votes—a scant two-tenths of 1 percent of the popular vote.

After the ELECTION OF 1936, the CPUSA continued to work toward the creation of a strong Farmer-Labor Party. To attract prospective members and broaden its influence, the CPUSA stepped up its efforts on behalf of organized LABOR. Party members sometimes played important roles in helping establish the fledgling CONGRESS OF INDUSTRIAL ORGANIZATIONS (CIO) and held important positions in some CIO unions. The CPUSA criticized the Roosevelt Administration for applying the NEUTRALITY ACTS to the Spanish Civil War and was instrumental in forming the Abraham Lincoln Brigade, comprised of several thousand American volunteers who went to fight against Franco in Spain.

Throughout the Popular Front period, Browder also tried to "Americanize" communism. His 1936 campaign slogan claimed that "Communism is Twentieth-Century Americanism," and CPUSA rallies of the time placed Washington and Lincoln on the same pedestal with Lenin and Marx. While the CPUSA's foray into coalition building never convinced many workers to become communists, it did win for communism more American support than it had ever had before. In the years between 1935 and 1939, CPUSA membership grew considerably and reached its highest number ever, with estimates ranging as high as 100,000. The CPUSA also sponsored or infiltrated peace, youth, and religious groups in an effort to expand its influence.

In the fall of 1939, following the signing of the NAZI-SOVIET PACT in August, the Communist Party leadership in Moscow announced that the Popular Front strategy was to be abandoned. Many people, including some top CPUSA leaders, were shocked and angered by the reversal in policy. This sense of betrayal, together with the CPUSA's renewed criticism of Roosevelt and the DEMOCRATIC PARTY, reduced party membership and increased anticommunist sentiment. In the next two years, the CPUSA sided with ISOLATIONISTS in opposing a FOREIGN POLICY that was increasingly anti-AXIS.

After the German invasion of the Soviet Union in June 1941, the Communist Party again sounded the call for antifascist unity. The Soviet people's bravery and sacrifice while fighting the Nazis, together with the formation of the GRAND ALLIANCE after U.S. entry into the war, helped to partially rehabilitate communism's image. This second "popular front" also proved to be short-lived, however, for the end of World War II brought the beginning of the cold war and the escalation of anticommunism in American politics.

Further reading: Harvey Klehr, *The Heyday of American Communism: The Depression Decade* (New York: Basic Books, 1984).

—Pamela J. Lauer

population trends

Events of such great magnitude and diverse consequences as the GREAT DEPRESSION and WORLD WAR II almost inevitably affect population trends. Overall, the 1929–45 era divides into three segments in terms of the impact on population. The early years of the depression generally slowed existing trends, most obviously in marriages, births, divorces, and MIGRATION. From the mid-1930s to the beginning of World War II, population trends largely resumed previous patterns. And then during the war, population change sped up, sometimes dramatically, particularly in marriages, births, and migration. But there were variations and exceptions to these generalizations, and dynamics already underway before 1929 often continued to shape demographic trends.

Population growth slowed dramatically in the 1930s, partly because of falling birth rates but also because of a sharp reduction in IMMIGRATION as a result of the depression and of the immigration restriction legislation of the 1920s. Between 1930 and 1940, the U.S. population increased by just 7 percent (from 123 million to 132 million)—the lowest growth rate for a decade ever registered since the nation's founding. Population growth in the 1940s was about twice that, in line with the 1910–30 rate, as it picked up during the war and then still more afterward.

The depression and then the war had a significant impact on MARRIAGE AND FAMILY LIFE. Economic insecurity produced by high UNEMPLOYMENT and low incomes meant the postponement of many marriages early in the depression, and the marriage rate (measured by the number of marriages per 1,000 unmarried women aged 15 and over) fell from 67.6 in 1930 to just 56 in 1932. It then increased, to 72.5 in 1935, to 82.7 in 1940, and to a wartime high of 93.6 in 1942. It fell to 84.5 in 1945 and then shot up to a peak of 120.7 in 1946. (It declined to the still substantial level of 90.2 by 1950.)

Because the marriage rate had been above 90 in 1920, the sharp drop early in the depression may have been in part a continuation of 1920s trends. But the increase after the mid-1930s, and especially during the war, is clear; deferred marriages from the early 1930s and then war marriages evidently account for the trend. Having generally fallen in the first three decades of the century, the median age of first marriage held steady for men (24.3) and rose only slightly for women (increasing from 21.3 to 21.5) in the 1930s, before decreasing with wartime and postwar marriages (to 22.8 for men and 20.3 for women by 1950).

Divorce rates also showed significant changes in the era. The divorce rate (divorces per 1,000 married women) had risen from 4 in 1900 to about 5 in 1910 and then to 8 in 1920 before falling slightly in the 1920s to 7.5 by 1930. In the early years of the depression, the divorce rate dropped to 6.1 in 1932 and 1933, then rose to 7.8 in 1935 and 8.8 in 1940, and then increased more rapidly still to 14.5 in 1945 before peaking at 17.8 in 1946. Clearly, the end of the war brought the dissolution of war marriages that had not worked, as well as enabling marriages that had been deferred.

Both the depression and World War II affected birth rates. Continuing their long-term decline, birth rates had fallen from 30.1 per 1,000 people in 1910 to 21.3 in 1930. They then fell further, to 18.4 in 1933; and the rate of decline from 1930 to 1933 was about three times that of the 1910–30 rate. Birthrates then generally moved up in the mid- and late 1930s, reaching 19.4 in 1940 and peaking in 1943 at 22.7 before falling back to 20.4 in 1945. The true "baby boom" began in 1946, when the birth rate reached the mid-20s, where it would remain for a decade and more; but the war years began the increases in marriages and births that would characterize postwar America.

The depression and the war also had a significant impact on migration within the United States. Overall, the era brought a significant redistribution of the population toward the SUNBELT states of the SOUTH and West Coast, toward metropolitan areas, and toward SUBURBS. Much of this essentially reinforced ongoing trends, as rural and small-town America continued their long-term decline and metropolitan areas and the West their long-term growth.

In migration, the three-part division of the era is especially obvious. From 1930 to 1935, population movement and redistribution slowed dramatically. Given the widespread ravages of the depression, there seemed little to be gained by moving from one region to another or by moving from rural areas to CITIES or vice versa, although there was more urban to rural movement than in previous decades. In the late 1930s, population movement increased and resumed pre-depression patterns, away from the rural South and Midwest toward metropolitan areas and toward the Pacific Coast.

World War II then greatly accelerated migration. More than 30 million people, or nearly one-fourth of the population, moved during the war, as some 15 million civilians moved to a different county, and about 16 million GIs served in the armed forces. Approximately 12 million people—almost one-tenth of the population—moved permanently to another state. The depopulation of rural America accelerated, as did the growth of the sunbelt, which housed so many wartime defense industries and military bases. Suburbs attracted more people because of a lack of space in the central cities. Impressive though the numbers are, however, the basic geographic patterns were largely consistent with previous ones.

Wartime migration did more than simply redistribute the general population: It had other important consequences as well. The growing importance of the sunbelt states on American culture and politics would be especially evident in the postwar era. (In the last third of the 20th century, every elected president came from a sunbelt state.) The renewed migration of AFRICAN AMERICANS out of the rural South and toward cities, especially in the North and West, was of crucial importance for American race relations and the status of blacks. Crowded war-boom cities often experienced tensions, including racial tensions and sometimes conflict, as newcomers moved in and seemed to challenge and change old ways. In bringing different people into contact with one another, migration also had the effect of reinforcing trends toward cultural diffusion and homogenization.

The reduction of immigration, long a major source of American population increase, also contributed importantly to population trends and influenced various aspects of American life from 1929 to 1945 and afterward. The slowed population growth rate of the 1930s stemmed partly from the effect of the restrictive immigration laws of the 1920s in curtailing immigration and of the depression in tarnishing the economic lure that had traditionally made America so attractive to immigrants. World War II also held down immigration.

The decline in immigration led to the diminishing presence of immigrants in the United States. The number of foreign-born people in the population fell from close to 12 percent in 1930 to 9 percent in 1940 to 7 percent in 1950. Of course, the children and grandchildren of immigrants made up a substantial part of the population, and ethnic groups and ethnicity thus remained central to virtually every aspect of American life. But until the changes in immigration law in the 1960s, immigrants made up a far smaller part than previously of the population.

Some other population trends bear scrutiny. Average life expectancy continued its long-term rise, going from 47.3 years in 1900 to 50 in 1910, to 54.1 in 1920, to 59.7 in 1930, to 62.9 in 1940, and to 68.2 in 1950. Median population age rose from 26.5 to 29 in the 1930s, higher than the trend line and partly a result of declining birth rates, and then to 30.2 in 1950 before turning down in the 1950s because of the baby boom. Death rates trended down overall in the 1930s (from 11.3 per 1,000 people in 1930 to 10.8 in 1940) and then averaged 10.6 from 1941 to 1945. In part reflecting the fact that almost all of the 400,000 American military deaths in World War II were men, women comprised slightly more than half the population in 1950 after being under half down to the mid-1940s. Changes in immigration patterns also affected the gender ratio, for the heavy immigration in the century's first three decades had been about 60 percent male, while the reduced immigration from 1930 to 1950 was almost 60 percent female.

By the end of World War II, the United States was, in significant ways, different from what it had been at the outset of the Great Depression. Important changes had come to the nation's ECONOMY and to its GOVERNMENT and politics. But American society had also changed, not least because of population trends of the era. In all of those areas, the changes often involved continuing or reinforcing long-term trends, but the Great Depression and World War II had important effects as well.

Further reading: *The Statistical History of the United States from Colonial Times to the Present* (Stamford, Conn.: Fairfield Publishers, 1965) (It should be noted that compilations of statistical data tend to vary slightly from one another, but the general levels and patterns are quite consistent.); Theodore Caplow, Louis Hicks, and Ben J. Wattenburg, *The First Measured Century: An Illustrated Guide to Trends in America, 1900–2000* (Washington, D.C.: AEI Press, 2001).

postwar planning

American planning for the postwar era was shaped by the experiences of the GREAT DEPRESSION and WORLD WAR II. The decade-long depression and the understanding that economic recovery had come only with war MOBILIZATION engendered planning efforts by GOVERNMENT, by BUSINESS, and by LABOR to maintain a prosperous, full-employment ECONOMY when the war was over. The collapse of the international economy and the breakdown of the peace in the 1930s led to planning for postwar FOREIGN POLICY to maintain global peace and prosperity. There were other planning efforts as well, conducted by countless public agencies and private organizations from their own perspectives and for their own purposes. But the dominant priorities of postwar planning in the United States—and the overriding goals of the American people as revealed by PUBLIC OPINION POLLS during the war—were to achieve the security of prosperity and peace in the postwar era.

Even before American entry into the war, President FRANKLIN D. ROOSEVELT directed the NATIONAL RESOURCES PLANNING BOARD (NRPB) to initiate domestic postwar planning. The NRPB developed a far-reaching set of proposals for government programs to underwrite full-employment prosperity and economic security. Reflecting the postwar agenda of LIBERALISM, the NRPB reports had no chance in the conservative wartime CONGRESS, which largely ignored them and killed the NRPB itself in 1943. But other administration agencies, including the Bureau of the Budget and the Social Security Board, continued the NRPB's planning for postwar fiscal policy based on KEYNESIANISM to underwrite full-employment prosperity and for social policies to ensure economic security. Given the strength of the CONSERVATIVE COALITION in Congress and the emphasis of public opinion on jobs rather than social welfare, only the fiscal policy approach had significant support. The FULL EMPLOYMENT BILL of 1945 (which became the attenuated Employment Act of 1946) was the most concrete manifestation of administration postwar planning.

Meanwhile, such war agencies as the WAR PRODUCTION BOARD, the OFFICE OF WAR MOBILIZATION AND RECONVERSION, and the SELECTIVE SERVICE system planned for RECONVERSION to a peacetime economy and for DEMOBILIZATION of the armed forces. Congress enacted postwar policies to assist business in making the transition from war to peace. Drawing in part on NRPB recommendations, Congress and the administration agreed upon the GI BILL OF RIGHTS, signed by Roosevelt in June 1944, to ease the readjustment of veterans to civilian life by providing a variety of benefits including education grants and home loans.

But government at all levels, not just in Washington, conducted postwar planning. States, larger CITIES, and also smaller jurisdictions established planning efforts, particularly with an eye to ensuring continuing business and employment opportunities, but also for other purposes as well. Innumerable business and service organizations in the private sector also launched planning initiatives. ADVERTISING, working with business, portrayed visions of a bountiful future hoping to stimulate spending that might produce prosperity as well as profits.

Not all of the domestic planning involved the economy. Racial prejudice, tensions, and sometimes conflict during the war, for example, led not only AFRICAN AMERICANS but also many whites to plan to ameliorate such patterns of RACE AND RACIAL CONFLICT. In the SOUTH, the Commission on Interracial Cooperation became the Southern Regional Council and aimed to bring equal opportunity to blacks. In the North, interracial commissions were created by a number of state and local governments to study the causes of racial tensions and propose corrective action. Concern about wartime ANTI-SEMITISM also figured in the work of such agencies.

The federal government also conducted important planning for postwar foreign policy, efforts manifesting the nation's determination to play a leading role in world affairs in the postwar era. The BRETTON WOODS CONFERENCE of 1944, and the resulting International Monetary Fund and World Bank, reflected the conviction of American officials that high tariffs, currency devaluation, and other breakdowns of economic cooperation in the 1930s had not only harmed the international economy but had contributed to the coming of World War II.

But the most important postwar planning in foreign policy involved efforts to create an effective international collective security organization to keep the peace. (The military also initiated planning for the postwar period—and for the next war, should it come.) Wanting to avoid the errors of the Woodrow Wilson administration in designing the League of Nations during World War I, the Roosevelt administration stayed in close contact with Congress in planning for a new collective security organization. The UNITED NATIONS conference in San Francisco in April 1945, and the Senate's overwhelming ratification of the United Nations charter in July 1945, brought that planning exercise to a successful conclusion.

Further reading: Stephen Kemp Bailey, *Congress Makes a Law: The Story behind the Employment Act of 1946* (New York: Columbia University Press, 1950); Robert A. Divine, *Second Chance: The Triumph of Internationalism during World War II* (New York: Atheneum, 1967); Philip W. Warken, *A History of the National Resources Planning Board, 1933–1943* (New York: Garland, 1979).

Potsdam Conference (July–August 1945)

The Potsdam Conference, held outside of Berlin, Germany, from July 17 to August 2, 1945, was attended by U.S. president Harry S. Truman, Soviet premier Joseph Stalin, British prime minister Winston Churchill, and, after Churchill's election defeat, new British prime minister Clement Attlee. Potsdam was the first meeting of the "Big Three" leaders of the United States, Britain, and the Soviet Union without FRANKLIN D. ROOSEVELT present, the first since the surrender of Germany in May 1945, and the only conference where Truman and Stalin met. This meeting was held to clarify issues discussed at the YALTA CONFERENCE of February 1945 including Germany, Poland, and ending the war against Japan. It concluded with the Potsdam Declaration, which called for the unconditional surrender of Japan.

Much of the discussion at Potsdam involved policy toward postwar Germany. As agreed at Yalta, Germany was divided into four occupation zones (American, British, French, and Soviet), with a joint Allied Control Council to address general issues. Truman reluctantly conceded German territory east of the Oder and Neisse Rivers to Poland (which had lost its eastern section to the Soviet Union). Stalin had called for German reparations in the amount of

Clement Attlee, Harry S. Truman, and Joseph Stalin at Potsdam, 1945 *(National Archives)*

$20 billion at Yalta, but Roosevelt and Churchill had deferred decision on reparations. At Potsdam it was agreed that each occupying power could take reparations from its zone, with the Soviets to get special consideration because of their enormous losses during the war. The Big Three agreed that Germany would be de-Nazified and demilitarized, but did not fully settle the political or economic future of Germany, which would remain a cause of contention as the cold war developed. The conference established a Council of Foreign Ministers to draft peace treaties with Germany and her allies and to implement agreements made at Potsdam and Yalta.

With respect to Poland's government, the United States and Britain understood that the Soviet Red Army was in control of Poland, and Truman agreed to recognize the new Polish government, controlled by Moscow, provided that free elections were held as originally agreed to at Yalta. Like Germany, Poland remained a source of controversy in SOVIET-AMERICAN RELATIONS and in the developing cold war.

With the war in Europe over, the war against Japan figured even more prominently than at Yalta in the discussions. As Roosevelt had done, Truman sought to insure the involvement by Soviet Union, still party to a nonaggression pact with Japan, in the WORLD WAR II PACIFIC THEATER, so that the war could be brought to an end as quickly as possible. Essentially reaffirming his Yalta pledge to enter the war within two or three months of Germany's surrender, Stalin guaranteed Soviet entry into the campaign by mid-August.

At Potsdam, however, Truman's calculations and performance were affected by news that the ATOMIC BOMB had been successfully tested at Alamogordo, New Mexico. While it was not at all obvious just what the impact of the bomb would be on the war against Japan or on Soviet-American relations, it plainly would be a significant factor in both. Truman had known in advance of the conference that word of a successful test might come, and his advisers had discussed whether he should inform Stalin and whether a successful test should change the policy of unconditional surrender. Toward the end of the conference, Truman, as he later put it, "casually mentioned to Stalin that we had a new weapon of unusual destructive force." Stalin (who knew of the atomic bomb project from Soviet ESPIONAGE) gave little reaction.

On July 26, Truman and Attlee issued the Potsdam Declaration, calling upon Japan to surrender unconditionally by August 3 or face "prompt and utter destruction." The surrender terms included an end to Japanese militarism, disarmament, the evacuation of all Japanese territories except for the home islands, the punishment of war criminals, and the Allied occupation of Japan. It contained no mention of the emperor and his status, although it did say that the Allies would establish a democratic system. The Japanese did not accept these terms at first, which led to the dropping of atomic bombs on HIROSHIMA AND NAGASAKI on August 6 and 9.

See also FOREIGN POLICY; GRAND ALLIANCE.

Further reading: Herbert Feis, *Between War and Peace: The Potsdam Conference* (Princeton, N.J.: Princeton University Press, 1960); Charles L. Mee Jr., *Meeting at Potsdam* (New York: M. Evans, 1975).

—Anne Rothfeld

presidency

From 1929 to 1945, the presidency grew significantly in size and power and took on a larger role than ever before in American GOVERNMENT. This resulted from both the extraordinary demands of the GREAT DEPRESSION and WORLD WAR II and from the leadership of President FRANKLIN D. ROOSEVELT. The executive branch grew very slowly during the HOOVER PRESIDENCY from 1929 to 1933, expanded rapidly during the NEW DEAL years of the 1930s, and then nearly quadrupled in size during World War II. Even after postwar retrenchment, the executive branch remained far larger than it had before 1933, and both the CONGRESS and the public looked much more to the president for policy direction than had been the case prior to Roosevelt's presidency.

At the beginning of his term as president in 1929, HERBERT C. HOOVER intended to energize the executive branch and apply modern organizational techniques to national issues. A powerful secretary of commerce in the 1920s, Hoover believed in an active presidency, although he wanted—consistent with his convictions about the role of the federal government—an office that would catalyze and coordinate efforts to address national problems rather than directing and controlling them. Appointing like-minded "Hoover men" to cabinet and subcabinet positions, he initiated action on a number of issues, began studies of social and economic trends, and planned conferences on social and economic problems.

But inertia and Hoover's reluctance to push too hard or change things too fast limited such undertakings, and by late 1929 the onset of the Great Depression and the collapsing ECONOMY commanded his attention. Although the Hoover presidency did more than any previous administration had done during economic hard times, those efforts were constrained by Hoover's steadfast opposition to a regulatory or welfare state. By the end of his term, Hoover used the power of the presidency largely to restrain Congress from doing or spending too much. Hoover also lacked the temperament to take on the political and symbolic roles of the presidency, and his gloomy

NUMBER OF EXECUTIVE BRANCH EMPLOYEES

1929	567,721
1933	590,984
1940	1,022,853
1945	3,786,645
1950	1,934,040

outlook and growing unpopularity diminished the authority of the White House. "This office," he said, "is a compound hell."

Franklin D. Roosevelt saw the presidency much differently. "I want to be a *preaching President*," he once declared; and he wanted to be a powerful president as well. Confident in his abilities, comfortable in the White House, and ready to use the federal government to deal with the Great Depression, Roosevelt from the first expanded the size and power of his office. He served far longer than any other president and, during his 1933–45 tenure, played a decisive role in the evolution of the modern presidency. Under FDR, the president became more than ever before the center of national government, setting the agenda for public policy, sending proposals to Congress, and then implementing the resulting programs. Congress increasingly responded to the president's agenda rather than initiating its own, and the SUPREME COURT ultimately approved the expansion of federal and executive-branch power. Although Roosevelt has often been criticized for his untidy administrative style, he infused the executive branch with energy, focused its efforts, and expanded its role and authority in both domestic and foreign policy. His adept use of the NEWS MEDIA contributed still further to the new power of the presidency in national affairs.

In the first months of his presidency, Roosevelt oversaw the remarkable first Hundred Days that began the New Deal's unprecedented array of programs to combat the depression. As the subsequent proliferation of new programs greatly enlarged the size and reach of the executive branch, he also wanted to reorganize the presidency in order to provide more efficient policy planning and coordination. Although the CONSERVATIVE COALITION that stymied much of his second-term agenda considerably weakened the final measure, Roosevelt in 1939 won passage of the EXECUTIVE REORGANIZATION ACT, which established the Executive Office of the President and provided more presidential control over the executive branch. During World War II, the size and powers of the presidency grew even faster and further than during the depression. Congress delegated great authority to the president to coordinate war MOBILIZATION, and Roosevelt also exercised the military and diplomatic powers of commander in

chief to an unprecedented degree. Much of the wartime growth of the presidency was cut back once the war was over; but in 1950, the executive branch had nearly twice as many employees as in 1940, and more than three times as many as in 1933. The Executive Office of the President established in 1939 provided an institutional foundation for presidential power, while managing the regulatory welfare state implemented in the 1930s and overseeing the nation's new global role further entrenched the new size and authority of the presidency.

See also FOREIGN POLICY.

Further reading: Thomas E. Cronin, *The State of the Presidency,* 2d ed. (Boston: Little, Brown, 1980); Sidney M. Milkis, *The President and the Parties: The Transformation of the Party System since the New Deal* (New York: Oxford University Press, 1993); Richard E. Neustadt, *Presidential Power and the Modern Presidents: The Politics of Leadership from Roosevelt to Reagan* (New York: Free Press, 1990); Stephen Skowronek, *The Politics Presidents Make: Leadership from John Adams to George Bush* (Cambridge, Mass.: Belknap Press of Harvard University Press, 1993).

prisoners of war

According to the 1899 and 1907 Hague Conventions and the 1929 Geneva Convention, capturing powers in wartime were to remove prisoners from battle areas and give them medical care, housing, clothing, and food comparable to those of their own troops. When interrogated, prisoners of war (POWs) were to receive treatment commensurate with their rank, and could refuse to give any information except their name, rank, and service number. While in captivity, POWs were to be able to practice their religion, correspond, and expect humane treatment. The Geneva-based International Red Cross inspected camps to insure compliance. During WORLD WAR II, however, reality typically departed far from such guidelines, with the circumstances of the millions of POWs dependent on resources, the time and place of capture, and the attitudes of the capturing powers. The treatment of POWs by the United States was in general good, while American POWs received decent treatment from Germany and usually dreadful treatment by the Japanese.

Germany took more than 2 million prisoners in its conquests of Poland and France in 1939 and 1940, and then 5 million Red Army captives after the invasion of the Soviet Union in June 1941. Germany treated Soviet prisoners exceptionally badly. Unlike Allied POWs in the West, who were housed in camps built for the purpose, captured Soviets became inmates of the Nazi concentration camp system. More than 3 million Soviet prisoners died in German captivity. Because the Soviet government had not signed the Geneva Convention, the Germans held that Soviet prisoners were not covered by its terms. This attitude, when combined with Nazi racial policies defining Slavs as subhumans, sealed the fate of Soviet prisoners. German treatment was reciprocated by the Soviets toward their portion of the nearly 4.5 million Germans captured by the Allies. Of the nearly 3 million Germans in Soviet captivity, fewer than a million had returned to Germany by 1957, the remainder perishing in Soviet labor camps. Moreover, after the war, repatriated Russians, at Joseph Stalin's insistence, were imprisoned in the USSR as punishment for having been captured. The Western Allies repatriated all AXIS prisoners by 1947.

Germany and Japan captured 200,000 and 108,000 British and Commonwealth soldiers, respectively—most between 1940 and 1942 in Europe, North Africa, Burma, Malaya, and Hong Kong. Some 80,000 British troops were captured by the Japanese at Singapore alone in 1942, and were joined in squalid camps by 22,000 Dutch from the Netherlands East Indies. German treatment of British prisoners was far better than that by their Japanese allies, largely because of the German belief that the British would then treat well the growing numbers of Germans in British hands. The same logic and pattern held true for the 90,000 Americans captured by the Germans after 1942.

Particularly for those German and Italian POWs transported to the United States, the U.S. treatment of POWs was generally humane and within convention guidelines. In fact, the treatment of Axis prisoners sometimes drew civilian complaints that the enemy was being "mollycoddled" while American servicemen were dying abroad. The 670,000 Italian and German prisoners held in the 155 main camps and 500 subcamps in the continental United States were often used as farm labor. Sometimes POWs were permitted to leave camps in the United States for brief periods of recreation. AFRICAN AMERICANS complained that German and Italian POWs in the United States received better treatment and more access to public accommodations than did black Americans. Relatively few Japanese soldiers surrendered and became POWs in the bloody WORLD WAR II PACIFIC THEATER.

Japanese military and racial attitudes, coupled with Japan's lack of recognition of the Geneva and Hague Conventions, reinforced the Japanese belief that prisoners were dishonored and inferior weaklings, unworthy of respect, if not of life itself. This same attitude dominated the beliefs of Japanese soldiers and was the reason that fewer than 11,000 Japanese military personnel were taken prisoner by all of the Allied powers before August 15, 1945. The Japanese in turn were infamous for their brutal treatment of British prisoners and of the 15,000 Americans captured in the PHILIPPINES (site of the BATAAN DEATH MARCH of

American and Filipino POWs), at Guam, and at Wake Island. The Japanese captors ruthlessly demanded hard labor on military projects, and typically denied POWs adequate food, medicine, clothing, and proper care. In MANCHURIA, Unit 731 of the Japanese Army conducted heinous medical and biological warfare experiments on prisoners. Thousands of Allied prisoners were transported to Japan and Manchuria to perform slave labor in mines and war industries in direct violation of the Geneva Convention. More than 12,000 British and Commonwealth prisoners died from overwork, ill treatment, and disease constructing the Burma railway. All told, nearly 40 percent of the Allied prisoners in Japanese captivity died.

While it was considered the duty of prisoners to escape, only about 35,000 British, Commonwealth, and American prisoners escaped German captivity. The number of Axis prisoners escaping Allied custody, and Allied prisoners escaping the Japanese, was so low as to be statistically insignificant.

Further reading: Gavan Daws, *Prisoners of the Japanese: POWs of World War II in the Pacific* (New York: Morrow, 1994); Arnold Krammer, *Nazi Prisoners of War in America* (New York: Stein & Day, 1979).

—Clayton D. Laurie

propaganda

Propaganda is the use of the written and spoken word to persuade a population to adhere to a particular point of view or to follow the policies of a leader, group, or party. Propaganda used for military purposes, especially as refined during WORLD WAR II, is known as *combat propaganda* or *psychological warfare*. Propaganda has been used since ancient times, but its use in war and peace has increased dramatically in modern times with the advent of mass communications and literate audiences. During World War II, all belligerent powers used propaganda to build morale, unity, and support for the war effort in their own populations, while simultaneously using propaganda abroad to undermine enemy military and civilian populations.

Nazi Germany put enormous efforts into propaganda beginning in 1933. Led by Joseph Goebbels, who directed the Nazi Ministry of Propaganda and Popular Enlightenment, the Nazis thoroughly controlled all print and film media as well as all radio communications within Germany, while also seeking to influence overseas populations through radio broadcasts and print media, especially during the prewar years. The heavy emphasis on crude racial philosophies, and the inability of the Nazis to adapt their appeals to specific populations, severely limited the effectiveness of their efforts. The same was true for the propaganda efforts of the Soviet Union during the early years of World War II. Recognizing communism's unpopularity Joseph Stalin changed the emphasis of Soviet propaganda from defending the world communist movement to fighting a great patriotic war for the fatherland against fascism, a theme that appealed to all members of the GRAND ALLIANCE.

In Japan, government propaganda aimed at its own citizens succeeded in maintaining both civilian and military morale until late in the war, when the mounting evidence of an imminent and overwhelming defeat could no longer be denied. Otherwise, however, Japanese propaganda had virtually no success. Japanese propaganda efforts beyond the homeland were hampered by the broad expanses of territory needing coverage, the dearth of personnel with knowledge of the hundreds of languages found in Asia and the Pacific, and the lack of a mass literate audience with access to radios. The primary propaganda theme, "Asia for the Asiatics," initially had appeal to those desiring an end to decades of European colonial rule, but Japanese ruthlessness, brutality, and blatant racism quickly convinced most Asians that the Japanese had come as cold-blooded oppressors and not liberators. Propaganda directed toward Allied soldiers and sailors also failed badly. The efforts of "Tokyo Rose" (Iva Ikuko Toguri, a UCLA graduate trapped in Japan at the start of the war) provide a case in point. She delivered 15-minute daily radio broadcasts to Allied troops, who found the music entertaining but the crude propaganda messages entirely unconvincing.

Great Britain created a large and sophisticated propaganda bureaucracy by 1941 that emphasized the ideals of the ATLANTIC CHARTER. The Ministry of Information controlled all radio broadcasts and print media to populations in enemy, neutral, and Allied nations worldwide through the programs of the British Broadcasting Corporation. The British also formed the Political Warfare Executive in early 1941 to conduct Britain's psychological warfare campaign, in cooperation with British and Allied military services, against enemy populations, both civilian and military, worldwide. The British emphasis on what they termed "political warfare," either clandestine ("black") or overt ("white"), was so great that British officials often referred to such unorthodox means as the fourth dimension of warfare to be fully utilized in conjunction with conventional air, sea, and land forces.

The United States developed domestic and overseas propaganda organizations for civilian audiences as well as a sophisticated psychological warfare capacity for use against enemy military forces in the combat theaters abroad. The OFFICE OF WAR INFORMATION, formed in June 1942, consisted of both domestic and overseas branches. Domestically, the OWI produced literature portraying the war in clear good-versus-evil terms, and assisted film producers in portraying the conflict in similar ways. Although successful in enhancing national unity and morale, the domestic OWI was often criticized for glorifying FRANKLIN D. ROOSEVELT and his administration. The overseas OWI, in its publications, in literature placed in OWI-sponsored reading rooms in neutral, liberated, and Allied nations, and in Voice of America radio broadcasts heard worldwide, portrayed the American war effort and the nation's war aims in similar lofty and high-minded terms. The OWI emphasized the truth, although often in simplistic and vague news reports. In spite of its critics, however, who maintained that the office was attempting to globalize the NEW DEAL, the Overseas OWI did lift morale and promote unity among the populations of Allied and AXIS-occupied nations.

With respect to combat propaganda, the Overseas OWI cooperated with U.S. ARMY psychological warfare units in the combat theaters abroad. OWI assisted military propagandists with the production of "white" or overt propaganda leaflets and radio broadcasts that had some success in helping to weaken the morale and fighting ability of Axis military forces, especially in the latter days of the war. The OFFICE OF STRATEGIC SERVICES, in cooperation with the OWI and the British Political Warfare Executive, produced a variety of covert or "black" psychological warfare programs, although their effectiveness and utility were often in doubt.

Further reading: Clayton D. Laurie, *The Propaganda Warriors: America's Crusade against Nazi Germany* (Lawrence: University Press of Kansas, 1996); Allan M. Winkler, *The Politics of Propaganda: The Office of War Information, 1942–1945* (New Haven, Conn.: Yale University Press, 1978).

—Clayton D. Laurie

public opinion polls

During the 1930s and 1940s, important advances in sampling techniques and methods of data collection and analysis contributed to a substantial increase in the use and variety of public opinion polls by BUSINESS, GOVERNMENT, and political parties.

Beginning in the 1920s, scientific polls were increasingly used by business to gauge consumers' responses to new products and to ADVERTISING campaigns, and by the growing RADIO industry to determine the popularity of specific programs. Such surveys were conducted by scholars trained in the social sciences and employed systematic methods for gathering and interpreting data. Beginning in 1929, the federal government used surveys to assess the extent of the GREAT DEPRESSION and its impact on the public.

Many polls however, like those used as early as 1824, were designed simply to predict the outcome of an election by using what was called a "straw vote" survey in which newspapers and magazines published ballots or sent out postcards to be returned to the publisher and tallied in the final poll. This method, used in the 1920s by the *Literary Digest* as well as newspapers throughout the country, relied on those who took the time to return their ballot, or answered telephone surveys. Although publishers touted such polls as being scientific, many scholars criticized them in the 1930s for their large and unscientific sample size and their bias in favor of the middle and upper classes.

During the ELECTION OF 1936, disparities between the work of social scientists and some media pollsters highlighted the shortcomings of straw-vote polling methods. Before the *Literary Digest* began its polling, George Gallup, an influential innovator in survey research methods, correctly predicted that the *Literary Digest* would favor Republican nominee ALFRED M. LANDON to defeat incumbent president FRANKLIN D. ROOSEVELT. Gallup's own prediction—of a Roosevelt victory—was published by his organization, the American Institute for Public Opinion (AIPO), which, he argued, could give a more accurate prediction of the national and state-level results. Two other established polls, one by Archibald Crossley, a prominent market researcher, and one published by *Fortune* magazine and directed by Elmo Roper, also predicted Roosevelt's reelection. Roosevelt's victory with three-fifths of the popular vote confirmed the criticisms of the *Literary Digest* polls and prompted pollsters to reevaluate and refine their research methods.

The lessons of the *Literary Digest* debacle contributed to the proliferation of survey research among political strategists, policymakers, businessmen, and scholars. Both the DEMOCRATIC PARTY and the REPUBLICAN PARTY used opinion surveys in the ELECTION OF 1940 and especially the ELECTION OF 1944. Scholars also began to use survey research to study social and economic characteristics of the electorate.

The use of scientific surveys, however, was not limited to business and politics. Building upon the work of Gallup and Roper, psychologists such as Hadley Cantril used polls to measure general attitudes and analyze various aspects of "everyday life." In 1937, the Princeton Radio Research Project (later called the Office of Radio Research, or ORR) was established to study the cultural impact of radio. Among other studies, the ORR published *The Invasion from Mars* (1940), which used survey data to examine listener's reactions to ORSON WELLES's radio production of *War of the Worlds.*

In the late 1930s, as WORLD WAR II approached, researchers as well as politicians used polling data to measure American opinion on FOREIGN POLICY issues. In 1940,

Cantril together with social scientist Paul Lazarsfeld established the Office of Public Opinion Research at Princeton University. Cantril directed surveys of American attitudes on intervening in the war, and during the war served as a consultant to the White House and War Department. (In 1951, Cantril published *Public Opinion: 1935–1946,* an invaluable compendium of surveys in the era.)

After the attack on PEARL HARBOR and the official U.S. entry into the war, CONGRESS appropriated funds for survey research focusing on military morale, foreign morale, and civilian morale on the WORLD WAR II HOME FRONT. Roosevelt continued to use surveys both in the White House and in government agencies. Opinion researchers hoped to promote the use of polls as a guide for policymakers by providing them with a reasonably accurate assessment of the "will of the people." Near the end of the war, however, Congress, suspicious of the Roosevelt administration's use of social research to promote its own political interests, severely cut the budget of the OFFICE OF WAR INFORMATION as well as funding for other studies. Nevertheless, the wartime experiences of researchers served to broaden the scope of opinion research as well as reveal its practical applications.

Further reading: Hadley Cantril, ed., *Public Opinion 1935–1946* (Princeton, N.J.: Princeton University Press, 1951); Jean Converse, *Survey Research in the United States: Roots and Emergence, 1890–1960* (Berkeley: University of California Press, 1987).

—Shannon L. Parsley

Public Utility Holding Company Act (1935)

The Public Utility Holding Company Act led to the restructuring of the public utility industry by reducing the size and power of the giant holding companies that had dominated it. Part of the SECOND NEW DEAL of 1935, the legislation (also known as the Wheeler-Rayburn Act, after its principal congressional sponsors, Senator BURTON K. WHEELER of Montana and Representative Sam Rayburn of Texas) did not go as far as President FRANKLIN D. ROOSEVELT had desired. It was nonetheless one of the most significant ANTIMONOPOLY efforts of the NEW DEAL, and part of its increased regulation of BUSINESS.

The public utility (electric power) industry had attracted many critics and foes by the 1930s. The industry was dominated by a small number of large holding companies that owned local operating companies, often in complicated, multistate organizational structures. Reaping large profits from the local companies by selling them management services and receiving their stock dividends, the holding companies typically proved unresponsive to improved, cheaper, or expanded electrical service and avoided state regulation. Their reluctance to extend operations into rural areas caused Roosevelt to create the RURAL ELECTRIFICATION ADMINISTRATION in May 1935.

Roosevelt and other members of his administration thought the utility industry was perhaps the most egregious example of harmful monopoly power. If the holding company pyramids could be leveled, the local operating companies could be more responsive and less expensive. The president sent Congress a bill that would give the SECURITIES AND EXCHANGE COMMISSION (SEC) power to dissolve after January 1, 1940, any holding company that could not justify its existence in terms of economic efficiency and geographical integration.

The utility industry and its lobbyists put enormous pressure on Congress to defeat the bill, and especially its "death sentence" clause requiring the dissolution of holding companies that could not justify their existence. After a fierce battle, the Senate approved the bill with the death sentence clause by just one vote in June. In July the House defeated the death sentence clause but passed the rest of the bill. In August, Congress agreed upon a revised bill that eliminated holding companies more than twice removed from operating companies but required the SEC to justify dissolving other utility holding companies.

The Public Utility Holding Company Act seemed to many a modest victory for the Roosevelt administration, because the initial "death sentence" had been defeated. But the legislation did significantly expand the regulatory power of the GOVERNMENT over public utilities, even though the big companies fought it in the courts and the SEC made slow progress in rationalizing the industry. Eventually the law had a real impact on the structure of the electric power industry, and companies that were reorganized and geographically integrated were typically the stronger and more profitable for it.

Further reading: Philip Funigiello, *Toward a National Power Policy: The New Deal and the Electric Utility Industry* (Pittsburgh: University of Pittsburgh Press, 1973); Michael E. Parrish, *Securities Regulation and the New Deal* (New Haven, Conn.: Yale University Press, 1970).

Public Works Administration (PWA)

The Public Works Administration was created by the NATIONAL INDUSTRIAL RECOVERY ACT (NIRA) of June 16, 1933, one of the cornerstone measures of the FIRST NEW DEAL. Title I of the NIRA created the NATIONAL RECOVERY ADMINISTRATION (NRA), which was to help achieve recovery from the GREAT DEPRESSION by means of economic planning and controls for industry. Title II of the NIRA established the PWA and allocated the agency its initial $3.3 billion for large-scale public-works projects. These

PWA projects were to stimulate the ECONOMY by producing new jobs and BUSINESS activity and to build projects that would enrich the national domain. Directed by Secretary of the Interior HAROLD L. ICKES, the PWA was a major New Deal agency that achieved its aims of building important, well-engineered, and well-constructed public works projects. Like the NRA, however, it did not contribute significantly to economic recovery.

The public works achievements of the PWA were significant and sometimes spectacular. Spending more than $6 billion on some 35,000 projects in the 1930s, the PWA underwrote an astonishing array of projects, from public HOUSING, to hospitals, dams, and battleships, and allocated nearly $2 billion more to other federal projects and programs, including the CIVIL WORKS ADMINISTRATION (CWA). From 1933 to 1939, PWA helped construct some two-thirds of the nation's new schools and one-third of its hospitals and public health facilities. La Guardia Airport in New York City, the Skyline Drive in Virginia, the San Francisco–Oakland Bay Bridge in California, and the aircraft carriers *Enterprise* and *Yorktown* were all financed by PWA. Under Ickes's meticulous, prudent leadership there was almost none of the inefficiency and waste of some New Deal programs, and no hint of corruption. The PWA Housing Division pioneered the first federal housing projects, which though disappointing in the volume of housing built became in some ways a model for slum clearance and public housing projects to follow. PWA projects also signally advanced the conservation aims of the administration, and provided employment at prevailing wages for more than 1 million workers. By one accounting, all but three counties in the United States had at least one PWA project.

Yet the economic impact of the PWA was consistently disappointing. Not just insistent upon the most careful planning and management, but also deeply suspicious and greatly concerned about his own reputation for rectitude, Ickes spent money far too slowly to have the desired effect on recovery or employment. In the PWA's first six months, when the economic situation was most perilous, for example, Ickes expended just $110 million of the agency's $3.3 billion authorization. The Housing Division built only some 22,000 units of low-cost public housing from 1933 to 1937, leading impatient reformers such as New York senator ROBERT F. WAGNER to create the UNITED STATES HOUSING AUTHORITY. Ickes's priorities and performance also produced near-constant conflict over public works money with RELIEF administrator HARRY HOPKINS, who believed that government public-works and work-relief money should be spent as rapidly as possible and on labor-intensive projects like those of the CWA and the WORKS PROGRESS ADMINISTRATION (WPA) rather than on the capital-intensive projects of the PWA. In these often acerbic intra-administration battles, President FRANKLIN D. ROOSEVELT more often than not sided with Hopkins. But while Roosevelt shared Hopkins's preference for quick-impact projects that would directly provide jobs and income (and political benefit), he never embraced the emerging view of KEYNESIANISM that large-scale government deficit spending could produce economic recovery. The failure of PWA to spend sufficiently to underwrite recovery was thus by no means the responsibility of Ickes alone.

In the end, the PWA should be remembered for its accomplishments as well as for its limitations. Although it never achieved its aims or potential before being phased out in June 1941 (by which time defense spending had begun to confirm Keynesian doctrine of the importance of government spending to economic recovery), the PWA not only financed thousands of important and well-constructed projects but provided a model for prudent, efficient, effective federal funding of major construction and conservation projects.

Further reading: David M. Kennedy, *Freedom from Fear: The American People in Depression and War, 1929–1945.* (New York: Oxford University Press, 1999); Graham White and John Maze, *Harold Ickes and the New Deal: His Private Life and Public Career* (Cambridge, Mass.: Harvard University Press, 1985).

Pyle, Ernie (Ernest Taylor) (1900–1945)

Ernie Pyle, the most famous combat correspondent of WORLD WAR II, won the Pulitzer Prize for his reports that captured the hopes and fears of ordinary soldiers.

Born on August 3, 1900, in the small farming community of Dana, Indiana, Ernest Taylor Pyle was a quiet but restless youth with dreams of a future filled with travel and adventure. In 1923, he left Indiana University to work for a small paper in La Porte, Indiana, only to move a few months later to a desk job with the *Washington Daily News.* Pyle spent the next 12 years with this paper, where he worked as a reporter and copy editor, launched the country's first daily aviation column in 1928, and reluctantly become the paper's managing editor in 1932.

In 1935, Pyle sought and received a roving reporter position with the Scripps-Howard newspapers. Over the next seven years, Pyle and his wife Jerry crossed the United States some three dozen times and traveled to Canada, South America, and England as he wrote a daily column, which appeared in as many as 200 newspapers across the country. His reports were intertwined with nostalgic themes and provided stories of adventure and escape to readers who could never hope to make such journeys.

Pyle asked to work as a war correspondent in 1942. In covering the war over the next three years, he revealed his personal fears and hatred of war as he tried to interpret his own feelings as well as those of the GIs. Pyle's dispatches often contained the names and hometowns of the men who experienced the hardships, sacrifices, and homesickness he wrote about. His reports were collected in his best-selling books *Here Is Your War* (1943) and *Brave Men* (1944). He won the Pulitzer Prize in 1944 for his reporting from the WORLD WAR II EUROPEAN THEATER.

Tragically, on April 18, 1945, while covering the OKINAWA campaign in the WORLD WAR II PACIFIC THEATER, he visited the nearby island of Ie Shima and was killed by Japanese gunfire. His reporting, however, lived on. His coverage of the Italian campaign inspired the 1945 motion picture *G.I. Joe,* and a final book, called *Last Chapter,* was published in 1946.

Further reading: Lee G. Miller, *The Story of Ernie Pyle* (New York: Viking, 1950); James Tobin, *Ernie Pyle's War: America's Eyewitness in World War II* (New York: Free Press, 1997).

—Ronald G. Simon

R

race and racial conflict

The economic dislocations of the GREAT DEPRESSION and the contradictions of fighting for freedom abroad during WORLD WAR II while enforcing discrimination and segregation at home exacerbated racial and ethnic conflict throughout America. Lynchings of AFRICAN AMERICANS surged in the rural SOUTH in the early 1930s, and during the war rioting occurred in major CITIES, accompanied by other acts of communal discord. Despite this, the era offered hope for improved race relations as black activists and white liberals joined forces with renewed vigor to fight racial discrimination and protect CIVIL RIGHTS.

The era began on a discouraging note as lynching increased sharply during the depths of the depression. Organizations such as the NATIONAL ASSOCIATION FOR THE ADVANCEMENT OF COLORED PEOPLE (NAACP), the National Urban League, and the Commission on Interracial Cooperation (which had been founded in 1919 "to quench, if possible, the fires of racial antagonism" in the South) had helped reduce the practice. But in 1930, lynchings shot up from 10 to 21 per year, fell to six in 1932 and then jumped to 28 the next year. According to the Tuskegee Institute's lynching statistics, 20 lynchings took place in 1934, after which the annual number fell into the single digits.

The horrific 1934 lynching of Claude Neal in the Florida panhandle so shocked the nation that sentiment built against such actions. Claude Neal was arrested for the rape and murder of his 19-year-old white neighbor. In fact, she hadn't been raped and Neal's guilt in the murder was uncertain. The sheriff removed him to Alabama for safety. But a mob tracked him down, extracted him from the jail, and took him in a car caravan back to Florida, where he was castrated, made to eat his genitalia, and ultimately riddled with bullets. His body was dragged to the home of the victim, where a mob that included children stabbed, kicked, and cut pieces from the body for souvenirs. With the corpse hanging in the local courthouse square—its torso covered for modesty's sake—a race riot ensued that drove many blacks from their homes and jobs. Regional papers had advertised the impending lynching, RADIO stations broadcast its location, and the lynchers released a statement inviting all white people to the affair. Between 3,000 and 7,000 attended.

After researching lynching several years later, GUNNAR MYRDAL reported in his seminal 1944 work on race relations, *An American Dilemma,* that he encountered few people in the middle and upper classes in the South who approved of it. Yet few of them said they would try to stop a lynching or punish the perpetrators. In fact, prominent people often participated. At the national level, efforts of the NAACP and their supporters to persuade CONGRESS to pass antilynching legislation failed in the 1930s.

The "legal lynching" of the SCOTTSBORO BOYS in 1931 grew directly out of this sort of poisoned atmosphere. The trial of the nine young black men falsely accused of raping two white women in Alabama made a mockery of justice—although, because of SUPREME COURT rulings, all nine eventually regained their freedom.

In the Scottsboro case and other situations, COMMUNISTS tried during the depression to win support from working-class blacks in order to displace the NAACP, whose legal gradualism and middle-class bias also alienated those pressing more militant agendas. The Communist Party of the United States (CPUSA) gained control of the defense of the Scottsboro Boys and sought to use it to attract black support. The CPUSA's International Legal Defense obtained the *pro bono* services of Samuel S. Leibowitz, at the time perhaps the country's best criminal attorney. Communists were instrumental in freeing Birmingham coal miner Angelo Herndon, who had been jailed for inciting insurrection. His crime was trying to convince other blacks to join the Communist Party.

Despite such episodes, however, and the continuing Jim Crow system of segregation and disfranchisement in the South, African Americans overwhelmingly embraced the American system, rejected radical ideologies, and stayed well away from communists and communism. The National Negro Congress, for example, formed in 1936 by aggressive young black intellectuals, fell apart when leaders like Ralph Bunche and A. PHILIP RANDOLPH resigned in protest at Communist threats to take over its agenda.

Although public protest led to a reduction in lynchings, heinous acts continued sporadically. In the 1942 lynching of 25-year-old Cleo Wright in Sikeston, Missouri, the county prosecutor and local police were present at the jail when a mob seized Wright and dragged him behind a car to the black section of the community, poured gasoline over him, and set him afire. Local whites responded to the horrible affair by advocating more segregation—for the "protection" of African Americans.

Also alarming during this 15-year period was the spread of rioting. White mob actions were similar to those in industrial centers during and after World War I. In the early 1930s, Arkansas whites burned homes and crops and fired upon black sharecroppers active in the SOUTHERN TENANTS FARMERS UNION. Elsewhere, black farmers who were thought to have fallen under radical LABOR influences were harassed and attacked. ANTI-SEMITISM led to violence in depression-racked New York City when gangs of young IRISH AMERICANS and GERMAN AMERICANS roamed the streets of Washington Heights, Flatbush, and the South Bronx robbing and harassing JEWS, occasionally vandalizing their stores.

Indicative of a rising anger and determination in black America, insurrectionary rioting also emerged in which African Americans resorted to mass violence to express outrage over continued subordination. A riot erupted in Harlem in 1935 after police scolded (and released) a black youth caught shoplifting candy. Rumors spread that they had killed the boy. Fueled by simmering bitterness, blacks dismissed police denials and retaliated against symbols of their subordination. One white was killed, and 200 white-owned stores were trashed.

In 1941, black soldiers rioted in North Carolina when they were not allowed on a bus with white soldiers. One black and one white were killed. Many of these men came from the North and had no experience in the ways in which Jim Crow governed day-to-day race relations in the South. A similar incident took place in El Paso, Texas, in 1943. In Camp Stewart, Georgia, rumors of a black man raping a white woman led ultimately to a riot by black troops that took two battalions to suppress.

Fisk University reported 242 separate incidents of racial violence in 1943. Race riots broke out in several major cities, often setting African Americans against ethnic whites. Tulsa, Chicago, East St. Louis (Illinois), Philadelphia, Buffalo, and Beaumont (Texas) all experienced racial disturbances. In Mobile, Alabama, whites rioted because 12 black men had been promoted into skilled jobs in the shipyards, the preserve of whites. The mob drove away every black worker it could find.

The most violent riots of 1943 occurred in Harlem and Detroit, where whites resented black economic incursions, and blacks resented continuing discrimination. The Detroit riot began over racial taunting at the Belle Isle public park and lasted for three days. In typical fashion, whites invaded black neighborhoods and blacks fought back. Thirty-four people, including 25 African Americans, were killed before the police, supported by the military, were able to quell the disturbance.

In Harlem a few weeks later another riot broke out, triggered by a confrontation involving a white policeman, as had been the case in 1935. This time, a uniformed black soldier was shot in a hotel lobby by a patrolman. Rumors that the serviceman died led to a riot in which six people were slain and 150 stores were looted. The two Harlem riots set the pattern for the ghetto insurrections of the "long hot summers" of the 1960s, in which the urban African-American poor resorted to violent protest over their powerlessness.

The Port Chicago, California, incident of July 1944—the worst war-related disaster in the territorial United States—exemplified the depths of racial disharmony. While poorly trained African-American sailors were loading ammunition onto Liberty Ships, a huge explosion obliterated two ships, killing 320 men, 202 of whom were black. Fifty black sailors were court-martialed for refusing to return to this duty, claiming that only African Americans were assigned such dangerous work. This affair contributed to the decision of the U.S. NAVY to begin integrating before the war ended.

Los Angeles' infamous "Zoot-Suit Riot" broke out in June 1943 when a white mob comprising soldiers, sailors, and civilians descended upon Mexican barrios invading theaters, streetcars, and even homes. The riot received its name from the fancy, high-waisted suits that many young male MEXICAN AMERICANS were wearing. With police acquiescence, mobs attacked these individuals, stripped them of their clothes, and beat them, often quite severely. After the Hearst newspapers wrote prejudicial stories about ZOOT-SUITERS, the Los Angeles City Council made wearing the garb a misdemeanor.

During the Second World War, nativist and racial hostility led to the relocation of JAPANESE AMERICANS and the incarceration of more than 110,000 first- and second-generation Japanese Americans in internment camps. These unfortunate families often lost their homes, businesses, and investments in the government's haste to protect national security—and to respond to political pressure. In the camp at Manzanar in the California desert, which opened in June 1942 surrounded by barbed wire with guard towers, searchlights, and machine gun emplacements, two inmates died and eight were injured in a riot against the War Relocation Authority's use of informants within the camp.

The war galvanized black determination to enter the American mainstream, and led to more attention to minorities and to civil rights. Leading black newspapers popularized the "Double V" campaign—victory at home over Jim Crow as well as victory abroad over the AXIS. The NAACP grew from 50,000 to 450,000 members during the war, and black protest increased. The MARCH ON WASHINGTON MOVEMENT organized by A. Philip Randolph in 1941 led President FRANKLIN D. ROOSEVELT to issue EXECUTIVE ORDER 8802 banning racial discrimination in GOVERNMENT and in industries with government defense contracts and establishing the FAIR EMPLOYMENT PRACTICES COMMITTEE.

At the same time, an increasing number of concerned whites became convinced that the problems of racial prejudice, tension, and conflict heightened by the Great Depression and highlighted by the war effort had to be addressed. As early as 1938, the Southern Conference for Human Rights sought to improve conditions for the underprivileged. This organization spoke out boldly against lynching, Jim Crow voting laws, and other forms of racial discrimination. More important, in response to the violence of 1943, the Commission on Interracial Cooperation was reformed into the Southern Regional Council to bring to African Americans "the equal opportunity that every other citizen of the United States has."

Outside the South, too, new initiatives were undertaken. In Chicago that same year the American Council on Race Relations was formed to advise communities on racial problems. Local and state interracial commissions were created to look into the causes of racial tensions and to address prejudice and discrimination. In California, the governor implemented an effort to investigate and improve the situation of Mexican Americans following the zoot-suit riots. Such initiatives sought to build upon the foundation of government protection of minority rights (NATIVE AMERICANS also won attention from reformers in the era) and helped lay groundwork for the restoration of civil rights in the postwar era. Gunnar Myrdal's influential *An American Dilemma,* Supreme Court decisions eroding the legal foundations of Jim Crow in education and voting, and the growing prominence of civil rights in the agenda of LIBERALISM also contributed to the momentum of such efforts.

Further reading: Paul A. Gilje, *Rioting in America* (Bloomington: Indiana University Press, 1996); Herbert Shapiro, *White Violence and Black Response: From Reconstruction to Montgomery* (Amherst: University of Massachusetts Press, 1988).

—Howard Smead

radio

The difficult years of the GREAT DEPRESSION and WORLD WAR II coincided almost exactly with what has since become known as radio's golden age. The irony of radio's glory days occurring during such a troubled period is not hard to understand. In a time of economic privation and insecurity, radio offered cheap entertainment and information for virtually every American household. And in an era of great social and political upheaval, radio provided a sense of cohesiveness to a national audience of listeners in the privacy of their own homes.

By 1930, radio had become the "electronic hearth" in 12 million of the country's 30 million homes. By 1945, virtually every home and millions of automobiles were equipped with radio sets. All across the nation, listeners shared the daily ritual of tuning in a favorite program and listening to familiar voices. Part of the ritual quality of radio listening had to do with the phenomenon of millions of people tuned into the same show simultaneously. By the start of the 1930s, three national networks and hundreds of local broadcasters had blanketed the country with daily programming fare consisting chiefly of classical and popular music, coverage of SPORTS events, and a few enormously popular dramas and comedies like *The Goldbergs* and *Amos 'n' Andy.* Popular memory and contemporary journalistic accounts relate the common anecdote of a pedestrian walking down a public street and listening to a single broadcast as it issued from the windows of every home. Without breaking stride, the pedestrian could listen to an entire broadcast of *Amos 'n' Andy* or a fireside chat of President FRANKLIN D. ROOSEVELT. This story also suggests the curious way that radio blurred the boundaries between the public world of politics and entertainment and the private world of the home. As radio brought the public world inside the private one, Americans had to adjust to the ubiquity of strange voices in their home. Inundated with advertising chatter about laxatives, soap operas, and the voice of the president, the American home became an important crossroads for public and private modes of speech.

The best radio performers understood the significance of radio's incursion into the privacy of the home and adjusted their voices accordingly. Many of radio's first and best performers migrated from the vaudeville and Broadway theater traditions and had to learn to speak softly and conversationally into microphones. Politicians and preachers, used to the stump or the pulpit, had to make similar adjustments. Roosevelt's fireside chats are perhaps the most famous example of the power of an intimate, informal vocal presentation to deliver public addresses over the airwaves. These broadcasts were among the most listened-to in radio history, as determined by the new ratings services that began to measure radio's audience and, thus, its commercial value to advertisers. Fictional dramas and comedies set in the family home—soap operas and situation comedies—provided another means for making radio appropriately intimate. Finally, audience participation programs—quiz shows, interview programs, and amateur hour shows—lent the informal sound of everyday voices to radio's daily repertoire.

Radio broadcasts also made an indelible impression on the historical memory of the nation. Replacing newspapers as the most important of the NEWS MEDIA for information about current events, radio in the 1930s and 1940s became the central conduit through which millions of Americans experienced the MUNICH CONFERENCE crisis in 1938, the BATTLE OF BRITAIN in 1940, the attack on PEARL HARBOR in 1941, news from the battlefronts, and the death of Roosevelt in 1945. Radio was also the means by which listeners shared other kinds of information. The infamous *War of the Worlds* broadcast by ORSON WELLES in 1938, for example, scared some listeners with its fictional, dramatized news bulletins of an inva-

sion from Mars. More significantly, this broadcast drew attention to the broad cultural authority radio had attained as a source for news of the world. It also renewed criticisms of radio's negative effect on the rationality of its mass audience.

The essentially commercial, centralized nature of the broadcasting industry was shaped by the Federal Radio Act of 1927 and reaffirmed and made permanent by the Communications Act of 1934, which established the FEDERAL COMMUNICATIONS COMMISSION (FCC) as a continuing federal regulatory agency. These laws confirmed the dominance of the airwaves by CBS, NBC Red, and NBC Blue, precursors to the big three television networks that emerged at the end of the 1940s, and a handful of smaller networks and for-profit regional stations. The basic structure of radio broadcasting—network domination, commercial sponsorship, a handful of recognizable genre formulas, and oversight by the FCC—has exerted enormous influence on the shape of television in the United States. And radio's tendency to blur the boundaries of public and pri-

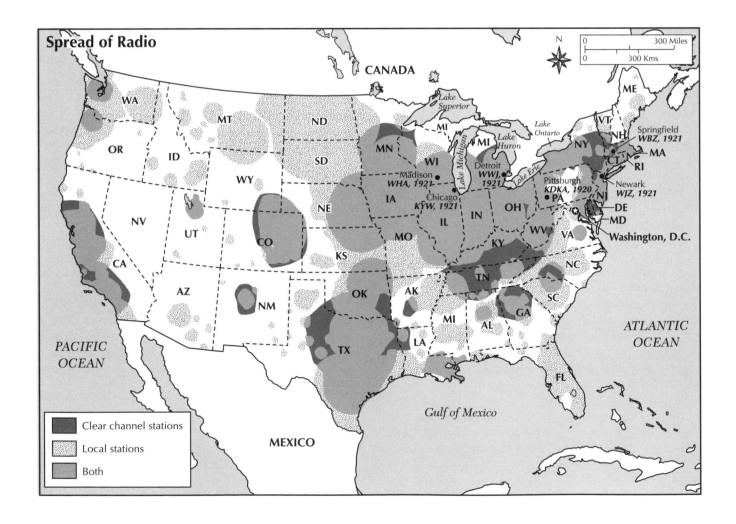

vate space has become its most significant legacy in the world of mass-mediated POPULAR CULTURE. This legacy is most evident in such recent technological developments as cell phones, the Internet, miniature cameras, and wireless voice and data devices, and in such cultural phenomena as confessional talk shows, personal webpages, and the "reality programming" fad.

Further reading: Erik Barnouw, *A Tower in Babel: A History of Broadcasting in the United States to 1933* (New York: Oxford University Press, 1966); ———, *The Golden Web: A History of Broadcasting in the United States, 1933–1953* (New York: Oxford University Press, 1968); Michele Hilmes, *Radio Voices: American Broadcasting, 1922–1952* (Minneapolis: University of Minnesota Press, 1997); Jason Loviglio and Michele Hilmes, eds., *Radio Reader: Essays in the Cultural History of Radio* (New York: Routledge, 2001).

—Jason Loviglio

Randolph, A. Philip (1889–1979)

A LABOR and CIVIL RIGHTS leader, A. Philip Randolph spent much of his life working for equality for AFRICAN AMERICANS.

Asa Philip Randolph was born in Crescent City, Florida, on April 15, 1889. The son of a minister of the African Methodist Episcopal Church, Randolph was raised to appreciate education. He graduated from high school in 1907, and in 1911 moved to Harlem, where he continued his education through night classes and became familiar with the principles of socialism. He met and married a widow, Lucille Green, who introduced him to a Columbia University student named Chandler Owen. Together, Randolph and Owen joined the Socialist Party in 1916 and began speaking on street corners. They encouraged unionization of black laborers and discouraged black men from fighting in World War I. They created and published a magazine titled the *Messenger,* called the "only radical Negro magazine in America."

In 1925, Randolph was persuaded to become head of the newly formed and all-black Brotherhood of Sleeping Car Porters. Randolph was a good choice for this position because of his gift for oratory, his understanding of unionization, and the fact that he was not an employee of the Pullman Company—and thus the company could not fire him, as it had done to leaders of prior attempts at organization. In 1937, the Brotherhood was finally recognized as the representative body for the porters, rather than the Pullman Company union. This was a triumph for labor, for African Americans, and for Randolph himself, who became one of the most influential black leaders in the country.

In 1941, Randolph organized the MARCH ON WASHINGTON MOVEMENT, in an attempt to persuade the GOVERNMENT to allow black Americans to participate fully in defense industry and the armed forces during WORLD WAR II. The march, intended to mobilize 100,000 African Americans to come to the nation's capital to protest, was scheduled for July 1, 1941. President FRANKLIN D. ROOSEVELT met with Randolph and other black leaders, attempting to convince them to call off the march, but was initially unsuccessful. It was only with the issuance of EXECUTIVE ORDER 8802, ordering an end to discrimination in government and firms with defense contracts, and establishing the FAIR EMPLOYMENT PRACTICES COMMITTEE, less than a week before the march was to be held, that Randolph agreed to cancel the scheduled march.

In 1948, Randolph organized a campaign of civil disobedience for the cause of a desegregated military, an effort that contributed to President Harry S. Truman's decision to ban segregation in the armed forces. Randolph remained a visible labor leader, in 1955 taking a place as the vice president of, and the only black representative on, the executive council of the AFL-CIO, and creating the Negro American Labor Council in 1960.

In the 1960s, Randolph's preference for pacifism and nonviolent protest in the search for civil rights led to criticism from younger, more militant, black leaders. However, in 1963, Randolph helped to organize the March on Washington. He spoke at this event, in front of the Lincoln Memorial, sharing the podium with Rev. Martin Luther King, Jr. As Randolph grew older, he became less active, though he established the A. Philip Randolph Institute to use political means to encourage social change. Randolph retired as head of the Brotherhood of Sleeping Car Porters in 1968, and he died in 1979.

Further reading: Jervis Anderson, *A. Philip Randolph: A Biographical Portrait* (New York: Harcourt Brace Jovanovich, 1973); Paula F. Pfeffer, *A. Philip Randolph: Pioneer of the Civil Rights Movement* (Baton Rouge: Louisiana State University Press, 1990).

—Joanna Smith

rationing

Economic MOBILIZATION for WORLD WAR II created the need to ration consumer goods on the WORLD WAR II HOME FRONT. Military material and production requirements meant limited supplies of a variety of consumer goods, as did also the inability to import sufficient quantities of some raw materials. The higher incomes created by wartime prosperity and the price controls imposed to restrain inflation meant that people could afford consumer goods—and they wanted to buy them after a decade of deprivation. A rationing system was thus necessary to ensure that essential goods were allocated fairly. Wartime rationing, administered by the OFFICE OF PRICE ADMINISTRATION (OPA), was generally effective, but it was never popular.

The OPA implemented rationing when requested by various supply agencies, with the WAR PRODUCTION BOARD ultimately gaining the authority to determine which goods would be rationed, when, and in what amounts. Ten rationing programs were begun in 1942, with more following in the remainder of the war. They involved a number of products for a variety of reasons. Rationing of tires, for example, came because of the near total cutoff of the importation of rubber from Japanese-controlled Asia and the need for rubber for the military and essential civilian uses. Gasoline rationing was implemented largely to save rubber and tires, fuel oil because of the needs of railroads as well as the military. Shoes were rationed because of military needs. Canned foods rationing came because of military requirements for tin; coffee and sugar rationing, because shipping was diverted to other purposes; meat and butter rationing, to ensure adequate supplies for the military and for LEND-LEASE ACT shipments to the Allies. Some goods in short supply were not rationed. Automobile production, for example, was shut down during the war as the AUTOMOBILE INDUSTRY converted to wartime production, and no rationing was needed. Clothing (except for shoes) was not rationed, nor were fresh fruits and vegetables, nor whiskey and cigarettes.

Consistent with the OPA's grassroots organization principles, every county had a rationing board and tens of thousands of volunteers implemented a changing system of ration books, coupons, colored stamps, stickers, and certificates for various goods and amounts. Merchants could not get new supplies until they turned in coupons, certificates, and so forth for the inventories they had sold. OPA also employed a complicated and variable point system to try better to balance supply and demand.

While most Americans understood the need for rationing and supported the principle, the system seemed complicated and confused and susceptible to arbitrary and unfair decisions. And inevitably, board members sometimes (many Americans thought *usually*) showed favoritism to friends and family, or to those with influence.

Moreover, rationing seemed somehow un-American, depriving people of their right to buy what they wanted in the amounts they wanted, especially after the decade-long GREAT DEPRESSION. The scarcity and rationing of some items was especially galling—above all, perhaps, for gasoline and meat, which struck at driving and eating preferences. Indeed, President FRANKLIN D. ROOSEVELT postponed gasoline rationing until after the 1942 elections because he knew how unpopular it would be. Rationing

gave rise to the flourishing BLACK MARKET of the American home front, most notably in such items as gasoline and meat. Panicked buying and hoarding preceded the imposition of rationing on sugar, coffee, meat, canned foods, and other items.

The wartime mantra of shortages and sacrifice was "use it up, wear it out, make it do or do without"—but few Americans wanted to do without, and when they used it up or wore it out they wanted to buy more. Often they could not buy more—not only was automobile production stopped but other consumer durables requiring metal (refrigerators and other appliances, for example) were in short supply, and rationing restricted purchases of many other items. Still, overall consumer spending and production of consumer goods increased during the war, despite the shortages and rationing, and despite grumbling about deprivation. The United States devoted only about 40 percent of its GNP to war production, as compared to more than half in Germany and Britain. Quality and choice often declined, but buying did not, and nutritional standards rose. Where annual per capita meat consumption fell in Britain from 132 to 115 pounds during the war, for example, it rose from 134 to 162 in the United States. Corrected for inflation, consumer spending rose by 12 percent in the United States from 1939 to 1943 and fell by about 30 percent in Britain.

Rationing, then, became an accepted though never popular feature of wartime American life, accepted in principle but criticized and sometimes resisted or evaded in application. And while rationing produced inconvenience and frustration, it did not prevent generally rising living standards, and it created little real hardship.

Further reading: Richard Lingeman, *Don't You Know There's a War On? The American Home Front, 1941–1945* (New York: Putnam, 1970).

recession of 1937–38

The recession of 1937–38, also known as the "Roosevelt Recession," was a sharp downturn of the ECONOMY following some recovery from the depths of the GREAT DEPRESSION. Caused largely by a turn to tighter fiscal and monetary policies in 1937, the recession of 1937–38 had important political as well as economic consequences.

Although the NEW DEAL programs and spending of President FRANKLIN D. ROOSEVELT's first term did not bring full recovery from the depression, they did contribute to economic improvement. Between 1933 and 1937, unemployment fell from about 25 percent to 14 percent of the labor force, while the gross national product (GNP) rose by an average of nearly 16 percent annually, and national income by about 21 percent annually. Measured in constant 1929 dollars to correct for the falling price levels of the depression, the GNP actually exceeded 1929 levels by 1937. Those gains constitute one of the most impressive peacetime expansions ever, although that was largely because economic indexes had fallen so far by 1933. In 1937, the economy still languished well below full-production, full-employment prosperity.

Roosevelt and Secretary of the Treasury HENRY MORGENTHAU, JR., thought that the improving economy provided a chance to reduce the budget deficits incurred during the first term, a priority of both men. The administration therefore slashed spending—the WORKS PROGRESS ADMINISTRATION was cut sharply, removing more than a million people from its rolls—at the same time that new payroll taxes under the SOCIAL SECURITY ACT took money from consumers. Worried like Roosevelt and others in the administration about inflation, the Federal Reserve Board imposed tighter monetary policy by raising reserve requirements for banks, and the Treasury Department "sterilized" incoming gold by putting it in inactive accounts instead of using it to increase the money supply. In addition, New Deal LABOR and TAXATION policies from 1935 to 1937 had the effect of further worrying and alienating BUSINESS and thus inhibiting private investment.

In the late summer and fall of 1937, the economy abruptly turned down; indeed, indexes dropped faster (though not farther nor for as long) than at the outset of the Great Depression. The Dow Jones industrial stock average sank from 190 to 115 in three months; steel production fell off by 75 percent; corporate profits plummeted by 80 percent; and unemployment shot up some 25 percent, to nearly 10 million, in the winter. By the spring of 1938, payrolls and industrial production were down by more than one-third, and the Dow Jones was off by nearly 50 percent. Unemployment for 1938 was 19 percent of the labor force.

The new economic collapse led to a serious reconsideration of economic policy within the administration. Morgenthau continued to urge balanced budgets to restore economic health and confidence, while Postmaster General (and Democratic National Committee chairman) JAMES A. FARLEY and others recommended moderating regulation, tax, and other polices that disturbed business and impeded investment and production. Advocates of ANTIMONOPOLY policy, led by LEON HENDERSON, maintained that economic concentration had led to restrictions on production and to higher prices, resulting in reduced investment, production, employment, and income. They argued for stepping up antitrust policy. Others, led by MARRINER ECCLES and HARRY L. HOPKINS, advocated returning to the deficit spending that had evidently produced the 1933–37 expansion. The antimonopoly and spending approaches were not mutually exclusive, for Henderson was among the New Dealers converted by 1938 to KEYNE-

SIANISM, the idea that GOVERNMENT deficit spending could compensate for inadequate private spending and stimulate the economy.

In mid-April 1938, Roosevelt announced an emergency increase in RELIEF spending, and then at the end of the month requested that Congress form a special committee to look into economic concentration. In June, Congress established the TEMPORARY NATIONAL ECONOMIC COMMITTEE (TNEC). As the economy began to expand again, especially with the beginning of heavy spending for WORLD WAR II, Keynesian ideas reoriented LIBERALISM toward seeking full-production, full-employment prosperity by means of government compensatory spending—a change in the liberal agenda that was central to what some scholars have called the THIRD NEW DEAL of Roosevelt's second and third terms. Meanwhile, antimonopoly efforts faded.

But the recession had political implications beyond the reorientation of the New Deal and liberalism. It weakened Roosevelt's popularity and power, emboldened conservative critics, and contributed to the formation of the CONSERVATIVE COALITION in CONGRESS that would henceforth thwart significant expansion of the New Deal and roll back some New Deal reforms when it could. The recession of 1937–38 was thus in several ways one of the most important episodes in Roosevelt's eventful second term.

Further reading: Alan Brinkley, *The End of Reform: New Deal Liberalism in Recession and War* (New York: Knopf, 1995); Dean L. May, *From New Deal to New Economics: The American Liberal Response to the Recession of 1937* (New York: Garland, 1981); Kenneth D. Roose, *The Economics of Recession and Revival: An Interpretation of 1937–38* (New Haven, Conn.: Yale University Press, 1954).

Reciprocal Trade Agreements Act (1934)

President FRANKLIN D. ROOSEVELT proposed the Reciprocal Trade Agreements Act of 1934 as part of the NEW DEAL policy to combat the GREAT DEPRESSION. The legislation was designed to stimulate foreign trade by authorizing the president to increase or decrease existing tariff rates up to 50 percent for nations that would reciprocate with similar terms for American products.

The Reciprocal Trade Agreements Act superseded the HAWLEY-SMOOT TARIFF ACT of 1930, which had sharply raised tariff rates in the United States between 1930 and 1932. While the Hawley-Smoot act was in effect, some two dozen trading partners retaliated by increasing their tariffs, contributing to a precipitous reduction in U.S. exports. Though FDR criticized the Hawley-Smoot act in the 1932 presidential campaign, he said that international trade relations were secondary to the establishment of a solvent domestic economy. FDR's emphasis on the domestic economy was reflected as well by his "bombshell message" that wrecked the LONDON ECONOMIC CONFERENCE of 1933 by declaring that the U.S. would not participate in currency exchange rate stabilization. FDR also prevented Secretary of State CORDELL HULL from submitting a reciprocal tariff agreements proposal to CONGRESS. However, as the Great Depression wore on, FDR and his administration looked increasingly to international trade as a means of alleviating the economic problems in the United States.

Hull, an advocate of free trade, favored the idea of reciprocity in which the president would have the power to negotiate agreements with other nations to reduce tariffs without the interference of Congress. Support of Hull's position by Secretary of Agriculture HENRY A. WALLACE and by HENRY L. STIMSON, secretary of state during the HOOVER PRESIDENCY, helped lead FDR to ask Congress for such power in March 1934. Republican congressmen and BUSINESS interests opposed the bill, and were especially hostile to the most favored nation clause, which stated that the United States would negotiate tariffs with another nation at rates equal to those applied to any other nation with whom it traded. Opponents thought that the United States should not make any concessions unless certain privileges were received in return. Ultimately, the bill was passed in June despite these objections.

As a result the Reciprocal Trade Agreements Act of 1934, Hull negotiated 18 reciprocity treaties in the next four years. The act, which remained in effect until amended in the Trade Expansion Act of 1962, helped prevent further drastic decline in the world economy, even though the most prominent and immediate economic effect was limited to Latin America. The long-term effects of lowering tariffs included expanded world trade in the post–WORLD WAR II era and the General Agreement on Tariffs and Trade signed in 1947.

See also FOREIGN POLICY.

Further reading: Robert Dallek, *Franklin D. Roosevelt and American Foreign Policy, 1932–1945* (New York: Oxford University Press, 1979).

—Michael T. Walsh

Reconstruction Finance Corporation (RFC)

The Reconstruction Finance Corporation (RFC) was created by CONGRESS in January 1932 at the request of President HERBERT C. HOOVER and continued through the presidency of FRANKLIN D. ROOSEVELT. Under the leadership of JESSE H. JONES, it played important roles in NEW DEAL efforts to stimulate the ECONOMY during the GREAT DEPRESSION and in the economic MOBILIZATION for WORLD WAR II.

The RFC came about because of the crisis of the banking system in the early 1930s. Initially resisting bankers' requests for federal assistance, President Hoover prevailed upon them late in 1931 to establish the National Credit Corporation, with a fund of $500 million to lend to banks needing cash to sustain their operations. But Hoover also agreed to provide federal help if the NCC proved inadequate; and when it did, Congress in January 1932 created the Reconstruction Finance Corporation and authorized it to lend up to $2 billion to commercial banks, savings banks, credit unions, and other financial institutions. RFC loans went especially to major banks and institutions, but with little apparent impact upon the collapsing banking system, and the HOOVER PRESIDENCY came under fire for the RFC's ineffectiveness as well as for its apparent favoritism to large banks.

In the summer of 1932, the RFC took on new responsibilities in public works and RELIEF. As the depression worsened, Congress increasingly supported spending on public works and relief to spur the economy and alleviate distress. Hoover rebuffed or vetoed most such efforts, but in July 1932 reluctantly agreed to the compromise RELIEF AND RECONSTRUCTION ACT, which authorized the RFC to lend states up to $300 million for relief and up to $1.5 billion for self-liquidating public works projects (for example, toll roads and bridges). To qualify for federal loans, states had to certify that they had reached their financial limits, and the combination of this "pauper's oath" and the reluctance of the Hoover administration to spend on relief and public works meant that little of the money was expended.

President Franklin D. Roosevelt thus inherited an agency with significant potential but little accomplishment. Roosevelt energized and redirected the RFC. The EMERGENCY BANKING ACT OF 1933 allowed the RFC to buy preferred commercial bank stock, thus increasing the working capital of banks instead of lending them money and increasing their indebtedness. FDR also named Texas banker Jesse Jones, who served as an RFC director under Hoover, to head the agency. Believing that the RFC had favored conservative eastern banks over smaller banks in other regions, Jones wanted to make the RFC a far more venturesome and expansive agency.

While other New Deal agencies took over government relief and public works functions, the RFC became a major source of money for GOVERNMENT agencies and private businesses and banks. It became, in effect, the largest bank and the largest investor in the nation, and by 1945 had distributed more than $35 billion in loans, investments, and other expenditures. Among its many operations, the RFC helped to underwrite such key agencies as the FEDERAL EMERGENCY RELIEF ADMINISTRATION and the RURAL ELECTRIFICATION ADMINISTRATION, directed the Commodity Credit Corporation and the Export-Import Bank and financed the various federal mortgage agencies, including the HOME OWNERS LOAN CORPORATION, the FARM CREDIT ADMINISTRATION, and the FEDERAL HOUSING ADMINISTRATION. The RFC also made BUSINESS loans in an effort to stimulate the economy, and by 1940 had expended some $8 billion in business and banking loans. Although the New Deal failed to bring full economic recovery, the RFC under Roosevelt and Jones became a powerful and innovative agency.

The RFC then played an important role in economic mobilization during World War II. The Defense Plant Corporation, a subsidiary of the RFC, spent more than $9 billion in constructing more than 2,000 factories, while the Defense Supply Corporation spent a similar amount in acquiring materials necessary for the war effort. As ubiquitous during the war as in the 1930s, the RFC also undertook such diverse activities as overseeing the synthetic rubber industry, financing defense housing, and buying up materials needed by the AXIS nations. RFC overseas efforts led to a bitter dispute between Jones, who had become secretary of commerce in 1940 in addition to his duties as RFC chairman, and Vice President HENRY A. WALLACE, which ultimately led to Jones's resignation from government in early 1945. The agency itself continued into the postwar era, though without the significance or impact of the Roosevelt-Jones era of 1933–45.

Further reading: James S. Olson, *Saving Capitalism: The Reconstruction Finance Corporation and the New Deal, 1933–1940* (Princeton, N.J.: Princeton University Press, 1988); Bascom N. Timmons, *Jesse H. Jones: The Man and the Statesman* (New York: Henry Holt, 1956).

reconversion

As early as spring 1943, with Allied victory in WORLD WAR II increasingly likely, GOVERNMENT and military officials began seriously considering plans for returning the United States to a peacetime ECONOMY after the war—a process called reconversion. Reconversion included terminating wartime contracts that were no longer needed, helping returning veterans and former war workers find civilian employment, disposing of surplus government property, assisting BUSINESS to resume production of civilian products, and relaxing WAGE AND PRICE CONTROLS, RATIONING, and other wartime restrictions.

Most people agreed that early planning for reconversion was a necessary part of POSTWAR PLANNING. America's unplanned demobilization after World War I had disastrous consequences for the U.S. economy, and policymakers hoped that early planning would allow the United States to avoid making the same mistakes again. Moreover, Americans realized that the wartime economic recovery was

based largely on the money spent on war MOBILIZATION, and many feared that without carefully planned reconversion the United States might slip back into the GREAT DEPRESSION once the stimulus of wartime spending had disappeared. Yet, despite the agreement that timely and effective planning for reconversion was necessary, policy clashes ensued over how and when reconversion should take place.

Although the NATIONAL RESOURCES PLANNING BOARD and the WAR PRODUCTION BOARD had done some work on reconversion, CONGRESS did not give reconversion significant attention until 1943, when the tide of war had clearly turned in favor of the Allies. In March 1943, the Senate created a special committee on Postwar Economic Policy and Planning chaired by Walter F. George of Georgia, followed 10 months later by a parallel House of Representatives committee headed by William Colmer of Mississippi.

By then, however, DEMOBILIZATION and reconversion had already become controversial issues. Liberals and LABOR argued that an early, incremental, and well-planned reconversion would limit the number of worker layoffs as well as protect small businesses as war production declined. On the other hand, the military argued that early reconversion would disrupt the production of war goods and wanted to delay reconversion for as long as possible. Big war contractors wanted to delay reconversion because they feared that early reconversion would allow competitors to resume civilian production, while they would still be producing war materials. Businesses also did not want to dispose of surplus government property, or terminate wartime contracts, without receiving generous compensation from the U.S. government.

In November 1943, JAMES F. BYRNES, director of the OFFICE OF WAR MOBILIZATION (OWM), announced that BERNARD M. BARUCH and John M. Hancock had agreed to head a special unit within OWM to develop a unified approach for dealing with postwar reconversion. The Baruch-Hancock Report, made public in February 1944, proposed creating a Joint Contract Termination Board within OWM to unify all government contract termination efforts, as well as a Surplus Property Administrator to dispose of surplus property. It also suggested creating a "work director" to supervise the discharge of personnel from the armed forces, coordinate efforts to care for disabled veterans, and provide job placement assistance and educational training to returning service personnel.

Many of these provisions went into effect. President FRANKLIN D. ROOSEVELT set up the Surplus War Property Administration within OWM, as well as a new unit called the Retraining and Reemployment Administration, which became the "work director" proposed in the Baruch-Hancock Report. Roosevelt also signed the GI BILL OF RIGHTS in June 1944, and in October 1944 Congress created the

OFFICE OF WAR MOBILIZATION AND RECONVERSION (OWMR). Yet as many people had feared, the so-called human side of reconversion, such as the training and placement of discharged veterans, took a back seat to the interests of the military and big business. Indeed, OWMR, its Surplus Property Administration, and other reconversion agencies allowed war manufacturers to purchase government-owned factories and other surplus property at greatly discounted rates, offered them lucrative bonuses to settle wartime contracts, and protected them from competitors.

Nevertheless, because of careful planning, generally efficient retooling of factories, higher incomes and savings, and pent-up demand during the war years, the nation did not slip back into depression after the war as many had feared. Despite some difficulties, such as labor unrest that impaired production and inflationary price rises for many items, consumer spending increased significantly once the war was over and wartime restrictions were lifted. The resulting surge in demand helped maintain prosperity and enabled returning service members and war workers to be reintegrated into America's peacetime economy.

Further reading: Herman Miles Somers, *Presidential Agency: OWMR, the Office of War Mobilization and Reconversion* (Cambridge, Mass.: Harvard University Press, 1950).

—David W. Waltrop

recreation

Recreation in the United States expanded during the 1920s, largely because of the increasing amounts of free time and discretionary income in urban areas. The commercial recreation industry was badly hurt by the onset of the GREAT DEPRESSION, but recreation and leisure activities increased later in the 1930s and during WORLD WAR II. Personal consumption expenditures for recreation grew from a depression low of $2.2 billion in 1933 (down from $4.3 billion in 1929) to more than $6.1 billion in 1945.

In response to growing interest and demand, President HERBERT C. HOOVER directed his 1929 Committee on Social Trends to pay special attention to recreation. The following year, during the White House Conference on Children and Youth, Hoover declared that all CHILDREN should receive "wholesome physical and mental recreation" from birth through adolescence. Little came of these efforts, however, and even though CITIES provided recreational outlets for citizens, UNEMPLOYMENT and underemployment produced a greater need for facilities and programs provided by voluntary and municipal agencies. The National Recreation Association received a substantial private grant to expand its work in 1932, but the federal GOV-

ERNMENT did not begin more fully to address the seriousness of the situation until the Roosevelt administration.

Though focused on economic problems, the NEW DEAL of President FRANKLIN D. ROOSEVELT created work RELIEF programs that established affordable recreational opportunities for the public. New Deal agencies such as the FEDERAL EMERGENCY RELIEF ADMINISTRATION, the CIVILIAN CONSERVATION CORPS, and the WORKS PROGRESS ADMINISTRATION (WPA) provided jobs constructing community centers, libraries, parks, picnic areas, roads, and trails. WPA arts projects introduced many Americans to the worlds of MUSIC, LITERATURE, ART, and the theater. The WPA, along with the NATIONAL YOUTH ADMINISTRATION, also employed recreation leaders and held instructional institutions to train new recreation workers. The growing demand for trained administrators encouraged development of college programs across the country devoted to recreation management.

Public usage of national parks, monuments, and related areas increased from fewer than 4 million visitors in 1932 to approximately 15 million visitors in 1937. Another major development occurred in 1936 when the National Park Service (created by Roosevelt in 1933) established Lake Mead as the first national recreation area and initiated 46 Recreational Demonstration Areas that helped increase the popularity of the outdoor sports of hunting and fishing. The federal government spent an estimated $1.5 billion on the development of recreational facilities as some 881 new parks, 1,500 athletic fields, 12,700 playgrounds, 750 swimming pools, 3,500 tennis courts, 123 golf courses, 1,000 ice skating rinks, and 28 miles of ski trails were created.

Such activities as listening to the RADIO, attending MOVIES and SPORTS events, dancing, parlor games, and prize contests were popular throughout the 1930s. After movie attendance dropped in the early 1930s, the remainder of the decade saw an increase to an average of about 85 million weekly moviegoers. By 1935, swing music and the big band sound of the swing era had left behind the more sedate dancing of the early 1930s for jitterbugging. With the repeal of Prohibition, thousands of new bars and taverns installed jukeboxes to provide the latest tunes, and the listeners dropped approximately 5 million nickels each day by the end of the decade, producing a multimillion dollar industry.

An early 1930s craze for contract bridge brought about an increase in playing card manufacturing as an estimated 20 million people began to play the game, and no major newspaper was without a bridge column by the middle of the decade. Another game that became popular during the depression years was bingo, with variations such as beano or keno. Low-cost bingo contests offered prizes such as a tin of coffee, a ham, or cash. Get-rich quick dreams also inspired the 1935 introduction of the nation's best-selling game, Monopoly, which sold an estimated 6 million copies by early 1937.

In January 1931, the Department of Commerce reported that miniature golf had become a $125 million industry and provided employment for 200,000 workers, as some 30,000 newly built roadside courses became almost as common as hotdog stands and filling stations. By year's end, this fad had burned out, leaving courses to be reclaimed by weeds, but by the mid-1930s other recreation sports such as bowling and softball began to gain in popularity. The number of bowling teams reportedly grew from a 1933 low of around 30,000 to more than 130,000 in 1940, while an estimated 2 million people played softball in 1935 and more than 5 million people played in 1939. By the end of the decade, young boys were also provided with a chance to participate in organized sports with the creation of Little League Baseball (1939).

Despite a growing interest in recreational events, professional sports attendance suffered during the depression as spectator sports admissions dropped from $66 million in 1929 to a low of $47 million in 1932; but by 1941, paid admissions rebounded to an estimated $107 million. To reverse the decline in baseball attendance, owners implemented new ideas including doubleheaders, radio broadcasts (St. Louis, 1935), and the advent of night baseball (Cincinnati, 1935). Such changes and the improved economy brought an increase of some 1.6 million spectators between 1936 and 1940. Other sports, including professional and college football, horse, dog and automobile racing, and prize fighting, also drew larger crowds in the late 1930s.

Americans spent an estimated $4 billion—roughly 7 percent of personal income—on all recreational activities in 1935. Vacation travel associated with the automobile accounted for more than half of this figure. Travel to foreign countries dropped by nearly half from 1930 to 1933, but by 1937 it rebounded to the level of 1926. Inspired by economic realities and by new advertising slogans, such as "See America First," traveling by automobile became a principal source of recreation for many Americans. Holiday and vacation travel, trips to the beach, and simple recreational driving were all now within practical reach. Statistically, the greatest growth in travel by Americans was to national parks and monuments. Motor courts became an important industry by late in the decade. The invention of the mobile home in 1929 also increased travel, as it offered an alternative to the cost of dining and lodging. By 1936 an estimated 160,000 mobile homes were on the road.

Americans on the WORLD WAR II HOME FRONT once again faced restrictions on their leisure activities, this time because of gas RATIONING, blackouts, dimouts, food shortages, travel restrictions, and occasional curfews. Encour-

Crowd waiting to enter movie theater in Littleton, New Hampshire *(Library of Congress)*

aged by the government, civilians nonetheless continued to pursue leisure and entertainment opportunities. Neighborhood teen centers, adult education programs, and home gardening all flourished. More than 2,000 war plants provided dancing facilities during breaks, and parlor games such as chess, checkers, and card playing grew in popularity. A 1942 survey reported that 87 percent of Americans played cards at home, and playing card sales increased by 1,000 percent during the war.

Aided by the introduction of the inexpensive paperback book in 1939, reading—especially of nonfiction, mysteries, and comic books—became a more important part of leisure time as well. Book sales jumped from $255 million in 1941 to $520 million at the end of 1945, and membership in the Book-of-the-Month Club (established in 1936) doubled during the war. Read by tens of millions of civilians, LIFE MAGAZINE and other news periodicals saw an increase of nearly $330 million in income over the same period. Radio listening increased by 20 percent just from 1941 to 1942 and continued to grow throughout the war as people tuned in for the latest news.

The government renewed its emphasis on promoting better mental and physical health through recreation when large numbers of draftees were judged to be unfit for service. Organizations such as the American Red Cross and the UNITED SERVICE ORGANIZATIONS (USO), along with the U.S. military, promoted programs on the battlefield, in camps, and in rest centers to relieve tension and bolster morale among servicemen. The armed services alone employed 12,500 recreation directors. The American Red Cross established close to 750 clubs worldwide, with another 250 mobile entertainment units, while the USO established community drop-in centers for servicemen looking for food, dancing, books, or conversation and promoted tours starring Hollywood stars for servicemen around the world.

Youth agencies were also busy on the home front, as Boy Scouts, Girl Scouts, and Camp Fire Girls collected scrap metal, sold WAR BONDS, and made supplies for USO centers. Besides aiding the war effort, these groups helped provide adolescents with things to do. Together with recreational centers and teen canteens that sprang up across the country, these organizations wanted to provide a chaperoned environment to deter the growing problem of teen delinquency. Larger cities also developed privately owned teen clubs.

At the end of the war, recreational facilities, expenditures, and participation continued to grow rapidly. The strong economy and a new knowledge of the world inspired people to broaden their horizons and to travel, as they never had before. The automobile and other consumer goods began to catch up with the growing demands of veterans and industrial workers ready to spend their savings on pent-up desires of travel and leisure.

See also POPULAR CULTURE.

Further reading: Gary Dean Best, *The Nickel and Dime Decade: American Popular Culture during the 1930s* (Westport, Conn.: Praeger, 1993); Foster Rhea Dulles, *A History of Recreation: America Learns to Play*, 2d ed. (New York: Appleton-Century-Crofts, 1965); Richard Lingeman, *Don't You Know There's a War On? The American Home Front, 1941–1945* (New York: Putnam, 1970).

—Ronald G. Simon

refugees

Nazi persecution of JEWS and other minorities during the HOLOCAUST and the effects of WORLD WAR II precipitated a refugee crisis in Europe. IMMIGRATION policies of the U.S. GOVERNMENT significantly shaped the American response to this crisis, as did concerns in the 1930s about immigrants taking jobs during the high UNEMPLOYMENT of the GREAT DEPRESSION. ANTI-SEMITISM in the United States also contributed to the reluctance to accept refugees from Europe. Even so, perhaps as many as a quarter million refugees were accepted by the United States by the early postwar years, far more than by any other nation.

In 1924, CONGRESS enacted legislation that sharply reduced immigration and apportioned it according to national origins. The onset of the Great Depression led to an unsuccessful effort in Congress to further restrict immigration, but in 1930 President HERBERT C. HOOVER directed immigration officials to stringently exercise their authority under the law to deny visas to those who might become public charges. Within a year, this move decreased the number of visas granted by 90 percent.

Although Hoover established a precedent for executive action that President FRANKLIN D. ROOSEVELT would later exploit, FDR's ability to maneuver was circumscribed by a restrictionist Congress and a nativist and increasingly anti-Semitic American public fearful of having to compete with refugees for scarce jobs. Worry about a backlash that might cause Congress to eliminate immigration altogether made Jewish and refugee aid organizations hesitant to call for measures to circumvent the quota system to aid refugees.

The United States did accept about one-third of the initial 150,000 refugees fleeing Nazi persecution in accordance with existing law. As the numbers of the primarily Jewish refugees grew larger, Roosevelt convened an international conference in Evian, France, in 1938, but the conference yielded few tangible results. Available options such as resettling refugees or negotiating with the Nazi regime for the safe passage of refugees foundered, as no nation, including the United States, would agree to amend its immigration laws to admit refugees. Responding to the German annexation of Austria in 1938, FDR pledged unilaterally to merge and fill German and Austrian quotas for entry into the United States. He also used his executive power to mitigate Hoover's public charge visa criteria for admission and enabled refugees on temporary visas to remain. Over 120,000 refugees, comprising nearly 100 percent of available quotas, were allowed entry into the United States from 1938 to mid-1940.

The proposed Wagner bill of the late 1930s, an effort to admit some 20,000 primarily Jewish German children outside the quota system, demonstrated the limits of FDR's power to affect refugee policy, and also his unwillingness to challenge restrictionists in Congress. Debate over the bill mobilized strong public opposition led by veterans' and patriotic organizations. According to PUBLIC OPINION POLLS, most of the public also opposed the bill. The administration did little to promote passage of the measure, which failed even to reach the floor for a vote. Congress did in 1940 easily approve a bill to temporarily admit English children to the United States so they could escape the bombing attacks launched by Germany in the BATTLE OF BRITAIN.

The swift conquest of western Europe by the Nazi BLITZKRIEG in the spring and summer of 1940 activated Roosevelt's Presidential Advisory Committee (PAC) on Refugees, a nongovernmental group, to secure emergency visas for a select group of intellectuals and political refugees. State Department officials, notably Breckinridge Long, however, acted in concert with consular officers abroad to restrict visas issued to those on the PAC's list.

Eventually about 2,000 political refugees were allowed into the United States, fewer than one-third of those approved by the PAC. State Department officials justified the creation of a series of increasingly restrictive bureaucratic hurdles to immigration between 1940 and 1943 as necessary to counter the threat of a "fifth column" of infiltrating Nazi and Communist spies. These hurdles imposed by the State Department slashed immigration to levels that a restrictionist Congress had not been able to achieve by legislation. At the height of Nazi atrocities in Europe, America's immigration quotas thus went unfilled.

Toward the end of the war some change began, when Secretary of the Treasury HENRY MORGENTHAU, JR., showed Roosevelt evidence of State Department obstructionism on refugees, and the president established the War Refugee Board in January 1944. Although the WRB may have helped rescue as many as 200,000 Jews, a new national policy on refugees and others displaced by World War II did not come until after the end of the war.

Further reading: Richard Breitman and Alan Kraut, *American Refugee Policy and European Jewry, 1933–1945* (Bloomington: Indiana University Press, 1987); David S. Wyman, *The Abandonment of the Jews: America and the Holocaust, 1941–1945* (New York: Pantheon, 1984).

—Julie Whitcomb

relief

Relief, as the term was used in the 1929–45 era, meant assistance—money, food and clothes, jobs—to the needy. Before the GREAT DEPRESSION, relief had been the responsibility of state and local GOVERNMENT and of private charitable agencies. But the catastrophic impact of the Great Depression on the nation's ECONOMY, creating unprecedented levels of UNEMPLOYMENT, transformed the provision of relief in the United States during the presidency of FRANKLIN D. ROOSEVELT. Though limited in their levels of coverage and assistance, NEW DEAL relief programs of the 1930s accepted federal responsibility for aiding the unemployed and destitute, provided essential help to tens of millions of needy Americans, and helped initiate the modern American welfare state.

Almost from the beginning, the Great Depression pushed traditional sources of relief assistance to their limits, and beyond. Private organizations and local government simply lacked the ability—and in the case of local government sometimes the legal authority—to provide adequate assistance to the needy. Only a tiny fraction of the unemployed and impoverished received assistance in the early years of the depression, and what they got was typically meager indeed—sometimes just a few dollars a week for those lucky enough to receive anything at all. Soup kitchens and breadlines became more prevalent and visible but, like other sources of public and private aid, provided nothing close to adequate support.

With the need so great and the customary sources of relief assistance so overmatched, attention turned to the federal government. President HERBERT C. HOOVER addressed the issue in a way consistent with his general principles about the role of the national government, convictions that also shaped his other responses to the Great Depression. Help for the needy, Hoover thought, should come from the local level and private sources, not from Washington. He feared that federal relief programs would make the poor dependent upon the government and would dry up voluntary giving and private and local charity. He believed that heavy spending on relief was in any case fiscally irresponsible and would help create a too-powerful bureaucratic central government. The federal government did in his view have a role, but, as in other areas, it was to encourage, publicize, and, as much as possible, help coordinate private and local efforts. In October 1930, Hoover established the President's Emergency Committee for Employment, which was replaced in 1931 by the President's Organization for Unemployment Relief (POUR). But these agencies lacked the power or the will to do much and consistently underestimated need and overestimated what was being done to help.

With the HOOVER PRESIDENCY thus constrained by its ideology, the CONGRESS, controlled by Democrats and progressive Republicans after the election of 1930, seized the initiative. Senators ROBERT F. WAGNER of New York and ROBERT M. LA FOLLETTE, JR., of Wisconsin took the lead in calling for large relief and public works program to assist the unemployed. Hoover denounced and resisted such efforts. His sharp objections to a proposal that would have created a new federal agency to aid the states in providing relief assistance helped kill that bill in February 1932, and in July 1932 he vetoed the Garner-Wagner relief bill, which would have created an expensive federal public works and loan program for the unemployed. Later in July Hoover did sign as a compromise the RELIEF AND RECONSTRUCTION ACT, which authorized the RECONSTRUCTION FINANCE CORPORATION to lend states up to $300 million for relief and up to $1.5 billion for self-liquidating public works projects (toll roads, for example). But in the remaining months of the Hoover presidency, little of that money was expended, partly because states had to certify that they had exhausted their borrowing and taxing powers in order to qualify for the loans, and partly because the administration had agreed to the bill only under pressure from Congress.

By the ELECTION OF 1932, relief had become one of the important differences between Hoover and his opponent, Franklin D. Roosevelt. As governor of New York,

Red Cross workers give boxes of seed to crowds of farmers in Mississippi, 1930. *(Hulton/Archive)*

Roosevelt had been among the most innovative governors in the nation, establishing the state's Temporary Emergency Relief Administration in 1931 and declaring that relief "must be extended by Government, not as a matter of charity, but as a matter of social duty." And perhaps nothing so diminished Hoover's popularity and image by 1932 as his adamant resistance to federal relief. The "Great Humanitarian" of World War I relief efforts in Europe now seemed not just tightfisted but hard-hearted, symbolized in the public mind not just by his opposition to relief assistance but also by his handling of the BONUS ARMY of the summer of 1932, when World War I veterans came to Washington for help and were driven out by federal troops.

Relief was one of the highest priorities of the New Deal, and marked one of the great changes in government between Roosevelt's administration and Hoover's. Roosevelt and his relief administrator, HARRY HOPKINS, implemented a number of major relief programs, designed to tide over the unemployed until the economy recovered and

there were jobs enough in the private sector. In fact, both men shared some of Hoover's misgivings about relief, fearing in FDR's words that direct relief or the "dole" (payments in cash or food and clothing) could be a "narcotic, a subtle destroyer of the human spirit" that robbed recipients of dignity and independence. Like Hopkins, FDR preferred work relief—jobs for the unemployed and destitute on government work projects—that would preserve self-respect and a sense of productivity at the same time that it produced valuable work for the nation. Roosevelt, who was sincere in his concern about budget deficits in the 1930s was concerned as well that heavy spending on relief would have adverse fiscal consequences. And Roosevelt, together with most other New Dealers, much preferred private to public employment and wanted the government to "quit this business of relief" as quickly as possible. But Roosevelt also saw relief as a "social duty" of government—and as politically potent as well, so long as it was needed—and the New Deal included a number of large-scale and expensive relief programs. Where Hoover would not act, Roosevelt did.

The first relief programs came in the first Hundred Days of Roosevelt's administration, during the so-called FIRST NEW DEAL. The CIVILIAN CONSERVATION CORPS, (CCC) both a conservation and a work-relief program, came first, followed by the FEDERAL EMERGENCY RELIEF ADMINISTRATION (FERA), which provided for direct relief to unemployed people who qualified via a means test. But these programs only began to address the needs of massive unemployment and poverty, and as the winter of 1933–34 approached, with the specter of widespread suffering that might rival that of the preceding winter, Roosevelt and Hopkins established the CIVIL WORKS ADMINISTRATION (CWA). Beginning in November 1933, the CWA spent some $900,000 and put more than 4 million people to work on a variety of work relief projects. When Roosevelt terminated the CWA in the spring of 1934, worried about its costs and about criticisms of it, some of its work-relief programs were transferred to the FERA.

In 1935, New Deal relief programs took a new turn, beginning the SECOND NEW DEAL of the spring and summer of that year. Unemployment remained high, and pressure had built for more effective federal action to help the jobless and needy. Roosevelt, moreover, was increasingly concerned about the federal government's role in providing direct relief and perhaps creating a class of people dependent upon the federal government. Restructuring New Deal relief efforts, the EMERGENCY RELIEF APPROPRIATION ACT approved by Congress on April 8, 1935, authorized almost $5 billion—the largest single appropriation ever to that point in American history—for work relief and public works programs. Under the bill's provisions, the federal government would assume responsibility only for those jobless people who were on relief rolls and who were able to work and thus "employable." "Unemployables" (those too old or infirm to work, for example) would again be the responsibility of state governments. (Later in 1935, the SOCIAL SECURITY ACT authorized federal matching grants to the states for such unemployable and dependent people in addition to its much larger and better-known old-age pensions and unemployment compensation programs.)

The Emergency Relief Appropriation Act spawned a number of major new agencies. Most important among them was the WORKS PROGRESS ADMINISTRATION, the most significant and expensive of the New Deal relief agencies. Before its termination in 1943, the WPA employed more than 8 million workers, spent more than $10 billion, and accomplished a huge and varied number of projects, including tens of thousands of buildings and bridges and hundreds of thousands of miles of roads and highways. But the WPA did not only provide needed jobs and income to

manual workers for construction projects. It also employed white-collar workers in a variety of projects to save their skills and dignity. It created the FEDERAL WRITERS' PROJECT, the FEDERAL THEATRE PROJECT, the FEDERAL ART PROJECT, and the FEDERAL MUSIC PROJECT to help unemployed writers, actors, artists, and musicians. The NATIONAL YOUTH ADMINISTRATION, by 1939 an independent agency, also began under the WPA and provided both jobs and training for out-of-school youth and money to help other young people stay in school.

Despite their impressive range and impact, and the changes they marked in the role and responsibility of the federal government, New Deal relief agencies had real limits and encountered increasing resistance and criticism. Funding was never adequate to meet the needs of the jobless and destitute, and Roosevelt continually worried about the psychological and fiscal impact of relief spending. Even the WPA, by far the largest and best-financed of the relief programs, never employed more than about one-third of the unemployed at any given time, could not count on predictable funding from CONGRESS, and paid wages well below prevailing rates in private enterprise. In varying degrees and ways, relief programs discriminated against AFRICAN AMERICANS, other minority groups, and women. After 1935, unemployables, the most vulnerable of the poor, were returned to state and local government responsibility. Relief agencies, and particularly the WPA, were often used for nakedly political purposes, to win support from working-class voters and to reward local politicians with patronage. Attacked by conservatives for doing too much, New Deal relief programs were attacked from the left for doing too little, and for subordinating the needs of the poor to politics and private enterprise. Not just critics but also New Deal relief administrators complained that recipients were too often made to feel like charity cases by submitting to a means test; or by receiving not work or even cash, but, rather, prescribed grocery and food orders; or, on most work-relief projects, by receiving only a fraction of prevailing wages in the private sector.

Yet the limits and shortcomings of the relief programs were only partly the responsibility of Roosevelt and the New Dealers. They reflected also constraints arising from the very structure of American government including a central government that in 1933 was small and had little established administrative capacity and a federal system where much power lay with state and local government.

Congress was loath to delegate too much power to the executive branch. Conservative resistance in Congress thus limited relief programs and their funding, while reluctant, tightfisted, and sometimes inept or racist administration by local officials shaped the implementation of federal relief programs. Local politicians and Republicans, not just New Dealers and Democrats, used relief programs for political purposes. The limits of New Deal relief programs reflected as well the continuing power of CON-SERVATISM during the New Deal years, especially by the late 1930s, and of widespread concerns—sometimes shared by relief recipients themselves—about government spending, government support of the poor, and a too powerful central government. It required the devastating impact of the Great Depression and the reformist impulses of Roosevelt and the New Deal to take relief programs as far as they went. Once prosperity returned with WORLD WAR II, the relief agencies seemed unnecessary, popular support waned rapidly, and conservative opponents in Congress attacked and reduced appropriations for the relief programs, which were largely liquidated by 1943. Nonetheless, the magnitude and the importance of New Deal relief programs should not be minimized. Spending billions of dollars on millions of people and hundreds of thousands of projects, they provided essential sources of income and often of self-respect, produced work of enduring value, and constituted a major new departure in American government.

Further reading: Searle F. Charles, *Ministry of Relief: Harry Hopkins and the Depression* (Syracuse, N.Y.: Syracuse University Press, 1962); Donald F. Howard, *The WPA and Federal Relief Policy* (New York: Russell Sage Foundation, 1943); Richard Lowitt and Maurine Beasley, eds., *One Third of a Nation: Lorena Hickok Reports on the Great Depression* (Urbana: University of Illinois Press, 1981); James T. Patterson, *America's Struggle against Poverty, 1900–1980* (Cambridge, Mass.: Harvard University Press, 1981); Bonnie F. Schwartz, *The Civil Works Administration, 1933–1934: The Business of Emergency Employment in the New Deal* (Princeton, N.J.: Princeton University Press, 1984).

Relief and Reconstruction Act (1932)

The Relief and Reconstruction Act of July 1932 authorized the RECONSTRUCTION FINANCE CORPORATION to lend states up to $300 million to spend on RELIEF assistance to the unemployed and to lend states and municipalities up to $1.5 billion to finance self-liquidating public works projects (for example, toll roads).

President HERBERT C. HOOVER reluctantly signed the measure as a compromise between his own opposition to federal financial assistance to the unemployed and his concern for fiscal prudence on the one hand and the growing readiness of the CONGRESS to spend on relief and on public works projects on the other. Hoover had earlier in July vetoed the far more expansive Garner-Wagner bill providing direct federal relief to the unemployed and committing the government to a large public works program. His administration then implemented the Relief and Reconstruction Act slowly and grudgingly, lending only a portion of the money authorized to states and localities.

By mid-1932, as the GREAT DEPRESSION neared its nadir and UNEMPLOYMENT continued to soar, the question of relief had become an important political issue, with Hoover and most Republicans still opposing direct relief from the federal government and Democrats increasingly supporting the idea. Hoover's opposition to federal relief was among the factors that made him increasingly unpopular as the ELECTION OF 1932 approached. The large-scale federal relief and public works programs of the NEW DEAL would mark one of the major differences between the HOOVER PRESIDENCY and that of FRANKLIN D. ROOSEVELT.

Further reading: David Burner, *Herbert Hoover: A Public Life* (New York: Knopf, 1979).

religion

The American religious landscape at the end of the 1920s reflected the rapidly increasing complexity of American society. Modernizing social and cultural change since the late 19th century involved a number of developments that continued to influence American religion in the era of the GREAT DEPRESSION and WORLD WAR II. These included the continuing growth of religious pluralism beyond the previously simpler patterns of Anglo-Protestant and Roman Catholic Christianity; the maturation of an increasingly ethnic Roman Catholicism into a political and cultural power, especially in industrialized CITIES; the fragmentation of Anglo-Protestantism into fundamentalist and modernist wings; the influential emergence of the neo-orthodox (or Christian Realism) movement; the continuing expansion of non-Anglo ethnic/religious groups (for example, Lutherans and Dutch Reformed throughout the Midwest and various wings of Judaism in urban areas); the development and expansion of a recently emergent Pentecostal form of Christianity; increasing regional and cultural/moral religious tensions (for example, urban vs. small town/rural, northeastern cosmopolitan vs. southern evangelical, and differing views on Prohibition); the continuation of racially based religious divisions; the continued dominance of the white Southern Baptist Convention as a religious force in the SOUTH; and, a noticeable growth in cosmopolitan secularism and religious indifference, especially in heavily urbanized areas. The events of the Great Depression and World War II posed major challenges to existing patterns of belief and religious adherence. But these events did not dramatically redirect the changes set in motion during previous decades; and, despite the challenges, organized religion and religious belief remained potent factors in American life.

By the end of the 1920s, the United States had implemented legislation restricting large-scale IMMIGRATION and thus ending the massive influx of Roman CATHOLICS and JEWS from southern and eastern Europe typical of the early years of the 20th century. However, this interlude allowed the estimated 20 million Roman Catholics, especially urban Irish, Italian, and Polish immigrants, to become more settled and Americanized, as well as to become a potent political force during the NEW DEAL era. While still the objects of anti-immigrant and anti-Catholic nativism, (as evidenced by the failed 1928 presidential campaign of the Roman Catholic Al Smith), ethnic Roman Catholics became key participants in LABOR movements as well as fervent supporters of President FRANKLIN D. ROOSEVELT and the NEW DEAL.

Roman Catholic religion itself became a more accepted and "respectable" form of American religion, especially in cosmopolitan areas, and influential bishops and church leaders obtained new political and social clout. The depression helped to produce the social empowerment of Roman Catholic clergy and lay voters, as Roman Catholics began to effectively utilize mass media, especially the RADIO. Some Roman Catholic broadcasters, most notably the controversial preacher Father CHARLES E. COUGHLIN, became nationally recognized figures, as much known for their political and social commentary as their purely doctrinal and ecclesiastical commitments. Meanwhile, women, such as Dorothy Day, who was a founding figure in the Catholic Worker movement, became active in the public arena as well, especially as related to labor and social issues that affected Roman Catholics. At the grassroots level, Roman Catholic piety was characterized by Marian devotion, neighborhood festivals in urban areas, and more frequent reception of the Eucharist by the laity in worship services. At the onset of World War II, most Roman Catholics fervently and patriotically supported the war effort, further cementing their sociocultural status as "real" Americans.

Jewish religion during this period continued to display the dominance of Orthodox Judaism (the most traditionalist, rabbinical, and ethnically self-conscious branch) over the Conservative (less traditional with respect to Americanization and doctrinal issues) and Reform (the most nontraditional and Americanized) wings. The continuing power of Jewish Orthodoxy came about especially because of large-scale, urban Orthodox immigration from eastern Europe in previous decades. This predominant status was reinforced by the emergence of Yeshiva College (later University) in New York City as a vibrant intellectual center of Orthodoxy. By the late 1930s, Orthodox Judaism registered approximately 200,000 families, Con-

servative Judaism 75,000 families, and Reform Judaism 50,000 families.

Both increased secularism and Americanization on the one hand, and the development of traditionalist, fervently mystical, and insular piety on the other, especially among Hasidic Jews (a more mystically inclined wing of Orthodoxy), flourished during this period. This set the stage for later controversies over the nature of Judaism and Jewish identity in modern America. Out of Jewish circles came several profoundly influential theologians and intellectuals, including Martin Buber (who also had a major impact in Christian circles). Also, Abraham Heschel became an influential participant in emerging Jewish/Christian dialogue, especially at the social level. And Mordecai Kaplan, who wrote the influential work *Judaism as a Civilization* (1934), advocated a comprehensive Jewish culture as a means of slowing the tide of secularism and religious indifference that was increasingly evident in the Jewish-American community of the day.

Of all the increasingly diverse groups in America during the era of the Great Depression and World War II, long-established white Anglo-Protestant religion suffered the most controversy, fragmentation, and continued upheaval. Some historians have labeled this period the era of the final "disestablishment" of Anglo-Protestant Christianity. This religious outlook had been the dominant religious and cultural framework of the nation from its founding until the early 20th century. Many factors contributed to this outcome, including the immigration patterns discussed previously. But conflict within mainstream Protestantism itself contributed greatly to its ebbing hegemony.

Most significantly, the fundamentalist/modernist controversy of the 1920s had split many Anglo-Protestant denominations, such as the Presbyterians, the Baptists, and the Methodists, with the smaller Episcopal Church eventually embracing modernism for the most part. Theological disputes centered upon the key question of how Protestant groups should respond to the challenging perspectives of modern science and biblical criticism, as well as to the growing spirit of rationalistic anti-supernaturalism among intellectuals. On the surface, a progressive-minded and optimistic modernism received the most positive exposure from the national media, academia, and intellectuals, as the movement attempted to accommodate and reinterpret traditional Christian doctrines in the light of a more modern mind-set. However, rapidly developing underground networks of evangelical and fundamentalist (two groups with similar theological perspectives but differing views on the question of engagement with broader, pluralistic society) organizations emerged that would lay the groundwork for the future public role of Protestant evangelicalism and fundamentalism. For example, the public evangelicalism of Billy Graham from the late 1940s onward would significantly influence American cultural and political ideology, especially in connection with anticommunism during the cold war era.

Less visible groups (at least from the vantage point of the Anglo-Protestant oriented media) included such ethnic and regional religious forces as the varied Lutheran bodies, often divided by Germanic and Scandinavian ethnic identities, and the Dutch Reformed churches, with both groups having important cultural and religious influences throughout much of the Midwest. Many white southerners continued to be profoundly influenced by the region's sociocultural and revivalist powerhouse, the Southern Baptist Convention. However, newly emergent Pentecostal groups, such as the Assemblies of God, would further lay the groundwork for the future, rapid expansion of this charismatic variety of Christianity throughout the South and beyond. And African-American religion, virtually ignored outside of black circles, would continue its status as a crucial institution for blacks in a still highly segregated America. Black churches and religion especially offered hope to those in the South suffering under the ongoing burdens of Jim Crow life.

Theologically, the most noteworthy developments centered upon the continuing emergence of the Neo-Orthodox, or Christian Realism, movement through the 1940s and beyond. This movement, sparked in Europe by such thinkers as Karl Barth and Emil Brunner (both from Switzerland), challenged the prevailing theological and cultural optimism that pervaded much of early-20th-century liberalism and modernism. Advocating the reappropriation of such Protestant Reformation–era themes as original sin, as well as the necessity of absolute human dependence upon divine grace for all aspects of existence, the theologian brothers Reinhold and H. Richard Niebuhr became profound spokespersons for the Neo-Orthodox movement in America. H. Richard Niebuhr explored the complex interactions of religion, culture, and the role of institutional Christianity in America. Reinhold Niebuhr examined overarching political and economic themes from the vantage point of a theological realism that severely criticized the optimistic (and what he believed to be naïve) assumptions of modernistic Christianity. Reinhold Niebuhr would especially gain widespread exposure through the mass media as well as through his influential list of publications. The earlier optimism of religious liberalism was sent into widespread retreat by the emergence of the Neo-Orthodox movement, though religious liberalism continued to survive in certain quarters.

With such religious diversity prevalent throughout the increasingly fragmented Protestant world, the Great Depression mounted further challenges to mainstream Protestantism. The situation was further destabilized by rampant poverty and the growing despair of individuals who, in former times, might have looked to especially Protestant benevolent and charitable societies to provide effective RELIEF assistance. Protestant churches and organizations were quickly overwhelmed by the scope of the Great Depression, and, with the advent of Franklin Roosevelt's comprehensive New Deal programs, individuals in the future would look increasingly to a rapidly expanding federal government for economic stability and confidence. But the anxieties and challenges of both the depression and World War II conversely led many people to seek comfort and ultimate explanations in religion.

By the time of World War II, more and more Americans embraced an increasingly generic monotheism (a broadly Protestant–Roman Catholic–Jewish nexus) in contrast to the dominant Protestant evangelical outlook of the 19th and early 20th centuries. While concern for "civil" religion continued to be stressed (a general faith in a less-defined God and the corresponding need for community morality and "decency"), foundations were being laid for a more secular nation in the years to come. On the other hand, and no doubt reflecting wartime and subsequent cold war fears, church membership actually grew from about 49 percent of the population in 1940 to 57 percent in 1950, and both church membership and church attendance in the United States were higher than in other Western nations. By the close of World War II, Americans appeared to be more willing to accept the proposition that the nation would be increasingly pluralistic religiously in the years to come.

See also IRISH AMERICANS; ITALIAN AMERICANS; MEXICAN AMERICANS; POLISH AMERICANS.

Further reading: Sydney E. Ahlstrom, *A Religious History of the American People* (New Haven, Conn.: Yale University Press, 1972); Winthrop S. Hudson, *Religion in America*, 6th ed. (Upper Saddle River, N.J.: Prentice Hall, 1999); Martin E. Marty, *Modern American Religion: The Noise of Conflict, 1919–1941* (Chicago: University of Chicago Press, 1991); ———, *Modern American Religion: Under God, Indivisible, 1941–1960* (Chicago: University of Chicago Press, 1996).

—J. Henry Allen, Jr.

Republican Party

When HERBERT C. HOOVER won the presidency in 1928, the Republican Party (sometimes colloquially called "the Grand Old Party," or GOP) had been the majority party in American politics since the 1890s, and had elected all but two of the presidents since 1860. With their decisive victory in the election of 1928, the Republicans seemed poised to retain control of CONGRESS and the White House for the foreseeable future. In a few short years, however, the

GOP's dominance ended dramatically and the Republican Party struggled in the mid-1930s to remain a viable political force. By the end of WORLD WAR II, Republicans remained the minority party, but a changed, strong, and combative one.

The onset of the GREAT DEPRESSION and the response of the HOOVER PRESIDENCY to it sharply eroded the Republican Party's support, exposed rifts within the GOP, and galvanized opposition in the DEMOCRATIC PARTY, which had been divided during the 1920s. Voter constituencies that had previously supported the GOP, such as AFRICAN AMERICANS and many farmers and workers, were being drawn away from the Republicans. Hoover's opposition within the Republican Party came primarily from such midwestern and western progressives as WILLIAM E. BORAH, ROBERT M. LA FOLLETTE, JR., and GEORGE W. NORRIS, who all were unhappy with the president's response to the economic crisis. After the mid-term elections of 1930, the Republicans retained a tiny one-vote majority in the Senate, and the election-day tie of 217 elected members for each party in the House of Representatives shifted to a slim Democratic majority when several GOP members died during the interim period between congressional sessions.

In the ELECTION OF 1932, with America in the depths of the depression, the Republicans, with neither enthusiasm nor any real alternative, renominated the embattled Hoover. The Republicans offered little new in the party platform to solve the economic crisis, and GOP progressives either remained neutral or endorsed FRANKLIN D. ROOSEVELT, the Democratic nominee. In the election, Roosevelt carried 57.4 percent of the popular vote and 42 of 48 states as Hoover won only 59 electoral votes in suffering the worst reversal ever for an incumbent president. The rout of the GOP was made complete in the Congress as Democrats held commanding margins of 60 to 35 in the Senate and 310 to 117 in the House.

The situation got worse for the party in 1933 and 1934, when NEW DEAL programs—many backed by Republican progressives—were passed in such rapid succession that GOP leaders were left dazed, often bewildered, and unable to mount a well-organized response to Roosevelt and the Democrats. The Republicans' congressional leadership—Senate minority leader Charles McNary, an Oregon progressive, and House minority leader Bertrand Snell, an upstate New York conservative—reflected divisions within the Republican Party on how to respond to the New Deal. The "old guard," led by Hoover, his hand-picked Republican National Committee chairman, and congressional conservatives, primarily from the Northeast, persisted in a direct assault on the New Deal and what they claimed were its threat to American traditions. Western progressives wanted to affirm basic agreement with the New Deal and proposed further reform in AGRICULTURE, regulation of BUSINESS, and RELIEF programs. The mid-term election of 1934 was disastrous for the Republicans, as Hoover's high-profile attacks on the New Deal reminded voters of his discredited presidency, and the GOP progressives' embrace of Roosevelt spelled doom for the party. The Democrats increased their margins in the Senate to 69-25 and in the House to 319-103, while also achieving a 39-7 majority among the nation's governors.

Increasingly in 1935, when FDR and the SECOND NEW DEAL moved leftward by passing legislation beneficial to LABOR unions and workers, business broke with the president, and through groups such as the AMERICAN LIBERTY LEAGUE hoped to ally with the Republican Party in the ELECTION OF 1936. As 1936 approached, several candidates appeared as GOP presidential contenders. Borah was the progressives' choice; Hoover, still lashing out at the New Deal, was ready to run again; and two former "Bull Moose" supporters of Theodore Roosevelt—Chicago newspaper publisher Frank Knox and Kansas governor ALFRED M. LANDON, who had been elected and then reelected in the Democratic landslides of 1932 and 1934—had support. Hoover's potential renomination frightened many Republicans, even the old guard, who foresaw the Democrats focusing on his failed administration; Borah's candidacy, opposed by conservatives and hampered by his age (71), ran aground early in the primary season; and Knox had not built a large base of support.

The Republicans therefore turned to Landon, nominating him in Cleveland, on a platform that attempted an awkward combination of condemning the New Deal while at the same time quietly endorsing aspects of it. In addition, the GOP platform advocated a noninterventionist FOREIGN POLICY, hoping to win back Republican progressives, most of whom were ISOLATIONISTS. Landon at first campaigned as a moderate, seeking to unite both wings of the party, but with the influence of the conservative Republican National Committee chairman, and the infusion of money and rhetoric from William Randolph Hearst and his newspapers and from the Liberty League—which sent out spokesmen such as Al Smith to denounce Roosevelt—the Kansas governor soon began attacking the New Deal more harshly. Although one poll, in the *Literary Digest*, predicted a Landon victory, many observers, at least in private, conceded that Roosevelt would win. In the election, Roosevelt scored one of the biggest landslides in presidential election history as he won all but two states—Maine and Vermont, with a total 8 electoral votes—and held Landon to 36.5 percent of the popular vote. Democrats achieved near total domination of Congress as the Republican Party emerged from 1936 with only 89 of 435 House seats and 16 of 96 in the Senate. Never had the party's fortunes fallen so low.

The Republicans entered 1937 seemingly close to extinction and unlikely to be competitive for years, as they held 105 total seats in Congress, a handful of governorships, and had lost much of the eastern urban, Midwest farmer, and African-American base that had formed the core of the party prior to 1932. But Roosevelt's COURT-PACKING PLAN, a political misstep by the president, split the Democrats and reenergized Republican hopes. Southern Democrats, often skeptical already of New Deal programs, and some western Democratic progressives such as BURTON K. WHEELER spoke out against the court plan. In the Senate, GOP leader McNary urged his small group of colleagues to "let the boys across the aisle do the talking." Landon urged other Republicans to adopt a "strategy of silence," which Hoover, a rival to the Kansan for leadership in the party, reluctantly acceded to. The GOP strategy worked, as leading dissident Democrats joined with Republicans to defeat court-packing, inaugurating the CONSERVATIVE COALITION in Congress, which would apply the brakes to the New Deal.

The court-packing plan, the RECESSION OF 1937–38, unpopular labor unrest, and the emergence of the congressional conservative coalition led to a GOP comeback in the 1938 mid-term election, as Republicans gained 7 Senate seats, 75 House seats, and won 18 of 27 governorships outside the SOUTH, giving the party hope of capturing the presidency in 1940. Meanwhile, the Republican Party was being reoriented geographically and ideologically. The party's former alignment of eastern conservatives and western progressives was being transformed into a coalition of an eastern moderate wing, interventionist in foreign policy, and, reflecting their urban base, accepting much of the New Deal, and a midwestern and western anti-New Deal, conservative, isolationist wing that reflected the deaths, defeats, and defections of the old GOP progressives.

Roosevelt's decision to seek a third term, and the advent of war in Europe affected the ELECTION OF 1940. GOP isolationists such as ROBERT A. TAFT wanted the party to nominate a noninterventionist, while a growing number of Republicans believed that in order to defeat the Democrats, an internationalist had to head the ticket. The early front-runner was Thomas E. Dewey, a New York district attorney, who had narrowly lost the governor's race in 1938; but another group of eastern Republicans, backed by publisher HENRY LUCE, promoted utilities executive WENDELL L. WILLKIE, a nominal Democrat but a vocal critic of the New Deal. Roosevelt himself undercut the Republicans by naming two of their own to his cabinet: HENRY L. STIMSON as secretary of war, and Frank Knox, the 1936 GOP vice presidential candidate, as secretary of the navy. As the Republican convention approached, the fall of France occurred, highlighting the youth and inexperience of Dewey and the isolationism of Taft. At the Philadelphia convention, anxieties about the war helped create a groundswell that led to Willkie's nomination.

Although Willkie ran an energetic campaign as the first candidate of the eastern, moderate, internationalist wing of the Republican Party, GOP conservatives and isolationists were cool to him, and Roosevelt's continuing popularity and experience in the face of possible war gave the incumbent president an insurmountable advantage. In the election, Roosevelt won 54.8 percent of the popular vote and all but 82 electoral votes, although Willkie won back the midwestern farm vote for the Republicans, and received more of the popular vote than any previous GOP candidate. The party lineup in Congress remained about the same as it had been after the 1938 election.

After PEARL HARBOR, most Republicans closed ranks behind Roosevelt and supported the war effort, although many joined the conservative coalition with southern Democrats to stymie and scale back the New Deal. In the 1942 mid-term election, Republicans nearly captured the House, winning 46 seats for a total of 208 seats, just a dozen fewer than the Democrats won; gained 9 seats in the Senate for a total of 37; and won a key governorship in New York, where Dewey was elected.

Dewey then emerged as the early front-runner for the Republican nomination in the ELECTION OF 1944. After Taft declined an opportunity to run from the conservative wing, and Willkie, now a party pariah because of his liberal domestic and foreign policy stances, was bumped from the race by the early primaries, Dewey became the nominee. Running in the midst of the war and wartime prosperity against the popular Roosevelt, Republicans had little to campaign on beyond alleging communist tendencies in the New Deal, and raising veiled questions—accurate in retrospect—about the president's declining health. In the election, Roosevelt won 53.5 percent of the popular vote and 432 of the 531 electoral votes, and Democrats made a modest recovery in the Congress from the Republican gains of two years earlier.

By the end of World War II, the Republican Party had made great strides in recovering from its perilous situation in the middle 1930s. Its new dominant eastern moderate wing had accepted the heart of the New Deal regulatory welfare state and an internationalist foreign policy for a larger American role in the world. The western, conservative, isolationist wing did remain a vocal and persistent minority with particular strength in the GOP's congressional delegations. Despite gaining control of Congress in 1946 and 1952, and the presidency in 1952, the Republican Party would have to wait several decades until the Democratic New Deal coalition would fragment, opening the door to GOP parity at the national and state levels.

See also POLITICS IN THE ROOSEVELT ERA.

Further reading: Ronald L. Feinman, *Twilight of Progressivism: The Western Republican Senators and the New Deal* (Baltimore: Johns Hopkins University Press, 1981); Donald Bruce Johnson, *The Republican Party and Wendell Willkie* (Urbana: University of Illinois Press, 1960); George H. Mayer, *The Republican Party 1854–1966,* 2d ed. (New York: Oxford University Press, 1967); Malcolm Moos, *The Republicans: A History of Their Party* (New York: Random House, 1956); Clyde P. Weed, *The Nemesis of Reform: The Republican Party during the New Deal* (New York: Columbia University Press, 1994).

—William J. Thompson

Resettlement Administration (RA)

The Resettlement Administration, a NEW DEAL agency created by President FRANKLIN D. ROOSEVELT in May 1935 under the auspices of the EMERGENCY RELIEF APPROPRIATION ACT, sought to assist and relocate struggling farmers and to provide new HOUSING for urban workers. Limited funding, opposition from conservatives, large farmers, and real estate interests, and sometimes resistance from the groups it tried to help, impeded the agency's ability to accomplish its goals.

Headed by REXFORD G. TUGWELL, the Resettlement Administration (RA) focused on tenants, sharecroppers, and small farmers in its efforts in AGRICULTURE. These groups, Tugwell and others thought, had not received sufficient aid from the AGRICULTURAL ADJUSTMENT ACT, yet they had suffered disproportionately from the GREAT DEPRESSION and other ills of American agriculture. The RA took over the Department of the Interior's Subsistence Homestead Division and the FEDERAL EMERGENCY RELIEF ADMINISTRATION's rural rehabilitation efforts as part of its programs.

The RA sought both to provide technical advice and other assistance to struggling rural people to improve land-use practices where they lived and to relocate poor farmers and workers from unproductive and overused land to more fertile sites with new housing and community services. The RA also built camps for migrant workers and moved some farmers into new suburban areas. The agency established communal farms in New Madrid, Missouri; Casa Grande, Arizona; and Lake Dick, Arkansas. Some families were unwilling to relocate to new areas or to trust agency personnel despite impoverished conditions, and CONGRESS proved unwilling to finance the RA adequately. The RA relocated less than 1 percent of the more than half million farm families it planned to move.

The Resettlement Administration also sought to improve housing for urban workers. The primary project involving disadvantaged urban laborers was the "greenbelt" program. RA planners intended to transplant urban workers from crowded inner cities into new suburban settlements designed to include cooperative services and democratic involvement in community management. Nine such communities were proposed, but only three were built: Greenbelt, outside of Washington, D.C.; Greenhills, near Cincinnati; and Greendale, close to Milwaukee.

These greenbelt towns did not attract the anticipated numbers of needy workers from the inner cities. Site selection contributed to the shortcomings of the program, for the locations chosen were outside cities that were already taking action on housing and other urban ills. Other problems included a lack of funds needed to build enough houses to support community services, rent levels too high for low-income workers, and the rapid turnover of younger tenants, which limited participation in neighborhood management. While these difficulties limited the number of workers assisted, many middle-class families were able to take advantage of the opportunity offered by the greenbelt towns to move to a suburban setting. The ideas and concepts behind the greenbelt towns also provided information for later government housing planning projects.

The Resettlement Administration faced sharp criticism and stiff opposition throughout its short existence. Some detractors focused on Tugwell as too radical to head the agency, and labeled the agency's efforts "socialistic." To counteract such criticism, Tugwell created an Information Division to produce favorable publicity about the RA's efforts. PHOTOGRAPHY proved an important medium for this task, leading to a collection of documentary photographs of the difficulties of rural life. Despite his efforts at creating a positive image for the Resettlement Administration, Tugwell resigned in 1936 in order to protect the agency from further objections due to his presence. The RA's programs also faced opposition from conservatives, larger farmers, and local real estate organizations who protested federal interference in agriculture and housing. With the enactment of the Bankhead-Jones Farm Tenant Act in 1937, the Resettlement Administration became part of the FARM SECURITY ADMINISTRATION.

Further reading: Paul K. Conkin, *Tomorrow a New World: The New Deal Community Program* (Ithaca, N.Y.: Cornell University Press, 1959); Bernard Sternsher, *Rexford Tugwell and the New Deal* (New Brunswick, N.J.: Rutgers University Press, 1964).

—Courtney D. Mattingly

Revenue Act of 1935

The Revenue Act of 1935 was the first major effort of President FRANKLIN D. ROOSEVELT and the NEW DEAL to reform federal TAXATION. Part of the SECOND NEW DEAL of 1935, it became known as the "Wealth Tax," because Roosevelt sought a more progressive tax structure that would take proportionately much more from BUSINESS and the wealthy. In its final form, however, "Wealth Tax" was a misnomer, for it fell far short of Roosevelt's proposal and had little if any impact on the distribution of wealth. It nonetheless did have important political implications.

Roosevelt had contemplated reform of the tax structure since early in his presidency. Partly his concern was to raise revenue to meet growing GOVERNMENT expenses under the New Deal, especially given his dedication to balancing the budget. But Roosevelt also wanted a more progressive (graduated) tax system that would take relatively more from business and the very wealthy to pay for social and economic reform that would benefit the struggling and needy. Secretary of the Treasury HENRY MORGENTHAU, JR., shared those concerns and priorities.

But more lay behind the proposed Revenue Act of 1935 than policy considerations. By 1935, Senator HUEY P. LONG was building a national following for his "Share Our Wealth" program that called for heavy taxes on the very wealthy to be redistributed so that all Americans could have a home, health and education benefits, and adequate income. Long and others on the left complained that the New Deal had done more to help business and the well-off than to help the poor. And by 1935, the cooperation between the New Deal and business that Roosevelt had hoped to establish had turned into sharp conflict. Politically, then, FDR might profit from appealing to the followers of Long and others without fear of losing business and conservative support that was already vanishing.

In June 1935, Roosevelt sent CONGRESS what soon became known as the "Wealth Tax" (some called it the "soak-the-rich tax") bill. In addition to reforming the tax structure and raising revenues, FDR believed that his plan would free up money held by wealthy individuals and corporations and thus enhance economic opportunity and efforts at recovery from the GREAT DEPRESSION. The bill called for a graduated tax on corporate incomes, a corporate excess profits tax, and an intercorporate dividends tax. It proposed sharply increasing the maximum tax rate on high incomes and adding a federal inheritance tax to the existing estate tax. And it recommended a constitutional amendment to allow the federal government to tax the interest earned on state and municipal bonds, used by the wealthy to avoid taxes.

The tax bill encountered stiff opposition in the Congress, and the legislation finally passed more than two months later by Congress and signed by Roosevelt did not go nearly as far as the original proposal. The proposed tax rates for wealthy individuals were pared back, and the taxes on corporate income and intercorporate dividends were slashed even more. Congress increased the estate tax but defeated the proposed inheritance tax and the constitutional amendment.

The Revenue Act of 1935 had more important political than policy and economic consequences. Roosevelt could take political credit for proposing the bill and thus steal some of the thunder from critics on the left—and in fact Morgenthau thought that Roosevelt meant the bill mostly as a "campaign document" and worried about what seemed the president's lukewarm commitment to it. The proposal contributed to the emerging split in the DEMOCRATIC PARTY between liberals and conservatives, worsened anti-Roosevelt sentiment among the wealthy, and increased the estrangement of business from Roosevelt and the New Deal. Yet despite the storm over the tax, it did little to either redistribute income or raise revenue.

Further reading: John Morton Blum, *Roosevelt and Morgenthau: A Revision and Condensation of* From the Morgenthau Diaries (Boston: Houghton Mifflin, 1970); Mark Leff, *The Limits of Symbolic Reform: The New Deal and Taxation, 1933–1939* (New York: Cambridge University Press, 1984).

Revenue Act of 1942

The Revenue Act of 1942 greatly expanded the number of people who paid income taxes and led to the withholding system that has been central to the United States tax system ever since.

President FRANKLIN D. ROOSEVELT wanted the 1942 Revenue Act to do three things: raise money to help pay the MOBILIZATION costs of WORLD WAR II; combat inflation by reducing spending power; and make the tax structure more progressive by sharply raising taxes on high personal incomes and corporate profits. CONGRESS, consistent with its previous responses to the TAXATION proposals of the Roosevelt administration, resisted steeply graduated taxes. In the end, the Revenue Act of 1942 did raise personal and corporate income taxes, though not as much as Roosevelt had desired. It also taxed all incomes over $624 (median annual family income was about $2,000) as a compromise substitute for a sales tax desired by many in Congress. Lowering the minimum taxable income to that level meant that a much higher proportion of the population paid federal income taxes—and the number of taxable incomes soared from roughly 4 million in 1939 to nearly 43 million by the end of the war. By 1944, personal income taxes had replaced corporate taxes as the most important source of federal revenue.

With so many more people paying taxes than ever before, the Treasury Department wanted a way to simplify and ensure collection, and recommended initiating a payroll deduction plan. But beginning the withholding system in 1943 would mean that taxpayers would have money deducted from their pay for 1943 taxes at the same time that they had to pay their 1942 tax bills. The solution was to forgive most of the 1942 tax obligations and have the 1943 payroll deductions provide the government's revenue in 1943. The proponent of this idea Beordsley Ruml, chairman of the New York Federal Reserve Bank and treasurer of R.H. Macy and Company, likened it to daylight savings time: It would just move "the tax clock forward, and cost the Treasury nothing until Judgment Day." And on Judgment Day, said one politician, "no one will give a damn." Roosevelt opposed absolving taxpayers of so much of their 1942 taxes, believing that it amounted to an undeserved windfall for the wealthy and deprived the GOVERNMENT of needed revenue, but Congress approved the 1942 tax forgiveness plan in 1943.

Further reading: W. Elliott Brownlee, ed., *Funding the Modern American State, 1941–1995: The Rise and Fall of the Era of Easy Finance* (New York: Cambridge University Press, 1996).

Robeson, Paul (1898–1976)

A world-renowned and critically acclaimed African-American singer and actor, Paul Robeson was a political activist for the rights of AFRICAN AMERICANS and took controversial stances in support of communism and the Soviet Union. He was famous for his rich baritone renditions of African-American spirituals, his MOVIES, and his numerous stage appearances during the 1930s and 1940s, as well as for his political beliefs.

Robeson was born April 9, 1898, in Princeton, New Jersey, to Reverend William Robeson, who had escaped from slavery at age 15, and Maria Robeson, a schoolteacher. At Rutgers College, he won awards for scholarship, oration, and athletics, and was class valedictorian and an All-American football player. While attending Columbia Law School he supported himself by playing professional football, and married fellow Columbia student Eslanda "Essie" Goode, with whom he later had one son, Paul Robeson, Jr. Encouraged by Essie, he began acting in amateur theater and in 1922 made his professional debut in the play *Taboo*. After graduation from law school Robeson became the only African American at a prominent New York law firm, but resigned and ended his law career when a white secretary refused to take dictation from him because he was black.

Between 1924 and 1930 Robeson became a celebrity, starring in plays and musicals in New York and London including Eugene O'Neill's *All God's Chillun Got Wings, Porgy and Bess, Show Boat* (singing his famous interpretation of "Ol' Man River"), and *Othello*. He also performed solo concerts of African-American spirituals across Europe and the United States.

During the 1930s, Robeson began focusing more of his attention on political issues and the examination of other cultures, studying African languages and history and including the folk songs of Russian serfs in his performances. In 1934, he spoke out against Nazi oppression of Jews and was invited by the Russian filmmaker Sergei Eisenstein to visit the Soviet Union. During his visit in 1935, Robeson described the USSR as a society free from racial discrimination and said, "Here, for the first time in my life, I walk in full human dignity."

In the second half of the 1930s, Robeson began studying socialism, helped found the Council on African Affairs (an organization promoting African self-rule) and supported the antifascist forces fighting in the SPANISH CIVIL WAR. In 1939 he defended the NAZI-SOVIET PACT, arguing that it was important for the USSR's national security.

Throughout the 1940s, Robeson supported a variety of liberal and leftist causes. He promoted antilynching legislation, refused to sing before racially segregated audiences, and announced that he would no longer act in Hollywood movies because of their demeaning and condescending portrayal of blacks. His starring role in *Othello*

Paul Robeson *(Hulton/Archive)*

on Broadway was acclaimed as a landmark in race relations and the show was the longest-running Shakespeare play in Broadway history. In 1941, the FEDERAL BUREAU OF INVESTIGATION (FBI) placed Robeson under surveillance as a suspected member of the Communist Party.

In the 1950s, Robeson continued to defend the Soviet Union despite revelations of Stalin's purges and brutalities. He also refused to answer the questions of the House Committee on Un-American Activities and the State Department about his political affiliations. Consequently, his passport was taken away and his career was severely damaged. He was blacklisted by recording companies, banned from television and from performing in certain areas of the country, and the leading journals and newspapers refused to review his autobiography, *Here I Stand*. Despite his deteriorating health he spent several more years as a political activist before retiring completely. He died on January 23, 1976.

Further reading: Martin Duberman, *Paul Robeson* (New York: Knopf, 1988).

—Aimee Alice Pohl

Roosevelt, Eleanor (1884–1962)

Eleanor Roosevelt was first lady of the United States longer than any other woman, and in the 12 years from 1933 to 1945 she changed the nature and status of the position. The stances she took on such issues as race and social justice earned her both tremendous praise and sharp criticism. By the time of the death of her husband, President FRANKLIN D. ROOSEVELT, Eleanor Roosevelt had become the most important and controversial first lady the nation had seen.

Born Anna Eleanor Roosevelt in New York on October 11, 1884, she was the oldest child and only daughter of Anna and Elliott Roosevelt and the niece of President Theodore Roosevelt. Her mother died when Roosevelt was a young girl, while her father, before his early death, was an important, if distant, part of her life. Following the wishes of her mother, she was provided an expansive education for a girl of her time, and her time spent at the Allenswood School near London proved to be a major influence on the shy, awkward girl. At Allenswood, Roosevelt was exposed to the world beyond her affluent upbringing in New York; the experience also gave her a new sense of confidence. Returning to New York in 1902, Roosevelt was deemed ready to enter society and begin her search for a husband.

As her grandmother wanted, Roosevelt began to socialize among her peers, but she resisted attempts to marry quickly. Instead, she became involved in the settlement house movement in New York, working with young immigrant girls at the Rivington Street Settlement House. In the meantime, she had begun seeing Franklin D. Roo-

sevelt, her fifth cousin from Hyde Park, New York. Over the objections of Franklin's mother, Sara Delano Roosevelt, who remained an active and often interfering part of their lives until her death in 1941, the two were married in 1905. Eleanor spent the first years of the marriage concentrating on her family, which grew to six children, of whom five survived infancy. As her husband's career as a Democratic politician developed in the 1910s, she busied herself in the role of an upper-class wife and mother, including charity work, reading, and domestic life. But she was dissatisfied with not being able to utilize the intellectual talents she had nurtured at Allenswood. The turning point in her life came nearly two decades into her marriage when two life-altering events occurred; the revelation in 1918 of her husband's affair with Lucy Mercer, and Franklin's attack of polio in 1921.

By the 1920s she had taken a more assertive role, both within her marriage and in her public activities. FDR's polio, which had left him paralyzed from the waist down, made Eleanor Roosevelt his public representative, keeping his political aspirations alive through her appearances on his behalf. She also moved to expand her own life. In addition to becoming more active in charity work, Roosevelt went to work, taking a teaching position at the Todhunter School for Girls in New York and pursuing her interests in social causes. The expansion of her world brought together both her political training as her husband's surrogate and her interest in women's issues so that she became a champion of female participation in the public sphere. While she never had an interest in achieving public office, she was a major advocate of women's involvement in politics and of their holding GOVERNMENT positions.

Franklin Roosevelt made his political comeback when he was elected governor of New York State in 1928 and then won the presidency in the ELECTION OF 1932. While FDR was governor, Eleanor Roosevelt continued to nurture her own interests and influence her husband, becoming his "social conscience." She was reluctant to have her husband run for president, worried about how the more public role of being the president's wife might restrict her activities. But when FDR entered the presidency in 1933, Roosevelt turned her energy to using her public stature to advocate for policies she cared deeply for. Her interests were seemingly everywhere, from CIVIL RIGHTS to rural poverty to obtaining prominent government positions for women as part of the WOMEN'S NETWORK.

Eleanor Roosevelt's championing of civil rights for AFRICAN AMERICANS was a prominent and controversial example of how she stepped beyond the customary bonds of the first lady's role. Several incidents garnered her criticism, especially sharp from Republicans and southerners, such as when she was photographed at a ceremony dedicating a public HOUSING unit accepting flowers from a

Eleanor Roosevelt *(National Archives)*

young African-American girl and then giving the girl a flower from the bouquet. Roosevelt's awareness of racial disparities had been awakened when she struck up a friendship with educator MARY MCLEOD BETHUNE in the late 1920s. Further motivated by friendships she developed with other prominent black leaders, including WALTER WHITE, president of the NATIONAL ASSOCIATION FOR THE ADVANCEMENT OF COLORED PEOPLE, Roosevelt pressured her husband to gain access for African Americans in NEW DEAL programs. Her efforts, along with those of like-minded liberals, including HARRY HOPKINS and HAROLD ICKES, helped to increase black participation in programs such as the WORKS PROGRESS ADMINISTRATION, as well as in the creation of the Division of Negro Affairs in the NATIONAL YOUTH ADMINISTRATION, headed by Bethune. One of the issues that Roosevelt came to passionately champion was antilynching legislation. While the measure failed in CONGRESS in the 1930s, she continued to lobby for it in the decades to follow.

The United States's entrance into WORLD WAR II augmented Roosevelt's highly public role. Representing the president, she toured military bases both at home and abroad, visited wounded soldiers, and, in a much-publicized event, flew in an army air force fighter plane. The war also reenergized her commitment to fighting for social justice. Roosevelt provided a major voice in the White House when she thought that domestic needs were being overshadowed by the emphasis on winning the war. Her major regret from the war years was that she backed down from her opposition to the relocation of JAPANESE AMERICANS, one of the few times that her public voice was stifled by her husband, when she followed the president's wishes to not to speak out against this violation of CIVIL LIBERTIES.

After FDR died in April 1945, Roosevelt embarked in a new stage in her life. Many of her associates suggested that she enter electoral politics. But she did not feel it was appropriate for a former first lady, nor was she particularly interested in public office. Instead, Roosevelt spent the next two decades championing causes that she strongly supported while remaining a major force within the DEMOCRATIC PARTY.

Without the limitations of being first lady, Roosevelt's activities included supporting international cooperation, giving more vocal support to civil rights and civil liberties, participating in Democratic Party politics, and continuing to write the newspaper column that had caused her so much criticism in the 1930s, *My Day*. In 1945, she was a selected as a delegate to the UNITED NATIONS, where she worked with the United Nations Human Rights Commission and was instrumental in the passage of the Universal Declaration of Human Rights. Roosevelt also remained active in party politics, often disagreeing with the positions of Harry S. Truman's cabinet members, whom she saw as too conservative. After Dwight D. Eisenhower's presidential victory in 1952, Roosevelt submitted her resignation from the United Nations, and accepted a position with the American Association for the United Nations to defend the international organization. She also spoke out critically about the anticommunist campaigns of the 1950s, and served as honorary chairman of the Americans for Democratic Action, a liberal organization she helped found after World War II. A supporter of Adlai Stevenson's unsuccessful campaigns for the presidency in 1952 and 1956, she maintained her influence within the Democratic Party, as demonstrated when John F. Kennedy courted her public support during the 1960 presidential election.

Finding a more active role when Kennedy won in 1960, Roosevelt once again became a UN delegate while also chairing the President's Commission on the Status of Women. But just as she found another role for herself, Roosevelt began to slow down, suffering from anemia and a rare form of bone marrow tuberculosis. Eleanor Roosevelt died on November 7, 1962, leaving behind the legacy of an activist first lady who turned attention to important social issues.

Further reading: Blanche Wiesen Cook, *Eleanor Roosevelt, 1884–1933* (New York: Viking, 1993); ———, *Eleanor Roosevelt: The Defining Years, 1933–1938* (New York: Viking, 1999); Doris Kearns Goodwin, *No Ordinary Time: Franklin and Eleanor Roosevelt, The Home Front in World War II* (New York: Simon & Schuster, 1994); Lois Sharf, *Eleanor Roosevelt—First Lady of American Liberalism* (Boston: Twayne, 1987); Eleanor Roosevelt, *The Autobiography of Eleanor Roosevelt* (New York: Harper & Brothers, 1961).

—Katherine Liapis Segrue and Susan F. Yates

Roosevelt, Franklin D. (1882–1945)

Franklin Delano Roosevelt, the 32nd president of the United States, is widely acknowledged to have been the most important American public figure of the 20th century. Elected to the White House four times from 1932 to 1944, FDR, as he was commonly called, led the nation through two of the century's greatest crises, the GREAT DEPRESSION and WORLD WAR II. His presidency launched both the nation's modern regulatory welfare state and the internationalist FOREIGN POLICY of World War II and after. The NEW DEAL and POLITICS IN THE ROOSEVELT ERA produced large and lasting changes in American GOVERNMENT and politics and profoundly affected the nation's ECONOMY and society. Historians count Roosevelt, with Washington and Lincoln, as one of America's three greatest presidents.

Franklin D. Roosevelt was born January 30, 1882, in Hyde Park, New York, the son of James and Sara Delano Roosevelt. A distant cousin of Theodore Roosevelt, Franklin grew up in the genteel security of 19th-century "old money" wealth. The protective world of Hyde Park gave young Roosevelt a sunny confidence and serene self-assurance that served him well later in facing his own polio and the challenges of the Great Depression and World War II. His childhood evidently contributed also to his social conscience and sense of noblesse oblige. Roosevelt attended Groton, an exclusive prep school, and Harvard University. After graduating from Harvard in 1904, Roosevelt enrolled at Columbia University law school, left after one year, but passed the bar and joined a New York City firm.

In 1905, Franklin married his fifth cousin ELEANOR ROOSEVELT, a niece of Theodore, and the couple had five children who lived to adulthood. Intimacy within the marriage ended in 1918 with Eleanor's discovery of Franklin's affair with Lucy Mercer, her former social secretary. The affair terminated after ultimatums from Eleanor and from his mother, a doting and at times obtrusive presence in Franklin's (and Eleanor's) life until her death in 1941. Thereafter, the marriage became an effective partnership that served them both well, with Eleanor supporting Franklin's political ambitions and FDR encouraging Eleanor in her various activities and causes.

Roosevelt was ambitious, and, wanting to emulate Theodore Roosevelt, decided to enter politics. Despite his mother's opposition, Roosevelt ran for and won a seat in the New York State Senate in 1910 and won reelection in 1912. In 1912, he also supported Woodrow Wilson's campaign for the White House, and Wilson appointed Roosevelt assistant secretary of the navy in 1913. In 1920, Roosevelt was nominated for vice president on the Democratic national ticket headed by Ohio governor James M. Cox.

Following his return to private life after the decisive Democratic defeat in the election, Roosevelt was felled by acute poliomyelitis in August 1921. For three years, Roosevelt valiantly but unsuccessfully attempted to regain use of his legs and for the remainder of his life used heavy metal leg braces as well as a wheelchair. Perhaps deepening Roosevelt's sensitivities, polio made him more dependent upon Eleanor as his envoy. When he reentered public life, the extent of his handicap—although not the fact that he had been stricken by polio—was hidden from the public by a compliant press corps, in what scholars have labeled "FDR's splendid deception."

Although his mother wanted him to retire to the life of a country squire, Eleanor and political adviser Louis Howe encouraged Roosevelt to return to politics. In 1924, he nominated New York governor Alfred E. Smith for president at the Democratic National Convention, a speech that reestablished Roosevelt as an important national figure in the DEMOCRATIC PARTY. In 1928, Roosevelt narrowly won election as governor of New York. Reelected overwhelmingly in 1930, Roosevelt was noted as governor for his progressive initiatives, including establishing a model agency of its kind for giving RELIEF help to the unemployed.

As governor of the nation's most populous state and an innovative chief executive in dealing with the Great Depression, Roosevelt emerged as the early favorite for the 1932 Democratic presidential nomination. Helped by a campaign team headed by JAMES A. FARLEY, Roosevelt ultimately gained the nomination on the fourth ballot. With unemployment at 25 percent, he decisively won the ELECTION OF 1932, capturing some 57 per cent of the vote against the embattled incumbent president, HERBERT C. HOOVER.

Accepting his nomination, Roosevelt pledged a "new deal" for the American people, but he was often vague and even contradictory about his plans during the campaign. In fact, there was never a master plan, as Roosevelt allowed himself wide leeway to accommodate his constantly changing thinking. Experimentation and flexibility would be hallmarks of Roosevelt's leadership and administrative styles. He once wrote, "I dream dreams but am, at the same time, an intensely practical person." "Take a method and try it," Roosevelt said. "If it fails, admit it frankly and try another. But above all, try something." Indeed, FDR's ideas were often as difficult to pin down as his frequently enigmatic personality, and even his closest associates were sometimes dismayed by his changes of mind and his deviousness.

But although he was no rigid ideologue, Roosevelt did have consistent convictions and principles about the purpose of government and clear priorities as president. He believed that government should promote the general welfare and help the "forgotten man at the bottom of the economic pyramid." A "little left of center," in his own words, he tended to accept incremental and moderate reform rather than wholesale or radical change. Believing deeply in American democratic capitalism, he wanted to reform the system in order to strengthen and preserve it. He sought in the 1930s to bring recovery from the depression (although it was war MOBILIZATION, not the New Deal, that ended the depression), humanitarian assistance to the unemployed and impoverished, and reform to the nation's institutions. During the war, he sought victory above all, and victory that might lead to lasting peace. Roosevelt was also a politician, sometimes a manipulative and polarizing one, as he sought to build his own political power and to make the Democratic Party the liberal and enduring majority party of the nation.

When Roosevelt took office on March 4, 1933, America was at the nadir of the Great Depression. After declaring that the "only thing we have to fear is fear itself," the new president called CONGRESS into special session, launching the first Hundred Days of remarkable legislative achievement. Contrary to legend, Roosevelt did not simply bend Congress to his will in framing the New Deal. Rather, the House and the Senate sometimes took the lead on legislation and particularly after his first term also denied him reform measures he wanted.

But Roosevelt was a powerful chief executive, not only in his dealings with Congress but also with the public. In speeches and in his fireside chats, Roosevelt effectively used the RADIO to explain his programs and build support for them. He also used the radio to buttress national confidence during both the depression and the war, as his buoyant, optimistic voice reached and offered reassurance to millions of listeners. He cultivated the press through frequent press conferences, holding court for reporters by offering up what information he wanted the public to know. He was from the beginning a confident and effective leader. Supreme Court Justice Oliver Wendell Holmes supposedly said that Roosevelt had "a second-rate intellect, but a first-rate temperament."

The programs of the FIRST NEW DEAL of 1933, perhaps especially RELIEF assistance for the unemployed and efforts to effect economic recovery and social reform, made

Roosevelt enormously popular. In the election of 1934, Democrats increased their margins in both houses of Congress, an obvious show of support for the president and his policies. In 1935 came a second wave of reform, known as the SECOND NEW DEAL, including the SOCIAL SECURITY ACT, the NATIONAL LABOR RELATIONS ACT, and the REVENUE ACT OF 1935.

As he sought reelection in 1936 on the basis of his first-term record, Roosevelt exploited criticism from conservatives and business, denouncing "economic royalists" and saying that he hoped it would later be said that "the forces of selfishness and of lust for power met their match" in his first term and "met their master" in his second. With chin pointing upward, cigarette holder jutting forward, and a ready grin, Roosevelt inspired confidence and hope among unemployed, working-class, and middle-class voters. Critics thought him a dangerous demagogue. In the ELECTION OF 1936, Roosevelt won 46 of 48 states and captured more than three-fifths of the popular vote in putting together a coalition of voters based upon great strength in the CITIES and the SOUTH, and among LABOR unions, AFRICAN AMERICANS, CATHOLICS, and JEWS, that would make the Democrats the majority party for decades to come.

Following his landslide reelection, Roosevelt intended to address the plight of what he called at his second inauguration the "one-third of a nation ill-housed, ill-clad, ill-nourished." But early in his second term, he encountered a series of problems that prevented him from achieving much of his second-term agenda. First came the storm of controversy over his COURT-PACKING PLAN to protect the New Deal from the SUPREME COURT, which had overturned a number of key New Deal programs. Then, the severe RECESSION OF 1937–38, labor unrest, and FDR's unsuccessful attempt to "purge" anti–New Deal Democrats in the 1938 primaries compounded his difficulties. In 1938, the REPUBLICAN PARTY made a strong resurgence, and, beginning in the late 1930s, congressional Republicans and conservative Democrats often cooperated in a CONSERVATIVE COALITION that would hinder liberal reform for a quarter century.

During the second half of Roosevelt's second term, events in Europe and Asia increasingly shifted the president's focus to foreign policy. By heritage and experience, Roosevelt was an internationalist with a keen interest in foreign affairs, but during his first term, foreign policy took a backseat to pressing domestic concerns. Recognizing the strength of ISOLATIONISTS and the opposition to interventionism in Congress and among the public, Roosevelt acquiesced in the NEUTRALITY ACTS of the mid-1930s. By the late 1930s, however, and especially after the beginning of World War II in Europe in late 1939, FDR shifted toward anti-AXIS interventionism. Winning

This 1941 photograph shows President Franklin D. Roosevelt asking Congress to declare war on Japan the day after Pearl Harbor. *(Library of Congress)*

revision of the Neutrality Acts in 1939, he increased military appropriations and gained approval of SELECTIVE SERVICE in 1940.

With the war approaching, Roosevelt decided to seek an unprecedented third term in the ELECTION OF 1940 and defeated WENDELL L. WILLKIE, winning 55 percent of the vote. The war figured importantly in the election, but even more important were Roosevelt's record in the first two terms and the loyalty he had won from his supporters and the continued enmity of his opponents. Following his reelection, Roosevelt continued his increasingly anti-Axis foreign policy, including the LEND-LEASE ACT of early 1941.

After the Japanese attack on PEARL HARBOR on December 7, 1941, which the president memorably called "a date which will live in infamy," Roosevelt focused on economic mobilization, military and diplomatic strategy, and national morale. The president's management of mobilization resembled his earlier untidy administering of the New Deal and contributed to the early difficulties of economic mobilization. Ultimately, American production both ended the depression and helped win the war. In military affairs, Roosevelt was an active commander in chief, acting decisively and closely monitoring strategy, while placing trust in his commanding generals and admirals, especially GEORGE C. MARSHALL. To boost national morale, the president depended once again, as during the depression, on

his unique combination of personal dynamism and buoyant optimism.

As chief diplomat, Roosevelt bypassed Secretary of State CORDELL HULL and largely conducted wartime diplomacy himself. Wanting to keep the GRAND ALLIANCE together after the war, he forged a close relationship with British prime minister Winston Churchill, and tried with less success to do the same with Soviet leader Joseph Stalin. At the TEHERAN CONFERENCE and the YALTA CONFERENCE, the "Big Three" leaders discussed both war strategy and the postwar world order. In pursuing a new internationalism of ongoing American leadership in world affairs, Roosevelt also supported the development of the UNITED NATIONS as a collective security organization to keep the peace and the BRETTON WOODS CONFERENCE to produce mechanisms for global prosperity. He also authorized the MANHATTAN PROJECT that produced the ATOMIC BOMB.

By 1943, Roosevelt had largely shelved "Dr. New Deal" for "Dr. Win-the-War," frustrating liberals hoping to expand programs in wartime, and delighting conservatives in Congress who succeeded in rolling back domestic initiatives. Roosevelt's record on CIVIL RIGHTS and CIVIL LIBERTIES was mixed at best, issuing under pressure from African Americans EXECUTIVE ORDER 8802 that established the FAIR EMPLOYMENT PRACTICES COMMITTEE, but also acquiescing in restricting the immigration of Jewish REFUGEES from Europe and in the RELOCATION OF JAPANESE AMERICANS. In 1944 FDR espoused the ECONOMIC BILL OF RIGHTS that reflected the reorientation of LIBERALISM during his presidency.

By 1944, Roosevelt's health was failing, and he was diagnosed with hypertension and congestive heart failure. But with the war in progress, Roosevelt felt obligated to see the conflict to conclusion. So he ran again for president, as problems with his health were kept secret from the American public (although photographs showed a visibly aged president, and friends and associates were shocked by FDR's ashen complexion, hand tremors, and mental drift). At the 1944 Democratic National Convention, conservatives, with Roosevelt's acquiescence, forced out liberal vice president HENRY A. WALLACE and selected the more moderate Harry S. Truman as FDR's running mate. In the fall, Roosevelt defeated GOP nominee Thomas E. Dewey.

Returning home from the Yalta Conference in February 1945, the president, obviously frail, spoke to Congress and the American people while sitting at a desk in the House chamber. In early April, Roosevelt went to Warm Springs, Georgia, for a period of rest and relaxation. He died there of a cerebral hemorrhage on April 12, 1945, three weeks before the war ended in the WORLD WAR II EUROPEAN THEATER and four months before hostilities ceased in the WORLD WAR II PACIFIC THEATER. His death was a shock to the tens of millions of Americans who could scarcely remember or imagine anyone else as president, and the impact of his presidency resonated throughout the remainder of the century and beyond.

Further reading: James MacGregor Burns, *Roosevelt: The Lion and the Fox* (New York: Harcourt Brace, 1956); ————, *Roosevelt: The Soldier of Freedom* (New York: Harcourt Brace Jovanovich, 1970); Robert Dallek, *Franklin D. Roosevelt and American Foreign Policy, 1932–1945* (New York: Oxford University Press, 1979); Frank Freidel, *Franklin D. Roosevelt: A Rendezvous with Destiny* (Boston: Little, Brown, 1990); Doris Kearns Goodwin, *No Ordinary Time: Franklin and Eleanor Roosevelt: The Home Front in World War II* (New York: Simon & Schuster, 1994); Eric Larrabee, *Commander in Chief: Franklin Delano Roosevelt, His Lieutenants, and Their War* (New York: Harper & Row, 1987); Joseph P. Lash, *Eleanor and Franklin: The Story of Their Relationship* (New York: Norton, 1971); Patrick Maney, *The Roosevelt Presence: A Biography of Franklin D. Roosevelt* (New York: Twayne, 1992); Sean J. Savage, *Roosevelt: The Party Leader, 1932–1945* (Lexington: University Press of Kentucky, 1991).

—William J. Thompson

Rosie the Riveter

The iconographic image of Rosie the Riveter, perhaps best known through a 1943 *Saturday Evening Post* cover by Norman Rockwell and similar portrayals in wartime efforts to attract women to industrial jobs, has largely defined popular American perceptions about women's roles during WORLD WAR II. While the long-term impact of wartime industrial employment on WOMEN'S STATUS AND RIGHTS has often been exaggerated, women defense workers represented by "Rosie" played a significant role in wartime production and the experience provided countless women with greater independence and self-confidence.

Successful wartime recruitment of women into the industrial workforce occurred only after 1942, when severe shortages of male workers who had entered the military forced employers to look for alternative sources of labor, and when more women were willing to take such jobs. By 1945, the proportion of women working rose from 28 to 37 percent—nearly one-third of them in blue-collar positions. Yet, while the war expanded the range of jobs that women held, employment patterns frequently followed old norms. Many more women worked in secretarial, clerical, sales, and service employment than in heavy industry (and were more likely to keep such work after the war); relatively few women with young children entered the labor force; and marriage and family held higher priorities for most women than did employment. As the historian David M. Kennedy has put it, "Rosie the Riveter might therefore more appro-priately have been named . . . Sally the Secretary, or even, as events were to prove, Molly the Mom."

On the job, real-life Rosies faced a number of obstacles. Women workers were generally relegated to the least-skilled and worst-paid jobs in wartime industry—and in fact, comparatively few were given work in riveting, which required skill and training. Women often faced patronizing or blatantly hostile male coworkers. Black women suffered from additional discrimination, as industrial employers frequently refused to consider them for anything but janitorial and similar low-level positions. Employers were slow to address the needs of their new female workers, who often maintained full responsibilities at home in addition to their jobs, contributing to higher rates of absenteeism and turnover among women. Unions admitted female members, but rarely fought against discriminatory practices in promotion and wages on behalf of women. Once an Allied victory appeared imminent, women were the first employees laid off as the United States prepared to absorb returning veterans into the peacetime economy. While some women lamented at being forced from their relatively high-paying industrial jobs, others had expected only to work "for the duration" and willingly returned to their domestic responsibilities at the end of the war.

Despite these issues, however, many women defense workers considered their wartime experiences to be positive. These women had obtained their jobs for a variety of reasons and appreciated the sense of personal and economic self-sufficiency obtained in doing what previously had been deemed "men's work." Both those women who remained in the workforce and those who never again held employment outside the home shared the belief that, in the words of one former "Rosie," their wartime work had proven they were able "to hold their own with men."

Further reading: Sherna Berger Gluck, *Rosie the Riveter Revisited: Women, the War, and Social Change* (Boston: Twayne, 1987); Susan M. Hartmann, *The Home Front and Beyond: American Women in the 1940s* (Boston: Twayne, 1982).

—Mary E. Carroll-Mason

Rural Electrification Administration (REA)

With the onset of the GREAT DEPRESSION, the situation of the nation's farmers became even more dire than it had been in the 1920s. By 1932, net farm income was about one-third of what it had been in 1929, and throughout the agricultural regions of the country, farm families lived lives of poverty, tedium, and endless toil. The Rural Electrification Administration (REA) was one of many NEW DEAL agencies aimed at ameliorating the harsh conditions found in rural areas.

As late as 1930, only about one out of 10 farms in the United States had electricity. In Mississippi, the figure was as low as one out of 100. The cost of installing and maintaining power lines in areas with few customers, together with the expectation that small farms would never use enough electricity to offset costs, discouraged private utility companies from extending service to most rural communities. Many people, however, were committed to the idea that access to electrical power would greatly enrich the lives of the rural poor. The programs sponsored by the Rural Electrification Administration, like those of the TENNESSEE VALLEY AUTHORITY (TVA) before it, were based upon this idea. Electricity would help improve the health of rural populations by permitting running water and proper storage of food. It would also improve other aspects of life in rural America by allowing the use of such labor-saving and leisure-enhancing devices as washing machines and radios. Finally, it would enable agricultural diversification, giving farmers the opportunity to produce commodities such as poultry and dairy products on a larger scale, which could in turn lead to improved economic prospects.

The REA was actually an outgrowth of the TVA. Plans to follow the success of the TVA by establishing seven "little TVAs" were halted by wary congressmen who were afraid of too much government interference and anxious to retain the support of the private utility interests. Proponents of rural electrification had to formulate a new plan. They found a model in Alcorn County, Mississippi, where one of the TVA's first customers, an electricity cooperative, had made money so quickly that it was able to pay back its TVA loan much earlier than required. This cooperative was successful in large part because of the Electric Farm and Home Authority, an agency that gave farmers the chance to purchase electrical appliances with low-cost loans; ownership of such appliances obviously boosted the farmers' use of electricity. Because the Alcorn County cooperative had met with such success, the electrical cooperative was seen as a promising means of continuing the work of electrifying rural America. With the passage of the EMERGENCY RELIEF APPROPRIATION ACT of 1935, the REA was set up to fund these cooperatives, at first under the WORKS PROGRESS ADMINISTRATION in 1935, and later, in 1936, as an independent agency.

Private utility companies often tried to hinder the work of the REA. Attempting to undercut REA revenues, they strung so-called spite lines along REA lines and served any large customers in an area, leaving only the smaller consumers of electricity to be serviced by the REA. Private companies also tried to discourage farmers from applying to the REA and used their influence in state governments to thwart the electrical cooperatives. Nonetheless, the REA successfully extended access to low-cost electricity to millions of people.

Although the REA, like the other New Deal attempts to aid AGRICULTURE, did not reverse the declining economic and cultural importance of the family farm in American society, it was largely successful in achieving its primary goal—delivering electrical service to rural areas. By 1941, two out of every five farms had electricity. Although the REA's funding was sharply decreased in 1943, it had set in motion the electrification of rural America. By 1950, 90 percent of farms had access to electricity, and this access did indeed help to alleviate the hardships of farm life. In fact, the historian William Leuchtenburg claims that the REA "revolutionized rural life."

See also PUBLIC UTILITY HOLDING COMPANY ACT.

Further reading: D. Clayton Brown, *Electricity for Rural America: The Fight for the REA* (Westport, Conn.: Greenwood, 1980); Philip Funigiello, *Toward a National Power Policy: The New Deal and the Electric Utility Industry* (Pittsburgh, Pa.: University of Pittsburgh Press, 1973).

—Pamela J. Lauer

S

Schechter Poultry Corporation v. United States
(1935)

On May 27, 1935, "Black Monday" to the administration of President FRANKLIN D. ROOSEVELT, the SUPREME COURT in the *Schechter* case struck down the NATIONAL INDUSTRIAL RECOVERY ACT (NIRA), one of the cornerstone agencies of the FIRST NEW DEAL. Subsequent Court decisions would overturn other major NEW DEAL programs, but perhaps no decision was so important as *Schechter* in the escalating conflict between the judicial and executive branches that led to the COURT-PACKING PLAN of 1937.

The Schechter Poultry Corporation was a Brooklyn, New York, company that specialized in kosher chickens. In 1934, the company had been convicted of selling diseased chickens, of not killing its chickens in the required fashion, and of not complying with wage and hour requirements—all violations of the Live Poultry Code of the NATIONAL RECOVERY ADMINISTRATION (NRA). A number of lawsuits against the NRA worked their way through the judicial system, and as part of its effort to end unwanted GOVERNMENT regulation, the Iron and Steel Institute financed the Schechter company's appeal to the Supreme Court. By a unanimous 9-0 decision, the Court found the NIRA unconstitutional on two grounds. First, the Constitution authorized the federal government only to regulate commerce between states—but the Schechter company operated only within the state of New York. Second, the NRA codes (which regulated such matters as production, prices, and wages) were an unconstitutional delegation of legislative authority to the executive—"delegation running riot," as one justice put it.

The *Schechter* (or "Sick Chicken") decision caused consternation in the Roosevelt administration. It indicated the Court's readiness to use the commerce clause and the distinction between interstate and intrastate commerce to invalidate other New Deal measures. It threatened the administration's efforts to extend the authority of the executive branch and the role of independent rule-making agencies. And although by May 1935 the NRA was unpopular and ineffective, it was a major New Deal program that embodied an approach to recovery to which Roosevelt was still committed. In fundamental ways, then, the decision seemed to challenge the New Deal itself.

Angry at the decision and distressed by its unanimity, Roosevelt at a press conference four days later called it the most important ruling since the *Dred Scott* case. He wondered whether the Court thought the federal government had control over any national economic problem and declared that the ruling put the nation back to "the horse-and-buggy definition of interstate commerce." Beyond this initial response, the *Schechter* decision was crucial to the dynamics producing the SECOND NEW DEAL of 1935 as well as Roosevelt's court-packing plan of 1937.

See also PRESIDENCY.

science

Continuing trends that accelerated throughout the 20th century, science from 1929 to 1945 became ever more closely related to TECHNOLOGY and dependent on large and expensive instruments. Science and technology were individually transformed and advanced in numerous ways in the hothouse environment of WORLD WAR II, and also brought into even closer interaction. Supported almost entirely by private foundations and conducted in limited facilities before the war, science became woven into the federal agencies and increasingly dependent on GOVERNMENT support during and after the war, and it became dominated by large, resource- and labor-intensive projects sometimes referred to as "big science."

In MEDICINE, new vaccines and antibiotics appeared during the 1930s, and mass-production techniques made them increasingly available in large quantities and high purity. Intravenous anesthetics, improved blood transfusion methods, and X-ray and other electrical diagnostic machines made surgery more of a reliable cure for some conditions and less of a last resort. Wartime urgencies pushed such methods rapidly into common use, and thousands of medical practitioners gained an accelerated experience in treatment of battlefield and other injuries and conditions.

Biology as a holistic discipline encompassing all scientific understanding of living things had been promoted by various leaders in the life sciences since the 19th century. In the early 1920s, new biology departments and programs at a number of major research universities, including the California Institute of Technology and Harvard, replaced a somewhat tangled and quaint variety of approaches with a scientific discipline fully established on a solid foundation of laboratory work and connections to physics and chemistry. The mechanisms, role, and power of heredity and environment in shaping individuals constituted a vital issue in science no less than in social theory and public policy. Quantitative and qualitative theories from many areas merged to form consistent and satisfying elaborations of the process of individual embryological development as well as evolution.

As the basic chemistry of biological processes became clearer, biologists and chemists were able to synthesize artificial versions of some vitamins and other biological substances, strongly influencing pharmacology and medical practice. In this they drew on new optical and electric diagnostic instrumentation that provided new insights into molecular structure. Theoretical chemistry explored the use of quantum physics in illuminating the mechanisms of chemical reactions, while, on the more practical side, a host of synthetic plastics, polymers, and artificial fibers and synthetic rubbers such as neoprene issued from laboratories, making industrial and organic chemistry one of the most productive and publicly appreciated areas of science.

In astronomy, the great optical telescopes, dominated by the Carnegie Institution's 100-inch-diameter reflector opened on Mount Wilson in 1917, provided a continuing string of discoveries. Edwin Hubble during the 1920s demonstrated that many of the so-called spiral nebulae were actually whole galaxies themselves, all rushing away from one another as if from a central explosion. By 1929 he had developed the basis of the so-called expanding universe. Within just a few short years the size and complexity of the universe had grown dramatically, and its ultimate history and fate seemed within the grasp of knowledge. A completely new kind of telescope, the radio antenna, was developed during the 1930s; and with wartime improvements in antennas and receivers, radio astronomy blossomed after the war and finally allowed the radio sky to be compared to the optical sky in some detail.

Physicists used balloons and aircraft, and then rockets, to hoist their detectors to higher altitudes where they could detect cosmic rays and other energetic radiation absorbed in the lower layers of the atmosphere. Solar astronomers using various telescopes contributed to physicists' attempts to understand the nuclear reactions that powered the Sun in terms of quantum physics. Continuous wartime monitoring of the Sun to predict conditions of radio transmission and reception helped solar astronomers understand better the interaction of various particles and radiation with the upper atmosphere and magnetic field of the earth.

Physicists investigating the smallest particles of matter and working out the theories of Einstein and of the new quantum physics turned to astronomical data and to laboratory apparatus of increasing size, complexity, and power. In the early 1930s, high voltage electrostatic generators, such as those of van de Graaff and Tesla, could only dissociate matter so far, even with the 5 million volts reached by Westinghouse in 1937. E. O. Laurence at Berkeley developed the first "atom smasher," or cyclotron, in 1932, which relied less on brute force and more on great velocities to bring particles into mutual collision and reach higher voltages. By the late 1930s, controlled laboratory splitting of uranium atoms showed the feasibility of atomic power, and several nations began development of crude reactors and of the ATOMIC BOMB during the war. Physicists were beginning to understand the series of fission and fusion nuclear reactions that power the Sun and stars, and were making headway in grappling with the picture of the early universe implied by Edwin Hubble's studies of galaxies and the expanding universe.

Through the 1930s, geology was joined—and sometimes challenged—by the hybrid discipline of geophysics, which sought to understand the deeper interior of the earth and the physical processes that operated on short and long time scales. Global measurements of magnetism, gravity, and other parameters as well as long series of time-based measurements, such as those of seismology, slowly revealed the structure of the earth below its surface, a planet with a solid core with a molten covering, surrounded by a mantle of rock, and a thin crust, similar to the other interior planets of the solar system. Like oceanography, geophysics would find enormous demand as well as lucrative possibilities during the war. Geologists, geophysicists, and oceanographers in the course of their war work and travels were almost constantly on a field survey or expedition.

Scientific research moved increasingly from private foundation support to dependence on the federal government, particularly during and after World War II. A uniquely American phenomenon, private philanthropic foundations, established earlier by wealthy capitalists such as Andrew Carnegie, Henry Ford, John D. Rockefeller, and others for a variety of altruistic and self-serving motives, supported many research and educational ventures. During the 1920s, emphasis was on training researchers and equipping institutions, while the 1930s targeted emerging new disciplines or interdisciplinary areas, such as molecular biology and cultural anthropology.

Science during the interwar years was vigorous and exciting, and drew broad public support and interest. Major discoveries in numerous fields, as well as intriguing syntheses and theories, made scientists in all areas reluctant to interrupt their work. However, they enlisted in the war effort quickly and wholeheartedly, where they made many unexpected discoveries and contributions, often outside their own fields of study. Transformed by the unprecedented mobilization of science for the war, and with the solid achievements of the interwar years as a basis, science and scientists were poised in 1945 for the well-funded, hectic, and productive postwar period.

Further reading: A. Hunter Dupree, *Science in the Federal Government: A History of Policies and Activities* (Baltimore: Johns Hopkins University Press, 1986); Marc Rothenberg, *The History of Science and Technology in the United States: An Encyclopedia* (New York: Garland, 2001); Trevor I. Williams, *Science: A History of Discovery in the Twentieth Century* (New York: Oxford University Press, 1990).

—Joseph N. Tatarewicz

Scottsboro Boys

On March 25, 1931, nine African-American teenagers were arrested near Scottsboro, Alabama, for the rape of two white women who had been riding on a freight train with the defendants when the alleged assault took place. By April 9, eight of the youths had been tried, convicted, and sentenced to death for the alleged crime; the trial of the youngest defendant ended in a mistrial. Although all of the accused ultimately regained their freedom, what many saw as a "legal lynching" became a symbol for the unjust treatment of AFRICAN AMERICANS in the SOUTH. The case of the "Scottsboro Boys" (as everyone called them because of their youth) contributed to the growing visibility of CIVIL RIGHTS issues and to increasing attention to RACE AND RACIAL CONFLICT. The Scottsboro appeals and retrials also strengthened the use of the court system to gain civil rights for African Americans.

The International Labor Defense (ILD), the legal branch of the Communist Party of the United States (CPUSA), took charge of the defense because the NATIONAL ASSOCIATION FOR THE ADVANCEMENT OF COLORED PEOPLE (NAACP) reacted cautiously to the legal needs of the defendants. Despite attempts to take the case from the ILD and the hiring of the renowned defense attorney Clarence Darrow, the NAACP never gained the trust of the defendants.

The
SCOTTSBORO BOYS
MUST NOT DIE!
MASS SCOTTSBORO DEFENSE MEETING
At St. Mark's M. E. Church
137th Street and St. Nicholas Avenue
Friday Eve., April 14th, 8 P. M.
Protest the infamous death verdict rendered by an all-white jury at Decatur, Alabama against HAYWOOD PATTERSON

The Meeting will be addressed by:

Mrs. JANIE PATTERSON, mother of Haywood Patterson, victim of the lynch verdict; SAMUEL LEIBOWITZ, chief counsel for the defense; JOSEPH BRODSKY, defense counsel; WILLIAM PATTERSON, National Secretary of the I. L. D.; RICHARD B. MOORE; Dr. LORENZO KING; WM. KELLEY of the Amsterdam News; and others.

THUNDER YOUR INDIGNATION AGAINST THE JUDICIAL MURDER OF INNOCENT NEGRO CHILDREN!

COME TO THE MASS PROTEST MEETING
AT ST. MARK'S M. E. CHURCH
137th Street and St. Nicholas Avenue

FRIDAY EVENING, APRIL 14th, 8 P. M.

Emergency Scottsboro Defense Committee
119 West 135th Street, New York City

This poster represents the reaction of the African-American community to the Scottsboro Boys case. *(New York Historical Society)*

The involvement of the COMMUNISTS led to a backlash against those sympathetic to the defense. In Camp Hill, Alabama, a meeting of African Americans to protest the Scottsboro trials was mistaken for a radical gathering and violently broken up by sheriffs. In addition, the distrust of southerners for northerners resulted in death threats directed at the defense attorney, Samuel Leibowitz, a skillful noncommunist attorney from New York retained by the CPUSA to counter anticommunist sentiment.

The United States SUPREME COURT overturned the convictions in 1932 and in 1935, citing lack of counsel during the first trials and a scarcity of African-American representation on the jury during the initial retrials. Despite a recantation by one of the accusers, the last set of retrials resulted in one death sentence (never carried out) and four long-term imprisonments. In July 1937, charges against the other four defendants were dropped. In the 1940s, four more of the Scottsboro Boys were released, although two served additional prison terms because of parole violations. The ninth escaped from prison in 1948.

See also COMMUNISTS.

Further reading: Dan T. Carter, *Scottsboro: A Tragedy of the American South,* rev. ed. (Baton Rouge: Louisiana State University Press, 1979); James E. Goodman, *Stories of Scottsboro* (New York: Pantheon, 1994).

—Traci L. Siegler

second front

On June 6, 1944, Allied forces crossed the English Channel and attacked the German-held beaches of Normandy in France. Known popularly as D day, the INVASION OF NORMANDY opened the second front in the WORLD WAR II EUROPEAN THEATER and helped produce the surrender of Nazi Germany within a year. (The "first" front was the eastern front, where Soviet and German forces had fought since mid-1941.) In addition to its military importance, the question of a second front was a significant factor in the strained relations among the United States, Great Britain, and the Soviet Union in the wartime GRAND ALLIANCE.

Soon after the American entry into the war in December 1941, Soviet leader Joseph Stalin demanded a second front to draw German troops away from the eastern front and relieve pressure on the Red Army and on the Soviet Union. (Ultimately, the Soviet Union lost at least 20 million people during World War II.) The United States supported the idea of opening a second front as soon as possible, and in April 1942, General GEORGE C. MARSHALL, the U.S. ARMY chief of staff, and HARRY L. HOPKINS, a close adviser of President FRANKLIN D. ROOSEVELT, arrived in London to seek British agreement for an attack across the English Channel into France. Their proposal, which won apparent acceptance by Winston Churchill, involved three stages, code-named Bolero, Roundup, and Sledgehammer. Operation Bolero would consist of an initial buildup of men and munitions in Britain that would culminate in Operation Roundup, a substantial cross-Channel invasion. Operation Sledgehammer would be a smaller landing to seize a bridgehead in the Cherbourg Peninsula.

Churchill had reservations about this strategy because he feared a repeat of the heavy British losses that had occurred in land battles on the western front in World War I. When Soviet foreign minister Molotov traveled to London and to Washington, D.C., to get an agreement on a second front in May 1942, he was tersely informed in London that Britain was not prepared for such an extensive operation. In Washington, the United States told Molotov that a second front would be initiated in 1942, though LEND-LEASE ACT materials for the Soviets would have to be

decreased as a result of the military buildup. After Molotov's visits, Churchill met with FDR to discourage a second front in 1942. Churchill preferred a peripheral strategy, which called for a NORTH AFRICAN CAMPAIGN instead. Although U.S. military advisers opposed this approach, Churchill was able to convince FDR to agree to the campaign, on the basis that the United States was still not fully prepared to mount a successful cross-Channel attack in 1942.

The CASABLANCA CONFERENCE of January 1943 brought together U.S. and British delegations to revitalize the talks on a second front. Stalin refused to leave the Soviet Union during the pivotal Battle of Stalingrad for this conference. After initial U.S. reluctance to postpone a cross-Channel invasion again, the British and Americans decided that they would not immediately undertake an invasion into France after the North African campaign ended. Instead, they would forge ahead into the Mediterranean for an invasion of SICILY in the spring of 1943. At the Trident Conference in Washington in May 1943, Churchill and Roosevelt concluded that the second front would have to be delayed until 1944 because the buildup of Operation Bolero was proceeding slowly. Roosevelt was able to extract a British commitment to a cross-Channel invasion, now called Operation Overlord, for May 1, 1944.

The TEHERAN CONFERENCE (November 28 to December 1, 1943) provided an opportunity for the Grand Alliance to devise a strategy to end World War II as well as to make preliminary plans for the postwar period. Roosevelt feared that unless a second front were opened in the near future, much of postwar Europe would be controlled by the Soviet Union, while Stalin continued to complain about the American and British delay. Distrust in the Grand Alliance and in SOVIET-AMERICAN RELATIONS over these and other issues foreshadowed the cold war. When Stalin agreed to enter the Pacific war against Japan after Germany was defeated, Roosevelt set the date of May 1, 1944, for opening the second front, and Churchill could offer no other effective alternative to further postponing it. The Allies then devised a military strategy that involved a joint British and American invasion of France coupled with a simultaneous Soviet offensive against the Germans from the east that would force the Germans to spread out their forces on two fronts.

The projected date of Overlord was changed and postponed until June 5, to ensure more equipment and weapons for the landing force. A storm on June 5 delayed the invasion for another day. Early on June 6, under the leadership of General Dwight D. Eisenhower, the cross-Channel invasion began. The successful opening of a second front signaled that war was nearing its finale in the European theater. The pincer movement by Allied forces from the east and west forced Germany to surrender in May 1945.

Further reading: Robert Dallek, *Franklin D. Roosevelt and American Foreign Policy, 1932–1945* (New York: Oxford University Press, 1979); Warren F. Kimball, *Forged in War: Roosevelt, Churchill, and the Second World War* (New York: William Morrow, 1997).

—Michael T. Walsh

Second New Deal

The so-called Second New Deal of 1935 marked a shift in domestic policy from the GOVERNMENT planning and controls that provided the foundation for the FIRST NEW DEAL of 1933 to a greater emphasis on social reform. The Second New Deal was characterized also by a heightening of anti-BUSINESS rhetoric in President FRANKLIN D. ROOSEVELT's appeals to an increasingly class-conscious electorate.

As with notions of a First New Deal and a THIRD NEW DEAL, scholars disagree about the extent to which the Second New Deal represented either a dramatic ideological shift or a substantial change in policy. While some argue that in 1935 the agenda of the Roosevelt administration moved left, becoming increasingly antibusiness and pro-LABOR, others contend that the Second New Deal marked a conservative retreat from national planning and restructuring of the American ECONOMY, to traditional progressive ANTIMONOPOLY policy. Still others argue that the Second New Deal maintained strong continuities with the First New Deal and was really a practical reshaping of NEW DEAL policy in response to limitations of the First New Deal and to the changing political climate of the mid-1930s and the election of a more liberal CONGRESS in 1934.

Although the Second New Deal appeared to represent a break from the ideology and methods that characterized the First New Deal, its goals of providing economic security and making efforts to protect the rights of organized labor were broadly consistent with those of earlier New Deal programs. The most prominent pieces of Second New Deal legislation were the EMERGENCY RELIEF APPROPRIATION ACT (ERAA), the SOCIAL SECURITY ACT, and the NATIONAL LABOR RELATIONS ACT (or Wagner Act). The ERAA provided an alternative to the direct handouts of the FEDERAL EMERGENCY RELIEF ADMINISTRATION by placing a greater emphasis on the work-RELIEF programs of the new WORKS PROGRESS ADMINISTRATION, though it drew upon earlier work-relief programs. The Social Security Act continued to expand the role of government in social welfare by establishing long-term programs for economic security. And the Wagner Act provided statutory authority to guarantee labor the right of collective bargaining as first outlined in Section 7(a) of the NATIONAL INDUSTRIAL RECOVERY ACT (NIRA) of 1933.

While relief efforts and the Wagner Act had precursors in the First New Deal, and the Social Security Act had been under development since 1934, the REVENUE ACT OF 1935 and the PUBLIC UTILITY HOLDING COMPANY ACT (PUHCA) represented a move toward the left on the part of FDR. Facing political challenges from grassroots movements, notably the Share Our Wealth movement, led by HUEY LONG, Roosevelt sided with members of CONGRESS who were proponents of "soak-the-rich" tax legislation. The PUHCA, designed to use the SECURITIES AND EXCHANGE COMMISSION to disentangle and reorganize complex webs of utility holding companies, prompted harsh criticism of the Roosevelt administration among businessmen and conservatives alike.

According to the "two New Deal" framework, the Second New Deal continued into WORLD WAR II when, according to Roosevelt, "Dr. New Deal" gave way to "Dr. Win-the-War." However, some scholars argue that during the late 1930s, a Third New Deal began, marking a substantial change in economic policy that was strongly influenced by the principles of KEYNESIANISM.

Further reading: William E. Leuchtenburg, *Franklin D. Roosevelt and the New Deal, 1932–1940* (New York: Harper, 1963); William H. Wilson, "The Two New Deals: A Valid Concept?" *The Historian* 28 (February 1966): 268–88.

—Shannon L. Parsley

Securities and Exchange Commission (SEC)

A federal GOVERNMENT regulatory agency created as part of the NEW DEAL in June 1934 by the Securities and Exchange Act, the Securities and Exchange Commission (SEC) enforced standards for securities markets and brought protection for individual investors. It did this by regulating securities trading practices and requiring the full disclosure and registration of information for securities traded on the nation's exchanges.

Despite the disastrous STOCK MARKET CRASH of 1929, Wall Street traders and investment bankers continued to claim that the American securities industry operated well. In fact, it had a number of legal and functional problems. Chief among these was that much trading was done in ignorance. Many companies issued no financial reports or published ones with information that was misleading or unaudited. Certain investment banks and firms held a near monopoly on reliable information concerning securities and the companies issuing them. This ignorance made individual investors and securities firms vulnerable to abuses such as misrepresentation, insider trading, and uncontrolled speculation. In 1933, the Senate's Banking and Currency Committee, under the leadership of its chief counsel, Ferdinand Pecora, held hearings revealing criminal fraud and improper trading practices in securities markets that had contributed to the Crash. Calls for reforms of the securities industry followed the hearings.

The first step in regulating the securities industry came when CONGRESS passed the Securities Act of 1933. The act mandated that all new securities offerings must be accompanied by accurate public information filed with the Federal Trade Commission. Then, in February 1934, President FRANKLIN D. ROOSEVELT asked for legislation to take the next step and establish a regulatory agency to monitor the operations of the nation's securities exchanges. The proposed securities and exchange bill provoked strong opposition from the securities industry, which claimed that the act would turn Wall Street into a "deserted village." The New York Stock Exchange, said its president, Richard Whitney (later sent to prison for mishandling funds), "is a perfect institution."

Though compromising on some of the bill's more stringent proposals, FDR arrived at an understanding with moderates on Wall Street and the leaders of the country's numerous regional exchanges, who were more sensitive to the need for regulation. This coalition eased the way for the passage of the Securities and Exchange Act on June 6, 1934. In addition to establishing the Securities and Exchange Commission to carry out the provisions of both the 1933 and 1934 securities legislation, the act mandated full disclosure of an issuing company's financial information, required the verification of such data by independent auditors using accepted, standard accounting procedures, and established federal control of trading practices on the stock markets. The SEC thus had authority to regulate securities registration, exchanges, dealers, and trading. The Securities and Exchange Act also gave the Federal Reserve Board authority to regulate the sort of credit purchasing of stock that had fueled speculation leading to the 1929 Crash.

Roosevelt appointed JOSEPH P. KENNEDY, a wealthy businessman and Wall Street investor, as the first SEC chairman. This surprising appointment, at first likened by many observers to putting the fox in charge of the henhouse, worked well. Kennedy and his immediate successors, lawyers James M. Landis and WILLIAM O. DOUGLAS, proved effective administrators who helped ensure that securities markets operated along rational and legal lines so that investment decisions could be based upon reliable information. In the decade of the 1930s, the SEC prevented the issue of some $150 million of fraudulent securities, and by 1941 it operated 10 regional offices to oversee 20 stock exchanges and 7,000 brokers and dealers. Protecting purchasers, it also won the support of most of the financial community. The later study of government agen-

cies by HERBERT C. HOOVER noted that the SEC was an "outstanding example of the independent commission at its best."

Further reading: Michael E. Parrish, *Securities Regulation and the New Deal* (New Haven, Conn.: Yale University Press, 1970).

—Robert J. Hanyok

Selective Service

On September 16, 1940, President FRANKLIN D. ROOSEVELT signed the Selective Training and Service Act that created the Selective Service System. Authorizing the conscription of 900,000 men between 21 and 36 years of age, the legislation marked the nation's first attempt to mobilize a military force before it declared war, and was approved for one year. It narrowly won extension a year later, and then, with further amendment, enabled the huge expansion of the armed forces after the United States entered WORLD WAR II.

The original impetus for the 1940 draft came from outside the GOVERNMENT rather than from President Roosevelt or the War Department. The Military Training Camps Association, a private organization that stressed preparedness, lobbied CONGRESS to use conscription as the means to prepare the nation for war. Conservatives who opposed the draft argued that it tampered with the nation's traditional antimilitary, antistatist, and pro-individualist ideals and feared it would become a first step toward totalitarianism. Supporters, however, argued that the traditional volunteer system would not work.

The Nazi BLITZKRIEG that overran western Europe in the spring and summer of 1940 lent momentum to preparedness sentiment, and the selective service bill passed 47 to 25 in the Senate and 232 to 124 in the House. October 16 was set as the date when all males from 21 to 36 years old would register. It appeared that conscription might become a major issue in the ELECTION OF 1940, one reason that Roosevelt was slow to back the measure, but Republican presidential nominee WENDELL L. WILLKIE also supported the draft.

The Selective Service System administered the draft through 6,443 local boards and 505 appeal boards. It oversaw the registration of men, selection by lottery, requests for deferments or conscientious objector status, and appeals. Planners looked to the lessons of World War I and the Civil War to avoid flaws in the system, and consequently citizens rather than federal bureaucrats or military officers ran local draft board offices. Using the principle of a rational and orderly use of manpower, the Selective Service System attempted to balance military with domestic needs and to decide whether each man could do the country the most good as a soldier or as a civilian worker. Efforts to put the Selective Service System under the control of the WAR MANPOWER COMMISSION, however, created a bureaucratic battle that Selective Service director Lewis Hershey fought to a standoff and that left him with authority over the draft.

During World War II, the FEDERAL BUREAU OF INVESTIGATION checked on 373,000 draft evaders and obtained 16,000 convictions. In addition, 4.5 million of the 36 million men classified by local boards million appealed their classifications, mostly in hope of avoiding service. By war's end, of the 22 million registrants between ages 18 and 38, some 10 million—or about 45 percent—had received deferments for a variety of reasons, mostly for family status, infirmity, or occupation. The military preferred men under 26, and fathers generally were not drafted until late in the war.

The Selective Training and Service Act of 1940 exempted from combat men who "by reason of religious training and belief" opposed war. CONSCIENTIOUS OBJECTORS served in noncombat roles in the military or performed national service in lieu of military duty. Many of these men worked as civilians in public service camps on conservation projects. Some served as human guinea pigs in experiments on diet, endurance, and control of diseases and infections. In all, about 40,000 men were classified as conscientious objectors.

Although the Selective Service Act included an antidiscrimination clause, it did not initially reduce discrimination against AFRICAN AMERICANS in the armed forces. Top military officials refused to expand black units sufficiently to allow the induction in proportion to their numbers in the population, and a higher rejection rate for blacks than for whites suggests that the mostly white draft boards often discriminated against blacks. Several incidents of black resistance to the draft occurred in Chicago and other cities. Roughly 400 African-American men refused to serve, viewing the war as a white man's war or refusing to serve in a

President Franklin D. Roosevelt is seen looking on as a blindfolded Secretary of War Henry L. Stimson draws the first numbers in the Selective Service lottery. *(National Archives)*

Jim Crow army or fight for a country that denied them their CIVIL RIGHTS.

The Selective Service System performed well during World War II and ensured that the military received the number and quality of men it requested rapidly and efficiently. The massive effort directed by the agency from 1940 until 1945 was unprecedented. In September 1939, U.S. ARMY strength stood at about 190,000 men, which made it the world's 17th-largest force. Five years later, the army stood at more than 8.2 million and American armed forces were the world's most powerful. During the war, local draft boards registered about 50 million men and inducted more than 10 million of them. In all, the agency conscripted nearly two-thirds of the 16 million men who served in the armed forces during the war. The rest were volunteers, as were the women who served in the military.

While they did not intend it, the lawmakers who passed the 1940 Selective Service Act created a historical precedent. After World War II ended, policymakers used this first "peacetime" draft act to justify extending the draft in the cold war until 1973.

Further reading: John Whiteclay Chambers II, ed., *Draftees or Volunteers: A Documentary History of the Debate over Military Conscription in the United States, 1787–1973* (New York: Garland, 1975); George Q. Flynn, *The Draft, 1940–1973* (Lawrence: University Press of Kansas, 1993); George Q. Flynn and Lewis B. Hershey, *Mr. Selective Service* (Chapel Hill: University of North Carolina Press, 1985).

—Edwin D. Miller

shipbuilding

WORLD WAR II had two important effects on shipbuilding in the United States. First, the war pulled the shipbuilding industry out of its doldrums of the 1920s and 1930s by catalyzing the construction of new shipyards and the production of thousands of ships. Second, it led to innovations in shipbuilding that made the process faster, more efficient, and more profitable.

During the interwar years, the American shipbuilding industry fell upon hard times. Demand for new vessels shrank because of high production during World War I (ships typically have long life spans) and because of naval arms limitation agreements. The GREAT DEPRESSION dealt the industry another blow. Then, in the late 1930s, the naval rearmament in the United States and Europe brought new business to shipyards. British and then American losses to German U-boats—which reached more than 100 ships per month by early 1942—in the BATTLE OF THE ATLANTIC increased the need for both merchant ships and surface combat vessels. Large appropriations for expanding

the U.S. NAVY began in 1940 and 1941, as the nation committed itself to a two-ocean navy. After PEARL HARBOR and the American entry into the war, further appropriations came, and the merchant marine as well as the navy underwent dramatic expansion.

New innovations in shipbuilding helped meet the exploding demand for new vessels. HENRY J. KAISER, an industrialist who had made his fortune with construction and public works projects, came up with a way to increase the volume and efficiency of ship construction. When his company took GOVERNMENT contracts to build new merchant vessels, popularly called liberty ships, Kaiser built an entirely new type of shipyard in Richmond, California, on San Francisco Bay. First, he put all of the necessary supply operations, such as a steel mill and rolling plant, on the same property as the shipyard, which eliminated time spent waiting for the delivery of steel plates. He prefabricated as many of the ship's parts as possible, again saving precious time. And he instituted an assembly line technique that put together the ships quickly and efficiently.

Kaiser was able to reach astounding speed and volume of production. It had taken traditional East Coast shipyards a year to build a liberty ship in 1941; by 1942, Kaiser had pared the time to two months, and subsequently to a few weeks. Once, as a demonstration, the Kaiser yards built a liberty ship in less than five days. Accounting for about one-third of the nation's shipbuilding in 1943, Kaiser became known as "Sir Launchalot." Kaiser's employees were motivated not just by patriotism but also by the high wages and good benefits that he provided, including a health plan for his workers and child-care centers to help working women.

Kaiser was not the only innovator in the shipbuilding industry. Based in New Orleans, Andrew Jackson Higgins used mass-production techniques in his new shipyards for the construction of landing craft that became known as Higgins Boats. These were the small motorized boats carried by AMPHIBIOUS WARFARE assault ships that transported the troops, equipment, and vehicles ashore during the INVASION OF NORMANDY and the various amphibious assaults in the WORLD WAR II PACIFIC THEATER. Higgins also built the small, fast, and maneuverable PT-boats that played an important role in the Pacific.

Using the new mass-production methods of prefabrication and assembly line techniques in modern shipyards, American shipbuilding accomplished remarkable feats during the war. In addition to speeding up the production process, the new shipyards turned out a prodigious quantity of construction. By war's end, the United States had produced some 5,800 merchant ships, with a cargo-carrying capacity of nearly 60 million tons, and 1,500 naval vessels.

The war brought changes in the labor force as well new shipbuilding processes. The workforce in American shipyards had always been racially diverse, but with racial stratification that gave white workers the best jobs, AFRICAN AMERICANS the lower-status and lower-paying jobs. The production demands and labor shortage of the war years eroded such disparities and brought black workers new opportunities in shipyards. African Americans began to take on jobs as welders and electricians, for example, although the advances were limited and sometimes brought white resentment and troubled race relations. Women entered the shipyards in large numbers during the war (helping give rise to the popular image of ROSIE THE RIVETER), and at the Kaiser yards in Richmond, California, made up 40 percent of the welders.

Contributing to the growth of the SUNBELT states during the war, the U.S. shipbuilding industry expanded enormously, from Seattle to San Francisco to San Diego on the Pacific Coast, from Houston to New Orleans to Mobile to Tampa on the Gulf Coast, and from Charleston to Norfolk on the South Atlantic Coast. The new yards were more efficient and cost effective, and in the SOUTH there was less LABOR union organization and cheaper labor. As the war drew to a close, shipbuilding slowed and the industry began to contract again.

See also MOBILIZATION; WOMEN'S STATUS AND RIGHTS.

Further reading: Robert A. Kilmarx, ed., *America's Maritime Legacy: A History of the U.S. Merchant Marine and Shipbuilding Industry since Colonial Times* (Boulder, Colo.: Westview Press, 1979); Clinton H. Whitehurst, *The U.S. Shipbuilding Industry: Past, Present, and Future* (Annapolis, Md.: Naval Institute Press, 1986).

—Nicholas Fry

Sicily

The decision to invade Sicily, a large Italian island in the Mediterranean across the Strait of Messina from the mainland, was made at the CASABLANCA CONFERENCE in January 1943. While the Americans wanted to open a SECOND FRONT in the WORLD WAR II EUROPEAN THEATER by launching a cross-Channel invasion of German-occupied France, they agreed to continue pursuing the British peripheral approach strategy with further Mediterranean operations. The invasion of Sicily in July 1943 drove AXIS forces from Sicily by August and led to the invasion of mainland Italy in September that began the ITALIAN CAMPAIGN.

The invasion of Sicily, code-named Operation Husky, was given to British general Harold R. L. G. Alexander's newly formed 15th Army Group. Comprising Lieutenant General Bernard L. Montgomery's British Eighth Army and Major General GEORGE S. PATTON's U.S. Seventh Army, the 15th Army Group totaled eight divisions, including airborne, commando, and ranger units. The British sea

and air commanders, Admiral Andrew B. Cunningham and Air Marshall Arthur Tedder, worked with Alexander under the overall command of U.S. ARMY lieutenant general Dwight D. Eisenhower at Allied Forces Headquarters in Algiers. Planning for the invasion was poor and was complicated by Anglo-American disagreements, a lack of close interservice and interarmy cooperation, and a general high level of acrimony. The American and British armies that invaded Sicily largely acted independently of each other in both planning and operational stages.

The invasion took place at dawn on July 10, 1943. It was the second largest AMPHIBIOUS WARFARE assault in Europe during the war (the later INVASION OF NORMANDY was the largest), involving 180,000 troops, more than 2,500 ships, and 3,700 aircraft. Axis air power was destroyed at the outset, but strong winds made the first large airborne operation of the war a disaster as many of the gliders carrying airborne units were forced down in the ocean, drowning many of the troops. The amphibious landings, in spite of the bad weather, went smoothly. Montgomery's forces landed on the eastern coast, between Pozallo and Syracuse, where they encountered only slight opposition. Syracuse was captured the first day. The Americans landed on the southwestern coast, between Cape Scaramia and Licata, and were more exposed to the weather. The opposition they encountered was also stronger, but all three divisions were ashore by the end of the first day, with U.S. NAVY warships providing much needed fire support.

Although ordered to protect Montgomery's flank as his Eighth Army advanced north toward Messina to cut off the Axis retreat, General Patton, already frustrated with the plodding pace of the British advance, formed a provisional corps for an advance on Palermo at the opposite end of the island. When Alexander again ordered him to continue protecting Montgomery's flank, Patton flew to see him in protest, while continuing his advance. New instructions from Alexander allowed the Americans to reach Palermo on July 22 after a stunning advance. Although the rugged Sicilian terrain confined armored and motorized units to a few narrow winding roads, the Americans made rapid progress, unlike their British allies, who moved very slowly, allowing Axis troops to retreat in good order before them. Only two German divisions were in Sicily, the Hermann Göring Division and 15th Panzer Grenadier Division, but both offered stubborn resistance. Overall Axis morale, however, including that of 250,000 Italian troops, was low.

Hitler initially opposed any retreat; but when Italian dictator Benito Mussolini was ousted from power on July 25, Hitler ordered plans for an evacuation. On July 27, the Germans began withdrawing across the island, although continuing to offer resistance. The Italians had virtually given up. German field marshal Albert Kesselring ordered a full evacuation on the night of August 11, 1943. In a brilliantly planned and executed move, as many as 40,000 German and 62,000 Italian troops, including most of their equipment and supplies, escaped unmolested to Italy. Although Ultra INTELLIGENCE had given the Allies 10 days warning of Axis intentions, cooperation and coordination were so poor that no real effort was made to intervene. A final dash by the Americans put them in Messina before the British, with one patrol entering the city on August 16. Axis casualties numbered some 164,000, of which 32,000 were German. American casualties were 7,300, and British casualties 9,350.

Although the Sicily campaign failed to knock Italy out of the war, it did provide a base for invading the Italian mainland and gave the Americans much-needed fighting experience.

Further reading: Carlo D'Este, *Bitter Victory: The Sicily Campaign, 1943* (New York: Dutton, 1988); Albert N. Garland and Howard M. Smyth, *Sicily and the Surrender of Italy* (Washington, D.C.: U.S. Army Center of Military History, 1965).

—Clayton D. Laurie

Sinatra, Frank (Francis Albert) (1915–1998)

During WORLD WAR II, Frank Sinatra became perhaps the most popular singer in the country, and his remarkable career ultimately spanned more than half a century. He played a major role in shifting the focus of popular MUSIC from the bands that had dominated "swing era" jazz of the 1930s to the singers themselves.

Francis Albert Sinatra was born on December 12, 1915, in Hoboken, New Jersey, the son of Italian immigrants. He often ignored his studies, and eventually dropped out of school at the age of 16. Determined to make a living with his voice, Sinatra played nightclubs, roadhouses, Democratic Party meetings, and gatherings of the Hoboken Sicilian Cultural League in the 1930s.

Sinatra's break came in February 1939, when he was hired by popular band leader Harry James. A year later, in January 1940, Sinatra signed a contract with the Tommy Dorsey Band. In May, the band released "I'll Never Smile Again," which catapulted Sinatra to stardom. By January 1942, Sinatra began considering severing his ties with Dorsey. Creative and personal differences along with the success of "Night and Day" and other songs made Sinatra desire a solo career. He played his final show with the Tommy Dorsey Band in September 1942, although he was not finally released from his contract until March 1943.

In December 1942, Sinatra gave a solo performance at New York's Paramount Theater that helped catapult him to still greater fame and popularity. The audience was comprised mostly of teenage girls known as bobbysoxers,

who welcomed his performance with extraordinary enthusiasm. "Sinatramania" had begun and persisted through the war, with Sinatra playing to packed audiences and enjoying huge record sales. An inner ear dysfunction exempted him from the armed forces, and although his general popularity did not suffer, he was held in low esteem by many GIs.

Called by some the greatest popular singer of the 20th century, Sinatra went on to a long and influential career, and he also won plaudits from critics and fellow musicians for the craftsmanship he brought to his singing, especially his phrasing of lyrics. Sinatra also acted in Hollywood films, and won an Academy Award in 1953 for his acting in *From Here to Eternity*, a film about World War II adapted from a novel by James Jones. His life, both private and public, was often tempestuous and controversial.

Further reading: John Lahr, *Sinatra: The Artist and the Man* (New York: Random House, 1997).

—Daniel J. Fury

Smith Act (1940)

In June 1940, CONGRESS overwhelmingly approved the Alien Registration Act, popularly known as the Smith Act after its principal author, Virginia Democratic representative Howard W. Smith. The registration of ENEMY ALIENS during WORLD WAR II was carried out under the provisions of the Smith Act.

The Smith Act mandated the registration and fingerprinting of all resident aliens (hence its official name), and authorized the deportation of any alien who belonged to a revolutionary organization or expressed revolutionary sentiments. But much of the legislation aimed at limiting political expression. The act made illegal any speech that attempted to create disloyalty among members of the military. It also outlawed speech that "advocated the necessity, desirability or propriety of overthrowing the government by force." Organizations were forbidden to teach overthrow of the GOVERNMENT, and any printed matter intended for use in violation of the act was subject to seizure. Originally, the penalty for conviction of these offenses was a prison term of up to 10 years and/or a fine of up to $10,000, but these limits were later doubled.

Talk of an antisedition measure had begun in response to leftist activities in the 1930s, but increasing concerns about the war in Europe and the role there of fifth-column internal subversion and sabotage paved the way for the bill's passage. By June 1940, when Germany defeated France, many Americans, including President FRANKLIN D. ROOSEVELT, supported measures to limit political dissent, especially among supporters of fascism and the AXIS powers.

Only two cases were prosecuted under the Smith Act during World War II. In one case, 29 members of the Socialist Workers Party, a communist group centered in Minnesota, were indicted for conspiring to destroy the U.S. GOVERNMENT. Of the 29, 18 were convicted, 10 were acquitted, and one committed suicide. The other case, which became known as the Great Sedition Trial, involved 39 defendants who were alleged to be leaders of a fascist conspiracy. It resulted in no convictions.

In the early years of the cold war, prosecutions under the Smith Act became more common, because of fears of communism and accusations made by the House Un-American Activities Committee. In all, more than 150 persons have been indicted for violating this law. In 1951, the SUPREME COURT upheld the Smith Act in *Dennis v. United States;* the Court subsequently narrowed the law's scope, but has never found it unconstitutional.

See also CIVIL LIBERTIES; COMMUNISTS.

—Pamela J. Lauer

socialists

Led by NORMAN THOMAS, socialists during the 1930s and 1940s offered a left-wing alternative to the two major parties. Although the GREAT DEPRESSION offered opportunities for socialism to gain support, the American people chose to preserve capitalism instead of replacing it with a form of collectivism.

The primary means for advancing socialist political views was through the Socialist Party, led for many years by Eugene V. Debs until his death in 1926. The party, whose membership swelled to over 100,000 before World War I, had fallen on hard times during the 1920s, as the Red Scare early in the decade, prosperity throughout the decade, and the weakness of party organization had reduced the number to only 7,000 by 1928. In 1928, Norman Thomas, the Socialist presidential candidate, received 267,835 votes—less than 1 percent of the popular vote.

The collapse of the ECONOMY with the onset of the Great Depression gave socialists hope that Americans would turn their way for solutions to the economic crisis. The Socialist Party platform in the ELECTION OF 1932 called for federal RELIEF and public works, medical and old age insurance, the right of collective bargaining by unions, repeal of Prohibition, arms reduction, and American membership in the League of Nations. Despite internal rifts, Thomas was once again the Socialists' nominee in 1932, but received only the disappointing total of 881,951 votes (barely more than 2 percent).

The election of FRANKLIN D. ROOSEVELT and the enactment of NEW DEAL legislation seemed to steal much of the Socialists' thunder and undercut the party's potential base of support among LABOR and farmers. A number of Socialist-leaning labor leaders, such as SIDNEY HILLMAN and Walter Reuther, viewed the New Deal as a giant step forward for workers' rights, and passage of the NATIONAL LABOR RELATIONS ACT in 1935 moved union members to the DEMOCRATIC PARTY. Other socialists, led by Thomas, criticized much of the New Deal, especially the NATIONAL INDUSTRIAL RECOVERY ACT, which it called the framework for a fascist state. They also denounced the AGRICULTURAL ADJUSTMENT ACT for offering little to poor farmers, and the Socialist Party sponsored the formation of the SOUTHERN TENANT FARMERS UNION (STFU), a biracial group which sought to organize agricultural workers throughout the SOUTH, often at great personal risk.

The Socialist Party was also hurt by factional infighting between the moderate "old guard" (New York–based and European-born trade unionists) and two insurgent groups: progressives (including Thomas), who wanted to organize farmers and labor into a democratic socialist state; and militants (middle-class and recently converted socialists), who sought accommodation with American COMMUNISTS and cooperation with the SOVIET UNION. The split among Socialists was apparent at the party's 1934 convention, where militants pushed through a "Declaration of Principles" (supported by Thomas but opposed by the old guard), which called for war resistance through general strikes, and for organizing a socialist government if American capitalism collapsed. In the ELECTION OF 1936, with the old guard defecting to Roosevelt, Thomas was again the Socialist Party nominee, but he received only 187,720 votes (less than one-half of 1 percent). Party membership dropped to about 7,000.

With the old guard, including Hillman, moving into the Democratic Party, the militant socialists split into two groups, and were joined for a time by dissident ex-Communists until their expulsion from the Socialist Party in 1938. Thereafter, the Thomas-led progressives were in control of the party. Thomas became a leading spokesman for the ISOLATIONISTS, opposing the LEND-LEASE ACT and SELECTIVE SERVICE and appearing at AMERICA FIRST COMMITTEE rallies. In the ELECTION OF 1940, with party membership down to barely 2,000, Thomas ran for a fourth time as the Socialist Party nominee and received 99,557 votes (just one-fifth of 1 percent). After PEARL HARBOR, Socialists gave "critical support" to the war, but the party never adopted a clear statement on the conflict, as Thomas ran a fifth time for president in 1944, his vote down now to 80,518.

By the end of WORLD WAR II, the socialists, having failed to win farmers and labor, been undercut by the New Deal, and weakened by factionalism, had seen their greatest opportunity as a political force go unfulfilled. By the 1950s, they would nearly fade into oblivion.

Further reading: David A. Shannon, *The Socialist Party of America: A History* (New York: Macmillan, 1995); Frank A. Warren, *An Alternative Vision: The Socialist Party in the 1930s* (Bloomington: Indiana University Press, 1974).
—William J. Thompson

Social Security Act (1935)

The Social Security Act of 1935 was a landmark piece of NEW DEAL legislation that created the framework of the United States welfare system. The best-known feature of the legislation is what is known popularly today as "Social Security"—old-age insurance. In addition, the Social Security Act contained unemployment insurance as well as public assistance programs, including Aid to Dependent Children (renamed Aid to Families with Dependent Children in 1962), Aid to the Blind, and Old-Age Assistance (folded into Supplemental Security Income in 1972). Part of the SECOND NEW DEAL of 1935, the act was a first step to provide Americans with "freedom from want."

The social welfare system of the United States prior to the GREAT DEPRESSION had been the responsibility of state and local GOVERNMENT, together with private charities. But the economic collapse of the Great Depression quickly exhausted the resources of these traditional sources of RELIEF. When FRANKLIN D. ROOSEVELT was elected president in 1932, the nation was entering the worst winter of the depression, with UNEMPLOYMENT estimated at nearly 25 percent. As part of the FIRST NEW DEAL of 1933 of the Roosevelt presidency, CONGRESS enacted several measures to address the collapse of the ECONOMY. For desperate Americans and cash-strapped states, the FEDERAL EMERGENCY RELIEF AGENCY (FERA) was the most immediate response, providing direct assistance to the unemployed and destitute. Roosevelt, Secretary of Labor FRANCES PERKINS, and relief administrator HARRY L. HOPKINS, among others, saw FERA and direct federal relief as a temporary measure. The major work-relief program of the early New Deal, the CIVIL WORKS ADMINISTRATION provided needed jobs in the winter of 1933–34 but was terminated in the spring of 1934. By 1934, the administration wanted a permanent program that did not appear to be a handout.

The president created the Committee on Economic Security (CES) on June 29, 1934, to study and make recommendations on the problem of economic security. Headed by Perkins, the CES included Treasury Secretary HENRY MORGENTHAU, JR., and Agriculture Secretary HENRY A. WALLACE, as well as Hopkins. The committee concentrated on unemployment, old-age security, and national health insurance, and submitted its recommendations to Roosevelt on January 15, 1935. National health insurance was not included in the recommendations, for CES thought it too controversial to pass in CONGRESS, given the opposition of the American Medical Association. The CES report was sent to Congress on January 17, 1935, as the Economic Security Bill.

The legislation was part of a larger framework created in 1935 to address the continuing problems of unemployment and economic need. The Economic Security Bill was thus an omnibus measure also aimed at those considered "unemployable," meaning the elderly, CHILDREN, and the blind, and it included establishing a longer-term program for those temporarily in need when they were laid off from their job. The other side of the new 1935 framework was assistance for people able to work but who could not find jobs. The EMERGENCY RELIEF APPROPRIATION ACT (ERAA) of 1935 addressed this group by providing the unprecedented sum of nearly $5 billion to fund public works projects. Out of the ERAA came such programs as the WORKS PROGRESS ADMINISTRATION and the NATIONAL YOUTH ADMINISTRATION, as well as additional money for the CIVILIAN CONSERVATION CORPS and the PUBLIC WORKS ADMINISTRATION. Passed by Congress on April 8, 1935, the ERAA provided assistance to the unemployed through meaningful jobs, guided by the theory that the economy might be permanently stagnant and the federal government needed to step in and help provide jobs.

While working on the ERAA, Congress was also debating the Economic Security Bill, which passed the House in April by a margin of 372 to 33 and the Senate in May by 77 to 6. But in the final version of what Congress renamed the Social Security Act, the legislators did make changes to the act, some of which would have a significant impact on the course of social welfare. The old-age public assistance title was placed first, an acknowledgement of the increasing support for an old-age pension, coming most loudly from the followers of Dr. FRANCIS TOWNSEND. But a flat-grant pension such as Townsend advocated was voted down in favor of including the self-supporting old-age insurance program of the Social Security Act, providing a victory for Roosevelt and the CES bill's supporters.

The other significant changes made by Congress involved the public assistance titles. A provision allowing the federal government to determine whether each state's public assistance programs gave recipients "a reasonable subsistence compatible with decency and health" was deleted by southern conservatives, preventing effective federal control of state welfare programs. The other major change was administrative. Originally, the programs were to be administered by the Department of Labor, with Aid to Dependent Children and the maternal and child welfare programs placed in the Children's Bureau. In committee, however, Congress reorganized the administration by creating the Social Security Board (Title VII), a three-member independent agency that was given authority over all of the program except the Public Health Service and maternal and child welfare grants, both given to the Labor Department. (The board was replaced by Congress in 1946 with the Social Security Administration.)

The Social Security Act passed in the House by voice vote on August 8, 1935, and the next day passed in the Senate; it was signed into law by FDR on August 14, 1935. The first four titles of the act set up the core of the social security system. Title I, Old-Age Assistance (OAA), was public assistance for needy elderly, and like the other public assistance titles, was funded through a matching grant to the states and administered by the state welfare apparatus. Title II, Old-Age Benefits, was the centerpiece of the act, setting up a retirement system for covered workers funded by an employee payroll tax and matching contributions by employers. Unlike public assistance, this Old-Age Insurance (OAI) program as passed in 1935 was not supposed to use public funds to support the program and it was the only program to be federally administered. Title III, Unemployment Compensation (UC), set up a federal-state unemployment insurance program, funded through employee payroll deductions and employer contributions but administered by the states. Title IV, Aid to Dependent Children (ADC), provided public assistance to children deprived of parental support (usually the father's support) to allow their mothers to raise them at home. The act also included a maternal health, crippled children, and child welfare grant (Title V), which was a federal grant-in-aid to states that resurrected the defunct Sheppard-Towner Act to provide money for education and public health care for pregnant women, mothers, and young children; created the Public Health Service (Title VI); and established Aid to the Blind (Title X), a public-assistance program to support disabled individuals in the one group everyone then agreed was unable to gain employment. Taken together, the programs were aimed at two groups: the temporarily unemployed, the large group who were of working age and could not find suitable work in the current (or future) depression; and the unemployables, those groups who, due to age or disability, should be taken out of the workforce and given public support.

Together with the work-relief programs created by the Emergency Relief Appropriation Act, the Social Security Act aimed at providing Americans with what Roosevelt called protection "from cradle to grave." But just as the work-relief programs had shortcomings, the social insurance and public assistance programs also had important limitations in coverage. The most glaring was that old-age insurance and unemployment compensation excluded many worker categories, most notably agricultural and domestic workers. Also, public assistance was left to the states to establish eligibility criteria and benefits. The result was that the programs varied greatly and were vulnerable

A poster for Social Security, 1934   *(Library of Congress)*

to efforts of some states to exclude groups of Americans. Thus, AFRICAN AMERICANS, other minorities, and women, disproportionately employed in noncovered employment categories and subjected to state efforts to exclude them, received little immediate assistance from the programs of the Social Security Act. But on the positive side, proponents of an expanded social welfare system saw the act as the first step, with gaps and limitations to be addressed over the years.

The most controversial feature of the Social Security Act in 1935 was Old-Age Insurance, because of the payroll tax that funded the program. Critics argued that the payroll tax would take needed income out of the economy (payments were not scheduled to begin until 1942, when a large enough pool of funds had accumulated) and tended to favor a larger old-age pension program. Supporters of the act also feared that the SUPREME COURT would overturn the act based on the payroll tax feature, but the Court, in *Steward v. Davis* (1937) and *Helvering, et. al. v. Davis*

(1937), upheld the Social Security Act. Another potential threat to OAI was the popularity of flat grant pensions for the elderly. The idea of providing income maintenance for the elderly had been growing in popularity during the decade, and the Townsend Plan was the most visible of the many plans for the elderly. The Townsend Plan was introduced into Congress several times after 1935 as a replacement for OAI, although, because of the expense of funding a widespread pension out of general revenues, it never had a realistic chance of passage.

The Social Security Act received its first revision in 1939. One goal of Social Security officials was to strengthen the Old-Age Insurance program and thwart the old age pension movement. Benefit payments were accelerated to begin in 1940, and benefit amounts were also increased. In addition, a survivors' provision was added, making widows with underage children eligible for the employee's benefits if the employee died before retirement (Old-Age and Survivors Insurance, OASI). The amendments also made some changes to the public assistance programs, notably putting the Aid to Dependent Children program on par with Old-Age Assistance and Aid to the Blind with a 50-50 matching grant to the states.

Following the 1939 amendments, there remained gaps in the social security system that were addressed throughout the next several decades. For example, there was no national health insurance, and large numbers of workers were excluded from OASI, especially in categories that employed large numbers of women and minorities. Exclusions in coverage were addressed over the next several decades, as Congress made small changes to the programs, but the much more expansive welfare program developed by the Social Security Board during WORLD WAR II was not pursued by FDR or his successors, Harry S. Truman and Dwight D. Eisenhower.

The Social Security Act underwent its next significant revision in 1950, when disability assistance was added and a caretaker grant was put into the ADC program, greatly increasing its costs; and in 1956, disability insurance was added for those qualified for OASI (and renamed OASDI). And over time, OASDI coverage was expanded to include most workers. But while the insurance programs have remained largely intact, the public assistance programs have undergone major changes, beginning with their separation from Social Security in 1963, when the short-lived Welfare Administration was created (1963–67). In 1965, Medicare and Medicaid addressed the last major gap in coverage: providing health insurance for the retired and poor, respectively. Finally, the old-age and disabled assistance programs were folded together in 1972 to create Supplemental Security Income (SSI), while AFDC was changed to Temporary Aid to Needy Families (TANF) in 1996. Despite the flaws of the Social Security Act and its various revisions, it was a major step in the federal government providing economic security, with Social Security becoming the major source of retirement security for working Americans.

Further reading: Edward D. Berkowitz, *America's Welfare State: From Roosevelt to Reagan* (Baltimore: Johns Hopkins University Press, 1991); James T. Patterson, *America's Struggle against Poverty in the Twentieth Century* (Cambridge, Mass.: Harvard University Press, 2000); Alan Pifer and Forrest Chisman, eds., *The Report of the Committee on Economic Security of 1935 and Other Basic Documents Relating to the Development of the Social Security Act* (Washington, D.C.: National Conference on Social Welfare, 1985).

—Katherine Liapis Segrue

Solomon Islands

The fierce struggle for the Solomon Islands (and especially for GUADALCANAL) that lasted from August 1942 until December 1943 provided a significant victory for the United States over Japan in the WORLD WAR II PACIFIC THEATER.

Collectively, the Solomon Islands consists of a double chain approximately 600 miles long in the South Pacific, northeast of Australia. Green and Bougainville islands became Australian League of Nations mandates following World War I, while the islands to the southeast, including Choiseul, Rendova, Vella Lavella, Santa Isabel, Florida, the Treasury Islands, New Georgia, Tulagi, and Guadalcanal, were British protectorates. Japanese forces occupied the entire chain between January and July 1942. Guadalcanal, the southernmost island, became the construction site for a Japanese airfield that could threaten Allied supply lines to Australia.

Following the American victories at the Battle of the CORAL SEA in May 1942 and at the Battle of MIDWAY in June, General Douglas A. MacArthur and Admiral ERNEST J. KING decided to launch offensives in New Guinea and the Solomons to halt further Japanese expansion. MacArthur's forces began operations in Papua New Guinea in July 1942. In the neighboring South Pacific theater, Admiral Robert L. Ghormley, commanding U.S. NAVY and U.S. MARINES units under Rear Admiral Richmond K. "Kelly" Turner and Major General Alexander A. Vandergrift, ordered the First U.S. Marine Division to land on Guadalcanal and Tulagi islands on August 7.

While the marines surprised the Japanese on both islands, their actions brought the region to the attention of the Japanese high command, which quickly moved to reinforce Guadalcanal by sea. The marines completed the airstrip begun by the Japanese, renaming it Henderson

Field, and fought ever larger Japanese forces on the island. The Japanese, in turn, sought to control "the slot," the channel between the two Solomon chains, and harassed the marines on the island with air and naval attacks. They continued to stubbornly resist marine advances through insect-infested, thick tropical jungles into early fall. By October, the number of marines on Guadalcanal had increased to 23,000, following reinforcement by the Second Marine Division. By early December the Japanese were clearly on the defensive, the result of increased American AIR POWER and troop reinforcements, consisting of the U.S. ARMY American and 25th Infantry Divisions. This raised the number of Americans on the island to 58,000, nearly three times the Japanese strength. Between January 10 and February 7, 1943, a final American offensive secured the island following the evacuation by sea of the remaining 17,000 Japanese troops.

During the struggle for Guadalcanal, the U.S. Navy, with increased success, contested the Japanese presence in the waters of the Solomons. Following the Battle of Savo Island in August, the U.S. Navy engaged the Imperial Japanese Navy in a series of sea battles between late August 1942 and January 1943. These included the Battle of Cape Esperance, October 11–13; the Battle of the Santa Cruz Islands, October 26–27; the sea battles of Guadalcanal, November 12–15; the Battle of Tassafaronga, November 30, 1942; and the Battle of Rennell's Island, January 29–30, 1943. American control of the air and sea around the Solomons was a major reason for the Japanese withdrawal from Guadalcanal, for their position on the island became increasingly untenable.

Following the conquest of Guadalcanal, the major Japanese base at Rabaul became the next Allied objective, with forces in the Solomons coming under control of General MacArthur's Southwest Pacific theater command. MacArthur intended to reduce Rabaul through a two-pronged assault, one moving up through New Guinea, and the other advancing northwestward up the Solomons chain. American forces in the Solomons began their preparations in early 1943 under a new South Pacific commander, Admiral WILLIAM F. "BULL" HALSEY, before launching an attack that took the island of Rendova on June 30. Between July 2 and August 25, 1943, U.S. Army troops, with marine support, assaulted and secured New Georgia. The capture of Vella Lavella followed, with action taking place between August 15 and October 7. By October, the Japanese presence in the Solomons was confined to the Treasury Islands, which fell on October 27, and to the islands of Bougainville and Choiseul. These two islands were secured following a hard-fought campaign that started on November 1 and extended through late December 1943.

Although the Solomons were in Allied hands by the end of 1943, the U.S. Joint Chiefs of Staff made the decision to bypass, rather than reduce, the Japanese base at Rabaul, contrary to MacArthur's original plan. Although Allied naval and air power would continue to harass Japanese forces in the region, the Solomon Islands were no longer a scene of significant combat after 1943.

Further reading: Edwin P. Hoyt, *The Glory of the Solomons* (New York: Stein & Day, 1983); Eugene L. Rasor, *The Solomon Island Campaign, Guadalcanal to Rabaul* (Westport, Conn.: Greenwood Press, 1997).

—Clayton D. Laurie

South

Although the South remained the nation's most distinctive region in the 1929–45 era, the GREAT DEPRESSION, the NEW DEAL, and especially WORLD WAR II had a large impact on virtually every area of southern life. By 1945, a restructuring of southern AGRICULTURE, massive rural depopulation, industrial and commercial growth, and burgeoning CITIES were changing the face of the region. The Jim Crow system that segregated, disfranchised, and oppressed AFRICAN AMERICANS was beginning to undergo significant challenge, and the foundations of the Democratic "Solid South" in place since the era of the Civil War and Reconstruction were eroding.

The Great Depression exacerbated long-standing southern economic and social problems. Overwhelmingly rural, and dependent upon such staple crops as cotton and tobacco in an agricultural system where sharecropping and tenant farming mired millions in debt, poverty, and dependency, the South was in many ways a sort of agricultural colony producing raw materials and providing a market for the industrial North. The region's coal and textile industries were marked by overproduction, low prices, low wages, and dreadful conditions. In such key social or economic indexes as EDUCATION, health, and income, the South lagged well behind the rest of the nation. Economic and political power was concentrated in the hands of a small elite who resisted change. Intensifying such problems, the depression brought still more hardship upon the region and further impoverished southerners of both races.

A variety of New Deal programs—chief among them the AGRICULTURAL ADJUSTMENT ACT, the TENNESSEE VALLEY AUTHORITY, the NATIONAL RECOVERY ADMINISTRATION, and RELIEF agencies—brought attention and assistance to the South. Most southerners applauded the early New Deal, and in the ELECTION OF 1936, the South increased its overwhelming support for FRANKLIN D. ROOSEVELT to more than 80 percent of the vote. In CONGRESS, southerners in the House and Senate were at first more liberal overall than their northern counterparts. But partly because of the depth of the problems, partly because of the limits of the programs, especially when administered at the local level by people who resisted significant change, New Deal programs had but limited success. The Agricultural Adjustment Administration, for example, helped big farmers more than small ones and helped whites more than blacks, and its acreage reduction programs deprived many tenant farmers and sharecroppers of their means of subsistence. Although the New Deal energized southern liberals, efforts made by progressive white politicians and by such groups as the SOUTHERN TENANT FARMERS UNION, the Southern Conference for Human Welfare, and the CONGRESS OF INDUSTRIAL ORGANIZATIONS did little to change economic, social, or racial patterns. In releasing the National Emergency Council's *Report on Economic Conditions in the South* in 1938, which called for concentrated federal efforts for regional development in the South, President Roosevelt called the South the nation's number one economic problem.

It was World War II rather than the New Deal that brought dramatic change to the South. Billions of dollars poured into the region, which received nearly one-fifth of federal money spent on defense production and more than one-third of the money spent on military installations. Birmingham steel revived, the AIRCRAFT INDUSTRY in the Atlanta-Marietta and Dallas–Fort Worth areas burgeoned, petrochemical industries in the Gulf Coast grew rapidly, and coastal SHIPBUILDING from Norfolk to New Orleans accounted for one-quarter of the nation's ship production during the war. Most southern cities grew rapidly, as people flocked there from the rural South and from elsewhere in the nation. During and after the war, state governments initiated new development efforts to encourage industrial and commercial growth and to lure northern BUSINESS and dollars South. Although the South remained far behind the North in industrialization and urbanization, World War II catalyzed major change that increasingly would link the South to economic patterns elsewhere in the SUNBELT.

MIGRATION was another important factor changing the South and connecting it more to larger national patterns. More than 3 million people—one-fifth of the region's rural population—departed the rural South for the armed forces and for urban areas, often in the South but also in the North and West. Partly because of the exodus of so much of the farm population, farmers turned increasingly to mechanized production involving such equipment as tractors and the mechanical cotton picker. The mechanization of farming continued after the war, changing the structure of southern agriculture and contributing to the departure of millions more displaced sharecroppers and tenant farmers from the rural South in the postwar years. For their part, rural folk of both races who moved to new wartime jobs in urban areas often had no desire to return to the poverty and primitive conditions of tenant farming and sharecrop-

ping. Millions of people came South, too, especially to military bases but also to war production centers, and some of them remained or returned once the war was over.

World War II also had important implications for southern racial and political patterns. African Americans who stayed in the South or who returned there from war work or the armed forces, had tasted new opportunities and prospects. During and after the war they were increasingly ready to protest and work for change. Many northern veterans, both black and white, who passed through the South also supported CIVIL RIGHTS efforts in the postwar era because of what they had seen or experienced. Most white southerners resisted changes in the region's racial patterns, and racial tensions and conflict flared in the wartime South. There were at least six civilian riots, nearly two dozen military riots or mutinies, and dozens of lynchings. Partly because of the impact of the war upon the South, and partly because of larger national developments, including increasing support for civil rights in the North and in Washington, important challenges to the South's racial system were underway.

Even before the war, concern about challenges to Jim Crow, including proposed antilynching legislation, had contributed to a growing disaffection among southern political leaders with the national DEMOCRATIC PARTY, and as the party had increasingly pursued an agenda of urban liberalism, southern Democrats led the way in forming the CONSERVATIVE COALITION in Congress in the late 1930s and early 1940s. By the early 1940s, southerners in Congress were more conservative than northerners in the House and the Senate. Although the South gave Roosevelt 72 percent of its vote in 1944, that was down nearly 9 percentage points from 1936 and was the last time that the South voted solidly Democratic in a presidential election.

Further reading: James Cobb and Michael Namaroto, eds., *The New Deal and the South: Essays* (Jackson: University Press of Mississippi, 1984); Pete Daniel, "Going among Strangers: Southern Reactions to World War II," *Journal of American History* 77 (December 1980): 886–911; George B. Tindall, *The Emergence of the New South, 1913–1945* (Baton Rouge: Louisiana State University Press, 1967).

Southern Tenant Farmers Union (STFU)

During the GREAT DEPRESSION, the already dreadful conditions of sharecroppers, tenant farmers, and other small farmers and farm laborers in the SOUTH grew worse. These farm workers, disproportionately African American, were confronted with the loss of their livelihood as well as eviction from their homes because of a combination of low crop prices and the policies of the Agricultural Adjustment

Administration (AAA), which favored large landowners. In response, a small group of black and white sharecroppers and tenant farmers formed the Southern Tenant Farmers Union (STFU) in Arkansas in July 1934. Although met with violence, repression, economic retaliation, and threats of lynching by local officials and large landowners, the STFU, supported by NORMAN THOMAS, the Socialist Party, and the NATIONAL ASSOCIATION FOR THE ADVANCEMENT OF COLORED PEOPLE, attracted a membership of some 25,000 within a few years.

In an attempt to raise prices in AGRICULTURE, the AGRICULTURAL ADJUSTMENT ACT of 1933 subsidized farmers to limit crop production, but big landowners rarely shared these funds with the tenant farmers and sharecroppers who worked the land. Such farm workers were thus subject to both a major reduction in their already meager income and a lack of federal assistance. Additionally, when landowners were required to distribute part of the subsidies to those who lived and worked on their lands, they often evicted the workers to avoid giving them any share of the funds.

Over the next several years, the STFU organized strikes for greater compensation, led the struggles against evictions and for the direct distribution of AAA payments to tenant farmers and sharecroppers, and worked for antilynching legislation to help protect their members from violence. In January 1939, almost 2,000 tenant farmers and sharecroppers, many of them evicted from their homes, appealed for help from the federal GOVERNMENT by camping along Highway 61 in Missouri for nearly a week until they were forcibly removed. Despite such pleas, as well as requests by some federal investigators and NEW DEAL officials, neither CONGRESS nor President FRANKLIN D. ROOSEVELT responded favorably to the STFU agenda because of strong opposition by southern legislators.

Although beset by internal disputes as well as external opposition, and in sharp decline by the end of the 1930s, the STFU brought attention to the conditions of AFRICAN AMERICANS and the poor in the rural South and is considered a milestone in successful interracial LABOR organizing.

Further reading: Donald H. Grubbs, *Cry from the Center: The Southern Tenant Farmers' Union and the New Deal* (Chapel Hill: University of North Carolina Press, 1971); Gavin Wright, *Old South, New South: Revolutions in the Southern Economy since the Civil War* (New York: Basic Books, 1986).

—Aimee Alice Pohl

Soviet-American relations

The diplomatic relationship between the Soviet Union and the United States underwent considerable change from 1929 to 1945. While ideologically based tensions between the two nations—one a totalitarian marxist regime, the other a democratic capitalist state—never disappeared, Nazi Germany created pressing mutual concerns that led the United States and the Soviet Union to cooperate during WORLD WAR II. By 1945, however, old frictions and new issues produced discord, and the international structure of the postwar era would be defined largely by the developing cold war rivalry between the United States and the Soviet Union.

In 1929, the United States had no formal diplomatic relationship with the Soviet Union, having refused to recognize its Communist government as legitimate since the Bolshevik Revolution of 1917. This state of affairs did not change until President FRANKLIN D. ROOSEVELT extended official recognition to the Soviet Union in November 1933, in hope not only of normalizing relations but also of finding markets to help the American ECONOMY during the GREAT DEPRESSION. This change in FOREIGN POLICY, however, brought no significant change in the substance of Soviet-American relations.

The continuing distrust between the Soviet Union and the western democracies both helped produce and was exacerbated by the NAZI-SOVIET PACT of August 1939. The Soviets evidently felt they could not rely upon the United States, Britain, or France in the event of conflict with Germany. After signing the nonaggression treaty, they began their own campaign of territorial expansion, invading eastern Poland almost immediately and Finland in October. These actions increased anti-Soviet sentiment in the United States, as did the Soviets' signing of a neutrality pact with the Japanese in April 1941.

By late 1941, Soviet-American relations had changed dramatically. After Germany invaded the Soviet Union in June 1941, the United States extended aid to the Soviets under the LEND-LEASE ACT in the autumn. Then, with the Japanese attack on PEARL HARBOR and the American entry into the war, the Soviet Union became a part of the GRAND ALLIANCE with the United States and Great Britain and endorsed the war aims set forth in the ATLANTIC CHARTER. Because of the Japanese-Soviet neutrality pact, the Soviets did not become involved in the WORLD WAR II PACIFIC THEATER until August 1945, but the Soviet Union was included in strategic discussions throughout the remainder of the war.

The diplomatic relationship between the United States and the Soviet Union, however, was never as strong as the one between the United States and Great Britain. Significantly, the Soviets were not included in talks between the Americans and British about the potential uses of the ATOMIC BOMB and were not informed of American progress in the development of the weapon in the MANHATTAN PROJECT. (The Soviet Union did know about the project, however, as a result of its ESPIONAGE activities in the United States.)

A series of wartime conferences of the Grand Alliance illuminated differences and disagreements among its members. The "Big Three" leaders of the alliance—Franklin Roosevelt, Winston Churchill, and Joseph Stalin—met for the first time at the TEHERAN CONFERENCE in late 1943. Over British objections, Roosevelt agreed to set the invasion of Normandy for the spring of 1944 and thus open the SECOND FRONT in Europe long desired by Stalin to reduce German military pressure on his country. The decision brought Soviet-American relations to their highest point during the war, despite disagreements at Teheran about postwar plans.

By 1944, it was apparent that the United States and the Soviet Union would emerge from the war as the two remaining great powers, but the impending end of the war increased tensions. Disagreements about eastern Europe, liberated from Nazi control and then occupied by the Soviet Union, figured especially prominently. At the YALTA CONFERENCE of early 1945, Roosevelt seemed willing to allow the Soviets to create a "buffer zone" of Communist governments in eastern Europe in order to maintain Soviet-American cooperation, though with the hope that the Soviet Union would not exercise iron control over this sphere of influence. At Yalta, the Soviets agreed to take part in the postwar UNITED NATIONS and to enter the war against Japan within a few months after the surrender of Germany. In addition to eastern Europe, however, contention also arose concerning postwar Germany and other matters.

By the POTSDAM CONFERENCE in the summer of 1945, following the surrender of Germany, difficulties in the Soviet-American alliance were even clearer. Issues involving eastern Europe, Germany, and economic assistance for the Soviets remained unresolved, and Soviet-American relations were further complicated by the atomic bomb. New president Harry S. Truman continued to defend the principles of the Atlantic Charter, not wishing to be accused of selling out eastern Europe, as had happened to Roosevelt following Yalta. Stalin continued to defend the right of the Soviet Union to protect its borders from yet another invasion by surrounding itself with Communist puppet states. Such differences, partly ideological and partly involving national security concerns, became even sharper over the next year and would help dissolve the wartime alliance between the United States and the Soviet Union, replacing the world war with a cold war that would last 45 years.

See also ANGLO-AMERICAN RELATIONS.

Further reading: Robert Dallek, *Franklin D. Roosevelt and American Foreign Policy, 1932–1945* (New York:

Oxford University Press, 1979); John Lewis Gaddis, *The United States and the Origins of the Cold War, 1941–1947* (New York: Columbia University Press, 1972); Ralph B. Levering, *American Opinion and the Russian Alliance, 1939–1945* (Chapel Hill: University of North Carolina Press, 1976); William Hardy McNeil, *America, Britain, and Russia: Their Cooperation and Conflict, 1941–1946* (New York: Oxford University Press, 1953).

—Mary E. Carroll-Mason

Spanish Civil War

The Spanish Civil War, which lasted from July 1936 to April 1939, pitted Spain's existing government, the Republic, against a Nationalist movement led by General Francisco Franco. The conflict had repercussions far beyond Spain. The Soviet Union sent military equipment and advisers to its allies on the leftist Republican side, while Fascist Italy and Nazi Germany supported the fascist Nationalists with equipment and tens of thousands of troops, and used the situation to test new military technology and techniques. France and Britain, fearful of a wider conflict, gave no aid to the Republic. Reflecting the power of ISOLATIONISTS and the political influence of the anti-Republic Catholic Church, the United States remained officially neutral throughout the war and imposed an arms embargo against both sides.

Most Americans were apathetic toward or ignorant about the Spanish Civil War. Two-thirds of those polled in 1937 had no opinion about it. These responses reflected interwar isolationist tendencies and a preoccupation with the GREAT DEPRESSION. Having witnessed the catastrophes of World War I, the great majority of Americans opposed entry into another conflict in Europe. In addition, most Americans in the 1930s were more interested in the ECONOMY and their own circumstances than in FOREIGN POLICY and events overseas.

American support for Franco came largely from CATHOLICS aroused by reports of anticlerical acts committed by the Republic, which was seeking to lessen the power and influence of the Catholic Church in Spanish daily life. The American Catholic Church urged support of Franco, who, with papal backing, was seeking the reunification of church and state in Spain. In addition, many American Catholics were swayed by Franco's argument that he was fighting for the establishment of democratic government and against encroaching communism and socialism.

Support for the Republic in the United States came especially from Protestants and Jews on the political left. Seeing the conflict as one between fascism and democracy, they expected the Republic to establish a permanent liberal democracy, abolish unification of church and state, and improve education and the rights of women and children. They organized parades and other demonstrations of support for the Republic and raised money for relief supplies. Ernest Hemingway's novel, *For Whom the Bell Tolls,* provides a sympathetic account of the Republic's supporters.

The most radical leftists committed to the Republic volunteered to fight in Spain against Franco. Largely organized by the COMMUNISTS, the International Brigades, formed to support the Republic's army, drew men from across Europe and the United States. The most notable American contingent was the Abraham Lincoln Battalion of the XV International Brigade (popularly known as the Abraham Lincoln Brigade). The approximately 3,000 men who volunteered for the Lincoln Brigade from 1936 to 1938 came from a variety of occupational and ethnic backgrounds but what they shared was their passionate support of the Republic's liberal cause and the fight against fascism.

President FRANKLIN D. ROOSEVELT and Secretary of State CORDELL HULL maintained American neutrality during the Spanish Civil War. The president, although later regretful about what he understood to have been a mistaken course of action, was influenced both by Catholics, whose political support he wanted, and by the pervasive anti-interventionism that helped produce the NEUTRALITY ACTS of the mid-1930s. In any case, Spain was not among his priorities in the mid-1930s. The State Department, influenced by the British decision against intervention, sought neutrality partly because of concerns that the Soviet-backed and increasingly communist-dominated Republic might lead to the establishment of a communist state. Roosevelt initially urged a "moral embargo" on arms to both sides, and CONGRESS acceded to his subsequent recommendation that the arms embargo of the Neutrality Acts be extended to the Spanish Civil War.

As the war continued, American supporters of the Republic demanded lifting the embargo so that munitions and medical supplies could be sent to aid the failing Republican forces. As Franco's fascist intentions and brutal warfare, including the bombing of civilians, became clearer, others joined the campaign. Secretary of Commerce HAROLD ICKES said of Hull's refusal to issue passports to Americans who wanted to serve as ambulance drivers for the Republic, "It makes me ashamed." Even isolationist senator Gerald Nye, chairman of the NYE COMMITTEE, urged lifting the arms embargo. But the United States maintained the embargo until the end of the Civil War on April 1, 1939, when the Republic surrendered to Franco. For those Americans who actively supported one side or another, passions and animosities provoked by the conflict resonated for years.

Further reading: Allen Guttman, *The Wound in the Heart: America and the Spanish Civil War* (New York: Free Press, 1962); Douglas Little, *Malevolent Neutrality: The United States, Great Britain, and the Origins of the Spanish Civil War* (Ithaca, N.Y.: Cornell University Press, 1985).

—David Slak

sports

During the 1920s, American sports experienced a golden age, as stadiums and arenas filled with spectators cheering their teams and athletic heroes. Sports had become as central to American POPULAR CULTURE as ART, LITERATURE, MUSIC, and the MOVIES. The onset of the GREAT DEPRESSION and the decline or retirement of star golden age athletes, however, made the 1930s a decade of uncertainty—but ultimately also one of innovation—in American sports. Sports and the appearance of new stars and fan-friendly rule changes gave depression-era Americans a diversion from harsh economic realities. Financially, sports, like other sectors of the ECONOMY, struggled in the early 1930s, but recovered later in the decade. Annual spending on spectator sports, which had risen to $66 million by 1929, fell to $47 million in 1932 but then climbed steadily to $107 million in 1941.

WORLD WAR II brought new challenges for sports, but Americans from President FRANKLIN D. ROOSEVELT on down were determined that sporting pursuits should continue whenever possible as a morale booster for the nation. The subpar quality of competition arising from so many men away at war did not deter Americans from attending sporting events, although receipts fell to $62 million by 1943 before rising to $80 million in 1944 and a new record $116 million in 1945.

Baseball

During the 1920s, baseball, "the national pastime," had reached new heights of popularity, thanks in large part to the explosion of offense featuring Babe Ruth and the home run. Then, with the onset of the depression, attendance and revenue dropped, player salaries were cut, and the sport struggled financially.

Baseball remained resilient, however, and survived the decade's economic crisis, due in part to innovations that became integral parts of the game. The "farm system" of minor-league franchises allowed poorer baseball clubs to compete with wealthier rivals, who could buy top prospects, by developing talent at less cost. Night baseball, originating in the minor leagues, was brought to the reluctant majors, first in Cincinnati in 1935, then in Brooklyn in 1938, as a means to stimulate sagging attendance and to attract working-class and younger fans to ball games. The

1930s also saw the inauguration of the mid-season All-Star Game, featuring the American and National Leagues' best players, and the opening of the Hall of Fame Museum in Cooperstown, New York.

On the field, the New York Yankees, baseball's dominant team in the Ruth era of the 1920s, became so again by the mid-1930s, winning four consecutive World Series from 1936 to 1939, led by JOE DIMAGGIO. In the world of segregated baseball, the Negro Leagues survived the depression, due to stable financial backing—albeit much of it from gambling interests—and to talented players such as Josh Gibson and Satchel Paige, who were the equal of the best white major leaguers. But major league baseball remained resistant to integration, a situation unchanged until 1946, when Jackie Robinson was signed by the Brooklyn Dodgers.

After PEARL HARBOR, baseball was given the green light to continue by Roosevelt, who deemed it important to national morale. But baseball was adversely affected by the war as many players joined the military, leaving major league squads composed of aging veterans, inexperienced youngsters, and players rejected by draft boards because of assorted physical problems.

Football

Football's popularity during the 1920s lay primarily with the college game, as large crowds filled campus stadiums to root for regional favorites, or for "national" teams such as Army, Navy, and especially Knute Rockne's Notre Dame. Professional football, on the other hand, was small-town and blue-collar, with many teams located in smaller cities such as Green Bay, Wisconsin, and Canton, Ohio.

Notre Dame's dominance of college football ended for a time after Rockne's death in a 1931 airplane crash, and gridiron supremacy passed to Minnesota, Alabama, Stanford, and others. Among the top college players of the 1930s, Don Hutson of Alabama and Sammy Baugh of Texas Christian became important to the growing professional game, and Jay Berwanger of Chicago (who never played professionally) won the first Heisman Trophy in 1936 as the best collegiate in the nation. The economic health of college football remained strong, as evidenced by creation of the Orange, Sugar, and Cotton Bowls as rivals to the Rose Bowl.

World War II greatly affected college football, as more than 300 schools temporarily dropped the sport. The Rose Bowl was moved east from California, and teams played with 17 year-olds, wounded veterans, and young men rejected by the draft. The strongest wartime teams were schools with naval training programs, military bases such as Great Lakes Naval Training Station, and the service academies—especially Army, which went undefeated in 1944 and 1945.

The National Football League (NFL) gained respectability in the 1930s—helped by the 1927 signing of college star Red Grange (by the Chicago Bears, the era's dominant pro team)—and expanded into more of the larger cities. The NFL split itself into two divisions, with the winners meeting for the league championship. In addition, the college player draft was instituted in 1936 to allow more competitive balance, and rule changes were made to increase offense, such as allowing the *T* formation.

During World War II, dozens of NFL players saw military service, forcing teams to cut rosters and merge franchises. In 1943, the Philadelphia Eagles and Pittsburgh Steelers became the "Steagles"—and a year later, the Steelers and Chicago Cardinals merged into "Card-Pitt" (or because of their 0-10 record, "Carpets").

Basketball

Basketball had advanced since its peach-basket origins, but the style of play was slowed by center jumps after each basket, and it was still a regional sport, most popular in New York City, Philadelphia, the Midwest, and on the West Coast. In 1934, Ned Irish, a New York sportswriter, introduced the doubleheader at Madison Square Garden, and soon attracted college teams from around the country. The center jump after each basket was eliminated after 1937, opening up play, producing more offense, and enabling the emergence of star players such as Stanford's Hank Luisetti, who utilized the one-handed jump shot in an era still dominated by the two-handed set shot. The popularity of the Garden doubleheaders led to establishment of the New York–based, postseason National Invitation Tournament (NIT) in 1938, and the NCAA Tournament the following year.

Meanwhile, professional basketball languished in obscure eastern and midwestern leagues, denied access to Madison Square Garden and other major arenas, with teams owned by businessmen whose players often worked for the owner's company as their primary jobs. The best pro teams in the 1930s were barnstorming African-American teams, especially the Harlem Globetrotters. during World War II, basketball benefited from the increased height of players (many rejected for military service), bringing new interest to the sport and producing the first star "big man," 6'10" George Mikan of DePaul University and later the Minneapolis Lakers.

Boxing

Boxing in the 1920s was dominated by the rivalry between heavyweights Jack Dempsey and Gene Tunney, and most important bouts occurred at Madison Square Garden, the mecca of boxing. During the early 1930s, boxing experienced difficulties as Dempsey and Tunney faded from the scene, promoters lost money, and the sport's already suspect image was further enhanced by criminal wrongdoing, primarily in fixing fights.

The African-American boxer JOE LOUIS helped boxing rebuild its popularity and credibility with epic fights against the German Max Schmeling that coincided with the rise to power of Hitler and the Nazis. After losing to Schmeling by a 12-round technical knockout in July 1936, Louis dispatched Schmeling with a quick TKO only two minutes into the first round in June 1938. As the most prominent black athlete of his generation, Louis's accomplishments were welcomed with pride by AFRICAN AMERICANS.

Boxing was affected by World War II, as outdoor fights were virtually eliminated because of blackout regulations, prize purses were lowered, and percentages of money were given over to the war effort. Most star fighters were in military service, including Louis, whose celebrity was used to boost the war effort among African Americans by touring bases and staging exhibition bouts.

Golf

At the end of the 1920s, golf was played and governed primarily by the country club elite that considered the amateur, as personified by Bobby Jones, the outstanding player of the decade, as the true embodiment of the sport. Professional golf was a loosely organized seasonal activity, with uneven purses, and was looked down upon by the club amateurs.

The 1930s brought technical changes to golf and the growth of the professional tour. Two major innovations were the sand wedge, used to hit the ball out of course hazards, and the steel-shafted club, which replaced wooden shafts and gave golfers more driving power. The Professional Golfers Association (PGA) struggled early in the decade, but was energized by Bobby Jones's creation of the Master's Tournament in 1934, a year-round schedule, more sponsors putting up more money for purses and player endorsements, and rising young stars such as Byron Nelson and Sam Snead. Women's professional golf was boosted with the addition of Mildred "Babe" Didrikson, an Olympic track-and-field champion of 1932 and a great all-around athlete.

World War II affected golf, as many players served in the military, foreign tournaments were discontinued, and events in the United States were curtailed. In addition, purses were reduced or a percentage given to WAR BONDS, and the ball's quality diminished due to rubber shortages. Nelson's record 11 consecutive tournament victories in 1945 set the stage for golf's postwar resurgence.

Tennis

In the 1920s, tennis was even more of a preserve of amateurism than was golf, and the patricians who dominated eastern clubs barred professionals from major tourna-

Mildred "Babe" Didrikson (Zaharias) *(Hulton/Archive)*

ments. The 1930s brought a new group of talented young players who would transform men's and women's tennis. Although tennis was still run by the eastern elite, the best American players (especially the men) came from California: Bobby Riggs, Jack Kramer, and the top performer of the 1930s, Don Budge, who in 1938 won the Grand Slam by winning the sport's four major titles (the Australian, French, and U.S. Opens, and the tournament at Wimbledon). Women's tennis in the 1930s was dominated first by Helen Wills Moody—a star from the 1920s—then by Helen Jacobs, Alice Marble, and Sarah Palfrey. Tennis was affected by World War II as international tournaments were stopped, the professional tour was curtailed due to travel restrictions, most players were in military service, and the ball, made of reclaimed (that is, recycled) rubber, bounced poorly. After the war, while most top U.S. players turned professional, leadership in the still-dominant amateur game passed to the Australians for the next generation.

Track-and-Field

American prowess in track-and-field throughout the 1930s was concentrated in the sprint events—the 100, 200, and 400 meters, plus relays—and the long jump, where a number of African-American runners—Ralph Metcalfe, Eddie Tolan, Mack Robinson, and especially JESSE OWENS—dominated world and Olympic events. In 1932, the Olympic Summer Games were held in Los Angeles, and Americans dominated the track events, with the star performer being a woman, Babe Didrikson, who won two gold medals, in the javelin and 80 meter hurdles. Four years later, the games were held in Berlin as a showcase for Nazi superiority, a goal ruined by victories by Owens and the other African-American track stars. Track-and-field nearly ceased during World War II as athletes served in the military, meets were reduced, and international events were cancelled, including the Olympics of 1940 and 1944.

Hockey

Ice hockey, Canada's national sport, had arrived professionally in the United States during the 1920s with National Hockey League (NHL) franchises in Boston, Chicago, Detroit, and New York. The players, however, were predominantly Canadian, even as American franchises won a number of Stanley Cup titles. During World War II, American and Canadian players went into military service, and in 1944 the number of franchises was reduced to six, a number that would remain unchanged until the NHL expanded twenty-three years later.

Horse Racing

Thoroughbred racing in the 1920s was dominated by old wealthy families such as the Vanderbilts and Whitneys, with racetracks in only a few states, and few legal outlets for wagering (leaving betting in the hands of bookmakers). After suffering in the early years of the depression, racing experienced a resurgence by the mid- to late 1930s, for several reasons: States re-legalized betting under the parimutuel system (winnings divided in proportion to sums individually wagered); California legalized racing and a new track was built at Santa Anita, in Los Angeles; and the rivalry between War Admiral, the 1937 Triple Crown winner, and Seabiscuit, who became the all-time prize winner (with $437,730 in earnings). World War II saw a temporary decline in racing, a result of gasoline and tire shortages affecting transportation of thoroughbreds. In December, 1944, OFFICE OF WAR MOBILIZATION czar JAMES F. BYRNES ordered horse racing to suspend operations; racing did not resume until V-E DAY.

Further reading: Douglas Noverr, *The Games They Played: Sports in American History* (Chicago: Nelson-Hall, 1983); Benjamin G. Rader, *American Sports: From the Age of Folk Games to the Age of Televised Sports*, 3d ed. (Englewood Cliffs, N.J.: Prentice Hall, 1996).

—William J. Thompson

steel industry

Once the backbone of the American ECONOMY, the steel industry was hit hard by the GREAT DEPRESSION. Production, employment, and profits all plummeted in the early 1930s, and then the industry underwent internal conflict between LABOR and management. However, with the national MOBILIZATION for WORLD WAR II, the steel industry recovered and gave vital support to the U.S. war effort.

When the Great Depression struck, the steel industry saw its output drop by some 60 percent or more by 1933, primarily because of the decreased purchases of such consumer goods as automobiles and lower capital investment in factories and machinery on the part of American BUSINESS. UNEMPLOYMENT among steelworkers climbed to staggering figures, sometimes reaching 50 percent and more, and many of the remaining workers suffered from cuts in hours and wages. By the mid-1930s, the economy had improved from the depths of the depression, and steel mills increased production, partly because of GOVERNMENT public works projects established under the NEW DEAL. The industry still had considerable excess capacity, however.

Also in the mid-1930s, JOHN L. LEWIS of the Committee for Industrial Organization (later the CONGRESS OF INDUSTRIAL ORGANIZATIONS) saw an opportunity to unionize the steel industry. Helped by the NATIONAL LABOR RELATIONS ACT of 1935, Lewis established the Steel Workers Organizing Committee (SWOC) headed by PHILIP MURRAY as part of his effort to unionize the mass-production industries. The steel industry had in the past witnessed epic labor-management battles, and another seemed to loom ahead.

A struggle ensued, though steel was spared the worst of the potential labor conflict. After General Motors came to an agreement with autoworkers in February 1937 following the sit-down strike at GM's Flint, Michigan, plant, the powerful U.S. Steel Corporation quickly recognized the SWOC in order to avoid such an experience. The so-called Little Steel companies (Republic, Bethlehem, and others) resisted unionization until the early 1940s, and in the summer of 1937 their opposition led to bloody confrontations that resulted in the death of 18 steelworkers. Nonetheless, the agreement between U.S. Steel and the SWOC was crucial not just for the steel industry but for the unionization of American industry more generally.

The sharp RECESSION OF 1937–38 sent production and employment in the steel industry spiraling downward again, but real recovery at last began with the outbreak of World War II in Europe in 1939. The industry saw its production increase to meet the needs of other nations as well as the American rearmament effort, and by the early 1940s the industry far exceeded predepression levels. The production of steel ingots and castings, which had plunged from 56 million long tons in 1929 to 14 million in 1932, rose to 47 million in 1939 and then increased to 74 million by 1941 and 80 million by 1944. Like the AUTOMOBILE INDUSTRY, however, the steel industry resisted expanding and converting to defense production until after PEARL HARBOR, for it did not want to forego the recovering market for consumer goods and feared excess capacity.

When the United States. entered World War II, steel became a strategic material used in the production of a huge variety of equipment needed for the war effort. The SHIPBUILDING industry was a major consumer of steel because of the need for steel for U.S. NAVY combat vessels as well as the humble, but no less vital, "liberty ship" cargo vessels. The U.S. ARMY also needed large quantities of steel for ammunition, transport vehicles, weapons, and tanks, and all of the military services needed millions of helmets, mess tins, gas cans, canteens, and many other items requiring steel. Increased output during the war also meant expanded and modernized plants that made the American steel industry the most productive in the world.

This change to wartime production came at the expense of consumer goods. The automobile industry, for example, stopped production of new cars when it converted to war production. At the same time, the war brought full-employment prosperity to the nation and a desire to spend again after the deprivations of the depression decade. When World War II ended in 1945, this pent-up demand for consumer goods together with wartime savings and relatively quick RECONVERSION to peacetime production helped the steel industry avoid contraction. The postwar period was a time of continued health for the industry—until steel from newer mills in Germany and Japan that the United States had helped to build after the war led to the contraction of the American steel industry.

Further reading: John Barnard, *Walter Reuther and the Rise of the Auto Workers* (Boston: Little, Brown, 1983); Irving Bernstein, *The Turbulent Years: A History of the American Worker, 1933–1941* (Boston: Houghton Mifflin, 1970); Richard A. Lauderbaugh, *American Steel Makers and the Coming of the Second World War* (Ann Arbor, Mich.: UMI Research Press, 1980).

—Nicholas Fry

Steinbeck, John (1902–1968)

The celebrated writer John Steinbeck is best known for his Pulitzer Prize–winning novel, *The Grapes of Wrath* (1939), which quickly became the dominant fictional account of the impact of the GREAT DEPRESSION. One of the major figures in mid-20th-century American LITERATURE, Steinbeck also won the Nobel Prize in literature in 1962.

Born in Salinas, California, on February 27, 1902, Steinbeck began writing and submitting his work for pub-

lication at the age of 15. After finishing high school, he entered Stanford University but left before finishing a degree. As a young man, Steinbeck worked a number of jobs to support his writing career, including a stint in farming and processing sugar beets, which gave him insight into California farm life that would later serve as the background for many of his novels. He remained virtually unknown until the publication of *Tortilla Flat* in 1935.

During the 1930s, work as a journalist offered Steinbeck the opportunity to gather the material for his novels *In Dubious Battle* (1936), *Of Mice and Men* (1937), and *The Grapes of Wrath* (1939). His experiences interviewing farm-labor organizer Cecil McKiddy and countless "Okies" who had streamed into California's Central Valley from Oklahoma looking for work allowed him to depict the plight of rural Americans displaced by the depression with startling realism. The trials of the Joad family in *The Grapes of Wrath* gave many Americans their first glimpse of the suffering experienced by refugees from the DUST BOWL of the Great Plains. To this day, *The Grapes of Wrath* provides the archetypal portrayal of the American experience of the Great Depression. Steinbeck's stark realism and his sympathy for his hopelessly dispossessed subjects, however, left him open to accusations of leftist tendencies—and indeed the novel was one of social protest.

After the United States entered WORLD WAR II, Steinbeck worked for several government information agencies on a volunteer basis. At this time, he wrote the novel *The Moon Is Down* (1942), which once again embroiled him in controversy. While *The Moon Is Down* ultimately depicted Western democracy as superior to Nazi tyranny, Steinbeck's characterization of German officers as ordinary men in the service of an evil dictator through circumstance rather than conviction raised questions about his loyalties. These questions left Steinbeck unable to join the army air corps, and instead he accepted an assignment as war correspondent for the *New York Herald-Tribune*.

The years after World War II brought significant problems for Steinbeck personally and professionally. Literary critics dismissed his nostalgic novel *Cannery Row* (1945) as trite and sentimental, and his second marriage suddenly failed not long after. In addition, the painfully shy Steinbeck continued to be dogged by the demands of literary stardom and lingering questions about his political beliefs. These pressures caused a severe nervous breakdown.

Following his recovery, Steinbeck's fiction focused on the exploration of failed family relationships and the values of middle-class America with such works as *The Winter of Our Discontent* (1947) and *East of Eden* (1952). The literary establishment continued to disparage Steinbeck's work, even after he was awarded the Nobel Prize in literature in 1962. This course of events prompted Steinbeck to turn increasingly toward journalistic and travel writing. After serving for a brief time as a war correspondent in Vietnam, John Steinbeck died in New York City on December 20, 1968. His work, in its political content and literary quality, remains controversial for both popular and academic audiences.

Further reading: Jackson J. Benson, *The True Adventures of John Steinbeck, Writer: A Biography* (New York: Viking, 1984).

—Mary E. Carroll-Mason

Stimson, Henry L. (1867–1950)

Henry Lewis Stimson served as secretary of state from 1929 to 1933 under President HERBERT C. HOOVER and as secretary of war from 1940 to 1945 under Presidents FRANKLIN D. ROOSEVELT and Harry S. Truman. He had previously served as secretary of war from 1911 to 1913 under President William Howard Taft.

Born in New York City on September 21, 1867, Stimson was educated at Andover, Yale University, and Harvard Law School. After joining the law firm of Root and Clark in 1891, Stimson moved up through Republican political circles to a post on the New York County Republican Committee and served as the U.S. attorney for the southern district of New York between 1906 and 1909. After running unsuccessfully for governor of New York in 1910, Stimson joined the law firm of Bronson Winthrop before accepting President Taft's nomination as secretary of war. In this post, from May 11, 1911, to March 4, 1913, Stimson built upon reforms and reorganizations begun by his predecessor and law partner Elihu Root, and greatly increased the power and influence of the civilian secretary over the army high command. Following Taft's defeat for reelection in 1912, Stimson returned to the practice of law.

Stimson joined the army in 1917 and as a lieutenant colonel in the 31st Field Artillery served in France between December 1917 and August 1918. After practicing law again following his service in World War I, Stimson became a presidential emissary to Nicaragua in 1927 and was then governor-general of the PHILIPPINES between 1927 and 1929. Nominated in March 1929 by President Hoover to serve as secretary of state, Stimson held that post until March 1933. During his tenure, Stimson chaired the American delegation to the 1930 LONDON NAVAL CONFERENCE. Although his name was attached to the Stimson Doctrine of nonrecognition and nonintervention when the Japanese took control of MANCHURIA in 1931–32, Stimson wanted a stronger American response, and throughout the 1930s was an ardent opponent of fascism and an advocate of a more active FOREIGN POLICY against militarism. Following his

service as secretary of state, Stimson once again returned to his law practice.

In July 1940, wanting to give his cabinet a bipartisan look, President Franklin D. Roosevelt nominated Stimson as secretary of war. Immediately upon his confirmation, which was opposed by conservative and isolationist members of his own REPUBLICAN PARTY, Stimson began to give order and direction to a War Department badly in need of both after decades of retrenchments and neglect. He quickly surrounded himself with a group of able civilian aides, including Robert A. Lovett, Robert P. Patterson, and John J. McCloy, and established a good working relationship with chief of staff GEORGE C. MARSHALL. Stimson was a strong advocate of conscription and led the effort for the SELECTIVE SERVICE Act in the fall of 1940. Soon after the United States entered WORLD WAR II, Stimson became closely involved with the RELOCATION OF JAPANESE AMERICANS from the West Coast, a decision that disturbed him but which he nonetheless felt was necessary. Although he appointed a black adviser on racial matters and made Benjamin O. Davis the army's first African-American general, he opposed desegregating the U.S. ARMY.

As the war progressed, Roosevelt increasingly bypassed Stimson on questions of strategy, tactics, and operations, choosing to confer with General Marshall directly. The president, however, trusted Stimson's judgment on military and administrative matters and relied on Stimson's capacity for hard work and his able management of the War Department. (Stimson for his part thought FDR a poor administrator.) From the outset, Stimson pushed development of the ATOMIC BOMB, and shortly after Roosevelt's death on April 12, 1945, he advised incoming president Harry S. Truman about its existence and potential.

Although Stimson appeared stern, reserved, and forbidding, he was also considered a man of high moral principles and advocated absolute candor in public affairs. He was reputed to have opposed CODE BREAKING as a form of ESPIONAGE, saying that gentlemen did not read other gentlemen's mail. Stepping down as secretary of war on September 21, 1945, Stimson retired to his Long Island estate, where he died at age 83 on October 20, 1950.

Further reading: Godfrey Hodgson, *The Colonel: The Life and Wars of Henry Stimson, 1867–1950* (New York: Knopf, 1990); Elting E. Morison, *Turmoil and Tradition: A Study of the Life and Times of Henry L. Stimson* (Boston: Houghton Mifflin, 1960).

—Clayton D. Laurie

stock market crash (1929)

The collapse of prices on the American stock market in late October 1929 has come to symbolize the end of the prosperity of the 1920s and the beginning of the long decade of the GREAT DEPRESSION. But while the stock market crash was a shocking and significant event, the ECONOMY was already in trouble and the market crash itself did not cause the depression.

After declining early in the autumn of 1929, stock prices fell sharply on October 23. The next day, "Black Thursday," a record high 12.9 million shares were traded, as panicked selling drove stock prices down still further before major bankers succeeded in rallying prices and confidence. Then on "Black Tuesday," October 29, the bottom dropped out of the stock market, with more than 16 million shares changing hands in a stampede of liquidation. By November, the value of industrial stocks had plummeted to just half of their September high—and prices continued generally down for the next three years. By 1932, the total price of all stocks on the New York Stock Exchange had fallen by more than 80 percent. For the stocks of some of the leading industrial and commercial companies, the collapse of prices was devastating: General Electric and RCA fell by 98 percent from 1929 to 1932, for example; Sears, Roebuck by 95 percent; and U.S. Steel by 92 percent. It took the stock market until 1954 to regain 1929 levels.

The basic reason for the stock market crash is that by 1929 stock prices were so high, out of a sound relation to the real value of the stocks, that a decline was virtually inevitable. Throughout much of the 1920s, there had been a steady rise in stock prices, largely reflecting solid investments in companies doing well in an expanding economy. But in 1928, get-rich-quick speculation increasingly displaced careful investment, and trading and prices on the stock market exploded. The volume of sales on the New York Stock Exchange nearly doubled from 1927 to 1929, and the prices of the major industrial stocks doubled just between May 1928 and September 1929. Though by some analyses prices of most stocks were not hugely out of line with earnings and potential, many were seriously overpriced—and the general high price level rested on confidence that both individual firms and the "new economy," would continue to grow and prosper.

A number of factors had caused the spectacular bull market of 1928–29. The expansion of the American economy after the 1921–22 recession produced a confident expectation of continued prosperity. Worried about attracting too much gold to the United States and thus weakening the international financial system, the Federal Reserve Board lowered interest rates in 1927, facilitating heavy borrowing by investors and speculators. Stockbrokers' call loans were easy to get—often requiring a margin payment from their borrowers of only a small fraction of a stock's current price, with the stock itself serving as collateral for the loan. Major corporations by the late 1920s increasingly were putting their large cash reserves into the stock market rather than into plant expansion, while commercial banks put more and more money into the stock market instead of into commercial loans. The unregulated stock market enabled stock promoters to put out inflated (often simply dishonest) information and prospectuses. And as prices shot up in 1928 and 1929, a speculative buying momentum drove prices up still further, despite tighter money policies by the Federal Reserve. In retrospect, it is clear that market prices were dangerously high, and that a downward correction or readjustment was almost sure to come.

The readjustment, which became the crash, then occurred in the late summer and fall of 1929. Evidence that the economy was slowing led some stockholders to sell their shares in order to take their profits before prices fell. Instability on the London Stock Exchange unsettled the American market. As some prices began to fall, investors and speculators alike became concerned about the future, and an increase in orders to sell stocks caused sharp price declines. Nervous brokers began to call loans on declining stocks, which caused still more liquidation. What had been a speculative dynamic that sent prices up became a panicked dynamic driving them down in a ferocious bear market. The stock market buckled in mid-October, broke on "Black Thursday," and then collapsed on "Black Tuesday." The doubling of industrial stock prices that had occurred in the previous 16 months was wiped out in just two months. The market would continue to spiral down to its nadir some three years later.

The consequences of the Great Crash were serious, though often exaggerated or misunderstood. At most, some 2 or 3 percent of the population owned stock, and few were so heavily invested that the crash produced bankruptcy or impoverishment. Tales of suicidal leaps from tall buildings are essentially myth. And the Great Crash did not by itself cause or begin the Great Depression; indeed, some scholars assign it a relatively small role in the collapse of the economy. But the crash was a stunning event with large impact and evidently played some role in the development of the Great Depression. It dashed much of the economic confidence of the 1920s, illuminated weak spots in the economy, weakened the vulnerable banking system, inhibited consumer spending and private investment that might have helped buoy the economy, and helped to dry up American loans overseas that had supported the international economy. The stock market crash and investigations launched by CONGRESS also helped to bring about NEW DEAL reforms of the stock market and the creation of the SECURITIES AND EXCHANGE COMMISSION as the regulatory agency to enforce new standards.

Further reading: John Kenneth Galbraith, *The Great Crash* (Boston: Houghton Mifflin, 1955); Maury Klein,

Rainbow's End: The Crash of 1929 (New York: Oxford University Press, 2001).

submarines

Submarines played a major role in WORLD WAR II. The invention of electric motors in the 1880s and of internal combustion engines in the early 1900s made the submarine a practical vessel, and by the time of World War I, submarines had made major advances, able to reach surface speeds of 16 knots and 10 knots submerged, and carrying crews of 35 or more. Armed with torpedoes and deck guns, submarines revolutionized sea warfare and posed new dangers to merchant shipping. The Germans, in particular, excelled at such warfare and in World War I their U-boats threatened Allied commerce and the viability of the British blockade.

During World War II, the Germans, Americans, British, Japanese, and Italians launched several thousand larger and more powerful "blue water" boats capable of high seas operation and difficult to detect. Crew sizes, tonnage, and lethality doubled. Germany built more than 1,160 U-boats and seriously contested Allied control of the Atlantic between 1939 and 1943. During the BATTLE OF THE ATLANTIC, Germany lost some 785 submarines, more than any other belligerent—but the U-boats also sank nearly 2,600 Allied merchantmen totaling some 14.5 million tons gross weight.

British submarines sank 169 warships and 493 merchant vessels, while suffering 74 losses, about 33 percent of the total British submarine force during the war. In the Mediterranean, British submarines impeded the supply of AXIS forces in the NORTH AFRICAN CAMPAIGN, contributing significantly to their May 1943 defeat. Although Italy possessed some 150 submarines, vastly superior British anti-submarine tactics restricted their use, and 86 Italian submarines were lost with only six enemy warships and 500,000 tons of destroyed merchant shipping claimed in return.

U.S. NAVY submarines in the Pacific destroyed Japanese merchant shipping between 1943 and 1945 to the point that enemy offensive operations were made impossible. Although having to overcome early defects in torpedo design, the 288 U.S. submarines sank nearly 1,300 Japanese merchantmen as well as one battleship, eight aircraft carriers, and 11 cruisers. Fifty-two American submarines were sunk. The 200 submarines ultimately comprising Japan's submarine force did not register significant successes, although they sank a score of American warships and about 170 merchant and transport vessels while losing 128 of their own.

Little is known of Soviet submarines during the war, although they were active in the Baltic and Black Sea areas.

With Soviet submarines technologically inferior to the boats of other powers, it has been speculated that the Soviets lost one submarine for each enemy ship sunk.

Further reading: Erminio Bagnasco, *Submarines of World War II* (Annapolis, Md.: Naval Institute Press, 1977); Norman Friedman, *U.S. Submarines through 1945: An Illustrated Design History* (Annapolis, Md.: Naval Institute Press, 1995); Brayton Harris and Walter J. Boyne, *The Navy Times Book of Submarines: A Political, Social, and Military History* (New York: Berkeley, 1997).

—Clayton D. Laurie

suburbs

Residential suburbs grew in the 1920s because of prosperity, technological developments including the increased use of automobiles and electricity, and a desire by many Americans to live outside the CITIES. A declining housing market in the late 1920s, followed by the onset of the GREAT DEPRESSION, slowed suburban expansion, but a number of NEW DEAL programs under President FRANKLIN D. ROOSEVELT helped the housing industry and spurred suburban growth by the mid-1930s. Innovative ADVERTISING schemes and new TECHNOLOGY in HOUSING enhanced the allure of suburbs, and WORLD WAR II further accelerated economic and population growth in the suburban areas of metropolitan centers. As people sought to escape deteriorating and crowded conditions and undesirable housing in the central cities, the suburban population growth rate jumped from 12 to 32 percent from the 1930s to the 1940s.

Roosevelt's rallying cry of "get building going" was an attempt to increase construction and put builders back to work, but he also took steps to help homeowners who were in danger of foreclosure. The HOME OWNERS LOAN CORPORATION (HOLC) took the initiative by providing funds for assisting banks with defaulted loans and refinancing low-cost mortgages for middle-class homeowners. The success of the HOLC helped win support for other New Deal policies including the FEDERAL HOUSING ADMINISTRATION (FHA), which stimulated the building and purchasing of new homes in the suburbs. FHA policy also had the effect, not always intended, of reinforcing the white, middle-class character of the suburbs.

Under the auspices of the RESETTLEMENT ADMINISTRATION (RA), the Greenbelt New Towns program aimed to relocate urban workers to rental communities outside cities where they would be involved in decision-making for the neighborhood. The first such town, aptly named Greenbelt, was located 13 miles outside of Washington, D.C., on an undeveloped tract of 12,000 acres. Preplanned facilities included a town center, school, theater, centrally located artificial lake, and encircling the town, a green belt of grass for gardening and RECREATION. Only two other Greenbelt New Towns communities were constructed: Greenhills, a suburb of Cincinnati; and Greendale, on the outskirts of Milwaukee.

At the same time that the Greenbelt program was being created with government funds, many private developers were experimenting with suburban communities. The building firm of Abraham Levitt and Sons (later famous for the mass-produced postwar "Levittowns") began building Strathmore-at-Manhasset in assembly line fashion on Long Island, approximately 15 miles from Manhattan. They targeted the upper middle class with brand-name products and high-quality engineering. Rather than adopting the community decision-making policy of the Greenbelt towns, they instituted regulations concerning the appearance of properties. The firm used surveys and advertising to target a specific consumer base and effectively market their homes.

The look of the suburban home changed considerably after the early 1930s. Suburban lots in the older "streetcar suburbs" averaged 3,000 square feet, whereas new housing lots in the more distant "automobile suburbs," with lower per-acre land costs, averaged 5,000 square feet. New suburban houses were designed to be functional and representative of a simpler lifestyle. Frank Lloyd Wright's Usonian (United States of North America) designs were published in LIFE MAGAZINE in 1938 and billed as the home for "true Americans." These one-story homes, which could be prefabricated, averaged only some $5,000 to $6,000 in price and featured flexible, sunlit interiors. Making such functional, attractive, and low-cost housing available for middle-class Americans is sometimes counted Wright's most important achievement. Likewise, technological improvements such as the attached garage, automatic heating system, storm windows, and power lawn mowers added to the idea of the functional house.

The image of conformity in the suburbs resulted in large part from marketing strategies of the time. Developers created the "model home"—a prebuilt, prefurnished home for prospective buyers to peruse. In 1935, General Electric sponsored an architectural competition to inspire the creation of single-family homes replete with their electric appliances and gadgets. The *Ladies' Home Journal* sponsored an exhibit called the "House of Tomorrow" in 1937, which was a precursor to the 1939 NEW YORK WORLD'S FAIR exhibit of 21 single-family homes within the "Town of Tomorrow." In the same year, the FHA survey depicted the typical American home to be "bungalows or colonials on ample lots with driveways and garages." The *Ladies' Home Journal* furthered the conformity of housing design with the "dream homes" series from 1941 to 1946.

However, the image of these suburbs as socially homogeneous areas is not wholly accurate. Working-class Americans began to move to the nearer suburbs, and "industrial suburbs" began to encroach upon some middle-class residential suburbs. Other suburbs included a variety of occupational, religious, and ethnic groups. Nonetheless, suburbs were largely middle and upper class and mostly white, partly because of the results, intentional and unintentional, of FHA policies. FHA officials, seeking to minimize loan defaults, favored middle-class loan applicants wanting to build in the suburbs, and FHA guidelines sought to keep "inharmonious" groups apart. Private restrictive covenants barring sales to such groups as AFRICAN AMERICANS, JEWS, MEXICAN AMERICANS, and ASIAN AMERICANS also helped keep the suburbs racially homogenous in this era.

Further reading: Kenneth T. Jackson, *Crabgrass Frontier: The Suburbanization of the United States* (New York: Oxford University Press, 1985).

—Traci L. Siegler

Sunbelt

The Sunbelt has eluded precise geographical definition—or, perhaps more accurately, it has been defined in a variety of ways. Virtually everyone agrees that the Sunbelt includes areas on or near the Atlantic coastline of the SOUTH and the Gulf and Pacific coasts from Norfolk to Miami to Mobile to Houston to Los Angeles, plus noncoastal areas of Texas, New Mexico, and Arizona north of the Rio Grande. Many would include areas as far inland as the 37th parallel of latitude (roughly, a line running from North Carolina's northern border west to California), while others would include the entire West Coast (despite the cool, rainy climate of the Pacific Northwest). But whatever the exact boundaries of the Sunbelt, it expanded significantly in the 1929–45 era and became increasingly important in the nation's economic, cultural, and political life in the post–World War II era.

Although Sunbelt growth accelerated dramatically during WORLD WAR II, the expansion of some Sunbelt areas had long been underway. During the long decade of the GREAT DEPRESSION of the 1930s, with its low rates of population growth and of MIGRATION, for example, the population growth of California and Florida dwarfed that of other areas, chiefly because of high in-migration rates. California had a net in-migration of just over 1 million people, Florida of one-third million. Both states attracted migrants because of their climate and quality of life, while California's agriculture and industry were also lures. But except for urban California, the Southwest was sparsely populated and without much manufacturing, while President FRANKLIN D. ROOSEVELT called the South the nation's "number one" economic problem because of its widespread poverty, depressed agriculture, and limited manufacturing. For the most part, then, the Sunbelt shared the hard times and limited growth that marked the rest of the nation in the 1930s.

As wartime MOBILIZATION galvanized the nation, it had a particularly large impact on the Sunbelt, especially its metropolitan areas. Military bases along the southern Atlantic, Gulf, and Pacific coasts were built or expanded to take advantage of climate, open space, and access to sea transportation to the battlefronts. Tens of billions of federal dollars poured into Sunbelt states to finance war production. California alone received nearly 10 percent of all federal money spent during World War II. Pacific Coast shipyards and aircraft plants from Seattle to San Diego built about half of all ships and planes during the war, while the southern SHIPBUILDING industry from Norfolk to New Orleans built about one-fourth of all ships. The South also had a nascent AIRCRAFT INDUSTRY in the Atlanta-Marietta and Dallas–Fort Worth areas; Birmingham's steel industry boomed; and Gulf Coast petroleum industries played a vital role in synthetic rubber production and other vital needs. In the West, metals and electronics expanded. The MANHATTAN PROJECT that built the atomic bombs depended heavily upon installations in Los Alamos, New Mexico, and Oak Ridge, Tennessee. Not only did the war stimulate economic growth and expansion, then, but it did so in defense-related and technological industries that would be increasingly important in the postwar era.

The expansion of military installations and defense industries brought wartime migrants flocking to Sunbelt cities. Of the eight most congested metropolitan centers produced by wartime migration, three were in the South and the other five on the West Coast. Servicemen came from all around the nation, while defense workers and their families came especially from the rural South, Southwest, and Midwest. Many of those who had moved to Sunbelt cities remained after the war, while some servicemen who passed through returned, especially to California. Between 1940 and 1950, the nation's population increased by 15 percent—and California's by 53 percent. Such major metropolitan areas as Los Angeles, San Diego, Houston, Dallas–Forth Worth, Miami, and Atlanta grew by at least 50 percent, and sometimes much more, during the decade, as did a host of other Sunbelt cities.

Such economic and demographic change had major impact not just on the Sunbelt but also on the nation as a whole. Underwritten by federal money, wartime and postwar economic growth, especially in new aerospace, electronics, and other defense-related industries occurred to a substantial degree not in the old urban-industrial northeastern quadrant but rather in the Sunbelt. The Sunbelt also continued to attract the largest migratory streams, as people moved there to find good jobs, to enjoy the quality of life, or to retire. Wartime migrants had been young people for the most part, and they, with the postwar newcomers, lent a dynamic, optimistic aura to their new communities. The Sunbelt played an increasingly vital role in such areas as RELIGION, MUSIC, and politics. Every president elected from 1964 to 2000 was from a Sunbelt state. The World War II mobilization, though largely accelerating trends already under way, thus played a key role in the growing importance of the Sunbelt in national life.

Further reading: Richard M. Bernard and Bradley R. Rice, eds., *Sunbelt Cities: Politics and Growth since World War II* (Austin: University of Texas Press, 1983); Gerald D. Nash, *The American West Transformed: The Impact of the Second World War* (Bloomington: Indiana University Press, 1985).

Supreme Court

The Supreme Court underwent important change in composition and outlook in the 1929–45 era. After overturning a number of major NEW DEAL programs in 1935 and 1936, it ultimately upheld the New Deal regulatory welfare state that greatly expanded the size and power of the federal GOVERNMENT.

President HERBERT C. HOOVER inherited a Supreme Court that had in the 1920s generally taken conservative positions on economic policy, LABOR unions, and CIVIL LIBERTIES. During his presidency, Hoover made three appointments: Charles Evans Hughes as the successor to William Howard Taft as chief justice, and Benjamin Cardozo and Owen Roberts as associate justices. Although more than two dozen senators voted against Hughes because of his Wall Street ties, Hughes, in addition to serving as secretary of state in the 1920s, had been governor of New York in the Progressive Era and had already served as a generally progressive associate justice of the Supreme Court from 1910 to 1916 before resigning to run unsuccessfully for president as the Republican candidate in 1916. Roberts had won plaudits as a prosecutor in the Teapot Dome scandal, while Cardozo was one of the most highly regarded judges in the country. Hoover also nominated John J. Parker of North Carolina to the Court, but Parker's antilabor rulings and his efforts to weaken the role of AFRICAN AMERICANS in the southern Republican Party led to his narrow defeat by the Senate and to the subsequent nomination and confirmation of Roberts. Hoover's appointees pointed the Supreme Court in a more liberal direction, but the Court heard few significant cases from 1929 to 1933—a situation that changed dramatically with President FRANKLIN D. ROOSEVELT and the New Deal.

At first, a majority of the Supreme Court justices seemed ready to permit both state and federal governments latitude to deal with the emergency of the GREAT DEPRESSION. Narrow 5-4 decisions in 1934, for example, allowed state governments to impose a moratorium on mortgage payments and to fix prices, and early in 1935 the Court by a 5-4 margin upheld New Deal policies suspending gold payments on both private contracts and the public debt. But during the next year, the Supreme Court used its power of judicial review to invalidate a number of important New Deal programs. In early May 1935, the Court found against the Railroad Retirement Act by a 5-4 vote, on the grounds that the federal government's long-established authority over interstate railroads did not extend to mandatory pensions. On "Black Monday," May 27, 1935, in the famous case of SCHECHTER POULTRY CORPORATION V. UNITED STATES, the Court unanimously overturned the NATIONAL INDUSTRIAL RECOVERY ACT and by another 9-0 vote also invalidated the Frazier-Lemke Farm Bankruptcy Act. In the *Schechter* case, the Court ruled that the company had been involved in intrastate commerce, outside the authority of the federal government to regulate interstate commerce, and that the NATIONAL RECOVERY ADMINISTRATION (NRA) codes were an improper delegation of legislative authority to the executive branch.

In January 1936, the Court invalidated the AGRICULTURAL ADJUSTMENT ACT by a 6-3 vote in *United States v. Butler,* on the grounds that agriculture was local production, not interstate commerce, and that the AAA processing tax violated the Tenth Amendment by encroaching upon rights reserved to the states. In March, by another 6-3 vote, the Court in the *Carter Coal* case overturned the Guffey-Snyder Act, a "little NRA" for coal, holding that coal production was local production beyond the power of the federal government to regulate. Then, having limited the federal government's power, the Court declared by a 5-4 margin in the *Tipaldo* case that a New York minimum wage law violated freedom of contract.

These decisions revealed three major blocs on the Court. One comprised the conservative "Four Horsemen of the Apocalypse," as their liberal critics called them —George Sutherland and Pierce Butler (Harding appointees), James MacReynolds (a Wilson appointee), and Willis Van Devanter (a Taft appointee)—who opposed New Deal economic regulation and social welfare as violating economic liberty and exceeding the proper power of government. A second group included the three "liberal" judges—Cardozo, Harlan Fiske Stone (a Coolidge appointee) and Louis Brandeis (a Wilson appointee)—who believed that the Court should exercise judicial restraint and allow the executive and legislative branches of the government leeway to take action in the absence of clear constitutional prohibition. As Stone put it in dissenting from the majority decision in the AAA case, "Courts are not the only agency of government that must be assumed to have a capacity to govern." In the middle, as the crucial swing votes on 5-4 and 6-3 decisions, were Hughes and Roberts.

Hurriedly written, much New Deal legislation contained flaws that conservative jurists could seize upon. Particularly in interpretations of the commerce clause and of the due process clauses of the Fifth and Fourteenth Amendments, conservatives could also find precedents in previous decisions that had overturned economic and social reform. Liberals believed that the conservative Four Horsemen were interpreting the Constitution to make their decisions come out where they wanted them to for ideological reasons; liberals criticized, for example, rulings that agriculture or coal mining were local production when shipment and sales of agricultural products and coal clearly

Discouraged by the Supreme Court's rejection of key New Deal measures—and emboldened by his landslide reelection in 1936—President Franklin D. Roosevelt made a controversial move to add political allies to the Court bench. Claiming that he had to "save the Constitution from the Court and the Court from itself," Roosevelt announced a plan for the reorganization of the federal judiciary (1937), in which he proposed an additional justice for each existing justice aged 70 or over. The surprised man with Roosevelt in this cartoon is Harold Ickes, Roosevelt's secretary of the interior and leader of the Public Works Administration; the cartoon indicates that even some of Roosevelt's fellow New Dealers found his reorganization plan objectionable. In what would prove to be his greatest defeat in his four terms as president, Roosevelt's bill was voted down in Congress. Cartoon by Walter Berryman *(Library of Congress)*

JUSTICES OF THE SUPREME COURT, 1929–1945

	Term of Service
Oliver Wendell Holmes	1902–1932
Willis Van Devanter	1911–1937
James C. McReynolds	1914–1941
Louis D. Brandeis	1916–1939
William Howard Taft, *Chief Justice, 1921–1930*	1921–1930
George Sutherland	1922–1938
Pierce Butler	1922–1939
Edward T. Sanford	1923–1930
Harlan Fiske Stone, *Chief Justice, 1941–1946*	1925–1946
Charles Evans Hughes, *Chief Justice, 1930–1941*	1930–1941 (also 1910–1916)
Owen J. Roberts	1930–1945
Benjamin N. Cardozo	1932–1938
Hugo L. Black	1937–1971
Stanley F. Reed	1938–1957
Felix Frankfurter	1939–1962
William O. Douglas	1939–1975
Frank Murphy	1940–1949
James F. Byrnes	1941–1942
Robert H. Jackson	1941–1954
Wiley B. Rutledge	1943–1949
Harold H. Burton	1945–1958

---

involved interstate commerce. But whatever the motivation or reasoning of the decisions invalidating liberal reform, their cumulative impact was seemingly to hamstring the New Deal, which was above all concerned with economic regulation and social welfare. Roosevelt complained that the decisions seemed to create "a no man's land where no Government—State or Federal—can function." And both the SOCIAL SECURITY ACT and the NATIONAL LABOR RELATIONS ACT were working their way through the appeals process, and, on the bases of the 1935–36 decisions, seemed likely to be invalidated as well, as did the wages and hours regulation that Roosevelt desired.

Early in 1937, Roosevelt introduced the Judicial Procedures Reform Bill, which among other things would have permitted the president to name up to six additional justices to the Supreme Court and which quickly became known as the COURT-PACKING PLAN. His proposal, obviously intended as a way to appoint liberal justices, touched off a furor. Ultimately, FDR met an embarrassing defeat with the bill, and the struggle played a major role in the formation of the CONSERVATIVE COALITION in CONGRESS, which thereafter made it difficult for the pres-

ident's congressional supporters to pass further liberal legislation.

But the Supreme Court, by 5-4 votes with Roberts and Hughes voting in favor, upheld the National Labor Relations Act in April and the Social Security Act in May. The role of the court-packing bill in this apparent reversal remains unclear. Some analysis have found substantive consistency, not just a politically motivated "switch in time that saved nine" in the votes by Hughes and Roberts to uphold New Deal legislation; but the obvious public approval of the New Deal in the ELECTION OF 1936 and the court-packing challenge evidently played some role too. Some scholars also maintain that the trend of Supreme Court decisions had for some time been toward allowing greater government power in economic and social policy.

In May 1937, conservative justice Willis Van Devanter resigned, and he was replaced by liberal Alabama senator HUGO BLACK. During the remainder of Roosevelt's presidency, vacancies on the court allowed FDR to appoint seven additional justices, and he named Harlan Fiske Stone as chief justice when Hughes resigned in 1941. Despite the defeat of the court-packing proposal, the

Supreme Court had been reshaped as Roosevelt wanted, and the Court never again invalidated a major New Deal program. The modern regulatory welfare state was safe from judicial veto.

The "Roosevelt Court" proved liberal not only on social and economic policy but often also on CIVIL RIGHTS and sometimes on civil liberties. In the area of civil rights, it began to provide momentum toward the famous 1954 school desegregation decision of Brown v. Board of Education of Topeka by ruling in 1938 in the case of Missouri ex rel. Gaines v. Canada that a state's refusal to provide law-school education to a qualified African American was a violation of the Fourteenth Amendment. In 1943, the Court found unconstitutional a railroad union's discrimination against black workers, and in 1944 in Smith v. Allwright it declared the all-white primary prevalent in the SOUTH unconstitutional. In the half decade after the war, the Court struck down segregation on interstate buses, ruled against restrictive racial covenants in private contracts, and found against segregation in higher education.

The Roosevelt Court was less bold on civil liberties. In the 1930s, the Hughes Court had done much more than the Taft Court of the 1920s to protect First Amendment rights, and during WORLD WAR II the Court upheld the rights of Jehovah's Witnesses to worship as they wished, restored the citizenship rights of a naturalized citizen stripped of citizenship for being a Communist, protected freedom of expression for apparent German sympathizers, and established safeguards in prosecuting treason in 1945. But the Supreme Court also largely avoided safeguarding the rights of CONSCIENTIOUS OBJECTORS, overturned only in 1946 a 1943 measure sponsored by the House Committee on Un-American Activities to dismiss three federal employees on hearsay evidence of disloyalty, and in KOREMATSU V. UNITED STATES sustained the worst wartime violation of civil liberties, the RELOCATION OF JAPANESE AMERICANS. Despite its equivocal wartime record on civil liberties, however, the new Roosevelt Court marked important departures in upholding economic regulation and social welfare and in protecting civil rights.

Further reading: Peter Irons, Justice at War: The Story of the Japanese Internment Cases (Berkeley: University of California Press, 1983); William E. Leuchtenburg, The Supreme Court Reborn: The Constitutional Revolution in the Age of Roosevelt (New York: Oxford University Press, 1995); Richard A. Maidment, "The New Deal Court Revisited," in Nothing Else to Fear: New Perspectives on America in the Thirties, edited by Stephen W. Baskerville and Ralph Willet (Manchester, U.K.: Manchester University Press, 1985); Michael E. Parrish, "The Hughes Court, the Great Depression, and the Historians," The Historian 40 (1975): 286–308.

T

Taft, Robert A. (1889–1953)

A United States senator from Ohio from 1939 until his death in 1953, Robert Alphonso Taft became known as "Mr. Republican" for his fiercely partisan leadership roles in the REPUBLICAN PARTY in the 1940s and early 1950s.

Born in Cincinnati, Ohio, on September 8, 1889, Taft was the elder son of William Howard Taft, the 27th president of the United States (1909–13) and chief justice of the SUPREME COURT from 1921 to 1930. He was educated at Yale University and Harvard Law School. After practicing law in Cincinnati, Taft served an assistant counsel of the U.S. Food Administration during World War I and as a member of the American Relief Administration to aid European war survivors. Returning to Ohio, Taft entered politics, served in the state House of Representatives and then in the state Senate, and became the acknowledged leader of the Ohio GOP.

Taft won election to the U.S. Senate in 1938, and quickly became a prominent member of the CONSERVATIVE COALITION and a persistent critic of FRANKLIN D. ROOSEVELT and the NEW DEAL. Conservative on domestic policy, Taft was among the ISOLATIONISTS in FOREIGN POLICY, opposing the SELECTIVE SERVICE Act and the LEND-LEASE ACT. Yet Taft could also be pragmatic: He supported some federal aid to education and housing, a limited national health program after WORLD WAR II, and the establishment of the UNITED NATIONS. During the 1940s, Taft became the Republican Party's chief spokesman on domestic policy. He cosponsored the 1947 Taft-Hartley Act, which amended the NATIONAL LABOR RELATIONS ACT of 1935 by imposing restrictions on unions. During Harry S. Truman's presidency, he remained a critic of the Democratic agenda. After the Korean War began, Taft criticized what he saw as excessive presidential power in sending American troops to Korea; he attacked the Truman administration over the loss of China and for being soft on communism, but he supported the war.

Ambitious for the White House, Taft sought the Republican presidential nomination three times—losing in 1940 to WENDELL L. WILLKIE, in 1948 to Thomas E. Dewey, and in 1952 to Dwight D. Eisenhower. After Eisenhower's election and the Republican recapture of the Senate, Taft became majority leader in the Senate and established a good working relationship with the new president. But Taft was soon diagnosed with cancer, and he died in Washington, D.C., on July 31, 1953.

Further reading: James T. Patterson, *Mr. Republican: A Biography of Robert A. Taft* (Boston: Houghton Mifflin, 1972).

—William J. Thompson

tanks

Tanks were important armored vehicles used in WORLD WAR II by both the Allied and AXIS forces. From 1941 to 1945, the United States produced nearly 90,000 tanks, including the Locust, Grant, and Sherman models, though the combat performance of these tanks differed widely.

After World War I, the United States disbanded its tank corps until May 1940, when the Armored Forces were created in response to the effectiveness of the German BLITZKRIEG. Despite the creation of the Armored Forces and the objections of GEORGE S. PATTON, JR., who wanted a more central role for tank warfare, the U.S. ARMY viewed tanks as an auxiliary of the infantry. Tank doctrine included tactics that stressed exploiting breakthroughs, protecting and assisting unarmored units, and seizing and holding strategic positions.

Of the American tanks of World War II, the medium-sized Sherman tanks were especially important. The Shermans were designed specifically for speed, mobility, and easy modification, so that they could be updated as tank technology progressed. However, against Field Marshal Rommel's German Panzer divisions in the NORTH AFRICAN

CAMPAIGN, the Sherman tanks were revealed to be ill equipped for tank-to-tank duels. Inferior to tanks such as the German Mark V Panther or the Mark VI Tiger, they were dubbed "Purple Heart Boxes" because so many of their operators were wounded. The Sherman tanks, however, far outnumbered the German tanks, a testament to the American MOBILIZATION and production effort, and the sheer number of Allied tanks proved instrumental.

U.S. tanks continued to have mixed results in the later stages of the war. During the INVASION OF NORMANDY in June 1944, many Sherman tanks, which were equipped to "swim" to the shore of Omaha Beach, sank far from their beach destination, causing thousands of casualties among the infantry. But once they were ashore, two-bladed steel prows called hedgehogs were attached to the front of the tanks and successfully sliced through the hedgerows that had provided a natural defense for the Germans. At OKINAWA, flame-throwing tanks fired jellied gasoline at Japanese defenses, eventually causing those defenses to break. After the war, a general board assessed the performance of U.S. tanks and recommended improvements in design.

Further reading: Robert M. Citino, *Armored Forces: History and Sourcebook* (Westport, Conn.: Greenwood, 1994); Kenneth Macksey, *Tank Warfare: A History of Tanks in Battle* (New York: Stein & Day, 1972).

—Michael T. Walsh

Tarawa (November 1943)

On November 20, 1943, the U.S. MARINES 5th Amphibious Corps, under Major General Holland Smith, invaded two small atolls in the Gilbert Islands—Tarawa and Makin. These invasions marked the beginning of the Central Pacific offensive of the U.S. NAVY in the WORLD WAR II PACIFIC THEATER. But the invasion of Tarawa was a costly learning experience for the marines and changed how they conducted future AMPHIBIOUS WARFARE operations.

Because of poor communications, the pre-invasion bombardment of Tarawa was too short, and it did little damage to the well-entrenched Japanese defenders. Furthermore, Admiral Raymond Spruance, the overall commander of the operation, mistakenly believed that the water would be deep enough for U.S. landing craft to pass over the coral reefs that surround the Gilbert Islands. New American amphibious landing craft ("amtracs"), which had the ability to climb over the coral reefs, landed the first three waves of marines on the beach with few casualties. But there were not enough amtracs, so the marines that followed had to use deep-draft landing craft, which became caught on the reefs. Some marines had to wade through shoulder-high water for hundreds of yards before reaching the beach, all the time under heavy Japanese artillery and machine gun attack.

By the end of the first day, the 2nd Marine division, under Major General Julian Smith, only held a small beachhead 300 yards deep, and 1,500 of the 5,000 troops that landed were dead or wounded. It took two more days of savage fighting before the marines finally secured the island on November 23, 1943. In total, the marines lost more than 1,000 dead and more than 2,000 wounded, a dreadfully high price to pay for such a small atoll. Only 17 Japanese soldiers survived out of a garrison of 5,000.

After Tarawa, the Navy continued its island-hopping campaign up the Central Pacific toward the MARIANA ISLANDS, while the U.S. ARMY, under General Douglas MacArthur, advanced up the southwestern Pacific toward the PHILIPPINES. Because of the experience at Tarawa and the lessons learned from it, the marines subsequently had better information on the strength and location of the enemy defenses, more effective command-and-control procedures, and greater awareness of the tides and other factors that could affect their amphibious assaults.

Further reading: Joseph H. Alexander, *Utmost Savagery: The Three Days of Tarawa* (Annapolis, Md.: Naval Institute Press, 1995).

—David W. Waltrop

taxation

Taxation in the United States changed dramatically from 1929 to 1945. In 1929, the total of local, state, and federal taxes amounted to roughly $10 billion (about one-tenth of the gross national product); by 1945, total taxes had risen to approximately $50 billion (about one-fourth of GNP). While state and local taxes rose by roughly 50 percent in that period, federal internal revenue collections soared from just under $3 billion to nearly $44 billion. The federal individual income tax also came to include far more people than ever before: in 1929, some 2.5 million individuals filed taxable federal returns; in 1945, nearly 43 million did so.

The most significant changes in taxation thus came at the federal level, because of the NEW DEAL, the economic MOBILIZATION for World War II, and the great expansion of the federal GOVERNMENT during the administration of President FRANKLIN D. ROOSEVELT. Although the New Deal brought some reform to the federal tax system, the war years had a far larger impact on taxation: from 1939 to 1945, the number of people paying income taxes increased from some 4 million in 1939 to almost 43 million; individual income tax payments became a more important source of federal revenue than corporate income taxes; and the withholding tax system was adopted. The changes in the federal income tax enabled fiscal policy based on KEYNE-SIANISM to be implemented more easily during and after World War II.

At the outset of the HOOVER PRESIDENCY in 1929, state and local taxes exceeded federal taxes by about a two-to-one ratio, and local property taxes accounted for approximately half of the total tax incomes of government at all levels. During World War I, the administration of President Woodrow Wilson had extended the income tax (authorized by the Sixteenth Amendment to the Constitution in 1913) rather than sales taxes to help pay for the war. It had also made individual and corporate income taxes more progressive (that is, more graduated, with higher tax rates for higher incomes). During the 1920s, the Republican administrations scaled back individual and corporate income taxes. Local governments continued to rely chiefly on property taxes in the decade, while state governments expanded sales taxes much more than income taxes to help pay for their increasing costs of constructing roads and schools.

As the GREAT DEPRESSION developed, federal individual and corporate income taxes fell sharply in the early 1930s because of plummeting BUSINESS and personal income. With the great majority of federal tax revenues coming from income taxes (about 80 percent in the first years of the HOOVER PRESIDENCY), the federal deficit approached $3 billion in 1932—more than half of the government's expenditures. President HERBERT C. HOOVER, sharing the orthodox belief that balanced budgets were essential to economic health, asked CONGRESS for increased taxes. Congress, led by Republican representative FIORELLO LA GUARDIA of New York, defeated Hoover's request for a national sales tax, but it did make the Revenue Act of 1932 the largest peacetime tax increase in American history to that point. Excise taxes (levies on the production, sale, or consumption of commodities and services) were increased significantly, and by 1933 they accounted for half of federal tax income.

When Franklin D. Roosevelt became president in 1933, the budget situation remained as worrisome as it had been in 1932. He and many of his advisers (including HENRY MORGENTHAU, JR., treasury secretary from 1934 to 1945) also believed in the balanced budget, although they were willing to incur budget deficits if necessary to provide help for impoverished and unemployed Americans. Raising revenues thus became a priority, especially as New Deal programs increased the costs of government. One reason for supporting the end of Prohibition was to levy excise taxes on alcohol. A key part of the AGRICULTURAL ADJUSTMENT ACT of 1933 was the processing tax paid by processors of farm goods (millers, canners, and so forth) to help support agricultural subsidies. The NATIONAL INDUSTRIES RECOVERY ACT of 1933 included an excess profits

tax and a small tax on capital stock. In 1935, the SOCIAL SECURITY ACT imposed payroll taxes on employers and employees to pay for benefits.

But the major New Deal tax efforts involved the income tax. Roosevelt, Morgenthau and his Treasury staff, and others in the administration wanted to reform the income tax system, not only to increase revenues to pay for government programs but also to make taxes more progressive and to make use of money held by wealthy individuals and corporations. In the early years of the New Deal, regressive excise taxes increased by the 1932 legislation contributed more to federal revenues than did individual and corporate income taxes combined. The Revenue Act of 1934 raised taxes on higher incomes and on gift and estate taxes, but this only marked the beginning of New Deal attempts to restructure the tax system.

The first major effort to reform the income tax structure came with the REVENUE ACT OF 1935, which became known as the "Wealth Tax" because it sought to levy much higher taxes on high incomes and corporate profits. It was the result not only of administration analysis of the tax system, but also of the political atmosphere of 1935, in particular the success of Senator HUEY P. LONG in capturing a large national following with his Share Our Wealth program of heavy taxes on the wealthy to be redistributed to the general public.

In June 1935, Roosevelt sent a revenue bill to Congress asking for increased taxes on high personal incomes, for graduated corporate income taxes, and for new taxes on excess corporate profits, intercorporate dividends, and inheritances, as well as for a constitutional amendment to allow the federal government to tax interest earned on state and municipal bonds. Business and the wealthy bitterly opposed the proposal, and conservatives in Congress diluted it. Roosevelt, who often seemed more interested in gaining political credit for proposing the bill than in fighting for it, settled for some increase in personal and corporate taxes, for a scaled-down intercorporate dividend tax, and for a new estate tax. Hardly a wealth tax at all in its final form, the Revenue Act of 1935 did little to redistribute income or even raise revenues. Still, it began the efforts for significant tax reform.

In 1936, Roosevelt and Morgenthau proposed another tax reform bill, this one involving a graduated tax on undistributed corporate profits. The undistributed profits tax would replace other corporate taxes and thus eliminate what seemed "double taxation," whereby corporations paid taxes on profits and then individuals paid taxes on dividends received from corporate profits. It would close an important loophole—by preventing dividend distributions, wealthy corporate directors were able to avoid taxes on higher incomes. And the tax would increase revenues—a necessity after the SUPREME COURT had invalidated the

Agricultural Adjustment Act and its processing tax and after Congress had authorized prepaying bonuses to World War I veterans.

As the administration saw it, the bill also had two other virtues: It might reduce the concentration of economic power by forcing big business to seek money for expansion in the money market instead of relying on its pools of undistributed profits, and it might stimulate the ECONOMY by forcing idle money out of corporate coffers and into the hands of smaller stockholders who would spend it or invest it. Following another battle with Congress, the Revenue Act of 1936 ultimately implemented a smaller undistributed profits tax than Roosevelt had requested, though it retained the corporate income tax. It constituted a significant reform and further embittered business against the administration.

The Revenue Act of 1937 then closed a number of additional loopholes (involving, for example, personal holding companies, artificial losses on property sales, and non-resident taxpayers), again with the aim of making the tax system more productive as well as fairer. Roosevelt and Morgenthau wanted still further reforms in 1938, including an increase in the undistributed profits tax and the imposition of a graduated tax on capital gains. But by 1938, Congress was in the hands of the CONSERVATIVE COALITION, and the RECESSION OF 1937–38 (the so-called Roosevelt Recession) had emboldened conservative and business critics of the New Deal. The Revenue Act of 1938 eliminated the graduated corporate income tax and reduced the undistributed profits tax, and the Revenue Act of 1939 then eliminated the undistributed profits tax.

The Revenue Acts of 1935 to 1937 constituted the high water mark of New Deal tax reform. The legislation did make federal taxes somewhat more progressive, imposed new taxes on business, and at least partly closed a number of loopholes. But the tax measures did not bring about any real redistribution of income, wealth, or economic power, and were weakened significantly in the late 1930s. Moreover, the increasing reliance of state governments on sales taxes (which more than doubled in the 1930s) and the imposition of the new Social Security payroll tax outweighed any small increase in the progressivity of the federal income taxes.

But although tax reform was essentially dead by the late 1930s, major revision of the tax system did come during World War II because of the need to raise money to meet the enormous costs of mobilizing for war. The federal government spent some $300 billion during the war, which it financed by a combination of increased revenues and massive borrowing. Wartime mobilization created a full-production, full-employment economy with rising personal and corporate incomes and thus more money to be taxed. And in addition to producing revenue to help pay for the war, taxes helped to siphon money from consumers and thus combat inflation. During the war, the tax system underwent significant change, particularly in greatly expanding the reach of the federal income taxes. Tax measures early in the 1940s began the process by lowering the threshold for paying federal income taxes.

The major tax legislation of the war years, and one of the most important in American history, was the REVENUE ACT OF 1942. It taxed all incomes over $624, vastly enlarging the number of Americans paying income taxes; and it led to the adoption in 1943 of the withholding system of payroll deductions to simplify the collection of taxes from so many more people. The number of taxable incomes soared from 7.4 million in 1940 to 40.2 million by 1943. And by 1944, for the first time, individual income taxes exceeded corporate income taxes. The expanded tax base and the withholding provision also made it much easier for the government to increase or decrease revenues and implement Keynesian fiscal policy during and after the war.

Wanting to increase revenues further, Roosevelt in 1943 sent the Congress legislation that would have produced $10.5 billion more in taxes. Congress, controlled more firmly than before by the conservative coalition after the election of 1942, provided for an increase of only some $2 billion, and rather than hiking taxes on the wealthy and on business profits gave generous tax benefits to business. Angrily calling it "not a tax bill but a relief bill providing not for the needy but for the greedy," Roosevelt vetoed the bill in February 1944—and, for the first time in history, Congress passed a tax bill over the president's veto.

By the end of World War II, the American tax system, and especially the federal income tax, was far different from what it had been a decade and a half earlier. Federal taxes, about half the size of state and local taxes in 1929, were more than four times their size by 1945. Individual and corporate income taxes, which contributed less than half of federal tax revenues in 1933, produced about 80 percent in 1945. Individual income taxes, with their enormously expanded base, exceeded corporate income taxes. The new withholding system allowed for the easy and routine collection of taxes. The modern American tax system—mass-based more than class-based—had been created, with the demands and politics of World War II playing a more important role than the reforms of the New Deal.

Further reading: John Morton Blum, *From the Morgenthau Diaries*, 3 vols. (Boston: Houghton Mifflin, 1959, 1965, 1967); W. Elliot Brownlee, *Federal Taxation in America: A Short History* (New York: Cambridge University Press, 1996); ———, *Funding the Modern American State, 1941–1995* (New York: Cambridge University Press, 1996); Mark Leff, *The Limits of Symbolic Reform: The New Deal and Taxation, 1933–1939* (New York: Cambridge University Press, 1984); Herbert Stein, *The Fiscal Revolution in America* (Chicago: University of Chicago Press, 1969); John Witte, *The Politics and Development of the Federal Income Tax* (Madison: University of Wisconsin Press, 1985).

technology

In spite of the GREAT DEPRESSION, the 1930s were increasingly technological times for most Americans. They rode automobiles, trains, and even airplanes. Most had electricity and running water, a few appliances, and access to a telephone. More families had a RADIO than had a telephone, and even in the midst of the depression, one could find cheap entertainment by going to the MOVIES—sometimes to see color films in an air-conditioned theater. Television broadcasts could be received in New York and Chicago, although only a handful of households had television sets. Electrical devices were becoming more common in physicians' offices, either for diagnosis or therapy. A host of new consumer products, made cheaply from various chemicals and resins, imitated older, more expensive products or evolved into new forms of commercial design. The 1939–40 NEW YORK WORLD'S FAIR gave many Americans the opportunity to celebrate hope for the future based on SCIENCE and technology. During WORLD WAR II, the United States GOVERNMENT aggressively and deliberately fostered many areas of technology, and trained troops and home-front workers in the most modern methods of production and logistics. This new capacity and knowledge helped fuel postwar prosperity and social change.

While coal and gas still dominated heating, government-sponsored electrification brought service to most Americans by World War II, and to more than half the rural areas by 1946. By 1931, 1 million electric refrigerators had been produced, and electric dishwashers, clothes dryers, and a host of smaller appliances followed rapidly. At war's end the microwave oven, descended from radar, appeared, as did the fully automatic washing machine, although the former did not become a common household appliance until the 1980s. Air conditioning and refrigeration systems found growing commercial use throughout the 1930s, and began to transform daily life, particularly in the SOUTH.

The automobile entered a mature phase, with styling and options augmenting Henry Ford's initial austere approach, although Ford still commanded much of the market. Paved roads multiplied, and gasoline engines improved with higher compression, longer life and reliability, and easier maintenance that made driving more accessible to a greater variety of people. The AUTOMOBILE INDUSTRY alone during the war produced approximately 4 million engines of all types, 6 million guns, 3 million tanks and trucks, and 27,000 aircraft. In AGRICULTURE, mecha-

nization proceeded with tractors for small farmers, and huge self-contained combination harvesters and pickers brought economies of scale in food production that fed the war effort and European reconstruction thereafter.

Charles Lindbergh's solo flight across the Atlantic in 1927 and other impressive feats by famous aviators had demonstrated aviation's utility and safety. In 1935, the Douglas DC-3 offered middle-class patrons the first truly comfortable air TRANSPORTATION, and this reliable twin-engine aircraft captured 80 percent of domestic service by 1941. Throughout the era, the National Advisory Committee on Aeronautics (NACA) operated federal laboratories and cooperated with the AIRCRAFT INDUSTRY to introduce improvements, and the federal GOVERNMENT regulated routes, prices, safety, and other areas to help establish civil aviation. Starting well behind even the other allies, the massive U.S. production of aircraft during World War II bequeathed a surplus of planes, pilots, mechanics, and infrastructure to the postwar period. The jet engine, developed just before the war, began to dominate in the 1950s, and by the end of the decade air travel finally surpassed rail in the number of domestic passenger-miles.

Telephone service improved with better switching and transmission, and U.S. telephone access became the highest in the world. Throughout the 1930s commercial radio, which had been launched in 1920, blossomed. Entertainment comedy and drama programs, game shows, daytime soap operas, and news and public affairs filled the programming schedule. President FRANKLIN D. ROOSEVELT used his famous fireside chats to inform the country, buoy spirits, and build support for his programs during the depression. All areas of communications technology were targeted for development during the war, and afterward legions of technically adept young developers emerged to make good use of the technology in peacetime. The 1947 invention of the transistor made possible smaller and more portable radio sets and other entertainment and communications devices.

Automated punch card systems and mechanical calculators were commonly used in BUSINESS and government in the era. Beginning in the late 1930s several electronic computers, using vacuum tubes in place of mechanical switches, were built and found early use during the war in CODE BREAKING, ballistics calculations, the ATOMIC BOMB project, and other applications. These leviathans were hundreds of feet long, contained tens of thousands of tubes, and consumed about 100 kilowatts of electricity each. In 1946, mathematician John von Neumann, a close adviser to the war effort, added the notion of changeable stored programs to produce the basis for the modern computer, with the construction of a prototype in 1947.

While science underwent dramatic changes in direction and intensity from the interwar years through World

War II, technology enjoyed a more incremental yet no less impressive advance. In the interwar years, it was perceived as fueling prosperity and, with scientific management, as the basis for unlimited possibilities. It was a crucial tool in some NEW DEAL programs. Like scientists, engineers and industrial managers joined the war effort, though typically working somewhat closer to their prewar areas of expertise. Many of the most distinguished and powerful engineers and industrial leaders served as DOLLAR-A-YEAR MEN and engaged their firms and companies in war MOBILIZATION. Crucial engineering refinements, supplanted by applying scientific principles and research in selected areas, led to a panoply of clever and impressive devices that were ready for postwar civilian use.

The thousands of engineers who had worked to develop these devices, and the many thousands more young soldiers who were trained in technology and science to operate them, would form the basis of a postwar social transformation and economic boom. The INTELLIGENCE-gathering technologies and the many and powerful instruments of war would also find an enduring role to play and opportunities for steady development in the cold war.

See also POPULAR CULTURE.

Further reading: Ruth Schwartz Cowan, *A Social History of American Technology* (New York: Oxford University Press, 1997); Marc Rothenberg, *The History of Science and Technology in the United States: An Encyclopedia* (New York: Garland, 2001); Trevor I. Williams, *A Short History of Twentieth-Century Technology, C. 1900–C. 1950* (New York: Oxford University Press, 1982).

—Joseph N. Tatarewicz

Teheran Conference (November 28–December 1, 1943)

From November 28 to December 1, 1943, U.S. president FRANKLIN D. ROOSEVELT, British prime minister Winston Churchill, and Soviet premier Joseph Stalin, the "Big Three" leaders of the GRAND ALLIANCE fighting the AXIS, met in Teheran, Iran. Focusing on major issues of military strategy, geopolitics, and postwar planning, the discussions and decisions at Teheran were important not only for the conduct of WORLD WAR II but also for the postwar world.

The conference marked the first meeting between Roosevelt and Stalin, and Roosevelt tried hard to establish a good working relationship with the Soviet leader, even staying at the Soviet embassy and sometimes siding with Stalin against Churchill. Reflecting the relative power of the three nations by late 1943, Churchill's influence was waning, and Roosevelt and Stalin dominated the conference. The clear Allied ascendancy in both the WORLD WAR II EUROPEAN THEATER and the WORLD WAR II PACIFIC THEATER by late 1943 underlay the general good spirits at Teheran but also underlined the need to make decisions about the future.

Military discussions primarily involved the long-delayed SECOND FRONT in Europe. Stalin, who had long insisted that the United States and Great Britain open the second front to relieve pressure on Soviet forces on the eastern front, demanded that Operation Overlord, the cross-Channel invasion of German-occupied France, take place as soon as possible. At Roosevelt's insistence, Churchill acquiesced in a date of May 1, 1944, in conjunction with an attack on southern France. The Soviets agreed to launch an eastern offensive at the same time so that the Nazis could not concentrate forces on the new western front. Stalin also indicated that the Soviets would enter the war against Japan (the Soviet Union and Japan were still bound by a neutrality treaty signed in 1941) after the defeat of Germany—a pledge that FDR had long wanted in order to help bring the Pacific war to an end as quickly as possible.

But the geopolitical and postwar issues brought no such agreement—and reflected disagreements and suspicions that would trouble the Grand Alliance for the remainder of the war and lead to its dissolution in the early postwar period. There was some discussion and vague agreement about a postwar world organization, and other issues were addressed as well, but Poland and Germany were central to the agenda. Stalin insisted that the Soviet Union should retain the borders established by the NAZI-SOVIET PACT of 1939, in particular as they affected Soviet control of eastern Poland and the Baltic states. Roosevelt and Churchill agreed that the Soviet Union might retain the eastern section of Poland, with Poland's western border extended west into what was then eastern Germany. As to the postwar government of Poland, Stalin refused to recognize the anti-Communist Polish government-in-exile in London. Roosevelt explained that the millions of Polish-American voters (and much smaller number of voters from the Baltic states of Latvia, Lithuania, and Estonia) made it difficult for him publicly to acquiesce in their domination by the Soviet Union. Final decisions were left for the future, though it seemed clear enough that the Americans and British would not challenge Soviet interests—or troops—in those areas.

The question of what to do about Germany also loomed large at Teheran, as it would for the remainder of the war and after. Deeply concerned about German power and intentions, the Soviets wanted Germany dismembered into smaller states and left without the economic or military power to threaten other nations. Roosevelt and Churchill did not agree to such draconian action, although they did seem amenable to some dismemberment to weaken Germany. Specific decisions about postwar Germany were left for future resolution.

The major issues discussed at the Teheran conference proved significant to the outcome of World War II and the postwar world. Operation Overlord was the decisive D day INVASION OF NORMANDY in June 1944. The questions left unanswered, in particular those surrounding Poland and Germany, continued to plague the Grand Alliance and SOVIET-AMERICAN RELATIONS and were taken up again at the YALTA CONFERENCE in early 1945. Although the Teheran Conference from some perspectives marked the apex of Big Three comity and agreement, the issues and disagreements also evident at the conference would help disrupt the Grand Alliance and lead to the cold war.

See also FOREIGN POLICY.

Further reading: Robert Dallek, *Franklin D. Roosevelt and American Foreign Policy, 1932–1945* (New York: Oxford University Press, 1979); Keith Sainsbury, *The Turning Point: Roosevelt, Stalin, Churchill and Chiang Kai-Shek, 1943: The Moscow, Cairo, and Teheran Conferences* (New York: Oxford University Press, 1985).

Temporary National Economic Committee (TNEC)

On the recommendation of President FRANKLIN D. ROOSEVELT, CONGRESS established the Temporary National Economic Committee (TNEC) in June 1938 to analyze the poor performance of the American ECONOMY during the GREAT DEPRESSION. Arising from a concern about the impact of monopoly BUSINESS power on the economy, the TNEC held hearings from December 1938 to March 1941 and eventually published dozens of volumes of testimony and studies of the economy. The TNEC hearings unexpectedly provided a more important forum for KEYNESIANISM and compensatory fiscal policy than for ANTIMONOPOLY policy.

The impetus for the TNEC had both long-term and short-term roots. To some degree it reflected the antimonopoly component of LIBERALISM going back to the Progressive Era and advocated by a number of New Dealers. It stemmed also from the long depression of the 1930s and related concern about big business and concentrated economic power. But the proximate reason for the creation of the TNEC was the severe RECESSION OF 1937–38 and the policy debates within the administration about what had caused it and what to do to restore the economy to full production and full employment.

As the debates proceeded in the winter and spring of 1938, several viewpoints existed. Some in the administration, led by LEON HENDERSON and others, believed that monopoly power kept prices high, restricted production, produced unemployment, and sharply restricted consumer spending. They believed that the administration must turn to antitrust policy to stimulate the economy. Another group, led by MARRINER ECCLES and HARRY L. HOPKINS, argued that compensatory fiscal policy based on Keynesianism could provide the stimulus required to move the economy toward full production and full employment. (These two approaches were not mutually exclusive; Henderson, for example, advocated both antimonopoly and compensatory fiscal policy.) Some in the administration, led by Secretary of the Treasury HENRY MORGENTHAU, JR., advocated fiscal prudence and the balanced budget as the way to right the economy, and others argued for more thorough regulation of business. But the main contest was between antimonopoly and spending as the focus of government economic policy.

In April 1938, Roosevelt seemed to avoid making a final decision by taking both approaches. In the middle of the month, he announced a renewed spending program. Then, at the end of the month, he recommended to Congress a "thorough study of the concentration of economic power in American industry." In June, Congress passed legislation, signed by Roosevelt, establishing the TNEC. FDR had anticipated an administration committee to conduct the investigation, but Congress wanted half the committee to come from Congress, half from federal agencies. Chaired by Wyoming Democratic senator Joseph C. O'Mahoney, the committee included a variety of viewpoints, and was charged to study economic policy broadly, not just economic concentration and its consequences. Leon Henderson served as executive secretary and managed the committee's operations.

The TNEC began its hearings in late 1938, and ultimately heard from some 552 witnesses. Some argued for vigorous antitrust policy, some for compensatory spending, some for accepting concentrations of economic power but imposing more stringent regulation. The committee also developed a wealth of detail about the economy. But as the committee labored on, it became increasingly peripheral, as attention in Washington and the nation focused on global events and FOREIGN POLICY. Perhaps the most significant testimony came from a number of Keynesians who argued in the spring of 1939 for the importance of compensatory fiscal policy to achieve economic recovery. They reflected the direction of the Roosevelt administration in the so-called THIRD NEW DEAL of the second and third terms, and their viewpoint was corroborated when massive deficits during WORLD WAR II produced full-production, full-employment prosperity.

Although the TNEC's testimony and studies were full of useful information, its final report and recommendations in 1941 were anticlimactic, unfocused, and largely ignored, partly because they came in the much different context of war in Europe, economic MOBILIZATION, and returning prosperity. Seemingly of great potential importance as it began its work, the TNEC together with its reports and recommendations quickly became little more than a footnote to history. The economic recovery of the war years brought the ascendancy among liberals of the Keynesian approach to economic policy over both antimonopoly and increased regulation and control.

Further reading: David Lynch, *The Concentration of Economic Power* (New York: Columbia University Press, 1946).

Tennessee Valley Authority (TVA)

The Tennessee Valley Authority (TVA) was created by CONGRESS in May 1933 to breathe new life into the economically depressed Tennessee River region. Part of the first Hundred Days legislation of the NEW DEAL, the TVA represented the commitment of President FRANKLIN D. ROOSEVELT to depressed regions in America, and culminated years of legislative struggle for Nebraska senator GEORGE W. NORRIS, the champion of public power.

The Tennessee River basin encompassed seven states, extending 650 miles from Knoxville, Tennessee, near the Great Smoky Mountains, to the Ohio River at Paducah, Kentucky. Widespread poverty characterized the region, and timber companies left the area scarred and workers unemployed. Farmers, hampered by poor soil, eked out a bare existence. Few had electricity, and the area received more than 50 inches of rain annually, creating floods that devastated crops.

The Tennessee River dropped 130 feet over a distance of 40 miles in the area of Muscle Shoals, Alabama, creating rapids that had great potential for economic development but that constituted a navigational nightmare. During World War I, the federal government built the Wilson Dam and two partly completed power plants at Muscle Shoals, but throughout the 1920s the Republican administrations wanted to sell or lease the complex to private interests. Norris stopped an attempt by Henry Ford to lease Muscle Shoals, and introduced six bills for Tennessee Valley public power development. Twice the legislation passed Congress, only to be vetoed by Presidents Calvin Coolidge and HERBERT C. HOOVER, who said that government ownership of Muscle Shoals was a "negation of the ideals upon which our civilization has been based."

In the ELECTION OF 1932, Roosevelt, the Democratic presidential nominee, endorsed public development of the Tennessee Valley for water power, flood control, soil conservation, reforestation, agricultural innovation, and industrial growth, a stand that earned Norris's endorsement. On April 10, 1933, Roosevelt submitted to Congress a message calling for creation in the Tennessee Valley of a "corporation clothed with the power of government, but possessed of the flexibility and initiative of a private enterprise." Both houses of Congress passed Tennessee Valley legislation, with the House of Representatives' version limiting government power to build dams and transmission lines for electricity—restrictions that Senator Norris would not accept. Roosevelt, after ensuring that the final bill provided the stronger federal role preferred by Norris, signed the Tennessee Valley Authority Act on May 18, 1933.

The TVA was to be an independent agency responsible directly to the president and Congress, and governed by a three-person board with one member as chairman. The first chairman of the TVA was Arthur E. Morgan, an engineer and former college president, who advocated centralized economic planning, the elimination of poverty from the valley, and cooperation with private utilities in the region. The other board members were Harcourt Morgan, an agricultural scientist and advocate for larger farming interests who was suspicious of Arthur Morgan's utopian schemes, and DAVID E. LILIENTHAL, a Harvard-trained lawyer and member of the Wisconsin Public Service Commission, who wanted TVA electricity to compete directly with private utilities. Arthur Morgan's desire to turn the TVA into a social planning agency created conflict with Harcourt Morgan and Lilienthal, and led to his dismissal by Roosevelt in 1938 after the chairman publicly attacked his colleagues.

The private utilities, led by Commonwealth and Southern, which controlled electric power in the region, had assets of over $1 billion, and was headed by New Deal critic WENDELL L. WILLKIE, mounted legal challenges to the TVA's constitutionality. In the *Ashwander* case, which began as a lawsuit by private utility stockholders in Alabama, the SUPREME COURT in February 1936 affirmed the TVA's constitutional authority to market power from Wilson Dam to local municipalities, but sidestepped issues of the TVA's overall legality.

Under the TVA, dams were built on the Tennessee and its tributaries that turned the river into a series of large lakes providing a 300-foot wide channel for shipping. Although falling well short of Arthur Morgan's grand goals of transforming the Tennessee Valley's society and economy by comprehensive GOVERNMENT planning, the TVA provided flood control, fertilizer manufacture, reforestation, soil erosion prevention, agricultural experimentation, industrial development, and public works projects. The main goal of the TVA, however, was to bring electric power to the Tennessee Valley, and from 1933 to 1945 the percentage of farms with electricity jumped from 2 percent to 75 percent. During WORLD WAR II, the TVA, which had become the largest producer of power in the United States, produced nitrates for munitions and provided electricity for the Oak Ridge plant of the MANHATTAN PROJECT that produced the ATOMIC BOMB. Although the Tennessee Val-

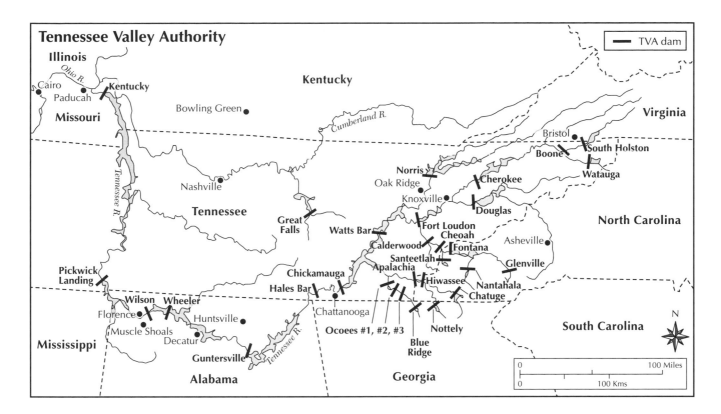

ley Authority would be studied throughout the world as a model for developing agriculturally poor regions, its success was never copied at home, despite Roosevelt's desire to develop other American rivers.

Further reading: Erwin C. Hargrove and Paul K. Conkin, eds., *TVA: Fifty Years of Grass-Roots Democracy* (Urbana: University of Illinois Press, 1983); Thomas McGraw, *Morgan vs. Lilienthal: The Fight within the TVA* (Chicago: Loyola University Press, 1970); ———, *TVA and the Power Fight* (Philadelphia: Lippincott, 1971).

—William J. Thompson

Third New Deal

The "Third New Deal" refers to domestic policy developments in the second and third terms of President FRANKLIN D. ROOSEVELT. A distinction between a FIRST NEW DEAL of 1933 that emphasized recovery and RELIEF, and a SECOND NEW DEAL of 1935 concerned especially with social reform, has long provided one important framework for understanding the NEW DEAL. The period after 1935 seemed far less significant, as a more conservative CONGRESS and then the prosperity and global priorities of WORLD WAR II stymied efforts to expand the New Deal.

But a number of New Deal scholars now recognize a Third New Deal that began to take shape in Roosevelt's

second term and that was perhaps as important to postwar American GOVERNMENT as the bursts of liberal reform in 1933 and 1935 that created the modern regulatory welfare state. As with the First and Second New Deals, scholars do not always agree on precisely what the Third New Deal entailed. Some, for example, emphasize efforts to enhance the policy planning and coordination capacity of the executive branch by such means as the EXECUTIVE REORGANIZATION ACT of 1939 and the NATIONAL RESOURCES PLANNING BOARD. But a consensus has come to emphasize two related aspects of a Third New Deal: a more conservative political atmosphere in Washington and the nation that prevented significant expansion of the New Deal; and a new focus of LIBERALISM on government spending to produce full-employment prosperity.

The key event leading to this Third New Deal was the RECESSION OF 1937–38. Together with such other events as the COURT-PACKING PLAN of 1937 and LABOR unrest, the 1937–38 recession eroded President Roosevelt's popularity and power, helped produce a CONSERVATIVE COALITION of Republicans and conservative Democrats in Congress, and fueled Republican gains in the 1938 elections. Henceforth, Roosevelt would not have Congresses nearly so cooperative as those of 1933 and 1935. But the recession also persuaded a growing number of New Deal economists and policymakers that deliberate deficit spending based on KEYNESIANISM was the way out of the GREAT DEPRESSION and that spending on social programs could underwrite both recovery and reform.

World War II then confirmed and reinforced patterns under way in the late 1930s. Particularly after the 1942 congressional elections, the conservative coalition became even more powerful in Washington. As war priorities became paramount, and as the massive wartime deficit spending brought full employment and rising living standards, several New Deal relief agencies were terminated, and liberals stood little chance of expanding social welfare programs or enacting new ones. Wartime MOBILIZATION efforts, though ultimately successful, showed the difficulties of federal micromanagement of the ECONOMY—and also the ability of BUSINESS and the military to "capture" government agencies designed to regulate the economy. At the same time, wartime prosperity proved the resiliency of the American economy and corroborated the theory that deficit spending could produce prosperity. Moreover, fiscal policy—taxing and spending—did not entail government control of the economy, was politically more feasible than major new economic and social reform, and brought obvious gains to working- and lower-class Americans by producing full-employment prosperity. Although Roosevelt and other liberals talked about a far-reaching ECONOMIC BILL OF RIGHTS toward the end of the war, the FULL EMPLOYMENT BILL proposed in 1945 embodied the change in liberal priorities from the more aggressive economic reform and regulation of Roosevelt's first term. The emphasis on fiscal policy and full-employment prosperity of the Third New Deal would continue (along with a new emphasis on CIVIL RIGHTS) to characterize liberalism in the postwar era.

Further reading: John W. Jeffries, "A 'Third New Deal'? Liberal Policy and the American State, 1937–1945," *Journal of Policy History* 8, no. 4 (1996): 387–409.

Thomas, Norman (1884–1968)

Pacifist, civil libertarian, writer, and longtime leader of American SOCIALISTS. Norman Thomas headed the U.S. Socialist Party from 1928 until his death in 1968 and was a six-time candidate for the presidency on its ticket.

Norman Mattoon Thomas was born in 1884 in Marion, Ohio, into a family of Presbyterian ministers. He graduated from Princeton University and then from Union Theological Seminary, where he became a disciple of the Social Gospel movement. Ordained in 1911, Thomas had become a pacifist by 1916. In 1917, motivated by the poverty he had witnessed, he identified himself as a Christian Socialist. During World War I, Thomas helped found the National Civil Liberties Bureau, predecessor of the AMERICAN CIVIL LIBERTIES UNION. He joined the Socialist Party in 1918,

and in 1921 he became associate editor of the *Nation,* a major journal of the left. During the 1920s and early 1930s, Thomas worked for reform in New York City, running for mayor twice. He first ran for president as a Socialist Party candidate in 1928, polling less than 300,000 votes.

In the ELECTION OF 1932, Thomas won almost 900,000 votes, a disappointing total (just 2 percent of the popular vote) for the Socialists in the midst of the GREAT DEPRESSION. Many NEW DEAL policies reflected important parts of Thomas's platform, including RELIEF for the unemployed and impoverished and support for the rights of LABOR. When President FRANKLIN D. ROOSEVELT achieved some of the goals of the Socialist platform, many of Thomas's followers left the Socialist Party for the DEMOCRATIC PARTY. In the ELECTION OF 1936, Thomas polled some 190,000 votes. Increasingly frustrated with both the church and marxism in the 1930s, Thomas resigned his ordination, condemned Stalinism, and tried to build up the non-marxist wing of the Socialist Party. He continued to be active in the fight to protect CIVIL LIBERTIES, working for the release of Communist Party leader Earl Browder and for CIVIL RIGHTS, supporting antilynching legislation and the SOUTHERN TENANT FARMERS UNION.

Although Thomas opposed U.S. entry into WORLD WAR II before PEARL HARBOR, he supported the U.S. war effort afterward. During the war he condemned the relocation of JAPANESE AMERICANS, aided CONSCIENTIOUS OBJECTORS, and protested racial inequality. He remained active until he died in 1968 at the age of 82, helping victims of anticommunist legislation, founding the antinuclear organization Committee for a Sane Nuclear Policy (SANE), and protesting against the Vietnam War.

Further reading: W. A. Swanberg, *Norman Thomas, The Last Idealist* (New York: Scribner's, 1976).

—Aimee Alice Pohl

Townsend, Francis E. (1867–1960)

Francis Everett Townsend, a retired physician in Long Beach, California, mobilized many of the ELDERLY during the GREAT DEPRESSION into a mass movement demanding a retirement pension. The passage of the SOCIAL SECURITY ACT of 1935 led to the decline of Townsend's movement. While Townsend continued to advocate his plan of a $200 per month pension for the elderly, what had seemed to be a potent challenge to President FRANKLIN D. ROOSEVELT and the NEW DEAL in the mid-1930s dwindled away as Social Security programs benefited Townsend's constituency.

Born on January 13, 1867, Townsend had grown up in Nebraska and, until he entered medical school in 1897, had failed at several ventures, including farming and sales.

Setting up his medical practice in South Dakota, Townsend spent the next several decades with a comfortable practice. But concerns about his health led him to relocate in 1919 to the more comfortable climate of Long Beach, California, where he set up a new practice and lived in relative obscurity.

Townsend claimed that the idea for his plan to help the elderly came from a vision he had when he watched three elderly women searching for scraps in garbage cans near his home in 1933. But however it came about, Townsend began to publicize his idea for a $200 per month pension for all persons over age 60. The Townsend Plan, as it came to be called, was to be funded through a 2 percent sales tax, with pension recipients to spend the entire $200 by the end of each month. Townsend promoted his plan as pumping money back into the economy, taking "surplus workers" out of the labor market, and providing economic security for the nation's elderly. The plan was economically unsound, for, as Townsend's critics pointed out, estimates indicated that the plan would have cost up to half of the nation's income and possibly doubled the tax burden on younger generations. But despite the flaws in the plan, Townsend had hit upon an issue that carried tremendous appeal.

Following Townsend's publication of his plan in the *Long Beach Press-Telegraph* in September 1933, the Townsend movement grew explosively. Townsend formalized his organization on January 1, 1934, when he created the Old-Age Revolving Pensions, Ltd., and launched a weekly newsletter. The organization began circulating a petition for a federal old-age pension and quickly spread beyond California. By mid-1935, perhaps as many as 25 million people had signed the petition, while about 5,000 local Townsend clubs (which claimed to have more than 2.2 million members) had sprung up around the nation. There were at least 500,000 dues paying members, and it appeared that Townsend had wide support in CONGRESS for his pension plan.

In early 1935, a Townsend-supported congressman introduced the Townsend Plan in Congress. The plan was easily defeated, with many congressmen recognizing its impracticality and expense. (Many also did not want to be on record as voting against it, and some 200 members of the House of Representatives were absent when the vote came up.) Coming just before President FRANKLIN D. ROOSEVELT sent Congress the Economic Security Bill (which became the Social Security Act), the popularity of Townsend's plan may have helped the old-age programs of Social Security gain increased support in Congress as a more realistic method to assist the elderly.

The passage of the Social Security Act in August 1935 did not end Townsend's quest for an across-the-board pension, for he felt the act did not do enough to support the elderly. Partly because Roosevelt had opposed the Townsend plan, the doctor became a major, though soft-spoken, opponent of the president as the ELECTION OF 1936 approached. Recognizing that many of his supporters were also drawn to Senator HUEY P. LONG and Father CHARLES E. COUGHLIN, Townsend made overtures to these two men about forming a loose alliance. But his distaste for them was apparent in his lukewarm support for the UNION PARTY, formed by Father Coughlin and supported by Long's organization to challenge Roosevelt in the 1936 election. While Townsend lent his endorsement to the Union Party in the 14 states where it was on the ballot, he preferred REPUBLICAN PARTY candidate ALFRED M. LANDON. The dismal showing by the Union Party allowed Townsend to distance himself from Coughlin, and he returned to advocating his pension plan.

Townsend spent the next several decades trying to replace Social Security with his plan. But the Social Security Act had sapped much of his support and his attempts to reintroduce it in Congress never went very far. Townsend died on September 1, 1960, having failed to achieve his plan but contributing to the organization of one of the largest lobbying groups in American politics, the elderly.

Further reading: Abraham Holtzmann, *The Townsend Movement: A Political Study* (New York: Brookman Associates, 1963).

—Katherine Liapis Segrue

transportation

The 1930s and 1940s brought dramatic changes in the transportation of goods and people in the United States. A number of significant developments in automobiles, aircraft, and railroads combined to change the way Americans moved freight and passengers on local, national, and international levels. These changes contributed to the important role of transportation in supporting economic and military MOBILIZATION and interstate MIGRATION during WORLD WAR II.

In the interwar years, America's railroads faced new competition for business from automobiles, buses, and trucks. Automobiles allowed people to travel at their pleasure rather than at times and by routes dictated by the rigid schedules of the railroads, and railroad passengers and passenger mileage declined in the 1920s, while automobile travel increased. The early years of the GREAT DEPRESSION reduced passenger traffic still further, and by causing American industries to curtail production also reduced shipments of raw materials and finished goods. From 1929 to 1933, the number of railroad passengers fell from 786 million to 435 million, passenger miles fell from 31.2 to 16.4 billion, and freight tonnage fell from 1.34 billion to 699 million. In those four years, American railroads went from a net income of $977 million to $27 million (after net losses of $122 million in 1932).

Federal regulation prevented the railroads from raising rates and abandoning routes to stem the loss of income, so a new way of increasing revenue had to be found. On September 29, 1932, the Burlington Railroad and a Philadelphia metal maker began construction of the first streamlined train, the Burlington Zephyr, as part of the railroad's plan to regain passengers lost to cars and buses. The streamliner provided fast transportation for its passengers in air-conditioned comfort and at lower cost to the railroad. The streamliners so enchanted the public that the Zephyr had to turn away passengers during its first year of service. Soon other railroads introduced new diesel streamliners of their own, or streamlined their older trains like the New York Central's 20th Century Limited, and the Baltimore and Ohio's Royal Blue. Passenger travel and revenue rose slowly after 1933.

With the outbreak of World War II, railroads experienced a rapid resurgence of their freight traffic as defense plants began to produce war material that needed to be moved from the factories to embarkation points along the coasts. On December 18, 1941, President FRANKLIN D. ROOSEVELT established the Office of Defense Transportation to coordinate all transportation for the war effort. Railroad freight traffic, both raw materials and finished products, increased during the war. So did rail passenger traffic when gasoline RATIONING made traveling long distances by automobile impractical and millions of GIs and defense workers and their families had to move across the country. Soon, American railroads were transporting war material, supplies, soldiers, and civilians across the country and in unprecedented amounts. In 1944, railroad passenger miles peaked at their all-time high of 95.7 billion as railroads carried more than 900 million passengers, and freight tonnage reached a new record 1.5 billion. The net income of American railroads also reached new levels during the war.

Sales of new cars by the AUTOMOBILE INDUSTRY collapsed early in the depression, plummeting from nearly 4.5 million cars sold in 1929 to a low of 1.1. million sold in 1932. Nevertheless, the automobile became still more popular during the 1930s because of the personal freedom that it gave to travelers. Despite widespread economic hardship, Americans did not give up the cars they already owned, and passenger vehicle traffic held roughly steady early in the 1930s and then increased significantly in the second half of the decade; the number of vehicle miles traveled in 1940 was nearly 50 percent higher than in 1930. As travel for pleasure picked up in the late 1930s, it sparked the development of the nascent motor court industry. Automobile sales picked up after 1932, but just as they neared predepression levels in 1940 and 1941, the automobile

Pictured here is the McDonnell Douglas DC-3, the workhorse of commercial aviation in the 1930s *(Library of Congress)*

industry had to switch to military production because of World War II.

During the 1920s, efforts to improve road surfaces across America gained momentum in order to facilitate the growing use of trucks to transport goods over short and medium distances as well as automobile and bus traffic. When the Great Depression hit, road-building projects suffered as state and municipal finances were strained. But President Roosevelt's NEW DEAL funded federal highway projects such as the Pennsylvania Turnpike and U.S. Route 66, while more local "farm to market roads" were built to assist farm recovery efforts as part of the WORKS PROGRESS ADMINISTRATION. These roads were to make up for the loss of railroad transportation that had previously served farmers' shipping needs, and they enabled farm products to be shipped cheaply to the market via trucks. During the war, such roads facilitated the transportation of goods, especially of foodstuffs from farms to canneries and packing plants and then on to markets and ports for shipment to war zones.

Railroads and automobiles also facilitated population migration, especially during the war years. Although the early years of the Great Depression greatly reduced population movement, migration picked up in the second half of the 1930s as people moved away from the rural Midwest, Southwest, and South toward metropolitan areas and the Pacific Coast in search of work. An unknown but highly visible number of Americans became hoboes, taking to the rails and riding freight trains in the hope that they would be taken somewhere where work was available. Whole families left the DUST BOWL of the Midwest and Southwest and headed to California in their family cars looking for a better life. Later, with the need for more workers in factories during World War II, millions of Americans headed to the war production centers of the industrial Northeast, Midwest, and West, and joined military personnel on the crowded trains and buses of the war years.

While the automobile and railroad industries had become fairly well established in America, the AIRCRAFT INDUSTRY was still in its infancy at the beginning of the depression. There were few customers for new airplanes, especially for large commercial aircraft. However, as the 1930s progressed and the speed and convenience of air travel became more obvious, more and more people began traveling by air. Not only did cross-country air travel increase, but international flights also enabled more and more people to fly across the oceans for pleasure and business. In 1930, the aircraft industry transported fewer than 400,000 passengers; in 1940, it carried more than 2.5 million passengers. Twenty-three million paying passenger miles were flown in 1929, 56 million in 1935, and a record-breaking 110 million paying passenger miles were flown in 1940. Despite such dramatic increases, particularly late in the decade, passenger traffic in commercial aircraft in the 1930s was dwarfed by travel on railroads and automobiles. After the war, however, and the enormous wartime expansion of the aircraft industry, airplanes took an increasing share of the railroads' long-distance passenger traffic, while automobiles took many of the local passengers.

Further reading: Keith L. Bryant, ed., *Railroads in the Age of Regulation, 1900–1980* (New York: Facts On File, Inc., 1988); George S. May, ed., *The Automobile Industry, 1920–1980* (New York: Facts On File, Inc., 1989); John B. Rae, *Climb to Greatness: The American Aircraft Industry, 1920–1960* (Cambridge, Mass.: MIT Press, 1968).

—Nicholas Fry

Truman, Harry S.   See Volume IX

Tugwell, Rexford G. (1891–1979)

Rexford Guy Tugwell was a noted economist, a member of the BRAIN TRUST of President FRANKLIN D. ROOSEVELT, governor of Puerto Rico, and historian of the NEW DEAL.

Tugwell was born near Buffalo, New York, in 1891, and received his bachelor's, master's, and Ph.D. degrees from the University of Pennsylvania. In 1920, he joined the Economics Department of Columbia University in New York, and taught progressive ideas of activist government and cooperative labor-management relations. A respected scholar, Tugwell's central tenet was the "magnificence of

[government] planning," which he believed could produce prosperity by ensuring balanced investment, production, and consumption.

After the GREAT DEPRESSION struck, Tugwell criticized the approach of the HOOVER PRESIDENCY. Believing that the depression had resulted from structural flaws in the U.S. ECONOMY, he maintained that underconsumption was the primary cause of the depression and that recovery must start in AGRICULTURE. In 1932, RAYMOND MOLEY asked Tugwell to join Roosevelt's inner advisory circle, which soon was known as the "Brain Trust." Witty, confident, assertive, and a resourceful thinker, Tugwell had FDR's ear even when they disagreed. He was regarded as the most radical member of the Brain Trust and saw the key to recovery in government economic planning and controls.

After Roosevelt's victory in the ELECTION OF 1932, Tugwell was appointed assistant secretary of agriculture and became undersecretary in 1934. He was instrumental in drafting the NATIONAL INDUSTRIAL RECOVERY ACT (NIRA) and the AGRICULTURAL ADJUSTMENT ACT (AAA), both of which reflected his belief in government planning, though neither of which went nearly as far as Tugwell desired. In 1935, Roosevelt appointed Tugwell to head the RESETTLEMENT ADMINISTRATION, which sought to resettle farmers from depleted to arable farmland and also sponsored model "greenbelt" towns—planned communities designed to avoid urban congestion.

Tugwell resigned from the GOVERNMENT after Roosevelt's reelection in 1936. Though still on good terms with FDR, he was unhappy with the limits of the NIRA and the AAA, indeed with the more general limits of the New Deal to provide the sort of planning, controls, and policy he thought essential, and he had become a controversial target of conservatives. He had lost a battle in 1935 to have AAA payments go to tenants and sharecroppers, and he had also argued unsuccessfully for a national system of unemployment compensation and health insurance as part of the SOCIAL SECURITY ACT. Two years later, New York City mayor FIORELLO LA GUARDIA appointed him chairman of the New York City Planning Commission. In 1941, Tugwell was named governor of Puerto Rico, serving in that position until 1946. In later years, Tugwell was a prolific and influential writer on the history of the New Deal, writing prize-winning studies of Roosevelt and of the brain trust. He died in 1979.

Further reading: Bernard Sternsher, *Rexford Tugwell and the New Deal* (New Brunswick, N.J.: Rutgers University Press, 1964).

—Robert J. Hanyok

U

unemployment

Unemployment was one of the chief defining characteristics of the GREAT DEPRESSION of the 1930s. By 1933, at least one-fourth and perhaps as much as one-third of the American labor force was unemployed. Unemployment generally declined for the rest of the 1930s, and NEW DEAL programs provided RELIEF and other assistance to the unemployed; but as late as 1940, nearly 15 percent of the labor force remained unemployed. Spending for World War II finally ended the Great Depression, produced a full-production, full-employment economy, and returned unemployment to low levels.

Unemployment had for the most part been low in the 1920s, after the sharp recession at the outset of the decade, and only about 1.6 million workers, just 3.2 percent of the civilian labor force, were unemployed in 1929. The Great Depression then began late in 1929, and unemployment (see the table accompanying this entry) soared over the next four years—to nearly 13 million workers and one-fourth of the civilian labor force by 1933, when the economy reached its nadir. These figures, moreover, are really little better than informed estimates, probably on the low side; some scholars believe that the real unemployment rate was nearer to one-third of the labor force. Nor do the net figures for unemployment adequately reflect the depression's impact on employment, for millions more were underemployed, working part-time instead of full-time or at lower-level jobs than before, and thus with sharply reduced income. And some workers simply left the labor force as the depression wore on, and thus were not counted in unemployment figures.

The overall figures on unemployment also fail to show how the Great Depression affected particular areas, industries, and groups. By 1933, manufacturing unemployment was off by at least one-third, and perhaps by as much as two-fifths; and in some industries and cities unemployment rates were 50 percent and higher. The troubled industries of the 1920s, coal and textiles, were joined in high unemployment rates by the automobile, construction, and other consumer durable industries that had sparked the economic growth of the 1920s. In Detroit, for example, that symbol of American production and prosperity in the 1920s, more than half the labor force was unemployed by 1933. In Akron, Ohio, unemployment was estimated at 60 percent in 1932; in Dayton, Ohio, the figure was 80 percent. Most farmers, of course, kept their jobs, working harder than before though earning less money as AGRICULTURE suffered; but the impact of the depression and of the New Deal's AGRICULTURAL ADJUSTMENT ADMINISTRATION meant significant unemployment among tenant farmers, sharecroppers, and migrant farm workers.

The depression hit other groups, especially minority groups, with particular force. AFRICAN AMERICANS, last hired during the prosperity of the 1920s and even then with relatively high unemployment rates, were first fired in the hard times of the 1930s and experienced significantly higher unemployment rates than whites. By 1932, more than one-half of black workers in southern cities were jobless. In Pittsburgh, one-third of white workers were unemployed in 1933—and half of black workers. MEXICAN AMERICANS also had unemployment rates well above the disastrous national and local averages. Young and ELDERLY workers also had disproportionately high unemployment rates, with workers under 20 and those over 60 being twice as likely to be unemployed.

The story of unemployment for women was complicated. Initially, women tended to lose jobs faster than men, since domestic and unskilled manufacturing workers were often laid off first and married women with employed husbands were sometimes fired in an effort to spread jobs around. But there were countervailing forces, ironically sometimes the result of longstanding disparities, that worked in favor of women's employment: women were concentrated in "women's jobs" in the service and clerical sectors, which recovered or expanded faster than manufacturing, and in teaching and light industry, which had lower unemployment rates than heavy industry; and they typically were paid lower wages, which made them more attractive to employers. Many women had to work, because their husbands were unemployed—and the percentage of married women working rose by some 50 percent in the 1930s.

A sense that poverty and unemployment were somehow personal failings, and that GOVERNMENT should not do too much to help the jobless and destitute, proved widespread and strongly ingrained. The continuing strength of CONSERVATISM even in the reformist 1930s included an emphasis on personal responsibility and a concern about too-costly or too-powerful government. A keen feeling of personal inadequacy often dogged the unemployed themselves, even when it was obvious that the economic system had collapsed and that millions of hard-working, responsible people were out of work through no fault of their own. Many people receiving relief assistance were ambivalent about it and worried about the new role of the federal government in directly helping the unemployed. Although the New Deal reforms of the 1930s eroded such feelings, they did not end them. As unemployment declined sharply during World War II, so did popular support for relief programs for the unemployed and destitute, which most Americans, including

most New Dealers, had envisioned only as temporary stopgaps.

The table accompanying this entry charts unemployment totals from 1929 to 1945. After its explosive growth from 1929 to 1933, unemployment declined steadily during the early New Deal, and was down from 24.9 percent to 14.3 percent by 1937 as the ECONOMY expanded from the low point of 1933. The RECESSION OF 1937–38 then sent unemployment soaring again, to nearly one of five workers in 1938; and despite some economic improvement as the Roosevelt administration began to turn in the late 1930s to an expansive fiscal policy based upon KEYNESIANISM, nearly 15 percent of the civilian workforce (a rate not much below that of 1931) remained unemployed in 1940–10 long years after the onset of the Great Depression. However, by 1941, with the impact of defense spending as the nation began the MOBILIZATION of its productive and military resources, unemployment declined sharply as industry began to produce and hire more and as the armed forces drew people from the work force. During the war the nation's economic problem was how to find workers for jobs, not the 1930s problem of how to find jobs for workers—which offered new opportunities (sometimes slowly) for African Americans and other minority groups, to women, to young and old workers, to displaced farm work-

UNEMPLOYMENT, 1929–1945*

	Unemployed Workers	% Unemployed of Civilian Labor Force	Civilian Labor Force Employment	Armed Forces
1929	1,550,000	3.2%	47,630,000	255,031
1930	4,340,000	8.7	45,480,000	255,648
1931	8,020,000	15.9	42,400,000	252,605
1932	12,060,000	23.6	38,940,000	244,902
1933	12,830,000	24.9	38,760,000	243,845
1934	11,340,000	21.7	40,890,000	247,137
1935	10,610,000	20.1	42,260,000	251,799
1936	9,030,000	16.9	44,410,000	291,356
1937	7,700,000	14.3	46,300,000	311,808
1938	10,390,000	19.0	44,220,000	322,932
1939	9,480,000	17.2	45,750,000	334,473
1940	8,120,000	14.6	47,520,000	458,465
1941	5,560,000	9.9	50,350,000	1,801,101
1942	2,660,000	4.7	53,750,000	3,858,791
1943	1,070,000	1.9	54,470,000	9,044,745
1944	670,000	1.2	53,960,000	11,451,719
1945	1,040,000	1.9	52,820,000	12,123,455

*Source: The Statistical History of the United States, from Colonial Times to the Present (Stamford, Conn.: Fairfield Publishers, 1965)

ers. With some 54 million Americans employed in civilian jobs and another 11.5 million in the military, barely two-thirds of a million people and just 1.2 percent—a stunningly low level—of the civilian labor force were unemployed in 1944. Because of the searing impact of unemployment during the Great Depression, a concern about unemployment would be central to POSTWAR PLANNING and to politics and policy during and after the war; but the war had ended the unemployment crisis of the 1930s and begun a quarter century of remarkable economic growth and prosperity.

Further reading: Caroline Bird, *The Invisible Scar* (New York: McKay, 1966); Lester Chandler, *America's Greatest Depression* (New York: Harper & Row, 1970); Richard Lowitt and Maurine Beasley, ed., *One Third of a Nation: Lorena Hickok Reports on the Great Depression* (Urbana: University of Illinois Press, 1981); Robert McElvaine, *The Great Depression: America, 1929–1941* (New York: Times Books, 1984).

Union Party

The Union Party was a short-lived phenomenon, created in the summer of 1936 and withering away after its weak showing in the ELECTION OF 1936. William "Liberty Bill" Lemke, a North Dakota congressman unhappy that the NEW DEAL was doing too little for impoverished farmers, ran for president on the Union Party ticket. The party was formed by FATHER CHARLES E. COUGHLIN, a bitter foe of President FRANKLIN D. ROOSEVELT by the mid-1930s, who tried to forge a coalition of his followers with those of other critics of the limits of the early New Deal—in particular, Dr. FRANCIS TOWNSEND, who had rallied millions of elderly people behind his old-age pension plan, and HUEY P. LONG, whose Share Our Wealth clubs had enlisted millions of supporters. Townsend agreed to support the new party, as did Gerald L. K. Smith, who had assumed leadership of the Share Our Wealth clubs after Long's assassination in 1935.

But by 1936, the potential strength of those groups had faded. Not only was the magnetic Long dead, but the SECOND NEW DEAL of 1935, by passing such measures as the SOCIAL SECURITY ACT and the REVENUE ACT OF 1935 (or "Wealth Tax"), had seemed to meet key demands of Townsend and Long. Roosevelt in 1936 proved again an adept campaigner, aggressively reaching out to lower-income voters who had seemed dissatisfied a year earlier. With no real organization, indeed with no common cause apart from its leaders' enmity for Roosevelt, the Union party fell into bitter disarray. Townsend distanced himself from the campaign, and Smith and Coughlin became increasingly intemperate. Calling Roosevelt a "betrayer and

liar," a communist, and a "scab president," Coughlin was denounced by his superiors in the Catholic Church. When Coughlin began calling Lemke "Liberty Bell Lemke," critics reminded voters that the Liberty Bell was cracked. Lemke (educated at Georgetown and at Yale Law School) campaigned gamely on, but with no success. Coughlin had claimed that the party would win at least 9 million votes; in fact, it won only 882,479, just 1.9 percent of the vote. Coughlin veered into the ANTI-SEMITISM that marked the rest of his career. Lemke tried to keep the party alive, but he gave up the effort by the end of the decade.

Further reading: David H. Bennett, *Demagogues in the Great Depression: American Radicals and the Union Party, 1932–1936* (New Brunswick, N.J.: Rutgers University Press, 1969); Alan Brinkley, *Voices of Protest: Huey Long, Father Coughlin, and the Great Depression* (New York: Knopf, 1982).

United Nations (UN)

As WORLD WAR II drew to a close in the spring of 1945, the leaders of the Allied nations sought to establish an international organization to ensure lasting world peace. Representatives of 50 nations met in San Francisco in April 1945 to flesh out an agreement on the charter of the United Nations based especially on the principle of collective security to combat aggression. Reflecting the wartime change toward internationalism in American FOREIGN POLICY, the U.S. Senate ratified the UN Charter on July 28, 1945, by a vote of 89 to 2.

From the beginning of World War II, the Allied nations opposing the AXIS took steps toward international cooperation to defeat Germany and then to preserve peace in the postwar era. Representatives of nine European nations joined with Britain and members of the Commonwealth in signing the Inter-Allied Declaration in 1941, which united these countries in their efforts to liberate Europe from Hitler so that its people could live in peace and security. While the European allies took the initial step toward a United Nations with the Inter-Allied Declaration, the ATLANTIC CHARTER, issued by President FRANKLIN D. ROOSEVELT and British prime minister Winston Churchill in August 1941, linked the United States to this mission of freedom and cooperation—though Roosevelt at this stage opposed a public declaration of a new collective security organization. The Declaration by United Nations (January 1942), the first official use of the phrase *United Nations*, sanctioned the goals of the Atlantic Charter and was signed by some two dozen nations, including the United States, Great Britain, and the Soviet Union. Later, at the TEHERAN CONFERENCE (1943), Roosevelt, Churchill, and Soviet premier Joseph Stalin agreed to the idea of an international organization charged with preserving world peace.

Because of lessons learned from the coming of World War II, and because of the efforts of President Roosevelt and his administration, American public opinion and foreign policy shifted decisively toward internationalism during the early and mid-1940s. Roosevelt, like other Americans, believed that the weaknesses of the League of Nations had contributed to unchecked aggression and the breakdown of peace in the 1930s and that a new collective security organization would have to be based on a more realistic readiness to use force to stop aggression and prevent war. Learning from Woodrow Wilson's mistakes, Roosevelt also made certain to include Republicans in the planning process.

Further discussions among the Allied nations in the fall of 1944, at the Dumbarton Oaks Conference in Washington, led to several concrete proposals that were eventually included in the UN Charter, including a major role for the Security Council in preventing conflicts and brokering peace agreements. Disagreements between American and Soviet negotiators at these meetings reflected the emerging rift in SOVIET-AMERICAN RELATIONS. In February 1945, Roosevelt, Churchill, and Stalin met at the YALTA CONFERENCE, where they announced plans for the United Nations Conference on International Organization.

The conference opened in San Francisco on April 25, 1945. Delegates from 50 nations worked out the details of the UN Charter, amid major disagreements over the veto power of the larger nations. Though unable to curb the role of the major Allied powers on the Security Council, the smaller nations were successful at increasing the relative importance of the other more egalitarian organs such as the General Assembly and the Economic and Social Council.

Article 1 of the United Nations Charter enunciated its objectives: to maintain international peace and security; to develop friendly relations among nations based on mutual respect for the principle of equal rights and self-determination of peoples; to achieve international cooperation in addressing international problems of an economic, social, cultural, or humanitarian nature; and to operate as a center for harmonizing the actions of nations in order to reach these ends. The charter enumerated six principal organs: the General Assembly, the Security Council, the Economic and Social Council, the Trusteeship Council, the International Court of Justice, and the Secretariat. Chiefly responsible for keeping the peace, the Security Council was delegated the most critical task.

The five major Allied powers—the United States, the Soviet Union, Britain, France, and China—became permanent members of the UN's peacekeeping arm, the Security Council, each holding the right to veto its actions. The charter took effect on October 24, 1945, the date cele-

brated annually as United Nations Day. In January 1946, the first session of the 51-member Assembly convened in London, before voting to move the UN headquarters to New York, its present location. Cold war tensions between the United States and the USSR sometimes threatened to paralyze the United Nations, casting doubt over its ability to maintain international peace and security.

In the decades after 1945 the United Nations grew to include almost every country in the world, expanding rapidly during the postwar period from 51 countries in 1945 to nearly 190 in 2002. As its budget, its mission, and its sometimes controversial role in the arbitration of conflicts between nations spread, the UN helped to establish the independent states of Israel and Pakistan in the late 1940s. Dominated by the Americans, UN forces waged the Korean War from 1950 to 1953. In addition to numerous peacekeeping missions around the world in subsequent years, various UN agencies have worked to improve health and environmental standards for the world's people.

See also CORDELL HULL.

Further reading: Robert A. Divine, *Second Chance: The Triumph of Internationalism during World War II* (New York: Atheneum, 1967); Townsend Hoopes and Douglas Brinkley, *FDR and the Creation of the U.N.* (New Haven, Conn.: Yale University Press, 1997).

—Joseph C. Gutberlet

United Service Organizations (USO)

The United Service Organizations (USO) was created in 1941, after President FRANKLIN D. ROOSEVELT urged six private welfare organizations to meet the off-duty recreation and relaxation needs of members of the armed forces. The six agencies that pooled their resources to form the USO were the Salvation Army, the National Catholic Community Services, the Young Men's Christian Association, the Young Women's Christian Association, the National Travelers Aid Association, and the National Jewish Welfare Board. This combined enterprise sought to avoid the contention and overlapping efforts that plagued such private-sector agencies in World War I, though not with total success. Often concerned about their own welfare and visibility, and with differing goals and constituencies, the agencies sometimes quarreled or complained about the assignment of specific USO sites and responsibilities.

Such interagency disagreements did not, however, prevent the USO from successfully meeting its aim of helping to sustain the morale of the armed forces during WORLD WAR II. By 1944 there were approximately 3,000 local USO sites, providing facilities for a variety of activities from washing up to writing letters, to simply resting in lounges. USO personnel also gathered local sightseeing information,

Seen here are the Andrews Sisters—La Verne, Maxene, and Patty—an extremely popular singing trio who performed in USO productions for troops around the world.
(National Archives)

and provided local clergy for personal counseling. Perhaps the best-known activities of the USO, but not necessarily the most important, were the camp shows. Organized with the help of the entertainment industry, the USO camp shows brought live entertainment to bases in the United States and overseas. Star entertainers such as Bob Hope and the Andrews Sisters were especially prominent in bringing first-rate performances to troops stationed around the world.

The USO played a significant role in the war, both on the home front and overseas. Providing RECREATION, relaxation, and entertainment, the USO also reminded the men and women in the armed forces that the nation supported them, thus helping to sustain the morale of youth pursuing essential, challenging, and often dangerous military tasks far from home.

Further reading: Maxene Andrews, *Over Here, Over There: The Andrews Sisters and the USO Stars in World War II* (Washington, D.C.: Zebra Books, 1993); Gretchen Knapp, "Experimental Social Policymaking during World War II: The United States Organizations (USO) and American War Community Services (AWCS)," *Journal of Policy History* 12, no. 3 (2000): 321–38.

—Amanda Lea Miracle

United States Housing Authority (USHA)

The United States Housing Authority (USHA) was created by the United States Housing Act of 1937. The first agency specifically concerned with urban HOUSING, the USHA was charged with clearing slum units and building low-cost, livable housing for low-income Americans. Like many NEW DEAL social programs, the USHA suffered from insufficient funding because of conservative opposition in CONGRESS to such an expansion of the role of the federal GOVERNMENT. But while the initial accomplishments of the agency were limited, the USHA did set the precedent for federal efforts to alleviate the shortage of adequate housing in America's CITIES and for a much larger government role in the postwar period.

The first New Deal efforts to address urban housing came from the PUBLIC WORKS ADMINISTRATION. The agency allocated funds for new home construction in 1933, but the PWA's director, HAROLD ICKES, was extremely careful in expending his funds, wanting to make sure every PWA project was an efficient use of government money. By 1937, the Housing Division of the PWA had built only 25,000 new housing units.

Ickes's caution was not the major impediment to New Deal housing policy. President FRANKLIN D. ROOSEVELT was not a major supporter of public housing, and the New Deal was interested first and foremost in reviving the sagging home mortgage industry through the HOME OWNERS LOAN CORPORATION and the FEDERAL HOUSING ADMINISTRATION. Primarily aimed at middle-class homeowners, neither agency actively engaged in promoting affordable home construction in cities. In addition, there was considerable opposition to federally funded public housing by southern Democrats and conservative Republicans with ties to BUSINESS. Neither group saw public housing as benefiting important parts of their constituencies—rural residents of the SOUTH and banking and realty interests in the North. But as the shortcomings of the PWA's Housing Division came clear by 1935, New York senator ROBERT F. WAGNER began pushing for a more comprehensive public housing program.

Wagner introduced his housing bill several times before he received the reluctant support of President Roosevelt in 1937. As created by the United States Housing Act (sometimes known as the Wagner Public Housing Act) of 1937, the USHA emerged as a compromise agency, with provisions that limited the agency's spending to 10 percent in any one state to make sure that USHA did not operate only in large northern cities, capped building expenditures per unit, made local financial participation a condition to receiving USHA funds, and cut the initial appropriation to half of the $1 billion Wagner had proposed. But while the record of public housing building by the USHA never produced nearly the amount of low-cost housing units that Wagner had envisioned, the agency did provide the first precedent for federally funded public housing.

The first years of the agency reflected the limitations placed upon the USHA and the lukewarm reception given to public housing. Municipalities and other local units of government who chose to participate were required to set up local housing authorities to administer their public housing as well as financially contribute to the units' cost. By 1939, there were only 221 local housing authorities created to take advantage of the USHA's funds and fewer than 150,000 new housing units built, with the building rate decreasing rapidly after 1939, when Congress cut the USHA's appropriation.

Under President Harry S. Truman, the USHA was given new life in 1949, when recognition of a severe housing shortage created an alliance of urban Democrats and Republicans. But while the 1949 Housing Act allowed for 810,000 new public housing units, just over 350,000 were built in 1910. Overall, the USHA built only one-tenth of the estimated number of public housing units needed from 1939 to 1960. When the Department of Housing and Urban Development (HUD) was created in 1965 as a cabinet-level agency, it reflected the growing role of the federal government in the problems faced by American cities in the latter half of the 20th century.

Further reading: Mark I. Gelfand, *A Nation of Cities: The Federal Government and Urban America, 1935–1965* (New York: Oxford University Press, 1975); Gail Radford, *Modern Housing for America: Policy Struggles in the New Deal Era* (Chicago: University of Chicago Press, 1997).

—Katherine Liapis Segrue

V

V-E Day

V-E Day is the term that designates the day of Victory in Europe in WORLD WAR II. Germany surrendered unconditionally to the Allied Powers on May 7, 1945, but May 8 was the date of the official announcements and celebrations of V-E Day. U.S. president Harry S. Truman, British prime minister Winston Churchill, and Soviet premier Joseph Stalin, representing the wartime GRAND ALLIANCE that had defeated Germany, decided to coordinate a time when they would formally announce the victory in Europe to their countries. Churchill and especially Truman (the Soviet Union was not yet at war with Japan) hoped to limit the excitement and keep their citizens from losing sight of the war in the WORLD WAR II PACIFIC THEATER, where Japan was reeling but not expected to surrender soon.

World reaction to V-E Day varied according to country. Truman kept his speech restrained by expressing great satisfaction over Germany's surrender, but also warning the country to stay focused on the war in the Pacific. Generally low-key celebrations took place in the United States, and within a week attention to the end of the war in Europe had faded and American newspapers were emphasizing the Pacific theater. Churchill, like Truman, reminded his nation that the war in the Pacific would likely be long and difficult. Still, compared to the somewhat restrained reaction in the United States, British reaction was jubilant—not surprisingly, since Britain had been directly attacked by Germany, had undergone such anxiety and loss in the war, and was not so heavily involved as the United States in the Pacific theater. For the British, the WORLD WAR II EUROPEAN THEATER was the dominant part of their war, and V-E Day was a time of great celebration in London and throughout the United Kingdom. France, defeated by Germany in 1940 and liberated by the Allies in 1944, responded joyously as well, as did the Soviet Union, which had suffered so grievously from the German invasion, losing 20 million or more soldiers and civilians.

There was much work to be done after V-E Day, in rebuilding Europe, winning the war in the Pacific, and working to establish a permanent peace. Accordingly, Americans looked at V-E Day as a significant event to be celebrated, a giant but not the final step to the end of the war, and only the beginning of a period of readjustment at home and abroad.

See also V-J DAY.

—Prathyusha B. Reddy

V-J Day

Victory over Japan Day (V-J Day) was celebrated on August 14 and into August 15, 1945, after President Harry S. Truman announced the surrender of Japan to end WORLD WAR II, although it was officially observed on September 2, when the surrender documents were signed.

On the morning of August 10, 1945, just days after the dropping of the ATOMIC BOMBS on HIROSHIMA AND NAGASAKI and the Soviet declaration of war against Japan, President Truman received a letter from the War Department containing an informal message relayed through the Swiss government that Japan was ready to surrender, but with the emperor remaining in power. This conflicted with the unconditional surrender demanded by the POTSDAM CONFERENCE, and the war continued until a satisfactory solution was reached by an agreement that the emperor's powers were "subject to the Supreme Commander of the Allied Powers."

On August 14, at 7 P.M. Eastern War Time in Washington, President Truman announced, simultaneously with Great Britain and the Soviet Union, the surrender of Japan. The true V-J Day, Truman said, "must wait until formal signing of the surrender terms by Japan." Americans said differently, and joyous demonstrations erupted across the country on August 14. Los Angeles celebrated with spontaneous parades; crowds in Salt Lake City danced in the rain; and in Washington, D.C., jubilant conga lines formed in front of the White House. Nothing was so memorable as the scene in New York City, where an estimated 2 million Americans thronged around Times Square, hugging and kissing and together celebrating the end of the war. Celebrations, sometimes more organized, continued on August 15.

The end of the war was officially observed on September 2, 1945, when surrender documents were signed aboard the USS *Missouri* in Tokyo Bay. The actual signing was anticlimatic because the war had been over for nearly three weeks, and Americans were attempting to adjust to the new world that World War II had created. On the home front, Americans faced the challenges of DEMOBILIZATION and RECONVERSION. In the area of international relations, postwar efforts to avoid yet a third major conflict provided a primary focus. Growing tension and suspicions in SOVIET-AMERICAN RELATIONS added to concerns, especially among American policymakers. And the world had now entered the atomic age. Americans had much to celebrate on V-J Day, but also much to ponder.

See also V-E DAY.

—Jonathan R. Mikeska

W

wage and price controls

Because the economic MOBILIZATION for World War II raised employment and income and diverted production to needed war goods, a potentially dangerous "inflationary gap" threatened to open because of increasing disposable income and the restricted availability of consumer goods. In order to head off inflation, the GOVERNMENT imposed price controls and wage controls. (RATIONING helped to ensure the fair allocation of essential items.) By 1943, a generally effective system of wage and price controls had been implemented, and wartime inflation was held within reasonable bounds. It must be noted, however, that economists and economic historians have produced a number of divergent estimates of wartime price levels and that official figures underestimate, perhaps seriously, the real inflation of the war years.

As with rationing, the public understood the need for wage and price controls but typically disliked them nonetheless. As always, moreover, personal circumstances and interests shaped opinion. BUSINESS liked wage controls much more than price controls; LABOR had just the opposite reaction. Farmers might applaud price controls on manufactured goods, but farm products were another matter. Landlords approved of price controls but not of rent controls.

The development of a satisfactory system of wage and price controls took several years and mirrored the early difficulties overall in economic mobilization. In April 1941, President FRANKLIN D. ROOSEVELT established the Office of Price Administration and Civilian Supply (OPACS) headed by LEON HENDERSON. Like other agencies created before PEARL HARBOR and the American entry into the war, the OPACS had little authority and effectiveness. In August 1941, FDR replaced it with the OFFICE OF PRICE ADMINISTRATION (OPA), also under Henderson; then, in January 1942, CONGRESS gave the OPA authority to set maximum prices on nonfarm goods and rents with the Emergency Price Control Act.

In April 1942, the OPA froze most prices at the highest level reached in March 1942. (The order was called the General Maximum Price Regulation—or, in the wartime atmosphere, "General Max.") But General Max could not regulate farm prices or wages, involved various discrepancies and inequities, and failed to stop price rises. Congress allowed agricultural prices to reach 110 percent of the parity level of the AGRICULTURAL ADMINISTRATION ACT of the NEW DEAL. Manufacturers found ways around price controls by introducing slight changes in packaging or content of items that allowed them to call them "new" items not falling under the authority of General Max. The OPA did have more success with rent controls.

As the OPA tried to implement effective price controls, the administration turned to the other side of the equation—wage controls. In July 1942, the NATIONAL WAR LABOR BOARD (NWLB) enacted the so-called Little Steel formula (developed in working with the smaller steel companies) allowing a 15 percent increase in hourly wage rates after January 1, 1941 (to compensate for the rise of prices between then and May 1942). The formula applied to regular hourly wages, but not to overtime or incentive pay, benefits, or job upgrades. Average weekly earnings ultimately increased by some two-thirds.

Together the "General Max" and "Little Steel" policies helped check the upward movement of prices and wages. In October 1942, Roosevelt persuaded Congress to pass the Economic Stabilization Act and arranged for SUPREME COURT justice JAMES F. BYRNES to head the new Office of Economic Stabilization, with power over farm prices and wages. In April 1943, FDR issued a "hold-the-line" order on wages and prices.

By 1943, inflation had largely been brought under control. The consumer price index rose only by about 4 percent for the rest of the war, after having increased by some 24 percent from 1939 to 1943. The wage and price control programs were by no means perfect or altogether equitable. Some prices and incomes rose faster than others.

While the NWLB turned down requests to allow raising wages of the lowest-paid workers—in 1944, one-fourth of manufacturing workers earned less than 60¢ per hour—conservatives in Congress beat back administration efforts to cap salaries of the well-off. The consumer price index, in addition to underestimating wartime inflation, did not take into account such hidden price increases as diminished quality, choice, discounts, and services, or the prices paid on the wartime BLACK MARKET. Yet despite the problems, the efforts did have important success; and although controls were never very popular, most Americans understood the need for wage and price controls and accepted the principle.

Further reading: Lester V. Chandler, *Inflation in the United States, 1940–1948* (New York: Harper & Row, 1951); Harold G. Vatter, *The U.S. Economy in World War II* (New York: Columbia University Press, 1985).

Wagner, Robert F. (1877–1953)

Robert Ferdinand Wagner, a Democratic United States senator from New York from 1927 to 1949, became the leading voice and symbol of urban LIBERALISM. He was an important supporter of the NEW DEAL, an assertive advocate of LABOR, and an architect of significant reform legislation.

Wagner was born in Germany in 1877, and his family immigrated to the United States in 1886, settling in New York City. The youngest of seven children, he was able to attend City College through the efforts of his family. He then went on to New York Law School and became involved in local politics as a student. In 1904, Wagner won his first election, to the state assembly, as the Tammany Hall candidate. He spent the next two decades involved in New York politics, elected a state senator in 1908 and then a state supreme court judge in 1918. Over the years Wagner became increasingly liberal, and with state assembly leader Al Smith provided New York with one of the most progressive labor laws of the time following the tragic 1911 Triangle Shirtwaist Company fire. When Wagner was elected to the United States Senate in 1926, he brought his concern about the working class to CONGRESS.

During the HOOVER PRESIDENCY, Wagner became one of the most vocal proponents of measures to address rising UNEMPLOYMENT. After the GREAT DEPRESSION struck in 1929, Wagner pushed hard for his "three bills" legislation—to collect better unemployment data, to fund public works projects, and to strengthen the United States Employment Service. His efforts led to the RELIEF AND RECONSTRUCTION ACT of 1932, which authorized the RECONSTRUCTION FINANCE CORPORATION to lend states and municipalities up to $1.5 billion for self-liquidating public works projects

and states up to $300 million for RELIEF assistance to the unemployed.

By 1933, Wagner was disappointed by what had been done to alleviate the Great Depression. He was an early supporter of the candidacy of New York governor FRANKLIN D. ROOSEVELT for president in 1932, although his friendship with Al Smith kept him from publicly campaigning for FDR. When Roosevelt was elected, Wagner worked closely with the administration and sometimes went well beyond it in advocating labor, public HOUSING, and other reforms aimed especially at the urban working class. A proponent of antilynching legislation efforts during the 1930s, Wagner also supported CIVIL RIGHTS for AFRICAN AMERICANS.

Wagner is perhaps best known for successfully championing landmark legislation for labor unions. When the NATIONAL INDUSTRIAL RECOVERY ACT (NIRA) of 1933 was being drafted in Congress, Wagner ensured that it not tilt too far toward BUSINESS by insisting that collective bargaining, minimum wage, and maximum hours provisions were included in Section 7(a) of the legislation. But Section 7(a) did less than he had hoped to underwrite labor organization, despite his efforts to strengthen its enforcement. In 1935, after the SUPREME COURT had declared the NIRA unconstitutional, Wagner pressed for the NATIONAL LABOR RELATIONS ACT (also known as the Wagner Act). Despite lukewarm support from FDR and Secretary of Labor FRANCES PERKINS, the NLRA passed Congress in June 1935, and was signed by Roosevelt in July. Establishing the NATIONAL LABOR RELATIONS BOARD with the power to oversee union elections and investigate unfair business practices, the Wagner Act was justly called the magna carta of labor for guaranteeing its right to organize and bargain collectively.

Another of Wagner's major concerns was the lack of adequate and affordable housing for low-income Americans. Early New Deal programs, such as the HOME OWNERS LOAN CORPORATION and the FEDERAL HOUSING ADMINISTRATION were concerned more with the sagging construction and mortgage industries than with providing affordable housing. Beginning in 1935, Wagner began introducing legislation to provide federal money to build low-income public housing, again with only reluctant support from FDR. The resulting U.S. Housing Act of 1937 (sometimes known as the Wagner Public Housing Act) created the UNITED STATES HOUSING AUTHORITY, which provided money to local housing authorities to build low-income housing units.

During WORLD WAR II, Wagner had less success in advancing liberal reform. He was particularly concerned about the postwar period, fearful that the economic depression would reemerge once the nation began DEMOBILIZATION. In 1943, the Wagner-Murray-Dingall bill was introduced, which would have greatly expanded the welfare state set up by New Deal programs such as the SOCIAL SECURITY ACT of 1935. It also included national health insurance. After it died in committee, a less expansive version was reintroduced in 1945 and also went nowhere. Despite these setbacks to social welfare policy for the postwar era, Wagner persevered, cosponsoring the FULL EMPLOYMENT BILL of 1945, which declared the right to a job for all Americans. It was passed as the watered-down, though still significant, Employment Act of 1946.

By the late 1940s, Wagner finally began to accept that neither Congress, controlled since the late 1930s by a CONSERVATIVE COALITION, nor the nation, prosperous again, was prepared for more sweeping liberal reform. In ill health since 1940, Wagner resigned from the Senate on June 29, 1949, and returned to New York. He passed away on May 4, 1953.

Further reading: J. Joseph Huthmacher, *Senator Robert F. Wagner and the Rise of Urban Liberalism* (New York: Atheneum, 1968).

—Katherine Liapis Segrue

Wallace, Henry A. (1888–1965)

Secretary of agriculture and vice president of the United States under President FRANKLIN D. ROOSEVELT, Henry A. Wallace was a major proponent and architect of NEW DEAL policies of the 1930s and an insistent advocate of liberal domestic and FOREIGN POLICY in the 1940s. He ran unsuccessfully for president as the Progressive Party candidate in 1948.

Born on October 7, 1888, and raised in Iowa, Wallace was the son of a Republican secretary of agriculture in the 1920s, Henry C. Wallace. Young Wallace demonstrated an independent streak both in politics and farming. Creative by nature, he was an early proponent and developer of scientific farming. Wallace conducted experiments in the hybridization of corn, and this early work was later credited as a major catalyst for the "green revolution" of the 20th century. In 1926, Wallace founded a hybrid seed company. By 1928, he had broken with the REPUBLICAN PARTY over its farm and tariff policies.

Roosevelt tapped Wallace, who had supported him in the ELECTION OF 1932, as his first secretary of agriculture. Controversial throughout his years in Washington, Wallace served as agriculture secretary during Roosevelt's first two terms. His principal responsibility was the AGRICULTURAL ADJUSTMENT ACT, a cornerstone of the FIRST NEW DEAL of 1933, which sought to resolve the crisis in AGRICULTURE through subsidies and production controls. But his views and goals expanded from his efforts to rescue commercial farming and he became increasingly concerned with small

and struggling farmers. Along with such presidential advisers as HARRY HOPKINS, HAROLD ICKES, and ELEANOR ROOSEVELT, Wallace also advocated the implementation and expansion of adequate RELIEF programs, public works projects, progressive TAXATION, and other liberal New Deal programs to help not just farmers but also destitute and struggling Americans of all types.

In the ELECTION OF 1940, Roosevelt prepared to seek an unprecedented third term as president and personally selected the liberal Wallace as his running mate despite the disgruntled reaction of many Democrats. As vice president, Wallace helped organize MOBILIZATION efforts during WORLD WAR II, headed the Board of Economic Warfare, and served as one of the leading voices of LIBERALISM. But he was often frustrated with what he saw as the administration's increasing conservatism and became increasingly outspoken. He advocated liberal domestic programs and also a "Century of the Common Man," in which the United States would assist the underprivileged and attempt to spread democratic beliefs. Wallace's progressivism was not popular with many in the DEMOCRATIC PARTY, and his often eccentric and impolitic ways alienated party professionals. In the ELECTION OF 1944, when Roosevelt ran for a fourth term, Wallace was removed from the ticket with FDR's acquiescence and replaced by Senator Harry S. Truman, who was regarded as more moderate.

Still loyal to Roosevelt and the party, Wallace accepted a post as secretary of commerce at the beginning of FDR's new term in 1945. He continued to clash with the administration's conservative members, particularly former commerce secretary JESSE H. JONES, a pro-BUSINESS Texas banker. Following Roosevelt's death in April 1945, Wallace retained his cabinet position under Truman, but the often-strained relationship between the two men deteriorated badly. Amid rising anticommunism and cold war fears, fostered in part by the Truman administration, Wallace's call for a conciliatory stance toward the Soviet Union rankled the president. Throughout 1946, Wallace publicly criticized the ATOMIC BOMB tests on Bikini atoll, the proliferation of air bases throughout Europe and Asia, and increasing American militarism in general. In September 1946, Truman fired Wallace after the commerce secretary delivered a particularly fierce attack on the administration's foreign policy. Wallace remained politically active and later that year became editor of the liberal *New Republic*.

In 1948, Wallace challenged Truman for the presidency. As the Progressive Party candidate, Wallace proposed a minimum wage, federal aid to EDUCATION, and a national health care system, and made a special appeal to minorities with the inclusion of a CIVIL RIGHTS plank. He also explicitly condemned Truman's employee loyalty program, which had forced applicants for federal jobs to reveal their political activities and renounce communism. While mainstream liberals embraced "Vital Center" liberalism, with its emphasis on anticommunism and attacks on the tyranny of Soviet leader Joseph Stalin, Wallace and the Progressives argued that cooperation with the Soviet Union, even the sharing of atomic technologies, was possible—and were accused of being a communist front. Wallace and the Progressives garnered only 1.2 million votes out of some 49 million cast in Truman's upset victory over Republican candidate Thomas E. Dewey.

Following his poor showing in 1948, Wallace remained largely absent from the political scene, and he died in relative obscurity in 1965.

Further reading: John C. Culver and John Hyde, *American Dreamer: The Life and Times of Henry A. Wallace* (New York: W. W. Norton Press, 2000); Graham J. White and John Maze, *Henry A. Wallace: His Search for a New World Order* (Chapel Hill: University of North Carolina Press, 1995).

—Douglas G. Weaver

war bonds

Soon after the entrance of the United States into WORLD WAR II, Secretary of the Treasury HENRY MORGENTHAU, JR., announced that war bonds would be available for purchase by the American public. The bonds, redeemable for a higher price after being held for a fixed period of time, were sold for the multiple purposes of providing funds for the GOVERNMENT, involving the public in the war effort, and combating inflation by providing a savings outlet for the higher incomes and greater spending power of the war years.

Bond purchases by the public accounted for a far smaller part of government borrowing (which paid for more than half the costs of the war) than did such commercial enterprises as banks and corporations. However, Morgenthau and President FRANKLIN D. ROOSEVELT felt that it was important that Americans feel connected to the war effort. Morgenthau saw selling bonds as an opportunity to "sell the war," and war bond campaigns became in part a form of PROPAGANDA, encouraging Americans to buy bonds as part of their patriotic duty. Morgenthau and Roosevelt also preferred a voluntary savings program provided by bonds to a compulsory one and hoped for heavy public purchases. Stars of MOVIES and SPORTS, as well as other celebrities, traveled the nation and performed for free at events at which war bonds were promoted and sold, and ADVERTISING agencies contributed their expertise to the bond campaigns.

Americans of all income levels bought war bonds, thanks to the small-denomination Series E bonds, and to the war stamps that could be bought for pennies and then collected and redeemed for bonds. Many people had money regularly taken out of their paychecks for the purchase of bonds, and in 1944 sales of E bonds absorbed about 7 percent of after-tax personal income. Although sales to the public were not as high as the administration had hoped, estimates of individual bond sales range as high as $50 billion, or up to one-sixth of the costs of fighting the war.

—Joanna Smith

War Manpower Commission (WMC)

President FRANKLIN D. ROOSEVELT created the War Manpower Commission (WMC) on April 18, 1942, about four months after PEARL HARBOR and the American entry into WORLD WAR II. With the NATIONAL WAR LABOR BOARD and the WAR PRODUCTION BOARD, the WMC was charged with facilitating full production by the nation's war industries. More specifically, the WMC was to ensure there were enough workers for war and essential civilian industries in the war MOBILIZATION effort.

President Roosevelt's decision that the United States would provide military forces in both the WORLD WAR II EUROPEAN THEATER and the WORLD WAR II PACIFIC THEATER while also serving as the "arsenal of democracy" for the GRAND ALLIANCE that fought the AXIS created a manpower dilemma. In early 1942, planners estimated that defeating the Axis powers might require a combined military and civilian work force of up to 60 million people, or about 45 percent of the U.S. population. Balancing military and production requirements would be difficult if the military grew larger than 8.2 million, some military planners said. Yet by 1945, approximately 16 million men had joined the military, and in 1942 millions of men began reporting for military duty, sometimes leaving key industries and also AGRICULTURE facing shortages of workers.

The massive mobilization of the labor force was hardly flawless. Throughout the war, a number of problems highlighted the difficulty of coordination in an increasingly complex and interdependent modern society. Agencies with overlapping mandates often refused to cooperate or to coordinate their efforts. Many of these problems fell at the feet of Roosevelt, who demonstrated an unwillingness to delegate broad authority to any single agency to manage the mobilization effort. Ultimately, however, the nation's military and production needs were met.

FDR named former Indiana governor Paul V. McNutt to head the WMC and direct manpower policy. McNutt soon tried to consolidate the functions of about 20 agencies responsible for different aspects of the manpower effort. The president, however, did not place SELECTIVE SERVICE, which administered the military draft, under the WMC until McNutt complained in December 1942. The WMC faced similar problems with other agencies and departments. In January 1943 it lost control over the agricultural labor supply to the Labor Department. The Civil Service Commission began recruiting workers independently to fill the expanding wartime bureaucracy. As the war continued, the WMC also lost authority over railroad workers and merchant marine sailors.

Putting Selective Service under the WMC did not alleviate McNutt's problems. Throughout the war, the military attempted to keep the WMC and other civilian-run agencies from dictating either manpower or procurement policies. Although the Selective Service System technically reported to the WMC, the War Department continued to treat the agency as its own and expected it to represent military interests. The Selective Service System, and its director, General Lewis Hershey, responded and fought to ensure that the military always received the number and quality of men it asked for, sometimes over WMC objections. In late 1943, CONGRESS, overruling FDR, made the Selective Service System an independent agency free of WMC control. Congress effectively had prevented the president from integrating the draft into the overall manpower program.

The primary means the WMC used to manage industrial manpower became the draft deferment, which excused from military service certain groups of civilian workers, including farmers, deemed essential to the war effort. In all, some 5 million such deferments were granted. But factories often competed for skilled workers, which led to high turnover and production inefficiencies. Compounding the situation was the government's refusal to outlaw strikes and its rejection of national service and "work or fight" programs that would have allowed it to draft workers for jobs in industry or agriculture.

In May 1943, Roosevelt decided he needed a more powerful agency to better allocate resources, coordinate the mobilization effort, and ameliorate the political bickering among the agencies. He created the OFFICE OF WAR MOBILIZATION, (OWM), which toward the end of the war became the OFFICE OF WAR MOBILIZATION AND RECONVERSION (OWMR). The president named JAMES F. BYRNES, a former Supreme Court justice and U.S. senator from South Carolina, as the new agency's director.

Although subordinate to the OWM and then the OWMR, the WMC operated with little interference from Byrnes, whose philosophy was that the OWM must not administer anything or interfere with the normal operations of existing agencies. For the remainder of the war, the WMC recruited and trained labor for the war effort, analyzed manpower utilization practices to increase labor efficiency, and issued lists of deferrable and nondeferrable jobs that were sometimes not followed by local draft boards. The WMC was dissolved on September 19, 1945, after

Japan's formal surrender earlier in the month. McNutt soon was named high commissioner for the Philippines.

Further reading: George Q. Flynn, *The Mess in Washington: Manpower Mobilization in World War II* (Westport, Conn.: Greenwood Press, 1979); Herman M. Somers, *Presidential Agency: The Office of War Mobilization and Reconversion* (Cambridge, Mass.: Harvard University Press, 1950).

—Edwin D. Miller

War Production Board (WPB)

President FRANKLIN D. ROOSEVELT established the War Production Board (WPB) in January 1942, just a month after the Japanese attack on PEARL HARBOR. The agency was designed to coordinate America's economic MOBILIZATION for WORLD WAR II and to resolve the difficult problems of setting material and production priorities. However, because its director, DONALD M. NELSON, was not a strong leader and lacked authority over important segments of the ECONOMY, the WPB's power and effectiveness fell far short of Roosevelt's intentions.

In 1940, with America's entry into World War II seeming increasingly likely, the United States began a massive effort to mobilize its industrial and economic resources for war. But until the creation of the OFFICE OF WAR MOBILIZATION in 1943, the agencies involved were poorly organized and frequently at odds with each other. Moreover, down to Pearl Harbor, several key industries, such as the AUTOMOBILE INDUSTRY and the STEEL INDUSTRY, were reluctant to convert to wartime production. To encourage American BUSINESS to convert to wartime production, the GOVERNMENT from the beginning of its mobilization efforts walked a fine line between coercion and persuasion, and often gave government subsidies, low-cost loans, and quick tax write-offs to businesses that agreed to invest in defense production.

Although Nelson had been a Sears, Roebuck executive and had directed other mobilization efforts from 1940 to 1942, he lacked both the authority and the diplomatic and administrative skills needed to unify American business and organize America's mobilization efforts. The WPB did not have power over LABOR and manpower issues, and the OFFICE OF PRICE ADMINISTRATION was in charge of price controls. The U.S. ARMY and U.S. NAVY insisted upon their power to approve military contracts. President Roosevelt continued to create additional war mobilization agencies as well as several independent "czars" over manpower, rubber, and petroleum—areas that were beyond Nelson's control. Making things still more difficult, the mild-mannered and often indecisive Nelson had difficulty asserting his authority, especially over the single-minded and often battle-hardened officials in the War and Navy Departments, who were not likely to knuckle under to pressure from anyone outside their normal chain of command.

Before the WPB was created, CONGRESS had expressed the need for a strong central authority to administer America's mobilization efforts. As it became clear that Nelson and the WPB were not meeting the president's high production goals, several congressional committees urged the administration to replace the WPB with a more effective agency. Some members of Congress were also concerned, as they would be throughout the war, about what seemed the excessive influence of big business in the WPB and mobilization policy. Realizing that something needed to be done, and wanting to avoid undue congressional involvement in something he considered to be firmly within his authority, the president issued an executive order in May 1943 creating the Office of War Mobilization (OWM) to coordinate economic mobilization. The OWM was headed by JAMES F. BYRNES, who quickly succeeded Nelson as the director of the mobilization program.

The WPB became one of the OWM's subordinate agencies. Under this new organizational structure, the WPB helped to implement more efficient mobilization policies. The Controlled Materials Plan, which had been developed in late 1942 and which allowed the army and navy to continue awarding contracts while the WPB had power to allocate materials, proved especially effective. Nelson remained head of the WPB until June 1944, when he resigned after losing a fight with the military and business over his proposal to begin limited RECONVERSION to civilian production. The WPB itself was dissolved in November 1945 and the Civilian Production Administration was established to take over its remaining reconversion duties.

Further reading: Bruce Catton, *The War Lords of Washington* (New York: Harcourt Brace, 1948); Donald M. Nelson, *Arsenal of Democracy: The Story of American War Production* (New York: Harcourt, Brace, 1946); Eliot Janeway, *The Struggle for Survival: A Chronicle of Economic Mobilization in World War II* (New Haven, Conn.: Yale University Press, 1951).

—David W. Waltrop

Welles, Orson (1915–1985)

Known as the "Boy Wonder" of Hollywood for his early work as an actor and director there, Orson Welles was an innovator in RADIO, MOVIES, and the stage. His best-known works were the 1938 radio adaptation of H. G. Wells's *War of the Worlds*, which caused a nationwide panic, and the groundbreaking and controversial 1941 film *Citizen Kane*.

Orson Welles *(London Illustrated News)*

Welles was born in Wisconsin, in 1915, the son of upper-middle-class parents. After five years of schooling, Welles acted professionally from 1930 to 1934, moving to Broadway in 1934. While playing supporting roles on stage, he became a radio actor to help make ends meet and became famous as the voice of the mysterious crime fighter on the radio show *The Shadow*. Despite his radio work, Welles's main source of income remained the theater. With other theater workers and actors, Welles felt the effects of the GREAT DEPRESSION, and he became involved in the FEDERAL THEATRE PROJECT of the NEW DEAL's WORKS PROGRESS ADMINISTRATION. There, working with John Houseman, Welles mounted avant-garde dramas, including a production of *Macbeth* with a cast comprised entirely of AFRICAN AMERICANS.

In 1937, Welles and Houseman founded the Mercury Theater. Following some stage hits, the company moved on to radio and was reborn as the Mercury Theater of the Air, which broke new ground in radio with dramatic acting and innovative sound effects. On October 30, 1938, the Mercury Theater group performed its infamous broadcast of *The War of the Worlds*. Welles's production, portions of which were similar to a news bulletin, caused listeners across the United States to believe that Martians were invading Earth. Panic erupted, and some listeners even armed themselves to battle the Martians. The ensuing public uproar led to an investigation by the FEDERAL COMMUNICATIONS COMMISSION.

The Mercury Theater folded soon after the *War of the Worlds* broadcast, and the troupe moved to Hollywood, signing with RKO Pictures. Then Welles undertook his most ambitious project, *Citizen Kane,* whose plot centered on a publishing magnate resembling William Randolph Hearst. *Citizen Kane* broke new technical ground in a number of ways. It used impressionistic camera angles, sophisticated mood lighting for scenes, deep focus photography, new sound and editing methods, and flashbacks. Though now regarded as a historic and classic film, *Citizen Kane* was released in 1941 to mixed reviews and disappointing box-office business.

Hurt by Hollywood's refusal to accept him as a director (he demanded complete control over all aspects of his film productions), Welles turned to acting to finance his own low-budget movies. Over the years Welles appeared in such films as *The Third Man, Touch of Evil,* and *A Man for All Seasons.*

Further reading: Frank Brady, *Citizen Welles: A Biography of Orson Welles* (New York: Anchor Books, 1990); Simon Callow, *Orson Welles: The Road to Xanadu* (New York: Viking, 1996).

—Nicholas Fry

Welles, Sumner (1892–1961)

Sumner Welles, a friend and FOREIGN POLICY adviser of President FRANKLIN D. ROOSEVELT, served in several important posts in the State Department and was an architect of the GOOD NEIGHBOR POLICY toward Latin America in the 1930s.

Benjamin Sumner Welles was born in New York City on October 14, 1892. After graduation from Harvard University, he entered the foreign service in 1915. He became acting head of the Latin American Division in the State Department in 1921, and worked to improve the image of the United States in the region by reducing the American military presence there. After leaving the State Department in 1925, he maintained his interest in the region, and wrote a book about the Dominican Republic.

Welles was appointed assistant secretary of state in 1933, and played a leading role in implementing the Good Neighbor policy. Continuing his involvement in Latin American affairs as World War II approached, he was deeply involved in developing a common Western Hemisphere policy toward Nazi Germany at the Buenos Aires Inter-American Conference in 1936, and then later at the Rio de Janeiro Conference in 1942.

In 1937, Roosevelt appointed Welles under secretary of state over the objections of Secretary of State CORDELL HULL, and the president increasingly relied upon Welles's advice. Welles accompanied Roosevelt to the August 1941 Atlantic Conference, assisting in the preparation of the ATLANTIC CHARTER. He also played an important role in early State Department planning that led to the postwar UNITED NATIONS.

Hull resented Welles's close relationship with Roosevelt and his access to the president, believing that Welles was usurping his authority as secretary of state. In 1943, Hull told Roosevelt that either Welles would have to leave the administration or Hull himself would. Welles's own position was further complicated by innuendos regarding possible homosexual activity on his part. Though Welles had become a political liability, Roosevelt did not want to embarrass him; the president asked for his resignation and offered to send him on a special mission to Moscow. Welles refused this proposal but resigned on September 25, 1943.

Following his departure from the State Department, Welles continued to write on issues affecting diplomatic matters. Welles was married three times. He died in New Jersey in 1961.

Further reading: Irwin F. Gellman, *Secret Affairs: Franklin Roosevelt, Cordell Hull, and Sumner Welles* (Baltimore: Johns Hopkins University Press, 1995).

—Edwin C. Cogswell

Wheeler, Burton K. (1882–1975)

Burton Kendall Wheeler was a progressive four-term Democratic senator from Montana who became known best for his isolationist opposition to the FOREIGN POLICY of President FRANKLIN D. ROOSEVELT.

Born in Hudson, Massachusetts, on February 27, 1882, Wheeler settled in Butte, Montana, and opened a law practice there in 1905, after card sharps had left him broke while he was on his way west to pursue a legal career. He became active in local Democratic politics, served as Montana's U.S. attorney, and in 1922 was elected to his first of four terms in the U.S. Senate. Wheeler quickly came to national prominence, serving as a chief investigator of the scandals in the Warren G. Harding administration and running as the vice presidential candidate on the Progressive Party ticket of Robert M. La Follette in 1924.

A progressive Democrat who was inspired by William Jennings Bryan, Wheeler was among the first advocates of Roosevelt's presidential candidacy in 1932, and he supported most of the early NEW DEAL, especially in the areas of banking, securities, and utilities regulation. By the late 1930s, however, he was increasingly at odds with the president and his programs. Like other western Democrats still suspicious of excessive power in the central GOVERNMENT, Wheeler came to think the New Deal was going too far. He broke publicly with the president over the COURT-PACKING PLAN and played a decisive role in its defeat. Roosevelt excluded Wheeler from White House discussions of New Deal legislation and from Montana patronage decisions, and Wheeler compared Roosevelt to "a king trying to reduce the barons."

By the end of the decade, Wheeler became one of the most important and outspoken of the ISOLATIONISTS critical of Roosevelt's anti-AXIS foreign policy. He opposed the SELECTIVE SERVICE ACT, and he called the LEND-LEASE ACT the "New Deal's Triple-A foreign policy," saying "it will plough under every fourth American boy"—a statement that Roosevelt termed "the rottenest thing that has been said in public life in my generation." After considering a presidential bid for himself in 1940, Wheeler refused to campaign for Roosevelt's third term in the ELECTION OF 1940. Instead, he devoted his energy to speaking on behalf of the isolationist AMERICA FIRST COMMITTEE and opposing the president's interventionist foreign policy.

During WORLD WAR II, Wheeler's isolationism reduced his influence in the Senate. Ultimately, his isolationist and maverick ways split the Montana Democratic party, and he was denied renomination in 1946. Wheeler remained in Washington, D.C., until his death in 1975.

Further reading: Burton K. Wheeler, with Paul F. Healey, *Yankee from the West: The Candid, Turbulent Story of the Yankee-born U.S. Senator from Montana* (Garden City, N.Y.: Doubleday, 1962).

—William J. Thompson

White, Walter (1893–1955)

A leading advocate of CIVIL RIGHTS, and executive secretary of the NATIONAL ASSOCIATION FOR THE ADVANCEMENT OF COLORED PEOPLE (NAACP), Walter White devoted his life to seeking equality for AFRICAN AMERICANS.

Walter Francis White was born July 1, 1893, in Atlanta, Georgia. He attended Atlanta University, where he was elected class president, and graduated in 1916, after which he worked selling insurance. He chose to live his life as an African American, although only a small percentage of his ancestry was black, and his appearance was that of a white man. (He had light skin, blue eyes, and blond hair.) After joining the NAACP in 1916, he impressed the executive secretary, James Weldon Johnson, and was hired as an assistant secretary in 1918. White moved to New York, where the association was headquartered, but spent much of his time over the next several years traveling. He made speeches throughout the country and investigated

lynchings in the SOUTH, under the guise of a white reporter from Chicago. He published two novels in the 1920s—*The Fire in the Flint* (1924) and *Flight* (1926). Both dealt with issues of RACE AND RACIAL CONFLICT, as did his frequent magazine articles, his two syndicated newspaper columns, and his three other books. In 1930, he led the successful effort to prevent Judge John J. Parker, who favored racial segregation, from being appointed to the U.S. SUPREME COURT.

White succeeded Johnson as executive secretary of the NAACP in 1931. In that position, he devoted much energy to securing federal antilynching legislation, nearly succeeding in 1938 before the bill was finally defeated. He worked with A. PHILIP RANDOLPH to induce President FRANKLIN D. ROOSEVELT to establish the FAIR EMPLOYMENT PRACTICES COMMITTEE in 1941, their goal being to give blacks an opportunity to take part in the defense MOBILIZATION for WORLD WAR II. He continued to speak to large audiences worldwide, and although he was primarily concerned with American race relations, he also found time to serve as a government adviser on issues of the Virgin Islands and the UNITED NATIONS. In addition, he worked from 1943 to 1945 as a special war correspondent for the *New York Post*.

Walter White continued to lead the NAACP and remained active in pursuing its goals until his death in 1955.

Further reading: Walter Francis White, *A Man Called White: The Autobiography of Walter White* (New York: Viking, 1948).

—Joanna Smith

Willkie, Wendell L. (1892–1944)

The REPUBLICAN PARTY nominee for president in the ELECTION OF 1940, Wendell Lewis Willkie was born in Elwood, Indiana, on February 18, 1892. He graduated from Indiana University in 1913, taught high school in Kansas, worked at a Puerto Rico sugar factory, attended law school, and enlisted in the army after America entered World War I, though he did not see combat. After the war, Willkie moved to Akron, Ohio, where he established his own legal practice, and soon became one of the city's leading citizens. Active in DEMOCRATIC PARTY politics, Willkie was a delegate to the party's 1924, 1928, and 1932 national conventions and supported FRANKLIN D. ROOSEVELT for president in the ELECTION OF 1932.

In 1929, Willkie moved to New York to become counsel for Commonwealth and Southern, a public utility holding company with assets over $1 billion. He became president of the company in 1933 and chief executive officer the following year. Willkie gained national attention with his attacks on the NEW DEAL, especially the TEN-

NESSEE VALLEY AUTHORITY, a direct competitor of Commonwealth and Southern, and the PUBLIC UTILITY HOLDING COMPANY ACT. In the ELECTION OF 1936, Willkie, still nominally a Democrat, backed Republican ALFRED M. LANDON for president.

Over the next several years, anti-Roosevelt Democrats and eastern Republicans urged Willkie to switch parties and run for president in 1940 on the GOP ticket. By early 1940, HENRY LUCE and other internationalist, eastern Republicans, many of them from Wall Street, had begun a concerted effort to draft Willkie for the Republican nomination. Germany's advance across western Europe during the spring of 1940 in the early stages of WORLD WAR II increased the appeal within the GOP for Willkie, instead of the youthful Thomas E. Dewey or ROBERT A. TAFT, one of the U.S. Senate's leading ISOLATIONISTS. By the time of the Republican convention in July in Philadelphia, Willkie's popularity had grown, although he still seemed a long shot for the nomination. But with his partisans packing the upstairs convention hall galleries and chanting "We want Willkie," he surged into second place by the third ballot and won his improbable nomination on the sixth.

Willkie proved to be an effective campaigner. His boyish looks, tousled hair, and rousing stump style enabled him to draw large crowds to rallies, where he often ad-libbed his speeches. Luce's *Time* magazine declared him the first candidate since Theodore Roosevelt whom Republicans "could yell for and mean it." On the issues, Willkie promised to keep New Deal programs intact and expand the SOCIAL SECURITY ACT, although he criticized Roosevelt and the New Deal for anti-BUSINESS policies that had prevented economic recovery and said that FDR's attempt for an unprecedented third term would lead to dictatorship. Willkie's FOREIGN POLICY views differed little from Roosevelt's interventionist, anti-AXIS approach, and he endorsed the SELECTIVE SERVICE Act and did not make a major issue of the DESTROYERS-FOR-BASES DEAL. Near the end of the campaign, however, Willkie attacked Roosevelt as a "warmonger" who would have the United States at war by April 1941, a statement that prompted the president to declare: "Your boys are not going to be sent into any foreign wars." Despite Willkie's best efforts, Roosevelt won 38 states with 449 electoral votes, to Willkie's 10 states and 82 electoral votes. Willkie received more than 22 million votes, at that time the most ever for a Republican presidential candidate.

During World War II, Willkie became a traveling ambassador for Allied unity and international cooperation. He urged Congress to pass the LEND-LEASE ACT, and visited Great Britain in 1941, and the Middle East, China, and the Soviet Union in 1942, as Roosevelt's personal emissary. He wrote a best-selling book entitled *One World*, which urged a more liberal and internationalist American foreign policy, and he became an advocate of CIVIL RIGHTS. In the ELECTION OF 1944, Willkie again sought the Republican presidential nomination, but by then he was too liberal for the GOP on both foreign and domestic policy and ended his campaign after a crushing defeat in the Wisconsin primary. By September 1944, Willkie was considering backing Roosevelt, but an endorsement never came—he suffered a series of heart attacks, the last of which was fatal, on October 8, 1944, in New York City.

Further reading: Donald Bruce Johnson, *The Republican Party and Wendell Willkie* (Urbana: University of Illinois Press, 1960); Steve Neal, *Dark Horse: A Biography of Wendell Willkie* (Garden City, N.Y.: Doubleday, 1984).

—William J. Thompson

Women Accepted for Volunteer Emergency Service (WAVES)

Approximately 85,000 WAVES served as officers and enlisted personnel in the U.S. NAVY from mid-1942 to the end of WORLD WAR II. These women performed a number of duties, including technical activities in INTELLIGENCE, navigation, and aviation, as well as "traditional" women's roles of office and clerical work. WAVES faced many of the difficulties with respect to acceptance by men and restrictions in their duties as did women serving in the WOMEN'S ARMY CORPS (WAC) of the U.S. ARMY and the WOMEN AIRFORCE SERVICE PILOTS (WASP), a quasimilitary organization working with the U.S. ARMY AIR FORCES. Like other women in the military, the WAVES had also to deal with civilian attitudes of hostility, condescension, and skepticism about their morals.

Women had served in private or semiofficial capacities for the U.S. Navy since the 19th century, at first almost exclusively in nursing. In 1917, Secretary of the Navy Josephus Daniels approved enlisting women in the naval reserve as yeoman (F) in order to release men from shore duty to service in the fleet. Eventually, 12,500 of these "yeomanettes" served in a number of departments such as intelligence and censorship, and held jobs as translators, draftsmen, electricians, and other specialties. Except for nurses, women were demobilized from the navy after World War I and were subsequently prevented from enlisting.

By 1940, with the increased fleet building program because of World War II, the navy faced a potential manpower shortage. Yet, the Navy Department was uncertain how to proceed. Many admirals did not want women to join at all. Other officers suggested that women join an auxiliary arm, not unlike the army's Women's Auxiliary Army Corps (later the WAC). The navy's aviation branch pushed for direct service for women. In early 1942, President FRANKLIN D. ROOSEVELT, after urging from his wife, ELEANOR

ROOSEVELT, intervened in favor of including women in the navy. On July 30, 1942, Public Law 689 established the navy's Women's Reserve; Mildred McAfee, the president of Wellesley College, served as the first director of the WAVES. The act specified that women serve only on shore duty within the continental United States. As in 1917, the purpose in recruiting women was to release men for duty at sea by replacing them in shore stations.

Eligibility standards for the Women Accepted for Volunteer Emergency Service (WAVES) were more restrictive than for men in the navy. The minimum enlistment age was 20. Women with children under 18 were not accepted. The educational requirement for enlisted personnel was graduation from high school or technical training. Female officers had to be college graduates or have the equivalent years of experience. As a practical concern, physical requirements for women were less than those for men. Generally, WAVES were older than their male counterparts. AFRICAN AMERICANS were rejected until FDR ordered them included in 1944, and even then only about 100 served. The navy maintained a more prudish outlook toward its women than for its men, and discharged WAVES for actions that violated the moral standards of the period. Even so, rumors circulated about their sexual promiscuity, both heterosexual and lesbian.

Initially, the navy believed that WAVES would be restricted to duties identified as "women's jobs." Yet, as men were shipped overseas, demands increased for WAVES to replace them in a wider range of assignments. By 1944, women held virtually every occupation outside of direct combat. These jobs included such diverse ones as radio operators, parachute riggers, aircraft engine mechanics, and navigation instructors. Some WAVES participated in classified projects such as manning long-range navigation stations, developing a navy night fighter, and CODE BREAKING of German U-boat radio traffic. Late in 1944, women were finally allowed to serve overseas at naval facilities in the Western Hemisphere and the territories of Hawaii and Alaska. Ultimately, some 4,000 WAVES went overseas, mostly to Hawaii.

By war's end, some 85,000 WAVES and another 11,000 nurses, in the separate Navy Nurse Corps, served in the U.S. Navy. The chief of naval operations, Admiral ERNEST J. KING, praised their efforts. By one estimate, the WAVES had freed up enough sailors to man a large carrier task force of 25 ships. More importantly, the WAVES' accomplishments and attitude had convinced the Navy leadership to retain them in the naval reserve beyond the DEMOBILIZATION at the end of the war. On June 12, 1948, President Truman signed the Women's Armed Services Integration Act that established permanent places for women in all four branches of the armed services.

See also WOMEN'S STATUS AND RIGHTS.

Further reading: Julius A. Furer, *Administration of the Navy Department in World War II* (Washington, D.C.: U.S. Government Printing Office, 1959); Susan M. Hartmann, *The Home Front and Beyond: American Women in the 1940s* (Boston: Twayne, 1982).

—Robert J. Hanyok

Women Airforce Service Pilots (WASP)

The Women Airforce Service Pilots (WASP), a quasimilitary civilian organization that worked for the U.S. ARMY AIR FORCES during WORLD WAR II, provided an example of the unprecedented ways women contributed to the war effort—and of the difficulties that they often faced in making those contributions.

The WASP was created in July 1943. Two prominent women aviators, Jacqueline Cochran and Nancy Harkness Love, had maintained since 1939 that women pilots should be used in noncombat roles, but not until the army air forces ran short of male pilots for such duties did the War Department take steps in that direction. In September 1942, Cochran was authorized to form the Women's Flying Training Detachment and Love to form the Women's Auxiliary Ferrying Squadron. In July 1943, those two organizations were merged to form the WASP, which was headed by Cochran.

Some 25,000 women applied to the WASP (for fewer than 2,000 places), and they faced stringent requirements. In addition to being high school graduates between the ages of 18 and 34, they had to have accumulated 200 flying hours, possess a pilot's license, and pass an interview with a recruiting officer. The initial high number of flying hours required (the requirement was eased later) helped to alleviate some of the criticism the program would have received for using women pilots. Ironically, the WASP, which encountered disparities in pay and treatment as compared to men, discriminated against AFRICAN AMERICANS, and the organization remained all white.

WASP aviators at first ferried planes from factories or bases to pilots waiting at embarkation points, but they subsequently assumed other responsibilities. They towed targets so recruits could practice shooting at moving objects and performed searchlight and tracking missions. Despite being told at first that bombers were too big and too difficult for them to operate, they flew the B-17 Flying Fortress, the B-25, and the B-26, sometimes as test pilots. They engaged in smoke laying, participated in radio-control flying, and taught basic instrument instruction. They were sometimes responsible for test-flying previously damaged planes for pilots who would use them in combat—an extremely hazardous assignment, in which the women would put great stress on the planes to ensure they were ready for combat. They also test-piloted unproven and often dangerous new planes, including fighters. In performing such tasks, the women compiled more than 60 million miles in the air. Thirty-eight of the roughly 1,000 women who ultimately served in the WASP died, although the women's accident rate was somewhat lower than that of comparable civilian male pilots.

Despite their contributions and accomplishments, the WASP never gained military status. Wanting to keep the WASP a separate unit, Cochran resisted having it become part of the WOMEN'S ARMY CORPS (WAC) when the WAC was given full army status in 1943. Then in 1944, when the army air forces requested that CONGRESS give the WASP full military status, circumstances worked against the women. Thousands of male flight instructors and trainees called to active duty wanted to be pilots, not crew members, and many combat veterans wanted the stateside ferrying jobs that women held. Petitioned by male trainees and pilots, and lobbied by the aviation industry and the American Legion, Congress defeated the WASP militarization bill and chose instead to disband the organization. WASPs did not receive veteran status or benefits until a special act of Congress in 1977.

See also WOMEN'S STATUS AND RIGHTS.

Further reading: Molly Merryman, *Clipped Wings: The Rise and Fall of the Women Airforce Service Pilots (WASPs) of World War II* (New York: New York University Press, 1998).

—Amanda Lea Miracle

Women's Army Corps (WAC)

Approximately 200,000 women served in the U.S. ARMY during WORLD WAR II. Some 60,000 served in the Army Nurse Corps, while the others served first in an auxiliary status in the Women's Army Auxiliary Corps (WAAC), and then in regular military status in the Women's Army Corps (WAC) that succeeded the WAAC. Women in the WAC filled a variety of noncombat roles, mostly in administrative and clerical positions but also in mechanical and technical jobs requiring extensive training. Like their counterparts in the WOMEN'S AUXILIARY VOLUNTEERS FOR EMERGENCY SERVICE (WAVES) of the U.S. NAVY and the quasimilitary WOMEN AIRFORCE SERVICE PILOTS (WASP) that worked with the U.S. ARMY AIR FORCES, Wacs faced discriminatory practices that were pervasive in the nation's culture.

With the country's impending involvement in World War II by the early 1940s, women's organizations urged that women be fully included in wartime efforts. In large part because of the persistence of Massachusetts Republican congresswoman Edith Rogers in working to overcome resistance in the army and the CONGRESS, the WAAC was created in May 1942. A major premise for approving the WAAC was that women could free men for combat by performing a number of the clerical, communications, and service duties essential to modern warfare.

The Waacs, as members of the WAAC were called, soon began to serve in a variety of capacities and places, but numerous questions arose with respect to how existing army policies and procedures would apply to the Waacs. Rogers then introduced a bill to grant full military status to Waacs, and despite some continuing opposition and a campaign of slander against the group, focusing especially on allegations of heterosexual promiscuity and of lesbianism, the WAC was created in 1943. Army regulations were amended in matters such as clothing, housing, military justice, and discharge for pregnancy.

The typical Wac was in her mid-20s, a high school graduate with clerical experience, single, without children, and desirous of being actively engaged in the war effort to a degree that civilian status did not allow. AFRICAN AMERICANS were accepted into WAAC and WAC in the same proportion (about 10 percent) as in the army, but they served in racially segregated units and generally were given lower-status positions. Women with children under 14 could not serve. Wacs were explicitly forbidden to serve in combat units or in positions in units with a combat mission (though nurses did see service in the war theaters, often near combat lines).

The U.S. Army Air Forces' (USAAF) relatively progressive attitude toward the employment of women provided nearly 40,000 positions for Wacs. The USAAF was the first Army command to substantially integrate women, admitting them to all noncombat schools. Wacs served as radio operators, mechanics, and photographers on B-17 training flights. Others filled positions as clerical staff, instructors, weather observers, cryptographers, business machine operators, control tower operators, and medics. Thousands of Air Wacs served overseas in Alaska, Hawaii, Great Britain, Africa, and India.

The Army Ground Forces (AGF) did not have the same success with utilizing Wacs, largely because its units were tactical in nature and accordingly women were excluded from many positions. AGF lost one-third of its women during the conversion period from the WAAC to the WAC because of poor morale caused by malassignment and underutilization. Eventually, women were placed into more meaningful assignments such as clerks, dispatchers, drivers, radio mechanics, parachute riggers, control tower operators, and instructors. Difficulties in integration persisted, since the Wacs were not allowed to wear the insignia of the AGF and had problems receiving advancements. However, as the manpower shortage increased, the AGF WAC units became the backbone at many of the replacement depots across the country.

Women in military service: Shown here is the first contingent of 253 female marines who reported for duty at U.S. Marine headquarters, 1943 *(Library of Congress)*

The Army Service Forces (ASF) requested the use of women in the Signal Corps, which led to the creation of the WIRES plan (Women in Radio and Electrical Service). However, until the conversion to military status took place, the ASF faced difficulties utilizing the women without violating their auxiliary status. From that point on, women played crucial roles in such areas as the Signal Corps, Chemical Warfare Service, and the Corps of Engineers. At first, the Medical Department of the ASF did not make use of the women, but eventually Wacs successfully completed training courses and worked as psychiatric social workers, therapy assistants, laboratory and surgical technicians, stenographers, and clerks.

Once DEMOBILIZATION began, the future of WAC became a significant question. Recognizing the contributions of the WAC to the American effort in World War II,

Congress in 1948 passed the Women's Armed Forces Integration Act, which made the WAC part of the regular army, albeit with a number of restrictions on the numbers and roles of women. WAC veterans received generally the same benefits as men, including those provided by the GI BILL OF RIGHTS.

See also WOMEN'S STATUS AND RIGHTS.

Further reading: D'Ann Campbell, *Women at War with America: Private Lives in a Public Era* (Cambridge, Mass.: Harvard University Press, 1984); Susan M. Hartmann, *The Home Front and Beyond: American Women in the 1940s* (Boston: Twayne, 1982); Mattie E. Treadwell, *The Women's Army Corps* (Washington, D.C.: Office of the Chief of Military History, Department of the Army, 1954).

—Traci L. Siegler

women's network

The term "women's network" refers to an interconnected group of women with important positions in the administration of President FRANKLIN D. ROOSEVELT.

The growth of the federal GOVERNMENT under the NEW DEAL greatly expanded the federal workforce and provided unprecedented opportunities for women. Most of the women who worked for the federal government had traditional "pink-collar" jobs as entry level clerks, phone operators, and secretaries. But for the first time, a substantial number of women also held top-level federal positions. This group of women included Secretary of Labor FRANCES PERKINS; Democratic Party Women's Division director and then Social Security board member MARY W. "MOLLY" DEWSON; Jane M. Hoey, director of the Bureau of Public Assistance; Assistant Secretary of the Treasury Josephine Roche; and about two dozen other highly placed women. Taken together, this group of women has been termed the women's network.

The women's network members had much in common. Many were not only colleagues but had been friends before coming to Washington. As they strived to establish their careers in the 1910s and 1920s, they had formed bonds based on their experiences in trying to forge professional careers in a culture that still thought of women as primarily wives and mothers. They also tended to come from a similar professional background, beginning their careers in the social welfare field. This was one area where women were seen as having particular expertise, and the women of the women's network had the opportunity to build careers in social welfare in the private sector and state and local governments. Perkins, for example, began her career in Chicago's Hull-House before moving to New York and entering a public service career concerned with the conditions of LABOR. Dewson was involved in consumer advocacy before entering electoral politics and raising awareness of women's issues with the DEMOCRATIC PARTY. At the local level, Jane Hoey rose to become the assistant secretary of the New York City Welfare Council, the largest city social welfare agency at the time, as well as building political connections through state advisory committees on prison conditions and reform.

The central figures of the women's network were ELEANOR ROOSEVELT, Frances Perkins, and Molly Dewson. Roosevelt, the only one without an official position but at the heart of the network through her status as first lady and her relationships with most of the other women, was the network's conduit to the White House. She lobbied President Roosevelt to appoint women to major government positions, raised women's issues with her husband and his senior staff, and worked to raise awareness about social problems through her public appearances and newspaper column. Perkins, as the first female cabinet secretary, gave more attention to women's issues than had the secretaries of labor who preceded her. The women who worked for her at the Department of Labor included Grace Abbott and then Katharine Lenroot, who were directors of the Children's Bureau, and Mary Anderson, who headed the Women's Division. Dewson worked in the political arena, carving out a role for women in the Democratic Party through the Women's Division as well as campaigning tirelessly for female appointments in the Roosevelt administration.

Given their background in social welfare field, the largest policy impact of the women's network was the SOCIAL SECURITY ACT of 1935. Perkins was the major advocate pushing FDR to formulate a system of social security that would include old-age and unemployment insurance. Women in the Children's Bureau provided input on children's issues, presenting their plan to federalize the state-level Mother's Pension programs, which became the Aid to Dependent Children program (changed to Aid to Families with Dependent Children in 1962). Without the interest of the Children's Bureau in having the omnibus Social Security Act include a program for dependent children, the act likely would not have provided for children who lacked parental financial support.

The legacy of the women's network is mixed. This group of approximately 30 women achieved many firsts for women in the federal government, including the first cabinet secretary and first female ambassador (Ruth Bryan Owen, minister to Denmark, 1933–36). They also brought valuable experience to the federal government as it began entering the social welfare field and influenced New Deal policy and politics. But these women did not see themselves as only advocates for women nor did they view themselves essentially as feminists; they were working for the betterment of all Americans. On this basis, many opposed the Equal Rights Amendment, fearing it would erode protective labor legislation. That they did not pursue a more feminist agenda has been a source of criticism aimed at the women's network. Nonetheless, it took decades for women to match the achievements of the women's network in terms of position and influence.

See also WOMEN'S STATUS AND RIGHTS.

Further reading: Susan F. Ware, *Beyond Suffrage: Women and the New Deal* (Cambridge, Mass.: Harvard University Press, 1981); Susan F. Ware, "Women and the New Deal," in *Fifty Years Later: The New Deal Evaluated,* edited by Harvard Sitkoff (New York: McGraw Hill, 1985).
—Katherine Liapis Segrue

women's status and rights

During the GREAT DEPRESSION and WORLD WAR II, the status and rights of women in the United States continued to expand, following trends dating back to the beginning of the 20th century and before. Progress was made in spite of the fact that the women's movement had fragmented during the 1920s, after the unifying goal of suffrage was achieved. More of the legal and other constraints on women, including some preventing married women from working, fell during these years. In the 1930s and 1940s, married women entered the workforce in increasing numbers as acceptance of their presence grew, and by 1945 there were more wives in the paid workforce than single women. These lasting changes, however, were not simply the result of either the depression or the war but reflected long-term developments as well.

Throughout the 1930s, the great majority—about three-fourths—of American women were not employed outside the home. A 1936 Gallup Poll revealed that 82 percent of Americans believed that married women, especially those with children, should remain at home. Both the depression and traditional American values influenced this attitude. Throughout the depression, with its high UNEMPLOYMENT rates, employers often tried to reserve available jobs for men and might fire women to create openings. Many organizations, including government agencies, banks, and schools, had rules against employing married women. For much of the decade, the federal GOVERNMENT prohibited two members of the same family from holding civil service jobs, a rule that chiefly affected women workers.

In spite of pressures to stay home, about 25 percent of American women, both single and married, were members of the paid workforce by the end of the decade, continuing the increase of previous decades. Although only about one-fifth of white women were employed, almost two-fifths of black women worked, mostly as domestic servants or agricultural laborers. Women usually took jobs because they or their family needed the money. Removing women from the workforce did not always create work for men. Women were frequently segregated into jobs perceived as "women's work" including clerical work, light industry, or domestic service. Men were reluctant to take these jobs even during hard times and even though such jobs were cut back less than "men's jobs" in heavy industry. Job segregation thus sometimes worked to women's benefit, keeping jobs open to them throughout the depression. So did the lower wages typically earned by women, and the numbers of women and of married women working rose during the 1930s.

Some professional women faced the added difficulty of competing with men for education and jobs. Admission to medical and law schools remained extremely difficult and, for the most part, reserved for men. Women dropped from almost 44 percent to about 40 percent of the college student population, and those who managed to graduate had a difficult time finding and keeping a job, given employer's prejudices. Teaching and nursing standards rose during these years due to stiff competition for few positions. Rare professional victories did occur, as when Florence Allen was named the first female judge on the U.S. Court of Appeals.

Women made significant gains in the public arena during the 1930s. Although they had held appointive office in the past, never before had they attained such numerous or influential positions. The NEW DEAL brought social problems similar to those women reformers had long been involved with at the local level and in private organizations. Now they sometimes held key positions in the new federal agencies. There was a small increase in the number of women in Congress, and about a quarter of the newly appointed postmasters were women. Women holding other important offices included Secretary of Labor FRANCES PERKINS (the first woman cabinet member ever); Assistant Secretary of the Treasury Marion Glass Banister; Director of the U.S. Mint Nellie Tayloe Ross; and the ambassador to Denmark, Ruth Bryan Owen. Perkins, ELEANOR ROOSEVELT, and MARY W. "MOLLY" DEWSON, head of the Women's Division of the DEMOCRATIC PARTY National Committee, led the WOMEN'S NETWORK that advocated bringing women into GOVERNMENT and advised President FRANKLIN D. ROOSEVELT on women's issues. This increased presence in government, however, declined after the 1930s.

While few New Deal programs explicitly included women, women did benefit from many of them. Some held jobs or were in circumstances that qualified for SOCIAL SECURITY ACT benefits. Minimum wage laws and the NATIONAL LABOR RELATIONS ACT assisted some as well. However, RELIEF programs were difficult for women to enter. Since only one person per household qualified for federal relief programs, women did not get on the rolls very often. And, when they did, it was sometimes hard to place them; women could not work as laborers on construction jobs, for example. But despite such limits, which were greater in the case of AFRICAN AMERICANS, the New Deal did help women. New Deal programs and Molly Dewson's work in mobilizing the women's vote helped make women an important component of the "Roosevelt Coalition" that made the Democrats the new majority party of the nation.

MARRIAGE AND FAMILY LIFE were also affected by the depression. Most men did not lose their jobs, but even those who did not often suffered significant salary cuts. Not only the loss of a husband's salary, but also a smaller salary coming into the household forced women to provide goods and services that had previously been bought or hired. Although the depression often reinforced the traditional family division of labor, women's work at home became more valuable during these years. How a wife managed the household might determine whether or nor her family successfully navigated the hard times. The greater responsibilities that women had in the home when men lost job or experienced pay cuts sometimes changed family dynamics, giving women a larger voice.

In the early years of the depression, cash-strapped Americans postponed marriage and childbearing, and the rates of both dropped significantly. However, marriage and birth rates began to rise by the middle of the decade, and then increased more rapidly when World War II brought economic improvement. The number of marriages continued to rise after the United States entered the war. Babies followed, and there were more babies born in 1943 than any other year to that point in the 20th century. By the early postwar years, a higher proportion of Americans were married and they were marrying younger than any time in the century; the resulting baby boom continued for almost two decades.

At first, World War II changed few attitudes about women. Most Americans continued to believe that women, especially wives and mothers, belonged at home. As job prospects improved, employers continued to favor male workers. Yet, as men were drafted and the number of jobs continued to increase, a severe labor shortage developed, and attitudes did undergo some change. President Roosevelt urged reluctant employers to forget their prejudices and hire women. Companies and the government launched campaigns to encourage women to take jobs "for the duration." By 1944, the portion of American women working had increased from about a quarter to more than one-third. Many of the new workers were women over 35 whose children no longer needed their constant care. Nearly one out of four wives had jobs. The number of working wives with small children increased only marginally, and American society continued to discourage them from seeking employment outside the home. By 1945, more than 35 percent of women worked. And since women had high turnover rates, it is possible that almost half of American women were employed at some point during the war,

The enduring symbol of the World War II woman worker, ROSIE THE RIVETER, nonetheless is misleading. While women did take on a greater number and array of jobs, sometimes as riveters, fewer than 10 percent of female workers labored in defense plants, where they were usually considered short-term, unskilled employees and not given training for skilled jobs such as riveting. More frequently, women held clerical and service positions during the war, and both the number and the type of white-collar jobs available to women expanded during the war. There was an increased need for secretaries and record keepers, and about 20 to 25 percent of the women workers were so employed. However, women also moved into jobs that were previously held by men including bank tellers, store clerks,

This poster was issued by the Office of War Information in 1943 to encourage the participation of women in the war effort. By 1944, approximately 3.5 million women worked side by side with 6 million men on the factory assembly lines. (National Archives)

and some middle management positions. Unlike the industrial jobs, women were more likely to keep these jobs after the war.

World War II brought some changes in the employment of female AFRICAN AMERICANS as well. During the war, they began to move out of agricultural work and domestic service into other jobs. Some took cleaning, cooking, or serving jobs in offices, hotels, or restaurants. Others were employed in laundries and foundries, and in factories where federal standards required fair treatment. The number of black women working for the federal government increased significantly, and more than half of these new employees held white-collar jobs. However, such women were a very small minority of the population, and wherever African-American women were employed, racial barriers continued to restrict hiring and promotions.

The war also affected women's EDUCATION. Many dropped out of school to take war-related jobs, although high school completion rates continued to rise and exceeded men's. At the same time, with fewer male students, traditionally male disciplines enrolled more women. The number of women majoring in mathematics, science, and engineering increased by 29 percent. Females now made up 14 percent of all medical students. However, this trend reversed after the war when colleges turned away new female students and gave preference to veterans.

Perhaps the most significant new departure involved women entering the military. Although nurses had been made a permanent part of the army and navy years before, other women had not. Some women joined the WOMEN'S ARMY CORPS (WAC), the navy's WOMEN ACCEPTED FOR VOLUNTEER EMERGENCY SERVICE (WAVES), the coast guard's SPARS (from *Semper Paratus,* the coast guard's motto), or the women's branch of the marines. Others volunteered for the WOMEN AIRFORCE SERVICE PILOTS (WASP), although they never achieved full military status. Only the WAC initially accepted African Americans. At first, women performed jobs perceived as "women's work"; four-fifths of women who were not nurses held clerical positions. However, as the demand for their labor grew, they were given a wide variety of noncombat roles. Although the 350,000 women involved were not initially accepted by most of their male counterparts, their competency, efficiency, and bravery soon changed many men's minds. After the war, women remained part of the military.

The women's movement saw some progress at both the state and federal levels during these years. A few states passed equal pay laws. Several states made women eligible for jury duty. In many places, rules prohibiting the employment of married women were thrown out. Although the Equal Rights Amendment (ERA) gained a few key endorsements during the 1930s, it generally lost momentum during the depression decade. Women's contributions to the war effort then rallied supporters to force Congress to finally consider the amendment seriously, but when it came to a vote after the war, it did not receive the necessary two-thirds majority. While this interest kept the ERA alive, real action did not come until the 1960s.

Many women who did not take a paid job participated in wartime volunteer work. Although all races, ages, and classes were involved, the majority of the volunteers were white middle-class wives. The OFFICE OF PRICE ADMINISTRATION used volunteers to help administer prices, rents, and RATIONING. Women grew victory gardens and helped in the scrap and WAR BONDS drives. They worked as hostesses or dance partners at Red Cross or UNITED SERVICE ORGANIZATIONS recreation centers. Probably as many as one in four women were involved with such activities.

No matter what a woman's situation was, her home life was most likely disrupted by the war. More women than in any previous decade in the United States found themselves head of a household while their husbands were absent for the duration. Many problems and decisions that he might have dealt with were suddenly her responsibility. Women were usually the ones forced to cope with rationing, merchandise shortages, and unavailable items. If she had a war job, household chores could be even more onerous and were frequently performed with little help from her husband, if he was home. Shops often closed before she finished work. There was some day care, but many women did not want to leave their children with strangers. Although services improved during the war, wives and mothers sometimes skipped work to nurse a sick child, catch up on housework, or simply to rest.

When the war ended, many women wanted to keep their jobs. However, businesses and the government often urged women to return home, reminding them that they had only been hired for the duration. Many lost jobs to returning soldiers. Others quit because they wanted to stay home full time. In spite of the jobs lost at the end of the war, many women who wanted paid employment were back at work by 1947, although usually in traditionally feminine jobs.

Further reading: D'Ann Campbell, *Women at War with America* (Cambridge, Mass.: Harvard University Press, 1984); William H. Chafe, *The Paradox of Change: American Women in the 20th Century* (New York: Oxford University Press, 1991); Claudia Goldin, *Understanding the Gender Gap: An Economic History of American Women* (New York: Oxford 1990); Susan Hartmann, *The Home Front and Beyond: American Women in the 1940s* (Boston: Twayne, 1982); Susan Ware, *Holding Their Own: American Women in the 1930s* (Boston: Twayne, 1982).

—Jill Frahm

Works Progress Administration (WPA)

The largest, most important, and most innovative of the RELIEF programs of the NEW DEAL, the Works Progress Administration (WPA) was created under the auspices of the EMERGENCY RELIEF APPROPRIATION ACT of April 8, 1935. President FRANKLIN D. ROOSEVELT created the Works Progress Administration by executive order on May 6, 1935, and New Deal relief administrator HARRY HOPKINS headed the new agency until he resigned to become secretary of commerce in December 1938.

The Emergency Relief Appropriation Act and its funding of nearly $5 billion escalated a struggle going back to 1933 for works projects funds between Hopkins and public works administrator HAROLD ICKES. Ultimately, the great majority of the funds went to Hopkins and his emphasis on labor-intensive work relief projects rather than to

Poster for the Works Progress Administration *(Library of Congress)*

Ickes's capital-intensive heavy public works projects that would employ fewer workers and dispense money more slowly. The WPA reflected the desires of Roosevelt and Hopkins to replace direct relief programs (payments in cash or food and clothing) still being carried out by the FEDERAL EMERGENCY RELIEF ADMINISTRATION (FERA) with work relief programs (jobs on government projects) of the sort begun by the CIVIL WORKS ADMINISTRATION (CWA) and then partly continued by the FERA when the CWA was terminated. In the new organization of relief, the federal government would assume responsibility for employable jobless workers, while unemployables on relief (handicapped, aged, infirm, dependent children) would become the responsibility of the states (which subsequently would receive federal matching funds for such groups via the SOCIAL SECURITY ACT of August 1935). The WPA projects were to be useful, employ workers on relief rolls, spend money promptly, and put as much of the spending as possible into wages.

As always, Hopkins acted quickly, and by December the WPA had plans to employ 3.5 million workers. Paying its workers wages that were higher than direct relief assistance, yet were below prevailing wages so as not to compete with the private sector for workers, the WPA continued and enlarged the variety of projects building the nation's infrastructure begun by the CWA and the FERA in their work relief efforts. Within three years, the WPA had employed 5 million workers, some 3.3 million at its height

during the RECESSION OF 1937–38. By the time the agency was terminated in 1943, the WPA had spent more than $10 billion, employed more than 8 million workers, constructed some 40,000 buildings, 80,000 bridges and viaducts, 8,000 parks, and 350 airports, and improved hundreds of thousands of miles of roads and 85,000 public buildings.

But the impact of the WPA went beyond its achievements in construction projects and work relief for manual workers. The agency also launched an array of programs aimed at preserving and enhancing the skills of a variety of white-collar workers, artists, actors, authors, professionals, and young people, and it gave unusual attention as well to AFRICAN AMERICANS and women. It created the FEDERAL ART PROJECT, the FEDERAL THEATRE PROJECT, the FEDERAL MUSIC PROJECT, and the FEDERAL WRITERS' PROJECT (together known as "Federal One"). The WPA also launched the NATIONAL YOUTH ADMINISTRATION (NYA), which provided young people assistance to stay in school (and out of the job market) as well as employment and training for out-of-school youth. Hopkins and other officials made the WPA one of the New Deal agencies most sensitive to and supportive of blacks, including establishing the NYA's Division of Negro Affairs headed by MARY MCLEOD BETHUNE. The Women's and Professional Division of the WPA gave substantial attention to helping working women.

Despite such achievements, the WPA had real limitations. It never employed more than about one-third of the unemployed at any one time, paid low wages, and proved unable to surmount various forms of prejudice and discrimination. Such limitations stemmed largely from obstacles that the WPA encountered. It never received funding from CONGRESS sufficient in size or predictability to meet Hopkins's larger aims. Like other New Deal programs, its implementation depended in part on state and local governments that were often inefficient and resistant to federal direction.

Although criticized from the left for doing too little for the unemployed, the WPA faced criticism from conservatives for doing and spending too much, and in the late 1930s it came under fire from the emerging CONSERVATIVE COALITION in the Congress. Critics alleged that WPA workers engaged in useless "boondoggle" projects and that *WPA* really stood for "We Poke Along." A special Senate committee uncovered evidence of inappropriate political activity. The House Committee on Un-American Activities and other congressional committees investigated the agency—especially the theater and writers' projects—for "un-American" activities. The House Subcommittee on Appropriations eliminated the Federal Theatre Project, reduced funding for a number of projects, and required workers to sign an oath of loyalty to the United States. In 1939, Roosevelt changed the agency's name to the Works

Projects Administration to draw attention to its projects, but as prosperity returned with increased defense spending, the WPA like other relief agencies lost favor with the public and encountered growing opposition from conservatives and the Congress. In December 1942, with Congress sharply reducing appropriations for the WPA, Roosevelt reluctantly gave the agency its "honorable discharge" and ordered its termination by the end of 1943.

Further reading: Searle F. Charles, *Minister of Relief: Harry Hopkins and the Depression* (Syracuse, N.Y.: Syracuse University Press, 1963); Donald S. Howard, *The WPA and Federal Relief Policy* (New York: Russell Sage Foundation, 1943); George T. McJimsey, *Harry Hopkins: Ally of the Poor and Defender of Democracy* (Cambridge, Mass.: Harvard University Press, 1987).

World Disarmament Conference (1932–1934)

The World Disarmament Conference opened in Geneva, Switzerland, under the auspices of the League of Nations, in February 1932. Following the partial success of the LONDON NAVAL CONFERENCE of 1930 in extending naval arms limitation agreements, there was hope that new agreements could be reached to curtail arms expenditures and production. The GREAT DEPRESSION, and the desire of the United States and other nations to spend less on armaments so that more could be devoted to domestic economic and social programs, also provided part of the context for the discussions of arms reduction. The conference nonetheless proved a disappointing failure, unable to achieve any significant agreement on disarmament.

In approaching the general question of disarmament, the conference faced the specific issue of Germany's demand for parity in armaments and France's concerns about Germany and its own national security on the European continent. Hopes of a disarmament agreement turned on the willingness of the French to scale down their armaments, thus sacrificing the arms superiority over Germany granted by the Versailles treaty. France required that other nations, in particular Great Britain, provide guarantees of security and assistance in the event of conflict, but the British said they could not take on new commitments.

The United States played a significant role at the conference. In June 1932, President HERBERT C. HOOVER took the initiative by proposing a general one-third reduction in armaments, but he failed to gain sufficient support. In what some called the Hoover Plan, the United States proposed a reduction especially in offensive weapons. As he had in the London Naval Conference, Hoover wanted to reduce arms expenditures so that nations could stabilize their domestic economies as well as reduce the chances for armed conflict, and he also hoped that linkages might be made between the disarmament conference and the planned LONDON ECONOMIC CONFERENCE.

In 1933, new U.S. president FRANKLIN D. ROOSEVELT said that disarmament was "one of the principal keys to the world situation," and he pledged to use "every possible means" to help the disarmament conference have some success. In May 1933, he promulgated an "Appeal to the Nations of the World for Peace and for the End of Economic Chaos" and drew attention to both the World Disarmament Conference and the London Economic Conference. But FDR helped torpedo the London conference by refusing to support currency stabilization and a return to the gold standard. Committed to working for arms control, despite the lack of significant progress at Geneva and his own growing pessimism about the discussions, Roosevelt did try to salvage something from the disarmament conference. But opposition from ISOLATIONISTS in Washington led FDR to withdraw even an offer to link arms reduction to American cooperation with League of Nations economic sanctions against an aggressor nation.

In October 1933, Adolf Hitler, who had become Germany's new chancellor in January 1933, withdrew Germany from the World Disarmament Conference and the League of Nations. Germany's withdrawal, and its clear intention to rearm, killed hopes of any meaning disarmament agreement. Like Germany, Japan also withdrew from the League of Nations and pursued both rearmament and territorial aggrandizement as the decade wore on. The United States, though having played active roles in such interwar arms reduction efforts as the Washington Naval Conference of 1921–22, the London Naval Conference, and the World Disarmament Conference, followed a noninterventionist FOREIGN POLICY until the outbreak of WORLD WAR II.

Further reading: Hugh R. Wilson, *Disarmament and the Cold War in the Thirties* (New York: Vantage, 1963).

—Michael Leonard

World War II

World War II was an enormous conflict that had great impact on the global role of the United States and on the American home front. It has inevitably given rise to an abundance of interpretations of its events and meaning.

Some of the important interpretations and debates involve specific events and developments. Did President FRANKLIN D. ROOSEVELT know about the Japanese attack on PEARL HARBOR beforehand and welcome it as a "back door" to war? (Most scholars find little credible evidence for that view.) Was the two-pronged American campaign in the WORLD WAR II PACIFIC THEATER by the U.S. ARMY and the U.S. NAVY the wisest course of action? (Perhaps not—but it worked.) Why did the United States use the

ATOMIC BOMB in August 1945? (Most scholars agree that it was for the primary purpose of bringing the war to an end as quickly as possible, though with the secondary purpose of impressing the Soviet Union and making it more cooperative after the war.) Did the atomic bombings of HIROSHIMA AND NAGASAKI end the war and prevent an invasion of Japan that would have cost up to a million American dead? (The conventional view has been yes, but a number of scholars suggest that there were other alternatives to invasion and that the estimate of so many American deaths is inflated.)

There are many important interpretive questions. Why did SOVIET-AMERICAN RELATIONS sour and the GRAND ALLIANCE dissolve at the end of the war? (Most scholars point to longstanding tensions antedating the war and to wartime disagreements arising from conflicting worldviews and war aims.) Why did the United States do so little to rescue victims of the HOLOCAUST? (There is no clear consensus, but many scholars continue to hold that evidence was more fragmentary and even more unbelievable than it now seems, although ANTI-SEMITISM played a role, too.) What led to the RELOCATION OF JAPANESE AMERICANS and their incarceration? (Historians emphasize racism as the key factor, but also point to unfounded military fears and to the small numbers and lack of political power of Japanese Americans.)

These and other questions continue to attract the attention of scholars of World War II. But beyond the interpretations of such specific issues, there are also two overriding interpretations about the meaning and significance of World War II for the United States that have come to shape general understandings of the war—and that have also provoked debate among historians. One is that it was the "Good War" that defeated the AXIS, saved democracy, and brought unity, prosperity, and social advance in the United States. The other is that World War II was a watershed in history that changed the world, transformed American FOREIGN POLICY, and in numerous ways made the United States a far different place from what it had been before the war.

The interpretation of World War II as the "Good War" fought and won by America's "greatest generation" has taken firm hold as the prevailing public view of the war. Shaping the 50-year celebrations of the war from 1989 to 1995, the idea of the Good War focuses partly on the global significance of the Second World War, partly on the benefits it evidently brought the United States. In this analysis, the Grand Alliance against the AXIS vanquished Nazi Germany and Imperial Japan, liberated conquered areas from their control, and saved democracy. At home, the "Good War" unified the nation, restored prosperity, provided new opportunities, and laid groundwork for the postwar CIVIL RIGHTS and women's movements—and without the home

front destruction and casualties of the other nations at war. In retrospect, many wartime Americans thought the war years the best and most rewarding time of their lives.

There have always been qualifications to or dissent from the idea of the Good War. But concurrently with, and partly in reaction to, the celebratory semicentennial observations of World War II, the idea of the Good War came under sharp attack from a number of scholars. They have stressed for one thing the degree to which racism and prejudice shaped the American conduct of the war—including the relocation of Japanese Americans, discrimination against and segregation of AFRICAN AMERICANS, limited chances for MEXICAN AMERICANS and NATIVE AMERICANS, the disturbing anti-Semitism of the war years, discrimination against GAYS AND LESBIANS, especially in the armed forces, and the limited and often short-lived gains for WOMEN'S STATUS AND RIGHTS.

This alternative interpretation also points out that home-front shortages, RATIONING, and restrictions gave rise to complaints, selfishness, favoritism, and a BLACK MARKET; that social tensions flared in crowded war-boom communities; that MARRIAGE AND FAMILY LIFE was disrupted; and that juvenile delinquency became a national concern. Racial violence sometimes erupted, most notably in the summer of 1943. And in this view, the American home front was marked by an illiberal, enforced conformity in which the incarceration of innocent Japanese Americans was simply the worst and most obvious violation of CIVIL LIBERTIES. Government CENSORSHIP and manipulation of war news and images shaped NEWS MEDIA reporting and PHOTOGRAPHY and infringed upon First Amendment rights.

Even the idea of the virtuous Good War abroad against the Axis has experienced some challenge. A few Americans lamented from the beginning the alliance with the Soviet Union and the Soviets' increased power in the world as a result of the war. More have regretted and questioned the use of the atomic bomb against Japan. Increasing evidence has surfaced about the brutal warfare on all sides, including the bombing of civilian populations, not just in the Pacific theater but also in the WORLD WAR II EUROPEAN THEATER. Although almost no one disputes the notion that defeating the Axis was a good thing, more accounts now point to questionable or even unworthy means toward that end.

The other prevailing interpretation of World War II is that it was a watershed event that transformed both the world and the United States. The argument is compelling with respect to America's world role and FOREIGN POLICY. Because of World War II, the United States became by far the world's richest and most powerful nation and embarked upon a course of active leadership in world affairs, including a major role in the new UNITED NATIONS.

The watershed interpretation of the WORLD WAR HOME FRONT holds above all that the war ended the depression and triggered unprecedented prosperity. It also expanded the middle class, and strengthened and diversified the economies of the SOUTH and the West. It enlarged the size of organized LABOR and integrated unions into the policymaking machinery. It restructured AGRICULTURE, especially by accelerating the growth of large, mechanized, commercial agribusiness.

The war, moreover, greatly increased the size and reach of the federal GOVERNMENT—especially the PRESIDENCY and made KEYNESIANISM central to fiscal policy. Wartime SCIENCE and TECHNOLOGY (underwritten by the government) produced not only such instruments of war as radar and the atomic bomb but also the computer revolution and the development of sundry wonder drugs, new insecticides, and synthetic materials.

The interpretation of World War II as a watershed in national life also focuses on the social consequences of the war. For African Americans, the war produced massive movement out of the rural South, new opportunities in industry and the armed forces, rising expectations, and the determination to use the war as a lever of social change. For women, too—for whom the abiding and partly misleading symbol is ROSIE THE RIVETER—the war brought new opportunities and new roles. For white ethnic groups, the war evidently hastened inclusion into the social and economic mainstreams. Servicemen—and sometimes women—encountered extraordinary new circumstances and experiences, gained vital new training and skills, and profited from the GI BILL OF RIGHTS. And World War II brought important demographic change. MIGRATION sped the growth of the SUNBELT states of the South and West, of metropolitan areas, and of SUBURBS. The war also affected POPULATION TRENDS by helping to launch a marriage and baby boom of great proportions and still greater implications.

Yet for all the strength of the "watershed" interpretation, which is only sketched here, there is another side, one stressing continuity as well as change and suggesting that the "watershed" interpretation oversimplifies or exaggerates the war's impact. In important areas of American life, for example, longer historical perspective suggests that many of the changes associated with the war had long been under way. These include new roles for women, altered circumstances and civil rights activism for blacks, the rise of suburbs and the Sunbelt, the growing size and role of the federal government, the assimilation of white ethnic groups, and the global power of the United States. The war may have reinforced or accelerated such changes, but it did not necessarily produce them.

Nor did World War II complete or consummate many of the changes commonly attributed to it. The Civil Rights movement took more than a decade after 1945 to gain great momentum, the women's movement more than two decades; and both blacks and women remained in significant ways on the margins of American society at the end of the war. Similarly, the baby boom, the mushrooming of the suburbs, the decline of small farming and of the farm population, and the impact of new technologies were more evident after than during the war.

Not all areas of American life experienced dramatic change during the war. Examinations of New England and the Midwest, for example, often show basic continuities, and important studies have recently contended that even in California the war largely reinforced longstanding patterns of population and economic growth. There was nationally no great change in the distribution of wealth and little in the distribution of power. In politics, existing party appeals, voting patterns, and domestic policy changed little during the war, despite the resurgent strength of CONSERVATISM.

One reason for the incompleteness and slowness of social change, moreover, was the continuing hold of old values, old norms, old patterns of life with respect to race, to gender, to family and community life, and to much else besides. Most wartime Americans—African Americans were an obvious exception—tended to visualize the postwar era as a more prosperous version of prewar America. The transformations that most people wanted were in personal circumstance and opportunity, not broad social patterns and norms.

Several perspectives can help in sorting through the claims and counterclaims with respect to World War II as a watershed or as the Good War. For one thing, the issues are to an important extent ones of balance and focus. One can find both change and continuity in the war years, both huge successes and troubling shortcomings.

With both the watershed and the Good War frameworks, moreover, comparative analysis can be illuminating. The World War II American home front, for example, was not so repressive or illiberal as the World War I home front or as those of other World War II belligerents. Nor did the war affect American life as it did the other nations at war.

As compared to the watershed interpretation, the idea of the Good War turns more on value judgments than on dispassionate analysis. In this respect, the two interpretive frameworks have quite different dimensions and raise different issues. In another sense, however, they are often mirror images of one another. To a significant extent the view of the war as a watershed suggests that it was a good war: It restored prosperity; it provided new opportunities; it improved the roles, status, and prospects of women, of African Americans, of the working class. By contrast, challenges to the Good War thesis are also often, implicitly at least, challenges to the notion of the war as a great divide:

Longstanding prejudice limited the gains of blacks, of women, and of other groups on the margins of status and power; the already rich and powerful—not workers or unions or small business or small farmers—profited from the war.

For the nature and significance of World War II—as for virtually any important and complicated question in history—there is no single, all-purpose interpretation. For wartime America, different people, different groups, different regions, had different experiences, true for them but not necessarily representative of the whole. The war also had diverse and differential effects on the various components of American life and government. Students of the Second World War will thus continue to come to different interpretations about its meaning and impact, as well as about its leading events and personalities.

See also WORLD WAR II EUROPEAN THEATER; WORLD WAR II HOME FRONT; WORLD WAR II PACIFIC THEATER.

Further reading: Michael C. C. Adams, *The Best War Ever: America and World War II* (Baltimore: Johns Hopkins University Press, 1994); John Morton Blum, *V Was for Victory: Politics and American Culture during World War II* (New York: Harcourt Brace Jovanovich, 1976); Paul Fussell, *Wartime: Understanding and Behavior in the Second World War* (New York: Oxford University Press, 1989); John W. Jeffries, *Wartime America: The World War II Home Front* (Chicago: Ivan R. Dee, 1996); David M. Kennedy, *Freedom from Fear: The American People in Depression and War, 1929–1945* (New York: Oxford University Press, 1999); William L. O'Neill, *A Democracy at War: America's Fight at Home and Abroad in World War II* (New York: Free Press, 1993); Studs Terkel, *"The Good War": An Oral History of World War II* (New York: Pantheon, 1984).

World War II European theater

The European theater of World War II broadly encompassed those land, sea, and air operations taking place between the GRAND ALLIANCE headed by the United States, Great Britain, and the Soviet Union, and the AXIS powers of Germany and Italy and their allies, in northwestern, central, and eastern Europe, in the Atlantic Ocean, in North Africa and the Mediterranean Sea, and in the Soviet Union. In terms of intensity, the amount of manpower and national resources expended, and the number of casualties and the destruction incurred, World War II in the European theater dwarfed the war against Japan in the WORLD WAR II PACIFIC THEATER.

After a series of Axis BLITZKRIEG campaigns conducted between September 1939 and August 1942, the Germans and Italians dominated the European continent from Norway to the Mediterranean Sea (and also North Africa) and from the Bay of Biscay off the western coast of France to the breadth of European Russia. With Axis forces well entrenched, and opposing powers struggling either to survive or to rearm and mobilize, moves to liberate Europe from fascist rule came only following a long and costly war of attrition. When combined with the necessity of defeating Imperial Japanese forces in the Pacific, World War II became a global "total war" of unprecedented proportions.

At a post-PEARL HARBOR conference in Washington, D.C., held between December 14, 1941, and January 15, 1942, the United States and Great Britain built upon earlier joint military staff talks held in August 1941. They developed a combined Anglo-American command, control, and logistical structure for their growing military forces as well as the broad outlines of a strategy to liberate the continent and defeat the Axis. An agreement was reached that the defeat of the European Axis, especially Nazi Germany, would take top priority in the years ahead, for Germany was considered the most powerful and dangerous of the Axis powers, requiring the greatest amount of effort to overcome. The Anglo-American talks also produced a statement of support for the Soviet war effort against Germany—the USSR was already receiving American assistance under the LEND-LEASE ACT—and a decision to engage Axis forces as soon as possible on the continent itself, using all available air, land, and sea capabilities. Once the European Axis was defeated, Allied attentions would focus on defeating Imperial Japan. Until such time as Allied predominance in Europe was assured, however, the war against Japan would take secondary priority and would consist of holding actions and limited offensives. Five subsequent wartime conferences held between 1943 and 1945, involving American president FRANKLIN D. ROOSEVELT, British prime minister Winston S. Churchill, and Soviet dictator Joseph Stalin (known together as the "Big Three") and their military and diplomatic staffs, further refined Allied strategy in consideration of ever changing events.

Yet even with the broad consensus gained in Washington, significant disputes remained among the Soviet, American, and British allies. The United States favored an immediate cross-Channel assault on Axis-occupied France to speed the ultimate goal of invading Germany and destroying its war-making capability. Soviet premier Stalin also favored the immediate opening of a SECOND FRONT, both to ease pressure on the Red Army fighting in the east, and to gain reassurance of the commitment of the Western Allies to the Grand Alliance. Great Britain, however, mindful of American military inexperience, and of the bloody stalemate of the Western Front during World War I, opposed an early direct assault on "Fortress Europe,"

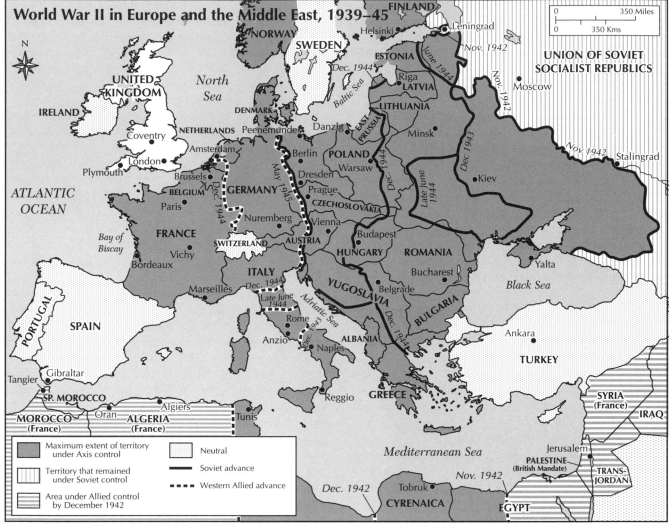

World War II in Europe and the Middle East, 1939–45

preferring a peripheral approach until the Axis was sufficiently weakened to insure Allied success at the lowest possible cost.

While the Americans continued to favor a direct assault in either 1942 or 1943, building up the necessary manpower and war production needed to guarantee Allied superiority was going to take years. As a result, the Americans agreed to follow the British peripheral approach, while securing the Atlantic sea lanes, conducting a campaign of psychological warfare and aid to resistance movements, and mounting an ever more powerful strategic AIR POWER campaign against Germany. In spite of repeated calls by Stalin for an immediate second front, the British strategic view prevailed until 1944, when American war production and military power allowed the United States to determine overall strategy for the Western portion of the Grand Alliance.

As the Western Allies mobilized to conduct a total war, the decision was made to build upon British and Commonwealth efforts against Italian and German forces in North Africa (in the Western Desert in Libya and Egypt) that had commenced in late 1940, providing a foothold for the NORTH AFRICAN CAMPAIGN. Anglo-American planning began immediately in the summer of 1942 to invade Vichy French territories in Northwest Africa, specifically in Morocco and Algeria, with a subsequent thrust toward Tunisia, thus placing Axis forces in a large east-west pincer movement. Once the Allies had defeated Axis forces in North Africa, they would be poised to launch an offensive on the European continent through the perceived "soft underbelly" of Italy or the Balkans.

Operation Torch, the Anglo-American invasion of North Africa, took place on November 8, 1942, with Anglo-American forces landing in Casablanca, Algiers, and

Oran. The Anglo-American forces quickly overcame resistance by Vichy French forces and effected a cease-fire on November 10, but soon bogged down in the advance toward Tunisia due to poor weather, logistical difficulties, and the relative inexperience of American forces. This allowed the Germans to significantly bolster their armies in Tunisia, and to undertake offensive operations against the Allies—most notably at the Kasserine Pass, where U.S. Army forces were dealt a defeat in February 1943. Yet, with British Commonwealth forces pressing retreating Axis armies from the east, following the Second Battle of El Alamein in October 1942, the increased Allied pressure succeeded in forcing Axis troops into Tunisia, where they surrendered on May 13, 1943.

With preparations for the cross-Channel attack on France still ongoing, the Allies decided at the January 1943 CASABLANCA CONFERENCE to continue Mediterranean operations by invading SICILY. At the midsummer Quebec Conference, the Western Allies decided to continue this line of advance to the Italian mainland itself, having dismissed both the possibility of an invasion of France in 1943 and of other peripheral attacks in the Balkans. The conquest of Sicily by August provided the Allies with a major base for the September 1943 invasion of Italy. Earlier, in July, fascist dictator Benito Mussolini was ousted from power; Italy surrendered on September 8. While it was hoped that the Germans would withdraw beyond the Alps, German forces (with fascist Italian support) instead occupied the entire Italian peninsula. Following Anglo-American invasions on September 3 and 9 at Salerno, Taranto, and Reggio, the ITALIAN CAMPAIGN turned into a drawn-out war of attrition through the remainder of 1943 and into 1944, moving northward up the Italian peninsula toward Rome. Attempts to break the German defensive belt known as the Gustave line south of Rome failed even after the Anglo-American amphibious invasion at Anzio in January 1944.

In the meantime, the Soviet Red Army continued to battle for survival against the bulk of Axis military forces on the 1,800 mile-long eastern front. Following the beginning of Operation Barbarossa, the German invasion of the Soviet Union, on June 22, 1941, the Germans killed or captured 3 million Red Army troops in a series of stunning blitzkrieg operations that took them deep into the Ukraine, to the gates of Leningrad in the north, and to the outskirts of Moscow by December 1941. Weather, Axis logistical difficulties, and sizeable Soviet manpower reserves, however, slowed and then halted the German advance, while a massive counteroffensive on December 5, 1941, pushed German forces 100 miles away from Moscow. Although German forces again went on the offensive in the spring of 1942, with the goal of capturing the Caucasus oil fields, a midsummer diversion to seize Stalingrad resulted in one

of the longest urban battles of attrition in military history. German forces succeeded in capturing two-thirds of the city by late October, but a Soviet counteroffensive on November 19 succeeded in surrounding and isolating Axis forces, and a lengthy siege forced their surrender in late January 1943. While the Germans would launch one further (yet limited and failed) offensive, in the summer of 1943 at Kursk, the tide of the war in the east had clearly turned, and growing Soviet military and industrial power promised to overwhelm the increasingly weaker Axis forces.

Planning for a second front in the west continued through 1943 with the decision made at the TEHERAN CONFERENCE in the fall of 1943 to launch the invasion in Normandy in May 1944. The subsequent INVASION OF NORMANDY on June 6, 1944, succeeded in establishing a beachhead, and was followed by a breakout in July. Combined with a second Anglo-American invasion in southern France in August 1944, the Allies succeeded in liberating the bulk of French territory by September 1, 1944. Although the Allies attempted to pierce German frontier defenses on the Siegfried line, or West Wall, in the fall of 1944, these attempts, as well as offensives in the Huertgen Forest, and an airborne operation in the Netherlands to seize Rhine River crossings, failed to produce the expected breakthroughs. In Italy, American forces liberated Rome on June 4, 1944, and, with British forces, pushed the Germans north of Florence before the offensive again stalled for yet another winter on the Gothic line. A mid-December 1944 second Ardennes offensive, known popularly as the BATTLE OF THE BULGE, produced temporary German gains against American forces in Belgium, but was quickly reversed by overwhelming Allied ground and air forces by mid-January 1945.

A major Soviet offensive in the east in June 1944, timed to coincide with the Normandy and French Riviera landings, sent Axis forces along the entire eastern front reeling, resulting in the liberation of European Russia, Poland, and the Balkans by September 1944. Red Army advances prompted the surrender of Romania, Bulgaria, Hungary, and Finland by the late fall of 1944. By February 1945, Red Army forces were on the Oder River 50 miles from Berlin, and were besieging Budapest in Hungary, and were closing in on Austria. The final offensives in the west began in March 1945, with Anglo-American armies forcing multiple crossing of the Rhine River and capturing the German industrial Ruhr Valley by April. In eastern Germany, the final Soviet offensive annihilated the remaining German forces, and the city fell to Soviet forces on May 2, 1945. On the same day, Axis forces in Italy surrendered. In the west, German commanders signed the instrument of surrender in General Dwight D. Eisenhower's headquarters in Rheims, France, on May 7, 1945, in a ceremony repeated the following day, May 8, 1945, in Berlin. Victory in Europe Day, or V-E DAY, was marked officially on May 8, 1945.

Further reading: Stephen E. Ambrose, *The American Heritage New History of World War II* (New York: Viking, 1997); Charles B. MacDonald, *The Mighty Endeavor: The American War in Europe* (New York: DaCapo Press, 1999); Gerhard L. Weinberg, *A World at Arms: A Global History of World War II* (Cambridge, U.K.: Cambridge University Press, 1995); Alexander Werth, *Russia at War, 1941–1945* (New York: Carroll & Graf, 1999).

—Clayton D. Laurie

World War II home front

As compared to its huge and sometimes catastrophic impact on the home fronts of the other major combatants, WORLD WAR II had smaller, generally salutary, but nonetheless significant effects on the American home front. Most obviously, MOBILIZATION returned the ECONOMY to full-production, full-employment prosperity after the long decade of the GREAT DEPRESSION. To manage the war effort, GOVERNMENT grew much larger and more expensive. More than 30 million people—nearly one out of every four—took part in the massive wartime MIGRATION, and the SUNBELT and metropolitan areas saw their populations surge. Women and AFRICAN AMERICANS gained new opportunities, as Americans joined in common cause to defeat the AXIS and win the war. In significant ways, the United States at 1945 looked and felt different—and better—from the way it had just five years earlier.

But there was another side to the home front experience. Migrants often were greeted with suspicion and even hostility in their new communities, and prejudice and discrimination continued to affect American life. People complained about shortages of some consumer goods and other apparent sacrifices, and many turned to the BLACK MARKET for items they wanted. Wartime CENSORSHIP and other government actions sometimes eroded CIVIL LIBERTIES. Old attitudes and values shaped both home front life and hopes for the future, and wartime change often essentially continued prewar trends. Some things scarcely changed at all. Not just the complicated military and diplomatic history of the war but also the fascinating, kaleidoscopic home front experience has contributed to the variety of interpretations of World War II.

Mobilization for war was the fundamental fact and factor on the home front. Producing the war goods and military force that made the United States the "arsenal of democracy" galvanized the nation's economy and society and brought a dual victory—over the Great Depression as well as over the Axis. As late as 1940, UNEMPLOYMENT stood at a depression-level 14.6 percent; by 1944, it had shrunk to a remarkable 1.2 percent. The gross national product and national income more than doubled in those same four years. After a somewhat stumbling start, the mobilization effort worked well and inflation was brought under control. Despite wartime shortages and RATIONING, spending on consumer goods rose, as did living standards.

Mobilization opened new opportunities and experiences, and, with them, heightened aspirations and expectations for millions of Americans. In the 1930s, the pressing national issue had been how to find jobs for all the nation's workers; on the home front, it was how to find workers for all the jobs that needed doing, especially with 16 million men joining the armed forces. As a result, BUSINESS, encouraged by government, eventually turned to other sources of workers—including young people, the ELDERLY, and especially women and African Americans, who gained access to a greater range and higher level of jobs than before. For the first time, married women and women over 35 outnumbered the unmarried and under-35 women in the workforce. Young men (and women) joining the armed forces gained experience, training, and broadened perspectives, and in the postwar period benefited from the GI BILL OF RIGHTS. Organized LABOR grew in numbers and influence.

Mobilizing industry and the armed forces sent GIs, defense workers, and their families to military bases and war plants around the country, but particularly in the Sunbelt states along the Pacific, Gulf, and Atlantic coasts. CITIES, and especially their suburbs, grew rapidly, while the long-term depopulation of rural America accelerated. By the end of the war, one-tenth of the nation's population had moved permanently to a different state. For African Americans, moving out of the rural SOUTH to cities in the North and on the West Coast had especially important long-term consequences. And unlike the dispirited travels of the depression decade, wartime migration and the crowded public TRANSPORTATION facilities of the war years were marked by a bustling excitement and vitality, if often by understandable apprehension as well. Marriage and birth rates picked up early in the war—partly out of hopes that husbands and fathers would be deferred from the military draft by SELECTIVE SERVICE—and set the stage for the great postwar baby boom.

Wartime changes often came with old constraints, however. Despite EXECUTIVE ORDER 8802 that created the FAIR EMPLOYMENT PRACTICES COMMITTEE, the defense industry did not begin to hire blacks in significant numbers or in better jobs until the middle of the war. The somewhat misleading symbol of ROSIE THE RIVETER notwithstanding, women were sometimes reluctant to enter the workforce, encountered prejudice and limited opportunity, and made their most lasting employment increases in white-collar clerical and secretarial work. Prosperity raised income and living standards, but there was virtually no change in the distribution of wealth or economic power—though it often felt that way because national income was so much higher and so many more people were doing better.

Mobilization also brought social strains and even conflict. Arriving migrants were often greeted with some apprehension and distaste, because they seemed to tax community resources and challenge community standards. Worrisome misbehavior by some young people made juvenile delinquency a concern. Divorce rates increased toward the end of the war, reflecting hurried, inappropriate marriages and sometimes wartime tensions in MARRIAGE AND FAMILY LIFE. ITALIAN AMERICANS were treated with distrust early in the war, and ANTI-SEMITISM sometimes flared on the home front. GAYS AND LESBIANS faced new discrimination in the military. MEXICAN AMERICANS encountered prejudice as they took part in the migration to urban areas, and in Los Angeles in 1943 Mexican American ZOOT-SUITERS were the target of ugly rioting. In Detroit, New York, and elsewhere race riots involving African Americans also broke out in the summer of 1943. And the RELOCATION OF JAPANESE AMERICANS and their incarceration constituted by far the worst violation of civil liberties during the war.

Social change and home front life had positive and uplifting sides, too, of course. The war ultimately hastened the assimilation of Italian Americans and other white ethnic groups into the mainstream of American society. African Americans pursued what some black newspapers called the "Double V" campaign—victory at home over Jim Crow as well as abroad over the Axis—and laid crucial groundwork for the postwar Civil Rights movement. Many women, in the workplace or (with husbands away) at home had new experiences and autonomy.

Shortages and rationing of consumer goods, especially of gasoline and meat, may have rankled and led to violations of policy, but most people went along. Indeed, they often found common cause in the grumbling and limited sacrifice as well as in efforts on production lines, military units, and wartime communities. Home front Americans pitched in with such diverse activities as civil defense efforts, scrap drives, victory gardens, and WAR BONDS sales. From the first shocking news of the Japanese attack on PEARL HARBOR, moreover, Americans were sure of their cause and confident of victory. The complaints about home front disruptions and the frustrations with the rocky beginning of mobilization did not in any serious way impair home front morale.

Americans on the home front also found time to enjoy themselves, engaging in RECREATION, watching SPORTS events, going to the MOVIES, listening to MUSIC at home and at live performances, and enjoying RADIO and other aspects of POPULAR CULTURE. Spared the often devastating impact of war on home fronts of their British and especially Russian allies and of their German and Japanese foes, home front Americans often did have a "good war," despite some sacrifices and real anxieties about family and friends in the armed forces. Tens of millions found solace and reassurance in RELIGION. Although worries existed about the postwar economy, the new jobs, training, experiences, and higher living standards of the war years restored confidence and optimism to Americans and raised hopes for the future. Many would later look back to the wartime experience as the best years of their lives.

In addition to its economic and social impact, wartime mobilization also had important consequences for American government. To acquire and allocate the material, manpower, and money required for the war effort greatly increased the power, size, and cost of the federal government—far beyond the growth in the NEW DEAL years of the 1930s. Staffing the mobilization agencies quadrupled the number of civilian federal employees to nearly 4 million. Paying for the gigantic war effort increased the expenses of the government from $9 billion to almost $98 billion between 1939 and 1945. In addition to drafting men for the wartime military, the government conscripted money to help meet wartime costs—and wartime TAXATION, especially the REVENUE ACT OF 1942, greatly expanded the reach of the income tax and produced the withholding tax system. The number of taxable individual incomes soared from 4 million in 1939 to nearly 43 million by war's end.

The mobilization effort had important consequences for the political economy. Not only did the government's size, power, and costs grow, but so too did its scope—in underwriting SCIENCE and TECHNOLOGY, for example, especially through the OFFICE OF SCIENTIFIC RESEARCH AND DEVELOPMENT. Because there were not enough experienced bureaucrats to manage economic mobilization, DOLLAR-A-YEAR MEN and other businessmen came to Washington to head or serve on key agencies, and in the process helped to increase the economic and political power of big business. Some scholars see World War II as the crucial period for the development of the so-called military-industrial complex—or the military-industrial-scientific complex. Organized labor and big AGRICULTURE also gained new power during the war, as the modern political economy of big government, big business, big labor, and big farming took clearer shape.

Wartime government spending had important consequences for fiscal policy. From PEARL HARBOR to V-J DAY, the government spent about $300 billion—twice as much as in all its previous history, from 1789 down to 1941. Despite the increase in taxes, current revenues paid for less than half of the costs of mobilization. The rest the government funded by borrowing. The massive deficits not only paid for the war but underwrote full-production, full-employment prosperity and thus confirmed the central argument of KEYNESIANISM that government deficit spending could produce growth and prosperity. Together with the much enlarged tax structure of the war years, this provided the basis for postwar fiscal policy. It also helped consummate a shift in LIBERALISM toward Keynesian fiscal policy.

Despite the large impact of the war on the nation's economy, society, and government, politics changed surprisingly little from 1940 to 1945. Indeed, unlike even Great Britain, which called off elections for the duration, the normal rhythms—and the fierce partisanship—of American politics continued. President FRANKLIN D. ROOSEVELT won an unprecedented third term in the ELECTION OF 1940, and then a fourth in the ELECTION OF 1944. Voting patterns closely resembled those of the previous decade, and depression-era party images and issues continued to shape voter preferences, with the DEMOCRATIC PARTY still seen as the party of prosperity and economic security. But, particularly in the congressional elections of 1942, the REPUBLICAN PARTY regained some of the strength lost in the 1930s—partly because of unhappiness with shortages, rationing, and the OFFICE OF PRICE ADMINISTRATION. In CONGRESS, the CONSERVATIVE COALITION of Republicans and conservative Democrats that had emerged in the late 1930s grew stronger still and prevented any expansion of liberal reform.

As victory in the war came in sight by 1944, Americans began to look ahead to the postwar era. POSTWAR PLANNING revealed the emphasis on full employment and postwar prosperity evident in PUBLIC OPINION POLLS, while ADVERTISING showed visions of the good life of abundance that people wanted. Polls and ads also demonstrated the emphasis on marriage and family that would characterize the postwar decades. Apprehension—what some called "depression psychosis"—nonetheless persisted about what would happen to the economy once the stimulus of war mobilization was gone.

The end of the war in August 1945 brought jubilant V-J Day celebrations, but also concern about the challenges at home and abroad. RECONVERSION and DEMOBILIZATION went generally effectively, however, and despite early problems and disruptions, prosperity continued. The nation shifted more easily into the postwar period than many had feared during the war. Postwar America would be different from prewar America, different because of World War II and its impact on the home front. But along with those differences were powerful continuities in social, political, and economic patterns and in the nation's bedrock values and attitudes.

See also POLITICS IN THE ROOSEVELT ERA; WOMEN'S STATUS AND RIGHTS.

Further reading: Mark Jonathan Harris, Franklin Mitchel and Steven Schechter, *The Homefront: America during World War II* (New York: Putnam, 1984); John W. Jeffries, *Wartime America: The World War II Home Front* (Chicago: Ivan R. Dee, 1996); Richard R. Lingeman, *Don't You Know There's a War On? The American Home Front, 1941–1945* (New York: G.P. Putnam's Sons, 1970); Richard Polenberg, *War and Society: The United States, 1941–1945* (Philadelphia: J. B. Lippincott, 1972); Allan M. Winkler, *Home Front U.S.A.: America during World War II*, 2d ed. (Wheeling, Ill.: Harlan Davidson, 2000).

World War II Pacific theater

As compared to the WORLD WAR II EUROPEAN THEATER, the Pacific theater opened more than two years later, encompassed a far greater geographic expanse, and involved fewer troops and nations at a lower cost in casualties, physical destruction, and material expended. Although many nations participated, the ultimate victory over Japan was overwhelmingly the result of American naval, air, and ground operations.

Imperial Japan began a campaign of Asian conquest in MANCHURIA in September 1931, followed by the invasion of China in July 1937, which had bogged down by 1940. Events in Europe, however, provided the military-controlled Japanese government with the opportunity to profit from Dutch, French, and British weakness in Asia, where these powers controlled lightly defended, yet resource-rich colonies in the Netherlands East Indies, Indochina, Burma, Malaya, and elsewhere. These regions could provide Japan with resources it needed as a modern industrial power, as well as its own empire, the "Greater East Asia Co-prosperity Sphere." Japanese expansion would end Western hegemony in Asia and Western support of the Nationalist Chinese regime.

While Japanese diplomacy produced an alliance with Thailand, the Rome-Berlin-Tokyo AXIS, and bases in French Indochina, American opposition to Japanese activities strained relations and prompted an American embargo on Japan in September 1940, which was followed by an Anglo-American freezing of Japanese assets in July 1941. In response, and despite negotiations between the United States and Japan to maintain the peace, the Imperial Japanese military decided in July 1941 to launch a campaign of conquest in the Pacific by December. As the United States was the only power that could interfere with these plans, Japan planned to destroy the U.S. Pacific Fleet at PEARL HARBOR, Hawaii. Before the United States could recover from this devastating blow and mobilize its forces,

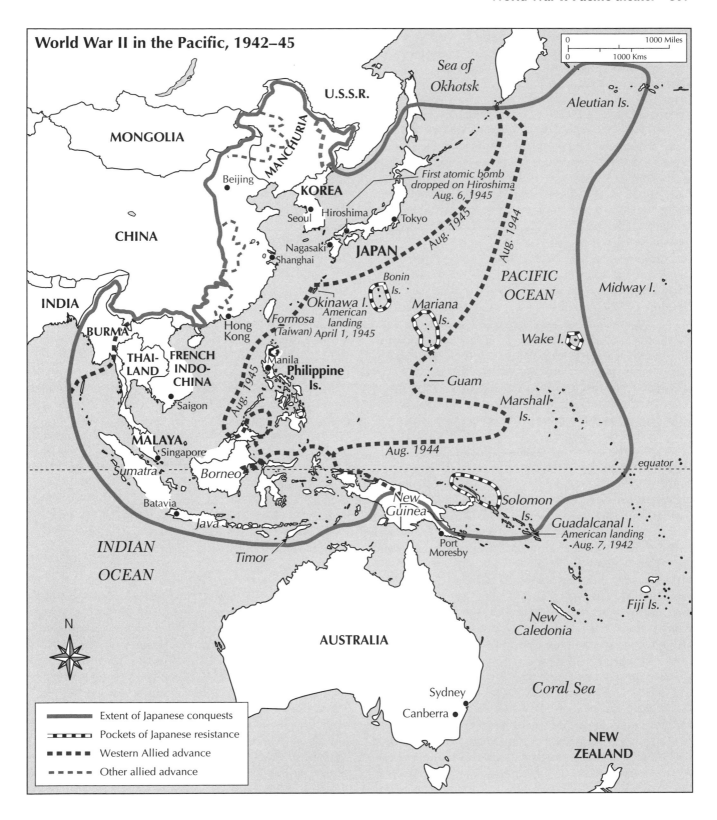

World War II in the Pacific, 1942–45

MONGOLIA

U.S.S.R.

Sea of Okhotsk

Aleutian Is.

Beijing

MANCHURIA

KOREA

CHINA

Seoul   Hiroshima   Tokyo

First atomic bomb dropped on Hiroshima Aug. 6, 1945

Nagasaki

Shanghai

JAPAN

Aug. 1945

Aug. 1944

Bonin Is.

Mariana Is.

PACIFIC OCEAN

Midway I.

INDIA

BURMA

Hong Kong

Formosa (Taiwan)

Okinawa I.
American landing April 1, 1945

Wake I.

THAI-LAND

FRENCH INDO-CHINA

Manila

Aug. 1945

Philippine Is.

— Guam

Marshall Is.

Saigon

MALAYA   Singapore

Sumatra

Borneo

Aug. 1944

equator

Batavia

Java

New Guinea

Solomon Is.

Port Moresby

Guadalcanal I.
American landing Aug. 7, 1942

Timor

INDIAN OCEAN

Fiji Is.

New Caledonia

N

AUSTRALIA

Coral Sea

Sydney

Canberra

NEW ZEALAND

Extent of Japanese conquests
Pockets of Japanese resistance
Western Allied advance
Other allied advance

Japan expected to have vanquished China and created a fortified empire in Asia and the Pacific. The United States, the Japanese believed, would then negotiate a settlement leaving the new Japanese empire intact rather than fight over former European colonies of little interest or value to Americans.

The surprise Japanese attack on Pearl Harbor on December 7, 1941, opened hostilities, and coincided with similar attacks throughout Asia and the Pacific. Moving aggressively against disunited, demoralized, and weak British, Dutch, American, and Australian forces, a relatively small Japanese army of 250,000 troops, supported by powerful naval and air forces, quickly conquered Hong Kong, Singapore, the PHILIPPINES, the Dutch East Indies, Burma, Malaya, Indochina, and New Guinea. By late spring 1942, Japanese forces had pushed deep into the Pacific as far as the Gilbert, Solomon, and Aleutian Islands, and were poised for invasions of Australia, India, and southern China, having cut the Burma-Ledo Road supplying Nationalist Chinese forces.

Although the United States and Great Britain had decided on a strategy to defeat the European Axis first, the attack on Pearl Harbor enraged Americans, and the rapid Japanese advance resulted in a shift of most Allied manpower and material produced during 1942 to Asia and the Pacific. The number of powers with diverse holdings in the Pacific theater also caused unique problems in supply, planning, and coordination. The primary aim of the Dutch and the British (and, to a lesser extent, of the French and Australians) was to liberate their colonies, while the United States had as its priority the destruction of Japanese military power in the Pacific.

Unlike the European theater, which enjoyed a unity of command and purpose, with the early designation of supreme allied commanders in the Mediterranean and northwestern Europe, no similar allied command situation existed in the Pacific. Instead, the British established an India theater headquarters, later expanded to a Southeast Asia Command under Lord Louis Mountbatten, operating in Burma. These British and Indian forces served in the China-Burma-India (CBI) theater in conjunction with Nationalist Chinese and American forces, under Generalissimo Chiang Kai-shek and his American military adviser, U.S. Army lieutenant general Joseph W. Stilwell. Operations in the CBI were distinct from operations conducted by the American-supplied Nationalist Chinese Army in the China theater directly controlled by Chiang.

In the greater Pacific Ocean Area, command and control was even more diffuse due to interservice U.S. rivalries. In Australia, U.S. Army general Douglas A. MacArthur commanded a mixed American and Australian force in what became known as the Southwest Pacific theater. MacArthur was unwilling to allow U.S. NAVY commanders to control army air or ground forces, but he also needed their support for his planned advance in New Guinea. In 1942, the Joint Chiefs of Staff decided to conduct a two-pronged Pacific offensive. Admiral CHESTER W. NIMITZ, designated commander in chief of U.S. Forces, Pacific

Ocean Areas, was authorized to conduct a westward advance through the North, Central, and South Pacific theaters with the U.S. Navy and U.S. MARINES, using U.S. ARMY air and ground support where necessary. MacArthur was granted similar navy and marine support for his operations. Although the American strategy defied the axiom about never dividing one's forces, the multiple front nature of the Pacific war strained Japan's limited resources and logistics capabilities, hastening their defeat.

American ground operations began in August 1942 with the marine invasion of GUADALCANAL and Tulagi in the SOLOMON ISLANDS in the South Pacific theater under Admiral WILLIAM F. "BULL" HALSEY. In a hard fought campaign involving marine, army, and navy units, Japanese forces were defeated on the ground and at sea by February 1943, while U.S. forces continued to move up the Solomons to Bougainville. Simultaneously, U.S. Army and Australian forces under MacArthur began operations in Papua New Guinea from Port Moresby. Following the conquest of Buna, and a series of leapfrog amphibious operations up the New Guinea coast at Lae, Salamaua, Finschafen, Hollandia, Biak, and Morotai, MacArthur prepared to invade the Philippines by September 1944. In the process, he bypassed the Japanese base at Rabaul, now surrounded and ineffectual.

In the China-Burma-India theater and the China theater, Allied troops tried without success to push back Japanese forces. This area, starved of manpower and material by the demands of other fronts and the relative lack of military prowess shown by Nationalist Chinese forces, was maintained almost solely by airlifted supplies coming over the Himalayas (or "the Hump"). The CBI and China theaters remained regions of secondary and diminishing importance as opposed to the faster moving offensives in the Southwest and Central Pacific.

The long-awaited U.S. Navy and Marine Corps Central Pacific advance began in November 1943 with the invasion of TARAWA atoll in the Gilbert Islands chain. Tarawa was the first of several island-hopping AMPHIBIOUS WARFARE assaults conducted by naval and marine forces, where each island taken served as a jumping-off point for further advances west. In relatively quick succession, the U.S. Navy and Marine Corps team, with U.S. Army support, secured the Marshall Islands in February 1944, followed by the June–July 1944 conquest of Saipan, Tinian, and Guam in the MARIANA ISLANDS. The storming of Peleliu in the Palau Group in September 1944, and the bypassing of the Japanese-held Caroline Islands with its major stronghold at Truk, which was left to wither on the vine, brought American forces close to the Philippines by fall 1944.

The Central Pacific advance was only possible because of the significant expansion of the U.S. Navy and its ability to defeat Imperial Japanese sea and air power in a series of engagements. After Pearl Harbor and the Allied defeat at the Battle of the Java Sea in February 1942, U.S. Navy forces had succeeded in halting Japanese expansion toward Australia in the BATTLE OF THE CORAL SEA in May 1942 and then decisively turned the tide with their stunning victory at the BATTLE OF MIDWAY in June 1942. Japanese efforts to repel U.S. forces in the Marianas during the July 1944 invasions resulted in their further defeat in the BATTLE OF THE PHILIPPINE SEA, which brought the final destruction of Japanese naval air power. Although the Japanese navy would again attempt to contest American landings in the Philippines, the BATTLE FOR LEYTE GULF in October 1944 resulted in the destruction of the remaining elements of Japanese naval strength and gave naval supremacy in the Pacific to the United States. The successful efforts of U.S. SUBMARINES against the Japanese merchant fleet showed both the glaring deficiencies in Japanese maritime power and the inability of its military to keep its far-flung forces adequately supplied. Increasingly, after 1943, Japanese forces were literally starved for food, medical supplies, and war materials necessary to defend the empire.

With the conquest of the Mariana Islands, it became possible to launch a strategic air campaign against the Japanese home islands using the new, long-range B-29 Superfortress bomber, which moved from less effective bases in India and China in October 1944. The U.S. Marine landings on IWO JIMA in February 1945, the bloodiest battle in marine corps history, succeeded in gaining a fighter escort base and emergency landing field for B-29s returning from their firebombing raids on Japan. The bombing raids caused an estimated 500,000 Japanese civilian deaths between March and July 1945.

The original American strategy in the Pacific called for an invasion of Japan from bases in Formosa (Taiwan) and the Chinese coast, but the lack of Chinese progress in liberating these potential base areas by 1944 made it imperative that alternatives be found. Following MacArthur's invasion of the Philippines, at Leyte in October 1944 and at Luzon in January 1945, it was determined that OKINAWA, in the Ryukyu chain, some 350 miles south of Japan, would provide a suitable base. While the Australians invaded Borneo, the British and Indians liberated Burma, the U.S. Army continued to fight the Japanese in the Philippines (in a campaign that would last until the end of the war), and American forces invaded Okinawa in April 1945. The bloody Okinawa campaign, taking nearly three months, demonstrated Japanese tenacity and seeming willingness to fight to the last man. Costly attacks by Japanese kamikaze suicide aircraft on U.S. Navy forces offshore convinced American military leaders that Japan would fight to the bitter end during any invasion of the home islands, now scheduled for October 1945 and January 1946.

The successful test of the ATOMIC BOMB by the United States on July 16, 1945, however, offered an opportunity to end the war quickly without an invasion. Although questioned in later years, the use of the atomic bomb brought the surrender of Japan and saved the many American and Japanese lives that would have been lost had there been a grinding, drawn-out campaign of attrition in Japan. Following the atomic bombings of HIROSHIMA AND NAGASAKI on August 6 and 9, and the Soviet declaration of war against Japan on August 8, Japanese emperor Hirohito called on his forces to lay down their arms on August 15. The official document of surrender was signed aboard the USS *Missouri* in Tokyo Bay on September 2, 1945, ending the war in the Pacific, as well as World War II.

Further reading: Eric Bergerud, *Touched with Fire: The Land War in the South Pacific* (New York: Penguin, 1985); John Costello, *The Pacific War, 1941–1945* (New York: William Morrow, 1983); Ronald H. Spector, *Eagle against the Sun: The American War against Japan* (New York: Random House, 1985).

—Clayton D. Laurie

Wright, Richard (1908–1960)

Richard Wright powerfully depicted the prejudice and discrimination facing AFRICAN AMERICANS in *Native Son* (1940), his gripping novel about black life in Chicago, and in *Black Boy* (1945), his autobiographical account of growing up in the deep SOUTH. These and other of his writings illuminated the circumstances of African Americans and contributed to black protest and activism on behalf of CIVIL RIGHTS. *Native Son*, his major and most influential work, was a selection of the Book of the Month Club, and thus had a particularly widespread readership and impact.

Wright was born on September 4, 1908, near Roxie, Mississippi, not far from Natchez. His father was an illiterate sharecropper, his mother a teacher. After a difficult childhood because of poverty, racism, and the desertion of his father, he moved to Chicago when he was 19 years old. Although he had little formal education, he read widely, and his reading helped shape his understanding of the plight of the urban poor, especially in the black community. In 1933, Wright was introduced to the John Reed Club, a Communist literary group, and attracted by the Communist Party's writings about radical change and equality for the lower classes, he joined the party in 1934. He was supported by the FEDERAL WRITERS' PROJECT of the NEW DEAL while also writing for left-wing literary magazines. His first book, *Uncle Tom's Children*, a collection of his stories, was published in 1938. Increasingly disillusioned by the COMMUNISTS, he publicly broke with party during WORLD WAR II, and his 1944 essay explaining his decision was reprinted in *The God That Failed* (1950).

But Wright was also disillusioned and disheartened by the patterns of RACE AND RACIAL CONFLICT in the United States, and he moved to France after the war. In addition to continuing to write, he also became a spokesman for Africa and anticolonialism. He died in Paris in 1950.

See also LITERATURE.

Further reading: Hazel Rowley, *Richard Wright: The Life and Times* (New York: Henry Holt, 2001).

Y

Yalta Conference (February 1945)

The Yalta Conference was held February 4–12, 1945, in Yalta, in the Soviet Union province of Crimea on the Black Sea. It involved the "Big Three" leaders of the GRAND ALLIANCE against the AXIS in WORLD WAR II: Soviet premier Joseph Stalin, British prime minister Winston Churchill, and U.S. president FRANKLIN D. ROOSEVELT. The meeting took up issues previously discussed at the TEHERAN CONFERENCE, including the surrender and postwar status of Germany; the postwar status of eastern Europe, especially Poland; the establishment of an international organization to maintain postwar peace; and the final stages of the war in the WORLD WAR II PACIFIC THEATER. Issues not settled at Yalta were left to later meetings, and ongoing questions involving Poland, eastern Europe, and Germany played an important role in the unraveling of the Grand Alliance and the development of the cold war. Particularly in the United States, decisions made at the conference were controversial from the beginning.

At Yalta, Stalin wanted to ensure secure borders for the Soviet Union in eastern Europe and to receive heavy German reparations to help rebuild the postwar Soviet Union. His advantages for negotiating at the conference included the immense Soviet contribution to the war effort and the position of the Red Army, which by February 1945 had wrested eastern Europe from Nazi control and was driving toward Berlin. Roosevelt's objectives included Soviet agreement to joining the postwar UNITED NATIONS and a Soviet declaration of war on Japan. He wanted to avoid overt Soviet domination of eastern Europe and to ensure cooperative SOVIET-AMERICAN RELATIONS and Stalin's constructive participation in the postwar world.

The Big Three confirmed the CASABLANCA CONFERENCE policy of Germany's unconditional surrender and agreed to the division of Germany into four zones of occupation. The Soviets, Americans, British, and French would each administer their own zone, with a central control commission in Berlin overseeing all four zones. With respect to reparations from Germany, Stalin wanted $20 billion, but the British and the Americans only agreed to use that sum as a working number, with the Soviets to receive no more than half. The final amount would be decided at a subsequent conference.

Discussions of Poland focused on the country's borders and its government. Churchill and FDR agreed to the Soviet acquisition of eastern Poland, with the prospect, to be decided later, of Poland being compensated by receiving part of eastern Germany to the Oder and Neisse Rivers. The question of Poland's government proved especially difficult. Stalin insisted upon recognizing the Soviet-sponsored government located in the Polish city of Lublin, rather than the rival anticommunist Polish government-in-exile in London. FDR was concerned about the possible political backlash from Polish-American voters and was not ready to accept the new Lublin government. The Big Three agreed to a provisional government, which was to include members of the London government-in-exile and to hold free elections. No date or enforcement procedures were established, and the Soviets, who occupied Poland, would oversee the process. FDR was unable to receive firmer guarantees from Stalin and explained to his chief of staff, Admiral WILLIAM D. LEAHY, that "it's the best I can do for Poland at this time."

The Big Three also agreed to a Declaration on Liberated Europe, which committed them to "arrange and conduct free elections" so that liberated countries could democratically meet their political and economic problems. Interim governments would be created that would be "broadly representative of all democratic elements," including both Communists and non-Communists, until free elections were held. The terms of this were also vague and open to interpretation.

Roosevelt had success on two issues of paramount importance to him. Stalin agreed to help establish the postwar United Nations, on condition of big-power veto authority on action items in the Security Council and the

Winston Churchill, Franklin D. Roosevelt, and Joseph Stalin at Yalta *(Library of Congress)*

membership of two Soviet republics in the General Assembly. Roosevelt also wanted Stalin's commitment to declare war against Japan (still linked to the Soviets by a mutual nonaggression treaty) so that the war in the Pacific theater could be brought to an end as quickly as possible. Stalin agreed to enter the war within two or three months of Germany's surrender in exchange for postwar annexation of the Kurile Islands, southern Sakhalin Island, restoration of rights lost in Manchuria in the 1904–05 Russo-Japanese War, and recognition of Soviet-controlled Mongolia. Stalin also agreed to deal with the Chiang Kai-shek's Nationalists as the legitimate government in China.

After Yalta, Roosevelt was criticized by conservatives and by Polish Americans for betraying Poland, Eastern Europe, and China, and such charges played a significant role in the postwar McCarthy era. Historians have dis-

agreed about Roosevelt's performance at Yalta, including the degree to which his failing health hampered him. Most historians agree, however, that he received important concessions from Stalin on the United Nations and the war against Japan and that Soviet influence over eastern Europe was inevitable, given Soviet security concerns and the Red Army's control of the area.

See also POTSDAM CONFERENCE.

Further reading: Diane Sharer Clemens, *Yalta* (New York: Oxford University Press, 1970); Robert Dallek, *Franklin D. Roosevelt and American Foreign Policy, 1932–1945)* (New York: Oxford University Press, 1979); Athan G. Theoharis, *The Yalta Myths: An Issue in U.S. Politics, 1945–1955* (Columbia: University of Missouri Press, 1970).

Z

Zionism

Support of Zionism, the international movement to create a Jewish state in Palestine, increased in the 1930s because of the plight of Jewish REFUGEES from Nazi Germany. During WORLD WAR II, mounting evidence of the HOLOCAUST further augmented Zionist sentiment. By the middle of the war, most American JEWS, including such prominent figures as Supreme Court justice FELIX FRANKFURTER and Secretary of the Treasury HENRY MORGENTHAU, JR., had apparently become supporters of a Jewish state in Palestine; so too had many people outside the Jewish community, including Vice President HENRY A. WALLACE.

At a conference in New York in May 1942, American Zionist leaders called for an independent Jewish state in Palestine and subsequently stepped up pressure for support from the American GOVERNMENT. Congressional resolutions for a Jewish state in Palestine were reviewed and supported by the House Foreign Affairs Committee, but they encountered opposition from the State Department, which feared that an official acceptance of these resolutions would create problems with the Arab nations where the United States was building oil pipelines. ANTI-SEMITISM among some State Department officials also militated against Zionist aims.

Zionists also sought support from President FRANKLIN D. ROOSEVELT, who seemed open to providing assistance. The Roosevelt administration helped organize the Conference on Refugees in Bermuda in 1943, but the conference failed when Britain continued to oppose the immigration of Jewish refugees from Europe to Palestine. Even though Roosevelt, concerned about American-Arab relations and about stability in the Middle East and deferring to British policy, continued to avoid formal backing of a Jewish state in Palestine, Zionists supported him in the ELECTION OF 1944. But following the election, Roosevelt, despite some sympathy for Zionist goals, still refrained from endorsing a Jewish homeland in Palestine.

At the end of World War II, Zionists had thus failed to win official support of their goal of a Jewish state in Palestine. Concerns about oil and relations with the Arab states, especially Saudi Arabia, had proved more powerful than the lobbying and political influence of Zionist supporters. But a highly effective publicity campaign by the American Zionist Emergency Council helped persuade some three-fourths of all Americans to support a Jewish homeland in Palestine by late 1947 and produced growing pressure on new president Harry S. Truman to support Zionist aspirations. When the British mandate over Palestine ended in May 1948, Palestinian Jews declared the independence of the new state of Israel. Reflecting among other things sympathy for Jewish suffering during the Holocaust and the importance of the Jewish vote to the DEMOCRATIC PARTY, President Truman gave de facto recognition to Israel. His action helped secure the success of the Zionist aim of an independent Jewish state in Palestine.

Further reading: Henry L. Feingold, *The Politics of Rescue: The Roosevelt Administration and the Holocaust, 1938–1945* (New Brunswick, N.J.: Rutgers University Press, 1970); Melvin I. Urofsky, *American Zionism from Herzl to the Holocaust* (Garden City, N.Y.: Doubleday, 1975).

—Ann Adams

zoot-suiters

Zoot-suiters, mostly young male AFRICAN AMERICANS and MEXICAN AMERICANS, earned their name by wearing an ostentatious style of suit, zoot suits, in the early 1940s. Newspapers across the nation sensationalized the outfit, and the term "zoot-suiter" quickly gained a negative association with unpatriotic and criminal activity. Backlash against the "zooters"—rooted in deeper racial and ethnic animosities—reached a zenith in the summer of 1943 with the "zoot suit riots," a series of mob attacks on minority youth in several American cities.

Zoot suit coats were characterized by wide padded shoulders, sleeves reaching the fingertips, baggy fit, wide lapels, and an extended length, often reaching to the knees. This was paired with loose-fitting pants with very narrow cuffs, and with string ties, gold watch chains, and wide brimmed hats with narrow crowns. The brighter and bolder the color of the suit, the more stylish and noticeable it was—characteristics highly desired by zoot-suiters.

The origin of the zoot suit is found in the vigorous improvisational MUSIC of swing, a highly danceable type of jazz. The narrow cuffs of the zoot suit prevented catching ones shoes while performing the athletic movements of the jitterbug and lindy hop. Swing inspired many young people of all races to spend evenings dancing at large urban dancehalls such as Minton's in Harlem. Musicians' use of improvisation in playing was also echoed in the jive or slang language adopted by zoot-suiters. Originating in Harlem, the zoot suits spread across the country to the West Coast.

Many African Americans relocated from rural communities in the SOUTH to northern CITIES in search of new employment opportunities produced by the economic MOBILIZATION for WORLD WAR II. Similarly, Mexican Americans moved to West Coast defense industries, especially in and around Los Angeles. The renewed energy created by this economic change inspired young urban Americans to spend more of their earnings on entertainment and on fashionable clothing like the zoot suit. The influx of African Americans and Mexican Americans also produced racial tensions and sometimes conflict in crowded war boom areas.

Clothing regulations issued by the WAR PRODUCTION BOARD, including allowable usage of natural materials such as wool, contributed to the disparagement of the zoot suiters. The WPB promoted the so-called victory suit—and with its slim pants, narrow lapels, and conservative styling, the victory suit was an obvious opposite of the zoot suit. The WPB found zoot suits unpatriotic because of the flagrant excess amount of fabric used and ordered an end to production of the suits.

Newspapers across America amplified antipathy against the zoot suit and its wearers through accounts connecting zoot-suiters to gangsters and moral deficiencies. Zooters were described as shiftless hustlers who dodged the draft and assaulted white women. While some zoot-suiters did engage in criminal behavior, most did not. In Los Angeles and elsewhere, many belonged to gangs, though often for social, not unlawful, activities. For many of these youth, the zoot suit exemplified an independent spirit.

Violence against zoot-suiters erupted in Los Angeles, California, in June 1943. White U.S. servicemen, fueled by rumors that Mexican-American zoot-suiters harassed and molested white women, assaulted zoot-suiters and destroyed and stripped the suits off of them. Bystanders cheered as zoot- suiters were beaten and then arrested by local police. More than 100 Mexican Americans suffered serious injuries, in contrast to only 20 servicemen in the L.A. riot. Racism was a clear motive of the violence, as many victims of the riot were not even wearing zoot suits. Newspaper articles recounted the riot with an air of festivity, further stimulating anti-Mexican sentiment.

Violence against zoot-suiters, part of a more general pattern of racial conflict in the summer of 1943, also broke out in other cities such as New York and Detroit, where violence was directed at young African Americans. The zoot suit's popularity declined sharply after the rash of riots in the summer of 1943. In California, the zoot suit riots produced an effort led by the governor to combat prejudice and enhance the prospects of Mexican Americans. Similarly, the general outburst of race riots suits in the summer of 1943 sparked efforts elsewhere to address the problems of racial discrimination and conflict.

See also RACE AND RACIAL CONFLICT.

Further reading: Mario T. Garcia, *Mexican-Americans: Leadership, Ideology, and Identity, 1930–1960* (New Haven, Conn.: Yale University Press, 1989); Mauricio Mazon, *The Zoot-Suit Riots: The Psychology of Symbolic Annihilation* (Austin: University of Texas Press, 1984).

—Courtney D. Mattingly

Chronology

1929

William Faulkner publishes *Sartoris* and *The Sound and the Fury*.

Comedian Groucho Marx and his brothers appear in their first movie, *The Cocoanuts*.

The Agricultural Marketing Act of 1929 establishes the Federal Farm Board to promote the sale of agricultural products through cooperatives and stabilization corporations.

Thomas Wolfe publishes his first novel, *Look Homeward, Angel*.

The United States and 19 Latin American states sign the Inter-American Treaties of 1929, which oblige the signatories to submit all disputes of an international nature to arbitration and conciliation commissions.

The New York stock market crashes on Black Tuesday. The crash helps usher in the Great Depression in the United States.

Mexico and the United States establish the Mexican Repatriation Program to resettle Mexican Americans in Mexico during the Great Depression. Some 500,000 Mexican Americans resettle through the program by 1940, as many as half of them American citizens.

1930

Sinclair Lewis is the first U.S. citizen to receive the Nobel Prize in literature. In his acceptance speech, he attacks the conservative American literary establishment as antithetical to the revolutionary nature of the United States.

The Nation of Islam is founded in Detroit.

Herbert Hoover signs into law the Hawley-Smoot Tariff Act of 1930, which raises U.S. protective duties to their highest rate ever.

Drought takes hold in the Great Plains; over the next decade more than 300 dust storms rob the region of billions of tons of topsoil, crippling agriculture and producing the Dust Bowl.

The National Association for the Advancement of Colored People (NAACP) leads a successful protest to block the nomination of Judge John Parker to the U.S. Supreme Court because of racist statements.

1931

The "Scottsboro Boys" trial begins and attracts national attention, illuminating the rural southern judicial system.

The economic depression deepens; unemployment skyrockets, and hundreds of U.S. banks close.

The Empire State Building opens; it is the tallest skyscraper in the world.

Journalist Walter Lippman begins writing his influential column for the *New York Herald*.

In *Near v. Minnesota*, the U.S. Supreme Court upholds the right of the press to criticize public officials.

Imperial Japan invades Manchuria. In response, the U.S. secretary of state enunciates the Stimson Doctrine, which states that the United States will refuse to recognize any territorial gains brought about by use of armed force in violation of international law.

1932

The Reconstruction Finance Corporation is created to give financial assistance to failing banks; it later funds self-liquidating state public work projects under the Relief and Reconstruction Act.

The League of Nations hosts the World Disarmament Conference in Geneva, Switzerland; negotiations fail to bring about significant arms reductions before Germany and Japan withdraw.

Comedian Jack Benny begins his radio show; it remains on the air, via radio and, later, television for 23 years.

The American Civil Liberties Union (ACLU) issues *Black Justice*, a report detailing the extent of institutional racism in America.

Pilot Amelia Earhart becomes the first woman to fly solo from the United States to Europe.

In *Powell v. Alabama,* the U.S. Supreme Court overturns the conviction of the "Scottsboro Boys," who were tried and sentenced for rape without the defense of legal counsel.

The Norris–La Guardia Act of 1932 prevents the government from issuing injunctions to restrain strikes, boycotts, or picketing, except where such strikes affect the public safety, or to enforce antiunion "yellow dog" contracts.

The United Conference of Mayors forms to seek federal aid for the urban unemployed.

In Tuskegee, Alabama, the U.S. Public Health Service begins a 40-year study on the effects of untreated syphilis, using approximately 400 African-American men. The men are never informed of their disease, nor are they given treatment.

Approximately 20,000 World War I veterans and their family members set up camp in Washington, D.C., seeking early payment of service bonuses; President Hoover refuses to pay bonuses early and has the military forcibly disperse the "Bonus Army."

Amid growing dissatisfaction with government efforts to bring the country out of the depression, incumbent president Herbert Hoover is defeated by Democrat Franklin D. Roosevelt.

1933

Franklin Roosevelt is sworn in as president on March 4; he had pledged a "new deal" for the American people and initiates numerous economic stimulus and relief programs in his first hundred days in office.

The Emergency Banking Relief Act of 1933 gives the president broad powers over the national banking system.

The U.S. Congress ratifies the Twentieth and Twenty-first Amendments to the U.S. Constitution; the Twentieth Amendment adjusts the length of congressional and presidential terms of office, and the Twenty-first Amendment ends Prohibition by repealing the Eighteenth Amendment to the U.S. Constitution.

Dorothy Day founds the *Catholic Worker,* a monthly newspaper that aims to raise society's consciousness regarding the poor.

Benny Goodman records Billie Holiday and introduces her distinctive singing style to the American public.

The U.S. Congress passes the Agricultural Adjustment Act of 1933, which raises farm income and commodity prices—and reduces surpluses of basic commodities—by curtailing production.

The U.S. Congress creates the Federal Emergency Relief Administration to help support unemployed Americans until economic recovery can provide jobs.

The U.S. Congress creates the Tennessee Valley Authority to stimulate the economically depressed Tennessee River region.

The Gold Repeal Resolution of 1933 moves the United States away from the gold standard. Currency is no longer tied to the amount of gold held in reserve by the U.S. Treasury.

With unemployment of at least 25 percent of the American workforce, the U.S. Congress passes the National Industrial Recovery Act in an attempt to encourage industrial and business recovery, reduce unemployment, foster fair competition, and provide for the construction of public works.

President Franklin Roosevelt names Frances Perkins secretary of labor; she becomes the first female cabinet member.

U.S. Congress passes the Securities Act of 1933, which is designed to ensure full disclosure to purchasers of most stocks and bonds offered for public sale.

Fiorello La Guardia is elected mayor of New York City; his 12 years in office are marked by government reform and the expansion of public services.

President Roosevelt extends U.S. recognition to the Soviet government.

The Banking Act of 1933 separates commercial and investment banking and creates the Federal Deposit Insurance Corporation (FDIC) to protect deposits in the event of bank failure.

1934

The Civil Works Administration provides work relief to help otherwise unemployed Americans through the winter of 1933–34.

The Indian Reorganization Act reverses federal policy designed to assimilate Native Americans.

Elijah Muhammad assumes leadership of the Nation of Islam.

Actress Shirley Temple receives a special Academy Award at age six.

The Communications Act of 1934 creates the Federal Communications Commission to regulate interstate and foreign communications by telegraph, cable, and radio.

The U.S. Congress passes the Securities and Exchange Act of 1934, which establishes the Securities and Exchange Commission (SEC) to regulate American stock exchanges and to enforce the Securities Act of 1933.

The Reciprocal Trade Agreements Act of 1934 authorizes the president to negotiate agreements to reduce tariff rates, up to 50 percent, with foreign countries that would reciprocate with similar concessions for American goods.

The Tydings-McDuffie Act of 1934 pledges independence for the Philippine Islands by 1945.

The U.S. Congress passes the Frazier-Lemke Farm Bankruptcy Act of 1934 to assist farmers threatened with foreclosures on their mortgages by enabling them to get credit extensions.

The U.S. Congress passes the National Housing Act of 1933, which creates the Federal Housing Administration, an agency designed to revive the housing industry by insuring long-term mortgages and stimulating construction of new homes.

1935

Senator Huey P. Long delivers his "Share Our Wealth" speech, in which he advocates the liquidation of large personal fortunes and the redistribution of funds so that every American family can buy a house, a car, and a radio.

The U.S. Congress passes the Emergency Relief Appropriation Act, which funds nearly $5 billion for work relief and public works programs, the largest single appropriation to date in U.S. history.

The Works Progress Administration (WPA) is created; it provides work relief in the areas of art, theater, writing, and music; provides assistance to young people to stay in school and out of the workforce; and gives millions of people jobs on government projects.

The Resettlement Administration begins to relocate struggling farmers to new, fertile lands; photographer Dorothea Lange memorably records their plight.

In *Schechter Poultry Corporation v. United States*, the U.S. Supreme Court overturns the National Industrial Recovery Act, a key piece of New Deal legislation.

The U.S. Congress passes the National Labor Relations Act of 1935, which guarantees workers the right to organize and to bargain collectively through their chosen representatives.

The U.S. Congress passes the Social Security Act to provide old-age retirement insurance, unemployment insurance, and public assistance.

Huey P. Long, a controversial senator from Louisiana, is assassinated.

The Committee for Industrial Organization is founded by John L. Lewis and the heads of eight member unions of the American Federation of Labor in order to organize unskilled laborers.

1936

In *United States v. Butler et al.*, the U.S. Supreme Court invalidates another piece of New Deal legislation, the Agricultural Adjustment Act of 1933.

The U.S. Congress passes the Walsh-Healey Government Contracts Act of 1936, which specifies working conditions and wages for employees of companies that had U.S. government contracts greater than $10,000.

Playwright Eugene O'Neill is awarded the Nobel Prize in literature.

Construction begins on architect Frank Lloyd Wright's Falling Water, a modernist-style country house.

German dictator Adolf Hitler is infuriated when African-American athlete Jesse Owens wins four gold medals at the Olympic games in Berlin.

In *United States v. Curtiss-Wright Export Corporation,* the U.S. Supreme Court confirms the federal government's power to conduct foreign relations and the U.S. president's exclusive authority to exercise that power.

The U.S. Congress passes the Soil Conservation and Domestic Allotment Act of 1936 to control soil erosion and limit agricultural production.

British economist John Maynard Keynes asserts the importance of government spending in fostering full-production, full-employment prosperity in his book *General Theory of Employment, Interest, and Money.*

Ty Cobb becomes the first player elected to the National Baseball Hall of Fame.

In one of the largest landslide victories in American political history, Franklin D. Roosevelt is reelected to the presidency over Republican challenger Alfred M. Landon. Public opinion polls are used to accurately predict this outcome.

Life magazine begins weekly publication November 19; the first photojournalistic magazine in America, it is an immediate success.

The United Automobile Workers (UAW) conducts a sit-down strike at General Motors' Flint, Michigan, plant; after 40 days, GM recognizes the UAW in February 1937, setting a precedent for the automobile and steel industries.

1937

William H. Hastie becomes the first African-American jurist to be appointed to the federal bench.

In order to protect New Deal legislation, Roosevelt tries to "pack" the Supreme Court; his efforts are blocked by U.S. Congress.

Under the Bankhead-Jones Farm Tenant Act, Secretary of Agriculture Henry A. Wallace establishes the Farm Security Administration (FSA), which grants low-interest, long-term loans to farm tenants, sharecroppers, and farm workers who wish to purchase their own farms.

The Wagner-Steagall Act establishes the U.S. Housing Authority (USHA), under the Department of the Interior, to build public housing for low-income people.

Despite opposition due to his former membership in the Ku Klux Klan, Hugo Black becomes a U.S. Supreme Court justice.

The U.S. Supreme Court upholds the National Labor Relations Act and the Social Security Act.

Congressmen critical of the New Deal draft the *Conservative Manifesto* opposing the federal regulatory welfare state; they form a strong opposition known as the conservative coalition.

In summer the economy takes a sharp downturn, leveling many New Deal economic gains and beginning the recession of 1937–38.

Walt Disney releases *Snow White and the Seven Dwarfs,* the first full-length animated film.

1938

Benny Goodman's swing band performs in Carnegie Hall, helping legitimize jazz as a music form.

American novelist Pearl S. Buck wins the Nobel Prize in literature.

Terminally ill, Lou Gehrig retires from baseball after playing 2,130 consecutive major league games with a batting average of 340.

In *Missouri ex rel. Gaines v. Canada,* the U.S. Supreme Court rules that a state's refusal to provide law school education for a qualified African American was a violation of the Fourteenth Amendment.

The Vinson Naval Act expands the U.S. Navy in response to the hostilities developing in Europe.

The Civil Aeronautics Act creates a supervisory body to regulate the commercial aviation industry.

The Food, Drug, and Cosmetic Act of 1938 prohibits the sale of foods dangerous to health as well as foods, drugs, and cosmetics packaged in unsanitary or contaminated containers.

In a widely publicized boxing rematch, African-American Joe Louis knocks out German Max Schmeling in the first round.

The Fair Labor Standards Act of 1938 establishes a minimum wage, caps the work week at a maximum of 44 hours, and outlaws employment of individuals under age 16 in the manufacture of materials shipped across state lines.

The United States protests the violation of American treaty rights incurred by the Japanese invasion of China in 1937.

The House Committee on Un-American Activities is formed.

Orson Welles's radio adaptation of H. G. Well's *War of the Worlds* causes a nationwide panic.

Led by John L. Lewis, the 10 unions of the Committee for Industrial Organization break away from the American Federal of Labor (AFL), becoming known as the Congress of Industrial Organizations.

Twenty-one countries in North and South America adopt the Declaration of Lima, which asserts Western Hemisphere solidarity against foreign intervention.

1939

The film *Gone With the Wind* is released, starring Clark Gable and Vivien Leigh.

The Grapes of Wrath, John Steinbeck's Pulitzer Prize–winning novel about depression-ravaged migrants, is published.

Albert Einstein informs President Roosevelt that it is possible to construct a new type of extremely powerful bomb.

The New York World's Fair opens, showcasing "The World of Tomorrow."

The Soviet Union signs a nonagression treaty with Nazi Germany.

After being refused the use of Constitution Hall by the Daughters of the American Revolution, opera singer Marian Anderson gives a concert on the steps of the Lincoln Memorial in Washington, D.C.

Germany invades Poland; Britain and France declare war on Germany. The conflict escalates into a world war. The United States remains neutral.

The Neutrality Act of 1939 restates the U.S. policy of neutrality but revision allows Great Britain and France to buy arms and munitions on a cash-and-carry basis.

The Declaration of Panama of 1939 creates a safety zone around the Panama Canal to be protected by U.S. and Latin American navies.

The Hatch Act of 1939 prevents federal officeholders from participating in election campaigns.

1940

Benjamin O. Davis, Sr., becomes the first African-American general in the U.S. armed forces.

In *Minersville School District v. Gobitis,* the U.S. Supreme Court upholds a Pennsylvania state law requiring daily flag salutes by all public school students.

In spring the Nazi blitzkrieg, or "lightning war," overruns western Europe.

The U.S. Congress passes the National Defense Appropriation Act of 1940, which initiates appropriation of billions of dollars for defense.

In *Cantwell v. Connecticut,* the U.S. Supreme Court upholds the right to the free exercise of religion protected by the First Amendment to the U.S. Constitution.

The U.S. Congress passes the Smith Act of 1940, which mandates the registration and fingerprinting of all resident aliens and authorizes the deportation of suspected revolutionaries.

Canadian prime minister L. Mackenzie King and President Roosevelt issue the Ogdensburg Declaration of 1940, which announces the establishment of the Permanent Joint Board of Defense. The board's purpose is to plan for the cooperative defense of North America in case of any foreign attack.

In the destroyers for bases deal, the United States trades World War I destroyers for 99-year leases on British bases in the Western Hemisphere.

The America First Committee is formed; it is the most prominent organization to oppose American intervention in World War II.

The U.S. Congress passes the Selective Training and Service Act of 1940, which establishes the first peacetime program of compulsory military service in the United States.

Germany, Italy, and Japan sign the Tripartite Pact committing the Axis nations to mutual action against attack.

Republican Wendell Willkie loses the presidential race to Franklin D. Roosevelt; Roosevelt becomes the only president elected to a third term.

Richard Wright's novel *Native Son* examines the effects of racial discrimination on blacks.

1941

Despite opposition from isolationists, the U.S. Congress passes the Lend-Lease Act of 1941, which allows for the shipment of war materials to Britain (and later the Soviet Union).

In *Edwards v. California,* the U.S. Supreme Court invalidates a California law designed to exclude poor immigrants from the state.

A. Philip Randolph threatens to march on Washington, D.C., with 100,000 African Americans to protest racial discrimination and segregation in defense industry and the military. In response, President Roosevelt issues Executive Order 8802, which bans discrimination in defense industries and in government.

Joe DiMaggio, "the Yankee Clipper," sets a baseball record by hitting safely in 56 consecutive games.

Former U.S. attorney general Harlan Fiske Stone becomes chief justice of the United States.

The United States and Britain issue the Atlantic Charter, which states their common standards for world peace.

President Franklin Roosevelt's message to Emperor Hirohito urges the Japanese monarch to do his part to avoid hostilities with the United States.

Orson Welles releases *Citizen Kane;* the film breaks new technical ground in cinematography, lighting, sound, and editing, but fails to win over contemporary audiences and critics.

The Japanese attack the U.S. naval base at Pearl Harbor, Hawaii; the United States declares war on Japan.

Italy and Germany declare war on the United States; the United States responds in kind.

Six agencies pool their resources to form the United Service Organizations (USO) to sustain the morale of the armed forces during World War II.

1942

The U.S. Congress gives the Office of Price Administration (OPA) authority to set maximum prices on nonfarm goods and rents with the Emergency Price Control Act. The OPA freezes prices at March 1942 levels and implements rationing programs for the duration of the war.

President Roosevelt issues Executive Order 9066, which enables the relocation of Japanese Americans from the West Coast to military-supervised camps. More than 110,000 Japanese Americans are incarcerated under the order.

Admiral Chester Nimitz is named commander of the U.S. Pacific Fleet; General Douglas MacArthur is named supreme commander of the armed forces in the southwest Pacific.

William Donovan becomes director of the Office of Strategic Services, which coordinates military intelligence in World War II and is a forerunner of the Central Intelligence Agency (CIA).

Despite resistance by Filipino and American forces, the Philippines falls to Japan. Japanese forces drive 60,000 Filipinos and 10,000 Americans to prison camps in the Bataan Death March.

The Office of War Information is established to manage dissemination of government information at home and abroad during World War II.

Physicist J. Robert Oppenheimer leads research on atomic weapons at Los Alamos, New Mexico.

U.S. naval forces halt the Japanese in the Battle of Midway, and U.S. troops land on Guadalcanal in the Solomon Islands.

The Congress of Racial Equality (CORE), a civil rights organization committed to the nonviolent confrontation of racism and segregation, is established.

The United States and Mexico establish the bracero program to import Mexican seasonal farmworkers to alleviate U.S. agricultural labor shortages.

Humphrey Bogart and Ingrid Bergman star in the movie *Casablanca.*

U.S. troops invade North Africa; they are led by General Dwight D. Eisenhower and General George S. Patton.

In one of his fireside chats, President Roosevelt urges U.S. citizens to help participate in a scrap-rubber drive to help locate rubber that can be used in the war effort.

The Revenue Act of 1942 greatly expands the number of people who pay taxes and leads to the system of withholding. Within two years, individual income tax revenues exceed corporate tax revenues for the first time.

1943

At the Casablanca Conference, President Roosevelt and Prime Minister Churchill decide against opening a second front against the Germans. Instead, Allied forces plan to focus on Sicily and on ending the German U-boat threat in the Atlantic. The Soviet Union continues to take the brunt of the German offensive. Roosevelt announces the doctrine of unconditional surrender.

African-American actor Paul Robeson plays the title role in a record-breaking run of Shakespeare's *Othello* on Broadway; the production is acclaimed as a landmark in race relations.

After six months of combat, the U.S. Marines secure Guadalcanal Island; the U.S. Navy and Marines employ an island hopping strategy to gain control of the Pacific.

Axis forces surrender North Africa to the Allies.

Navy personnel in Los Angeles assault Mexican Americans wearing zoot suits while authorities stand by in the Zoot Suit Riots. Race riots also break out in New York City and Detroit that summer.

The Allies, led by General Omar Bradley, land in Sicily; Italy surrenders.

Leonard Bernstein conducts the New York Philharmonic Orchestra for the first time.

Folksinger Woody Guthrie publishes *American Folksongs,* a collection of his best-known works.

In *West Virginia State Board of Education v. Barnette,* the U.S. Supreme Court rules that the state cannot compel students to declare a belief, stating that "no official . . . can prescribe what shall be orthodox in politics, nationalism, religion, or other matters of opinion or force citizens to confess by word or act their faith therein."

In the Moscow Conference Declarations of 1943, the United States, the Soviet Union, China, and Great Britain pledge to continue the war against the Axis powers, to establish an international organization to maintain peace and security, and to cooperate with one another to bring about an agreement to control armaments in the postwar period.

The U.S. Congress passes the Smith-Connally Anti-Strike Act of 1943, which gives the president the power to seize any plant or industry where a labor dispute might interfere with war production.

At the Teheran Conference, President Franklin Roosevelt, Premier Joseph Stalin, and Prime Minister Winston Churchill schedule the opening of the long-awaited second front against Nazi Germany.

The leaders of the United States, Great Britain, and China issue the Cairo Conference Statement, which charts Allied military strategy for the war in the Pacific theater.

1944

The War Refugee Board is established to assist European Jews and other foreign nationals displaced by World War II.

The U.S. Congress authorizes the Missouri River Basin Project; the building of dams and reservoirs becomes an important issue between Native American reservations and the government.

Allied forces liberate Rome.

The U.S. Congress passes the GI Bill of Rights, which authorizes economic and educational assistance for World War II veterans.

Evangelist Billy Graham holds the first of his masive revival meetings.

Representatives of 44 countries meet in Bretton Woods, New Hampshire; the resulting Bretton Woods Agreement lays the foundations of the International Monetary Fund and the International Bank for Reconstruction and Development.

The D day invasion of Europe begins on June 6; the Allies penetrate the Normandy coastline of German-occupied France.

The Allies liberate Paris.

Along with saxophonist Charlie Parker and others, trumpeter Dizzy Gillespie launches the bebop movement in jazz.

In *Smith v. Allwright,* the U.S. Supreme Court rules that the exclusion of African Americans from the Texas Democratic Party is a violation of the Fifteenth Amendment to the U.S. Constitution.

Swedish sociologist Gunnar Myrdal publishes *An American Dilemma,* his study of race relations in the United States.

U.S. forces begin to liberate the Philippines from Japan. President Roosevelt is reelected for a fourth term over Republican challenger Thomas Dewey.

In *Korematsu v. United States,* the U.S. Supreme Court upholds the wartime relocation and incarceration of Japanese Americans. On the same day, the Court rules in *Ex parte Endo* that the government cannot hold loyal American citizens.

German forces launch an offensive effort to retake Belgium in the Battle of the Bulge; surprised American forces repel the attack.

1945

President Roosevelt, Soviet leader Joseph Stalin, and British prime minister Winston Churchill meet at the Yalta Conference to discuss postwar plans for Europe.

The U.S. Marines capture Iwo Jima and Okinawa.

President Roosevelt dies; Vice President Harry S. Truman succeeds him.

Twenty-one countries in North and South America sign the Act of Chapultepec, which expands the Monroe Doctrine's unilateral guarantee against intervention in the Western Hemisphere into a mutual security system.

Berlin falls and Germany surrenders.

Truman, Stalin, and British prime minister Clement Attlee attend the Potsdam Conference; the Soviet Union agrees to declare war on Japan.

The United States, Great Britain, and the Soviet Union demand the unconditional surrender of Japan; Japan refuses.

The United States drops atomic bombs on Hiroshima and Nagasaki; Japan surrenders, ending World War II.

The United Nations is created; Eleanor Roosevelt is named U.S. delegate to the United Nations and becomes chairperson of the Committee on Human Rights.

President Truman's Statement on Fundamentals of American Foreign Policy outlines a 12-point policy based on U.S. military strength as a means to preserve world peace.

W. E. B. Du Bois helps write a constitution for the NAACP. The document is created in response to attacks against the organization's conservative approach to civil rights reform.

Documents

President Franklin Roosevelt's First Inaugural Address, 1933

Henry Steele Commager and Milton Cantor, eds. *Documents of American History*, 10th ed. (Englewood Cliffs, N.J.: Prentice Hall, 1988), pp. 239-242

March 4, 1933

I am certain that my fellow Americans expect that on my induction into the Presidency I will address them with a candor and a decision which the present situation of our Nation impels. This is preeminently the time to speak the truth, the whole truth, frankly and boldly. Nor need we shrink from honestly facing conditions in our country today. This great Nation will endure as it has endured, will revive and will prosper. So, first of all, let me assert my firm belief that the only thing we have to fear is fear itself—nameless, unreasoning, unjustified terror which paralyzes needed efforts to convert retreat into advance. In every dark hour of our national life a leadership of frankness and vigor has met with that understanding and support of the people themselves which is essential to victory. I am convinced that you will again give that support to leadership in these critical days.

In such a spirit on my part and on yours we face our common difficulties. They concern, thank God, only material things. Values have shrunken to fantastic levels; taxes have risen; our ability to pay has fallen; government of all kinds is faced by serious curtailment of income; the means of exchange are frozen in the currents of trade; the withered leaves of industrial enterprise lie on every side; farmers find no markets for their produce; the savings of many years in thousands of families are gone.

More important, a host of unemployed citizens face the grim problem of existence, and an equally great number toil with little return. Only a foolish optimist can deny the dark realities of the moment.

Yet our distress comes from no failure of substance. We are stricken by no plague of locusts. Compared with the perils which our forefathers conquered because they believed and were not afraid, we have still much to be thankful for. Nature still offers her bounty and human efforts have multiplied it. Plenty is at our doorstep, but a generous use of it languishes in the very sight of the supply. Primarily this is because the rulers of the exchange of mankind's goods have failed, through their own stubbornness and their own incompetence, have admitted their failure, and abdicated. Practices of the unscrupulous money changers stand indicted in the court of public opinion, rejected by the hearts and minds of men.

True they have tried, but their efforts have been cast in the pattern of an outworn tradition. Faced by failure of credit they have proposed only the lending of more money. Stripped of the lure of profit by which to induce our people to follow their false leadership, they have resorted to exhortations, pleading tearfully for restored confidence. They know only the rules of a generation of self-seekers. They have no vision, and when there is no vision the people perish.

The money changers have fled from their high seats in the temple of our civilization. We may now restore that temple to the ancient truths. The measure of the restoration lies in the extent to which we apply social values more noble than mere monetary profit.

Happiness lies not in the mere possession of money; it lies in the joy of achievement, in the thrill of creative effort. The joy and moral stimulation of work no longer must be forgotten in the mad chase of evanescent profits. These dark days will be worth all they cost us if they teach us that our true destiny is not to be ministered unto but to minister to ourselves and to our fellow men.

Recognition of the falsity of material wealth as the standard of success goes hand in hand with the abandonment of the false belief that public office and high political position are to be valued only by the standards of pride of place and personal profit; and there must be an end to a conduct in banking and in business which too often has given to a sacred trust the likeness of callous and selfish wrongdoing. Small wonder that confidence languishes, for it thrives only on honesty, on honor, on the sacredness of obligations, on faithful protection, on unselfish performance; without them it cannot live.

Restoration calls, however, not for changes in ethics alone. This Nation asks for action, and action now. Our greatest primary task is to put people to work. This is no unsolvable problem if we face it wisely and courageously. It can be accomplished in part by direct recruiting by the Government itself, treating the task as we would treat the emergency of a war, but at the same time, through this employment, accomplishing greatly needed projects to stimulate and reorganize the use of our natural resources.

Hand in hand with this we must frankly recognize the overbalance of population in our industrial centers and, by engaging on a national scale in a redistribution, endeavor to provide a better use of the land for those best fitted for the land. The task can be helped by definite efforts to raise the values of agricultural products and with this the power to purchase the output of our cities. It can be helped by preventing realistically the tragedy of the growing loss through foreclosure of our small homes and our farms. It can be helped by insistence that the Federal, State, and local governments act forthwith on the demand that their cost be drastically reduced. It can be helped by the unifying of relief activities which to-day are often scattered, uneconomical, and unequal. It can be helped by national planning for and supervision of all forms of transportation and of communications and other utilities which have a definitely public character. There are many ways in which it can be helped, but it can never be helped merely by talking about it. We must act and act quickly.

Finally, in our progress toward a resumption of work we require two safeguards against a return of the evils of the old order; there must be a strict supervision of all banking and credits and investments; there must be an end to speculation with other people's money, and there must be provision for an adequate but sound currency. There are the lines of attack. I shall presently urge upon a new Congress in special session detailed measures for their fulfillment, and I shall seek the immediate assistance of the several States.

Through this program of action we address ourselves to putting our own national house in order and making income balance outgo. Our international trade relations, though vastly important, are in point of time and necessity secondary to the establishment of a sound national economy. I favor as a practical policy the putting of first things first. I shall spare no effort to restore world trade by international economic readjustment, but the emergency at home cannot wait on that accomplishment.

The basic thought that guides these specific means of national recovery is not narrowly nationalistic. It is the insistence, as a first consideration, upon the interdependence of the various elements in all parts of the United States—a recognition of the old and permanently important manifestation of the American spirit of the pioneer. It is the way to recovery. It is the immediate way. It is the strongest assurance that the recovery will endure. In the field of world policy I would dedicate this Nation to the policy of the good neighbor—the neighbor who resolutely respects himself and, because he does so, respects the rights of other—the neighbor who respects his obligations and respects the sanctity of his agreements in and with a world of neighbors.

If I read the temper of our people correctly, we now realize as we have never realized before our interdependence on each other; that we cannot merely take but we must give as well; that if we are to go forward, we must move as a trained and loyal army willing to sacrifice for the good of a common discipline, because without such discipline no progress is made, no leadership becomes effective. We are, I know, ready and willing to submit our lives and property to such discipline, because it makes possible a leadership which aims at a larger good. This I propose to offer, pledging that the larger purposes will bind upon us all as a sacred obligation with a unity of duty hitherto evoked only in time of armed strife.

With this pledge taken, I assume unhesitatingly the leadership of this great army of our people dedicated to a disciplined attack upon our common problems.

Action in this image and to this end is feasible under the form of government which we have inherited from our ancestors. Our Constitution is so simple and practical that it is possible always to meet extraordinary needs by changes in emphasis and arrangement without loss of essential form. That is why our constitutional system has proved itself the most superbly enduring political mechanism the modern world has produced. It has met every stress of vast expansion of territory, of foreign wars, of bitter internal strife, of world relations.

It is to be hoped that the normal balance of executive and legislative authority may be wholly adequate to meet the unprecedented task before us. But it may be that an unprecedented demand and need for undelayed action may call for temporary departure from that normal balance of public procedure.

I am prepared under my constitutional duty to recommend the measures that a stricken nation in the midst of a stricken world may require. These measures, or such other measures as the Congress may built out of its experience and wisdom, I shall seek, within my constitutional authority to bring to speedy adoption.

But in the event that the Congress shall fail to take one of these two courses, and in the event that the national emergency is still critical, I shall not evade the clear course of duty that will then confront me. I shall ask the Congress for the one remaining instrument to meet the crisis—broad Executive power to wage a war against the emergency, as great as the power that would be given to me if we were in fact invaded by a foreign foe. For the trust reposed in me I will return the courage and the devotion that befit the time. I can do no less.

We face the arduous days that lie before us in the warm courage of the national unity; with the clear consciousness of seeking old and precious moral values; with the clean satisfaction that comes from the stern performance of duty by old and young alike. We aim at the assurance of a rounded and permanent national life.

We do not distrust the future of essential democracy. The people of the United States have not failed. In their need they have registered a mandate that they want direct, vigorous action. They have asked for discipline and direction under leadership. They have made me the present instrument of their wishes. In the spirit of the gift I take it. In this dedication of a Nation we humbly ask the blessing of God. May He protect each and every one of us. May He guide me in the days to come.

Social Security Act (1935)

United States Statutes at Large (74th Cong.,
1st sess., chap. 531), pp. 620–647

An Act

To provide for the general welfare by establishing a system of Federal old-age benefits, and by enabling the several States to make more adequate provision for aged persons, blind persons, dependent and crippled children, maternal and child welfare, public health, and the administration of their unemployment compensation laws; to establish a Social Security Board; to raise revenue; and for other purposes.

Be it enacted by the Senate and House of Representatives of the United States of America in Congress assembled,

Title I—Grants to States for Old-Age Assistance

Appropriation

Section 1. For the purpose of enabling each State to furnish financial assistance, as far as practicable under the conditions in such State, to aged needy individuals, there is hereby authorized to be appropriated for the fiscal year ending June 30, 1936, the sum of $49,750,000, and there is hereby authorized to be appropriated for each fiscal year thereafter a sum sufficient to carry out the purposes of this title. The sums made available under this section shall be used for making payments to States which have submitted, and had approved by the Social Security Board established by Title VII (hereinafter referred to as the "Board"), State plans for old-age assistance.

State Old-Age Assistance Plans

Sec. 2. (a) A State plan for old-age assistance must (1) provide that it shall be in effect in all political subdivisions of the State, and, if administered by them, be mandatory upon them; (2) provide for financial participation by the State; (3) either provide for the establishment or designation of a single State agency to administer the plan, or provide for the establishment or designation of a single State agency to supervise the administration of the plan; (4) provide for granting to any individual, whose claim for old-age assistance is denied, an opportunity for a fair hearing before such State agency; (5) provide such methods of administration (other than those relating to selection, tenure of office, and compensation of personnel) as are found by the Board to be necessary for the efficient operation of the plan; (6) provide that the State agency will make such reports, in such form and containing such information, as the Board may from time to time require, and comply with such provisions as the Board may from time to time find necessary to assure the correctness and verification of such reports; and (7) provide that, if the State or any of its political subdivisions collects from the estate of any recipient of old-age assistance any amount with respect to old-age assistance furnished him under the plan, one-half of the net amount so collected shall be promptly paid to the United States. Any payment so made shall be deposited in the Treasury to the credit of the appropriation for the purposes of this title.

(b) The Board shall approve any plan which fulfills the conditions specified in subsection (a), except that it shall not approve any plan which imposes, as a condition of eligibility for old-age assistance under the plan—

(1) An age requirement of more than sixty-five years, except that the plan may impose, effective until January 1, 1940, an age requirement of as much as seventy years; or

(2) Any residence requirement which excludes any resident of the State who has resided therein five years during the nine years immediately preceding the application for old-age assistance and has resided therein continuously for one year immediately preceding the application; or

(3) Any citizenship requirement which excludes any citizen of the United States.

Payment to States

Sec. 3. (a) From the sums appropriated therefor, the Secretary of the Treasury shall pay to each State which has an approved plan for old-age assistance, for each quarter, beginning with the quarter commencing July 1, 1935, (1) an amount, which shall be used exclusively as old-age assistance, equal to one-half of the total of the sums expended during such quarter as old-age assistance under the State plan with respect to each individual who at the time of such expenditure is sixty-five years of age or older and is not an inmate of a public institution, not counting so much of such expenditure with respect to any individual for any month as exceeds $30, and (2) 5 per centum of such amount, which shall be used for paying the costs of administering the State plan or for old-age assistance, or both, and for no other purpose. . . .

Title II—Federal Old-Age Benefits
. . .

Old-Age Benefit Payments

Sec. 202. (a) Every qualified individual (as defined in section 210) shall be entitled to receive, with respect to the period beginning on the date he attains the age of sixty-five, or on January 1, 1942, whichever is the later, and ending on the date of his death, an old-age benefit (payable as nearly as practicable in equal monthly installments) as follows:

(1) If the total wages (as defined in section 210) determined by the Board to have been paid to him, with respect to employment (as defined in section 210) after December 31, 1936, and before he attained the age of sixty-five, were not more than $3,000, the old-age benefit shall be at a monthly rate of one-half of 1 per centum of such total wages;

(2) If such total wages have more than $3,000, the old-age benefit shall be at a monthly rate equal to the sum of the following:

(A) One-half of 1 per centum of $3,000; plus

(B) One-twelfth of 1 per centum of the amount of which such total wages exceeded $3,000 and did not exceed $45,000; plus

(C) One-twenty-fourth of 1 per centum of the amount by which such total wages exceeded $45,000

(b) In no case shall the monthly rate computed under subsection (a) exceed $85.

(c) If the Board finds at any time that more or less than the correct amount has theretofore been paid to any individual under this section, then, under regulations made by the Board, proper adjustments shall be made in connection with subsequent payments under this section of the same individual.

(d) Whenever the Board finds that any qualified individual has received wages with respect to regular employment after he attained the age of sixty-five, the old-age benefit payable to such individual shall be reduced, for each calendar month in any part of which such regular employment occurred, by an amount equal to one month's benefit. Such reduction shall be made, under regulations prescribed by the Board, by deductions from one or more payments of old-age benefit to such individual.

Payments Upon Death

Sec. 203. (a) If any individual dies before attaining the age of sixty-five, there shall be paid to his estate an amount equal to $3^{1/2}$ per centum of the total wages determined by the Board to have been paid to him, with respect to employment after December 31, 1936. . . .

Title III—Grants to States for Unemployment Compensation Administration

Appropriation

Section 301. For the purpose of assisting the States in the administration of their unemployment compensation laws, there is hereby authorized to be appropriated, for the fiscal year ending June 30, 1936, the sum of $4,000,000, and for each fiscal year thereafter the sum of $49,000,000, to be used as hereinafter provided. . . .

Title IV—Grants to States for Aid to Dependent Children

Appropriation

Section 401. For the purpose of enabling each State to furnish financial assistance, as far as practicable under the conditions in such State, to needy dependent children, there is hereby authorized to be appropriated for the fiscal year ending June 30, 1936, the sum of $24,750,000, and there is hereby authorized to be appropriated for each fiscal year thereafter a sum sufficient to carry out the purposes of this title. The sums made available under this section shall be used for making payments to States which have submitted, and had approved by the Board, State plans for aid to dependent children. . . .

Payment to States

Sec. 403. (a) From the sums appropriated therefor, the Secretary of the Treasury shall pay to each State which has an approved plan for aid to dependent children, for each quarter, beginning with the quarter commencing July 1, 1935, an amount, which shall be used exclusively for carrying out the State plan, equal to one-third of the total of the sums expended during such quarter under such plan, not counting so much of such expenditure with respect to any dependent child for any month as exceeds $18, or if there is more than one dependent child in the same home, as exceeds $18 for any month with respect to one such dependent child and $12 for such month with respect to each of the other dependent children. . . .

Definitions

Sec. 406. When used in this title—

(a) The term "dependent child" means a child under the age of sixteen who has been deprived of parental support or care by reason of the death, continued absence from the home, or physical or mental incapacity of a parent, and who is living with his father, mother, grandfather, grandmother, brother, sister, stepfather, stepmother, stepbrother, stepsister, uncle, or aunt, in a place of residence maintained by one or more of such relatives as his or their own home;

(b) The term "aid to dependent children" means money payments with respect to a dependent child or dependent children.

Title V—Grants to States
for Maternal and Child Welfare
Part 1—Maternal and Child Health Services

Appropriation

Section 501. For the purpose of enabling each State to extend and improve, as far as practicable under the conditions in such State, services for promoting the health of mothers and children, especially in rural areas and in areas suffering from severe economic distress, there is hereby authorized to be appropriated for each fiscal year, beginning with the fiscal year ending June 30, 1936, the sum of $3,800,000. The sums made available under this section shall be used for making payments to States which have submitted, and had approved by the Chief of the Children's Bureau, State plans for such services.

Allotments to States

Sec. 502. (a) Out of the sums appropriated pursuant to section 501 for each fiscal year the Secretary of Labor shall allot to each State $20,000, and such part of $1,800,000 as he finds that the number of live births in such State bore to the total number of live births in the United States, in the latest calendar year for which the Bureau of the Census has available statistics.

(b) Out of the sums appropriated pursuant to section 501 for each fiscal year the Secretary of Labor shall allot to the States $980,000 (in addition to the allotments made under subsection (a)), according to the financial need of each State for assistance in carrying out its State plan, as determined by him after taking into consideration the number of live births in such State.

(c) The amount of any allotment to a State under subsection (a) for any fiscal year remaining unpaid to such State at the end of such fiscal year shall be available for payment to such State under section 504 until the end of the second succeeding fiscal year. No payment to a State under section 504 shall be made out of its allotment for any fiscal year until its allotment for the preceding fiscal year has been exhausted or has ceased to be available.

Approval of State Plans

Sec. 503. (a) A State plan for maternal and child-health services must (1) provide for financial participation by the State; (2) provide for the administration of the plan by the State health agency or the supervision of the administration of the plan by the State health agency; (3) provide such methods of administration (other than those relating to selection, tenure of office, and compensation of personnel) as are necessary for the efficient operation of the plan; (4) provide that the State health agency will make such reports, in such form and containing such information, as the Secretary of Labor may from time to time require, and comply with such provisions as he may from time to time find necessary to assure the correctness and verification of such report; (5) provide for the extension and improvement of local maternal and child-health services administered by local child-health units; (6) provide for cooperation with medical, nursing, and welfare groups and organizations; and (7) provide for the development of demonstration services in needy areas and among groups in special need.

(b) The Chief of the Children's Bureau shall approve any plan which fulfills the conditions specified in subsection (a) and shall thereupon notify the Secretary of Labor and the State health agency of his approval. . . .

Part 2—Services for Crippled Children

Appropriation

Sec. 511. For the purpose of enabling each State to extend and improve (especially in rural areas and in areas suffering from severe economic distress), as far as practicable under the conditions in such State, services for locating crippled children, and for providing medical, surgical, corrective, and other services and care, and facilities for diagnosis, hospitalization, and aftercare, for children who are crippled or who are suffering from conditions which lead to crippling, there is hereby authorized to be appropriated for each fiscal year, beginning with the fiscal year ending June 30, 1936, the sum of $2,850,000. The sums made available under this section shall be used for making payments to States which have submitted, and had approved by the Chief of the Children's Bureau, State plans for such services. . . .

Part 3—Child-Welfare Services

Sec. 521. (a) For the purpose of enabling the United States, through the Children's Bureau, to cooperate with State public-welfare agencies in establishing, extending, and strengthening, especially in predominantly rural areas, public-welfare services (hereinafter in this section referred to as "child-welfare services") for the protection and care of homeless, dependent, and neglected children, and children in danger of becoming delinquent, there is hereby authorized to be appropriated for each fiscal year, beginning with the fiscal year ending June 30, 1936, the sum of $1,500,000. Such amount shall be allotted by the Secretary of Labor for use by cooperating State public-welfare agencies on the basis of plans developed jointly by the State agency and the Children's Bureau, to each State, $10,000, and the remainder to each State on the basis of such plans, not to exceed such part of the remainder as the rural population of such state bears to the total rural population of the United States. The amount so allotted shall be expended for payment of part of the cost of district, county or other local child-welfare services in areas predominantly rural, and for developing State services for the encouragement and assistance of adequate methods of community child-welfare organization in areas predominantly rural and other areas of special need. . . .

Part 4—Vocational Rehabilitation

Sec. 531. (a) In order to enable the United States to cooperate with the States and Hawaii in extending and strengthening their programs of vocational rehabilitation of the physically disabled, and to continue to carry out the provisions and purposes of the Act entitled "An Act to provide for the promotion of vocational rehabilitation of persons disabled in industry or otherwise and their return to civil employment", approved June 2, 1920, as amended (U.S.C., title 29, ch. 4; U.S.C., Supp. VII, title 29, secs. 31, 32, 34, 35, 37, 39, and 40), there is hereby authorized to be appropriated for the fiscal years ending June 30, 1936, and June 30, 1937, the sum of $841,000 for each such fiscal year in addition to the amount of the existing authorization, and for each fiscal year thereafter the sum of $1,938,000. . . .

Title VI—Public Health Work

Appropriation

Section 601. For the purpose of assisting States, counties, health districts, and other political subdivisions of the States in establishing and maintaining adequate public-health services, including the training or personnel for State and local health work, there is hereby authorized to be appropriated for each fiscal year, beginning with the fiscal year ending June 30, 1936, the sum of $8,000,000 to be used as hereinafter provided. . . .

Investigations

Sec. 603. (a) There is hereby authorized to be appropriated for each fiscal year, beginning with the fiscal year ending June 30, 1936, the sum of $2,000,000 for expenditure by the Public Health Service for investigation of disease and problems of sanitation. . . .

Title VIII—Taxes with Respect to Employment

Income Tax on Employees

Section 801. In addition to other taxes, there shall be levied, collected, and paid upon the income of every individual a tax equal to the following percentages of the wages (as defined in section 811) received by him after December 31, 1936, with respect to employment (as defined in section 811) after such date:

(1) With respect to employment during the calendar years 1937, 1938, and 1939, the rate shall be 1 per centum.

(2) With respect to employment during the calendar years 1940, 1941, and 1942, the rate shall be 1 1/2 per centum.

(3) With respect to employment during the calendar years 1943, 1944, and 1945, the rate shall be 2 per centum.

(4) With respect to employment during the calendar years 1946, 1947, and 1948, the rate shall be 2 1/2 per centum.

(5) With respect to employment after December 31, 1948, the rate shall be 3 per centum.

Deduction of Tax from Wages

Sec. 802. (a) The tax imposed by section 801 shall be collected by the employer of the taxpayer, by deducting the amount of the tax from the wages as and when paid. . . .

Excise Tax on Employers

Sec. 804. In addition to other taxes, every employer shall pay an excise tax, with respect to having individuals in his employ, equal to the following percentages of the wages (as defined in section 811) paid by him after December 31, 1936, with respect to employment (as defined in section 811) after such date:

(1) With respect to employment during the calendar years 1937, 1938, and 1939, the rate shall be 1 per centum.

(2) With respect to employment during the calendar years 1940, 1941, and 1942, the rate shall be 1 1/2 per centum.

(3) With respect to employment during the calendar years 1943, 1944, and 1945, the rate shall be 2 per centum.

(2) With respect to employment during the calendar years 1946, 1947, and 1948, the rate shall be 2 1/2 per centum.

(3) With respect to employment after December 31, 1948, the rate shall be 3 per centum. . . .

Title X—Grants to States for Aid to the Blind

Appropriation

Section 1001. For the purpose of enabling each State to furnish financial assistance, as far as practicable under the conditions in such State, to needy individuals who are blind, there is hereby authorized to be appropriated for the fiscal year ending June 30, 1936, the sum of $3,000,000, and there is hereby authorized to be appropriated for each fiscal year thereafter a sum sufficient to carry out the purposes of this title. The sums made available under this section shall be used for making payments to States which have submitted, and had approved by the Social Security Board, State plans for aid to the blind. . . .

Neutrality Act of 1937

United States Statutes at Large (75th Cong., 1st sess.), pp. 121–128

Joint Resolution

To amend the joint resolution entitled "Joint resolution providing for the prohibition of the export of arms, ammunition, and implements of war to belligerent countries; the prohibition of the transportation of arms, ammunition, and implements of war by vessels of the United States for the use of belligerent states; for the registration and licensing of persons engaged in the business of manufacturing, exporting, or importing arms, ammunition, or implements of war; and restricting travel by American citizens on belligerent ships during war", approved August 31, 1935, as amended.

Resolved by the Senate and House of Representatives of the United States of America in Congress assembled, That the joint resolution entitled "Joint resolution providing for the prohibition of the export or arms, ammunition, and implements of war to belligerent countries; the prohibition of the transportation of arms, ammunition, and implements of war by vessels of the United States for the use of belligerent states; for the registration and licensing of persons engaged in the business of manufacturing, exporting, or importing arms, ammunition, or implements of war; and restricting travel by American citizens on belligerent ships during war", approved August 31, 1935, as amended, is amended to read as follows:

"Export of Arms, Ammunition, and Implements of War

"Section 1. (a) Whenever the President shall find that there exists a state of war between, or among, two or more foreign states, the President shall proclaim such fact, and it shall thereafter be unlawful to export, or attempt to export, or cause to be exported, arms, ammunition, or implements of war from any place in the United States to any belligerent state named in such proclamation, or to any neutral state for transshipment to, or for the use of, any such belligerent state.

"(b) The President shall, from time to time, by proclamation, extend such embargo upon the export of arms, ammunition, or implements of war to other states as and when they may become involved in such war.

"(c) Whenever the President shall find that a state of civil strife exists in a foreign state and that such civil strife is of a magnitude or is being conducted under such conditions that the export of arms, ammunition, or implements

of war from the United States to such foreign state would threaten or endanger the peace of the United States, the President shall proclaim such fact, and it shall thereafter be unlawful to export, or attempt to export, or cause to be exported, arms, ammunition, or implements of war from any place in the United States to such foreign state, or to any neutral state for transshipment to, or for the use of, such foreign state.

"(d) The President shall, from time to time by proclamation, definitely enumerate the arms, ammunition, and implements of war, the export of which is prohibited by this section. The arms, ammunition, and implements of war so enumerated shall include those enumerated in the President's proclamation Numbered 2163, of April 10, 1936, but shall not include raw materials or any other articles or materials not of the same general character as those enumerated in the said proclamation, and in the Convention for the Supervision of the International Trade in Arms and Ammunition and in Implements of War, signed at Geneva June 17, 1925.

"(e) Whoever, in violation of any of the provisions of this Act, shall export, or attempt to export, or cause to be exported, arms, ammunition, or implements of war from the United States shall be fined not more than $10,000, or imprisoned not more than five years, or both, and the property, vessel, or vehicle containing the same shall be subject to the provisions of sections 1 to 8, inclusive, title 6, chapter 30, of the Act approved June 15, 1917 (40 Stat. 223-225; U.S.C., 1934 ed., title 22, secs. 238-245).

"(f) In the case of the forfeiture of any arms, ammunition, or implements of war by reason of a violation of this Act, no public or private sale shall be required; but such arms, ammunition, or implements of war shall be delivered to the Secretary of War for such use or disposal thereof as shall be approved by the President of the United States.

"(g) Whenever, in the judgment of the President, the conditions which have cause him to issue any proclamation under the authority of this section have ceased to exist, he shall revoke the same, and the provisions of this section shall thereupon cease to apply with respect to the state or states named in such proclamation, except with respect to offenses committed, or forfeitures incurred, prior to such revocation. . . .

"Financial Transactions

"Sec. 3. (a) Whenever the President shall have issued a proclamation under the authority of section 1 of this Act, it shall thereafter be unlawful for any person within the United States to purchase, sell, or exchange bonds, securities, or other obligations of the government of any belligerent state or of any state wherein civil strife exists, named in such proclamation, or of any political subdivision of any such state, or of any person acting for or on behalf of the government of any such state, or of any faction or asserted government within any such state wherein civil strife exists, or of any person acting for or on behalf of any faction or asserted government within any such state wherein civil strife exists, issued after the date of such proclamation, or to make any loan or extend any credit to any such government, political subdivision, faction, asserted government, or person, or to solicit or receive any contribution for any such government, political subdivision, faction, asserted government, or person: *Provided,* That if the President shall find that such action will serve to protect the commercial or other interests of the United States or its citizens, he may, in his discretion, and to such extent and under such regulations as he may prescribe, except from the operation of this section ordinary commercial credits and short-time obligations in aid of legal transactions and of a character customarily used in normal peacetime commercial transactions. Nothing in this subsection shall be construed to prohibit the solicitation or collection of funds to be used for medical aid and assistance, or for food and clothing to relieve human suffering, when such solicitation or collection of funds is made on behalf of and for use by any person or organization which is not acting for or on behalf of any such government, political subdivision, faction, or asserted government, but all such solicitations and collections of funds shall be subject to the approval of the President and shall be made under such rules and regulations as he shall prescribe.

"(b) The provisions of this section shall not apply to a renewal or adjustment of such indebtedness as may exist on the date of the President's proclamation.

"(c) Whoever shall violate the provisions of this section or of any regulations issued hereunder shall, upon conviction thereof, be fined not more than $50,000 or imprisoned for not more than five years, or both. Should the violation be by a corporation, organization, or association, each officer or agent thereof participating in the violation may be liable to the penalty herein prescribed.

"(d) Whenever the President shall have revoked any such proclamation issued under the authority of section 1 of this Act, the provisions of this section and of any regulations issued by the President hereunder shall thereupon cease to apply with respect to the state or states named in such proclamation, except with respect to offenses committed prior to such revocation.

"Exceptions—American Republics

"Sec. 4. This Act shall not apply to an American republic or republics engaged in war against a non-American state or states, provided the American republic is not cooperating with a non-American state or states in such war.

"National Munitions Control Board

"Sec. 5. (a) There is hereby established a National Munitions Control Board (hereinafter referred to as the 'Board') to carry out the provisions of this Act. The Board shall consist of the Secretary of State, who shall be chairman and executive officer of the Board, the Secretary of the Treasury, the Secretary of War, the Secretary of the Navy, and the Secretary of Commerce. Except as otherwise provided in this Act, or by other law, the administration of this Act is vested in the Department of State. The Secretary of State shall promulgate such rules and regulations with regard to the enforcement of this section as he may deem necessary to carry out its provisions. The Board shall be convened by the chairman and shall hold at least one meeting a year.

"(b) Every person who engages in the business of manufacturing, exporting, or importing any of the arms, ammunition, or implements of war referred to in this Act, whether as an exporter, importer, manufacturer, or dealer, shall register with the Secretary of State his name, or business name, principal place of business, and places of business in the United States, and a list of the arms, ammunition, and implements of war which he manufactures, imports, or exports.

"(c) Every person required to register under this section shall notify the Secretary of State of any change in the arms, ammunition, or implements of war which he exports, imports, or manufactures; and upon such notification the Secretary of State shall issue to such person an amended certificate of registration, free of charge, which shall remain valid until the date of expiration of the original certificate. Every person required to register under the provisions of this section shall pay a registration fee of $500, unless he manufactured, exported, or imported arms, ammunition, and implements of war to a total sales value of less than $50,000 during the twelve months immediately preceding his registration, in which case he shall pay a registration fee of $100. Upon receipt of the required registration fee, the Secretary of State shall issue a registration certificate valid for five years, which shall be renewable for further periods of five years upon the payment for each renewal of a fee of $500 in the case of persons who manufactured, exported, or imported arms, ammunition, and implements of war to a total sales value of more than $50,000 during the twelve months immediately preceding the renewal, or a fee of $100 in the case of persons who manufactured, exported, or imported arms, ammunition, and implements of war to a total sales value of less than $50,000 during the twelve months immediately preceding the renewal. The Secretary of the Treasury is hereby directed to refund, out of any moneys in the Treasury not otherwise appropriated, the sum of $400 to every person who shall have paid a registration fee of $500 pursuant to this Act, who manufactured, exported, or imported arms, ammunition, and implements of war to a total sales value of less than $50,000 during the twelve months immediately preceding his registration.

"(d) It shall be unlawful for any person to export, or attempt to export, from the United States to any other state, any of the arms, ammunition, or implements of war referred to in this Act, or to import, or attempt to import, to the United States from any other state, any of the arms, ammunition, or implements of war referred to in this Act, without first having obtained a license therefor.

"(e) All persons required to register under this section shall maintain, subject to the inspection of the Secretary of State, or any person or persons designated by him, such permanent records of manufacture for export, importation, and exportation of arms, ammunition, and implements of war as the Secretary of State shall prescribe.

"(f) Licenses shall be issued to persons who have registered as herein provided for, except in cases of export or import licenses where the export of arms, ammunition, or implements of war would be in violation of this Act or any other law of the United States, or of a treaty to which the United States is a party, in which cases such licenses shall not be issued.

"(g) Whenever the President shall have issued a proclamation under the authority of section 1 of this Act, all licenses theretofore issued under this Act shall ipso facto and immediately upon the issuance of such proclamation, cease to grant authority to export arms, ammunition, or implements of war from any place in the United States to any belligerent state, or to any state wherein civil strife exists, named in such proclamation, or to any neutral state for transshipment to, or for the use of, any such belligerent state or any such state wherein civil strife exists; and said licenses, insofar as the grant of authority to export to the state or states named in such proclamation is concerned, shall be null and void.

"(h) No purchase of arms, ammunition, or implements of war shall be made on behalf of the United States by any officer, executive department, or independent establishment of the Government from any person who shall have failed to register under the provisions of this Act.

"(i) The provisions of the Act of August 29, 1916, relating to the sale of ordnance and stores to the Government of Cuba (39 Stat. 619, 643; U.S.C., 1934 ed., title 50, sec. 72), are hereby repealed as of December 31, 1937.

"(j) The Board shall make an annual report to Congress, copies of which shall be distributed as are other reports transmitted to Congress. Such reports shall contain such information and data collected by the Board as may be considered of value in the determination of questions connected with the control of trade in arms, ammunition, and implements of war. The Board shall include in such reports a list of all persons required to register under the provisions of this Act, and full information concerning the licenses issued hereunder.

"(k) The President is hereby authorized to proclaim upon recommendation of the Board from time to time a list of articles which shall be considered arms, ammunition, and implements of war for the purposes of this section.

"American Vessels Prohibited from Carrying Arms to Belligerent States

"Sec. 6. (a) Whenever the President shall have issued a proclamation under the authority of section 1 of this Act, it shall thereafter be unlawful, until such proclamation is revoked, for any American vessel to carry any arms, ammunition, or implements of war to any belligerent state, or to any state wherein civil strife exists, named in such proclamations, or to any neutral state for transshipment to, or for the use of, any such belligerent state or any such state wherein civil strife exists.

"(b) Whoever, in violation of the provisions of this section, shall take, or attempt to take, or shall authorize, hire, or solicit another to take, any American vessel carrying such cargo out of port or from the jurisdiction of the United States shall be fined not more than $10,000, or imprisoned not more than five years, or both; and, in addition, such vessel, and her tackle, apparel, furniture, and equipment, and the arms, ammunition, and implements of war on board, shall be forfeited to the United States.

"Use of American Ports as Base of Supply

"Sec. 7. (a) Whenever, during any war in which the United States is neutral, the President, or any person thereunto authorized by him, shall have cause to believe that any vessel, domestic or foreign, whether requiring clearance or not, is about to carry out of a port of the United States, fuel, men, arms, ammunition, implements of war, or other supplies to any warship, tender, or supply ship of a belligerent state, but the evidence is not deemed sufficient to justify forbidding the departure of the vessel as provided for by section 1, title V, chapter 30, of the Act approved June 15, 1917 (40 Stat. 217, 221; U.S.C., 1934 ed., title 18, sec. 31), and if, in the President's judgment; such action will serve to maintain peace between the United States and foreign states, or to protect the commercial interests of the United States and its citizens, or to promote the security or neutrality of the United States, he shall have the power and it shall be his duty to require the owner, master, or person in command thereof, before departing from a port of the United States, to give a bond to the United States, with sufficient sureties, in such amount as he shall deem proper, conditioned that the vessel will not deliver the men, or any part of the cargo, to any warship, tender, or supply ship of a belligerent state.

"(b) If the President, or any person thereunto authorized by him, shall find that a vessel, domestic or foreign, in a port of the United States, has previously cleared from a port of the United States during such war and delivered its cargo or any part thereof to a warship, tender, or supply ship of a belligerent state, he may prohibit the departure of such vessel during the duration of the war.

"*Submarines and Armed Merchant Vessels*

"Sec. 8. Whenever, during any war in which the United States is neutral, the President shall find that special restrictions placed on the use of the ports and territorial waters of the United States by the submarines or armed merchant vessels of a foreign state, will serve to maintain peace between the United States and foreign states, or to protect the commercial interests of the United States and its citizens, or to promote the security of the United States, and shall make proclamation thereof, it shall thereafter be unlawful for any such submarine or armed merchant vessel to enter a port or the territorial waters of the United States or to depart therefrom, except under such conditions and subject to such limitations as the President may prescribe. Whenever, in his judgment, the conditions which have caused him to issue his proclamation have ceased to exist, he shall revoke his proclamation and the provisions of this section shall thereupon cease to apply.

"*Travel on Vessels of Belligerent States*

"Sec. 9. Whenever the President shall have issued a proclamation under the authority of section 1 of this Act it shall thereafter be unlawful for any citizen of the United States to travel on any vessel of the state or states named in such proclamation, except in accordance with such rules and regulations as the President shall prescribe: *Provided, however,* That the provisions of this section shall not apply to a citizen of the United States traveling on a vessel whose voyage was begun in advance of the date of the President's proclamation, and who had no opportunity to discontinue his voyage after that date: *And provided further,* That they shall not apply under ninety days after the date of the President's proclamation to a citizen of the United States returning from a foreign state to the United States. Whenever, in the President's judgment, the conditions which have caused him to issue his proclamation have ceased to exist, he shall revoke his proclamation and the provisions of this section shall thereupon cease to apply with respect to the state or states named in such proclamation, except with respect to offenses committed prior to such revocation.

"*Arming of American Merchant Vessels Prohibited*

"Sec. 10. Whenever the President shall have issued a proclamation under the authority of section 1, it shall thereafter be unlawful, until such proclamation is revoked, for any American vessel engaged in commerce with any belligerent state, or any state wherein civil strife exists, named in such proclamation, to be armed or to carry any armament, arms, ammunition, or implements of war, except small arms and ammunition therefor which the President may deem necessary and shall publicly designate for the preservation of discipline aboard such vessels. . . ."

Albert Einstein's Letter of 1939 to President Franklin D. Roosevelt

Courtesy Franklin D. Roosevelt Library, PSF: Box 5, PSF: Safe File, Sachs

Sir:

Some recent work by E. Fermi and L. Szilard, which has been communicated to me in manuscript, leads me to expect that the element uranium may be turned into a new and important source of energy in the immediate future. Certain aspects of the situation which has arisen seem to call for watchfulness and, if necessary, quick action on the part of the Administration. I believe therefore that it is my duty to bring to your attention the following facts and recommendations:

In the course of the last four months it has been made probable—through the work of Joliot in France as well as Fermi and Szilard in America—that it may become possible to set up a nuclear chain reaction in a large mass of uranium, by which vast amounts of power and large quantities of new radium-like elements would be generated. Now it appears almost certain that this could be achieved in the immediate future.

This new phenomenon would also lead to the construction of bombs, and it is conceivable—though much less certain—that extremely powerful bombs of a new type may thus be constructed. A single bomb of this type, carried by boat and exploded in a port, might very well destroy the whole port together with some of the surrounding territory. However, such bombs might very well prove to be too heavy for transportation by air.

The United States has only very poor ores of uranium in moderate quantities. There is some good ore in Canada and the former Czechoslovakia, while the most important source of uranium is Belgian Congo.

In view of this situation you may think it desirable to have some permanent contact maintained between the Administration and the group of physicists working on chain reactions in America. One possible way of achieving this might be for you to entrust with this task a person who has your confidence and who could perhaps serve in an inofficial capacity. His task might comprise the following:

a) to approach Government Departments, keep them informed of the further development, and put forward recommendations for Government action, giving particular attention to the problem of securing a supply of uranium ore for the United States;

b) to speed up the experimental work, which is at present being carried on within the limits of the budgets of University laboratories, by providing funds, if such funds be required, through his contacts with private persons who are willing to make contributions for this cause, and perhaps also by obtaining the co-operation of industrial laboratories which have the necessary equipment.

I understand that Germany has actually stopped the sale of uranium from the Czechoslovakian mines which she has taken over. That she should have taken such early action might perhaps be understood on the ground that the son of the German Under-Secretary of State, von Weizsacker, is attached to the Kaiser-Wilhelm-Institute in Berlin where some of the American work on uranium is now being repeated.

Yours very truly,
[signed]
(Albert Einstein)

Atlantic Charter, 1941

Henry Steele Commager and Milton Cantor, eds. *Documents of American History.* 10th ed. (Englewood Cliffs, N.J.: Prentice Hall, 1988), p. 451

August 14, 1941

The President of the United States of America and the Prime Minister, Mr. Churchill, representing His Majesty's Government in the United Kingdom, being met together, deem it right to make known certain common principles in the national policies of their respective countries on which they base their hopes for a better future for the world.

First, their countries seek no aggrandizement, territorial or other;

Second, they desire to see no territorial changes that do not accord with the freely expressed wishes of the peoples concerned;

Third, they respect the right of all peoples to choose the form of government under which they will live; and they wish to see sovereign rights and self government restored to those who have been forcibly deprived of them;

Fourth, they will endeavor, with due respect for their existing obligations, to further the enjoyment by all States, great or small, victor or vanquished, of access, on equal terms, to the trade and to the raw materials of the world which are needed for their economic prosperity;

Fifth, they desire to bring about the fullest collaboration between all nations in the economic field with the object of securing, for all, improved labor standards, economic advancement and social security;

Sixth, after the final destruction of the Nazi tyranny, they hope to see established a peace which will afford to all nations the means of dwelling in safety within their own boundaries, and which will afford assurance that all the men in all the lands may live out their lives in freedom from fear and want;

Seventh, such a peace should enable all men to traverse the high seas and oceans without hindrance;

Eighth, they believe that all of the nations of the world, for realistic as well as spiritual reasons must come to the abandonment of the use of force. Since no future peace can be maintained if land, sea or air armaments continue to be employed by nations which threaten, or may threaten, aggression outside of their frontiers, they believe, pending the establishment of a wider and permanent system of general security, that the disarmament of such nations is essential. They will likewise aid and encourage all other practicable measures which will lighten for peace-loving peoples the crushing burden of armaments.

SIGNED Franklin D. Roosevelt
Winston S. Churchill

"Four Freedoms" Speech (1941)
President Franklin Roosevelt

Franklin D. Roosevelt, *The Public Papers and Addresses of Franklin D. Roosevelt.* Vol. 9. *War—And Aid to Democracies,* 1940 (New York: Macmillan, 1941), pp. 663–672

Mr. President, Mr. Speaker, Members of the Seventy-seventh Congress:

I address you, the Members of the Seventy-seventh Congress, at a moment unprecedented in the history of the Union. I use the word "unprecedented", because at no previous time has American security been as seriously threatened from without as it is today.

Since the permanent formation of our Government under the Constitution, in 1789, most of the periods of crisis in our history have related to our domestic affairs. Fortunately, only one of these—the four-year War Between the States—ever threatened our national unity. Today, thank God, one hundred and thirty million Americans, in forty-eight States, have forgotten points of the compass in our national unity.

It is true that prior to 1914 the United States often had been disturbed by events in other Continents. We had even engaged in two wars with European nations and in a number of undeclared wars in the West Indies, in the Mediterranean and in the Pacific for the maintenance of American rights and for the principles of peaceful commerce. But in no case had a serious threat been raised against our national safety or our continued independence.

What I seek to convey is the historic truth that the United States as a nation has at all times maintained clear, definite opposition to any attempt to lock us in behind an ancient Chinese wall while the procession of civilization went past. Today, thinking of our children and of their children, we oppose enforced isolation for ourselves or for any other part of the Americas.

That determination of ours, extending over all these years, was proved, for example, during the quarter century of wars following the French Revolution.

While the Napoleonic struggles did threaten interests of the United States because of the French foothold in the West Indies and in Louisiana, and while we engaged in the War of 1812 to vindicate our right to peaceful trade, it is nevertheless clear that neither France nor Great Britain, nor any other nation, was aiming at domination of the whole world.

In like fashion from 1815 to 1914—ninety-nine years—no single war in Europe or in Asia constituted a real threat against our future or against the future of any other American nation.

Except in the Maximilian interlude in Mexico, no foreign power sought to establish itself in this Hemisphere; and the strength of the British fleet in the Atlantic has been a friendly strength. It is still a friendly strength.

Even when the World War broke out in 1914, it seemed to contain only small threat of danger to our own American future. But, as time went on, the American people began to visualize what the downfall of democratic nations might mean to our own democracy.

We need not overemphasize imperfections in the Peace of Versailles. We need not harp on failure of the democracies to deal with problems of world reconstruction. We should remember that the Peace of 1919 was far less unjust than the kind of "pacification" which began even before Munich, and which is being carried on under the new order of tyranny that seeks to spread over every continent today. The American people have unalterably set their faces against that tyranny.

Every realist knows that the democratic way of life is at this moment being directly assailed in every part of the world—assailed either by arms, or by secret spreading of poisonous propaganda by those who seek to destroy unity and promote discord in nations that are still at peace.

During sixteen long months this assault has blotted out the whole pattern of democratic life in an appalling number of independent nations, great and small. The assailants are still on the march, threatening other nations, great and small.

Therefore, as your President, performing my constitutional duty to "give to the Congress information of the state of the Union," I find it, unhappily, necessary to report that the future and the safety of our country and of our democracy are overwhelmingly involved in events far beyond our borders.

Armed defense of democratic existence is now being gallantly waged in four continents. If that defense fails, all the population and all the resources of Europe, Asia, Africa and Australasia will be dominated by the conquerors. Let us remember that the total of those populations and their resources in those four continents greatly exceeds the sum total of the population and the resources of the whole of the Western Hemisphere—many times over.

In times like these it is immature—and incidentally, untrue— for anybody to brag that an unprepared America, single-handed, and with one hand tied behind its back, can hold off the whole world.

No realistic American can expect from a dictator's peace international generosity, or return of true independence, or world disarmament, or freedom of expression, or freedom of religion—or even good business.

Such a peace would bring no security for us or for our neighbors. "Those, who would give up essential liberty to purchase a little temporary safety, deserve neither liberty nor safety."

As a nation, we may take pride in the fact that we are soft-hearted; but we cannot afford to be soft-headed.

We must always be wary of those who with sounding brass and a tinkling cymbal preach the "ism" of appeasement.

We must especially beware of that small group of selfish men who would clip the wings of the American eagle in order to feather their own nests.

I have recently pointed out how quickly the tempo of modern warfare could bring into our very midst the physical attack which we must eventually expect if the dictator nations win this war.

There is much loose talk of our immunity from immediate and direct invasion from across the seas. Obviously, as long as the British Navy retains its power, no such danger exists. Even if there were no British Navy, it is not probable that any enemy would be stupid enough to attack us by landing troops in the United States from across thousands of miles of ocean, until it had acquired strategic bases from which to operate.

But we learn much from the lessons of the past years in Europe—particularly the lesson of Norway, whose essential seaports were captured by treachery and surprise built up over a series of years.

The first phase of the invasion of this Hemisphere would not be the landing of regular troops. The necessary strategic points would be occupied by secret agents and their dupes—and great numbers of them are already here, and in Latin America.

As long as the aggressor nations maintain the offensive, they—not we—will choose the time and the place and the method of their attack.

That is why the future of all the American Republics is today in serious danger.

That is why this Annual Message to the Congress is unique in our history.

That is why every member of the Executive Branch of the Government and every member of the Congress faces great responsibility and great accountability.

The need of the moment is that our actions and our policy should be devoted primarily—almost exclusively—to meeting this foreign peril. For all our domestic problems are now a part of the great emergency.

Just as our national policy in internal affairs has been based upon a decent respect for the rights and the dignity of all our fellow men within our gates, so our national policy in foreign affairs has been based on a decent respect for the rights and dignity of all nations, large and small. And the justice of morality must and will win in the end.

Our national policy is this:

First, by an impressive expression of the public will and without regard to partisanship, we are committed to all-inclusive national defense.

Second, by an impressive expression of the public will and without regard to partisanship, we are committed to full support of all those resolute peoples, everywhere, who are resisting aggression and are thereby keeping war away from our Hemisphere. By this support, we express our determination that the democratic cause shall prevail; and we strengthen the defense and the security of our own nation.

Third, by an impressive expression of the public will and without regard to partisanship, we are committed to the proposition that principles of morality and considerations for our own security will never permit us to acquiesce in a peace dictated by aggressors and sponsored by appeasers. We know that enduring peace cannot be bought at the cost of other people's freedom.

In the recent national election there was no substantial difference between the two great parties in respect to that national policy. No issue was fought out on this line before the American electorate. Today it is abundantly evident that American citizens everywhere are demanding and supporting speedy and complete action in recognition of obvious danger.

Therefore, the immediate need is a swift and driving increase in our armament production.

Leaders of industry and labor have responded to our summons. Goals of speed have been set. In some cases these goals are being reached ahead of time; in some cases we are on schedule; in other cases there are slight but not serious delays; and in some cases—and I am sorry to say very important cases—we are all concerned by the slowness of the accomplishment of our plans.

The Army and Navy, however, have made substantial progress during the past year. Actual experience is improving and speeding up our methods of production with every passing day. And today's best is not good enough for tomorrow.

I am not satisfied with the progress thus far made. The men in charge of the program represent the best in training, in ability, and in patriotism. They are not satisfied with the progress thus far made. None of us will be satisfied until the job is done.

No matter whether the original goal was set too high or too low, our objective is quicker and better results.

To give you two illustrations:

We are behind schedule in turning out finished airplanes; we are working day and night to solve the innumerable problems and to catch up.

We are ahead of schedule in building warships but we are working to get even further ahead of that schedule.

To change a whole nation from a basis of peacetime production of implements of peace to a basis of wartime production of implements of war is no small task. And the greatest difficulty comes at the beginning of the program, when new tools, new plant facilities, new assembly lines, and new ship ways must first be constructed before the actual materiel begins to flow steadily and speedily from them.

The Congress, of course, must rightly keep itself informed at all times of the progress of the program. However, there is certain information, as the Congress itself will readily recognize, which, in the interests of our own security and those of the nations that we are supporting, must of needs be kept in confidence.

New circumstances are constantly begetting new needs for our safety. I shall ask this Congress for greatly increased new appropriations and authorizations to carry on what we have begun.

I also ask this Congress for authority and for funds sufficient to manufacture additional munitions and war supplies of many kinds, to be turned over to those nations which are now in actual war with aggressor nations.

Our most useful and immediate role is to act as an arsenal for them as well as for ourselves. They do not need man power, but they do need billions of dollars worth of the weapons of defense.

The time is near when they will not be able to pay for them all in ready cash. We cannot, and we will not, tell them that they must surrender, merely because of present inability to pay for the weapons which we know they must have.

I do not recommend that we make them a loan of dollars with which to pay for these weapons—a loan to be repaid in dollars.

I recommend that we make it possible for those nations to continue to obtain war materials in the United States, fitting their orders into our own program. Nearly all their materiel would, if the time ever came, be useful for our own defense.

Taking counsel of expert military and naval authorities, considering what is best for our own security, we are free to decide how much should be kept here and how much should be sent abroad to our friends who by their determined and heroic resistance are giving us time in which to make ready our own defense.

For what we send abroad, we shall be repaid within a reasonable time following the close of hostilities, in similar materials, or, at our option, in other goods of many kinds, which they can produce and which we need.

Let us say to the democracies: "We Americans are vitally concerned in your defense of freedom. We are putting forth our energies, our resources and our organizing powers to give you the strength to regain and maintain a free world. We shall send you, in ever-increasing numbers, ships, planes, tanks, guns. This is our purpose and our pledge."

In fulfillment of this purpose we will not be intimidated by the threats of dictators that they will regard as a breach of international law or as an act of war our aid to the democracies which dare to resist their aggression. Such aid is not an act of war, even if a dictator should unilaterally proclaim it so to be.

When the dictators, if the dictators, are ready to make war upon us, they will not wait for an act of war on our part. They did not wait for Norway or Belgium or the Netherlands to commit an act of war.

Their only interest is in a new one-way international law, which lacks mutuality in its observance, and, therefore, becomes an instrument of oppression.

The happiness of future generations of Americans may well depend upon how effective and how immediate we can make our aid felt. No one can tell the exact character of the emergency situations that we may be called upon to meet. The Nation's hands must not be tied when the Nation's life is in danger.

We must all prepare to make the sacrifices that the emergency—almost as serious as war itself—demands. Whatever stands in the way of speed and efficiency in defense preparations must give way to the national need.

A free nation has the right to expect full cooperation from all groups. A free nation has the right to look to the leaders of business, of labor, and of agriculture to take the lead in stimulating effort, not among other groups but within their own groups.

The best way of dealing with the few slackers or trouble makers in our midst is, first, to shame them by patriotic example, and, if that fails, to use the sovereignty of Government to save Government.

As men do not live by bread alone, they do not fight by armaments alone. Those who man our defenses, and those behind them who build our defenses, must have the stamina and the courage which come from unshakable belief in the manner of life which they are defending. The mighty action that we are calling for cannot be based on a disregard of all things worth fighting for.

The Nation takes great satisfaction and much strength from the things which have been done to make its people conscious of their individual stake in the preservation of democratic life in America. Those things have toughened the fiber of our people, have renewed their faith and strengthened their devotion to the institutions we make ready to protect.

Certainly this is no time for any of us to stop thinking about the social and economic problems which are the root cause of the social revolution which is today a supreme factor in the world.

For there is nothing mysterious about the foundations of a healthy and strong democracy. The basic things expected by our people of their political and economic systems are simple. They are:

Equality of opportunity for youth and for others.

Jobs for those who can work.

Security for those who need it.

The ending of special privilege for the few.

The preservation of civil liberties for all.

The enjoyment of the fruits of scientific progress in a wider and constantly rising standard of living.

These are the simple, basic things that must never be lost sight of in the turmoil and unbelievable complexity of our modern world. The inner and abiding strength of our economic and political systems is dependent upon the degree to which they fulfill these expectations.

Many subjects connected with our social economy call for immediate improvement.

As examples:

We should bring more citizens under the coverage of old-age pensions and unemployment insurance.

We should widen the opportunities for adequate medical care.

We should plan a better system by which persons deserving or needing gainful employment may obtain it.

I have called for personal sacrifice. I am assured of the willingness of almost all Americans to respond to that call.

A part of the sacrifice means the payment of more money in taxes. In my Budget Message I shall recommend that a greater portion of this great defense program be paid for from taxation than we are paying today. No person should try, or be allowed, to get rich out of this program; and the principle of tax payments in accordance with ability to pay should be constantly before our eyes to guide our legislation.

If the Congress maintains these principles, the voters, putting patriotism ahead of pocketbooks, will give you their applause.

In the future days, which we seek to make secure, we look forward to a world founded upon four essential human freedoms.

The first is freedom of speech and expression—everywhere in the world.

The second is freedom of every person to worship God in his own way—everywhere in the world.

The third is freedom from want—which, translated into world terms, means economic understandings which will secure to every nation a healthy peacetime life for its inhabitants— everywhere in the world.

The fourth is freedom from fear—which, translated into world terms, means a world-wide reduction of armaments to such a point and in such a thorough fashion that no nation will be in a position to commit an act of physical aggression against any neighbor—anywhere in the world.

That is no vision of a distant millennium. It is a definite basis for a kind of world attainable in our own time and generation. That kind of world is the very antithesis of the so-called new order to tyranny which the dictators seek to create with the crash of a bomb.

To that new order we oppose the greater conception— the moral order. A good society is able to face schemes of world domination and foreign revolutions alike without fear.

Since the beginning of our American history, we have been engaged in change—in a perpetual peaceful revolution—a revolution which goes on steadily, quietly adjusting itself to changing conditions—without the concentration camp or the quick-lime in the ditch. The world order which we seek is the cooperation of free countries, working together in a friendly, civilized society.

This nation has placed its destiny in the hands and heads and hearts of its millions of free men and women; and its faith in freedom under the guidance of God. Freedom means the supremacy of human rights everywhere. Our support goes to those who struggle to gain those rights or keep them. Our strength is our unity of purpose.

To that high concept there can be no end save victory.

Executive Order 8802 (June 25, 1941)
President Franklin Roosevelt
Franklin D. Roosevelt Library, Official File, of 4245-G.

Reaffirming Policy of Full Participation in the Defense Programs by All Persons, Regardless of Race, Creed, Color, or National Origin, and Directing Certain Action in Furtherance of Said Policy.

Whereas it is the policy of the United States to encourage full participation in the national defense program by all citizens of the United States, regardless of race, creed, color, or national origin, in the firm belief that the democratic way of life within the Nation can be defended successfully only with the help and support of all groups within its borders; and

Whereas there is evidence that available and needed workers have been barred from employment in industries engaged in defense production solely because of considerations of race, creed, color, or national origin, to the detriment of workers' morale and of national unity;

Now, therefore, by virtue of the authority vested in me by the Constitution and the statutes, and as a prerequisite to the successful conduct of our national defense production effort, I do hereby reaffirm the policy of the United States that there shall be no discrimination in the employment of workers in defense industries or government because of race, creed, color, or national origin, and I do hereby declare that it is the duty of employers and of labor organizations, in furtherance of said policy and of this order, to provide for the full and equitable participation of all workers in defense industries, without discrimination because of race, creed, color, or national origin;

And it is hereby ordered as follows:

1. All departments and agencies of the Government of the United States concerned with vocational and training programs for defense production shall take special measures appropriate to assure that such programs are administered without discrimination because of race, creed, color, or national origin;

2. All contracting agencies of the Government of the United States shall include in all defense contracts hereafter negotiated by them a provision obligating the contractor not to discriminate against any worker because of race, creed, color or national origin;

3. There is established in the Office of Production Management a Committee on Fair Employment Practice, which shall consist to a chairman and four other members to be appointed by the President. The chairman and members of the Committee shall serve as such without compensation but shall be entitled to actual and necessary transportation, subsistence and other expenses incidental to performance of their duties. The Committee shall receive and investigate complaints of discrimination in violation of the provisions of this order and shall take appropriate steps to redress grievances which it finds to be valid. The Committee shall also recommend to the several departments and agencies of the Government of the United States and to the President all measures which may

be deemed by it necessary or proper to effectuate the provisions of this order.

Franklin D. Roosevelt

The White House,

June 25, 1941.

"Day of Infamy" Speech (1941)
President Franklin D. Roosevelt
Public Papers of the Presidents, Franklin Delano Roosevelt, 1941, p.300–301

The Capitol, December 8, 1941

Yesterday, December 7, 1941—a date which will live in infamy—the United States of America was suddenly and deliberately attacked by naval and air forces of the Empire of Japan.

The United States was at peace with that nation and, at the solicitation of Japan, was still in conversation with its Government and its Emperor looking toward the maintenance of peace in the Pacific. Indeed, one hour after Japanese air squadrons had commenced bombing in the American Island of Oahu, the Japanese Ambassador to the United States and his colleague delivered to our Secretary of State a formal reply to a recent American message. And while this reply stated that it seemed useless to continue the existing diplomatic negotiations, it contained no threat or hint of war of armed attack.

It will be recorded that the distance of Hawaii from Japan makes it obvious that the attack was deliberately planned many days or even weeks ago. During the intervening time the Japanese Government has deliberately sought to deceive the United States by false statements and expressions of hope for continued peace.

The attack yesterday on the Hawaiian Islands has caused severe damage to American naval and military forces, I regret to tell you that very many American lives have been lost. In addition American ships have been reported torpedoed on the high seas between San Francisco and Honolulu.

Yesterday the Japanese Government also launched an attack against Malaya.

Last night Japanese forces attacked Hong Kong.

Last night Japanese forces attacked Guam.

Last night Japanese forces attacked the Philippine Islands.

Last night the Japanese attacked Wake Island.

And this morning the Japanese attacked Midway Island.

Japan has, therefore, undertaken a surprise offensive extending throughout the Pacific area. The facts of yesterday and today speak for themselves. The people of the United States have already formed their opinions and well understand the implications to the very life and safety of our nation.

As Commander-in-Chief of the Army and Navy I have directed that all measures be taken for our defense.

But always will our whole nation remember the character of the onslaught against us.

No matter how long it may take us to overcome this premeditated invasion, the American people in their righteous might will win through to absolute victory.

I believe that I interpret the will of the Congress and of the people when I assert that we will not only defend ourselves to the uttermost but will make it very certain that this form of treachery shall never again endanger us.

Hostilities exist. There is no blinking at the fact that our people, our territory and our interests are in grave danger.

With confidence in our armed forces—with the unbounding determination of our people—we will gain the inevitable triumph—so help us God.

I ask that the Congress declare that since the unprovoked and dastardly attack by Japan on Sunday, December seventh, 1941, a state of war has existed between the United States and the Japanese Empire.

Executive Order 9066, 1942
Federal Register 7, no. 38 (February 25, 1942): 1407

Executive Order
Authorizing the Secretary of War to Prescribe Military Areas

Whereas the successful prosecution of the war requires every possible protection against espionage and against sabotage to national-defense material, national-defense premises, and national-defense utilities as defined in Section 4, Act of April 20, 1918, 40 Stat. 533, as amended by the Act of November 30, 1940, 54 Stat. 1220, and the Act of August 21, 1941, 55 Stat. 655 (U.S., Title 50, Sec. 104):

Now therefore, by virtue of the authority vested in me as President of the United States, and Commander in Chief of the Army and Navy, I hereby authorize and direct the Secretary of War, and the Military Commanders whom he may from time to time designate, whenever he or any designated Commander deems such action necessary or desirable, to prescribe military areas in such places and of such extent as the or the appropriate Military Commander may determine, from which any or all persons may be excluded, and with respect to which, the right of any person to enter, remain in, or leave shall be subject to whatever restrictions the Secretary of War or the appropriate Military Commander may impose in his discretion. The Secretary of War is hereby authorized to provide for residents of any such area who are excluded therefrom, such transportation, food, shelter, and other accommodations as may be necessary, in the judgment of the Secretary of War or the said Military Commander, and until other arrangements are made, to accomplish the purpose of this order. The designation of military areas in any region or locality shall supersede designations of prohibited and restricted areas by the Attorney General under the Proclamations of December 7 and 8, 1941, and shall supersede the responsibility and authority of the Attorney General under the said Proclamations in respect of such prohibited and restricted areas.

I hereby further authorize and direct the Secretary of War and the said Military Commanders to take such other steps as be or the appropriate Military Commander may deem advisable to enforce compliance with the restrictions applicable to each Military area hereinabove authorized to be designated, including the use of Federal troops and other Federal Agencies, with authority to accept assistance of state and local agencies.

I hereby further authorize and direct all Executive Departments, independent establishments and other Federal Agencies, to assist the Secretary of War or the said Military Commanders in carrying out this Executive Order, including the furnishing of medical aid, hospitalization, food, clothing, transportation, use of land, shelter, and other supplies, equipment, utilities, facilities, and services.

This order shall not be construed as modifying or limiting in any way the authority heretofore granted under Executive Order No. 8972, dated December 12, 1941, nor shall it be construed as limiting or modifying the duty and responsibility of the Federal Bureau of Investigation, with respect to the investigation of alleged acts of sabotage or the duty and responsibility of the Attorney General and the Department of Justice under the Proclamations of December 7 and 8, 1941, prescribing regulations for the conduct and control of alien enemies, except as such duty and responsibility is superseded by the designation of military areas hereunder.
Franklin D. Roosevelt
The White House,
February 19, 1942.

Yalta Agreement (1945)

Franklin D. Roosevelt, *The Public Papers and Addresses of Franklin D. Roosevelt.* Vol. 13, *Victory and the Threshold of Peace, 1944–45,* (New York: Random House, 1950), pp. 531–537.

February 11, 1945

Yalta Agreement

The Defeat of Germany
We have considered and determined the military plans of the three Allied powers for the final defeat of the common enemy. The military staffs of the three Allied Nations have met in daily meetings throughout the Conference. These meetings have been most satisfactory from every point of view and have resulted in closer coordination of the military effort of the three Allies than ever before. The fullest information has been interchanged. The timing, scope, and coordination of new and even more powerful blows to be launched by our armies and air forces into the heart of Germany from the East, West, North, and South have been fully agreed and planned in detail.

Our combined military plans will be made known only as we execute them, but we believe that the very close working partnership among the three staffs attained at this Conference will result in shortening the war. Meetings of the three staffs will be continued in the future whenever the need arises.

Nazi Germany is doomed. The German people will only make the cost of their defeat heavier to themselves by attempting to continue a hopeless resistance.

The Occupation and Control of Germany
We have agreed on common policies and plans for enforcing the unconditional surrender terms which we shall impose together on Nazi Germany after German armed resistance has been finally crushed. These terms will not be made known until the final defeat of Germany has been accomplished. Under the agreed plan, the forces of the three powers will each occupy a separate zone of Germany. Coordinated administration and control has been provided for under the plan through a central control commission consisting of the Supreme Commanders of the three powers with headquarters in Berlin. It has been agreed that France should be invited by the three powers, if she should so desire, to take over a zone of occupation, and to participate as a fourth member of the control commission. The limits of the French zone will be agreed by the four Governments concerned through their representatives on the European Advisory Commission. It is our inflexible purpose to destroy German militarism and Nazism and to ensure that Germany will never again be able to disturb the peace of the world. We are determined to disarm and disband all German armed forces; break up for all time the German General Staff that has repeatedly contrived the resurgence of German militarism; remove or destroy all German military equipment; eliminate or control all German industry that could be used for military production; bring all war criminals to just and swift punishment and exact reparation in kind for the destruction wrought by the Germans; wipe out the Nazi Party, Nazi laws, organizations and institutions, remove all Nazi and militarist influences from public office and from the cultural and economic life of the German people; and take in harmony such other measures in Germany as may be necessary to

the future peace and safety of the world. It is not our purpose to destroy the people of Germany, but only when Nazism and militarism have been extirpated will there be hope for a decent life for Germans, and a place for them in the comity of Nations.

Reparation by Germany

We have considered the question of the damage caused by Germany to the Allied Nations in this war and recognized it as just that Germany be obliged to make compensation for this damage in kind to the greatest extent possible. A commission for the compensation of damage will be established. The commission will be instructed to consider the question of the extent and methods for compensating damage caused by Germany to the Allied countries. The commission will work in Moscow.

United Nations Conference

We are resolved upon the earliest possible establishment with our allies of a general international organization to maintain peace and security. We believe that this is essential, both to prevent aggression and to remove the political, economic, and social causes of war through the close and continuing collaboration of all peace-loving peoples.

The foundations were laid at Dumbarton Oaks. On the important question of voting procedure, however, agreement was not three reached. The present Conference has been able to resolve this difficulty.

We have agreed that a conference of United Nations should be called to meet at San Francisco in the United States on April 25, 1945, to prepare the charter of such an organization, along the lines proposed in the informal conversations at Dumbarton Oaks.

The Government of China and the Provisional Government of France will be immediately consulted and invited to sponsor invitations to the conference jointly with the Governments of the United States, Great Britain, and the Union of Soviet Socialist Republics. As soon as the consultation with China and France has been completed, the next of the proposals on voting procedure will be made public.

Declaration on Liberated Europe

The Premier of the Union of Soviet Socialist Republics, the Prime Minister of the United Kingdom, and the President of the United States of America have consulted with each other in the common interests of the peoples of their countries and those of liberated Europe. They jointly declare their mutual agreement to concert during the temporary period of instability in liberated Europe the policies of their three Governments in assisting the peoples liberated from the domination of Nazi Germany and the peoples of the former Axis satellite states of Europe to solve by democratic means their pressing political and economic problems.

The establishment of order in Europe and the rebuilding of national economic life must be achieved by processes which will enable the liberated peoples to destroy the last vestiges of Nazism and Fascism and to create democratic institutions of their own choice. This is a principle of the Atlantic Charter—the right of all peoples to choose the form of government under which they will live—the restoration of sovereign rights and self-government to those peoples who have been forcibly deprived of them by the aggressor Nations.

To foster the conditions in which the liberated peoples may exercise these rights, the three Governments will jointly assist the people in any European liberated state or former Axis satellite state in Europe where in their judgment conditions require (a) to establish conditions of internal peace; (b) to carry out emergency measures for the relief of distressed peoples; (c) to form interim governmental authorities broadly representative of all democratic elements in the population and pledged to the earliest possible establishment through free elections of governments responsive to the will of the people; and (d) to facilitate where necessary the holding of such elections.

The three Governments will consult the other United Nations and provisional authorities or other Governments in Europe when matters of direct interest to them are under consideration.

When, in the opinion of the three Governments, conditions in any European liberated state or any former Axis satellite state in Europe make such action necessary, they will immediately consult together on the measures necessary to discharge the joint responsibilities set forth in this declaration.

By this declaration we reaffirm our faith in the principles of the Atlantic Charter, our pledge in the declaration by the United Nations, and our determination to build in cooperation with other peace-loving Nations world order under law, dedicated to peace, security, freedom, and general well-being of all mankind.

In issuing this declaration, the three powers express the hope that the Provisional Government of the French Republic may be associated with them in the procedure suggested.

Poland

A new situation has been created in Poland as a result of her complete liberation by the Red Army. This calls for the establishment of a Polish provisional government which can be more broadly based than was possible before the recent liberation of western Poland. The provisional government which is now functioning in Poland should therefore by reorganized on a broader democratic basis with the inclusion of democratic leaders from Poland itself and from Poles abroad. This new government should then be called the Polish Provisional Government of National Unity.

M. Molotov, Mr. Harriman, and Sir A. Clark Kerr are authorized as a commission to consult in the first instance in Moscow with members of the present provisional government and with other Polish democratic leaders from within Poland and from abroad, with a view to the reorganization of the present government along the above lines. This Polish Provisional Government of National Unity shall be pledged to the holding of free and unfettered elections as soon as possible on the basis of universal suffrage and secret ballot. In these elections all democratic anti-Nazi parties shall have the right to take part and to put forward candidates.

When a Polish Provisional Government of National Unity has been properly formed in conformity with the above, the Government of the U.S.S.R., which now maintains diplomatic relations with the present provisional government of Poland, and the Government of the United Kingdom and the Government of the U.S.A. will establish diplomatic relations with the new Polish Provisional Government of National Unity, and will exchange ambassadors by whose reports the respective Governments will be kept informed about the situation in Poland. The three heads of government consider that the eastern frontier of Poland should follow the Curzon line with digressions from it in some regions of five to eight kilometers in favor of Poland. They recognized that Poland must receive substantial accessions of territory in the North and West. They feel that the opinion of the new Polish Provisional Government of National Unity should be sought in due course on the extent of these accessions and that the final delimitation of the western frontier of Poland should thereafter await the peace conference.

Yugoslavia

We have agreed to recommend to Marshal Tito and Dr. Subasic that the agreement between them should be put into effect immediately, and that a new government should be formed on the basis of that agreement.

We also recommend that as soon as the new government has been formed it should declare that:

1. The anti-Fascist Assembly of National Liberation (Avnoj) should be extended to include members of the last Yugoslav Parliament (Skupschina) who have not compromised themselves by collaboration with the enemy, thus forming a body to be known as a temporary Parliament; and,

2. Legislative acts passed by the anti-Fascist Assembly of National Liberation will be subject to subsequent ratification by a constituent assembly.

There was also a general review of other Balkan questions.

Meetings of Foreign Secretaries

Throughout the Conference, besides the daily meetings of the heads of governments and the Foreign Secretaries, separate meetings of the three Foreign Secretaries, and their advisers have also been held daily.

These meetings have proved of the utmost value and the Conference agreed that permanent machinery should be set up for regular consultation between the three Foreign Secretaries. They will, therefore, meet as often as may be necessary, probably about every three or four months. These meetings will be held in rotation in the three capitals, the first meeting being held in London, after the United Nations Conference on World Organization.

Unity for Peace as for War

Our meeting here in the Crimea has reaffirmed our common determination to maintain and strengthen in the peace to come that unity of purpose and of action which has made victory possible and certain for the United Nations in this war. We believe that this is a sacred obligation which our Governments owe to our peoples and to all the peoples of the world.

Only with the continuing and growing cooperation and understanding among our three countries and among all the peace-loving Nations can the highest aspiration of humanity be realized—a secure and lasting peace which will, in the words of the Atlantic Charter, "afford assurance that all the men in all the lands may live out their lives in freedom from fear and want."

Victory in this war and establishment of the proposed international organization will provide the greatest opportunity in all history to create in the years to come the essential conditions of such a peace.

Signed: Winston S. Churchill
Franklin D. Roosevelt
J. Stalin

President Truman's Announcement of the Atomic Bombing of Hiroshima, 1945

Public Papers of the Presidents (Harry S. Truman, 1946, pp. 197–200)

Statement by the President Announcing the Use of the A-Bomb at Hiroshima

Sixteen hours ago an American airplane dropped one bomb on Hiroshima, an important Japanese Army base. That bomb had more power than 20,000 tons of T.N.T. It had more than two thousand times the blast power of the British "Grand Slam" which is the largest bomb ever yet used in the history of warfare.

The Japanese began the war from the air at Pearl Harbor. They have been repaid many fold. And the end is not yet. With this bomb we have now added a new and revolutionary increase in destruction to supplement the growing power of our armed forces. In their present form these bombs are now in production and even more powerful forms are in development.

It is an atomic bomb. It is a harnessing of the basic power of the universe. The force from which the sun draws its power has been loosed against those who brought war to the Far East.

Before 1939, it was the accepted belief of scientists that it was theoretically possible to release atomic energy. But no one knew any practical method of doing it. By 1942, however, we knew that the Germans were working feverishly to find a way to add atomic energy to the other engines of war with which they hoped to enslave the world. But they failed. We may be grateful to Providence that the Germans got the V-1's and V-2's late and in limited quantities and even more grateful that they did not get the atomic bomb at all.

The battle of the laboratories held fateful risks for us as well as the battles of the air, land and sea, and we have now won the battle of the laboratories as we have won the other battles.

Beginning in 1940, before Pearl Harbor, scientific knowledge useful in war was pooled between the United States and Great Britain, and many priceless helps to our victories have come from that arrangement. Under that general policy the research on the atomic bomb was begun. With American and British scientists working together we entered the race of discovery against the Germans.

The United States had available the large number of scientists of distinction in the many needed areas of knowledge. It had the tremendous industrial and financial resources necessary for the project and they could be devoted to it without undue impairment of other vital war work. In the United States the laboratory work and the production plants, on which a substantial start had already been made, would be out of reach of enemy bombing, while at that time Britain was exposed to constant air attack and was still threatened with the possibility of invasion. For these reasons Prime Minister Churchill and President Roosevelt agreed that it was wise to carry on the project here. We now have two great plants and many lesser works devoted to the production of atomic power. Employment during peak construction numbered 125,000 and 65,000 individuals are even now engaged in operating the plants. Many have worked there for two and a half years. Few know what they have been producing. They see great quantities of material going in and they see nothing coming out of these plants, for the physical size of the explosive charge is exceedingly small. We have spent two

billion dollars on the greatest scientific gamble in history—and won. But the greatest marvel is not the size of the enterprise, its secrecy, nor its cost, but the achievement of scientific brains in putting together infinitely complex pieces of knowledge held by many men in different fields of science into a workable plan. And hardly less marvelous has been the capacity of industry to design, and of labor to operate, the machines and methods to do things never done before so that the brain child of many minds came forth in physical shape and performed as it was supposed to do. Both science and industry worked under the direction of the United States Army, which achieved a unique success in managing so diverse a problem in the advancement of knowledge in an amazingly short time. It is doubtful if such another combination could be got together in the world. What has been done is the greatest achievement of organized science in history. It was done under high pressure and without failure.

We are now prepared to obliterate more rapidly and completely every productive enterprise the Japanese have above ground in any city. We shall destroy their docks, their factories, and their communications. Let there be no mistake; we shall completely destroy Japan's power to make war.

It was to spare the Japanese people from utter destruction that the ultimatum of July 26 was issued at Potsdam. Their leaders promptly rejected that ultimatum. If they do not now accept our terms they may expect a rain of ruin from the air, the like of which has never been seen on this earth. Behind this air attack will follow sea and land forces in such numbers and power as they have not yet seen and with the fighting skill of which they are already well aware. The Secretary of War, who has kept in personal touch with all phases of the project, will immediately make public a statement giving further details.

His statement will give facts concerning the sites at Oak Ridge near Knoxville, Tennessee, and at Richland near Pasco, Washington, and an installation near Santa Fe, New Mexico. Although the workers at the sites have been making materials to be used in producing the greatest destructive force in history they have not themselves been in danger beyond that of many other occupations, for the utmost care has been taken for their safety.

The fact that we can release atomic energy ushers in a new era in man's understanding of nature's forces. Atomic energy may in the future supplement the power that now comes from coal, oil, and falling water, but at present it cannot be produced on a basis to compete with them commercially. Before that comes there must be a long period of intensive research.

It has never been the habit of the scientists of this country or the policy of this Government to withhold from the world scientific knowledge. Normally, therefore, everything about the work with atomic energy would be made public.

But under present circumstances it is not intended to divulge the technical processes of production or all the military applications, pending further examination of possible methods of protecting us and the rest of the world from the danger of sudden destruction.

I shall recommend that the Congress of the United States consider promptly the establishment of an appropriate commission to control the production and use of atomic power within the United States. I shall give further consideration and make further recommendations to the Congress as to how atomic power can become a powerful and forceful influence towards the maintenance of world peace.

Bibliography

Adams, Michael C. C. *The Best War Ever: America and World War II.* Baltimore: Johns Hopkins University Press, 1994.

Allswang, John M. *The New Deal and American Politics.* New York: John Wiley & Sons, 1978.

Badger, Anthony. *The New Deal: The Depression Years, 1933–1940.* New York: Hill & Wang, 1989.

Ballard, Jack S. *The Shock of Peace: Military and Economic Demobilization after World War II.* Washington, D.C.: University Press of America, 1983.

Bernstein, Alison R. *American Indians and World War II.* Norman: University of Oklahoma Press, 1991.

Bernstein, Irving. *Turbulent Years: A History of the American Worker, 1933–1941.* Boston: Houghton Mifflin, 1970.

Bernstein, Michael. *The Great Depression: Delayed Recovery and Economic Change in America, 1929–1939.* New York: Cambridge University Press, 1987.

Best, Gary Dean. *The Nickel and Dime Decade: American Popular Culture during the 1930s.* Westport, Conn.: Praeger, 1993.

Blum, John Morton. *V Was for Victory: Politics and American Culture during World War II.* New York: Harcourt Brace Jovanovich, 1976.

Bordo, Michael D., Claudia Goldin, and Eugene N. White, eds. *The Defining Moment: The Great Depression and the American Economy in the Twentieth Century.* Chicago: University of Chicago Press, 1998.

Brinkley, Alan. *The End of Reform: New Deal Liberalism in Depression and War.* New York: Knopf, 1995.

Buchanan, A. Russell. *The United States in World War II*, 2 vols. New York: Harper & Row, 1964.

Burns, James MacGregor. *Roosevelt: The Lion and the Fox.* New York: Harcourt, Brace, 1956.

———. *Roosevelt: The Soldier of Freedom.* New York: Harcourt, Brace Jovanovich, 1970.

Cantril, Hadley, ed. *Public Opinion, 1935–1946.* Princeton, N.J.: Princeton University Press, 1951.

Chandler, Lester V. *America's Greatest Depression, 1929–1941.* New York: Harper & Row, 1970.

Chapman, Richard N. *Contours of Public Policy, 1939–1945.* New York: Garland, 1981.

Cobb, James, and Michael Namaroto, eds. *The New Deal and the South: Essays.* Jackson: University Press of Mississippi, 1984.

Cohen, Lizabeth. *Making a New Deal: Industrial Workers in Chicago, 1919–1939.* New York: Cambridge University Press, 1990.

Cole, Wayne S. *Roosevelt and the Isolationists, 1932–1945.* Lincoln: University of Nebraska Press, 1983.

Cook, Blanche Wiesen. *Eleanor Roosevelt*, vols. 1 and 2. New York: Viking, 1992, 1994.

Dallek, Robert, Jr. *Franklin D. Roosevelt and American Foreign Policy, 1932–1945.* New York: Oxford University Press, 1979.

Divine, Robert A. *Roosevelt and World War II.* Baltimore: Johns Hopkins University Press, 1969.

———. *The Illusion of Neutrality.* Chicago: University of Chicago Press, 1962.

Dower, John. *War without Mercy: Race and Power in the Pacific War.* New York: Pantheon, 1986.

Fraser, Steve, and Gary Gerstle, eds. *The Rise and Fall of the New Deal Order.* Princeton, N.J.: Princeton University Press, 1989.

Freidel, Frank. *Franklin D. Roosevelt: A Rendezvous with Destiny.* Boston: Little, Brown, 1990.

French, Warren, ed. *The Thirties: Fiction, Poetry, Drama.* Deland, Fla.: Everett Edwards, 1967.

Fussel, Paul. *Wartime: Understanding and Behavior in the Second World War.* New York: Oxford University Press, 1989.

Gaddis, John Lewis. *The United States and the Origins of the Cold War, 1941–1947.* New York: Oxford University Press, 1972.

Galbraith, John Kenneth. *The Great Crash.* Boston: Houghton Mifflin, 1955.

Gelfand, M. I. *A Nation of Cities: The Federal Government and Urban America, 1933–1965.* New York: Oxford University Press, 1975.

Goodwin, Doris Kearns. *No Ordinary Time: Franklin and Eleanor Roosevelt: The Home Front in World War II.* New York: Simon & Schuster, 1994.

Greenfield, Kent Roberts. *American Strategy in World War II.* Baltimore: Johns Hopkins University Press, 1963.

Hartmann, Susan. *The Home Front and Beyond: American Women in the 1940s.* Boston: Twayne, 1982.

Hawes, Joseph M. *Children between the Wars: American Childhood, 1920–1940.* New York: Twayne, 1997.

Hawley, Ellis W. *The New Deal and the Problem of Monopoly.* Princeton, N.J.: Princeton University Press, 1966.

Hess, Gary R. *The United States at War, 1941–1945.* Arlington Heights, Ill.: Harland Davidson, 1986.

Howard, Donald S. *The WPA and Federal Relief Policy.* New York: Russell Sage Foundation, 1943.

Iriye, Akira. *The Globalizing of America, 1913–1945.* New York: Cambridge University Press, 1993.

Jackson, Kenneth T. *Crabgrass Frontier.* New York: Oxford University Press, 1985.

James, D. Clayton, and Anne Sharp Wells. *From Pearl Harbor to V-J Day: The American Armed Forces in World War II.* Chicago: Ivan R. Dee, 1995.

Jeffries, John W. *Wartime America: The World War II Home Front.* Chicago: Ivan R. Dee, 1996.

———. *Testing the Roosevelt Coalition: Connecticut Society and Politics in the Era of World War II.* Knoxville: University of Tennessee Press, 1979.

Karl, Barry D. *The Uneasy State: The United States from 1915 to 1945.* Chicago: University of Chicago Press, 1983.

Keegan, John. *The Second World War.* New York: Viking, 1989.

Kennedy, David M. *Freedom from Fear: The American People in Depression and War, 1929–1945.* New York: Oxford University Press, 1999.

Kimball, Warren F. *The Juggler: Franklin Roosevelt as Wartime Statesman.* Princeton, N.J.: Princeton University Press, 1991.

Klein, Maury. *Rainbow's End: The Crash of 1929.* New York: Oxford University Press, 2001.

Koppes, Clayton R., and Gregory D. Black. *Hollywood Goes to War: How Politics, Profits, and Propaganda Shaped World War II Movies.* New York: Free Press, 1987.

Ladd, Everett C. Jr., with Charles D. Hadley. *Transformations of the American Party System. Political Coalitions from the New Deal to the 1970s,* 2nd ed. New York: Norton, 1978.

Larabee, Eric. *Commander-in-Chief: Franklin Delano Roosevelt, His Lieutenants, and Their War.* New York: Harper & Row, 1987.

Leff, Mark. *The Limits of Symbolic Reform: The New Deal and Taxation, 1933–1939.* New York: Cambridge University Press, 1984.

Leuchtenburg, William E. *The Supreme Court Reborn: The Constitutional Revolution in the Age of Roosevelt.* New York: Oxford University Press, 1995.

———. *Franklin D. Roosevelt and the New Deal, 1932–1940.* New York: Harper & Row, 1963.

Lichtenstein, Nelson. *Labor's War at Home: The CIO in World War II.* New York: Cambridge University Press, 1982.

Lindenmeyer, Kriste. *"A Right to Childhood": The U.S. Children's Bureau and Child Welfare, 1912–1946.* Urbana: University of Illinois Press, 1997.

Linderman, Gerald F. *The World within War: America's Combat Experience in World War II.* New York: Free Press, 1997.

Lingeman, Richard R. *Don't You Know There's a War On? The American Home Front, 1941–1945.* New York: G. P. Putnam's Sons, 1970.

Lowitt, Richard, and Maurine Beasley, eds. *One-Third of a Nation: Lorena Hickok Reports the Great Depression.* Urbana: University of Illinois Press, 1981.

MacDonald, Charles B. *The Mighty Endeavor: The American War in Europe.* New York: DaCapo Press, 1999.

Maney, Patrick J. *The Roosevelt Presence: A Biography of Franklin Delano Roosevelt.* New York: Twayne, 1992.

McDonald, William F. *Federal Relief Administration and the Arts: The Origins and Administrative History of the Arts Projects of the Works Project Administration.* Columbus: Ohio State University Press, 1969.

McElvaine, Robert S. *The Great Depression: America, 1929–1941.* New York: Times Books, 1984.

McNeill, William Hardy. *America, Britain & Russia: Their Cooperation and Conflict, 1941–1946.* New York: Oxford University Press, 1953.

Nash, Gerald D. *The American West Transformed: The Impact of the Second World War.* Bloomington: Indiana University Press, 1985.

O'Neill, William L. *A Democracy at War: America's Fight at Home and Abroad in World War II.* New York: Free Press, 1993.

Overy, Richard. *Why the Allies Won.* New York: Norton, 1995.

Parrish, Michael E. *Anxious Decades: America in Prosperity and Depression, 1920–1941.* New York: Norton, 1992.

Patterson, James T. *The New Deal and the States: Federalism in Transition.* Princeton, N.J.: Princeton University Press, 1969.

———. *Congressional Conservatism and the New Deal: The Growth of the Conservative Coalition in Congress, 1933–1939.* Lexington: University Press of Kentucky, 1967.

———. *America's Struggle against Poverty in the Twentieth Century.* Cambridge: Harvard University Press, 2000.

Philp, Kenneth R. *John Collier's Crusade for Indian Reform, 1920–1954.* Tucson: University of Arizona Press, 1977.

Plotke, David. *Building a Democratic Political Order: Reshaping American Liberalism in the 1930s and 1940s.* New York: Cambridge University Press, 1996.

Polenberg, Richard. *War and Society: The United States, 1941–1945.* Philadelphia: J. B. Lippincott, 1972.

Rhodes, Richard. *The Making of the Atomic Bomb.* New York: Simon & Schuster, 1986.

Saloutos, Theodore. *The American Farmer and the New Deal.* Ames: Iowa State University Press, 1982.

Schlesinger, Arthur M., Jr. *The Crisis of the Old Order.* Boston: Houghton Mifflin, 1957.

———. *The Coming of the New Deal.* Boston: Houghton Mifflin, 1959.

———. *The Politics of Upheaval.* Boston: Houghton Mifflin, 1960.

Schwarz, Jordan A. *The Interregnum of Despair: Hoover, Congress, and the Depression.* Urbana: University of Illinois Press, 1970.

———. *The New Dealers: Power Politics in the Age of Roosevelt.* New York: Knopf, 1993.

Sherry, Michael. *The Rise of American Air Power.* New Haven, Conn.: Yale University Press, 1987.

Sherwin, Martin. *A World Destroyed: The Atomic Bomb and the Grand Alliance.* New York: Knopf, 1975.

Sitkoff, Harvard. *A New Deal for Blacks: The Emergence of Civil Rights as a National Issue.* New York: Oxford University Press, 1978.

Sitkoff, Harvard, ed. *Fifty Years Later: The New Deal Evaluated.* New York: McGraw-Hill, 1985.

Smith, Gaddis, *American Diplomacy During the Second World War, 1941–1945,* 2nd ed. New York: Knopf, 1985.

Spector, Ronald H. *Eagle Against the Sun: The American War Against Japan.* New York: Random House, 1985.

Stein, Herbert. *The Fiscal Revolution in America.* Chicago: University of Chicago Press, 1969.

Sweeney, Michael S. *Secrets of Victory: The Office of Censorship and the American Press and Radio in World War II.* Chapel Hill: University of North Carolina Press, 2001.

Terkel, Studs. *"The Good War": An Oral History of World War II.* New York: Pantheon, 1984.

———. *Hard Times: An Oral History of the Great Depression.* New York: Pantheon, 1970.

Tuttle, William. *"Daddy's Gone to War": The Second World War in the Lives of America's Children.* New York: Oxford University Press, 1993.

Vatter, Harold G. *The U.S. Economy in World War II.* New York: Columbia University Press, 1985.

Ware, Susan. *Holding Their Own: American Women in the 1930s.* Boston: Twayne, 1982.

Weed, Clyde P. *Nemesis of Reform: The Republican Party during the New Deal.* New York: Columbia University Press, 1994.

Weiss, Nancy J. *Farewell to the Party of Lincoln: Black Politics in the Age of FDR.* Princeton, N.J.: Princeton University Press, 1983.

Wilcox, Walter. *The Farmer in the Second World War.* Ames: Iowa State University Press, 1947.

Wilson, Joan Hoff. *Herbert Hoover: Forgotten Progressive.* Boston: Little, Brown, 1975.

Winkler, Allan. *Home Front U.S.A.: America during World War II,* 2nd ed. Wheeling, Ill.: Harlan Davidson, 2000.

Worster, Donald. *Dust Bowl: The Southern Plains in the 1930s.* New York: Oxford University Press, 1979.

Wynn, Neil A. *The Afro-American and the Second World War,* rev. ed. New York: Holmes & Meier, 1993.

Young, Roland. *Congressional Politics in the Second World War.* New York: Columbia University Press, 1956.

Zieger, Robert H. *The CIO: 1935–1955.* Chapel Hill: University of North Carolina Press, 1995.

Index

Boldface page numbers denote extensive treatment of a topic. *Italic* page numbers refer to illustrations; *c* refers to the Chronology; and *m* indicates a map.